Chthonic deities under the earth
or beings

afflatus – inspiration

# THE
# GEOGRAPHY
## OF THE
# IMAGINATION

FORTY ESSAYS BY GUY DAVENPORT

North Point Press · San Francisco · 1981

FOR HUGH KENNER

# Table of Contents

Acknowledgments                                    ix
The Geography of the Imagination                    3
The Symbol of the Archaic                          16
Another Odyssey                                    29
The House That Jack Built                          45
Prehistoric Eyes                                   61
Whitman                                            68
Olson                                              80
Zukofsky                                          100
Marianne Moore                                    114

Spinoza's Tulips                                                    123
Do You Have a Poem Book on E. E. Cummings?                          131
Seeing Shelley Plain                                               135
Persephone's Ezra                                                  141
The Pound Vortex                                                   165
Ezra Pound 1885–1972                                               169
"Trees"                                                            177
Jonathan Williams                                                  180
Ronald Johnson                                                     190
*Poetry*'s Golden                                                  205
Where Poems Come From                                              209
Ishmael's Double                                                   215
Louis Agassiz                                                      230
That Faire Field of Enna                                           250
Charles Ives                                                       272
Ozymandias                                                         278
Christ's Cunning Rimesmith                                         282
Joyce's Forest of Symbols                                          286
The Man Without Contemporaries                                     300
Narrative Tone and Form                                            308
Tchelitchew                                                        319
Jack Yeats the Elder                                               326
Wittgenstein                                                       331
Hobbitry                                                           336
Dictionary                                                         339
No, But I've Read the Book                                         343
The Anthropology of Table Manners from Geophagy Onward             345
The Indian and His Image                                           353
Finding                                                            359
Ralph Eugene Meatyard                                              368
Ernst Machs Max Ernst                                              373

# Acknowledgments

Most of these essays were called into being by editors and occasions. "The Symbol of the Archaic" was read at the University of Louisville as part of the Conference on Twentieth-Century Literature in 1974, and later that year at the University of Illinois. "The House that Jack Built" was the inaugural lecture to open the Yale Center for the Study of Ezra Pound and His Contemporaries, 30 October 1975. "The Geography of the Imagination" was the Distinguished Professor Lecture at the University of Kentucky for 1978. "Joyce's Forest of Symbols" was the Eberhardt Faber Lecture for 1973 at Princeton.

For permission to reprint I am grateful to *Perspective* and *The Georgia Review* for slightly different versions of "The Symbol of the Archaic"; to *Salmagundi* for "The House that Jack Built"; to *Arion,* Eva Hesse, Faber and Faber, and the University of California Press for "Persephone's

Ezra"; to *Parnassus* for "In Gloom on Watch-House Point" and *Bound-ary 2* for "Scholia and Conjectures for Olson's 'The Kingfishers'" (these two studies are combined here under the title "Olson"); to *National Review* and the Jargon Society for "Do You Have a Poem Book on E. E. Cummings"; to *National Review* for "*Poetry*'s Golden" (where it appeared as "National Poetry Festival: A Report"), part of the essay on Zukofsky which appeared there as "Happy Birthday, Wm. Shaxpar," a review of *Bottom*, part of the essay on Tchelitchew, which appeared there as "Romantic in an Unromantic Age," "Seeing Shelley Plain," "No, But I've Read the Book," "Wittgenstein," "Dictionary," and "The Pound Vortex"; to *Vort* for "Narrative Tone and Form"; to W. W. Norton and Co. and Sand Dollar Press for the two pieces on Ronald Johnson that are here combined as a single essay; to *The Iowa Review* for "Joyce's Forest of Symbols"; to *Arion* for "Another Odyssey" and "Ezra Pound 1885–1972; to *Aperture* for "Ralph Eugene Meatyard"; to *Parnassus* and *Paideuma* for two sections of "Zukofsky"; to *The Ballet Review* for part of "Tchelitchew"; to *The Hudson Review* for "Prehistoric Eyes," "The Indian and His Image," "The Man without Contemporaries," and "Where Poems Come From?" to *Parnassus* for "Whitman" and "Charles Ives"; to Beacon Press for "Louis Agassiz"; to the University of North Carolina Press and New Directions for "Jonathan Williams"; to *Inquiry* for "Christ's Cunning Rimesmith" and "Jack Yeats the Elder"; to *The New York Times* for "Ozymandias," "Trees," and "Hobbitry"; to *Perspective* for "Spinoza's Tulips"; to *New Literary History* for "Ernst Machs Max Ernst"; to *Antæus* for "Finding" and "The Anthropology of Table Manners from Geophagy Onward" and to New Directions for all the quotations throughout from Ezra Pound.

# The Geography
# of the Imagination

# The Geography
# of the Imagination

The difference between the Parthenon and the World Trade Center, between a French wine glass and a German beer mug, between Bach and
John Philip Sousa, between Sophocles and Shakespeare, between a bicycle and a horse, though explicable by historical moment, necessity, and
destiny, is before all a difference of imagination.

Man was first a hunter, and an artist: his earliest vestiges tell us that
alone. But he must always have dreamed, and recognized and guessed
and supposed, all skills of the imagination. Language itself is continuously an imaginative act. Rational discourse outside our familiar territory
of Greek logic sounds to our ears like the wildest imagination. The Dogon, a people of West Africa, will tell you that a white fox named Ogo
frequently weaves himself a hat of string bean hulls, puts it on his impudent head, and dances in the okra to insult and infuriate God Almighty,

and that there's nothing we can do about it except abide him in faith and patience.

This is not folklore, or a quaint custom, but as serious a matter to the Dogon as a filling station to us Americans. The imagination; that is, the way we shape and use the world, indeed the way we *see* the world, has geographical boundaries like islands, continents, and countries. These boundaries can be crossed. That Dogon fox and his impudent dance came to live with us, but in a different body, and to serve a different mode of the imagination. We call him Brer Rabbit.

We in America are more sensitive than most to boundaries of the imagination. Our arrival was a second one; the misnamed first arrivers must still bear a name from the imagination of certain Renaissance men, who for almost a century could not break out of the notion that these two vast continents were the Indies, itself a name so vague as to include China, India, and even Turkey, for which they named our most delicious bird.

The imagination has a history, as yet unwritten, and it has a geography, as yet only dimly seen. History and geography are inextricable disciplines. They have different shelves in the library, and different offices at the university, but they cannot get along for a minute without consulting the other. Geography is the wife of history, as space is the wife of time.

When Heraclitus said that everything passes steadily along, he was not inciting us to make the best of the moment, an idea unseemly to his placid mind, but to pay attention to the pace of things. Each has its own rhythm: the nap of a dog, the precession of the equinoxes, the dances of Lydia, the majestically slow beat of the drums at Dodona, the swift runners at Olympia.

The imagination, like all things in time, is metamorphic. It is also rooted in a ground, a geography. The Latin word for the sacredness of a place is *cultus,* the dwelling of a god, the place where a rite is valid. *Cultus* becomes our word *culture,* not in the portentous sense it now has, but in a much humbler sense. For ancient people the sacred was the vernacular ordinariness of things: the hearth, primarily; the bed, the wall around the yard. The temple was too sacred to be entered. Washing the feet of a guest was as religious an act as sharing one's meals with the gods.

When Europeans came to the new world, they learned nothing on the way, as if they came through a dark tunnel. Plymouth, Lisbon, Amsterdam, then the rolling Atlantic for three months, then the rocks and pines, sand and palms of Cathay, the Indies, the wilderness. A German cartographer working in Paris decided to translate the first name of Amerigo Vespucci into Latin, for reasons best known to himself, and call the whole thing America. In geography you have maps, and maps must have the names of places on them.

We new-world settlers, then, brought the imagination of other countries to transplant it in a different geography. We have been here scarcely a quarter of the time that the pharaohs ruled Egypt. We brought many things across the Atlantic, and the Pacific; many things we left behind: a critical choice to live with forever.

The imagination is like the drunk man who lost his watch, and must get drunk again to find it. It is as intimate as speech and custom, and to trace its ways we need to reeducate our eyes. In 1840—when Cooper's *The Pathfinder* was a bestseller, and photography had just been made practical—an essay called "The Philosophy of Furniture" appeared in an American magazine. Dickens made fun of Americans for attending lectures on the philosophy of anything, the philosophy of crime on Monday, the philosophy of government on Wednesday, the philosophy of the soul on Thursday, as Martin Chuzzlewit learned from Mrs. Brick. The English, also, we know from Thomas Love Peacock's satirical novels, were addicted to the lecture. The great French encyclopedia, its imitators, and the periodical press had done their work, and audiences were eager to hear anybody on any subject. Crowds attended the lectures of Louis Agassiz on zoology and geology (in 1840 he was explaining the Ice Age and the nature of glaciers, which he had just discovered); of Emerson, of transcendentalists, utopians, home-grown scientists like John Cleve Symmes, of Cincinnati, who explained that the globe is open at the poles and another world and another humanity resident on the concavity of a hollow earth; and even Thoreau, who gave lectures in the basements of churches.

This "Philosophy of Furniture" was by an unlikely writer: Edgar Allan Poe. In it he explains how rooms should be decorated. "We have no aristocracy of the blood," says this author who was educated at a university founded by Thomas Jefferson, "and having therefore as a natural, and indeed as an inevitable thing, fashioned for ourselves an aristocracy of dollars, the *display of wealth* has here to take the place and perform the office of the heraldic display in monarchial countries."

We are familiar with Poe's anxiety about good taste, about the fidelity of the United States to European models. What we want to see in this essay is a clue to the structure of Poe's imagination, which Charles Baudelaire thought the greatest of the century, an imagination so fine that Paul Valéry said it was incapable of making a mistake.

Poe's sense of good taste in decoration was in harmony with the best English style of the early Victorian period; we recognize his ideal room as one in which we might find the young Carlyles, those strenuous aesthetes, or George Eliot and Elizabeth Gaskell—a glory of wallpaper, figured rugs, marble-top tables, tall narrow windows with dark red curtains, sofas, antimacassars, vases, unfading wax flowers under bell jars, a rosewood piano, and a cozy fireplace. The amazing thing is that Poe emphasizes lightness and grace, color and clarity; whereas we associate his imagination with the most claustrophobic, dark, Gothic interiors in all of literature.

On our walls, Poe says, we should have many paintings to relieve the expanse of wallpaper—"a glossy paper of silver-grey tint, spotted with small arabesque devices of a fainter hue." "These are," he dictates, "chiefly landscapes of an imaginative cast—such as the fairy grottoes of Stanfield, or the lake of the Dismal Swamp of Chapman. There are, nevertheless, three or four female heads, of an ethereal beauty—portraits in the manner of Sully."

In another evocation of an ideal room, in a sketch called "Landor's Cottage" he again describes a wall with pictures: " . . . three of Julien's exquisite lithographs à trois crayons, fastened to the wall without frames. One of these drawings was a scene of Oriental luxury, or rather voluptuousness; another was a 'carnival piece', spirited beyond compare; the third was a Greek female head—a face so divinely beautiful, and yet of an expression so provokingly indeterminate, never before arrested my attention."

Poe titled the collection of his stories published that year *Tales of the Grotesque and Arabesque*. These two adjectives have given critics trouble for years. *Grotesque,* as Poe found it in the writings of Sir Walter Scott, means something close to *Gothic,* an adjective designating the Goths and their architecture, and what the neoclassical eighteenth century thought of mediæval art in general, that it was ugly but grand. It was the fanciful decoration by the Italians of grottoes, or caves, with shells, and statues of ogres and giants from the realm of legend, that gave the word *grotesque* its meaning of *freakish, monstrous, misshapen.*

*Arabesque* clearly means the intricate, nonrepresentational, infinitely graceful decorative style of Islam, best known to us in their carpets, the geometric tile-work of their mosques, and their calligraphy.

Had Poe wanted to designate the components of his imagination more accurately, his title would have been, *Tales of the Grotesque, Arabesque, and Classical.* For Poe in all his writing divided all his imagery up into three distinct species.

Look back at the pictures on the wall in his ideal rooms. In one we have grottoes and a view of the Dismal Swamp: this is the grotesque mode. Then female heads in the manner of Sully: this is the classical mode. The wallpapaer against which they hang is arabesque.

In the other room we had a scene of oriental luxury: the arabesque, a carnival piece spirited beyond compare (Poe means masked and costumed people, at Mardi Gras, as in "The Cask of Amontillado" and "The

Masque of the Red Death"): the grotesque, and a Greek female head: the classical.

A thorough inspection of Poe's work will disclose that he performs variations and mutations of these three vocabularies of imagery. We can readily recognize those works in which a particular idiom is dominant. The great octosyllabic sonnet "To Helen," for instance, is classical, "The Fall of the House of Usher" is grotesque, and the poem "Israfel" is arabesque.

But no work is restricted to one mode; the other two are there also. We all know the beautiful "To Helen," written when he was still a boy:

Helen, thy beauty is to me
Like those Nicaean barks of yore,
That gently, o'er a perfumed sea,
The weary, way-worn wanderer bore
To his own native shore.

On desperate seas long wont to roam,
Thy hyacinth hair, thy classic face,
Thy Naiad airs have brought me home
To the glory that was Greece
And the grandeur that was Rome.

Lo! in yon brilliant window niche
How statue-like I see thee stand,
The agate lamp within thy hand!
Ah, Psyche, from the regions which
Are Holy Land!

The words are as magic as Keats, but what is the sense? Sappho, whom Poe is imitating, had compared a woman's beauty to a fleet of ships. Byron had previously written lines that Poe outbyrons Byron with, in "the glory that was Greece / And the grandeur that was Rome." But how is Helen also Psyche; who is the wanderer coming home? Scholars are not sure. In fact, the poem is not easy to defend against the strictures of critics. We can point out that *Nicaean* is not, as has been charged, a pretty bit of gibberish, but the adjective for the city of Nice, where a major shipworks was: Marc Antony's fleet was built there. We can defend *perfumed sea,* which has been called silly, by noting that classical ships never left sight of land, and could smell orchards on shore, that perfumed oil was an extensive industry in classical times and that ships laden with it would smell better than your shipload of sheep. Poe is normally far more exact than he is given credit for.

That window-niche, however, slipped in from Northern Europe; it is Gothic, a slight tone of the grotto in this almost wholly classical poem.

And the closing words, "Holy Land," belong to the Levant, to the arabesque.

In "The Raven" we have a dominant grotesque key, with a vision of an arabesque Eden, "perfumed from an unseen censer / Swung by Seraphim whose footfalls tinkled on the tufted floor," and a grotesque raven sits on a classical bust of Pallas Athene. That raven was the device on the flag of Alaric the Visigoth, whose torch at Eleusis was the beginning of the end of Pallas's reign over the mind of man. Lenore (a name Walter Scott brought from Germany for his horse) is a mutation of Eleanor, a French mutation of Helen.

Were we to follow the metamorphoses of these images through all of Poe—grotesque, or Gothic; arabesque, or Islamic; classical, or Graeco-Roman—we would discover an articulate grammar of symbols, a new, as yet unread Poe. What we shall need to understand is the meaning of the symbols, and why they are constantly being translated from one imagistic idiom to another.

The clues are not difficult, or particularly arcane. Israfel for instance is an arabesque, and Roderick Usher a grotesque Orpheus; Orpheus himself does not appear in Poe in his native Greek self. But once we see Orpheus in Usher, we can then see that this masterpiece is a retelling of his myth from a point of view informed by a modern understanding of neuroses, of the inexplicable perverseness of the human will. That lute, that speaking guitar, all those books on Usher's table about journeys underground and rites held in darkness—all fit into a translation by Poe of a classical text into a Gothic one. "The Gold Bug," as Northrop Frye has seen, is strangely like the marriage of Danaë; the old black who lowers the gold bug is named Jupiter. Danaë was shut up in a treasure house and a riddle put her there.

Where do these images come from? The Mediterranean in the time of Columbus was from its western end and along its northern shore Graeco-Roman, what historians call the Latin culture, and at its eastern end, and along its southern shore, Islamic. So two thirds of Poe's triple imagery sums up the Mediterranean, and fed his imagination with its most congenial and rich portion. The Gothic style has its home in northern Europe, "my Germany of the soul" as Poe put it. He was always ambiguous about the culture with which, ironically, he is identified. Death, corruption, and dreariness inhere in the Gothic. Poe relates it to melancholia, hypersensitivity, madness, obsession, awful whirlpools in the cold sea, ancient houses spent and crumbling. Is there some pattern here from his own life? There is a real House of Usher, still standing, not in a gloomy Transylvanian valley by a black tarn, but in Boston, Massachusetts, where Poe was born, and where his barely remembered mother played the first Ophelia on an American stage, a rôle definitively Gothic in Poe's scheme of modes.[1]

Poe's sense of Islam, which we can trace to Byron and Shelley, derived as well from the explorers Burckhardt, Volney, and John Lloyd Stephens. The angel Israfel is not, as Poe wants us to believe, in the Koran, but from George Sale's introduction to his translation of the *Koran* by way of Thomas Moore.

The classical was being restated before Poe's eyes in Charlottesville by an old man who said he loved a particular Greek temple as if it were his mistress. Jefferson had the undergraduates up to dinner at Monticello two at a time, in alphabetical order. *P* is deep in the alphabet; Poe was expelled and the old man dead before the two most astute readers of Alexander von Humboldt in the United States could face each other over a platter of Virginia ham.

Poe's imagination was perfectly at home in geographies he had no knowledge of except what his imagination appropriated from other writers. We might assume, in ignorance, that he knew Paris like a Parisian, that Italy and Spain were familiar to him, and even Antarctica and the face of the moon.

The brothers Goncourt wrote in their journal as early as 1856 that Poe was a new kind of man writing a new kind of literature. We have still to learn that his sensibility was radically intelligent rather than emotional.

When he compares the eyes of Ligeia to stars, they are the binary stars that Herschel discovered and explained in the year of Poe's birth (the spectroscopic double Beta Lyra and the double double Epsilon Lyra, to be exact), not the generalized stars of Petrarchan tradition. We have paid too little attention to this metaphysical Poe; and we scarcely understand Europeans when they speak of the passion they find in his poetry. What are we to think of the Russian translator of Poe, Vladimir Pyast, who, while reciting "Ulalume" in a St. Petersburg theater, went stark raving mad? Russians treasure the memory of that evening.

Night after night, from 1912 to 1917, a man who might have been the invention of Poe, sat in a long, almost empty room in a working-class district of Berlin, writing a book by candle light. *Might have been the invention of Poe*—he was basically a classicist, his doctoral thesis was on Heraclitus, his mind was shaped by Goethe, Nietzsche, von Humboldt, and Leo Frobenius, the anthropologist and cultural morphologist. Like Poe, he thought in symbols.

He was Oswald Spengler. His big book, *The Decline of the West,* was meant to parallel the military campaigns of the Wermacht in 1914–1918,

[1]Fiske Kimball, *Domestic Architecture of the American Colonies and of the Early Republic* (New York: Dover, 1966), p. 275.

which by pedantic adherence to tactics and heroic fervor was to impose German regularity and destiny upon Europe. Spengler's book, like the Wermacht, imposed only a tragic sense that history is independent of our will, ironically perverse, and, a nightmare.

The value of *The Decline of the West* is in its poetry of vision, its intuition of the rise, growth, and decline of cultures. By culture Spengler meant the formative energy of a people, lasting for thousands of years. A civilization is the maturity of a culture, and inevitably its decline. His feeling for the effeteness of a finished culture was precisely that of Poe in "The Fall of the House of Usher" and "The Murders in the Rue Morgue"—both stories about the vulnerability of order and civilized achievement.

Spengler's most useful intuition was to divide world cultures into three major styles: the Apollonian, or Graeco-Roman; the Faustian, or Western-Northern European; and the Magian, or Asian and Islamic. Historians instantly complained that the cultures of our world may not be divided into three but into seventy-six distinct groups.

What interests us, however, is that Spengler's categories are exactly those of Edgar Allan Poe.

And those of James Joyce. Look at the first three stories of Joyce's *Dubliners*. The first is concerned with a violation of rites that derive from deep in Latin culture by way of the Roman Mass, the second takes its symbols from chivalry, the moral codes of Northern knighthood, and the third is named "Araby." This triad of symbolic patterns is repeated four more times, to achieve fifteen stories. The first three chapters of *Ulysses* also follow this structure, even more complexly; and the simplest shape to which we can summarize *Ulysses* is to say that it is about a man, Leopold Bloom, in a northern European, a Faustian-technological context, who is by heritage a Jew of Spengler's Magian culture, who is made to act out the adventures of Ulysses, exemplar of classical man.

"We have museum catalogues but no artistic atlases," the great French historian and cultural geographer Fernand Braudel complains in his *The Mediterranean and the Mediterranean World in the Age of Philip II,* "We have histories of art and literature but none of civilization."

He suspects that such a map of the arts would disclose the same kind of historical structure that he has demonstrated for food, clothing, trade routes, industrial and banking centers; and that our understanding of our imaginative life would take on as yet unguessed coherence and hitherto uncomprehended behavior.

Such a map would presumably display such phenomena as the contours of the worship of Demeter and Persephone, coinciding with grain-producing terrain, and with the contours of Catholicism. This would not surprise us. It might also show how the structure of psychology and drama nourished by grain-producing cultures persists outside that terrain, continuing to act as if it were inside, because its imaginative authority refuses to abdicate.

How else can we explain a story like O. Henry's "The Church with the Overshot Wheel"? In this poignant little tale, set in the pinewoods of North Carolina, a miller's daughter named Aglaia (a name commensurate with the style of naming girls in the Fancy Names Belt) is kidnapped by shiftless rovers who take her to Atlanta. The miller in his grief moves away to the Northwest, becomes prosperous and a philanthropist, naming his best brand of flour for his lost daughter whom he supposes to be dead. In her memory he has his old mill rebuilt as a church, endowing it handsomely, but keeping its overshot wheel. The community becomes a summer resort for people of modest means; and of course O. Henry has the orphan daughter come to it as a grown woman, and in a typical denouement, her memory of a song she used to sing as a child, together with an accidental spill of flour over her father, who is visiting the old mill, reunites them. O. Henry, perhaps unconsciously, has retold the myth of Persephone, using a name, Aglaia, "the bright girl," which was one of the epithets of Persephone, deification of wheat, and all the elements of the myth, transposed to twentieth-century America: the rape that brought devastation, the return and reunion that brought healing and regeneration.

I find an explanation of this story according to the theory of Jungian archetypes—patterns imprinted in the mind—unsatisfactory. It is better to trace O. Henry's plot and symbols backward along geographical lines, through myths brought across the Atlantic from the Mediterranean, through books and schoolrooms, through libraries and traditions, and to assess his story as a detail in the structure of a culture of strong vitality which decided on the expressiveness of certain symbols five thousand years ago, and finds them undiminished and still full of human significance.

The appeal of popular literature must lie precisely in its faithfulness to ancient traditions. The charming little children's book by Carlo Collodi, *Le Avventuri di Pinocchio,* can scarcely claim to be included in a history of Italian literature, and yet to a geographer of the imagination it is a more elegant paradigm of the narrative art of the Mediterranean than any other book since Ovid's *Metamorphoses,* rehearses all the central myths, and adds its own to the rich stock of its tradition. It reaches back to a Gnostic theme known to both Shakespeare and Emily Dickinson: "Split the stick," said Jesus, "and I am there." It combines Pygmalion, Ovid, the book of Jonah, the Commedia dell'Arte, and Apuleius; and will continue to be a touchstone of the imagination.

The discovery of America, its settlement, and economic development, were activities of the Renaissance and the Reformation, Mediterranean tradition and northern acumen. The continuities of that double heritage have been longlasting. The *Pequod* set out from Joppa, the first Thoreau was named Diogenes, Whitman is a contemporary of Socrates, the *Spoon River Anthology* was first written in Alexandria; for thirty years now our greatest living writer, Eudora Welty, has been rewriting Ovid in Mississippi. "The Jumping Frog of Calaveras County" was a turn for a fifth-century Athenian mime.

A geography of the imagination would extend the shores of the Mediterranean all the way to Iowa.

Eldon, Iowa—where in 1929 Grant Wood sketched a farmhouse as the background for a double portrait of his sister Nan and his dentist, Dr. B. H. McKeeby, who donned overalls for the occasion and held a rake. Forces that arose three millennia ago in the Mediterranean changed the rake to a pitchfork, as we shall see.

Let us look at this painting to which we are blinded by familiarity and parody. In the remotest distance against this perfect blue of a fine harvest sky, there is the Gothic spire of a country church, as if to seal the Protestant sobriety and industry of the subjects. Next there are trees, seven of them, as along the porch of Solomon's temple, symbols of prudence and wisdom.

Next, still reading from background to foreground, is the house that gives the primary meaning of the title, *American Gothic,* a style of architecture. It is an example of a revolution in domestic building that made possible the rapid rise of American cities after the Civil War and dotted the prairies with decent, neat farmhouses. It is what was first called in derision a balloon-frame house, so easy to build that a father and his son could put it up. It is an elegant geometry of light timber posts and rafters requiring no deep foundation, and is nailed together. Technically, it is, like the clothes of the farmer and his wife, a mail-order house, as the design comes out of a pattern-book, this one from those of Alexander Davis and Andrew Downing, the architects who modified details of the Gothic Revival for American farmhouses. The balloon-frame house was invented in Chicago in 1833 by George Washington Snow, who was orchestrating in his invention a century of mechanization that provided the nails, wirescreen, sash-windows, tin roof, lathe-turned posts for the porch, doorknobs, locks, and hinges—all standard pieces from factories.

We can see a bamboo sunscreen—out of China by way of Sears Roebuck—that rolls up like a sail: nautical technology applied to the prairie. We can see that distinctly American feature, the screen door. The sash-windows are European in origin, their glass panes from Venetian technology as perfected by the English, a luxury that was a marvel of the eighteenth century, and now as common as the farmer's spectacles, another revolution in technology that would have seemed a miracle to previous ages. Spectacles begin in the thirteenth century, the invention of either Salvino degl'Armati or Alessandro della Spina; the first portrait of a person wearing specs is of Cardinal Ugone di Provenza, in a fresco of 1352 by Tommaso Barisino di Modena. We might note, as we are trying to see the geographical focus that this painting gathers together, that the center for lens grinding from which eyeglasses diffused to the rest of civilization was the same part of Holland from which the style of the painting itself derives.

Another thirteenth-century invention prominent in our painting is the buttonhole. Buttons themselves are prehistoric, but they were shoulder-fasteners that engaged with loops. Modern clothing begins with the buttonhole. The farmer's wife secures her Dutch Calvinist collar with a cameo brooch, an heirloom passed down the generations, an eighteenth-century or Victorian copy of a design that goes back to the sixth century B.C.

She is a product of the ages, this modest Iowa farm wife: she has the hair-do of a mediæval madonna, a Reformation collar, a Greek cameo, a nineteenth-century pinafore.

Martin Luther put her a step behind her husband; John Knox squared her shoulders; the stock-market crash of 1929 put that look in her eyes.

The train that brought her clothes—paper pattern, bolt cloth, needle, thread, scissors—also brought her husband's bib overalls, which were originally, in the 1870s, trainmen's workclothes designed in Europe, manufactured here by J. C. Penney, and disseminated across the United States as the railroads connected city with city. The cloth is denim, from Nîmes in France, introduced by Levi Strauss of blue-jean fame. The design can be traced to no less a person than Herbert Spencer, who thought he was creating a utilitarian one-piece suit for everybody to wear. His own example was of tweed, with buttons from crotch to neck, and his female relatives somehow survived the mortification of his sporting it one Sunday in St. James Park.

His jacket is the modification of that of a Scots shepherd which we all still wear.

Grant Wood's Iowans stand, as we might guess, in a pose dictated by the Brownie box camera, close together in front of their house, the farmer looking at the lens with solemn honesty, his wife with modestly averted eyes. But that will not account for the pitchfork held as assertively as a minuteman's rifle. The pose is rather that of the Egyptian prince Rahotep, holding the flail of Osiris , beside his wife Nufrit—strict with pious rectitude, poised in absolute dignity, mediators between heaven and earth, givers of grain, obedient to the gods.

This formal pose lasts out 3000 years of Egyptian history, passes to some of the classical cultures—Etruscan couples in terra cotta, for instance—but does not attract Greece and Rome. It recommences in northern Europe, where (to the dismay of the Romans) Gaulish wives rode beside their husbands in the war chariot. Kings and eventually the merchants of the North repeated the Egyptian double portrait of husband and wife: van Eyck's Meester and Frouw Arnolfini; Rubens and his wife Helena. It was this Netherlandish tradition of painting middle-class folk with honor and precision that turned Grant Wood from Montparnasse, where he spent two years in the 1920s trying to be an American post-Impressionist, back to Iowa, to be our Hans Memling.

If Van Gogh could ask, "Where is my Japan?" and be told by Toulouse-Lautrec that it was Provence, Wood asked himself the whereabouts of his Holland, and found it in Iowa.

Just thirty years before Wood's painting, Edwin Markham's poem, "The Man with the Hoe" had pictured the farmer as a peasant with a life scarcely different from that of an ox, and called on the working men of the world to unite, as they had nothing to lose but their chains. The painting that inspired Markham was one of a series of agricultural subjects by Jean François Millet, whose work also inspired Van Gogh. A digging fork appears in five of Van Gogh's pictures, three of them variations on themes by Millet, and all of them are studies of grinding labor and poverty.

And yet the Independent Farmer had edged out the idle aristocrat for the hand of the girl in Royal Tyler's "The Contrast," the first native American comedy for the stage, and in Emerson's "Concord Hymn" it is a battle-line of farmers who fire the shot heard around the world. George III, indeed, referred to his American colonies as "the farms," and the two Georges of the Revolution, Hanover and Washington, were proudly farmers by etymology and in reality.

The window curtains and apron in this painting are both calico printed in a reticular design, the curtains of rhombuses, the apron of circles and dots, the configuration Sir Thomas Browne traced through nature and art in his *Garden of Cyrus,* the quincunxial arrangement of trees in orchards, perhaps the first human imitation of phyllotaxis, acknowledging the symmetry, justice, and divine organization of nature.

Curtains and aprons are as old as civilization itself, but their presence here in Iowa implies a cotton mill, a dye works, a roller press that prints calico, and a wholesale-retail distribution system involving a post office, a train, its tracks, and, in short, the Industrial Revolution.

That revolution came to America in the astounding memory of one man, Samuel Slater, who arrived in Philadelphia in 1789 with the plans of all Arkwright's Crompton's, and Hargreaves's machinery in his head, put himself at the service of the rich Quaker Moses Brown, and built the first American factory at Pawtucket, Rhode Island.

The apron is trimmed with rickrack ribbon, a machine-made substitute for lace. The curtains are bordered in a variant of the egg-and-dart design that comes from Nabataea, the Biblical Edom, in Syria, a design which the architect Hiram incorporated into the entablatures of Solomon's temple— "and the chapiters upon the two pillars had pomegranates also above, over against the belly which was by the network: and the pomegranates were two hundred in rows round about" (1 Kings 7:20) and which formed the border of the high priest's dress, a frieze of "pomegranates of blue, and of purple, and of scarlet, around about the hem thereof; and bells of gold between them round about" (Exodus 28:33).

The brass button that secures the farmer's collar is an unassertive, puritanical understatement of Matthew Boulton's eighteenth-century cut-steel button made in the factory of James Watt. His shirt button is mother-of-pearl, made by James Boepple from Mississippi fresh-water mussel shell, and his jacket button is of South American vegetable ivory passing for horn.

The farmer and his wife are attended by symbols, she by two plants on the porch, a potted geranium and sanseveria, both tropical and alien to Iowa; he by the three-tined American pitchfork whose triune shape is repeated throughout the painting, in the bib of the overalls, the windows, the faces, the siding of the house, to give it a formal organization of impeccable harmony.

If this painting is primarily a statement about Protestant diligence on the American frontier, carrying in its style and subject a wealth of information about imported technology, psychology, and aesthetics, it still does not turn away from a pervasive cultural theme of Mediterranean origin—a tension between the growing and the ungrowing, between vegetable and mineral, organic and inorganic, wheat and iron.

Transposed back into its native geography, this icon of the lord of metals with his iron sceptre, head wreathed with glass and silver, buckled in tin and brass, and a chaste bride who has already taken on the metallic thraldom of her plight in the gold ovals of her hair and brooch, are Dis and Persephone posed in a royal portrait among the attributes of the first Mediterranean trinity, Zeus in the blue sky and lightning rod, Poseidon in the trident of the pitchfork, Hades in the metals. It is a picture of a sheaf of golden grain, female and cyclical, perennial and the mother of civilization; and of metal shaped into scythe and hoe: nature and technology, earth and farmer, man and world, and their achievement together.

# The Symbol of the Archaic

Four years ago[1] there was discovered near Sarlat in the Dordogne the rib of an ox on which some hunter engraved with a flint burin seventy lines depicting we know not what: some god, some animal schematically drawn, a map, the turning of the seasons, the mensurations of the moon.

We have found in this lovely part of France many such prehistoric artifacts, carved bones, mysterious sceptres, rocks written over with lunar counts and seasonal notations and decorated with salmon, reindeer and seals, the lines of which are worn faint from being carried for ages in the hands of hunters.

Many of these objects, the engraving of which is not in the least primitive or unsophisticated, are fifty millennia old.

[1]In 1970. See François Bordes, *A Tale of Two Caves* (New York: Harper and Row, 1972), p. 62.

The ox rib found at Sarlat was published before a learned community in Toronto by Alexander Marshack (in a paper given to the American Anthropological Association in December 1972). Professor Hallam Movius, Professor Emeritus at the Peabody Museum of Archeology and Ethnology, Harvard, and a protégé of L'Abbé Henri Breuil, the most distinguished of prehistorians, believes it to be 100,000 years old. Alexander Marshack whose reading of prehistoric notation (*The Roots of Civilization*) is as brilliant and surprising as that of André Leroi-Gourhan (*Treasures of Prehistoric Art*), dates the Sarlat ox rib at 135,000 years, and its discoverer, François Bordes, Director of the Laboratory of Prehistory at the University of Bordeaux, places it at 230,000.

It is man's oldest known work of art, or plat of hunting rights, tax receipt, star map, or whatever it is.

Just a little over a century ago, John William Burgon, then an undergraduate at Worcester College, Oxford, wrote a poem about the desert city Petra, which the traveller Johann Ludwig Burckhardt had come upon thirty years before. Except for these magic lines, much anthologized, the poem has been forgotten, along with its poet:

> Not saintly grey, like many a minster fane
> That crowns the hill or sanctifies the plain:
> But rosy-red, as if the blush of dawn
> Which first beheld them were not yet withdrawn:
> The hues of youth upon a brow of woe,
> Which men called old two thousand years ago!
> Match me such marvel, save in Eastern clime,
> A rose-red city—half as old as time!

Shelley had put Petra in a poem as soon as Burckhardt discovered it: it is one of the places the wandering youth visits in *Alastor*; the others are taken from Volney's *Les Ruines* (1791), which had also inspired *Queen Mab* and *The Daemon of the World*. Burgon, stealing half a line from Samuel Rogers' *Italy*, makes Petra "half as old as time," for creation was still an event dated 4004 B.C.

The eighteenth century taught us to look at ruins with a particular *frisson*, to thrill to the depths of years in which we can stand. Volney at Persepolis and Palmyra, Gibbon in the Colosseum, Champollion at Thebes, Schliemann at Hissarlik and Mycenae were as symbolic of the attention of their age as Command Pilot Neil Armstrong on the moon of ours. The discovery of the physical past generated a deep awe and Romantic melancholy, positing a new vocabulary of images for poetry. Petra, carved in red Nabataean stone, became an image resonant with meaning. Without its name, and with a sharper *Angst* than Romantic wonder, it can still move us in Eliot's evocation in *The Waste Land:*

> . . . you know only
> A heap of broken images, where the sun beats,
> And the dead tree gives no shelter, the cricket no relief,
> And the dry stone no sound of water. Only
> There is shadow under this red rock
> (Come in under the shadow of this red rock). . . .

From the visits in 1678 and 1691 of English merchants to Palmyra, which they supposed to be the Biblical Tadmor, providing Gibbon with a sceptical footnote, Thomas Love Peacock with a fashion-setting poem, and the Romantic poetry of Europe with a new kind of image, to the present diligent science of archeology, a meditation on ruins has been a persistent theme. In our time we have Charles Olson's "The Kingfishers," the central poem in the Projectivist School of poets and a meditation on ruins, demonstrating that the form is far from exhausted. It is even *Volneyesque,* and, for all Olson's stringent modernity, can be read as an inquiry into the rise and fall of civilizations that continues a subject taken up in the earliest days of Romanticism.

Like his master Pound, Olson sees civilizations grow and perish against a continuum of nature, though he is modern enough to know that nature's moments are not really eternal; they are simply much longer than those of civilizations. Nature herself has her ruins, deserts, and flooded lands. Olson was writing poems about the drift of continents when he died.

Olson's "The Kingfishers" was inspired in part by Pablo Neruda's *Alturas de Machu Picchu,* a masterpiece among poems about ruins by a travelled poet who had been to Angkor Wat and the Athenian acropolis, Yucatan and Cuzco.

At the heart of Olson's poem is "the E on that oldest stone" meaning the epsilon on the omphalos stone at Delphi, which Plutarch puzzled over at the behest of Nero. We are still not certain whether it is part of the word, *Gea,* Earth, or part of a Greek citizen's name; Plutarch, always willing to be Pythagorean, gives many symbolic explanations, but for Olson the import of that conical, ancient stone was precisely that it is so ancient that we have lost the meaning of the writing upon it. When we discover what it means, we will still be dissociated forever from the complex of ideas in which it occurs.

And that is the center of Olson's concern in this poem, that culture is both historically and geographically discrete. "We are alien," Olson said, "from everything that was most familiar." This is a random statement from his late, inarticulate lectures, and like so many of the poet's Delphic utterances lies unexplained in a tangle of *non sequiturs.* Perhaps he felt that it was already elaborated by poets as different as Keats and Rimbaud, who had intuitions of a deep past which we have sacrificed for a tawdry and impious present; by Neruda and Prescott, men appalled by the brutality with which the indigenous cultures of the Americas were murdered. Olson was writing his poem while Europe still lay in ruins from the Second World War.

Olson was a poet with a frightening sense of where he was in time. He was one of the most original explicators of Melville, whose *Clarel* is among the great (and greatly neglected) meditations on ruins (of Christianity as well as of cultures which he suspected he might have found more congenial than his own, if mankind had allowed them to survive), and whose *Moby-Dick* was Olson's model for his vision of the long continuum of nature, the majesty of which belittles the diminutive empires of man—man, whose bulk is one twelve hundred and fiftieth of that of a whale, whose lifespan is a third of that of a goose, and whose advantages over his fellow creatures are all mechanical and therefore dependent on the education of each generation: meaning that an intervening generation of barbarians destroys all that has been carefully accumulated for centuries.

The unit of civilization is the city. The classical ages knew this so well that they scarcely alluded to it intellectually. Emotionally it was a fact which they honored with rites and a full regalia of symbols. The city appeared on their coins as a goddess crowned with battlements. She was the old grain goddess Cybele-Demeter, and it is clear that ancient men thought of the city as a culmination of a process that began among the cityless hunters who learned to pen cattle and live in the enclosure with them, who developed agriculture (the goddess's second gift, after the bounty of the animals) and made the city a focus of farms and roads.

About the time the Romantic poets were being most eloquent about ruined cities, the city itself was undergoing a profound change. The railroad was about to cancel the identity of each city, making them all into ports of trade, into warehouses and markets. Eliot's *Waste Land,* Joyce's *Ulysses,* Pound's *Cantos,* Bëly's *Petersburg,* all epics of city, appear at the same time as the automobile, the machine that stole the city's rationale for being, and made us all gypsies and barbarians camping in the ruins of the one unit of civilization which man has thus far evolved.

The city lasted from Jericho, Harappa, and the Çatal Hüyük to its ruin in Paterson, New Jersey (as one poet specified), from Troy to Dublin: Joyce's long chord. Pound in the *Cantos* makes another chord of meaning with the beginning and end of Venice, Europe's first outpost against the barbarians.

All of this is part of what Olson meant by saying that we are alienated from all that was most familiar. Basically he meant that we no longer milk the cow, or shoot the game for our dinner, or make our clothes or houses or anything at all. Secondly, he meant that we have drained our symbols of meaning. We hang religious pictures in museums, honoring a residual meaning in them, at least. We have divorced poetry from music, language from concrete particulars. We have abandoned the *rites de passage* to casual neglect where once we marked them with trial and ceremony.

Thirdly, he meant that modernity is a kind of stupidity, as it has no critical tools for analyzing reality such as the ancient cultures kept bright and sharp. We do not notice that we are ruled by the worst rather than the best of men: Olson took over a word coined by Pound, *pejorocracy*. Poetry and fiction have grieved for a century now over the loss of some vitality which they think they see in a past from which we are by now irrevocably alienated.

Joyce found in Vico cause to believe that Western civilization is at an end. Olson felt with Mao Tze Tung that the new vitality will come from the East. Pound considered us to be in a blank hiatus between cultures. So did Yeats, and perhaps Eliot. D. H. Lawrence looked for restorative forces deep in blood and genitals, longing for the color and robustness of the Etruscans.

All this pessimism and backward yearning has usually been counterbalanced and complemented by a kind of fulfillment. for in any characterization of the arts in our time we shall always want to say that if we have had a renaissance in the twentieth century, it has been a renaissance of the archaic.

Every age has had its sense of archaic time, usually mythological, usually at variance with history. It is man's worst ineptitude that he has not remembered his own past. Another way of saying this is that only at certain moments in cultures does man's past have any significance to him.

Go back to the Sarlat bone, possible 230,000 years old, with which we began. What would it have looked like to a seventeenth-century antiquarian? John Aubrey, we remember, thought Stonehenge to be the ruins of a Roman temple, and his patron Charles was satisfied with this information. When the Abbé Breuil petitioned UNESCO for funds after the Second World War to study the 20,000-year-old paintings in the Lascaux cave near Montignac (discovered in 1940 by Jacques Marsal's dog Robot, who was chasing a rabbit,) UNESCO refused, on the grounds that the paintings were obviously fraudulent.[2] Breuil had encountered the same incredulity for forty years.

There was, however, a silent believer from the beginning of his career, who saw prehistoric art with eyes which would influence all other eyes in

[2]That UNESCO thought Lascaux a hoax was conveyed to me by Mr. Lester Littlefield, who was an official there at the time of the Abbé Breuil's request.

our time. When Breuil was copying the ceiling of bulls in the Spanish cave Altamira, a young man from Barcelona crawled in beside him and marvelled at the beauty of the painting, at the energy of the designs. He would in a few years teach himself to draw with a similar energy and primal clarity, and would incorporate one of these enigmatic bulls into his largest painting, the *Guernica*. He was Pablo Picasso.

If we say, as we can, that the archaic is one of the great inventions of the twentieth century, we mean that as the first European renaissance looked back to Hellenistic Rome for a range of models and symbols, the twentieth century has looked back to a deeper past in which it has imagined it sees the very beginnings of civilization. The Laocoön was Michelangelo's touchstone; the red-stone *Kouros* from Sounion was Picasso's.

What is most modern in our time frequently turns out to be the most archaic. The sculpture of Brancusi belongs to the art of the Cyclades in the ninth century B.C. Corbusier's buildings in their cubist phase look like the white clay houses of Anatolia and Malta. Plato and Aristotle somehow mislaid the tetrahedron from among Pythagoras's basic geometric figures. Recovered by R. Buckminster Fuller, the tetrahedron turns out to be the basic building block of the universe. Pythagoras said that where two lines cross, the junction is two lines thick; Euclid said that lines can cross infinitely without any thickness at all. R. Buckminster Fuller constructs his tensegrities and geodesic domes with the firm notion that at their junction crossed lines are two lines thick.

Fuller, then, is our Pythagoras. Niels Bohr is our Democritus. Ludwig Wittgenstein is our Heraclitus. There is nothing quite so modern as a page of any of the pre-Socratic physicists, where science and poetry are still the same thing and where the modern mind feels a kinship it no longer has with Aquinas or even Newton.

*Ethos anthropoi daimon*, said Heraclitus, which may mean that our moral nature is a *daimon,* or guiding spirit from among the purified souls of the dead. Or it may be utterly primitive and mean that the weather is a god. *Character,* R. Buckminster Fuller seems to translate it, *is prevailing wind.* Pound: *Time is the evil.* Novalis: *Character is fate.* Wyndham Lewis: *The Zeitgeist is a demon.* Wittgenstein was paraphrasing it when he said (as if he were an Erewhonian): *Character is physique.*

In Heraclitus our most representative writers discovered a spirit congenial to their predicament as modern men. The neo-Epicurean philosopher Gassendi revived him, Nietzsche admired the elemental transparency of his thought, and we can now find him as a *genius loci* everywhere, in Hopkins, Spengler, Pound, William Carlos Williams, Eliot, Olson, Gertrude Stein.

It is not entirely Heraclitus's intuitive fusion of science and poetry that has made a modern philosopher of him; it is also his primacy in western thought. He has lasted.

The heart of the modern taste for the archaic is precisely the opposite of the Romantic feeling for ruins. Heraclitus, like the paintings at Lascaux, like the eloquent fragments of Sappho and Archilochos, has survived and thus become timeless. Picasso liked to say that modern art is what we have kept. To his eyes Brancusi *was* Cycladic; Stravinsky in the *Sacre du printemps* was a primitive Russian. Conversely, the bisque-colored, black-maned prancing tarpan of Lascaux, the very definition of archaic painting, is one of the most characteristic works of twentieth-century art, for quite literally ours are the first eyes to see it ever. It was painted in the deep dark of a cave by torchlight, an uncertainty to the man or woman who painted it. The best way to see it has always been as a color reproduction in a book; and now this is the only way to see it; twenty years of tourists' breaths caused bacteria to grow in the paint, and Lascaux, the most beautiful of the prehistoric caves, has been closed forever.

It has taken half the century for modern eyes to see the archaic. Cocteau dated this aesthetic adjustment from the year 1910, when Guillaume Apollinaire placed a Benin mask on his wall. Suddenly an image both ugly and disturbing, still bearing the name *fetish* which the Portuguese exploiters of Africa had given it, became a work of art which could hang in a museum beside a Hogarth or Rembrandt.

Apollinaire was not all that original. He was taking his cue from the German anthropologist Leo Frobenius, who had begun to argue that African art was neither primitive nor naive; it was simply the African style. Even before Apollinaire broadened his vision to see the sophistication and beauty of African art, the French sculptor Henri Gaudier-Brzeska had also read his Frobenius and was working in styles derived from Polynesia, Egypt, and ancient China. All he required of a style was that it be archaic; that is, in the primal stage of its formation, for Gaudier and his friend Pound had conceived the notion that cultures awake with a brilliant springtime and move through seasonal developments to a decadence. This is an idea from Frobenius, who had it from Spengler, who had it from Nietzsche, who had it from Goethe.

Archaic art, then, was springtime art in any culture. We can now see how Pound proceeded to study and imitate the earliest Greek poetry, the earliest Italian, the earliest Chinese. Pound culminated his long career by translating the Chinese *Book of Odes,* the first poems of which are archaic folksongs collected by Confucius.

And look at Canto I. It is a translation of the most archaic part of the *Odyssey:* the descent of Odysseus into Hades, a motif that goes all the way back to the Gilgamesh epic. And how does Pound translate it? Not from the Greek, but from the Latin of Andreas Divus, the first Renaissance translator of Homer, thereby working another archaic fact into his symbol. And into what kind of English does he translate it? Into the rhythms and diction of *The Seafarer* and *The Wanderer:* archaic English.

The modern grasp of the archaic happened first not in the appreciation of modern art but in the attempt to recover the archaic genius of the language itself: in the sense William Barnes and Frederick James Furnivall developed of a pure, mother English which would eschew Latinisms and Renaissance coinages—a kind of linguistic Pre-Raphaelitism that wanted to circumvent the Europeanization of English.

The first fruits of this enthusiasm were Gerard Manley Hopkins, whose English is purer even than Spenser's, and the great unknown of English letters, Charles Montagu Doughty, who suspected all writers after Chaucer of whoring after strange dictionaries, who went into the Arabian desert (or "Garden of God")—the most archaic act of modern literature—to save, as he said, the English language.

That salvation is still one of the best of books, the *Travels in Arabia Deserta,* though we have neglected his masterpiece, *The Dawn in Britain,* with its archaic theme and its archaic English.

When in *Ulysses* Joyce writes a chapter in English that evolves from its most archaic to the most modern and slangy styles, he conceals in his parody of Carlyle, the Victorian archaicist, the phrase "A doughty deed, Purefoy!" to let us know that he is keeping the faith. Joyce's rigorous sense of correspondences places him foremost, or at least alongside Picasso, in the century's equation of archaic and modern. Like Pound and Kazantzakis he wrote his epic across the most ancient pages of Western literature, the *Odyssey,* and in *Finnegans Wake* writes across the fact of the Indo-European origin of European languages, seeing in the kinship of tongues the great archeological midden of history, the tragic incomprehensibility of which provides him with a picture of the funeral of Western culture.

One sure principle of *Finnegans Wake* is that it always holds in its puns the modern and the archaic. A street full of traffic is also a panorama of prehistoric places and animals: *". . . the wallhall's horrors of rollsrights, carhacks, stonengens, kisstvanes, tramtrees, fargobawlers, autokinotons, hippohobbilies, streetfleets, tournintaxes, megaphoggs, circuses and wardsmoats and basilikerks and aeropagods. . . ."*

While Joyce was discovering how to make a Heraclitean circle of the modern and the archaic, joining the end to the beginning, Velimir Khlebnikov in Russia was making a similar fusion of old and new, opening words etymologically, reviving Old Russian, and treating themes from folklore, all in the name of the most revolutionary modernity. His friend Vladimir Tatlin, who liked to call himself the Khlebnikov of constructivist art, spent thirty years trying to build and fly Leonardo da Vinci's ornithopter. And what is the only surviving example of Russian Futurism, Lenin's tomb, but the tumulus of a Scythian king combined with an Egyptian *mastaba,* complete with mummy?

Behind all this passion for the archaic, which is far more pervasive in the arts of our time than can be suggested here, is a longing for something lost, for energies, values, and certainties unwisely abandoned by an industrial age. Things, Proust says, are gods, and one way our arts seem to regard our world is to question what gods have come to dwell among us in the internal combustion engine, the cash register, and the computer.

One answer to this question lies in a single rich symbol which is of such ambiguity that we can read only part of its meaning. It is an elusive symbol, to be traced on the wing. We can begin with the mysterious painting *Hide and Seek* by the Russian painter Pavel Tchelitchew. This enormous painting (now in the Museum of Modern Art) is a pictorial equivalent of the method of *Finnegans Wake.* All of its images are puns which resolve into yet other punning images. First of all, it is a great oak tree against which a girl presses herself: she is the *it* in a game of hide-and-seek. The hiders are concealed in the tree itself, so many children, who are arranged like the cycle of the seasons, winter children, summer children.

These children, seen a few paces back, become landscapes, and eventually two folded arms, as the tree itself resolves into a foot and hand; and, further back, the face of a Russian demon, mustached and squint-eyed. Further back, the whole picture resolves into a drop of water— Leeuwenhoek's drop of water under the microscope in which he discovered a new world of little animals; the drop of crystal dew on a leaf at morning which acts like Borges's *aleph* or Blake's grain of sand or any Leibnizean monad mirroring the whole world around it; Niels Bohr's drop of water the surface tension of which led him to explain the structure of the atom.

This is a very modern picture, then, a kind of metaphysical poem about our non-Euclidean, indeterminate world. But at its center there is the one opaque detail in the painting: the girl in a pinafore hiding her face against the tree.

She is, let us say, the same girl who as Alice went into the Freudian dark called Wonderland and through the looking glass into the reflected, dimensionless realm of word and picture. She is Undine, Ciceley Alexander, Rima, Clara d'Ellébeuse, Grigia, Ada. She is Anna Livia Plurabelle, the Persephone of Pound's *Cantos,* Brancusi's "Maiastra" birds, the women in Antonioni's films. She is a symbolic figure who serves in the imagery of modern art as the figure of Koré in the rites of Demeter of the ancient world.

A catalogue of her appearances will disclose that she emerges in Romantic literature toward the beginning of the nineteenth century. If we say that she is a symbol of the soul, we do not mean that she is consciously so except in the imagination of writers who, like Dino Campana, Proust, Joyce, and Pound, were aware of her persistence and pervasiveness. She appears as a half-acknowledged ghost in Poe, who knew that she came from the ancient world and named her Ligeia and Helen. She is all but wholly disguised in Ruskin, where her name is Rose and where her new Hades, the industrial world, is accurately identified.

Picasso depicts her with proper iconography, a girl carrying a dove—the Sicilian Persephone—and places her near a Minotaur, his symbol for a world half brutal. She is a constant figure in the fiction of Eudora Welty, who is aware of her transformation into Eurydice, Helen, Pandora, Aphrodite, Danaë, Psyche. She is the magic female phantom in Jules Laforgue and Gérard de Nerval, in Rilke and Leopardi.

An ambiguous symbol of life and death, she is Odette de Crécy as Swann imagines her in love: a girl from Botticelli, a lyrical phrase in Vinteuil's sonata, a flower. But she is also the depraved Odette whose music is not Vinteuil but Offenbach's *Orfée aux enfers,* a witch of sensuality and deception, a *fleur du mal.*

In an age when the human spirit is depressed and constrained, this symbol of the soul is a depiction of Persephone or Eurydice in Hades. In a euphoric or confident time, she is above-ground: a Beatrice, an Aphrodite. Knowing this, we can read Rossetti's paintings and Swinburne's poems as hymns to the soul underground, the soul sunk in ungrowing matter, allied with sterile gold and crystal, but itself, like Persephone, a seed with the power to reach upward to the light.

This light is the principle counter to dark, the sun, Demeter's torch, Orpheus's lyre, man's regard for the earth's resources and the Themis of heaven. Where the soul is depressed beyond hope, we have a Poe writing a black parody of the myth of Orpheus and Eurydice: Roderick Usher with his hypersensitive lute and his schizophrenic, Hamlet-like indecision, whose will is rotten and perverse, who is terrified by existence itself and diabolically puts his Eurydice in Hades and spinelessly leaves her there.

In Roderick Usher we see the emergence of the symbolic gear of the complementary myth which runs alongside that of Persephone-Eurydice in modern art. That lute will turn up on the Cubist table-top, in the iconography of Cocteau and Apollinaire, in Rilke and de Nerval.

It will, with idiotic faithfulness, turn up on the study table of Sherlock

Holmes, along with Usher's opium and erudite books about subterranean journeys. But then we remember that Holmes is Roderick Usher all over again, with Auguste Dupin thrown in (Dupin, who could not find a Persephone named Marie Roget, but could identify the dark power which raped the ladies on the Rue Morgue), and that Holmes is also derived from the man who drew the gaudiest picture of subterranean Persephone in the nineteenth century, saying that she is older than the rocks among which she sits, that like the vampire she has been dead many times and learned the secrets of the grave: the man who retold the myth of Cupid and Psyche for the nineteenth century, Walter Pater.

Orpheus, then, is one archaic ghost we have revived and put to work bringing us out of the sterile dark; and Persephone in many disguises is our way of seeing the soul lost and in trouble.

Persephone's most powerful evocations are in Joyce and Pound, as Molly Bloom and Anna Livia, and as Pound's Homeric array of women, Pre-Raphaelite of beauty and Pre-Raphaelite of distress. For Pound these women are symbols of the power of regeneration. Lucrezia Borgia is among them, a literal queen of death who had her springtime at the end of her life, the reformed Este Borgia. Madame Hylé, Pound calls her: Lady Nature, who takes the shape of tree or animal only through a cooperation with light.

For Joyce the regeneration of the spirit is a cyclic female process, like the self-purifying motion of a river. One of Joyce's strong themes is the human paralysis of will that stubbornly resists regeneration, and Anna Livia at the end of *Finnegans Wake* is resisting her plunge into the sea much as Eveline in *Dubliners* balks at changing her life, though the triumphant Molly Bloom, Demeter and Persephone together, cries out at one point to her creator, "O Jamesy let me up out of this!"

Once this theory is sorted out and anatomized, we shall see that the artists for whom the soul in plight can be symbolized as Persephone surround her with an imagery of green nature, especially the flowering tree which was one of her forms in the ancient Mediterranean world. Joyce, Tchelitchew, and Pound are clear examples of this correspondence of tree and maiden; so are Ruskin and Lewis Carroll, Francis Jammes and Proust, Yeats and Jules Supervielle.

The poets who replace Persephone with Eurydice work under the sign of the lute of Orpheus: Laforgue, Rilke, Poe, and we should not hesitate to add Braque, Orff, and Picasso.

And if we ask why our artists have reached back to such archaic symbols to interpret the distress of mind and soul in our time, there are partial but not comprehensive answers. One reason, I suggest, is the radical change in our sense of what is alive and what isn't. We have recovered in anthropology and archeology the truth that primitive man lives in a world totally alive, a world in which one talks to bears and reindeer, like the Laplanders, or to Coyote, the sun and moon, like the plains Indians.

In the seventeenth century we discovered that a drop of water is alive, in the eighteenth century that all of nature is alive in its discrete particles, in the nineteenth century that these particles are all dancing a constant dance (the Brownian movement), and the twentieth century discovered that nothing at all is dead, that the material of existence is so many little solar systems of light mush, or as Einstein said, ". . . every clod of earth, every feather, every speck of dust is a prodigious reservoir of entrapped energy."

We had a new vision that death and life are a complementary pattern. Darwin and Wallace demonstrated this, but in ways that were more disturbing than enlightening, and Darwin's vision seemed destitute of a moral life. The nearest model for a world totally alive was the archaic era of our own culture, pre-Aristotelian Greece and Rome. From that world we began to feel terribly alienated, as the railroad tracks went down and the factories up, as our sciences began to explain the mechanics of everything and the nature of nothing.

The first voices of protest which cried that man is primarily a spirit, the voices of Blake, Shelley, and Leopardi, sounded sufficiently deranged, and we had to hear the equally dubious voices of Nietzsche, Freud, and Jung before we could begin seriously to listen.

It was, however, the artists who were performing the great feat of awakening an archaic sense of the world. The first effort was a clear outgrowth of Renaissance neoclassicism and led to a revolution in which the themes were subversively rejuvenated: Shelley's Platonism, for instance, and Blake's kitchen-forged mythology, the metacultural visions of a Novalis or Baudelaire.

The second effort can be called the Renaissance of 1910, which recognized the archaic. Hilda Doolittle, Pound, and Williams could catalyze poetry by returning to the Greek fragment, to archaic simplicity, to a sense of reality that was fresh because it had been so long neglected. Brancusi, Gaudier-Brzeska, Modigliani, Picasso turned to the energy and liveliness of primitive art. The piano, Stravinsky announced, was a percussion instrument, like a drum from the jungle. The artist Wyndham Lewis said, looking at prehistoric paintings that seemed to be excused from the ravages of time, the artist goes back to the fish.

Whether, indeed, the century's sense of the archaic served to alleviate our alienation from what was once most familiar, or whether it put our alienation into even starker contrast to ages in which we romantically suppose man to have lived more harmoniously and congenially with his gods and with nature, it is too early to say. Certainly it has deepened our tragic sense of the world, and set us on a search to know what the beginnings of our culture were. Only our age has prepared itself to feel the significance of an engraved ox rib 230,000 years old, or to create and respond to a painting like Picasso's *Guernica*, executed in allusion to the style of Aurignacian reindeer hunters of 50,000 years ago.

On the other hand, our search for the archaic may have contributed to our being even more lost. For the search is for the moment now over in the arts, and our poets are gypsies camping in ruins once again. Persephone and Orpheus have reverted to footnotes in anthologies. The classic sense of the city perished rather than revived in the Renaissance of 1910, which had spent its initial energies by 1914, and was exhausted by 1939, the year of the publication of *Finnegans Wake* and of the beginning of the second destruction of the world in twenty-five years.

Some of the masters lived on. Pound wrote two more masterpieces. Picasso continued, filling eighty years of his life with work, completing a painting every seventy-two hours of that time.

Men have walked on the moon, stirring dust that had not moved since millennia before the archaic hand carved the images on the Sarlat bone which mean nothing to our eyes. The world that drove Ruskin and Pound mad has worsened in precisely the ways they said it would. Eliot's wasteland has extended its borders; Rilke's freakshow outside which the barker invites us to come in and see the genitals of money is a feature of every street. Never has an age had more accurate prophets in its writers and painters.

The donation remains, to be assessed and understood, and the discovery, or invention, of the archaic is as splendid a donation as that of Hellenism to the Renaissance. We are just now seeing, amidst the fads and distractions, the strange fact that what has been most modern in our time was what was most archaic, and that the impulse to recover beginnings and primal energies grew out of a feeling that man in his alienation was drifting tragically away from what he had first made as poetry and design and as an understanding of the world.

Here are Ezra Pound's last lines:

Poetry speaks phallic direction
Song keeps the word forever
Sound is moulded to mean this
And the measure moulds sound.[3]

This is a translation from an archaic Chinese text, explaining that poetry is a voice out of nature which must be rendered humanly intelligible, so that people can know how to live.

[3]Hugh Kenner, *The Pound Era* (Berkeley and Los Angeles: University of California Press, 1971), p. 104.

# Another Odyssey

Salvatore Quasimodo translates the three lines that begin the third book
of the *Odyssey:*

> Il sole, lasciata la serena distesa dell'acqua,
> si levò verso il cielo di rame a illuminare gli dèi
> e gli uomini destinati alla morte sulla terra feconda.

What Eélios departs from here is not *thálassa* or *póntos* but *límne,* an
inlet of the sea. The word later comes to mean a marsh or pooled tidewa-
ter, and is also used to mean a lake. Telemakhos and Athena are sailing
into the Bay of Navarino where they see the sacrifices at Pylos of the
Sands; the poet calls the bay a *límne,* and adds that it is very beautiful,
*perikalléa.* Signor Quasimodo folds these two images together as *la
serena distesa dell'acqua* as smoothly as he takes *polýkhalkon* as a color

29

adjective describing the glaring dawn sky. Richmond Lattimore gives *límne* the first meaning offered by the Revs. Liddell and Scott, "standing water":

> Helios, leaving behind the lovely standing waters, rose up.[1]

As for the sky, Professor Lattimore calls it "brazen," as do Samuel Henry Butcher and Andrew Lang, Robert Fitzgerald, William Cullen Bryant, and William Morris. Chapman understands the adjective to include both the hardness and gleam of bronze:

> The Sunne now left the great and goodly Lake,
> And to the firme heav'n bright ascent did make.

English words, Joseph Conrad complained, say more than you want them to say. "Oaken," for instance, has overtones which force one to say in remarking that a table is *de chêne,* that it is also solid and British. "Brazen" and "standing waters" are not phrases that a stylist, poet or prose writer, would consider without making certain that he wanted the overtones as well. Except, of course, when he is asking the reader to agree that he is writing in a high style the dignity of which prevents one from imagining anything but the purest lexicographic content of every word. Such a request might be backed up by asking the reader to keep well in mind at all times that the text before him tranlates a great poem, said by people who know to be magnificent. With such an understanding between translator and reader, the translator can then write "immortals" where Homer has *athánatoi* and "mortals" where Homer has *thnetoî* and forget that the two words were worn out years ago. A translator who dares not ask such an agreement feels compelled to convey the sharpness of the Greek. Signor Quasimodo has seen the interplay in the homily, has thought about it, and puts it into seamless contemporary words: the sun shines on the gods and on men who must someday die and on the fecund earth. Chapman manages to keep the two possible meanings of *zeídoros,* giver of life or giver of *zeia,* one of the most primitive of grains:

> To shine as well upon the mortall birth
> Inhabiting the plowd life-giving earth
> As on the ever-tredders upon Death.

Lattimore's "mortal men," Quasimodo's "gli uomini destinati alla morte," Chapman's "ever-tredders upon Death"—which replaces a Greek word with a dictionary equivalent and which tries to unfold the Greek sense?

"Show me," Wittgenstein liked to say, "how a man uses a word and I'll

[1]Richmond Lattimore, trans., *The Odyssey of Homer,* (New York: Harper and Row, 1967).

tell you what he really thinks about it." No word in a context can have more meaning than the writer thinks into it. When a writer does not care about the meaning of a word, we know it. We also know *how* a man cares about words; we know from his words what he honors, what he is unaware of, and how he modifies with his individual use of it the culture in which he exists. When, for instance, William Cullen Bryant translates the passage we are looking at,

> Now from the fair broad bosom of the sea
> Into the brazen vault of heaven the sun
> Rose shining for the immortals and for men
> Upon the foodful earth,

we see the translator shying away from particular description. He has a bay and a plowed field that he is content to render invisible; he introduces a bosom and a vault; and he is not afraid that in recitation the audience will hear "foodful" as a tongue-twisted "fruitful." There is a kind of thanksgiving piety in Bryant. The sea is a bosom (Homer elsewhere calls it unharvestable); the firmament is a bit of decorative architecture which we should no doubt stand in awe of; and the sun shines *for* gods and men. Homer merely says that it shines on them. Professor Lattimore has the sun shining on gods and men but *across* the grain field—a gratuitous angle that shows us that a grain field for Professor Lattimore is a pretty landscape primarily and the source of life secondarily.

Robert Fitzgerald sees the generosity of the sun:

> —all one brightening
> for gods immortal and for mortal men
> on plowlands kind with grain,

and hides altogether the idea of death and fecundity occurring together under the eyes of the gods and the indifferent sun. Mr. Fitzgerald likes to freeze time when he comes to the lovely passages, savoring a still beauty; Homer's very beautiful bay is "the flawless brimming sea." He removes Homer's shadows and makes the scene golden, "kind with grain."

If you don't care about words at all, it can be translated thus:

> As the sun rose from the beautiful mere of the sea
> To climb to the brazen heaven and shine with his light
> On gods and on men that inhabit the grain-giving earth.

This is simply a rewording (executed in 1948 by S. O. Andrew) of William Morris's

> Now uprose the Sun, and leaving the exceeding lovely mere
> Fared up to the brazen heaven, to the Deathless shining clear,
> And unto deathful men on the corn-kind earth that dwell.

Morris was at least trying to keep the reader aware that the poem is of an age. Mr. Andrew has sealed himself up in himself and is having a wonderful time.

But back to Professor Lattimore. Here is the beginning of the account of the hunt on Parnassos where Odysseus was scarred by the boar:

> But when the young Dawn showed again with her rosy fingers,
> they went out on their way to the hunt, the dogs and the people,
> these sons of Autolykos, and with them noble Odysseus went.

Is it not a bit chewing-gummy to say that Dawn showed? Johnson gives ten definitions of "show," none of which sanctions this suppressed reflexive, and Fowler clucks his tongue if consulted on the matter. Webster's Third International describes the intransitive "show" and takes its example of usage from H. A. Sinclair: "I'm glad you showed, kid." And "out on their way"? As for the "went," that's where Homer put it. And dear rosy-fingered Dawn, she turns up in *The Faerie Queene* about the time Chapman was putting her into his *Iliads;* it's a toss-up as to who stole her from whom. She is the Kilroy of Homeric translation.

Professor Lattimore continues:

> They came to the steep mountain, mantled in forest,
> Parnassos, and soon they were up in the windy folds.

(Colonel Lawrence has "wind-swept upper folds"; Morris, "windy ghylls.")

> At this time
> the sun had just begun to strike on the plowlands, rising
> out of the quiet water and the deep stream of the Ocean.
> The hunters came to the wooded valley, and on ahead of them
> ran the dogs, casting about for the tracks, and behind them
> the sons of Autolykos, and with them noble Odysseus
> went close behind the hounds, shaking his spear far-shadowing.
> Now there, inside that thick of the bush, was the lair of a great boar.
> Neither could the force of wet-blown winds penetrate here,
> nor could the shining sun ever strike through with his rays, nor yet
> could the rain pass all the way through it, so close together
> it grew, with a fall of leaves drifted in dense profusion.
> The thudding made by the feet of men and dogs came to him
> as they closed on him in the hunt, and against them he from his woodlair
> bristled strongly his nape, and with fire from his eyes glaring
> stood up to face them close.

"Plowlands" is an archaic word, once an exact measure. "The quiet water . . . of the Ocean" avoids the traditional "soft-blowing," but what does it mean? Surely Homer meant to describe a calm sea, not to calculate the amount of noise it was making. "Casting about for the tracks"—here Professor Lattimore should have kept to Liddell and Scott, who say "casting about for the scent." Dogs do not follow tracks, a visual skill, but the smell of their prey. Why "noble" Odysseus? He is no nobler than his uncles, and to single him out with such a word seems to put him in contrast to his very family. He's a stripling here; surely Homer means "charming" or "handsome."

Professor Lattimore in his faithfulness places himself at the mercy of the merciless Greek language. His boar "bristled strongly his nape, and with fire from his eyes glaring / stood up to face them close." The verb is most certainly "bristled" and the noun "nape," but a boar is a very special kind of animal whose bristling is a thing unto itself, and his nape, like a snake's neck, is more a word than a reality. The very same words might be used of a cat, and we would have to translate "camelled his back and bushed." A boar bunches his shoulders. He *hackles.* He *burrs up.* Mr. Fitzgerald has:

> with razor back bristling and raging eyes
> he trotted and stood at bay.

Splendid, that "trotted and stood." Professor Lattimore has the boar lying down until the dogs are at his door, which is a bit cool even for such an insolent beast as this one.

Here is how Mr. Fitzgerald begins the boar hunt:

> When the young Dawn spread in the eastern sky
> her finger tips of rose,

(Both Chapman and Pope ducked having to do something with a *rhododaktylos Eos* here, Chapman looking to the sun's heat and Pope to its color for a paraphrase. Chapman knows his out-of-doors, and has not forgotten that the hunters have just spent the night on the ground; Pope saw the dawn through windows; Fitzgerald, writing in a century whose every gesture is timed, adds motion to the venerable epithet.)

> the men and dogs
> went hunting, taking Odysseus.

(Odysseus loses his *dios,* and the sons of Autolykos their patronymic: no matter—that information is well-established, and Mr. Fitzgerald doesn't need *formulae.*)

> They climbed
> Parnassos' rugged flank mantled in forest,

(Pope's "Parnassus, thick-perplex'd with horrid shades" has alternately an English and a Latin word: what we are looking at is a line of Vergil every other word of which has been glossed into English. Homer, we might note, is at some distance, and his more cultivated imitator has the stage.)

> entering amid high windy folds at noon
> when Hêlios beat upon the valley floor
> and on the winding ocean whence he came.

(The "amid" is not current English; "fold" is not good American, but British [Lawrence: "wind-swept upper folds"]; and is it at noon or just after sunrise that they reach the high gorges? The "winding" is taken from Homeric cosmography rather than from the text, which says "deep." But what a clear, solidly paced three lines! Bryant's ". . . airy heights. The sun, new risen / From the deep ocean's gently flowing stream, / Now smote the fields" misses the look of a great mountain, tries [like Fitzgerald] to tuck in Homer's earth-encircling ocean and makes a mess of it—the kind of paralytic total miss with an image that drives clever children and the literal-minded away from poetry altogether. Yet genteel readers in Bryant's day took that "stream" as a refinement, and the "gently," their experience of the sea to the contrary, as evidence of Bryant's higher soul. The version reaches solid ground with the Biblical "smote." But Bryant is simply Wordsworthing around here; four words on he's talking about "a dell.") Fitzgerald continues:

> With hounds questing ahead, in open order,
> the sons of Autólykos went down a glen,
> Odysseus in the lead, behind the dogs,
> pointing his long-shadowing spear.

Fitzgerald deploys dogs and hunters in a forward motion: "questing ahead . . . in the lead . . . pointing"; Professor Lattimore scatters the motion: "casting about . . . behind them . . . close behind . . . shaking." There is an outwardness to Fitzgerald's rhythms that makes Lattimore sound distinctly bumpy.

Translation involves two languages; the translator is in constant danger of inventing a third that lies between, a treacherous nonexistent language suggested by the original and not recognized by the language into which the original is being transposed. The Greek says "of Odysseus the loved son," and Professor Lattimore translates "the dear son of Odysseus." Who uses such language in English? Chapman's "Ulysses' lov'd sonne" seems more contemporary. Bryant says "dear son," perhaps with an impunity that we feel we ought to withhold from Professor Lattimore. I once dined with Professor Lattimore and he did not speak like William Cullen Bryant. He spoke a charming and fluent and even racy colloquial English.

If we take everything in Greek in a literal, grammar-book sense, obviously we are going to come up with some strange locutions. If Homer says "And in his hand he had a bronze spear," by what determined deafness to English must Professor Lattimore write "in his hands holding a bronze spear?" The verb is "have," not "hold." One may say "in his hand a bronze spear," or "holding a bronze spear," but not a mixture of the two. And why "hands"? The Greek is "hand." To read Professor Lattimore's *Odyssey* we must simply accept the curious fact that he is writing in a neutralized English wholly devoid of dialect, a language concocted for the purpose of translating Homer. It uses the vocabulary of English but not its rhythm. It has its own idiom. One can say in this language such things as "slept in that place in an exhaustion of sleep" (for Homer's "aching with fatigue and weary for lack of sleep"), and "the shining clothes are lying away uncared for" (for "your laundry is tossed in a heap waiting to be washed").

Professor Lattimore adheres to the literal at times as stubbornly as a mule eating briars. When, for instance, the Kyklops dines on Odysseus's men, he washes his meal down with "milk unmixed with water." But why would anyone, except a grocer, water milk? The word that makes the milk seem to be watered is the same as the one that turns up in the phrase "unmixed wine," meaning neat. But even there the wine is unmixed because it is for dipping bread into; so the word comes to take on the latter meaning. What the homely Kyklops was doing was dipping the meat in his milk.

There is a chill puritanism about Professor Lattimore's program: which is to render the *Odyssey ad verbum* into English. Tone be damned, rhythm and pace be damned, idiom (like the milk for dunking) be damned; this version is going to be punctiliously lexicographic. I need not labor the truism that the literal translator can be at a great spiritual distance from his original, and I realize that this is something of a galling paradox. Of the two most exciting translations from Homer in recent years, one, Robert Fitzgerald's, is as accurate as that of Professor Lattimore's, but it is not obsessed with a verbal game as desperate as Russian roulette; the other, that of Christopher Logue, departs from Homer's words altogether (so do all other translators, for that matter) and reconstructs the action as his genius dictates. Look at a passage near the beginning of the nineteenth book of the *Iliad* as translated by Lattimore and Logue. Lattimore:

> The goddess spoke so, and set down the armour on the ground
> before Achilleus, and all its elaborations clashed loudly.
> Trembling took hold of all the Myrmidons. None had the courage
> to look straight at it. They were afraid of it. Only Achilleus

looked, and as he looked the anger came harder upon him
and his eyes glittered terribly under his lids, like sunflare.

Logue:

> And as she laid the moonlit armour on the sand it chimed:
>     and the sounds that came from it
> followed the light that came from it,
>         like sighing,
>             saying,
>                 Made in Heaven.
> And those who had the neck to watch Achilles weep
> could not look now. Nobody looked. They were afraid.
>
>     Except Achilles. Looked,
> lifted a piece of it between his hand; turned it;
> tested the weight of it; then,
> spun the holy tungsten like a star between his knees,
> slitting his eyes against the flare, some said,
> but others thought the hatred shuttered by his lids
>     made him protect the metal.
>
> His eyes like furnace doors ajar.

We have all been taught to prefer the former, out of a shy dread before
Homer's great original; we instinctively, if we have ever felt a line of
poetry before, prefer the latter. And the kind of paranoia fostered by
graduate schools would choose to have Professor Lattimore give his
imagination more tether and Mr. Logue rein his in, so that we could be
certain that it's all Homer that we are enjoying.

Chapman translates the tale of the boar:

>                 When the Sun was set
> And darknesse rose, they slept, till daye's fire het
> Th'enlightned earth, and then on hunting went
> Both Hounds and all Autolycus' descent.
> In whose guide did divine Ulysses go,
> Climb'd steepe Parnassus, on whose forehead grow
> All sylvan off-springs round. And soone they rech't
> The Concaves, whence ayr's sounding vapors fetcht
> Their loud descent. As soone as any Sun
> Had from the Ocean (where his waters run
> In silent deepnesse) rais'd his golden head,
> The early Huntsmen all the hill had spread
> Their Hounds before them on their searching Traile.
> They neere, and ever eager to assaile,
> Ulysses brandishing a lengthfull Lance,
> Of whose first flight he long'd to prove the chance.

> Then found they lodg'd a Bore of bulke extreame
> In such a Queach, as never any beame
> The Sun shot pierc'st, nor any passe let finde
> The moist impressions of the fiercest winde,
> Nor any storme the sternest winter drives,
> Such proofe it was: yet all within lay leaves
> In mighty thicknesse, and through all this flew
> The hounds' loud mouthes. The sounds, the tumult threw.
> And all together rouz'd the Bore, that rusht
> Amongst their thickest: all his brissels pusht
> From forth his rough necke, and with flaming eyes
> Stood close, and dar'd all. On which horrid prise
> Ulysses first charg'd, whom above the knee
> The savage strooke, and rac't it crookedly
> Along the skin, yet never reacht the bone.

There were still queaches near Hitchin in Chapman's day from which the more sanguine gentry might rout a boar. He blurs the mountain scenery ("Concaves, whence ayr's sounding vapors fetcht") but deploys the hounds and moves in on the kill with a clear sense that the *tremendum* of the scene is in the ruckus of the dogs and the fury of the boar. William Cullen Bryant, the Henri Rousseau of Homer's translators, has the hunt unfold at a genteel pace:

> Up the steeps of that high mount
> Parnassus, clothed with woods, they climbed, and soon
> Were on its airy heights. The sun, new risen
> From the deep ocean's gently flowing stream,
> Now smote the fields. The hunters reached a dell;
> The hounds before them tracked the game; behind
> Followed the children of Autolycus.
> The generous youth Ulysses, brandishing
> A spear of mightly length, came pressing on
> Close to the hounds. There lay a huge wild boar
> Within a thicket, where moist-blowing winds
> Came not, nor in his brightness could the sun
> Pierce with his beams the covert, nor the rain
> Pelt through, so closely grew the shrubs. The ground
> Was heaped with sheddings of the withered leaves.
> Around him came the noise of dogs and men
> Approaching swiftly. From his lair he sprang
> And faced them, with the bristles on his neck
> Upright, and flashing eyes.

The boar dies "with piercing cries amid the dust." Bryant smacks of Currier and Ives; Chapman is closer to a Mantegna drawing. Bryant's "thicket," "covert," and "shrubs" are wispy and feathery, and he has a humanitarian tenderness toward the badgered boar that is in contrast to Chapman's bloody delight in the kill ("And shew'd his point gilt with the gushing gore"—Chapman's world still thought of hunting as providing food for the family. And Bryant rejoiced when he got to a line he could silver over: "And sacred rivers flowing to the sea" (10.422). His Homer is Vergilian, or at least Wordsworthian.

Pope, Fenton, and Broome give us:

> Soon as the morn, new rob'd in purple light,
> Pierced with her golden shafts the drear of night,
> Ulysses, and his brave maternal race
> The young Autolyci, essay the chase.
> Parnassus, thick-perplexed with horrid shades,
> With deep-mouth'd hounds the hunter-troop invades;
> What time the sun, from ocean's peaceful stream,
> Darts o'er the lawn his horizontal beam.
> The pack impatient snuff the tainted gale;
> The thorny wilds the woodmen fierce assail:
> And, foremost of the train, his cornel spear
> Ulysses wav'd, to rouse the savage war.
> Deep in the rough recesses of the wood,
> A lofty copse, the growth of ages, stood;
> Nor winter's boreal blast, nor thunderous shower,
> Nor solar ray, could pierce the shady bower.
> With wither'd foliage strew'd, a happy store!
> The warm pavilion of the dreadful boar.
> Rous'd by the hounds' and hunters' mingling cries,
> The savage from his leafy shelter flies;
> With fiery glare his sanguine eye-balls shine,
> And bristles high impale his horrid chine.

One would like to know how Pope imagined that one could make a fifteen-foot spear out of a cherry branch; *dolikhoskios* ("long of shadow") isn't all that hard to make sense of. But if one has set out, Handel-like, with purple light fleeing from golden arrows, a cherry-wood spear is no matter. In such a rendering, worthy of Salvator Rosa, all reality is subsumed in stage sets, costumes, and music; it is opera, and Italian opera at that. When Eurykleia speaks, the words come in a contralto burst: "My son!—My king!" (Is that the Eurykleia who lifts her skirts and dances in the gore of the suitors, cackling with laughter?) Odysseus's reproof is baritone and Rossini:

> Thy milky founts my infant lips have drain'd:
> And have the Fates thy babbling age ordain'd
> To violate the life thy youth sustain'd?

An exile have I told, with weeping eyes,
Full twenty annuals suns in distant skies.

Here's the hunt as a Victorian painting by Landseer, the prose version
of Butcher and Lang:

> Now so soon as early Dawn shone forth, the rosy-fingered, they all went
> forth to the chase, the hounds and the sons of Autolycus, and with them
> went the goodly Odysseus. So they fared up the steep hill of wood-clad Par-
> nassus, and quickly they came to the windy hollows. Now the sun was but
> just striking on the fields, and was come forth from the soft flowing stream of
> deep Oceanus. Then the beaters reached the glade of the woodland, and
> before them went the hounds tracking a scent, but behind came the sons of
> Autolycus, and among them goodly Odysseus followed close on the hounds,
> swaying a long spear. Thereby in a thick lair was a great boar lying, and
> through the coppice the force of the wet winds blew never, neither did
> the bright sun light on it with any rays, nor could the rain pierce through, so
> thick it was, and of fallen leaves there were a great plenty therein. Then the
> tramp of the men's feet and of the dogs' came upon the boar, as they pressed
> on in the chase, and forth from his lair he sprang towards them with crest
> well bristled and fire shining in his eyes, and stood at bay among them all.

A boar is never "at bay"—he attacks from the beginning. A stag at bay
is one who is either trapped or winded and turns in desperation to fight.
Homer's boar greets his enemies at his door, disdainful of their folly. In a
boar hunt, technically it is always the hunter who is at bay, for one discovers the boar tracking the hunt and turns on him. He is a fearless and
ill-tempered beast. Words to Butcher and Lang are invariably decorative,
swatches of color all. So that dogs *tramp*. And when there is a paucity of
adjectives for fringe, Butcher throws in a "yea" ("many were the men
whose towns he saw and whose minds he learnt, yea") and Lang throws
in a "lo" ("lo, the dogs withhold him from his way").

It was Samuel Butler who conceded that "Wardour Street has its uses"
(what if "The Ancient Mariner" were called "The Old Sailor"?), but his
*Odyssey* (1900) is an obvious movement away from the gorgeous antiqu-
ing of Butcher and Lang (1879) and of William Morris (1887). Butler
hoped for biscuit-plainness and sinew. "Here was the lair of a huge boar
among some thick brushwood so dense that the wind and rain could not
get through it. . . ." Odysseus has simply "a long spear in his hand";
Butler slices away its shadow and whatever Odysseus was doing with the
spear (shaking, swaying, brandishing, waving). Butler tidies up; he
knows the difference between poetry and prose. Yet he remains respectful
toward Homer's stock images and is not embarrassed by them. He keeps
"the child of morning, rosy-fingered Dawn" while his successor Colonel
Lawrence thinks it too literary and writes instead a pukka "at dawn."

Ennis Rees is equally eager to hide Homer's *formulae* and atheizes rosy-toed Eos into "the first red streaks / Of morning." Butler's boar "raised the bristles of his neck, and stood at bay with fire flashing from his eyes." Lawrence's has a "bristling spine and fire-red eyes." Rees: "bristling back and eyes aflame."

A strange entropy runs through the translations of Homer into English, from Chapman to Colonel Lawrence. The descent might be plausibly ascribed to the revolt of the masses, the democratizing of literature. Another cause is just as plausibly a settled desire for gentility, for wistful sweetness, for taming. Both Butler and Lawrence concocted Homers of their own imagining, and both wanted to see him as a literary bloke up to no discernible good; and both were men who delighted to do things which they protested weren't worth doing, while secretly hoping that they would be praised for ascribing virtues to Homer that we can no longer see. Butler's novelistic Homer and Lawrence's bookish rescinder of ancient tales are masks that we don't care to bring down from the attic any more. The end of entropy is to fall into one's own source of energy and die. The death throes came with W. H. D. Rouse—the drift toward making Homer an old salt's yarn complete. The names became Dickensian; every episode was gilded over with a William Morrisy coziness, and Homer was perhaps irretrievably a northern European, a Romancer, a Bard.

And yet northern Europe was not all this time armoring itself in obtuseness against the ravishments of Homer. Far from it. At the moment we are watching the resurgence of a new cycle: the relocation by Robert Fitzgerald and Christopher Logue of the translator's energies. Homer *the poet* seems about to have his day again.

Between Bryant and Fitzgerald we have had no *Odyssey* from a major English poet. If we are willing to discount Pope's *Odyssey* as a work by Pope and take it as a work by apprentices capable of constructing with the master's example and direction a poem in the manner of his *Iliad,* we can then note an even wider span: two *Odysseys* only from poets in the history of English literature, Chapman's and Fitzgerald's. There are, at a guess, some fifty English *Odysseys*.

Morris *ought* to have given us an *Odyssey*. His *The Earthly Paradise*, a neglected masterpiece of English literature sorely needing restoration to the curriculum, is poetry of the highest order and displays a narrative skill beautifully suited to the rendering of a Pre-Raphaelite *Odyssey*, a verbal equivalent of Burne-Jones's *Circe*. He gave us instead a verbal equivalent of Burne-Jones at his most turgid: Tennyson gone high and about to wriggle into the fanciest convolutions of Art Nouveau. Morris satisfied all his need to do an *Odyssey* when he made his *Life and Death of Jason.* The land of Morris's heart's desire was northern, a barbaric forest or Iceland or the Troll King's country.

The force that broke the palsied spell the Victorians and their German cousins cast over Homer was Samuel Butler. But the force flowed not from his plain-prose *Iliad* and *Odyssey*. It flowed from his fierce impatience with humbug.

Butler's real translation of the *Odyssey* is *The Authoress of the Odyssey,* a great burst of Sicilian light upon Homeric studies that made the classicists secure their dark glasses the firmer. Butler's offering an intelligent (and extremely funny) girl as a replacement of the Bard is a symbol of astounding importance. It was an event that has not yet been assessed, but its consequences are scarcely hidden. From Butler come many gifts that found their way to the worktable of James Joyce. The *Portrait of the Artist as a Young Man* derives from Butler's *Ernest Pontifex* (that we have to know under the un-Butlerian title *The Way of All Flesh*), and Butler's resurrection of the *Odyssey* precedes *Ulysses*. From Butler comes Giuseppe Tomasi di Lampedusa's *Il Professore e la Sirena,* a transmutation into fable of the essence of *The Authoress of the Odyssey* so pointed that it ought to be designated the highest moment of Homeric criticism in the twentieth century.

"The *Odyssey,*" Butler perceived while he was still in school, "is the wife of the *Iliad.*" And years later that astute perception grew into the insistent news that the *Iliad* and the *Odyssey* are not ruins, but alive. But the century wanted Homer to be a ruin; romantic distance was the sole perspective from which it could appreciate the two poems. The Renaissance was over; the Hon. William Gladstone, who was known to correspond with Schliemann and whose hobby was archaeology, took up the translating of Homer, thus:

> And the heralds ordered silence;
> And, on chairs of polished stone,
> Ranged in venerable circle
> Sate the Elders. One by one
> Each the clear-toned herald's sceptre
> Took, and standing forth alone
> Spake his mind. Two golden talents
> Lay before them, to requite
> Only him, among the Judges,
> Straightliest who should judge the right.

No wonder Butler flipped back his cuffs and made a plain prose translation, and went even further and imagined a sprightly girl to replace the harper of Khios, so that the Elder Statesman's wheezings would be the ultimate affront to her *élan*.

For the next half-century we get a curious pattern among writers involved with Homer either as translators or imitators. Charles Doughty is careful to make his epic *Dawn in Britain* half *Odyssey* and half *Iliad*, like the *Aeneid*, with the *Iliad* getting the lion's share, as he had already written his *Odyssey*, the *Travels in Arabia Deserta*. Colonel Lawrence translated the *Odyssey* as a companion piece to his *Iliad, The Seven Pillars of Wisdom*. Kazantzakis both translated the *Odyssey* into modern Greek and wrote a sequel. In just a few years, when a detached consideration of our age is possible, Joyce's *Ulysses* and Pound's *Cantos*, both versions of the *Odyssey*, will take their place in a complex of meaning that we can now only suspect. And at the heart of the complex will be the two Homeric poems.

And now real poets like Fitzgerald and Logue are returning to the poems themselves; which is to say that from the diffuse appearance of Homer in practically every form of art except translation, Homer is drifting back to his own pages. The dust of Butler's demolition settles nicely, and in place.

And Professor Lattimore's *Odyssey*, where does it fit in all of this? Like his *Iliad*, it will please professors and serve as a standard textbook, for to the professorial eye it is *accurate*. It fits almost word for word over the Greek text; it can be used as a crib by the student. Its architecture is this: there was an extensive wall made of Greek bricks. Brick by brick Professor Lattimore has taken down this structure, replacing each Greek brick with an English one, or perhaps a Basic English one. This is a mode of translation plumped for by Vladimir Nabokov, a translator of formidable talent and effectiveness (though it perhaps ought to be noticed, if only to catch in an inconsistency a man so sure of himself, that when Nabokov translates his own poems he takes his liberties). It is the mode by which hopeful Christians assume the Bible was translated.

And yet, and yet. This is a *new Odyssey;* it takes its place beside other *Odysseys* on the library shelf. There it sits, beside many *Odysseys* obviously less competent and in various Wardour Street and Walter Scott styles; and beside burly, noble Chapman; beside good old leafy William Cullen Bryant; beside the graceful and inventive Robert Fitzgerald. Not far down the shelf are the passages of the *Iliad* rendered by Christopher Logue, a miracle of the imagination. Professor Lattimore is aware that he does not have access to a language as rich as Chapman's, and says so in his introduction. No one has; that age is gone. Ours, he sighs, is not a heroic culture. So he feels he must make do with a diction all but featureless, all but denatured. Yet this is the age of Eliot and Pound and Joyce.

The curious thing about so many of Professor Lattimore's words and phrases is that they aren't very different from those of the Victorians, or from those of the consciously mannered Colonel Lawrence. He demands, to be sure, a stark neutrality of his words, and keeps the *Zeitgeist* well out of it, so that nowhere do we smile at homely touches such as Bryant's having Odysseus visit "the capitals of many nations," as if he were Emerson on a tour. This neutrality is not total; the King James Bible rings in from time to time ("his time of homecoming," "nor among his own people"). There are, happily, grand lines throughout that reach for their resonance into the deepest traditions of English poetry; watch the alliteration and assonance in this:

> slaughter his crowding sheep and lumbering horn-curved cattle;

the Milton in this:

> and descended in a flash of speed from the peaks of Olympos.

Yet we must come across these lines in a style that by now can only be called Ageless Homeric Pastiche:

> My child, what sort of word escaped your teeth's barrier?

And:

> Then in turn the goddess gray-eyed Athene answered him.

Professor Lattimore is like an engraver copying a painting. The color of the original must everywhere appear in his work as monochrome shades. This need not have been, but Professor Lattimore chose to have it that way. He is *not* writing an English poem; he is writing a translation. He does not relish the half-compliment that Pope had to suffer; he has not written a very pretty poem that must not be called Homer. He has written a sprawling poem that imitates Homer along certain aesthetic lines. It is sometimes severely controlled, stately, grave; it is also a mussy poem, flaring out of control, losing contact with both Greek and English.

Professor Lattimore's careful erudition and earnest solicitude for accuracy led him to believe that the *Odyssey* would somehow write itself. If he stuck to his business, the poem would stick to its. Why should it not? The method is logical but wildly improbable, for the simple reason that words are not numbers, nor even signs. They are animals, alive and with a will of their own. Put together, they are invariably less or more than their sum. Words die in antisepsis. Asked to be neutral, they display allegiances and stubborn propensities. They assume the color of their new surroundings, like chameleons; they perversely develop echoes.

Words also live in history, aging, or proving immune to the bite of time. Much that was thought clever in recent translations is already wilt-ing and going quaint. A neutral vocabulary stands well against time and like the basic geometric figures never goes out of style. It is plausible that Professor Lattimore's *Odyssey* may weather our age and the next while translations more interesting to us at the moment will soon begin to sound like William Morris. But posterity is one audience, and we here and now are another. Homer, in defiance of Heraclitus, remains.

# The House that Jack Built

A hundred years before the death of Ezra Pound, a week short of the very day, John Ruskin sat down in his red room at Brantwood, among his geological specimens and Scott manuscripts, to instruct the English working man in the meaning of labyrinths, the craftsman Daedalus, and the hero Theseus. He was writing Letter XXIII of *Fors Clavigera*, his monthly tracts against usury and banks. This incremental work, a splendid pottage of autobiography, pamphleteering, preaching, and haphazard digressions worthy of Sterne, gave lessons in aesthetics and economics, morals and literary criticism.

*Fors* is a kind of Victorian prose *Cantos*, arranging its subjects in ideogrammatic form, shaping them with a poetic sense of imagery, allowing themes to recur in patterns, generating significance, as Pound did, by juxtaposition and the intuition of likenesses among dissimilar and unexpected things.

Ruskin, who sounded as provincial to Matthew Arnold as Pound to
Gertrude Stein, was yearning in *Fors Clavigera* for a cleansing and reor-
dering of civilization, in almost the same way Pound did in *The Cantos*.
Both works trace a heritage of wisdom and tradition now obscured or
abandoned. Both works direct our attention to the monetary historian
Alexander del Mar, to the capacious minds of Louis Agassiz and Alexander von Humboldt, architects of systems of knowledge. Both works ana-
lyze the cultures of Venice and Florence, admire the energy of fifteenth-
century *condottiere,* and draw morals from various kinds of Italian
banks. Both teach us how to see the roots of the Renaissance in mediæval
art. Both are works by men with an extraordinary range of concerns who
have the same, almost insurmountable problem of organizing their material into a large work.

And because both issued their work piecemeal (*Fors* in monthly installments from 1871 to 1887, *The Cantos* sporadically in magazines and
books since 1917, with Cantos LXXII and LXXIII yet to be published),
the assumption has been fairly common that *Fors* and *The Cantos* are
serial commentary basically random in organization. Yet both works are
strenuously unified. They both insist that economics must be a part of our
literacy and a legitimate and pressing subject for the artist.

Watch how Ruskin in *Fors XXIII* goes about fixing the meaning of
Theseus in our minds, and you will see how Pound built ideograms of
images and ideas.

A great captain, says Ruskin, is distinguished by Fortune's "conclusive
stroke against him." We see this proof of adversity in the loss of Ariadne.
But of Theseus, more later: we must turn to an engraving by Botticelli
representing the seven works of mercy, "as completed by an eighth work
in the center of all; namely, lending without interest, from the Mount of
Pity accumulated by generous alms. In the upper part of the diagram we
see the cities which first built Mounts of Pity; Venice, chief of all—then
Florence, Genoa, and Castruccio's Lucca; in the distance prays the monk
of Ancona, who first taught, inspired by Heaven, of such wars with
usurers."

Ruskin then rambles around in what seems to be a shambles of subjects: Victorian fund raising, national defense, reforms in punishment,
Maria Edgeworth's novel *Helen*, until he can get back to Theseus, this
time to his image in the British Museum, where he is a stolen antiquity
only, unless we can see his meaning. Theseus's stamp is common in our
world, in, for example, the Greek fret we can see everywhere. The meaning of this design is now lost, conveying nothing to our eyes. It was,
however, the Greek life-symbol, and ours.

Best try to understand it by remembering the cathedral doors at Lucca, near which, in the church porch, we can find this sixteen-hundred-year-old inscription:

*Hic quem creticus edit Dedalus est Laberinthus*
*de quo nullus vadere quivit qui fuit intus*
*ni Theseus gratis Adriane stamine iutus.*

(This is the labyrinth which the Cretan Daedalus built, out of which nobody can find his way except Theseus, nor could he have done it unless he had been helped by Ariadne's thread, for love.)

This, Ruskin goes on, can be reduced from mediæval sublimity to the nursery rhyme "The House That Jack Built."[1] The cow with the crumpled horn will then be the Minotaur. The maiden all forlorn will stand for Ariadne, "while the gradual involution of the rhyme and the necessity for clear-mindedness as well as clear utterance"—

This is the farmer sowing his corn
That owned the cock that crowed in the morn
That waked the priest all shaven and shorn
That married the man all tattered and torn
That kissed the maiden all forlorn
That milked the cow with the crumpled horn
That tossed the dog that worried the cat
That killed the rat that ate the malt
That lay in the house that Jack built—

are a vocal imitation of the deepening labyrinth.

"Theseus, a pious hero, and the first Athenian knight who cut his hair short in front, may not inaptly be represented as the priest all shaven and shorn; the cock that crew in the morn is the proper Athenian symbol of a pugnacious mind; and the malt that lay in the house fortunately indicates the connection of Theseus and Athenian power with the mysteries of Eleusis, where corn first, it is said, grew in Greece."

There was a Greek spirit in Shakespeare, Ruskin continues, compelling him to associate English fairyland with the great Duke of Athens. And Jack the builder neatly equals Daedalus, "Jack of all trades."

Ruskin is just getting warmed up. Coins of Cnossos bore the symbol of the labyrinth. Symbols are natural shapes elevated to significance. The Greek fret existed before Theseus, but he gave it the meaning of a labyrinth. The spiral is the shape a worm draws with its coiling bore, a fern with its bud, and a periwinkle with its shell. Completed in the Ionic capital, and arrested in the fending point of the acanthus in the Co-

---

[1] *The Oxford Dictionary of Quotations,* 2nd ed. (1956), p. 369, traces this rhyme to *Nurse Truelove's New-Year's-Gift (1755), but it is probably older.*

rinthian, it has become the prime element of architectural ornament in all ages. In Athenian work the spiral mirrors wind and waves; in Gothic, the serpent Satan. But Satan is a power of the air, as in the story of Job and the story of Buonconte di Montefeltro in Dante.

Ruskin next compares labyrinths, coins, modes of justice, judges of the dead, until he can demonstrate that Dante's hell is a labyrinth, until he can triumphantly identify the Minotaur with greed, lust, and usury, like Ezra Pound, whose symbol for usury is Dante's monster of deceit, Geryone: "Hic est hyperusura."

Modern criticism has X-ray eyes to see that the house that Ruskin makes Jack-as-Daedalus build is the house that Jack Ruskin built: his cycle of books around the violence of greed in his world and the violence of lust within. His Ariadne was named Rose, whose name he finds, and conceals, everywhere in the text of *Fors*. Between Ruskin and Browning, Pound's first master, we can see the invention of Daedalian art in literature: the discovery that only in that intricacy which the Greeks called *poikilía*—cunning craftsmanship—can complexities of meaning beyond inherited styles of narrative and poetry be summoned into play. A terrible beauty, Yeats said, was born into the world.

Did Pound know *Fors*? He at least knew Ruskin's method, and called it by the Greek word *paideuma*. His early "I Gather the Limbs of Osiris" was perhaps an imitation of Ruskin's manner. Yeats's last prose work, *On the Boiler*, was a conscious attempt to repeat *Fors Clavigera*.

In Charles Olson's Gloucester there still lived an old man who had heard Ruskin lecture at Oxford. Between his house and Olson's there is an inlet in which lay a sunken battleship completely covered with Gloucester sewage. The symbolism of this pleased Olson immensely.

James Joyce certainly knew Ruskin's *Fors*, for the doubling of the labyrinth as the house that Jack built became a Joycean mode of building symbols. Professor Herbert Marshall McLuhan has recently announced his discovery that the fifteen stories in *Dubliners* correspond symbolically to the fifteen books of Ovid's *Metamorphoses*.[2] What he is observing is the mythological dimension of those stories, whereby they are made to correspond to the adventures of Odysseus, to episodes in the Bible, and to various archetypal parables and fables. To find the outlines of Joyce's symbolic structures it is always best to follow the rules of symmetry. The tale of Daedalus, for instance, is midmost Ovid's text. "A Little Cloud" is midmost *Dubliners*. And if you look, you will find nothing overt about Daedalus in "A Little Cloud" (unless you want to see Little Chandler as a man trapped in an emotional labyrinth, tempted by Gallaher to fly away,

[2]Letters to the Editor, *The James Joyce Quarterly,* Vol. 12, no. 4 (1975): 342.

or allusions to great height and molten wax in the title and the name Chandler). You will, however, find phrases from "The House that Jack Built," the word *malt* and the phrase *crumpled horn.*

In the spiral labyrinth of The Cattle of the Sun chapter in *Ulysses* you will find an elaborate web of allusions to Daedalus and the labyrinth, and an equally elaborate web of allusion to "The House that Jack Built."

In the center of *Finnegans Wake* there is a corresponding evocation of the nursery rhyme: "the jackhouse that jerry built." Its address is *32 West 11th streak* (an entropic Fibonacci progression, the way nature runs down). Throughout his work Joyce puts Jack at the center of the house he built, Daedalus at the center of the labyrinth, from which the design spirals out or radiates.

This symbolic figure from a childish, and therefore primal source in our knowledge of literature, is Joyce's signature, his labyrinthine thumbprint on his work. *Finnegans Wake* is the house Jack Joyce built, but it is a reading of the Old Testament, the house that Jacob built, and of the New Testament, the house that the carpenter Jack Christ built. It is a world of involuted meaning like the house that Jack Ruskin built, Ruskin being the Shaun to Charles Dodgson's Shem. The *Wake* dreams through ultimate absurdities of symbols, such as our dreams make us suffer, and through the tragic limitations of language which imprison us when we would be meaningful, and betray us, whatever our caution.

Contemplating the sonorous midden of the *Wake*, William Carlos Williams decided to make an American model. He singled out a river even filthier than the Liffey, the yellow Passaic, and a New Jersy town with a name half Latin, *pater,* and half English, *son;* in America our parentage is European; and as Pound's *Cantos* begin—like H. G. Wells's *Outline of History*—with the word *and,* Williams's poem *Paterson* begins with a colon, a device Joyce could not have used, as his art does not omit the material implied to the left of that colon. In a sense, Joyce is on one side of that colon, Williams on the other.

He takes from the *Wake* one sleeping giant, one hamadryad, and the radical idea that words go numb. And he also took, whether intentionally or not, the idea that where understanding fails the result is that we perceive a monster instead of an intelligible reality.

This idea seems to have been precipitated from a painting by the Russian Pavel Tchelitchew. Williams met him in 1942 and saw the massive canvas called "Phenomena" in progress. This painting is iconographically a Temptation of St. Anthony, with monsters of all sorts, monsters which, as Dr. Williams, a pediatrician, observed to the painter, are all teratologically exact. Williams saw the point, and took away with him the courage to write about the decay of an American city as the gradual metamorphosis of humanity into monstrosity. He ordered the original plan of *Paterson* with the four classical elements, earth, air, fire, and water, and saw in their flux a tragic entropy that nevertheless fell back into itself to begin again. A poet whose lifelong business it was to bring babies into the world could never see nature as anything but counter-entropic.

And a monster of monsters, the atomic bomb (which, incredibly, its mushroom cloud shaped like a skull, appears in the deep background of Tchelitchew's "Phenomena," painted nine years before Hiroshima)—the atomic bomb and the radioactivity of matter gave Williams his sense that the world is regenerative in a way we had not expected.

He then added two more books to *Paterson,* one for love, and one for genius, which he symbolized by the figure of Henri de Toulouse-Lautrec, sensualist and monster, an artist who gazed on the ugly and lifted it with love and understanding into the realm of the radiant, into the articulateness of exact statement. The Minotaur may, after all, be the heart of the labyrinth.

The painter Tchelitchew later took to concealing Minotaurs in his Joycean style of punning with multiple images inside the same outline, and even painted a "Riddle of Daedalus," an anatomical drawing of the nasal labyrinth where we breathe and smell: our animal intake of knowledge. This picture resolves, if you look carefully enough, into a bull's face and into genitals male and female.

Just last month Louis Zukofsky, our greatest living poet, finished his long poem "*A*" that he began fifty years ago.[3] It was written under the double tutelage of Pound and of Pound's tutors, by a student stubbornly faithful and stubbornly original. "*A*" is a dance of words to Bach and to the music of Shakespeare's thought. It is a dance of imagery that follows the laws of Orphic Daedalus. It ties and unties knots in a harmony of emblems the way Ben Jonson's Daedalus instructs his dancers to do in the "Masque of Pleasure Reconciled to Virtue":

Then, as all actions of mankind
Are but a laborinth, or maze,
So let your daunces be entwin'd
Yet not perplex men, unto gaze.
But measur'd, and so numerous too,
As men may read each act you doo.
And when they see the Graces meet,
Admire the wisdom of your feet.

[3]This paper was read 30 October 1975, at Yale, to inaugurate the Beinecke Rare Book and Manuscript Library's Center for the Study of Ezra Pound and His Contemporaries.

The daedalian artist infolds, he makes a *complicatio*. We beholders are involved in an *explicatio;* we unfold to read. Or, with Zukofsky, we un-fold to hear, for, as with Joyce, it is the labyrinth of the ear in which Zukofsky likes to move. His images pun with a playful energy we have not seen since Shakespeare. He has made a pun in English on every Latin word of Catullus; he has made sawhorses in a Brooklyn street (emblems of the letter A) gallop with manes made of the Latin word *manes* and with heads made of the number 7.

He has made all of his work tributary to the poem *"A."* His *oeuvre* is tied in an elegant and fanciful knot. To see the beauty of *"A,"* we must know the maze-like commentary on Shakespeare called *Bottom.* For at the center of Zukofsky's daedalian labyrinth is a puckish Minotaur in-deed, the ass-headed Bottom and his fellow daedalian craftsmen "in a quaint maze in the wanton green." (Remember that Ruskin accepts the Theseus of "A Midsommer Nights Dreame" as the proper English under-standing of the Athenian maze-treader).

The labyrinth, as we could continue to demonstrate, became a life-symbol of our century (witness Borges and his labyrinths, Gide's *Theseus,* Cortázar's *Hop-Scotch,* Kafka, Kazantzakis). And so did Daedalus, Icarus, and their wings.

A pioneering and all but complete edition of the writings of Leonardo da Vinci appeared in London in 1883. Queen Victoria, the Kaiser, and even the National Library of Dublin are listed among the subscribers (but not Chester A. Arthur or the Library of Congress). This handsome edi-tion omits those beautiful drawings of ornithopters and pages on the theory of flight that are to our eyes some of the most fascinating in da Vinci's notebooks. The omission is tacit and the reason obvious. Da Vinci the anatomist was of living interest (though Victoria covered them with decent blank paper in her copy); da Vinci the botanist, the geographer, the military engineer: these faces of his genius were of sound cultural interest. We must assume that the pages about flight were so much Baron Munchausen in 1883.

They had forgotten Daedalus. A one-year-old baby in Dublin would eventually remind them. And in five more years a steam-powered mono-plane named the *Aeolus* would fly 150 feet outside Paris, Clément Ader its designer and pilot, only to hiss down with a plop and await the perfec-tion of the internal combustion engine, until another example of its species would mount the air again.

This was to be the pattern of the twentieth century—a labyrinth as Ezra Pound would call it in *The Cantos*—history would develop a maze-like pattern full of sudden surprises and tragic blind alleys. A man searching for a way out, or attempting to plot the confusion, would rarely agree with, or even know about, other men on a similar search.

*The Cantos* are a maze by plan and in subject. The second canto does not follow from the first, but takes up anew; and so do the third, fourth, and fifth. At LXXIV the poem discloses a direction unplanned by the poet, and the last three divisions of the epic are meditations on ways of getting out of the labyrinth of history into the clear air of certainty.

If the Victorians could see only unhinged frivolity in da Vinci's pages on flight, they were very much alive to other mythological symbols. Ruskin, lecturing at Oxford on sculpture, taught his students that the lesson of Daedalus is an ambiguous one. He placed the labyrinth in contrast to that golden honeycomb with which Daedalus crowned his lifetime of invention. They are similar structures, but in one lurks a symbol of bestiality and violence, in the other bees and honey, signs congenial to the royal houses of Mycenae and China, to John Bunyan and Napoleon. Prophetically Ruskin disclosed symbols that would appear in work after work of twentieth-century art. Joyce in *Dubliners* depicts the city as a labyrinth (including, as we have seen, Daedalus the craftsman under the name of Jack). In *A Portrait of the Artist as a Young Man* he introduces his own Daedalus, fused with the figure of Icarus. *Ulysses* is a labyrinth within a labyrinth, and *Finnegans Wake* is his golden honeycomb.

Daedalus. He would have had the scrupulous, the piercing eye of Wittgenstein, who was also architect, engineer, craftsman, and aviator. He would have had the lean, nautical body of Vladimir Tatlin, architect, engineer, craftsman, and an aviator who proposed to assume wings powered by the human body, and pedal through the air. He had, as the myths tell us, the sudden temper and inept solicitude for apprentices that Leonardo himself displayed, da Vinci who was also architect, engineer, craftsman, and an aviator who designed a bat of lathes and struts in which he hoped to swim through the Tuscan air. He would have had the laconic inwardness and heroic alertness of Wilbur Wright, who was also architect, engineer. craftsman, and an aviator who, on Monday the 14th of December 1903, at a little after three in the afternoon, from Kill Devil Hill at Kitty Hawk, North Carolina, flew. He was ready the day before to take mankind on its first flight, toward Fiume, London, Coventry, Berlin, Sheffield, Dresden, Hiroshima, Hanoi, except that the day before was the Sabbath, which he declined to break.

O sinewy silver biplane, nudging the wind's withers!

(as Hart Crane wrote in "The Bridge")

Warping the gale, the Wright windwrestlers veered
Capeward, then blading the wind's flank, banked and spun

What ciphers risen from Prophetic script,
What marathons new-set between the stars!

*"Je n'ai cherché pendant toute ma vie,"* said Pound's friend Brancusi, *"que l'essence de vol. Le vol, quel bonheur!"*

Henri Rousseau around 1906 painted a charming landscape of the Pont de Sèvres, and placed a balloon in the sky—there had been balloons in the skies of France since Benjamin Franklin's day. Next year, the ruddered dirigible *La Patrie* took to the air, and Rousseau added it to his landscape. Next year, Wilbur Wright flew at Le Mans while Blériot watched in tears of ecstasy, and Rousseau added the Wright Flyer No. 4 to his sky: the world's first painting of an aeroplane.

In Dublin that year James Joyce invented a young man named Stephen Dedalus. Ezra Pound had just begun a long poem on which he would write for sixty-seven years, and never finish.

Guillaume Apollinaire, addressing the Tour Eiffel, told her, shepherdess as he imagined her to be of bridges and automobiles:

La religion seule est restée toute neuve la religion
Est restée simple comme les hangars de Port-Aviation

And seeing in the aeroplane something as new as the unaging newness of Christianity, compared the new aviators to Christ and His priests:

C'est le Christ qui monte au ciel mieux que les aviateurs
Il détient le record du monde pour la hauteur

and later, in *Zone:*

et changé en oiseau ce siècle comme Jésus monte dans l'air

Henry James, out walking his dachshund on the South Downs, saw Blériot complete his Channel crossing in 1909. Kafka saw Curtiss and Rougier fly at Brescia. Gertrude Stein included Wilbur Wright among her *Four in America;* Robert Frost wrote a "Kitty Hawk."

And there was a day when Ezra Pound brought James Joyce to the studio of Constantin Brancusi, who had metamorphosed a mythological Roumanian bird, the Maiastra, into an image of pure flight, and who had sculpted a tombstone for Rousseau on which Apollinaire had written the epitaph.

Brancusi's portrait of Joyce is a spiral labyrinth, an ear. He kept it pinned to his wall, and told people that it was a symbol opposite to that of *"la pyramide fatale,"* by which he meant the idea of fitful material progress.

The Minotaur enters Picasso's work in 1927, to become a constant icon thereafter. In 1931 he made a set of etchings for Ovid's *Metamor-*

*phoses,* for Albert Skira, specifying the work himself as the only one he was interested to illustrate. A few years later he did the most finished and mythological etching of his career, the mysterious "Minotauromachy," in which brutal violence stands opposed to an innocent girl holding flowers and a candle. For the rest of his life, for another forty years, he would meditate on the Minotaur. Sometimes the Minotaur is as ambiguous a symbol in Picasso's iconography as the bullfight itself, which he insisted was prehistoric ritual, as disturbing as the animal-headed creatures from the imagination of Jean Cocteau, horse-headed *daimons* of the underworld, cat-headed beasts which, if loved, turned into prince charmings, as ambiguous as Gide's Minotaur, which was beautiful but brainless.

Picasso's Minotaur is a symbol of creative energy, chthonic inspiration, the prehuman past, the animal in man; and our century has maintained an argument in its art as to the harmony between our bestiality and our humanity. What beast is there at the center of the labyrinth? It is sex embracing death, said Freud. It is, said Ezra Pound, the moth called over the mountain, the bull running upon the sword. It is the dolphin leaping in its element, said Yeats.

Not until his old age did Picasso turn to the daedalian part of our myth. Commissioned to do a mural for the UNESCO building in Paris, he chose the fall of Icarus for his subject, making Icarus's body out of lines he had seen in prehistoric caves in the Dordogne, the raised arms that can be traced through stone-age art to the Egyptian hieroglyph for praise, spindly and uncertain lines with which the earliest artists drew man's body as distinct from the masterful lines and religious awe with which they drew their splendid animals.

Picasso includes in his mural an Ariadne abandoned, and three figures on land beside the empty blue sea into which Icarus is falling: two reclining figures in warm earth colors, and a perplexed figure with joined hands, the gesture of the thinker, of man considering, of vapid theorizing at the very edge of plunging tragedy. Picasso's first mural depicted violence hurled from the skies upon a Spanish town; his second contrasted war and peace; this, his fourth and last, displays how he finally saw our century: a woman in distress, youth falling from an awful height, a man lost in thought.

The first mural is in a museum, the second and third in a church, the "Fall of Icarus" in a building that administrates educational programs. Like his other murals, it is unsigned, the sole works to which he did not put his name, as if to say that words have nothing to do with pure emblems, as if to remind himself, triumphantly and in a veritable temple of words, that he never mastered the alphabet.

It was a mural, according to a famous passage in Yeats, that served Pound as a plan for *The Cantos:* the Sala dei Mesi in the Palazzo Schifanoia that Francesco del Cossa, Cosimo Tura, and their assistants painted for the Este family. The photograph Pound showed Yeats at Rapallo was of the east wall of the room which is made to say in Canto XXIV: "Albert made me, Tura painted my wall."

The Schifanoia palace was built in 1391 by Alberto d'Este; the Room of the Months, painted from floor to ceiling in three horizontal bands, is one of the few painted rooms to survive moth, rust, and thieves, and only two walls of it, at that.

The uppermost zone shows in twelve divisions the triumphs of the Olympian gods, together with allegorical figures signifying the virtues and skills over which the gods preside.

The middle zone shows in twelve panels the signs of the zodiac and the Decan symbols, figures appropriate to the three groups of ten days that make up the month over which each sign of the zodiac rules. Hence each of the middle panels contains four figures, or groups of figures, one for the zodiac, one for each Decan.

The bottom zone, also in twelve parts, depicts the life of Ferrara in the time of Borso d'Este, who figures in the first thirty cantos as a symbol of good will and just government.

Reading downward, we see that allegory, symbol, and scene from history correspond. Thus, if the top shows Minerva, or Justitia, with scholars, poets, priests, and women at their looms around her, the zodiacal band shows emblems of industry, and at the bottom we see a vineyard, a hunt (for food, not sport: dukes in those days provided for their own tables, and later in *The Cantos* we see pharoahs sowing crops, and John Quincy Adams at the plow receiving news of his election to the presidency), the law courts at Ferrara, and Borso d'Este trying a case.

Yeats tells us that the upper panels, the Triumphs, represent archetypal persons in *The Cantos,* the center panels "a descent and metamorphosis" and the lower panels, in Yeats's wonderfully vague phrase, "certain modern events."

It has been argued that Yeats got everything wrong, even if he heard correctly, and that Pound never followed this plan, or that he abandoned it long before the Pisan group.

Some years ago I had the privilege of helping Ezra Pound move his effects from one house to another in Rapallo. With a Max Ernst in one hand and the poet's Spartan cot on my head ("*Ecco il professore di greco,*" sang out a jovial Rapallese, "*con il letto del poèta sulla testa!*" —what a symbol of critics and poets) I noticed at my feet the sepia reproduction of the east wall of the Schifanoia *freschi*, the very print that Pound had shown Yeats. Turning it over, I found these words on the back, in Pound's hand:

> Intention of Cantos
> To run parallel (this found later)
> The Triumphs
> The Seasons
> The contemporary, with activities of the seasons
>                                           *Estate 63.*

Forty years after explaining the plan to Yeats, the poet had taken down the framed print (the war intervening, an exile within an exile intervening) and confirmed what Yeats had reported in *A Vision*. I asked, and was given permission to copy it.

*The Cantos* do indeed follow the triumphs, the seasons, and the activities of the seasons. To know the triumphs we must know the past, which is told in many tongues in many places; to know the past we descend, like Odysseus, into the House of Hades and give the blood of our attention (as translators, historians, poets) so that the dead may speak. To know the seasons we must understand metamorphosis, for things are never still, and never wear the same mask from age to age. The contemporary is without meaning while it is happening: it is a vortex, a whirlpool of action. It is a labyrinth.

The clue to this labyrinth, Pound knew, was history. *The Cantos,* therefore, are labyrinthine in structure, a zigzag of subjects, modifying and illuminating each other by proximity, treating time as if it were a space over which one can move in any direction. We begin in Greek time, move into Roman time, and then into mediaeval time, not naively, like the Connecticut Yankee to King Arthur's court, but in the hands of guides. The descent into hell is Odysseus', out of Homer, Homer paraphrased by a Latin hand in the Renaissance, with the language guided by archaic English, the tone of which is a music familiar to our ears.

We move as if from room to room of a house, from *stanza* to *stanza*, for a poem has always been thought of as a house, and verses are *versus,* our turning at a door or stair, and we tread in meter. *The Cantos* were originally conceived as a Browningesque movement from room to room of a painted palace.

We have left the metamorphic House of Circe as we begin, to go to *domus Hadês.* A ghost named Robert Browning fades into Proteus, who fades into Homer, who fades into Ovid.

The third canto begins in the labyrinth of Venice and ends in the Gonzaga palace in Mantua. Between Cantos IV and V Troy fades into the circular city Ecbatan, with many a transformation on the way. As the epic proceeds, houses begin to be the most substantial images: the House of Malatesta, the dynasties of China, the House of Adams. And, as Joyce might have punned, many houses that jack built, meaning banks.[4]

Basically three kinds of houses appear in the epic: the House of Hades (the phrase is Homer's) or repository of history, tradition, and myth, the houses of great families (Italian, Chinese, American), and the "quiet houses" (Ithaca, "thy quiet house at Torcello," the mountain retreats, as of Confucius on T'ai Shan, Pumpelly's at Chocorua: places on hills where the traveller who has seen the cities and known the minds of men can "make it all cohere").

The pattern from the Schifanoia *freschi* turns out to be the same as the plan given in Canto LXXIV:

between NEKUIA where are Alcmene and Tyro
  and the Charybdis of action
  to the solitude of Mt. Taishan

This is emblematically the plan of the *Odyssey* as well, and of *The Divine Comedy*. It is also Confucian, implying a reverence for ancestors and past wisdom brought forward, a philosophical balance in the midst of turmoil, a return to a spiritual homeland.

We have many brilliant readings of Pound; he is as much a magnet (and a battlefield) now as he was for more than half a century. *The Cantos* have that intricacy of architecture and minutely finished detail which have kept us reading both Homer and Dante. They have that original energy and freshness of Cubist canvases, the best of Gaudier and Brancusi, a page of *Ulysses* or *Finnegans Wake,* the brightness of Rimbaud, Apollinaire, and Cocteau, that has not aged. Pound spent his scholarly life looking at art so beautifully made that it cannot deteriorate. That vitality of line and image was his supreme lesson to us, and his best guide.

But we have only begun to read him, just as we have only begun to read and to see and to hear the whole Tribe of Daedalus: Eliot Cummings, Hilda Doolittle, William Carlos Williams, Henri Gaudier-Brzeska, Wyndham Lewis, Joyce, Zukofsky. Their art has changed all our previous concepts of art, and much of our concept of reality.

The essence of daedalian art is that it conceals what it most wishes to

[4]In Ray W. Irvin's *Daniel D. Tompkins: Governor of New York and Vice President of the United States* (New York Historical Society, 1976) one can see a reproduction of a broadside of the time of Madison parodying "The House that Jack Built." The house is the New York State Treasury and *jack* is used in the sense of *money.*

show: first, because it charges word, image and sense to the fullest, fusing matter and manner; and secondly, to allow meaning to be searched out. There are flying *Daidaloi* and falling *Ikaroi* on all pages of *A Portrait*. When, in *Ulysses,* people make change, with money, a metamorphosis occurs. The word *Stephen* is concealed in the opening phrase of *Finnegans Wake* ("rivverun, past *Eve and* Adam's . . .") and the word *stephanos,* a garland or victor's wreath, is hidden in rainbows and Viconian circles down the page.

But who has begun to see that *The Cantos* begin with a descent into Hell, a transformation involving wine, and a child amid ruins, as in a Renaissance nativity scene? And are about the driving of moneychangers from the temple? That Minos and his labyrinth are neatly concealed in Pound's portrait of the artist as a young man, *Hugh Selwyn Mauberley,* a poem moreover in which a Venus rises from the sea, as in Joyce's *Portrait?* When can we begin to see the parallels between *The Cantos* and *Ulysses,* both rewritings of the *Odyssey?* When shall we appreciate that the words in which both works are written are as formulaic as Homer's? Joyce accepted Homer's formulae in the comic mode, as cliché, and parodied all the English there is; Pound understood the formulae to be words shaped by masters: all those quotations are not quotations (and they usually turn out to be misquotations, from memory, if you look them up); they are the formulaic gists of ideas in maximum verbal focus.

Homer, as best we know, did not invent a version of the wanderings and return of Odysseus. From the best phrases he knew, all tried and tested by singers over the centuries, he took the firmest and finest, dialect be hanged, and built them into a strong, incredibly elegant symmetry.

When shall we begin to see Joyce's radical invention, the interior monologue, random phrases and capricious images (seemingly, though held firmly in a logic of association, correspondence , and symbol), as an invention parallel to, and strangely like, Pound's radical invention, the ideogram? The ideogram is a complex word, however many phrases long, a new kind of word, which we must learn to read in reverse etymology, from components to the whole idea.

The next step in reading *The Cantos* is to master the labyrinth of its images so that we can see it with new eyes for what it is, not the Cretan maze but the last, triumphant labyrinth of Daedalus the Master, a golden honeycomb. But until we tread the maze wisely, it will remain a perplexity. It is alive. It will change from labyrinth to honeycomb only after you have seen its architecture and learned the harmony of its ways.

The English artist Michael Ayrton, disciple of Wyndham Lewis and a sculptor who specialized in Minotaurs and who wrote a novel about

Daedalus, was commissioned a few years ago by the mountain-climber and bee-keeper Sir Edmund Hilary to see if he could discover how Daedalus made a honeycomb of gold. The lost-wax process, perhaps its very invention, was obviously involved. Michael Ayrton proceeded to make a golden honeycomb. Moreover, when Sir Edmund put it in his garden in New Zealand as a gleaming piece of sculpture, bees came, accepted it as a hive, and filled it with honey and their young.

Just this week, my student Bruce Wiebe pointed out in a seminar on Joyce that in the fifth chapter of *Ulysses,* the Lotos Eaters, where the symbolism is concerned with flowers, Leopold Bloom is a bee gathering nectar (look at *Gold Cup, Sceptre,* the calyx of the rolled newspaper, and Bloom's characteristically apian figure-eight amble). Molly, in the preceding chapter, is the queen of the hive. Stephen is a larva, and the whole novel is a daedalian golden honeycomb, the ultimate remaking and refinement of the labyrinth (which it also is). The original labyrinth was political, the final one, the honeycomb, is a gift to Aphrodite.

Crystal, we beseech thee,

(we read in Canto C)

Clarity, we beseech thee
from the labyrinth.

And in Canto LXXXIII, written in the concentration camp at Pisa:

and Brother Wasp is building a very neat house
of four rooms, one shaped like a squat indian bottle
La Vespa, *la* vespa, mud, swallow system

and further along in the Canto:

and in the warmth after chill sunrise
an infant, green as new grass
has stuck its head or tip
out of Madame La Vespa's bottle

and:

The infant has descended.
from mud on the tent roof to Tellus,
like to like color he goes amid grass-blades
greeting them that dwell under XTHONOS    ΧΘΟΝΟΣ
OI ΧΘΟΝΙΟΙ;          to carry our news
    εις χθονιους          to them that dwell under the earth,

begotten of air, that shall sing in the bower
of Kore,                    Περσεφόνεια
and have speech with Tiresias, Thebae

Cristo Re, Dio Sole

in about ½ a day she has made her adobe
(la vespa) the tiny mud-flask

and that day I wrote no further.

# Prehistoric Eyes

When the Dogon of Upper Volta and Mali, some of the most primitive people to survive into our age, build a new sanctuary, they decorate the façade with a tall painted oblong to the right of the door, and with one to the left. The one on the right is filled in top to bottom with two zigzag lines superimposed, making a kind of totem pole of lozenges, with a dot added to the center of each lozenge. The oblong to the left is divided into rectangles, each corresponding to the lozenges in the other oblong, and each with a dot in its center. Nothing could be simpler: we doodle such designs on our scratchpads at committee and board meetings, and we are aware that pottery the world over bears such repetitious designs. So does embroidery, wallpaper, furniture, jewelry. Encountering such designs, we have the aestheticians to tell us that they are rhythmic ways of filling space and of pleasing the eye. Archeologists will tell you that they are memories of the days when the first clay pots were imitations of woven baskets. The theories run on: these linear patterns spring from a love of symmetry, from a sense of infinity, from generosity of spirit, from a passion for intricate decoration.

But the Dogon are with us, lively and thriving, and if asked will explain their intent in painting a column of dotted lozenges to the right of a sanctuary door and a column of dotted rectangles to the left.

The column to the right represents the descent of a heavenly ark from deep in space to the African earth. On board were the 266 things which constitute all of life. The lozenges are actually the same as the rectangles on the left of the door, but tilted, to indicate that the ark in its fall spun like a leaf. Space is four-cornered (witness the solstices and equinoxes); hence lozenges. The dots are stones for the primal field. The left-hand column also represents the ark and the stages of its descent. Its rectangles are the lozenges oriented properly, as space when the ark had landed settled down to a constant up, a constant down, and the cardinal directions were then established.

The Dogon's explanation of this innocent-looking pattern goes on; you can consult 544 pages of it in the first fascicle of volume 1 of a projected sixteen volumes.[1] Similar explanations the world over of such designs are equally startling, equally discouraging to our attempts to read symbols.

And if the symbols are 30,000 years old? We are then faced with the letter in *Finnegans Wake* scratched up from a midden—Joyce's symbol for the deep, forgotten past, a past recorded sensitively and beautifully on cave walls, on bone, in sculpture, on flint tools, rings of megaliths, and mounds of earth depicting running horses, ithyphallic giants, and serpents. We have a vocabulary of responses to these signs, possibly all wrong, and probably projections of our way of seeing the world. We live in a decorated world, a frivolously decorated world, and thus see the Dogon graph of the primal ark's descent as a primitive pattern, something daubed by simple black souls.

In the deep background of Alexander Marshack's brilliant speculative study of prehistoric symbolism[2] is our gratuitous assumptions about the creature we call Cave Man. It was William Randolph Hearst, I believe, who gave us the shaggy, cow-browed, club-wielding lout dragging his wife behind him. We have received the curious notion that perhaps he grunted rather than spoke, and hunkered around a stick fire looking dazed and immensely stupid.

---

[1] Marcel Griaule and Germaine Dieterlen, *Le Renard pâle* (Paris: Institut d'Ethnologie, Musée de l'Homme, 1965).

[2] Alexander Marshack, *The Roots of Civilization: The Cognitive Beginnings of Man's First Art, Symbol and Notation* (New York: McGraw-Hill, 1972).

Yet in 18,000 B.C. he stitched his clothes together with an eyed needle, and when he fished he took along a fishhook and braided twine. He painted magnificent pictures of animals and gods, he sculpted with naturalistic skill. He had summer camps and winter camps.

He has even left us a picture of himself at Marsoulas, a face engraved in rock. It looks like nothing so much as a caricature by the French cartoonist Siné. The head is light-bulb-shaped. The eyes are shaky spirals crossed by an eyelid line. The nose is sharp and French, a triangle with a sagging hypotenuse. Two more lines: septum and mouth, at right angles, *et voilà!* There is a hairdo, probably plaits. Is it a woman? If not, our Cave Man shaved.

This George Price janitress (or god, or demon) is something we literally cannot see. We do not know if it is ugly or handsome, caricature or pious icon, male or female. Our eyes helplessly see it as witty and playful. It is Alley Oop by Alley Oop. And from it we can deduce an artist, a chisel, a mallet, and an audience that liked to look at pictures.

But Mr. Marshack starts his book with the fact that this creature watched the moon, noting its regularity of waxing and waning by notching bones, as if to be able to ascertain by double-checking that indeed every 29.5 days it repeats its dramatic metamorphosis from dark to sickle to circle to sickle to dark again.

This is Mr. Marshack's beginning. He was trying to make mathematical sense of the thousands of prehistoric objects on which prehistoric men kept track of something, like a western sheriff notching the handle of his gun for every horse thief brought down, or Robinson Crusoe with his calendrical stick. Some scholars said these incised lines were decoration; some have tried to see the birth of mathematics in them.

All, says Buckminster Fuller, is angle and incidence. Of primitive man's grasp of angles we know nothing. He would know that going downhill is easy, uphill hard, and would have perceived the use of the simplest machine, the inclined plane, down which things roll of their own accord. Some *vorarchimedisch* Archimedes would have stepped on the up end of a log leaning across a log and seen the principle of the fulcrum.

But it is incidence that Mr. Marshack tracks on the carved bones and calibrated rocks of the Upper Paleolithic. He offers dramatic and detailed arguments for reading the phases of the moon in series of notches which have been hitherto understood as decorations. Practically all the reviews of this part of his book have been scholarly cautious, many of them unconvinced. With reputations at stake, it is understandable that fellow prehistorians are not going to endorse Mr. Marshack straight off. Science is a matter of redoing experiments. In a sense it does not matter whether these markings are moon calendars or not. Mr. Marshack's point is that they are accounts in primeval numbers of something (animals killed in the hunt perhaps, or years in office of a phylarch, or days between menstrual periods).

When language emerges, the verb to *draw* is the same as *to write*. We can see, and to some extent read, the drawings of primitive man. Mr. Marshack's triumph in this book is that he goes a long way in showing us that the writing of the old stone age is indeed writing, and that there are plausible ways of reading it. From the notches which tend to come in groups of thirty and thus look suspiciously like lunar counts, he turns to engraved artifacts which have been around for years in museum cases and proceeds with a brilliantly useful idea—that of incidence, or as he says, "time-factoring"—to find coherences in symbols which had been interpreted before as totemistic, magic, or sexual.

A mackeral engraved on a bone, its mouth closed, becomes after Mr. Marshack's reinvestigation with microscope a salmon with its mouth open. Moreover, he identifies the pip that appears in the salmon's mouth at the spawning season. And why is the salmon pictured with a seal? Because, Mr. Marshack explains, seals at this time (as we know from fossils) followed the salmon far up inland rivers. And a squiggle of tiny lines in the composition with the salmon and seal turns out under the microscope to be a flower. The images become a story: spring, spawning, the earth coming to life again. Mr. Marshack is the first student of prehistory to detect floral imagery in these archaic pictures. Indeed, one needs a microscope to see the miniature blossoms and buds. Many "feathers," "spears," and "phalluses" of previous readings may well be primitive grains, or even trees.

Trees. The acacia tree to the Dogon is an animal, not a vegetable, or, as they say, "a person." It is surprising that ethnologists have not applied their knowledge of primitive thought to the reading of prehistory. It is among primitive metaphysics that the symbolic grammar of paleolithic signs will have survived, if it has survived. (Anthropologists like Leo Frobenius and Bertha von Dechend assume that it has.) Why not take a Dogon cosmologist to these mysterious bones and ask him to read them? If the master Dogon metaphysician Ogotemmêli, the blind old wizard who explained the earth, fate, and the stars (star by star) to the French ethnologist Marcel Griaule, could have been enticed into an *aliplani* (as he called it) and taken to the caves of the Dordogne, God knows what he could have explained.

Coming so soon after M. André Leroi-Gourhan's study of paleolithic cave painting, *Treasures of Prehistoric Art* (1968), and Annette Laming's *Lascaux* (1959), Mr. Marshack's pioneering theories arrive as part of a renaissance of prehistoric inquiries. Prehistory (Glyn Daniel has written a charming account of it in an available Penguin, *The Idea of Prehistory*) began among the antiquarians of England and France who kept stumbling upon it as inexplicable data (John Aubrey explained to King Charles that Stonehenge was a Roman temple). Some of the stone-age caves in France were discovered in the eighteenth century, though the discoverers hadn't a clue what they had discovered: they scrawled their initials and the date across the paintings and walked away, much as the chucklehead Bjarni Hrolfsson sailed by the coast of Massachusetts in 1000 and did not think it interesting enough to land upon.

John Frere had begun by 1790 to collect flint weapons from a pit in Suffolk; in 1838 Boucher de Perthes had a collection of stone axes; and the great search sets out in 1838 when Brouillet found in a cave at Vienne an engraved bone: the first example of ice-age art (Darwin was at the same time grasping the principles of evolution in the Galapagos).

Prehistory became a science in the hands of Henri Breuil and Émile Cartailhac and their circle. Even before their theories became current knowledge, Breuil's disciple Leroi-Gourhan, whose training was anthropological rather than antiquarian, found a way of making sense of the cave paintings. Starting with a survey of some 600 caves, he began to see patterns in the grouping of the animals: if a horse here, then a cow there. Human figures are always at the entrance or deepest part of the caves. Breuil had established the vocabulary of the images; Leroi-Gourhan gives us a coherent theory of the grammar. Mr. Marshack offers us a theory of inflections, of morphology.

Context has been the great problem of understanding: how these images figured in man's life. Breuil, a priest, tended to see them as religious; Leroi-Gourhan posited a sexual context of survival and creation. Marshack places them in time, in the seasons, and relates them to the hunt (man followed the herd animals; the Lapps still do), the sacrifice (the microscope discloses that images of animals have been "killed" several times over with lines in mortal places), the rutting and birth periods.

The microscope can determine that a small object, an incised bone with images and time-notations, was carried in men's hands for years and years. It can also reveal that worn images were "refreshed" with new engraving after years of handling. This is a new concept for prehistory: suddenly we have migrant men with objects in their hands which are not axes or knives, but chronometers with persistent symbols—a horse and salmon together was one of the most common. The hunter hunted with an image of the dying, pierced animal in his hand.[3]

[3]François Bordes, Professor of Prehistory at the University of Bordeaux, announced in December 1972 that he had discovered an engraved bone near the Pech de l'Aze Cave, in the environs of Sarlat, a region of the Dordogne rich in prehistoric caves and artifacts, which he estimates to be 230,000 years old. This is 200,000 years older than any previously known graphic notation by a human hand. The bone is the thigh of an ox, and the marks are arcs, bands, and double chevrons (like a gull's wings in flight). Mr. Marshack flew to France to

The little goddesses, all fat behind and bosom, turn out to be annotated, and this makes the moon count wonderfully plausible, for she is
our sole link between the wandering tribes and man the agriculturalist in
his first cities. That she is a moon goddess is one of the very few sure
guesses we can make about the religion of ice-age man.

For years now two disciplines have been tunneling toward each other
through deep time: the prehistorians, who see their subject melt into thin
air before 10,000 B.C., and the archeologists, who see their subject arising
around 6,000 B.C. A few faint and tenuous lines are beginning to cross
those blind years. The images on rock in the Val Camonica in the Tyrol
seem to be continuous from prehistory to Roman times: in the earliest,
horned men with strange paddles in their hands mate with reindeer cows,
and in the later, they own wagons and chariots and bronze swords. James
Mellaart's discoveries at Çatal Hüyük in Anatolian Turkey connect history and prehistory: the bulls of Lascaux and Altamira are still in the
religious symbolism, and the big-bosomed goddess is there, flanked by
leopards, recognizably the Mama of Sumeria and the Cybele of ancient
Syria. Zuntz's *Persephone* (1972) traces the rise of this old goddess (who
will become the field-goddess Demeter of the Greeks and the city-goddess
Cybele-Astarte-Fortuna of the Roman Empire) in Malta, where her prehistoric underground shrines were kidney-shaped, dark, and devoted to
the idea that birth and death are complementary events: Eleusis thousands of years before Eleusis.

"The repertoire of images found across the Upper Paleolithic of
Europe," Mr. Marshack writes

> . . . suggests a storied, mythological, time-factored, seasonal, ceremonial and
> ritual use of animal, fish, bird, plant, and serpent images, and it apparently
> also includes at times what seem to have been selective and seasonal killing
> and sacrifice, either of the image, in rite, or of the real animal. The complex-
> ity and interrelation of these storied meanings cannot easily be explained by

determine by microscopic analysis if indeed the bone is engraved rather than scratched or
cracked. His conclusion, which he presented before the American Association of Archeologists at the end of the year, is that it is engraved by two different chipped flint instruments. Prof. Hallam Movius, the distinguished protégé of Henri Breuil and Professor of
Archeology at Harvard, agrees that the bone is engraved deliberately (as distinct from idle
whittling). He would, however, shave 100,000 years from the bone's antiquity, and Marshack himself believes the bone to be no more than 135,000 years old. I learned about the
bone from the French press and, remembering its flair for the sensational, called both Profs.
Movius and Marshack to see just what had been found. Prof. Marshack feels that markings
are neither art nor notation of the kind he elucidates in *The Roots of Civilization*, but is
certain that they are signs. The dating of the bone is by geological stratum. Except for the
sureness that the bone is pre-Neanderthal, there is no information whatever to point to
what kind of people might have engraved it. No marked object older than 35,000 years was
known before its discovery.

any generalizing theories propounding concepts of hunting magic, fertility ritual, or sexual symbolism. Instead, the art and symbol suggest a broad range of cognitions, cultural and practical, and a profound understanding of processes in nature and of the varieties of living creatures. (p. 260)

And of the men who left us this art Mr. Marshack has wanted to determine their "evolved human cognition." And there the mystery is concealed: for we are on the moon studying geology and cosmology while acting, as nations and as individuals, with a savagery and brutality that may not even have been known (certainly not possible) to primitive man. Man, it would seem, does not evolve; he accumulates. His fund of advantages over nature and over the savage within is rich indeed, but nothing of the old Adam has been lost; our savagery has perhaps increased in meanness and fury; it stands out ever more terribly against a modern background.

Art, for instance, has not evolved. It has always been itself, and modern artists have notoriously learned more from the archaic discovered in our time than from the immediate centuries. Heraclitus was more precious to Wittgenstein than Plato. One can move from Pythagoras to Buckminster Fuller without needing the intervening geometricians as a connection.

And cognition? I would swap eyes, were it possible, with an Aurignacian hunter; I suspect his of being sharper, better in every sense. History is not linear; it is the rings of growth in a tree; and it is tragic. Mr. Marshack's study of mind twenty millennia back is a touching of ghosts in the dark, the ghosts of people from whom we are descended, whose genes we carry in our bodies. Our most diligent sciences look inward into the cell and atom, to stave off death. The historical sciences do not so obviously stave off death, but it seems to me that searching for man in his past and finding him not brutal and inarticulate but a creature of accomplished sensitivity and order, sane and perhaps more alive than we, is a shield against the forces among us that stave off life.

The Dogon, most primitive of men, can point to the star (western man found it only recently, with a telescope, and catalogued it with a number, and published the fact in the back pages of a newspaper, which was then used to wrap garbage) that contains the plan for the spiral inside the crabgrass seed, the source of life. I imagine the reindeer hunters of the Dordogne could, too. The real meaning, it seems to me, of such a book as this, is not what we have grown from as men living together, but what we have lost.

# Whitman

His rooms in Camden were shin-deep in wadded paper; nonchalance was one of the household gods. Visitors, wading in, knew the others so numinously there around the old man with so much white hair and beard, so freckled and so barbaricly slouched on a buffalo robe: the ghosts of Rossini and Scott, of Lincoln and Columbus, of Anacharsis Cloots and Elias Hicks, and two supreme goddesses, Artemis Philomeirix and Eleutheria whose *eidolon* was erected in his sixty-third year on Bedloe's Island, a gift from the French, three hundred and two feet tall, statue and pediment together, the work of Frédéric-Auguste Bartholdi, at the sight of which millions of eyes would water in grey dawns with an anguish of hope which only Whitman's poetry can duplicate ("Not a grave of the murdered for freedom but grows seed for freedom . . . in its turn to bear seed, / Which the winds carry far and re-sow, and the rains and the snows nourish"), Liberty.

Lincoln on horseback tipped his hat to him in Washington one day, a gazing stranger whom Lincoln must have supposed was some office seeker or underling in one of the departments, perhaps a geologist with that grizzled a beard. It was the republican equivalent of Napoleon looking in on Goethe to talk history and poetry.

He attended Poe's funeral, standing toward the back of the mourners. He comforted the dying in the war (like Henry James) and wrote letters home for them (like Ezra Pound at Pisa). Not until he was an old man did anyone care or know who he was. George Collins Cox came and photographed him hugging children (and copyrighted the photograph, as if Walt were Niagara Falls or Grand Canyon); Thomas Eakins came and did a masterpiece of a portrait. Young men came and learned what they might do with their lives, John Burroughs being the star pupil.

Like Poe, he has always been suspect in his own country. To name the Walt Whitman Bridge the authorities had to sidestep the objections of Christians and Patriots that his morals were un-American. Emerson, who once strolled through the Louvre without stopping in front of a single picture, was at pains to have it known that he was not a close friend of Whitman's. Thoreau wrote in his journal, December 1, 1856: "As for the sensuality in Whitman's 'Leaves of Grass', I do not so much wish that it was not written, as that men and women were so pure that they could read it without harm."

"Whitman," Kafka told his friend Gustav Janouch, "belongs among the greatest formal innovators in the modern lyric. One can regard his unrhymed verse as the progenitor of the free rhythms of Arno Holz, Émile Verhaeren, and Paul Claudel. . . . The formal element in Walt Whitman's poetry found an enormous echo throughout the world. Yet Walt Whitman's significance lies elsewhere. He combined the contemplation of nature and of civilization, which are apparently entirely contradictory, into a single intoxicating vision of life, because he always had sight of the transitoriness of all phenomena. He said: 'Life is the little that is left over from dying.' So he gave his whole heart to every leaf of grass. I admire in him the reconciliation of art and nature. . . . He was really a Christian and—with a close affinity especially to us Jews—he was therefore an important measure of the status and worth of humanity."[1]

"Have you read the American poems by Whitman?" Van Gogh wrote to his sister-in-law in September 1888. "I am sure Theo has them, and I strongly advise you to read them, because to begin with they are very fine, and the English speak about them a good deal. He sees in the future, and even in the present, a world of healthy, carnal love, strong and frank—of friendship—of work—under the great starlit vault of heaven a something

[1]Gustav Janouch, *Conversations with Kafka*, trans. Goronwy Rees (New York: New Directions, 1971), p. 167.

which after all one can only call God—and eternity in its place above this world. At first it makes you smile, it is all so candid and pure; but it sets you thinking for the same reason.

"The 'Prayer of Columbus' is very beautiful."[2]

The range of sensibilities that responded to his is impressive and a bit puzzling: Henry James, Melville, Swinburne, Tennyson, Victor Hugo, John Hay, Yeats, the Rossettis. He was a force useful to talents as diverse as those of William Carlos Williams and Dino Campana, Guillaume Apollinaire and Hart Crane. He had freed poetry from exclusive commitments to narrative and the ode. He closed the widening distance between poet and audience. He talks to us face to face, so that our choice is between listening and turning away. And in turning away there is the uneasy feeling that we are turning our backs on the very stars and on ourselves.

He succeeded in making himself a symbol of American idealism as bright and in many ways far more articulate than Jefferson or Jackson. But as an ideal figure he turned out to be risky currency. Thoreau and Emerson were safer, more respectable, and more apt to remain in the realm of ideas.

Whitman, Jack Yeats complained, was bad for the American spirit because it seemed to him that we indulged all too naturally in what Whitman urged us to wallow. Beerbohm caricatured this view of Whitman (". . . inciting the American eagle to soar"), and the young Ezra Pound in his Pre-Raphaelite suit thought Whitman much too much, while intelligently suspecting that there was something there that the critics weren't seeing.

There are lots of things the critics haven't seen. It is for instance worthwhile reading Whitman against the intellectual background he assumed his readers knew and which is no longer remembered except sporadically: the world of Alexander von Humboldt, from which Whitman takes the word *cosmos,* Louis Agassiz, for whom Thoreau collected turtles, Volney's *Ruins,* the historical perspective of which is as informative in Whitman as in Shelley; Fourier, Scott. A great deal that seems naif and spontaneous in Whitman has roots and branches.

His age still read Plutarch as part of its education, and Whitman's understanding of erotic camaraderie looks different (less personal and eccentric) beside a knowledge of the Theban Sacred Band under Pelopidas and Epameinondas, whose conversations in Elysium with Freud one would like to hear, those heroes whose names were terror to the Spartan infantry, who were Pythagoreans who believed, in the Master's

[2]*Complete Letters of Vincent van Gogh,* vol. 3 (New York: Graphic Society, 1958), p. 445.

dictum, that a friend is another self, who were sworn to chastity, and who passed daily the palace of an old king named Oedipus.

And they were, as they said in their language, democrats.

Whitman's fond gaze was for grace that is unaware of itself; his constant pointing to beauty in common robust people was a discovery. Custom said that beauty was elsewhere. Women in his time, as now, were pathologically interested in their own looks, especially in well-to-do families, because that would be their sole achievement, aside from motherhood, on this earth. They were laced breathlessly into corsets, caged in hoopskirts, harnessed into bustles. The body was girt about with bodices, drawers, bloomers, stockings, gloves, petticoats. Their shoes were always too small. They took no more exercise than aged invalids. Their hair was curled with irons heated in an open fire, then oiled, then shoved into a bonnet it would tire a horse to wear. Their flesh never met the light of the sun. They fainted frequently and understandably. How in the world did they pee?

In Plutarch you could read about Spartan girls who wrestled with boys, both naked. It was the opinion of the Spartans that clothing on such an occasion would be indecent. (We know of a Philadelphia woman in the time of Dr. Benjamin Rush who chose to die in modesty rather than let a doctor see her breasts).

One suspects that Thoreau would have married a woodchuck or a raccoon, if the biology of the union could have been arranged; Whitman might, given the opportunity, like Clarence King or Lafcadio Hearn, have married a black woman. It was one of his fantasies that he had had one for a mistress.

Freud's replacing one Calvinism with another pretty much the same should not fool us into thinking we can say that Whitman's love for handsome boys was a psychosis which we can then subtract from his book, like Victoria looking at da Vinci's notebooks with the anatomical drawings decorously covered by brown paper. That love is the very heart of his vision. He was reinventing a social bond that had been in civilization from the beginning, that had, in Christian Europe, learned various dodges, and met its doom in Puritanism and was thus not in the cultural package unloaded on Plymouth Rock.

As in the ancient world Whitman had no patience with the pathic (as his word was), the effeminate. He wanted in men and women a love that was unaware of itself, as heroism is unaware of itself, as children are unaware of their own beauty. What Whitman was observing as the mating habits of the species was a debased form of Courtly Love that the industrial revolution had intwined with commerce (a pretty wife was an asset to a rich man, indeed, she was part of his wealth). Women were caught in a strange new myth, as if Pluto were the most eligible husband for Persephone.

There was accuracy in Whitman's turning to those spirits that were free to be lively, lusty, inventive. He loved, as Nietzsche said of the Greeks, the health of the race. His race was like none before. It stood at a unique place in history. It joined the two halves of the world. Whitman's great vision culminates in his celebration of the spanning of our continent with rails, the closing of the gap between Europe and America with the transatlantic cable, and the opening of the Suez Canal. These completed the circle of which Columbus had drawn the first brave arc. More than commerce would flow along that new route that at last belted the whole earth. Why should not ideas as archaic as man himself immigrate along that line?

One reason Whitman is so interesting right now is that we do not yet know if that band around the earth is an umbilicus or a strangling cord. Albert Speer explained at Nuremberg that radio and telephone had amplified Hitler's scope and accelerated the implementation of his orders so far beyond any such power available to previous tyrants that we need a new kind of imagination to grasp how so much evil could have been done in those twelve infernal years. The first hell allowed by the world belt was Whitman's own Civil War, an old feud of the English that infected the new world and broke out with renewed vigor, Round Head and Cavalier, North and South, industrialist and planter.

Whitman's fellow nurse in the Union hospitals, Henry James, would live until 1916, another hell caused by easy scope of movement. Modernity seems to sink Whitman's vision of a cohesive society further and further back into the past while isolating its essential purity and brilliance. The final sterilizer of his vision would seem to be the internal combustion engine, which has made all movement restless and capricious.

And at the center of all Whitman's poetry there is movement. His age walked with a sprier step than ours; it bounced in buckboard and carriage; a man on a horse has his blood shaken and his muscles pulled. A man in an automobile is as active as a sloth; an airplane ride offers no activity more strenuous than turning the pages of a magazine. Dullness, constant numbing dullness, was the last thing Whitman would have thought of America, but that is what has happened.

In his second letter to Emerson Whitman objected at length to "writers fraudulently assuming as always dead what every one knows to be always alive." He meant sex; I wonder if the assumption might not now be valid of the mind. From Whitman onward there is a distrust of the poet in the United States. The art of genteel America was to be fiction, the movies, and *Schlagsahne*. There is a bewildering irony in New England Transcendentalism's fathering both Whitman and the current notion that poetry is cultural icing, spiritual uplift, wholly unrelated to anything at all. What was useful to middle-class frumpery was trivialized for anthologies, and the rest dismissed to the attention of professors and idealists.

Within a few miles of each other in the 1880s, Whitman was putting last touches to his great book, Eadweard Muybridge was photographing movements milliseconds apart of thousands of animals, naked athletes, and women, and Thomas Eakins was painting surgeons, boxers, musicians, wrestlers, and Philadelphians. Mary Cassatt, who might have been among them, had moved to France, permanently. In a sense Muybridge and Eakins were catching up with Whitman's pioneering. Their common subject, motion, the robust real, skilled and purposeful action, was distinctly American, an invention. Eakins and Muybridge worked together; Eakins came over to Camden and photographed and painted Whitman. Their arts ran parallel, shared a spirit and a theme. Muybridge's photographs, the monumental *Zoopraxia,* kept Degas and Messonier up all night looking at it. There has been no finer movement in American art, nor a more fertile one (from Muybridge, through Edison, the whole art of the film), and yet their impact was generally felt to be offensive. Eakins and Muybridge were forgotten for years; Whitman persisted.[3]

Grass: "a uniform hieroglyphic." Meaning in *Leaves of Grass* is an interpretation of symbols. The poet's work encompasses the undertaking of the most primitive transcriptions of nature into signs as well as contemporary decipherings of science, which had "great saurians" to explain, electricity, new planets. The double continuum of time and space became in Whitman's imagination a coherent symbol with perspectives to range.

Emerson's "He seems a Minotaur of a man" and Thoreau's "He occasionally suggests something a little more than human" (both remarks

[3]Muybridge, eccentric soul that he was, inscribed the double-folio *Zoopraxia: Men and Animals in Motion* as a gift to Haverford College. The good Quakers wrapped it in brown paper and hid it on the shelves of the library among outsized books, omitting to list it in the card catalogue. I found the bulky parcels there in an idle moment in 1964. Once I saw what I'd found, I commanded three hale students to help me carry it to my apartment. I then called the great kinesiologist Ray L. Birdwhistell, Jr., who dropped everything and came out. We spread the sheets all over the floor and in hours of looking I listened to Birdwhistell's analysis of how nineteenth-century people moved, what they did with shoulders, elbows, hips, eyebrows, toes, knees. Sherlock Holmes would have fallen down and worshiped. Any reading of Whitman is vastly enriched by a knowlege of Eakins and Muybridge; their arts can now be seen as complementary. Whether the Quakers have catalogued their Muybridge, sold it for the thousands of dollars it is worth, or put it back in its plain brown paper on the back shelves of the library, I have never asked.

were in letters to friends, not public print) catch Whitman in what would become traditional opinions: that his idealism was inappropriate to his rough matter, and that the roughness of his matter offended the idealism of his cultivated readers. No woman, it was assumed, could ever read him; Lowell insisted that the book, if placed in libraries, be kept from seminarians.

Is he so big that no one has yet taken his size? The cooperative struggle to measure Melville revealed greatness upon greatness. Where Whitman's tone is rich we can see his mastery: there is nothing anywhere like "Out of the Cradle Endlessly Rocking" (Hugo at his most resonant and symbolic sounds thin beside it; Leopardi, a plausible rival, could not have achieved the wildness, the lonely openness of the poem). Nor does "When Lilacs Last in the Dooryard Bloom'd," for all its Tennysonian color and voice, have an equal.

There are 390 poems in *Leaves of Grass* as Whitman left it. Modern editions add 42 others that he had rejected or not yet included; the Blodgett and Bradley Comprehensive Reader's Edition (Norton, 1965) adds 123 more pages of fragments, deletions, and notebook drafts.

He threw away:

I am that halfgrown angry boy, fallen asleep,
The tears of foolish passion yet undried upon my cheeks

and

Him of The Lands, identical, I sing, along the single thread . . .

in which the full timbre of his voice is undiminished. Had Whitman written entirely in his strong, aria-like, lyric mode, he would have fared far better with the critics (who speak of his formlessness) and fellow poets (who complain of the catalogues, the dross, the talk), but he would have been little more than an American Victorian, Tennyson with a twang.

We have paid too little attention to Whitman's subjects, especially when they smack of the prosaic. Consider "Outlines for a Tomb (G. P., Buried 1870)" which imagines various tableaux for a millionaire philanthropist's tomb, a poem thoroughly traditional, a classical eulogy to which Chaucerian pictured rooms have been added. The poem comes into stereoptic focus when we go to the trouble to discover that G. P. is George Peabody (1795–1869). The curious "buried 1870" becomes clear when we know that Peabody died in London and was brought home in a British war ship, with full honors. An apprentice to a drygoods firm at eleven, he worked his way up in the world until, as head of a banking firm with offices in Baltimore, Philadelphia, New York, and London, he was able to become one of the first great merchant philanthropists. He gave two million to the English for housing for the poor, a museum to Harvard, and a museum to Yale. Yale got her museum to house the paleontological collection of Othniel Marsh, who was Peabody's nephew; Harvard got hers to house Agassiz's biological specimens. Harvard was not originally a beneficiary; it was only after the pious Peabody discovered that Marsh was a Darwinian that he tried to counteract this heresy by bestowing equal funds on Harvard, where Agassiz, Darwin's superior as a zoologist, declined to accept the great theory without further proof. Yet you will not find George Peabody in the *Britannica*.[4]

As Whitman's world faded into dimness, a great deal of his poetry was rendered meaningless except as general or abstract statement. Things vivid to him and his readers, such as Transcendentalism, the philosophy of Fourier and Owen, the discovery of dinosaurs in the west by Cope and Marsh, phrenology, photography, telegraphy, railroads, have fused into a blur. A technological era was beginning to articulate itself and Whitman was its poet. It was not a time to which one inside it could easily give a name, or a direction. Whitman's only certainty was that he was living in a new kind of society, that tore itself asunder in the tragedy of the Civil War, but did not thereby abandon its orignal intention to be a democratic republic.

> Quicksand years that whirl me I know not whither,
> Your schemes, politics, fail, lines give way, substances mock and elude me,
> Only the theme I sing. . . .

The theme. A music of sensations, songs containing catalogues of things, as if creation could be summoned and praised by chanting the name of everything there is, the constructing of a context, like Noah's ark, where there is a place for everything, a compulsion to confront every experience with innocent eyes—no one phrase is ever going to label Whitman's theme. The base on which it stands is Christian: a sympathy whose scope is rigorously universal, a predisposition to love and understand. Young admirers fancied him an American Socrates, but of course he is the very opposite. He was like those Greeks in love with the immediate, the caressable (always with the eye), the delicious, who, to St. Paul's distress, worshiped each other when free from placating and begging from a confusion of gods.

And he was decidedly pagan, always ready with a good word for "the

---

[4]You will in *The Columbia Encyclopedia*. For an account of Peabody in his scientific context, as well as for a splendid history of paleontology in the age of Whitman, see Robert West Howard's *The Dawnseekers* (New York: Harcourt Brace Jovanovich, 1975). You can also see in this book a photograph of Edgar Allan Poe inspecting the fossil skeleton of a prehistoric horse: a photograph still unknown to the Poe scholars.

rhythmic myths of Greece and the strong legends of Rome." A pagan is not a godless man; he is a man with many gods. Whitman could easily (as he liked to imagine) kneel with the Muslim, hear the Law with the Jew, sit in silence with the Quaker, dance with the Pawnee.

This splendid sympathy with forms knits his book together. Grass is the one universal plant, absent only in the deserts of the poles. Classifying and naming the grasses of the world has kept botanists overworked since Linnaeus, and the end is nowhere in sight. Leaves: we use the word for the pages of books, and the first paper was leaves of grass, papyrus. Grass is a symbol for life throughout the Bible, integral with the metaphor of shepherd and sheep.

There were "nations ten thousand years before these States"; we are carrying something on. And of this past "not a mark, not a record remains—and yet all remains." From the people in the deep forgotten past,

Some with oval countenances learn'd and calm,
Some naked and savage, some like huge collections of insects,

our heritage is unknown, but there is no doubt of there being a heritage.

Charles Fourier, who thought civilization a mistake, said that man's first duty to keep the Sacred Flame, which he understood to be both our kinship to God and those livelinesses of spirit man himself had invented—the dance, poetry, music, mathematics, communal genius like French cuisine, Cretan stubbornness, Scotch scepticism, Dutch house-keeping. Whitman knew Fourier only in the washed and bowdlerized versions of his thought discussed at Brook Farm, and in the writings of Blaine, Greeley, and Margaret Fuller. Perhaps he believed Emerson's warning that Fourier was basically unsound. Yet Whitman and Fourier were of the same historical moment, and much of their thought rhymes, though with many a dissonance. Fourier died (in Montmarte, while saying his prayers, kneeling against his bed, surrounded by his cats) when Whitman was eighteen. In those eighteen years Fourier was writing texts that would have interested Whitman immensely—they were not published until 1957, and some are still unpublished. They describe a world, the New Harmony as Fourier called it, that has kept the flame. It is a world divided up into beehives of communities, each of which is a family of human beings and animals. All work is done by everybody, an hour at a time. The days are rhythmic and contain a little of everything good. All sexual predilections are arranged for and honored for their diversity. Ceremonial honors are given to those whose passionate nature encompasses the widest range. All are friend and servant to all. Children learn every skill by age ten, yet the dominant note of the community is play.

Fourier's vision was an opposite to the commercial world in which he lived and suffered. In utopian design his is the most extreme yet achieved. It can be explained by noting that Fourier's every detail intends to save the individual from that dullness and quiet despair which was the immediate and alarming result of the Industrial Revolution.

If the world was to belong to the rapacious, civilization was then little more than the jungle. Rapacity, in any case, as Fourier thought, was alternative action symbolizing and disguising warmer passions unacceptable to civilization. Marriage, for instance, is a reproductive not a social unit. A true family is an enormous gathering of people, like a primitive tribe, where congeniality can have a large scope, and where everybody knows he belongs. The city was to disappear, and we may already have cause, watching the cities rot and revert to the jungle, to wonder whether Fourier's small communities could possibly by this time have rotted with such Spenglerian gangrene as Detroit and St. Louis.

*To keep the sacred flame.* The image is taken from antiquity, when the household fire was a god, part of which was given to each member of the family as they went away to new homes. Symbolically this fire was the family spirit, guardian of its integrity and survival. Fourier talks about it as if it were spirit itself, and he designed his Harmony to preserve the liveliness of the child into old age; he saw no reason why it should drain away. He is the only philosopher interested in happiness as the supreme human achievement. A good nature should be the whole concern of government.

It was compliant, insouciant, easy good nature that Whitman admired most in society. And nineteenth-century industrial culture had begun to erase the possibilities of Whitmanian good nature. Ruskin noted the characteristic sulk on American girls' faces, the pout, the petulance. Look at the Steichen photograph of J. P. Morgan, 1903, the one with the dagger. Slow-burning rage, not charming insouciance, was to be the standard American state of mind.

An American publisher remembered in old age "a large-boned old man in a sombrero" shuffling into the Hotel Albert (the anecdote is Ford Madox Ford's, and is therefore suspect). "I am Walt Whitman," said the old man, "if you'll lend me a dollar you'll be helping immortality to stumble on." (The dollar would have been equally useful upstairs in the hotel, where Ryder hovered over his visions: American culture has the eerie habit of passing itself, in narrow corridors, ghostlike). Whitman's personal loneliness and destitution became part of the legend quite early. "A fine old fellow in an iron land" begins Ruben Darío's sonnet to Whitman. Garcia Lorca:

Not for a single moment, handsome old Walt Whitman,
have I lost the vision of your beard full of butterflies,

your corduroy shoulders wasted by the moon
your thighs of virginal Apollo,
your voice like a column of coarse ashes;
old man beautiful as mist.[5]

Crane in *The Bridge* lets his evocation of Whitman walking on the beach "Near Paumanok—your lone patrol . . ." blend with another beach, Kitty Hawk. Even if the Gasoline Age had not changed the world into the Slope of Sisyphus, it would still be arguable if any society could have lived up to Whitman's idealism. Like Thoreau's, it is an idealism for individuals rather than conglomerates. For all its acceptance of the city crowds and the bustle of commerce, it is in essence pastoral, following natural rhythms, with sympathies that depend on the broad and easy freedom of country people. Never again could a major American poet comprehend, much less repeat, Whitman's vision. Yet many began there and were nourished on its honey before they ate of the tree of the knowledge of good and evil. Charles Ives did, set some of the poems as songs, but abandoned his *Walt Whitman Overture,* if he ever indeed began it. Pound's *Cantos* are a version of "A Passage to India" written in finer historical detail and transposed into a tragic mode. *Paterson* is Whitman's vision after a devastating rain of acid vulgarity. Olson's *Maximus* records the awful fact that Whitman's prophecy for a coherent democratic society remains unfulfilled in any sense, as we now live in an incoherent industrial society that has discovered that death is much better for business than life. The largest American business is the automobile, the mechanical cockroach that has eaten our cities; that and armaments.

Of the delights celebrated in "A Song of Joys," most are accessible now only to the very rich, some are obsolete, some are so exploited by commerce as to be no longer joys for anybody except the stockbroker, two are against the law (swimming naked, sleeping with "grown and part-grown boys"), and one is lethal ("the solitary walk").

Whitman is a kind of litmus paper, perhaps a seismograph. Reading him, we become aware of an awful, lost innocence, and are not certain whether the innocence was real or in Whitman's imagination. He gave his whole life to a book, he freed literature to go courses that were until Whitman unsuspected. He had the power to move even unwilling hearts (witness Gerard Manley Hopkins reading him because he couldn't not read him, knowing the author to be "a scoundrel" and the poetry to be wicked). Pound in the cage at Pisa remembered a University of Pennsylvania philologist who was suprised at attitudes toward Whitman, as "even the peasants in Denmark know him." The Japanese publish a jour-

[5]Geoffrey Dutton, trans., *Whitman* (New York: Grove Press, 1961), p. 111.

nal devoted to him. The Russian Futurists and Mayakovsky considered Whitman to be the founder of their school.

Many excellent books have been written about him, his place in world literature is assured. He is still, however, a renegade, disreputable still. That he was a master of words and rhythms is affirmed and denied with equal passion. His cults come and go. He is, like Goethe in Germany and Victor Hugo in France, inextricably part of our histroy. Like Jefferson and Franklin he has been woven into our myth. He is our archetypal poet, our great invention in literature, our lyric voice. I like to think that eventually he will shame us into becoming Americans again.

# Olson

It is now almost seven years since the enormous presence of Charles Olson arrived rumpled and wild upon the yellow distances of the Plain of Elysion, on the outermost ring of the circle river Okeanos, estate of heroes and poets, where he would have had to bend deeply to embrace his belovéd Keats, twenty-one inches shorter than Olson, who in his stocking feet was taller by half again than Alexander the Great.

At Olson's funeral, Allen Ginsberg, chanting kaddish with an anguished uncertainty of the words ("*Yisgadal v'Yiskadash shmay raba* ..."), stepped in his confusion on the pedal that would lower the outsized coffin into the grave. A soft whirr, the coffin tilted, lurched, and stuck before Ginsberg could leap away from the pedal. He continued chanting the ancient Aramaic words "*yhai shlama raba min-shmaya v'hiyim. . . ."* In the silence that followed, the undertaker's functionary who pressed his foot on the pedal that would lay Olson forever to rest discovered that Ginsberg had jammed the mechanism. The coffin was wedged neither in nor out of the grave.[1]

Keeping as it does the tradition of funerary chaos among American men of letters—a locomotive jumped its track and smashed Poe's tombstone (this is the *"calme bloc ici-bas chu d'un désastre obscur"* of Mallarmé's "Tombeau d'Edgar Poe"), Bret Harte's funeral was followed by a taggle of dogs throwing his entrails into the air (evisceration was a problem for early embalmers, and Harte was the first American author to be embalmed), and Melville, dying forty years after the world had forgotten him, was buried as "a formerly well-known author" whose best book, said the obituaries, was *Typee*—Olson's funeral is a symbol of his reputation as a poet.

His poetry is inarticulate. His lectures achieved depths of incoherence. His long poem *Maximus* was left unfinished, like most of his projects and practically all of his sentences. He put food in his pockets at dinner parties. He was saved from starving by Hermann Broch. He once ate an oil rag. He was, like Coleridge, a passionate talker for whom whole days and nights were too brief a time to exhaust a subject. He wrote a study of American musical comedies, was a professional dancer, served in the State Department under Roosevelt, went to the rain forests of Yucatan, was rector of a college. He was taller than doors and had the physique of a bear. He was an addict as he grew older to both alcohol and drugs.

He was interested in everything. Stan Brakhage visited him in Gloucester, May 1963. Their first conversation was twelve hours long; Brakhage wrote down what he could remember of it for his wife Jane. "This last year . . . most difficult ever . . . but that's changing, changing so fast . . . I see that change—yes, I HEAR you . . . how it takes form in terms of money; but then remember, this IS America—in three weeks this whole picture could be changed for all of us. . . ."

He was still interested in a *collegium* of scholars and teachers. Black Mountain, he felt, and the small college in general, was no longer the way. The universities were *centers* ("you can use them, you know . . .") where something like education just might happen, if you could get the right men together.

He took Brakhage round the town, pointing. He explained that he had been raised on the first point of the mainland of America, "that point geographically furthest out, I mean where I could be most easterly-

---

[1]This account, I'm told, is not wholly accurate. I had it from Stan Brakhage, who had it secondhand. I leave it as an example of the kind of folklore about himself that Olson inspired and encouraged.

westerly . . . how I was, as my father before me, letter-carrier; my first job as a boy—right here, where we're standing." He took Brakhage to stand where, under them, out of sight and out of most memories, a battleship's hull is buried, its pumps functioning as the town's sewerage disposal.

And the talk went on. Drama needed the mask again. Women actors ought not to have been introduced onto the stage. There were no more plays. "Yes, yes, we must, must, *must* get rid of drama, at all costs—I mean, even get rid of narrative—the temptation, you hear?"

"With you, Brakhage, it is at this point a question of focus, is it not. . . ? I'm an authority on cave painting, as you surely know. . . . Stop trying to defend the fact that you ARE, are you not, myopic, that is, NEAR-sighted; and wall-eyed . . . as am I . . . as is Robert Duncan . . . right?"

"I have, even tho' I suffer from claustrophobia, crawled around IN those tunnels, seen how, very often, the Pleistocene man HAD, that is chose, to paint where he couldn't have seen more than six inches from where he was painting, eyes THAT close."

"I mean what IS all that out there which we CALL focus? What IS focus, Brakhage? Hey?"[2]

Thousands and thousands of hours of such talk shaped his mind. His attention was constantly changing focus, from the rods and cones in a pigeon's eye to the drift of continents. A good half the time in the classroom his students didn't know even remotely what in the name of God he could be talking about. Surviving lecture notes have such entries as "journals of the Amiel brothers"—Olson's or the student's fusion of Amiel's *Journal* with that of the brothers Goncourt? Black Mountaineers remember the persistence of the names Frobenius and Bérard; one wonders what they could have read to follow up? You couldn't step twice into the same Olson lecture. Mark Heddon's Black Mountain diary records that Olson wanted his students to achieve vertically the entire horizon of human knowledge.[3]

Knowledge to Olson was a compassionate acquisition, an act of faith and sympathy. He meant primarily that knowledge is the harvest of attention, and he fumed in great rages that the hucksters prey on our attention like a plague of ticks. In his first thoroughly Olsonian poem, "The Kingfishers," a *canzone* that divides decisively modern from postmodern poetry, the theme states that when our attentions change, our culture

[2]Stan Brakhage, *Metaphors on Vision,* ed. and with an introduction by P. Adams Sitney, *Film Culture,* no. 30 (Fall 1963), pages unnumbered: passages quoted here all occur in the last five pages.

[3]Martin Duberman, *Black Mountain: An Exploration in Community* (New York: Dutton, 1972), p. 373.

changes. He uses the firm example of the Mayan cultures, overgrown with jungles. The Mayan shift in attention was culturally determined: every fifty-two years they abandoned whole cities in which the temples were oriented toward the planet Venus, which edges its rising and setting around the ecliptic. The new city was literally a new way to look at a star (this is one meaning of "polis is eyes").

There is history (Waterloo, Guadalcanal) and there is the history of attention (Rousseau, Darwin). The kind of knowledge that shifts attention was Olson's kind of knowledge. He was interested in the past because it gives us a set of contrasts by which to measure events and qualities.

The awe with which he told Brakhage about entering prehistoric caves and looking at the paintings done there is a sensitivity achieved with enormous learning and insight. The first prehistoric paintings to be discovered were assumed to be a few hundred years old, the work perhaps of rude shepherds passing the time. It took a corps of scientists (Cartailhac, Breuil, Movius, Peyrony, the Bégouïns ... ) half a century to prepare our attention to grasp the spiritual content of these eloquent pictures, and to teach us the value of knowing what they are.

Look what happens when you have neither knowledge nor sense of awe. By 1846 only a few of the French caves in the Dordogne had been discovered, and there was only a rudimentary understanding of the prehistoric: Sallèles-Cabardès, Rouffignac, Le Portel, and perhaps Niaux were known. (Altamira is 1879, Les Trois Frères 1916, Lascaux 1940). With whatever scant knowledge, a sonneteer in 1846, annoyed by the proliferation of illustrations in Victorian magazines, shamed mankind for reverting to the crudity of communication by pictures. Here is the sonnet—it is the first mention in English poetry of Cro-Magnon polychrome painting (40,000 to 25,000 B.C.), the renaissance of which by modern artists (Picasso, Gaudier, Braque, Pound) constitutes the basis of the sharpest sensibility of our century:

Discourse was deemed Man's noblest attribute,
And written words the glory of his hand;
Then followed Printing with enlarged command
For thought—dominion vast and absolute
For spreading truth, and making love expand.
Now prose and verse sunk into disrepute
Must lackey a dumb Art that best can suit
The taste of this once-intellectual Land.
A backward movement surely have we here,
From manhood—back to childhood; for the age—
Back toward caverned life's first rude career.

Avaunt this vile abuse of pictured page!
Must eyes be all in all, the tongue and ear
Nothing? Heaven keep us from a lower stage!

Wordsworth, of all poets, is the author of this sonnet. One gauge of the kind of attention Olson meant is to imagine Wordsworth in Lascaux. ("Don't laugh," Degas said at a Cubist exhibition, "this is as hard to do as painting.") Would he have seen it as art at all? What sensibilities could he have relied on to make a focus for his attention? Olson's argument throughout his poetry is that awareness is an event caused by multiple forces, setting multiple forces in action. No force is ever spent. All events are lessons. No event can be isolated.

Olson therefore evolved a kind of poem that would at once project historical ponderables (for history is the ground for all his poetry) and allow him free play for contemplation and response. The poems in *Maximus III* were written "in gloom on Watch-House Point" from 1963 to 1969. They constitute the third volume of perhaps one long poem, "Books VII and After" (Olson's working title), comparable in American literature to *The Cantos* and *Paterson;* perhaps a suite of poems (the early format of "letters from Maximus" allowing for the versatility and spontaneity of a correspondence) like *Leaves of Grass.* The first volume, *The Maximus Poems,* came out in 1960, as Number 24 of Jonathan Williams's Jargon series,[4] the second as *Maximus Poems IV, V, VI* (New York: Cape Goliard/Grossman, 1968).

If we allow for the sections of these poems that quote historical documents, and for the occasional jeremiad, we can go a long way toward understanding them by noting that they are variations of Keats's nightingale ode. They are for the large part written at night (by a Timonish Endymion *en pantoufles,* or an insomniac bear with clipboard wandering about Gloucester, caught from time to time in the spotlight of a police cruiser), they share the imagery of bird and flower (cormorant and nasturtium here), fierce seas and bonging bells (buoys on Cape Ann), and they meditate on resonances of the past that can still be heard.

The first poem—

having descried the nation
to write a Republic
in gloom on Watch-House Point

[4]There had been two previous editions: *The Maximus Poems 1–10* (Stuttgart: The Jargon Society, 1953) and *Letters 11–22* (Stuttgart: The Jargon Society, 1956), both published by Jonathan Williams. *Maximus I* was revised for the 1960 volume. You could still have bought the 1953 volume in Highlands, North Carolina, last year for its original price of $2.25 (the going price outside North Carolina is $100). Olson himself placed the books with The Book Mart there, five copies, which took twenty-one years to sell.

—contains the Keatsian verb *descry* (to spy out, to examine at a distance:
Johnson), an eventful phrase ("to write a Republic" invites us to understand "to write a *Republic,* like Plato and Machiavelli," "to write a letter
to the Republic"), and a place the name of which is transparently symbolic.

The second is in a congenial voice—

Said Mrs Tarantino,
occupying the yellow house
on fort constructed like
a blockhouse house said
You have a long nose, meaning
you stick it into every other person's
business, do you not? And I couldn't
say anything
but that I
do

And her name is *Tarantino,* citizen of Tarentum, the colonial city
where Greek and Roman cultures first met and fused; Greek name,
Taras. Spartans founded Taras in 706 B.C. following the edict of the Oracle at Delphi to "colonize this rich land and be a trial to the barbarians."[5]
Tarentine history was brilliant under the archonship of the great Platonic
philosopher and physicist Archytas. Over the centuries the Tarentine
cavalry was the terror of southern Italy. After Pyrrhus's eponymous victory over the Romans in 275 (about which Stephen Dedalus is questioning his class at the opening of the second chapter of *Ulysses*), the citizens
threw in their lot with "the barbarians," and by 213 were so far from
their Spartan heritage that they invited Hannibal to be their overlord.
When the Romans retook the city in 209, they burnt it, *für Schreck-
lichkeit,* sold the entire population into slavery, and carried off the
statues of the gods (all but the "angry ones"). The principal temple was
to Demeter and Persephone, but the city had been under the protection of
Bona Dea, Athena of Cities. The third poem begins with her name.
Gloucester was colonized in 1623, a town, like Taras, of fishermen and
godly people; in 1776 it dissolved its ties with its mother country and
joined the federation: ". . . this filthy land / in this foul country where /
human lives are so much trash"[6] we read by page 120.

[5]J. Bérard, *Le Colonization grecque de l'Italie méridionale et de la Sicile dans l'antiquité*
(Paris, 1957), p. 162. This is not Olson's Bérard that he was always talking about; that is
Victor Bérard, who derived the *Odyssey* from Phoenician sailing maps.

[6]Automobile accidents, for example, claim 50,000 lives a year, and maim 75,000 bodies. To
act out the fantasies of various liars, scoundrels, and politicians 56,869 young Americans
died in Vietnam.

Olson's spiritual barometers and seismographs give readings that we have to live with for awhile before they begin to render up sense. His view of mankind reaches into the backward abysm. Geologically the world is in the Pleistocene still, the age that evolved the horse, elephant, and cow more or less as we know them. And man. And the arrangement of the continents as they are now.

From *Maximus IV* forward Olson has introduced the subject of continental drift. This is the discovery of the German geologist Alfred Wegener, though the likelihood was first suggested by the United States geologist Frank B. Taylor between 1908 and 1910.[7] Francis Bacon observed that the continents seemed to be a jigsaw puzzle, as did François Placet and Alexander von Humboldt.

Two hundred million years ago there was one continent, so the theory runs, named Pangaea, and one ocean, Panthalassa. (Has geology ever sounded more Ovidian?) A northern landmass, Laurasia, split away from the southern landmass Gondwana a hundred and thirty-five million years ago. Another twenty-five million years, and India wandered away from Africa. The last of the continents to divide was the one that became Antarctica and Australia.

The long and perilous voyage that brought Europeans into America as a second migration, 150,000 years after the Indian came here from Asia, could at one time (if any men were about) have been made by taking a single step.

Throughout these last Maximus poems Olson keeps gazing at the offshore rocks, especially Ten Pound Island. That it was once at the bottom of an ice sheet that lay across Europe is a fact rich in mythological tone. The severing of the continents is itself a comprehensive symbol of disintegration, of man's migratory fate, of the tragic restlessness of history (". . . and Gloucester still moves *away* from the Canaries—she was Terceira 'lightest' of those islands. . . .").

What has happened to American culture (Melville observed that we are more a world than a nation) is a new disintegration that comes hard upon our integration. A new *daimon* has got into the world, a daimon that cancels place (American cities all look like each other), depletes the world's supply of fossil fuel (if anybody's around to make the statement, our time can be put into a sentence: *the Late Pleistocene* ate *the Eocene*), transforms the mind into a vacuum ("Do they grow there?" a New Yorker asked of the offshore rocks at Gloucester) which must then be

[7]Dover Publications has just reissued Wegener's *The Origin of Continents and Oceans* (New York, 1929), translated by John Biram. Edwin H. Colbert's *Wandering Lands and Animals* (New York: Dutton, 1973) is an excellent exposition of the subject. A shorter account can be found in Samuel W. Matthews, "This Changing Earth," *National Geographic,* Jan. 1973, pp. 1–37.

filled with evaporating distractions called entertainment.[8] Olson was too intelligent to give a name to this daimon; he was aware of the names Ruskin and Pound had given it, but a cooperation between greed and governments is far too mild a monster for Olson's vision. He was of De Gaulle's opinion that we are the first civilization to have bred our own barbarians: De Gaulle was alluding to the masked rioters stomping down the Boulevard St.-Germain in May of '68; Olson would have meant the automobiles with their hind ends up like the butts of hemorrhoidal jack-rabbits that squawl their tires and are driven by a hunnish horde of young who have been taught nothing, can do nothing, and exhibit a lemming restlessness. Their elders are scarcely more settled or more purposeful to themselves or their neighbors.

A shift in attention allows the jungle in.

The *polis* is gone; no one can imagine that there are any American cities left. The towns have died at their centers and thrown up a circular scab around themselves, a commercial carnival. We know all too well what Olson is talking about, if not what he is trying to teach us. These poems are more frightening in their implications than the last of *The Cantos,* than Dr. Williams's diagnoses.

I am not able here to given any notion of the wideness of these last Maximus poems—the horizon they survey is vast—nor of their depth, which goes back into various histories (the Hittite, Egyptian, Greek, Roman, paleolithic) in new and bright ways (Olson's eyes were open to everything and very little got by him). Nor can I adequately represent their religious concern. A movement is closed by them, a movement that began with Thoreau and Whitman, when America was opening out and possibilities were there to be stumbled over or embraced. Olson is the other term of this movement. He is our anti-Whitman (like Melville before him). He is a prophet crying bad weather ahead, and has the instruments to prove it.

## II. SCHOLIA AND CONJECTURES FOR "THE KINGFISHERS"

"The Kingfishers" is itself a paradigm of the process of continuity and change which it tracks with a kind of philosophical radar.

This most modern of American poems, the most energetically influential text in the last thirty-five years, is a resuscitation of a poetic form worked to death between the late eighteenth and mid-nineteenth cen-

[8]At a recent trial of some members of the American Nazi Party, the jurors proved to be unprejudiced, for the simple reason that they, all middle-aged, had never heard of *any* Nazis. And a child for whom I was drawing animals the other day asked me to draw him a *jaws.*

turies, from the age of Peacock's "Palmyra," Shelley's "The Demon of the World" and "Ozymandias," and Volney's *Les Ruines,* to the masterwork of all meditations on ruins, Melville's *Clarel.* That there was life and a new relevance in a genre which had been a standard feature of the Victorian sensibility was proved three years before "The Kingfishers" by the Chilean poet Pablo Neruda, whose *Alturas de Macchu Picchu* provided Olson with a chord of images (honey, stone, blood), the balanced historical moments of brutal conquests and the Marxist revolutions of the present, the continuity of natural and the discontinuity of human history, and perhaps a line: "Not one death but many" (*y no una muerte, sino muchas muertes*). Perhaps: for those words also occur in a dialogue of Plutarch's which is yet another instigation for the poem's composition.

"The Kingfishers" is also a response to *The Pisan Cantos,* which had been published the August before (Olson completed the poem 20 July 1949);[9] its opening line is modelled on the fifth line of Canto LXXIV, "That maggots shd/ eat the dead bullock," Olson mistaking the slash after "shd" (a device Pound took from the letters of John Adams, along with the abbreviation, both of which were common practice in Adams's time) for a new kind of punctuation, "a pause so light it hardly separates the words."

The Republic of China was proclaimed 1 October 1949, three months after Olson wrote "The Kingfishers." The imminent fall of China to the Communists is also a theme in the *Pisan Cantos.* Both Pound and Olson mark the event as a momentous one, and they are equally uncertain as to its meaning. One of the continued themes from the poetry of Pound to that of the Projectivist School is a new sense of history. It is a sense that is always in touch with archaic beginnings. Pound's Mao is "a snotty barbarian ignorant of T'ang history." Olson places Mao against ancient considerations that seem to have nothing to do with his revolution: the fate of the Mayans, the Hellenistic empire in the time of Nero and Plutarch, the Khmer dynasty of Cambodia.

And then "The Kingfishers" is as well a Romantic ode, like Keats's "Nightingale" and Shelley's "Skylark"—a philosophical lyric with a bird *daimon* at its center. Add to this that it is a Pythian dialogue in the manner of Plutarch ("The Praises" is another such dialogue among philosophers skilled in the traditions of their subject, the "Leskenoi," devotees of Apollo Leskhenorios, "Apollo the Conversationalist") and we can begin to grasp the intricacy and energy of the vector field Olson has constructed.

[9]Published in *The Montevallo Review,* no. 1 (Summer 1950), ed. Robert Payne.

A new kind of poem then, asking for a new kind of reading. It cannot be avoided that we as readers are asked to become Leskenoi along with the poet, to leave the polychrome images and finely modulated rhythms of the poem, learn some things, and then return as a worthy participant.

A superficial reading will show some of the perspectives, and something of the harmonies.

The kingfisher. Audubon's *Birds of America,* plate 77, is a handsome representation of the fowl. It is about a foot long. *Megaceryle Alcyon.* It is a lake and river bird, ecologically welcome, as it feeds on enemies of the trout. There are no rivers in Yucatan, and John Lloyd Stephens in his catalogue of Mayan fauna lists no kingfishers, though they winter in other parts of Mexico. The European counterpart is a persistent image in classical poetry, from the *Iliad* forward. It is also everywhere in Romantic poetry. Is Olson presenting it as a symbol? (William Carlos Williams, who was fond of the poem, and habitually called it "The Woodpeckers," hoped not.) "The trouble with symbol, it does not trouble" ("The Post Virginal"). We must take the kingfisher as a totem image, a hieroglyph. It is an element in an ideogram. And the poem, like a canto of Pound, is a single ideogram, its components working in synergy.

1.

The opening line is a translation of Heraclitus's Fragment 23 (quoted by Plotinus in the *Enneads* IV.viii.1). *Metabállon anapaúete:* "Change is at rest." Or: "Change alone is unchanging." Sensing in the etymology of *metabállon* the idea of wilfullness (*bállo,* I throw, is kin to *boúlomai,* I will), Olson translates *metabállon* as "the will to change."

There follows a narrative passage reminiscent of the room full of birds in Malraux's *La Condition humaine,* but which is probably a transcription from life (Ronald Johnson assures me that Olson frequently slept in his clothes). Fernand is a mystery: a survey of Olson's circle and scholars has failed to turn up any identification at all. Léger at Black Mountain? He is a man who knew Josef Albers (b.1888), the painter, who was on the faculty at Black Mountain when the poem was written, and knew something of the Khmer ruins at Angkor Vat, something of the Aztec-Mayan commerce in kingfisher feathers, and something of the well of sacrifice ("The pool is slime") at Chichen Itza which Bishop Landa described in the sixteenth century and which was dredged by Edward Thompson in 1904–1907. The sacrificial victims thrown into this well by the Mayans (they were messengers with requests carefully memorized to recite to the gods once they were in the kingdom of the dead) wore head-dresses (*corozas*) of feathers.

2.

The "E on the stone" is the epsilon carved on the omphalos, or navel stone, at the oracle of Delphi in Boiotia. It is probably not an epsilon, but some Pythagorean mystical symbol that looks like an E.

In September, 1913, the French Archaeologist Francois Courby unearthed this "omphalos" at Delphi, the stone which was thought to sit directly under the Pole Star and was "the navel of the earth."[10] Plutarch's essay *The E at Delphi* (written toward the end of the first or in the early years of the second century A.D.) discusses various conjectures as to what the mysterious E might signify.[11] It is abundantly evident that the meaning of the E had been lost by Plutarch's time, and Pausanias seemed not to realize that the omphalos he was shown at Delphi was not the archaic one with its enigmatic E, but a replica in white marble bound in a network of fillets. This public omphalos was discovered by Bourguet just before Courby found the archaic one.[12]

Plutarch's seven different explanations of the E on the stone depend on the name of the letter in Plutarch's time (*ei*, rather than *epsilon*), which is then taken to be a cryptic allusion. *Ei*, for instance, is the Greek for *if*, and this is a likely component of questions asked the Delphic Oracle. *Ei* (or epsilon) is the second vowel in the alphabet; the sun is the second planet; the sun is Apollo's planet, and the Delphic Oracle is Apollo's

[10]F. Courby, *Comptes rendus de l'Académie des inscriptions et belles lettres* (1914), pp. 263–66; and in *Fouilles de Delphes* ii.I.76.

[11]Plutarch, "De E apud Delphos," in *Moralia* (Cambridge, Mass.: Harvard University Press; Loeb Classical Library, 1962) vol. V, pp. 198–253.

[12]For a full account of what Olson knew about Courby's stone, see A. B. Cook, "The Delphic Omphalos," in *Zeus* (Cambridge, England: Cambridge University Press, 1925) vol. II, pp. 169–93.

sacred place. *Ei* means "thou art," and affirms the existence of Apollo. And so on, increasing our conviction that the meaning of the E was lost knowledge by Hellenistic times, even to the High Priest at Delphi, which position Plutarch held.

It is plausible that the stone itself was lost by this time, and that Plutarch had not seen it. The stone Courby dug up has an E on it, and it also has more letters, which A. B. Cook read as GAS, "of the earth." He argued that the E is not an epsilon, but a hieroglyph of a temple or shrine, perhaps the peculiar symbol of Delphi itself, the center of a circular world under a circular sky. This stone, then, is one end of the world's axis; the Pole Star is the other.

Modern criticism tends to be skeptical. "The crude inscription," Professor R. E. Wycherley says in his edition of Pausanias,[13] "once interpreted as being E (a scared symbol at Delphi) and GAS "of earth," proves to be part of the name of one Papaloukas."

Mr. Papaloukas is even more mysterious than the E, but has not kept the museum at Delphi from placing Courby's stone on top of Bourguet's, where it seems to fit.

To think of the "E cut so rudely on the oldest stone" is to contemplate a sign of central importance in a world we have lost the meaning of wholly. It is as eloquently mute as the prehistoric cave paintings in which Olson found so deep a meaning.

What Mao said—"The dawn light is before us, let us rise up and act"—is in his speech of 1948 to the Chinese Communist Party shortly before the government fell into their control.

Two descriptions of the kingfisher from the *Encyclopædia Britannica* (13th edition) intersperse Mao's words ("The features . . . inconspicuous" and "it does nest . . . fetid mass"), and are themselves interrupted by the poet's "But not these things were the factors."

The process by which the kingfisher became the architect of a nest which it always builds superbly well was developed over millions of years of evolution. Against this continuous line of natural onwardness the rise and fall of human empires are swift and of indifferent interest to the living universe. The stone that marked the center of the earth for the Boiotians held the scientific and religious gaze of a handful of Panhellenic tribes for a few thousand years only. The Chinese meld into western history as a Marxist-Leninist revolutionary begins a dynasty in the world's oldest civilization.

All three ideogrammatic elements are held in a relation to the sun: the Delphic stone religiously, Mao metaphorically and rhetorically, the kingfisher mythically.

---

[13]Pausanias, *Description of Greece*, ed. W. H. S. Jones and R. E. Wycherley (Cambridge, Mass.: Harvard University Press; Loeb Classical Library, 1918) vol. V, p. 170.

3.

The beginning remembers Canto XX:

> Jungle:
> Glaze green and red feathers, jungle,
> Basis of renewal, renewals;
> Rising over the soul, green virid, of the jungle,
> Lozenge of the pavement, clear shapes,
> Broken, disrupted. . . .

The ideogrammatic elements are all taken from William H. Prescott's *History of the Conquest of Mexico* (1843). The "fine ear" is possibly Robert Southey's, whose description of the magnificent Tlascalan army is quoted by Prescott in a note.[14] The passage beginning "of green feathers" (p. 197) is a description of gifts given to Cortés by Montezuma as recorded in Albrecht Dürer's diary, 27 August 1520, when he saw them in Brussels, displayed by Charles V, then on his way to Aix-la-Chapelle to be crowned Holy Roman Emperor. The other two passages, parts of Prescott's account of the massacre at Cholula, (p. 273) are a mixture of quotation and paraphrase.

The ideogram can be turned, like a mobile structure; one perspective juxtaposes tilled fields and the jungle: culture (the word first means tilling fields) and its opposite, nature without the order of humanity. Another perspective discloses the wealth and splendor of the Mexicans and the rapacity and cruelty of the conquistadores. There is a deeper perspective in historic time: the Delphic stone knew its waves of conquerors— Persians, Spartans, Romans. Let us say that this element in the ideograms can be tagged: the unwilled change of war. And do not miss, out of ideological blindness, the fact that Mao, like Cortés, was exterminating a civilization, with comparable cruelty.

4.1

"Not one death but many" reflects both Pablo Neruda's long poem, the *Alturas de Macchu Picchu,* which Olson's poem resembles and was inspired by, and Plutarch's Pythian dialogue, "The E at Delphi." In Neruda the line means that men with a life as hard as the Peruvians in their isolated mountain fastnesses die difficulty by difficulty. Plutarch's meaning is Heraclitean: one self dies and is replaced by another as our concerns and fortunes change.

To quote a part of Ammonius's words in the dialogue will locate the next seventeen lines of this section:

[14](New York: Random House, n.d.), p. 235.

"It is impossible to step twice in the same river" are the words of Heracleitus, nor is it possible to lay hold twice of any mortal substance in a permanent state; by the suddenness and swiftness of the change in it there "comes dispersion and, at another time, a gathering together"; or, rather, not at another time nor later, but at the same instant it both settles into its place and forsakes its place; "it is coming and going."

Wherefore that which is born of it never attains unto being because of the unceasing and unstaying process of generation, which, ever bringing change, produces from a seed an embryo, then a babe, then a child, and in due course a boy, a young man, a mature man, an elderly man, an old man, causing the first generations and ages to pass away by those which succeed them. But we have a ridiculous fear of one death, we who have already died so many deaths, and still are dying! For not only is it true, as Heracleitus used to say, that the death of heat is birth for steam, and the death of steam is birth for water, but the case is even more clearly to be seen in our own selves: the man in his prime passes away when an old man comes into existence, the young man passes away into the man in his prime, the child into the young man, and the babe into the child. Dead is the man of yesterday, for he is passed into the man of today; and the man of today is dying as he passes into the man of tomorrow. Nobody remains one person, nor is one person; but we become many persons, even as matter is drawn about some one semblance and common mould with imperceptible movement. Else how is it that, if we remain the same persons, we take delight in some things now, whereas earlier we took delight in different things; that we love or hate opposite things, and so too with our admirations and disapprovals, and that we use other words and feel other emotions and have no longer the same personal appearance, the same external form, or the same purposes in mind?[15]

Something of the previous state, however, survives every change. This is called in the language of cybernetics (which took it from the language of machines) *feedback,* the advantages of learning from experience and of having developed reflexes. Olson learned this word from a book published the year he was writing "The Kingfishers," Norbert Wiener's *Cybernetics.* "Feedback," Wiener says in *The Human Use of Human Beings: Cybernetics and Society,* "is a method of controlling a system by reinserting into it the results of its past performance."[16]

Men (and history), then, are both discrete and continuous; the kingfisher's history, for instance, is continuous (and eventless), evolution being a process by which all advantageous feedback is built henceforth into the design. Human culture is discrete, discontinuous: this is the sub-

[15]Plutarch, "The E at Delphi," in Moralia, trans. Frank Cole Babbitt (Cambridge, Mass.: Harvard University Press, 1962), vol. V, pp. 241–43.

[16](New York: Doubleday, 1954), p. 61.

ject of Pound's *Cantos* and the concern of most historians after Vico and Michelet. Nature phasing out the brontosaurus was adjusting a totality of ecological design; the fall of Alexander's empire was tragedy.

Olson takes the words "discrete" and "continuous" from the mathematician Riemann, and the reader who wishes to feel the full content of these words should go to Olson's essay "Equal, That Is, to the Real Itself."[17]

Change, therefore, is always a message, a statement of attention and intention. Change is the mute, as language is the articulate, discourse of history, and the two are frequently at grievous divergence from each other. Nature's feedback is the study of science; man's feedback ought to be the study of history, except that history is blocked by ignorance and loss. The search for the past is arduous, and when found it is difficult if not impossible to read.

"This very thing you are" can only be said, in the terms of Plutarch's dialogue, to a god, an imagined stability of Being. (Ammonius's discourse, quoted from above, is based on the interpretation of the E as *ei*, "thou art.") Said to a man, it can only mean that what he is can be identified as a variant of a common model. The model, then, is the heart of every culture, the degree of excellence it offers the individual.


4.2

Prescott again: the opening lines are from a passage about the mother goddess Cioa-coatl (a kind of Artemis). I have not found a source for the detail of the Mongolian louse (either in books about the Mayas or from Mayan anthropologists I've consulted), though the Asian origin of the American Indian is a widely held hypothesis.

"The light is in the east": we are at a dawn moment in history. The Cold War was beginning, a new age of technology (atomic power, polymers, jet flight, plastics) was beginning; empires (British, Soviet, Chinese) were changing character and boundaries.

The "guide" is Ezra Pound, and his "rose" (an image from Dante) is the model civilization meditated on in *The Pisan Cantos* which history has consistently betrayed through greed and loss of vision, but which remains as an ideal, "now in the mind indestructible." Olson perceives that Pound's clearest vision of this ideal was in Confucius, and echoes the first page of the Pisan group ("what whiteness will you add to this whiteness, what candor?"), itself a paraphrase of the *Analects*.

But the Heraclitean paradox remains, that justice is born from contention, peace from war, benevolence from violence.

[17]*Selected Writings*, ed. Robert Creeley (New York: New Directions, 1966).

The meeting of East and West in post-Columbian Mexico is again evoked. The conquistador who "healed" is Cabeza de Vaca; the one who "tore the eastern idols down" is Hernando Cortés. The excuse for his violence was the greater violence of human sacrifice. Prescott, perplexed by the anomoly of human sacrifice among the splendid Mexicans, searches for parallel examples among civilized people in a gory footnote (p. 698): "Marco Polo notices a civilized people in South-eastern China, and another in Japan, who drank the blood and ate the flesh of their captives; esteeming it the most savory food in the world—"*La più saporita et migliore, che si possa truovar al mondo*' (*Viaggi*, lib. '2, cap. 75; lib. 3, 13, 14)."

But do we judge the flower by the root; is the analogy in anywise apt? The rhetorical questions are anguished and damning. "*Pudor*" and "*Pejorocracy*" are from Pound's vocabulary; and Shakespeare's bitterest voice speaks through the mask of the despairing Timon:

> Sonne of sixteen,
> Plucke the lyn'd Crutch from thy old limping Sire
> With it, beate out his Braines, Piety, and Feare,
> Religion to the Gods, Peace, Justice, Truth,
> Domesticke awe, Night-rest, and Neighbour-hood,
> Instruction, Manners, Mysteries, and Trades,
> Degrees, Observances, Customes, and Lawes,
> Decline to your confounding contraries.[18]

Civilization "flowers" (the image is a cliché among historians); Olson embeds puns alluding to this image (which his masters Pound, Eliot, and Williams redeemed from triteness): "whence it arose," "what stalks." The sardonic last ten lines of this movement are Latinate, unarguably just in their charge, and balance with their lyric and rhetorical clarity the busy energy of the interrupted articulateness and fragmented images that precede them.

## 4.3 [Coda]

"That I am no Greek has not the advantage I would like." Is this the meaning? Klaus Reichert, the German translator of "The Kingfishers," misreads the line as: *Kein Grieche bin ich, den vorzug hab ich nicht* (and Olson did not object). I suspect a syncopated quotation here. Paraphrase: My culture and my language give me scant advantage for speaking as I would like.

Pound in the *Guide to Kulchur:* "It is my intention . . . to COMMIT

---

[18]*Timon of Athens* IV.I.1, 13–20. I am indebted to Mr. Gerrit Lansing for pointing out this quotation.

myself on as many points as possible, that means I shall make a number
of statements which very few men can AFFORD to make, for the simple
reason that such taking sides might jeopard their incomes (directly) or
their prestige or 'position' in one or other of the professional 'worlds'.
Given my freedom, I may be a fool to use it, but I wd. be a cad not to."

Pound, then, is the kinsman whose commitment and courage the poet
wishes to emulate. (Pound at the time was serving the fourth year of a
thirteen-year prison sentence for speaking his mind over Radio Rome).

If the failure of culture and language cannot give the poet words to
complete his poem, he can at least plead that he is aware of the violence
underlying every feature of civilization's mask. Olson wrote "The
Kingfishers" just before going to Yucatan: in a strange economy of anticipation he wrote his meditation on the ruins before he ever saw them.
So he chose to quote, as a coda to his meditation, a poet who left civilization for the jungle and the desert, Rimbaud.

The couplet Olson quotes occurs twice, first in a poem calles "Fêtes de
la Faim" (written August 1872),

> Ma faim, Anne, Anne,
> Fuis sur ton âne.

Si j'ai du *goût,* ce n'est guères
Que pour la terre et les pierres.
Dinn! dinn! dinn! dinn! Mangeons l'air,
Le roc, les charbons, le fer . . .

and as a passage in *Une Saison en enfer* (1873),

Si j'ai du goût, ce n'est guères
Que pour la terre et les pierres.
Je déjeune toujours d'air,
De roc, de charbons, de fer.

Mes faims, tournez. Passez, faims,
    Le pré des sons.
Attirez le gai venin
    Des liserons.

Manges les cailloux qu'on brise,
Les vieilles pierres d'églises;
Les galets des vieux déluges,
Pains semés dans les vallées grises.

                        * * *

Le loup criait sous les feuilles
En crachant les belles plumes
De son repas de volailles:
Comme lui je me consume.

Les salades, les fruits
N'attendent que la cueillette;
Mais l'araignée de la haie
Ne mange que des violettes.

Que je dorme! que je bouille
Aux autels de Salomon.
Le bouillon court sur la rouille,
    Et se mêle au Cédron.

Which is, roughly:

If I have any taste,
It is for earth and stone.
I take for my meals
Rock, coal, iron.

Hungers, leave. Graze, hungers,
    In fields of sound.
Suck the morning glory's
    Gay poison.

Eat crunched pebbles,
Ancient church stones,
Boulders from the flood,
Bread cast in grey valleys.

\* \* \*

The wolf bayed under the leaves,
Spitting pretty feathers
Of the birds he'd eaten.
Like him, I consume myself.

Salads, fruit,
They wait to be picked;
But the grass spider
Eats violets only.

Let me sleep! Let me stew
On Solomon's altars.
The gravy spills down the rust
And runs into the Kedron.

This "taste for stone" is a theme in modern literature that emerges in the early days of Romantic writing and flows like a submerged river of meaning through practically all serious works in the nineteenth and twentieth centuries. It stems from the classical feeling that stone was a dead substance and therefore belonged to a separate realm of being. Hades, for instance, was stone, as was the dead moon. The firm Greek sense that stone does not grow distinguished it radically from things that do. And yet it was of mineral substance that everything is made: an organism was an interpenetration of matter and spirit.

Put the understanding another way: science and poetry from the Renaissance forward have been trying to discover what is alive and what isn't. In science the discovery spanned three centuries, from Gassendi to Niels Bohr, and the answer is that everything is alive.

Poetry has had a similar search, and its answer is not yet formulated, as it cannot understand nature except as a mirror of the spirit. One can read *The Cantos* as a subtle meditation on whether stone is alive, and a generation of French poets found in the mineral world a correlative of art itself: Baudelaire, Laforgue, and Mallarmé chiefly. That is why Rimbaud is asked to witness at the end of "The Kingfishers"—his hunger for stone is the modern question all over again: "What is alive, and how?" Though Olson can ask the question in the nineteenth-century manner—is man an alien spirit in a world that has its own, separate existence?—in such a poem as "The Praises" and in the Maximus poems, he puts the brunt of his question in "The Kingfishers" as Pound (or a classical Greek) would put it. In what way does meaning inhere in things?

Does meaning drain from art, for instance, "when the attentions change?" Is the Mayan culture lost to us forever, like the meaning of the E on the Delphic navel stone? Is there really a feedback operative in history, so that men learn from experience? (This question was being asked three years after we had found the mountains of corpses at Buchenwald and Auschwitz, and while the Red Guards were oiling their carbines).

The poet's taste (a pun in Rimbaud's French: appetite, correct discrimination) is a characteristically Olsonian insistence on the physiology of things: he means intellectual passion. And in it he conceals a quarrel with his master Pound, who set out in *The Cantos* to say how cultures rise and fall. Olson's very silence on the economic vision which Pound gives as an explanation states his indifference to it. Hence the pointed question, which is a way of asking what can survive as salvageable meaning from Fascism ("that maggots shd/ eat the dead bullock," the dead bullock being Mussolini hanging by his heels at Milan). The question is also Samson's riddle: "Out of the eater came foorth meate, And out of the strong came foorth sweetness" (Judges 14:14).

History is fable. Its meaning is always the harmony of meaning which we can make out of it. It is the lion slain in the sun; it is a stone carved with an enigmatic E. It is the Mayan ruins, Angkor Vat, Macchu Picchu.

The kingfishers: they quelled the winds and brought the new year in, their feathers crowned the messengers to the gods, they are fixed as bright emblems of spirit in the poetry of the Chinese. A modern scientist will tell you that they control insects and the enemies of the trout. They are an order of being.

There is history, Olson says in *Maximus V* ("A Later Note on Letter #15"), and there is the dream of history: fact and interrupted fact, or fable. Objective history is always a lie, for it cannot disclose the truth. "No event" (Olson is quoting Whitehead) "is not penetrated, in intersection or collision with, an eternal event."

"The Kingfishers" is a projection (Latin, "propelling forward") of intersecting events which would never otherwise have come into relation to each other except for the poet's imagining them in this conjunction. Like Pound's ideogrammatic forms, it is poetry that demands consideration among several people, and thus easily becomes social discourse, rich material for classes in schools. Its seeming inarticulateness is not a failure to articulate, but a declining to articulate images and events which can be left in free collision.

# Zukofsky

## I. "A"

For forty-six years, from 1928 to 1974, Louis Zukofsky wrote, with awesome care and skill, a long poem called "A." Its first twelve parts were set in type by Japanese compositors and printed in Kyoto in 1959. The first thirty of Pound's *Cantos* were set by French, the eighty-fifth through ninety-fifth by Italian compositors; the first half of Olson's *Maximus* was printed in Germany, the second half in England; Walt Whitman himself set *Leaves of Grass;* Melville paid for the printing of *Clarel* out of his own pocket; *The Columbiad* sold because of its handsome binding and typography and engravings by Robert Fulton.[1] Only Williams's *Paterson*

---

[1]Steamboat Fulton. Someone must someday write about the affinity between steamboats and poets. Robert Burns was on the maiden voyage of the first steamboat, and Shelley when he was drowned was just about to found a steam-ship company plying between London and Genoa.

100

came in an untroubled and ordinary way from a publisher. It cannot be demonstrated that the American public has ever clamored to read a long poem by an American poet.

"*A*", *1–12* was issued in America in 1967 (a photocopy of the Japanese compositors' work). This edition was financed by *The Paris Review* and is now out of print. "*A*", *13–21* was published in England in 1969. "*A*"–*24*, the final section of the poem, was published in New York—*New York!*—1962. Parts 22 and 23, written in Port Jefferson, N.Y., the poet's final home after a lifetime in Manhattan and Brooklyn, were published in 1975.[2] The whole poem was brought together and published as Zukofsky lay dying in 1978.[3] He never saw a copy.

Every skilled poet finds the innocent world pregnant with analogies. If saw-horses have been set up outside one's Brooklyn apartment and one has the seventh part of a long fugal poem to compose, there are things to be seen in those horses with their lettering on their crosspieces, lanterns hung on their ends. These wooden horses lack heads and necks, for instance, but with horses so archaically elemental, won't the number 7 itself supply that want? And the poet will supply the manes, the *di manes* of his shamanistic art. And what presence will emerge in the trance? Two horses together make an M (each horse singly, an A). As the poet is working in counterpoint like his great master Bach, whose spirit presides over the whole poem, the theme M inverted is W (the theme of *manes* trotting across itself inverted, the theme of William, the one named Shakespeare; as the theme A simultaneously moves across its extreme in the alphabet, Z). The theme A doubled suggests doubling lines; lines get doubled in a sestina, so we begin to make a sestina. When we double theme A in its seventh progression, the number 14 pops up, and that is a Shakespearean number, the lines of a Shakespearean sonnet, so our sestina must blend into a cycle of sonnets. How many? Seven, of course.

One would expect these wooden horses to bear Greeks into Troy; they bring, instead, Roman soldiers to the agony in the garden: Christian Friedrich Henrici's libretto for Bach's *St. Matthew Passion* has figured in the poem from the beginning.

Does "*A*" begin in a thoroughly Marxist way, positing man's economic anguish as an agony in what might have been, had greed and misdirection not ruined it, the garden of the world? The poem begins on Passover 1928 at a performance of the *St. Matthew Passion* at Carnegie Hall; Easter is four days away. The banks are soon to close; the country is deep into the Depression. Women in diamonds have come to hear

[2]Louis Zukofsky, "*A*"–*24* (New York: Grossman, 1972). "*A*" *22 & 23*, same publisher, 1975.

[3]Louis Zukofsky, "*A*" (Berkeley and Los Angeles: University of California Press, 1978).

underpaid musicians. Zukofsky always counterpoints his themes with the precision of a baroque master. Passover: Easter. Leipzig 1728: New York 1929. Jew: Christian. Christ on the cross: industrial workers crucified on their machines. Lenin had been dead only four years. The poet's parents spoke no English and he grew up speaking Yiddish with a Russian accent. It was the opinion of the Communist Party cell which he attended with a view to joining (his sponsor was his classmate at Columbia, Whittaker Chambers) that he was not CP material but a young man ambitious to move to the West Side.

Gibbon would eventually temper, correct, and supplement Marx; Thomas Jefferson, Lenin. But Shakespeare and Bach would become the *lares penatesque* of this most passionately intellectual of American poets. Only Emily Dickinson has kept to her hearth more than Zukofsky. When he left home, a home intensely a focus of his whole existence, he traveled, like Basho, with his own weather, coals from his fire, a splendid sense that by drawing this chair here and that chair there he could summon the exact skirts of the tent that kept out the sand and desert cold on the marches across Sinai, the straw curtains that screened the family from the chatter and blasphemy of Babylon, the lamplit walls of Polish rooms, the shades one draws against Brooklyn.

This inwardness is the ground for all the glittering themes and their variations which dance in "A." Dance, for the essence of the poem is in play, intellectual play, a play of words and music. Zukofsky is the most Apollonian of our poets, but his Apollo cavorts with Pan and Priapos. So did the Apollo of Bach, Shakespeare, and Catullus. Zukofsky's honor for olden and abandoned spirits is one of his most strenuous pieties. There are many ways of talking about Zukofsky's particular marshalling of spiritual dominions and powers. "A," for instance, is about a marriage in which the wife has the Elizabethan name Celia, hence lyrics for the lute throughout); it is crucial, however, to an understanding of his art to single out the wonder of his playfulness, for it sets his work aside (and above) as distinctly as his superb mastery of sound and measure.

Consider the pantomimic brio here:

Man in the moon stand and stride
On his forked goad the burden he bears
It is a wonder that he does not slide,
For doubt lest he fall he shudders and sheers. (*"A"*–13)

This *buffo glissando* clowns on for forty lines, achieving the most spirited aria Pierrot ever sang to the moon ("Hop out Hubert in your hose magpie!"). Is it Pierrot baying at the moon and crying for the sun? Is it Zukofsky watching astronauts on TV? Is it a bumpkin from Shakespeare drawling what would be fine euphuistic rhetoric except that its socks keep falling down around its ankles?[4]

All, and more. For by the middle and later parts of "A" Zukofsky had found a way (like Charles Ives, as we shall see) to harmonize counterpointed themes that is something like the deferential richness of a Latin line of poetry (the genitives, datives, and ablatives generously and promiscuously attaching themselves to the words around them, though we are supposed to reserve our sense of relationships until the whole line is in place), something like Pound's and Williams's imagistic gisting of English phrases into a Chinese aesthetic of terseness, and something of Zukofsky's heroic endeavor to marry words to a music, the more impossible the program, the better. In the eccentric *Catullus,* the Latin is the music, and the English is the words set to it. *"A"*–21 is so many English words set to Plautus's Latin; *"A"*–15 begins with the English words set to the Hebrew of *Job.* Sharp ears can hear Mallarmé in *"A"*–19.[5]

This interpenetration of meaning and meaning ("once She now Eunuch reigned"—*"A"*–21, for example, refers to the reign of Justice in Ovid's Golden Age, though an obvious theme of our time gets alluded to, and the grammar can read, "We are ruled by eunuchs rather than by just men") has a parallel in Ives, one of whose best interpreters is the poet's son Paul.

Ives's "Concord Sonata" begins with what sounds like variations on the initial theme of Beethoven's Fifth Symphony; we discover later that the joke is Louisa May Alcott trying to play Wagner's piano redaction of the noble symphony, making a mangle out of it and faking difficult passages with phrases from the Calvinist hymns with which her fingers are most comfortable; but a musicologist can tell us that the phrase isn't Beethoven at all, but a Scots folk melody that sounds like Beethoven, just as in the grand theme of the Second Symphony we are convinced we are hearing the National Anthem ("Columbia, Gem of the Ocean" at that time) whereas we are hearing yet another Scots tune, "My Bonnie Lies Over the Ocean." This is all very Zukofskian.

(I once asked Zukofsky what the "mg. dancer" is who dances in *"A"*–21, a milligram sprite, a magnesium elf, a margin dancer, or Aurora, as the dictionary allows for all of these meanings. "All," he replied.)

[4]It is Zukofsky's translation into modern English of a Middle English lyric about Hubert, the man in the moon, Harley MS 2253. For one medieval text see J. A. W. Bennett and G. V. Smithers, *Early Middle English Verse and Prose,* (Oxford: Oxford University Press, 1960).

[5]See Kenneth Cox's essay, "Zukofsky and Mallarmé" in John Taggart's excellent collection of Zukofskian studies, *Maps 5: Louis Zukofsky,* (1973). These ten essays make as intelligent an introduction to Zukofsky as is available at the moment: pioneer work, all.

Consider ("A"–21, again):

sleepless in a city
of thieves

who cannot foretell evening
from morning.

Both robbed and robber are the sleepless. The thieves cannot tell in the morning if they will be alive by nightfall (addicts, desperate men, hunted men, starving men: the words will accommodate all these senses). The thieves are in such a world of their own confusion that they cannot tell morning from evening.

The passage continues:

from morning   trafficked streets
still cobbled   Could be
a sphere

of pyramidal honeycomb, the
sphere enclosing the most space
with the least surface
strongest against

internal pressure   the honeys
enclosing the least space   most
surface best to withstand
external pressures

could be one lean buck
take heart grow fuller
knowing like transported cargo
smells of

portage the winter-wrapped tree
elsewhere May   a summer's
dory unstowed so much
so little

each one's house just
float off   nations just stops
and wander that needs
no feet.

The "sphere of pyramidal honeycomb" is the geodesic dome which R. Buckminster Fuller has proposed to build over Manhattan and thus control its weather: his name is concealed further down in "one lean buck / take heart grow fuller." Fuller gets into the poem (or rather, into Plautus's Rome which is the mask New York is made to wear at this point) because of the dangerous streets, which, like Rome's, signalled the collapse of her culture. Fuller is a systems designer; he is like the buck in winter who knows that May will come again; Zukofsky likes Fuller's ideas of portable houses and of finding life-support systems in nature for the rejuvenation and continuance of our city life, but worries (taking the lyric as a whole, of which I have quoted only the latter section) whether a culture can stand so much nomadism, and wonders if the modern city isn't more a matter of nomads and hordes wandering than of people living in a settlement. New York died as a city in which one can live while Zukofsky was writing his poem.

Now that almost the whole structure is available to us, we can see that it is a series of metamorphoses in which thought turns into music. That's what happens in Shakespeare's sonnets; thought becomes one of the figures in a richly patterned music. The thought itself is accidental, like the plot of a short story. It comes from the outside: the war in Vietnam, saw horses in the street. There is enough narrative and anecdotal *matter* in "*A*" to make a shelf of novels.

The ending of the poem is 239 pages of music, Handel's *Pieces pour le Clavecin* copied out in Celia's neat hand. Against this music actors perform a masque by reciting from Zukofsky's essays (the volume *Prepositions*), his play of 1936, *Arise, Arise* (the title is the *International* talking at the same time as John Donne), the book of stories *It Was,* and previous portions of "*A*."

The masque begins this way: the harpsichord opens with a fine arpeggio. A voice begins to read from an essay called "A Statement of Poetry":

And it is possible in imagination to divorce speech of all graphic elements, to let it become a movement of sounds.

(The ghost of Mallarmé nods agreement from the azure.)

While we hear this voice speaking about the movement and tone words, a second voice, lower, speaks disjunct lines, as if at random from the script, from the play *Arise, Arise:* ("My mother hit her mother?"). Simultaneously a third voice recites from the story "It Was." The loudest voice, coming in at the second bar of the music, speaks the lyric "Blest / Infinite things" from "*A*"–14.

This goes on for an hour and ten minutes—four voices speaking simultaneously to a constant glory of Handel.[6] Nothing, let us note, is being

---

[6]Maurice Edwards staged a performance at the Cubiculo on West 51st Street, June 14–23, 1973, with Douglas Coe at the harpsichord. The parts were spoken by Keith Aldrich, Bill Maloney, Luane Rohrbacher, Helene Friedman, Cordell Reagon, and Gary Smith. A discussion after the Friday performance amounted to a public conversation between the poet and Hugh Kenner.

obscured by all these voices talking at once. We have no more right to complain that we can understand nothing (as indeed we can't) than to complain of Ives's *Putnam's Camp, Redding, Connecticut* that we can't make out what two military bands are playing (separate tunes simultaneously on top of some lovely ragtime and a bit of *Tristan*). The elements exist elsewhere, and can be consulted. This is *Celia's Masque for LZ*: she knows the parts by heart, and if it pleases her to hear them this way, then that is the symbol, the figure as she makes it out in the carpet. She typed all these words in a house with a violinist practicing.[7]

Polyphonic voices is not a musical form we are used to, though any American room will usually have two conversations going at once while the television set maintains its diarrhea of words and crappy music. I suspect that ultimately Zukofsky wanted "A" to culminate and fulfill itself at a family reunion of his work, inside and outside of the poem, a grand Jewish family affair, with everybody cheerfully talking at once. The *surface* of the poem then achieves its maximum turbulence within such forms as the harpsichord can impose; the reciters must watch the score, and follow the measure.

Total familiarity with the piece will begin to disclose remarkable dissonances and harmonies. The scholars will want to ask *why* the voices have been put together in just this way. Why, for instance, the essay on Henry Adams is made to move alongside a reprise of "A"–7, while other voices are talking about graves.

Familiarity is the condition whereby all of Zukofsky's work renders its goodness up. Zukofsky's surface is apt to appear spare and a bit cold, as *Finnegans Wake* is apt to seem a briar-patch of words. Many of Zukofsky's phrases seem to be knots tied too elaborately: they seem to ask to be picked apart. Once we know that every phrase is an ultimate condensation of what the same concepts would be in a windier poet, we can then gear our wits to Zukofsky's finer machinery than we could possibly be used to.

It has been complained of Zukofsky that he confuses obscurity and profundity. He *is* profound (but never arcane); he is profound as music is profound, for his words are powerful enough to stir response, sympathy, and revery. They reward attention, and keep rewarding attention. His obscurity is in the reader's mind, not in the poem. And it is an obscurity which disappears as we learn our poet, his precision and skill. His passion.

Zukofsky's work has been published for fifty years and the reviewers and scholars, except for a few, have been silent and indifferent. Only

---

[7]*Some* in his young years. Paul Zukofsky defies the rule of constant practice to which other violinists adhere with perhaps as much superstition as benefit.

recently has the poet begun to appear in reference works of American poets, and in an occasional anthology. He has had the pleasure of riding along a London street under a banner tied from lamp post to lamp post on which he could read WELCOME TO CAMBERWELL LOUIS ZUKOFSKY. He has with incredible and disgusting difficulty seen his *Bottom: On Shakespeare* and his *Catullus* into print, agonies comparable to Joyce's, the details of which constitute a formal indictment of the American publishing industry on charges of critical dullness, terminal stupidity, and general mopery.

Perhaps, at the moment, when the life of the mind is in more peril than ever in the Republic, Zukofsky must seem to be not so much a poet's poet as a poet's poet's poet, and may be the last man of the great generation of the Men of 1914, the inventors of the art of the century. Our greatest living poet is usually a man as unknown to the professariat as to the corps of reviewers and the deaf custodians of the laurels. It was true of Whitman in 1873, and is true of Zukofsky in 1973.

## II. SCRIPTA ZUKOFSKII ELOGIA

1    Eighteen songs, set to music by his wife, and fifty-three lines of type in six blocks of prose: this is Zukofsky's *Autobiography,* not his most eccentric work but certainly foremost as an eccentricity among the world's autobiographies.

1.1    The first of these songs is a buffoonery that Mr. Punch, Groucho Marx, Zero Mostel, and Buck Mulligan might sing in Elysium. It is a motet.

> General Martinet Gem
> Coughed Ahem, and Ahem, and Ahem
> Deploying the nerves of his men
> Right, and about face, to his phlegm.
> Their whangs marched up to the sky,
> His eyes telescoped in his head
> A pillow that as pillar of Europe
> He flung to his rupture Ahead.

1.2    The song is Zukofsky's world. Wrangel, Haig, Tojo, Goering.

1.3    The city in which Zukofsky lived he pictured by translating Catullus, as effective a recreation of the color, odor, and tone of its original as Orff's *Carmina Catulli* or Fellini's *Satyricon*.

1.4    The home in which Zukofsky lived is "A". It contained two musicians, a poet, many books, and a television set.

2    "Has he published?" a professor asked at the committee meeting where I was trying to have a thousand dollars appropriated to bring Zukofsky to the University of Kentucky for a reading. But this same professor had probably never heard of Ausonius, Ts'ao Chih, or Stevie Smith.

2.1   How to answer the ignorant professor? The greatest of elegies for JFK ("A"–15

> The fetlocks ankles of a ballerina
> 'Black Jack' Sardar with black-
> hilted sword black dangled in silver scabbard from
> the saddle rider less rider
> his life looked back
> into silver stirrups and the
> reversed boots in them.
> . . .
> John to John-John to Johnson).

2.2   The most original meditation on Shakespeare since Coleridge.

2.3   A translation of all of Catullus, all but unreadable except with great sympathy and curiosity, in which the English sounds like the Latin and is in the same meter. The beauty of this strange text is that it catches Catullus's goatish nasty with dignity, honesty, and a decent eye.

2.4   "A".

2.5   Four volumes of lyrical poems, some of which rank among the finest of our century.

2.6   Some critical prose distinguished by its good sense and a pure style, some narrative prose distinguised by its whimsy, wit, and individual tone. LZ wrote prose as a race horse walks: nervous, skittery, itching for the bugle and the track.

3    His Shakespeare was a quattrocento Florentine.

4    Spinoza, Heraclitus, Wittgenstein, Bach, Jefferson, LZ: men with brotherly minds.

5    The engineering of his poetry, when revealed and demonstrated, will bring him close to Joyce.

6    He taught at a polytechnic institute, saw the Brooklyn Bridge daily for thirty years, was fascinated by the shapes of the letter A (tetrahedron, gable, strut) and Z (cantilever), and designed all his poetry with an engineer's love of structure, of solidities, of harmony.

7 *Le Style Apollinaire.* LZ is a scrupulous punctuator, with correcter parentheses, dashes, and semicolons than anyone else. Punctuation became dense as the railroad tracks went down, corresponding to their points, switches, signals, and semaphores. With the airplane, trackless and free, we get Apollinaire with no punctuation at all, Eliot, Pound, Cummings.

7.1 *"A"*—16 has no punctuation: it is airborne and speaks of the windflower. *80 Flowers* has no punctuation. But LZ's punctuation remains that of the city man for whom traffic signals are crucial. *"A"*—13 is a poem imitating a partita by Bach; I—75 is a four-lane highway.

8 The elegant engineering of *"A"* is an integral symbol.

9 The invention that distinguishes Zukofsky is the play of his wit. His instructors here were Shakespeare and the Baroque fiddle: a continuum of sense that nevertheless interrupts itself all along the line to play, juggle quibbles, pun, dance in and out of nonsense, sustain cadenzas of awesome virtuosity, and switch the ridiculous and the sublime so fast that we are taught their happy interchangeability in a beautifully poised sensibility.

10 Jewish humor assumes a sweet intelligence. We feel the non-Euclidean rightness of Sam Goldwyn's "Include me out" and "A man who goes to a psychiatrist ought to have his head examined." It was Freud who thought humor was the tension of anxiety released in a cryptogram that was sociable and congenial though threatening to the psyche as a decoded statement. As soon as we reach the anecdote of the rabbi and the telephone in *"A"*, we know we are in good hands.

11 Zukofsky as a child thought that the uncircumcised couldn't urinate and was troubled to understand the radically different physiology of the *goyim.* Hence the concealed jokes about urine throughout *"A"*.

> Or as the Queen of British barmaids
> Before the Jury of her Pee-ers, Call
> Me Hebe, that means goddess of youth, Dears! (*"A"*—13)

Freudian blips zing across cockney fun: *Jewry* across *jury, hebe* (Hebrew) across *Hebe,* and in *Dears!* you can hear Fagin's lisp.

12 LZ was a prodigious and searching reader. He accepted books as his inheritance and spent a lifetime assaying the bequest.

13 He had the gift of the laconic. To Pound praising Mussolini in 1939, he said, "The voice, Ezra, the voice!" There must be hundreds of critical

·postcards like ones I've had from him. Of my Archilochos, "Something new!" Of *Flowers and Leaves,* "Yes, but where's the passion?" Of my "Herakleitos," "Jes' crazy!"

14  Hearing that he frequently saw Djuna Barnes when he was out for a morning paper, I asked him if they exchanged pleasantries. "No," he said. "What do you say to the Minister's Black Veil?"

15  Fellow artists have treated him as a phenomenon, a force, a man (like Mallarmé or Whistler) to make obeisance to whether you understand his work or not. His appearance in Brakhage's *23rd Psalm Branch* is characteristic of such homage. In a sequence about the Nazi concentration camps, Zukofsky's face is introduced as a motif. He was the kind of man who would have suffered Mandelstam's fate in Russia, Max Jacob's in France.

16  Joseph Cornell, Lorine Niedecker, Ronald Johnson, Charles Ives, Albert Pinkham Ryder, Emily Dickinson, Walt Whitman.

17  LZ was wise in the ways of a family as William Carlos Williams in the ways of a community, Pound in the splendors of cultures. LZ was the most civilized of the three, an accomplished city dweller, a practical critic of place and history.

18  He would not talk on the phone if Celia were not there to hear the conversation.

19  Exploring the prehistoric caves at Les Eyzies in the Dordogne, he went into some that were too uncomfortable for Celia but described them so well that she felt she'd seen them.

20  A music of thought.

21  The precision of his mind demanded a heterogeneous and improbable imagery. Surmounting difficulties was his *daimon.* When enough people become familiar with *"A"* so that it can be discussed, the first wonder will be how so many subjects got built into such unlikely patterns, and what a harmony they all make.

22  Two lives we lead: in the world and in our minds. Only a work of art can show us how to do it. The sciences concerned with the one aren't on speaking terms with those concerned with the other. Lenin once said that Socialism would inspire in the working man a love of natural beauty. One of my colleagues, a professor, once observed in front of my crackling, cozy fireplace that it was such a day as one might want to sit in front

of a crackling, cozy fireplace if only people had such nice things anymore. I thought I was losing my mind: he really did not notice that he was sitting in front of a fire. His talk runs much to our need to expand our consciousness. LZ in his poetry is constantly knitting the two worlds together, fetching a detail from this one to match one in the other. And he saw into other minds with a lovely clarity.

23   Spinoza with a body.

24   He propounded no theory, stood on no platform, marched in no ranks. He thought, he observed, he loved, he wrote.

25   Carmen 95 of *Catullus* is "to Ezra Pound." "Purvey me my intimate's core," it ends, "dear monument's all that there is, / let th' populace (tumid or gaudy) eat Antimacho." *Parva mei mihi sint cordi monumenta sodalis, / at populus tumido gaudeat Antimacho.*

BOTTOM

Born in a country market town, educated at the grammar school, regarded by his villagers as capable of taking over, in time, his father's business in beef and hides, he married Anne Whateley or Hathaway (the records are confused) and seemed to settle down as a burgher with a family. But then, inexplicably though perhaps precipitated by a tangle with the poaching laws, he set out for London with his friend Robert Davenport. Two decades later he had become the only writer of English whose imagination and mastery of words rivaled Chaucer's. For the first time in the history of the West, the supreme poet was not Homer but Homer or Shakespeare, as you would. Homer had grasped the human spirit in its perennial truths. It is all there, the world agreed, all that need be said of man. It remained to Shakespeare to render another description of man, this time of his imagination and its inward world. Look at Telemachus; look at Hamlet. Listen to Hermes in the *Odyssey;* listen to Ariel. Compare Priam and Lear in their anguish; the one, we say, needing no other words, is Homeric, the other Shakespearean; and nothing has reached such greatness.

Of all birthday presents of the quatercentenary, none has come close to the poet Louis Zukofsky's offering, a discursive book of 470 pages called *Bottom: On Shakespeare,* boxed with a second volume by his wife, the composer Celia Zukofsky, a musical setting for *Pericles.*

The body of Zukofsky's book is a cycle of essays, or "an alphabet of subjects," from A to Z. The momentum that carries the reader fascinated through this poet's notebook of perceptions is generated in the introduction, 90 pages ostensibly about eyes ("Let the audience look to their eyes," cries Bottom). What emerges is a kind of dance of imagery and words which Zukofsky, with pure delight, has set in motion. It is Shakespeare's peace of mind that intrigues him, the balance of the poet's argument within itself. An elaborately cultivated imagination has limits and contours—one begins to wonder if Shakespeare's have ever been found—but there are interior harmonies that act like music in their repetitions and contrasts and which visually are inexhaustible of interest. Zukofsky reports from a lifetime's study of these harmonies, and before we are well into the book we meet a Shakespeare classrooms and theatres have never heard of.

Floated on footnotes, tastefully edited by professors, dried into jerked beef for the Hymarx Series, strained for teenagers and the delicate, Shakespeare has survived, has communicated. One feat Zukofsky has performed without saying a word: he has wrested Shakespeare from two centuries of embattled siege by the English professors. (Olivier's placing of Shakespeare in the film *Henry V*, deep in the background of the dressingroom scene, in dark glasses and shirt sleeves, leafing through a prompter's script, did more than three whole lectures on the bard to make him a flesh-and-blood being, though I've never met another soul who *saw* him there.)

Occasionally a Landor or a Hazlitt has helped us to see the breathing Englishman, hazel-eyed, superbly deep but always clear of thought, with the heart of man helplessly naked to his gaze. But the student begins to think of him very soon as an institution vaguely religious, vaguely pedagogical, inscrutable, endless of corridor, governed by generations of quarreling wardens. The institution endows chairs, gives assistant professors grants for studies of kingship, Tudor allusions, image clusters, stage history. As if all this grind and cough had never existed, Zukofsky has written a book about a poet whose precision of word and eye can be talked about endlessly.

It is a book that belongs to that scarce genre which we can only call a *book*, like Boswell's *Johnson*, Burton's *Anatomy*, Walton's *Compleat Angler*. Zukofsky gives us a lover's insight into the way he reads Shakespeare; he makes lines that we have read all our lives turn to gold before our eyes. All that poets and men of good talk have said about Shakespeare is there; the index runs to thirty pages; on page 346 we get the innocent quotation, "Od's me! Qu'ai-j'oublie?" (*Merry Wives* I.iv.64) and the typist's ad lib *Nothing!* has been let stand, and with justice.

For Zukofsky Shakespeare is an elaborate argument that flows, a voice all its own, in and out of characters, from play to play. It is an argument about love, about understanding, about truth. "It argues with no one," he says, "only in itself." With the humblest touchstone—Bottom's wildly innocent fantasia on Shakespeare's great theme that love is to reason as eyes are to mind—here is the greatest meditation, certainly the most intricately lucid and beautiful, ever built around the thousand forms of a single thought.

# Marianne Moore

In Marianne Moore's poems—there are but seventy-one of them, five more than the restrained Eliot has published—we are asked

> Does yonder mouse with a
>   grape in its hand and its child
> in its mouth, not portray
>   the Spanish fleece suspended by the neck?

And we are told of the jerboa that

> Its leaps should be set
> to the flageolet.

We are taken into this kind of confidence:

>       If tributes cannot
>   be implicit,

give me diatribes and the fragrance of iodine,
the cork oak acorn grown in Spain;
the pale-ale-eyed impersonal look
which the sales-placard gives the bock beer buck.

This "fine careless rapture," as Ezra Pound called it in 1918 (it was his first letter to Miss Moore, seven pages of strenuous excitement), has been sustained for forty years now, and to it has been added the translations of La Fontaine. "Definiteness of your delineations is delicious," Pound wrote in his second letter to her. He was judging from the verse that went into the *Observations* of 1923, much of which was deleted or revised in later years. The *Collected Poems* of 1951 has, for example, a much finer version of "Poetry." Titles have grown terser and wittier, and poems which would do credit to a lesser poet have been stricken from the canon.

It is a poetry anxious to reproduce textures and the peculiar qualities of plants, animals, and places with an accuracy of simile and a precision in words. The pangolin's armor is "scale / lapping scale with spruce-cone regularity." Virginia pansies are "dressed, but for a day, in over-powering velvet; and / grey-blue-Andalusian-cock-feather pale ones, ink-lined on the edge, fur- / eyed, with ochre / on the cheek." Miss Moore has said of poetry that

[not] till the poets among us can be
   'literalists of
    the imagination'—above
      insolence and triviality and can present

for inspection, 'imaginary gardens with real
    toads in them',
     shall we have
it.[1]

It is curious, at first glance, that Miss Moore would speak of poetry this way: her own poetry seems real gardens with real toads, so meticulously accurate is her description.

But then we realize that she means just what she says. The poet or painter who transcribes literally—"an externalist," as Miss Moore says elsewhere—is reproducing only a segment of experience; he must be literal about the imagination also. "Literalists of the imagination" is a

---

[1]The 1951 version of this poem is twenty-five lines longer than the 1923 one. To the list of bat, wolf, base-ball fan, and statistician has been added "the immovable critic twiching his skin like a horse that feels a flea"—a telling note in a revision made between 1924 and 1950, and one that apparently dictated that "these phenomena are pleasing" to be changed to "these phenomena are important." The recasting of this poem is as revealing a gauge as one would want of Miss Moore's craftsmanship and scrupulous care in composition.

phrase adapted from Yeats's essay on Blake's illustrations to Dante.[2] Doré's Dante is dull because it is literal; it provides the very simulacra an unimaginative reader could supply for himself. Blake, despising the realistic painting "of Venice and Holland" which has not the limpid bounding lines of Michelangelo or Dürer, gives us in his watercolors to Dante an imaginative response—they are transmuted forms but they are alive precisely where Doré's are dead. Wallace Stevens has pointed out that the ostrich of "He 'Digesteth Harde Yron'" can be found in encyclopedias, too, and proceeds to compare an encyclopedia entry with Miss Moore's poem.[3] The difference is a delightful shock. The encyclopedia is blind; the poet can see. Put it any way you like. The encyclopedia is literal; Miss Moore is imaginative. The encyclopedia is disinterested, is indifferent, is academic. But it is clear that the poet's mind is, paradoxically, more interested in the ostrich than the ornithologist who wrote "Ostrich" for the *Britannica*.

Let us look fairly closely at a single poem of Marianne Moore's in order to understand her as well as we can. "His Shield" is an essay on freedom. First, to simplify the matter of the poem in bare outline, the roughest kind of paraphrase: Hedgehogs, echinoderms (sea urchins and the like), porcupines and rhinoceroses are examples of heavily armored animals. It is better, by way of armor, to be clad in asbestos and iron shoes, like the fabled emperor Presbyter John. His mythical land had abundant gold and rubies; his people knew neither greed nor flattery. For all his magical armor, however, his true armor was his humility. This took the form of his giving up instantly what anyone wanted to take from him; that is true freedom. My advice, then, is: arm yourself well, do nothing to make your neighbors envious, never evaluate, never criticize, be dull—that is your protection.

What the poem says is not merely satirical or merely sarcastic: it is scornful. And the prose paraphrase shows well that statement abstracted from an imaginative structure of sound, rhythm, and image is perforce inadequate and by no means equivalent to any part of the poem. The beginning is a cacophonous indecision, like a man picking his way through thorns. A pattern of assonance and consonance distresses us as much as the five bristly animals their neighbors. We guess part of the poet's meaning already: heavy armor is a ruinous price to pay for well-being. Whether or not we begin to expand the meaning at this point is of

[2]W. B. Yeats, "William Blake and His Illustrations to the 'Divine Comedy'," *Ideas of Good and Evil* (London: Macmillan, 1908).

[3]Wallace Stevens, "About One of Marianne Moore's Poems," *The Necessary Angel* (New York: Knopf, 1951).

no consequence. Certain clichés come to mind. Switzerland, mountain-fortressed and peaceful, has been a dull little country culturally and historically. The hedgehog and the porcupine figure in the imagination as formidable and inviolable, but our affection is for the graceful deer and the witty monkey. The rhinoceros has no fans. Such animals are dull as battleships are dull.

The sound of the opening lines is as fanciful as the images. The second line, for instance, has this succession of vowels: ɝ ɛ a ɨ ɔ ɛ a ɨ ɔ ɨ ɛ ɨ au. Note that [ɛ ɑ ɨ ɔ] is repeated exactly. The music of [ɨ ɔ ɨ ɛ ɨ au] is the same kind of see-sawing of sound we get in Chédevilles's

Even the rhyme-scheme ( a b c a b c ) seems satiric. The words—Miss Moore, like any poet with a distinctive style, seems to have words all her own—are deliberately ambiguous because ambiguity is part of the poem's subject: how much freedom does one have when he is the prisoner of his own security? Neither *pin-swin* nor *spine-swine* are listed in the OED; they are coinages, perhaps, or dialect words, as is *edgehog* ("sword-point pig"). *Pig-fur* may be leather or it may be, as in "permanent pig on the instep," pig iron. Salamander skin is fire-proof. The section of the poem about Prester John is taken, as information, from the *Encyclopædia Britannica* and, as with "He 'Digesteth Harde Yron'", the transformation of the material is a lesson in itself.

"His Shield" is a typical poem of Miss Moore's in that it exercises many of her devices. It is an essay, for it treats its subject discursively and offers informal illustrations of it. It is built in the spirit of a bestiary: such and such an animal has certain qualities from which we can derive a practical lesson. Its language creates a texture and an atmosphere: the poem is bristly and hostile. To be literal about it, armor of one sort or another is mentioned thirty-seven times. Its rhythm is complex and designed to slow the eye—and the voice—to a meditative pace. One would like to call it Baroque; much of it is counterpointed in the manner of Hopkins.

what one would keep; ‖ that is freedom. ‖ Become

There are two caesuras to this line; at each one the feet reverse: this is the principle of counterpoint that Hopkins found in *Samson Agonistes*.

Marianne Moore's literalness sets her poetry apart in modern verse.

Pound and Williams are literal in much the same way, and all three have avoided the pervasive surrealism that mars so much minor poetry of the period and which has been pushed to levels of excellence in Dylan Thomas, Lawrence Durrell, and Wallace Stevens. Take Pound's

> the female
> Is a chaos
> An octopus
> A biological process.[4]

We understand the lines as being imaginatively literal; there is folklore (and Remy de Gourmont) to testify to the first equation. The second is a richly ambiguous metaphor, and the third, less inventive, lives in the momentum built up by the first two. Historically such language stems from Rimbaud (particularly *Une Saison en enfer*), although there are examples of it in Hebrew and Persian poetry.

But Miss Moore's literalness is apt to be more rigorous still. "An Octopus" is about "an octopus of ice." At a first reading we have no way of knowing that the "octopus" is the snow-cap of a mountain, not a real octopus frozen or one carved from ice. The poem is a fine description of animals and scenery in the Rockies, yet the metaphorical octopus is kept as an allusion throughout. Metaphor, no matter how simple, always makes a double image. To work out and sustain an image of an octopus-like snow-cap is an extension of the use of metaphor to what must be one of its ultimates.

"The Jerboa" is a poem in two parts: "Too Much" and "Abundance." Ostensibly both parts treat of the jerboa, a small desert rat whose agility and courage are proper cause for admiration. We can imagine the jerboa easily and with delight. Here he is feeding and running:

> By fifths and sevenths,
> in leaps of two lengths,
>     like the uneven notes
> of the Bedouin flute, it stops its gleaning
> on little wheel castors, and makes fern-seed
> foot-prints with kangaroo speed.

---

[4]Canto XXIX. These lines are doubly pertinent to our subject in that they were first a jovial parody of Miss Moore, sent to her in a letter (London, 1 Feb. 1919).

> The female is a chaos,
> the male
> is a fixed point of stupidity . . . stupidity. . . .

One recognizes it as the method used in "The Mind Is an Enchanting Thing" and "To a Steam Roller." See Paige, ed., *The Letters of Ezra Pound 1907–1941* (New York: Harcourt, Brace, 1950).

In a recent moving picture, Walt Disney's "The Living Desert," there were sequences in which the American desert rat—cousin of the jerboa—triumphed over a sidewinder. The photography was with telescopic lens, in sharp focus, and of an excellence that would convince one that he had been in as intimate a position to observe the spunky little rat as ever he could be. But there was no imaginative control of the subject such as Miss Moore gives us. Disney used a musical accompaniment, but accompaniment is precisely what it was. To compare the jerboa's alternating long and short leaps to the sound of a Bedouin flute is another matter altogether. Bedouin music and a Bedouin rat are yoked in an imaginative trope that camera and sound-track can only approximate. "Fern-seed foot-prints" is hyperbolic; fern-seeds are well nigh microscopic. This, however, is one Miss Moore's most powerful devices. She is describing the jerboa with what seems to be the accuracy of an Agassiz or a Fabre. She isn't. She describes with an accuracy that is literal about the imagination only, but manages to make us see a jerboa more sharply than Disney's camera, a *National Geographic* article, or even our seeing one in a zoo.

But what is the poem saying? It opens with a description of an ugly Roman fountain, proceeds to talk of Egyptians and their animals, of "Pharoah's rat," the tamable mongoose, and lastly of the jerboa. "Abundance," the second part, opens with the jerboa, takes up Jacob's vision of the ladder, and mirages. The last seven stanzas are sharp descriptions of the jerboa. Yet it is a poem about freedom, or, more accurately, about liberty. A very great many of Miss Moore's poems are. But it is not "about" its subject in the way that John Stuart Mill's *On Liberty* is, or Spinoza's "Concerning Human Bondage." It is probably convenient to think of "The Jerboa" as an essay, for its structure is closer to discourse than to narrative or lyric. It is also an elaborate entry in a bestiary. The jerboa is a symbol of freedom for Miss Moore, as the ostrich is one of justice, the hedgehog of dullness, the skunk of wit, and so on. The free, in whatever sense, keep the enslaved alive. The "enslaved" in the poem are Romans and Egyptians; they have "power over the poor" and even though they are enslaved in spirit only, they look to the completely free spirit with an astonished admiration. That is why the Romans were proud of their bronze fir-cone fountain executed by a freed slave. It became automatically a symbol of freedom. The Egyptians with their rigid cities and ceremonial life dedicated the mongoose to Pharoah, who gave his name to "basalt serpents and portraits of beetles," "and he was named for them." The jerboa, however, is "free-born," and thus became a potent symbol of freedom—as Ananse to the West Africans and Brer Rabbit to the southern Negro. This ability to create folklore while anatomizing with an essayist's thoroughness a difficult abstraction is certainly not the least of Marianne Moore's achievements.

"Marriage" is an essay in verse—and to say so is not to deprecate it as poetry. Its wit comes not so much from its brilliant satire as from its swift changes of point of view. One opinion on wedlock displaces another; image follows image with the jolt of incongruity or the delight of the exact phrase or of the perfectly appropriate sentiment. Hymen is "a kind of overgrown cupid"; the ritual of marriage has in its lavishness fiddle-head ferns, lotus flowers, optunias, white dromedaries, a hippopotamus ("nose and mouth combined / in one magnificent hopper") and a snake and potent apple. The reader is not apprehensive over the lotus flowers of marriage or its optunias, but just what the hippopotami of marriage might be is a speculation that plunges us into the heart of Marianne Moore's poetics. Is it an image of unwieldiness (marriage as more than one can handle); is it a rough equivalent of Pound's "Et quant au troisième / Il est tombé dans le / De sa femme . . ." (Canto XXVII)? And marriage's white dromedaries? All of this is a mixture of sense and nonsense—for nonsense is very much a part of Miss Moore's business. "What monarch would not blush / to have a wife / with hair like a shaving-brush?"

The poem's laconic ending is a fine example of its method. Abruptly into the subtle arguments pro and con is inserted Daniel Webster's "Liberty and Union / now and forever" (the inscription on the base of his statue in Central Park), followed by an image of Webster himself, grim and authoritative. The effect is hilarity itself.

Ultimately it is to Miss Moore's language that we turn in order to appreciate the extent of her genius.

> The lemur-student can see
>    that an aye-aye is not
>
> an angwan-tíbo, potto, or loris. The sea-
>    side burden should not embarrass
> the bell-boy with the buoy-ball
>    endeavouring to pass
> hotel patronesses; nor could a
>    practised ear confuse the glass
>       eyes for taxidermists
>
> with eye glasses from the optometrist.

A student of lemurs, or a student with lemur eyes? Is the bell-boy embarrassed because of an accident of sound? It is a rule, seemingly, of Miss Moore's craft to carry a subject to extremes. This poem, "Four Quartz Crystal Clocks," elaborates a theme from Jean Giraudoux—that scientific observation is more and more confused with wisdom, so that accuracy of measurement threatens to replace native wit and acumen. In the passage above Miss Moore is laughing hard at confusions which no one is likely to be guilty of. But from the ludicrous extreme to the just mean is not so easy, and the reader who doesn't see that the accuratest of clocks is being laughed at also is misreading the poem.

There is what we might call Miss Moore's genius for illustrations. A cross section of one's correspondence would seem to imply that we are "citizens of Pompeii arrested in action" ("Bowls"). Apropos the Irish, she refutes the adage that water seeks its own level, by observing, "You have seen it, when obstacles happened to bar / the path, rise automatically" ("Sojourn in the Whale"). The cat "takes its prey to privacy, / the mouse's limp tail hanging like a shoelace from its mouth" ("Silence"). This aptness is the result of a precisionist's searching for words: brief words exactly right, and with a rare terseness.

There is her ability to reproduce color and texture with the success of an Audubon:

> A brass-green bird with grass-
> green throat smooth as a nut springs from
> twig to twig askew, copying the
> Chinese flower piece,—businesslike atom
> in the stiff-leafed tree's blue-
> pink dregs-of-wine pyramids
> of mathematic
> circularity. . . .
>   ("Smooth Gnarled Crape Myrtle")

There is the ability to construct an atmosphere of place and time. Here is a graveyard in Virginia:

> A deer-
> track in a church-floor
> brick, and a fine pavement tomb with engraved top, remain.
> The now tremendous vine-encompassed hackberry
> starred with the ivy-flower,
> shades the church tower;
> And a great sinner lyeth here under the sycamore.

Marianne Moore's poetry is a body of such consistently good poems, and good in so many ways, that a summary description of them capsizes in richness. Few poets have made an aesthetic so pliable or versatile. Each poem is a complex of experiences appropriate to that poem only, so that in her work there are no "periods," no sequences of poems, no poems using a theme or subject—or form—used in any other. Her subjects are

those of a mind intent on seeing things not only for what they are precisely, but how they act in and with the imagination. That is why her
animals are uncannily real and why they lose none of their reality when
they become symbols or points of departure into speculation.

One probably never reads a poem of Miss Moore's in a large enough
context. Within a minute description of a Swedish carriage there is

Washington and Gustavus
Aldophus, forgive our decay.

And the carriage thereby becomes much more than an image of past elegance. An heirloom has outlasted the heirs. Miss Moore is neither a sentimental collector nor a dabbler in wildlife. Behind her work is a love
of—it is unfair to have to speak for her—things cunningly made: for one,
armored anteaters, and for another, Egyptian pulled glass bottles. Things
that seem to defy description but which her art labors well to describe
well: icosaspheres and paper nautiluses. Beauty—her triumph is that she
has found it where few have before, and convinced us of it. Conciseness
and symmetry. Liberty. Tough, even cantankerous individuality. Justice:
there is "Virginia Britannia" and the poems written during the last war.
The "inwardly" of

I inwardly did nothing
    O Iscariotlike crime!

is a key to all her poems. One has to learn to read a poetry with so
engaging a surface from the inside out. The alternative is the externalist's.
But the full quotation is:

I inwardly did nothing
    O Iscariotlike crime!
Beauty is everlasting
    and dust is for a time.

*A man's paradise is his own good nature.*
                    (VI Dynasty, *Massime degli antichi*
                    *Egiziani*, Boris de Rachewiltz, 1954)

*Look down now, Cotton Mather, from the blank.*
*Was heaven where you thought? It must be there.*
*It must be where you think it is, in the light*
*On bed-clothes, in an apple on a plate.*
*It is the honey-comb of the seeing man.*
                    ("The Blue Buildings in the Summer Air")

# Spinoza's Tulips

Between Glauco Cambon's Stevens, *"un acrabata interiore che vol-*
*teggiava fra bellezza e verità"* and Mr. Winters's Stevens, a brilliant but
ineffectual smith of gaudy verse—these being characteristic extremes of
explaining away a poet not wholly understood—there is the Stevens who
is the poetic cousin of Spinoza and Santayana. It is this Stevens, the
philosophical poet, or, considering the imagery that objectifies most often
the philosophy in Stevens, the philosophical landscapist, that I intend to
discuss. Writing after Mr. William Van O'Connor's *The Shaping Spirit,*
one feels free to inspect Stevens at any point without needing to explain
or eulogize his entire work. To keep my argument close to a single poem I
have chosen for analysis the poem that, in a sense, "makes all the difference" between Stevens and his forbears and contemporaries, "The Comedian as the Letter C." The extreme of sensuous coloring in Stevens's

poetry, its vocabulary of intense seriousness, hilarity and wit, its brilliant but difficult and seemingly capricious ordering of sense and imagery have all been subjected to a variety of considerations. My purpose is not to elucidate his poetics but to single out his injunction to discount the poem and to look to the concrete particulars of which it is an abstract, to turn Spinozan materialist, in fact, and learn to live in a world stripped of its illusions.

Stevens grows from a philosophical spirit rather than from any one philosophy, but that spirit can be identified and shown to be of vital worth in the understanding of him. "To define poetry as an unofficial view of being," Stevens says in "The Figure of the Youth as Virile Poet," "places it in contrast with philosophy and at the same time establishes the relation between the two. . . . We must conceive of poetry as at least the equal of philosophy."

Santayana, addressing an audience at the Hague on the tercentenary of Spinoza's birth, asked his listeners "to imagine the truth to be as unfavorable as possible to your desires and as contrary as possible to your natural presumptions; so that the spirit in each of us may be drawn away from its accidental home and subjected to an utter denudation and supreme trial."

Compare this, then, with the opening passages of "Notes toward a Supreme Fiction":

> Begin, ephebe, by perceiving the idea
> Of this invention, this invented world,
> The inconceivable idea of the sun:
>
> You must become an ignorant man again
> And see the sun again with an ignorant eye
> And see it clearly in the idea of it.

Without following just now what I hope will appear as a philosophical kinship among Stevens, Santayana, and Spinoza—Spinoza, too, for instance, had an experience with the sun, which in his deliberately becoming an ignorant man again seemed "about two hundred feet away"—it should be seen that the results of their three intense speculations on the nature of being are wonderfully different, no matter how close the processes of inquiry; that, briefly, the "imageless ontology of Spinoza," as Friedrich Schlegel called it, and "Fat girl, terrestrial, my summer, my night . . . my green, my fluent mundo" of Stevens are almost from separate orders of thought. Their kinship needs Santayana to illuminate it, even though *The Realms of Being*, which has for greenery that one passage from Wordsworth quoted to be disapproved of diligently, is almost as imageless as the *De Ethica*. It is when Santayana asks what "inmost allegiance, what ultimate religion, would be proper to a wholly free and disillusioned spirit?" that we see the root of the drama in "The Comedian as the Letter C" and the central idea in "Sunday Morning," "L'Esthétique du Mal," and "Notes toward a Supreme Fiction." And, once it is understood, as Crispin has it, that "the soil is man's intelligence," that Santayana's *Realm of Matter* is the prose parallel of much of Stevens (note, for example, "The Blue Buildings in the Summer Air"), Stevens's use of landscape in practically every poem can be seen as the mundus eternally feeding the mind, the vital and proper traffic between reality and the imagination.

Wordsworth's "one impulse from a vernal wood" is not Santayana's complex of essences, but the reverse: the spirit outside of man "whose dwelling is the light of setting suns" is but another fiction impeding perception, an accidental predilection of the imagination positing its imagery and arbitrary vocabulary upon the dumb image of landscape. It is ironic that Wordsworth was excited by and possibly deeply interested in Spinoza and what he thought was his pantheism, for what he achieved as a poet of nature is as alien to Spinoza's *Deus siva Natura* as it is to Stevens's theme of landscape. The distinction is insisted upon in "Notes toward a Supreme Fiction":

Never suppose an inventing mind as source
Of this idea nor for that mind compose
A voluminous master folded in the fire.

Iamblichus's sun, as metaphor, is not uncongenial. I have shown Stevens's attitude toward such "honeycombs of the seeing man" in my superscription. That the imaginative conception of the real—the poet's business—is ultimately superior to the imaginative treatment of the imaginary is discussed at length in "The Noble Rider and the Sound of Words." The mind struggles with two worlds, fictive and real. Stevens's major theme is his philosophical propounding of this struggle. He has joined Spinoza and Santayana in their honest materialism and made a body of poetry brilliantly distinct from that of any other of the moderns. The struggle is dramatized more concisely than elsewhere in "The Comedian as the Letter C," concerning one Crispin, a European valet who comes to settle in the Carolinas.

Part I, "The World without Imagination" introduces Crispin who "created, in his day, a touch of doubt" as to whether man, "the intelligence of his soil" is also "preceptor to the sea." As with Melville, for whom the sea was an old chaos of the unabated deluge where man's

predicament in a disordered civilization and an inscrutable world can be
seen in greater relief than in the confusing speciousness of land, the sea in
Stevens is an elemental landscape,

> Ubiquitous concussion, slap and sigh,
> Polyphony beyond his baton's thrust.

Crispin as a character comes into French literature in 1654, in Scar-
ron's *Écolier de Salamanque*, *"un valet,"* as the *Larousse* sums him up,
*"goguenard, peureux, fanfaron, fripon, frotte de latin et de philosophie
comme ses maîtres, toujours prêt à les flatter ou à les jouer, habille
presque comme eux (petit chapeau et vêtement noirs, fraise blanche, bot-
tes molles, ceinture de buffle et longue rapière), apte à tous les metiers."*
Behind the initial poses of Crispin, at the beginning of the poem, there are
echoes of plays about him: "Preceptor to the sea" (*Crispin précepteur* of
La Thuillérie, 1679), "musician of pears" (*Crispin musicien* of
Hauteroche, 1674), "this nincompated pedagogue" (*le Fou raisonnable*
of Poisson, 1664), "this same wig of things" (*Crispin chevalier* of
Champmesle, 1671, and *Crispin gentilhomme* of Montfleury, 1677).

To identify him, moreover, as another Candide is not far amiss, and if
we draw attention to his likeness to Peer Gynt or indeed to any of the
sophomores of satiric *contes* in which a clown or Harlequin—Pinocchio,
for a good example—is forced by the buffeting of fortune to become a
tragic or "serious" figure we will have a basis for understanding the origin if not the subsequent development of Crispin.

Crispin as virtuoso servant, amateur savant and dilettante is meant to
epitomize the ruses of the time: politic for honest behavior, *la politesse*
for intelligence, polish for sensibility. Verities in the hands of vigorous
men ran counter to such daintiness. It was as a servant of state and
church that Swift came to grief; Johnson's brusqueness registered a protest. After the eighteenth century the "wig of things, this nincompated
pedagogue" could no longer function, the "eye most apt in gelatines and
jupes, / Berries of villages, a barber's eye" with its aesthetic of Pope and
Christopher Wren became a fiercer searcher of man's rôle in nature.
Crispin's metanoia upon the sea, his change from eighteenth to nineteenth-century man can be seen in the Turner family, where the father
was a lady's barber, a specialist in gossip and the roiled coiffures of the
age, the son the greatest of England's romantic seascapists. The barber-
valet imagery—touched first, as a theme, in Crispin's name (*crispus,*
curled) and brought to ironic fulfilment in *And Daughters with Curls*—
affects the opening experiences of the sea-change ("silentious porpoises,
whose snouts / Dibbled in waves that were mustachios, / Inscrutable hair
in an inscrutable world.")

"The valet in the tempest was annulled," and nothing remained of Crispin but "some starker, barer self." The attendant god is Triton, or the idea of Triton, for he, too, long before, had gone the way of Crispin so that "memorial gesturings" only were left, "hallucinating horn . . . A sunken voice." This device of mythological context is repeated in Part II, "Concerning the Thunderstorms of Yucatan,"

> the note
> Of vulcan, that a valet seeks to own. . . .

In Yucatan the violence of earthquake parallels the storm at sea of Part I. Now stripped of his civilized finesse and polished manners, Crispin discovers that he is "aware of exquisite thought" and that he has become a "connoisseur of elemental fate." The office of Vulcan has succeeded that of Triton; Crispin's adventures are at a peak.

Yucatan serves Crispin as a landscape a degree more human than the sea, "most inhuman of elements." His voyage plunged him into primeval chaos; the jungle is but a little less overpowering. If Crispin's fate is a fable, in part, of the adjustment of the European *homo faber* to his American wilderness, then Yucatan, the seat of an extraordinary and obscure culture that was already in ruins when the Spaniards first saw it and utterly forgotten when it was rediscovered in 1839, has been selected as a fine example of landscape in high contrast to anything Europeans had seen. Confusion, having broken up previous concepts into elemental awe, soon became a basis for renewal. The primitive Mayans, partly savage and partly westernized (there are but 200 of them living nowadays), still praying to the night-bird and running to the cathedral in time of disaster, leave Crispin with a chthonic respect for nature. The pattern is not unfamiliar: Gauguin in the South Seas, Hudson in the Amazon basin, von Humboldt, after seeing America, recognizing the sixteen basic kinds of landscape. Landscape itself became in the nineteenth century a medium of expression of considerable impact, functioning in painting as Stevens makes it function in his poetry. We have but to look at Edward Lear's profound disturbance on first seeing India after a lifetime of doing "views" of Italian passes and Adriatic bays and promontories, or at Ruskin's analyses of landscape in terms of moral edification to appreciate Stevens's remarkable recovery and consummate application of an art that has become in our day moribund and symptomatically insignificant.

"Approaching Carolina," the third part of the poem, is a second voyage for Crispin, another "sweating change." At first he hopes that the Northern spring ("America was always north to him") with its "legendary moonlight" and "green palmettoes in crepuscular ice" might give him "the relentless contact he desired" and be

The liaison, the blissful liaison,
Between himself and his environment,
Which was, and is, chief motive, first delight
For him, and not for him alone. . . .

But immediately he realizes that "the book of moonlight" will not do,
that it's "wrong as divagation to Peking," a "passionately niggling nightingale." He must have a robust landscape about him, "prickly and obdu-
rate. " The spring that he comes upon on the Carolina coast is

A time abhorrent to the nihilist
Or searcher for the fecund minimum.
The moonlight fiction disappeared. . . .

He savors the "burly smells" of the docks , becomes infatuated with
"the essential prose / As being . . . the one integrity" and decides that
"prose shall wear a poem's guise at last." It is not difficult to see in the
poem thus far the pattern of discovery that brought Spinoza to his initial
skepticism and Santayana to his stoic materialism. The world has had
few men "disillusioned" enough to accept the world stripped of all fictive
ornament, "the same insoluble lump" as Crispin calls it. But such an idea
is bed-rock, else the poem would end here. Santayana's philosophy, beyond its Spinozan metaphysics, is an elaborate ethics and aesthetic: the
essential prose, to be tolerable, and because it leads, with Spinoza, to
man's love for his world, and because, with Santayana, it grows from an
"animal faith," must wear a poem's guise. It must be "chief motive, first
delight." We recognize a similar experience in Melville's saying that a
whaling ship was his Harvard and his Yale, and in much of Thoreau. One
might compile a select company of such uncompromising artists who will
have no illusions about them, who want for paradise nothing but their
own good natures; they are not many. And in the history of ideas they
must be seen as renegades from the seemingly unbreakable tradition of
nineteenth- and twentieth-century pessimism, beside which they stand
out as hearty, jovial aristocrats of the heart. If no confusion between
pessimism and ill will botch the rightness of the comparison, or, for that
matter, between good will and optimism, an excellent symbol would be
Captain Ahab and Ishmael. Crispin belongs to the family of Ishmael,
although Ishmael, agreeing that much docrine is to be concocted from the
rout of things and that the flavor of the world comes in "Seraphic proclamations of the pure / Delivered with a deluging onwardness," would
emend Crispin's final deduction to "the sea is man's intelligence."

Part IV, "The Idea of a Colony," shows us Crispin acting to make his
"new intelligence prevail." Mr. O'Connor points out that "The Comedian as the Letter C" is autobiographical, that it can be read as Stevens's

poetic manifesto. It is also a microcosm of the intellectual development of that part of America which was transplanted from eighteenth century Europe, enriched by the shock of inundation by a savage terrain, and which flourished as a hive of liberalism and individuality in the milieu of Jefferson, Franklin, and their republican fellows until, like Crispin, it settled complacently into quiet mediocrity. Crispin's "singular collation" of plans for a colony in the new world is mock-Jeffersonian:

> The melon should have apposite ritual,
> Performed in verd apparel, and the peach,
> When its black branches came to bud, belle day,
> Should have an incantation.

But (and here we have the only hint as to why Crispin made his voyage):

> These bland excursions into time to come,
> Related in romance to backward flights,
> However prodigal, however proud,
> Contained in their afflatus the reproach
> That first drove Crispin to his wandering.

Stevens chides gently the fervor of the colonizer, a "clown, perhaps, but an aspiring clown." Left to make a world for himself, he makes, after all, a replica, as best he can, of the world he left. But he does it with his new intelligence, with a vigor for him unprecedented. Whereas before he wrote his annual poem to the spring (a proper bow to what the paideuma of his former culture held to be the nature of things), he now knows the spring for what it is, "the essential prose . . . the one discovery still possible to make / To which all poems were incident. . . ."

Mr. Stevens himself makes the comparison with Candide, but with the difference that Cripsin has "a fig in sight." It is worth noting that "The Comedian as the Letter C" is not only an elaboration of such *contes philosophiques* as *Candide,* where the ability to come to terms with one's world is ultimately parochial and isolationist, but an implicit criticism of traditional pessimism: Crispin is to be seen as a better manipulator of his destiny than his literary brothers. Where Peer Gynt is lost and fit only to be recast as molten material—the parallels are perhaps not accidental: it was in Carolina that Peer stripped himself of all integrity and in tropic landscapes that he realized his worthlessness—Crispin continues to struggle at reclamation. His advantage over a Peer Gynt or a Gulliver is his ability to make his heart a honeycomb, to be both disillusioned and a man of imagination. Nowhere does Stevens saddle him with being shocked at the truth; on the contrary, he's delighted with it, but intelligently always. Stevens's faith in his bandy-legged, comically enthusiastic hero would distress a Swift and bring a charge of levity from an Ibsen. It is on this account that one should recognize in Stevens a preëminence both in modern philosophy and poetry for his rigorous sanity and honied good nature.

There is a proper questioning of Crispin's achievement in the final parts of the poem. Is he a failure as innovator for returning to salad beds? Has he wasted his efforts in ending contentedly with a nice shady home and four curly-haired daughters? When he becomes a "fatalist" Stevens uses the word with irony, for what Crispin has learned is "not doctrinal/ In form though in design." It is, after all, in a real world, "autumn's compendium," "perfectly revolved." If Crispin has concluded "fadedly," he has at least done so honestly, has illuminated—as the poet must— "plain and common things" "from a fancy gorged / By apparition." It is a comedy with which we are dealing; it resolves itself, unlike tragedy, only in relation to its audience. The closing line is doctrinal: "So may the relation of each man be clipped." Crispin as persona of the poet wears a Harlequin's mask and thus acts out but part of the drama in Stevens's poetry. His tableau is at once a fable of our landscape and what we have made of it (or, as Spinoza and Santayana would say, what it has made of us, what it has, by its power to be congenial or hostile to the spirit, caused us to feel and to think), and of Blake's Fool who persisted in his folly and came upon a paradise all the same.

There is a tale that Spinoza found the onions of Amsterdam particularly tasteless and accepted their insipidity as part of the price one pays for exile, for being able to live as he pleased. But he discovered one day that all along he had been eating tulip bulbs, not onions. Crispin's voyage is an elaboration of this moral tale; the intelligent man's intelligence of his vegetables is prologue to intelligence of his world, "veracious page on page, exact." One hardly needs to add that few men have attempted Crispin's voyage or had his energy or heart, or that Wallace Stevens's poetry is of a freshness and sanity all too scarce in contemporary writing.

# Do You Have A Poem Book
# on E. E. Cummings?

The poet—"one who writes in measure," as Johnson laconically defines him—and poetess ("a she poet") have always had a rough time of it in the Republic. It has ever been their endemic luck to starve, become a Harvard professor, commit suicide, lose their reading glasses before an audience of sophomores, go upon the people *à la* Barnum, and serve as homework in state universities, where they could in nowise get a position and where their presence usually scatters the English faculty like a truant officer among the Amish. But the very worst has happened to him, and in the last couple of decades. It has been forgotten in high places what he is, and every school child is taught the most godawful rot as to why he writes as he does in measure.

The things of the world are always at one's doorstep; the miseries of the American poet were nicely defined while I was on my errands this morning deep in Kentucky. At the grocer's, as I was throwing *Time* into my cart, a lady broke into a motherly smile. "Thar you go," she said, "buyin' th' magerzine book of your choice for the month: ain't it grand to read?" It was at the local paperback emporium that a teen-ager, obviously a time-server in summer school, asked for "a poem book on E. E. Cummings." The lady admirer of literacy is a guitarist and sings "Great Speckled Bird" and "The Murder of James A. Garfield" on the radio. She is, in her way, a poet; and one of the things utterly forgotten about poets is that they come in hierarchies and orders.

Edgar A. Poe and Edgar A. Guest spoke, to be very sure, from different sensibilities, but their greatest difference is that they spoke *for* different sensibilities. The young man with his poem book on E. E. Cummings will have been taught by the time this gets into print that Mr. Cummings's poems are the expression of Mr. Cummings's inward reflections and ideas. Mr. Cummings had Personality, and was capable of Self Expression. He was a book author. Lord help us, he even used Symbols. If Mr. Cummings speaks with another man's voice, as he does in poem after poem, the teen-ager's teacher will explain that the poet is Undercutting with Irony.

That the poet speaks for people who cannot speak, that he makes sentences for people to *say,* is as outmoded a concept in pedagogy as whacking the behind for laziness and insolence. The poet, poor fellow, has become a Personality, and the only authority for his raving is that he stands in his shoes. That pair of shoes over there: in them stands a man who for lack of Personality might be as famous as the poet.

One can think of statements that seem to explain so wry a misunderstanding of the poet as an issuer of personal pronunciamentos. Behavioral psychology, squirted into the ears of students from Head Start through the Ph.D., can account for no action not grounded in self-advancement; it follows that the poet as a voice for other people is suspect. He *must* be expressing himself, don't you see? Poor Whitman. He wrote a corpus of poems for an entire nation, to give them a tongue to unstop their inarticulateness. He wrote in their dialect, incorporating the nerve of their rhetoric and the rhythms of the Bible from which their literacy came. He wrote two elegies for Lincoln, one for grownups ("When Lilacs Last in the Dooryard Bloom'd") and one for school children ("O Captain! My Captain!"). He tried to understand the voiceless American and to speak for him, and as much as any poet has ever succeeded, he did. Yet he has been idiotically deposed from the fulcrum he so carefully selected. He wrote not a single personal poem and yet every word is taught to students as the self-expression of an elate disk-jockey who made his scene with a poetry book, Way Back Yonder (but still pertinent, as he used symbols and sometimes undercut with irony).

Thus the editors of *Time* have no trouble doing an article on the most

significant modern American poet. Marianne Moore? Louis Zukofsky?
Ezra Pound? Robert Kelly? Ronald Johnson? Robert Duncan? Naw.
Robert Lowell. Mr. Lowell has, indeed, worked hard at being a poet. He
has been severe in his output, and knows, with Brahms. that writing is all
too easy. What's hard is to throw most of what you've written in the
trash-basket. He has been smart and modern in metric and diction. And
he has been bleak, agonized, and serious, terribly serious. He seems to
have always had a headache. He is respected at Bennington. Mr. Pound
(as *Time* does not seem to know) has read from his poems at Spoleto.
And *Time* has singled him out as *the* significant poet.

And he is, if we define poetry as essentially self-expression. And if Mr.
Lowell's response to the world were as eloquent as, say, Stan Laurel's or
François Villon's or Mahalia Jackson's—that is, if there were some juice
or even some mud between the toes—the report from his inwards might
instruct us in grief and support us when we're doleful. One need not
diminish Mr. Lowell's excellence to say what's out of joint in *Time*'s
report on current American poetry; but since they set him up as representative, it is necessary to say with some firmness that he is not. He is a
thoughtful, serious, melancholy academic poet; if he is representative of
anything beyond himself, it is of a broody school of professor-poets
whose quiet, meticulous verse is perhaps the lineal and long-winded descendant of the cross-stitch sampler.

Poets, *Time* says, are moony minded, seeing camels and bunny rabbits
in clouds. (Shiver and snuggle up, dear reader, *Time* is going to walk right
up to a poet, give him an Ed Sullivan hug, and get him to express himself
about his self-expression.) Shelley, by golly, saw a cloud as a cloud, but
never mind. "Poets," Mr. Lowell says, "are a more accepted part of society." Mr. Lowell is a Harvard professor, and would no doubt, if he
taught physiology, explain to his students that the tongue is an admirable
and useful organ, and that society is almost reconciled to its being a part
of the body. When Ezra Pound ("the father of modern poetry," says
*Time*) became a more accepted part of society, after thirteen years in the
pokey where society put him in a moment of rejection, he was detained
momentarily by reporters asking the usual silly questions. "Ovid had it a
lot worse," he said, and while they were looking at each other's note-
pads to see how to spell Ovid, he clapped his hat on his head, and walked
off to take a ship to Italy.

Mr. Lowell is a poet and presumably knows his fellow poets, and when
he says that they are integrated and accepted and living it up in what
*Time* calls "an ambience of instant feeling," I still wonder about an excellent poet who I happen to know is a bus boy in a short-order kitchen, and
another who cleans shower stalls at a gym, and another who is a janitor
in a Boston tenement—all thoroughly sane and serious people whose

ambitions are simply more poetical than material, but scarcely to be described as within the grateful embrace of society.

"Poetry books," *Time* assures us, "trip ever more briskly off the presses." A major American poet, whom I shall not embarrass by naming has sought a publisher for a major work for two years now, and the hope of finding one is still thin. The poet and publisher Jonathan Williams stumps the country annually, reading, showing slides, and importuning financial sources for the wherewithal to publish American poets. His list of those to be accommodated is staggering. What *Time* ought to have said about the state of American poetry is that it is extremely diverse, bouncing and healthy, and that the public who might buy it and read it is so dismally stupid, sheepish, and tediously ignorant—I mean the less than 1 per cent of the population that buys books and the fraction of them that read them—that it is a kind of miracle that we have a single poet in the country.

The blue-haired followers of Kahlil Gibran read Dylan Thomas, their Thammuz and their Adonis. Allen Ginsberg and Peter Orlovsky, who look like the ghosts of Karl Marx and Raymond Duncan, have their raggletaggle following. As Mr. Lowell says, the world is swimming with poets. But he neglected to inform *Time* of their names, so that their readers, imagining themselves informed about American poetry, have never been quite so miserably misinformed. Louis Zukofsky is not mentioned. A simple telephone call to Henry Rago, editor of *Poetry* would have ascertained that Zukofsky, alongside Marianne Moore and Ezra Pound, is one of the three most distinguished living American poets. And the elate and brassy Michael McClure, as American as a six-shooter, *Time* has not heard tell of him, either. Or the masterful lyricist Robert Kelly, or the visionary Ronald Johnson. Or Jonathan Williams and J. V. Cunningham, whose poems are as well made as wristwatches. The scope for educating *Time* is large; one could go on. Journalism, the purpose of which is to inform and to disseminate, isn't doing its job; neither are the schools. Thirty years of liberal twiddling with the lines of communication has made it almost impossible to broadcast anything but received propaganda.

All the arts are in the same predicament, so that what's happening in the minds that keep other minds alive and give them the courage to live is reported, if at all, in a dangerously denatured and official trickle of news. The arts can look after themselves; they are used to neglect and obfuscation. It is the people who suffer from the dullness and ignorance of the press. The diligent goddess Nemesis is an ironic old girl. Time was, the journals were literate in America and cried out for poets to grace the nation. Now the journals when they babble about poetry are illiterate, and can't even find out the poets' names.

# Seeing Shelley Plain

Wordsworth pushing a wheelbarrow containing Coleridge with blistered heels; the grave infant Milton watching lean Will Shakespeare and fat Ben Jonson staggering home from the Mermaid; Rousseau hiding all day in his own attic because he'd had the servant say to Boswell that he was out and the intrepid Scot shoved his way in to sit stubbornly until the philosopher showed; Joyce and Proust in a taxi, the one lowering the windows because of his claustrophobia, the other raising them because of his asthma, up and down, down and up, all the way to Maxim's; Eliot and Pound lifting their feet to accommodate the imaginary vacuum cleaner of a lunatic while they conversed in a cell in St. Elizabeths Hospital—the literary anecdote, as Donald Hall observes in the introduction to his *Remembering Poets,* is a genre all to itself "at the edges of literature."

Hazlitt was a master of the form; what would the English Romantics look like without his account of them? It was gossipy Henry Crabb Robinson who gave us our images of the Blakes reading *Paradise Lost* in their back garden, naked, pink, and chubby. And what else was Boswell doing but compiling an epic portrait of Johnson out of anecdotes?

Now that literature itself has become paperborne, the literary anecdote may be the last survivor of the oral tradition. It would, I think, be awkward for a poet nowadays to offer a recitation of his verses at a dinner party (something you went to dinner parties *for*, once upon a time, when a duke's wink from deep inside a ruff of squirrel fur activated a page, who brought a candle to the shoulder of Maister Chaucer, who unfolded a sheaf of parchment and began to speak in octosyllables), but if he has spent a drunken evening with Cal Lowell, or sat at the colossal knees of Robert Kelly, or played billiards with Sam Beckett, he has an audience all ears.

Gossip is a social art form, it is intimate, and it is a tradition as old as eating in company. It does not go easily into print (one of Professor Hall's triumphs as a writer is that his style keeps the feel of *telling*). If it's literary gossip, it has few occasions for native expression; you can't tell an anecdote about an obscure poet, and you must also have the sense that you are satisfying curiosity. I would venture a grander role for the anecdote than Donald Hall modestly claims; it is the folklore that plays around a high seriousness, the saints' legends of a religion, and usually has the truth of myth rather than of fact.

Hall omits the anecdote of Dylan Thomas's question to Harry Levin, who he had just learned was a professor of Comparative Literature: "What," Thomas asked in his best Welsh White Trash voice, "do you compare it to?" The deliciousness of this cannot be explained to the uninitiated (but it isn't a snob's anecdote; snobs can't tell literary anecdotes worth a damn): Harry Levin is a gracious and civilized soul with a poise that one cannot imagine being discomfited, and yet his immense usefulness to the world is explaining literature, and here he is, in Cambridge congeniality, being cheeked by a poet. The *Urgestalt* of the anecdote is Diogenes asking Alexander the Great to get out of his light.

Donald Hall, poet, short-story writer, critic, teacher, and *raconteur,* tells us what it is like to have known Eliot, Thomas, Frost, and Pound, not for any length of time—know a great man too well and you can't write about him at all—but in intense intermittences: a hair-raising day of pub-crawling in London with Thomas, and an overnight stay with his pitiful family in Wales; visits to Eliot's lair at Faber and Faber; sessions with Frost at writing conferences; Fellini-like visits to the ancient Ezra Pound in his decade of ghostly silence. And with all, business. Hall is no lion-hunter (they can't tell anecdotes, either); he is, as best one can make out from his book, a literary diplomat. To him we must pay our gratitude for the very last fragments of *The Cantos*.

One of the ironies of the literary life is that capable Boswells turn up just when the subject is on its last pins, either drinking himself to death like Thomas, or ill and frail like Eliot and Pound, or wearing a public mask like Frost. Still, our curiosity about a great creative figure grows with his eminence. The clever old codgers write a script for the interviewer, every chuckle in the same place—Sir P. G. Wodehouse was the master of this, so was Frost, a mysterious and secret man who put on his Norman Rockwell face for any public whatever. (Hall's "Mortimer Snerd" is a bit harsh; it was more like Uncle Remus up at the big house, Tomming it to a fare-thee-well.)

Professor Hall was a student of his poets' writings; underneath his very human curiosity about them as men with children to feed and mortgages to pay off was his concern for seeing into the work with the leverage of the person. Talk about pitching mercury with a fork!

In meeting great men a wholly uninspected and peculiar chemistry transforms the psyche, provided, of course, that one has the hero worship, the awe, the plangently romantic giddiness of anticipation and fulfillment. I wonder that some psychological boffin has not anatomized for science this longing of admirers to see distinguished men; somewhere deep in the phenomenon is a clue to faith, loyalty, and all the gaudier kinds of enthusiasm.

Lord knows I have known enough of the giddiness of such excitement to be the perfect reader of Donald Hall's book. I met T. S. Eliot five times over the years; four of them involved (as you will find in the sheets of the Recording Angel when the scrolls are opened) the exchange of the words "Pleased to meet you," together with a handshake. The fifth encounter was chummier. I had accomplished the fifth "Pleased to meet you," and handshake, in the Common Room of Eliot House, and had the honor of steering him toward the dining room where all Harvard that was anybody and enterprising awaited his presence. To the right of the door leading out of the Common Room hangs a portrait of Eliot by Wyndham Lewis, or rather, a first draft of Lewis's first portrait of him, the circumspect banker who was known in both South Kensington and Bloomsbury, the *TLS* crack reviewer, the chameleon American who could chat Gibbon with Strachey on Lady Ottoline Morrell's lawn or Benda with Hulme at a chop house, a man with an ether addict for a wife.

Eliot drew up short before the portrait, held his lapels and craned forward the eagle's profile. "I seem," he said to me, "to have changed."

I have had even briefer *rencontres* with the great. My father and I saw Franklin Roosevelt fall from a train, sprawling onto the station floor (Gainesville, Georgia, 1936, FBI goons snatching cameras left and right); and I have assisted in extinguishing Jean-Paul Sartre when he was on fire. Pete Maas and I, in our salad days, were at the Deux Magots of an evening. "Guy," said the affable Pete, "that old wall eye over the way put his lit pipe in his jacket pocket awhile ago and in just a bit will be in flames, wouldn't you say? Go tell him."

We tried out various phrases, selecting *Monsieur, vous brûlez* as the most expressive. Pete is a more forward person than I, and it was he who went over, begged the pardon of Sartre, and told him that his jacket pocket was on fire. Nothing happened. The conversation raged on, arms flailing, Existentialism as thick in the air as the smoke from Sartre's *confection*. Sartre did not deign to notice Pete, though Pete ventured a polite tug at his sleeve. Nor did Monsieur Camus or Monsieur Richard Wright give the least heed. Whereupon I offered Pete our carafe of water, and this he poured into the philosopher's pocket, which hissed.

My fate has been the tangential brush. I have listened to Roy Campbell drunk and Mann sober, all in respectful silence. My sessions with J. R. R. Tolkien were an exquisite misery: he was trying to teach me Anglo-Saxon. I have helped Marianne Moore look for her lost glasses, and have shaken hands with Gerald Ford (by mistake, he thought I was somebody else). I have said "Pleased to meet you" to Eleanor Roosevelt and mounted the steps of Widener as Prince Karim Khan and the King of Belgium descended them, and nodded, futilely, to both. I have heard Faulkner's voice through a closed door; I have been the one on KP, on my knees at the time, sweeping ashes from under a range, who noticed that in our midst General Mark Clark was wandering about, presumably looking for a cup of coffee, and shouted the stentorian "TEN-shun!!!" and presented arms with a broom, the propriety of which in military politeness is still a dubious point with me.

And Frost. "The man from Porlock!" he said of me the one time I went to his house in Cambridge, though I was scarcely interrupting the composition of a second "Kubla Khan," only a *Saturday Evening Post* cover tableau of the freckled old apple-cheeked New Hampshire Poet by a crackling fire, the inevitable Andrew Wyeth (a barn in January light) over the mantlepiece and Harvardlings at his feet.

I had brought the piece of paper that would release Ezra Pound from 13 years in a madhouse. Eliot had already signed it, twice, as it turned out, once in the wrong place and once in the right. Faulkner had signed it, Hemingway had signed it on a yacht off the coast of Cuba (naturally).

MacLeish had signed it. Wallace Stevens had refused. ("I don't want Ezra on my back step, do you?") And now Frost was to sign it. A year before, Attorney General Rogers had been willing quietly to *nol pros* the Pound case, on the grounds that a case 13 years cold could not be tried, but the press got wind of the matter and raised such a ruckus that nothing could be done. Now MacLeish was trying again, as he had for years. Rogers had asked for a big name to cow the press, and everyone agreed that Frost was just about as good as the Statue of Liberty.

Frost took the paper, disappeared into another room with it, meditating a whole ten minutes. The Harvardlings glared at me. I dripped from a snowstorm outside, and my purse did not run to overshoes. The old man shuffled back into the room, frowning.

"Eisenhower will never consent to this," he said. "It's a waste of all our time. Why didn't Archie come himself?"

Professor MacLeish, I explained, had left the day before for Antigua. I pronounced it as a Spanish word.

"They used to call it An-TIG-yu-ah," he said, holding the door for me to leave. "They've changed everything."

He had never visited Pound in the asylum. Professor Hall's account of Frost's efforts to free Pound are not quite right. Archibald MacLeish, for all practical purposes alone, got Pound out. Frost played his part, as requested. He may even, as Hall hints, have imagined that he thought it all up himself.

The portrait of Pound in this wonderfully readable book is the most thorough, the most moving, and the one with the most cooperative subject. (Hall's *Paris Review* interviews with Pound and Eliot are included in an appendix.) With Thomas, Eliot, and Frost Professor Hall had a worn path to beckon him on, but the way to Pound had been initially blocked by Pound's besmirched reputation as an antisemite, bootlicker of Mussolini, Fascist, obscurantist, and traitor. But get around these he did, to find a man perhaps more complex and pesky than the scary one.

The Pound he knew was in the depths of guilt and, frequently, despair, accusing himself of having wrecked his and his family's life. He brooded terribly. He practiced a candor of terrifying honesty. ("How are you, Mr. Pound?" "Senile.") He clawed the back of his hands. He watched his world die and fade utterly away. Still, in his ruin, he was more interesting than ten hale newly minted literati together. He could swim like a dolphin at eighty. He walked upright, dressed with dapper taste (though he became so thin that his trousers fell off at the opera, an accident that made him so furious with the nature of things that he simply stood and glared while he was ringed about by friends).

The value of reports from the horse's mouth is that public opinions get revised; propinquity corrects the distant, third-hand view. Here we have an arrogant Frost and a contrite Pound, the opposite of received opinion. The gilt flakes off Thomas. Eliot remains as inscrutable as ever, a whole theater of mimes, the king of the possums.

Donald Hall is a fine reporter, a clear-headed witness, and judging by his friendly association with these four difficult men, a worthy companion.

# Persephone's Ezra

## THE FLOWERED TREE AS KORÉ

Of the twenty-three poems in Ezra Pound's first book of verse, the unpublished *Hilda's Book* now in Houghton Library at Harvard, written between 1905 and 1907 for Hilda Doolittle in whose posession it was during most of her lifetime, only "Donzella Beata," "Li Bel Chasteus," and "The Tree" were salvaged for *A Lume Spento* in 1908. "Donzella Beata" prefers a live girl to a Blessèd Damozel waiting in heaven, and "Li Bel Chasteus" depicts Tristram and Iseult high above the common world in their rock haven. "The Tree," however, begins a theme that has remained in Pound's poetry for sixty years. It is the first poem of the *Personae* canon, and is echoed as late as Canto CX ("Laurel bark sheathing the fugitive"). It is a poem under the spell of Yeats, kin to "The Song of Wandering Aengus" and other evocations of an enchanted wood. The Pre-Raphaelite Yeats is everywhere in *Hilda's Book*.

141

Autumn is over the long leaves that love us,
And over the mice in the barley sheaves;
Yellow the leaves of the rowan above us,
And yellow the wet wild-strawberry leaves

begins Yeats's "The Falling of the Leaves" (*Crossways,* 1889). The first poem of *Hilda's Book* opens with a hint of Whitman but proceeds as if by Yeats:

Child of the grass
The years pass Above us
Shadows of air All these shall love us
Winds for our fellows
The browns and the yellows
Of autumn our colors.

But Celtic twilight and Yeatsian diction are but part of the strange beauty of "The Tree." That a tree can be a persona at all is startling. Joyce, years later, will have a tree speak in his poem "Tilly" (*Pomes Penyeach,* 1927). Pound's poem trembles between the imitative and a strong originality. It is as precious as the early Yeats while having the masculine boldness of William Morris. It is both Ovidian and Thoreauvian. It is seed-rich in matters that will occupy Pound for years: the theme of metamorphosis and the mimetic act of assuming a mask and insisting on the most strenuous empathy. Daphne and the figures of Baucis and Philemon will appear throughout *The Cantos.* The most fructive theme, however, is that of chthonic nature as a mystery, the Eleusinian theme. To understand "many a new thing. . . . That was rank folly to my head before" is to find a mode of perception other than one's own. *Omniformis omnis intellectus est,* Psellus says in *The Cantos,* quoting Porphyry. But why begin with the nymph's supernatural, intranatural sense of things? The question is a large one, for trees are everywhere in Pound's poetry, and become symbols of extraordinary power and beauty in *Rock-Drill, Thrones,* and the cantos drafted for the poem's conclusion.

   *Hilda's Book* is green with trees, poem after poem. "*Dulce myrtii floribus,*" we read; "sweeter than all orchards breath"; "She swayeth as a poplar tree"; "the moss-grown kindly trees"; "some treeborn spirit of the wood/About her." *A Lume Spento* was originally titled *La Fraisne,* the ash tree; and the poem of that name is a variant of "The Tree," as is "A Girl" in *Ripostes.*

   In 1960 Pound chose for the translator Alfredo Rizzardi a selection of his poems to be published in Arnoldo Mondadori's *Poeti dello Specchio* series. From the twenty-three poems of *Ripostes* as that book is preserved in the *Personae* canon, he chose "N.Y.," that charmingly ironic-romantic poem in which he persists in having the New York of "a million people surly with traffic" appear as a girl praised by Solomon, "a maid with no breasts, / . . . slender as a silver reed"; "A Girl" ("The tree has encountered my hands"); "The Cloak," a poem about the claims of love and death and a paraphrase of Sappho's poem reminding a girl who refused her gift of roses that death is long and loveless (Fragment 55, Lobel and Page); Δώρια, another poem of love and death ("The shadowy flowers of Orcus / Remember thee."); and "Apparuit," a ghostly and splendid evocation of Persephone, in sapphics and with the touch of Sappho more finely upon it than any translation yet of Sappho into English. A glance at *Ripostes*—a book dedicated to William Carlos Williams, with the Propertian tag *Quos ego Persephonae maxima dona feram,* to which Williams replied in his *Kora in Hell* (1920)—will show that Pound selected for his Italian translator only those poems that contained the theme of Persephone as the sign of youth radiant before its doom or as the indwelling spirit of springtime. Conversely, Pound chose from the early *Personae* volumes (1908–1910) only those poems that are about Aidonian Persephone whose beauty is destructive, Helen and Iseult, the figure that will become Circe in *The Cantos.*

Pound was not without clues as to how to move from the neurasthenic dark of the nineteenth-century Circe-world and its hell-like *cul de sac*; he has acknowledged his debt to Whitman and Whistler. He had the end of the thread when he wrote "The Tree." But he preferred to go back to the very beginning of literature, to see its growth from sensibility to sensibility, and to arrive, if possible, with its masters who knew the art best. We find him instinctively turning toward robustness and clarity. There are many ways of studying Pound's evolution; his own criticism will probably remain the surest record. But everywhere we turn in his poetry there is the clear emergence of Persephone and her springtime as a persistent image and symbol. The first great search concentrated on the springtime of styles and cultures; with what sureness does he introduce the archaic Minoan undulations and Cretan basketwork braids into the Edwardian fog of *Mauberly!* (and he was working, except for the *Illustrated London News* and Sir Arthur Evans's *Mycenaean Tree and Pillar Cult* of 1901, well ahead of the world's knowledge of Knossan art; *Mauberley* was published a year before Evans's *The Palace of Minos*).

As if Persephone were his guide toward the light he sought, as if she, the power of renewal, had chosen him and not he her (as in the conceit in Canto LXXVI where we have "Dafne's Sandro," the fleet laurel nymph choosing Botticelli as her painter rather than the other way round), his eye went to the master poets whose manner is limpid, sharp, clear and simple: Homer, Ovid, Dante, and Chaucer. So carefully did he study each that one can plausibly trace Pound's style wholly to Homer, or wholly to Dante, as it would seem; what we would be looking at is the unbroken tradition of the Homeric phrase in western literature, clear equally of metric, sound, image, and thought. We would also be looking at a special propensity to find conjunctions of trees and radiant girls, reminiscent of the Cretan and Mycenaean assimilation of pillar and tree as the goddess's sign. It is an atmosphere that can best be described as Botticellian or Ovidian. In Arnault Daniel,

> Ges rams floritz
> De floretas envoutas
> Cui fan tremblar auzelhon ab lurs becs
> Non es plus frescs,

in Cavalcanti,

> Avete in voi li fiori, e la verdura,

in Dante,

> Tu mi fai rimembrar dove a qual era
>     Proserpina nel tempo che perdette
>     la madre lei, ed ella primavera,

in Li Po

> While my hair was still cut straight across my forehead
> I played about the front gate, pulling flowers,

he found a mode of poetry that moved him with a force easier to illustrate than to attempt a theory versatile enough to encompass all its dimensions. In "The Alchemist" he brings such illustrious women as Odysseus saw at Persephone's request in Hades in conjunction with American trees, "under the larches of Paradise / . . . the red gold of the maple, / . . . the light of the birch tree in autumn. . . ." The heart of the poem is a prayer to Persephone ("Queen of Cypress") in her other kingdom, the world under earth or ocean:

> From the power of grass,
> From the white, alive in the seed,
> From the heat of the bud,
> From the copper of the leaf in autumn,
> From the bronze of the maple, from the sap in the bough;
> Lianor, Ioanna, Loica,
> By the stir of the fin,
> By the trout asleep in the gray-green of water;
> Vanna, Mandetta, Viera, Alodetta, Picarda, Manuela
> From the red gleam of copper,

Ysaut, Ydone, slight rustling of leaves,
Vierna, Jocelynn, daring of spirits,
By the mirror of burnished copper,
    O Queen of Cypress,
Out of Erebus, the flat-lying breath,
Breath that is stretched out beneath the world:
Out of Erebus, out of the flat waste of air,
    lying beneath the world;
Out of the brown leaf-brown colourless
        Bring the imperceptible cool.

Apart from the satires and the studies of the forces counter to Persephone, such as the Hell cantos, which are about the abuses of nature, and
the great "Sestina: Altaforte," in which Bertran de Born welcomes Easter
as good weather for a military campaign, there is little in Pound that is far
away from Persephone and her trees.

It is curious that Michael Ventris was born when Pound was drafting
his first Canto. A man with *The Cantos* in his head sees this correlation of
*periploi*—Odyssean voyages—as being within the *numen* that Pound,
more than any man of our time unless it be Picasso and his Ovidian eyes,
has recovered and charged with meaning. Canto I, set in Persephone's
kingdom which is not the dead past but the communicable spirit of being,
metamorphosed from the temporal to the eternal, is Homer's most archaic matter, his deepest plumbing of "rite and foretime" (in David
Jones's resonant phrase). It is the hero's necessary recognition of his life's
roots in the powers that sustain him.

Poured ointment, cried to the gods,
To Pluto the strong, and praised Proserpine.

These words contain strata, like a geological cross-section, or, to take
an even more pertinent image, like the rings of growth in a tree, for they
are Homer's words (first discernible date: the beginning of Mediterranean literature), Andreas Divus's words,

Excoriantes comburere: supplicare autem Diis,
Fortique Plutoni, et laudatae Proserpinae,

(second date: the Renaissance), cast in the Anglo-Saxon rhythms of *The
Seafarer* (third date: the Renaissance of 1910, the linguistic renovations
of which are still not understood, but which grow out of Morris's and
Doughty's new sense of the genius of English), and they are words
written with the intuition that their chthonic matter would continue to
speak, as Ventris, Chadwick, and Palmer found Persephone and Demeter
in the Linear B tablets; Frobenius, "the car of Persephone in a German
barrow" (*Kulchur*, 244).

Persephone weathered the decline of antiquity, and survived the Middle Ages to emerge in the Renaissance. Ovid and Vergil had kept her in Italian tradition. Chaucer brought her to the north, "Proserpyne, / That quene ys of the derke pyne." Arthur Golding's Ovid of 1567 (when Ovid still, as for Chaucer, meant the *Metamorphoses*) renders her myth with particular beauty; she is made accessible to the age as far more than a bit of classical iconography around which to shore up emblematic patterns (as in Francesco Colonna's *Hypnerotomachia* of 1499). Ovid's plastic terseness becomes an English narrative voice of lively extravagance:

> By chaunce she let her lap slip downe, and out the flowres went.
> And such a sillie simplenesse her childish age yet beares,
> That even the very losse of them did move hir more to tears.

Milton's typological mind began the impressive baroque flourish that foreshadows Eve's temptation with an evocation of Persephone:

> Not that faire field
> Of *Enna,* where *Proserpin* gathring flours
> Her self a fairer Floure by gloomie *Dis*
> Was gatherd

And Shakespeare, enchanted by flowers, gave Perdita the speech that outdoes Poliziano in the imitation of Ovid's floral imagery:

> O *Proserpina,*
> For the Flowres now, that (frighted) thou let'st fall
> From *Dysses* Waggon: Daffadils,
> That come before the Swallow dares, and take
> The windes of March with beauty: Violets (dim,
> But sweeter then the lids of *Juno's* eyes
> Or *Cytherea's* breath. . . .

Thereafter she is everywhere, as firmly within English poetry as Latin or Greek. But as the Renaissance fades, she disappears from poetry. Neither the eighteenth century nor the early nineteenth thinks it sees anything in her myth, except to reflect the subterranean existence of her *Paradis artificiel* in such figures as La Motte Fouqué's *Undine* or Poe's *Ligeia.* Then all at once she is again in the open air, whether awakened by Sir James Frazer's *Golden Bough* or the new, charismatic interest in natural beauty that begins with scientific eyes (Humboldt, Agassiz, Darwin, Hugh Miller, Gosse) and is rapidly taken up by poetic ones (Thoreau, W. H. Hudson, Ruskin), or because of the new and pervasive interest in myth generated by archaeology, new texts and folklore.

Like Sappho and Chaucer, Ruskin wrote about girls as if they were flowers, about flowers as if they were girls (so that his botanical treatise called *Proserpina* has more of an archaic Greek flavour than any of the period's translations), and Lewis Carroll's Alice is a kind of Persephone. There is Tennyson's sombre, Vergilian "Demeter and Persephone," Swinburne's "The Garden of Proserpine" and "Hymn to Proserpine." The young Pound grew up in an ambiance congenial to myth; the power it had over the minds of his generation can be seen in Frederic Manning's "Koré," to which Pound wrote a reply that T. S. Eliot kept in the Faber *Selected Poems* but which Pound cancelled in the *Personae* canon.

Persephone enters Pound's poetry early and remains, and she is always there in an Ovidian sense, embodied in a girl or flower or tree, so that his most famous *haiku* is like a face Odysseus sees in Hades, reminding him of the springtime above in an image combining tree and girl: *petals on a wet, back bough.* In "Heather"

> The milk-white girls
> Unbend from the holly-trees.

"O Nathat-Ikanaie, 'Tree-at-the-river,'" we read in "Dance Figure," and in "The Spring" (that subtle mistranslation of Ibykos), "Cydonian Spring with her attendant train, / Maelids and water-girls. . . ." Her most poignant epiphany is as a ghost, Persephone bound in hell awaiting the spring

> Les yeux d'une morte
> M'ont salué,

begins "Dans un Omnibus de Londres," where the *frisson* depends on our recognizing Persephone by her Ovidian swans, which Pound has given Plutonian colours (Neare *Enna* walls [as Golding puts it] there stands a lake *Pergusa* is the name. / Cayster heareth not mo songs of Swannes than doth the same.):

> Je vis les cygnes noirs,
> Japonais,
> Leurs ailes
> Teintées de couleur sang-de-dragon,
> Et toutes les fleurs
> D'Armenonville.
>
> Les yeux d'une morte
> M'ont salué.

These are the eyes of Jacopo's Venus in "The Picture" and its pendant, "Of Jacopo del Sellaio," that belonged to a model long dead and are now pure vision,

> The eyes of this dead lady speak to me.

They are the eyes at the end of *Mauberley* that do not know they are dead. They are the ghostly eyes of *The Pisan Cantos,* where they stand in relation to a continuum of images that reaches back to the

> Souls out of Erebus, cadaverous dead, of brides
> Of youths and of the old who had borne much:
> Souls stained with recent tears, girls tender

of Canto I, the murdered bride Inez de Castro of Canto III, the Ione and "Eyes floating in dry, dark air" of Canto VII. These eyes in Hades are one of the concomitants of Persephone's theme. Another is the alignment of girl and tree, as in

> And Sulpicia
> green shoot now, and the wood
> white under new cortex
> (Canto XXV)

or the appearance of Nausicaa, a type of Persephone, in a canto about women whose souls are chaotic, establishing a contrast between neurosis and health, confusion and clarity:

> Beauty on an ass-cart
> Sitting on five sacks of laundry
> That wd. have been the road by Perugia
> That leads out to San Piero. Eyes brown topaz,
> Brookwater over brown sand,
> The white hounds on the slope,
> Glide of water, lights and the prore,
> Silver beaks out of night,
> Stone, bough over bough,
>      lamps fluid in water,
> Pine by the black trunk of its shadow
> And on hill black trunks of the shadow
> The trees melted in air.
> (Canto XXIX)

This theme prepares itself in the first thirty cantos, recurs less frequently but rhythmically through the American and Chinese cantos (XXXVI: woman radiant, a *ric pensamen* to the mind , *inluminatio coitu* to the heart; XXXIX: Circe, the richly dark, chthonic nature of woman—the two cantos form a diptych, and are brought together in XLVII, which is about the harmonizing of intelligence and the fixed order of nature: "First must thou go the road / to hell / And to the bower of Ceres' daughter Proserpine"), and becomes in the *Rock-Drill* and *Thrones* sections a synergetic presence.

Beyond the poem's beginning in her underworld, Persephone is apt to be just off-stage, or invisibly contained. She is the spirit of natural metamorphosis; in the first thirty cantos her absence is as significant as her presence. In Canto XXI she, Pallas, and Pan, Titania and Phaetusa, Aetna's nymph at the entrance to the under-realm, are set in contrast to Midas, Plutus, and gold: the power to grow toward renewal, to think, to reproduce—against greed and ungrowing matter. At the end of XXI her rape is staged like Icarus's fall in Brueghel's painting, unnoticed, its implications unsuspected:

> Dis caught her up.
> And the old man went on there
> beating his mule with an asphodel.

The loss of form through aimlessness, through moral slither, through the continued use of form without content, or by influences hostile to the organic nature of a form is a metamorphosis that is seedless, a stasis.

> Life to make mock of motion:
> For the husks, before me, move.
> (Canto VII)

One can follow throughout *The Cantos* the force that reclaims lost form, lost spirit, Persephone's transformation back to virginity. As Homer shows us a chastened and chaste Helen in the Odyssey, so the first thirty cantos end with the moral regeneration of Lucrezia Borgia, that archetype of the Circe-world of the late nineteenth century from which every major artist of the time had to extricate himself in order to discover the moral nature of reality. She appears with the drunken gaiety of Botticelli's Primavera, Dea Flora, and the Graces, "foot like a flowery branch," "Madame ''ΥΛΗ,'" a woman obedient to all of nature's appetites, but with the balance and rhythm of nature's seed-cycle regeneration.

Through the *Pisan Cantos* Persephone is the promise of rebirth from the dark, an Ariadne in the labyrinth. "When night is spent," ends the Pisan group, in which Persephone was prayed to throughout. Pisa parallels the Homeric episode of Odysseus captured by the Kyklops (of whom the brute violence of war is an example), and the evocations of Persephone are under the sign of Δημητὴρ δακρύων, nature impotent and dying.

> with a smoky torch thru the unending
> labyrinth of the souterrain
> or remembering Carleton let him celebrate Christ in the grain
> and if the corn cat be eaten
> Demeter has lain in my furrow.
> (Canto LXXX)

But faith in all that Persephone has meant in the poem is unwavering.

> Elysium, though it were in the halls of hell,
> What thou lovest well is thy true heritage
> What thou lovest well shall not be reft from thee.
>                      (Canto LXXXI)

In watching a baby wasp, born in a nest in the corner of Pound's tent at Pisa, the poet brings the theme to one of its most resonant statements:

> When the mind swings by a grass-blade
>     an ant's forefoot shall save you
> the clover leaf smells and tastes as its flower
>
> The infant has descended,
>     from mud on the tent roof to Tellus,
> like to like colour he goes amid grass-blades
>     greeting them that dwell under XTHONOS XΘONOΣ
> OI XΘONIOI, to carry our news
>     εις χθονιους to them that dwell under the earth,
> begotten of air, that shall sing in the bower
>     of Kore,                   Περσεφόνεια
> and have speech with Tiresias, Thebae.
>                      (Canto LXXXIII)

"Man, earth," says Canto LXXXII, "two halves of the tally." Man is under Fortuna, the *Pisan Cantos* say repeatedly, and the DTC at Pisa is "a magna NOX animae" (Canto LXXIV), a very dark night of the soul, a hell out of which some spiritual recovery like the earth's from winter must happen.

The placing of events in time is a romantic act; the *tremendum* is in the distance. There are no dates in the myths; from when to when did Heracles stride the earth? In a century obsessed with time, with archaeological dating, with the psychological recovery of time (Proust, Freud), Pound has written as if time were unreal, has, in fact, treated it as if it were space. William Blake preceded him here, insisting on the irreality of clock time, sensing the dislocations caused by time (a God remote in time easily became remote in space, an absentee landlord) and proceeding, in his enthusiastic way, to dine with Isaiah—one way of suggesting that Isaiah's mind is not a phenomenon fixed between 742 and 687 B. C. Pound's mind has to be seen for the extraordinary shape it has given to itself. To say that *The Cantos* is "a voyage in time" is to be blind to the poem altogether. We miss immediately the achievement upon which the success of the poem depends, its rendering time transparent and negligible, its dismissing the supposed corridors and perspectives *down* which the historian invites us to look. Pound cancelled in his own mind the dissociations that had been isolating fact from fact for centuries. To have closed the gap between mythology and botany is but one movement of the process; one way to read *The Cantos* is to go through noting the restorations of relationships now thought to be discrete—the ideogrammatic method was invented for just this purpose. In Pound's spatial sense of time the past is here, now; its invisibility is our blindness, not its absence. The nineteenth century had put everything against the scale of time and discovered that all behavior within time's monolinear progress was evolutionary. The past was a graveyard, a museum. It was Pound's determination to obliterate such a configuration of time and history, to treat what had become a world of ghosts as a world eternally present.

Whatever the passions and predilections that we detect in *The Cantos,* they are dispositions of mind that Pound is reflecting, not programs he is advocating, not even matters on which he has passed judgment. The botanist may have a preference for conifers but he does not therefore omit mushrooms from his textbook. Pound's understanding of the world is always directed toward making us share the understanding he has found in other minds; we hear St. Ambrose and John Adams condemn usury, not Pound; Confucius speaks for rectitude and probity; a good thousand voices speak. It was Pound's skill, the duty he assumed, to keep us from imagining that we are listening to ghosts, or that we are hearing dimly over vast time, or that the voices are meaningless.

Persephone, as a word, was, in the historical account of things, current among certain Greeks, Cretans, Sicilians, and Romans between such-and-such a year and such-and-such a year. Ethnology can also tell us that she is also known as Koré (The Girl), Flora, Persephatta, Persephoneia, and Proserpina. Any actual modern reference to her, in, say, the Greek hills, is a quaint bit of folklore, like the Cretans's still placing in the corpse's hand some token for Charon. The springtime, however, is eternal, though man's emotional response to it depends upon his sensibilities and education. And everything we call civilization depends upon that response. Man is aware of or blind to the order in which he lives by keeping or losing the tone of that response. From the beginning Pound was intuitively drawn to speaking of women and trees as if the one transparently showed something of the beauty of the other. From poem to poem this image grew; it is possible to point to where this or that detail was added in the enrichment, until coming across a late passage such as

The purifications
    are snow, rain, artemisia,
    also dew, oak, and the juniper

And in thy mind beauty, O Artemis,
      as of mountain lakes in the dawn.
Foam and silk are thy fingers,
           Kuanon,

and the long suavity of her moving,
      willow and olive reflected
          (Canto CX)

we find the ideogram to be a focus for meanings (the purpose of the ideogram in the first place) rather than a surface from which the eye uneducated by all that has come before it in the poem can discern anything beyond the beauty of the words.

For these words are not primarily lyric: nor are they a detail of memory, as they would be in Wordsworth, nor the epiphany of a visionary state, as they would be in Yeats. They are lines from an epic poem, their muse is Calliope, and their concern is with men in action. Calliope is The Muse with the Beautiful Eyes, and her business is to have looked and seen.

Tell me of that man, Musa, who took the uneasy turn
At all the crossroads, who came homeward in disaster
From the plundering of the holy acropolis of Troia;
Many towns has he seen, known the minds of many men,

begins the *Odyssey,* a poem about a man who thought trees were as beautiful as girls, girls as beautiful as trees; whose patrimony was an orchard and vineyard, whose peace, given him by Athena, is permanently before him and his children in the signature of the olive tree, who in the darkest trope of his wandering was sent by the witch-master of the lore of flowers and leaves, Circe, to the dwelling of Persephone, whose mystery is the power of eternal regeneration, in order that he find his way home.

In *Thrones* Persephone's tragedy is over: she has returned; her trees are in blossom. The voices that speak of her are easy, colloquial, at peace:

And was her daughter like that;
Black as Demeter's gown,
                eyes, hair?
Dis' bride, Queen over Phlegethon,
      girls faint as mist about her?

The strength of men is in grain.
          (Canto CVI)

She is the power of moving from dark to light, from formlessness to form, from Circe, whose inhuman mind is instructive but tangential to the life of man, to Penelope, whose virtues are domestic, an unwavering continuum:

> this is the grain rite
> near Enna, at Nyssa:
>> Circe, Persephone
> so different is sea from glen that
>> the juniper is her holy bush.

In 1958, after the thirteen Odyssean years in a fastness that had been an aboretum (and has kept its trees) before it became a prison, Ezra Pound, a free man, went first to the sea whose greatest poet he is in our time, and secondly to a particular apple tree in Wyncote, Pennsylvania, in whose boughs he read the lines of Yeats's that moved him to write "The Tree" that stands foremost in his poems:

> I have been a hazel tree and they hung
> The Pilot Star and the Crooked Plough
> Among my leaves in times out of mind

The stars by which Odysseus navigated!

### THE TREE AS TEMPLE PILLAR OR DEMETER

> Jardins audacieux dans les airs soutenus,
> Temples, marbres, métaux, qu'êtes-vous devenus?
>> (André Chénier, Élegie XCVI)

At the end of Canto XXX, before the laconic notation of Alessandro Borgia's death—for the opening three decades of the poem are essentially a vortex of turbulence and misdirection to which Alessandro's dark squalor makes a fitting signature—we are shown the colophon of a book printed in July of 1503 (Alessandro died the next month of that year). Girolamo Soncino, one of a family of Jewish printers who came to Italy from Nürnberg in the late fifteenth century, and Francesco Griffo da Bologna the type designer (who also cut type for Aldus Manutius, the Venetian printer whose editions of the classics spread the Renaissance beyond the scholars' walls) were brought to Fano by Cesare Borgia to found a press for books in Hebrew, Greek, Latin, and Italian. The text which is "taken . . . from that of Messire Laurentius / and from a codex once of the Lords Malatesta" is Petrarch's *Rime* which Soncino printed for Cesare Borgia in 1503—seventy-eight years before the edition of the Petri at Basel which bibliographies are apt to list as Petrarch's earliest printing.

With characteristic obliquity in the angle of his gaze Pound stations the *Realpolitik* of the Borgias within the humanist tradition that has come

down to us as a distinct activity. We can also observe that Pound is placing Cesare's patronage of the arts alongside Malatesta's and the Medici's. And that Canto XXX is in spirit Machiavellian, from its opening
*planh* against Pity to its alignment of Petrarch and the attempts of the
Borgias to unify Italy; for *Il Principe,* like Canto XXX, ends with a
melancholy hope that depends on both a dream of Petrarch's and the firm
hand of a Borgia or a Medici: ". . . acciò che, sotto la sua insegna, e
questra patria ne sia nobilitata, e sotto li sua auspizii si verifichi quel
detto del Petrarca":

> Virtù contro a furore
>> Prenderà l'arme; e fia el combatter corto:
>> Ché l'antico valore
>> Nelli italici cor non è ancor morto.

The lines are from the "Italia mia" canzone of Petrarch's and the word
before the one that begins Machiavelli's quotation is "pity." But it is pity
by which *virtù* takes up arms against Italy's enemies; it is solicitude for
Italy. The theme of Italy as a high culture is more lyrically and directly
stated throughout the poem (and Italia serves here as a type of the *patriae*
and *urbes* that illustrate the theme of the city as the sacred reservoir of the
continuity of civilization, and we should remember that Petrarch's allegorical Italia began her history as the city-goddess Roma).

Between a matrix of stars above and a matrix of stone and water beneath, the earth is given its form. "Zeus lies in Ceres' bosom" (Canto
LXXXI)—light shapes the dark seed into the wheat ear. The profoundest
diagram of this process, no less for civilization's rhythm of inevitable
decay and conscious renewal than for the green world, is the myth of
Persephone. Yet her myth is of the kinesis of growth and germination, of
loss and return. Her mother Demeter has been from the beginning the
sign of the process's maturity, the harvest. Persephone is the living tree;
Demeter is the tree carved, shaped, painted, capitalled with acanthus,
translated into marble, even turned upside down (as at Knossos).

Ecbatana, Deioces' city as Herodotus describes it (Cantos IV, V,
LXXIV, and LXXX) reflected in its seven concentric walls the circuits of
the planets, and its acropolis was (as in the ziggurats of Sumeria and the
Parthenon at Athens) a place of the meeting of man and god, and Pound
remembers that mountains first served this purpose (Sinai, T'ai Shan,
Olympus). The Prophet Ezra honours Cyrus's anxiety to restore the temple at Jerusalem ("for Yahweh is the god of that place"). Nineveh took its
ground-plan from Ursa Major; Jerusalem began as a model in heaven,
was translated into brick and stone for an historical existence and was by
John of Patmos's time a heavenly paradigm again. Sigriya in Ceylon is an

earthly model of the celestial city Alakamanda. (Leo Frobenius's *Erlebte Erdteile* is still the fullest and most perspicacious study for the sacred origins and designs of the walled, temple-centered city, though the subject has received brilliant attention in the fifty years that Pound has been building the subject into *The Cantos:* see especially Dumézil's *Jupiter, Mars, Quirinus,* and *Tarpeia,* Giedion's *The Eternal Present,* and Eliade's *Cosmos and History*).

The figure of Italia (or Roma) persists on Italian money and postage stamps: a woman's head crowned by battlements. She is the city "now in the mind indestructible" of Canto LXXIV. Toward this allegory Pound tends to move all the goddesses he evokes in *The Cantos,* until he has constructed one of the richest symbols in the whole poem. Persephone's wreath of meadow flowers will become interchangeable with Demeter's coronal of wheat. The goddess crowned with an image of her city is the Mediterranean's oldest emblem of sovereignty (the high priest of Babylon wore a replica of a ziggurat that is the model for the Pope's tiara today; the Pharaoh's double crown of the Two Kingdoms represented a pyramid). And the emblem was not only of the holy acropolis, with which Pound associates the tower of Danaë, human receptacle of divine seed and archetype for the poem of the women who bear children to gods, but of the outer limits as well—the man-made stone wall and the outer, magic, invisible wall which was put into place with music and incantation (like the Knossan maze and the wall that Achilles destroyed when he drove Hector counter-clockwise around Troy, undoing the spell that bound the city to Pallas's protection, or the walls of Alba Longa [*Aeneid* V. 583–602].

It was Cybele, the Phrygian Demeter, who, as far as we know, first wore a crown of battlements, for she was not only the goddess of mountains, forests, and the wealth of nature, but was the giver of towers and city walls to mankind. In her is that marriage of flower and stone toward which Pound's early poetry moved, not quite knowing its way, seeing in stone something sinister (as had the major poets and painters of the nineteenth century) rather than the under-matrix of nature. Once we realize this double nature of Demeter's patronage, her protection of both field and city, we can see with what care Pound has chosen his pictures of her in all her transmutations. She first appears in the poem as Venus, with the towers and walls (*munimenta*) of mountain copper (*orichalchi*) at Cyprus as her allotted place. This initial conjunction of city and goddess is deliberately portentous and auspicious. From it will grow the definition of civilization everywhere implicit in *The Cantos.* In the Homeric Hymn to Aphrodite from which Pound takes "Cypri munimenta sortita est," Venus appears disguised as a Phrygian princess, to beget with Anchises the city-builder Aeneas, transplanter of a culture to which, in time, an oracle will cause Cybele's turret-crowned image to be brought. Ovid in the *Fasti* (IV. 179–376) describes her arrival in Rome, and explains her diadem of towers:

> at cur turrifera caput est onerata corona?
> an primus turris urbibus illa dedit?
> (IV. 219–20)

Yet the goddess was already in Rome. She was the Etruscan Vortumna, Goddess of the Turning Year, an indigenous Demeter whose name would get changed to Fortuna, and who was to be fused with the allegorical Roma. In the *Aeneid* we can feel the subtle confusion of Roma and Fortuna, for practically every mention of Fortuna involves the destiny of Rome's walls.

> Qua visa est Fortuna pati Parcaeque sinebant
> Cedere res Latio, Turnus et tua moenia texi.
> (*Aeneid* XII. 147–48)

Vergil of course was aware of the Phrygian origin of the wall-crowned goddess:

> Et hujus, nate, auspiciis incluta Roma
> Imperium terris, animos aequabit Olympo
> Septemque una sibi muro circumdabit arces,
> Felix prole virum: qualis Berecyntia mater
> Invehitur curru Phrygias turrita per urbes
> Laeta Deum partu centum complexa nepotes,
> Omnes caelicolas, omnes supera tenentes.
> (*Aeneid* VI. 781–87)

Lucretius describes the goddess:

> Muralique caput summum cinxere corona,
> Eximiis munita locis quod sustinet urbes.
> (*De rerum naturae* II. 606–7)

The Greek Tyché also wears a crown of towers, whence Fortuna got hers. Doughty found somewhere in his erudition cause to describe an allegorical figure of Claudius Caesar's triumph over Britain as

> (Minerva seems!) *Colonia Nova*, Claudia;
> Like shielded goddess, with high turrets crowned.
> (*The Dawn in Britain*, XVII)

The resonant *krédemnon* of Canto XCVI—the goddess Ino-Leucothea's headdress—may be a doubled image, for *krédemna* were the battlements of a city, and Leucothea is under the sign of Fortuna. (*Kré-demnon:* something that binds, a turban or magic precinct around a city.)

Fortuna, evoked so lyrically in *Thrones* and *Rock-Drill,* is another mask of the pervasive Mediterranean diety whom anthropology has traced through a thousand guises by now and who—as Pound sees her—always emerges, whatever her name or attributes, as the chthonic, mysterious force whose harmony man must search out and adhere to or perish. As Castalia she comes crystal and clear from the dark earth (Canto XC, and as Arethusa and other spring nymphs throughout *Rock-Drill* and *Thrones*), inspiration of poets and Pound's further extension of the rivers of light in Dante's *Paradiso* and the opposite of the destructive floods in *Thrones* (rhyming with Petrarch's flood-imagery in the "Italia mia" canzone, where the floods are the barbaric ravagers of Italy). Or she comes from the chaos of the sea (Aphrodite, Leucothea) as civilization itself grows from the dark forest and wildness to the ordered perfection of a city.

An altar to Tyché stands at Eleusis, facing the sea. Fortuna eluded all the forces of time and Christianity that disguised or banished the other gods. She lived quite respectably in the mediæval mind, where (as in Alan de Lille and Bernardus Silvestris) she becomes identified with Natura and moves suavely in and out of theology and philosphy. Goliardry and the *Carmina Burana* fashioned her into a striking figure, though her reputation, as now, vacillated between that of a strumpet and a powerful force worthy of placation and circumspect deference. In *Inferno* VII Vergil chides Dante for so misunderstanding Fortuna:

> He whose wisdom transcends all made the heavens and gave them guides, so that every part shines to every part, dispersing the light equally. In the same way He ordained for worldly splendours a general minister and guide who should in due time change vain wealth from race to race and from one to another blood, beyond the prevention of human wits, so that one race rules and another languishes according to her sentence which is hidden like the snake in the grass. Your wisdom cannot strive with her. She foresees, judges, and maintains her kingdom, as the other heavenly powers do theirs. Her changes have no respite. Necessity makes her swift, so fast men come to take their turn. This is she who is so reviled by the very men that should give her praise, laying on her wrongful blame and ill repute. But she is blest [*ma ella s' è beata*] and does not hear it. Happy with the other primal creatures she turns her sphere and rejoices in her bliss [*e beata si gode*].[1]

This is reflected in Canto XCVII as:

[1]Trans. John D. Sinclair (London: John Lane the Bodley Head, 1948).

Even Aquinas could not demote her, Fortuna,
    violet, pervenche, deep iris,
        beat'è, e gode,

and as:

All neath the moon, under Fortuna,
        splendor' mondan',
beata gode, hidden as eel in sedge,
        all neath the moon, under Fortuna.

Fortuna is the goddess of *forsitan:* of perhaps. Her virtue is in "ever-shifting change" (Canto XCVII), the constant motion that Thoreau thought was the very definition of life. Pound claims Fortuna as a positive force under the theme of metamorphosis (even if she wears the Gorgon mask of Nemesis); her unceasing turbulence is a natural mode, and all of man's actions are within it.

That Fortuna should come to the fore in the Pisan group and remain as a lyric presence grows from the Homeric ground-plan. All of Odysseus's adventures are either hairbreadth escapes or subtle enchantments. In the first half of the poem we find the adventures of enchantment, Sirens, Lotos Eaters, Circe. The Pisan DTC begins the adventures of entrapment and physical endurance, Scylla, Charybdis, Kyklops, and the shipwreck before Phaeacia. The mimesis of action, however, is Great Bass, as Pound calls it. We listen to it to calculate the aptness of the counterpoint, remembering that we are experiencing an *epos* of ideas released in interlocked phrases each of which is a musical phrase, an image, and as much of a grammatical coherence as the poet can allow. There is a larger grammar, where entire cantos count as ideograms; to see the meaning of the goddesses we must read the larger grammar. We have seen that Persephone and her green world move through the poem.

Cantos I–XXX are under the sign of Circe. XXXI–XLI are under the sign of three goddesses insofar as they have power over wild beasts; that is, are civilizing and taming forces: Aphrodite, Circe, and the Egyptian Aphrodite (roughly) Hathor. XLII–LI are under the sign of Demeter, as are LII–LXXI. The *Pisan Cantos* bring to a crescendo the theme of Demeter and Persephone, introduce Fortuna, and evoke Athena, Artemis, and Fortuna's planet the moon. *Rock-Drill* introduces Leucothea (an agent of Fortuna), and carries forward the amplified theme of all the natural goddesses, adding many from cultures other than the Mediterranean, Kwannon, the Buddhist goddess of Mercy, for instance. The visionary eyes of the goddess, flowing crystal, light "almost solid," mermaids, nymphs, and many historical figures (Elizabeth I, Theodora, Jeanne d'Arc) embody the bright theme of the lady of spiritual power. *Thrones* approaches the imagery of the *Paradiso* in its translucent brilliance.

These images are not only radiant; they act as mirrors to each other in patterns of increasing clarity the more we understand the poem. Many distinct but congenial themes flow through the matters we have just been looking at (the half-visible parallel to Christianity, for instance, reaching from Eleusis, as Tadeusz Zielínski argues in *The Religion of Ancient Greece,* to the saintly ecstasies of the twelfth century), but what we are interested to watch emerge is the articulation of the offices of Demeter and Persephone into an image of extraordinary meaning and beauty.

A culture, in the sense that Leo Frobenius understood it (and hence Pound), has two dominant symbols, the male one of action, the female one of stillness and place (*Ruhe und Raum*). The male symbol is of direction, expansion, intensity, considering space as distance to traverse and measure, and is therefore volatile, unstable, destiny-ridden.

> Moth is called over mountain
> The bull runs blind on the sword, *naturans.*
> > (Canto XLVII)

And in the same canto, and again of Odysseus:

> First must thou go the road
> > to hell
> And to the bower of Ceres' daughter Proserpine,
> Through overhanging dark, to see Tiresias,
> Eyeless that was, a shade, that is in hell
> So full of knowing that the beefy men know less than he,
> > Ere thou come to thy road's end.
> > Knowledge the shade of a shade,
> Yet must thou sail after knowledge
> Knowing less than drugged beasts. . . .

Canto XLVII aligns even the indomitable Odysseus with the fate of the yearly slain: Tammuz, Adonis, Osiris, for man the seed-scatterer is staccato, discontinuous. He runs on the sword; he perishes as the moth. The female is on the other hand a mountain, a cave, the fecund earth, considering space as a room. Woman for Pound is the stillness at the heart of a culture.

*The Cantos,* for all their ability to make the past transparent, are ultimately about their own century. Pound's despair over his own time, rarely stated personally in the poem, is nevertheless an astringent theme. The man who wrote the Hell Cantos (XIV–XVI) and who wrote in Canto XCVI

> Good-bye to the sun, Autumn is dying
> Χαῖρε ὁ ῾Ήλιος
> Χαῖρε clarore

said to the journalist Grazia Livi in 1963: "The modern world doesn't exist because nothing exists which does not understand its past or its future. The world of today exists only as a fusion, a span in time."[2] We are, in Pound's image, inundated; we have "heaped fads on Eleusis" (Canto XCVI). We have lost our clarity. The tragedy outlined in such hard detail in *The Cantos* begins deep in the nineteenth century when Europe was preparing a spiritual metamorphosis of extraordinary dimensions. The nature of this metamorphosis can still be seen only in symbolic configurations, although we can with some certainty translate the symbols into what we imagine to be historical facts. André Chénier (1762–94), writing a suite of elegies that can be seen as the end of the meditative tradition of sweetly melancholy verse that begins with Petrarch or as the first Romantic inventions of an imaginary past of golden splendor, begins to construct a vision that is both past and future—we recover from the high cultures a spiritual reality that we hope to claim. Like Watteau imagining a magical Cytherea he could say:

> Partons, la voile est prête, et Byzance m'appelle.
> (*Élégie* XLVIII)

> "Constantinople" said Wyndham "our star,"
> Mr. Yeats called it Byzantium.
> (Canto XCVI)

Chénier hungered for the physical recovery of what there might be left of the past:

> L'herbe couvre Corinthe, Argos, Sparte, Mycène;
> La faux coupe le chaume aux champs où fut Athènes.
> (*Élégie* XCVI)

Yeats's two great visions of Byzantium are derived from the imagery of Shelley's *The Revolt of Islam,*

> this vast dome,
> When from the depths which thought can seldom pierce
> Genius beholds it rise, his native home.
> (I. L. 1–3)

The nineteenth century was obsessed with visions of paradises and utopias: Blake's Jerusalem, Coleridge's Xanadu, Shelley's Bosch-like lands of the spiritually cleansed, Rimbaud's and Henri Rousseau's jungle gardens. Two poles of attraction, we have seen, seemed to control these visions. One was Arcadian and natural, with some of its roots in Christian thought, and was a node for those Romantics who were seeking a

world-order consonant with nature (Wordsworth, Ruskin, the Transcendentalists). The other was deliberately artificial, arcane, symbolic.
Novalis's *Heinrich von Ofterdingen* searching for his blue flower, des
Esseintes immured among his bibelots and curios, Yeats longing to be
refined into a mechanical nightingale in a Byzantium under the spell of
faery—Baudelaire (the spiritual heir of Novalis, Hoffman, and Poe) gives
a name to the century's predilection for a counterfeit world, *les paradis
artificiels,* a phrase that Pound saw as the ultimate etiolation of Villon's
*Paradis paint, où sont harpes et lus.* Baudelaire was principally concerned
to contrast the healthy mind with the drugged one, natural vision with
that induced by opium. Helplessly he preferred the natural, but as the
drunkard commends sobriety. He was committed to his *"nouveauté sublime et monstrueuse"* (as Guillaume Apollinaire called it). Practically all
its practitioners saw the Décadence as a religious force, specifically an
inverted, mirror-like parody of Christianity; Baudelaire, especially, saw
*Les Fleurs du mal* as a kind of hymnal or missal. It contains litanies,
prayers, meditations.

> Ô vierges ô démons, ô monstres, ô martyres,
> De la réalité grand esprits contempteurs,
> Chercheuses d'infini, dévotes et satyres,
> Vous que dans votre enfer mon âme a poursuivies.
>                                 (*Femmes damnées*)

What, to Pound's mind, the century was doing was imagining Persephone's reign in hell. And the artist is a prophet. He shows the first
symptoms of what will become contagion. Persephone's hell is one of
nature's modes—the dwarf world, as folklorists know it, a world with
phosphorus for light, with strange parodies of growing nature (geode for
fig, gems for flowers, crystal for water). Image after image betrays an
unconscious longing to be released from the sterility of this gorgeously
artificial Hades, though its evil consists solely in one's mistaking it for
reality's wholeness. Poe symbolized its psychology by placing his demon
raven atop a bust of Pallas: the irrational dominating the intellect. Rossetti's paintings became an endless series of portraits of Persephone in
hell. The "Veronica Veronese" of 1872 shows a young lady in plush
(Miss Alice Wilding, the model) in a room hung with heavy cloth. She is
reproducing on a violin the notes of her caged canary. Flowers made of
jewels hang from her wrist; shells of ivory, gold, and pearl figure in her
necklace. Once Pound had perceived that the major artists of the late
nineteenth century had, for the most part unconsciously, taken Persephone grieving for another world as a dominant symbol, he was in a
position to write both *Hugh Selwyn Mauberley* and the first thirty cantos.
He had identified the chthonic Persephone with Circe, and the mirror-

world in which nineteenth-century art had locked itself as a counterfeit paradise, a *paradis artificiel*. One of his responses was to write "An Idyll for Glaucus," casting the problem of increasingly arcane subjectivity as that of a girl trying to communicate with the metamorphosed Glaucus (he has eaten a magic herb and become a sea-creature).

Three English writers began almost simultaneously to transmute this precious, ungrowing world of the imagination (reflecting what malady of the soul practically every artist of the twentieth century has tried to say) into visions of growth and organic fufilment, to find again the ancient conjunction of flower and stone, underworld, world, and empyrean ("Topaz, God can sit on," Canto CIV). All three, Joyce, Eliot, and Pound, were close students of Dante, and all three, however differently, were involved in the recovery of the Mediterranean past by archaeology and anthropology. In Dantesque terms, Eliot managed an *Inferno (The Waste Land)* and fragments of a *Purgatorio (Ash Wednesday , The Four Quartets)*. Joyce constructed in *Ulysses* the century's *Inferno* and in *Finnegans Wake* a *Purgatorio*—a cyclic *Purgatorio* from which one cannot escape. Pound has attempted a *Paradiso,* a vision of the world's splendor encompassing, as he configures the design, both of Persephone's kingdoms, "the germinal universe of wood alive, of stone alive" (*Spirit of Romance,* p. 72). It is in religion eclectic and is as interested in justice and piety, as reflected in collective human behavior, as in the fufilment of the soul's inwardness. Eliot's and Joyce's city is unquestionably hell. Pound chose to traverse the dark vision completely and posit the city as the one clear conquest of civilization.

Each of the first thiry cantos either ends with the image of a city wall or tower or contains such an image: even the comic Canto XII ends with the word "Stambouli." The darkest of these images are of ruin (III, IV, XVIII, XX) or treachery (V, VI, VII, XXVIII). The brightest are of Aphrodite's copper walls, Danaë's tower, Sigismundo's Rimini, Chinese dynastic temples, and Florence, Venice, and Ferrara at their height. Yet everything in *The Cantos* is seen in tragic deterioration up until Pound discloses in the Pisan group the enveloping idea of the past as a symbol alive in the present and holding within it the seeds of the future. It is here that he brings in the city "now in the mind indestructible" and the oldest myth in the entire poem, that of Wagadu in Africa, a Soninke legend of a city, Wagadu, that was lost as a reality but remained in men's hearts.

"Four times Wagadu stood there in her splendour. Four times Wagadu disappeared and was lost to human sight: once through vanity, once through falsehood, once through greed, and once through dissension. Four times Wagadu changed her name. First she was called Dierra, then

Agada, then Ganna, then Silla. . . . Wagadu, whenever men have seen her, has always had four gates, one to the north, one to the west, one to the east, and one to the south. These are the directions from whence the strength of Wagadu comes, the strength in which she endures no matter whether she be built of stone, wood or earth, or lives but as a shadow in the mind and longing of her children. For, really, Wagadu is the strength which lives in the hearts of men, and is sometimes visible because eyes see her and ears hear the clash of swords and ring of shields, and is sometimes invisible because the indomitability of men has overtired her, so that she sleeps. . . . Should Wagadu ever be found for the fifth time, then she will live so forcefully in the minds of men that she will never be lost again, so forcefully that vanity, falsehood, greed, and dissension will never be able to harm her."[3]

In Canto XVI, emerging from the hell of the decivilizers, we have as a counter-vision:

> entered the quiet air
>     the new sky,
>   the light as after a sun-set,
>     and by their fountains, the heroes,
> Sigismundo, and Malatesta Novello,
>     and founders, gazing at the mounts of their cities.

In Canto XVII: "and the cities set in their hills." In Canto XXVI there is a Jerusalem painted by Carpaccio, which was also a city foursquare, many times lost and now a vision in the mind, as it (or she) was iñ the time of Isaiah and Jeremiah, in whose pages the myth of Wagadu would be perfectly at home. In the figure of the city that has become a throne—a spiritual power of greatest force—Pound sees the one inclusive symbol of civilization. Here the odysseys of men come to rest and cohere with the Penelope-work at the still center. By Canto CVII Demeter has become Queen of Akragas, and the cities through whose histories *The Cantos* have moved become temples containing light, and the processes of architecture the music by which Amphion lifted the enchanted stones into place to ring Thebes with a wall.

> Amphion not for museums
>     but for her mind
>         like the underwave.
>         (Canto CVII)

[3]Leo Frobenius and Douglas C. Fox, *African Genesis* (London: Faber and Faber, 1938), pp. 109–10.

The museum, twentieth-century parody of a temple, is all that we have, physically, of the past; and Joyce begins *Finnegans Wake* in a museum. The early interpreters of *The Cantos* tended to see the poem as a study of the man of willed and directed action, as a persona of Odysseus. It is now clear that the poem rests most firmly in a deeper, stiller sense of humanity, the city and its continuity, symbolized by the goddess of field and citadel wearing the sanctuary of her people as a crown.

# The Pound Vortex

A little past one o'clock on the fifth of June 1915, Corporal Henri Gaudier of Seventh Company, 129th Infantry, Capitaine Ménager commanding, ordered his squad to fix bayonets and deploy themselves in diamond formation around him as they went over the top. The artillery cover began to crack its flat thunder behind them, whining over their heads to blow yet more of the grey stone houses of Neuilly St. Vaast to rubble, where the Germans were dug in.

In the charge Corporal Gaudier was cut to pieces by machine-gun fire. He was twenty-three years old. He was descended from sculptors who had worked on Chartres. The preceding November he had lain in mud and watched a cathedral burn, the lead of its molten roof dropping in great white globs through Gothic tracery.

This Corporal Gaudier, cited for bravery, remembered by his fellow soldiers for his intelligence, was one of the greatest sculptors of our century. He signed his work Henri Gaudier-Brzeska, adding the name of his Polish mistress to his own. Though it is futile to guess what work he would have done had he lived, it is now clear that he died with the century.

What we call the twentieth century ended in 1915. Those artists who survived the collapse of civilization at that point completed the work they had planned before then, when they looked forward to a century of completely different character. Joyce wrote his *Ulysses* and *Finnegans Wake,* both implicit in the nineteenth-century idea of literature. Proust, aware that tanks were crawling like monsters out of H. G. Wells and Jules Verne over the poplar-lined road to Illiers, completed his account of the world which the war obliterated as the brimstone Sodom.

What the war blighted was a renaissance as brilliant as any in history which we can only know by the survivors and by the early work of the dead—the Alain-Fourniers (Battle of the Meuse, 1914), Sant' Elias (Monfalcone, 1914), Apollinaires (1918), Gaudiers.

No man was more aware of this renaissance than Ezra Pound, one of its most vigorous instigators and the center of its vortex. Gaudier had carved his bust (after sixty years it is still as smartly and strangely modern as the day it was finished; there is something classical in its ability to resist becoming a period piece); Gaudier had read *Cathay* to his troops. *Cathay* ("Pound is the inventor of Chinese poetry for our time"—T. S. Eliot), *Personae* (actors' masks!), *Cantos;* Pound's poetry was very new and very old at once. The man seemed to live deep in history and yet he was the present for writers alive with the idea of being modern. Even now Pound's genius for the ancient and the modern together has not been generally grasped. Our ignorance of the past blinds us to his finest accomplishments. Unless he designates that a poem is a paraphrase of Latin, we miss it, Latin having dropped from classrooms. Nor is it a settled matter that Pound is a master poet. The great paradox which Mr. Kenner must struggle with in this first full-scale study of Pound and his era is that Pound was the first to arrive in the modern renaissance, and his reputation will be the last to arrive in its proper place in the world's opinion.

Mr. Kenner's *The Pound Era* (a history book, a book of explication, "an X-Ray moving picture," as he calls it) was ten years in the writing. It is not so much a book as a library, or better, a new kind of book in which biography, history, and the analysis of literature are so harmoniously articulated that every page has a narrative sense. Mr. Kenner's prose, always a miracle of compression and robust grace, is here brought to a perfection. Has anyone since De Quincey written English with such verve and color? Has any scholar ever been so thorough?

Mr. Kenner's peculiar genius is the ability to move into a subject as Tolstoy constructs an episode: with the authority of a sure hand, with the steady accumulation of detail a sense of effect demands, and always, always, the perfect awareness that something is being explained and that somebody is following. There is a touch of the magician in Mr. Kenner; he knows when to produce the dove from a clap of empty hands, when to make his audience suck in its breath with surprise.

*Era,* an age; *the Pound era.* It began in Philadelphia, in classrooms of philology ("we studied until we dropped," Pound once said) and in the now gone and impossible idealism of students at the turn of the century. (There were, for instance, but two students in the Catullus class at Penn in 1904. Thirty-five years later those two students were knocking on the doors of two very different statesmen, to instruct them how to behave themselves. Pound failed to get an audience with Roosevelt to demonstrate to him how to avoid the Second World War, though the other student of Catullus, the Quaker saint George Walton, was admitted to the presence of Reichskanzler Hitler, to whose face he said, "Thee are not a kind man.")

Learning, then, great, ardent learning, and idealism. Pound has always gone on the principle that if a thing can be thought it can, by golly, be done. One can animate the dead past and make it live again in a poem (*The Cantos*), one can find out the causes of wars, one can educate the people and make them noble, one can protect men of genius and see to it that they are known and that they get enough to eat. But all this fervent activity, maintained at fever pitch for sixty years (even for thirteen years in a mad house, one of Pound's most productive and busy periods) can be put into a phrase: *to find the best in the past and pass it on.*

That is what Mr. Kenner demonstrates, the sifting of the past and the ways found for passing it on—and not in abstractions and mumblings through a hat, but with a passion for showing how things work (such as how a poem is translated, word by word, process by process, from the Chinese, from Greek, from Provençal) and how things correlate: thus we have in *The Pound Era* the interwoven careers of Eliot, Joyce, Wyndham Lewis, William Carlos Williams, and others, even Amy Lowell (whose war with Pound over Imagism is germane to the plot, and Mr. Kenner's account of that battle makes the funniest pages in literary criticism since Mark Twain threw Cooper down and danced on him).

*The Pound Era* is a book to be read and reread and studied. For the student of modern letters it is a treasure, for the general reader it is one of the most interesting books he will ever pick up in a lifetime of reading. This is because Mr. Kenner's mind is both thorough and particular. If the modern sense of words has a history (it does), he can work that history (another scholar's fat book, were another scholar to write it) into his narrative without dropping a single strand of his complex web. The elegantly relevant digressions in *The Pound Era* might be the work of a community of scholars rather than the diligent labor of Hugh Kenner.

And the *authority* of detail, of place, of time; how does he do *that?* For one thing, he has been and looked. He has been to the site of the concentration camp at Pisa and waited until the mountain beyond looked like Taishan, the Chinese sacred mountain. And then he has photographed it (he is a superb photographer) just as Pound saw it and described it in *The Cantos.* (There are fifty-seven other illustrations, all an integral part of the narrative). Mr. Kenner has also talked with most of the characters in the book: Eliot, Lewis, Beckett, Williams, Zukofsky, Marianne Moore, Pound ("Marvellous *raconteur,* Professor Kenner," Miss Rudge, Pound's companion, once explained to me, who had known that fact for twenty years, and Pound nodded gravely, in assent).

But why the Pound Era? Why did Mr. Kenner, who has written similarly thorough studies of Wyndham Lewis, Joyce, Eliot, Beckett (even Chesterton), and delightful studies of invisible movements among things and people, styles and metamorphoses of the spirit (*The Stoic Comedians, The Counterfeiters*), why has he cast his masterpiece around Pound and the genius he fostered? One reason is obviously Pound's difficulty (caused not by Pound but by the withering of the audience for which he thought he was writing) and consequent need of lucid explication. Another is that Pound was indeed the center of literature in English for those sixty years, as Picasso was the center of painting, Brancusi the center of sculpture, Wittgenstein the center of philosophy. Pound alone was vocal and mobile. He alone wrote stacks of letters daily, saw everyone, knew everyone, and eventually suffered the tragedy in real which all the greatest of modern artists suffered symbolically or cast into their art.

For they were all exiles, the borders of their homelands closed to them. Picasso spoke to Fascist Spain with the *Guernica,* Joyce to Ireland with *Ulysses,* Pound to the United States over short-wave radio, maddened by the spectacle of another war.

His tragedy (concentration camp, jail, insane asylum, and in his last years a Trappist silence and a formal repudiation of his writing) is the tragedy of the artist in the century that did not turn out as its best minds planned or hoped. It was the First World War that drove Pound to study the economic theories that made him a casualty in the Second. His fate was the same as Gaudier's, after all. Gaudier's was swift, Pound's slow; they both failed to complete the work only they could have done; they both saw the cathedrals burn.

# Ezra Pound 1885–1972

From the absolution by a black-stoled Benedictine with aspergillum and censer (*te supplices exoramus pro anima famuli tui Ezra*) four gondoliers in their Sunday best brought the coffin through the Palladian doors of San Giorgio Maggiore where it had lain before the altar in a solemnity of Gregorian chant and Monteverdi, and set it with tricky skill among heaps of flowers in a black gondola from the stern of which thirty-five fat coral roses rode in high solitary splendor as it moved across the *laguna,* nodding and dipping their red into the Adriatic.

With its burden of weightless flowers and a frail old man who had died in his sleep, chrysanthemums crowded yellow and white along the coffin's right side, long fronds of palm arching out of banked ruffles of color, the gondola made its cadenced progress through the canals of Venice to the *campo santo* on San Michele. Here the gondoliers shouldered the coffin and set it on the ropes with which it was lowered into the grave, where it lay at a slight angle to the sides. *In paradisum deducant te Angeli,* the priest sang, *in tuo adventu suscipiant te Martyres, et perducant te in civitatem sanctam Jerusalem.*

This burial among exiles is temporary. Ezra Pound specified in his will that he wished to be buried in Hailey, Idaho, where eighty-seven years before he was born. His portrait bust by Henri Gaudier-Brzeska is to be his tombstone. This summer he consulted Isamu Noguchi about a pediment and setting for his Gaudier.

In the last week of his life he attended a Noh play and the Peter Brook production of *A Midsummer Night's Dream,* flatly refusing to wear his topcoat to either. He was a stubborn old man, locked into a silence out of which he could rarely be enticed. His last words in public were during the intermission the evening of the Shakespeare. A woman had come over to pay her respects. After she left, he said to his party, "Beautiful." Silence. Then: "And smart, too."

He could get through whole days without saying a word. I have seen him sit in an agony of silence in a restaurant, the waiter standing with courteous patience while Olga Rudge, Pound's charming companion, cajoled and pleaded, trying one argument after another, to little avail. The alternative to not saying what he wanted was to go without lunch while the rest of us ate. The agony deepened, and with it the silence. It was like a saint breaking a vow when he sagged and gave in. *"Gnocchi,"* he said.

When he did venture a remark, it was apt to be a Proustian obliquity. On a sweet August evening after we had all been swimming and Miss Rudge had invited me, the film-maker Massimo Bacigalupo, and the archaeologist Steven Diamant to dine with her and Pound at a favorite *trattoria* in the hills of San Ambrogio, the old poet broke hours and hours of silence to say, "There's a magpie in China can turn a hedgehog over and kill it."

The silence was now ours. Miss Rudge, the master of any situation, picked it up. *"Wherever,"* she laughed, "did you find anything so erudite?"

"In Giles's *Dictionary,"* he said, a flicker of mischief in his eyes. Then he glared at me, and went back into the silence until a good hour later, over dessert, when he said, "Coffee is the one thing you mustn't order here."

The Chinese magpie, as I remember, kept its secret until the next day. Steve, Massimo, and I worked it out, with some help from Miss Rudge. Three days before I had given Pound a copy of my translation of Archilochos. It was the Hedgehog and Fox fragment he was alluding to, and this was his way of acknowledging that he had read the translation. He had read it to Miss Rudge, and we learned thereby that the silence ended at night, when he liked to read aloud. That week, in fact, he was reading Miss Rudge Sartre's *Les Mots,* which had just been published.

A book less likely to interest Pound cannot be imagined, and yet he was always capable of suprising our notions of what he did and didn't like. His last journey was by yacht to the Schloss Duino. Rilke! Who could have forseen that act of homage?

His last critical admonition was to bid us look at Laforgue again and appreciate his depths. His last translation might have been of Henri Michaux's *Idéogrammes en Chine,* a prose poem written as an introduction to Léon Chang's *La Calligraphie chinoise* (1971), except that he gave it up after a few starts.

This silence at the end of his life follows the design of his major works, which begin with *forte* movements and end *pianissimo. The Cantos* open with the noise of the sea and clattering oars; the fragments with which they end evoke quiet houses, the stillness of nature, the silence of mountains. *Mauberley* ends with a gazing face, *Propertius* on the Styx. The Confucian Odes begin with crying hawks, gongs and horse-bells; their concluding poems fold together images of autumnal stillness, sacrificial drums that are tapped softly with sticks, a palace "high in the air and quiet."

His generation had assumed that a life was a work of art, and it helps us understand the thirteen years in which Pound was locked up with catatonics. Only a man with deep resources could have survived that ordeal. Like Pascal with his account of his vision of Christ hung around his neck, Pound wore a similar document: it was from a friendly stranger, a psychiatrist who had taken the trouble to write out instructions for a sane man condemned to live among the insane.

Art is a matter of models; life is a matter of models. In St. Elizabeths he remembered C. Musonius Rufus, condemned first to a waterless Aegean island by Nero (he survived by discovering a spring for himself and his fellow prisoners) and finally to slinging a pickaxe in the chain gangs that dug the canal across the isthmus of Cornith. He remembered Tasso and Raleigh writing in their cells. As for the charge of treason, he shared that with William Blake, Dante, and Socrates. And the charge of madness was all but the common property of poets, deserved and undeserved. In an age of sober realism a Christopher Smart on his knees praying in the middle of London traffic must be taken to Bedlam, and a poet shouting over the radio that armaments manufacturers have the morals of cockroaches must be locked up in St. Elizabeths.

A theme that runs through the poetry of the madhouse days is mindlessness, especially the vacuum which had once been among educated men a knowledge of history and the classics. How strange his condemnation of usury sounded to a world that had forgotten the rage of Ruskin against the shrinking of all values into the shilling, the passionate voices of Fourier, Thoreau, and Marx that men were becoming the slaves of factories and banks.

Nothing characterizes the twentieth century more than its inability to pay attention to anything for more than a week. Pound spent the last third of his life learning that the spirit of the century was incoherence. Men who forget the past are doomed to repeat it, and the century has idiotically stumbled along repeating itself, its wars, its styles in the arts, its epidemics of unreason. Joyce, not Pound, was the voice of the century.

This paradox is cruel. Pound began under the protection of Apollo Leskhenorios, patron of poets and philosophers who can speak in the ancient traditions, who could refine, modify, and augment the traditions once they had mastered them. In Plutarch we hear these Pythian discourses with their wealth of allusion: everyone knows Homer by heart, the playwrights, the poets, the schools of philosophy. Their anthologies did not have footnotes to identify Zeus, Jehovah, the yew tree, Diana of the Ephesians, and Kublai Kahn.

The great Leskhenorian of the nineteenth century was Browning, and Pound intended to play Brahms to his Beethoven. He would add China to the tradition, he would recover the springtime of all the arts and imitate them in their fullest vigor. His audience would be educated men. They would recognize a tag from Homer (as a matter of fact the Greek line in "Mauberley" has not yet in fifty-odd attempts been set accurately in type); they would know Capaneus and his significance (can one university student in 5000 identify Capaneus?); certainly an American audience would see the relevance of an epic poem beginning with the word "And." (They have not even noticed the Homeric pun.)

So a tradition rotted not in but around Pound. Joyce knew that the tradition had begun to rot a long time ago. He believed Flaubert. Joyce therefore locates his work in the heart of the century, its grief and alienation, and speaks for it. Pound spoke to it. A page of *Finnegans Wake* is the voice of the century, the polyglot murmur from Buchenwald, the Babel in the corridors of the UN, the Russian short-wave voice jamming a Hungarian poem.

Stephen Dedalus is as much the young Pound as the young Joyce. Dedalus was to assume the mantle of the poet-priest-shepherd and be the conscience of his race, a proud and arrogant magus. What became of him we know not; presumably like that James Joyce whose nephew wrote *The Horse's Mouth* and *Herself Surprised* he bored his fellow Irishmen to death with his talk about being a writer and drank himself to death without writing a word.

In the Möbius trickery of the biographies of artists we know that Stephen Dedalus was killed in Joyce and was replaced by an artist who could understand Leopold Bloom as civilization's failure and humanity's triumph.

Pound could do neither. He kept his Dedalus inside himself, maturing around him, utterly unable to see the acumen of Odysseus distributed among all the poeple, recognizing it only in those examples of Odyssean cunning which in Joyce's opinion were best bred out of man. Pound kept his attention on rulers, Joyce on the ruled.

Pound's eye was on the sources of energy, guiding us to the neglected ones, guarding them from contamination. Joyce was interested in energy as it is actually used. Thus Joyce the Catholic saw nothing in saints so long as religion seemed to be all bigotry and superstition, while Pound the Protestant saw everything in saints, and was in love with so many religions that we have to accept him as a pagan who couldn't have too many gods on his hearth.

Joyce's books are perfections. Pound's all tend to resemble the Renaissance building which he celebrates in *The Cantos* and which is one of his richest symbols, the Tempio Malatestiano in Rimini. The Tempio is a shell of neoclassical marble encasing a Gothic church. Like *The Cantos* it is unfinished, is a monument to the skill and sensitivity of its creator, and yet is a realized, useful part of the world: one can go to mass in the Tempio, one can read *The Cantos*.

*The Cantos.* "Fragments shored against our ruin," a poem about empires (Alexander's, Rome, China, The United States), a poem about the advantages moral, spiritual, and technological of having an accessible and pervasive sensibility, a poem about the wealth of the sterile and the poverty of the productive, *The Cantos* are an epic restatement of Ruskin's *Fors Clavigera,* the thesis of which is that the usefulness of a government is its power to issue money.

What drove Pound mad was the simple fact that the United States issues no money at all but borrows money issued by a private bank. The hideous and obscene taxes which we pay our government are actually interest on this perpetual loan, ineradicable and unpayable. To explain this Sisyphean economic insanity, Pound convinced himself that it was all a plot of international Jewish bankers. Pound further believed that if the people could ever know that the United States gave up in 1913 its Constitutional directive to issue money (with the founding of the Federal Reserve Bank) they would rise up in revolution, purify the government, and return to a simple, taxless federation of states, ruled by laws locally passed and locally enforced. The Jews, financers and provokers of world wars, would then be powerless to manipulate national treasuries and would presumably revert to being private usurers. Such was the geometry of his vision.

"Usury," I heard him say one afternoon at St. Elizabeths, "I wish I'd never heard the damned word." I had two degrees after my name when I met Pound, and was working toward a third and a fourth, and the corrosion of civilization by usury was a subject lightly touched on if at all by my teachers. Pound sent me to study under dear old John Talbot, of Kirkwood, Mo., who had tutored William Jennings Bryan and Wendell Wilkie, and who was past ninety and deaf. I read Ruskin. I read Thomas Hart Benton the elder (and managed to introduce Benton to Perry Miller, who pounced on it with that mind and that energy). I read Alexander Del Mar. I learned all sorts of things I would probably never have heard of otherwise. Like many another, I saw in Pound the very archetype of the man who cared about things.

I had first read The Cantos years before meeting Pound. One fine summer Christopher Middleton and I walked about Italy and France with two books only, a Donne and a Cantos. Neither of us, I think, had much notion as to what the long poem was about, except that it had strangeness and beauty in great measure. It, like Donne, was always something to read, passing magic. I had also got onto Gaudier before I knew anything about Pound. Thank God the universities let contemporary literature alone in those days!

My Pound was first of all a man who had written a rich, barely comprehensible poem, a man whose portrait bust had been chiselled by Gaudier. My first response was to learn Italian and Provençal, and to paint in the quattrocento manner. All real education is such unconscious seduction.

I have had to become aware of many other versions of Pound since, though only Hugh Kenner's in his two books about him and his many essays (and our many conversations) bears any resemblance to the Pound I first knew. The man himself did not alter my view of him. He talked as I suspected he would talk. And it was from Pound himself that I first saw how whacky the anti-Semitism was. It made no sense that I could see. I had paid attention to the war, I knew refugees, I understood Treblinka and Buchenwald, I had seen Europe in ruins.

Southerners take a certain amount of unhinged reality for granted, and I was grateful for a day at St. Elizabeths when Pound gave me a copy of Frobenius's Kulturgeschichte Afrikas.

"How are you leaving?" he asked, reaching for the book.

When I said I was leaving by train, he reversed the dust jacket, so that it was blank. I understood. An agent of the Rothschilds' could spot me by that study of African anthropology and be driven to fury that learning was being freely transported about the Republic. *Paranoia,* said I, and was grateful for the disclosure, and further felt that a man caught in such a fate (escape from a Partisan firing squad, concentration camp where he was caged like an animal, and then in his eighth year in a madhouse) was entitled to all the paranoid fantasies he was pleased to nurse.

A few years after his return to Italy, suddenly old and silent, he went into the garden one day and sat down at his typewriter. He wrote letters. He had not written anybody in years. Were the old fires flaring up again? The despondency and fatigue "deep as the grave" rolling away? He mailed the letters himself. Within a week they began to return. They were addressed to James Joyce, Ford Madox Ford, Wyndham Lewis, William B. Yeats.

The great silence began. The Italians did not like it, they who fulfill themselves with words. It was "a slap in the face with a fish." It was all but total, this refusal to speak. At a celebration of the D'Annunzio Centennial which he was attending with his friend Salvatore Quasimodo, he was recognized and applauded until he stood. "Tempus loquendi," the frail voice said with its typical rising quaver, "tempus tacendi," quoting Ecclesiasticus, Malatesta, and Thomas Jefferson simultaneously, and explaining, in his way, that he had said quite enough. What he had to say about D'Annunzio, for instance, had been said forty-three years before.

Did he see in silence a new way of talking? Did he fear that he was old and a bore to the world, and would spike that by one last revolutionary invention?

At the very last he had regained a kind of sprightly composure, a kind of uneasy peace. He had the Gaudier bust brought from Brunnenburg to Venice and set it in his small, tidy apartment. He planned an American reading tour, and his friends were terrified that he would mount the podium before hordes of hippies and the curious and say absolutely nothing. He ate vealburgers in Harry's Bar, and over his ice-cream was a good time to tease him out of his glaring silence. Miss Rudge knew the formulae.

"Ezra!"

"?"

"What was Mr. Joyce wont to break into?"

A smile, a long pause before speaking:

"My friend Mr. Joyce was wont to break into *song.*"

He was born the year of Brahms's Fourth and of *Diana of the Crossways;* of *The Mikado* and the second volume of *Das Kapital;* in the reigns of Grover Cleveland and Victoria. At his death every school of poets

writing in Engish was under his influence, and his name was spoken with
awe by every man of letters in the world. I have seen students learn
Chinese because of him, or take up mediæval studies, learn Greek, Latin,
music; the power of his instigation has not flagged.

Joyce said that he was more in his debt than to any other man. He was
a mentor to Eliot, Ford, Wyndham Lewis, Hilda Doolittle, Marianne
Moore, Louis Zukofsky, William Carlos Williams, Charles Olson.

Once he was through his epigonic work (which belongs to Pre-
Raphaelitism) he saw that the art of the century would take its energy
from the primal and archaic, and he set about donning the masks of early
Chinese poets, of the masters of mediæval poetry, of Homer, of Dante.
Like Stravinsky and Picasso and Joyce, he had styles rather than a style.

As his reputation recedes in time, his radical Americanness will probably emerge from all the foreign masks. His rage at usury is a deep American theme, and is derivable from transcendentalist passions and ideals as
well as from the firmest traditions stemming from Jefferson and Adams.
His poetry is by its nature intricate, and will generate curiosity and explication for as long as we continue to study poetry. There will be many
revisionist views of Pound the man. Whatever view we take of his work,
we cannot diminish its inventiveness or mastery of language, or the pervasive intelligence which drove him to both his tragedy and his greatness.

He wrote to Henry Rago, when *Poetry* awarded him its Fiftieth Anniversary prize as its most distinguished contributor, that he was content
to be remembered as "a minor satirist who contributed something to a
refinement of the language." The modesty of those words well up from
old age and disillusion. He was a renaissance.

# "Trees"

In June, 1918, the Cincinnati poet Eloise Robinson was in the wasteland of Picardy handing out chocolate and reciting poetry to the American Expeditionary Forces. Reciting poetry! It is all but unimaginable that in that hell of terror, gangrene, mustard gas, sleeplessness, lice, and fatigue, there were moments when bone-weary soldiers, for the most part mere boys, would sit in a circle around a lady poet in an ankle-length khaki skirt and Boy Scout hat, to hear poems. In the middle of one poem the poet's memory flagged. She apologized profusely, for the poem, as she explained, was immensely popular back home. Whereupon a sergeant held up his hand, as if in school, and volunteered to recite it. And did.

So that in the hideously ravaged orchards and strafed woods of the valley of the Ourcq, where the fields were cratered and strewn with coils of barbed wire, fields that reeked of cordite and carrion, a voice recited

"Trees." How wonderful, said Eloise Robinson, that he should know it. "Well, ma'am," said the sergeant, "I guess I wrote it. I'm Joyce Kilmer."

He wrote it five years before, and sent it off to the newly founded magazine *Poetry,* and Harriet Monroe, the editor, paid him six dollars for it. Almost immediately it became one of the most famous poems in English, the staple of school teachers and the one poem known by practically everybody.

Sergeant Alfred Joyce Kilmer was killed by German gunfire on the heights above Seringes, the 30th of July, 1918. The French gave him the *Croix de Guerre* for his gallantry. He was thirty-two.

"Trees" is a poem that has various reputations. It is all right for tots and Middle Western clubwomen, but you are supposed to outgrow it. It symbolizes the sentimentality and weak-mindedness that characterizes middle-class muddle. It is Rotarian. Once, at a gathering of poets at the Library of Congress, Babette Deutsch was using it as an example of the taradiddle Congressmen recite at prayer breakfasts and other orgies, until Professor Gordon Wayne coughed and reminded her that the poet's son, Kenton, was among those present. No one, however, rose to defend Kipling and Whittier, at whom La Deutsch was also having.

It is, Lord knows, a vulnerable poem. For one thing, it is a poem about poetry, and is thus turned in on itself, and smacks of propaganda for the art (but is therefore useful to teachers who find justifying poetry to barbarian students uphill work). For another, the opening statement is all too close to Gelett Burgess's "I never saw a Purple Cow," lines that had been flipping from the tongues of wits since 1895.

And if the tree is pressing its hungry mouth against the earth's sweet flowing breast, how can it then lift its leafy arms to pray? This is a position worthy of Picasso but not of the Cosmopolitan Cover Art Noveau aesthetic from which the poem derives. Ask any hard-nosed classicist, and she will tell you that the poem is a monster of mixed metaphors.

And yet there is a silvery, spare beauty about it that has not dated. Its six couplets have an inexplicable integrity, and a pleasant, old-fashioned music. It soothes, and it seems to speak of verities.

The handbooks will tell you that Yeats and Housman are behind the poem, though one cannot suspect from it that Kilmer was one of the earliest admirers of Gerard Manley Hopkins. Poems of great energy are usually distillations of words and sentiments outside themselves. Poems are by nature a compression. Another chestnut, Longfellow's "A Psalm of Life," was generated by the Scotch geologist Hugh Miller's *Footprints of the Creator* and *The Old Red Sandstone,* books made popular in America by Longfellow's colleague at Harvard, Louis Agassiz. It is an example of the miraculous (and of the transcendentally vague) how

Longfellow, reading about fossils in Miller, latched onto the sandstone and the vestiges thereupon, to intone "Lives of great men all remind us / We can make our lives sublime / And in passing leave behind us / Footprints on the sands of time."

Poets work that way, condensing, rendering down to essence. Another poem, as popular in its day as "Trees," Edwin Markham's "The Man with the Hoe" lived in Ezra Pound's mind until it became the opening line of *The Pisan Cantos*—"The enormous tragedy of the dream in the peasant's bent shoulders."

"Trees" is, if you look, very much of its time. Trees were favorite symbols for Yeats, Frost, and even the young Pound. The nature of chlorophyll had just been discovered, and *Tarzan of the Apes*—set in a tree world—had just been published. Trees were everywhere in art of the period, and it was understood that they belonged to the region of ideas, to Santayana's Realm of Beauty.

But Kilmer had been reading about trees in another context that we have forgotten, one that accounts for the self-effacing closing lines ("Poems are made by fools like me, / But only God can make a tree"), lines that have elevated the poem into double duty as a religious homily. Kilmer's young manhood was in step with the idealism of the century. One of the inventions in idealism that attracted much attention was the movement to stop child labor and to set up nursery schools in slums. One of the most diligent pioneers in this movement was the Englishwoman Margaret McMillan, who had the happy idea that a breath of fresh air and an intimate acquaintance with grass and trees were worth all the pencils and desks in the whole school system. There was something about trees that she wanted her slum children to feel. She had them take naps under trees, roll on grass, dance around trees. The English word for gymnasium equipment is "apparatus." And in her book *Labour and Childhood* (1907) you will find this sentence: "Apparatus can be made by fools, but only God can make a tree."

# Jonathan Williams

Jonathan Williams, poet. He is an entertaining array of other things, too, but they are for the historian of publishing to talk about, the connoisseur of fine books, the biographer, the *raconteur,* the chronicler, if any ever comes forward, of the poets who in our new intellectual ecology have risked their stomachs, nerves, and reputations to read in colleges, YMCA's, high schools, YWCA's, filling stations (yes, filling stations), universities, YMHA's, churches, and even department stores. There is a reason for this goliardry, to which we shall return. It was R. Buckminster Fuller, on his way from Carbondale to Ghana (and deep in Kentucky at the time) who remarked of Jonathan Williams that "he is our Johnny Appleseed—we need him more than we know." He publishes poets, introduces poets to poets, poets to readers, professors to poets, poets (perilous business) to professors, and he photographs poets. The color slide, descendant of the magic lantern, is still the most charming disseminator of culture, and Jonathan Williams is its master. He is the iconographer of poets in our time, and of the places and graves of poets gone on to Elysium. He is an ambassador for an enterprise that has neither center nor hierarchy but whose credentials are ancient and respected. He is also a traveller, hiker, botanist, antiquarian, epicure, and much else to engage our attention if we wish to look at the poet rather than the poetry. And so, quickly, before the poet gets in our line of sight, the poetry.

Its weightlessness is that of thistledown and like the thistle it bites. Its coherence is that of clockwork, at once obvious and admirable. Its beauty is that of the times: harsh, elegant, loud, sweet, abrupt all together. The poet in our time does what poets have always done, given a tongue to dumbness, celebrated wonderments, complained of the government, told tales, found sense where none was to be perceived, found nonsense where we thought there was sense; in short, made a world for the mind (and occasionally the body too) to inhabit. Beauty, poets have taught us, is the king's daughter and the milkmaid, the nightingale and the rose, the wind, a Greek urn, the autumn moon, the sea when it looks like wine. None of which appear often in the confusion of our world. Yet, perhaps all too rarely, poets keep to their traditional loyalties:

dawn songs in the dews of young orange trees;
and ranging orisons; and wordless longings

sung in tranquillity's waters sliding in sun's light;

and benisons sung in these trees. . . .

That cello passage is Jonathan Williams meditating on Frederick Delius. The imagination of the poet converses with the imagination of the composer. The language for talking to Delius is Delius. And what if the poet wants to talk back to the TV set? It is there that he encounters of a morning rockets blasted toward a star his ancient craft has sung for two thousand years (and probably longer). He switches from cello to clarinet, piano, snare drum, and trombone:

Woke up this mornin',
Cape Canaveral can't get it up . . .
Woke up this mornin',
Cape Canaveral can't get it up . . .

But sent a cable to Great Venus—
told her, better watch her ass!

*"Unravished bride of quietness,"*
blasts off in my head . . .
*"Unravished bride of quietness,"*
blasts off in my head . . .

Liable to be a whole lot more people
than just John Keats dead!

Lonnie Johnson and Elmer Snowden, accomplished singers of the
blues, were enlisted in this enterprise, for their tradition of eloquent dismay before a world independent of their will and opaque to their evaluation of life has been under refinement for three centuries, and their sly
alignment of technology's troubles with a ribaldry both venerable and
primitive is worthy of Brer Fox. The art of Méliès is there, too—the poet
is remembering *The Rocket to the Moon,* in which Verne's astronauts
smack into the planet's outraged eye. And Keats's great ode. Poets are
licensed idiots and can be counted on without fail to note the change
when the silent moon—Sappho's wild-rose-fingered moon born from the
violet sea, Vergil's friend of silence, Shakespeare's moist starre—becomes
a junkyard.

The poet, like a horse, is a mythological creature. The accoutrements
of both are the same now as in the days of Hsiang Yü, Mimnermos, and
Caedmon. Their duties are the same, their *numen,* their intractable identity and presence. They are, they always have been. The horse is as archaic as he is modern, forever the "neighing quadruped, used in war, and
draught and carriage" that Johnson said he was, independent of time and
fashion: which is why the poet Christopher Fry called him the last
mythological beast. Eternity seems to have made a separate contract with
him, and extended the same gracious codicil to the poet, who also is
neither archaic nor modern, or rather is most modern when he is most
archaic. For the work of the poet is continuous, while all other modes of
discourse—mathematics, physics, politics—are wildly discontinuous, repeating stupidities because they forgot the past, stopping and starting
because of barbarians, rebellions, and simple loss of vision. The poet
works his melodies into the very grain of existence.

An eidetic Ezra Pound, we learn from the poem "Some Southpaw
Pitching," once appeared to the poet Charles Olson to say, "*Let the song
lie in the thing!*" Our other recorded appearance of Ezra Pound as "a
familiar compound ghost" was to Air Raid Warden Eliot during the Blitz
when he could be discerned "in the waning dusk," along with Dante and
Mallarmé, saying

> . . . our concern was speech, and speech impelled us
> To purify the dialect of the tribe
> And urge the mind to aftersight and foresight.

Eliot of course is here reimagining Dante's encounter with his teacher
Brunetto Latini—the meeting to which the title of Jonathan Williams's
first book alludes in its elate way, *The Empire Finals at Verona* (1958).

Poi si rivolse, e parve di coloro
   che corrono a Verona il drappo verde
   per la campagna; e parve di costoro
quelli che vince, non colui che perde.

The ghost also said to Mr. Eliot: "Next year's words await another voice." Another master to whom Jonathan Williams has listened with care wrote: "No ideas but in things." That was William Carlos Williams (no kin) who appears in his poetry saying (in "Dangerous Calamus Emotions"):

him and that Jesuit, them with the variable feet—
they changed it!

Walt Whitman, he means, and Gerard Manley Hopkins. What they changed is what Jonathan Williams (with help and in good company) is still changing: poetry. "Next year's words await another voice." By paying careful attention to William Carlos Williams, who insisted that the poet's business is to let the world speak for itself, Jonathan Williams learned to make such poems as this:

Mister Williams
lets youn me move
tother side the house

the woman
choppin woods
mite nigh the awkerdist thing
I seen.

The title to this poem is a verbal gesture alerting us to cock our ears: "Uncle Iv Surveys His Domain from His Rocker of a Sunday Afternoon as Aunt Dory Starts to Chop Kindling." The poem defines a culture. Edwin Markham was satisfied to let the man with the hoe remain as voiceless as the Barbizon painting in which he found him. That the world they have been so diligently describing might have a voice seems to be a late idea to American poets. James Joyce offered as the purpose of literature the simple but radically unassailable office of making the dumb to speak. And not in paraphrase. The poet locates himself between reality and the poem, and trains himself to be the medium through which reality flows into the poem.

*I found the poems in the fields*
*And only wrote them down*

That is John Clare as he speaks in Jonathan Williams's "What the Flowers in the Meadow Tell Me." And there is a response:

John, *claritas* tells us the words are *not* idle,
the syllables are able
to turn plaintains into quatrains,
tune *raceme* to *cyme*, *panicle* and *umbel* to
form corollas in light clusters of tones . . .

Sam Palmer hit it:
"Milton, by one epithet
draws an oak of the largest girth I ever saw,
'Pine and *monumental* oak':

I have been trying to draw a large one in
Lullingstone; but the poet's tree is huger than
any in the park."

Muse in a meadow, compose in
a mind!

Any poem worth its salt is as transparently complex as

air in a hornet's nest
over the water makes a
solid, six-sided music

wherein every quality is mirrored in another (and an *aria* and a *horn* are camouflaged into the richness); that the lines are typographically isometric, seven-syllabled, and inwardly ornamental (-net's nest; solid/sided; *s, m,* and *n* so placed as to make a bass line to the treble) is as native an instinct to the poet as the hornet's hexagonal architecture.

Native, to be certain, but only after much work. Man is the animal that chooses its instincts through emulation, and all his learning has roots and branches. Jonathan Williams's first masters would seem to be Charles Olson, whose *Maximus* poems he later published, and whose master was Ezra Pound. We cannot draw a direct line of descent from Pound to Olson, however, for there is an intervening generation. Louis Zukofsky and William Carlos Williams are at its center, its Mallarmé and its Whitman. Their admonitions to the young stressed objectivity, technique, honesty, clarity, realism. The European poem was not to be continued in America; it was not republican. Rhyme was feudal; recurring metrical patterns warped thought and natural speech. Images must come not from books but the world. The poet must therefore find a new shape for every poem, and liberty turned out to make far harder demands than the sonnet. Hence Olson's heroic struggle with balance of phrasing, William Carlos Williams's plain carpentry and boyish honesty, and Zukofsky's daredevil integrity and fierce control of rhythm and design—a passionate mathematics engraved on steel with a diamond. Never before had American poetry worked with such fine tools or insisted upon such craftsmanship. Professors of literature, ever conservative, cautious, and lazy, will discover all this in their own sweet time.

The young poets who went to school to these hard masters—Robert Creeley, Robert Duncan, Jonathan Williams, Robert Kelly, Ronald Johnson—have by now each evolved a style of his own. The spare asceticism of their training remains, however, as an armature within. Johnathan Williams learned how to write a poem as trim and economical as a tree. And like a tree his poems have roots, exist against a background, and convert light into energy. And take their shape not only from inner design but also from the weather and their circumjacence.

Which brings us to the fact that the honey bee has a lethal sting. Were it not for a long and distinguished history of poets who have balanced a love affair and a feud with the world—Archilochos, Catullus, Horace, Villon, Pope, E. E. Cummings—Jonathan Williams's double-threat handiness with a lyric would seem charmingly schizoid. *Odi et amo.* A settled hatred for one's species (Little Harp's excuse for his *terreur,* and his last words) is traditionally counterpoised in the satirist by a rich sensuality before all that's innocent.

The satire has been there from the first; wit and sense do not exist apart from each other in Jonathan Williams's mind. Pathos must appear in comic socks or not at all. Incongruity seems to be the stuff of existence, and outrage may be our surest response to the universe. There is a moral discourse of some consequence in the poet's reply to political rhetoric:

Hush, L'il Guvnuh,
don't you fret. . . .

The genius of Jonathan Williams's satire is as old as tyranny. The slave learns to speak in riddles and sly enigmas; *The Blue-Tailed Fly,* homely folksong as it seemed, was in fact a song of emancipation. Look hard at his satires: their pungency and sass are not irresponsible, nor their wit flippant. In "Faubus Meets Mingus during the Latter's Dynasty" the particular politician and composer easily translate into the struggle between power and art anywhere. It is Jonatahn Williams's surest instinct that poetry is not ideas or rhetoric. He locates meaning specifically. To the child's question,

whut fer
thesehyar
animules
be,
Granny?

the reply is:

haint fer
to name! why Adam's
Off-Ox
in thishyar
Garden
haint got
no name
neither
yet

but the Lord's
liable to call
thishyar
tree
Arber
Vity

hit's got
thishyar
sarpint
in it.

"And out of the ground the LORD GOD formed every beast of the field, and every foule of the aire, and brought them unto Adam, to see what he would call them: and whatsoever Adam called every living creature, that was the name thereof. . . ." The child who inquired about the gingham and calico animals in the patchwork quilt will have heard these words in Sunday School and may never hear Milton's

The grassie Clods now Calv'd, now half appeered
The Tawnie Lion, pawing to get free
His hinder parts, then springs as broke from Bonds,
And rampant shakes his Brinded main; the Ounce,
The Libbard, and the Tyger, as the Moale
Rising, the crumbl'd Earth above them threw
In Hillocks; the swift Stag from under ground
Bore up his branching head

nor Jules Supervielle's

Sombres troupeaux des monts sauvages, étagés,
Faites attention, vous allez vous figer.
Ne pouvant vous laisser errer à votre guise
Je m'en vais vous donner d'éternelles assises.
Les chamois bondiront pour vous . . .

but has his vision all the same of the Garden, its Tree, and its Serpent.

As we read Williams's poems we become aware that whereas the satirist's predilections are as esoteric as the headlines in this morning's newspaper, the lyricist's predilections begin to display a wonderful strangeness. A pattern of artists emerges—Blake, Ives, Nielsen, Samuel Palmer, Bruckner—and (if we have our eyes open) a whole world. It is a world of English music, especially the Edwardian Impressionists and their German cousins Bruckner and Mahler, of artists oriented toward Blake and his circle but going off by centrifugal flight into wildest orbits, men like Fuseli, Calvert, and Mad Martin. The poet's admiration for Edith Sitwell will have had something to do with this exploration of English eccentricity, and the poet's Welsh temperament, and, most clearly, William Blake himself. The artist is aware of a heritage not only because, like the rest of us, he recognizes in it his origins and values, but because he is consciously adding to it. What Jonathan Williams found in England, Wales, and Scotland was not a second heritage (as it might seem to a casual glance) but the heritage in which he was raised from the beginning. When, for instance, he met the Scotch poet Ian Hamilton Finlay, among whose work we can find (in the Glaswegian tongue):

```
hooch
a heilan coo
wis mair liker
it
      the hiker
s
hoo hoos
ferr feart
o ma
herr-do
```

he was, as perhaps only a citizen of Appalachia can know, solidly within his heritage. Finlay probably got his matter out of the air (the *heilan coo* can be found in his *Glasgow Beasts, an a Burd, Haw, an Inseks, an, Aw, a Fush*) without necessarily knowing that he was retelling a song that can be traced to Taliesin (the *Câd Goddeu*), is known in Spanish, Italian, Roumanian, Greek, and Serbian versions, and is sung in Jonathan Williams's neck of the woods as "She looked out o the winder as white as any milk."[1] Finlay has remarked of the Glaswegians that their dialect parodies itself, so that arch comic banter has become the preferred mode of discourse. The same observation describes Appalachia, the linguistic horizon that Jonathan Williams has never cared to stray very far from.

English eccentricity goes back to the Druids and beyond—the Sutton Ho jewelry discovered in 1939 looks remarkably as if it were what Jonathan Williams calls Theosophical Celtic Art Nouveau. From Blake's

[1] Ian Hamilton Finlay's little book is based on the transformation theme. The protagonist shifts shape from one animal to another for various reasons. See Buchan, *Ancient Ballads and Songs,* 1, 24, and Child's *English and Scottish Ballads,* 1, 244.

Ancients (Samuel Palmer and Edward Calvert) stems a tradition. The Rossettis belonged to it; Browning paid it his respects; but for the most part it is a tangled and untraced path in and out of official literature and art. There's Charles Doughty, whom entire departments of literature university after university have not read, a state of affairs roughly analogous to a department of physics sublimely ignorant of Proteus Steinmetz. There's Stanley Spencer, J. R. R. Tolkien, Edith Sitwell. And Bruckner and Bax and John Ireland. And Odilon Redon and James McGarrell. And more—we await the historian of these visionaries. Literature, as Harry Levin is wont to say, is its own historian, and Jonathan Williams's honor to his spiritual forebears may be the beginning of a resuscitation. Meanwhile, we must recognize that they constitute a tradition, and that he has taken up their torch, and carries it to and fro in the United States. His *Mahler,* responses movement by movement to the ten symphonies, will mark (once the dust has settled) the introduction of Blake's "Young Ancients" to our shores, a hundred and forty years late. If Walt Whitman had married the Widow Gilchrist as she proposed, we should not have had to wait so long, perhaps. And that speculation makes it clear that I have wandered far enough into an unwritten history.

Poetry is always inviolably itself, and it is always something more. Jonathan Williams offers us in every poem a lyric line of suave clarity and a highly involved verbal harmony. The poem itself finds and articulates a single image or action. This is an art like pole vaulting: the center of gravity is outside the trajectory. Build-up and follow-through are not the poem, though the poem depends upon them; the one is in the poet's control, the other in yours. We are not suprised to learn that the poet is an athlete.

And the poet is a wanderer. If his poetry defines and extricates a tradition from the past, his wandering (as Buckminster Fuller points out) defines the curious transformation of the shape of American culture. There is no American capital; there never has been. We have a network instead. A French poet may plausibly know all other French poets by living in Paris. The smallest of American towns contains major poets, and all other kinds of artists. In no other country does such a distribution of mind appear. Millidgeville, Ga., contained Flannery O'Connor (and at one time Oliver Hardy); Jackson, Miss., Eudora Welty; Minerva, O., Ralph Hodgson; Rollinsville, Col., Stan Brakhage. If you know where Charles Ruggles lives, Ray Bradbury, Michael McClure, or Edward Dorn, you may count yourself learned indeed. For a decade now Jonathan Williams has made it his business to go from point to point on the network: there has been nothing like it since the mediæval scholars who for want of any other means of communication wandered from university to university. His long zigzag trips can easily be explained by noticing that he is a publisher of books unwelcome to commercial publishers (who are closer to the grocery business than to that founded by Gutenberg); by invitations from universities to read, show slides, lecture on book design, architecture, and poetry; and by the fact that to know artists and poets one has to go to Pocatello, Idaho, and Pippa Passes, Ky. The true significance of all this gadding about is this: the poet with his preternatural, prophetic sense knows that this is the way he must live. Buckminster Fuller, who has also been on the road for the same decade, knew why Jonathan Williams is there too for the simple reason that they are each in his own way doing the same thing. Each has perceived that all other lines of communication are overloaded. Anything worth knowing passes from one person to another. The book is still a viable way of communicating, provided one has taught oneself to find the book one needs to read. It isn't easy. All the electronic media are a flood of noise. And no medium can replace what may be an essential need in the poet: an audience. Homer recited his poems to people who cheered and even gave prizes; at least they passed around wine. Chaucer read his poems in warm firelit rooms. Every line of Shakespeare was written to move a paying audience. The next time you read a slack, obscure, convoluted poem, reflect that it was written in an age when printing has replaced recitation, and that the poet cannot tell his good poems from his bad except by fortuitous criticism. Jonathan Williams's books have been published in fine editions, many of them collectors' items from the moment of their printing, and all of them by this time scarce. It is therefore not hyperbole to say that thousands of people have heard his poems at colleges and auditoriums (and at that one filling station) for every five who know them on the printed page. Their clarity to the ear and the inner eye has been tested in the classical weather of poetry, listening faces.

*The green gold is the living quality which the alchemists*
*saw not only in man but also in inorganic nature. It is an*
*expression of the life-spirit, the* anima mundi *or* filius
macrocosmi, *the Anthropos who animates the whole*
*cosmos. This spirit has poured himself into everything,*
*even into inorganic matter; he is present in metal and*
*stone.*

(Carl Jung, Memories, Dreams, Reflections)

# Ronald Johnson

## THE VALLEY OF THE MANY-COLORED GRASSES

The philosopher Wittgenstein, from whose formidable talents came a house, a sewing machine, and an airplane propeller as well as the books for which he is honored, said toward the end of his anguished life that he had always wanted to write a poem but could never think of a poem to write. Nor did Heraclitus write a poem, doubtless for the same reason. Nor Leonardo, that we know of. The miracle by which we have two poems from R. Buckminster Fuller, the Pythagoras *de nos jours,* rises from the transparent fact that Mr. Fuller's dymaxion prose has twice defied mortal comprehension and has twice been found to be readable when distributed on the page as poetry is, phrase by phrase, or "venti-lated," the texts in each instance being word for word the same. These austere extremes of the poetic imagination are useful if difficult evocations, for Ronald Johnson's transmutation of the English poem reaches down to the very roots of poetry itself. If a poem has ever occurred to Mr. Johnson, he has never written it. At least he has never published it.

A poem as it is generally understood is a metrical composition either lyric, dramatic or pensive made by a poet whose spiritual dominion flows through his words like the wind or the leaves or the lark's song through twilight. In the fourth part of "When Men Will Lie Down as Gracefully & as Ripe," Mr. Johnson performs for a passage of Emerson's what Buckminster Fuller did for his own prose. He spaces it out and makes a poem of it, though this bald-faced act scarcely answers to the received notion of how a poem is written. It is not Wordsworth in his blue sunglasses pacing his gravel walk and dictating to Dorothy. Nor Jaufre Rudel tuning his lute among the nightingales at Sarlat.

The lyric poem from Sappho to Voznesensky, with all its variants and transmutations, has become for us the model of all poems. The credentials of this ideal western poem tend to lurk not in the poems but in the personality of the poet. All that Byron wrote is somehow not as great as Byron. This illusion, fostered by the scandal-mongering of professors and the Grundyism of psychology, is a lazy and essentially indifferent view of poetry. The poet, who writes not for himself but to provide the world with an articulate tongue, longs to be as absent from his finished work as Homer. *Objective* and *subjective* are modes in the critic's mind; the poet scarcely knows what they mean.

If the finely textured geometry of words Ronald Johnson builds on his pages is not what we ordinarily call a poem, it is indisputably poetry. It is poetry written to a difficult music ("a different music," as the poet himself says). It is a poetry with a passion for exact, even scientific scrutiny. It incorporates in generous measure the words of other men. It does not *breathe* like most of the poetry we know. It is admirably un-self-conscious—the work of a man far too occupied with realities to have given much thought to being a poet. This objectivity is no doubt first of all a matter of temperament. It is no surprise to learn that the man writes cookbooks erudite enough to be published by university presses, seems to be something of a wanderer in a society where every man jack of us is bolted down and labelled, and that if he comes to visit he is apt to forget to go to bed and be up all night reading a book about the symmetry of the universe. It is perhaps unfair to give even so vague a glimpse as this of the poet, since he himself has shown us nothing more than his meticulous connoisseurship of the world as a system of harmonic advantages. "Nature," says the very first voice of philosophy, "loves to hide. What is hidden in nature is more harmonious than what we can easily see." The vision by which we discover the hidden in nature is sometimes called science, sometimes art. Mr. Johnson's books—*A Line of Poetry, A Row of Trees* (1965), *The Book of the Green Man* (1967), and *The Valley of the Many-Colored Grasses* (which incorporates a shortened and re-arranged version of the first book)—are about this vision in all its manifestations, from the scientific to the simple but difficult business of seeing the world with eyes cleansed of stupidity and indifference. Hence Mr. Johnson's special fascination with men who have sharpened their eyesight: explorers, anatomists, botanists, painters, antiquarians, poets, microscopists, mathematicians, physicists.

Poetry from the old age of Browning to the old age of Ezra Pound has had a passion for objectivity. Whitman made a note to himself to invent "a perfectly transparent plate-glass style, artless, with no ornaments." Mr. Johnson's immediate patrimony in letters comes from Jonathan Williams, the poet, publisher, and a long-time friend. But Jonathan Williams is himself a kind of polytechnic institute, and at the time Ronald Johnson met him, had already distilled from the confusing state of American poetry a clear sense that the masters were Pound, William Carlos Williams, and Louis Zukofsky, and had set about writing (and showing others, Ronald Johnson included, how to write) poems as spare, functional, and alive as a blade of grass. It was a poetry neither meditative nor hortatory but *projective*. It insisted that the world is interesting enough in itself to be reflected in a poem without rhetorical cosmetics, an arbitrary tune for melodramatic coloring, or stage directions from the literary kit and caboodle.

Art prepares its own possibilities for metaphysical shifts. We are at a point in the history of art when Robert Rauschenberg does not draw his drawings and is nonetheless a brilliant draughtsman. Charles Ives wrote his music, and we must quickly add that of course he didn't; these two statements exist in the realization that Ives is the most imaginative and accomplished of American composers. The quotations in Ronald Johnson's poems are simply a part of the world, like Wordsworth's daffodils, which the poet wishes to bring to us. The poet is at the edge of our consciousness of the world, finding beyond the suspected nothingness which we imagine limits our perception another acre or so of being worth our venturing upon.

It is always difficult to know how much of the world the artist has taught us to see; once we see it we are quick to suppose that it was always there. But there were no waterfalls before Turner and Wordworth, no moonlight before Sappho. The apple has its history. For it is not things which poets give us but the way in which they exist for us. The rich theme of The Green Man has always "been there" in the history of things, in folklore, in architecture, in poems. Some weeks after I read Mr.

Johnson's *Book of the Green Man* I was looking at Nelson Glueck's book about the ancient Nabataeans and was able to say of the strange leaf-bearded and leaf-haired demons depicted there, "Here's Ronald Johnson's Green Man way back in the Biblical Edom." Two days later the Jolly Green Giant suddenly lost his commercial enamel and stood there on his tin of beans as a household god thoroughly numinous.

"Every force," said Mother Ann Lee of the Shakers, "evolves a form." For the poet this is the opposite of supposing that a form can be filled with a force. The sentiments aroused by the moon painted by Ryder can be accommodated by a sonnet, but it is the sonnet in the end which is being accommodated, not the moon. In Ronald Johnson's poetry form seems to have been connected into diagrammatic elegance. What has happened is that the force of the subject matter has been allowed to shape the poem. The story of Edgar Allan Poe from which Mr. Johnson takes the title of this book has for an epigraph a tag from Lully which is a corollary to Mother Ann Lee's perception: *Sub conservatione formae specificae salva anima.* Nature, not culture, is for Mr. Johnson the constant mode of the world; his every poem has been to trace the intricate and subtle lines of force wherein man can discern the order of his relation to the natural world. These lines, as Heraclitus suspected, are largely invisible. About 2500 years ago poetry detached itself from the rituals of music and dance to go into the business of making the invisible visible to the imagination. This seeing where there is nothing to see, guided by mere words, is still the most astounding achievement of the human mind.

True imagination makes up nothing; it is a way of seeing the world. The imagination for Ronald Johnson is obviously a more complex process than we normally think it. There is the world to be seen, with its hidden harmony, and there is the poet (or painter, or composer) to perform the magic whereby we can possess the artist's vision. There is more. Throughout his poetry Mr. Johnson is interested to show us the world from multiple angles of vision, not only what he can show us but what others have seen also, so that we find ourselves not in the company of one poet but of many, and not only poets. All these voices quoted in Ronald Johnson's poems are other modes of vision which he is allowing to play over the subject along with his own. In the later poems we have to learn to read two poems at once, as in "The Different Musics," and to see with rapidly refocussed vision, as in "The Unfoldings."

There is a wild freshness about these poems that cannot be accounted for entirely by their newness of form and greenness of imagery. In avoiding the traditional forms of the poem, including the supertraditional form of Modern Poetry, Mr. Johnson also escaped the emotional clichés that cling to them like ticks to a dog. Things wholly new are perhaps impossible and a bit frightening; like all things fresh and bright, Mr. Johnson's newness is a reseeing of things immemorially old. In *The Book of the Green Man* he gives us a new look at Wordsworth, and adds Kilvert to the account; it is the conjunction, not the elements, that creates a new light. Much of Mr. Johnson's imagery that seems so wonderfully clean and new has been discovered in out-of-the-way places. Invention, we remember, really means *finding*. The knowledge he likes to teach us is indeed knowledge all but lost. We scarcely think of the poet any longer as a teacher, but Mr. Johnson does; and if we like to think of the poet as our conscience and our political guide and a figure speaking of contemporary and fashionable anxieties, we discover that Mr. Johnson might just as well be writing in any century you might arbitrarily name for all the mention he makes of his times. There is a brave innocence in this program, and an aptness that may not come readily to mind. It is characteristic of Mr. Johnson's generation and its immediate predecessors that a mind of one's own is preferable to tagging along with corporate thought. It was Louis Zukofsky, the friend of Whittaker Chambers at Columbia in its Reddest heyday, who read Gibbon with an eye to seeing what Marx would have done about it all and thus bade farewell to Marx and all his host. Stan Brakhage, the filmmaker, once banned the newspaper from his house and substituted Tacitus, which he read to his family daily. He had reached the assassination of Caesar on November 22, 1963. R. Buckminster Fuller, a friend of Mr. Johnson's, has noted that in nature there is no occasion on which the perimeter of a sphere is passed through its middle and has thus dismissed *pi* from his mathematics. One can note that we are looking at an awful lot of Transcendentalism here about which one could write quite an original book. In an essay we can do no more than alert ourselves to Mr. Johnson's transcendentalism and note that he came by it honestly, and read him accordingly. Transcendentalism holds that man must do his perceiving and his thinking for himself, and that he must learn how with much discipline and with constant awareness. Much that is new and rich in Ronald Johnson's poetry can be traced to his having seen the contents of his poems with his own eyes, out of his own curiosity. This charming doggedness, which Mr. Johnson shares with our best poets writing today, may have saved American poetry from a dismal return to the academic slush into which it is constantly threatening to sink. Sensitivity serves well for reading poems but not for writing them. The same Transcendentalism which flows from Emerson, Thoreau, and Whitman into the best of our poetry is the tradition also whereby it is assumed by ninety-nine out of a hundred practicing poets that sensitivity is the whole apparatus for making a poem. *Hélas*. The goodness of Ronald Johnson is in having got the real Transcendentalism from the very start, the kind that served Ives and

Buckminster Fuller, both of whom went back to the beginning of their arts as if time did not exist, and began anew. This is a tough and hazardous way of going about one's art, especially if there are two thousand years of tradition at one's back. And it requires enormous resourcefulness, sureness of hand, clarity of vision, and genius. But these Ronald Johnson has.

RADI OS

Art is man's teacher, but art is art's teacher. A poet usually finds his poetry in another poet. This process used to be called emulation, was admired and encouraged, but tumbled into disrepute from the Romantics to our day, when the red banner of Originality was carried to the barricades where it still stands. And, inevitably, it was long ago discovered that emulation is one of the most revolutionary forms of originality. The word *invention*, which once meant *finding* rather than making from scratch, now means *finding* again. Look at Eliot, Ives, Pound, Joyce, Picasso, Stravinsky. (The most original writer of our time, Gertrude Stein, still begins *The Making of Americans* with a passage from the Nichomachaean Ethics, and conceals the word *eros* in "A rose is a rose is a rose."

Ronald Johnson's finding his poem *Radi os* inside *Paradise Lost* is startlingly modern and thoroughly traditional. Insofar as he is making a version of the epic he is in the good company of Wordsworth, Blake, and the Joyce of the *Wake*. And of Milton himself, for to the craftsman's eye, Milton found his poem in the Bible, in Homer, in Virgil, in Joshuah Sylvester's translation of Guillaume de Salluste du Bartas's *La Semaine,* called *Divine Weekes and Workes,* and (as Milton scholars tend not to know) in Serafino della Salandra's *Adamo Caduto*. It would be as accurate to say that Milton found his epic in that fierce spirit of the Baroque that had begun all over Europe to state the tension between exuberance and restraint, between form and content, between the two winds of thought that made the weather of Milton's mind, Greece and Israel. The attempt to harness them both to one tumultuous chariot gave us Racine and Michelangelo, Dürer and Montaigne.

Nor is this the first poem to be precipitated from *Paradise Lost. The Prelude* is another, with its translation of the theme into the psychology of Romanticism and its transmutation of the Miltonic phrase to its own ends, whereby Wordsworth can begin his poem with Satan's words appropriated and set in a new context:

                                  escaped
From the vast city, where I long had pined
A discontented soujourner; now free,

Free as a bird to settle where I will.
What dwelling shall receive me?

Whether Wordsworth wanted us to hear Satan's voice inside his own here (and identify London with Jerusalem on high, and see Satan's wings in that bird, and hear the anguish of the outcast in the question) is the same consideration Ronald Johnson invites throughout his text. At least two voices are speaking: Milton's and Ronald Johnson's.

Blake also rewrote *Paradise Lost,* once as the unfinished epic called *Vala* or *A Dream of Nine Nights* or *The Book of Moonlight,* and once as his poem *Milton.* Blake was correcting and amplifying Milton; he was *opening him up,* as he said. Some day someone will explain why the Romantics wanted to rewrite *Paradise Lost* and the moderns to rewrite the *Odyssey.* And then we will have a clearer understanding of why Ronald Johnson returned, as a signal act of the postmodernist period (The Age of Olson the books will get around to naming it), to Milton. Part of the answer will be that Ronald Johnson began as a latter-day disciple of Blake.

His first poems are modelled on the visionary concerns of a group of young men who used to visit Blake in his old age.

It was an October afternoon in 1824—the year of Byron's death, Beethoven's Ninth, and the completion of the Erie Canal—that the portraitist John Linnell took the young Samuel Palmer to meet William Blake. (If you translate Palmer into a poet, you have Ronald Johnson, not exactly, but close enough.) They found him working in bed on the illustrations to Dante which Linnell had commissioned. (He also commissioned the Job engravings.)

For Palmer, a Baptist and an artist, his mind shaped by scripture, Bunyan, and Milton, it was one of those radiant encounters in which a disciple found his master. Blake had but three years to live. He was old, troubled by piles and gallstones, but his mind was as bright and as fertile as ever. In another, more prosperous, part of London Charles Babbage was building the grandfather of all computers. The steam locomotive had been invented and was already wobbling along a few short rails. The world said that it was now rational, scientific, progressive. When Palmer stepped into Blake's simple house at Fountain Court it was as if he had erased three thousand years of history and stepped into the tent of Isaiah.

Palmer, in turn, brought his mystical friend the pagan painter and engraver Edward Calvert, and eventually an enclave of enthusiastic young men who began to call themselves The Ancients—Palmer's cousin John Giles, the Rev. Arthur Tatham and his brother Frederick, the painter George Richmond, Francis Oliver Finch, Henry Walker, and Welby

Sherman. Only Calvert and Palmer survive in history; Linnell is half-remembered; the others deserve to have their names kept in the list, epic-fashion, because they brightened the last days of Blake and because they are the first members of a family that exists to this day.

Ronald Johnson is very much an Ancient of the tribe of William. The world into which he came (out of Kansas) offered encounters with Charles Olson and Louis Zukofsky, who both had been friends of Ezra Pound, channel of traditions (from him you could be one remove from James, Yeats, Ford, Joyce, or if you were so minded, Brancusi, Gaudier-Brzeska, Cocteau, Gourmont, or again, Wyndham Lewis, Eliot, H. D., John Quinn). At this writing Zukofsky, our greatest living poet, is not considered to be our greatest living poet; Olson is slowly being read and studied. Our liveliest literary tradition, as usual, is an unknown, even an unsuspected one. It is Ronald Johnson's tradition, his family, and the custodian of the things he honors. He came to it through his Iolian friend of a decade, Jonathan Williams, lyrical and satiric master of rhythms and images, whose masters are Olson, Zukofsky, Catullus, Bunting, and the great god Apollo himself.

Ronald Johnson's fund of imagery and tones goes back to Ruskin's precision in description and Thoreau's exact knowledge of nature, back to the visionary eyes of Palmer, Dove, and Burchfield. All that is particular in its splendor belongs to his imagination, Audubon and John Ireland, Cheval the French postman who built an Ideal Palace out of rocks picked up for twenty years, Satie, Arnold Bax, Victorian diarists. He once described my lawn in Kentucky as "all Klimt with violets."

From book to book he has grown more responsive to light and pattern in nature; he believes that light evolved the eye to see itself, an idea that would have made a stir among the Platonists at Chartres in the twelfth century, or in the study of Bishop Grosseteste at Lincoln. The major books are *A Line Of Poetry, A Row of Trees* (1963), *The Different Musics* (1967)—both collected in *Valley of the Many-Colored Grasses* (1969)—*The Book of the Green Man* (1967), *Songs of the Earth* (1970), and the great work now in the writing, *Ark,* part 1 of which is finished, part 4 of which may be *Radi os*.

The paradox of originality houses many rooms, and the views from the windows are all different. What the artist seems to create has, as the artist is the first to appreciate and acknowledge, already been created. Design and arrangement are the artist's passion. *Place* is all. The painters of Lascaux found their horses in the rock. Wherever there was a bulge in the cave wall that suggested equine solidity, they surrounded it with an elegance of mane, legs, and tail. The nose was drawn first, then, in a masterful stroke, the beautiful line from face to butt, the horizon of horse. We have found this line all by itself, whether unfinished or sufficient to say "horse" we shall never know. This line survives in the Chinese ideogram meaning horse, *ma,* together with the prancing legs that are man's first graph of the verb *to move.* Poetry and painting have a passport through time; historical styles which are the essence of a work of art to the historian are the artist's last consideration. So there is no anomaly in Ronald Johnson's choosing Milton to fuse into a new poetic symbiosis. The choice, however, was pure genius.

Toward the end of the nineteenth century Milton was already going out of fashion. Men with the surest command of English—especially the two masters Doughty and Hopkins—were turning away from the Renaissance donation of English diction and going back to native words and phrases. Yeats and Pound (outlanders, note) completed the process toward a natural, genial diction, and Milton was damned for writing no English at all. He was artificial. He was Latinate. (This is illusion. Eighty per cent of the words in *Paradise Lost* are of Anglo-Saxon derivation. Milton used far fewer Latinisms than Gibbon, and only sixty percent of Shakespeare's words are of English origin. And he was the most sparing of stylists—the word *afternoon* occurs but once in all his writing, *abrupt, inconvenient,* and *American*).

Milton was indeed artificial. His sonorous, highly pictorial style was evolved to impose classical form on one of the most energetic languages since Greek. A meticulously conscious artist in an age that knew the usefulness of art, Milton understood exactly where he was in history, and what he had to do to give his art its step in the pace of time.

Time, Pythagoras had said, is the mind of the stars. The book in which you could have found that sentence was printed in Paris in 1552, a translation into Latin of Plutarch's *On the Generation of the Soul.* Within the decade men would be born in England who would invent a poetry which they imagined was like that of the ancient world. All Europe by this time knew that a lost world was being recovered, a world that contained Plato and Homer, Pythagoras and Plutarch, Diodorus the Sicilian, St. Jerome and Virgil, Ovid and Catullus.

The first bright dawn of the Renaissance in England did not take time to study the economy of tone of the Greek and Latin which it was eager to have in English. With the old genius of British poetry the first translators went at their matter undaunted, godlike. Here is Arthur Golding doing Ovid:

She scarce had said these words, but that she leaped on the wave,
And getting to the ships by force of strength that Love hir gave,
Upon the King of *Candies* Keele in spight of him she clave.
Whome when hir father spide (for now he hovered in the aire,

And being made a Hobby Hauke did soare between a paire
Of nimble wings on yron Mayle) he soused down a maine
To seaze upon hir as she hung, and would have torn hir faine
With bowing Beake.

George Chapman translating Homer:

This shield thus done, he forg'd for him such curets as outshin'd
The blaze of fire. A helmet then (through which no steele could find
Forc't passage) he composde, whose hue a hundred colours tooke;
And in the crest a plume of gold, that each breath stirr'd, he stucke.
All done, he all to Thetis brought, and held up all to her.
She tooke them all, and like t' the hawke (surnamed the Osspringer),
From Vulcan to her mightie sonne, with that so glorious show,
Stoopt from the steepe Olympian hill, hid in eternall snow.

This robustness and headlong meter would be tamed by Marlowe, Shakespeare, Jonson, Spenser, each in his own tone (Shakespeare in a hundred tones), yet the energy remained, and the idiom remained English, glorious English. In this second perfection of the language (the first was Chaucer), the Bible was translated with a majesty of phrasing, a music of nuance and pause, a strength of diction that has never been equalled in any version of scripture:

Lift up your heads, O yee gates,
And be ye lift up ye everlasting doores;
And the King of glory shall come in.
Who is this king of glory?
The LORD strong and mightie,
The LORD mighty in battell.

The poet who would achieve a new vision of English poetry and turn it irrevocably toward the pure models of Greek and Latin was the latecomer Milton. As a baby he could have looked out the window and seen Shakespeare and Jonson in their tall, dove-gray felt hats and royal blue capes, for he lived on the street that one took to get to the tavern with a mermaid on its shingle.

We have no notion what served Shakespeare for religion, the scholarly and stubborn Jonson was sometimes Protestant, sometimes Catholic; English intellectuals were apt to run to Corinthian manners until reminded by the cannon's mouth or the headsman's ax that they were Christians. The young Milton was pious and grave, a Puritan with something of a private theology (as his greatest emulator Blake knew very well). Like other Puritans he was a humanist, cherishing pagan lore for its beauty and wisdom (Cotton Mather read his Ovid along with his Calvin). He dyed his mind with Latin, Greek, and Hebrew at Cambridge, did the grand tour (Galileo let him look through his telescope, and probably assured him in whispers that Copernicus was right: the earth is a planet among others that circles the sun, which great light, like God, moves all without itself moving).

He became Latin secretary to Protector Cromwell (on whose guns was inscribed "God is Love"), and here he read and wrote himself blind. When the king returned, he withdrew into a houseful of daughters and composed his epic. We are told that he got the lines straight in his head upon waking, and in the freshness of the morning announced that he was ready to be milked. He sat across a chair, his back against one arm, his knees over the other. One visitor described him in a suit of rusty green, and we are told that before bedtime he regaled himself with the pleasure of a pipe of Virginia tobacco and a cold glass of water. Even in his blindness he wore his sword.

The great poem he dictated—twice, as he expanded it amost immediately after its first edition from ten to twelve books—was the greatest verbal expression of the Baroque style which culminates the Renaissance, aggrandizing its spirit to a lyric grandeur. Music to Shakespeare was the lute; to Milton, the organ.

While he dictated, the long rule of Louis XIV began, no rain fell in India for three whole years, Velazquez painted the Spanish court and Vermeer Dutch housewives pouring milk, the Turks cut their way through Hungary and Transylvania toward Vienna, and certain children were born and baptized Daniel Defoe, Henry Purcell, Matthew Prior. In the American colonies Michael Wigglesworth published *The Day of Doom,* which sold more copies than any book of poetry ever published in this country.

And 310 years later a poet in San Francisco sits down with the text and begins to erase it. So that it now begins "O tree into the world, Man the chosen Rose out of Chaos: song." Trees come into the world (from seeds underground) in answer to light, and once there they convert our breath into oxygen which we breathe again, and they digest light in order to ferment water and minerals which they have brought up from the earth into a nourishing green, which we can eat, or eat the animal that has eaten the green. No tree, no man. We rose out of chaos together, and the rose is an order of petals symbolizing the opposite of chaos.

The poem we are reading is still Milton's, but sifted. The spare scattering of words left on the page continues to make a coherent poem, Milton *imagiste.* (Wordsworth and Blake did the same thing to the poem, except that they filled up the spaces again with their own words.) Strange and wonderful things happen on these pages. Here, for instance, Milton is made to anticipate the first Duino Elegy:

Who, from the terror of this
            empyreal
Irreconcilable
                    of joy
        answered
Too well I see
            : for the mind
swallowed up
                    entire,
    in the heart        to work in fire,
            words The Arch.

These pages at first glance look haphazard (as a Cubist painting seemed to first viewers to be an accident). They are not. There is a page that has the word *man* at the top, *flower* in the middle, and *star* at the bottom. There are other words on the page, and they help us see the relationship between man, flower, and star. One order of words gives: "man passed through fire / His temple right against the black." It is, for instance, electrochemical energy in brain cells derived from photosynthetic sugars in vegetables whereby we can see a star at all, and the fire of the star we call the sun thus arranged that it could be seen and thought of by nourishing the brain. Is that system closed? Did the sun grow the tree that made the paper you are holding, and the ink on it, so that it can read this book through your eyes?

The eye as a kind of scanner for the sun is an idea with a glimpse of God in it. It is knowledge. In Milton's myth man was created to be like a lion, with instincts. Such a creature fulfills itself by being an excellent lion (the rose knows nothing but to be a rose). He feels, breeds, fights, eats, sleeps. He will never know the harmony of numbers or compose a partita. He will never build an Ideal Palace or tell a folktale to his nieces or nephews. But he lives in a paradise. If he were to lose that paradise, he would have to begin finding it again.

He would know he was in an alien state, and his knowledge would be tragic. The knowledge of good and evil that man chose turned out to be (as he could not have suspected) meaningless. He could know facts, which are neutral, heartless, apt to serve one opinion as well as another. To knowledge must be added grace. It is at this turning of Milton's plot that Ronald Johnson seems to have become interested in following Milton through his maze of words, intent on mining a particular ore, on isolating, for greater clarity, a single radiant quality.

When Satan (who is the essence of nothing) tempted man into knowedge, he exiled him from lionhood, from a harmony with creation. We can call this a blindness, and the search for understanding a hunger for vision. It was Blake who saw that seeing eyes can be perfectly blind, that they can see without that special gift of apprehension that he identified with Christ, redemption, and grace. Milton calls the mind "infinitude confined" (Ronald Johnson retains these words in his erasure).

Nature has no nothing. To feel that it has is what we call the devil, the enemy. In Blakean words, our predicament is that we can exist and still not be, for being requires an awakeness from the dream of custom and of ourselves. The self is by nature turned outward to connect with the harmony of things. The eyes cannot see themselves, but something other. The strange and paradoxical rule of nature is that we are fullest in our being by forgetting our being. To love nothing is to be nothing, to give is to have.

*Radii* are the lines outward from a center. We exist because of the radii of the sun (because of the radii of God, Milton would say). Radiance, wheel after wheel of it, whether of benevolence or music or attention, is a basic pattern of life.

Knowledge is a kind of ignorance, ignorance a kind of knowledge. This peculiarly American perception runs through our literature, welling up from our experience. Wind brought us over, pushing sails, and spirit brought us over, pushing minds, and our greatest efforts have always been to harness energy. With forgivable innocence and unforgivable arrogance we mistook the knowledge of others for ignorance as often as we mistook our ignorance for knowledge. Learning has always therefore been a conversion for us. Our literature is one of persuasion and discovery, of vision.

Behind the mask of custom there is a natural life, our poets have always said; inside history, light. Our calipers for taking the measure of nature have never been on a human scale. Melville saw that a spermatozoon is a microscopic whale. Gertrude Stein, remembering Emerson, said that moonlight in a valley is before and after history. Poe could find a symbol for all of European civilization—Alaric the Visigoth's black crow surmounting a bust of Athene—and make a ghost story of it. We have sought a thoroughly enigmatic and inclusive symbol of the world in all our art, showing fear in a handful of dust, affection in a handful of grass ("I guess it must be the handkerchief of the Lord"), death in the buzz of a fly.

Foragers by destiny, we like to go into familiar places and make a new report of the contents—Henry Adams to Chartres, Pound to China, Olson to Yucatan. All too characteristically we have no notion what we're looking for; we are simply looking. Something, we feel—the national hunch—is always there. Louis Zukofsky began writing "A" in 1925, finishing it fifty years later (the first long American poem to be finished since Melville's *Clarel*), making it up as he went along, like an architect who put in a foundation without any idea whether he would continue in glass or brick. So Olson wrote his *Maximus,* Williams his *Paterson,* Pound his *Cantos,* Whitman his *Leaves of Grass.*

Ronald Johnson is writing a long poem called *Ark,* various schema on his worktable, visions in his head. It is a poem that grows naturally out of the concerns of his earlier poetry, unfolding them like a sunrise maturing toward noontide. But no sooner had he moved into this complex and brilliant poem, a masterpiece of new forms and rhythms, than he (true American forager) found an idea along the way. He found a poem inside another poem. All he had to do was to remove the superfluous words.

Works of art in response to other works of art create a symbolic chord reaching across the two. Ulysses in Ithaca, Ulysses in Dublin: a web of meaning not entirely under Joyce's control bridges the extremes and begins generating ratios. We can recognize in Ronald Johnson's derived poem an image of America as a paradise lost; it is a theme of the times. We can recognize the constant American theme of wondering all over again what to do with the gift of creation. Milton had the sense that the Reformation was waking the human spirit to things it had abandoned through error and negligence. It is a valid and perhaps urgent purpose for poetry to speak to a people who, at worst, have no vision of the gift of being other than to make money, slide (or rip) around in an automobile, and to spend the rest of their time before a box that alternately informs them that Haley's M.O. unclogs the sluggish bowel and that fighting continues in the streets of Beirut.

*Radi os* is a meditation, first of all, on grace. It finds in Milton's poems those clusters of words which were originally a molecular intuition of the complex harmony of nature whereby eyesight loops back to its source in the sun, the earth, the tree, our cousin animals, the spiralling galaxies, and mysteriously to the inhuman black of empty space. Out of these elements ("creation" was Milton's word) arose our imagined gods and our social order. At the center of the Greek spirit was a meditation on the origin of wheat. (By analogy the center of the American spirit should be a temple to petroleum, but we don't have even that.)

As I write this a spaceship is circling Mars, its computer eyes looking for a place to land. It will report back, if it functions, that there is nothing there but desolation. A similar voyage to all the other planets will report nothing, nothing, nothing. That we are alone in a universe of red stars and white stars, a catastrophe of light and electric thunder of time, vibrant forever, forever bright, fifty-eight sextillion, seven hundred quintillion, seven hundred and sixty quadrillion miles wide (by Einstein's reckoning), is the plain fact our age will have to learn to live with, as Milton in his lifetime had to learn that the earth is a planet of the sun, a smallish star.

The astronomers are beginning to tell us about events in space called black holes and naked particularities. Some cycle has made a revolution and come around again to a point where Milton made a vision of the world and of man's place in it. That our new moment is still somehow Miltonic is Ronald Johnson's discovery, a discovery that only a poet could make, a discovery that enhances and sharpens our sense of poetry and opens our eyes in a new way to the world.

# *Poetry*'s Golden

While the First National Poetry Festival convened in Coolidge Auditorium of the Library of Congress to celebrate the fiftieth anniversary of *Poetry: A Magazine of Verse,* one of the hardier survivors of the Renaissance of 1910 (its founder and first editor Harriet Monroe died in 1936; its present editor is the poet Henry Rago), and to inaugurate an annual *Oktoberfest,* sponsored by the Republic, of recitations and critical scrutiny, Ezra Pound dozed under his editor's eyeshade on the Via MacKay in Rapallo; William Carlos Williams sat in the morning sun among his Demuths, Sheelers, and Audubons at 9 Ridge Road, Rutherford, N.J., T. S. Eliot was at his desk in Russell Square; Marianne Moore was painting watercolors in Greece. At the last minute Robert Penn Warren fell ill in Connecticut and Robert Lowell and John Hall Wheelock sent their regrets. Archibald MacLeish, Conrad Aiken, and Arthur

205

Freeman budged not from Cambridge. Kenneth Patchen, Allen Ginsberg, Lawrence Ferlinghetti, Gregory Corso, Carl Sandburg, Richmond Lattimore, and W. H. Auden moved in courses which did not transverse the Library of Congress, where one could hear a confused high-school girl saying to the battalion of poetic genius before her, "But, I mean, you're all *college professors!*"

The festival raged for three days, mornings, afternoons, and evenings. There were some heady moments, some beautiful fights, and in among the heavyweight talk some fine exchanges among masters of words, as when Muriel Rukeyser, embattled in a plea for volcanic spontaneity as the unfettered condition of poetry, brought J. V. Cunningham to his feet to say, "Madame, you are an eloquent and warm-blooded woman. I am a cold-blooded reductionist. Let us leave it at that." Whereupon Sir Herbert Read announced that form was shape, and that shape was economy. Cunningham rose again. "Sir Herbert," he said, "my meditations on form began in profound disagreement with you and I have had no occasion to change my mind."

The session, given over to worrying publicly about poetry's audience in America, began in antique ideas and soon foundered. Miss Babette Deutsch (Mrs. Avrahm Yarmolinsky), still on the barricades of the twenties, asked (glass of water in hand), "Who answers to the name of poet, what manner of man or woman?" Her water reminded her that Shelley, Hart Crane, Virginia Woolf, and Li Po all drowned. Then she assured us that no beatniks were present and that only Sir Herbert Read spoiled the gathering's being a proletarian bloc. As evidence of poetry's hard times Miss Deutsch produced *The Congressional Anthology,* offensive in the first instance through its sponsorship by the International Christian Leaders, a "pious and patriotic" club, and in the second by its generous connoisseurship of Edgar Albert Guest and Ella Wheeler Wilcox. Kipling's "If" and Joyce Kilmer's "Trees" also appear in this compendium (Kenton Kilmer, the poet's son, was in our audience) along with other *detrimenta.* Whereas, we are told, Russian poets of the first water enjoy a "large and enthusiastic public," Tovarishch Yevtushenko and his following being evinced as a more ideal relationship than the "American poet can claim" (except, of course, those who don't deserve it and get quoted by legislators). Langston Hughes jovially denied Miss Deutsch's contentions, giving his own lively career as counter-evidence.

Mr. Howard Nemerov spoke in despair. A sweet despair, to be sure, and having made a disclaimer of patriotism for himself and one for poetry as "a ministry of propaganda and culture," he animadverted on the delicate uselessness of poetry, shuddered to contemplate "the grim phalanx of poets" before him, announced that "life is hopeless and beautiful," and sat down.

Mr. Karl Shapiro wistfully reported that Yevtushenko's poetry sells in editions of 100,000, begged not to be mistaken for a patriot if he used the adjective "American," recommended euthanasia for American poetry, and revealed that the real poetry of the U.S. is its prose. "The dawn of American poetry still lies ahead."

There was an embarrassing moment when Mr. John Klapack asked, "What is a poem?" Richard Wilbur, to whom the question was directed, declined to answer. Mr. Nemerov offered an emendation of Archibald MacLeish: a poem should mean *and* be. Mr. Untermeyer also declined to answer the question but warned us that poets are not seers nor sages nor philosophers. Mr. Wilbur then proceeded to suggest that if one has to ask, one is never going to know what a poem is.

From time to time within the polemic, rhetorical questions, and incredibly opaque formal papers ("the *impulsion* to continue with the alexandrine," "a poetic hold of a focus of a range of reference") there were hopeful moments when it seemed that someone might say something significant. "I have never heard the beatniks read," John Crowe Ransom said, "but I understand that they sometimes read to musical accompaniment." Prof. James V. Baker, of the University of Houston, referred to Allen Ginsberg's *Howl* as "a verbal vomit" and hoped that Allen Tate would agree; but Mr. Tate refused "to authorize that identification." Miss Deutsch declared that our poets will be read when "superannuated ideas are not allowed to control twentieth-century weapons, and it must be soon," and when she was asked to retract her words, quoted Kierkegaard on the propensities of swine. Mr. Tate confessed publicly that he had recently refused to write for the *Saturday Evening Post* and now feels that he did wrong. And so it went, until one began to see that panel discussions will go down in history as one of the characteristic aberrations of our age, as peculiar to us as bull leaping to Cnossans.

Robert Frost, entering, brought the audience to its feet. The real tradition which for three days eluded the wits and embarrassed the critics was palpably present. With shuffling nonchalance the smiling poet began to construct the past that had cared for him in his beginning: Harold Munro, "a poet who ran a bookstore," his early publishers, Susan Hayes Ward, Thomas Byrd Mosher, Edward Thomas, Lascelles Abercrombie, Mark Van Doren. He saved until the end of his talk his eulogy to Harriet Monroe and Ezra Pound. Two themes figured in intricate contrast through his splendidly rambling talk. One was a modest but firm inspection of the spirit of his own poetry. "It's tone I'm in love with; that's what poetry is, tone." The other was a sly, shrewd commentary on his recent Russian visit, which he ironically called "an experiment in translation that turned out to be an absolute loss." "I couldn't see if my poetry was any good in Russian and they couldn't see if I was any good in English. It was like duelling with battle-axes at a hundred yards in fog." When he complained that *they* cannot distinguish grievance from grief, that is, politics from poetry, one felt that *they* were not merely "the Great Man" (he referred to Khrushchev in no other way throughout) and all his works and all he stands for, but the forces inimical to poetry everywhere. "A Liberal," he said, "is a man too broadminded to take his own side in a quarrel." And: "A Liberal would rather fuss with the Gordian knot than cut it." He remembered that the Great Man had said to him, "As Gorki remarked to Tolstoy," 'There's such a thing as a country's being too soft-hearted to fight.'" Then with mischief in his eyes: "Very intellectual, that Great Man!"

No one imagined that this grand old voice was anything but independence itself, nonpartisan except to his own tough mastery of poetry and a jealous love of freedom. He had, "out of courtesy," referred to "our two kinds of democracy" in the Great Man's presence and had been assured by him personally of Russia's dedication to peace. The Cuban rockets were being seated even as those words were spoken and as Frost spoke that night our fleet was on its way to effect the blockade. "I feel let down by him, you know."

But if the manipulators of grievances had let him down, so had the defenders against grief, the poets before him. It was tradition and its memory and care that he insisted on finally. He accused his learned audience of not knowing its real past. To prove it, he quoted lovingly a passage of poetry beginning "The old agitation of myrtles and roses . . ." and confidently but sadly said that no one there could identify it. And no one could.

# Where Poems Come From

Books have family resemblances and tribal affinities. Stanley Burnshaw's treatise on the poetic afflatus, *The Seamless Web* (1970), is a grandchild of Arthur Koestler's *The Act of Creation* (1964) and *The Ghost in the Machine* (1967) and is a cousin to René Dubos's *So Human an Animal* and all the recent books we've been getting from the New Biology and its attendant prophets—roughly Konrad Lorenz and his circle. The slightly sinister figure of Eugène Marais haunts these new Calvinists—Marais, the Roger Casement of biology. It was he, the obscure South African amateur scientist writing perversely in Afrikaans and wearing his misanthropy like an opera cape, who tore open the closed question of man's instincts and started the search for a definition of man that does not set out in blind faith that we are born blank-minded. Along with the news that we are born programmed with the instincts of the animal we are, has come a spill of attendant suspicions. If man is a brute only partially tamed, he is also an artist and a scientist. Might not the same spooky instincts that drive him to his aggression, jealousy, mad possessiveness, and other ape-like postures lie at the root of his creativeness? Mr. Koestler has pondered this notion with much learning, and now Mr. Burnshaw has searched through hundreds of books and come up with a raggle-taggle and breathless report on the source of poetry from deep down in the artesian wells and half-explored ravines of the central nervous system.

Or so he says. It is difficult to decide if the trouble with Mr. Burnshaw's book is that he labors his subject until we are on our knees crying for mercy, or if he has brought in so many quotations that his own perspicacity gets lost in the heap. In any case, Mr. Burnshaw has read entirely too many books. The result is a confusion of voices. Open *The Seamless Web* at random and you will find on a single page (106) quotations from Heraclitus, Yeats, A. C. Bradley, Goethe, Eckermann, Blake, Plato, Maritain, and Bacon. The next page begins with Bacon quoting Lucretius quoting Anaxagoras. Good company, God knows, but let loose all together they elbow each other a little, and Mr. Burnshaw is talking right along with them.

The reader must therefore find with some ingenuity the subject of Mr. Burnshaw's essay. Whatever it is, it is diffused through so many randomly posited testimonials, illustrations, and obliquities that it is rather finely shredded by the time one has hold of it. I think the question asked by the essay is this: What spiritual state generated poetry? And the further question: What good is poetry to man? The answer Mr. Burnshaw likes to this second question is one given by John Keble, who said that poetry keeps man sane. So do all the arts, I should think, from carpentry to music.

To answer his first question Mr. Burnshaw moves eclectically through the New Biology, the *obiter dicta* of hundreds of poets, and a library of criticism. He has found many a treasure, and the reading of this rich book ought perhaps to be a relaxed state in which one simply listens to Mr. Burnshaw's fervent monologue. It is like being in the room with a charmingly intelligent man who has found a big subject in several hundred books. He attacks the subject this way, that way, pointing out this astuteness and that perception, all the while taking down book after book and reading the relevant passage. Having heard him to the end, you are still a bit puzzled as to how you might condense it all for its coherence and thrust, but you are aware that it is an important discussion you've heard. And that may be the immediate usefulness of this book: it invites speculation, arouses new curiosities, and may fling down a gauntlet. I found myself being most grateful for Mr. Burnshaw's dismissing the current vulgar opinion that poetry is self-expression.

At the risk of offering a map in primary colors for what in reality is a densely wooded kingdom, I think we might say that Mr. Burnshaw wants to tunnel through the world of Descartes and Locke and get back to the primal sense of art as inspiration, possession, vision. And he wants to do it not with enthusiasm and wishful thinking but with the unviolated reason of science, or at least with the moral support of several advance scouting parties among the biologists. He wants to locate the origin of poetry neither in the desire for elegant self-expression nor in the rational, objective desire of the artist to be a steady fulcrum for the world's moral uplift. Poetry comes rather from a more intricate and unexplored source. It comes not from the mind but from the body.

Such an idea can be both maddeningly intractable and wonderfully useful. Mr Burnshaw finds in it the discernible heaves and throbs of the power of poetry to move us with variously modulated emotions. Metric derives from the dance; the music of poetry is therefore addressed to and originates in the muscles. The tongue dances right along with feet and arms, and there is obviously some plexus deep in the inwards of the central nervous system that is the heart of the dance. Every movement of a poem can be traced to corresponding physical resonances. Like music and painting, it arises from the total organism.

Mr. Burnshaw, with these potent matters before him, devotes the greater part of his energies to the fact that poetry, like any creative impulse, is more likely than not born in the anarchy of strong emotion, and must be tamed before being shaped into a symbol of universal comprehension. The poem is born raw and bloody, the darkness of dreams still clinging to it. It is frequently in conflict with the code of the tribe. If it is a successful poem, it has the business of modifying the sensibilities of the order into which it is introduced. Mr. Burnshaw's arguing of these perceptions proceeds with much heat and perhaps too much documentation and illustration. The reader finds himself longing for an outline, or for a succinct graph.

The reader will also find himself practically at every point wanting to join in the discussion. Any knowledge of the arts will never overlap another knowledge of the arts, and I must now continue this essay not as a formal response to a book which I have been asked to assess for the reading community, but as a response from a particular reader who has found the book to be extremely interesting but also a little confusing and sometimes wide of its aim.

First of all, I kept building up expectations that were not satisfied. I thought surely that Mr. Burnshaw would get around to the very modern thinkers and artists who seem to me to have contributed to his subject. Nowhere, for instance, do I find Ray L. Birdwhistell, Jr., the wizard kinesiologist who knows more about eyesight, the movements of the body, and the reverberations of emotion within the body than any man alive. If reading a poem makes the hair crawl on the back of your neck, Dr. Birdwhistell also knows that it is making your left toe twitch and the right eye dilate a minim. It will be a great day when Mr. Burnshaw meets Dr. Birdwhistell.

And Stan Brakhage. His *Metaphors on Vision* is as resourceful a set of insights into the creative process as we have had recently, and Brakhage's store of knowledge about the body and perception is (I suspect) way out in advance of science.

And Robert Kelly, that great singer of the body? And Gottfried Benn and his ideas about primal vision? And Louis Zukofsky and Charles Olson and their clarities about breathing? Thomas Mann figures in the network of quotations not for his fascinating analyses of the creative process but as the purveyor of a secondary source for a quotation of Dostoievsky. Joyce is passed over altogether. It is, of course, absurd to keep pointing out what one would like to see in a book. But these inattentions serve to define a curious thing about this book: it is flattened against the centrifuge of a passionate argument.

When Mr. Burnshaw writes such a sentence as, "To anyone personally acquainted with creative artists, the picture of poets busying themselves for the high purpose of producing objects to give other people pleasure or instruction or knowledge or moral guidance is simply too ludicrous to be borne," he discloses his determination to believe that poetry can only be the voice of a possessed initiate. He also condescends from an apparent vantage of great privilege; even so, I who am less privileged, would like to witness for the opposite view and say that it is not in the least ludicrous to imagine poets producing objects (curious phrase!) to give other people pleasure, instruction, knowledge, and moral guidance. In fact, it seems to me to be the great enterprise of modern poetry to do just that; we live amongst the most moralistic pack of versifiers ever to be set loose on a public since the days of Michael Wigglesworth. Allen Ginsberg is a minor Hebrew prophet, Robert Lowell a master of the didactic, Gregory Corso a friar scholastic, Robert Creeley an anguished moralist. Poetry is not yet capable of escaping from the context given it by Transcendentalism. I cannot think of a poet who does not think of himself as having a purpose and a high calling.

What in the world would the reviewers and professors *do* if we were to have a Catullus or a Sappho? There has been only one poet in English since Christopher Smart who was untouched by the moral fervor of Transcendentalism; there's no need to add that he's unread. In fact, there's greater purpose in not mentioning his name, as it would be tossing his crown of laurel into bewilderment and indifference.

That is, for all his careful inspection of the kinds of voice with which poems speak, Mr. Burnshaw sees *the poem* as a particular kind of poetry to the exclusion of other kinds. Poetry for him is lyric or elegiac almost wholly, and I think what moves him is *song,* the rich surge of emotion, the radiant glory of speech in flight. This is splendid, of course, but it tends toward a puritanism that diminishes our taste for the comic, the satiric, the grotesque, the narrative poem, the wholesome and drab.

Poetry is most certainly, as Mr. Burnshaw elucidates, the most intense of man's voices. To devote a long and intricate book to its source within the spirit, and to the tensions of its creation and reception, is an enterprise that can only be praised, particularly when it is written by a scholar as inexhaustibly curious and as well read as Mr. Burnshaw.

Yet I feel that there is a limiting asymmetry to this study—a missing room to the structure. An inspection of origins ought also to concern itself with final causes. Our century is time-bound in its psychological bias; future ages will marvel at our inwardness, at the fervor of our subjectivity. It would be useful to have a companion book to Mr. Burnshaw's treatise on the birth of poems—a study of poetry in the world, its effectiveness and its usefulness. I would like to think that the use of poetry is to teach. Within the arts we have the memory of mankind in a way no other continuum of culture has kept the useful past. Science is self-erasing and constantly under revision. The ecological skills shift as the age demands.

It is true that the arts keep us sane, but a larger bias for this perception is surely the fact that the arts keep us civilized. Once a poem is written, it belongs to the world, and its greatest destiny is its usefulness to the tribe. Language is perpetually refined by the poet, the eye is taught by the painter, the ear by the composer. The psychology of aesthetics is of limited interest when we note that poetry teaches with a greater force than it entertains. The tragedy of our time may be that the two fierce voices—Ruskin's and Pound's—which cried out that the arts are the teachers of morality first and foremost are precisely the easiest voices to discount as those of charming cranks. One might do worse than notice that these two cranks made the most extensive studies of the arts of their two centuries and guarded the highest excellence of the arts, and that they knew what they were talking about.

And (if my experience with the teaching of poetry to students is in any way typical) it is worthwhile adding that the power of the poem to teach not only sensibilities and the subtle movements of the spirit but knowledge, real lasting *felt* knowledge, is going unnoticed among the scholars and pedagogues. The body of knowledge locked into and releasable from poetry can replace practically any university in the Republic. First things first, then. The primal importance of a poem is what it can add to the individual mind.

Poetry is the voice of a poet at its birth, the voice of a people in its ultimate fulfilment as a successful and useful work of art.

*Ere Babylon was dust,*
*The Magus Zoroaster, my dead child,*
*Met his own image walking in the garden.*
*That apparition, sole of men, he saw.*
*(Shelley,* Prometheus Unbound*)*

*I too would pelt the pelted one:*
*At my shadow I cast a stone.*

*When lo, upon that sunlit ground*
*I saw the quivering phantom take*
*The likeness of St. Stephen crowned:*
*Then did self-reverence awake.*
*(Melville,* Shelley's Vision*)*

*. . . it chanced that the vapory fleece hanging low in the*
*East, was shot through with a soft glory as the fleece of*
*the Lamb of God seen in mystical vision and*
*simultaneously therewith, watched by the wedged mass*
*of upturned faces, Billy ascended; and, ascending, took*
*the full rose of the dawn.*
*(Melville,* Billy Budd, Foretopman*)*

---

# Ishmael's Double

---

I

"I felt a melting in me," Ishmael says, speaking of his first days in
Queequeg's company. "No more my splintered heart and maddened
hand were turned against the wolfish world. This soothing savage
had redeemed it" (*Moby-Dick*, ch. 10). Each of the well nigh nameless
protagonists of Melville's first six novels, all young voyagers—
"Tommee," "Typee," "Taji," Redburn, "White Jacket," Ishmael—is
furnished with a bosom friend. Four of them are companions in adventure, chums. One, Dr. Long Ghost of *Omoo,* is a kind of father to the
protagonist. Queequeg, in whom Melville's conception of the ideal companion reaches its fullest development, but not its end, is brother, father,
and by his own symbolic Polynesian code, marriage partner. "Now this
*chummying* among sailors," Taji says in *Mardi,* "is like the brotherhood
subsisting between a brace of collegians (chums) rooming together. It is a

Fidus-Achatesship, a league of offence and defence, a copartnership of chests and toilets, a bond of love and good feeling, and a mutual championship of the absent one" (*Mardi*, ch. 3).

The companion in fiction, especially heroic fiction, is, of course, very old indeed—Gilgamesh had his Enkidu—but our interest here is the distinctive rôle the companion fills in Melville's novels and tales. Melville's companions, I hope to show, eventually merge with the hero, or, rather, replace him and grow into Billy Budd, Melville's symbolic good man in combat with evil.

Melville's heroines grow into that powerful-willed wife of "I and My Chimney" and "The Apple-Tree Table" or into that clayey woman Goneril of *The Confidence-Man*. The very real Fayaway, though perhaps betraying in her punning name the impossibility of her existence, gives way to the phantom Yillah. Lucy, more properly at home in Hawthorne or Dickens, is replaced by the enigma Isabel. After that, there are only wretched wives, and wretched maids in a paper mill. There is a noble woman in *The Encantadas,* but she is less than a heroine. For Melville the *alter ego* was male and complementary, a hearty friend, never a mirror of folly like Sancho Panza or a conscience like Poe's William Wilson's double. In his old age Melville wrote:

> I dream of the hearts-of-gold sped—
> The Falernian fellows—
> Hafiz and Horace,
> And Beranger—all
> Dextrous tumblers eluding the Fall,
> Fled, can be sped?
> But the marigold's morris
> Is danced o'er their head;
> And their memory mellows,
> Embalmed and becharmed,
> Hearts-of-gold and good fellows![1]

One of the suppositions to be derived from the hero and his companion is that the imagination in creating a heroic character nevertheless conceives of a real character and spills those traits and impulses denied the hero into a character at once complementary and contrasting. This would seem true of the American cowboy and his side-kick: the wholly serious, chaste Gene Autrey and the faithful clown Smiley Burnette. It would seem true of many another popular hero in fiction and myth.[2] The shin-

---

[1] Herman Melville, *Poems* (London: Constable, 1924), p. 428.

[2] As early in the recorded human imagination as the Gilgamesh fragments, the hero's companion was given a license denied the hero—a situation that tumbles over into comedy quite often (lean Don Quijote and Sancho Panza, "holy tummy"). Enkidu, a wild, pastoral figure who understands the language of animals, is seduced by a city prostitute. This is his

ing improbability of the Lone Ranger is made up for by the good, friendly Tonto: almost an apology for so doughty and detached an instrument. Huck Finn's unlikely sexual innocence is answered for, tacitly, in Nigger Jim, who under the slave-holding code was not accountable for immorality so long as it was within his own race.

Melville seems to have conceived of the companion as an ideal climate for the protagonist's comfort. In *Omoo* the companion is comic; in *Typee* he is romantic; in *Mardi,* sea hardy; in *Redburn,* a gentleman; in *White Jacket,* heroic and a paragon of all things nautical, the sailor's sailor; in *Moby-Dick,* the epitome of that Polynesian life which lay fertile in Melville's heart, the pagan stoic, part Horatio, part Odysseus, kind, loyal, wise, self-controlled, at peace with his world. To serve such a function, the companion is almost wholly imaginary, created to fill a need that grows less urgent as each novel progresses. The companions, save in *Moby-Dick,* have their big scene in opening chapters and then fade into the background.

Melville's fascination with the *alter ego* is decidedly of its time. If Hugh Henry Brackenridge's John Farrago and his Irish servant Teague Oregan are in strict imitation of the picaresque tradition, and Cooper's pioneers and Indians create almost imperishable archetypes (the Indian and the Negro are neatly together as attendant companions in *The Redskins*), the subtler conceptions of the hero's *alter ego* begin to be developed in Poe, for whom the ego is an imperishable substance, capable of being divided against itself ("The Fall of the House of Usher"), of being passed on to other bodies ("Morella"), of being split into two beings ("William Wilson"), of entering into animals ("Metzengerstein"), of stopping bestially half-formed in its development ("The Murders in the Rue Morgue," "Hop Frog") and wrecking all before it with the savagery of the jungle. As Poe's characters go into or emerge from the dark, either companionless, or, excepting *Arthur Gordon Pym,* with insignificant companions, Melville's characters proceed to an *impasse*—Bartleby's wall, shipless

---

"civilizing," that he might serve as auxiliary strongman to Gilgamesh. After a week with the seductress he can no longer understand the animals, and can but to the city to serve. Yet he remains uncouth and Samson-ish beside his more polished comrade. See Alexander Heidel, *The Gilgamesh Epic and Old Testament Parallels,* 2nd. ed. (Chicago: University of Chicago Press, 1949).

Robinson Crusoe's Friday remains a disciple and body servant, even in Europe, and begins to play a comic rôle (the bear-baiting scene in the Pyrénées) which the dour Crusoe would never find a bent for. The subject of hero and companion is, of course, enormous. Note Stephen Dedalus and Buck Mulligan and the complex symbolism attached to them: Mithraic priest and acolyte, Sir Gawain and the Green Knight, Hal and Falstaff, etc. The situation is levelled out in Pantagruel and Panurge, and in Wu Ch'êng-ên's *Monkey* the companion usurps the stage, so that the novel's real hero, the monk Tripitaka, stands second to the doings of Monkey, a situation quite frequent in popular literature; for example, Walt Disney's *Ben and Me,* in which the Franklin myth is presented as the achievement of a prudent mouse who had Ben's ear.

Ishmael, Israel Potter before his moss-covered cord of wood—well provided with companions.[3] But between Poe and Melville there is the kinship of *Pym* and *Moby-Dick,* and the character of the half-breed Peters, replacing gradually the initial Toby-Harry-Bolton-like *alter-ego* Augustus, seems to foreshadow the movement in Melville from spirited, genteel companions to a tougher sort: Jack Chase and Queequeg. Yet Dirk Peters is all brawn and pioneer cunning; he does not, like Queequeg, stand by the hero to remind him of his innate nobility, although the germ of that idea may be in him. It remained for Hawthorne, in the years of Melville's silence, to create a faun-like creature incapable of evil because ignorant of it within himself, until seduced by it. Is Billy Budd Melville's answering version of him?[4] This type of character mirrors in those surrounding him their potential toward his reality: Toby, his discontent moving toward decisive action; Dr. Long Ghost, his ability to be prudent and to suffer good naturedly a mess of things; Jarl, his strength of convictions; Harry Bolton, his pluck, albeit foolish, to rise above bad times; Jack Chase, his *joie de vivre;* Queequeg, his philosophical power to work and observe, and to love. It remained for Henry James to push the *alter ego* into a purely psychological drama, in "The Jolly Corner" (1909), to turn the idea as Freud was beginning to shape it, and as Dostoievsky, whose work was completed twenty-eight years before, had done, in studying that special twist of the *alter ego,* the "double." James took the mirror function of the *alter ego* into the mercurial area of speculation: what a man might have been. Queequeg, we remember, was "George Washington cannibalistically developed" (*Moby-Dick,* ch. 10). Are Melville's companions elaborate metaphors for the will of the protagonist? Melville, in his poem "Shelley's Vision,"[5] grieves for his imagination's having martyred so many times his shadow. Are not Toby and Jarl and Queequeg sacrificed to hostilities that might well have destroyed Tommee and Taji and Ishmael? It is quite clear that Queequeg's death, more strictly his preparation for death, is Ishmael's salvation.[6] In the passage from Shelley at the head of this essay, the Platonic ideals are "underneath the grave"

---

[3]"How can the prisoner reach outside except by thrusting through the wall? To me, the white whale is that wall, shoved near to me" (*Moby-Dick,* ch. 36).

[4]When T. E. Lawrence in that uncannily Melville-like book, *The Mint,* asks uneasily, "Do fauns brood?" he seemed to put his finger on the shortcoming of Hawthorne's imagination, which Melville seems to be correcting in *Billy Budd.* Yeats's faun of Phase I, in *A Vision,* is wholly unaware, like Billy, of his extraordinary perfection, or of the nature of the world that makes it extraordinary.

[5]Melville, *Poems,* p. 272.

[6]Note the ritualistic tone of Queequeg's preparing his coffin. Slain Polynesian warriors are cooked and placed in canoes, by their enemies, as part of the victory feast. Warriors dead among their people, as Queequeg tells us (in contradiction to information in *Mardi*), are placed in their canoes and floated out to sea. Melville seems to have been remembering the

> where do inhabit
> The shadows of all forms that think and live
> Till death unite them and they part no more.[7]

In Melville's "Shelley's Vision" the death of the shadow awakens "self-reverence." In other terms, the sacrifice of the companion is the only gauge of one's worth. Melville seems to have realized in his poem the stature that the companions had added to his heroes, all personae of himself.

The first of the companions is Toby, of *Typee*. As this account of adventure is not a novel, there is no particular demand that Toby be a developed character, and he isn't. An accomplice to jumping ship, a companion as long as the narrator is searching for the Happars, his Byronic prettiness pales among the pagan beauty of the Typees. He is practically forgotten until his mysterious disappearance, and were it not for *The Story of Toby* which is now usually bound in with *Typee,* and the real Toby's entering into the public life of the romance, he would be as unobtrusive as Jarl, in *Mardi,* with whom he must be classed. Melville seems to have had an artistic reason for creating Toby and Jarl, a reason that failed him in composition. Harry Bolton, in *Redburn,* would be similarly neglected did he not become a surrogate greenhorn on the return voyage. Dr. Long Ghost of *Omoo* and Jack Chase of *White Jacket,* if not neglected quite as much, do not fulfill the expectation built up around them. Not until *Moby-Dick* does the companion achieve his potential: Queequeg remains the masterpiece of Melville's companions. Pierre's cousin, Glendinning Stanly, at last animates the companion to full participation in the plot and makes him, as even Queequeg is not, an indispensable part of the novel's structure. At this point in Melville's work a curious thing happens: the companion comes into the foreground as the protagonist. Israel Potter, so fittingly a side-kick to John Paul Jones or Ethan Allen, has the novel to himself. We are reminded of Thomas Deloney's *Iack of Newbury,* with Henry VIII and Cardinal Wolsey coming and going, or of Nashe's *Unfortunate Traveller.*

In *The Confidence-Man* the very nature of the ethic and psychology of the companion is questioned—the novel's theme demands it—and the confidence man (or men) becomes the companion of a conglomeration of mankind, turning the trusting relation of Taji and Jarl, Ishmael and Queequeg, into a nightmare travesty of itself. But the novel belongs to that federation of manipulators who would be confidants, for whatever

---

American Indian's being buried in his canoe, or, possibly, the fantastically carved deathship of the Balinese, Tempon Telon's Banama Tingang, which gathers up the souls of the dead as it passes from island to island. See Leo Frobenius, *The Childhood of Man* (London: Seeley and Co., 1909).

[7]*Prometheus Unbound,* I, 11. 197–199.

purpose, of everybody. Billy Budd is equally the friend of all, a kind of ship's mascot: the companion, at last, in Melville's work, the ultimate hero.

Toby is singled out by the narrator because of his "remarkably prepossessing exterior" amid a crew "as coarse in person as in mind." On watch he is good for "chat, song, and story." He is "active, ready, and obliging, of dauntless courage, and singularly open and fearless in the expression of his feelings." Jack Chase in embryo, but whatever else he is remains as well in embryo. Like the genteel sailors in Victorian paintings,[8] he is "singularly small and slightly made, with great flexibility of limb. His naturally dark complexion had been deepened by exposure to the tropical sun, and a mass of jetty locks clustered about his temples, and threw a darker shade into his large black eyes" (*Typee*, ch. 5). This is part of the aesthetic of the time, a correlative to Toby's melancholy and Ishmael-like character ("one of that class of rovers you sometimes meet at sea"), but, as cannot be denied with later examples of the companion, a certain amount of appetence is in play here.[9] Melville is his own best explicator: in *Pierre* he writes of "the friendship of fine-hearted, generous boys, nurtured amid the romance-engendering comforts and elegancies of life, sometimes transcend[ing] the bounds of mere boyishness, and revel[ing] for a while in the empyrean of a love which only comes short, by the degree, of the sweetest sentiment entertained between the sexes" (*Pierre* ch. 15).[10] For the nonce it would be a mistake to loose the analytical faculties of psychology upon what could so unobstructedly be a supposed homosexual potentiality in Melville, as though he were Whitman at sea.

[8]See, for example, Abraham Solomon's *First Class—The Meeting, 'And at First Meeting Loved'*; J. C. Horsley's *Blossom Time*; and particularly Arthur Hughes's *Home from the Sea*. All are reproduced in Graham Reynolds's *Painters of the Victorian Scene* (London: B. T. Batsford, Ltd., 1953).

[9]To see the extent, and to my judgement it is the extent, of Melville's *flânerie* with the handsomeness of sailors, compare these two passages from *Moby-Dick*. From chapter 5: "This young fellow's healthy cheek is like a sun-toasted pear in hue, and would seem to smell almost as musky. . . ." From chapter 6: "Elsewhere match that bloom of theirs [the women of New Bedford], ye cannot, save in Salem, where they tell me the young girls breathe such musk, their sailor sweethearts smell them miles off shore, as though they were drawing nigh the odorous Moluccas instead of the Puritanic sands." However, Melville's preoccupation with the good-looking sailor has been accounted for as the satisfaction of a latent homosexuality, notably in Newton Arvin's *Herman Melville* (New York: Duell, Sloane, and Pierce, 1950). See also W. H. Suden, *The Enchafèd Flood* (New York: Random House, 1950), p. 149, especially in relation to Billy Budd.

[10]Perhaps Melville's inability in his first five novels to develop the companion is shown in his deflecting discussion of homosexuality from its probable outcome, and proceeding into a *non sequitur*. In *Pierre* (New York: Hendricks House, 1949, ed. Henry A. Murray, p. 255), he begins to digress on "the confirmed bachelor" in America, in the very thick of his eulogy on "boy-love," but trails off in the evasive statement that the bachelor is "the victim of a too profound appreciation of the infinite charmingness of woman."

His imagination honestly stopped short "by one degree," and the later symbolic development of this relationship is too great an achievement to stamp with medical nomenclature.

If Toby was selected for an accomplice as much as for his satisfying a certain admiration as for his melancholy and Romantic brooding, that pleasure is quickly dissipated by the Typees and their "bouyant sense of a healthful physical existence" (*Typee,* ch. 17). In the description of "the noble Mehevi" in full warrior's costume (ch. 11), and of the "Polynesian Apollo" Marnoo (ch. 18) Melville finds a richer ideal of humankind. Pierre Loti, thirty years later, described his Nukuhevan friend with pretty much the same aesthetic. "*Houga est beaucoup . . . joli . . . ; il a vingt-cinq ans, un peu de favoris noirs, et des yeux d'une douceur charmante; sa figure, de forme grecque, n'est pas tatouée. . . .*"[11] It is, of course, the approximation to the Greek ideal of physique that Melville's heroes delight in. Gauguin, whose painting so curiously parallels Melville's South Sea romances,[12] saw in the Polynesians not Greek but Egyptian form, as many of his paintings indicate.

Dr. Long Ghost, "a tower of bones," over six feet tall and a lover of mischief, is a comic companion, the very opposite of Toby. *Omoo* is neither idyll nor adventure; like T. E. Lawrence's *The Mint* or E. E. Cummings's *The Enormous Room,* it chronicles the boredom and fun of men in ridiculous straits, from crippled whaler to the Calabooze Beretanee to beach combing.   Seedy Dr. Long Ghost plays a paternal rôle. The romance in *Omoo* is all in memory. Long Ghost has had his share: an amour in Palermo, lion hunting among the Caffres. He would have made good copy for *Life on the Mississippi.* Somerset Maugham will eventually come along and take him seriously. Like the nameless, cadaverous reporter in Faulkner's *Pylon,* his emaciation is a symptom of his spiritual exhaustion. There is much of the run-down about him; indeed, the original who sat for the portrait, Mr. Jay Leyda thinks, may have been the initial step in conceiving the figure of the confidence man.[13]

With Jarl, the avuncular chum of *Mardi,* we get an even more mature companion than Dr. Long Ghost. He has made a friend of Taji possibly because of "that heart-loneliness which overtakes most seamen as they grow aged." He is a Skyeman, of Norse descent, illiterate, and inscrutable. Beside the young *milord* curly-haired prettiness of Toby, and the comic paleness of Dr. Long Ghost, Jarl is a startling patch of color. "Over the ordinary tanning of the sailor, he seemed masked by a visor of japan-

---

[11]C. Wesley Bird, *Pierre Loti, correspondant et dessinateur 1872–1889, quelques fragments inédits de "Journal Intime"* (Paris: Impressions Pierre André, 1947), p. xxi.

[12]Charles Estienne, *Gauguin* (Geneva: Skira, 1953), pp. 62–65.

[13]Jay Leyda, *The Melville Log* (New York: Harcourt, Brace and Co., 1951), p. xxxiii.

ning dotted all over with freckles, so intensely yellow and symmetrically circular that they seemed scorched there by a burning glass" (*Mardi*, ch. 10). He is carefully characterized, given an important and interesting part—and, like Toby, dropped. First he is excluded from the tour of the islands by being little better than abandoned, then killed by Taji's pursuers. When his death comes we have almost forgotten him. That Melville (and Taji) lost interest in him is clear; he is erased from the picture to make room for King Media and his court. We see the anomaly in the novelist's imagination: how bored the taciturn old salt must have been with that floating salon.

In creating his Rabelaisian, peripatetic company of gods, demigods, and philosophers, Melville was no doubt aware of the religious revival in the Society Islands which had championed the gods Ta'aroa and Oro and which centered in the Arioi Society, a group of "literary artists with libertine morals"[14] who attempted to evangelize surrounding islands. This movement began in the poets and craftsmen's guild—the *tahu'a*—that apprenticed students in "literary composition, traditions, astronomy, black magic, medicine, religion and the construction of canoes, houses and maraes (temples)."[15]

> "*L'origine de cette secte demeure assez obscure,*" comment Patrick O'Reilly and Jean Poirier, "*une grande licence sexuelle était de rigueur entre les membres qui devaient d'autre part prendre l'engagement de mettre a mort tout enfant qui viendrait à naître à partir de leur agrégation à la société. Elle était devouée au culte d'Oro, mais son influence ne s'est exercée que dans les îles de la Polynésie centrale (Société). Moerenhout, qui n'appréciait guère les Aréoï, décrit dans les termes suivants leur fonction artistique et littéraire: 'Tantôt, comme les bardes et les scaldes de l'antiquité gauloise et scandinave, ils célèbrent en des hymnes inspirés, les merveilles de la création, la vie et les actions des dieux. . . .*'"[16]

The relationship between the Arioi and Media's jolly cult of Oro ought to be looked into.

Harry Bolton returns, in type, to Toby: the young gentleman reduced in circumstances. After he disappoints Redburn's expectations, pushing his folly to ruination and self-pity, Melville makes him act out the bitter experience of the greenhorn on the return trip. In his delicately smooth

---

[14]"Polynesian Mythology," *Dictionary of Folklore, Mythology, and Legend,* ed. Maria Leach (New York: Funk and Wagnalls, 1950).

[15]Ibid.

[16]"Littératures Océaniennes," *Historie des littératures, I, Encyclopédie de la Pléiade* (Paris: Gallimard, 1955).

masculinity there is a hint of the rake, of a possible nobility sapped by irresponsibility and selfishness. Toby is the only companion that we see, momentarily, against his own background, the plush gambling parlor. Other companions hold their homes in nostalgia. As Toby is lost, Dr. Long Ghost left beach combing, and Jarl sacrificed for Taji, so Harry Bolton is given the comeuppance that Redburn has already suffered. *Redburn,* for all its haste in composition, is a serious encounter with the world. The hero is still the voyager all eyes and ears, but he is beginning to understand his world. The companion of sudden impulses will be exchanged for one with impulses proceeding more from experience. The American and European gentry must give way to English stalwartness and primitive royalty.

Jack Chase is at once one of the most colorful and engaging of the companions, and the most static. He is simply there, a portrait. All action on his part grows so logically from his nobility as to seem anticlimactic. But he was Melville's particular favorite—*Billy Budd* is dedicated to him—"Jack Chase, Englishman . . . that great heart." He emerges from a medley of "The Spanish Ladies" and *Os Lusiados.* He has read "all the verses of Byron, and all the romances of Scott." He leaves one navy to fight for another with a more urgent cause. Handsome as Toby and Harry, learned as Long Ghost, crafty a sailor as Jarl, and as devoted as all, Jack Chase is clearly a friend the pariah White Jacket would long to have. And because the wish is so devout, the reality is lessened. The ideal companion of all is too symmetrically and completely conceived. To criticize him for such consummate skill of spirit and mind is, of course, to risk the stuffed owl's walking away, for if Melville used his real name he must have drawn carefully (with leeway for a sailor's rounding out of a tale). The pity is that the imagination was satisfied with the stance and demanded no action from it; Jack Chase belongs to the ode, not to the myth or ballad.

II

In describing Queequeg as he first saw him, Ishmael notes: "Still more, his very legs were marked, as if a parcel of dark green frogs were running up the trunks of young palms" (*Moby-Dick,* ch. 3). Melville's images are accretions. An original vividness on the retina gathers about it cohering significances until it becomes a complexity, the nucleus oftentimes lost to the reader but apparently active for Melville. Think of Mocha Dick and Moby-Dick. This nuclear image is the reverse of Blake's "world in a grain of sand"; it is the grain of sand become pearl. What was Melville remembering when he was reminded of frogs? Look at *Mardi:*

Farther on, there frowned a grove of blended banian boughs, thick-ranked manchineels, and many a upas; their summits gilded by the sun; but below, deep shadows, darkening night-shade ferns, and mandrakes. Buried in their midst, and dimly seen among large leaves, all halberd-shaped, were piles of stone, supporting falling temples of bamboo. Thereon frogs leaped in dampness, trailing round their slime. (*Mardi*, ch. 107)

A fertile scene—the frogs are breeding amid all that devil's collection of poisonous trees (save the banyan, which is the holiest of Polynesian trees, sacred to Hina)—in a fertile chapter. It is perhaps not beside the point that Queequeg in the hold of the *Pequod* when the burtons are upped is described "crawling about amid that dampness and slime, like a green spotted lizard at the bottom of a well." But back to the frogs. Melville describes the Polynesian god of the ocean Ta'aroa (or Tangaroa) carved as a creator of all other gods:

We stood before an obelisk-idol, so towering that gazing at it, we were fain to throw back our heads. According to Mohi, winding stairs led up through its legs; its abdomen a cellar, thick-stored with gourds of old wine; its head, a hollow dome; in rude alto-relievo, its scores of hillock breasts were carved over with legions of baby deities, frog-like sprawling. . . .[17] (*Mardi*, ch. 3)

We ought to make nothing more of this than that Melville intended Queequeg to be richly done iconographically, which is to make quite a lot of it.

If Queequeg is to be the pagan counterpart of George Washington, whose monument in Baltimore, Ishmael says in chapter 25, "marks that point of human grandeur beyond which few mortals will go," a "sea Prince of Wales," "Czar Peter content to toil in the shipyards of foreign cities" (ch. 12), and on and on, we must understand him under those signs.

He is a pagan by choice, having rejected Christianity good-naturedly. He is both king and warrior, bearing both with Washingtonian modesty. "Was there ever such unconsciousness?" Ishmael asks after the rescue in the Acushnet river. His teeth are filed and pointed (a cosmetic affair, though Melville wants us to see it as a kind of predatoriness, nobly controlled in Queequeg) and Ishmael describes him in the heat of the chase as though he had Grenadier steak in sight. His tomahawk pipe is a plowshare-sword image. Times and places meet in his appearance. His harpoon is carried everywhere: the Polynesian king's spear of office. His wallet is sealskin; his beaver, of brand-new New England make. The tat-

[17]"The figure represents the Polynesian god of the Ocean, Tangaroa, at the moment of creation of other gods and human beings." (Note on plate 82, showing the Rurutu, Tubai Islands, version of the god Melville is describing in *Mardi*). Herbert Tischner and Friedrich Hewicker, *Oceanic Art* (New York: Pantheon, 1954).

tooing on his arm is "a Cretan labyrinth of a figure." His bald head is "like a mildewed skull." Queequeg is the first of the companions to be met in distrust. There is much fun in so devilish-looking a creature's saying to the pale Presbyterian for the first time before him, "Who-e debel you?"

The identity is mistaken, but the advent of Queequeg has been long prepared for. When a child, Ishmael had played sweep in the chimney and had been put to bed in the daytime for it. Asleep, he woke to feel a supernatural hand placed in his. Quequeeg's unconscious hug reminded him of that clasp. Did not the black idol Yojo in the sooty chimney also? Yojo is an ancester, hunchbacked with venerable age, yet he reminds Ishmael of a "three days' old Congo baby." Into blackness, into experience, is treacherous, but there are companion goers of the way. Their "marriage"—one of those "extravagant friendships, unsurpassed by the story of Damon and Pythias: in truth, much more wonderful" which Melville describes in *Omoo* (ch. 39)—is elaborated in the symbolism of the monkey-rope, later in the novel, where their separate fates are made one.

The rudiments of Queequeg are first seen in Melville's work in the Marquesan nurse to Queen Pomaree's children, Marbonna. He was "a philosopher of nature—a wild heathen, moralizing upon the vices and follies of the Christian court of Tahiti—a savage scorning the degeneracy of the people among whom fortune had thrown him" (*Omoo*, ch. 81). But what a growth from Marbonna is Queequeg! Along Marbonna's tattooing the young princes trace their fingers, fascinated with its intricacy. Queequeg's tattooing becomes one of the most elaborate images in *Moby-Dick*. It is a Cretan labyrinth, the gods clinging to Ta'aroa, a personal hieroglyph (he uses a detail of it for a signature), the Zodiac. We discover in chapter 110 that it is "the work of a departed prophet and seer of his island, who, by those hieroglyphic marks, had written out on his body a complete theory of the heavens and the earth, and a mystical treatise on the art of attaining truth; so that Queequeg in his own proper person was a riddle to unfold; a wondrous work in one volume; but whose mysteries not even himself could read, though his own live heart beat against them. . . ." His coffin, made from timber "cut from the aboriginal groves of the Lackaday islands," was carved with replicas of his tattooing.

After Queequeg, there are only John Paul Jones and Billy Budd as examples of the sworn brother in Melville's work. The stories, like *Pierre* and *The Confidence-Man*, often tell of treacherous and pitiful companions. Bartleby, in a sense, is an unwelcome and undetachable companion to his employer, dousing his jovial commercialism with despair. The moralizing companions of "Poor Man's Pudding and Rich Man's Crumbs" are self-fooled idealists. The automaton of "The Bell Tower" destroys his maker. There are curious companionships struck up with a cock, a chimney, a mountain. But what is happening in these stories is this: there is no *alter ego* because the ego itself, the persona, has been transmuted, no longer Ishmael but an imagined, easily perturbable old codger, kin to Yeats's "sixty-year-old smiling public man." If you will, he is Ishmael old and grown domestic. All the protagonists through Pierre have been the same kind of person. In *Israel Potter* and the tales a sudden objectivity occurs. The protagonist becomes what I would like to dub The Ardent Simpleton. He is Bartleby's employer, if not Bartleby himself. He is the cock-fancier of "Cock-a-Doodle-Doo!," the worshiper and the theater-goer of "The Two Temples," the naive spectator of "Poor Man's Pudding and Rich Man's Crumbs" and of "The Paradise of Bachelors and Tartarus of Maids." He is beset by lightning-rod salesmen and crack-pot uncles with crack-pot inventions; he is a poet made a fool of by a complacent has-been; he grows sentimental over roses and peacocks on ruined wallpaper. He is the eternally innocent, brash, un-comprehending Captain Delano of "Benito Cereno." He defends his chimney and his apple-tree table; he wanders into Massachusetts mountains that remind him of Nukuhevan forests, looking for fairyland.

*The Confidence-Man*, like *Pierre*, scarcely allows that a companion can exist. But our subject is much in play here nevertheless; for, like Billy Budd, the confidence man is a companion to everybody; everybody will have none of him. There is indeed no protagonist in the novel with whom he could ally himself, save "that multiform pilgrim species, man."[18] Throughout the novel the little scene that unites companions in other novels is attempted again and again, ending in failure—or delusion. Yet here is Melville's most searching study of trust and the relation that must exist between men if the world is to survive—but the novel ends questioning that very survival.

Billy Budd, though an orphan and with no home save that of ships, is not an Ishmael. He is connected with no search, no journey, no chase. He is a creature entirely of the present, without nostalgia. Illiterate, ignorant of his age, he has no being except his calling and his friendliness. Melville has made for him a set of metaphors new in his work. To call Queequeg "this sea Prince of Wales" rings with the humor of farfetchedness—a

---

[18]There is no evidence that Melville had been rereading Chaucer while writing this most Chaucerian of his books (as he himself claims in the second chapter), but we might note that Chaucer has but three swearings of brotherhood among all his characters: between Palamon and Arcite in "The Knight's Tale," among the thieves in "The Pardoner's Tale," and between the summoner and the devil in "The Friar's Tale"—a veritable devil's advocate's collection for a misanthrope.

metaphor striking home in the spirit of its incongruity. To call Billy Budd a "sea-Hyperion" is a plea for myth. "Close-reefing topsails in a gale, there he was, astride the weather yard-arm-end, foot in the Flemish horse as 'stirrup,' both hands tugging at the 'ear-ring' as at a bridle, in very much the attitude of young Alexander curbing the fiery Bucephalus" (*Billy Budd,* ch. 1). Before our eyes a sailor working in a storm congeals into a Greek frieze: both images are strength enlisted toward order. "A superb figure, tossed by the horns of Taurus against the thunderous sky, cheerily hallooing to the strenuous file along the spar." The image becomes sailor and rigging again, but through the catalyst Taurus, the springtime constellation, the image with which The Handsome Sailor is introduced. He is "like Aldebaran among the lesser lights"; that is, like *alpha* in Taurus. In him his admirers "took that sort of pride in the evoker of it which the Assyrian priests doubtless showed from their grand sculptured Bull when the faithful prostrated themselves."

Billy is unfallen Adam—"a fine specimen of the genus homo," as Captain Vere remarks to Lieutenant Ratcliffe, "who in the nude might have posed for a statue of young Adam before the Fall"—Orpheus, young Joseph, young David. As we see him he is everybody's companion, the exact opposite of the confidence-man, rejected by all. The confidence man is all talk, all speculation; Billy is a stutterer, all action. Melville has chosen to portray him in passing from adolescence to manhood; he is about to be given a position of leadership when Claggart tempts him to murder. Queequeg was neither "caterpillar nor butterfly," neither civilized nor primitive. Billy is a "barbarian" and "Budd" is obvious.

Melville is sly when writing of matters sexual, and having to be sly tempts him to poker-faced mischief. The passage on the mating and birth of whales in *Moby-Dick,* written with such beauty and feeling that D. H. Lawrence turned part of it into a poem, has a footnote with this masterpiece of pedantic tact in it: "When overflowing with mutual esteem, the whales salute *more hominum.*" But "The Tartarus of Maids" and chapter 95 of *Moby-Dick,* "The Cassock," are bold enough for wide-awake readers. Dr. Henry A. Murray in his introduction to the Hendricks House edition of *Pierre* has pointed out passages in that book where the sexual life of the hero is plainly put, once we know the vocabulary. It is because of this slyness that one is tempted to read a passage in *Billy Budd* with active suspicion. The scene is following the hanging:

> . . . the Purser a rather ruddy rotund person more accurate as an accountant than profound as a philosopher said at mess to the Surgeon, "What testimony to the force lodged in will power" the latter—saturnine spare and tall, one in whom a discreet causticity went along with a manner less genial than polite, replied, "Your pardon, Mr. Purser. In a hanging scientifically

conducted—and under special orders I myself directed how Budd's was to be effected—any movement following the completed suspension and originating in the body suspended, such movement indicates mechanical spasms in the muscular system. Hence the absence of that is no more attributable to will-power as you call it than to horse-power—begging your pardon."

"But this muscular spasm you speak of, is not that in a degree more or less invariable in these cases?"

"Assuredly so, Mr. Purser."

"How then, my good Sir, do you account for its absence in this instance?"

"Mr. Purser, it is clear that your sense of the singularity in this matter equals not mine. . . . It was phenomenal, Mr. Purser, in the sense that it was an appearance the cause of which is not immediately to be assigned." (*Billy Budd*, ch. 27)

Largely the Surgeon and Purser are talking about the absence of muscular spasm in Billy's dying body, which would be what the Puritans would have called a "remarkable," a sign from God that Billy, in the divine scheme, was innocent. But is not Melville slyly telling us also that Billy inexplicably did not show that spasmodic erection of the penis resulting from the sudden crushing of the spinal cord which is usually a consequence of hanging? An answer is not easily given. It may well be Melville's insistence that Billy did not suffer a fall comparable to the Fall, if, indeed, he "fell" at all. Perhaps in spite of his treatment of Billy's physical beauty, Melville wanted him eventually to be pure goodness, pure spirit. Blake's ability in his drawings and in some of his poetry to achieve a similar effect comes to mind, and we know that Melville's mind was much on Blake during the composition of the novel.[19] Treacherous evil does not tempt Billy so much as it affronts him, face to face. For all the Christian overtones of *Billy Budd*, it is not at all clear wherein the connections lie. Billy dies "a barbarian." He is clearly sacrificed to order, but the order is military and inhuman and brought into being by war.[20]

[19]In April 1886 Melville wrote James Billson, "It pleases me to learn from you that [James] Thomson was interested in $W^m$ Blake," and when in 1888 Billson sent Melville Thomson's essay on Blake, he was extremely interested in it. Melville bought Gilchrist's *Life of William Blake* in 1870. See Jay Leyda, *The Melville Log*, pp. 712, 799, 811.

[20]To gauge the change in Melville's ideas of good and evil between *Benito Cereno* and *Billy Budd*—some thirty-four years—note that in *Benito Cereno* evil stains the innocent and guilty alike. The gray of the story stands for indifference, indifference as a mode of ignorance. It is Captain Delano who is gray, and he remains as untouched by the *Affaire San Dominic* as by the world before. But he has not *experienced* the evil of the situation or felt the horror of the human capacity for evil which the slaves symbolize. Don Benito is crushed by this evil, though innocent of it, except as a conveyor in the slave trade. He cannot look at Babo during the trial, because he is ashamed *for* him. In *Billy Budd* Claggart's evil warp of mind has no effect on Billy: significantly he sees it only as a *lie*. (True, Billy has no time to reflect on it reasonably, but would he?) *Benito Cereno* is a richly wrought tale, deep with insight, and stands beside *Pierre* and *The Confidence-Man* as a psychological and ethical study. *Billy Budd* is narrow, clear, and powerful, a statement rather than a study. *Benito* is analytical; *Billy Budd*, a synthesis, mythological.

From Toby to Billy Budd transverses a lifetime's imaginative creation, and this line of dissecting is a possibility among limitless ones. The subject could be extended to the *Pequod*'s mates and their harpooneers, to Ahab and Pip, to Ahab and Fedallah, to Israel Potter and John Paul Jones. The propensity for creating the companions is clearly a sizable part of the energy of Melville's imagination. Behind it may lie one of the poignancies of a troubled life—but that is the man, not the work. It seemed always for Melville that the heart could seek the idyll while the mind froze at the sight of the reality. Where else in Melville is there a scene as terrible as the battle between the *Serapis* and the *Bonhomme Richard*—a description that makes Paul Jones's own account, in the famous letter to Franklin, palely tame—and what do we find there among the batteries of guns firing point blank at each other, "surrounded by their buff crews as by fauns and satyrs"?

# Louis Agassiz

## I. BEYOND THE GLASS FLOWERS

> Brown Séquard tells me I must not think. Nobody can ever know the tortures I endure in trying to stop thinking.
>
> (Louis Agassiz, just before dying of fatigue)

> This is a man who, at the height of Napoleon's power, refused the directorship of the Garden of Plants, and a seat as senator of the empire. He might, with little pains, have been rich; but he is penniless, after much toil, and the very house over his head is mortgaged to support a museum which belongs to other people.
>
> Theodore Lyman, *Recollections of Agassiz*

In the 1904 Baedeker for the United States, the English tourist in Cambridge, Massachusetts, had recommended to him "the University Museum (Director, Professor Alexander Agassiz), containing valuable collections of comparative zoology," the starred attraction being "the glass flowers at Harvard" which, Marianne Moore's father observed, superior people never make long trips to see. Mr. Moore was at least half satiric in his observation, but his intuition was perfect in suspecting that the glass flowers were ridiculous. They are, in fact, a symbol of Agassiz's achievement as it survives. His great museum of natural history is an appendage to Victorian simulacra; his reputation is thought to be part of the American dullness in the late nineteenth century.

Among the contributors of specimens to Agassiz's great unfinished work in the natural history of the United States we find "Mr. D. Henry Thoreau, of Concord," who is not to be wholly identified with the transcendental hermit of the literary handbooks, author of *Walden* and one lesser book. The Thoreau to whom Agassiz made his acknowledgment was a scientist, the pioneer ecologist, one of the few men in America with whom he could talk, as on an occasion when the two went exhaustively into the mating of turtles, to the dismay of their host for dinner, Emerson.

"Several score of the best-educated, most agreeable, and personally the most sociable people in America united in Cambridge to make a social desert that would have starved a polar bear," Henry Adams says in the *Education*. "The liveliest and most agreeable of men—James Russell Lowell, Francis J. Child, Louis Agassiz, his son Alexander, Gurney, John Fiske, William James and a dozen others, who would have made the joy of London or Paris—tried their best to break out and be like other men in Cambridge and Boston, but society called them professors, and professors they had to be." One reason that Agassiz is the subject for many romantic biographies, many inspiring books for children, and a mysterious figure in American intellectual history is that he moved among people who paid him every compliment except comprehension. He lectured everywhere, brilliantly. His lectures took the highest reward of nineteenth-century fame: parody. Artemus Ward and Josh Billings gave splendid satires of them, assuring audiences who had sat through Agassiz's masterful zoologizing that the hen is a fool and the mule an oversight. These dedicated audiences enjoyed Agassiz and Artemus Ward with compartmentalized minds, never realizing the humor as a higher appreciation than their own desperate patronage.

Thoreau's finest thought remained in the privacy of his rich notebooks because of the dullness of the public interest, which he treated to inspired insults and ironic exhortations, daring to risk his meditations on its blank surface. Agassiz remained charmingly gracious to the same audience, vaguely aware that it was there. He would talk natural history with professor or stable boy; what mattered was that he could focus an idea out loud. Agassiz made a wild guess about the autumn leaf, calling its color a maturation. Dutifully all the poetlings and ladies' diaries took up the phrase, "the maturing of the leaf." Emerson displayed a conceit about the account of the Brazilian expedition, a collaboration between Agassiz and his wife, saying that the book was like a mermaid, so harmonious was the combination of ichthyology and travelogue. This promptly became a Boston riddle: "Why is the Agassiz Brazilian book like a mermaid?" "Because you can't tell where the lady begins and the fish leaves off."

Watch an English artist within this insipidity. Marianne North, the painter, visited the Cambridge of Agassiz just weeks before her incredible debut at the White House as the daughter of Lord North, Earl of Guilford (fl. 1776)—Ulysses Grant even inquired as to his lordship's health. She perceived a level of culture at the Adams's, but then she began to meet people who wept over Dickens, and people who were trying the mermaid riddle one more time, and ladies who "wept bitterly" when Miss North sang after dinner, and the Miss Longfellows introduced themselves on the street car, and took her to lunch. "The luncheon was worthy of a poet—nothing but cakes and fruit, and cold tea with lumps of ice in it." Longfellow was "full of pleasant unpractical talk, quite too good for everyday use."

But in Agassiz, though she had been told that he was "the clever old Swiss professor" who had married "a most agreeable handsome woman" and a Bostonian to boot, she found a man "more to my mind," who "gave me a less poetical dinner." Darwin had been a little like this, full of Linnaean binomials for everything, a man who had looked and seen. Agassiz was more congenial, seeming "entirely content with himself and everyone else." His museum was a catalogue of nature. He called himself the librarian of the works of God, scarcely a facile image in its implications.

For all her advantage as an outsider, Marianne North perceived only that Agassiz was a man far above the intellectual atmosphere in which she found him. And he has remained a figure of unquestioned stature in American intellectual history. Few, however, can attach any reality to his vaguely familiar, vaguely exotic name. William James and Henry Adams would have thought this impossible, certainly unlikely. But in neither F. O. Matthiesen's *American Renaissance* nor the comprehensive Spiller, Thorp, Canby and Johnson *Literary History of the United States* will one find Agassiz mentioned, much less related to the minds upon which he pressed such influence. The obscurest subject in the curricula of American colleges is the intellectual history of the United States. Like American history itself, intellectual achievement has been stylized into an episodic myth in which the mind has no real prominence. Patrick Henry has become a single sentence; John Randolph has disappeared. The American scholar who found in his eightieth year the vestige of mankind's first cultivation of cereals is as unknown to American history as the tactician who drove Cornwallis into Washington's hands. Everyone agrees that Agassiz is a heritage. But what kind of heritage? Once one has discovered that beneath the legend is a system of ideas, it becomes apparent how wrong it is that Agassiz's writing has lain unpublished for over a century.

## II. VERBAL PRECISION

> Philosophers and theologians have yet to learn that a physical fact is as sacred as a moral principle. Our own nature demands from us this double allegiance.                      *(The Natural History of the United States)*

Now that at mid-century we have Louise Hall Tharp's *Adventurous Alliance: The Story of the Agassiz Family of Boston* (Boston: Little, Brown, 1959) and Edward Lurie's *Louis Agassiz: A Life in Science* (Chicago: University of Chicago Press, 1960), the asperity is diminished in having to witness the survival of Agassiz's genius as a facile and homely myth except for the almost secret publication by John Kasper and Ezra Pound, of an abominably printed but wholly admirable collection of paragraphs entitled *Gists from Agassiz, or Passages on the Intelligence Working in Nature,* (Washington, Square Dollar Series, 1953). This inspired, ninety-six-page pamphlet was the fruit of both Pound's homework for the *Rock-Drill* cantos and Kasper's exploration, under Pound's tutelage, of an American writer of greatest caliber now lost from curricula, a neglected classic which, in the unflagging diligence that turned up Alexander Del Mar, Senator Thomas Hart Benton, John Randolph of Roanoke, and like treasure, Pound recovered for his pupils from his dismal quarters in those fourteen Washington years. Hence the publishers found it expedient to note that a classical education is not "the mere adjunct of an art shop or a collection of antiques, but a preparation for contemporary life." The first three lines of the *Paradiso* made its epigraph:

> La gloria di colui che tutto move
> > per l'universo penetra e risplende
> > in una parte più e meno altrove.

Behind that alignment of scientist and poet who were gazing at the same intricate design of nature there is an equally fine, invisible intelligence to be discerned, and without detracting from John Kasper's diligence, rather congratulating him that his teacher was pleased to collaborate anonymously, we can identify the unmistakable voice of Ezra Pound on the book's jacket:

> The boredom caused by "American culture" of the second half of the XIX[th] century was due to its being offered as "something like" English culture, but rather less lively; something to join Tennyson in "The Abbey" perhaps, but nothing quite as exciting as Browning, or Fitzgerald's *Rubaiyat*.

> Agassiz, apart from his brilliant achievements in natural science, ranks as a writer of prose, precise knowledge of his subject leading to great exactitude of expression.

Agassiz, who as a freshman at Heidelberg knew more about fish than he was able to find from his professors or in their libraries, and whose last act in a life as creative as that of Leonardo or Picasso, was to sail along the route of the *Beagle* before announcing his final and authoritative rejection of evolution,[1] would as soon have laid down his Pliny and Aristotle as his Baer or Cuvier.

Agassiz was a major figure in nineteenth-century American culture, as much a part of our literary history as our scientific. Agassiz assumed that the structure of the natural world was everyone's interest, that every community as a matter of course would collect and classify its zoology and botany. College students can now scarcely make their way through a poem organized around natural facts. Ignorance of natural history has become an aesthetic problem in reading the arts. Thoreau, though he wondered why the very dogs did not stop and admire turned maples, knew better what the American attitude was, and was to be, toward natural history. Nullity.

The place scientific writing might claim among the corpus of imaginative writing zoned off as literature by unstable rules for admission and rejection is a strong one, allowing for inevitable airs of condescension from the protectors of letters. The spirit of our age has been curiously

---

[1]See Elizabeth Cary Agassiz, "In the Straits of Magellan," *The Atlantic Monthly* 21 (1873): 89–95, and her "Cruise through the Galapagos," ibid, pp. 579–84. This voyage of the *Hassler* was mainly oceanographic. Agassiz saw the opportunity "to study the whole Darwinian theory free from all external influences and former prejudices," as he wrote to a German friend, Carl Gegenbaur, adding that "It was on a similar voyage that Darwin himself came to formulate his theories!" Edward Lurie's account of this voyage, pp. 372-77 of his *Louis Agassiz: A Life in Science*, (Chicago: University of Chicago Press, 1960), is particularly fine. The crystallized rejection of Darwinian theory was published in 1874, "Evolution and Permanence of Type," *The Atlantic Monthly* 33 (1874): 92-101. The student of iconogrpaphy is invited to compare the Galapagos as they appeared to Darwin, Mrs. Agassiz, and Melville, whose sustained vastation in *Las Encantadas* is a prophetic view of the impact of evolutionary data on the imaginative mind.

denying, although its search for purity is understandable. The American in particular regards his mind as a showroom for certain furnitures as content, and this silly idea gets defended by the vulgar error that if the mind is stuffed, there'll be no room for important things in their time. I first collided with this homely belief while teaching in St. Louis, that museum of Americana, and should have known that it came from Poor Richard or Sherlock Holmes. It is from Holmes. At a more crucial level our very schools and journals encourage neglecting everything but some approved matter at hand. Even in so fine a morphology of literary form as Northrop Frye's *Anatomy of Criticism,* the shape of scientific writing gets but a passing glance (a sharp one, however).

Agassiz's masterpiece was to have been the *Contributions to the Natural History of the United States.* Its four handsome volumes remain as a triumph of thought and scholarship. So carefully do they begin, holding entire libraries of fact in perfect balance with original research, that the mind marvels at the inconceivably fine book the finished work would have been; for in 1,600 pages Agassiz has but described the embryology of the North American turtles and the anatomy of the most elusive and perishable of creatures, the jellyfish and his kin. "Jellyfish?" a transcendentalist once asked Agassiz. "It seems to be little more than organized water."

"Agassiz's influence on methods of teaching," William James reported to the American Society of Naturalists in 1896, "was prompt and decisive,—all the more so that it struck people's imagination by its very excess. The good old way of committing printed abstractions to memory seems never to have received such a shock as it encountered at his hands."

The ability to combine facts, he said at the end of his life, is a much rarer gift than to discern them. This observation has weight. The man who said it had combined facts enough, and when he held fire on evolution he had, as Darwin knew, more facts than Darwin to combine, but he was also the man who discerned what a glacier was, and the evidence of the Ice Age, and who cancelled species after species identified by his colleagues by pointing out that the new-found creature was but the pup of a well-known animal.

It has been said too often, especially as a motive for shelving Agassiz as a romantic biologist, that he refused to see the truth of evolution because it wasn't his discovery. This is easy to believe, difficult to prove.

The accuracy of his eye is more important than five hundred anecdotes of Cambridge life, and anyway his role as upsetter of the Harvard ambience sounds like (and, one hopes, was) an unsuspected maliciousness of fumigatory intent rather than the amusing mishaps of a sweet, *distrait* scientist. The snakes that the Boston ladies found beside them on the set-tee in the Agassiz parlor, the lizards and toads produced at transcenden-tal dinners (one must overlook these deep thinkers), and the drunken bear stalking what is now Massachusetts Avenue (one of Professor Agassiz's specimens), and a thousand other inadvertences, can scarcely all have been unplanned. The Harvard in which Agassiz halfheartedly submitted to the bit part of tame professor, the Harvard of Longfellow and James Russell Lowell, elicited gestures of self-defense. It was the Harvard which dyna-mited Raphael Pumpelly's bride (an error in victims, the charge being intended for a local tease), thereby alienating a brilliant mind. Agassiz found the Cambridge High School's chemistry lab better than Harvard's and worked there; his major biological work he did for a while in an abandoned bath house on the Charles, and later in a wooden building which was twice moved to greater distances from the Yard. It was the Harvard which denied Thoreau the use of its library.

To watch Agassiz at his bedrock-mounted microscope, tipping a watch-glass in which yellow granular cells in unfertilized turtle *ova* are like "glass globes whirling along, freighted on one side with golden peb-bles" is to realize what science was in its heroic age. *To watch* is the verb; the verbal precision of Agassiz's prose, unmatched in American litera-ture, can sustain for fifty pages a lucid description of the inside of an egg. When the "hyaline masses" of these *ova* are swollen with water to learn the tensile strength of the "glass globe," one five-hundredth of an inch in diameter, the yolk grains "dance about their confined sphere in a zigzag quiver, and finally their delicate boundary wall, which by this time has become unequivocally demonstrated, bursts suddenly on one side, and extrudes at a single contractive effort nearly the whole horde of its viva-cious motes, assuming itself by this loss a wrinkled, unsymmetrical, much diminished shape, but still holding a few oscillating corpuscles."

Darwin's prose, beside Agassiz's, is wordy, undistinguished, indecisive as to its audience. Agassiz was both popular lecturer and essayist; we are not surprised to find his scientific prose elegantly exact, scrupulous in its details. It has the eloquence of information, but it also has a brilliance all its own which flashes from deep sensibility and sharp awareness of beauty.

In a long, formal essay on the embryology of the turtle, we find these sentences in a study of the eggshell:

> The outermost of these layers, next to the hard calcareous deposit, are com-posed of the smoothest and most uniform fibres, resembling at times exces-sively elongated tubular crystals. Before the shell is deposited, these layers may be recognized by the peculiarly brilliant nacreous appearance which strikes the eye. In Glyptemys insculpta, where this has been noticed most

frequently, the component fibres are of excessive tenuity and compactness among each other, the latter feature tending, no doubt, to heighten the polished aspect of the surface of the layer.

Agassiz wrote comfortably in French, German, and Latin; English he learned late; he was never at ease speaking it and rejoiced when, in Brazil or exploiting the pretensions of Cambridge society, he could lecture in French. His written English, like Conrad's, depended heavily on the easy cliché, hence "resembling at times," "may be recognized," "which strikes the eye," "the latter feature tending," and "aspect" in this passage, a judicious picking from that smooth Victorian literacy from which few native writers escaped, Ruskin alone, perhaps, toward the end of his life. A necessary verbal conciseness gives the passage "calcareous," "tubular crystals," "nacreous," "tenuity and compactness." It is Agassiz's clarity of mind that makes the sentence pleasant to read and allows it to be accessible to the reader who exults in precision as a quality of mind.

The earliest indication of a mesoblast is manifested by a slight haziness at one single point within the ectoblast, close against its wall.

When the Purkinjean vesicle has reached a size but a little larger than that of the last, the Wagnerian vesicles almost entirely cover the wall of their parent, simulating, by their clearness and roundness of contour, drops of dew lining a glass globe.

The clear transparent nature of the younger states of the Wagnerian vesicles is gradually lost in a certain measure, and superseded by a pearly or milky complection bounded by a rather dark, soft outline, calling to mind the appearance of the denser species of Medusae, or the bluish transparency of boiled cartilage; at the same time there appears a very bright, irrefractive, eccentric spot, the Valentinian vesicle.

Not the artist, but that fiction the public, considers the scientist an alien. An approved and perhaps journalistically hatched topic of the day is the dichotomy of humanist and scientist, and atomic physicists are treated as if they were Martians, humanists as from Arcadia, while the journalists who pit one against the other apparently went to school to the angelic intelligences, happy to explain humanism to the scientist, science to the humanist. But look! Photography, as Bouvard or Bloom will tell you, was a blow to art, rivaling, demoralizing, and displacing it. Yet we cannot find the frightened artist or the sanguine photographer to give substance to this *idée reçue*. We can find Renoir ecstatic over photographic tone, Stieglitz sponsoring a whole movement in modern painting, a company of French painters staying up all night looking at Muybridge's photographs, and on and on, not to mention the distinguished list of painter-photographers. We should be especially suspicious of the advertised antagonism between students of matter in terms of natural law and students of all things in whatever terms. One of the most provocative books on the biology of sex is by a poet, Remy de Gourmont; one of the finest on art, by a scientist, Leo Frobenius.[2] One could fill pages with the sensibility of da Vinci; a painter invented the electric telegraph; the great poem *Paterson* was written by a doctor.

The line of distinction is misdrawn. Redraw it to zone sensibility from barbarity, and such an intelligence as Agassiz's will need no apology. The fact that a misplaced distinction exists leads us into dissociating

Ribes Bracteosum, Dougl. Unarmed, glabrous; leaves on long petioles, cordate, deeply 5–7 lobed, sprinkled with resinous dots beneath, the lobes acuminate, coarsely doubly serrate or incised; racemes long, erect, manyflowered, on short peduncles; calyx rotate, glabrous; flowers white; fruit black, resinous-dotted and scarcely eatable,

from this definition of love by a poet:

Where memory liveth,
    it takes its state
Formed like a diafan from light on shade

Which shadow cometh of Mars and remaineth
Created, having a name sensate,
Custom of the soul,
    will from the heart;

Cometh from a seen form which being understood
Taketh locus and remaining in the intellect possible
Wherein hath he neither weight nor still-standing
Descendeth not by quality but shineth out
Himself his own effect unendingly
Not in delight but in the being aware
Nor can he leave his true likeness otherwhere.

The first, from Sereno Watson's *Botany* (United States Geological Exploration of the Fortieth Parallel, 1871) is as severely disciplined a record of a prairie gooseberry as Guido Cavalcanti's poem is a closely argued, scholastic definition of love's attributes. So confused is the present delinquency from verbal precision that many sophomores and many professors will unhesitatingly declare this paragraph a hopeless specimen of pedantry, "scientific jargon." It is unimaginable that these professors and sophomores cannot appreciate the diction which named a jellyfish *Medusa* or chose as Linnaean binomials for Wyoming flora *Artemisia*

[2] I mean Gourmont's *Physique de l'amour: essai sur l'instinct sexuel* (1904) and Frobenius's *Erlebte Erdteile*, esp. vol. IV: *Paideuma* (1928).

*frigida, Helenium autumnale, Fritillaria pudica, Helianthus exilis* and *Cilia ciliata.* Samuel Johnson is palmed off in classrooms as a harmless drudge of a lexicographer, yet open the *Dictionary* anywhere and find precision and eloquent plainness. "ROOST: *That on which a bird sits to sleep.* POETESS: *A she poet.* HORSE: *A neighing quadruped, used in war and draught and carriage.*" Watson's description of the gooseberry is within a tradition of exactitude which was never divorced from sensibility. Scientific language (which, like poetry, is cared for word by word) is as interesting to the artist as the language of fine prose and poetry to the scientist. Botanical nomenclature, for instance, is transparent, unbetrayed into the opacity of use by rote. *Viola saint-pauliana,* the African violet, was discovered and named by a Christian missionary. This is not a fact; cultures can be deduced from any fragment thereof.[3] *Helenium autumnale* bears its original Greek name, aligning flower and woman in the deep tradition that awed and pleased John Ruskin, and a nineteenth-century botanist added *autumnale,* specifying both its flowering season and the botanist's world-weary nostalgia over classical culture, so that one cannot distinguish between the poetry and the science of the name; they are fused—a name fitted with precision into a universal nomenclature for all the *flora* and an image of a tall, aging heroine. The common name for *Helenium autumnale* is sneezeweed, and one perceives a known culture in that, too.

The second passage is a translation (by Ezra Pound, in Canto XXXVI) of a medieval poem which defines love. It does not define with terms any less clear than those of a psychologist, and if we are willing we can easily see the scientific precision of the poet with the same eyes that detect the poetic precision of the botanist. To see Sereno Watson and a mediæval poet within one frame is not only an advantage and privilege to the perceptor; it is also an invitation to read with new eyes. The index to culture is sensitivity. Our culture can be gauged as exultantly in Agassiz's long study of the naked-eyed Medusa as in Marianne Moore's dilation upon the edge-hog. But where can we find the teachers to talk about the two in one context? Even Wallace Stevens, in a brilliant and congenial essay in *The Necessary Angel,* compared Miss Moore's ostrich not with an ostrich but with the article on ostriches in the *Britannica,* that *pons asinorum.*

In Lowell's stultifying elegy, *Agassiz,* we find:

[3]*Nequiquam, quoniam medio de fonte leporum surgit amari aliquit quod in ipsis floribus angat!* "I hate to disillusion you," Agassiz's successor writes with Agassizian kindness, "but the name was given by a professional botanist in Hannover, Wendland, who, as far as I know, never went abroad; the name is in honour of a German nobleman, Baron Walter von Saint Paul, who brought a specimen back from Africa."

> . . . in him perhaps
> Science had barred the gate that lets in dream,
> And he would rather count the perch and bream.

Lowell allows Agassiz "the poet's open eye," but metaphorically only, for he suspected that so great a grasp of nature must coincide somewhere with the Wordsworthian sensibilities he dealt in. It is fairly clear that Lowell had no way of conceiving of Agassiz and Wordsworth as writers within the same range of meditation. Lowell himself was two men, the one not on speaking terms with the other. His comic alter ego Bigelow had a viable diction and wit. The official poet called "James Russell Lowell" could only manipulate, with a variety of ineptitudes, a collection of verbal tags and imitated emotions from Wordsworth, Milton, and Gray. The elegy to Agassiz's memory, written in Florence and dispatched to *The Atlantic Monthly,* is almost a good poem. He cannot hide Agassiz with his pomposity. He knew the man too well, and good phrases get in despite the poem's commitment to a high diction. We accept as accurate "his broad maturity" (Lowell perceiving a mind that had actually arrived at ideas and was not merely hankering for them). We can see Agassiz in "his wise forefinger raised in smiling blame," and in similar clear passages. But we read the poem with bleak appreciation, though we learn from Lowell's every gesture why the real excellence of Louis Agassiz is unknown to American students, and why American intellectual life (that "level monotone," as Lowell called it) could make nothing at all of the genius e to live and work in it.

III. INTELLIGENCES

Agassiz tells his class that the intestinal worms in the mouse are not developed except in the stomach of the cat.

Picked up, floating, an *Emys picta,* hatched last year. It is an inch and one-twentieth long in the upper shell and agrees with Agassiz's description at that age. Agassiz says he could never obtain a specimen of the *insculpta* only one year old, it is so rarely met with, and young *Emydidae* are so aquatic. I have seen them frequently.

Agassiz says he has discovered that the haddock, a *deep-sea fish,* is viviparous.

*March 20.* Dine with Agassiz at R. W. E.'s He thinks that the suckers die of asphyxia, having very large air-bladders and being in the habit of coming to the surface for air. But then he is thinking of a different phenomenon from the one I speak of, which last is confined to the very earliest spring or winter. He says that the *Emys picta* does not copulate till seven years old, and then does not lay till four years after copulation, or when eleven years old. The *Cistudo Blandingii* (which he has heard of in Massachusetts only at Lancaster) copulates at eight or nine years of age. He says this is not a *Cistudo* but an *Emys*. He has eggs of the *serpentina* from which the young did not come forth till the next spring. He thinks that the Esquimau dog is the only indigenous one in the United States. He had not observed the silvery appearance and dryness of the lycoperdon fungus in water which I showed. He had broken caterpillars and found the crystals of ice in them, but had not thawed them. When I began to tell him of my experiment on a frozen fish, he said that Pallas had shown that fishes were frozen and thawed again, but I affirmed the contrary, and then Agassiz agreed with me. Says Aristotle describes the care the pouts take of their young. I told him of Tanner's account of it, the only one I had seen.

The river over the meadows again, nearly as high as in February, on account of the rain of the 19th.                    (Thoreau, *The Journals*)

From the Lakedaimonian cabin at Walden Pond, Thoreau sent to Agassiz fish, snapping turtles, snakes, whatever he thought the professor might not know. Throughout the *Journals,* and even in *Walden* and the *Week on the Concord and Merrimac Rivers,* we find Thoreau exulting to have found things as yet unclassified. Agassiz paid well and Thoreau needed the money. When funds were low, Thoreau would advertise the riches of Walden to Agassiz's assistant, the naturalist Elliot Cabot: minks, muskrats, frogs, lizards, tortoises, snakes, caddie-worms, leeches, muscles, "etc., or rather, *here they are.*" For the great *Natural History of the United States,* Thoreau on one occasion made up an impressive shipment of his elected neighbors. From the pond came fifteen pouts, seventeen perch, thirteen shiners, one land and five mud tortoises. From the river came seven perch, five shiners, eight bream, four dace, two mud and five painted tortoises. The cabin itself gave up a black snake and a dormouse.

Agassiz, forever lecturing, forever searching out money for his collections—"I am too busy to make a living"—regarded Thoreau's detachment from the world with envy. "My only business is my intercourse with nature," he wrote to Thoreau in 1849, "and could I do without draughtsmen, lithographers, etc., I would live still more retired. This will satisfy you that whenever you come this way I shall be delighted to see you—since I have also heard something of your mode of living."

No one sent in such fresh fish as Thoreau, or seemed to know so intuitively what would please Agassiz, who, soon aware that his collector was no mean naturalist, began to cast his orders as hints ("I do not know how much trouble I may be giving Mr. Thoreau"). And his letters to Thoreau began to take on professional tones: ". . . the small mud turtle was really the *Sternothoerus odoratus,* as I suspected,—a very rare species, quite distinct from the snapping turtle." More than once Agassiz came to the cabin at Walden "to look after new *Leucisci,*" and to inspect turtles.

Looking at these two a hundred and twenty-odd years away, we perceive a curious touching of worlds. It is not, even now, known who Thoreau was, what science, purposefully unseparated from meditation, lies in the notebooks and journals. One distillation from his extraordinary reading of nature is *Walden;* given other precipitates, we can coagulate other systems of stuff. He was clearly an ecologist; he was also a student of time, of cyclic movements in nature and of the miraculously synchronous organization of plants and animals. Hence his daily inspection of one woodscape, knowing every detail of its life. Agassiz knew oceans, continents, mountains; he had lived on a glacier as Thoreau lived at Walden. But Thoreau did not know Agassiz any more than Agassiz knew Thoreau. These two minds of intense brightness were equally familiar with the shyness of turtles; each knew the unsuspected mysteries of nature, seeing more than they would ever have time to record.

But notice, however remote these conversations of Agassiz and Thoreau must remain to us, that the two figures—portly, bald Agassiz, shaggy, nimble Thoreau—bent over a painted turtle at Walden, change a great deal of our attitude as to what the nineteenth century called Nature. Bryant, Whittier, Emerson; Lowell, Longfellow, Holmes—they knew their Romanticism; they knew how to arrive at the "Wordsworthian impulses." Yet they could also focus on leaf or meadow with something of the discipline of a Japanese poet (and spoil their gaze, to be sure, with an easy moralizing). Their work is now considered dull. Go back to it, however. Be patient or kindly blind to their interpretive gestures. Look with their eyes at the physical world that held their attention: it is the symbol of the age's profound attachment to biological fact. Not rusticity merely or picnic-day ebullience, their engagement was aesthetic, faithful, an intuition of ultimate authenticities. Thoreau's love affair with the scrub-oak, homeliest of trees, began to have the qualities of myth, the Greek feeling for the olive which we find in *Oedipus at Colonus.*

IV. METAMORPHOSIS: AGASSIZ AND DARWIN

Hindsight instructs us to wonder why Agassiz could not see the truth of Evolution. But hindsight also reminds us that Agassiz consistently located intelligence *in* or *behind* nature, long before Bergson, Whitehead, and Wittgenstein were forced by logic to return intelligence to nature, as man had assumed from the beginning of thought, rather than live with the miserable confusions of nineteenth-century mechanism. Darwin's superimposition of Progress upon the processes of Evolution taxes pure empiricism more than Agassiz's finding an intelligent plan or even a divinity in nature. If Darwin's mechanism of natural selection has the merit of doing away with a single act of creation, it nevertheless leads to the embarrassment of introducing both purpose in nature and cognition in the evolutionist as *dei ex machina*. This difficulty has sufficiently impressed some of the acutest twentieth-century scientists and philosophers of science to lead them into doctrines of multiple acts of creation and even into attributing spontaneity, awareness, and purpose to all natural process. But in order not to distort, from our privileged point in time, a "vanquished viewpoint," let us simply note that Agassiz's writings in natural history and systematic biology are equally imperative reading for us, and let us consider whether a passage such as the following, from Agassiz's "Essay on Classification," is a last and most explicit statement of pre-Darwinian teleology or whether it is a suggestive precursor of post-Darwinian teleology and natural philosophy:

> But, which is the truly humble? He who, penetrating into the secrets of creation, arranges them under a formula which he proudly calls his scientific system? or he who, in the same pursuit, recognizes his glorious affinity with the Creator, and, in deepest gratitude for so sublime a birthright, strives to be the faithful interpreter of that Divine Intellect with whom he is permitted, nay, with whom he is intended, according to the laws of his being, to enter into communion?. . . if, in short, we can prove premeditation prior to the act of creation, we have done, once and for ever, with the desolate theory which refers us to the laws of matter as accounting for all the wonders of the universe, and leaves us with no God but the monotonous, unvarying action of physical forces, binding all things to their inevitable destiny. I think our science has now reached that degree of advancement, in which we may venture upon such an investigation. . . . I disclaim every intention of introducing in this work any evidence irrelevant to my subject, or of supporting any conclusions not immediately flowing from it; but I cannot overlook nor disregard here the close connection there is between the facts ascertained by scientific investigations, and the discussions now carried on respecting the origin of organized beings.

The more we look into his work, the more we realize that, in a sense, he did see the truth of Evolution. He had Darwin's facts before him and saw with different eyes the pattern they made. He saw metamorphosis. For Agassiz, evolution meant the growth of the embryo in the egg, the exfoliation of form from the inexplicable potential within the fusion of sperm and ovum. This was the classic sense of the word until the Darwinians applied it to the entire organic world. Where science now sees a linear development in time, Agassiz saw a lateral spread of design, somehow modified over long undulations of the eons, as Cuvier had suggested (possibly by the creation, no one knew how, of new species to replace extinct creatures), and somehow involved with the encroachment and recession of continental sheets of ice.

The western world has had three students of metamorphosis: Ovid, Darwin, Picasso. Ovid took evolution on faith and metamorphosis for granted. Form flows into form. Eternal form, a god, must make his epiphany in matter. Beauty must manifest itself in beautful things. Agassiz inherited this ancient idea: that within nature there is an intelligence, the force which the Greek perceived as a god, the force which Ovid as a poet saw expressed in the myths, a system of metaphors.

An oak leaf is a thought. It is a manifest idea. All of nature is some intelligent being's meditation on being. And on becoming, one might add, but we need not limit ourselves to that angle of vision. The becoming is not growth but transformation. Oak, acorn; acorn, oak. Agassiz saw that there are several maturations, not any one final fructification. In copulation we free a mature being, an animal we have carried in us, spermatozoon. He is little more than *Chaos Chaos,* an amoeba with a tail. Loosed, he (not us) goes to breed. He does what we agonize to do, what poem, song, and saint's meditation long for. He penetrates another being (or dies in crystal desiccation) and fuses with it. And here the succession of our metamorphoses begins. The fetus is a recapitulation of structural ideas, of themes in creation, an elaborate series of puns. Each stage is complete yet transitional; zygote is fetus to the child, anarchist, and tyrant. The adolescent is not a recent child about to become an adult. He is completed, mature, with a life span, a mode of thought and response; he is, in fact, a separate animal. The child is to the adolescent, and the adolescent to the young man, as the tadpole to the frog. By being wholly psychological about this physical fact we have accumulated a fantasia of inadequate ideas and bruised our knowledge of reality.

At this point it may be worthwhile to indicate that Henry Adams saw in the science around him a hope that "sex and race" would at last be explained by trained minds, and he looked to a Clarence King and Raphael Pumpelly, Agassiz's second-generation men in the field, to correlate data. The world still waits. If the ideas on this page seem curious, the reader is invited to reflect that Agassiz, Pumpelly, and King are scholars whose neglect is disturbing to contemplate. Agassiz died mid-career leaving a parabolic undertaking in scientific knowledge, and students are perfectly free to take up where he left off.

Growth, Agassiz saw, takes place *within* metamorphic form. The transformation of form into form is not properly growth but a true metamorphosis involving the total organism. There is no single growing

up. The grown child metamorphoses into an adolescent (what understanding we might have if scientists would define these matters!); the
adolescent into what classical wisdom called a *juventus*. Hence the boredom of a Spengler or a Frobenius, master analysts of metamorphic form
and of the peculiar destinies inherent in form, with the tidy, insular minds
of Darwin and Huxley, who wanted the interlocked natural systems of
metamorphoses to be a progress (history is dramatic), a beautiful growth
from one breathtakingly important—and accidental—egg, an exfoliation
of all from a fortuity that held in potential the armadillo, the rose, the
leopard, John Dillinger, and Confucius.

Agassiz was not bored by Darwin; one wonders what a complex of
certainty and doubt sometimes appeared to Agassiz's intelligence that
never found expression. Spengler's finding Darwin insular derives from
an inspection of the form of ideas, and ultimately, at our remove, it is
precisely the characteristic contours of ideas which can lead us to an
understanding of the nineteenth-century heritage we are still struggling to
understand and to modify.

Ovid studied men turning into animals; Darwin, animals into men.
Between these two brilliantly imaginative perceptions the subject of
metamorphosis stands as one of the most lyric of natural facts. With one
gesture nature holds matter firmly within her patterns. *Gingko biloba*,
the oldest of surviving trees and high among the loveliest, is of a design so
primeval that nothing but ferns and slimes are so antique. Yet it is a
*Stammvater* tree, an archaic and oriental kinsman of the conifers. In
Darwin's great vision of descent it was fit and survived, and so were its
cedar and loblolly and fir cousins; that is, it is within a linear metamorphosis, branching into a deltoid pedigree, but most of all in deep time, a
metamorphosis eons long.

For Agassiz, who discovered the Ice Age, time was no strange subject.
But in the puzzle of seeming Ur-parents and infinitely varied descendants
he was more modern. He belongs to the spirit of Picasso and Tchelitchew, who have meditated on change as infinite variety within a form,
theme variations made at the very beginning of creation, simultaneous.
The ideas of nature were for Agassiz what an image is for Picasso. Genus
and species are perhaps ideal forms from which nature matures all the
possibilities. Time need not enter into the discussion. Snake and bird and
pteridactyl all came from the same workshop, from the same *materia*
available to the craftsman; they do not need to be seen as made out of
each other. An artist fascinated by a structural theme made them all.
Darwin placed them in a time-order, and invited scientists to find the
serpent halfway in metamorphosis toward being a pteridactyl, the pteridactyl becoming bird. Agassiz stood firm on the unshakable fact that

dogs always have puppies; swans, cygnets; snakes, snakes. The *Origin of Species* was a misnomer. Darwin's *Metamorphoses* would have been better, but then Agassiz was a rival poet and fairly soon we may find both on the shelf with Ovid, splendors of imagination.

Ideas of nature are moral ideas. Darwin sat in black vastation, contemplating the god, or void, he could never decide which, that allowed to evolve from the innocent matter such horrors as the tapeworm, the syphilis spirochaete, the poliomyelitis virus. Darwin's view was more macroscopic, of course; he was spared viruses, though by the end of his days optics were disclosing the subtle murderers. Darwin felt black enough about the way of a cat with a captured mouse.

We can detect in Agassiz, a notoriously good-natured man, a certain evasion in his taking a medical degree, to please his parents, and never looking at a patient. All applied science was repugnant to him. It was his calling to study the nature of reality. Lesser, practical men could fit knowledge to use. In these last days of the world we regard such an attitude with cold respect; we cannot be enthusiastic about it. Darwin was hurt that his theory destroyed faith. Was his plan of creation not as marvelous as Genesis? Was myth to be preferred to demonstrable truth? Agassiz's god we know less about. At least the eloquent intelligence discernible in nature was a palpable attribute of God. We do not anywhere find Agassiz an agnostic; we cannot discover any conflict in him between religion and science.

V. RADIENCE

> I have devoted my whole life to the study of Nature, and yet a single sentence may express all that I have done. I have shown that there is a correspondence between the succession of fishes in geological times and the different stages of their growth in the egg—that is all. *(Methods of Study in Natural History)*

But Agassiz adds: "It chanced to be a result that was found to apply to other groups and has led to other conclusions of a like nature." The method whereby Agassiz got from ignorance to knowlege of the Devonian and Silurian fossils to "other conclusions" was simply comparison. "The comparative method" is Agassiz's heritage, a discipline which filled American classrooms with scientists for two generations afterward and which has borne other fruit.

When Emerson, of all people, complained that Agassiz was emphasizing science to the detriment of Harvard as a university, Agassiz patiently replied that the rest of the curriculum should be brought up to the standards he had set for his zoology labs. "The education of a naturalist now consists chiefly in learning how to compare," Agassiz said (and the *now* is ominous). "By the same process the most mature results of scientific research in Philology, in Ethnology, and in Physical Science are reached."

The brilliant strokes of the intellect can be seen best in generalizations, in finding "the great laws of combination," but first the facts must be collected. Hence the diligence of the next generation, almost invariably Agassiz's pupils, in the field. Henry Adams has left us pictures of Clarence King in the Montana wilderness, and Pumpelly has left his own fine record of geologizing the world over. These two bring the matter of Agassiz's teaching into focus, for neither was his pupil; they took his inspiration from the air, and yet both acknowledge his leadership as if they had been his closest assistants.

Agassiz's influence has flowed beyond science, as he himself suggested that it might. If any man has repaid America's debt to Europe for giving us Agassiz, it is Ezra Pound, who, as we have seen, has acknowledged *his* debt to Agassiz. By transposing Agassiz's comparative method for critical use in literature, Pound created an extraordinary richness in contemporary criticism. In Pound's *The ABC of Reading* we find:

> The proper METHOD for studying poetry and good letters is the method of contemporary biologists, that is careful first-hand examination of the matter and continual COMPARISON of one "slide" or specimen with another.
>
> No man is equipped for modern thinking until he has understood the anecdote of Agassiz and the fish:
>
> A post-graduate student equipped with honors and diplomas went to Agassiz to receive the final and finishing touches. The great man offered him a sunfish and told him to describe it.
>
> Post-graduate student: "That's only a sunfish."
>
> Agassiz: "I know that. Write a description of it."
>
> After a few minutes the student returned with the description of the Ichthus Heliodiplodokus, or whatever term is used to conceal the common sunfish from vulgar knowlege, family of Heliichtherinkus, etc., as found in textbooks of the subject.
>
> Agassiz again told the student to describe the fish.
>
> The student produced a four-page essay. Agassiz then told him to look at the fish. At the end of three weeks the fish was in an advanced state of decomposition, but the student knew something about it.

When Pound completed and edited Ernest Fenollosa's *The Chinese Written Character as a Medium for Poetry,* he already had an intuitive grasp of Agassiz's intellectual heritage and saw in Fenollosa's inspection of Chinese poetry exactly the method which Agassiz had recommended to Emerson. Throughout Pound's critical work the guidelines suggested by Agassiz are discernible, and from this effort more brilliant ideas have been exposed than literary history will be able to follow up in a generation of scholars. Hence in the *Paradiso* of *The Cantos:*

> Out of von Humboldt: Agassiz, Del Mar and Frobenius.

Humboldt's *Kosmos* is still good reading, though, as with Agassiz, scholars give us biographies which generate interest in texts that remain unprinted and oftentimes inaccessible. "Agassiz never appeared to better advantage," Emerson wrote in his *Journal* in 1870, "as in his Biographical Discourse on Humboldt, at the Music Hall in Boston. . . .What is unusual for him, he read a written discourse, about two hours long; yet all of it strong, nothing to spare, not a weak point, no rhetoric, no falsetto;—his personal recollections and anecdotes of their intercourse, simple, frank, and tender in the tone of voice, too, no error of egotism or self-assertion, and far enough from French sentimentalism. He is quite as good a man as his hero, and not to be duplicated, I fear." Emerson the next year would include Agassiz among his Carlylean heroes ("My men"). Emerson could understand Agassiz as the heir of Humboldt and Cuvier (toward the end we find Agassiz looking to Baer the embryologist as his preceptor and writing in his introduction to the American edition of Hugh Miller's *Footprints of the Creator* that the next significant discoveries would have to be in embryology)[4] because he habitually saw genius as a spiritual gift from teacher to pupil. Behind "Out of von Humboldt: Agassiz . . ." there is a perception of radiant intelligence, certain qualities of humanity, a signature of the analytical faculties in concert with the searching mind.

Agassiz was a graft, analogous perhaps to Conrad in the history of the English novel. Japan had Lafcadio Hearn, Pumpelly, and Ernest Fenollosa, and from them learned to teach, to mine ores, and to splice a long tradition to a neglectful present, but each of these scholars enlisted native genius. Their task was not so much transformation as directing energy, catalyzing. Agassiz transformed Harvard from college to university, but the bulk of his contribution he brought with him: a detailed knowledge of nature which Darwin envied, which upset the settled conclusions of lesser investigators. Agassiz focused his transforming powers on the student; it was as a teacher that he wished most to be remembered. His

---

[4]Throughout the first edition of *The Origin of Species*, Darwin, whose German was notoriously shaky, made the Freudian error of writing Agassiz when he meant von Baer. This was shamefacedly corrected in later editions, but it tells us where Darwin was actually getting his knowledge of embryology. See Jane Oppenheimer, "An Embryological Enigma in *The Origin of Species*," in *Forerunners of Darwin 1745-1859*, ed. Glass, Temkin, and Straus (Baltimore: Johns Hopkins Press, 1959), pp. 292-322.

colleagues he urged to think as they would, within the capacities of a temperament which, inherited by Alexander Agassiz and aggravated by America, ran to horse-whipping utter strangers "for looking insolent," and pulling incautious drivers from the first automobiles and shaking them until their teeth rattled.

In an age of touchy formalities and pathological restrictions of spirit, Agassiz insisted that the teacher was both a dedicated scholar and a good-natured human being. The Agassiz intellect was as admirably liberal in its commerce with the world as intense and uncompromising in scholarship. Agassiz's father, Benjamin Rodolphe, hunted on Sabbath mornings, leaving his game and fowling-piece at the church door while he preached to his congregation at Motier, on Lake Morat. Agassiz himself broke every smoking rule at Harvard, fenced with his students, and once offered the Emperor of Brazil an assistant's position at the university museum.

Scholarship, imagination, energy, intellect, good nature. Theodore Lyman, watching the Harvard students bearing Agassiz's heavy casket to the chapel in the Yard, said: "He was younger than any of them."

*Persephone in a cotton-field*
Ezra Pound, "Canto 106"

---

# That Faire Field of Enna

---

I

Every September for thousands of years before Alaric the Visigoth rode through the pass at Thermopylae in 396 A.D. like a field of horses on a racetrack, as the historian Eunapios wrote, a procession of worshippers united by their common tongue, which by law had to be Greek, the language of the gods, and by their faith in the life of the soul after the death of the body, walked the dusty Sacred Way from Athens to Eleusis, resonant drums pacing their steps, fourteen miles.

The priests who led them wore long red cloaks, and their hair was bound with twists of cloth called *strophia,* and with laurel. They carried piglets, of which the goddess of grain, Demeter, was fond.

Alaric's flag that floated in the smoke as he burned the sanctuary of Eleusis bore an emblematic crow, and his army wore stranger symbols

250

still, the gibbets of the Latin people, as if they wished at all times to have the hideous fact of death by crucifixion in their minds. They moved on, with crow and cross, to burn Corinth and Sparta, and all in between, on, eventually, to Rome itself, which had not seen an invader for 800 years.

What they destroyed at Eleusis was the sacred place where the Greek mind—which continues to educate the world—believed civilization to have begun. Here the transition was made from the restless, alert life of the hunter to the settled ways of the farmer, a life that would blend with others and found cities, where in the congenial life of the street leisure and conversation would invent philosophy and mathematics, jurisprudence and history.

The year after the burning of Eleusis, Claudius Claudianus, court poet to the western emperor Flavius Honorius, wrote his *De Raptu Proserpinae,* a melancholy, magnificent, unfinished poem. Claudianus was Alexandrian, his language Greek, his poetry erudite and ornate. He could imitate the classical style; his sense of the world, however, is already mediæval, wrought, colored. Marlowe and Chapman might have translated the *De Raptu* as a twin to their *Hero and Leander.*

Claudianus's very first image is that of ships, which organized Mediterranean civilization into coherence; his next is (in Harold Isbell's Penguin translation):

> the black horses of that thief from the underworld, the stars blotted out by the chariot's shadow

—the subterranean horses of Dis, but also the horses of Alaric at Eleusis. Claudianus's poem sees the rape of Persephone in the fall of Eleusis and Rome to the Visigoths and Huns: horse people knowing nothing of ships, agriculture, or cities.

This sense of people who walk and people who are mounted on horses is deep within the symbolism of Miss Welty's first transmutation of the myth of Persephone, the novel *Delta Wedding.* Her Delta family must accept with what grace it can the marriage of a daughter to Troy Flavin, a son of the hill people whose culture is primitive and rough (a culture to which Miss Welty would later devote her masterpiece, *Losing Battles*).

Troy Flavin. Flavin is a yellow dye derived from the black oak; he is red-haired and rides a black horse. His name is a combination of black and yellow, of alien and familiar. His first name points to the rape of Helen by Trojans, for which that of Persephone by Dis was the archetype. His surname mirrors that of the Flavius at whose court at Milan (Huns just beyond the hills) Claudian wrote the *De Raptu.*

Everywhere in Miss Welty's fiction there is the same understanding as in Claudian's poem that Persephone's innocence and vulnerability are to be seen as a civilized order menaced by invasion. In "The Burning" the invaders are Union soldiers who ride their horses into the living room where Southern ladies are sewing. (This story is paralleled by the story "Circe," with all the values transposed into a different key. Performing variations on a theme is a major impulse in Miss Welty's aesthetic will.)

Another September, some two thousand years after the high eminence of Eleusis in the Graeco-Roman world, in Mississippi, three girls ride into the town of Fairchilds from Shellmound plantation (chapter 5, part 2, *Delta Wedding*). They travel by pony cart, two little girls, one in her teens, Laura, India, and Shelly. Tanagran figurines survive to show us that Greek ladies travelled thus. The resemblance seems charmingly deliberate.

Their errand is into the black part of town, "dead quiet except for the long, unsettled cries of hens walking around, and the whirr of pigeons now and then overhead. Only the old women were home. The little houses were many and alike, all whitewashed with a green door, with stovepipes crooked like elbows or hips behind, okra, princess-feathers, and false dragonhead growing around them, and China trees over them like umbrellas. . . ."

They arrive at the shack of old Partheny, long a retainer of the family. She is to be invited to the wedding, and to be asked if she knows anything about the whereabouts of a lost garnet broach.

Partheny wore "a tight little white cap on her head, sharp-peaked with a frilly top and points around like a crown." Inside the house India finds and snuggles a guinea pig, a pet of Partheny's. The scene is rich, several plot lines being developed simultaneously, and deliciously comic ("Got a compliment on my drawer-leg," she says of her cap to a neighbor after they leave). But if we ask why that crown of twisted cloth (the *strophia* of the Eleusinian hierophants), the piglet, the name (Parthenia, an epithet of Artemis and Athena: *virginity* or *girlhood*), and the garnet (from the Old French *pome grenate,* pomegranate) we begin to see how beautifully a vocabulary of images from a myth has been woven into Miss Welty's text.

> ". . . let Proserpina come
> To the upper world again, on one condition:
> She must, in the world below, have eaten nothing,
> Tasted no food—so have the Fates enacted."

(This is Jove explaining to Ceres how she can reclaim her daughter from Hades.)[1]

[1]Ovid, *The Metamorphoses* V, trans. Rolfe Humphries, (Bloomington: Indiana University Press, 1955), lines 529–532.

And Ceres, as he ended, was determined
To have her daughter back, but the Fates forbade it.
She had been hungry, wandering in the gardens,
Poor simple child, and plucked from the leaning bough
A pomegranate, the crimson fruit, and peeled it,
With the inside coating of the pale rind showing,
And had eaten seven of the seeds. . . .

Diodoros the Sicilian's account of the rape of Persephone in his *History of the World,* written in the girlhood of Mary and the reign of Gaius Octavius Caesar Augustus:

> The myths say that Kora was caught in the meadows of Enna. The place is just outside the city, famous for its violets and for wildflowers of every kind, the delight of the goddess. So rich is the odor of the flowers thereabout that, as the story goes, hunting dogs lose the spoor. It is level, low, and veined with streams, this meadow, but rises steeply, like a bowl around its edges. The Sicilians say that it is the very center of their island and call it Our Navel. There are holy trees nearby, across the marshes, and a deep cave that leads down into the earth. Its mouth, facing north, was where the Lord of the Dead, Plouton, rode out in his chariot to capture Kora.
>
> The violets and other flowers bloomed the year round in this meadow, giving it a weather of incredible sweetness.
>
> The myth says that Athena and Artemis had, like Kora, made a vow of virginity, and grew up in her company, and went with her to pick flowers. The three of them wove their father Zeus's coat. They loved Sicily beyond all other islands and lovely places, because of the time they were together there and because of their love for each other. . . .
>
> It was near Syrakousa that Plouton raped Kora away in his chariot, ripping the earth open to take her down into Hades. From this wound in the meadow rose the Blue Fountain. . . . After the rape of Kora, Demeter, her mother, looking everywhere for her, lit torches at the fires of Aitna the volcano, and wandered over the inhabited earth. To the people who were kind to her she gave grains of wheat, which were then unknown.
>
> The kindest welcome of all was at Athenai, whose citizens were the second to be given wheat, after the Sikeliotai. In her honor the Athenians began the great mysteries at Eleusis, which, for their holiness and ancientness, are talked about in wonder by the whole of mankind.

II

Unlike the Homeric parallels in *Ulysses,* where we can say that Bloom is Odysseus, Molly Penelope, Stephen Telemachus, and so on, and unlike Pound's ideogrammatic array of images, where we can say that meaning bonds this element with that because of affinity or subject-rhyme, the symbolic content of Miss Welty's fiction transverses the realistic surface like sound waves, or like starshake against the grain of wood. The effect is that of a *moiré* pattern.

A theme will cross another from an angle, vibrantly. In the first paragraph of "Going to Naples"—

> The *Pomona* sailing out of New York was bound for Palermo and Naples. It was the warm September of a Holy year. Along with the pilgrims and the old people going home, there rode in *turistica* half a dozen pairs of mothers and daughters—these seemed to take up the most room. If Mrs. C. Serto, going to Naples, might miss by a hair's breadth being the largest mother—there was no question about which was the largest daughter—that was hers. And how the daughter did love to scream! From the time the *Pomona* began to throb and move down the river, Gabriella Serto regaled the deck with clear, soprano cries. As she romped up and down after the other girls—she was the youngest too: eighteen—screaming and waving good-by to the Statue of Liberty, a hole broke through her stocking and her flesh came through like a pear.

— we can see Miss Welty's Persephone theme in the name of the ship (Pomona, goddess of fruit, an aspect of Demeter), in its destination (Sicily, where Persephone was raped, Naples, ancient realm of the siren Parthenope, is a *daughter* city to a Greek mother city, "metropolis," hence its name Neapolis, New Town), in the month September, time of the Eleusinian mysteries, in the Holy Year (commemorating the immaculate conception of Mary, whose image and *cultus* continue those of Demeter, and Her birthday is September 8), in the phrase "mothers and daughters," in the name Serto (a garland of flowers), in the screaming of Gabriella (". . . with a wailing voyce afright did often call / Hir Mother and hir waiting Maides, but Mother most of all"), and in the image of the pear of flesh bulging through a hole in Gabriella's stocking, richly and ambiguously suggestive.

And over all, easily missed because of its familiarity, Demeter with her torch presides: the Statue of Liberty.

(Iconographically, that statue, an allegory of Liberty, derives directly from Cybele, goddess of cities and mother of Demeter. The cap of her Phrygian devotees became the Liberty cap of both the French and American revolutions. Note the symbolic value it would have had for the Certos, an immigrant Italian family.)

This reticulation flows all the way through the story, a music inside a music. For Joyce's skill with a similar method the critic Hugh Kenner coined the phrase "double writing." In a sense, all writing and all language is double by nature, for words are all metaphors that have lost their resonance through use. Joyce demands of us that we know the archaic components of words; Miss Welty seems to count on our being a lot more awake than we usually are before a text. She expects us, for instance, to notice her design. The passage just quoted begins and ends with fruit: the tone, therefore, is going to be in harmony with these autumnal images ("the old people going home"), with a theme of fulfillment and maturation.

III

Myth is a tale anyone can tell: it is not the story itself in a particular form or with a particular finish, like a play by Shakespeare or a story by Chekov. An Alabama folktale called "Orpy and Miss Dicey," Cocteau's *Orphée,* Monteverdi's *Orfeo,* Gluck's *Orphée,* Poe's "The Fall of the House of Usher" are all versions of an immemorially ancient pattern of events which sensibilities as diverse as those of Guillaume Apollinaire ("Zone" and the *Cortège d'Orphée*), Anton Donchev (*Vreme Razdelno*), Rilke (*Sonnette an Orpheus*), and Eudora Welty were interested to retell.

The tragic singer who lost his wife twice and who was torn apart by madwomen has never been absent from the art of Europe since its archaic formulation in the mountains of Thrace. In our time the theme arises obliquely from various new sources. I suspect that Stendahl unconsciously awakened the theme with the severed head of Julien Sorel in *Le Rouge et le Noir* (1830), the romantic irony of which Flaubert reinterpreted in his "Hérodias" later in the century. Thereafter the head of Orpheus or St. John became an obsessive subject among painters (Moreau), poets (Wilde), and composers (Strauss).

The Orpheus myth is complementary to that of Persephone. Both are about loss and redemption, about grief and the progress of grief on to a triumph. In the myth of Orpheus the feminine spirit is absorbed and integrated with the masculine, and the archetypal poet is an organization of both.

A society like Morgana, Mississippi, urban and agricultural, takes its shape from the template of such societies the world over. Its inner myth is that of Persephone and Demeter, the death and birth of nature; Miss Welty's first two books of stories tend to be set at the equinoxes and solstices, to allude to antipodes (digging to China, chinaberry trees, China Grove), to project a mirage of Persephone's rape and return.

Orpheus was a shepherd, his people Thracian mountaineers (Miss Welty's "hillpeople"). That the female spirit can be redeemed by the male is an idea inimical to barley-rite people. Miss Welty's grasp and exploration of this idea has been brilliant, fructive, and infinitely subtle.

In the story "Moon Lake" Miss Welty writes her version of Orpheus and Eurydice. Loch Morrison is Orpheus. A Boy Scout lifeguard on duty for a week at Moon Lake for a camping party of Morgana girls and some girl orphans, he saves the life of Easter, an orphan.

His name is a play on the words *moon lake:* loch, a lake; Morrison is the word *Moon* with the Greek for a spit of land stretching out into a lake, *ris,* dropped into the middle of it, the way dancing water fractures the reflection of the moon on it. Like Orpheus, this adolescent who despises girls for their ineptness and clannish selfishness has their nature unsuspected within himself. He is the lake of lethal moonlight into which all that fall lose their selfishness and identity. Eurydice means *the justice of the world.*

Thus Loch is a symbolic Christ ("martyred presence. . . . Life saver . . . ordeal . . . dived high off the crosspiece nailed up in the big oak"); the girl he saves is named Easter. But that is her illiterate pronunciation of her real name, which is Esther, who, like her, was an orphan, but an orphan who redeemed her people in captivity. The name goes deeper: Esther is our spelling of the Akkadian Istar, the Biblical Astarte, a chthonic goddess whom the ancients thought to be the same as Venus.

Easter: the dawn of the year, Persephone's return, resurrection. Easter-Esther-Istar is the way Miss Welty wants us to understand her orphan. She is ill-bred, sassy, independent, and resentful of her fear of the other girls. She is the prisoner of their selfishness, pride and status. She seems unassailable until an unexpected tickle sends her into the lake to drown (symbolically a snake bite, as with Eurydice).

IV

The story "Sir Rabbit" repeats in a Morgana wood the seduction of Leda by Zeus as a swan. Yeats's sonnet in *A Vision* is worked into the fabric:

> A sudden blow: the great wings beating still
> Above the staggering girl, her thighs caressed
> By the dark webs, her nape caught in his bill,
> He holds her helpless breast upon his breast.

("When she laid eyes on Mr. MacLain close, she staggered, he had such grandeur, and then she was caught by the hair and brought down as suddenly to earth as if whacked by an unseen shillelagh.")

> How can those terrified vague fingers push
> The feathered glory from her loosening thighs,
> And how can body, laid in that white rush,
> But feel the strange heart beating where it lies?

("Presently she lifted her eyes in a lazy dread, and saw those eyes above hers, as keenly bright and unwavering and apart from her life as the flowers on a tree.")

> A shudder in the loins engenders there
> The broken wall, the burning roof and tower
> And Agamemnon dead.
>            Being so caught up,
> So mastered by the brute blood of the air,
> Did she put on his knowledge with his power
> Before the indifferent beak could let her drop?

("But he put on her, with the affront of his body, the affront of his sense, too. No pleasure in that! She had to put on what he knew with what he did—maybe because he was so grand it was a thorn to him. Like submitting to another way to talk, she could not answer his burden now, his whole blithe, smiling, superior, frantic existence. And no matter what happened to her, she had to remember, disappointments are not to be borne by Mr. MacLain, or he'll go away again.")

Yeats's sonnet opens that part of *A Vision* called "Dove or Swan," in which he compares the two annunciations, Leda and Mary, the pagan and the Christian ages. ("A dove feather came turning down through the light that was like golden smoke. She caught it with a dart of the hand, and brushed her chin; she was never displeased to catch anything. Nothing more fell.")

We can, with delight, follow Ovidian details through this story. King MacLain is dressed in white, swanlike, and fires his gun by way of hurling a thunderbolt.

The way of a god with a girl—but the story is deeper than that. Zeus is the sky (as his name means in Greek); he is the whole presence of light in the world. He is promiscuous because he is generous and impartial.

We can pick our way through the story looking at trees, for light falling on matter evolved the green world, which is a response to light. We see because photoelectric cells in the brain, which are nourished by carbohydrates made by leaves from light, water, and earth, are alive to the rain of light from the sun. Nature is far more complex than that, but a myth that celebrates celestial generation is wonderfully true.

The first tree is a hickory (the word is from the Indians of Virginia). Ran and Eugene MacLain look around it to tease Mattie Will Holifield, *née* Sojourner. It is a nut tree of a family kin to but smaller than the oaks. When King MacLain appears, it will be from behind an oak, Zeus's sacred tree. The Latin botanical name for the walnut family *Juglandaceae*, of which the hickory is a member, preserves an image of Zeus's testicles: *Juglans*. *Ju* (as in Jupiter, "Zeus the Father"), *glans,* nut. Ancient metaphor and folkish understanding survive and cooperate in the image, and the oak is Zeus's tree, containing his presence, at Dodona.

These faunish twins begin and end the story. At the beginning they shape the idea of Zeus Digonos, the begetter of twins (the phrase can just as well mean Zeus of the Two Testicles, and ancient Greeks normally called testicles "the twins"); at the end they assume in Mattie Will's mind an affectionate regard—"they were like young deer, or even remoter creatures . . . kangaroos. . . . For the first time Mattie Will thought they were mysterious and sweet—gamboling now she knew not where."

A cluster of plants symbolically balances another at the story's extremes. Before King MacLain's appearance, sunflower, dewberry, peach, pin oak; after the seduction, haw, cherry, cedar, sunflower. Each has a thicket (dewberry, haw), a sunflower, a fruit tree of the genus *Prunus* (peach, cherry). King MacLain trails his gunstock (which would be of walnut, *Juglans*) through periwinkle (which is our homely pronunciation of *per vincia,* "overcoming in all directions")! Note how the double-headed pinecone rhymes with the twins, with the testicle imagery, and (as we discover from the last story in the book) the twins Mattie Will gave birth to afterwards.

King MacLain is "up there back of the leaves"—light. Consider that O. Henry could not have conceived of writing this story, that it is utterly outside the consciousness of Poe. It is both resuscitation (Ovid) and invention, the most splendid triumph of manner over matter in American literature.

Rabbit, who comes from Dahomey and Nigeria with the slaves, to mingle with his cousin Wabos of the Menominee, Cadjwanecti of the Yuchi, Manidowens of the Chippewa, tricksters all. We know him as Brer Rabbit, Joel Chandler Harris's fusion of an African and Indian creature whose strategies of camouflage and Brechtian disavowal are derived from black plantation manners. (The song about him that Mattie Will remembers was found by Miss Welty in Zora Neale Hurston's collection of black folklore, *Mules and Men.*)

It would be like rabbit to seem to be two of himself, and very like him to serve as a vehicle for the great god Zeus, who usually mated with humankind in animal guise. So the first word of "Sir Rabbit," *he,* refers at first, in supposition, to King MacLain, until he, with godly improbableness, looks around both sides at once, and is recognized as the MacLain twins, Ran and Eugene.

Is Miss Welty basically summoning spirits she knows to be out there, so that her stories in their deepest music are incantations? It was at the Treaty of the Dancing Rabbit that the Indians of Mississippi deeded their land to General Jackson. Every marriage, Erich Neumann says in his *Amor and Psyche,* is a rape of Persephone. And every rabbit Pan.

V

The Russian painter Pavel Tchelitchew (1898–1956) began to conceal images within images in his pictures after he came to the United States in the 1930s. A "David and Goliath" exhibited at the Museum of Modern Art in 1942 (Miss Welty was then writing *Delta Wedding* and beginning the stories for *The Golden Apples*) is ostensibly a handsome Connecticut landscape: blue hills, autumnal foilage, streaming clouds. The title invites us to look again. The leafless tree to the left will render up a figure standing with its back to us, its contours coinciding with those of the tree limb's. The demonic, bearded face of Goliath can be found occupying the shadow side of a mountain. Clouds become the hair of David, whose profile fills the righthand side of the picture, the bounding line being the edge of trees against distant hills. There are other images that can be discovered, faces among leaves, for instance.

In Miss Welty's "June Recital" a sailor on leave who has been dallying with Virgie Rainy in an empty house is flushed out by the house's being set on fire. He encounters a confusion of people outside:

> Old Man Moody's party was only now progressing again, for the old woman had fallen down and they had to hold her on her feet. Further along, the ladies' Rook Party was coming out of Miss Nell's with a pouring sound. The sailor faced both these ranks.
>
> The marshall tagged him but he ran straight off into the wall of ladies, most of whom cried "Why, Kewpie Moffitt!"—an ancient nickname he had outgrown. He whirled about-face and ran the other way, and since he was carrying his blouse and was naked from the waist up, his collar stood out behind him like the lowest-hung wings.

The way we see Cupid bolting from Psyche in this passage is the way we find David and Goliath in Tchelitchew's landscape.

From 1940 to 1942 Tchelitchew painted the large composition for which he is best known, *Cache-Cache* (*Hide and Seek*). The idea for the painting seems to have germinated from some studies of an ancient tree in Sussex made in 1934, a tree in which the painter saw a likeness to a large, gnarled, open hand, with its fingers about to grasp. Its root system looked to him like a foot. Later he added children playing around it and in its branches.

The completed painting depicts a girl standing with her face to the tree, the It of *Hide and Seek*. Stand back, and her body makes the face of a winking demon: a butterfly near her right arm serves for his left eye; her left arm, his half-crossed right eye. Her dress is his nose, her legs his Viking moustache.

We can look at this amazing painting at one distance or another; its images change into other images as you approach or draw back. In the intervals between the branch-fingers of the tree-hand there are children drawn in headlong perspective (the way a camera distorts things too near it, or a telescope the wrong way around). These children are transparent; through them we can see landscapes with yet other children, wheatfields, branches in the middle distance which outline faces and have leaves that turn out to be boys in cloaks. One child's face resolves at closer inspection into mushrooms, dandelions, dew into vine tendrils, and these in turn can be identified as veins and arteries, tissues and muscles, and down among these are elfin children still. Organizing all this we can make out a cycle of the seasons, the ages of man, sexual organs human and vegetable, life as a game and biological process, a lyric and informed affirmation of the synthesis of flesh and spirit, and a network of allusions concerning the Tree of Life, innocence and vitality, natural design, fate.

The root idea of the painting may be some piece of Russian folklore, for in Kiev there is a similar, though much cruder, painting by A. A. Shovkunenko called *The Honorable End of the Old Oak Tree* with punning images of goblin creatures worked as visual puns into the leafage.[2]

Tchelitchew's first major American painting was a Temptation of St. Anthony, a subject that in our time, after its immense significance in the late middle ages and the Renaissance, elicited great attention and genius from Flaubert (*La Tentation de st. Antoine*), Joyce (the Circe chapter of *Ulysses*), Wyndham Lewis (*The Childermass*), and Samuel Beckett (*Happy Days*). The painting is called "Phenomena"; instead of the Bosch-like grylli and surrealistic hybrids native to the subject Tchelitchew has human teratological specimens. When the poet (and doctor) William Carlos Williams saw the picture, he delighted the painter by remarking on the accuracy of the monsters. And thereafter monsters began to figure in Williams's long poem *Paterson*, dwarves, hydrocephalics, and notably Henri de Toulouse-Lautrec, monster and genius, who is the poem's symbol for the artistic sensibility.

This seems far afield from Miss Welty's Ovidian Mississippi until we learn that Tchelitchew's monsters in "Phenomena" derive from the poet Charles Henri Ford's connoisseurship of side-show freaks (such as Miss Welty's Petrified Man and Keela, the Outcast Indian Maiden) in his na-

[2]See *The Soviet Encyclopedia*, vol. 48 (1954), p. 132, for an illustration of it.

tive Mississippi. Coincidence; but coincidence in a context. Southern writers, from Poe to Flannery O'Connor, have seen a kind of Sybil in the human monster (the phrase is Tchelitchew's); witness Faulkner's idiots, Carson McCuller's maimed characters, Harry Crews's ogres. Miss Welty likes to quote Flannery O'Connor's reply to someone who asked about this anomaly in Southern imagination. "Well," said Flannery, "we know a freak when we see one."

Dwarves belong to the world of Hades, inside Mountains. They are workers of stone and metal, the crops of Persephone's realm when she is Dis's queen. In the old Greek understanding this realm was a negative to the upper world of light and growing things. It has been an instinct of the European imagination to see the mineral world as finite, dead, and inert.

We can thus trace through art a set of symbols opposing tree to stone, buttercup to gold, light to dark.


VI

Morgana, Mississippi: "The town of Morgana and the county of Mac-Lain . . . are fictitious . . ." says the ritual disclaimer opposite the table of contents in *The Golden Apples*. There is a Morgan City in Mississippi, and a Morgantown, but as with Yoknapatawpha County (said to have been inspired by the Coconino County of "Krazy Kat"), there is no Morgana. Miss Welty has named her town that because the stories are all about the morganatic marriages of Zeus; *morganatic,* a legal term from the German *Morgan,* "morning," meaning a left-handed marriage of a noble with a commoner whose children cannot inherit. The marriages of Zeus with mortals was divine condescension, improving, as Greeks thought, the quality of the family.

But in the straits of Messina between Sicily, Persephone's island and the place most often doubled with Mississippi in Miss Welty's fiction, and Italy, you can see a mirage—the refractive qualities of dense, cold air are different from those of thin, hot air, and if there are two layers of air through which you are looking, one very hot, the other high and cold, you see two visions of distant objects, ships that appear to be in the air, upside down trees, watery cities shimmering above real cities—which the Sicilians call "the enchantment of the witch Morgana la Fata."

She comes from ancient tales of the Welsh, this Morgan le Fay. Many families that bear her name came to Mississippi; she is well known in Sicily because Norman knights brought the Arthurian legends with them. To see the Fata Morgana is to see what's before your eyes and something else also, reality and a vision together. (There is a painting of Tchelitchew's called "Fata Morgana" that depicts wooded hills which become, as we look, a nymph and a faun fallen apart in exhaustion after coupling; it was painted in 1940. Did Miss Welty see it and have her own idea about fusing a mirage with a Celtic name to local reality?)

Mirage is a way of talking about many of Miss Welty's effects. She arranges images so that we see them in sharpest focus and simultaneously as a ghost of reality. When, for instance, a child is rescued from an oncoming train in *Delta Wedding,* we are made to see (if our imagination has its eyes open), the black, fuming chariot of Dis swooping down on Persephone picking flowers. The scene is not exactly a symbolic enactment; it is a mirage of it. The train is called "The Yellow Dog." Troy Flavin, another Dis with another Persephone, has a name that means yellow (*flavin*). Yellow: daffodils, roses, sunflowers; but gold, too. Dis's realm parodies our own ("I have another sun and other stars," he tells Persephone in the *de Raptu*); the apples there, for instance, are golden. The pomegranate in *Delta Wedding* is of stone, a garnet.

VII

For the first time since Dante, symbols became transparent on Joyce's pages. Psychology in the study of dreams defined the symbol as essentially opaque, a confusion rather than an epiphany of meaning. The darker the symbol, the richer it was thought to be, and ambiguity became a virtue in literature. James may be partly responsible, but then James posited for our pleasure in such things an ambiguity that is true of experience (we do not know each other's inner dark of soul, nor what is written in letters locked in a cupboard, nor what people see when they say they've seen a ghost). The symbols of the French *symbolistes* and their school from Oslo to Salerno, from Dublin to Budapest, were not properly symbols at all, but enigmas derived from the German doctrine of elective affinities among things and from Fourier and Swedenborg. These symbols so-called in the sensibilities of Baudelaire and Mallarmé became an abstract art, paralleling the disappearance of intelligible images in the painting of Malevich and Kandinsky a generation later. You cannot interpret a *symboliste* symbol, you can only contemplate it, like a transcendentalist brooding on the word *nature*.

Joyce, who rethought everything, rethought symbolism. It must first of all be organic, not arbitrary or fanciful. It must be logical, resonant, transparent, bright. From Flaubert he had learned that a true symbol must be found in an image that belongs to the narrative. The parrot Loulou in *Un Coeur simple* acts symbolically to make us feel the devotion, loneliness, ecstasy, and inviolable simplicity of Félicité. In its colors we remember the map of America shown Félicité, where her nephew has gone, the windows of the cathedral, the dove incarnating the Holy Spirit; it would not be too much to say that the stuffed Loulou symbolizes Madame Aubain, Paul, Virginie, all that Félicité has loved. It is also her vision of God. Flaubert says none of these things; he makes us see them in a piece of gaudy taxidermy.

In Joyce a rolled up newspaper with the words *Gold Cup* and *Sceptre* among its racing news becomes a symbolic blossom around which two men, symbolic bees, forage. This is a deeper symbolism than more apparent ones in operation at the same time: Odysseus among the Lotus Eaters, a spiritually lost Jew longing to return to Israel ("and the desert shall blossom like the rose"), a man psychologically a drone to his queen-bee wife, a man named Flower enacting the suffering of a saint named Flower (Anthony) and his temptations; and on and on. Joyce's symbols are labyrinths of meaning, but they are logical, and they expand meaning.

They are, as mediaeval grammarians said, *involucra*—seed husks asking to be peeled.

VIII

Plutarch in the first structuralist study of myth, *Isis and Osiris,* demonstrates that there is no one way of telling the tales of the tribe. A myth is a pattern, not a script. Like Lévi-Strauss dismantling and laying out the components of the Oedipus myth to discover that it is about an excess and a lack of kinship, Plutarch sifts through motifs in Greek and Egyptian mythology and makes a philosophical harmony of them by isolating themes (the grief of Isis, the grief of Demeter) and framing concepts (time as the wife of water, space the wife of dryness) implicit in dramatic surfaces. ("The insidious scheming and usurpation of Typhon, then, is the power of drought. . . .") He shows how divergent and unsuspected features can fit into the same contours. His humanistic interpretation of Egyptian cosmology in terms of Hellenic philosophy is a triumph of analytical perception unequalled until Sir James Frazer made his great synthesis of primitive and classical ritual.

Plutarch's insight into the Egyptian mind comes into sharpest focus in his comprehending that Egyptian piety was essentially a sustained meditation of every minutest example of life, to find out what they could see therein of the divine. "Creation is the image of being in matter, and the thing created is a picture of reality." Nothing is trivial, nothing insignificant.

Thought at its beginning was always, as far as we know, nurtured by a fanatic search for analogies, creating a poem in which flowers, girls, trees of certain kinds, sea shells, the moon, song birds, embroidery, ribbons, cats, dill, the left hand, fire, virginity, and springs are all kin. (A Dogon of Upper Volta knows that lizards, foreskins, and the sun are the same thing under three guises, as are menstrual blood, crabgrass seed, and the star Sirius). Lévi-Strauss notes that such thought (which reason, *one* of the Greek modes of the mind, now denies the name of thought at all) survives as what we call art in civilization. He therefore identifies literature and myth, as if no separation had ever occurred.

There was, if not a separation, a going of two ways.


IX

Action is character, and character fate, but in Eudora Welty's fiction we are almost always invited to follow action without purpose, a busy idleness. She observes character when it is in the machinery of unsuspected forces. Hence the preponderance of rituals: funerals, weddings, meals, recitals, journeys. Action of the usual sort is of so little interest to Miss Welty that it pleases her to omit mention of motivations to which Balzac would devote pages.

The story "Going to Naples," for instance, is about an Italian-American mother taking her fat daughter to Sicily to be married. There her plumpness is an asset. Nowhere in the story is this said, and one guesses that the mother has not confided in the daughter. The novel *Delta Wedding* is about a headstrong, stubborn girl who is marrying beneath her, for spite, perhaps, for the perverse joy of having her way, perhaps. Very little is made of this in the novel, though it must be in everybody's mind.

The early stories tend to be about people who are unaware of what they are doing because of feeble-mindedness or invincible ignorance. Her characters are always locked into their worlds. This is sometimes, as with Uncle Daniel Ponder, whose innocence is inviolable, a blessing; sometimes comic, as with the narrator of "Why I Live at the P. O.," but usually it is the context for Miss Welty's ironic observation. Character is the design of our boundaries.


X

If one were asked what absolute distinction makes Miss Welty's fiction different, the answer would not be her alert, perfectly idiomatic, honest prose, nor her immense understanding of character, nor her transmutation of fact into universal symbol, but her unique study of inarticulateness.

She found the inarticulate early in her career, and has carried her study of it forward to her masterpiece *Losing Battles*. The first brilliant analysis of voiceless people for whom reason and caution are alien modes, is the story "The Wide Net." Here a young country wife leaves a note for her husband to find, saying that she is going to commit suicide in the river. He, home from an all-night binge, enlists the countryside in helping him drag the river with a wide net. Afterwards, he discovers (as we suspect he knew by intuition all along) that his wife was hidden behind the door while he was reading her note. The dragging of the river is Homeric in its energy, like a heroic game, involving a fish fry and much congenial fellowship. The river is turned inside out, rendering up a flea market of objects and alligators.

Throughout the story the dialogue addresses itself neither to the drama of the suicide, nor to the problem between husband and wife that might have caused it.

That life happens at all times in a context we do not understand, and that most of our actions go unexplained among ourselves, and that when we do try to be articulate we usually talk about one thing while meaning another, are things we all know. Fiction, however, can usually be caught out ignoring this obvious truth. Flaubert began to acknowledge it, making a distinction between conscious and unconscious motives. Miss Welty takes it for granted that her characters cannot know their predicament, and that they are wanderers full of expectation for they know not what. We feel that there is wisdom in the silence of the two characters in "No Place For You, My Love," the first story in *The Bride of the Innisfallen*, but it would be difficult to say what they are up to, what they expected of each other, why they part as they do. (The story is a descent into Hades, a crossing of the Styx, but are the characters Orpheus and Eurydice or Dis and Persephone?)

This is not to say that Miss Welty is inarticulate, or that she deliberately tells her stories ambiguously, like James or Conrad. She is the most articulate of writers, and her subject is the incoherent buzz of experience, the way we live.

XI

Comedy is the salt of civilization, its critical voice. Having, through Christian charity and Stoic dignity, forbidden cruel laughter (the ancient Roman, like the Pygmy and the Dobu, thought the pain of others to be hilarious), civilized man evolved a comic spirit concerned with his own necessary barbarity, animality, and lapses of breeding.

Being in love (a kindred of madness, as Aristotle said) is biologically no different from being a blissoming ewe or a clickety fox, but man is a social animal cramped by taboos (societies that know no more of genetics than a pullet will not let you marry your sister or your aunt), pride, property, race, and aesthetics (a handsome Spartan was fined for marrying a short, plain wife). Is it any wonder that comedy is said to have grown into an art at weddings?

The comic spirit is forgiving, stands up for freedom and elasticity, and counters the corrosive power of evil by refusing to acknowledge its claim to dominance over the human spirit. Its real enemy is custom drained of significance; it is the ability of life to assert its claims no matter what social forms dictate.


XII

*Losing Battles* ends with an Orpheus and Eurydice walking along a road hand-in-hand, singing "Bringing in the Sheaves." For the first time in Miss Welty's fiction, Eleusinian symbols fuse with Christian ones, and for the first time a love story has a happy ending.

Two-thirds of the way through this transcendently beautiful novel, Granny Vaughn, the ninety-year-old great-grandmother of the hero (the hero, not the protagonist, who is his wife Gloria), rises without preamble from her chair in the midst of a family reunion at a north Mississippi farm, pats her foot, and begins to sing. ("Is it *Frog Went A-Courting* or *Wondrous Love?*" Aunt Birdie whispered. "Sounds like a little of both.") Noah Webster Beecham sprints across children, dogs, and preachers, banjo in hand, to provide the accompaniment.

The joy of this homely aria springs from its rising like music out of music, one of those elate touches Mozart loves to introduce just to show us that even though he has the whole of creation dancing a jig, a shooting star accross the sky won't hurt anything. And by the time of *Losing Battles,* Miss Welty's prose had become pure Mozart. There is nothing consciously musical in it—she is the least affected of great stylists—but of the speech of Mississippi country folk she has made, adding scarcely any words of her own, a music that is as inventive and charmed as the perpetual harmonies of Baroque music.

Out of the talk of fifty members of a family from dawn to midnight, every word of it authentic, she precipitates a plot about which one can only say that it is one of the best stories in the world. It is romantic, it is comic, it is elegiac, it is tragic. It is as close to myth as her other work, with a transparent surface and a *moiré* of allusion. But never have the mythical details been more glittering in their fragmentation—for something wonderfully strange happens if we try to articulate the myth. Orpheus turns out to be female, Eurydice male, their roles reversed. Throughout all her work Persephone has slowly metamorphosed into Eurydice, and now Eurydice becomes Orpheus.

*Losing Battles* is mythological in that its concerns are timeless, its action as old as agriculture and sin. The Scotch and Welsh of northern Mississippi are matriarchal, clannish, and hero-worshipping. The novel's hero, Jack Jordan Renfro, who has busted out of Parchman, the state penitentiary, a day before his sentence is up, to be at Granny Vaughn's birthday party and grand reunion, might well have stepped out of Sir Walter Scott, blue eyes, golden smile, and all. But he is also the same Jack who toppled giants, and he is Orpheus and Parsifal. Like a proper hero he wins his battles by losing them; the truly heroic are hammered by fate. These hill people have been losing battles since Bonnie Prince Charlie went under at Culloden Moor. But they are still there, as permanent as grass.

Against the still music of the reunion Miss Welty has set a raucous countertheme of great hilarity. On a bluff above the reunion she poses a 1932 Buick, its motor running, its occupants fled, its front wheels hanging over nothing, its midriff balanced on an evangelical signpost, with one of Mississippi's most feather-brained citizens picking a guitar in the back seat to keep it from going over. A highly independent mule, a truck amateurishly reconstructed after an encounter with the Memphis Special, a charge of dynamite that eccentrically explodes at intervals, and a committee of Jack and some women and children, all fail for hundreds of pages to save this hapless Buick. ("Looks like a booger had a fit in it," says someone of its eventual state.)

A third, tragic theme interrupts the rich interplay of the pastoral and comic movements. This is the death of Miss Julia Mortimer, the community's teacher, whose selfless life has touched that of everyone at the reunion. Her funeral serves as a coda to the long day that fills most of the novel.

Infinite comic detail, inexhaustible invention: *Losing Battles* is the orchestration of all her former themes. *The Golden Apples* showed how grief and common trouble make the world kin, make a universe of humankind rather than a confusion of suffering individuals. *Losing Battles* insists on reciprocity. That is why Orpheus and Eurydice swap roles, each becoming the other.

XIII

The optimist of *The Optimist's Daughter* is a Mississippi judge named McKelva, and his optimism is hearty enough, foolish enough, generous enough, to lead him to marry in his old age a young wife, a woman from

Texas whom he'd met at a Bar Association convention. Wanda Fay Chisom is her name, and it says all, as Miss Lizzie Stark might remark. Had she come to the attention of Faulkner, her name would be Snopes, and if Flannery O'Connor had created her, she would have been named Shiflet. She is, in the pecking order of the South, white trash.

Miss Welty has been fascinated before by these rapacious, weak-witted, pathologically selfish daughters of the dispossessed, and likes to bring them in sharp contrast (as in *The Ponder Heart*) with the decrepit chivalry and good manners of Mississippi gentry. The result, however complex and sensitive Miss Welty's handling of the misalliance, comes close to being a wail that an older order is being replaced by one that is by contrast barbarous and without transition.

The novel modulates finely between satire and tragedy. It relishes the absurd and the incongruous, with the canny gift of translating both into tragic understanding. The power behind this rare ability is a firm moral sense of human conduct. This sense, humanist and Christian, is yet broader and deeper. It is archaic, from the beginnings of civilization.

In Laurel the judge's daughter, we can see the figure of Psyche (her husband-to-be was named Phil, that is, *Philos,* Love). Thus Wanda Fay is a concentrate of Psyche's nasty, hateful sisters. But, as always, this Psyche figure (named for the tree into which Daphne was turned) is basically Persephone, image of natural order. Laurel (matter shaped by light as a tree) is the living Persephone; Wanda Fay (wand + fay, a sprite) is the dead Persephone. How do we say this otherwise? That the spirit is dying in our time? That we live in a spiritual hell rather than a natural order?

In *The Optimist's Daughter* Miss Welty returns to the impetus that wrote "Petrified Man," her severest vision of conduct without morals or values, which have been replaced by greed in all its forms. The moral condemnation of that powerful story grows from a concern for life as archaic as the myths it alludes to.

Watch how carefully *The Optimist's Daughter* flows against a frieze of flowers, as if all the action were a ritual of spring. The people are all rootless (the Texas Chisoms live in trailers rather than houses), or withering. The vision is chilling and tragic, and yet it implies a cyclical pattern, however awful the loss. (The most eloquent Eleusinian symbol is the breadboard, which Wanda Fay mutilates out of ignorance and carelessness).

XIV

The meaning of the world, said Wittgenstein, is outside the world. Events and values are distinguishable only in relation to others. A totality of events and values, the world itself, requires another. Hence our recourse to symbols, which serve for a sense of otherness, and our inadequate ideas of time and death, of purpose and being. Into this inadequacy mankind introduced an imaginary world in which the elusive is made to stand still, and an order too extensive and too complex for our understanding is given limit and measure.

The artist shows the world as if meaning were inherent in its particulars. We dress biological imperative in custom and ritual; the artist dresses it in analogy, and finds design in accident and rhythm in casualness. That every event is unique and every essence distinct from all others rarely interests the artist, for whom event is pattern and essence melodic.

XV

We need a geography of the imagination to understand the appearance and significance of cultural vernaculars beyond their origins. Such a geography would find among its concerns the continuity of culture into civilization, its transformation there, and the physiology of its integration.

Anthropology has demonstrated for over a century now that cultures cohere in patterns of wholly imaginative assumptions about the world that constitute systems of law, kinship, language, and philosophy. Civilization when we are first aware of it accepts culture as its archaic moment, precisely when it has lost its feeling for that moment and can be critical of it.

It would be useful to know where we are in this historical progression; I doubt if we are anywhere near finding out. We have gotten as far as seeing the shores of the Mediterranean as the origin of the world as it now is. Even the technological inventions of cultures alien to the Mediterranean have passed through that culture to be appropriated by it and returned: printing, for instance, the elements of which, paper, ink and moveable type, are Chinese, but a modern Chinese printing plant is European, a reimportation.

Arabian optics and botany, Mesopotamian astronomy, northern European ship design and navigation, Hindu mathematics: all are known to us in Mediterraneanized idiom. Plato would recognize the survival of his ideas in the Marxist state, both Leninist and Maoist. It can be argued that there is but one civilization (while still understanding very little of the archaic root that branched into China and Europe) which now has absorbed all but the most primitive cultures.

History is still grandly dark. When Marcel Griaule died he was not sure if he had discovered that the Dogon had invented the zodiac, diffused by the dawn of history all over the world, or whether their version of it was a decayed knowledge which they took over from another culture thousands of years ago. Professor de Santillana's speculations on the evolution of myth into science, Foucault's prospectus for an archeology of knowledge, Frobenius's and Spengler's theories of diffusion and metamorphosis, Lévi-Strauss's formulae for cultural structures, Eliade's identification of rite and sacredness of place as a common denominator of religions—all contribute to, but do not enter upon, a geography of the imagination.

Geography—lands, seas, climates—is overlaid with the second geography of political groups, empires, linguistic conglomerates. The geography of the imagination would be a third construing of cultural divisions, showing, for instance, the areas of the portrait, the epic, the novel, the symphony. Inside what boundaries is the myth of Orpheus and Eurydice meaningful? The version of it that we first know arose in the Rhodope mountains of Bulgaria, though it has obvious derivations from Akkadia and Dilmun. Why was it an Ovidian and Miltonic theme, why has it remained so close to opera and the dance, why was it a major theme of Parisian culture in the twentieth century? Why was it so compelling a story for Poe? For Eudora Welty?

Folklore has been of service in tracing the spread of motifs; literary history and theory have made fortuitous and largely random tracings of certain routes; Jungian psychology has posited an obscurantist hypothesis of archetypes that can ignore both history and geography.


XVI

Eudora Welty shares with Samuel Beckett the mastery of English prose among writers now living; she is one of the greatest of American writers in all our history, taking her place beside Hawthorne, Poe, and O. Henry in the craft of the short story. She cannot be placed as a novelist for the simple reason that her novels are unlike any written in the United States. We have to turn to Flaubert and Joyce to find a family for them, and ultimately we have to note that as the culminator of a particular tradition in prose she is alone, a superb and triumphant artificer.

Her distinctness is still blurred by critics and anthologists. To isolate it we want to observe certain qualities in her art that are inventions as profound and successful as any in our literature, and progressions in the development of fiction after Joyce which must be seen alongside those of Faulkner and Beckett.

Art is the attention we pay to the wholeness of the world. Ancient intuition went foraging after consistency. Religion, science, and art are alike rooted in the faith that the world is of a piece, that something is common to all its diversity, and that if we knew enough we could see and give a name to its harmony.

An anecdote about Faulkner relates that once on a spring evening he invited a woman to come with him in his automible, to see a bride in her wedding dress. He drove her over certain Mississippi back roads and eventually across a meadow, turning off his headlights and proceeding in darkness. At last he eased the car to a halt and said that the bride was before them. He switched on the lights, whose brilliance fell full upon an apple tree in blossom.

The sensibility that shapes that moment is of an age, at least, with civilization itself.

# Charles Ives

At the end of Charles Ives's centennial year *The New York Times Book Review* devoted its December 1st issue to the important books of 1974. That it did not mention, either under Significant or Notable or Music or any rubric at all, David Wooldridge's *From the Steeples and Mountains: A Study of Charles Ives* is an oversight (it probably wasn't an oversight, but out of courtesy to the Republic's most distinguished journal of literature we will take it as an oversight) comparable to omitting Lincoln from a list of the presidents. The *Times*, indeed, was in fashion in pretending that Mr. Wooldridge's book does not exist; the reviewers slept through its publication, and its publishers are under the impression that they have published a flop. They have, on the contrary, published the only book on Ives worthy of its subject, the first thorough study of Ives's music, the first biography of our greatest composer.

A hundred years ago last October 20th—on Rimbaud's twentieth birthday and while *Une Saison en enfer* was going through the press of Poot et Cie. in Brussels—Charles Ives was born in Danbury, Connecticut. Naturally the site is now a parking lot; naturally the parking lot is owned by a bank. For his centennial, his country, whose greatest composer he was, and among its most distinguished patriots, issued no commemorative postage stamp, erected no monument, set no plaque, commanded no orchestra to play his music.

True, it was a year in which the country had to turn out a pack of scoundrels, porch climbers, thieves, bullies, liars, and bores from the Executive Branch of the government, a year in which the sludge of usury which forms the basis of our economy began to slither and lurch, a year indistinguishable from any other in the national contempt for the arts.[1]

Ives would not have been shocked. The government was simply living up to his opinion of politicians. He was born in the administration of Grant. He had his first heart attack after shouting at Franklin Roosevelt a principle of democracy which Roosevelt couldn't understand. He wanted to amend the Constitution so that two thirds of the states had to ratify a declaration of war. Ten years after his death we were capable of getting into a war that cost a million dollars a day and fifty thousand American lives without anybody in the government being able to say just how we got into it.

Perversely he read the London *Times* to find out the news. He did not listen to the radio, paid scant attention to books. He got through a long life without reading Robert Frost; he looked into Gertrude Stein and called her a Victorian. Like Pound, his junior by eleven years, he considered Browning to be the great modern poet, and wrote a handsome, majestic overture in his honor—in twelve-tone rows, a dozen years before Schoenberg invented them.

His creative life occupies only nineteen years, 1898 to 1917, of his seventy-nine. In that intense period, Mr. Wooldridge shows, with great depth of biographical detail and sharpness of critical attention, that Ives "wrote more music, of greater stature, than most composers in a lifetime."

By this time all literate people know the strange history of that music, how Ives's reticence would have kept it from being played at all, how Nicolas Slonimsky played it in Boston, San Francisco, Paris; how German musicologists complained that it hurt their ears; how small groups heard some of the string works and songs; how John Kirkpatrick began his long task of teaching audiences to hear the Concord Sonata in Spar-

---

[1] The O. Henry centennial was similarly denied a commemorative stamp, though not by the Union of Soviet Socialist Republics.

tanburg, South Carolina, where a large cement apple sits on a pedestal in the Square. And Mr. Wooldridge has uncovered evidence that Mahler played the Third Symphony in Munich in 1910!

David Wooldridge, in the face of such a strange history, has had to write not one but three books about Ives, interweaving them as he proceeds. One is a brilliant, Olson-like essay on American music and American culture, so that we can see the courage and breathtaking dare of what Ives was doing, and knew he was doing. He was staging, almost alone, a transcendental movement in music paralleling the same movement in literature: a musical declaration of independence from Europe. Because he was therefore out of phase with what seemed to be American cultural history, he was like a lost battalion of an army which still had its own battle to fight, long after the war was over. He was not trying to be the Jefferson of music, but its Emerson and Thoreau.

The second book within Mr. Wooldridge's work is a study of the music. Both composer and conductor, he writes from that advantage as well as from a deeply philosophical sense of what Ives was inventing, why, and how.

The third book is Ives's dark, tragic life. Just before Mr. Wooldridge's study I had read the fifty-six accounts of Ives in Vivian Perlis's *Charles Ives Remembered: An Oral History*, a collection of reminiscences for which Ms. Perlis ought to be awarded a medal by Congress, and the effect had been that of reading about fifty-six extraordinarily interesting men all named Charles Ives. Mr. Wooldridge focusses the kaleidoscope into a single, resolved image—a genius who made two million dollars in the insurance business, composing on weekends, strangely anxious that no one see him as an artist, accepting occasions for music as they fell into his hands (the explosion of the *General Slocum* on which Leopold Bloom brooded, the sinking of the *Lusitania*.) He was a man needlessly defensive and pathologically touchy; he came to guard his obscurity as if it were his genius.

Mr. Wooldridge's study belongs to that small category of books written with passion and precision out of a need to understand, and make others understand, a subject of great importance and great complexity. It is a chapter in our cultural history which had hitherto been blank.

If I have any reservations about so accomplished and splendid a book, it is a slight quarrel over some points of interpretation having to do with Ives's subtlety. Far from being mawkishly sentimental, the little trilogy of songs of which "Tom Sails Away" is the center seems to me to be a triumph of bitter contempt—the kind of satire that comes equally from heart and spleen. I concede Mr. Wooldridge his stricture while reserving my choice to listen to those songs as if they were wickedly satirical. Ives is a composer where frame of mind while listening is crucial. His superb variations on *America* can be heard in innocence or as a glorious take-off on church organists and their styles (Methodist Gloom, Presbyterian Correctness) and Ives the Imp—for one of the variations is not *America* but a Persian dance that sounds like it.

Invited to celebrate Ives, I have thus far proceeded by disguising my celebration as a review of David Wooldridge's study, as that pioneering book fell under the evil spirit that has kept Ives himself a shy ghost in American art. How long it took us to see Melville! We still have no notion of Poe's greatness. Our Whitman and our Thoreau are not Whitman and Thoreau. We have a wrong, vague, and inadequate appreciation of Stephen Foster. And the great Formalist painter Grant Wood, who in Europe would have founded a school.

Did Mann hear about Ives from Schoenberg and conceive of his *Doktor Faustus* then and there? Faustus is a rich composite, an allegory of the German spirit, but we still have to account for descriptions of imaginary music corresponding so eerily to the Fourth Symphony. Hearsay is a powerful instigation to the creative mind. What a symbol it would make, and what a closing of the circle: Goethe, Transcendentalism, Ives, Mann, Goethe.

June 1863: a bandmaster in shako and sash snaps out the cake-walk rhythms of "Dixie" while Lee rides ahead of the flags across the Mason and Dixon Line. The troops shout a great *Huzzah!* It is a moment: *iacta alea est*. Military music haunted Ives all of his career; it was the tangible memory of his father, it was an art that strangely went to war, where its presence was as right and congenial as singing in church. "When the cannonade was at its height," Col. Fremantle wrote in his account of Gettysburg, "a Confederate band of music, between the cemetery and ourselves, began to play polkas and waltzes, which sounded very curious, accompanied by the hissing and bursting of shells." Before the line of tanks at El Alamein marched a line of highland pipers, Custer rode into Little Big Horn to "The Girl I Left Behind Me," Raleigh sailed into Cadiz harbor, *played an insulting fanfarol on the trumpet,* and sailed out again; the redcoats at Yorktown laid down their muskets, company by company, to a jig called "The World Turned Upsidedown"; D'Annunzio rode into Fiume at the head of his army of veteran *garibaldini* and Boy Scouts preceded by a symphony orchestra playing Verdi. Music is what the Ogboni call "words of power." It is both a spirit and a summoner of spirit; woe to them who trivialize words of power.

One way of beginning to hear Ives is to listen to how he summons spirits: his martial music incorporates the chains of the caissons, the rattle of gear, distant bugles, tolling bells of churches near the battle. When he summons various songs and noises all at once, he is working the synergy of heightened quotation: the same effect Borges savors when he has a character drench himself in Cervantes's psychology and style until, after a lifetime of trying, he can write a page of the *Quijote.* The page is identical with one of Cervantes's, but "much richer." The lines Eliot appropriates for *The Waste Land,* Pound for *The Cantos,* Wordsworth for *The Prelude* operate in this way. It is one of the century's modes. As value inheres in money alone, the arts shore up against their ruin.

Ives always quotes with perfect love and perfect contempt.

Ives has remained in classic American obscurity because:
  He is ironic.
  He is comic, satiric, lyric, contentious all at once.
  His music is a matter of ideas.
  Practically every composition is in a new form.
  He despised music which beguiles, overpowers, or exists for itself: and this is our sole conception of music. It is practically impossible to discover people listening to music. We have it everywhere, dribbling, droning, booming. We converse to it, drive to it, wait to it, have our teeth drilled to it. It is simply another narcotic. A person who assumes a predilection for music finds himself dumbfounded before Ives, where listening is required. Conversely people who use music for sensual pleasure find Ives flat and unmoving. I see an analogy in Browning, where you have to keep awake line by line: you can't read him, as people manage to read Keats or Tennyson, "for the beauty of it."

The first American composer and the last great composer in the western tradition that descends from Bach, Ives is in the unique position of being a great inventor who ends rather than begins a series. He is therefore like R. Buckminster Fuller, fellow transcendentalist and spiritual twin: their content goes back to archaic beginnings, their methods are profound inventions. Both have been repeatedly dismissed as cranks, though success thorough and indisputable vindicates their every venture. You can't argue with a geodesic dome or with the tragic grandeur of Ives's Fourth Symphony.

Ives aligns with the most significant art of his time: with Pound and Eliot in the reuse of extant compositions (Mann again, in ascribing to Leverkuhn as to his own narrative prose the mode of exposition by serious parody as *the* mode of the twentieth century), with Joyce in the hermetic diffusion of symbolism throughout a work, with Picasso in exploring the possibilities of extending forms and techniques.

But practically all of Ives is like nothing else. There is beneath every passage a grasp of vision completely Ives's. I hear in it a lifelong grief for all that is tragic in our history: the caissons going into place at Shiloh, Foster's taking up the abolitionist cause in his songs, the primal force of music as a word of power (the black regiment that marched through a burning Richmond singing "The Day of Jubilo," the bagpipers who led the tank attack at El Alamein, the band that played "Nearer My God to Thee" as the *Titanic* went down). Music, we are told, was born from tragedy; nearly all of Ives's grand themes allude to tragedies, particularly to that of the Civil War, and to his father's role in it as a musician.

The surface of Ives's music is music, just as the surface of Joyce's *Ulysses* is a tissue of clichés in one convention or another. Pound's *Cantos* was to have been an unbroken surface of voices from the past until at Pisa in the cage the design broke and the poet spoke in his own voice and in expectation of death before a firing squad.

Collage is retrospective in content, modern in its design. Kept up, it will recapitulate and summarize the history of its own being. One can go through Ives noting the voices (the Alcotts trying to speak Beethoven and Culture from Europe, Thoreau speaking through a hymn played on his flute against the voice of his woods, Fourth of July bands speaking with a martial air beside the voice of ragtime; Browning, Arnold, Whitman). Ives got as far as Isaiah asking *What is Man?* in the Fourth Symphony. History answers in the spiritual articulation of music, and finally a chorus of unidentifiable voices answers, in inarticulate words.

# Ozymandias

On a winter afternoon as brown as the dingy sheep driven early to fold down the high street beyond the darkening garden, a gentleman banker from London, Horace Smith by name, is sitting in the long library of a pleasant house in the village of Marlow, a few miles up the Thames from Henley. He is writing a sonnet.

There is something of the prismatic tidiness of Dombey about him and something of the rubicund joviality of Mr. Pickwick. He wears the last century's small clothes still, but his coat is already the alpaca of the age to come. The novels he writes under the name Horatio Smith are like his clothes: they begin in the eighteenth-century manner and end like nineteenth-century novels. The world has forgotten them, and him, though he was a talented, wonderfully humorous, and generous man. He accepts a pinch of snuff from his host's silver box, dips his quill, and begins to write on a block of paper the top sheet of which bears his host's drawing of a pine forest, an imp, and a labyrinth. There is, however, room for a sonnet.

Outside the leaded diamond panes a thoroughly dreary Saturday afternoon makes the firelit room even more comfortable. A white haze from the river sifts through the rusted garden. It is but two days after Christmas of the year 1817, and the banker has walked up the Tyburn Turnpike from London to Uxbridge, and thence by various country roads to the lacemaking town of Marlow.

Our banker's host, a mere boy to judge from his snub nose, spindly six feet, and wild hair (he ducks his head in a pail of water from time to time, for the freshness of it, as he explains), has been reading Gibbon all week and talks about history, to our banker's straight face, as if it were nothing but a succession of tyrants gnawing the elbows of the poor. His wife, a wide-eyed young lady, reads Tacitus for hours on end. She, too, has written a novel, now at the printer. *Frankenstein, or The Modern Prometheus,* she calls it.

The talk of the three turns from history to certain modern travelers who have been looking at, and theorizing on, cities and empires that have disappeared from the earth with scarcely a trace—to Count Constantin François de Chasseboeuf de Volney, whose *Voyage to Egypt and Syria* of 1787 and *Ruins, or Meditations on the Destiny of Empires* of 1791 were books much discussed in Europe and America, and to Johann Ludwig Burckhardt, who had refound the "rose-red city" Petra and the colossal statues of Rameses II at Abu Simbel, and who died earlier that year, buried as a Mohammedan somewhere in the wastes of Egypt.

Our banker has been reading the historian Diodorus, and it is on a description he has found there of a toppled monument that he is about to write a meditative sonnet.

Some 3,300 years before, the grandest Pharaoh of them all, Rameses II, set up a statue of himself at Thebes. It was sixty feet tall, weighed a thousand tons, and had inscribed on it: "I am User-ma-Ra, ruler of rulers, king of Upper and Lower Egypt, He of the Sedge and Bee, the mighty justice of Re, the chosen of Re. If a man wishes to know the greatness of me, here I lie, let him surpass what I have done."

Six hundred years later, the Greek traveler Hekataios visited Egypt and wrote an account of Rameses' great statue, doing the best he could with his name but making a hash of it. "Osymandyas" was how "User-ma-Ra" sounded to his Greek ears. His book is lost, but Diodorus, which our banker has open before him, included his description in his forty-volume history of the world written in the time of Augustus Caesar.

Here the inscription runs: "King of Kings Osymandyas am I. If any want to know how great I am and where I lie, let them outdo my deeds if they can."

So by lamplight and the failing winter sun Horace Smith the literary banker writes:

In Egypt's sandy silence, all alone,
Stands a gigantic Leg, which far off throws
The only shadow that the desert knows.
"I am great Ozymandias," saith the stone,
"The King of kings; this mighty city shows
The wonders of my hand." The city's gone!
Naught but the leg remaining to disclose
The sight of that forgotten Babylon.
We wonder, and some hunter may express
Wonder like ours, when through the wilderness
Where London stood, holding the wolf in chase,
He meets some fragment huge, and stops to guess
What wonderful, but unrecorded, race
Once dwelt in that annihilated place.

Before he has finished, his boyish host joins him across the table. He proposes to write a sonnet on the same theme. And writes:

There stands by Nile a single pedestal.
On which two trunkless legs of crumbling stone
Quiver thro sultry mist; beneath the sand
Half sunk a shattered visage lies, whose frown
And wrinkled lips impatient of command
Betray some sculptor's art whose

Here he quits, nibbles his quill, and strikes out the first line and the first word of the second line.

Smith has finished his sonnet. His host takes a new sheet and begins over:

I met a traveller from an antique land,
Who said—"Two vast and trunkless legs of stone
Stand in the desart. . . . Near them, on the sand,
Half sunk a shattered visage lies, whose frown,
And wrinkled lip, and sneer of cold command,
Tell that its sculptor well those passions read
Which yet survive, stamped on these lifeless things,
The hand that mocked them, and the heart that fed;
And on the pedestal, these words appear:
My name is Ozymandias, King of kings.
Look on my Works, ye Mighty, and despair!

Nothing beside remains. Round the decay
Of that colossal Wreck, boundless and bare
The lone and level sands stretch far away."

Thus, in ten minutes flat (or thereabouts), Shelley wrote one of the masterpieces of English poetry. But look how a Pharaoh, a committee of historians and explorers, and the luckless Horace Smith, wrote it for him. Genius is perhaps being in the right place at the right time, prepared for the moment. They sent their sonnets off to a newspaper, which printed both. The honest Smith called his "On a Stupendous Leg of Granite, Discovered Standing by Itself in the Deserts of Egypt, with the Inscription Inserted Below." Shelley called his "Ozymandias." Genius may also be knowing how to title a poem.

# Christ's Cunning Rimesmith

The winter of 1875 was one of ferocious gales on the English Channel. In the early hours of the 7th of December, a German liner named the *Deutschland,* sailing from Bremen to New York, foundered and broke up on the Kentish coast. As it lurched and rolled, its keel caught in liquid sand, its decks flooded, and its passengers and crew climbed as best they could in pitch-dark and howling, finger-freezing wind, into the swaying rigging. Many could not mount there, and held onto the gunwales and masts until waves clawed them into the sea. Among these were five Franciscan nuns who held hands in a circle and prayed until they were drowned. A survivor reported that the tallest of them cried out at the last, "O Christ, come quickly!"

To ponder the divergent claims of this pitiful calamity on the attention of a Victorian father and son drops us into the rift between matter and spirit which so many earnest nineteenth-century sensibilities ached to close. For Manley Hopkins, Anglican, spiritual advisor to the Hawaiian Islands, and broker in marine insurance, the disaster was a financial as well as a deplorable event. For his son Gerard Manley, a Jesuit who had renounced poetry along with the world, it was the signal that his love of words and worldly beauty had a place in his priesthood.

He spent a year composing "The Wreck of the Deutschland," as impassioned a poem as we have in English. Even now, when it is normal to expect all serious poetry to be difficult to construe, Hopkins's archaic "sprung rhythm" (a syncopation of metric which he heard in everyday talk—"do it; it needs to be done, don't it?"—and in nursery rhymes— "One, two: buckle my shoe / Three, four: shut the door") and "chiming of consonants" imitated from Welsh verse, require sharp attention to follow. To the editors of the Jesuit magazine, *The Month,* where he sent it for publication, it was bewildering. They accepted it, tried tampering with it, and finally shelved it. Forty-two years would pass before the world could see it in print.

Hopkins's poems became the ward of his friend and confidant, the Poet Laureate Robert Bridges, who cautiously (and with much misgiving) published them in 1918, thirty years after Hopkins's death.

By then, at least, there was some comprehension of the movement afoot among philologists and poets to effect a renaissance in English diction by anglicizing the language. This movement would lead to the Early English Text Society and the Oxford English Dictionary, would influence Hopkins, Hardy, Yeats, Pound, and many another. It was the feeling, both patriotic and aesthetic, of certain scholars like F. J. Furnivall, R. C. Trench, William Barnes, and James Murray, that English can say anything it wants to in a native way without coining from French, Latin, or Greek.

We ought, for instance, to say *foreword* rather than *preface*—it is a measure of the movement's partial victory that we now use both words. We should say *sunprint* for *photograph, inwit* for *conscience, wordhoard* for *vocabulary.* The most rigorous of the anglicizers was not Hopkins but Charles Montagu Doughty, whose allegiance to pure English in his *Travels in Arabia Deserta* (whose first champion was Robert Bridges) and his great unknown epic, *The Dawn in Britain,* has had a lasting impact on style—by way of Henry Green to John Updike, for instance; by way of Joyce to Eudora Welty, for another.

Hopkins saw in this predilection for real roots, as against grafting or borrowing, the same spirit that moved him in Duns Scotus and Heraclitus. His conversion to Catholicism, indeed, follows, as he would say, the same *instress* and *inscape.* His was not a mind for half measures or compromises. He grew up, as Paddy Kitchen shows us in an admirably brief biography,[1] in a thoroughly Victorian world. It was a world of decreed hierarchies, it recognized only a world-design of its own making, and rejected all that did not conform to its sense of comfort, wealth, or propriety.

The Oxford to which the young Hopkins was sent to be made into a Victorian gentleman was, as it turned out, a try-pot for rendering minds of susceptible plasticity into various contending idealisms. As we know from Geoffrey Faber's study of the Oxford Movement (of which Paddy Kitchen gives a rather too breathless summary as her introductory chapter), there was concealed in the High Church cause an epicurean philosophy which on inspection turns out to be a blend of pederasty, aestheticism, Anglo-Catholicism, and good breeding.

Walter Pater, connoisseur of male adolescent charm and the very fine fine arts, was Hopkins's tutor. Young men walked arm-in-arm in those pre-Freudian days, swore eternal friendship, and sighed wistfully that these times were not those of Alcibiades and Lysis. Their prep-school years had been one constant sideswiping by buggery and sadistic caning that all too frequently was masochistically received. Paddy Kitchen sees the stain of Oxford sexual mores throughout Hopkins's poetry (in "The Bugler's First Communion," "The Loss of the Eurydice," and "Epithalamion"—Hopkins's Whitmanesque description of boys bathing in a pool).

But surely if ever an appetence was refined into purest essence, Hopkins's habitual awareness of the sexuality of man and nature is the most chaste we are likely to know. It is Hopkins's delineation of beauty that leads most of us to him in the first place. He wrote when words still had to serve science in its descriptions of nature. The photograph and half-tone cut had not yet arrived to assist geologists like Hugh Miller and Agassiz. A generation of exact prose invented the discipline with which Hopkins described the textures and shapes of things. (A scholar might do worse for the next thesis on Hopkins than compare Miller's descriptions of fossil fish of the Old Red Sandstone, Ruskin's descriptions of flowers and rocks, and Agassiz's descriptions of turtle embryos with Hopkins's verbal precision—which, of course, has other instigations as well in scholasticism and in Greek poetry.)

One would like to follow more closely than Kitchen's biography does Hopkins's sweet mind from Victorian Oxford to his theological training with the Jesuits, and to have some understanding of his researches into Scotus and the pre-Socratics. He was, in every sense, extraordinary. It is chilling to remind ourselves that Joyce's Jesuits were, some of them,

[1]Paddy Kitchen, *Gerard Manley Hopkins* (New York: Atheneum, 1979).

Hopkins's colleagues in his last days in Dublin. What did Hopkins look like to the Jesuit who conducts the businessmen's retreat in Joyce's story "Grace"?

Once we have learned to be on our guard against Paddy Kitchen's style (she says "vulnerable" when she means "susceptible," "as" when she means "while," and is apt to introduce Jungian jargon), we can appreciate the goodness of her biography. It is tersely narrated, and packs in a wealth of details about Hopkins's uneventful outward life. It is charming to know that Hopkins helped direct a Jesuit performance of *Macbeth* in which, for propriety's sake, Lady Macbeth becomes Uncle Donald, and that a sermon of Hopkins's was so ludicrous that it was drowned out by the laughter of fellow seminarians. Hopkins had thought he could make sacred geography imaginable by comparing the Sea of Galilee to a left ear. He then located Nazareth by saying that it would be near the corresponding nose, the Jordan would run down through the hair of the head, and so on. We learn that Hopkins was batted out of a Jesuit spelling bee (an American contest that had become all the rage in Europe) by the word "allegiance." It is interesting to know that he had socialist hopes for the future, that he knew the Yeats family in Dublin, that he admired Whitman while thinking him depraved, that he did not like Browning, that he met John Tyndall, the evolutionist, on a walking tour of Switzerland, that he tried his hand at composing music.

He was still young when the filthy drinking water of Dublin did him in: typhoid. His last years were his most trying. He was at the peak of his creativity, he had hopes of contributing to the scholarship of Greek prosody, and all his time was claimed by a somnambulism of classroom drill and paper grading. His sensitive nature had suffered in ministering to parishes in Liverpool, London, and Glasgow. Drunkenness and poverty distressed him to behold. He was not an effective preacher. Except for a short, golden period at Oxford, his ministry was the trial of his soul he knew it would be when he took his vows. But Dublin seemed to be the sum of all that he found most uncongenial. It was drunken, inert, and poor; and the university was a treadmill.

At his funeral there was no one to suspect that the obscure professor of Greek interred at Glasnevin Cemetery (where fifteen years later an imaginary mourner named Leopold Bloom would opine that priestly mumbo jumbo alleviates grief, as it is a kind of poetry) would be recognized in the next century as one of the greatest of English poets. "I am so happy," were his last words.

# Joyce's Forest of Symbols

In Book 10 of *The Republic* we learn that we can all be artists by turning a mirror round and round, like Buck Mulligan in the first chapter of *Ulysses,* and that a man named Er, the son of Armenius, came to life at his own funeral and explained metempsychosis. This Er turns up in *Finnegans Wake* fused with Arminius and Comenius, quarrelers with Fate, wearing the mask of his namesake, the thundergod Er. "Airmienious" Joyce calls him, and we know him by the company he keeps, Hurdlebury Fenn and other attendants of their own obsequies.

This Finneganish Er, who when his heroic age is over will learn to sit by his wick in his wick, civilized enough to have a house and a lamp, and be known as Earwicker, says that in witnessing souls ready for reincarnation he saw Orpheus choose to return as a swan, Ajax choose to be a lion, and Ulysses choose to be a private citizen minding his own business.

Giambattista Vico could have advised Ulysses that he had made his choice in harmony with the course of history, for the age of heroes and kings gives way to the age of the common man, just as the age of the gods had given way to that of heroes and kings.

We can locate Bloom by other roads. The hero of the Aegean epic becomes in Athens the center of his nobility rather than a man who places his nobility at the center of events. In the truest genius of Roman literature the hero becomes the privileged spectator, like the charming scapegraces of Apuleius and Petronius.

The gods give way to magic, virtues and vices become civic rather than tragic and individual, and literature shifts from its concern for the relationship between God and man to a concern for the relationship between man and society. Yet the hero remains a hero, whether venturing into the lands of faery or into hell and purgatory.

Not until Sancho Panza began to be as interesting as his metempsychotic master was the age of heroes really over. And then, to speed up literary history to a blur, the children of Sancho emerge as Mr. Pickwick and Tartarin de Tarascon, who are products of metempsychosis by enthusiasm, and thence to the ultimate enthusiasts, Francois Denys Bartholomée Bouvard and Juste Romain Cyrille Pécuchet, who believe that the verities are not on Olympus, or in the club arm of a Hercules, or on a throne, but in the Bureau of Statistics and in the university, or in their equivalent, the encyclopedia.

The fourth age of Vico has arrived, and the man of acumen feeds the printing press with matter, puffs the winds of trade, and participates in all the events of history insofar as they have survived; rather, *as* they have survived—the prehistoric triple legs of the Manx arms, the ancient symbols persisting, the Sirens still at their station, Polyphemus still drunk and throwing things, Ulysses still seeking his home.

No book, unless it is *Don Quijote,* has been more aware than *Ulysses* of its place in time. *Oolysaze* (so Joyce said his title, a pronunciation that reflects better the genitive of *Ulex,* the mountain gorse that grows in the nostrils of the giant Finnegan, the heroic barbarity from which Bloom is descended and refined away from), *Ulysses* projects all its images transparently upon other images, which in turn lie transparently over other images, several piles deep. To read these multiple images we must learn to suffer the ridiculous image to disclose itself within the tragic, the mythic in the trivial, the ironic in the poignant. You do not read *Ulysses;* you watch the words. Reading is possible only after we have mastered Joyce's method and can share with him the tragic grief and comic fury that charge every word. So complex a fusion of meanings becomes a picture of meaning itself in all its darkness of ambiguity, ironic duplicity, and triumphant articulation of dead symbols, signifying that symbols, like seeds, come alive in due season and place.

Comic fury: the advantages of flexibility held up for comparison with the paralysis of Dublin. Tragic grief: that a history containing the bright sanity and comprehensive forgiveness of Homer, the virtue of Epameinondas, the minds of da Vinci and Edison, the ministry of Christ, the ear of von Flotow, has come to this.

*Ulysses* is more of a poem than a novel, or rather is a poem inside a novel. If tragedy educates our hearts against pain, and comedy makes us good-natured, Joyce's art acts like Galvani's electrical current touched to the dead frog's heart. We quicken. We feel the charm of the matter and the manner. With our attention thus fixed, the charm can work its transformation.

Most serious readers feel that they have by now mastered the prose, prose which fifty years ago gave intelligent people trouble. Shaw, Wells, Virginia Woolf, Yeats could not read it. Thomas Wolfe and Wyndham Lewis misread it. Thomas Mann longed to read it. Ezra Pound's interest soon waned after an initial excitement over its Flaubertian qualities.

*Stately,* the book begins; followed by *plump,* two adjectives modifying one Buck Mulligan who, like Scipio Africanus, shaves every day. *Stately, plump:* these two words, studied for what we might call the Kells effect, the symbolic content of illuminated lettering serving a larger purpose than its decoration of geometry, imps, and signs, contain the word that ends the book, Molly's ambiguous but eloquent *yes* (so that *Ulysses,* like the *Wake,* is circular, as is the *Portrait,* for the fabulous artificer at the end made artificial cows like the fabulous cow of the beginning—"anybody can be an artist by turning a mirror round and round").

When we are ready to scrutinize the Kells decoration, we can see that *stately* and *plump* encapsulate the whole first chapter. *Stately* is an adjective for kings, *plump* for plebeians. The etymologist Skeat, whose dictionary Stephen Dedalus carried in his pocket, gives "rude and clownish" for the original connotation of *plump.* It is the plump Falstaff who sings

O, won't we have a merry time
Drinking whisky, beer, and wine
On coronation,
Coronation day?

And it is the putatively stately Hal who must dismiss the spirit-stealing Falstaff before he can be a kingly man. Behind Hal and Falstaff are Everyman and Misrule. Joyce builds the chapter around a spectacle of authority usurped by disorder, Telemachus's plight, Hamlet's plight.

Stephen, melancholy, ineffectual, depressed, stands in contrast to Mulligan's rough ebullience. The one has power and spirit, the other longs for them. Mulligan, bearing his bowl of lather on which a mirror and razor lie crossed, is in fact a priest, but the god whose altar he approaches, intoning playfully the opening of the Latin Mass, is not the Christian God. He is the Shavian god whose mask Nietzsche had placed on the face of the *Zeitgeist,* Zoroaster's god Ahura-Mazda, the sun, whose processes of light, daily resurrection, and serpentine course through the zodiac were symbolized in the ancient world as a Kronos with a lion's head, or as we can say, *Leopold.*

Mulligan wears the yellow robe of the Mithraic hierophant and carries the sacrificial bowl containing the sperm of a slain bull, the razor with which he slew, and the mirror with which the priest of Mithra flashed tidings of the sun to bless the earth: south, east, and west, omitting Dublin (to the north) in his blessing. He growls at Stephen in the ritual lion greeting of Mithraics, and presides at a feast of milk and honey, the Mithraic eucharist. And all this is happening on the Mithraic sabbath, the sixteenth of every month.

Stephen longs and does not long for Mulligan's euphoric and pagan allegiance to the age's *élan vital,* and is thus pictured as an aspirant to Mithraic orders, the stages of initiation being distributed symbolically through the chapter. With diligence and perspicacity one can espy the Mithraic orders: that face gilded with marmalade is one, Mulligan's flapping his arms is another. The degree of lionhood is concealed in a song:

I am the boy
That can enjoy
Invisibility

—that is, Ariel, Lion of God.

But Shakespeare's Ariel also, for Mulligan is a kind of Caliban playing havoc with Stephen's melancholia. Stephen should therefore be Ariel, though Mulligan, borrowing a witticism of Wilde's, calls him Caliban. Correspondences in this first chapter are frequently topsy-turvy: Stephen has the pagan name, Mulligan is the pagan. Stephen has Ariel's soul and Caliban's status. As in a comedy, affairs are upside-down and must be righted. They are not, but the process of righting has begun when the novel ends.

The Mithraic correspondences in the first chapter can be accounted for. After Bloom appears in the fourth chapter, there is a Biblical scheme of correspondences, Old and New Testaments linked together typologically. The "Telemachiad" must therefore be extra-Biblical, and Joyce chose to mirror in these three chapters the three forces that most threatened Christianity: the rivalry of Mithraism in its early years in

Rome, the barbaric marriage of chivalry and Christianity, and the struggle with Islam.

To our surprise, we might notice that the first three stories of *Dubliners* answer to this same correspondence: there is a vision of Persia in "The Sisters," and the old priest's sin is not simony, of course, as the childish narrator has misheard, a sin scarcely available to an Irish parish priest, but sodomy; the chivalry in "An Encounter" is the Wild West variety; and the evocation of Islam in "Araby" is obvious.

But Joyce's correspondences are not linear parallels; they are a network. The tension between Stephen and Mulligan in the first chapter leads to an ineffectual telegram: "The sentimentalist is he who would enjoy without incurring the immense debtorship for a thing done." This is from Meredith's *The Ordeal of Richard Feveral*. Go back, however, to the opening chapters of *The Ordeal of Richard Feverel* and see Richard the Zoroastrian, fire-worshiper and burner of hayricks. No reticulation in the network of correspondences, it seems, was to be left untied.

One can search along the network of symbolic correspondences by asking questions. Why, for instance, does *Ulysses* have eighteen chapters? The *Odyssey* has twenty-four, as many as the letters of the Greek alphabet. Stephen, we learn in the Proteus chapter, once considered writing books with letters for titles. A good rule for solving Joycean riddles is to go directly to the Irish connection, which in this case will render up an Irish alphabet, one of such antiquity that its letters are the names of trees with magic properties, making it possible for Joyce to strike a great chord of correspondences, Irish alphabet to trees to Greek epic, and thus place Baudelaire's *forêt des symboles* as a sustained transparency of symbols over his novel. Joyce found this alphabet in a book with the serendipitously Homeric title *Ogygia,* published in Latin in 1785 by Roderic O'Flaherty, antiquarian, and translated into English in 1793 by the Rev. James Hely.

That name, Hely, an anagram for *hyle,* Greek for "forest," wanders through *Ulysses* on so many signboards carried by admen of peristaltic gait, as if Joyce wanted a symbol of a symbol, or wanted to signal to us that this Hely, a stationer, is named Wisdom, implying that the forest of symbolic trees, which determine the number and the pattern of correspondences of each chapter, is, like the seven trees that supported Solomon's tabernacle, Baudelaire's *"temple où de vivants piliers / Laissent parfois sortir de confuses paroles."*

The first letter of the Irish alphabet is *Beth,* the birch tree, the branches of which expel evil spirits and are used for beating the bounds of territories, for purification; and it is a tree propitious to inceptions, such as starting out on a quest. For Hamlet-Telemachus-Ariel-Stephen, who must set his house in order and go in quest of a good daimon, it is a most appropriate symbol.

The second is *Luis,* the rowan, which compels demons to answer difficult questions. This second chapter is made up entirely of questions and answers.

The third is *Nion,* the ash, which is sacred to Manannán McLir, the Celtic Poseidon, and is a charm against drowning. The background of this chapter is the sea; its struggle is with the shapelessness of water and with aquacity of thought.

The fourth is *Fearn,* or alder, the circling tree which confines and protects a sanctuary, as Calypso's magic island was hidden by ringed alder trees, and as Bloom's back-garden Eden is by spearmint. Here is one of those correspondences, Homer's Ogygian alder for the alder of the Irish alphabet, which makes one believe that God designed the world for Joyce's convenience.

The fifth is *Saille,* or willow, which protects one from charms, as Bloom must be protected from the narcosis of the lotus which drugs this chapter. This is the chapter in which Bloom is most deft with words, and inadvertently prophetic. The willow is the poet's tree.

The sixth is *Uath,* the hawthorn, which blooms in the season when Hermes Psychopompos leads the dead to Hades, and is sacred to the goddess of the dead, Maia. This is the chapter of the burial of Paddy Dignam.

The seventh is *Duir,* the oak, the tree of the weather and the door of the seasons, the equinoxes and solstices, when winds change their direction; and this is the Aeolus chapter, as windy as a canyon, and full of doors.

The eighth is *Tinne,* the holly, the oak tree's twin and rival. A strange and involuted symbolism here seems to say that the cannibalistic Lestrygonians are the abuse of the mouth as a door inward to the body, as in the preceding chapter the tongue is in windy rhetoric the door outward from the body, and that as the oak and holly vie for the rule of the year, like the oak knight and the holly knight, the one always decapitating the other, so belly and voice vie to debauch our senses and sense. Certainly Joyce does some decapitating of his own, for why should Bloom in this most Zolaesque of chapters eat gorgonzola if Joyce were not, Perseus-like, holding up for our inspection the head of his false twin, the Gorgon Zola?

The ninth is *Coll,* or hazel, which gives one the power to curse. This chapter is sulfurous with ritual curses, mainly upon both the houses of Aristotle and Plato, and particularly upon the care of literature in the hands of precious dilettantes and refined librarians. One of the darker curses is not easy to detect, as it is concealed in an awful pun: AE, IOU; that is, I am in debt to you, George Russell, but in the language of Mediterranean magic the minimally literate prophylactic retort to the Devil is the recitation of the vowels in order.

The tenth is *Muin*, the grapevine, the symbolism of which is Bacchic. Joyce seems to have taken the symbol to be a spiral, or a wandering around, and this suggested to him the microcosmic scenes which crisscross each other. The vine has a varied symbolism; it is sacred to Osiris, for instance, and the Osiris of *Ulysses*, Corny Kelleher the undertaker, is here; and since the vine is not native to Ireland (suggesting that the alphabet isn't, either), Joyce wraps his darkly satirical and bitter spiral around the alien force of the British governor, who, with liberal help from Bacchus, has contributed in large part to the paralysis of the island.

The eleventh is *Gort*, the ivy, the convivial companion to the vine, and the scene is the Ormond Hotel Bar, with Sirens and music.

The twelfth is *Peith*, or dwarf elder, the wood of which makes arrows for slaying giants, and this is the Polyphemus chapter, with its Rabelaisian gigantism of language.

The thirteenth is *Ruis*, the elder, the tree of witches. This is Gerty MacDowell's chapter, and the weirdness of the tree alerts us to the dimension of superstition, which is apt to go unnoticed among more prominent themes.

The fourteenth is *Ailm*, or the fir, tree of childbirth. This is the lying-in hospital chapter.

The fifteenth is *Onn*, the furze, which blooms at the spring equinox, and is the sun's signal to begin the year. This is Circe's chapter, a *Walpurgisnacht*. Stephen undergoes a ritual death and resurrection, or at least prepares for a metanoia.

The sixteenth is *Ura*, the heather, which is associated with the mating of bees. The *hieros gamos* of Stephen and Bloom in this chapter has yet to be explained, but we can see how the symbolism was commanded by the alphabetic correspondence.

The seventeenth is *Eadha*, the poplar, tree of resurrection, and the closing symbol of this chapter, with its secular communion of cocoa, is one of freedom from bondage, the hope of new beginnings.

The eighteenth is *Idho*, the yew, protector of sleep and graves, and the wood from which bows are made.

This scheme of alphabetical trees, giving Joyce the number of chapters he could write, is more than just another pattern among many used as armature or blueprint for the work. Joyce was attracted to it not only because it is archaically Irish but also because it extends an invisible forest over his cityscape, thereby tenting over the whole novel with

Dante's *selva oscura,* Calypso's magically restraining trees, the lost Eden, the forest of Europe from which our culture arose.

If lightning caused man, as Vico thought, to see god in the flash, the bounty of nature provided an idea of God's benevolence. Vico showed Joyce how to make grand linguistic chords by looking at the forest-floor existence of man in primal words that are still spoken today, completely drained of their original meaning. Bloom solicits ads for a newspaper. That *licit* root goes deep back through many words and meanings, words having to do with law (*lex, legis*), teaching (*lecture*), gathering (*collection*), until we get back to the forest floor, picking up the sacred acorns of Zeus, collecting—*collegere,* to *legere* from the *ilex,* the holm-oak.

*College sports:* words Bloom designs a poster for in his head in chapter 5. He would put a large bicycle wheel on his version of the poster, with the word *sports* repeated as the spokes, and at the hub he would put the word *college.* This is a nicely modern design for 1904, and it is an Art Nouveau poster Bloom is redesigning, wherein a cyclist is doubled up like a cod in a pot. Never mind for the moment that that fetal cyclist is Stephen, and that the sunburst design Bloom prefers is Bloom himself, a mature and accomplished man. Bloom's design is as archaic as the forest of Europe. It is Robin Goodfellow's phallic Maypole. *Hub* has Viconian connections with *Hob,* or *Rob,* as does *sport* with *spurt* and *disperse,* and there is the oak god's acorn-gathering word again: *college.* Whose voice are we listening to? That Old Artificer's, I think, who received Stephen's prayer at the end of the *Portrait,* to stand him in good stead.

It is a ghostly voice, and we must train our ears to hear it. It is a poet's voice, speaking along with the mimicry of the prose voice. Homer, as far as we know, shaped his poems out of nothing he originated. He told the stories men had told over and over; like Shakespeare ("He said he has beat them all," Nora Joyce said when the *Wake* was being written, "except that feller Shakespeare") he gave stories elegant, strong, geometrical shapes. He gave them the rhythm and integrity of narrative that they needed for greatest resonance.

So Joyce. He is an instrument through which the past can speak. Joyce's past, like Homer's, is not history. If the success of man as a political, companionable animal whose culture has thus far progressed to families living in cities, that achievement of humanity is dying, Joyce saw. Life at family level goes on pretty much as in the bronze age. Man's idea of God, though, is in trouble; his idea of the state is in trouble; and an awful restlessness begins to disturb the inert, paralyzed, darkened life of the people. *Ulysses* was written between 1914 and 1921, dates that end a world.

By asking what decorum can allow Joyce to weave correspondences of such intricate obscurity through his realistic prose, we come to the depths of the novel implied by these correspondences, and upon the principle of their effectiveness.

"Mr. Leopold Bloom ate with relish the inner organs of beasts and fowls" is the Dickensian sentence that introduces our typological Ulysses, who, moreover, has a sweet tooth for kidneys cooked just so. The symbols of this fourth chapter will flow from this innocent statement, and will all support the radical idea that Bloom is a man, not a god, and that given a choice, nay tempted, as Ulysses was by Calypso to become a god, he will defiantly choose to be a man. Ulysses's possible divinity would have come from his eating ambrosia and drinking nectar: in the bronze age you are what you eat.

Bloom's breakfast kidney is a correspondence to the zodiacal position of the sun on the 16th of June; because he burns it, it is a sacrifice to his former god Jehovah; and it is the chapter's corresponding organ, as Joyce indicated in the scheme he wrote out for Linati. *Kidney,* in the heroic age of English, meant something like *belly-pod,* the *innards.*

The chapter's symbol, Joyce specified, is the vagina, which in Greek is "fertile field," and the chapter extends itself between visions remote in space and time, and places darkly inward: the jakes, bowels, kidneys, the inside of hats, the fastnesses of Edwardian skirts and Molly under the bedcovers, sniffing herself, saying her first word in the novel: "Mn," less articulately than her *alter ego* the cat had said, "Mrkgnao."

This Calypso-Molly is Bloom's disillusioned view of womankind, a queen ant, fat and snug, served by her feeders. The oldest identifiable temples in the world are the subterranean earth-hives of Malta, all kidney-shaped. Here man worshipped the primeval Cybele, or Demeter, and Homer may have based his knowledge of Ogygia on what he had heard of Malta, for *Calypso* means *the hider,* and *Ogygia* means *the ancient place.*

Molly, then, is a uterine creature, demanding and selfish. She is a vain Eve so little understanding herself or her husband that she whorishly tucks the tempter's letter under her pillow, a toad close by her ear. Bloom does not even know his own disgust for her, though Joyce lets us see it. Nor does Bloom know that his vision of a model farm in Palestine, of a maiden with a zither, of a happier Utopian existence, is his deeply Hebraic longing for an ideal Molly, a virtuous Penelope, a resurrected Jerusalem, Isaiah's desert blossoming like the rose. His name, after all, is Bloom.

Bloom, Greek, *anthos.* Joyce follows mediæval tradition rather than good etymology in deriving the name "Anthony" from the Greek for "flower." Of all Bloom's guises, that of St. Anthony—Flaubert's St.

Antoine—would seem to be the one that has most poignantly intensified in the fifty years of the book's existence. Bloom the antihero has become a cliché, the second Chaplin of the century; Bloom as Charles Bovary, as Bouvard-Pécuchet, as a Krafft-Ebing case history, as the true existential Christian, as the Wandering Jew, as a Dublin Walter Mitty, as *l'homme moyen sensuel*—all of these rôles have been richly pondered.

Joyce with prophetic accuracy saw that Flaubert's most beautiful but least read masterpiece, *La Tentation de saint Antoine,* was the symbolic statement that would last out the century, and probably the next, and worked it into *Ulysses* as a configuration of prime symbolic import. The Circe chapter, the longest in the book, is Joyce's *Temptation,* the work's great fantasia of themes, its Descent of Orpheus into Hades, its Faust among the witches.

Because so many of its symbolic correspondences are in stage directions, where we do not expect them, we have missed seeing that this grand movement begins with a man named Antonio emerging with a swan from fog: St. Anthony and Orpheus, champions of stubborn faith and of art over the death of the spirit. They are masks of Bloom, who has portion enough of their genius, and has besides Ulysses's *moly,* magic flower, or Molly. Stephen enters next, serving mass as always (the bread and wine are concealed in the stanza of Omar Khayyam, which he tries to illustrate with gestures). He, too, is an Orpheus whose Eurydice is Old Gummy Granny herself, Ireland; and in another sense, his Eurydice is his own soul, which he has seen once before, a girl standing in the sea, like Venus, her skirt rucked up so that she resembled a wading bird, the ibis Thoth, inventor of writing. Stephen dies his spiritual death in this chapter; Joyce slays the Stephen Dedalus within himself, archetype of the sterile artist.

Bloom, however, stands forth in an epiphany that in many ways is more important than his astounding epiphany in the next chapter, where he appears in the newspaper (the daily *Odyssey* of Vico's fourth age), betrayed by a typographical error—he is revealed to be what Stephen guessed God always was (with a hint from Vico): thunder: L. Boom, El, boom!

If in this last phase of a cycle that began in the bronze age (Zeus Thunderer, its god) man is man's god, the *multus* the *unum,* Bloom is the age's portrait of that shouter in the street, a unit of the traffic along the Nevsky Prospekt, the Boulevard Raspail, or Grafton Street. If there is high comedy in Bloom as God, there is eloquent prophecy in Bloom as St. Anthony. The sense in which the world is his temptation is our sense of living in a world, spectators and consumers all, which invites us deeper and deeper into matter, whether we have the mastery to shape it into significant form or not. That *yes* at the end of the novel is matter's assent to form, female matter agreeing to be shaped by god or governor, whichever strategy Ulysses chooses. She is Circe, Calypso, Siren, or Penelope.

Bloom as Anthony derives from Flaubert's ultimate statement of the plight of the saint, from *Bouvard et Pécuchet,* inheritors of the Enlightenment and the French Revolution, the world's first generation to see and hear everything if they want to, the voices of the world's parliaments left at their doorsteps daily, art attractively arranged in museums, the wisdom of the ages (translated) available in paperback books (Penguin Books were established soon after the publication of *Ulysses,* to put the classics and all useful and uplifting knowledge in the workingman's hands at sixpence the volume), in short, the man two thousand years of civilization groaned to evolve.

Flaubert's first book was the *Tentation,* his last *Bouvard et Pécuchet,* which is a rewriting of the *Tentation,* much as Ezra Pound rewrote his *Hugh Selwyn Mauberley* as the *Homage to Sextus Propertius,* so that we would understand one version or the other. The *Tentation* is the modern world's first statement of its directionlessness, of its loss of coordinates, of its proliferating choices and versions of reality. We can appreciate with grim agreement the end of the *Tentation,* where Anthony is carried aloft by the devil and lectured on modern physics and scientific naturalism. Anthony is terrified. "Down?" says the devil. "Which way is down? Anyway at all." "*Descends au-dessous de la terre pendant des milliards de milliards de siècles, jamais tu n'arriveras au fond.*" So would our astronauts feel, were their computer-aimed trajectory to slip its course.

Bouvard and Pécuchet, uninformed by facts and unable to add a cubit to their height by thought, are transparencies through which we see St. Anthony; and so is Bloom.

It is this Temptation of St. Bloom, Joyce's phantasma of symbols, that shows us that all the adventures of Bloom have been temptations (only half the adventures of Homer's hero were), and that an alternative title to *Ulysses* might have been *The Temptation of St. Anthony.*

The reality before Anthony was the empty desert; solitude and the adoration of God fulfilled his being. But he never saw this reality, for the devil veiled it with monsters, philosophers, professors, and the flesh. What reality there is before Bloom is harder to see, for Joyce hides it like a Heraclitean principle. As the elbow is neither the joined ends of bones, nor the ligatures, nor the space between, but all together, a weightless, abstract event happening in an arm, so Bloom's reality is neither the words on the page (which are invariably parodies), nor the symbolic energy released through punning images and complex meanings, nor invisibilities that epiphanize when we can free the pattern from its background with which it blends in camouflage, but all these energies cooperating with each other.

What Bloom senses is temptation, idle, distracting, and deflecting. The world is opaque to him; people are capricious forces; he has no friends; he is self-contained. His education has melted, the wealth of knowledge he has learned from books and newspapers is in disarray, sex is underwear, he is a Jewish Catholic Protestant Agnostic, he is solicitous about the lying-in of a woman whose name he remembers alternately as Beaufoy and Purefoy.

Bloom is a dictionary of the age's mythology. The ideas of Fourier and Marx flicker in his mind; like Van Gogh he believes that a home medical guide will improve the national hygiene; he believes in advertising, callisthenics, special trams for funerals, planned parenthood, Irish home rule, and enlightenment through travel. He is a graduate of the university of life.

This comic surface of Bloom would be glorious, anarchic, and ragbag, except that Joyce has given it poetic order. We can trace Bloom's thoughts as they zigzag down a page in strict conformity to Freud's discipline of linked association, and even supply Bloom's next thought as surely as we can complete a Homeric formulaic phrase.

At the same time Joyce weaves into Bloom's interior monologue and its interjacent narrative prose other threads of correspondences. Almost constantly (I suspect absolutely constantly) Joyce recites in one disguise or another the adventures of Ulysses. In with this there is each chapter's special symbolism, coloring all the other matter with its peculiar tint.

In the Hades chapter, for instance, Joyce has had to find in Dublin geography those details that reflect Homer's matter. In and out of this runs the endlessly repeating list of the adventures. This complexity is then figured over with correspondences to hearts, in many senses. Then it pleased Joyce to allegorize the characters into the seven deadly sins doing a *Totentanz* around Bloom. And then, for good measure, Joyce makes the words, all of them in the chapter, rehearse over and over the sins themselves, with the exception of pride, for which he substitutes a meekness on Bloom's part.

Genius, Kafka remarked, is the ability to pay attention to two things at once. But then he had not read *Ulysses*.

There are other correspondences that need to be looked into by the scholars. I suspect, for instance, that every chapter is a mass, or sacrifice, of a different kind. We can best understand the great lyricism of Molly's monologue by grasping how strangely primitive a sacrifice it seems to symbolize: an utterly archaic spilling of blood. It is with Molly's (as with

Penelope's) consent that the suitors are slain. The arrows are released in the preceding chapter (Ithaca), question and answer being the opposite forces of the bow and the string. The slaughter is within Molly's monologue, and its gore is reflected in Molly's menstrual flow (negating the afternoon's lust), in the poppies and other red flowers, and in the blood-red Mediterranean at sunset, the apocalyptic transformation of the sea. This last chapter clearly corresponds to Revelation, as chapter 4 corresponds to Genesis, chapter 14 to the birth of Christ (the three Magi of the first chapter are there, stable animals, and a baby born to a woman named Pure Faith).

Bloom's dialogue, interior and exterior, is charmingly clear; so is his mind. Molly (what we hear her say) is not an articulate conversationalist but can replay experience with the genius of Proust. And now look again at Stephen. We can follow his metaphysical mind in its interior musings, and he is quite an accomplished poet in his abstruse thoughts (though Joyce in the *Scribbledehobble* calls him "a gentleman wordsmith"). But what critic has dared to notice that when he opens his mouth nonsense flies out?

Nonsense. Throughout *Ulysses* Stephen tells parables or riddles or conundrums, and none of them make any sense. He is so eloquent of thought and so skilled in sarcasm that we expect his words to make sense. Go and look at them, all of them, and see what sense can be made of them. All his words are self-collapsing systems, cancelling themselves and interfering with their own logic. Ask yourself why Stephen says what he does. Why does he sing "Hugh of Lincoln" to Bloom? What does his telegram to Mulligan mean? What do his speeches in the Circe chapter mean?

Bloom is articulate of speech, inarticulate of mind. For Molly, mind and speech are the same—she talks to herself to think, and thinks out loud to speak. Together they complement each other, and make a poem that speaks in three voices at once, as Hamlet when he speaks is a distraught prince of Denmark, a poet as enigmatic as Stephen Dedalus, and, ineluctably, the voice of Shakespeare.

Is not Joyce in many ways more like Bloom than Stephen? Professor Ellmann has found a real Martha Clifford; Nora Barnacle's letters are as much like Molly's monologue as Joyce's city-dwelling habits are like Bloom's.

Looked at this way, the novel becomes a solipsistic poem which accepts its inability to know another mind, and thus boldly stands forth not only as an epiphany of kinds of life in our time, uncompromisingly objective, but as an epiphany of art itself, the work of one mind and one sensibility, uncompromisingly subjective.

Opposites cooperate, said Heraclitus; opposites meet, said Blake; unity, says R. Buckminster Fuller, involves at least two things. I am suggesting, then, that the important voice in *Ulysses* is not the naturalistic one, which can stand beside that of Joyce's masters, Jacobsen, Tolstoy, Ibsen, and Flaubert. It is rather the inner voice of the novel, the poetic voice of the symbols, that gives the work its coherence and its profoundest harmony.

*It cannot be said that it was all smooth and unruffled
sailing in this huge, new socialist experiment undertaken
by the first workers' and peasants' state in the world.
There is a page in the biography of the Soviet Union
which is generally referred to as the period of the cult of
personality. It is bound up with the name of Joseph
Stalin.* [1]

> Albert P. Nenarokov,
> *Russia in the Twentieth Century*

# The Man Without Contemporaries

Osip Emilievich Mandelstam, a poet as obliquely allusive as Mallarmé, as honed, chiselled, and compact as Zukofsky, and such a master of form and imagery that he may well be the greatest Russian poet of our time, spent the last fifteen years of his life—from age thirty-two—banned, starving, homeless, and at times insane with desperation. In 1938 he was sentenced to a labor camp in Siberia, where he died after a few months. His brother was notified of his death three years later.

His widow, Nadezhda Yakovlevna, shared Mandelstam's persecutions while he was alive, survived what might have been a similar persecution except for luckier breaks and the death of Stalin, lived for years in the corner of someone else's kitchen, and now lives in a room of her own. She

[1]Except for the added sentiment that Stalin's "distortions, for all their gravity, did not alter the nature of socialist society, nor did they shake the pillars of socialism," this is the sole reference in a Soviet history book to the thirty-year Terror.

has no assurance that she will not be expelled from the country, and wrote both volumes of her memoirs expecting the knock of the police on the door.

Mandelstam's very existence has been a secret for which time itself through a complex gear of destinies evolved the disclosure. His wife says that she would not have twice braved the risk of *samizdat* (post-Gutenberg distribution of manuscripts in carbon copies) and publication in the West if the invisible and unapproachable commissars of Litkontrol had published her husband's poetry. (She could scarcely have guessed that among more Kafkaesque reasons for biding their time they were also waiting for the copyright to run out: why pay royalty checks to an old woman whose husband insulted Stalin and slapped the face of Comrade Alexei Tolstoi?)

While Mrs. Mandelstam was writing her 1100 pages of memoirs without a title (the English titles, punning on her name, which means "hope," were furnished by the publisher), Professor Clarence Brown, of Princeton, was finishing a twenty-year study of the poet. In 1955 there began to appear, in Russian, a New York edition of Mandelstam's poetry, collected and edited by two exiled scholars, Gleb Struve and Boris Filippov. This now runs to three volumes.

Our first substantial knowledge of Mandelstam's writing was Clarence Brown's translation of three prose pieces (*The Noise of Time, Theodosia, The Egyptian Stamp*)[2]—three delightful, lapidary, bright narratives. They seem to have been achieved by applying the severest rules of Imagism to the art of the novel. Mandelstam's economy with words was Spartan. He envied the mediæval philosophers their clarity and precision. Fragmentary and capricious as his prose seems, it has a sense of wholeness.

A page of Mandelstam's prose is a kind of algebra of ironies over which the same hand has drawn comic furniture and objects with a life of their own à la Chagall. *The Noise of Time* is a spiritual inventory of the mode of life swept away by the Revolution—men condemned to stations on the moon might write such books about life on the earth: a book that would teach us that the usual and the routine look like miracles once you have lost them forever.

Mandelstam wrote anywhere and everywhere. We can scarcely begin to realize his world in which the pencil stub and the three pieces of paper you have is all the pencil and all the paper you are ever going to have. He composed in his head, dictated to his wife, or wrote on a chair seat while kneeling. Some poems (like the offending Stalin lyric) were not written down at all.

---

[2]*The Prose of Osip Mandelstam* (Princeton: Princeton University Press, 1965).

After Mandelstam's death his wife memorized everything for which she had a text, prose and poetry together. She was in Voronezh. The tanks of the Wehrmacht were threatening from one direction, the NKVD from another.

Such persecution would be understandable up to a point if Mandelstam had been a man of power, like Trotsky, or an open opponent of the Bolsheviks. On the contrary, he was an all but invisible lyric poet. In the stupidity of the official minds that ordered his harassment and eventually his sentence to Siberia there must have been some dim notion that he was an aesthete, an idealistic Jew who had suspiciously converted to Christianity, a man who considered Marx and Lenin so much hot air, a poet who wasn't ever going to write paraphrases of the *Internatsionál* or an Ode to Stalin.

Nothing is so helpless as the liberal spirit face to face with fundamentalism. Such brute power can only be met with an equal and opposite moral strength, like that of the Jehovah's Witnesses who prayed for the souls of the machinegunners before whom they fell at Buchenwald, the singing Christians Nero nailed to crosses in the Circus, or Mandelstam's colleague the poet Gumilyov who crumbled under the volleys of a Soviet firing squad, clutching a Bible and a Homer to his heart.

Nadezhda Mandelstam's second volume of memoirs[3] is, like the first, designed as a Formalist novel, its components arranged according to a sense of kinship amongst its subjects rather than according to chronology. The Formalists (their art has been outlawed as un-Soviet since 1932) took Sterne for their model—they saw *Tristam Shandy* as something like a cubist novel, and they were excited by the idea of a narrative the architecture of which was more prominent than the conventional unfolding of a plot. (They were also influenced by the man they call O. Genry.) The Formalist matrix gives Mrs. Mandelstam the flexibility to move backward and forward along a plot line which we can reconstruct in our imagination.

In the first volume of the memoirs (opening in the typical Formalist fashion with Mandelstam slapping Alexei Tolstoi's face, the explanation of which is many pages away) Mrs. Mandelstam records the last four terrifying years of Osip's life. In digressions she posits enough of his biography to give us a full sense of his life. In this second volume she presents a sustained digression (621 pages) to the first volume.

For all the seeming despair of the title (not hers, anyway), the spirit behind every sentence is indomitable. Terror and grief made *Hope Against Hope* one of the most chilling accounts of Soviet authoritarianism (a book to authenticate Solzhenitsyn's *First Circle* and to sup-

[3]*Hope Abandoned,* trans. Max Hayward (New York: Atheneum, 1974).

plement Elizaveta Almadingen's terrifying *Tomorrow Will Come*). Now there is time, in this second volume, to meditate, to sift, to fill in details.

Mrs. Mandelstam's tone can range from that of Christian stoic—forgiving and devastating with the same fell epithet—to a Brechtian trooper who can call a man a son of a bitch and make the phrase have the hiss of a tiger whose eyes have just turned to fire and whose claws have all unsheathed at once. The hope she has abandoned is for any justice or sense in the miserable régime under which she has suffered for over half a century. Her contempt has become eloquent, and she is capable of cackling with a kind of tragic gaiety at the obscenities she has had to abide.

She was dismissed, for instance, from the only solid teaching position she had after her husband's death. This was at a school remote in the provinces where she was hailed at night to a kangaroo court (People's Court, they call it) and charged with making allusions about the rising young (viz., that in the English language the young infinitive is replacing the old gerund), with teaching a nonexistent (i.e., forbidden) law of sound changes (that of Grimm), and with sitting on a window ledge (*kulturny* Communist ladies sit demurely in chairs).

She has written a book of multiple purposes: a book that comments on Mandelstam's poems; that preserves his ideas, his complex personality, and *obiter dicta;* that surrounds the poet with his people—fellow Acmeists, notably Gumilyov and Anna Akhmatova, Khlebnikov, Ehrenburg, Gorodetski, a whole generation of Russian intellectuals and artists—that expounds her wonderfully wise and individual philosophy, part Christian, part pragmatic; that condemns the whole Soviet rigmarole and all its cruel absurdity.

This great document of the human condition is in essence, under all the details, the Leskovian wit, the Dostoyevskian passion, the Brechtian cheek, an extended statement by a modern Antigone. It rings with Antigone's moral authority, and it has Antigone's sense of a freedom to speak no matter what the consequences.

Professor Brown was telling me recently that while he was having tea with the Siniavskis this spring in Paris, the phone rang. It was Nadezhda calling from Moscow. Obviously the KGB were listening. But what in the world could they add to their file of either that wasn't already there in great measure? They were listening to the widow of Mandelstam and a political prisoner in perpetual exile. Did they realize that they were listening to two victims of their tyranny from whom tyranny had taken all that it can, leaving them free to say what they pleased?

Clarence Brown's combined biography and study of Mandelstam[4] involved several journeys to the Soviet Union and to people who knew

[4]*Mandelstam* (Cambridge, England: Cambridge University Press, 1973).

Mandelstam. The research was peculiarly difficult for obvious reasons. There were also myths to elude, especially that of a Mandelstam diminished to an elfin sprite remembered for his bird-like gestures and fin-de-siècle poses. The same thing happened to Shelley, a six-foot robust man who was mythologized into a frail wind spirit delicate as a lily.

The Mandelstam who emerges in Professor Brown's biography is a complex figure, a poet of genius, a man of great integrity. He becomes tragic becuase of the historical context in which he lived on the edge of being. The violence of the times demanded patience and heroism from him at immense cost to his poetry. The wonder is that he wrote anything at all after *Stone,* his first book of poems.

He seems to have developed a useful stoicism ("Who says that we were meant to be happy?") and the art of living nowhere and with no resources. The number of bone-wracking train journeys he had to make is appalling. It is no comfort to realize that the events of his life can be paralleled with wearying repetition from Dostoyevsky to Solzhenitsyn; nightmares get worse as they persist.

The engaging difference between Professor Brown's biography and the usual way of reconstructing a life from conflicting and obscure evidence is that he irons nothing out and indicates all the problems and blank spaces. He refrains from sentiment and guesswork, frequently showing us the processes of research (interviews, visits to Mandelstam's school and places of exile) in lieu of suppositions and sleight-of-hand narrative. Unpublished documents are for the most part given in full, and the discussions of the Acmeist School are rigorous and lucid.

Professor Brown shows how Acmeism (which can be defined roughly as the poetry of Mandelstam, Gumilyov, and Akhmatova) is curiously like Imagism as Pound and Hulme preached it. Both movements were a return to finely perceived realities ("to the world," Mandelstam said), after rich, and richly vague, Symbolist movements degenerating into a rhetoric of mysticism and an aesthetic of bogus philosophy and private vocabularies.

Mandelstam is not quite like any other poet, so that analogies run into instant trouble. My feeling that there is a great deal of Rimbaud in him is apparently wrong, as neither Professor Brown nor Mrs. Mandelstam mentions him. By Rimbaud I mean the gnarled image which suggests a chord of meanings rather than a simple metaphor or simile, a respect for classical form together with a bold originality, a hardness of poetic phrasing that defies translation into prose.

Mandelstam's "contemporaries" (he said that he had none in the literal sense) were Ovid, Villon, Dante, Racine, Poe. He was also aware that he was an Orpheus trying to reclaim a lost spirit: in the poems of the late

1920s Persephone becomes an eloquent symbol. It is as if Mandelstam saw how prophetically he had named his first book—*Stone*. His St. Petersburg was etymologically "the city of stone." The art of living in cities (which is what "civilization" means) begins with the shaping of stone, and civilization becomes for Mandelstam a metaphysical nostalgia. Civilization figures in his mind as the opposite of Socialism. Stone takes on an added ambiguity: Russia has become stone, Hades, an underworld, a prison for the spirit. The beautiful and mysterious poem "Solominka" is full of women who returned from the dead: Lenores and Séraphitas.

A Mandelstam poem lives inside itself. As in Keats, Mallarmé, or Shakespeare, the words breed meaning. Again and again Professor Brown makes anguished statements about the impossibility of translating Mandelstam into English. In order to make the attempt he turned to the poet W. S. Merwin (who knows bushels of languages but not Russian) and entered into one of the happier collaborations of literary history.[5]

In Professor Brown's *Mandelstam* we find this literal translation:

ringing little straw, dry Solominka,
you have drunk up all of death and become tenderer.

Merwin turns this into:

dry Solominka, little ringing straw
who sipped up the whole of death—it has made you gentle.

(Note how Merwin moves *ing* and *ink* in from the extremes of the line, and cancels the possibility of *unk* clinking against *ink*. I suppose it is Mandelstamian for "straw" to suggest "sip.")

We cannot bear strained silence—
The faultiness of souls is offensive, after all!
The reader had been confused when he first appeared
And was gleefully greeted with cries of "Please!"
I knew it, I knew who was invisibly there:
A man out of a nightmare was reading "Ulalume."
Meaning is mere vanity and the word is only noise
While phonetics is the seraph's handmaiden.
Edgar's harp would sing of the House of Usher,
The madman drank some water, blinked and said no more.
I was on the street. The silk of autumn whistled
And the silk of a tickling scarf warmed my throat.

That is Professor Brown's trot, intended for information only. Here's the Brown and Merwin version:

[5]Osip Mandelstam, *Selected Poems*, trans. Clarence Brown and W. S. Merwin (New York: Atheneum, 1974).

He can't speak, and we can't bear it!
It's like watching a mutilation of the soul.
A reciter stood on the stage, wild-eyed,
And they went mad, shouting "Please, please!"
I knew that another was there, invisible,
a man from a nightmare, reading "Ulalume."
What's meaning but vanity? A word is a sound—
one of the handmaidens of the seraphim.
Poe's harp-song of the House of Usher. Then the madman
swallowed some water, came to himself, was silent.
I was in the street. The silk of autumn was whistling. . . .

(The poem is "about" an evening in St. Petersburg when the poet Vladimir Pyast went mad while reciting Poe's "Ulalume.")[6]

The Russian rhymes *abba* and has in it glorious sounds (as best as I can make out) not imitated in either translation—the third stanza begins O *domye Esherov Edgara pyela arfa,* which elegant knot of words seems to make Edgar a member of the House of Usher (an astute bit of reading on Mandelstam's part) and to give him Roderick Usher's lute (and therefore "heart-strings"). The poem is a diagram (autumn of culture, a house split down the middle, the poet possessed by a prophetic meaning, a spirit lost and longed for: grief, madness, hysteria). It was written in 1913: four more years until the locomotive bearing its flags of bilious yellow and angry red would hiss into the Finland Station.

Mallarmé and Baudelaire learned English to read Poe: Proust learned it to read Ruskin and George Eliot. Surely it is time for us to begin Russian to read Mandelstam (and Khlebnikov and Akhmatova), for it is evident from these studies that the school of Russian poets flourishing (if that can be the word) in the Revolution and Soviet period is not merely an outgrowth of European poetry—not a branch but a new tree altogether. The Russian genius of this time could take western matters, transform them, and give back a whole new entity.

For years it had seemed that the Bauhaus was the *fons et origo* of practically all the international modern styles. Not so: it was the gift of modernism returned from Russia, reshaped and refined by Tatlin and Malyevich. The catenary arch now in St. Louis was designed for Red Square. These are random examples of a time of invention that counts as one of the great Renaissances in the West.

The remainder of the twentieth century (most miserable of ages since the Barbarians poured into Rome) might profitably be spent putting together the human achievements which tyranny has kept behind walls.

[6]Neither Clarence Brown nor Bill Merwin can spell the name which the sculptor Archipenko, at least, used to pronounce Headgear Olyan Paw. Edgar Poe incorporated into his name the name of his foster father John Allan.

Nadezhda Mandelstam's two volumes of memoirs would have been published in a cultural vacuum were it not for Professor Brown's monumental study of the poet. Both books (plus the Brown-Merwin translation of some of the poems) do more than import a major poet; they *find* Mandelstam for us. There is no greater success for scholarship than to recover, establish, and interpret an unknown figure. It is a recompense for a luckless life that Mandelstam is served in posterity by two masters of prose, for the critics are already noting that Nadezhda Mandelstam is a very great writer. And Clarence Brown is a prose stylist of the first rank, if so few people might constitute a rank, for what is rarer than a scholar who can write lucid, strong, and graceful prose? He has a great deal of the Mandelstamian wit and sense of the absurd; he has the unflagging curiosity to have tracked down everything trackable down; and has mercy on the Russianless reader, and always makes allowances for him. But the triumph is to have written a book, every detail of which is new and strange to the majority of its readers, which keeps matters clear, efficiently organized, and handsomely rendered.

# Narrative Tone and Form

The style of a narrative is a kind of dialect. The laws it obeys are of its own nature. Feeling that a style is natural and inevitable is like being among people with whom we share traditions and prejudices. Style can therefore be invisible, blending with our ignorance. To see it properly the critic frequently has to take it away from its background and put it against another, or find some other way to insist that narrative is artifice, deliberate, and shaped according to a style. The artist, too, lives with this problem, which can suggest to Kafka that he will be clearer about his own predicament if he calls Jews Chinese and their keeping the Law building the Great Wall. His narrative voice is therefore freed. Narrative is first of all interested in the functional liberty of the lie. *When I was a small boy at the beginning of the century I remember an old man who wore kneebreeches and worsted stockings, and who used to hobble about the street of our village with the help of a stick.* This is inviting, congenial, grandfatherly, British: English Novel Formulaic. We read it, assuming we know we have begun a novel, waiting for the effect to take, as if we were breathing the Pythian fumes. What we are doing is learning style: the hang of how this story is going to be told. Most novels begin with inconsequential remarks (short stories rarely, poems, never) to give us a chance to tune our ears to the style.

   *Mr. Hackett turned the corner and saw, in the failing light, at some little distance, his seat.* These are the rhythms of a Dublin storyteller. The voice is practiced. Narrative is its art: it knows how to drop prepositional phrases between the verb and its object, so that we have both to pay attention and wait. *En un lugar de la Mancha, de cuyo nombre no quiero acordarme, no ha mucho tiempo que vivía un hidalgo de los de lanza en astillero, adarga antigua, rocín flaco y galgo corredor.* Is it only the unexpected adjective for the nag that transposes the ritualness of this opening sentence into another key altogether? Style is character. The success of the sentence is our realizing that the narrator is keeping a grave face while wanting to break into a smile.

Twentieth-century narrative has tended to dispense with the beguiling opening sentence. Gertrude Stein's *The Making of Americans* begins: *Once an angry man dragged his father along the ground through his own orchard. "Stop!" cried the groaning old man at last, "Stop! I did not drag my father beyond this tree."* Something to figure out. Even if we recognize that the lines are lifted from the *Nicomachaean Ethics,* we are no wiser as to what they mean at the beginning of a novel. (Morphologically, an epigraph has been absorbed into the narrative).

   Narrative voice (tone, attitude, confidence) is as characteristic of its epoch as any other style. We do not, however, live in an epoch; we live between epochs.

   Literature, once a river defined by banks, is now a river in an ocean. Johnson and Voltaire read, or looked into, everything that came from the presses. A scholar's learning nowadays is certified by the ignorance with which he surrounds his expertise. It is therefore almost impossible to tell if the twentieth century has a style variously perceived by a variety of sensibilities, or the greatest diversity of styles known to cultural history.

SOME CERTAIN LANDMARKS:

The style of *Bouvard et Pécuchet,* the full development of Flaubert's hard, detached style, where banality appears as a kind of Swiftian sarcasm through sheer tone of voice. The phrases are innocent: the opening lines give a thermometer reading, note that an industrial street between the Bastille and the Jardin des Plantes is deserted because of the summer heat, describe a canal and its traffic, and focus on two ordinary men, one of whom has pushed his hat to the back of his head, unbuttoned his vest, and removed his tie. The other wears a brown suit and a cap. Flaubert has learned to make *things* articulate. Everything that the novel means is in that thermometer reading: Flaubert had perceived the transposition of significance (sign, symbol, signal of value or rank) from one set of signifiers to another. One series of human values was being displaced by a new series; the displacement was an accident. Who could have foreseen that the culmination of the Enlightenment would be Leopold and Molly Bloom, Charles and Emma Bovary, Bouvard and Pécuchet? Flaubert does not know (or is reluctant to risk his own reservations) why the age turned out so; hence his immense care to animate objective description with damning detail that can be trusted to speak for itself. This style Joyce (including *Finnegans Wake*), Beckett, Eudora Welty. It becomes a twentieth-century norm, admitting of such variants as Gertrude Stein (*Three Lives* is a Cubist *Trois contes*), Pound (facts and quoted phrases serving as atoms for his ideogrammic molecules), Kafka, Mandelstam, Mann.

The style of Kafka is a marriage of Flaubert and the folktale. The beginning of *Amerika* is good Flaubertian prose, restrained and objective, right up until the second sentence, which describes the Statue of Liberty. *The arm with the sword rose up as if newly stretched aloft, and round the figure blew the free winds of heaven.* That is the most brilliant imaginative touch in modern literature. Note how different it is from Columbus's seeing mermaids, nightingales, and lions in the new world. Or how different it is from the American looking for Notre Dame in London. It is the narrative voice saying for the first time in centuries that the world described in fiction is not the world of the same name in which we have our being. It is a kind of deliberate mistake of the kind committed by Homer when he misread a description of Vesuvius and turned it into a one-eyed giant who bellowed and threw rocks, or by mediæval artists who had to paint camels for the Magi from inadequate accounts of that beast. Kafka worked alongside Max Ernst, who had a similar genius for tinkering with reality, and alongside Henri Rousseau, whose lion in *The Sleeping Gypsy* is simply a dog with a mane, and was even more canine of anatomy until he noticed (or was told) the different genital arrangements of dogs and cats. The essence (and the power) of Kafka's narrative is its receptivity to unexpected intrusions of irreality. Only Walser had done this before outside the frame of either dream vision (Chaucer, Lewis Carroll) or illusion (Flaubert's *Tentation* and Joyce's imitation of it in the Circe chapter of *Ulysses*.)

THE STYLES OF LUDWIG WITTGENSTEIN AND GERTRUDE STEIN:

Strangely simultaneous in their stylistic concerns, the two were at work from 1917 onwards on identical linguistic phenomena: the splashed meaning of chattered language, language which is gesture, politeness, or social formula. We are aware of the fascination of such language for Henry James and Ionesco, who ask us to listen to talk with an intensity we cannot afford in useful and casual conversation. (Ivy Compton-Burnett achieves a dramatic richness in her dialogue by having characters pay spiteful attention to each other's remarks: Wittgensteinian analysis in the raw.) When Wittgenstein asks us to think hard about the philosophical implications of saying "I *have* a pain" and "I think I understand what you are driving at," he is being a dramatist at a primal level, trying to get us to wake up in the midst of dreaming.

Gertrude Stein's play, *An Exercise in Analysis* (1917), is a Wittgenstein drama of clichés and formulae. To notice that they make nonsense is to take the first step toward seeing why she assembled them. Unlike Ionesco, Gertrude Stein is not interested in the absurdity of language but in the astounding implications that can be flushed from its ordinariness. *Here is plenty of space.* This sentence crowds us in a logical corner out of which we can squirm only by insisting (and this is what she wants us to feel) that you have to understand what language means in spite of what it says—and this is not what we understand language to be at all. *He was a boy. Now I understand. Extra size plates.* These three seemingly innocent phrases are incautious matches struck in a murk of stupidity. *Can you recollect missing him.*

One reason William Carlos Williams seems flat beside a poet using language charged according to traditional poetic diction (Wallace Stevens, for example) is that we do not see the Steinian slant of his language. When he quotes, early in *Paterson,* a sign saying that dogs are not allowed in a park except on leashes, he wants to catch us in the Steinian-Wittgensteinian moment of seeing that, yes, the sign has a kind of purpose, but as dogs can't read, the sign exists in a sleep of reason.

I see a pattern here: a movement from assuming the world to be transparent, and available to lucid thought and language, to assuming (having to assume, I think the artists involved would say) that the world is opaque. This would seem to be the assumption of Joyce, Borges, Beckett, Barthelme, Ionesco.

The radical change in twentieth-century narrative is of form. There has been a new understanding that literature is primarily literature and not a useful critique of manners. And there has been a vigorous search for new patterns to the novel. Cubism, a nonsense word for a style of painting invented by Picasso and Braque, was essentially the return to an archaic mode that understands painting to be the same thing as writing. Prehistoric painters abbreviated images. A tarpan, for instance, was drawn by beginning with the dorsal line of profile that flows from ears to scut. Then the head was added, eyes, and ears. Then the tail. Next, front legs, belly line, and hind legs. The design could be abandoned at any point in the process; the graph would still mean *tarpan*. That dorsal line is still the Chinese for *horse*, with leg lines added.

Cubism must have developed when the artist considered how much of his sketch must be finished. Finishing involves a stupidity of perception. Graceful, spontaneous lines go dull or get lost altogether. Ruskin felt that Turner ruined each of his paintings as he filled in all parts of the canvas. Picasso and Braque tried to avoid this stultification of picturing by following archaic models. The Haida artist always depicts the *other side* of the animal he is drawing, so that his whales look like wings hinged at a medial point. Cubists include visual information which would require several points of view. Perspective commits itself to one point of view. *The Sound and the Fury* is therefore a Cubist narrative. *Les Fauxmonnayeurs,* Fowles's *The Collector* and *The French Lieutenant's Woman,* Mandelstam's *Noise of Time,* Cortázar's *Hop-Scotch.* Gertrude Stein's *The Making of Americans.*

The architectonics of a narrative are emphasized and given a rôle to play in dramatic effect when novelists become Cubists; that is, when they see the possibilities of making a hieroglyph, a coherent symbol, an ideogram of the total work. A symbol comes into being when an artist sees that it is the only way to get all the meaning in. Genius always proceeds by faith. We see the novel emerging in Roman literature when the particulars of reality rise to flood-tide. Apuleius wanted to write a new kind of myth: sensuality, brutality, Eleusis, Platonism, Mithraism, travel, trade, Cupid and Psyche—somehow all these touched each other and the tale-teller *could draw them altogether.* So with Petronius. This happens again with Cervantes, again with Dickens and Dostoievsky.

The twentieth-century experimenters wanted to learn how to syncopate, hyphenate, get the essence with a gist: to draw as much of the tarpan as would interplay with intelligence. Art has always known that reality can escape from artistic hubris back into the very natural camouflage from which the artist had hoped to isolate it. Rosa Bonheur's horses are horses; Picasso's horses are Picasso's horses. The one has praised God, the other understood Him.

The action of the *Iliad* lasts fifty-five days. The twenty-eighth day (Book X), or time-center of the epic, finds the Argives on their night raid into the Trojan lines. Agamemnon dresses in a lionskin, Menelaos in that of a leopard; Odysseus wears the helmet of his thieving grandfather Autolykos (The Wolf). Dolon, the Trojan spy they encounter, wears a wolf's hide. Greek and Trojan alike have become stalking nocturnal animals. Homer has measured out the days of his poem so that there are twenty-seven days + a day on which men dress as animals and act with brutal cunning + twenty-seven days. At the extremes of this elegant Bronze Age geometry we find the first and last words of the poem, *blind fury* and *horsetamer*. The meaning of the *Iliad* is thus written in its design: it is a poem about taming the animal in man.

The symmetry of the *Iliad* is rigorous (the duel of Paris and Menelaus balancing the duel of Hektor and Akhilleus, the one in the third book, the other in the third book from the end, Zeus's plan to dishonor the Greeks occupying the central ten books); its balanced, archaic strictness is bound by laws of repetition and rhythmic recurrence.

The *Odyssey* is more eccentric of design, though the adventures of Odysseus fall into a pattern. The descent to Hades is the center; six adventures fall away on each side, and pair off symmetrically. The Kikones and Phaiakians are opposites: earthly and supernatural societies. The Lotus Eaters and Kalypso (adventures 2 and 12) tempt Odysseus with deflections of the will. The Kyklops and the Cattle of Hyperion (3 and 11) involve sins against the gods. Aiolos and Skylla and Kharybdis (4 and 10) are forces of nature. The Laistrygonians and the Sirens (5 and 9) are cannibals. The two visits to Kirke (6 and 8) straddle the descent to Hades, the center of the symmetry. These can be arranged as concentric circles around the descent, a symbolic whirlpool, so that we can say of the *Odyssey* that it has the shape of water in a vortex, water being its pervasive symbol. The symbol of the *Iliad* is fire, which, like Akhilleus, can get out of hand, rage, and burn itself out.

The eighteenth century saw the design of the Homeric epics as rude and Ossianic, though demurrers were beginning to stir. When the Rev. Donald McQueen (the same who rowed Dr. Johnson along the coast of Scalpa in the Hebrides) "alleged that Homer was made up of detached fragments," Johnson insisted that "you could not put a book of the *Iliad* out of its place"; and he believed the same might be said of the *Odyssey*.[1] It is our opinion nowadays that not a line of either poem can be put out of its place.

The beauty of architectonics is both in and out of favor in our time, which is a way of saying that we are confused about design. The structure of Joyce's works is now known to be of an astounding intricacy; it has taken criticism half the century to learn to see the architectonics of *A*

---

[1]James Boswell, *The Journal of a Tour to the Hebrides with Samuel Johnson,* ed. L. F. Powell (London: J. W. Dent, 1958), p. 104.

*Portrait* and *Ulysses.* The bones of *Finnegans Wake* lie undected under its flesh of words; we cannot even find the outer shape, and suspect it of being a monster. My guess is that the shape of the *Wake* will turn out to be as strong and simple as Flaubert's *Trois contes,* a triptych of saints bound by a common allusion to a church window. Pound's *Cantos* seem to defy mapping. Our age is unlike any other in that its greatest works of art were constructed in one spirit and received in another.

There was a Renaissance around 1910 in which the nature of all the arts changed. By 1916 this springtime was blighted by the World War, the tragic effects of which cannot be overestimated. Nor can any understanding be achieved of twentieth-century art if the work under consideration is not kept against the background of the war which extinguished European culture. (Students reading Pound's "eye-deep in hell" automatically think it is an allusion to Dante until you tell them about trenches.) Accuracy in such matters being impossible, we can say nevertheless that the brilliant experimental period in twentieth-century art was stopped short in 1916. Charles Ives had written his best music by then; Picasso had become Picasso; Pound, Pound; Joyce, Joyce. Except for individual talents, already in development before 1916, moving on to full maturity, the century was over in its sixteenth year. Because of this collapse (which may yet prove to be a long interruption), the architectonic masters of our time have suffered critical neglect or abuse, and if admired are admired for anything but the structural innovations of their work.

In 1904 a man who concealed his name behind that of the French pharmacist Etienne-Ossian Henry (a name he would have seen daily in the *U. S. Dispensary,* a reference work druggists keep handy, a name that deflates deliciously to O. Henry) published a novel called *Cabbages and Kings.* The setting is a Central American banana republic. The Panama Canal had been begun earlier in the year; our author has an eye for topicality. And as the author's pseudonym mischievously hides the fact that he was very recently the pharmacist at the *Ohio State Penitentiary,* the title alludes to (among other things) the resemblance of the fat, moustached Secretary of War William Howard Taft to a walrus, Taft the designer and executor of American imperialism ("Dollar Diplomacy") in Central American affairs. The full joke of the title is that the cabbages and kings of Anchuria are bananas and vain dictators, the latter deriving their sovreignty from the American exporters of the former. *Anchuria:* land of the lazy, the happy, the expansive spirit. O. Henry does not explain his pseudonym for Honduras: it was apparently another private joke that he was describing an anti-United States.

Earlier in 1904 *Nostromo* had been published. So in a sense O. Henry, who had recognized his plight in Lord Jim's (". . . we both made one fateful mistake at the supreme crisis of our lives," he said to Alphonso Smith, "a mistake from which we could not recover"),[2] was repeating Conrad's novel about the disappearance of an enormous sum of money against a background of Latin American revolution.

It was the 23-year-old Witter Bynner's idea that O. Henry try his hand at a novel; perhaps only a man so young and so fresh from Harvard would have suggested to a 42-year-old master of the short story (he wrote 66 in 1904) that he turn to a longer form. Bynner suggested that certain stories already in print could be stitched together into a longer narrative. A story ("Money Maze") was sliced up and its parts interspersed with new material. O. Henry calls the form a "vaudeville," and asks us to imagine the last three scenes of the novel as three filmclips from the "Vitagraphoscope," an art then in the formative hands of Méliès, Edison, and the Lumière brothers.

Indeed, the moving picture must have been much in O. Henry's mind when he wrote this spliced-together novel. It has the rapid cutting which we accept as more characteristic of the moving picture than the prose narrative. It exploits the advantages of mime: the mistakes by which we misunderstand what is happening are largely misreadings of visual information. The novel opens by asking us to look at a grave and read the headstone. We are then shown a man tending the grave, but we are not told who he is or for whom he is working. The entire "Proem" (which is, as if to alert the perspicacious reader to the architecture of the book, "By the Carpenter") is a sustained presentation of misinformation. Is it within the business of criticism to note that the convicted embezzler O. Henry is one of literature's masters of sneaking beautifully falsified information past the reader?

Misunderstanding is the mainspring of the plot. A telegram alerts a businessman in a coastal town that the dictator of a country has absconded with the national treasury in suitcases. With him is his mistress, an opera star. Thereafter follows a chain of events so intricately misrepresented that de Maupassant (or Dostoievsky) would have envied it as plotwork. But de Maupassant and Dostoievsky would have used O. Henry's tricky plot to shape conflicts and tensions rising from the wills and passions of characters. O. Henry's characters are New Comedy types, humors, figures from joke, anecdote, and musical comedy.

*Cabbages and Kings* is an architectonic novel: a narrative built out of discrete pieces of imagery, anecdote, and short stories (of which there are five, three of which span two characters each). To its audience in 1904 it was a light, witty comedy interspersed with delicious jokes; if it had any

[2]C. Charles Alphonso Smith, *The O. Henry Biography* (New York: Doubleday, 1916), pp. 144–45.

deeper meaning it was an apology on behalf of the comic spirit to
Panama for McKinley's grey gunboats swinging at anchor in her harbors.
We can now read it as a disguised confession and perhaps a rationaliza-
tion of his crime and flight to Honduras. What gives the novel constant
energy is its versatile playing with appearance and reality.

The Russian Formalist critic Boris M. Ejxenbaum notes in his "O. Henry
and the Theory of the Short Story"[3] that in Russia O. Henry is
thought of as a master of anecdote and picaresque adventures; that is, the
robust American flavor. The theoreticians of Formalism (e.g., Shklovsky)
admired him for his mastery of form and technique, seeing in his tricky
plots and swift narrative a deep allegiance to the primal roots of the short
story in folktale and legend.

Brevity Ejxenbaum takes to be American energy, brio. He notes
that the golden period of the American short story (1830–50) coincides
with the perfection of the long Victorian novel. He then notices that
short stories tend to accumulate along thematic lines (he argues a unity of
theme—and I would add, of imagery—for each of O. Henry's short-
story collections), taking *Cabbages and Kings* to be O. Henry's one attempt to make thematic unity more obvious than a collection. There is a
parallel in Eudora Welty, whose books of stories all have abundant
thematic unity, though only *The Golden Apples* draws attention to its
architectonic structure. Ejxenbaum sees *Cabbages and Kings* as a return
to the earlier forms of the novel in which the plot is a cycle of anecdotes.
He might have said also that the American novel would create a tradition
of the novel as a diverse compendium of elements. Hugh Kenner, thinking of Melville and Hemingway, has remarked that the instruction manual seems to be the model for American novels. Certainly a love of skills
and technologies runs through all the American arts: Eakins (who
painted sportsmen and technicians), Whitman, Faulkner.

Architectonic form absorbs and displaces narrative. This begins to happen on both sides of the Atlantic, with Pound in *The Cantos* (an architectonic epic made of thematically interacting images rather than a plot with
characters), Mandelstam and Shklovsky in Russia, Hermann Broch in
Germany, Gide and Cocteau in France. After the War, the movement
subsided; except for *Ulysses* and some notable exceptions (Dos Passos's
*USA,* Cummings's *EIMI,* Bëly's *Petersburg*), narrative streamlined and
simplified the traditional novel. Pound remained an exemplum to American artists. Williams's masterpiece, *Paterson,* may be the only wholly

[3]Trans. I. R. Titunik, in Ladislav Matejka and Krystyna Pomorska, eds., *Readings in Russian Poetics: Formalist and Structuralist Views* (Cambridge: MIT Press, 1971), pp. 27–69.

accessible architectonic form in our literature. Olson's *Maximus* and Zukofsky's *"A"* are too symbolically and verbally complex, respectively, to command large audiences, especially in an age when a college degree is becoming a certificate of illiteracy.

Fifteen years ago there began to emerge a school of American artists working exclusively with architectonic form—the New American Cinema (Maya Deren, Gregory Markopoulos, Jonas Mekas, James Broughton), the genius of which is Stan Brakhage, whose *Anticipation of the Night* is the first architectonic film. Its "narrative" (said by Brakhage to be influenced by Pound and Stein) is a succession of images that do not tell a story but define a state of mind. His *Dog Star Man* goes even further; it is a long poem in images something like *Paterson* and *The Cantos*. It is useful to know about the American film-makers because they created an atmosphere in which prose writers could turn to architectonic form.

Paul Metcalf's *Genoa* is the only fully realized prose work of this new architectonic movement. (It was published in 1965 by Jargon Books and received two reviews). It has no plot—it carefully draws a hieroglyph before our eyes, a strangely dark symbol. As if introducing and developing musical themes, Mr. Metcalf speaks through a character who, we are to understand, is fictional in several different ways. This character, a Dr. Mills, is (like Paul Metcalf) descended from Herman Melville. At the same time, his brother is the notorious Carl Mills, who, with Bonnie Brown Heady, kidnapped and murdered Bobby Greenlease in 1953. So two relatives are joined in a fiction.

The narrative is built up by interweaving the careers of Columbus and Melville, each of whom grasped the fact of space in his own way. Mr. Metcalf posits his material with a minimum of narrative connections, using passages from Columbus's and Melville's writing to establish a highly defined psychological identity for each. There are further elements interspersed: passages from embryological works (especially teratology), passages from explorers and people in Melville's ambience. Alone among critics of Melville, Mr. Metcalf has seen that Ahab and his men swarm upon Moby-Dick as spermatozoa upon an ovum (a curiously complex image, as Melville has emphasized the sperm whales' resemblance to spermatozoa).

Given the achieved richness of *Genoa* (an essay, three lives, a poem with a biological theme, a meditation on what it would feel like to be Carl Mills's brother, a history of certain ideas), it would seem inevitable that the form would be architectonic. I would like to think that the form derives ultimately from Melville. Of what other novel than *Moby-Dick* can you say that a chapter on any subject under the sun might fit into it?

In *Genoa* every sentence is controlled by the form of the chapter. In the chapter entitled "Charybdis" every image, idea, and action has to do with whirlpools. (*Ulysses* is so unified.) No architectonic work is paraphrasable, for it differs from other narrative in that the meaning shapes into a web, or globe, rather than along a line.

Metcalf represents our most radical shift in the form of narrative; his tone belongs to the twentieth-century norm, beautifully realized but not different. A change in tone will be an achievement indeed. Donald Barthelme has gone a long way in this direction, as has Kenneth Gargemi. Mandelstam was a change in tone; his friend Shklovsky said that the duty of the writer is to make the familiar strange. European and American writing has largely spent the century trying to make the strange familiar.

# Tchelitchew

The public, an invention of nineteenth-century gentility, laid it down as one of its working maxims, once it took up Culture, that it doesn't know anything about art but that it knows what it likes, thus assuming as its own folk wisdom what the emperor Caligula had assumed for it. On the first Sunday that the public was allowed into the British Museum, a portly greengrocer backed into the amphora that inspired Keats's ode and smashed it to rubble. With a discarded cigar the public burnt all of Frederick Catherwood's drawings of the Mayan cities of Yucatan. The public has scratched out the eyes of paintings in the Uffizi, and one fine day a member of the public put the *Mona Lisa* under his arm, carried it out of the Louvre with great cool, and hung it at the foot of his humble bed.

Tax gatherers and philanthropists are not dismayed, however, and the public has its surprises. It took to Whistler's austere and decidedly grim *Arrangement in Grey and Black No. 1,* renamed it *Whistler's Mother,* and hugged it to its breast. It singled out Stuart's oil sketch of Washington, to the exclusion of all other portraits, including five by Stuart. It prefers Van Gogh to Mantegna. It goes to the National Gallery to see Dali's *Last Supper.* And, *mirabile visu,* its favorite painting at the Museum of Modern Art is by a painter whose name eludes pronunciation and whose other paintings have no claim on the public's attention. It is the *Cache-Cache* of Pavel Fyodorovitch Tchelitchew, but to the public it is "that picture you see things in," called *Hide and Seek,* and is the work of Pavvle Chelly Chew. The public is wiser than it can perhaps ever know to see it as a very special picture.

The critics, less creatures of impulse and love than the public, have always been embarrassed by *Cache-Cache.* And Edith Sitwell, the painting's sole audience as far as the painter was concerned, sat before it for a solid half-hour, having sailed to New York to see it just after it was finished, without saying—ever—a single word about it. Indeed it is like no other picture. Its punning images (Tchelitchew did not like people to say) are developed from the Renaissance painter Arcimbaldo, from da Vinci, and from those games, dear to children and artists, where faces are hidden in the branches of trees.

*Cache-Cache* depicts an ancient, gnarled tree against which a little girl, the "it" in a game of hide-and-seek, leans and counts. The tree is also a hand, and its root system a foot. Children's faces fill the contours of the branches, and on closer inspection these faces are made out of yet other faces. Landscapes visible beyond the tree make shapes also; in fact, the entire surface of the painting is a continuous pun that develops into thousands of images—this is not hyperbole but fact. It is quite simply a painting that can be looked at forever. The cycle of the seasons is in it, the human body in every possible anatomical depth, often in strangely beautiful transparencies where one is looking at skin, bone, veins, and muscles all at once, though one might have begun by looking at a child's ear that is also the space between two branches. The metamorphoses of the embryo are here, defined in flowers; boys playing in wheat become a lion's face; children seen through a lattice of apples and leaves become a spaniel.

But not until Parker Tyler—poet, historian of the movies, and friend of Tchelitchew—set himself the task of interpreting *Cache-Cache*[1] was there any response to this richest of modern paintings, other than the intuitive appetite to understand that everyone who has ever looked at it has felt. Out of what kind of mind did it come? What process led to its

[1]Parker Tyler, *The Divine Comedy of Pavel Tchelitchew* (New York: Fleet, 1917).

creation? Mr. Tyler has written a luminous and deep book; no other kind would have served to approach Tchelitchew. He has also written a new kind of book. It is a biography and it is also a novel, but it is, as well, a discursive book that explains the paintings, traces their growth, and analyzes their meaning. He calls it a divine comedy because Tchelitchew consciously divided his work into images of hell, purgatory, and heaven, and culminated each mode in an enormous painting, much as Picasso has always terminated his periods with one definitive painting into which all the skill and meditation of many individual paintings are brought to a perfection.

The hell painting is so terrible that few have looked at it, or been given the opportunity to. It hung for years in the Ringling Brothers Museum in Sarasota (since it depicts side-show freaks). With whatever irony and point, Tchelitchew willed it to his native Russia, to "the Soviet People," who, when he last saw them, had just appropriated his father's estate and vast forests. The Tchelitchews crossed Russia like a band of gypsies, reaching the Black Sea, where they made a brief stand with the White armies. Then they fled to Turkey. Tchelitchew's life thereafter was exile: Berlin (where he began to design for the theater), Paris (where he was taken under Gertrude Stein's wing), London (here Edith Sitwell became his patron), New York, Connecticut, and eventually Rome, where he died in 1957, just short of his fifty-ninth birthday. No one knew quite what to do when it was discovered that he wished Russia to own the panorama of freaks and monsters he called *Phenomena*. Lincoln Kirstein undertook to deliver it during a cultural exchange tour of the New York City Ballet. The Russians accepted it with cold and troubled politeness. They loaned it to the Gallery of Modern Art, which opened in 1964 with a retrospective show of Tchelitchew's. It presently sits in the basement of that museum. The Russians do not reply to offers to have it returned.

The purgatory painting is the *Cache-Cache*, which in every sense is the opposite of *Phenomena*. They both depict nature with an accuracy and wealth of information that no artist between da Vinci and Tchelitchew has mastered, unless it be such technical masteries as those of Stubbs and Audubon. *Phenomena* is satiric, but the satire springs from a pervasive dumb grief that nature could ever be grotesque and mean. *Cache-Cache* celebrates the metamorphic structure and growth of nature in all of its springtimes: childhood, new leaf and blossom, the transmutations of seed into plant and animal. Only the tree is old—and, if you stand back far enough—the barbarian face with cunning wink into which the entire picture resolves.

The third great painting, entitled *The Unfinished Picture*, may or may not be the evocation of Paradise Tchelitchew had spoken of. Mr. Tyler thinks that it is, and presents a convincing and fascinating argument. It grows out of the suprising style Tchelitchew developed after *Cache-Cache,* a style that is geometric, abstract and pure. Mr. Tyler's account of Tchelitchew's career begins with this picture, the last to be painted, showing how its swirls of light are intelligible.

Like most artists, Tchelitchew has no biography distinguishable from that of the labor of painting. The man himself was elate and fey, with periodic seizures of Russian gloom. Quite early he had invented a mask to wear before the world: a personality that Nabokov might have thought up for a novel satirizing Russian spleen and passion. Mr. Tyler carefully incorporates this play-acting into his biography—Tchelitchew terrified of a mouse aboard a Russian battle-cruiser during the Revolution, Tchelitchew going off in a Daimler to be examined for induction by an American draft board, a handkerchief soaked in perfume across his forehead, a distressed lady holding his hand. But Mr. Tyler is also careful to make it clear that the Tchelitchew who painted the pictures, designed stage sets, and protected his career like the general of a besieged fort, was about as wishy-washy as a mother tiger looking to the safety of her cubs.

Tchelitchew was an enigma even to his closest friends, and perhaps to himself as well. He was a Romantic in an age that spurned Romanticism; like few European artists who came to America as exiles he had the ability to put down deep roots—his New England landscapes in which he has hidden Biblical and mythical motifs seem to have been evoked from our past rather than his. He was both shrewdly practical and deeply superstitious. His vision of natural metamorphosis was at once scientific, magical, and religious. Most accounts and reference books of modern art omit him altogether. The volatile attention of the *beau monde* and the hysterical critical ambience that once surrounded Tchelitchew is already thinned out enough for us to begin to see the artist and his achievement with some clarity. Men immune to fashion have already paid their homage: *Cache-Cache* inspired parts of Eliot's *Burnt Norton;* William Carlos Williams's *Paterson* owes much to "Phenomena"; and some of the most mysteriously beautiful passages in Cocteau's *Léone* derive from Tchelitchew's doubled images.

Mr. Tyler has written, ironically, the first brilliant biography of any American artist, though America, whose citizen he was proud to be, can scarcely claim Tchelitchew; nor can the art of biography claim so inventive a study as Mr. Tyler's as simply the account of a life. It is scholarship at its very best, perceptive and painstakingly thorough, and it is storytelling of a high order. Like Tchelitchew himself, Mr. Tyler has the ability to control multiple levels of narrative, bringing into prominence now this, now that theme. His book is the product of many years of labor and research, and achieves what very few scholars have even approached, a lucid study in depth of a contemporary artist that is also as exciting to read as a novel, and which is in itself a wholly new and imaginative way of writing.

Tchelitchew's vision of death came early—a woman in white who glided down a vista of Russian trees. Like Nabokov, and Stravinsky, and Chagall, he took with him into his lifetime's exile a Russian childhood that became mythological over the years and served him as the Greek and Roman myths served Ovid in his exile in the Caucasus. Tchelitchew's last painting was of the white woman, Death. The trees among which she glided and the shape of the lake nearby are remembered in the *Cache-Cache*. The leaf-children, the idiot Tsars, the notion of art as an icon of forces worldly and other-worldly, the interpenetration of man and landscape, the artist as a passionate and suffering seer—all are profoundly Russian. Tchelitchew's devious route to our eyes, to the distracted and shallow New York of the 1940's, has prevented the ahistorical American mind from doing more with the strange Russian genius than perceiving that in his immediate past was the equally odd England of the Sitwells, and before that the Paris of Gertrude Stein. And before that, Berlin and Constantinople.

Parker Tyler therefore begins his biography with Tchelitchew's death, which happened at a remoteness as great as his birth and adolescence, at a psychological and spatial distance that only the tragic ironist can regard with any sense. That is why Parker Tyler's biography is first of all a novel kin to Dostoievsky in defining the life of a genius whose work flowed straight forward with great power and whose heart went crabwise in an agonized spiral. Tchelitchew's work, graphed dispassionately by an art historian, demonstrates a steady progression from style to style; his life without the art sounds like a novel by Nabokov: a decidedly half-mad Russian whose impractical aristocracy keeps him trapped in a world of masculine women and feminine men. Parker Tyler's first triumph is to show, as well as any artist is likely to, the harmony of man and painter. It is a strange and beautiful pattern; only Mann's *Doktor Faustus* is anything like it. Mr. Tyler achieves his biography by one of the feats of literature in our time: he combines novel, biography, and scholarly study. He hides none of his sources, is even willing to weave autobiography into his strong design, and is determined to illuminate his subject with every resource he can bring to bear upon it. Hence this is a biography with no closed doors, and yet there is nothing clinical or prurient about it. Every detail, whether it is Tchelitchew's tapeworm or some esoteric finesse of appetence, has its place in the design. It is almost as if Mr. Tyler, like Mann, had thought up an artist. But who could have thought up Tchelitchew?

Mr. Tyler, when he set out on this biography, had before him essentially two books to write. One would elucidate the paintings, the other would find some pattern in Tchelitchew's life. Both tasks were formidable. The life, for instance, had not been observed by any one person; the biographer had to recover its segments, frequently from sources guardedly secret. Tchelitchew's life was in one sense a great anguish, like Byron's, and in another a continuous gesture. The gesture was not only Romantic; it was Russian as well. Moreover, it was an actor's (should we say a dancer's?) gesture, both defending and hiding the absurd duality of his nature. The tense balance Tchelitchew maintained seems to have been an agreement whereby a feminine will, stubborn, dark, and capricious, ruled the man; and a masculine will, easy, bright, and accomplished, painted the pictures. These two wills began to cooperate quite early; the painter came to depend on the feminine self for its inspiration—an inspiration that was thoroughly mediæval (or perhaps simply Russian) in its intricate maze of zodiacal lore, white magic, superstition, and practically anything, so long as it was sufficiently incredible. The phenomenon is not uncommon: Cocteau saw it as a matter of putting down roots into the dark in order to blossom in sunlight. Tchelitchew, as Mr. Tyler goes to pains to show, was more aware than even Cocteau of the need to plumb the dark, and was just as aware that the work of art thus fed must be wholly free of its origins. The artist who does not free himself simply imposes his obsessions on his audience, and his art is morbid and puzzling. Each of the three masterpieces of Tchelitchew—*Phenomena, Cache-Cache,* and *L'Inachevé*—breaks from an awful darkness into the full clarity that a work of art creates both for itself and for the world.

The fullest triumph of Mr. Tyler's biography is that he can demonstrate the dark processes by which the paintings came into being, and can demonstrate with equal facility the coherence and clarity of the completed work. The biographer of an artist frequently finds himself in possession of dramatic facts—Shelley's covey of wives, Turner's eccentricities, and so on—which he knows must somehow be pertinent to the artist's work. The trick is to show how. Has anyone seen Leonardo the military engineer in the *Mona Lisa,* or Van Gogh the evangelist in *L'Arlesienne?* Mr. Tyler has the kind of mind that refuses to let a relationship elude it. Tchelitchew's work is always harmonic, and his explicator had to master that harmony; and master it he has. Iconography, that subtlest and most painstaking of modern humanistic disciplines, came to its maturity just when Mr. Tyler began his biography. Edgar Wind himself recognized at a glance that the *Cache-Cache* was a masterpiece, and must have sighed at the thought of an iconographer accounting for the multiple transparences organized in such a harmony of astounding strangeness. De Chirico, to be sure, is just as strange, but in looking at a de Chirico the scholar is aware that the vista down which he searches is ultimately as warm and familiar as the past of Italy. It is quite another thing to look down a vista that recedes into the forests of Russia, as well as into a mind that, unlike de Chirico's, belonged to no school, had no peer, and was committed to a poetic vision all but wholly inward and private.

Mr. Tyler reproduces among the hundred and twenty-eight pictures that illustrate his book a photograph by George Platt Lynes of fourteen European artists then in exile in the United States. (The photograph was made in March, 1942.) Only one face peers undisturbed and supremely confident from these troubled masks. It is the face of Max Ernst, that would be just as composed in the anthrax forests of Mars. Eugène Berman, Mondrian, and Chagall are visibly distressed; Breton and Masson are being brave, unsuccessfully. The rest, except for Tchelitchew, are putting up a good show as best they can. Tchelitchew's face is defiant; it is also filled with grief. His eyes alone are unfocussed; he alone has no sense of being photographed. Whatever Ernst is, Tchelitchew is the opposite. If Ernst is sane (and art has rarely known a saner mind), then Tchelitchew is wildly insane, an observation one feels he would have agreed with, nervously. The sane artist moves toward vision (Blake was sane, Flaubert was sane); the artist who has dared to allow the irrational into his art moves rather toward a recovery of reality, but on his own terms. Tchelitchew summarized years of work in two enormous paintings: one is devoted to the irrational within man and the irrational outside of him. Here natural design has gone hideously wrong, and the mind too has gone wrong. The face Tchelitchew gives himself in *Phenomena* is the one that appears in Lynes's photograph of the exiled artists. There is both fury and grief in that face, but it is also a face on which a great inwardness is written.

Is there a portrait of Tchelitchew in the *Cache-Cache?* Has anyone looked? His symbolic signatures are there, as Mr. Tyler shows us, but I suspect that his grieving face has no place in a painting that has obliterated the artist more than any other in our time. The *Cache-Cache* was not painted anymore than Bruckner's Ninth was written, or Brancusi's *Maiastra* was sculpted. It came into being through a process to which painting was incidental. It grew and was half a lifetime in the growing. If Picasso is a painter, Tchelitchew is a force of nature.

# Jack Yeats the Elder

Of time, the tyrant and obsession of the rest of the world, the Irish know nothing and care less. Dublin, a Catholic city for 1500 years, has never gotten around to building a cathedral. They intend to, of course. From its inception the Republic of Eire (or The Irish Free State, or Ireland, or Poblacht na h-Éireann, or whatever name they decide on, in time) has issued postage stamps depicting a map of the country that jauntily includes a largish portion of the United Kingdom. Never mind; the day will come when it will be Ireland's again. The clock in the Joyce household, we remember, disagreed by hours with Dublin's other clocks.

John Butler Yeats, one of the most gifted portraitists in the history of art, the father of Jack Yeats, Ireland's greatest painter, and of William Butler Yeats, Ireland's greatest poet, spent his eighty-three years as if time did not exist. When the Rebellion began with an orgy of dynamite in

1916, one of the casualties was a studio full of his unfinished oil portraits. And he, always the level philosopher, would have been the first to admit that he probably wouldn't have finished them anyhow. At his death in 1922 there was a self-portrait on his easel that had been commissioned for the incomparable collection of John Quinn. It had been on the easel for fifteen years. A generation of American painters watched him work on it. He would charge his palette with colors, take up a brush, fiddle with an effect, and begin to talk.

His skill as a raconteur, as a conversationalist, as a speaker at dinners or on any occasion, was magnificent, Irish, and inexhaustible. G. K. Chesterton remembered an offhand example of his mastery of the sentence: "Mr. Joseph Chamberlain has the character, as he has the face, of a shrewish woman who ruins her husband by her extravagance; and Lord Salisbury has the character, as he has the face, of the man who is so ruined."

Such balance of phrase, melody of words, and pungent imagery were accomplishments as admired as they were expected in J. B. Yeats's world. He talked with William Morris and Sam Butler, Father G. M. Hopkins and Edward Dowden, with Lady Gregory and John Quinn, with Ellis the editor of Blake and John O'Leary. He spoke briefly on the street one day with James Joyce. It tells us much about J. B. Yeats's ambience that he remarked to Quinn in later years that he was aware the people Joyce wrote about in *Dubliners* and *Ulysses* existed, but of course one had not met them.

The Yeatses were Anglo-Irish with eighteenth-century manners. They abided the Catholics but drew the line at Scots-Irish Protestants, who were apt to be ill-bred, bigoted, and enthusiastic. The young John Butler went off to a proper private school and Trinity College, and was setting out to be a barrister when he married the sister of a schoolmate, Susan Pollexfen of Sligo. Her family were merchants; in W. B. Yeats's poetry we hear much of them, their stalwart character, their virtue.

A great measure of Pollexfen endurance was indeed necessary to be the wife of John Butler Yeats, who in the first two years of his marriage earned exactly ten pounds, and that was a college prize for eloquence. Susan Pollexfen Yeats bore him two sons, and three daughters. To them we are indebted for many fine poems, paintings, and books (the daughters founded the Cuala Press and collaborated with Lady Gregory in a little renaissance of Irish folk crafts). But Susan remains a shadowy figure in all of this, a patient woman with a brilliant, unpredictable husband and talented children. Caught between the practicality of her own family and the irresponsibility of the Yeatses, she went quietly, pitifully, mad.

J. B. Yeats spent his entire career as a Dublin barrister drawing carica-
tures of the court. In the only deliberate decision of his life he moved to
London to study art, but when he arrived there he became the universal
model of dilatoriness. Everyone liked him, he had a preternatural gift for
catching a likeness, but he fitted into no editor's or sitter's schedule.
Robert Browning called, possibly wanting his portrait painted; we shall
never know, as J. B. Yeats never got around to arranging an appointment. Nor were Dante Gabriel Rossetti's overtures followed up.

Not until he was 61 did he have an exhibit, at which time Dublin
learned all at once, in the space of a week, that three Yeatses, old Jack,
young Jack, and Willie, were all geniuses. One suspects that the news was
equally astounding to old Jack, for whom this week of exhibits and plays
was merely an interval in his life of impassioned talk. If, as he heard, he
was a portraitist of the first rank, he had better set about finding a studio
and taking commissions.

Such was his intention (when he allowed himself an intention), but
another matter intervened. A man from New York, a lawyer from Ohio
with a taste for art and things Irish, had begun to come to Dublin to spray
dollars in all directions. He bought Yeats drawings, he bought Willie's
manuscripts, he bought books from the Cuala Press. It was of no interest
that this John Quinn also bought Brancusis, Picassos, Wyndham Lewises,
Rousseaus, Augustus Johns, and Matisses, or that he owned all of Conrad's manuscripts and a manuscript of Eliot's that would surface thirty
years later, the first draft of a very different *Waste Land* from the one we
know, transformed by Ezra Pound's editorial pencil.

When Quinn arranged for a show of Irish folk craft in New York, to be
exhibited by Lillie Yeats, old Jack thought it would be a fine idea if he
tagged along, to see the sights across the water. Quinn thought this an
awful idea, for what was he to do with an old man who could talk all day
and most of the night? What he did was introduce him around (people
loved him), commission a self-portrait for his collection of modern Irish
art, and abide his leisurely ways until it was time for his departure back
to Dublin.

Quinn was one of the busiest men in the world. He was a corporation
lawyer whose clients were apt to be Standard Oil of New Jersey and his
adversary in court The United States of America. He was involved with
the struggles of the avant-garde (sending almost daily checks and advice
to Pound, Joyce, Eliot, W. B. Yeats); he was the most astute and sensitive
collector of modern art in the U.S., making even Gertrude Stein seem an
amateur.

And here was old Jack Yeats come to visit. Quinn got him a room in a
Bohemian and wonderfully comfortable boarding house run by three

French sisters. Here old Jack became the mentor of young painters and poets. He was a success as an after-dinner speaker.Willlie looked in on his reading visits, letters floated back and forth to Dublin and London (letters so interesting that two selections of them, one by Pound, one by Joseph Hone, made him famous), and the drawing of portraits in pencil went on, as often given away as for a fee.

He never went home; he is buried in Chestertown, New York, in a cemetery plot donated by his friend Jeanne Foster, Quinn's last mistress. He never finished the self-portrait. If he never finished anything properly, neither did he use anything up. Life remained a wonderful round of talk, of drawing, of eating, of drinking, of reading, of speculation. He was always on the defense against every enticement to run smoothly in a groove. He wished Willie would give up his silly mysticism and John Sloan his silly politics. He lectured Quinn; he threw things at trained nurses who came to look after him in his bouts with the flu. His legacy is thousands of discerning, hastily rendered pencil portraits, some masterful oils, and his life.

It is William Murphy's surest understanding in his long and meticulously documented biography, *Prodigal Father: The Life of John Butler Yeats (1839–1922)*, that Jack Yeats's life, his daily round multiplying into a prodigy of years, is what we want to know about. A separate study (one is needed) of his art would have been quite a different book. A knowledge of his sitters would constitute a history of a large part of the intellectual life of Dublin, London, and New York for over half a century. To write biographies of other men one must helplessly make a generous space on the stage for old Jack Yeats. B. L. Reid found that this was so when he wrote his fine life of John Quinn, *The Man from New York* (1968). In books about W. B. and young Jack Yeats, in books about the Irish Renaissance, about realist painting in New York at the turn of the century, there he is, a firm old man talking and talking.

In Murphy's biography he is frequently offstage while necessary details are imparted—facts about Synge, the Armory Show, Lady Gregory pacing to and fro, Maude Gonne, Roger Casement—but he is always present in his absence. He was, as Murphy discovered, a spindle around which an incredible richness of strands was wound. He was strangely unaware of his prominence.Willie was an established poet before he realized it. It is questionable if he knew who his friend and patron Quinn really was.

Jeanne Foster, whose beauty inspired his finest drawings toward the end of his days and whose friendship he enjoyed, remembered a characteristic tale of old Jack's tenacious placidity. Quinn, busy with a case at law, was going mad with old Jack underfoot, imperturbably leisurely, good grammar and poised phrases leaping from him as thick as Dublin fleas. He secretly phoned Miss Foster, asked her to pretend she was going shopping, and begged the company of a gentleman.

"To be sure," agreed old Jack, always ready for a new turn to things. Quinn's Rolls came around, old Jack was tucked into it with a hot-water bottle and a lap rug. He was also, at his request, provided with a hot toddy to sip, for his health. As the great car, the chauffeur, the beautiful woman, and the eighty-year-old Irishman moved into the January slush of Fifth Avenue, old Jack turned to Jeanne Foster with a happy sigh. "One thing you've got to admit about Mr. Quinn," he said. "He knows how to live."

# Wittgenstein

Like the gentle Anton Bruckner, who counted leaves on trees to while away a Sunday afternoon, Ludwig Wittgenstein in odd moments calculated the height of trees by pacing off from the trunk the base of a right triangle, wheeling around and sighting along his walking stick (up the hypotenuse) to the tree's top, invoking then the majestic theorem of Pythagoras. Together with inventing a sewing machine (in his teens), designing a house in Vienna (still standing) that elicited the admiration of Frank Lloyd Wright, and following assiduously the films of the Misses Betty Hutton and Carmen Miranda, this is one of the few acts of the philosopher that was at all transparent. No mystery, however, surrounds either his life or his thought. If he was not the greatest philosopher of our age, he was the most significant. He founded (inadvertently) and disowned two major philosophies. He was "getting at something" when he died, just what we shall never know. At the end of his first book, the *Tractatus Logico-Philosophicus* (completed in a concentration camp during the First World War) he wrote: "My propositions serve as elucidations in the following way: anyone who understands me eventually recognizes them as nonsensical, when he has used them as steps to climb up beyond them." At the beginning of his other book, the *Philosophical Investigations,* he wrote: "It is not impossible that it should fall to the lot of this work, in its poverty and in the darkness of this time, to bring light into one brain or another—but, of course, it is not likely." Once, when a student posed a question during one of his classes at Cambridge, Wittgenstein said: "I might as well be lecturing to the stove." A box of slips of paper—*Zettel*—was found among Wittgenstein's effects. On each slip is written a thought. The order of the slips, if any, is of course unascertainable. To come to some understanding of them is not, as Sir Thomas Browne would cheer us on, beyond all conjecture, but we must go about it with the ghost of Wittgenstein whispering: "But, of course, it is not likely."

Wittgenstein before he came to philosphy was a mathematician, a musician, an architect, a sculptor, a mechanical engineer, a grade-school teacher, a soldier, and an aviator. He could have followed any of these careers doubtless with brilliant success; just before he came to Cambridge (they gave him a doctorate at the door) he was strongly inclined to "be an aeronaut." Every account of his strange life indicates that he *tried* to teach. He did not dine with the faculty, as the faculty in its grandeur always dines in academic gowns, black shoes, and neck tie. Wittgenstein was forever tieless and wore a suede jacket that opened and closed with that marvellous invention the zipper; and his shoes were brown. He held his lectures in his rooms, in the continental manner. As there was no furniture except an army cot, a folding chair, a safe (for the *Zettel*), and a card table, the students brought their own chairs. Philosophy classrooms in our century have frequently been as dramatic as stages: Santayana, Samuel Alexander, Bergson—men of passionate articulateness whose lectures fell on their students like wind and rain. But Wittgenstein, huddled in silence on his chair, stammered quietly from time to time. He was committed to absolute honesty. Nothing—nothing at all—was to be allowed to escape analysis. He had nothing up his sleeve; he had nothing to teach. The world was to him an absolute puzzle, a great lump of opaque pig iron. Can we think about the lump? What is thought? What is the meaning of *can,* of *can we,* of *can we think?* What is the meaning of *we?* What does it mean to ask what is the meaning of *we?* If we answer these questions on Monday, are the answers valid on Tuesday? If I answer them at all, do I think the answer, believe the answer, know the answer, or imagine the answer?

It was apparently not of the least interest to Wittgenstein that Plato had answered certain questions that philosophers need to ask, or that Kant or Mencius had answered them. He sometimes liked other philosophers' questions; he seems never to have paid any attention to their answers. Truth was stubborn; Wittgenstein was stubborn; and neither faced the other down. We have to look back to the stoic Musonius to find another man so nakedly himself, so pig-headedly single-minded. He actually taught for very little of his life. He was forever going off into the Norwegian forests, to Russia, to the west of Ireland where—and this is all we know of these solitudes—he taught the Connemara birds to come and sit in his hands. He mastered no convention other than speech, wearing clothes, and—grudgingly and with complaint—the symbols of mathematics. The daily chores of our civilization were wonders to him, and when he participated in them they became as strange as housekeeping among the Bantu. He liked washing dishes after a meal. He put the dishes and silverware in the bathtub, studied carefully the detergent, the temperature of the water, and spent hours at his task, and hours more in the rinsing and drying. If he was a guest for several days, all the meals had to be identical with the first, whether breakfast, lunch, or dinner. What he ate was of no matter, just so it was always the same. He listened carefully to human speech, and took it to pieces before one's eyes. Language, he decided, was a game men had learned to play, and he was always, like an anthropologist from Mars, trying to find out the rules. When he lay dying of cancer at his doctor's house, the doctor's kind wife remembered his birthday and baked him a cake. Moreover, she wrote on it with icing, "Many Happy Returns." When Wittgenstein asked her if she had examined the implications of that sentiment, she burst into tears and dropped the cake. "You see," Wittgenstein said to the doctor when he arrived on the scene, "I have neither the cake nor an answer to my question." Some days before, the doctor's wife, patient martyr in the history of philosophy, had shown Wittgenstein her new coat that she was to wear to a party that very evening. Silently he fetched the scissors, silently he snipped the buttons from the coat, silently he replaced the scissors. The sainted wife remarked that, yes indeed, come to think of it, the coat did look better without its buttons, but only when the seals are opened at Doom will the philosopher's skill with the scissors declare its meaning.

Except for the mathematician David Pinsent, to whom the *Tractatus* is dedicated and who was killed in the First World War, he was luckless in friends; he seems to have noticed women in order to know where to flee. The idea of a female philosopher made him close his eyes in despair. Insanity and suicide ran in his family. He pleaded with his students to take menial jobs (as he did from time to time, as a country schoolteacher and mechanic). Life was perhaps a strange disease which one suffered with heroism; thought was certainly a disease which philosophy, perhaps, could cure. Like Henry Adams he felt that a healthy intellect would be unaware of itself, and would get on with life's business, making beautiful machines, music, and poetry, without reflection. Whatever the truth of the world, it was simple in the sense that one can say, for instance, that death is not a part of life (one of the perceptions in the *Tractatus*) and that the world is independent of my will (another); and it was complex in the sense that all that happens is the result of many causes not all of which can ever be known.

It is only Wittgenstein's writing in the middle of his career that gives one fits—the part that gave birth (to his regret) to linguistic analysis, philosophy's darkest night. The early work—the *Tractatus*—is lucid and powerful. The newly discovered *Zettel* can only be compared to the fragments of Heraclitus. Indeed, Wittgenstein admired all his life the epigrams of the acid-tongued Lichtenberg, and felt that thought was basically perception. What the philosopher says about the world is not too different from the proverb, the old saw, the infinitely repeatable line of poetry. It is clear that the *Zettel* are a return to the manner of the *Tractatus,* back to the archaic period of philosophy, back before the talkative charm of Socrates. The philosopher, as Wyndham Lewis said of the artist, goes back to the fish. Physics in Wittgenstein's lifetime was going back to Heraclitus (a clue to cracking the atom was found in Lucretius by Niels Bohr); so was art; so was architecture. What could be more nakedly Pythagorean than the geodesic structures of Buckminster Fuller, what more household caveman than the paintings of Paul Klee? One definition of *modern* is a renaissance of the archaic (as *the* Renaissance was a reaching back to Hellenism, to Rome, to a ripened civilization rather than to the green springtime of that same civilization).

"The limits of my language are the limits of my world." "The most beautiful order of the world is still a random gathering of things insignificant in themselves." Which is Heraclitus, which Wittgenstein? "The philosopher," says one of the *Zettel,* "is not a citizen of any community of ideas. That is what makes him a philosopher." And: "What about the sentence—*Wie ist es mit dem Satz*—'One cannot step into the same river twice'?" That Heraclitean perception has always been admired for its hidden second meaning. *One* cannot step . . . ; it is not only the flux of the river that makes the statement true. But is it true? No, Wittgenstein would smile (or glare), but it is wise and interesting. It can be examined. It is harmonious and poetic.

The more we read Wittgenstein the more we feel that he is *before* Heraclitus, that he deliberately began an infinite recession (in order, of course, to go forward when he found a footing). He bowed out of the tradition whereby all philosophers digest all other philosophers, refuting and enriching, forming allegiances and enmities, and emitting their version of what they have learned from a conquered vantage which must be defended night and day. Wittgenstein declined to inspect the history of philosophy. It is questionable if when he died he had ever come to any understanding of the number 2. Two *what?* Two things would have to be identical, which is absurd if identity has any meaning. One of the *Zettel* wonders what the phrase "friendly hand" could mean. Another, if the absence of feeling is a feeling. Another, if his stove has an imagination and what it means to assume that the stove does not have an imagination.

Wittgenstein did not argue; he merely thought himself into subtler and deeper problems. The record which three of his students have made of his lectures and conversations at Cambridge discloses a man tragically honest and wonderfully, astoundingly absurd. In every memoir of him we meet a man we are hungry to know more about, for even if his every sentence remains opaque to us, it is clear that the archaic transparency of his thought is like nothing that philosophy has seen for thousands of years. It is also clear that he was trying to be wise and to make others wise. He lived in the world, and for the world. He came to believe that a normal, honest human being could not be a professor. It is the academy that gave him his reputation of impenetrable abstruseness; never has a man deserved a reputation less. Disciples who came to him expecting to find a man of incredibly deep learning, found a man who saw mankind held together by suffering alone, and he invariably advised them to be as kind as possible to others. He read, like all inquisitive men, to multiply his experience. He read Tolstoy (always getting bogged down) and the Gospels and bales of detective stories. He shook his head over Freud. When he died he was reading *Black Beauty.* His last words were: "Tell them I've had a wonderful life."

# Hobbitry

In the sad list of things that will always be beyond me, philology is toward the top, up with my inability to drive an automobile or pronounce the word "mirroring." The well-meant efforts of two universities to teach me to read (and in a recurring nightmare, to write and speak) Old English, or Anglo-Saxon as they sometimes called it, I have no intention of forgiving. Some grudges are permanent. On Judgment Day I shall proudly and stubbornly begrudge learning how to abandon a sinking ship, how to crawl under live machine-gun fire, and Anglo-Saxon.

The first professor to harrow me with the syntax and morphology of Old English had a speech impediment, wandered in his remarks, and seemed to think that we, his baffled scholars, were well up in Gothic, Erse, and Welsh, the grammar of which he freely alluded to. How was I to know that he had one day written on the back of one of our examination papers, "In a hole in the ground there lived a hobbit"?

Not until years later could I know that this vague and incomprehensible lecturer, having poked around on a page of the dread "Anglo-Saxon Chronicle" for an hour, muttering place names and chuckling over variant readings, biked out to Sandfield Road in Headington and moved Frodo and Sam toward Mordor.

Even when I came to read *The Lord of the Rings* I had trouble, as I still do, realizing that it was written by the mumbling and pedantic Prof. J. R. R. Tolkien.

Nor have I had much luck in blending the professor and the author in my mind. I've spent a delicious afternoon in Tolkien's rose garden talking with his son, and from this conversation there kept emerging a fond father who never quite noticed that his children had grown up, and who, as I gathered, came and went between the real world and a world of his own invention. I remembered that Sir Walter Scott's son grew up in ignorance that his father was a novelist, and remarked as a lad in his teens when he was among men discussing Scott's genius, "Aye, it's commonly him is first to see the hare."

Nor, talking with his bosom friend H. V. G. ("Hugo") Dyson, could I get any sense of the Tolkien who invented hobbits and the most wonderful adventures since Ariosto and Boiardo. "Dear Ronald," Dyson said, "writing all those silly books with three introductions and ten appendixes. His was not a true imagination, you know: He made it all up." I have tried for fifteen years to figure out what Dyson meant by that remark.

The closest I have ever gotten to the secret and inner Tolkien was in a casual conversation on a snowy day in Shelbyville, Kentucky. I forget how in the world we came to talk of Tolkien at all, but I began plying questions as soon as I knew that I was talking to a man who had been at Oxford as a classmate of Ronald Tolkien's. He was a history teacher, Allen Barnett. He had never read *The Hobbit* or *The Lord of the Rings*. Indeed, he was astonished and pleased to know that his friend of so many years ago had made a name for himself as a writer.

"Imagine that! You know, he used to have the most extraordinary interest in the people here in Kentucky. He could never get enough of my tales of Kentucky folk. He used to make me repeat family names like Barefoot and Boffin and Baggins and good country names like that."

And out the window I could see tobacco barns. The charming anachronism of the hobbits' pipes suddenly made sense in a new way. The Shire and its settled manners and shy hobbits have many antecedents in folklore and in reality—I remember the fun recently of looking out of an English bus and seeing a roadsign pointing to Butterbur. Kentucky, it seems, contributed its share.

Practically all the names of Tolkien's hobbits are listed in my

Lexington phone book, and those that aren't can be found over in Shelbyville. Like as not, they grow and cure pipe-weed for a living. Talk with them, and their turns of phrase are pure hobbit: "I hear tell," "right agin," "so Mr. Frodo is his first and second cousin, once removed either way," "this very month as is." These are English locutions, of course, but ones that are heard oftener now in Kentucky than in England.

I despaired of trying to tell Barnett what his talk of Kentucky folk became in Tolkien's imagination. I urged him to read *The Lord of the Rings* but as our paths have never crossed again, I don't know that he did. Nor if he knew that he created by an Oxford fire and in walks along the Cherwell and Isis the Bagginses, Boffins, Tooks, Brandybucks, Grubbs, Burrowses, Goodbodies, and Proudfoots (or Proudfeet, as a branch of the family will have it) who were, we are told, the special study of Gandalf the Grey, the only wizard who was interested in their bashful and countrified ways.

# Dictionary

Some years ago, on a particularly distraught evening, the drift of things into chaos was precipitated by my consulting Webster's Third International for the word *Mauser*. All I wanted to know was whether it sported an umlaut or not. It wasn't there. I paid $47.50 for my Webster's; it weighs as much as a six-year-old girl; and I had to build a table for it, as it is too bulky to go into a bookshelf, and will anyway come all to pieces unless it sits open day and night. And no *Mauser*. Indeed, Webster's is wary of trade names of any sort, not to mention all proper names whatever. They recognize *kleenex* (but not *Xerox*), *frigidaire* (but not *Jockey shorts*), *kodak* (but not *Bufferin*). One would like to have been a mouse in the rafters, to overhear the editorial battles at Webster's, as to what is and what isn't a word in the English language. Diction is thoroughly conservative; one word per object, admonishes the Muse. I once popped into *le drugstore* next door to the *Rhumerie martiniquaise* on the Boulevard St.-Germain. *"Et alors,"* I said, *"est-ce que vous avez mouchoirs de papier peut-être?"*

*"Ah!"* said the lady addressed, *"vous voulez dire le kleenex!"*

Stan Brakhage, the film-maker, was once shooting a TV commercial for Scotties, the purpose being to get people to recognize another name for *mouchoirs de papier.* "And now, sweetheart," said the formidable Brakhage to the moppet who was the star of his commercial, "when I hold up my hand, blow your nose on the kleenex." If, however, you put the word *kleenex* into print, you will receive by next mail a stern letter from the manufacturers of same pointing out that you should have written *Kleenex*—they have given up expecting *Kleenex (Reg. Trade Mark)*—and hinting that if you persist in writing *kleenex* rather than *Kleenex,* a big blue policeman will appear at your door. Ditto the Xerox people, who maintain a bumbailiff who does nothing but search public writ looking for *xerox;* then he pounces.

No wonder dictionaries have a nervous view of a whole family of words which the people use with utter abandon and licentiousness. In the new *American Heritage Dictionary of the English Language,* for instance, we find *Coke (Reg. Trade Mark)* but not *Coca-Cola.* (The senior members of my family down in South Carolina always refer to Coca-Cola as "a dope," and my intrepid mother calls it "a Pepsi," enough to make the public relations boys in Atlanta weep and wring their hands.) The AHDEL is generous with names aborning, but only within cautious limits. *Thermofax,* for instance, and *kotex* are not, as far as the American Heritage people are concerned, part of our language.

A dictionary should by definition be the vocabulary of a language, a task beyond both human effort and the might of computers. Languages are intractable for the simple reason that they are wildly alive, dropping words no longer useful and inventing new ones. (The AHDEL dutifully lists *quark,* a subatomic hypothetical particle, but mispells *Finnegans Wake* as *Finnegan's Wake* in giving the literary source from which a scientist whimsically took its name.) Actually a dictionary is a vocabulary restricted by the concept of diction: the range of words in use at a particular time, if—big *if!*—diction were of a coherence. It isn't.

The part of a language in use at any given time is hierarchically arranged in two great patterns, a vertical one rising to the pure and Olympian style of Santayana or Henry James, and sinking to the low and racy gabble of modern poets and used-car dealers. There is overlying this an horizontal gradation of dialect and professional jargon, together with the disastrous traumas of education wherein native dialects of great color and precision have been badgered into being "correct" English. Thus "between you and I" and "irregardless" and "I have saw," and all the other monsters whose inception can be laid at the sore feet of the English teacher. And then there was the stern hand of Noah Webster himself, who felt that everything in a word that could be pronounced should: hence, *falcon* pronounced so that its first syllable rhymes with *shall.* That dread bird is a *fawk'n.* And *forehead,* pronounced *ad litteram,* rather than *forrid.* The AHDEL mispronounces the one, but heroically holds to tradition with the other.

Along with a pervasive deterioration of idiom and the chronic mis-behavior of pronouns in the objective case, the most thoroughgoing abuse of English by American tongues is the pronunciation of words seen but apparently never heard, and I fear me that the AHDEL offers encour-agement to these ignorances by listing the mispronunciations (e.g. *hover, plover, kiln*), as a second and therefore good enough pronunciation.

The format of this dictionary follows that of the Larousse dictionaries and encyclopedias in France, placing the illustrations in an ample margin. These are for the most part sharply reproduced photographs, breaking the tradition, thank goodness, of the drawing and wood engraving. There is an annoying up-to-dateness in the selection of illustrations. One can see what U Thant looks like, but not Sir Walter Scott; Jomo Kenyatta, but not John Adams. Giorgio de Chirico is misspelled as "di Chirico."

The whole virtue of a dictionary, however, is in the precision with which it defines words. And it is here that the AHDEL loses its crisp appearance and sits in the muck beside Webster's Third and all the rest in our time, with the exception of the old Collier's New Century Dictionary, one of the nobler efforts of William James and his circle. But the art of definition seems to have died with Samuel Johnson, whose stern clarities can still be detected behind the graceless mangles of modern lexicog-raphy. For example, the AHDEL's definition of poker, "one that pokes; specifically, a metal rod used to stir a fire," is a spastic version of Johnson's "the iron bar with which men stir the fire."

*Scratch,* "a linelike mark produced by scratching" (AHDEL): "an inci-sion ragged and shallow" (Johnson). *Pastor,* "a Christian minister in his capacity of having spiritual charge over a congregation or other group" (AHDEL); "a clergyman who has the care of a flock; one who has souls to feed with sound doctrine" (Johnson). Johnson's science is of course imagistic rather than schematic; where modern dictionaries give us cold taxonomy (*Scorpion,* "any of the various arachnids of the order Scor-pionida . . ."), Johnson offered a homely poetry—*Scorpion,* "a reptile much resembling a small lobster, but that his tail ends in a point with a very venomous sting." And for all of Johnson's fame as a pedantic old grouch rumbling out latinate words, it is he and not a modern dictionary who can be counted on to blurt out a simple, blunt definition. For *shrub* the AHDEL gives "a woody plant of relatively low height." Johnson: "a bush, a small tree." And (the AHDEL having followed Webster's Third out of the Freudian jungle of words once taboo to gentility) look who leaps quickest to the safety of a euphemism: *piss*, "to urinate" (AHDEL); "to make water" (Johnson).

A good dictionary ought to be one's handy spelling-book, source of enlightenment for hard words, and guide to correct usage. The AHDEL will serve for all of these, but I don't see that it has added any new quality to lexicography. I shall take my copy to the office, to ornament the desk; my worktable at home shall keep its American Century and its Johnson, and when a hairy scientific word comes along or an impenetrable acronym, I shall still walk across the room to Webster's Third International, hoping that it isn't a registered trade name.

# No, But I've
# Read the Book

Since the days when Randolph of Roanoke tried to talk the Senate into outlawing the bowdlerized text of Shakespeare, such as high schools still use, American literacy in public places has drifted the other way. Now we have Tarzan tossed out of a California grade school, for living in sin with Jane. This happened over the Christmas holidays, and cries and counter-cries went up. Grosset and Dunlap assured the Republic that Lord Greys-toke and Miss Jane Porter, of Baltimore, were married with full rites of the Church of England, on page 313 of *The Return of Tarzan,* the second of the twelve-volume saga. The good folk of Downey, Calif., were think-ing of Hollywood's Tarzan.

In Burroughs's pages, when Miss Porter met Tarzan formally—she had seen him previously when he rescued her from the attentions of the ape Terkoz, a suitor unacceptable to La Porter—he could read and write

English (a trifle mushily), could speak "ape and a little elephant," and French. By the sixth volume of the epic Tarzan speaks Arabic, English, German, Bantu, a great deal of elephant, Swahili, French, monkey, Middle English, lion, Abyssinian, and has a fair understanding of American. So it goes. Open your *Frankenstein* and hear the monster quoting Aeschylus; see him Byronizing over the sublimity of the Alps; look at the poor critter in Hollywood's hands.

A grumpy stickler for consistency might complain that it's not fair to deteriorate both ways: to debase Tarzan with one hand and then ban him with the other for being a vulgar shadow of his chivalric self. And Tarzan, if you will, is immoral. To the student of ideas he is the man superciliously above the law, the superman with lifted nose. He is, in fact, Sherlock Holmes catalyzed by Rousseau and Fenimore Cooper and set in Darwin's imaginary jungle, fit and surviving. And Holmes is but Walter Pater dressed up like a sleuth so that the British public could participate, after all, in the arcane doings of the Aesthetes (Holmes the most dedicated and last Pre-Raphaelite of them all).

But you can't have everything as clear as you would like. Tarzan isn't ever going to be banned because the sensibilities in those novels are blunt and numb and are frequently in contempt of the kind of blundering justice which the rest of us have to make do with. As matters stand we can only urge Mr. Burroughs's authentic Tarzan on, good-hearted lunkhead and brilliant linguist that he is; for, compared to his diminuendo in film, comic book, and vacuum tube, he is a grand and noble creature indeed and, alas, worth a defense.

# The Anthropology of Table Manners
from Geophagy Onward

A businessman now risen to a vice-presidency tells me that in his apprentice days he used to cross deepest Arkansas as a mere traveling salesman,
and that there were certain farms at which men from his company put up
overnight, meals being included in the deal. Once, on a new route, he
appeared at breakfast after a refreshing sleep in a feather bed to face a
hardy array of buttery eggs, biscuits, apple pie, coffee, and fatback.

This latter item was unfamiliar to him and from the looks of it he was
damned if he would eat it. He knew his manners, however, and in passing
over the fatback chatted with the lady of the house about how eating
habits tend to be local, individual, and a matter of how one has been
raised. He hoped she wouldn't take it wrong that he, unused to consuming fatback, left it untouched on his plate.

The genial Arkansas matron nodded to this politely, agreeing that food is different all over the world.

She then excused herself, flapped her copious apron, and retired from the kitchen. She returned with a double-barreled shotgun which she trained on the traveling salesman, with the grim remark, "Eat hit."

And eat hit he did.

Our traveler's offense was to reject what he had been served, an insult in practically every code of table manners. Snug in an igloo, the Eskimo scrapes gunk from between his toes and politely offers it as garnish for your blubber. Among the Penan of the upper Baram in Sarawak you eat your friend's snot as a sign of your esteem. There are dinner parties in Africa where the butter for your stewed calabash will be milked from your hostess's hair. And you dare not refuse.

Eating is always at least two activities: consuming food and obeying a code of manners. And in the manners is concealed a program of taboos as rigid as Deuteronomy. We rational, advanced, and liberated Americans may not, as in the Amazon, serve the bride's mother as the wedding feast; we may not, as in Japan, burp our appreciation, or as in Arabia, eat with our fingers. Every child has suffered initiation into the mysteries of table manners: keep your elbows off the table, ask for things to be passed rather than reach, don't cut your bread with a knife, keep your mouth closed while chewing, don't talk with food in your mouth, and on and on, and all of it witchcraft and another notch upward in the rise of the middle class.

Our escapes from civilization are symptomatic: the first rule we break is that of table manners. Liberty wears her reddest cap; all is permitted. I remember a weekend away from paratrooper barracks when we dined on eggs scrambled in Jack Daniel's, potato chips and peanut brittle, while the Sergeant Major, a family man of bankerish decorum in ordinary times, sang falsetto "There Will be Peace in the Valley" stark naked except for cowboy boots and hat.

But to children, hardest pressed by gentility at the table, a little bending of the rules is Cockayne itself. One of my great culinary moments was being taken as a tot to my black nurse's house to eat clay. "What this child needs," she had muttered one day while we were out, "is a bait of clay." Everybody in South Carolina knew that blacks, for reasons unknown, fancied clay. Not until I came to read Toynbee's *A Study of History* years later did I learn that eating clay, or geophagy, is a prehistoric habit (it fills the stomach until you can bring down another aurochs) surviving only in West Africa and South Carolina. I even had the opportunity, when I met Toynbee at a scholarly do, to say that I had been in my day geophagous. He gave me a strange, British look.

The eating took place in a bedroom, for the galvanized bucket of clay was kept under the bed, for the cool. It was blue clay from a creek, the consistency of slightly gritty ice cream. It lay smooth and delicious-looking in its pail of clear water. You scooped it out and ate it from your hand. The taste was wholesome, mineral, and emphatic. I have since eaten many things in respectable restaurants with far more trepidation.

The technical names have yet to be invented for some of the submissions to courtly behavior laid upon me by table manners. At dinners cooked by brides in the early days of their apprenticeship I have forced down boiled potatoes as crunchy as water chestnuts, bleeding pork, gravy in which you could have pickled a kettle of herring, and a *purée* of raw chicken livers.

I have had reports of women with skimpy attention to labels who have made biscuits with plaster of Paris and chicken feed that had to be downed by timid husbands and polite guests; and my venturesome Aunt Mae once prepared a salad with witch hazel, and once, in a moment of abandoned creativity, served a banana pudding that had hard-boiled eggs hidden in it here and there.

Raphael Pumpelly tells in his memoirs of the West in the good old days about a two-gunned, bearded type who rolled into a Colorado hotel with a viand wrapped in a bandana. This he requested the cook to prepare, and seated at a table, napkined, wielding knife and fork with manners passably Eastern, consulting the salt and pepper shakers with a nicety, gave a fair imitation of a gentleman eating. And then, with a gleam in his eye and a great burp, he sang out at the end, "Thar, by God, I swore I'd eat that man's liver and I've done it!"

The meaning of this account for those of us who are great scientists is that this hero of the West chose to eat his enemy's liver in the dining room of a hotel, with manners. Eating as mere consumption went out thousands of years ago; we have forgotten what it is. Chaplin boning the nails from his stewed shoe in *The Gold Rush* is thus an incomparable moment of satire, epitomizing all that we have heard of British gentlemen dressing for dinner in the Congo (like Livingstone, who made Stanley wait before the famous encounter until he could dig his formal wear out of his kit).

Ruskin and Turner never dined together, though an invitation was once sent. Turner knew that his manners weren't up to those of the refined Ruskins, and said so, explaining graphically that, being toothless, he sucked his meat. Propriety being propriety, there was nothing to be done, and the great painter and his great explicator and defender were damned to dine apart.

Nor could Wittgenstein eat with his fellow dons at a Cambridge high table. One wishes that the reason were more straightforward than it is. Wittgenstein, for one thing, wore a leather jacket, with zipper, and dons at high table must wear academic gowns and a tie. For another, Wittgenstein thought it undemocratic to eat on a level fourteen inches higher than the students (at, does one say, low table?).

The code of Cambridge manners could not insist that the philosopher change his leather jacket for more formal gear, not could it interfere with his conscience. At the same time it could in no wise permit him to dine at high table improperly dressed. The compromise was that the dons sat at high table, the students at their humbler tables, and Wittgenstein ate between, at a card table, separate but equal, and with English decorum unfractured.

Maxim's declined to serve a meal to Lyndon Baines Johnson, at the time President of the United States, on the grounds that its staff did not have a recipe for Texas barbecue, though what they meant was that they did not know how to serve it or how to criticize *Monsieur le Président's* manners in eating it.

The best display of manners on the part of a restaurant I have witnessed was at the Imperial Ramada Inn in Lexington, Kentucky, into the Middle Lawrence Welk Baroque dining room of which I once went with the photographer Ralph Eugene Meatyard (disguised as a businessman), the Trappist Thomas Merton (in mufti, dressed as a tobacco farmer with a tonsure), and an editor of *Fortune* who had wrecked his Hertz car coming from the airport and was covered in spattered blood from head to toe. Hollywood is used to such things (Linda Darnell having a milk shake with Frankenstein's monster between takes), and Rome and New York, but not Lexington, Kentucky. Our meal was served with no comment whatever from the waitresses, despite Merton's downing six martinis and the *Fortune* editor stanching his wounds with all the napkins.

Posterity is always grateful for notes on the table manners of the famous, if only because this information is wholly gratuitous and unenlightening. What does it tell us that Montaigne glupped his food? I have eaten with Allen Tate, whose sole gesture toward the meal was to stub out his cigarette in an otherwise untouched chef's salad, with Isak Dinesen when she toyed with but did not eat an oyster, with Louis Zukofsky who was dining on a half piece of toast, crumb by crumb.

Manners survive the test of adversity. Gertrude Ely, the Philadelphia hostess and patron of the arts, was once inspired on the spur of the moment to invite home Leopold Stokowski and his orchestra, together with a few friends. Hailing her butler, she said breezily that here were some people for pot luck.

"Madam," said the butler with considerable frost, "I was given to understand that you were dining alone this evening; please accept my resignation. Good night to you all."

"Quite," said Miss Ely, who then, with a graciousness unflummoxed and absolute, set every table in the house and distributed splinters of the one baked hen at her disposal, pinches of lettuce, and drops of mayonnaise, not quite with the success of the loaves and fishes of scripture, but at least a speck of something for everybody.

I, who live almost exclusively off fried baloney, Campbell's soup, and Snickers bars, would not find table manners of any particular interest if they had not, even in a life as reclusive and uneventful as mine, involved so many brushes with death. That great woman Katherine Gilbert, the philosopher and aesthetician, once insisted that I eat some Florentine butter that Benedetto Croce had given her. I had downed several portions of muffins smeared with this important butter before I gathered from her ongoing conversation that the butter had been given her months before, somewhere in the Tuscan hills in the month of August, and that it had crossed the Atlantic, by boat, packed with her books, Italian wild flowers, prosciutto, and other mementos of Italian culture.

Fever and double vision set in some hours later, together with a delirium in which I remembered Pico della Mirandola's last meal, served him by Lucrezia and Cesare Borgia. I have been *in extremis* in Crete (octopus and what tasted like shellacked rice, with P. Adams Sitney), in Yugoslavia (a most innocent-looking melon), Genoa (calf's brains), England (a blackish stew that seemed to have been cooked in kerosene), France (an *andouillette*, Maigret's favorite feed, the point being, as I now understand, that you have to be born in Auvergne to stomach it).

Are there no counter-manners to save one's life in these unfair martyrdoms to politeness? I have heard that Edward Dahlberg had the manliness to refuse dishes at table, but he lost his friends thereby and became a misanthrope. Lord Byron once refused every course of a meal served him by Breakfast Rogers. Manet, who found Spanish food revolting but was determined to study the paintings in the Prado, spent two weeks in Madrid without eating anything at all. Some *Privatdozent* with time on his hands should compile a eulogy to those culinary stoics who, like Marc Antony, drank from yellow pools men did die to look upon. Not the starving and destitute who in wars and sieges have eaten the glue in bookbindings and corn that had passed through horses, wallpaper, bark, and animals in the zoo; but prisoners of civilization who have swallowed gristle on the twentieth attempt while keeping up a brave chitchat with the author of a novel about three generations of a passionately alive family.

Who has manners anymore, anyhow? Nobody, to be sure; everybody, if you have the scientific eye. Even the most oafish teen-ager who mainly eats from the refrigerator at home and at the Burger King in society will eventually find himself at a table where he is under the eye of his father-in-law to be, or his coach, and will make the effort to wolf his roll in two bites rather than one, and even to leave some for the next person when he is passed a bowl of potatoes. He will, naturally, still charge his whole plate with six glops of catsup, knock over his water, and eat his cake from the palm of his hand; but a wife, the country club, and the Rotarians will get him, and before he's twenty-five he'll be eating fruit salad with extended pinky, tapping his lips with the napkin before sipping his sauterne Almaden, and talking woks and fondues with the boys at the office.

Archaeologists have recently decided that we can designate the beginning of civilization in the concept of sharing the same kill, in which simple idea we can see the inception of the family, the community, the state. Of disintegrating marriages we note that Jack and Jill are no longer sleeping together when the real break is when they are no longer eating together. The table is the last unassailed rite. No culture has worn the *bonnet rouge* there, always excepting the Germans, who have never had any manners at all, of any sort.

The tyranny of manners may therefore be the pressure placed on us of surviving in hostile territories. Eating is the most intimate and at the same time the most public of biological functions. Going from dinner table to dinner table is the equivalent of going from one culture to another, even within the same family. One of my grandmothers served butter and molasses with her biscuits, the other would have fainted to see molasses on any table. One gave you coffee with the meal, the other after. One cooked greens with fatback, the other with hamhock. One put ice cubes in your tea, the other ice from the ice house. My father used to complain that he hadn't had any cold iced tea since the invention of the refrigerator. He was right.

Could either of my grandmothers, the one with English country manners, the other with French, have eaten on an airplane? What would the Roi Soleil have done with that square foot of space? My family, always shy, did not venture into restaurants until well after the Second World War. Aunt Mae drank back the tiny juglet of milk which they used to give you for coffee, and commented to Uncle Buzzie that the portions of things in these cafés are certainly stingy.

I was raised to believe that eating other people's cooking was a major accomplishment, like learning a language or how to pilot a plane. I thought for the longest time that Greeks lived exclusively off garlic and dandelions, and that Jews were so picky about their food that they seldom ate at all. Uncles who had been to France with the AEF reported that the French existed on roast rat and snails. The Chinese, I learned from a book, begin their meals with dessert. Happy people!

Manners, like any set of signals, constitute a language. It is possible to learn to speak Italian; to eat Italian, never. In times of good breeding, the rebel against custom always has table manners to violate. Diogenes assumed the polish of Daniel Boone, while Plato ate with a correctness Emily Post could have studied with profit. Thoreau, Tolstoy, and Gandhi all ate with pointed reservation, sparely, and in elemental simplicity. Calvin dined but once a day, on plain fare, and doubtless imagined the pope gorging himself on pheasant, nightingale, and minced boar in macaroni.

Honest John Adams, eating in France for the first time, found the food delicious if unidentifiable, but blushed at the conversation (a lady asked him if his family had invented sex); and Emerson once had to rap the water glass at his table when two guests, Thoreau and Agassiz, introduced the mating of turtles into the talk. Much Greek philosophy, Dr. Johnson's best one-liners, and the inauguration of the Christian religion happened at supper tables. Hitler's table-talk was so boring that Eva Braun and a field marshal once fell asleep in his face. He was in a snit for a month. Generalissimo Franco fell asleep while Nixon was talking to him at dinner. It may be that conversation over a shared haunch of emu is indeed the beginning of civilization.

To eat in silence, like the Egyptians, seems peculiarly dreadful, and stiff. Sir Walter Scott ate with a bagpipe droning in his ear and all his animals around him, and yards of babbling guests. Only the truly mad eat alone, like Howard Hughes and Stalin.

Eccentricity in table manners—one has heard of rich uncles who wear oilcloth aviator caps at table—lingers in the memory longer than other foibles. My spine tingles anew whenever I remember going into a Toddle House to find all the tables and the counter set; not only set, but served. One seat only was occupied, and that by a very eccentric man, easily a millionaire. He was, the waitress explained some days later, giving a dinner party there, but no one came. He waited and waited. He had done it several times before; no one had ever come. It was the waitress's opinion that he always forgot to send the invitations; it was mine that his guests could not bring themselves to believe them.

And there was the professor at Oxford who liked to sit under his tea table, hidden by the tablecloth, and hand up cups of tea and slices of cake from beneath. He carried on a lively conversation all the while, and most of his friends were used to this. There was always the occasional student who came to tea unaware, sat goggling the whole time, and tended to break into cold sweats and fits of stammering.

I was telling about this professor one summer evening in South Carolina, to amuse my audience with English manners. A remote cousin, a girl in her teens, who hailed from the country and had rarely considered the ways of foreigners, listened to my anecdote in grave horror, went home and had a fit.

"It took us half the night to quiet down Effie Mae," we were told sometime later. "She screamed for hours that all she could see was that buggerman under that table, with just his arm risin' up with a cup and saucer. She says she never expects to get over it."

# The Indian and His Image

"He is smart," the eighty-year-old Crow Plenty Coup said of the white man, "but not wise." At Little Big Horn the medicine men stole the wits of Custer's cavalrymen, Wooden Legs remembered, so that they went crazy and shot each other. The Cheyenne and Sioux, men trained to feign indifference to danger like the bear and to stare at their enemies like the wolf, had also assumed that the United States Army was usually dizzy with fire water. The *Columbia Encyclopedia* speaks of the " overwhelming numerical superiority of the Indians" without a word about their stone-age weapons.

Was the band still playing "The Girl I Left Behind Me" on fifes and drums when the indifferent, copper-faced Cheyennes lifted their chins, tossed their shoulders, and gave the coyote cries that froze a thousand Presbyterian bowels? By this time we can play Homer and expend richly

Romantic sympathies for the hearts that beat beneath breastplates of porcupine quills and those that beat beneath blue gabardine. We can cheer on the Sioux ponies plunging so rhythmically to the pounded shaman's drum and war cries, or we can be stirred by the frantic bugles trilling form and charge, by feathered spears or by the guidons dispersing three ways as captains standing in their stirrups tried to shape battle lines against a seamless and focussing horizon of Cheyenne and Sioux.

Custer, who had watched Lee hand his sword to Grant at Appomattox, must have known that his opponent on this occasion, a sachem of sachems who seemed to be a cross between a Roman senator and an owl with all its feathers blown backward, would merely grunt with disgust if he offered him his sword, and get on with the ticklish business of scalping so bald a man as George Armstrong Custer.

Sentimentality and cruelty are the ingredients of practically all our attitudes toward the redskin. He must be an official symbol in American lore, the presiding genius at Thanksgiving, the honorable and hieratic First American, the image for fifty years on our basic coin, the penny (1859–1909)—outlasting his fellow victim the buffalo, which was on our nickle for twenty-five years (1913–1938)—and at the same time he must disappear one way or another, either through outright extermination, or by assimilation. The Indian has refused both these exits from existence.

Elémire Zolla, professor of American literature at the University of Genoa,[1] examines in a long and meticulously detailed study[2] the historical rivalry of contradictory and consistently inadequate ideas with which Europeans approached the American Indian.

The villain of Professor Zolla's book is an idea: that of Progress. It was inherent in both the Puritan plan to convert and thus civilize the Indian, and in the Enlightenment programs of various kinds, which were not so much interested in saving the Indian's immortal soul as in introducing him to soap, decent clothes, education, and a steady job. Progress is a complex, self-deluding idea. It must suppose that the history of man is from some primitive condition to a civilized one, and civilization at the time of the New World's discovery was already transforming itself into a definition which uncritically included all technology while assuming that

---

[1] A man who has done pioneer research into matters American scholars have largely neglected (the sources and meaning of Melville's *Clarel*, for example). Novelist (*Minuetto all'inferno, Cecilia o della disattenzione*) and historian of ideas, he is best known for his *The Eclipse of the Intellectuals* (1959), a study of twentieth-century philosophy and art against the background of technology and the blinding idea of human progress. His study of alchemy, *Le meraviglie della natura: introduzione all'alchimia*, was published in 1975.

[2] Elémire Zolla, *The Writer and the Shaman: A Morphology of the American Indian*, translated by Raymond Rosenthal (New York: Harcourt Brace Jovanovich), 1973.

spiritual concerns were settled long before and would as if by a law of nature look after themselves.

The Puritans who thought they were bringing salvation to the Indian (the gift was more like gunpowder, rum, measles, and paranoia) were bringing instead the god Progress in whose superficial goodness and single-minded jealousy of its prerogatives was concealed the plan of genocide which in fact developed as the white man's only real attitude toward the Indian for three hundred years. There are pioneer Bibles in the library of the University of Texas bound in Indian skin. That symbol concentrates everything Professor Zolla has to say. *A neat idea!* Something to go look at on our vacation, Bibles bound in Indian skin. Genocide may well be an American invention.

And yet the Renaissance mind had trained itself to think of Ovidian Golden Ages, when man lived in a simple, natural nobility. Here it all is: discovered—a living past. America was Arcadia, the Indian a natural philosopher. But *that* idea concealed genocide, too, for it was a literary idea which no one seriously intended to do anything about. What happens to Golden Ages is that they are supplanted by ages symbolized by baser, more practical metals. So for a third of his book Professor Zolla must chart the impact of Renaissance ideas on the New World and show that there was little for the Indian to choose between the evangelists ("And why did you wait so long," said a Massachusetts Indian, "to come tell us?") and the capitalists.

The Indian's subtlest enemy was, and probably still is, humanitarianism bred of Enlightenment hope for reason in all things and universal *bon ton*. The Indian is a *child* of Nature; he is a creature of passion and instinct. He is primitive. To the Enlightenment mind he was in the precise sense of the word *retarded*. He was behind time on the linear scale of history; his future (as college presidents say at commencement) was all before him; given reason, he would move ahead to invent the electric chair, usury, landlords, polite conversation, and the machine gun.

Throughout the first three centuries of colonization the understanding of the Indian's mode of life was all but nil. The white man seemed determined to misunderstand. The Indian's chastity, which ought to have been admired by a Christian, was interpreted as frigidity. At the same time the Indian's nakedness was said to be salacious. The Indian's indifference to pain was not compared to Sparta and the Stoic creeds but to a perverse masochism. The Indian's intense religious observance was gratuitously identified as diabolism. He was to European eyes a shiftless creature. His womenfolk did all manual labor; he gambled, delighted in warfare, fell into trances, and imagined that he could converse with bears and racoons.

Much misguided energy went into determining *who* he was, as Scripture was silent on his existence. (That the red men were lost tribes of Israel was a long-held theory, and giddy Puritans were always trying to address them in Hebrew.) Racism is a precise prejudice; you never know who a man might not be. And prejudice must always have a man one's inferior or superior, never one's equal. The Indian is still caught in the schizoid view that he is superior (a *noble* savage) and that he is utterly inferior (evolutionary drop-out).

By the nineteenth century the white man began in the name of science to *listen* to the Indian, to find out what he thought, how he understood the world.

Though the man usually credited with beginning research into Indian ethnology is Henry Rowe Schoolcraft (from whose writings Longfellow would glean "Hiawatha"), Professor Zolla places him among the obstructionists. He ended by convicting the Indian one more time of the unforgivable sin of refusing Progress, and thus saw red men as an inferior race. Schoolcraft got it into his head (and was widely believed, especially by the United States Government) that the Indian is just that, a Hindu, a member of a "static" race which through fatigue and sloth had declined man's destiny of perpetual development. From Schoolcraft comes the idea of that benevolent concentration camp, the Indian Reservation.

Another early ethnologist, Lewis Henry Morgan, had even more far-reaching effects. His demonstration that the Indian was, in some slow way, evolving (he saw in the Iroquois the transition from tribe to primitive nation) fell into the hands of Engels and eventually into the hands of Lenin. Liberalism thereby acquired an ethnology, and Marxism even now looks forward to the greatest synthesis man can imagine: the noble savage simple, moral, kind, and pure of heart *in* the most advanced technological development.

The real pioneer in Indian ethnology was Charles Godfrey Leland (1824–1903), a Philadelphian educated at Princeton and Heidelberg, a kind of American George Borrow who was indifferent to appearances and immune to the idea of Progress. He was initiated into the tribe of the Kaw, joined the Gypsies, and died in Florence studying Etruscan lore and witchcraft. It was Leland who first understood the shamanistic nature of Indian religions, the sources of spiritual power, the sharp *difference* of the Indian mind and soul.

From mid-nineteenth-century anthropology onward the search into the reality of Indian life has gone forward (this account occupies the second half of Professor Zolla's study). The outline of the Indian's progress from Puritan writings to Cooper to Black Elk is fairly well known to reasonably literate people; it is the forgotten heroes of the process who are most interesting, essayists like Mary Austin (1868–1934) whose *The American Rhythm* Professor Zolla restores to its rightful place in American literature, as well as her novel, *The Land of Little Rain*. Ethnologists (Franz Boas, Ruth Benedict) and novelists (Willa Cather, William Faulkner) have had the lion's share of interpreting the Indian, and sometimes the two are combined, as in Jaime de Angulo. In cataloguing these latter-day portrayers of the Indian, Professor Zolla is commendably thorough and searching: this book deserves the adjective *authoritative*. It will assume the status of *the* survey of the American Indian in our literature, and many theses will be generated from its ideas, pro and contra.

Scholars will want to argue with some of the categorizing that Professor Zolla's neat mind posits (is Bartram, for instance, to be placed among the insensitive? or Mark Twain?) Professor Zolla has his off moments: he does not seem to understand that Thomas Berger's *Little Big Man* is an ironic novel. He does not know the work of Paul Metcalf (*Will West, Patagoni*). He does not talk nearly enough about the image of the Indian in the movies. His zoning out of his subject the Mexican and South American Indian may in many ways have distorted his subject (one thereby loses such signal statements as Charles Olson's "The Kingfishers" and Prescott's Incas and Aztecs).

On the other hand, it is refreshing to see that an Italian scholar is not taken in by the unresonating mind of Edmund Wilson, whose understanding of things spiritual (Indian or otherwise) tended to be extraordinarily flat.

Professor Zolla ends his book with an informed glance at Indian literature itself, and may be right in suspecting that there exists in it a treasure very like the lore of the Dogon which Marcel Griaule and Germaine Dieterlen found. For the Indian is still a prisoner on his own continent and his religion and lore are still an unknown matter. Whether they are about to become a depressed people is a question aside from that of their treaties and their civil rights. Indians are still shot for sport in Brazil. Most Americans probably suppose that they are already extinct, or that the Department of Indian Affairs can still be counted on to render them extinct if they raise a serious ruckus (like burring up to the Atomic Energy Commission or objecting to a new highway for the American God, the Automobile).

I spent my childhood collecting Indian arrows and tomahawks, and used to know practically every camping ground on the upper Savannah before the A.E.C. flooded them all. I was aware that two Indians, Anne Breadcrust and Jack Frost, used to live on the edge of the old homestead, the social inferiors of even the black fieldhands. The first real Indian I met (aet. 10) sold me a Cherokee bow ("Made in Czechoslovakia" was stamped in purple ink near one bownotch). For all my awareness of the real Indian, he might as well be a mythological creature, an Etruscan to our Rome, one of the Old Gods now so shy and cautious that they are rarely seen.

But of course this is not so. The Indians are probably more numerous now than at the time of Columbus's discovery. They are a vigorous people. After four hundred years of stubborn refusal to accept the gift of Europe which we have by now corrupted out of all resemblance to anything like a civilization, they should be brought to the council tables with all the old treaties in their hands. The idea that time cannot be reversed is mere Enlightenment dogma, liberal twaddle. And the sovereignty of the State is a totalitarian idea useful only to collect taxes. Let the Indian nations exist again within our borders.

Professor Zolla's study of the Indian in our literature is a book that means far more than it says. It is obviously a companion to his analysis of modern art and thought in a technological culture. The myth that was made to serve technology (the Renaissance myth of progress from primitive origins to a sophisticated and enlightened civilization) is coming to pieces before our eyes. It was perhaps an economic (and therefore immoral) myth to begin with; all its spirituality clotted into the idea of *convenience,* one of the strangest and tackiest ideas ever conceived by mankind. It may be the most corrupting social idea since that of slavery; and like slavery it is invisible while we are in its midst.

It is the prime duty of the moralist to point to examples of virtue; I have a feeling that this is what Professor Zolla is doing in this long study of the encounter between a people and a culture which they have held in utter contempt for four centuries. The wise man (better to say simply the sane man) will look at this contempt, to see what gives it its integrity and substance. The Indian is but one example of a people free of the myth of maniacally reiterated examples of convenient gimmickry which we mistake for progress. Any book that can penetrate the opacity of the technological myth is worth attention: this one is also a distinguished contribution to the history of ideas.

# Finding

Every Sunday afternoon of my childhood, once the tediousness of Sunday school and the appalling boredom of church were over with, corrosions of the spirit easily salved by the roast beef, macaroni pie, and peach cobbler that followed them, my father loaded us all into the Essex, later the Packard, and headed out to look for Indian arrows. That was the phrase, "to look for Indian arrows." Children detect nothing different in their own families: I can't remember noticing anything extraordinary in our family being the only one I knew of that devoted every Sunday afternoon to amateur archaeology.

We took along, from time to time, those people who expressed an interest in finding Indian arrows. Most of them, I expect, wanted an excuse for an outing. We thought of all neighbors, friends, and business associates in terms of whether they were good company or utter nui-

sances on our expeditions. Surely all of my attitudes toward people were
shaped here, all unknowing. I learned that there are people who see nothing, who would not have noticed the splendidest of tomahawks if they
had stepped on it, who could not tell a worked stone from a shard of flint
or quartz, people who did not feel the excitement of the whoop we all let
out when we found an arrowhead or rim of pottery with painting or
incised border on it, a pot leg, or those major discoveries which we remembered and could recite forever afterward, the finding of an intact
pipe, perfect celt, or unbroken spearhead elegantly core-chipped, crenu-
lated and notched as if finished yesterday. "I've found one!" the cry
would go up from the slope of a knoll, from the reaches of a plowed field,
a gully. One never ran over; that was bad form. One kept looking with
feigned nonchalance, and if one's search drew nigh the finder, it was
permissible to ask to see. Daddy never looked at what other people found
until we were back at the car. "Nice." he would say, or "That's really
something." Usually he grunted, for my sister and I would have a fistful
of tacky quartz arrowheads, lumpish and halfheartedly worked. Or we
would have a dubious pointed rock which we had made out to be an
arrowhead and which Daddy would extract from our plunder and toss
out the car window.

These excursions were around the upper Savannah valley, out from
places like Heardmont, Georgia, a ghost town in the thirties; Ware
Shoals, South Carolina; Coronaca (passing through which my grandmother Davenport always exclaimed, "Forty years come on Cornelia!"
and to my knowledge no one ever asked her why, and now we shall never
know), Calhoun Falls, Abbeville, and a network of crossroads (usually
named for their cotton gins), pecan groves, and "wide places in the road"
like Iva, Starr, and Good Hope Community. The best looking was in
autumn, when crops were in and frost had splintered the fields. It was
then that arrowheads sat up on tees of red earth, a present to us all. A
stone that has worked its way to the surface will remain on a kind of
pedestal, surrounding topsoil having been washed away. These finds
were considered great good fortune. "Just sitting right up there!" was the
phrase. But these were usually tiny bird arrowheads in blue flint. Things
worth finding were embedded, a telltale serif only showing. It was Daddy
who found these. My best find was a round stone the size of a quarter,
thick as three quarters, with Brancusi-like depressions on each surface, as
if for forefinger and thumb. I'd thought it was the stone on which Indians
twirled a stick with a bowstring, to make fire, yet the depressions did not
seem to have been designed for that, or caused by it.

Years later, at Harvard, I took the stone, at Daddy's suggestion,
around to an Indianologist at the Peabody Museum. He looked at it and
laughed. Then he pulled open a drawer full of similar stones. What were

they for? "We don't know," sighed the Indianologist. My father's guess that they were counters for some gambling game was probably right. The Cherokee whose stone artifacts we collected from their hunting grounds and campsites were passionate gamblers, and would stake squaw and papoose on a throw of the dice if all else were lost.

These Sunday searches were things all to themselves, distinctly a ritual whose *sacrum* had tacit and inviolable boundaries. Other outings, long forays into the chinquapin and hickory forests of Abbeville County, were for the pleasure of the walk and the odd pineknot, rich in turpentine, that one might pick up for the fire. There were summer drives for finding hog plums, wild peaches, and blackberries on the most abandoned of back dirt roads, autumn drives in search of muscadines and scuppernongs, the finding of which, gnarled high in trees like lianas, wanted as sharp an eye as an arrowhead. We were a foraging family, completely unaware of our passion for getting at things hard to find. I collected stamps, buttons, the cards that came with chewing gum, and other detritus, but these were private affairs with nothing of the authority of looking for Indian arrowheads.

Childhood is spent without introspection, in unreflective innocence. Adolescence turns its back on childhood in contempt and sometimes shame. We find our childhood later, and what we find in it is full of astounding surprises. As Proust has shown us, and Freud, its moments come back to us according to strange and inexplicable laws. If there is a penny on the sidewalk, I find it; I normally pick up seven or eight cents a week (I walk everywhere, rejecting the internal combustion engine as an effete surrender to laziness and the ignoble advantage of convenience), together with perfectly good pencils, firewood, and the rare dime. At Fiesole, when I should have been admiring the view, I unearthed with my toe a Mussolini nickel.

It is now shocking to me that I realized so few connections between things as a child. I vividly remember reading a book about Leonardo, and remember the important detail of his finding seashells in the mountains, but I thought that wonderful, wholly beyond my scope, failing to see any similarity between my amateur archaeology and Leonardo's. What controlled this severe compartmentalization of ideas was my sense of place. Books were read by the fire or by the Franklin heater in the kitchen; in the summer, under the fig tree, and what one read in books remained in the place where one read them. It did not occur to me that any of my teachers at school had ever heard of Leonardo da Vinci any more than of Tarzan, Victor Hugo, Robert Louis Stevenson, or the Toonerville Trolley, all of which were lumped together in my head as privacies in which no one else could be in the least interested.

The schoolroom was its own place, our home another, the red fields of the Savannah valley another, the cow pasture another, uptown, the movies, other people's houses: all were as distinct as continents in disparate geological epochs. The sociology of the South has something to do with this, I think. All occasions had their own style and prerogatives, and these were insisted upon with savage authority. At Grannyport's (thus her accepted name after its invention by us children) one never mentioned the moving pictures that played so great a part in my life, for Grannyport denied that pictures could move. It was, she said, patently illogical (she was absolutely right, of course, but I didn't know it at the time), and no dime could ever be begged of her for admission to the Strand (Hopalong Cassidy, The Lone Ranger, Roy Rogers) or the Criterion (Flash Gordon, Tarzan), for these places were humbug, and people who went to them under the pitiful delusion that pictures can move were certainly not to be financed by a grandmother who knew her own mind.

Nor could the movies be mentioned at Grandmother Fant's, for attending them meant going into public, a low thing that the Fants have never done. The Fants were French Huguenots, from Bordeaux. They were a kind of Greek tragedy in the third of a great trilogy. Once they were rich, with two ships that bore South Carolina cotton from Charleston to France. The United States Navy sank them both in the time of the War: there was a tale we heard over and over of Grandfather Sassard going down with the *Edisto,* standing impassively on her bridge, a New Testament clutched to his breast, his right arm saluting the colors of the Confederacy, which were soon to follow him beneath the waves of the Atlantic. His brother wore a friendship ring given him by Fitzhugh Lee, and this sacred ornament would be got out of a kind of jewel casket and shown to us. I don't think I ever dared touch it.

After the War my grandmother, born and raised in Charleston (she never said "the Yankees," but "the stinking Yankees," the one unladylike locution she ever allowed herself), married a Fant, who took her to Florida to homestead. There my uncles Paul and Silas were born, with teeth it was always pointed out, two tiny pink teeth each, for this was the *signum* of their fate. As they lay in their cradle a catamount sprang through the window and ate them. Sometimes it was an alligator that crawled into the house and ate them. As Granny Fant reached a matriarchal age, her stories began to develop structural variants. She used to ask me never to forget that we are descended from Sir Isaac Davis, though I have never been able to discover who Sir Isaac Davis was. Through him we were related to Queen Anne. And the stinking Yankees stole her wedding ring and gave it to the Holmans' cook, who wore it a day of glory and then returned it to Miss Essy.

Nor could I sing "The Birmingham Jail" at Granny Fant's, as Uncle

Jamie had once spent a night in that place. Nor could we (later on, in adolescence) mention new births in Uncle Jamie's presence, for at forty he still did not know the facts of life, and Granny Fant was determined to keep up the illusion that humanity is restocked by the stork. She was, as my father and I discovered to our amazement, wrong. It turned out that Jamie thought pregnancy came about by the passage of a testicle into some unthinkable orifice of the female. He remarked reflectively that if he'd married he could only have had two children. "And I don't think I could have stood the pain."

Nor could we mention looking for arrowheads—the thought that her daughter, son-in-law, and their children walked all over fields and meadows in public would have sent Granny Fant to her bed with a vinegar rag across her forehead. My point is that throughout my childhood place determined mood and tone. My schoolteachers knew nothing of our archaeology. Certainly the Misses Anna and Lillie Brown would somehow disapprove; they were genteel. I cannot remember any mention whatever of history in grammar school. All we learned of the Civil War is that our principal, Miss May Russell, was taken from her bed and kissed as an infant by the notorious renegade Manse Jolly, who had, to Miss May's great satisfaction, galloped his horse down the length of a banquet table at which Union officers were dining, collapsing it as he progressed, emptying two sixshooters into the Yankees and yodeling, "Root hog or die!" This was the rebel yell that Douglas Southall Freeman gave for a recording and dropped dead at the end of. This grotesque fact would not have fazed Miss May Russell; what finer way would a gentleman wish to die? We all had to learn it: the *root* is pitched on a drunken high note in the flattest of whining cotton-planter's pronunciation, the *hawg* is screamed in an awful way, and the *aw dah* is an hysterical crescendo recalling Herod's soldiery at work on male infants. We loved squawling it, and were told to remember how the day was saved at Bull Run, when Beauregard and Johnson were in a sweat until the Sixth South Carolina Volunteers under Wade Hampton rode up on the left flank (they had assembled, in red shirts, around our own court house and marched away to Virginia to "The Palmyra Schottische").

But school was school, as church was church and houses were houses. What went on in one never overflowed into any other. I was perfectly capable in Sunday school of believeing all the vicious bilge they wallowed in, and at home studying with glee the murders in the old *Sunday American,* and then spending the afternoon hunting arrowheads. After which came Jack Benny, and a chapter or two of Sir Walter Scott. To have mentioned religion while hunting Indian arrows would have been a breach of manners beyond conception or belief, insanity itself.

The rule was: everything in its place. To this day I paint in one part of my house, write in another, read in another; read, in fact, in two others: frivolous and delicious reading such as Simenon and Erle Stanley Gardner in one room, scholarship in another. And when I am away from home, I am somebody else. This may seem suspicious to the simple mind of a psychiatrist, but it seems natural enough. My cat does not know me when we meet a block away from home, and I gather from his expression that I'm not supposed to know him, either.

Shaw has Joan of Arc say that if everybody stayed at home, they would be good people. It is being in France that makes the English soldiers such devils. She and Shaw have a real point. A dog is a Turk only in his own yard. I am a professor only when I arrive in the classroom; I can feel the Jekyll-Hyde syndrome flick into operation. I have suffered the damnation of a heretic in rooms uncongenial and threatening. It takes a while to make a place for oneself in unfamiliar surroundings. It can be done; man can do anything. I have read Mann's Joseph novels beside the world's loudest jukebox in the recreation room of the XVIII Airborne Corps. A colleague remembers reading Tolstoy behind the field guns on Guadalcanal; another finished reading all of Shakespeare at the Battle of Kohima. Scholars took their work with them to the trenches in the First World War; Apollinaire was reading a critical journal when the shrapnel sprayed into his head. He saw the page all red before he felt the wound. Napoleon took a carriage of books with him to Waterloo. Sir Walter Scott, out hunting and with some good lines suddenly in his head, brought down a crow, whittled a pen from a feather, and wrote the poem on his jacket in crow's blood.

How capable we are off our turf ("far afield," "lost," "no place for me," the phrases run) may be one of the real tests of our acumen. I am a bad traveller. Even away from home with my family I could suffer acute nostalgia as a child. I know of no desolation like that of being in an uncongenial place, and I associate all travel with the possibility of uncongeniality—the Greyhound bus terminal in Knoxville with its toilets awash with urine and vomit, its abominable food and worst coffee in the universe (and their rule is that the more unpalatable the food, the higher the price), its moronic dispatchers, and the hordes of vandals in tight pink trousers and sleeveless T-shirts who patrol the place with vicious aimlessness; all airports; all meetings of any sort without exception; cocktail parties; lawn parties; dinner parties; speeches.

Some slackness of ritual, we are told, that hurt the feelings of the *dii montes,* the gnomes of the hills, allowed Rome to fall to the barbarians. These gods of place were *genii,* spirits of a place. All folklore knows them, and when a hero died who had wound his fate with that of a place, he joined its *genii* and thereafter partook of its life. Our word "congeniality" means kinship with the soul of a place, and places have souls in a way very like creatures.

In hunting Indian arrowheads we were always, it seemed, on congenial territory, though we were usually on somebody's land. We could trust them to know we were there; country people have suspicious eyes. My father was raised in the country and knew what to do and what not to do. Rarely would a farmer stroll out, in the way of peering at the weather or the road, and find out what we were up to. Likely as not, he would have some arrowheads back at the house and would give them to us. Never sell, give. He would be poorer than poor, but he would not sell a piece of rock.

Here at these unpainted clapboard sharecropper houses we would be invited to have a dipper of water from the well, cold, clean and toothsome. Sometimes a sweet-potato biscuit would be served by the lady of the house, a tall woman in an apron and with the manners of an English lady from the counties. We children would ask to see the pigs. Country people were a different nation, both black and white, and they exhibited *mores* long remembered. There was once an elder daughter who retired to a corner and tied herself into a knot of anguish. We assumed idiocy, as country people do not send their demented off to an asylum. But the mother explained, with simplicity, "She has been lewd, and she thinks you can see it in her."

And once we found a black family with our name, and traded family histories, blacks being as talkative and open as poor whites are silent and reticent, until we discovered that their folk had belonged to ours. Whereupon we were treated as visiting royalty; a veritable party was made of it, and when we were leaving, an ancient black Davenport embraced my father with tears in his eyes. "O Lord, Marse Guy," he said, "don't you wish it was the good old slavery times again!"

What lives brightest in the memory of these outings is a Thoreauvian feeling of looking at things—earth, plants, rocks, textures, animal tracks, all the secret places of the out-of-doors that seem not ever to have been looked at before, a hidden patch of moss with a Dutchman's Breeches stoutly in its midst, aromatic stands of rabbit tobacco, beggar's lice, lizards, the inevitable mute snake, always just leaving as you come upon him, hawks, buzzards, abandoned orchards rich in apples, peaches or plums.

Thoreauvian, because these outings, I was to discover, were very like his daily walks, with a purpose that covered the whole enterprise but was not serious enough to make the walk a chore or a duty. Thoreau, too, was an Indian-arrowhead collector, if collector is the word. Once we had found our Indian things, we put them in a big box and rarely looked at them. Some men came from the Smithsonian and were given what they chose, and sometimes a scout troop borrowed some for a display at the county fair. Our understanding was that the search was the thing, the pleasure of looking.

When, in later years, I saw real archaeologists at work, I felt perfectly at home among them: diggers at Mycenae and at Lascaux, where I was shown a tray of hyena coprolites and wondered which my father would have kept and which thrown away, for petrified droppings from the Ice Age must have their range from good to bad, like arrowheads and stone axes.

And I learned from a whole childhood of looking in fields how the purpose of things ought perhaps to remain invisible, no more than half known. People who know exactly what they are doing seem to me to miss the vital part of any doing. My family, praises be unto the gods, never inspected anything that we enjoyed doing; criticism was strictly for adversities, and not very much for them. Consequently I spent my childhood drawing, building things, writing, reading, playing, dreaming out loud, without the least comment from anybody. I learned later that I was thought not quite bright, for the patterns I discovered for myself were not things with nearby models. When I went off to college it was with no purpose whatsoever: no calling in view, no profession, no ambition.

Ambition was scorned by the Fants and unknown to the Davenports. That my father worked with trains was a glory that I considered a windfall, for other fathers sold things or processed things. If I am grateful for the unintentional education of having been taught how to find things (all that I have ever done, I think, with texts and pictures), I am even more grateful, in an inconsequential way, for my father's most astounding gift of all: being put at the throttle of a locomotive one night and allowed to drive it down the track for a whole five minutes. I loved trains, and grew up with them. I had drawn locomotives with the passion of Hokusai drawing Fujiyama. My wagon had been an imaginary locomotive more than it had been a rocket ship or buckboard. And here we were meeting the Blue Ridge one summer evening, and my father must have seen the look in my eyes as I peered into the cab of the engine. Suddenly I was lifted onto the step, and helped by the engineer—I believe his name was Singbell—into the ineffably important seat. The engine was merely switching cars in the yard, but it was my ten-year-old hand on the throttle that shoved the drivers and turned the wheels and sent plumes of steam hissing outward. Life has been downhill ever since.

But this is not the meaning of looking for Indian arrowheads. That will, I hope, elude me forever. Its importance has, in maturity, become more and more apparent—an education that shaped me with a surer and finer hand than any classroom, an experience that gave me a sense of the earth, of autumn afternoons, of all the seasons, a connoisseur's sense of things for their own sake. I was with grown-ups, so it wasn't play. There was no lecture, so it wasn't school. All effort was willing, so it wasn't work. No ideal compelled us, so it wasn't idealism or worship or philosophy.

Yet it was the seeding of all sorts of things, of scholarship, of a stoic sense of pleasure (I think we were all bored and ill at ease when we went on official vacations to the mountains or the shore, whereas out arrowhead-looking we were content and easy), and most of all of foraging, that prehistoric urge still not bred out of man. There was also the sense of going out together but with each of us acting alone. You never look for Indian arrows in pairs. You fan out. But you shout discoveries and comments ("No Indian was ever around *here!*") across fields. It was, come to think of it, a humanistic kind of hunt. My father never hunted animals, and I don't think he ever killed anything in his life. All his brothers were keen huntsmen; I don't know why he wasn't. And, conversely, none of my uncles would have been caught dead doing anything so silly as looking for hours and hours for an incised rim of pottery or a Cherokee pipe.

I know that my sense of place, of occasion, even of doing anything at all, was shaped by those afternoons. It took a while for me to realize that people can grow up without being taught to see, to search surfaces for all the details, to check out a whole landscape for what it has to offer. My father became so good at spotting arrowheads that on roads with likely gullies he would find them from the car. Or give a commentary on what we might pick up were we to stop: "A nice spearhead back there by a maypop, but with the tip broken off."

And it is all folded away in an irrevocable past. Most of our fields are now the bottom of a vast lake. Farmers now post their land and fence it with barbed wire. Arrowhead collecting has become something of a minor hobby, and shops for the tourist trade make them in a back room and sell them to people from New Jersey. Everything is like that nowadays. I cherish those afternoons, knowing that I will never understand all that they taught me. As we grew up, we began not to go on the expeditions. Not the last, but one of the last, afternoons found us toward sunset, findings in hand, ending up for the day with one of our rituals, a Coca-Cola from the icebox of a crossroads store. "They tell over the radio," the proprietor said, "that a bunch of Japanese airplanes have blowed up the whole island of Hawaii."

# Ralph Eugene Meatyard

When I moved to Lexington in 1964 the poet Jonathan Williams wrote me that there was a photographer here who took pictures of children and American flags in attics. His name was Ralph Eugene Meatyard. He was, Jonathan insisted, strange. I had learned to trust Jonathan's judgments. When he said strange he meant strange.

The next time Jonathan was in town, on one of his reading and slide-showing tours around the Republic in his Volkswagen, The Blue Rider, with its football decal on a window saying THE POETS (the football team of some Sidney Lanier High School in the pine fastnesses of Georgia), he and Ronald Johnson, Stan Brakhage and his six-year-old daughter Crystal, Bonnie Jean Cox and I set out to visit the Meatyards. The address was 418 Kingsway. We all piled out at 418 Queensway, and to this day I don't know the startled citizens who opened their door to find such a collection of people on the steps. Jonathan was got up as a Methodist minister in a three-piece suit, Stan was in his period of looking like a Pony Express scout out of Frederic Remington, and Bonnie Jean and Crystal were both gazing innocently up out from under bangs.

We fitted in well enough at the Meatyards' when we got there, a place where you were liable to find anything at all. There was an original drawing of Andy Gump crying "Oh, Min!" from a toilet stool: he has no paper. There were *Merzbilden*, paintings by the children, found objects, cats and dogs, books jammed into every conceivable space.

Gene Meatyard was a smiling, affable man of middle age and height. His wife Madelyn, Scandinavian in her beauty, had a full measure of Midwestern hospitality to make us feel comfortable. My own welcome was assured when we heard, as Melissa, the youngest Meatyard, showed her agemate Crystal Brakhage the kitchen, a little girl's piping voice saying, "Guy Davenport has ants and bugs in *his* kitchen." This gave me a chance to explain that I kept a saucer of sugar water for the wasps, hornets and ants that I liked to see in the house. To the Meatyards it meant that I couldn't be all bad.

Photographs were handed around. We talked about them. But not Gene. For nine years I would see the new pictures as they were printed and mounted, always in complete silence from Gene. He never instructed one how to see, or how to interpret the pictures, or what he might have intended. The room was full of keen eyes: Jonathan's lyric, bawdy eye; Ronald's eye for mystery; Stan's cinematic eye (a bit impatient with still images, as Gene was impatient with Stan's films—he never went to the movies, but would watch television if the program were sufficiently absurd); Bonnie Jean's stubborn, no-nonsense eye.

I did not know until after his death that he brought me the pictures to cheer himself up. "Guy knows what to say," he told Madelyn. I only said what the pictures drew out. I think he liked my having to fall back on analogies: that this print had a touch of Kafka, this a passage as if by Cézanne, this echoed de Chirico. In his last period he was fascinated by Cézanne and the cubists, by the verbal collages of William Carlos Williams.

We saw a wealth of pictures that evening. I remember thinking that here was a photographer who might illustrate the ghost stories of Henry James, a photographer who got many of his best effects by introducing exactly the right touch of the unusual into an authentically banal American usualness. So much of Gene's work requires the deeper attention which shows you that in a quite handsome picture of lawns and trees there are bricks floating in the air (they have been tied to branches to make them grow level; you cannot see the wires).

Light as it falls from the sun onto our random world defines everything perceptible to the eye by constant accident, relentlessly changing. A splendid spot of light on a fence is gone in a matter of seconds. A tone of light is frailer in essence than a whiff of roses. I have watched Gene all of a day wandering around in the ruined Whitehall photographing as diligently as if he were a newsreel cameraman in a battle. The old house was as quiet and still as eternity itself; to Gene it was as ephemeral in its shift of light and shade as a fitful moth.

He developed his film only once a year; he didn't want to be tyrannized by impatience, and I suspect that he didn't like being cooped up in the darkroom. He was a lens grinder by profession, which meant he was short of free time. His evenings were apt to be taken up with teaching, lecturing, arranging shows, and he longed to read more and more. There were books in his automobile, by his equipment in his office. He had more hobbies than could be kept up with, especially those that involved his family: hiking, cooking, collecting the poetic trash that served as props for his pictures. One could usually find the Meatyards up to something rich and strange: making violet jam (or some other sufficiently unlikely flavor), model ships, fanciful book covers; listening to a superb collection of antique jazz, or to recordings which Gene seemed to dream up and then command the existence of, like the Andrews sisters singing Poe's "Raven" ("Ulalume" on the flip side, both in close harmony). He had a recording of the wedding of Sister Rosetta Tharp. He had a looseleaf notebook of thousands of grotesque and absurd names. He was a living encyclopedia of bizarre accidents and Kentucky locutions. One evening he turned up to tell with delight of hearing an old man say of the moving pictures these days that by God you can see the actors' genitrotties.

And there was nothing behind him, nothing at all that one could make out. He had invented himself, with his family's full cooperation. One knew that he had been born in Normal, Illinois, because of the name. He had a brother, an artist, but it took forever to find this out. He had been to Williams. Williams! Surely this was an invention. Like hearing Harpo Marx had a degree from the Sorbonne. For whereas Gene seemed to read German, he pronounced French like Dr. Johnson—as if it were English. Greek nor Latin had he, though he once figured out with a modern Greek dictionary that a lyric of Sappho (which he had set out to read as his first excursion into the classics) had something to do with a truck crossing a bridge. Yet, by golly, he had been to Williams College. He was there with the Navy V-12 program. One even learned that he used to play golf. But he had no past. His own past had no interest whatever for him. Tomorrow morning was his great interest.

There was the London telephone book to be read (the scholar Tom

Stroup sent him one), new books of poetry to read between customers at the eyeglasses shop. He was an unfailing follower-up, which is why I think of him as the best educated man I have ever known. As a professor I must work with people for whom indifference is both a creed and a defense of their fanatic narrowness of mind, but Gene knew nothing of this. When he met Louis and Celia Zukofsky at my house, he went away and read Zukofsky. Not that he was an enthusiast. He simply had a curiosity that went all the way, and a deep sense of courtesy whereby if a man were a writer he would read what he had written, if a man were a painter he would look at his paintings.

Gene's extraordinary difference from any type sometimes puzzled people when they first met him. One evening the Montaigne scholar Marcel Gutwirth was in town, and he and Gene and I had a marvelous evening of talk while watching a new litter of kittens spring around the living room. When I walked Professor Gutwirth back to his hotel afterwards, he asked *who* this Monsieur Meatyard might be.

"Oh, Gene's wonderful," I said. "He knows more about modern literature than anyone at the university, but he's never read the *Odyssey.*"

"But, *ah!*" Marcel Gutwirth said. "What a reading the *Odyssey* will have when he gets around to it!"

Gene took up photography in 1954 and began to love it enough to submit to the demands it was making. He must have seen the difference between a photographer and an artist whose medium is photography. After a heart attack in 1961, he gave himself ten years to master his art. He was a great photographer well before that decade was up.

My first experience of Gene at work came when I asked him to do some pictures of me for the covers of a book. I had already selected a rich picture of his that I wanted for the front cover (the book was *Flowers and Leaves*), and we needed a portrait for the back. Gene drove me over to Interstate Highway 75 on a Sunday afternoon and put me out in the middle of traffic. He parked on the shoulder and began to photograph me trying to dodge a Greyhound bus and other dashing objects. I have never seen these pictures. Then he took me to an old churchyard and photographed me among the headstones. Finally, he drove to a house gutted by fire, and here he made the picture which we used. He never explained any of these settings. I only knew that he was after essence, not fact.

Usually he photographed people in so casual a manner that one did not know he was at work. I can remember three wonderful conversations with Thomas Merton, one of Gene's closest friends, which were recorded in this way. Gene never dropped out of the talk to find an angle, never asked anyone to pose. The camera was simply there. And, afterwards, the pictures.

He was rare among American artists in that he was not obsessed with his own image in the world. He could therefore live in perfect privacy in a rotting Kentucky town. He was forever sending off shows, he kept up with everything, he encouraged everybody. He was a quiet, diffident, charming person on the surface, a known ruse of the American genius (William Carlos Williams, Marianne Moore). This modesty amounted to there being at least two distinct Gene Meatyards in the world: an invisible Lexington businessman and a genius who achieved one of the most beautiful styles in twentieth-century art.

His death, heroic and tragic, proved to be the occasion for recognizing the two Gene Meatyards. For two funerals were required. The first was Protestant and, despite the distinguished people who came from all over the United States, thoroughly dull. I felt, as Cocteau had at another such obsequy, that Gene had not cared to attend. It was so formulaic and uninspired that I had to go and stand with my hands flat against the coffin to assure myself that I was at a funeral at all.

But there was another funeral, a true Meatyard funeral, one at which the rites were made up out of the family fund of inventiveness. A small group of us, Madelyn, the children (Mike with his wife and child, Christopher and Melissa), Joy Little, Bob May, Jonathan Greene, Bonnie Jean and I, went into the Red River Gorge which Gene had explored and photographed and tried to save from the ravagements of politics and greed. It was a fine spring Sunday. We climbed to an eminence that Gene had liked, a place as remote and quiet as any forest that has not yet heard the buzz saw and the bulldozer. Here we drank a wine that Gene had brewed. I read aloud a poem that Christopher had written, Mike emptied the canister that held all that could die and be burnt of Gene over the ledge of a high rock—a few dry bones which sifted into the tall treetops below. Melissa cast after them a bagful of flower petals.

Then we walked to another part of the forest and ate a feast, picnic fare of the outrageously copious and toothsome and rich kind which Gene fancied for a proper outing. Had Homer been a Sybarite, he would have described such a meal: chilled wines and cold chicken, crisp vinegary salads and homemade bread. I cannot describe it for I don't think I got to see it all, the choices were so great. I remember that when we could eat no more there were still plums swimming in port passed around in small round glasses.

And this funeral Gene attended.

# Ernst Machs Max Ernst

Mr. Richard Pevear, the gifted poet and translator, has remarked of my book of stories *Tatlin!* that although it contains "a wealth of narrative invention, the invention does not go outside the limits of fiction."[1] He is making a valid, if troublesome, distinction between storytelling and fiction, between narrative that is openly an invention (Apuleius, Malory, Rabelais are his examples) and narrative that is so plausible and lifelike that it is indistinguishable from an account of reality (Mrs. Gaskell, Balzac, Proust). He feels that storytelling is native to the human spirit, congenial, and social, rich in "interruption, quotation, dialectic."[2] Fiction,

---

[1]Richard Pevear, "*Tatlin!,* or the Limits of Fiction," *The Hudson Review,* 28 (Spring 1975): 141–46. For other studies, see Alan Williamson, "A Lateborn Modernist," *Shenandoah,* 26 (Spring 1975): 87–90; Richard Wertime, "*Tatlin!,*" *The Georgia Review,* 29 (Winter 1975): 948–57; and John Wilson, "*Tatlin!:* The Renaissance of the Archaic," Master's thesis, California State University, 1975.

[2]Pevear, p. 141.

on the other hand, casts a spell, is narcotic and propagandistic; it is an art of "continuity, coherence, persuasion."[3]

It is Mr. Pevear's observation that my writing keeps coming close to breaking out of fiction into storytelling, but that it never does. I read his article with much interest and a great deal of puzzlement. We had a long and instructive correspondence on the matter, which I initiated, as I had not once thought about the distinction while I was writing the stories, and because critical attention of such thoroughness and intelligence was something I could scarcely have anticipated.

Talking about oneself, said Menander, is a feast that starves the guest, and I hope in this essay to keep to the subject I was invited to consider, the confrontation of self in imaginative writing. I accepted the invitation with a wry trepidation, out of curiosity to see what could be discovered. My writing is primitive and contrived, and I have never written about myself in any conscious way: my stories are all set in places of which I have no personal knowledge and usually in times when I did not exist. I was forty-three when I wrote my first story since undergraduate days, "The Aeroplanes at Brescia,"[4] in which Kafka attends in the company of his friends Max and Otto Brod an airshow of archaic flying machines.

Kafka's account of this event is his first published writing, and as he could not in 1909 know the significance of what he had seen, I combined his newspaper article with Brod's memory of the occasion in his biography of Kafka, and with what I could discover of other people (D'Annunzio, Puccini) who were there, as well as of people who might well have been there (Wittgenstein). To realize certain details I studied the contemporary photographs of Count Primoli, read histories of aviation, built a model of Blériot's *Antoinette* CV25, and collected as rich a gathering of allusions to the times as I could. I presided over the story like a playful Calvinist God who knew what would happen in years to come. I knew that Kafka's first entry in his notebooks that led to writing *The Castle* was made at Merano, where he would have been gazing at the castle in which Ezra Pound was living at the time I was writing. What kind of symbol (if any) this constructs I do not know, but I felt that something was inside the image. It can be said of all my *involucra* that I hope there is a meaning inside, but do not necessarily know. I trust the image; my business is to get it onto the page.

A page, which I think of as a picture, is essentially a texture of images. In the stories "Tatlin!" and "Robot" drawings appear as integral parts of the text: sculpture by Tatlin that probably no longer exists, drawn

[3]*Ibid.*

[4]Guy Davenport, "The Aeroplanes at Brescia," *The Hudson Review*, 22 (Winter 1970): 567–85. (The text in *Tatlin!* is slightly revised.)

from poor photographs in bad reproductions; icons of Lenin and Stalin; quotations from Lascaux. The text of a story is therefore a continuous graph, kin to the imagist poem, to a collage (Ernst, Willi Baumeister, El Lissitzky), a page of Pound, a Brakhage film.

A writer's own sense of influences is spurious and frequently preposterous. When an influence dyes the mainstream it is all too obvious, disastrous, and tyrannical. As a true tributary it adds its lot and disappears into the flow. Who would suspect the influence of Delacroix on Van Gogh; of Dickens on Kafka, of Harriet Beecher Stowe on Tolstoy? My literary models (Kafka, Joyce, Flaubert, Welty) probably go unsuspected because of the ineptitude with which I have followed them, but my pictorial models are more deeply integrated, and perhaps more of an instigation than literary ones.

As a scholar I have always kept literature and painting together as a compound subject, the one complementing the other: Milton and Dürer, Joyce and Tchelitchew, Apollinaire and Picasso, Kafka and Klee, Whistler and Henry James.

I first saw a way to plot stories by studying the films of Stan Brakhage, where an architectonic arrangement of images has replaced narrative and documentation. What Brakhage is doing in his films is an invention that brings cinema close to poetry like the odes of Keats or the ideogrammatic mode of Pound, Zukofsky, William Carlos Williams, and Charles Olson, all of whom Brakhage claims as masters. How one art learns from another is a question better asked as what one art learns from another. The process begins in inspiration, which we might call the aesthetic will. Whistler's nocturnes and harmonies are a response to subject matter. His paradigmatic influences (Hiroshige, Degas, Velázquez) must fit into this process, along with symbolism and iconology, and the tacit and unsuspected dictates of vogue and epoch. Brakhage, I know, is writing a poem and composing a piece of music (his films are for the large part silent), at least, when he is making a film. He knows the history of film as well as Joyce knew that of literature or Picasso that of painting.

Things become quite complex, then, when we start looking at what activates the aesthetic will. And I suspect that the elements to be considered most profitably to understanding are the ones so familiar that curiosity passes them by in innocent stupidity. Words, for a beginning. Though I admire styles in which words are deployed in a practical economy. Bunyan, Caesar, Agassiz), my heart is with styles controlled by artifice. The prose of Doughty's *Travels in Arabia Deserta* is the most consistently interesting that I know, and his *Dawn in Britain* is a poem I read often, not only for the severity and archaic beauty of its diction, but also because it is the only epic in English.

My intent, then (to begin to answer Mr. Pevear's query as to whether I am a storyteller or fictioneer), has been to emulate Doughty in an artificial diction. Fiction demands a concealed and inconspicuous style; storytelling, a mimicry or a postured manner. Compare the *Tentation* with *Madame Bovary:* both styles are hallucinatory. The *Tentation,* however, is at every point a fabrication which we attend to because of its formal and imaginative qualities. We read *Madame Bovary* with quite different eyes.

The subjects I chose for the stories in *Tatlin!* are all in the position of being, as fact, almost not there. The story "Tatlin!" is built out of a mere handful of doubtful certainties. There is no biography of the man; his work is hidden or destroyed. All my information was at least thirdhand. The same is true of a day in 1909 at Brescia, of the discovery of Lascaux (no accounts agree, and though I talked with Jacques Marsal one beautiful July evening in Montignac, we did not talk about the discovery of the cave but about the tragedy of its having to be closed because of microorganisms growing under the twenty-thousand-year-old paint). Of Heraclitus's life no one knows anything. The story about Poe is a lie Poe told, which I take at face value, and there is no biography of Adriaan van Hovendaal, whom I think I saw one morning in Amsterdam fifteen years ago.

It is my sense that I am always telling a story rather than projecting an illusory, fictional world. I am aware of the trap in argument whereby we can seem to square a story with reality, and I felt wonderfully helpless when various critics jumped on my "mistakes." One brave Boston soul swore *he* was at that air show in Brescia, that Kafka wasn't there (the crowd was estimated by *La Sentinella Bresciana* to be 50,000), and that Blériot did not look like my description. A Russian has written to know why I have Lenin speaking in a dialect he wouldn't have used. And so on.

After the book was published, I had the strange and exciting experience of talking with a man who had known Tatlin. I heard details I would like to have known before: Tatlin's love of children, who were invariably fascinated by his own childlikeness; his atheism (which still shocked my interlocutor); his mistresses ("just women, one of them very beautiful"); his friendship with the watercolorist Bruni; his singing; the whiteness of his stark rooms in the bell tower of the New Maiden Monastery in Moscow. I learned that he never joined the Communist Party, that his eyes were slate gray, that he was a dark blond, that his voice was baritone, and that "he was a very complicated man, restless, disillusioned, silent, stubborn."

But verisimilitude of the kind invented by Scott and Flaubert, which achieved its apotheosis in D. W. Griffith's and Cecil B. De Mille's movie sets, I had sidestepped at the outset, trying instead for Kafka's description of America (skyscrapers symmetrically placed in wheatfields, the Statue of Liberty with a sword in her hand), for Rousseau's meticulous and pedantic mistakes. Euripides has the Egyptians living in pyramids; a character in Jardiel Poncela perversely consults a map of Barcelona to locate streets in Madrid; and I saw that my best hope of a sustained reality would be one like Max Ernst's world, which is always of verifiably real things that are not, however, where they are supposed to be. Surrealism knows no mistakes.

Writing in the twentieth century has for its greatest distinction the discovery of the specific. "Things," Proust said, "are gods." Compare Henry James and Joyce, Monet and Ernst. One could write a history of the specific and the vague; it would probably turn out to be a history of attention. If, as Barthes says, writing is an excess of historic intelligibility,[5] what writing is about and how it is written, especially with what regard to detail, constitute a parallel, companion history. We are aware of this kind of history, though much history has been written without instruction from it: Gibbon, for instance, in whose greatest of histories everything metamorphoses into style before our eyes. All is Gibbon, Gibbonesque. All is shaped in deference to polish, to a regularity of surface.

And all styles must do something like, or fail to be a style at all. I am not aware of having a style (hence my claim to primitiveness), but I am intensely aware of style when I write. I know how Joyce broke out of neoclassical rules, while seeming to obey them; how he dared to be angular, eccentric, barbaric. Style, "the man," remains unexplained, like different handwritings. It is imitation that has progressed into individuality; it is a psychological symptom kin to tone of voice and personality; it is a skill, an extension of character, an attitude toward the world, an enigma.

Let us say that style in writing is a subdivision of manners, its clarity solicitude to be understood, its form deference, and its choice of words decorum. This would be a classical definition. We know how Romanticism modified it. With realism came the *mot juste* and the rendering of description in the diction of the characters (Ford, Conrad, Joyce). The logical development of this would be parody and quotation, the stylistic program common to Joyce, Pound, Mann, and Eliot.

It is also the stylistic program of Max Ernst, who, like Joyce, discovered that quotation can be eloquent beyond its original statement, and can release meanings concealed in the original. Ernst discloses a nightmare presence in vernacular advertisements and illustrations; Joyce, an

[5]Roland Barthes, *Sade/Fourier/Loyola*, trans. Richard Miller (New York: Hill and Wang, 1976), p. 10

unsuspected wealth of psychological nuance in popular fiction (Doyle, Corelli, Dodgson).

This autopsy of writing corresponds to Ernst Mach's disturbing and fruitful analysis of science as a psychological history of scientists. Theories, he argued, and even the laws of nature as we know them, are rooted in individual psyches, like works of art. The theory of relativity is in the genius of its conception and in the style of its expression as much a projection of the uniquely individuated mind of Einstein as *Jerusalem* is of Blake's. A door thus opened admitted both Einstein (who regarded Mach as the liberating force that led to his great discoveries) and Joyce, who needed to see that the mind, whatever its activity, is a unity, its concerns all interdependent.

My understanding, then, of where writing's frontier was when I dared to try a contribution to it (rather like piping along on a pennywhistle while listening to Beethoven's Ninth), saw Joyce as a culmination, in the sense that Homer was a culmination of archaic Greece, Plato of the classical world, Plutarch of the Hellenistic, Dante of the mediæval, Shakespeare of the Renaissance. One can learn everything from Joyce except how to emulate him. Pound, Proust, Mann: the same holds true of them.

There are, however, corridors around these mountains. One is the hard path Kafka blazed. Another is the discovery by Ernst that Surrealism need not be Freudian: the raw, unexplained dream still has its power; the dream with legible symbols is a spent force. Hence the liveliness of Ernst, the dullness and triviality of Dalí.

Ernst shares with Mach the phenomenological doubt that we witness anything except in agnosis. What we understand of an event is very little compared to our ignorance of its meaning. The greater our sensibility, the sharper our skepticism, the more we are aware of the thinness of the light that is all we have to probe the dark. Ernst's surrealism dislocates our skilled, habitual reading of phenomena, awakening childish wonder, metaphysical dread, engaging us in a relationship with the world that forces us to confront a Heraclitean *logos* (what nature, desire, design, and God are saying) which we are free to ignore, "like men in a stupor," or to work with.

My little vision, then, could be generated by taking a few verbs and nouns of the *logos* (which, Heraclitus warns us, is wordless and requires translation from a language of harmonic design, trees, light, time, consciousness, attractions like gravity and reproduction) and speaking a simple statement. My first concern was to follow Mach and Ernst and see that the *logos* hides in technology in our time. *Tatlin!* begins with the invention of an archaic flying device, recognizable in other technological dialects as Pegasus, Chinese kites capable of reaching the moon, Daedalus's wings, the Wright Flyer, Eros as a *pteros* or winged phallos, da Vinci's ornithopter.

*Tatlin!* ends with Commander Neil Armstrong stepping onto the dust of the dead moon. The book therefore spans the history of flight, a sustained symbolic web woven throughout with images of birds, *pteroi*, machines—eight of the nine sentences in the first paragraph of "The Aeroplanes at Brescia" allude to things that fly, or to things like smoke and flags that seem to.

Composition as I understand it must be both a concrete and abstract continuum. It is not enough in a work of art to narrate; the narration must be made of words that constitute an inner and invisible harmony. The blossoms on the cherry, lyric white and as beautiful a sign as nature gives, must also be seen as a thousand new cherry trees *in potentia,* as a variant statement of the *logos* tree, a machine (in the language we now speak) that manufactures carbohydrates with sunlight and atoms.

One of my sure guides is Mother Ann Lee's Heraclitean dictum that every force evolves a form, together with the injunction from a Shaker hymn that we must "love to lay a good foundation / In the line of outward things." This rhymes with the Dogon understanding, more rigorously platonic than Plato, that forms exist in God's mind, realize themselves first in the world as points (the four corners of a house, the four corners of the universe: two solstices, two equinoxes), then as connected points (what we call a blueprint), and then as a three-dimensional schemata filled in with matter. They await, like Blake, the apocalyptic day when this scheme will turn itself inside out and disclose an ultimate harmony as yet hidden by God for His own good reasons.

This Dogon sense that man is a forager trying to find God's complete plan of the universe instructs (I hope) every page of *Tatlin!* (both Heraclitus, in the story named for him, and the Dutch philosopher Adriaan van Hovendaal, in "The Dawn of Erewhon," are made to be aware of this inner consistency of all dialects of the *logos;* Kafka and Wittgenstein in "The Aeroplanes at Brescia" have an intuition of it, as do the Abbé Breuil in "Robot," Poe in "1830"). A later story, "Au Tombeau de Charles Fourier,"[6] isolates this theme of foraging and proceeds like an Ernst collage to involve seven themes, or *involucra,* which when opened disclose the theme of foraging in various senses (Gertrude Stein and the cubists; wasps; the Dogon and their forager god Ogo; Charles Fourier and his utopian New Harmony; the flying machine, a bionic wasp as developed by Blériot and the Wrights; the French photographer Lartigue

[6]*The Georgia Review,* 29 (Winter 1975): 801–41; a second version in *Da Vinci's Bicycle* (Baltimore: Johns Hopkins University Press, 1979).

who made all his masterpieces with a child's intuition before he reached adolescence; and myself). That "myself" means nothing more than that I wanted to include a conversation of Samuel Beckett's about Joyce, and felt that this poignancy belonged to the pattern I was making and not to autobiography. The inscription on Fourier's tomb had been copied down in the cemetery at Montmartre the afternoon of the same day that I talked with Mr. Beckett at the Closerie des Lilas (in chairs once occupied by Apollinaire, Joyce, Picasso, Jarry, Braque); the story, or *assemblage,* was generated by this moment, with courage derived from the encounter. The sixteen drawings that are meant to be integral with the prose of this story (one hears a lot of the *logos* with one's eyes) turn the text into a *graph* ("to write" and "to draw" being the same Greek verb).

I do not know that this continuing of a theme through picture and word "works"; it is perhaps a skill of reading that has been abandoned for so long that we can't accept it. The method is implicit in Ernst (whose pictures are all texts to be read) and in the history of art: the prancing tarpan in Lascaux which I use as the first *sentence* of "Robot" has a glyph above it that clearly says "horse."

Inside the theme of a technological *logos* I see a question which I translate from both Samuel Butler's *Erewhon* (following van Hovendaal's essays on that astounding *involucrum* of a book) and Fourier; namely, is matter alive or dead? My symbols here are the living, green earth and the dead moon. Each of the stories states the question in its own way, and the final, long story, "The Dawn in Erewhon,"brings all the statements together.

And here my primitiveness as a writer asserts and defines itself, for I could manage no other way of exploring the theme of live earth and dead moon than to keep stating it with an imagistic inarticulateness that helplessly puts whole faith in the ability of the symbols to speak for themselves. The most meaningful of facts about nature seems to me to be that of the ten planets only the earth is alive. Next to this parareligious fact is the machine, which seems to be alive, but isn't. Hence the double theme from Fourier, who redesigned society so that we could make the best possible success of being alive on the only living planet, and from Butler, who with wise satire first claimed the machine as a living thing, showed its rivalry to natural evolution, and imagined a people who valued life enough to kill the machines.

Neil Armstrong's step onto a dead planet was the most pressing statement of the question as to the life of matter. He was a human being carried in a machine to posture as if in a charade (the photographs of him standing by that insectlike spacecraft, the American flag starched into a semblance of flying in a wind, the unerasable footprints, and none ever to be discovered of a Friday there before him, the absolute uniqueness of the event, dreamlike, had been anticipated by hundreds of Max Ernst drawings and paintings). The meaning of that charade is not only unknowable, it is unaskable.

The first appearance of the moon in "The Dawn of Erewhon" (the Ernst-like description of which is derived from the descriptions of an otherworldly landscape in Wyndham Lewis's *Childermass*) is intercut—Brakhage fashion—with scenes of Dutch children, in a setting of sterile sand that seems lush beside the dust of the moon, discovering the sexual attraction of each other's bodies. The human body in this story is a countersymbol to the machine. Butler, I feel, would have done much more with this in *Erewhon* if Victorian prudery had not stood in his way. I felt free to be as explicit as I could, for we have so misunderstood the animality of our bodies that we may deserve, as I have an Erewhonian Villiers de l'Isle Adam say, to have machines do our living for us.

"The Dawn in Erewhon," whose title is that of a Wyndham Lewis painting (an allusion by Lewis to Doughty's "The Dawn in Britain") is set in the Netherlands (the nether land, Hades), and the recurring images of the moon, where Plutarch and apparently the Pythagoreans thought Hades was, supply visions of a wasteland. Adriaan van Hovendaal (Hadrian, the garden keeper, *i.e.,* Epikouros) is in one dimension an Orpheus in the underworld trying to reclaim Eurydike, by whom I mean (following Ruskin, Proust, Pound, and Joyce, among others) a spirit lost to this world. What this spirit is—some liveliness, some principle of regeneration and care (I equate it with civilization)—has been the concern of western literature since around 1830. Hence a story with that title, and my endeavor to make Poe a nameless spirit identified with Byron, Novalis, and others who seem to record the rape of a Persephone or the death of a Eurydike. (Claudian wrote the *de Raptu Proserpinae* the year after the Goths burnt Eleusis; in 1830 the locomotive and other steam machinery began to appear—Hades's black horses in their Aetnaean smoke.)

Van Hovendaal's vision of a lost Eurydike is of both *koré* and *kouros,* because what he is recovering in his philosophy is an archaic understanding of the world, like his contemporary Wittgenstein. One is Kaatje, one Bruno. Each is meant to be a being from the world of Fourier's New Harmony, free of the restrictions and evasions of "civilization" (Fourier's name for what we call the Enlightenment and industrial revolution). They are epigonic extensions of Adriaan: when he is Fourier, they are members of the Little Hordes; when he is Higgs the traveler in Erewhon, they are Erewhonians. Together they illustrate a spontaneity and elasticity which a money-valued society must quickly breed out of our young in order to keep the world going in its murderous, despairing, narcotic way.

To achieve a richness of meaning I could manage no other way (again, primitively) than of constant rhyme in images, and of translation of meaning from one image to another, so that somewhere in the *textum* a thread would become vivid, or a portion of the design would become clear and lead the attentive reader on into the rest. On the surface I had only a sense that a page could be dense in various ways: through a knitting of sound patterns ("voluble pines and yellow villas of the Via Ponale"), through a knitting of imagery, and by evoking the names of people and things (there are ninety-three historical personages named in "The Aeroplanes at Brescia").

For making these particulars cohere I tried to learn from certain highly elliptical writers how much can be omitted from the texture of a page. If it is of any interest, the styles I find most useful to study are those of Hugh Kenner, Osip Mandelstam, Samuel Beckett, Wyndham Lewis, Ezra Pound, Charles Doughty. All of these are writers who do not waste a word, who condense, pare down, and proceed with daring synapses. From Viktor Shklovski I saw how narrative can be suggested rather than rendered, and how anything can be made startling by taking it out of "its series." Shklovski (and other Formalists) felt that art served a purpose by "making the familiar strange," a process of regeneration (of attention, of curiosity, of intelligence) the opposite of narcosis.

One of my concerns was to let nothing of myself get into these stories, whether for Flaubertian detachment or a reluctance to make a copy of myself or anyone I know, I can't say. Yet a friend who is also a very great critic has remarked with a degree of irony and wit that all the stories in *Tatlin!* are self-portraits. What he is perceiving is my engagement with the materials and people of which the stories are made, some as scholarly research, some as lines of inquiry crossing a diversity of activities: the story about Tatlin grew out of a political stance I took some years ago and have since modified, and out of a backtracking study in search of the origins of modernism in painting and sculpture; "The Aeroplanes at Brescia," "Robot," "Herakleitos," and "1830" all developed from studies of Kafka, prehistoric painting, early Greek writing, and Poe which exist in other forms (essays, critical studies, translations).

There is another sense in which autobiography enters into writing that is ostensibly objective far deeper than the coloration of attitude and characteristic attention. This entry is secret, sometimes personal, but not hidden (no one, for instance, could find it). In the story "Tatlin!" there is a grandfather to give some reality to, so I gave him details of my own (fused with the grandfather in Gogol's "Old World Landowners"), and gave Tatlin in his childhood activities and emotions I knew from my own childhood. This kind of piecing out (always to fill a vacuum of information) is in all of the stories. I confess that these minor details have a peculiar satisfaction for me; it is as if I had a fund of resources to be drawn on only when I could locate nothing in history. I could fill these lacunae with made-up material, except that I mistrust made-up material. This sounds like a paradox, but I have an incident to guide me here. Once, praising J. R. R. Tolkien to his friend Hugo Dyson, I was surprised to hear Dyson say that Tolkien would be a much better writer if he "hadn't made it all up." The lesson to be learned from this is that the writer assembles, finds, shapes. There is nothing to be gained by displacing the authentic. (And I would not agree that Tolkien did: the romantic epic is a game, and we do not confuse games with reality).

There is however, more to be seen here. My Tatlin is not Tatlin, nor my Poe Poe. But my stories are stories about them. We have lived for some two centuries now in a historical glare to which we are perhaps not yet, as a world, accustomed; we can no longer mythologize events. We do not know anything else to do with people. The Civil War is not a myth, but Lincoln is. *Tatlin!* begins with the last historical event—the Russian Revolution—to be mythologized by its participants. Into this soft place in the iron ring of history I moved my wedge. By ironically handling the Revolution I hoped to have the purchase to sustain a mythologizing of events, in order to have the advantage of storytelling (while keeping enough of the conventions of fiction to ward off a vatic tone), of the high hand that qualifies as "an excess of historic intelligibility."

So if we go back to the fiat of these stories, there is nothing there but the author, his aesthetic will, and the grist he needs for his work. I hope that every selfish expedient obeyed its explicit exclusion from the feast. All creation is so completely self-expression that the phantom, "the self," its quarrels with the world, its confessions, its admiration of its image in nemoral pools, should be unwelcome for what it is, a guest-invited guest, an intruder. The self, in any case, is a vacuum: nothing until it is filled. Continuity of perception, Mach said, is all we can call mind. A story, then, might be blatantly what it is under various guises of drama, propaganda, social significance, example, "entertainment"—an atomic spray of essences. The essences I choose (from forty years of attention to the world) can be displayed in words and pictures only, so already we have essences of essences, an absurdity, and must fall back and admit that stories are made of words: writing.

Far from wanting a word to be invisible, unassertive, the makeshift vehicle for something else ("idea," "thought"), I want every word to be wholly, thoroughly a word. If reality can be pictured in words, words must be seen as a set of essences in parallel series to the world. This sounds platitudinous until we notice how words are locked into the fomulae of *parole,* paralyzed in cliché, and used without a regard for color, tone, diction. Joyce brought writing closer to speech than it had ever been before, and at the same time distinguished writing from speech and returned it to its lost place among the arts that require genius and labor for their execution. The tenet of Romanticism that art can accommodate and be enriched by the vernacular has by now grown out of all proportion into the belief that the vernacular, unskilled, spontaneous, and unhindered by any discipline, is the only style natural to writing.

If I have a sensibility distinct from that of my neighbors, it is simply a taste, wholly aritificial and imaginary, for distant plangencies and different harmonies in which I can recognize as a stranger a sympathy I could not appreciate at my elbow: songs of the Fulani, a *ntumpan,* male and female, of ceremonial elephant drums of the Asantehene, dressed in silk, under a more generous sun and crowding closer upon the symbolled and archaic embroidery of the skirts of God, the conversations of Ernst Mach and William James, Basho on the road to the red forests of the North, Sir Walter Scott at dinner with Mr. Hinze, his cat, sitting by his plate.

All I have done in *Tatlin!* is to forage among certain events with multiple causes and effects, and to mythologize them as Max Ernst pictured the world in a temporary agnosis, to induce a stutter of recognition. My diction is labored and chiseled, out of a Shakerish concern for the *built,* and out of a desire to make it as sensitive as I could to "the pat of a shuttlecock, or the creaking of a jack" (a phrase recorded by Johnson in the *Dictionary*).

Design by David Bullen
Typeset in Mergenthaler Sabon
by Wilsted & Taylor
Printed by Maple-Vail
on acid-free paper

# A WORLD HISTORY OF ARCHITECTURE

# A WORLD HISTORY OF ARCHITECTURE

Michael Fazio

Marian Moffett

Lawrence Wodehouse

LAURENCE KING PUBLISHING

Published in 2008 by Laurence King Publishing Ltd
361–373 City Road
London EC1V 1LR
United Kingdom
Tel: + 44 20 7841 6900
Fax: +44 20 7841 6910
e-mail: enquiries@laurenceking.co.uk
www.laurenceking.co.uk

A catalogue record for this book is available
from the British Library.

ISBN: 978-1-85669-549-7

Senior Editor: Susie May
Designer: Andrew Lindesay
Cover Designer: Andy Prince
Picture Researcher: Jenny Faithfull
Maps by Advanced Illustration
Printed in China

Frontispiece: Christopher Wren, St. Stephen Walbrook interior,
London, 1672–87. Photo: A. F. Kersting.

# CONTENTS

PREFACE   x

INTRODUCTION   1

A Word about Drawings and Images   5

CHAPTER 1
THE BEGINNINGS OF
ARCHITECTURE   9

Prehistoric Settlements and Megalith Constructions   10
   Eastern Europe   10
   Western Europe   10
Ancient Mesopotamia   14
   Sumerians, Akkadians, and Neo-Sumerians   14
   *Essay: The Sumerian View of the World*   15
   Babylonians, Hittites, and Assyrians   18
   The Persians   19
Ancient Egypt   20
   The Early Dynastic Period and Old Kingdom   21
   *Essay: "Hydraulic" Civilizations*   22
   The First Pyramids   23
   Fourth-Dynasty Pyramids at Giza   25
   The Middle Kingdom   28
   The New Kingdom   29
Conclusions About Architectural Ideas   33

CHAPTER 2
THE GREEK WORLD   35

The Aegean Cultures   35
The Minoans   36
The Mycenaeans   39
Greece: The Archaic Period   44
Greece: The Classical Period   47
   The Parthenon, Athens   47
   Other Buildings on the Acropolis   50
   *Essay: Celebrating Athena's Birthday*   51
Greece: The Hellenistic Period   54
Greek City Planning   58
   The Athenian Agora   58
   Hellenistic Cities   59
Conclusions About Architectural Ideas   61

CHAPTER 3
THE ARCHITECTURE OF ANCIENT
INDIA AND SOUTHEAST ASIA   63

Religions of India   65
Early Buddhist Shrines   66
   *Essay: Bamiyan and the Colossal Buddha*   70
Hindu Temples   71
   Early Buildings   71
   Later Temples   72
   Angkor Wat   77
Conclusions About Architectural Ideas   78

CHAPTER 4
TRADITIONAL ARCHITECTURE OF
CHINA AND JAPAN   81

Chinese Architectural Principles   84
Principles of City Planning   87
Houses and Gardens   90
   *Essay: Elder Brother Rock*   91
Japanese Temple Architecture   94
   Buddhist Temples   94
   Shinto Shrines   97
Japanese Houses and Castles   98
Zen Buddhist Architecture and Its Derivatives   101
Conclusions About Architectural Ideas   103

CHAPTER 5
THE ROMAN WORLD   105

Entruscan Imprints   105
The Romans   107
Building Techniques and Materials   108
City Planning   111
   *Essay: The Engineering Might of the Romans*   117
Temples   118
Public Buildings   120
   Basilicas   120
   Public Baths   121
   Theaters and Amphitheaters   123
Residences   125
   Urban Housing   125
   Rural Villas and Urban Palaces   128
Conclusions About Architectural Ideas   130

CHAPTER 6
EARLY CHRISTIAN AND BYZANTINE
ARCHITECTURE   133

Early Christian Basilicas   134
Martyria, Baptistries, and Mausolea   135
    Essay: Eusebius and Constantine   138
Byzantine Basilicas and Domed Basilicas   139
Centrally Planned Byzantine Churches   143
Churches in Russia   146
Conclusions About Architectural Ideas   151


CHAPTER 7
ISLAMIC ARCHITECTURE   153

Early Shrines and Palaces   154
Conception of the Mosque   156
Regional Variations in Mosque Design   157
    Columned Hall or Hypostyle Mosques   157
    Iwan Mosques   160
    Multi-Domed Mosques   164
    Tombs   168
Houses and Urban Patterns   170
The Palace and the Garden   172
Conclusions About Architectural Ideas   175


CHAPTER 8
EARLY MEDIEVAL AND ROMANESQUE
ARCHITECTURE   177

Carolingian Architecture   178
    The Revival of Masonry Construction   178
    Monasteries   182
Viking Architecture   184
Early Romanesque Architecture   188
Romanesque Architecture
    of the Holy Roman Empire   190
Pilgrimage Road Churches   194
The Order of Cluny   198
    Essay: The Mystic Mill from Vézelay   200
Aquitaine and Provence   202
Cistercian Monasteries   205
Norman Architecture   208
Conclusions About Architectural Ideas   210


CHAPTER 9
GOTHIC ARCHITECTURE   213

Early Gothic   214
    The Abbey Church of St. Denis   214
    Early Gothic Cathedrals   216
High Gothic   220
    Chartres and Bourges   220
    The Sainte-Chapelle   224
English Gothic   226
    Early English   226
    Essay: A Wool Church   229
    Decorated and Perpendicular   232
German, Czech, and Italian Gothic   235
    Hall Churches   235
    Italian Gothic Variations   237
Medieval Construction   239
Medieval Houses and Castles   240
    Housing   240
    Castles   242
Medieval Cities   244
Conclusions About Architectural Ideas   248


CHAPTER 10
INDIGENOUS ARCHITECTURE IN THE
AMERICAS AND AFRICA   251

North America   251
    Tribes of the Great Plains and the Great Lakes   251
    Tribes of the Northeast   253
    Tribes of the Mississippi River Basin   253
    Essay: The Birthplace of the Choctaws   254
    Arctic and Subarctic Tribes   255
    Tribes of the Northwest and Northern California   256
    Tribes of the Southwest   257
Mexico and Central America   259
    The Olmecs of the Eastern Mexican Coast   259
    Teotihuacán in the Valley of Mexico   259
    The Zapotecs and Mixtecs at Monte Albán, Oaxaca   261
    The Maya   262
    Tikal   263
    Copán and Palenque   264
    Uxmal and Chichén-Itzá   266
    The Toltecs in the Valley of Mexico   267
    The Aztecs at Tenochtitlán   268
South America: The Andean World   269
    Early Cities on the North Coast of Peru   270
    Early Development in the
        Northern Peruvian Andes   270
    The Nazca on the Peruvian South Coast   272
    An Empire in the Western Bolivian Highlands   272
    The Chimor Kingdom   272
    The Inca   272

Africa   274
   Portable Fabric Structures   274
   Permanent Dwellings   274
   Urbanization and Fortification   276
   Palaces   280
   Churches and Mosques   281
Conclusions About Architectural Ideas   282


CHAPTER 11
RENAISSANCE ARCHITECTURE   285

Filippo Brunelleschi   286
   Florence Cathedral   287
   Other Florentine Buildings   288
Michelozzo Bartolomeo and the Palazzo Medici   291
Leon Battista Alberti   292
   Writings   292
   The Palazzo Rucellai, Florence   293
   Churches in Rimini, Florence, and Mantua   293
   The Ideal City   295
   *Essay: Pius's Resolutions*   296
The Spread of the Renaissance   297
   Urbino   297
   Milan   298
Leonardo Da Vinci   298
Donato Bramante   299
   The Tempietto, Rome   301
   St. Peter's, Rome   302
   The Belvedere Courtyard and the House of Raphael,
      Rome   303
The Late Renaissance and Mannerism   304
   The Villa Madama, Rome   305
   The Uffizi, Florence   306
   The Palazzo Del Te, Mantua   307
Michelangelo   308
   S. Lorenzo, Florence   308
   The Campidoglio, Rome   310
   The Palazzo Farnese, Rome   312
   St. Peter's, Rome   312
   Porta Pia, Rome   315
   Sforza Chapel, Rome   315
Andrea Palladio   315
   Buildings in Vicenza   316
   Villa Designs in the Veneto   317
   Churches in Venice   320
   The Teatro Olimpico   321
Palladio's Venice   321
Garden Design   324
The Renaissance in France   326
   Châteaux in the Loire Valley   326
   Sebastiano Serlio and Philibert de l'Orme   328
   The Louvre and the Place Royale   329

The Renaissance in England   330
   Elizabethan Country Houses   331
   Inigo Jones   333
Conclusions About Architectural Ideas   336


CHAPTER 12
BAROQUE ARCHITECTURE   339

The Reformation and Counter-Reformation   339
   Il Gesù, Rome   339
Pope Sixtus V and the Replanning of Rome   341
   St. Peter's   342
Gianlorenzo Bernini   343
   The Completion of St. Peter's   343
   S. Andrea al Quirinale, Rome   346
Francesco Borromini   346
   S. Carlo alle Quattro Fontane, Rome   347
   S. Ivo della Sapienza   348
Urban Open Spaces in Baroque Rome   350
   The Piazza Navona   350
   The Piazza del Popolo and the Spanish Steps   352
   *Essay: Piazza Navona—A Space for Spectacle*   354
The Spread of Baroque
     Architecture to Northern Italy   355
   Guarino Guarini   355
The Baroque in Central Europe   357
   Die Wies, Bavaria   359
The Baroque in France   363
   The Louvre, Paris   363
   François Mansart   364
   The Château of Versailles   366
   Jules-Hardouin Mansart   368
Christopher Wren and the Baroque in England   369
   The City Churches   370
   St. Paul's   370
   Housing in the Manner of Wren   372
Nicholas Hawksmoor, Sir John Vanbrugh, and James
     Gibbs   374
Conclusions About Architectural Ideas   376


CHAPTER 13
THE EIGHTEENTH CENTURY   379

The English Neo-Palladians   380
The Return to Antiquity   382
   *Essay: Piranesi's View of Rome*   383
Robert Adam and William Chambers   384
Etienne-Louis Boullée and Claude-Nicolas Ledoux   387
French Architects and the Aggrandizement of
     the State   390

Designs by the Pensionnaires   392
French Architectural Education and the Ecole des
    Beaux-Arts   394
The Challenge of the Industrial Revolution   395
Romanticism and the Picturesque   397
The Romantic Landscape   397
Picturesque Buildings   398
Conclusions About Architectural Ideas   399


CHAPTER 14
NINETEENTH-CENTURY
DEVELOPMENTS   401

Neo-Classicism   401
    Karl Friedrich Schinkel   402
    Sir John Soane   405
    Benjamin Henry Latrobe and Thomas Jefferson   406
The Gothic Revival   410
    A. W. N. Pugin   410
    The Ecclesiological Movement in England
      and America   411
    Eugène-Emmanuel Viollet-le-Duc   412
The Ecole des Beaux-Arts   413
    Richard Morris Hunt and the World's Columbian
      Exposition   413
    McKim, Mead, and White   414
Developments in Steel   416
    *Essay: The Coming of the Railroad*   418
Architectural Applications of Iron
    and Steel Construction   419
    Joseph Paxton   419
    Henri Labrouste   420
    Gustave Eiffel   422
    The First Skyscrapers   422
Skeletal Construction in Concrete and Wood   424
The Arts and Crafts Movement   425
    John Ruskin   425
    William Morris   426
    Richard Norman Shaw, C. F. A. Voysey, and Herman
      Muthesius   427
Art Nouveau   429
    Victor Horta and Hector Guimard   430
    Antonio Gaudí   433
    Charles Rennie Mackintosh   434
The Viennese Secession   437
The Search for an American Style   439
    Henry Hobson Richardson   439
    Louis Henri Sullivan and the Tall Building   442
Conclusions About Architectural Ideas   448

CHAPTER 15
THE TWENTIETH CENTURY
AND MODERNISM   451

The Idea of a Modern Architecture   451
    The War of Words   452
Adolf Loos   453
    *Ornament and Crime*   453
    The Raumplan and Loos's Buildings   453
The Modern Masters   455
Frank Lloyd Wright   455
    Developing the Prairie House   456
    Early Public Buildings   460
    The Flight from America   462
Peter Behrens and the Deutscher Werkbund   462
Futurism and Constructivism   463
Dutch and German Expressionism   466
Art Deco   472
De Stijl   477
Exploiting the Potential of Concrete   479
Le Corbusier   480
    The Dom-ino and Citrohan Houses   480
    The Villa Stein and the Villa Savoye   481
    Le Corbusier's "Five Points"   483
Walter Gropius   484
    Building Designs   484
    The Bauhaus in Weimar and Dessau   484
    *Essay: A Russian Painter at the Bauhaus*   485
Ludwig Mies van der Rohe   488
    The Barcelona Pavilion and the Tugendhat House   488
The Weissenhof Siedlung and
    the International Style   491
Later Work of Mies Van der Rohe   493
    Planning and Building at I.I.T.   493
Later Work of Frank Lloyd Wright   495
    Broadacre City   496
    Falling Water   496
    The Guggenheim Museum and Taliesin West   496
    Wrightian Protégés   499
Later Work of Le Corbusier   499
    Ronchamp and Sainte-Marie-de-la-Tourette   501
    Chandigarh   502
The Continuation of Traditional Architecture   503
Conclusions About Architectural Ideas   505

CHAPTER 16
MODERNISMS IN THE MID- AND LATE
TWENTY-FIRST CENTURY AND
BEYOND   507

Alvar Aalto   507
Eero Saarinen and His Office   512
Louis I. Kahn   513
Robert Venturi's Radical Counter-Proposal to Modernism
      517
Intellectual Inspirations for Post-Modernism   518
Philip Johnson   519
Charles Moore   521
Michael Graves   522
Robert A. M. Stern   524
Deconstruction   524
      Peter Eisenman   525
      Coop Himmelblau   526
      Zaha Hadid   526
      Frank Gehry   528
      Rem Koolhaas   532
Perseverance of the Classical Tradition   533
      Allan Greenberg   533
      Andres Duany and Elizabeth Plater-Zyberk   533
      Celebration, Florida   534
      Aldo Rossi   534
      Léon Krier   534
Modern Regionalism   535
      Luis Barragán   535
      Mario Botta   536
      Álvaro Siza   536
      Samuel Mockbee and the Rural Studio   537
Modernism and Japan   538
      Kenzo Tange   538
      Fumihiko Maki   538
      Arata Isozaki   539
      Tadao Ando   539
Form-Making in the United States   540
      The Boston City Hall   540
      The Vietnam Veterans Memorial   540
      The United States Holocaust Memorial Museum   541
      Tall Buildings in New York City   542
      Richard Meier   543
      Antoine Predock   544
      Steven Holl   544
      Morphosis   545
      Tod Williams and Billie Tsien   545
      Mack Scogin and Merril Elam   546
      Daniel Libeskind   547
      The DIA: Beacon   548
      The Museum of Modern Art   548
      Elizabeth Diller and Ricardo Scofidio   548
Form-Making Elsewhere   548
      Jørn Utzon   549

Arthur Erickson   549
Hans Hollein   549
Cesar Pelli   549
Justus Dahinden   550
Herman Hertzberger   550
Christian Portzamparc   550
Herzog and de Meuron   550
Raphael Moneo   551
Foreign Office Architects   552
European Architects and Technology   552
      Carlo Scarpa   552
      James Stirling   553
      Renzo Piano   555
      Santiago Calatrava   557
      Jean Nouvel   557
      Norman Foster   557
      Nicholas Grimshaw   559
Sustainable Design   560
      R. Buckminster Fuller   560
      MVRDV   560
      Glenn Murcutt   560
      The Center for Maximum Potential Building Systems
      564
Architects Working in China   564
Conclusions About Architectural Ideas   564


GLOSSARY   566

BIBLIOGRAPHY   571

PICTURE CREDITS   576

INDEX   577

# PREFACE

Marian Moffett, Lawrence Wodehouse, and I wrote this survey of world architecture not only for students taking introductory courses, but also for the general reader interested in buildings: specifically the stories they have to tell, the people who built them, and those who used them. We begin with prehistory and end with the turn of the twentieth century, covering the Western tradition as well as works in the Islamic World, the pre-Columbian Americas, Africa, India, China and Southeast Asia, Russia, and Japan.

Our aim has been to present this diverse sampling of the built environment in a straightforward but lively writing style that is rich with detail, so as to create a useful book for non-specialists with a passion for architectural history. The textbook contains extensive descriptive narrative leavened with focused critical analysis, a structure that both allows the book to stand alone and invites lecturers to impose their studied interpretations on the material without the danger of undue ambiguity or conflict. In a world that grows smaller by the day, it presents a global perspective, and in a discipline that concerns built objects that are often beautiful as well as functional, it is copiously illustrated, intelligently designed, and consistently usable.

Because architecture is at once utilitarian and a visual art, the text and its illustrations are inseparable. This book contains over 800 photographs and line drawings, most of which have discursive captions that can be read in conjunction with the text or appreciated independently. Short illustrated essays accompany each chapter (except for Chapter 7). An annotated bibliography at the end of the book provides suggestions for further reading.

## New to this Edition

- Chronologies allow readers to place the individuals, structures, and events in each chapter in a broader historical context.
- Longer chapter introductions and conclusions bring the architecture of each period or culture into sharper focus.
- Expanded treatment focuses on indigenous African architecture, Andean architecture, contemporary architecture, and urban planning and housing.
- More social, historical, and political context has been added to each chapter.
- Chapters 15 and 16 on modern architecture have been thoroughly revised and now examine more work by women and non-Western architects.
- Location arrows in plans and site plans identify camera positions for related figures.
- An Online Learning Center at www.mhhe.com/fazio3 provides additional study activities and resources, and links to additional images.

## Acknowledgments

In writing this book, we have received assistance from many sources. Our colleagues Lynn Barker, Robert Craig, Jack Elliott, Jay Henry, David Lewis, Daniel MacGilvray, Charles Mack, Mark Reinberger, C. Murray Smart, Jr., and Julia Smyth-Pinney contributed essays. The following reviewers read portions of the manuscript at various times and made comments that assisted us in clarifying and improving the text: Martha Bradley, University of Utah; Roger T. Dunn, Bridgewater State College; Fil Hearn, University of Pittsburgh; Lisa Reilly, University of Virginia; Mark Reinberger, University of Georgia; Pamela H. Simpson, Washington and Lee University; Murray Smart, Jr., University of Arkansas; Robert L. Vann, University of Maryland; and Craig Zabel, Penn State University. For their help with this edition in particular, thanks to Michael Charney, Kansas State University; Sabrina Johnson, Johnson County Community College; Joanne Mannell Noel, Montana State University; David A. Nurnberger, Wilbur Wright College; Shelley E. Roff, The University of Texas at San Antonio; Peter J. Wood, Prairie View A & M University; Robert Yoskowitz, Union County College; and Brian C. R. Zugay, Clemson University for their reviews. Others made suggestions for the revision of specific chapters in this edition: Yusheng Huang and Ming Zhang for chapter 4; Susan R. Henderson for chapter 7; John O'Brien for chapters 9, 11, and 12; and Michael Berk, Kimberly Brown, Leah Faulk, Robert Ivy, Chris Monson, and Mark Reinberger for chapter 16. Three graduate students in the School of Architecture at Mississippi State University—Yan Huang, Kai Pan, and Charlie Holmes—used their exceptional talents with graphics software to produce line drawings. Thanks also to librarian Susan Hall for bibliographical assistance.

My special thanks to Adam Beroud for his editorial guidance. At McGraw-Hill, Lisa Pinto, Betty Chen, and Meredith Grant provided important support. At Laurence King Publishing all editorial, design, illustrating, and scheduling issues were expertly managed by Susie May and Kara Hattersley-Smith. Andrew Lindesay laid out this new edition with great skill, and Jenny Faithfull researched most of the fine photographs. To these people and to our families we express our gratitude.

Photographs are acknowledged in the photo credits. In addition to photographs we have taken ourselves, we would also like to thank the following colleagues who supplied additional ones: Gerald Anderson, Robert Craig, Mark DeKay, Jeff Elder, Jason Labutka, David Lewis, Dan MacGilvray, Rachel McCann, Alison Moffett, Kenneth Moffett, R. Bruce Moffett, Max Robinson, J. William Rudd, Brenda Sartoris, Pamela Scott, Raiford Scott, Ronald Scott, Murray Smart, Jr., and Patrick Snadon.

*Michael Fazio*
*May 2006*

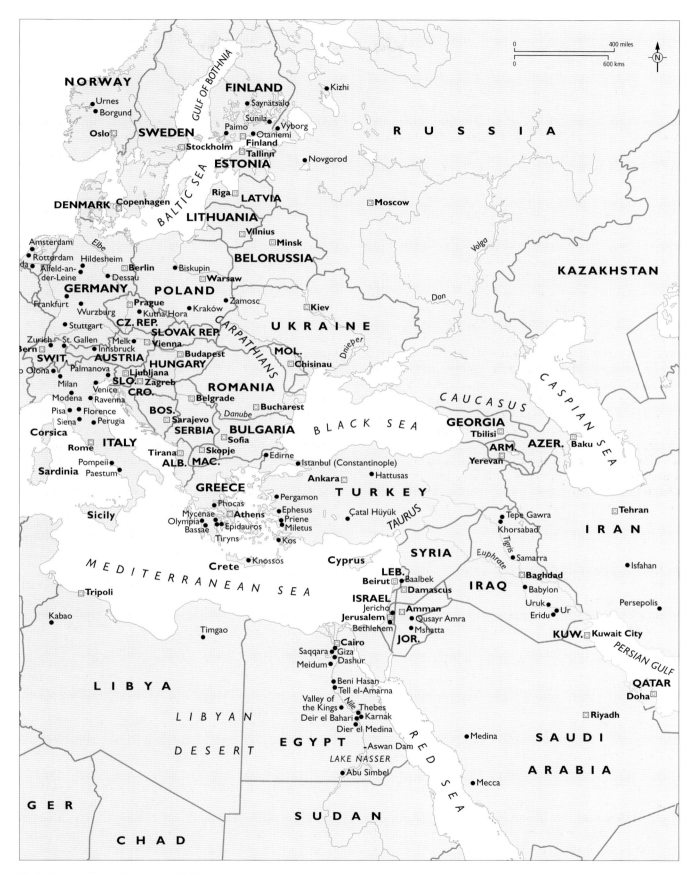

Map 1: Central and Eastern Europe and the Middle East

Map 2: Europe and North Africa

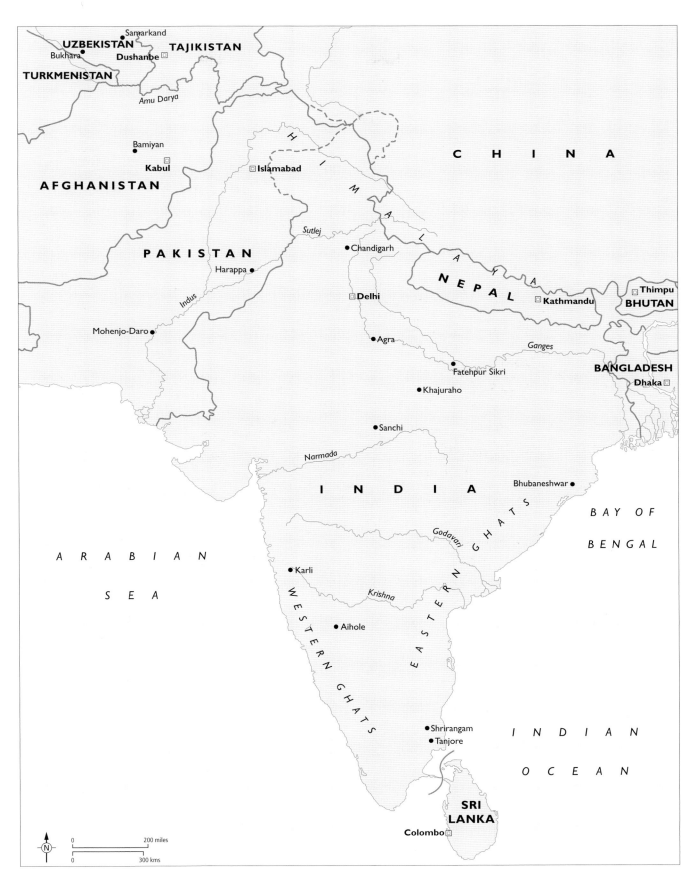

Map 3: Western Asia and India

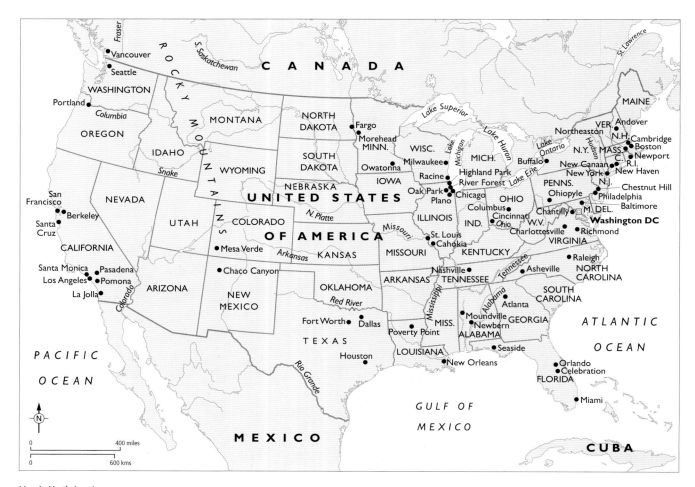

Map 4: North America

MEXICO
• Tula
Tenochtitlán
Teotihuacán
Mexico City
Uxmal • Chichén-Itzá
• Mitla
Monte Albán
Palenque
Bonampak • Tikal • Belmopan
GUAT. BELIZE
Guatemala City • Copán HONDURAS
San Salvador Tegucigalpa
EL NICARAGUA
SALV. • Managua
San José
COSTA Panama City
RICA PANAMA

GULF OF
MEXICO

CUBA
GREATER ANTILLES HAITI DOM. REP.
JAMAICA PUERTO RICO
CARIBBEAN SEA
LESSER ANTILLES

• Caracas
VENEZUELA Georgetown Paramaribo
Orinoco GUYANA SURINAM Cayenne
• Bogotá FRENCH GUIANA
COLOMBIA
Negro

ATLANTIC

OCEAN

Quito
ECUADOR
Marañón
Amazon
Huaca de los Reyes
at Cabalo Muerto
Chan Chan
Moche
Chavín de Huantar
PERU
Urubamba
Lima Machu Picchu
Cuzco
Saqsaywaman Lake Titicaca
Tiwanaku • La Paz
BOLIVIA
BRAZIL
São Francisco
BRAZILIAN HIGHLANDS
• Brasília

PARAGUAY
• Asunción
Paraná

ANDES

PACIFIC

OCEAN

CHILE

URUGUAY
Santiago Buenos Aires • Montevideo
ARGENTINA
Colorado

ATLANTIC

OCEAN

FALKLAND
ISLANDS (U.K.)

N

0        400 miles
0        600 kms

Map 5: Central and South America

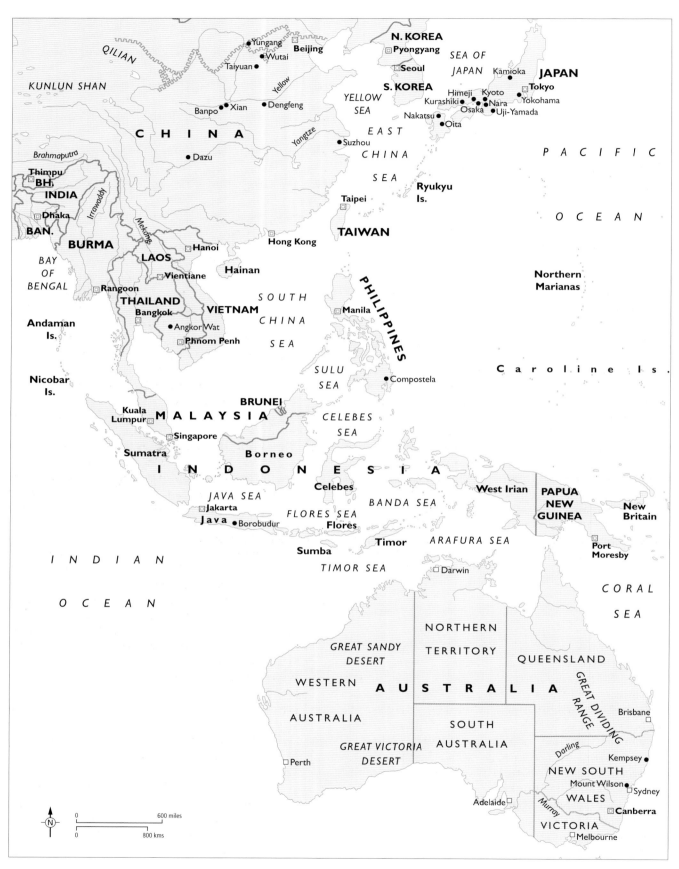

Map 6: Eastern Asia and Australia

# INTRODUCTION

You, the reader, are the reason for this book. We, the authors, have drawn on our cumulative experience in teaching and writing about architectural history to convey in words and images information about some of the world's most interesting and important buildings. This book surveys Western architecture in some depth and offers an introduction to non-Western architecture in Africa, India, China, Southeast Asia, Japan, the pre-Columbian Americas, and many Islamic settings. Together the text and illustrations encourage discussion, thought, and analysis. In this introduction, we offer a guide to the effective use of this book.

Architectural history begins with buildings. In order really to see these buildings, one needs to use precise descriptive language. Hence we have tried throughout to present clear, understandable, but provocative prose, and to define basic terminology when it is first introduced. Still, if left at the level of pure information, these words produce little true insight. We have therefore written this book in a way that encourages looking, but more than that, *seeing*; and the difference between the two is considerable. Seeing requires proceeding beyond the image projected on the retina to a process of analysis and the making of critical judgments. This, in turn, calls for placing buildings in their various contexts—social, political, economic, artistic, technological, and environmental—and determining whether they fulfill their obligations to their clients, to other users, and to society at large. To do this, it is necessary to enter the mind of the architect and to suspend modern biases so that we can evaluate the work as the product of a particular time and place.

What is architecture? Certainly it is shelter, but it can be much more. The phrase "frozen music" is often used, but such a description seems to imply that architecture has only an esthetic component. The "shaping of space for human use" seems more obviously useful, but it hardly explains the fascination of the Egyptian pyramids or the symbolism of a state capitol building. The Roman architect and engineer Vitruvius, active around 40 BCE, considered the essentials of architecture to be *firmitas*, *utilitas*, and *venustas*, commonly translated as firmness, commodity, and delight. Here firmness is structural stability, commodity is the meeting of functional requirements, and delight is beauty. One can hardly disagree with the need for firmness and commodity: any building that collapses or does not provide the right kind of space for the client's purposes must be considered a failure. Delight, or beauty, however, is a more elusive term, one with standards that have changed over time. Some have argued that beauty arises naturally from the fulfillment of functional requirements. Others have seen it as an inevitable result of the logical use of building materials and structural systems. Still others have found it in applied ornamentation.

Let us consider the first two terms in Vitruvius's triad in a slightly different way by asking, why and how is architecture produced? In order to erect buildings, people must have a motive—a will to build; materials and a knowledge of how to use them—a means to build; and systems of construction—an ability to build. The will to build certainly includes responses to functional requirements, but often goes well beyond these to address spiritual, psychological, and emotional needs. For some building types, such as industrial buildings, practical concerns naturally predominate. In others, such as civic or religious buildings, meanings may be dramatically revealed through symbolic forms. To most people, for example, the interior of a religious building should elevate the human spirit, while a warehouse must only protect material goods. However, utilitarian high-rise office buildings are usually designed to reflect the corporate image that the CEO and board of directors wish to project, and homeowners commonly modify their houses both inside and out, not only to accommodate changing functional demands but also to express their own personalities and values. All architecture reflects such values, and the best of it expresses the tastes and aspirations of the entire society. More money, finer workmanship and materials, and (often) better design have typically been expended on buildings that shelter activities important to large segments of society. Thus, for many periods, religious buildings have been the principal laboratories for architectural experimentation and have been built to endure, while residential architecture and even commercial buildings have been more transitory, which explains the abundance of religious buildings in a text such as this one.

At the beginning of an architectural project, the client and architect develop a program, or statement, of projected spatial uses, sizes, qualities, and relationships. The program for an apartment building, say, would itemize the number of apartments and their sizes, the common spaces such as lobbies, the service spaces such as mechanical rooms and storage, and also include an allowance for horizontal and vertical circulation (corridors, stairs, ramps, and elevators). Because many designs can satisfy such a program, it is the architect's responsibility to develop alternatives, to select the best ideas from among them, and to present the results in the form of drawings and models from which the building can be erected.

No matter how strong the will to build, people must

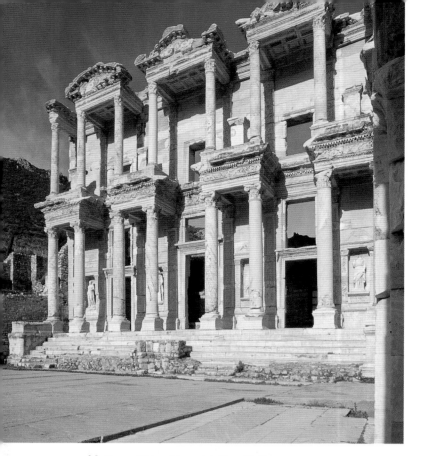

**0.1** Library of Celsus, Ephesus, Asia Minor, 114–17.

Constructed by the Romans, this is an example of post-and-lintel (column-and-beam) construction.

also have the resources with which to build, which historically has meant local building materials. In turn, materials have strongly influenced architectural character. One of the most fascinating aspects of studying everyday buildings from the past is noticing how the simplest materials, such as wood, clay, thatch, and stone, have been employed to create architecture. If clay alone was available in abundance, people used tamped earth or made bricks. If people lived in areas that were heavily forested, they built in wood. The ancient Greeks were among the most skilled carvers of stone, but they would hardly have become so without the abundant local marble that could be chiseled with extremely fine detail.

People must also have the ability to build. That is, they must be able to assemble materials into stable systems of construction. Structural materials can be classified according to the way they accept loads: in tension or compression, or a combination of the two. When in compression, the fibers of a material are pressed together; when in tension the fibers are pulled apart. Stone, brick, and concrete are all strong in compression but not in tension. Wood is strong in both tension and compression, as is iron; but iron is also brittle. In the nineteenth and twentieth centuries, metallurgists refined iron into steel, a material to which small amounts of other metals have been added to form alloys that are highly malleable. Because it combines the compressive strength of **concrete** with the tensile strength of embedded steel, reinforced concrete is also strong in both tension and compression.

All structures respond to the vertical pull of gravity in the form of live and dead loads, and to side loads or lateral forces created by the wind and earthquakes. Live loads are the people (and/or animals) that inhabit a structure. Dead loads are the weight of the building itself and of its inanimate contents such as furniture. Wind loads are accommodated primarily by diagonal bracing, and seismic loads through flexible connections.

Only in the past 150 years has it become possible to quantify the direction and magnitude of loads and to measure the ability of specific building materials to resist external forces, providing designers with the basis for producing mathematical models that predict structural behavior. For the vast majority of buildings considered in this book, however, achieving a stable structure was a matter of trial and error, based upon modifications of what had been done in the past.

Structural systems can be classified into five categories according to the geometric configuration of their members and the way in which loads are resisted: (1) post and lintel (or column and beam); (2) corbel and cantilever; (3) arch and vault; (4) truss and space frame; and (5) tensile. Post-and-lintel systems, formed by vertical and horizontal members, are perhaps the most common type, sometimes known as trabeated systems (Fig. 0.1). The possible distance between **posts** is primarily determined by the spanning capability of the **beams**. Under loading, the beams bend or deflect downward, stretching (or placing in tension) the fibers in the lower half of the member and pressing together (or placing in compression) the fibers in the upper half. Materials such as stone tend to fail quickly

**0.2** Arch, Kabah, Mexico, 850–900.

Built by the Maya of Central America, this is an example of corbeled construction. Note that the stones forming the triangular arch are laid in horizontal courses and slightly overlap one another as they rise.

**0.3** Barn, Cades Cove, Great Smoky Mountains National Park, Tennessee, 19th century.

This is an example of cantilevered construction. The second floor loft overhangs the log cribs of the base, supported on long, wooden cantilevers extending to the sides and front-to-back across the width of the barn.

**0.4** Street in Rhodes, 1100–1300.

Buildings here have been braced with arches as a result of earthquakes. Several different arch profiles can be seen, all constructed of wedge-shaped voussoirs.

if placed in tension, so one can hardly imagine a wire made of stone. Since materials for **lintels** should be equally strong in tension and compression, wood, steel, and reinforced concrete are widely used.

Stone was the most durable building material available to early societies. These civilizations found ways to overcome stone's inherent weakness in tension and at the same time used it to span greater distances than were possible in post-and-lintel construction. The earliest method was through **corbeling** (Fig. 0.2). Stones were laid in horizontal courses, with the last stone in each course projecting slightly beyond the one below it to form a corbeled **arch**. A corbeled **dome** is made up of rings of stones (or even wood), with each succeeding ring smaller and, therefore, projecting beyond the one below it. This same principle has been used in **cantilever** construction, where a beam or beams (often of wood) project beyond their supports to form an overhang, such as an **eave** below a roof or an overhanging second floor or **jetty** (Fig. 0.3).

Masonry arches and **vaults** are composed of wedge-shaped stones called **voussoirs** that must be supported on a temporary framework, called **centering**, until the arch or vault is completed, at which time the stones press tightly against one another and become self-supporting (Fig. 0.4). Such construction requires firm lateral bracing, as an arch or vault exerts not only a downward thrust but also a lateral thrust, which is an outward, overturning force that must be counteracted if the arch or vault is to remain in equilibrium. While all arches behave in a similar manner structurally, their profiles vary considerably. Semicircular (or Roman), **pointed**, horseshoe, and segmental arches are among the most important historically (see Fig. 9.44 for drawing of arch and vault types). Domes may also vary in profile, from shallow saucer shapes to semicircular or hemispherical to steeply pitched; the steeper the arch or dome's profile, the less the lateral thrust (Fig. 0.5).

The trussing method of spanning space calls for short wooden or metal elements to be connected in triangular configurations (Fig. 0.6). The Romans developed this technique for wooden bridges, but their experiments were not continued by subsequent societies. In the medieval period, **trusses** in church roofs depended on having one member, the bottom chord, equal in length to the span being covered. Early in the nineteenth century, bridge-builders reinvented the art of constructing trusses using short members, employing first wood and then iron and steel in various triangulated configurations, many of which were patented. The Warren truss, named for its designer and composed of equilateral triangles, is probably the most common today. A truss repeated in three dimensions is known as a space frame, a twentieth-century structural development that is particularly useful for long, clear-span roofs.

Some structures are based largely on tension. Fabric tents with upright posts are examples of tensile structures, as are suspension bridges (Fig. 0.7). In both cases, the load is partly carried by fibers or cables woven or spun together. Builders in China and the Andes of Peru used animal or vegetable fibers such as hair, vines, and sisal to build tension structures, but these were limited in durability by the inherent weakness of the fibers and their tendency to decay. Great progress has been made in the development of tensile construction in the nineteenth and twentieth centuries as engineers have used iron bars or spun thin strands of steel into cables to support the world's longest bridges. Cables have also been used to suspend floors of multi-story buildings. Pneumatic structures, like balloons, have lightweight membranes supported by pressurized air, and thus are also based on tension.

0.5 Goharshad Mosque, Mashhad, Iran, 1419.
This mosque design shows typical Islamic arch profiles and a handsome, bulbous blue-tiled dome.

0.6 Railroad bridge, Tennessee River, Knoxville, Tennessee, ca. 1906.
This bridge over the Tennessee River is composed of Warren trusses.

**0.7** Seventh Street Bridge, Pittsburgh, Pennsylvania, 1925–28.

This is an example of a suspension bridge structure where vertical loads are carried primarily in tension.

The possibilities of these structural systems are vast. In addition, there are hybrid systems such as cantilevered and arched trusses. The selection of any one of them for a particular building depends on available materials, economics, spatial requirements, and the esthetic sensibilities of the architect and client.

Finally, a few words about styles and precedents. During the eighteenth and nineteenth centuries, historians developed taxonomies classifying the architectural work of various periods according to perceived common characteristics. Today, we recognize that the story is often much more complex and that the lines between the chronological classifications are blurred. The reader should take this into account when studying a chapter on, say, the "Renaissance" or the "Baroque." These are convenient terms, but they should be seen as no more than that, conveniences, and should not obscure the diversity and complexity of the historical built environment. Likewise, the buildings discussed here have been carefully chosen. In most cases, they are the so-called "canonical" buildings, that is, the ones that have been recognized by many scholars over time as best representing a time and place or the work of an individual. The canon has changed and will continue to change, particularly for buildings outside the European context and those of the more recent past. Furthermore, not only historians but also architects themselves have participated in establishing the canon. Throughout history, architects have learned from those who preceded them. The buildings that they admired, studied, and emulated became design precedents. For instance, the exterior of McKim, Mead, and White's Boston Public Library (1887–93) (see Fig. 14.25) owes much to the principal façade of Henri Labrouste's Bibliothèque Ste. Geneviève in Paris (1844–50) (see Fig. 14.31), which, in turn, was based upon the side elevation of Leon Battista Alberti's church of S. Francesco in Rimini (begun ca. 1450) (see Fig. 11.14).

At S. Francesco, Alberti was inspired by the arches of the Tomb of Theodoric in nearby Ravenna (ca. 526). A similar backward trajectory can be established for the dome of the U.S. Capitol (1851–67), designed by Thomas U. Walter, who was inspired by Sir Christopher Wren's design for St. Paul's Cathedral in London (1675–1710) (see Fig. 12.47). Wren's probable precedent was François Mansart's dome of the Val-de-Grâce in Paris (see Fig. 12.37), which was in turn inspired by Michelangelo's dome for St. Peter's in Rome (see Fig. 11.42), which was itself based on Brunelleschi's dome for Florence Cathedral (see Fig. 11.3). Brunelleschi had looked for his inspiration to the Pantheon in Rome (see Fig. 5.19), erected about 125 CE for the Emperor Hadrian. Where Hadrian's architects got their ideas, we leave for you to discover. Throughout the ages, then, architects have been influenced by the works of their predecessors. We hope that you, our readers, whether you are concerned with history or design or both, will be equally informed and inspired by what is presented in the pages that follow.

## A WORD ABOUT DRAWINGS AND IMAGES

In this book, there are many drawings as well as photographs of interior and exterior views. Architects have long relied on the convention of orthographic projections—plans, elevations, and sections—to describe buildings. A plan represents a building as seen from above once a horizontal cutting plane has been passed through it, usually just above the height of the window sills, with everything above this cutting plane removed and the lines of the plan cast onto the cutting plane (Fig. 0.8). Elements that have been cut are usually defined by the darkest lines in the drawing or are blackened in completely. Elements below the cutting plane are drawn with thinner lines, and

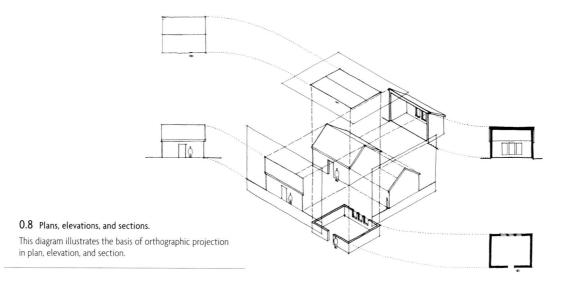

**0.8**  Plans, elevations, and sections.

This diagram illustrates the basis of orthographic projection in plan, elevation, and section.

doors may appear as arcs showing the direction of their swings. Dotted lines in a plan usually indicate ceiling elements above the cutting plane, such as vaults and **coffers**. Thus, in a single, economical drawing, a plan can indicate spatial distribution and dimensions on a particular floor and even give some idea of the structure above.

Elevations are obtained by passing a vertical cutting plane down through the ground a few feet in front of one exterior face of a building, with the image of the building then projected onto the cutting plane. Sections also result from a vertical cutting plane, but in this case one passed down inside a building with its image cast upon the plane. By convention, these cutting planes in elevation and section are placed parallel to the building's principal walls. In an elevation, the only line that is intersected by the cutting plane is the ground line, so this line is shown as the darkest in the drawing. In a section, as in a plan, all the building elements that have been cut are usually defined

by the darkest lines on the drawing or are blackened in completely, and elements beyond the cutting plane are seen in elevation and, therefore, are drawn with thinner lines. While it may take some experience to "read" orthographic drawings, they are very useful in the building process because dimensions can be scaled directly from them.

Let us see how drawings work by considering the pair of two-story houses shown in Figs. 0.9 and 0.10. They represent a common type built by early colonists in Connecticut, and both were enlarged by a one-story addition at the rear that was covered by extending the existing roof slope. The resulting form was dubbed a "saltbox" because it resembled the bulk salt containers found in nineteenth-century general stores. In Fig. 0.11, we see the plan and two elevations of another saltbox house as documented by the Historic American Buildings Survey, a national record of buildings begun in the 1930s and archived in the Library of Congress. From the plan it is easier to see the rear addition and to understand how the interior of the house was arranged. A perspective drawing, Fig. 0.12a, more closely resembles the photographs in Figs. 0.9 and 0.10, because

**0.9, 0.10**  (left) John Graves House, Madison, Connecticut, 1675; (right) Samuel Daggett House, 1750, Connecticut.

Although these colonial houses are not identical, they share a similar form and massing around a central chimney.

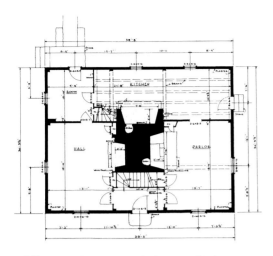

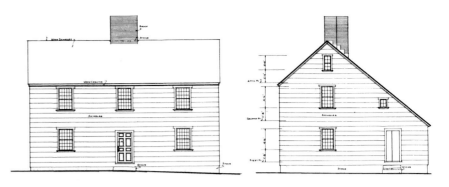

**0.11** Plan and front and right-side elevations of Ogden House, Fairfield, Connecticut, ca. 1700.

Fine lines on this drawing indicate dimensions taken from the building when it was measured for the Historic American Buildings Survey.

perspective drawings show all three dimensions through foreshortening, as photography does, with elements that are farther away (the front-left and back-right corners of the house, in this case) diminishing in size. We know that in fact both front corners of the house are the same height, but in a perspective the one closer to the viewer will be taller. Because most of us understand perspective drawing readily, this drawing type provides architects with a powerful tool for communicating the appearance of buildings not yet constructed in a way that non-architects can understand. An axonometric drawing, as in Fig. 0.12b, also depicts all three dimensions, but does so without distorting these dimensions as measured along the axes of height, width, and depth. Something must be distorted to capture a three-dimensional object in two dimensions, however, and in this case it is some of the angles at which these axes intersect. At the front- and right-side elevations, some 90° angles, like those at the right front corner, have become acute angles, while others are now obtuse angles.

One of the important uses of drawings is to show conditions that may not be visible in the finished building. Fig. 0.12c shows a perspective view of the structure of a saltbox house, allowing us to see the heavy timber frame that is covered by the exterior siding and also to understand how the massive stone chimney fits into the core. Images of buildings, no matter how detailed, are inevitably abstractions of reality. Even photographs do not show everything "as it really is." Therefore, having multiple images, drawings as well as photographs, aids in understanding a building's structure and spatial arrangement.

**0.12a** Perspective drawing of Ogden House.

This view is based on the dimensions of a house measured by the Historic American Buildings Survey.

**0.12b** Axonometric drawing of Ogden House.

This view is based on the dimensions of a house measured by the Historic American Buildings Survey. Compare this view with the perspective drawing (Fig. 0.12a) to see how these drawing types differ from one another.

**0.12c** Analytic perspective of a saltbox house.

With the exterior siding, doors, and windows removed, one can see the heavy timber frame and masonry chimney that comprise the structure of this building.

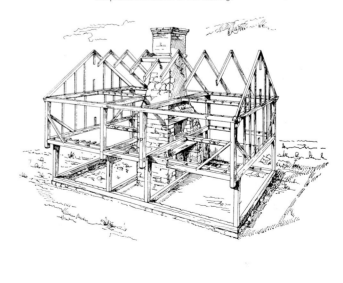

# CHAPTER 1

# THE BEGINNINGS OF ARCHITECTURE

Some readers may be discouraged by the prospect of a chapter about the "beginnings" of architecture or "prehistory," imagining that the really interesting constructions and provocative ideas lie many pages ahead; fortunately, this is not the case. The structures that appear in this initial chapter are rich and varied and often sophisticated. Moreover, because they are "ancient" and always local, they are in some ways more exposed to revelation than later structures. That is, they lay bare for consideration certain fundamental principles of architecture and, arguably, certain fundamental aspects of the human condition.

In 1964, polymath architect-engineer-historian Bernard Rudofsky organized a then surprising and ultimately extremely influential exhibition, "Architecture without Architects," at the Museum of Modern Art in New York City. The exhibition created something of a sensation, appearing as it did at a time of general cultural upheaval in the United States, and the subtitle of the book accompanying the exhibition, *A Short Introduction to Non-Pedigreed Architecture*, suggests why it was so sensational or perhaps more accurately, so iconoclastic. Illustrating, with obvious personal admiration, what he called "vernacular, anonymous, spontaneous, indigenous, rural" architecture, Rudofsky argued for a much more chronologically and geographically inclusive study of the built environment and one that did not cater exclusively to constructions for the wealthy and powerful and did not result exclusively from the efforts of what we might today call academically trained designers. The images of architectural objects that he displayed and analyzed ranged from earth mounds in China to rock-cut dwellings in Turkey, to reverse-action chimneys in Pakistan and much else in among them.

Reading Rudofsky's book and particularly the initial pages of this chapter, you will be directed away from matters of fashion and even style, in favor of "anonymous" but distinctive, even archetypal, forms, and you may come away with a deeper understanding of human responses to particularized environments, to specific local building materials, to elementary but expressively logical structural systems, and to early but nuanced social conditions. You will be able to embrace the essentials of function, space, and meaning by "beginning" with the architecture of prehistory, that is, the era before the appearance of written language.

Prehistory begins as early as 35,000 BCE and extends to about 3000 BCE in the lands of the eastern Mediterranean, and until well after 2000 BCE in parts of western Europe. On the timescale of humankind, these dates correspond to the earliest years of "modern" human evolution from cooperative hunting-and-gathering societies into agricultural civilizations with a fixed settlement area and a ruling class. In the absence of written records, archaeologists and historians must interpret the fragmentary evidence of ancient people—pottery, household implements and rubbish, burials, tombs, and building remains—found in locations scattered across Europe, Africa, and Asia. New technologies have assisted the dating of artifacts through the use of radioactive carbon 14, thermoluminescence, and dendrochronological analysis (the study of growth rings in trees), but both the methods and the hypotheses derived from them are subject to continual revision as researchers discover new evidence and reexamine old ideas. Reconstructions based on post-holes or masonry foundations help us visualize the simple buildings erected by early societies and provide clues to the more elaborate structures that come later.

Hypostyle Hall, Great Temple of Amun, Karnak, Egypt, ca. 1390–1224 BCE.

This vast roofed hall composed of closely spaced columns of large diameter was illuminated by sunlight filtered through clerestory grilles, one of which is seen here. Mysterious gloom inside the hypostyle hall contrasted with brilliant sunlight in the temple's open courts.

## Chronology

| | |
|---|---|
| beginning of prehistory | ca. 35,000 BCE |
| Sumerians develop a written language | 3500 BCE |
| construction of Stonehenge | ca. 2900–1400 BCE |
| Egyptian Old Kingdom | 2649–2134 BCE |
| construction of the pyramids at Giza | 2550–2460 BCE |
| construction of the Ziggurat at Ur | 2100 BCE |
| Egyptian Middle Kingdom | 2040–1640 BCE |
| Egyptian New Kingdom | 1550–1070 BCE |

## PREHISTORIC SETTLEMENTS AND MEGALITH CONSTRUCTIONS

### EASTERN EUROPE

Human settlement seems to have originated at the small clan or family level, with a sufficient number of people living together to provide mutual assistance in hunting and food gathering and joint protection against enemies. Among the earliest huts to be discovered are those at sites in the central Russian Plain (today's Ukraine), dated to about 14,000 BCE. Constructed of mammoth bones and pine poles, with a lining of animal skins and a central hearth, the largest dome-shaped hut incorporated skeleton parts from nearly a hundred mammoths in its framework. Archaeologists have also found clusters of skin-covered huts dated to about 12,000 BCE between Moscow and Novgorod. The largest of these huts, measuring about thirty-nine by thirteen feet in plan, had an irregular shape formed by three interlocking cones of inclined tree branches and was open at the top to allow smoke to escape from three hearths.

Excavations of town sites suggest that larger communities were a much later development. The existence of urban settlements depends on an agricultural surplus that enables some people to assume specialized roles (priest, ruler, merchant, craftworker) not directly tied to the production of food. Two of the earliest known urban communities were Jericho, Israel (ca. 8000 BCE) and the trading town of Çatal Hüyük (6500–5700 BCE) in Anatolia, part of present-day Turkey. Jericho was a fortified settlement, with a stone wall up to twenty-seven feet thick enclosing an area of about ten acres. Its earliest dwellings consisted of circular mud huts that may have had conical roofs. The inhabitants were farmers and hunters who buried their dead below the hut floors. Although by contrast Çatal Hüyük appears to have been unfortified, the town was a dense package of dwellings without streets (Figs. 1.1a,b). Residents gained access to the dwellings across roofs, while high openings in the walls were for ventilation. Mud-brick walls and a post-and-lintel timber framework enclosed rectangular spaces that abutted the neighboring houses so that together they established a perimeter town wall. Interspersed with the houses were windowless shrines containing decorative motifs of bulls and cult statuettes of deities. These seem to indicate that the themes of prehistoric cave art—hunting and fecundity—had not been discarded by this early urban society. The settlement at Çatal Hüyük is the precursor of more sophisticated communities that developed in the fertile valleys of the Tigris and Euphrates rivers at the beginning of the fourth millennium.

### WESTERN EUROPE

In western Europe the transition to urban communities was slower in coming, although the shift from hunting-

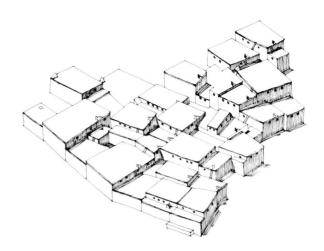

**1.1a**  Reconstruction view of buildings, Çatal Hüyük, Anatolia, ca. 6500–5700 BCE.

Notice how buildings abut one another, forming a continuous grouping broken occasionally by open courtyards. The buildings represent a mixture of dwelling houses, workshops, and shrines, all of which were accessed from the rooftops.

**1.1b**  Reconstruction of shrine room, Çatal Hüyük, Turkey, ca. 6500–5700 BCE.

The central figure on the left-hand wall represents a woman giving birth, while the horned bull skulls suggest masculine properties. Without written documentation, it is difficult to understand completely the significance of other architectural features, such as the stepped floor levels.

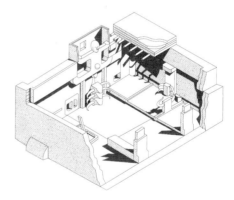

**1.2**  Megalith tomb, Er-Mané, Carnac, Brittany, France, ca. 4200 BCE.

This structure presents an early example of corbeled construction, in which stones are laid without mortar in layers, with each course projecting slightly beyond the previous one, to enclose space. The same area contains other prehistoric tomb chambers and nearly 300 standing and fallen megaliths set in rows aligned to indicate the direction of sunrise at summer and winter solstices and fall and spring equinoxes.

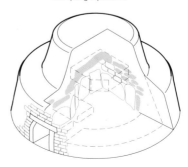

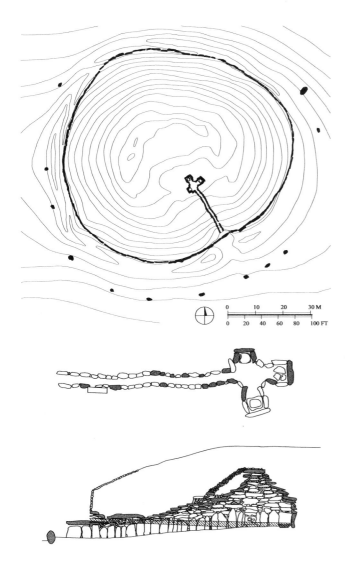

**1.3** Plans and section, Newgrange passage grave, County Meath, Ireland, ca. 3100 BCE.

The cruciform chamber of this communal grave is approached through a long passage created by upright stones. The near-horizontal shaded area represents the path of early morning sunlight on the winter solstice, which illuminates the passage and chamber floor, establishing a connection between the human and celestial worlds.

Ireland is particularly rich in megalith tombs, having over 500 documented sites. Constructing these communal graves for cremated or skeletal remains seems to have been not only an expression of reverence for ancestors but also a means of establishing claims to land, and megalith tombs are frequently located on prominent sites. Among the most impressive is the passage grave at Newgrange, County Meath, built about 3100 BCE on the crest of a hill overlooking the Boyne river. An earthen mound nearly 300 feet in diameter and thirty-six feet high covers the tomb, with the weight of the soil providing stability for the megaliths below. Decorated boulders surround the perimeter of the mound. (The white quartz facing is a modern reconstruction based on excavations, providing visibility from a distance.) The south-facing entry leads to a sixty-two-foot-long, upward-sloping passage covered by stone lintels terminating in a cruciform chamber covered by a beehive corbeled ceiling twenty feet high. Parts of the stonework in the passage and chamber are decorated with incised patterns, including diamond shapes and spirals, whose meanings are unknown (Figs. 1.3–1.4). The whole

**1.4** Entranceway, Newgrange passage grave, County Meath, Ireland, ca. 3100 BCE.

This view shows the stone façade as reconstructed by archaeologists. Note the rectangular opening that serves as a "transom light" over the portal, providing the path for sunlight on the winter solstice. Spiral designs on the stone that blocks direct entry may represent sun signs. The old stone door is visible to the right of the opening.

and-gathering societies to larger agricultural groups under the direction of a priest-king was similar to the experience of societies on the eastern rim of the Mediterranean Sea. The significant prehistoric architectural achievements of western Europe were megalith constructions, composed of large stones or boulders (**megalith** literally means "great stone"), many of which were erected for astronomical observatories or communal tombs for the privileged classes. Before 4000 BCE, chambered tombs of dry-wall masonry (stones laid without mortar) with corbeled roofs were constructed in Spain and France. One of the earliest of the megalith tombs, dated to 4200 BCE, is at Er-Mané, Carnac, in Brittany (Fig. 1.2). As with many other chambered tombs, this one was stabilized by a covering of earth.

**1.5** Stonehenge, Salisbury Plain, England, ca. 2900–1400 BCE.

Perhaps the most famous monument from prehistoric times, Stonehenge exemplifies the ability of some early civilizations to organize workers and materials to create evocative ceremonial places. The heel stone stands to the upper left beyond the circle.

construction is carefully oriented so that, in the five days around the winter solstice, light from the rising sun enters through the doorway and a **transom**-like light box, creeps along the passage, and illuminates the chamber within for about fifteen minutes (Fig. 1.4). To those fortunate enough to witness this annual event (the only time there is any light in the interior), the effect is magical and very moving. Constructing such a massive tomb (and there are two others on the same scale nearby) would have

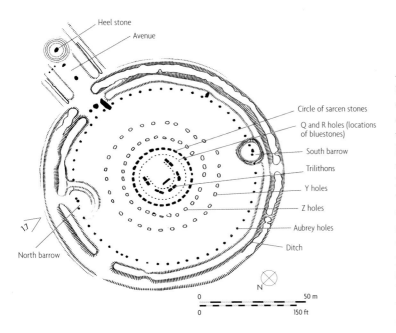

Heel stone
Avenue

Circle of sarcen stones
Q and R holes (locations of bluestones)
South barrow
Trilithons
Y holes
Z holes
Aubrey holes
Ditch

North barrow

N

| 0 | | 50 m |
| 0 | | 150 ft |

**1.6** Plan, Stonehenge, Salisbury Plain, England, ca. 2900–1400 BCE.

This plan includes the original earthworks. The trilithons set in a U-shape establish the axis of the avenue, which passes between perimeter stones to align with the heel stone set outside the circle. On the summer solstice, the sun rises precisely over the heel stone, when viewed from the center of the concentric circles.

required sustained effort over many years. Available technology provided nothing harder than copper or bronze tools for shaping stone, and there were no wheeled vehicles or draft animals to assist with transport. Nonetheless, ancient builders made the necessary astronomical observations and organized a work force sufficient to maneuver stones weighing up to five tons.

The ability to work large stones and to observe fundamental astronomical phenomena merged in the most celebrated of megalith constructions, Stonehenge, located on Salisbury Plain in southwestern England (Figs. 1.5–1.7).

At least three distinct building phases can be observed. The first phase began about 2900 BCE with excavation of two concentric circular ditches. Inside the perimeter, fifty-six evenly spaced holes (the Aubrey holes) were dug and filled with chalk, while a northeasterly line of sight to the horizon was established from the center across a pointed upright (the heel stone) outside the ditches. About 2400 BCE eighty-two coffin-sized stones of gray-blue dolerite, weighing about two tons each, were transported from quarries in the Pressely mountains of Wales and erected in a double ring of thirty-eight pairs, with six extra stones defining the northeast approach axis. At some point, perhaps before this second phase was completed, the bluestones were removed (their sockets are the so-called Q and R holes). The third and final phase involved transporting thirty-five lintels and forty sarcen stones (a form of sandstone) weighing up to twenty tons each. These were erected in a circle of thirty uprights enclosing five **trilithons** (two uprights capped by a single lintel) arranged in a U shape to focus on the Avenue, the axis leading northeast toward the heel stone. Knobs (**tenons**) left on the tops of the uprights fit into socket holes (**mortises**) carved into the undersides of the lintels, so that the stones lock together in a mortise-and-tenon joint when correctly positioned.

To many modern visitors, the sophisticated design and massive construction of the site has seemed beyond the capacities of prehistoric people. Thus the site has been interpreted variously as the work of giants, magicians, people imported from the Aegean, or even extra-terrestrials. The truth is more prosaic but ultimately more meaningful: archaeo-astronomer Gerald Hawkins demonstrated

**1.7** Stonehenge, Salisbury Plain, England, ca. 2900–1400 BCE.

This view from the north shows the present-day configuration of stones. Where the lintels are gone, the knobs (tenons) that held the horizontal stones in place can be seen on top of the uprights. The heel stone is the tall stone to the left.

that Stonehenge was a great observatory for determining the solstices (thus establishing the annual calendar) and predicting lunar and solar eclipses, knowledge that could have proved very useful in a society without almanacs. Its circular layout may well reflect a symbolic tie to the heavens, a link between human and celestial realms.

Experience gained in the construction and orientation of megalith tombs enabled early inhabitants of the British Isles to erect one of the most haunting architectural works of all time. Stonehenge represents the culmination of construction skill and scientific observation in the prehistoric era. Its builders met the challenge of moving and shaping massive stones. Bluestones from Wales were transported, largely by water, over 190 miles to the site, being dragged overland for the last leg of the journey. The larger sarcen uprights came from the Marlborough Downs, about fifteen miles from Stonehenge, and were probably dragged to the site. Modern experimentation with moving and erecting a trilithon on the scale of Stonehenge shows that erection could be accomplished with simple machines (lever and inclined plane), a sledge and greased track, wooden scaffolds, stout ropes, and about 130 people working together.

## ANCIENT MESOPOTAMIA

The distinction between the prehistoric world and historic times involves the development of written language, which was achieved by about 3500 BCE by the Sumerians in the Middle Eastern land of present-day Iraq and Iran. There, in the fertile lands between the Tigris and Euphrates rivers (named Mesopotamia or "between the rivers" by the ancient Greeks), the earliest literate civilizations developed in independent urban communities called city-states. Writing first developed as a means of documenting governmental transactions and was only later employed for what might be called literary purposes, communicating the legends, glorious deeds, hopes, and fears of the people. In about 3000 BCE, perhaps as a result of contacts with Mesopotamia, another center of civilization emerged in northeast Africa, along the banks of the Nile River in Egypt. These two regions, Egypt and Mesopotamia, are considered the cradles of Western history and architecture.

Despite on-going conflict in the Middle East, probably no culture seems more remote to the current student of architectural history than that of ancient Mesopotamia. There are strong religious images from Judeo–Christian scripture of flood stories and the Tower of Babel, both with Mesopotamian connections, but such textual images can only go so far, and Hollywood has not seen fit to dramatize the place and its people as they have Egypt and the ancient Egyptians. You can best begin, perhaps, by reading the accompanying essay for some sense of Mesopotamian culture, then consider the larger picture, and that picture begins with rivers.

Mesopotamia encompasses an area about 500 miles long by no more than 300 miles wide. Its southern boundary is the Persian Gulf, the shore of which was about 130 miles farther north during the third millennium than it is today. In addition, shifts in the river channels, climatic changes, and increased salinity of formerly irrigated lands have combined to bring about profound changes in the environment since antiquity. The Tigris and Euphrates rivers flow separately into the gulf. The Euphrates originates in the mountains of eastern Turkey and meanders across the plains in its lower reaches. The more easterly Tigris rises in the same mountains, but develops into a more swiftly flowing stream because of its numerous tributaries in the Zagros mountains. As a result, the Tigris was less navigable and did not have as great a unifying effect on settlements along its banks as did the Euphrates.

The Mesopotamian cultures did great things by exploiting their rivers. They regulated them as best they could and from them they constructed elaborate irrigation canals that made possible a fertile, even Edenesque landscape. Within this landscape, they cultivated sufficiently abundant crops to permit the large-scale storage of surplus grain. This relatively stable and plentiful supply of food, in turn, permitted the growth of large urban populations and that corollary of urbanism: specialization. Mesopotamian specialists included not only priests and merchants but also artisans, artists, and architects who could make beautiful objects, express their culture's worldview, and make gestures toward the connection of humankind to the cosmos.

### SUMERIANS, AKKADIANS, AND NEO-SUMERIANS

The Sumerians are generally credited with forming the world's first civilization, which began to take shape around 4000 BCE. At this time, the people of the fertile lands of southern Mesopotamia mastered arts of agriculture and developed irrigation systems to control the waters of the Euphrates River. Their civilization, which lasted until about 2350 BCE, is known as Sumerian, and the typical form of their settlements was the city-state, a political and religious center devoted to serving gods based on natural elements. These deities included the divine triad of Anu, god of the sky; Enlil, god of the earth; and Ea, god of water; supplemented by Nannar, god of the moon; Utu, god of the sun; and Inanna, goddess of fertility. The Sumerians believed that the sky and earth were two disks that had been blown apart and that all existence was governed by the gods, who represented the unpredictable elements affecting human life. They believed that human beings were created from the alluvial silt deposits in the river valleys to serve the gods and to relieve them of toil. Because the gods benefited from human praise, they had to remain in human favor. Thus there was a balance in the creative and destructive forces of the gods and a mutual inter-dependence between people and gods.

# THE SUMERIAN VIEW OF THE WORLD

by Michael Fazio

The Sumerians worshiped multiple gods of diverse rank and character and represented them in their art. This small object (Fig. 1.8) is the head of a ewe or female sheep carved by a Sumerian sculptor, perhaps in Uruk, more than five thousand years ago. Its current home is Louis Kahn's Kimbell Museum of Art in Fort Worth, Texas (see Figs. 16.15–16.17). Lovingly made, it renders more personal and more accessible these anonymous Sumerians who created a monumental architecture almost exclusively from mud.

We need to imagine the entire figure, its body intact, and so standing two to three feet high and having about the same length. Curators at the Kimbell interpret it as a symbol of the goddess Dittur, whose son Dumuzi was an important god of shepherding and milk (hence the sheep image), as well as the netherworld.

The ewe's head is worn, so again we need to imagine it as pristine, quite realistic and animate, and appreciate its sympathetic depiction in a society where such animals were essential to human survival. With its wide mouth, flaring nostrils, and alert ears that seem just to have heard the voice of the shepherd or shepherd god, it invites reverent touching, perhaps patting were it not so sacred. Again we can imagine the coarse warmth of its fleece and its quiet breath. We can imagine the artist working to communicate its "sheepness" and to communicate its meaning by drawing out the nature of the soft stone from which it is made.

Its home would have been a place like the White Temple (see Fig. 1.11). Here it would have been attended by priests and worshiped daily. The National Museum of Iraq in Baghdad, which was tragically ransacked during the war in 2003, contained sculpted images of such priests and other worshipful Sumerians (Fig. 1.9). These images are more formally abstract than the ewe, their upper and lower torsos wedge shaped, like the characters of Sumerian cuneiform writing, and their most striking features are extremely prominent eyes and ritually folded, almost wringing hands, seemingly expressive of a certain anxiety. The Sumerians struggled with a host of insecurities in a land where nature, particularly the weather, vacillated wildly between benevolence and malevolence. They asked the questions we still ask. Where had they come from? How could they exercise some measure of control over their environment? What awaited them after death?

**1.9** Sumerian statuette, Tell Asmar, ca. 2900–2600 BCE. Gypsum inlaid with shell and black limestone, approximately 16 inches.

Compare this statuette to the head of the ewe in Fig. 1.8. While the ewe is depicted realistically, the Sumerian worshiper is stylized. The same phenomenon is found in Egyptian art, where lowly subjects were often represented with a high degree of realism, while images of the pharaoh or of a god were abstracted, as if this abstraction might provide some insight into the more imponderable aspects of the human condition.

**1.8** Head of a ewe in sandstone, ca. 3200 BCE, 5¹⁄₄ inches by 5¹⁄₂ inches by 6¹⁄₄ inches.

The creator of this small, stony animal captured both its realistic "sheepness" and that enigmatic sense of the eternal to which great religious art aspires.

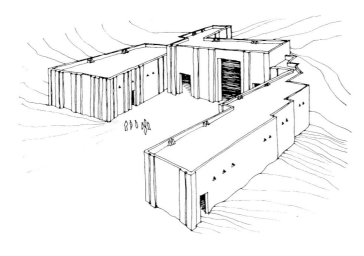

**1.10** Reconstruction of the Acropolis, Tepe Gawra, Sumer (Iraq), ca. 3800 BCE.

This religious structure was associated with a more complex urban society than those of prehistory. The scale of the building erected on the high point of the city reflects the importance of the society's religion and priestly class. Pilasters strengthened the mud-brick walls. The north temple stands at the upper left and measures about 25 feet by 40 feet.

Urban communities developed around religious shrines, the dwelling places of the gods and the repositories for surplus food stores, leading to the development of monumental temple complexes at the hearts of Sumerian cities. The earliest level of Eridu, the oldest city, had a small shrine with a brick altar in front of a wall **niche**, or recess, probably constructed to contain a cult statue, and altars and niches were found in all later Sumerian temples. Rebuildings of this temple at Eridu successively enlarged the relatively modest original shrine, and by about 3800 BCE the temple stood on a platform. Its **buttressed** walls enclosed a rectangular shrine room flanked by smaller side chambers. At about the same time Tepe Gawra, nearly 500 miles to the north, featured an **acropolis** with two temples, a shrine, and dwelling houses. Its major buildings formed a U-shaped open court. Their **façades** were articulated by buttressing **pilasters** (Fig. 1.10), a motif that will be seen again in early Egyptian architecture.

Most Sumerian buildings were laid up in sun-baked brick, a material easily obtained by shaping mud in molds and leaving it to dry for several weeks in the sun, but the resulting brick is not particularly resistant to weathering. As a result, much of Sumerian architecture is known only from foundations and lower sections of walls. Roofs were fabricated from lightweight wooden members or reeds that could not span great distances, so there were no large interior spaces. In both Sumerian and later Mesopotamian architecture, important buildings were given additional durability by having weather-resistant casings for the brick, and greater dignity by being raised on an artificial platform.

Such was the case at Uruk, where the so-called White Temple was built (ca. 3500–3000 BCE) on a forty-foot-high base of rubble from earlier buildings and provided with a protective coat of whitewash over its sloping walls of earth covered with sun-dried brick (Fig. 1.11). Entrance to the temple was made through a chamber in one long side, so that a "bent axis" led from the outside into the hall and sanctuary.

Contemporary structures excavated in the nearby precinct of Eanna (dedicated to Inanna) include two groups of temples flanking a courtyard ornamented by a **mosaic** of thousands of small **terracotta** cones. The base of each cone was dipped in black, white, or red glaze, and then its apex was inserted into the clay of the wall to form a polychromatic zigzag pattern with circular elements.

In 2350 BCE, Semitic-speaking peoples based principally in the cities of Sipar and Akkad, from which they take their name Akkadian, overthrew Sumerian civilization. Surviving evidence indicates that the Akkadians were fierce, governed not only by a priestly class but also by a warrior-king. They adopted many aspects of Sumerian culture, but their centralized form of government prefigured the hegemony of Babylon some 500 years later.

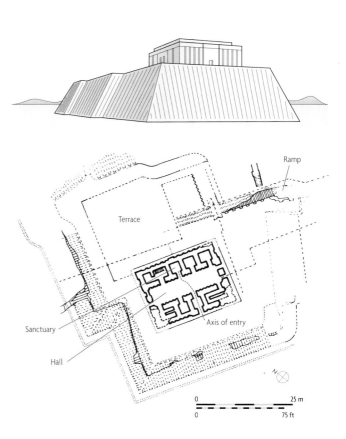

**1.11** View and plan of the White Temple, Uruk, Mesopotamia (Iraq), ca. 3500–3000 BCE.

Many temples in Mesopotamia were erected on raised platforms. The base of this temple was made in part with the rubble from previous buildings on the site, buttressed in a regular pattern and protected by layers of whitewash, hence the temple's name.

The Akkadian Empire was in turn overthrown in about 2150 BCE by the Guti, a group of tribes from the mountain regions of Iran. The military influence of the Guti weakened within a century, and political allegiances reminiscent of the first Sumerian city-states returned in what is termed the Neo-Sumerian period (ca. 2150–2000 BCE). This period witnessed the further development of urban temple forms, particularly the temple elevated on a tiered artificial mound, or **ziggurat**. Commonly constructed of sun-dried brick bonded together with bitumen, reed matting, or rope, ziggurats were finished with a weather-resistant exterior layer of kiln-fired brick. From a rectangular base, the ziggurat rose with battered or inward-sloping walls in a series of stepped platforms, culminating in a high temple at the top. A flight of stairs set in the center of one side afforded access to the temple. (Elements so placed in the center of a symmetrical form and aligned toward a terminus are said to be axial.) Ziggurats were designed to elevate the temples to the gods so that the latter might descend from the heavens and ensure the prosperity of the community. Symbolically, the ziggurat may have also represented the mountains whence the Sumerians came. To make their gods feel at home in the lowlands of the river valley, the Sumerians and their successors in Mesopotamia may have aspired to re-create their highland dwelling place. Raising the temple well above the elevation of the valley may also have reflected a desire to protect the sacred precinct from flood waters; it certainly gave it visual prominence in the city.

Little remains of the ziggurats constructed during the brief Neo-Sumerian interlude. Once the outer casing was removed by scavengers, the earthen core of ziggurats eroded considerably. Of those lofty artificial mountains that towered over Mesopotamian cities, only the ziggurat at Ur (ca. 2100 BCE) retains some of its architectural details (Figs. 1.12–1.13). One can still distinguish the three long stairways that converged on a tower gate at the level of the first platform. Shorter flights led to the second and third terraces, to which only the priests were allowed to ascend. These upper levels, together with the crowning temple, have been reduced to crumbled heaps, but archaeologists calculated that the original height was about seventy feet, with a base of about 200 by 150 feet. In contrast to the grand temple complexes, the houses of the ordinary population were set in densely packed neighborhoods. Plans were roughly orthogonal, and houses were constructed around open courtyards that provided light and fresh air to all rooms (Figs. 1.14a,b). To the street, the houses presented a blank wall, thereby ensuring privacy. Courtyard houses continue to the present day to be typical of Mediterranean and Middle Eastern communities.

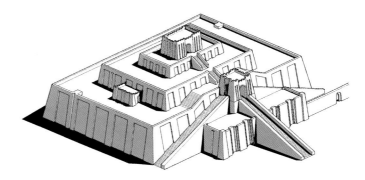

**1.13** Reconstruction of the ziggurat at Ur, Mesopotamia (Iraq), ca. 2100 BCE.

This drawing shows the original details that are now lost, including recessed panels defined by pilaster strips and parapets. The population below could observe the priestly processions up the successive flights of stairs to the temple on the uppermost platform.

**1.12** Ziggurat at Ur, Mesopotamia (Iraq), ca. 2100 BCE.

The best preserved of the massive temple mounds that once dominated every major Mesopotamian city, this ziggurat served to elevate a temple closer to the gods. Its core is sun-dried brick, overlaid with an outer layer of kiln-fired brick and bitumen as protection against weathering.

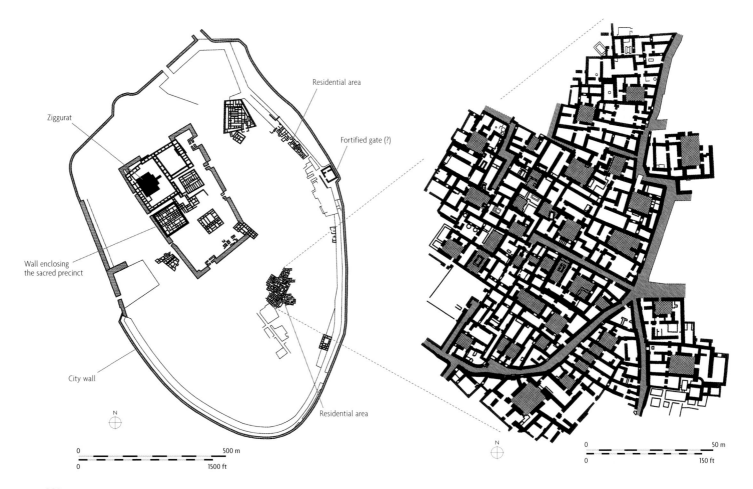

**1.14a** City of Ur, Mesopotamia (Iraq), ca. 2100 BCE.

This plan shows the walled precinct with the ziggurat and the enclosing city wall. A portion of the residential section that has been excavated can be seen to the southeast of the city center. Note the maze-like arrangement of the houses, contrasting sharply to the larger open spaces of the administrative and ceremonial center.

**1.14b** Plan of the residential quarter, Ur, Mesopotamia (Iraq), ca. 2100 BCE.

Surviving foundations indicate houses laid out on right-angled plans with living spaces organized around courtyards (shown hatched), a configuration that promoted urban density while also providing privacy and fresh air to each dwelling. Later versions of this house type can be found in Mohenjo-Daro (in the Indus Valley), Priene (in western Ionia), and in Islamic cities in the Middle East and North and East Africa.

## BABYLONIANS, HITTITES, AND ASSYRIANS

Beginning in 1800 BCE, the Amorite dynasty in the city-state of Babylon dominated Mesopotamia, with the most celebrated Babylonian king being Hammurabi (1728–1686). In 1830 BCE, the vigorous Indo-European Hittites overran Babylon and took over northern Mesopotamia. Farther south, the Semitic-speaking Assyrians took control and established capitals sequentially at Calah (present-day Nimrud), Dur-Sharrukin (Khorsabad), and Nineveh (Kuyunjik). Strongly fortified citadels built for each capital reflect the Assyrians' relentless warring as well as the ruthless character of their kings.

Khorsabad, the royal city built by Sargon II in ca. 720 BCE, illustrates the main characteristics of Assyrian architecture and planning (Figs. 1.15a,b). Projecting through one fortified wall of the city, the twenty-five-acre palace occupied a plateau fifty feet above the level of the town. Orthogonal geometry governed buildings in the palace area, which was organized by means of a series of courts. Rising on an axis with the ramparts was a seven-stage ziggurat, 143 feet square at the base, representing the cosmic order of the seven planets. The palace's courts were surrounded by rectangular rooms, including the throne room that was reached by a circuitous route, perhaps intended to confuse or frighten visitors and to heighten the sense of power and grandeur. Winged bulls with human heads carved in high relief from thirteen-foot-tall stone blocks guarded the entrances to the palace. Bone and muscle were realistically represented, while feathers, hair, and beard were stylized, forcefully conveying the strength of the monarch: as man, the lord of creation; as eagle, king of the sky; and as bull, fecundator of the herd. Other relief carvings within the palace depicted marching armies burning, killing, and pillaging to emphasize the folly of resisting Assyrian power. Without subtlety, Sargon II had the art and architecture of his palace communicate the overwhelming power residing in his person.

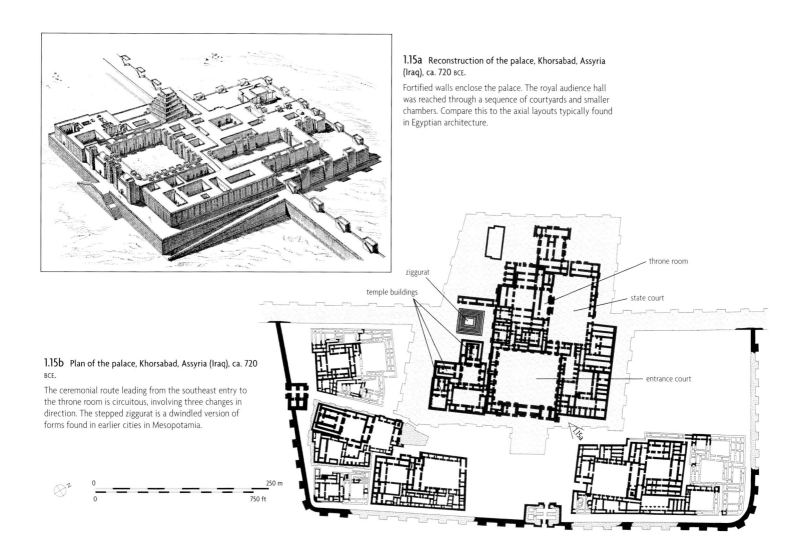

**1.15a** Reconstruction of the palace, Khorsabad, Assyria (Iraq), ca. 720 BCE.

Fortified walls enclose the palace. The royal audience hall was reached through a sequence of courtyards and smaller chambers. Compare this to the axial layouts typically found in Egyptian architecture.

ziggurat

temple buildings

throne room

state court

entrance court

**1.15b** Plan of the palace, Khorsabad, Assyria (Iraq), ca. 720 BCE.

The ceremonial route leading from the southeast entry to the throne room is circuitous, involving three changes in direction. The stepped ziggurat is a dwindled version of forms found in earlier cities in Mesopotamia.

0                    250 m
0                    750 ft

## THE PERSIANS

By 539 BCE, the Persian Empire was ruled by Cyrus II. The Persians had previously overthrown the Medes, and they continued to expand outward from their capital at Susa (in present-day Iran) to conquer all of Mesopotamia, Asia Minor, and even Egypt by 525 BCE. Within a century they controlled territory from the Danube to the Indus, and from the Jaxartes to the Nile, failing to subjugate only the Greek peninsula. The greatest surviving architectural contribution of the Persians is an impressive ruin at Persepolis (Fig. 1.16), the city founded in 518 BCE by Darius as a ceremonial capital to supplement Susa, the administrative capital, and Pasargadae as centers of court life. Lacking strong artistic traditions of their own, the Persians borrowed freely from the cultures they conquered. At Persepolis, there are echoes of Egyptian temple gates and **hypostyle halls**, Hittite audience chambers, and Mesopotamian sculpted animal motifs. The great palace, used primarily for ceremonies at the New Year and the

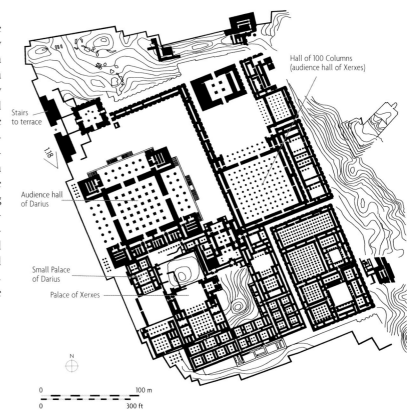

Hall of 100 Columns (audience hall of Xerxes)

Stairs to terrace

Audience hall of Darius

Small Palace of Darius

Palace of Xerxes

**1.16** Plan of the palace, Persepolis, Persia (Iran), ca. 518 BCE.

This great complex was created by at least three Persian monarchs as one of the capitals of the Persian Empire. Its ruins reveal architectural influences from other cultures in Mesopotamia, notably the Hittites and Assyrians, as well as the Egyptians.

0                    100 m
0                    300 ft

**1.17** View of the ruins of the palace, Persepolis, Persia (Iran), ca. 518 BCE.

Seen here are two columns with intact capitals remaining in the audience hall of Darius. The armies of Alexander the Great sacked and burned Persepolis.

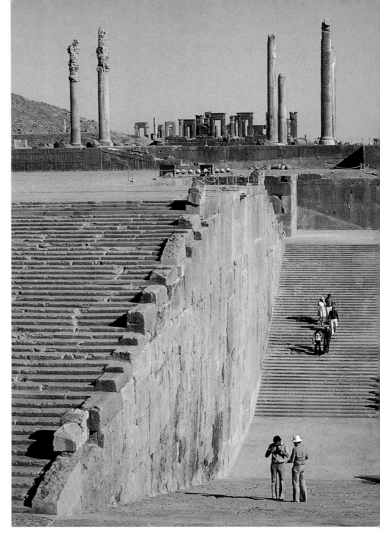

**1.18** Staircase to the upper terrace, Persepolis, Persia (Iran), ca. 518 BCE.

Isolated columns from the audience hall of Darius are visible, with doorways from Darius's palace in the background and the palace of Xerxes beyond.

beginning of spring, occupied a terrace 1500 by 900 feet; it contained reception courts, banquet rooms, and audience halls in a loosely organized orthogonal layout. King Xerxes's throne room, known as the Hall of a Hundred Columns and completed by Artaxerxes, was the largest roofed space in the palace, able to contain 10,000 people within its 250-foot square plan. Most of the construction was in stone. Stone **columns** supported wooden roof beams resting on the unique double-headed **capitals** carved in the form of bulls and lions (Fig. 1.17). Access to the terrace was gained via a flight of stairs flanked by relief sculptures representing delegations from twenty-three nations bringing tribute to the sovereign (Fig. 1.18). These stone figures, shown engaged in the same kind of activities as real-life visitors, provided a foretaste of the pageantry and banquets waiting in the palace above.

The conquests of Alexander the Great ended Persian dominance in 331 BCE. Alexander's armies eventually reached India, where Persian craftsmen appear to have accompanied them and then remained. They helped build the capital at Pataliputra (now Patna) for Chandragupta, where the many-columned halls and animal capitals recall the palace at Persepolis. Persian architecture became one of the major influences for the early stone architecture of India.

## ANCIENT EGYPT

Popular culture suffers from no shortage of ancient Egyptian images, be they from epic movies depicting Moses and the pharaohs or classic horror films where Boris Karloff, playing the mummy, wanders around menacingly, doling out ancient justice to naïve archaeologists and greedy tomb raiders. All of this is fun, as is wild speculation about the Egyptian pyramids being built by visitors from outer space using anti-gravity beams, but it threatens to obscure the real accomplishments of everyday men and women in the Nile Valley, albeit those of 5000 years ago. Like the Mesopotamians, the ancient Egyptians produced a great architecture by marshaling the forces of their entire civilization and directing those forces in the service of widely held cultural values. This architecture is much more varied than you may imagine, but it is not only largely understandable to the modern mind but also highly informative about design ideas applicable in any era.

The geography of Egypt is dominated by one great river, the Nile, which originates in the highlands of Uganda and passes through the Sudan and Ethiopia as it traverses more than 2000 miles before flowing out into the Mediterranean Sea to the north. Within the 600 lower miles of the river valley, agriculture is facilitated by the warm climate and the annual flood deposits of organic silt, which renew the fertility of the fields. On the margins of the valley in dynastic times there were marshes and open lands rich in game. (Today the desert encroaches on these areas.) Outside the rather narrow fertile band bordering the Nile, great expanses of inhospitable desert provided security from outside invasion, just as the Mediterranean served as a barrier for settlements on the Nile Delta. The culture that developed along the banks of the river was thus predominantly rural agricultural, in contrast to urban-oriented settlements in turbulent Mesopotamia. Egyptian life was organized around the annual flooding of the river, and the cyclical rhythm of the seasons fostered a civilization that remained remarkably stable for more than 2000 years. Two centers of Egyptian civilization, with differing cultural practices, arose in prehistoric times: Lower Egypt in the broad Nile Delta, and Upper Egypt in the more narrow southern river valley. At a very early stage, Egyptians also developed writing in the form of hieroglyphs, a system using both pictorial and phonetic symbols to record information.

The history of Egypt begins in about 3000 BCE with the union of Upper and Lower Egypt by Menes, the pharaoh king of Upper Egypt, who established his capital at Memphis, near the junction of the two lands. (Please note that dates in Egyptian history, especially for individual pharaohs in the early dynasties, are still matters of scholarly debate. All dates given here should therefore be treated as approximations.) Menes, like all his successors, was both a temporal ruler and a manifestation of the falcon-headed god Horus, the god of pharaohs. When the pharaoh died, he became identified with Osiris, father of Horus and lord of the underworld, and his successor as pharaoh assumed the Horus role. Egyptian theology linked both Osiris and Horus with the sun god Ra, whose symbol in the ancient temple at Heliopolis was the phallic, cone-shaped ben-ben stone, later stylized as a pyramid. The use of pyramid shapes at the top of stone shafts (**obelisks**) or as the building form itself (as in the pyramids) was thus a visual symbol of the connection between the ruler and the sun god.

## THE EARLY DYNASTIC PERIOD AND OLD KINGDOM (FIRST–EIGHTH DYNASTIES, ca. 2920–2134 BCE)

Egyptian history is divided into thirty dynasties, encompassing the period from Pharaoh Narmer's accession (ca. 3000 BCE) to the conquest of Egypt by Alexander the Great in 332 BCE. What we know of this early period comes largely from funerary monuments and inscriptions, where the focus is on the transition from the world of the living to that of the dead. Egyptians believed strongly in an afterlife in which the *ka*, or life-force, was reunited with the *ba*, or physical manifestation, to become an *akh*, or spirit. Elaborate rituals were performed inside tomb chambers to ensure that the transformation from life to death was successful. Preservation of the physical body (or at least a temporary forestalling of its putrefaction) after death was of great importance, as was the provision of household furnishings, surrogate servants, food, drink, and a suitable permanent chamber. The *ka* of an important person, especially the pharaoh, who was inadequately prepared for the afterlife might wander unsatisfied about the world and cause mischief for the living. It was therefore in society's interest to ensure that the pharaoh's body and spirit were well served. This goal led to the construction of enduring tombs for royalty and the development of mummification to preserve the body. Tombs, rather than temples or palaces, became the most lasting religious structures.

**Mastabas**, the earliest tombs, were built as eternal houses for the departed and were in all likelihood based on the design of the dwellings of the living. Ordinary houses were constructed of reed, thatch, and wood, materials wholly unsuited for a permanent residence, so the builders of mastaba tombs sought greater durability by using brick while retaining characteristic details provided by the customary bundled reeds and wooden supports. The basic mastaba (Fig. 1.19) was a blocklike structure above ground containing a small room for offerings and another chamber for the body and a statue of the deceased. Worldly goods entombed with the dead soon attracted thieves, so an early revision of mastaba design added a deep shaft under the building. The body was placed at its base, and the shaft was then filled with stone and rubble to deter would-be robbers. In the above-ground chamber, or **serdab**, a statue of the deceased would receive offerings. A later change toward increasing permanence involved using stone in the construction of the mastaba.

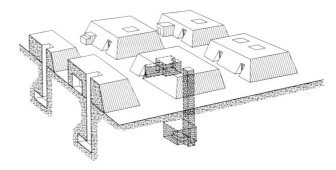

**1.19** Drawing of the mastaba tombs.

This aerial view shows the burial chambers beneath the structures and small chambers, or serdabs, provided at ground level for offerings to the spirit of the deceased. It is thought that these tombs, constructed of sun-dried brick or stone, were based on designs of actual dwellings constructed of less durable materials.

# "HYDRAULIC" CIVILIZATIONS

by Dan MacGilvray

*There is but little rain in Assyria. It is this which nourishes the roots of the corn; but it is irrigation from the river that ripens the crop and brings the grain to fullness: it is not as in Egypt, where the river itself rises and floods the fields: in Assyria they are watered by hand and by swinging beams. For the whole land of Babylon, like Egypt, is cut across by canals. The greatest of these is navigable: it runs . . . from the Euphrates to the Tigris . . .*

*. . . all the land . . . watered by the Nile in its course was Egypt, and all who dwelt lower down than the city Elephantine (Aswan) and drank of that river's water were Egyptians.*

*. . . there are no men, neither in the rest of Egypt, nor in the whole world, who gain from the soil with so little labour; they have not the toil of breaking up the land with the plow, nor of hoeing . . . the river rises of itself, waters the fields, and then sinks back again; thereupon each man sows his field and sends swine into it to tread down the seed, and waits for the harvest . . .*

1.20 Obelisk in a quarry, Aswan, Egypt.

The Greek historian Herodotus (484–425 BCE) traveled extensively throughout the ancient world and wrote the first narrative history. He was a keen observer of culture, and these quotations define one of the essential characteristics of Mesopotamian and Egyptian civilizations: their dependence on rivers. Water is an essential ingredient of all life, and flowing water is required for the development of civilization, not only for drinking and irrigation, but also to remove the human waste that accumulates in areas of dense population. Thus, all of the early civilizations from that of the Indus to the Mayans were founded on rivers. We refer to these as "hydraulic" civilizations.

Of necessity, a hydraulic civilization is a cooperative federation, in contrast to, say, a group of squabbling city-states. In a given watershed, strong centralized control is required for the construction of an inter-dependent system of canals to divert water for irrigation and drain swamps for cultivation, or dams and levees for flood control and water retention. Early hydraulic engineers learned the techniques of surveying and developed the skills to manage large-scale construction projects as they struggled to control the waters that brought both abundance and destruction. As Herodotus notes, the nation of Egypt defined itself by the Nile, and there is no doubt that the engineers of the pyramids learned to survey, to level, and to organize large work forces on the banks of the river. It has also been speculated that, because the farmers were inactive during flood times, they were available for conscription onto construction work gangs for massive projects like the pyramids.

The Tigris, Euphrates, and Nile rivers also served as the primary transportation arteries for the movement of goods between the various communities that lined them. Even today, in the age of jet travel, by far the cheapest means of moving freight per ton-mile is the river barge. In medieval times it was ten times cheaper to move cargo by boat than by ox-cart. And, because of the Nile, the ancient Egyptians had no use for wheeled vehicles or even paved roads; the chariot was a foreign import that arrived late to the water-borne Egyptians, who, not surprisingly, developed sophisticated construction techniques for boats of all sizes. In tomb paintings the largest are shown laden with granite obelisks, such as that in Figure 1.20, a cargo of up to 1000 tons.

**1.21** The step pyramid, Saqqara, Egypt, ca. 2630 BCE.

As the first monumental stone construction in Egypt, this tomb set the precedent for later pyramids of the pharaohs. Its architect, Imhotep, was remembered for his genius and later revered as a deity.

**1.22a** Plan of Djoser's funerary complex, Saqqara, Egypt, ca. 2630 BCE.

The step pyramid is the rectangular element in the center, dominating the Great Court, which is reached through the narrow Processional Hall at the lower left. The Egyptians provided the court's two B-shaped stone blocks so that Djoser's ka could continue to run the ceremonial race between them, symbolizing for eternity the governmental unity of Upper and Lower Egypt.

**1.22b** Section and plan of the step pyramid, Saqqara, Egypt, ca. 2630 BCE.

The section drawing shows the successive stages of construction, through which the original mastaba form was enlarged to become a pyramid, with the burial chamber under the center. The plan drawing shows the industry of later tomb robbers who tunneled in to recover treasure buried with Djoser.

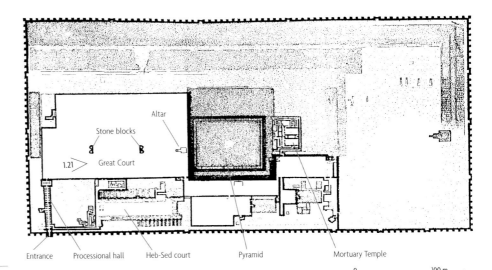

Altar

Stone blocks

B B

1.21   Great Court

Entrance   Processional hall   Heb-Sed court   Pyramid   Mortuary Temple

| 0 | 100 m |
| 0 | 300 ft |

N

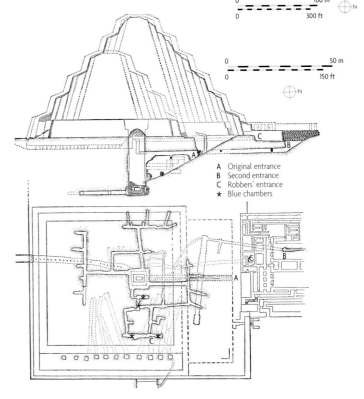

| 0 | 50 m |
| 0 | 150 ft |

N

A  Original entrance
B  Second entrance
C  Robbers' entrance
★  Blue chambers

## THE FIRST PYRAMIDS

As the religious ritual prescribed by the priesthood evolved to enhance further the significance of the pharaoh, the mastaba was likewise enlarged, eventually producing the pyramid. At death the pharaoh accompanied the sun god on his daily journey across the sky, so he needed to be lifted skyward. The pyramid, initially an upward-stepping form like the ziggurat, whose peak caught the first rays of morning light, was the emblem of the sun god as worshiped at Heliopolis. The shape also makes symbolic reference to the annual rebirth of nature, for as floods recede, the first signs of plant life appear on small hillocks. Thus the stepped and eventually the true pyramid's form represented both daily and yearly rebirth throughout eternity.

Imhotep, architect to the Third-Dynasty pharaoh Djoser (2630–2611 BCE), is credited with designing the first pyramid, for Djoser's funerary complex at Saqqara, outside Memphis (Fig. 1.21). This was also Egypt's first monumental construction in stone, no small factor in its survival through 4600 years. The complex is a large rectangle in plan, covering thirty-five acres, surrounded by a wall thirty-three feet high and a mile long (Figs. 1.22a,b). There is only

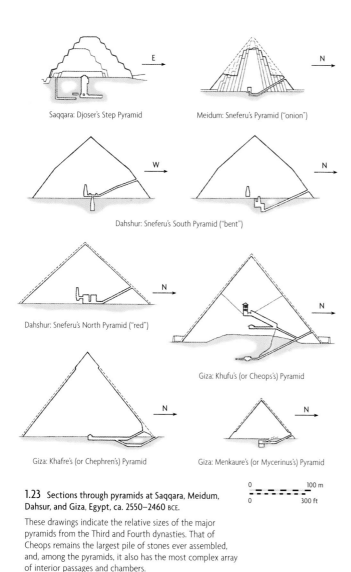

Saqqara: Djoser's Step Pyramid

Meidum: Sneferu's Pyramid ("onion")

Dahshur: Sneferu's South Pyramid ("bent")

Dahshur: Sneferu's North Pyramid ("red")

Giza: Khufu's (or Cheops's) Pyramid

Giza: Khafre's (or Chephren's) Pyramid

Giza: Menkaure's (or Mycerinus's) Pyramid

**1.23** Sections through pyramids at Saqqara, Meidum, Dahsur, and Giza, Egypt, ca. 2550–2460 BCE.

These drawings indicate the relative sizes of the major pyramids from the Third and Fourth dynasties. That of Cheops remains the largest pile of stones ever assembled, and, among the pyramids, it also has the most complex array of interior passages and chambers.

one entrance, a small door in the southeast corner that leads into a narrow colonnaded processional hall. At the end of the hall, one enters the main courtyard dominated by Djoser's stepped pyramid, which rises 197 feet above its 397-by-358-foot base. Begun as a mastaba, the pyramid was built up in several stages to attain its present shape, a mass rising in six steps. The exterior of the pyramid was faced with dressed limestone, while the courtyards and surrounding buildings are thought to be representations of Djoser's earthly palace in Memphis, rebuilt here to last for eternity. The appearance and typical details of the original materials are imitated in stone: reed-bundle and papyrus-stalk columns, log ceilings, even a stone hinge for an immobile stone door. North of the pyramid is the mortuary temple in which the pre-burial ritual was performed. A statue of Djoser looking outward sits in a small chamber, with a small aperture cut in the wall in front of the statue's stone eyes being the only access to the outside world.

Djoser's complex includes areas for the practice of rituals that are not completely understood today, but that were apparently important symbols of the bond between Upper and Lower Egypt. The great court was the scene of

the Heb-Sed race, run annually by the pharaoh to ensure fertility of the fields. The course consisted of four circuits of the court in each direction, clockwise for half of the kingdom and counterclockwise for the other half. Djoser had two burial chambers to symbolize his power and paternity over Upper and Lower Egypt. One chamber, located beneath the pyramid, contained his mummy in an alabaster coffin. The access passage was blocked by a stone plug six feet in diameter and weighing six tons, but this was inadequate protection against robbers, who nonetheless gained access to the tomb in antiquity. In 1928 excavators discovered the second chamber in the south side of the perimeter wall. Although it too had been plundered, the chamber originally contained the embalmed internal organs of the pharaoh, emblematic of his fertility and his protection of Lower Egypt. Grave robbers did not steal the handsome blue **faïence** wall decorations, which are now all that remains of the interior. These tiles are set into horizontal and vertical stone members to represent rush matting between wooden slats attached to larger wooden supports. On one wall is a relief carving depicting Djoser running the Heb-Sed race. Wearing the white crown of Upper Egypt, Djoser is portrayed in the manner peculiar to Egyptian art, with head, legs, and feet shown in profile and the torso shown frontally. In this one view Egyptian artists captured the essential features of the human body with great exactitude, even though the pose is not a "realistic" or natural one.

From its beginnings at Saqqara, the evolution of what we now think of as the "true" pyramid proceeds through at least three major projects before its culmination in the Fourth-Dynasty tombs at Giza, outside Cairo (Fig. 1.23). All three of these developmental pyramids were built or modified for one of the first pharaohs of the Fourth Dynasty, Sneferu (2575–2551 BCE), whose cult remained active for over 2000 years after his death. At Meidum, six miles south of Saqqara, Sneferu added an outer layer to the pyramid that may have been begun for Huni, the last pharaoh of the Third Dynasty. It began with a stepped core of seven stages, which was transformed into a true pyramid with the addition of two overbuildings. As the third and final outer casing of limestone was being installed, there is evidence that the upper portions of the work collapsed because the pyramid's stonework was insufficiently supported, given the relatively steep angle of inclination (51° 50′ 35″). Had it been completed as planned, the pyramid would have reached nearly 302 feet in height. As it stands, with its stepped core rising above the rubble, it has been given the descriptive name of an "onion" pyramid. Entrance was through a sloping corridor opening off the north side, descending below ground, and then rising a short distance vertically to the burial chamber at the center of the pyramid's base. Corbeled construction in the vault of this chamber marks the first time this technique was employed in stone by the Egyptians, although it had been used earlier in brick.

The collapse of the Meidum pyramid had an impact on another of Sneferu's pyramids under construction at the same time at Dahshur, about twenty-eight miles south of Meidum. There, a partially finished structure was transformed to create the so-called "bent" pyramid that began with a 616-foot-square base and sides inclined at 54° 27' 44". Observing the collapse at Meidum, the builders at Dahshur changed to a lower inclination angle of 41° 22' when the pyramid was half-built. Eventually reaching a height of 344 feet, the bent pyramid gains added stability from its firm limestone foundation and core, large stone casing blocks that are slightly inclined to the center, and the reduced angle of inclination. These stabilizing design features were incorporated from the beginning in the third pyramid of Sneferu, the north or "red" pyramid, also at Dahshur. (The color name derives from oxidation of the limestone used for its core, exposed after stone scavengers removed the white limestone casing.) From a base 722 feet square, the north pyramid rises at a constant 43° 22' angle to its apex 344 feet above the ground. Its profile is thus relatively low, a testimony to the conservative attitudes of its designers.

**1.24** Pyramids, Giza, Egypt, ca. 2550–2460 BCE.

Khufu's pyramid is the farthest back, to the right of Khafre's pyramid (distinguished by the remnant of outer casing stones at its peak). In front of Khafre's pyramid is that of Menkaure, while three much smaller pyramids in the foreground belonged to queens of Menkaure.

## FOURTH-DYNASTY PYRAMIDS AT GIZA

The trio of large pyramids at Giza (2550–2460 BCE) are the work of Sneferu's descendants, the Fourth-Dynasty pharaohs known as Khufu, Khafre, and Menkaure (or Cheops, Chephren, and Mycerinus in Greek transliteration) (Figs. 1.24–1.25). The largest pyramid, that of Khufu, who reigned 2551–2528 BCE, was built first and planned from the start to be a true pyramid of unprecedented proportions. The 755-by-755-foot base covers over thirteen acres; the sides rise at an angle of 51° 50' 40" to an apex at 481 feet. Most of the stone in the pyramid is limestone, although the large pharaoh's chamber in the center is made of granite. Nothing built in stone before or since has rivaled the Great Pyramid of Khufu for sheer size.

Khufu's pyramid is not completely solid, however. Three burial chambers are built within it, one excavated out of foundation bedrock and the other two constructed as the stone mountain was erected. Although these were once thought to represent changes made in design as work progressed, they are now interpreted as deliberate accommodations. The roughly finished lowest chamber is thought to represent the underworld. The middle chamber, the so-called Queen's Chamber, probably contained an over-life-sized statue of Khufu and served as his spirit chamber, or serdab. The top, or King's Chamber, beautifully constructed of red granite, contains a granite sarcophagus in which Khufu was in fact buried. To transfer the tremendous weight of the pyramid around the ceiling of the King's

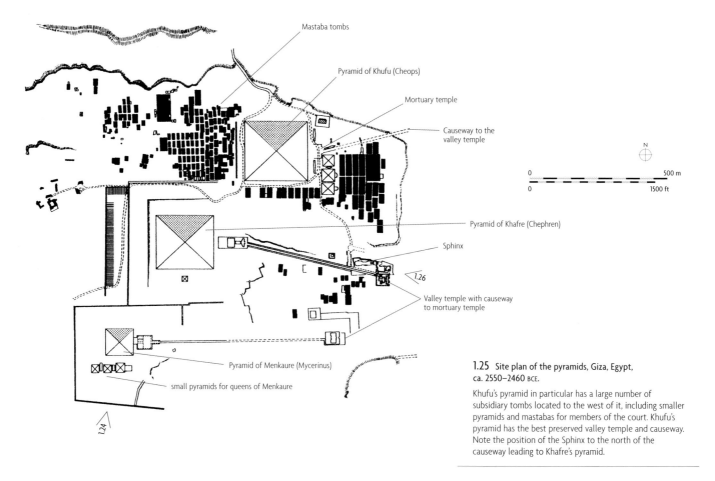

Mastaba tombs

Pyramid of Khufu (Cheops)

Mortuary temple

Causeway to the
valley temple

Pyramid of Khafre (Chephren)

Sphinx

Valley temple with causeway
to mortuary temple

Pyramid of Menkaure (Mycerinus)

small pyramids for queens of Menkaure

**1.25** Site plan of the pyramids, Giza, Egypt,
ca. 2550–2460 BCE.

Khufu's pyramid in particular has a large number of
subsidiary tombs located to the west of it, including smaller
pyramids and mastabas for members of the court. Khufu's
pyramid has the best preserved valley temple and causeway.
Note the position of the Sphinx to the north of the
causeway leading to Khafre's pyramid.

Chamber, eleven pairs of granite beams were set as a gabled brace or saddle roof extending into the mass of the pyramid above the chamber. Five massive sets of horizontal granite slabs form relieving chambers stacked between the saddle roof and the flat ceiling of the crypt as a means of reducing weight and pressure from above. The corbeled gallery leading to this chamber is also a construction marvel, rising twenty-six feet in height, a splendid contrast to a four-foot-high ascending passage to which it connects.

Both the King's and Queen's chambers have pairs of small shafts angling upward through the mass of the pyramid that may have been intended for ventilation. Their particular orientation implies connection to the pole star (north side) and Orion (south side), although the precise function and symbolic meaning of these ventilation shafts remain unclear.

Next in sequence of construction (and only slightly smaller in size) is the pyramid of Khafre, a son of Khufu, who reigned 2520–2494 BCE. Khafre's pyramid is 705 feet square at the base and rises at an angle of 53° 20' to an ultimate elevation of 471 feet. In many photographs of the Giza pyramids, this one seems the tallest of the three, but this is only because it stands on higher ground than that of Khufu. Khafre's monument is readily distinguished by the substantial fragment of the original smooth limestone casing that survives at the apex. On the inside there is a single tomb chamber in the center of the pyramid at the base level. A passageway in the north side provides access to the room, which, like all the tomb chambers in pyramids, was pillaged in ancient times.

The smallest of the Giza trio of major pyramids belonged to Menkaure, a son of Khafre who reigned 2490–2472 BCE. Containing less than one-tenth of the amount of stone of Khufu's pyramid, Menkaure's tomb seems to have been erected hurriedly and with less care than those of his predecessors. We know that it was not finished before Menkaure died. Its dimensions—335 by 343 feet at the base, a slope of 51° 20' 25", and 213 feet high—maintain the general proportions established by the neighboring tombs. Menkaure's successor, Shepseskaf, the last pharaoh in the Fourth Dynasty, chose not to have a pyramid burial, and although pyramids continued to be built by later rulers, the quality and scale of the Giza trio were never exceeded.

Associated with each of the pyramids were ancillary temples that are now largely ruins. Alongside the Nile was a lower or valley temple, where the boat bearing the pharaoh's body would land to disembark its royal cargo. The valley temple may have been the place where the process of mummification took place, although the evidence is not entirely clear on this point. A causeway connected this valley temple to the upper or mortuary temple at the base of the pyramid itself. Here the corpse would receive a final ritual cleansing prior to entombment.

Of all the Giza valley temples, the lower temple of Khafre remains in the best state of preservation. Essentially square in plan, with thick limestone walls encased in red granite, its central hall is an inverted T-shape. Red granite **piers** supported a roof with a **clerestory**; the windows were set so that sunlight coming through them illuminated the twenty-three statues of the pharaoh placed around the edges of the wall. Two levels of narrow storage rooms extended into the solid wall mass. Today the temple stands without a roof or its outer stone facing beside the Sphinx, a man-headed lion 187 feet long and sixty-six feet high, carved in situ out of a natural rock ledge (Fig. 1.26). (It has long been presumed that the head on the Sphinx was a likeness of Khafre, but this cannot be proven. Recent speculation that the **Sphinx** may be significantly older than the pyramids is not generally accepted by Egyptologists.) Khafre's mortuary temple at the base of the pyramid is connected to the valley temple by a causeway running at an oblique angle to the river. The mortuary temple is rectangular in plan, with a series of axially disposed interior spaces. Its limestone structure was probably cased with a finer material, and the floor was alabaster. At the center of the temple was a large courtyard surrounded by enormous pillars, in front of which stood twelve large statues of the pharaoh.

Pyramids, especially the impressive Giza group, have long provoked two questions: How could ancient peoples, working with simple technologies, have built such enormous structures, and why would they have built them? The answer to the first question can be reasonably surmised, although this is still an area of study. Even though the Egyptians lacked metals harder than copper and made no use of the wheel for transport, they were not primitive. Their knowledge of surveying, necessary for reestablishing field boundaries after the annual flood, enabled them to lay out the pyramid's base accurately and to orient the square plan to the cardinal directions. Khufu's pyramid deviates only 5½ minutes of arc from true north; its summit is only one foot off the center of the base; and there is only an eight-inch error in the length of one side of the base. The absence of wheeled vehicles was not a serious handicap, as much of the stone transport would have been made over water or across sand, where wheels would have provided no real advantage over the boats and sledges actually used. Quarrying was accomplished with metal saws for the softer limestones or sandstones, and by repeatedly pounding balls of very hard rock (dolerite) along seams in the harder stones such as granite. The finishing of cut surfaces could be accomplished with stone hammers, chisels, axes, and sand or grindstones. By any method, quarry work was tedious, and it was probably assigned to prisoners or conscripts. Much of the limestone in the core of the Giza pyramids was quarried on-site. Finer display stone and granite was transported from more distant locations.

Construction of the pyramids was probably done by large teams of laborers during the flood season when agricultural work was impossible. The muscles of men supplied the force to haul blocks into place. Studies of ruined or incomplete pyramids have revealed that there was no single construction method used; least of all is known about the most complete monuments, the Giza trio, because their interiors cannot be inspected closely. In some cases, ramps were erected along with the rising

**1.26** Khafre's pyramid and the Sphinx, Giza, Egypt, ca. 2550–2460 BCE.

Remains of the entrance to Khafre's valley temple are visible to the left.

masonry mountain to provide an inclined plane for dragging stone on sledges. It is also possible that the rising stepped core of the Giza pyramids served as a construction staircase for workers pulling and leveraging the blocks onto the upper levels, as the volume of material needed for additional ramps on these enormous buildings and the difficulty of hauling stone around corners would make inclined planes impractical. While the number of men and length of time required to see a major pyramid through to completion are still subject to debate, the Egyptians' ability to organize labor forces and quarrymen in seasonal building campaigns remains a fact and a tribute to the abilities of their engineers.

The question of why the pyramids were built has inspired both serious inquiry and speculative nonsense. Theories ranging from embodiments of standard measures (as defined in English units) to apocalyptic predictions of the end of the world have been offered to explain the dimensional configuration of Khufu's pyramid, but Egyptologists are convinced that the pyramids were first and foremost tombs for the pharaohs. Why people should devote so much effort to what we might regard as a fundamentally useless project is answerable only within the context of the Egyptian world view. Perhaps no other society before or since has invested so much time and labor to ensure survival after death for its most important personages. Virtually all Egyptian art and architecture was very practical, intended to assist one's passage to the next world and ensure comfort and pleasant living upon arrival. While the greatest attention was lavished on the setting for the pharaoh's afterlife, all Egyptians believed in their particular view of eternal life and so all had a stake in the creation of an architecture of death and rebirth, from the modest tombs of the poor to the monumental edifices of the rulers.

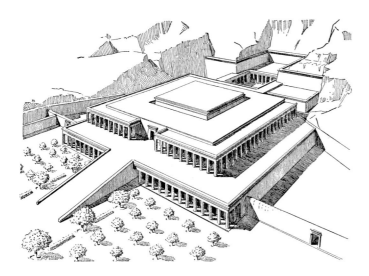

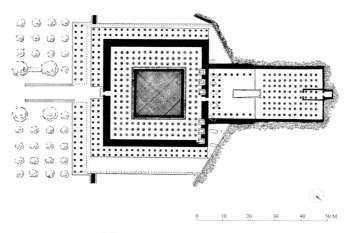

**1.27** Reconstruction and plan of Mentuhotep's mortuary temple, Deir-el-Bahari, Egypt, ca. 2061–2010 BCE.

This Middle-Kingdom temple represents an interesting synthesis of an axial temple, hypostyle hall, and burial chamber into a single composition. Its ramps and stepped terraces would be echoed in the New-Kingdom temple of Hatshepsut built about 400 years later on an adjoining site.

## THE MIDDLE KINGDOM (ELEVENTH–THIRTEENTH DYNASTIES, ca. 2040–1640 BCE)

The first eight Egyptian dynasties gave way to a period of upheaval when local feudal lords upset the unity achieved by Menes. This era of inter-regional strife is designated the First Intermediate period, and it was followed by a second phase of centralized government called the Middle Kingdom. During this period, the royal capital was relo-

cated from Memphis to Thebes, and the pharaoh's position was more that of a feudal lord over local vassals than an absolute and divine ruler in the Old-Kingdom tradition. Royal tombs were still of major architectural importance, but Middle-Kingdom tombs generally neither endured nor intimidated grave robbers.

The tomb of Mentuhotep II at Deir-el-Bahari (ca. 2061–2010 BCE) (Fig. 1.27) is an exceptional work of architectural innovation, combining temple and tomb chamber in a single composition. The complex, approached by an axial route from the Nile, had two levels of colonnaded terraces surrounding a masonry mass, long thought to have been a pyramid but more recently interpreted as a flat-roofed hall. (The building is a ruin today, so one cannot be sure of the initial design. The case for a flat-roofed hall is based on there being insufficient foundations to support even a modest pyramid.) The central **axis** continues through layers of square columns, through the flat-roofed hall, through a courtyard, and through a forest of columns until reaching Mentuhotep's actual burial vault carved in the rock cliff. The two levels of columns seen upon approach are dramatized by the contrast of their sunlit shafts with the shadowed recesses behind and anticipate Greek temples with their surrounding **colonnades**. Mentuhotep's tomb would serve as a prototype for the more elaborate adjoining funerary complex built by the New-Kingdom pharaoh Hatshepsut.

More typical of Middle-Kingdom tombs are those at Beni Hasan, which are cut into rock cliffs and provided with sheltering **porticoes** (Fig. 1.28). Reflecting the political importance of their builders, these tombs were constructed for minor nobles and court officials, who evidently enjoyed considerable influence and wealth. Most of the architectural character was created by excavation, and the builders replicated spaces and details associated with ordinary dwellings, that is, wooden and plastered reed structures with slightly arched roofs composed of mats laid on a frame.

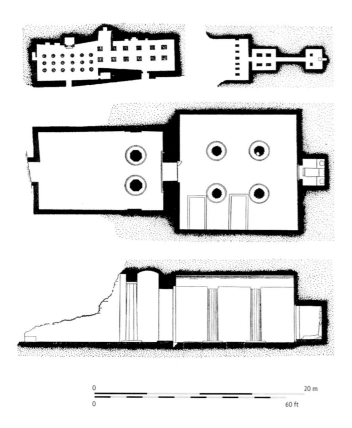

**1.28** Plan and section of rock-cut tombs, Beni-Hasan, Egypt, ca. 2000–1900 BCE.

Even when working amorphous rock, the builders chose to replicate rectangular geometries and to carve details reflecting the wooden and plastered reed construction that doubtless characterized houses. The lower of the two plans corresponds to the section.

## THE NEW KINGDOM (EIGHTEENTH–TWENTIETH DYNASTIES, ca. 1550–1070 BCE)

The Middle Kingdom was terminated by the arrival of the Hyksos, shepherd-kings who may have come from Asia. Whatever their origins, the Hyksos were the first successful invaders of Egypt in centuries, and they ruled for about 100 years in what is known as the Second Intermediate period. They introduced metallurgy, the two-person chariot, new deities, and new weapons to Egyptian culture, but their rule produced no lasting artistic innovations. With the expulsion of the Hyksos came the New Kingdom, which was characterized by an invigorated dynastic line of pharaohs and an increasingly powerful hereditary priesthood who brought Egypt to new heights of political and cultural brilliance.

The Eighteenth Dynasty, the first of the New Kingdom, continued the Middle-Kingdom tradition of burial in rock-cut tombs, going a stage further by eliminating all suggestions of monumentality. It had escaped no one's notice that all the dynastic tombs had been successfully penetrated by grave robbers. The Giza pyramids were probably plundered during the First Intermediate period. To preserve the worldly remains of the pharaoh and thwart the thieves, Eighteenth-Dynasty builders relied on concealment and improved policing of the royal necropolis. New-Kingdom pharaohs were interred secretly in the desert wilderness beyond Deir-el-Bahari, a region known as the Valley of the Kings, where very modest chambers were hewn out of the cliffs, and the entrances were hidden by dirt and sand. Spiritual nourishment for the deceased

**1.29** Mortuary temple of Queen Hatshepsut, Deir-el-Bahari, Egypt, ca. 1473–1458 BCE.

In its day, this great temple, with planted terraces and dignified carved colonnades framed by the cliff face, must have been a restful oasis in the dry landscape, a fitting monument to the peaceful reign of Hatshepsut, one of the rare woman rulers in antiquity.

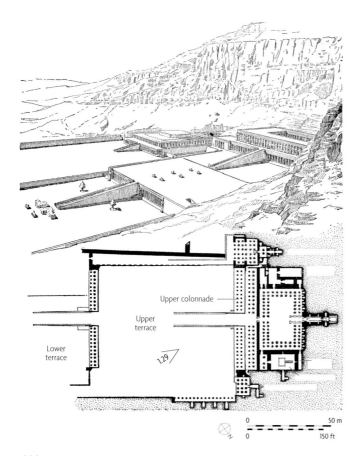

**1.30** View and plan of Hatshepsut's mortuary temple, Deir-el-Bahari, Egypt, ca. 1473–1458 BCE.

To thwart thieves, New-Kingdom pharaohs arranged for their bodies to be buried in concealed tombs in the Valley of the Kings (behind these cliffs), where priests guarded against robbers. Mentuhotep's earlier tomb is seen just beyond Hatshepsut's monument.

was provided at increasingly elaborate separately erected funerary temples.

Among the most splendid of the Eighteenth-Dynasty temples is the funerary complex of Queen Hatshepsut (1473–1458 BCE) at Deir-el-Bahari (Fig. 1.29), notable both for its architecture and for the fact that its patron was a woman. Succession to the throne passed through the female line, but the pharaoh was almost always male. Hatshepsut was the daughter of Thutmose I, and she married her half-brother, who became Pharaoh Thutmose II. During his reign she relegated him to a subsidiary role, and after his death she ruled independently, though ostensibly as regent for Thutmose II's son by a concubine, Thutmose III. Her court favorite was a commoner, Senmut, who was also responsible (perhaps as architect) for her funerary temple. Hatshepsut was buried on the other side of the mountain range in the Valley of the Kings, so the temple complex was a mortuary chapel dedicated to the god Amun, the sun god with whom the pharaoh was associated. Ramps lead up from the valley to three broad terraces, each defined by colonnades, which also serve as retaining walls for the next level (Fig. 1.30). The overall design was doubtless inspired by the neighboring temple of Mentuhotep, although Hatshepsut's temple is considerably larger and grander. Columns in the north colonnade of the second terrace are faceted in a manner suggesting the **flutes** of later **Doric** columns (Fig. 1.31). Relief carvings and wall paintings within the sanctuary spaces and in the great hall depict Hatshepsut's divine birth as the child of Amun and the activities of her peaceful reign, including trading expeditions to Punt (perhaps the Somali coast) bearing gold, ivory, baboons, and botanical specimens. Hatshepsut herself is usually depicted as a man, sometimes as the god Osiris, wearing the apron and headdress of a pharaoh.

Today they are sand-covered and barren, but in the Eighteenth Dynasty the terraces of Hatshepsut's temple were embellished with incense trees planted in earth-filled pits to create a garden for Amun's promenades. Buried irrigation pipes supplied water to sustain the plants, and priests placed tributes to the god in the shade beneath the branches. The entire setting of the temple, from the axial-ramp approach to the termination of the processional way at a false door painted on the wall of the final rock-hewn sanctuary, is a masterly blending of architecture into a dramatic landscape including rugged cliff faces. Although Hatshepsut reigned and died peacefully, her successors did

**1.31** Upper colonnade (detail), Hatshepsut's mortuary temple, Deir-el-Bahari, Egypt, ca. 1473–1458 BCE.

Behind the rectangular piers are cylindrical columns with fluting that has led to their being called proto-Doric. Certainly they are evidence of Egyptian precedent for what in Greek hands would become an aspect of the orders of architecture.

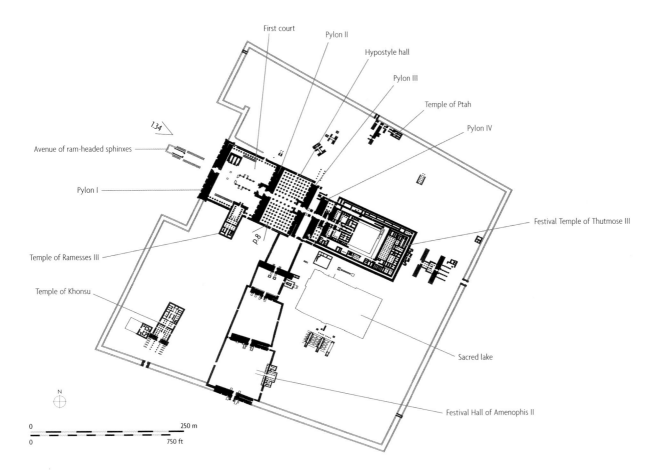

First court
Pylon II
Hypostyle hall
Pylon III
Temple of Ptah
Pylon IV

1.34

Avenue of ram-headed sphinxes

Pylon I

p.8

Temple of Ramesses III

Temple of Khonsu

Festival Temple of Thutmose III

Sacred lake

Festival Hall of Amenophis II

N

0              250 m
0              750 ft

**1.32** Plan of the Great Temple of Amun, Karnak, Egypt, begun ca. 1550 BCE.

This temple is celebrated more for its sheer size than for its architectural coherence. Dedicated to the sun god Amun, whose priesthood was powerful during the New Kingdom, the temple maintained a strong sense of axiality and monumental procession through all its additions.

everything possible to eradicate her memory, erasing her name from inscriptions, smashing almost all of her sculptural representations, and desecrating the burial site of Senmut.

In the course of the Eighteenth Dynasty, temple complexes built to honor both gods and pharaohs became more extensive and elaborate, aided by the establishment of Amun as the main "state" god and the increased power and influence of his priesthood. Successive rulers would add new portions or renovate older temples, creating designs whose chief attribute was overbearing grandeur, not coherence or esthetic delight. The temple at Karnak, across the Nile from Deir-el-Bahari, is an example of this process (Fig. 1.32). Begun about 1550 BCE, it was enlarged by Thutmose I, enriched by obelisks given by his daughter, Hatshepsut, and again expanded with a hypostyle jubilee festival hall constructed by Thutmose III for his own glorification. Yet another hypostyle hall, the largest of all, was built by Ramesses II.

Hypostyle halls are sizeable chambers created by rows of large columns placed closely together. The tight spacing was necessary to support the stone lintels of the roof, while the large column diameter reflected the substantial height of the stone cylinders. The net effect was a dimly lit interior without a sense of spatial expanse. Daylight admitted through slits in the stone clerestory grilles filtered through the incense smoke and the upper volume of the hypostyle columns to create a sense of mystery, the desired effect for religious ritual (see page 8). The temple was the habitation of the god, who was sheltered, clothed, and fed by the priests, by now a powerful and largely hereditary group. Each day the priests performed purification rites in the sacred lake within the temple precinct, dressed the statue of the deity in rich garments, and presented it offerings at the evening ritual. They carried small statues in processions, and placed others in the sun for rejuvenation in special festivals, such as those marking the beginning of the New Year. Monumental masonry entrance gates or **pylons** (Fig. 1.33) lined processional routes to represent the eastern mountains of Egypt through which the divine early-morning sunlight emanated. Despite their rambling plans and numerous additions, New-Kingdom temples maintained axial circulation spaces for the penetration of solar rays and

**1.33** Pylon gateway, Temple of Edfu, Egypt, 237–57 BCE.

While this pylon dates from the Ptolomaic period after Alexander the Great conquered Egypt, it is similar in form and purpose to those at Karnak. Such a spatial threshold signified the increasing sacredness of the space beyond. The four vertical slots once held obelisks.

**1.34** First court, Great Temple of Amun, Karnak, Egypt, begun ca. 1550 BCE.

Massive columns and colossal statues of Ramesses II define the axial path to the second pylon gate, built by Sethos I (1306–1290). Beyond is the Hypostyle Hall illustrated on page 8.

the movement of priestly processions (Fig. 1.34). The pylon gates were not only symbols of the entrance through which the sun was reborn each day, but also of the gates to the underworld through which the eternal spirit must pass.

Five generations after Hatshepsut, the pharaoh Amenophis IV (1353–1335 BCE) made a major break with Egyptian religious tradition by disavowing the multitudes of deities and instituting a monotheistic religion devoted to the sun disc Aten. Changing his name to Akhenaten, which means "all is well with Aten," Amenophis abandoned the old capital at Thebes about 1350 BCE to establish a new capital 300 miles to the north at Akhetaten (the modern Tell-el-Amarna). Judging from incomplete excavations of its ruins, Akhetaten was a linear town nearly seven miles long, bounded on the west by the Nile and on the east by mountains, and lacking a consistent overall plan. Transportation was facilitated by the

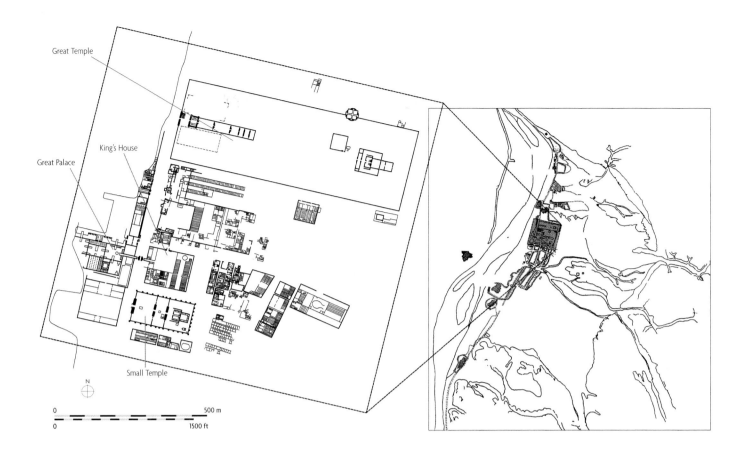

**1.35** Plan of the central section, Akhetaten (Tell-el-Amarna), Egypt, ca. 1350 BCE.

This was the new capital city of the pharaoh Akhenaten, located away from traditional religious centers in an effort to break the power of the established Egyptian priesthood. Rites for the sun disc Aten were celebrated in temples containing large open courtyards, lit directly by the sun's beneficent rays.

waterway, and a river road linked the various residential sections (Fig. 1.35). Temples had altars set in open court-yards, and there were no segregated areas for the priest-class. Private houses of the wealthy were commodious, walled off from public view, with rooms grouped around open courts with tree-planted gardens. Thick mud-brick walls moderated the extremes of heat and cold. No wall surrounded the city, protection being provided by free-standing guardhouses.

## CONCLUSIONS ABOUT ARCHITECTURAL IDEAS

Throughout this chapter, you have seen certain funda-mental architectural ideas appear that will be consistently used during every era in every geographical location covered by this text. These ideas have to do with such issues as demarcation, orientation, sequential movement, and surface articulation. A site like Newgrange encom-passes all of these, as it marks a significant spot, is aligned

with cosmic events, involves a path (in this case from profane to sacred space), and includes ornament. The zig-gurats and pyramid complexes exploited open terrain where the horizon was inescapable. Stepped, then true pyramids became manmade vertical foils for the natural horizontal, and in Egypt the pyramids were eventually superseded as vertical markers by the obelisk. Within both the ziggurat and pyramid environments, participants moved along an axis, toward a terminus, with architectural incidents like gateways providing a rhythm and signaling changes in spatial significance. The principles remained the same at both Middle and New Kingdom funerary com-plexes, where giant columns emerged as interior architec-tural features. While the pyramids exhibit a monolithic skin, the surfaces of ziggurats were articulated by means of brick bands and polychromatic glazes. At the funerary temple complexes of Mentuhotep and Hatshepsut, wall articulation evolved to the level of proto-columns, and columns will be the principal elements in the classical architectural language of the ancient Greeks and Romans discussed in coming chapters.

# CHAPTER 2

# THE GREEK WORLD

"Surely then," wrote the Greek philosopher Plato in *The Republic* (360 BCE), "to him who has an eye to see, there can be no fairer spectacle than that of a man who combines the possession of moral beauty in his soul with outward beauty of form, corresponding and harmonizing with the former, because the same great pattern enters into both." Plato was expressing a commonly held view in ancient Greece: that inward conditions could be expressed through outward appearances and so that moral and ethical matters were intrinsically related to art.

A fundamental means by which the Greeks attempted to communicate this unified view of the world was through proportional relationships. This effort is illustrated by a perhaps apocryphal story involving the Greek mathematician Pythagoras. As the story goes, he was walking past a blacksmith shop as the sounds of hammer to metal came from within. Listening to the tonalities and atonalities, he posed a question: could musical harmonies somehow have a mathematical basis? In order to form an answer, he experimented with the strings of a lyre and discovered that pleasing combinations resulted when two strings with their lengths related by simple ratios, such as 1:1, 1:2, 2:3, 3:4, and 4:5, were simultaneously struck. Here, in the mind of a mathematician, was a glimpse into the very ordering of the cosmos, and it was a short step from audible musical harmonies to dimensions and their ratios or proportions in the visual world.

While we may not accept this condition as an absolute today, we can first say without doubt that beauty mattered to the ancient Greeks and that their culture reached a consensus about it; witness, for instance, the "family resemblance" of so much Greek sculpture. Second, by extending this notion to architecture, we can see that the outward beauty of a Greek building was largely derived from the dimensions of its parts and their relationships to one another. Third, we can appreciate that when proportional beauty was achieved, it yielded in the Greek mind a kind of microscopic view into the inner workings of the cosmos. Heady stuff! Fourth and finally, we can also observe that the Greeks extended such philosophical thinking to the workings of their society. If proper propor-

tioning applied to outer physical beauty, and it also applied to inner moral beauty, this meant that the proper behavior of a Greek citizen (a freeborn male) demanded proper proportioning (or perhaps balance is the better term) in the actions of his life. That is, the good citizen was certainly not to become one of those specialists (like a stonemason or even an architect) made possible by urbanization, but was to participate fully and proportionally in the life of the **polis**, or city-state.

And so we can go full circle. The health of the polis demanded balanced lives from its citizens; this balanced life was encoded into the very fabric of ancient Greek temples through proper mathematical proportions and, in turn, these buildings reminded citizens of their proper moral and ethical behavior. The Greek temples became great billboards communicating and reinforcing commonly held values and reflecting the culture's greatest accomplishments and highest aspirations. With this in mind, we can begin our study of Greek architecture by turning first to those Aegean civilizations that preceded classical Greece.

## THE AEGEAN CULTURES

The Aegean Sea, bounded by the peninsula of Greece on the west, the mountains of Macedonia on the north, and the coast of Anatolia on the east, is studded with numerous islands. To the south is the island of Crete. By the beginning of the second millennium BCE (about the time of the Middle Kingdom in Egypt), the seafaring people of

North entrance of the palace, Knossos, Crete, ca. 1700–1380 BCE.

This section has been partially restored, including the unusual Minoan columns with bulbous capitals and downward tapering shafts.

### Chronology

| | |
|---|---|
| Minoan civilization | ca. 3000–1380 BCE |
| Bronze Age in the Aegean | ca. 2000–750 BCE |
| Mycenaean civilization | 1600–1100 BCE |
| Trojan War | ca. 1250 BCE |
| Iliad and Odyssey assume final form | 8th century BCE |
| Archaic Greek period | 700–500 BCE |
| Classical Greek period | 479–323 BCE |
| Pericles comes to power in Athens | 458 BCE |
| construction of the Parthenon | 448–432 BCE |
| life of Plato | ca. 427–347 BCE |
| conquests of Alexander the Great | 333–323 BCE |

this region had learned how to exploit natural resources—timber, stone, metallic ores, clay for pottery—to produce distinctive artifacts. With these, in addition to other agricultural products, they engaged in trade with Egypt and settlements along the eastern Mediterranean, where they constructed small fortified settlements and agricultural villages on islands and along the coast.

An examination of Aegean artifacts suggests strong influence from Mesopotamia as well as contact with Egypt. Early Cretans worshiped nature deities associated with mountains, trees, and animals (most notably snakes), as well as flowers, including lilies and poppies. Since there are no snakes on Crete, the snake cult appears to be an imported practice, probably derived from the Sumerian water god Ea, whose attributes included creativity, wisdom, magic, and slyness. Bull-baiting was a sport of the Sumerians, and bull-jumping seems to have become a ritual game in Crete. Lions were associated with royal symbolism in both Egypt and Mesopotamia, and lion images also came to be used in fortified royal settlements on the Greek mainland. Egyptian artifacts from the Eighteenth Dynasty have been retrieved from the harbor at Kairatos, Crete, and 1300 pieces of Aegean pottery dating from 1370 to 1350 BCE have been excavated from the rubbish heaps of Akhetaten.

Historians recognize two civilizations in the Aegean during the second millennium: that of the Minoans, based on Crete, and that of the Mycenaeans, established at several sites on the mainland of Greece. They share some artistic and cultural traits, including a reliance on trade with other communities in Egypt, Mesopotamia, Asia Minor, and Cyprus. Both produced luxury goods that were traded extensively around the eastern Mediterranean—Minoan envoys bearing characteristic pottery from Crete are included in Egyptian wall paintings from the reign of Queen Hatshepsut—and Mycenaean sites were involved in the Trojan War (ca. 1250 BCE), chronicled by Homer in the *Iliad*. Both civilizations contributed to the cultural patrimony of classical Greece.

## THE MINOANS

Most of what we know about the Minoan civilization comes from archaeologists, who are still making discoveries and reinterpreting older finds as a result of analysis with more sophisticated scientific tools. Not surprisingly, there is more than one theory related to the development and demise of the Minoans.

The civilization is named for Minos, which might be the name of an early king or simply the title (like pharaoh) that denoted a ruler. The later Greeks created legends associated with King Minos and his palace and **labyrinth** at Knossos, where the fearsome Minotaur, half-man and half-bull, that ate youths and maidens lived. Although numerous Minoan sites have been excavated on

Crete, Knossos remains the largest and best known. Four thousand years of Neolithic settlements lie under this Minoan site, which began in about 1900 BCE as a series of detached structures erected around a large rectangular court. When these were destroyed by a major earthquake in about 1700 BCE, the complex was rebuilt in a unified scheme on multiple levels, with ritual or ceremonial rooms, storage areas, and living accommodation connected by long corridors and staircases built around light-wells, open cores that admit sunlight to the lower levels. The courtyard continued as the primary element in the composition. Tablets inscribed in Linear A, a script that has still not been deciphered, appear in the archaeological record in about 1600 BCE. In about 1450 BCE, Knossos and all other Minoan palaces on Crete were destroyed, but Knossos alone was rebuilt. Traces of Mycenaean cultural influences, including writing in the script known as Linear B, an early form of Greek, are found in the rebuilt palace, suggesting either collusion or a forced alliance between Mycenaeans and the Cretans at Knossos. The final destruction of the site, this time by fire, came in about 1380 BCE.

Understanding the extensive ruins at Knossos is no easy task (Fig. 2.1). Sir Arthur Evans started excavations at the ceremonial center in 1900 CE. Archaeological investigation continues on the site today, and the associated town has yet to be unearthed. Evans was confident that he had found the palace of the legendary King Minos, but his chronology and efforts at reconstruction are now regarded as flawed and a recent assessment suggests that what Evans found was actually a sacred center. The function of the building may in fact have changed from a temple to a palace in its final years, but **frescoes** depicting priestesses and celebrants suggest the continuing centrality of religious practice. The charred remains of the final buildings present ambiguous evidence at best. While parts of the lower levels of the building were built in **ashlar** masonry, most of the upper floors were supported on walls built of rubble contained within squared timbers, wooden columns, and large wooden beams, the combustible portions of which were consumed in the conflagration. Evans relied on impressions of the **bases** and capitals where these touched stone to reconstruct the characteristic Minoan column, a downward-tapering shaft with a bulbous **torus** ring and **abacus** block capital (see page 34). (The columns on-site today are concrete.) On the basis of what he found, Evans also reconstructed major ceremonial rooms and several light-wells (Figs. 2.2–2.3).

Even after considerable study, however, the function of the whole complex is a matter of scholarly deliberation. Storerooms containing pottery jars for wine, oil, olives, and grain are unmistakable, but the function of other sections of the building, where several stages of construction can be detected, is still conjectural. The appearance and uses of the upper floors we cannot know, so photographs of the site today can only begin to suggest the grandeur that must have characterized the whole. When one realizes

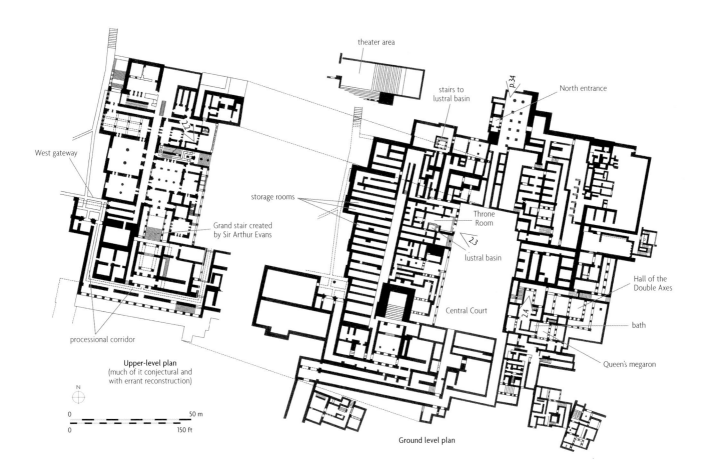

theater area

stairs to lustral basin

North entrance

p.34

West gateway

storage rooms

Throne Room

2.3

lustral basin

Central Court

Hall of the Double Axes

2.4

bath

Grand stair created by Sir Arthur Evans

Queen's megaron

processional corridor

**Upper-level plan**
(much of it conjectural and with errant reconstruction)

N

0 — 50 m
0 — 150 ft

Ground level plan

**2.1** Plan of the palace, Knossos, Crete, ca. 1700–1380 BCE.

The plan is organized around an open rectangular courtyard, off which major reception rooms open. As only the ground level of this three- or four-story building survived destruction, many aspects of its design are conjectural. The grand stair and associated axial sequence were an unfortunate Sir Arthur Evans creation. This portion of the palace is now being restored to its pre-Evans condition.

**2.2** Restored light-well, Knossos, Crete, ca. 1700–1380 BCE.

Located on the upper story, this light-well is located directly above the Throne Room (see Fig. 2.3). The fresco shown here is a restoration.

that the mainland Greeks of this period were living in far simpler buildings, it is possible that they preserved memories of the site in the legend of King Minos, using the term "labyrinth" to describe the large, rambling, and complicated plan that is the complex at Knossos. (Although the etymology of the word "labyrinth" is uncertain, the equivalent Egyptian term was applied to an enormous mortuary temple built during the Middle Kingdom for Amenemhet III [1844–1797 BCE] at Hawara.)

So far as we know, Knossos was unfortified. The

### 2.3 Throne Room, Knossos, Crete, ca. 1700–1380 BCE.

Named for the elaborate "throne," this room is provided with bench seating along the adjacent walls. Frescoes show griffins in lush foliage. Since a lustral basin adjoins this room, it is possible the space was used for religious ritual rather than royal audiences.

### 2.4 Reconstructed light-well staircase, Knossos, ca. 1700–1380 BCE.

As major ceremonial rooms were located partially under ground, stairs to reach them were constructed around open shafts to bring light and fresh air to lower levels. The original wooden columns and supporting beams were destroyed in the fire that consumed the palace about 1380 BCE.

palace/temple complex sat on a hill overlooking the harbor. Nearly four acres of buildings surround a central courtyard measuring 174 by 87 feet. In the three-story western wing, which contained ceremonial spaces, there is none of the axiality characteristic of Egyptian architecture. Instead, visitors to the palace during its final years entered through the west propylaea, or gateway, then followed a corridor lined with frescoes depicting priestesses and celebrants bearing offerings, before turning left twice to approach the courtyard from the south. On the left (west) wall near the north end of the courtyard was the entrance to the antechamber of a **lustral-basin** (depressed pool) sanctuary called the throne room because of an elaborate alabaster seat found there. On a lower level, along the southern edge of the throne room, was a lustral basin, one of several found in the complex that are thought to have been used in initiation rituals. This basin, which is only about eighteen inches deep, is concealed by a low wall and a screen of Minoan columns. Cult statues and votive offerings indicate that the site was sacred to a female deity linked to the earth and fertility. Long rows of underground storage rooms occupy the western side of this palace wing, dug into the slope of the hillside, with tall ceramic containers for olive oil, grain, and wine still in position.

Buildings on the eastern side of the courtyard have been interpreted as being residential, although some of the suites may have functioned as textile workshops and others were definitely used as storage areas. Some rooms here had views out over the valley below. The primary entrance to this section was made through a grand staircase approached from the middle side of the central court and illuminated by an open light-well. The stair led down to the Hall of the Double Axes, from which a corridor connected to the room Evans dubbed the Queen's **Megaron**, a pleasant space decorated with frescoes that include rosettes and flying dolphins. Smaller rooms behind the megaron contained a bathtub and a water closet (toilet) connected to the palace's drain system. Standards of water supply and drainage at the complex were exceptional for the time. Terracotta water pipes carried clean water through a series of settling tanks and siphons to supply baths, and sanitary sewers carried off waste water from basins and water closets, although the tub in the so-called "queen's apartments" had to be emptied by bailing.

At the northwest corner of the complex was the oldest and deepest (six feet) lustral basin, made accessible by a staircase with light-well (Fig. 2.4), and beyond this ran a series of broad steps, set into a slight rise in the ground and connected to the palace proper by a ceremonial road. This area has been labeled as a theater, although its precise use, as with so much else at Knossos, remains unclear. It seems that the large central courtyard provided the setting for theatrical ritual, including perhaps ceremonial games involving acrobatic feats by young men and women performed on running bulls. Frescoes preserved on some palace walls illustrate these amusements or rituals.

The naturalistic portrayal of the young men and women in these frescoes creates the impression that the Minoans were an energetic and cheerful people who took delight in their own beauty and that of the natural world. In contrast to the stiffness and formality of Egyptian art, frescoes and carvings at Minoan sites seem relaxed and open, emphasizing movement. Women held positions of high status, an unprecedented situation among contemporary civilizations. There is, however, a great deal that is still not clearly understood. The language(s) recorded in Minoan pictographs and on Linear A tablets remain undeciphered; the significance of the double-headed axe widely found in Minoan art is also a puzzle; and it is not known whether the appearance of Mycenaean culture in the final phase of Knossos came as a result of invasion or peaceful assimilation.

## THE MYCENAEANS

The Mycenaean civilization takes its name from Mycenae, the largest but not the only citadel in a trading society that appears to have been led by warrior-kings. Mycenaean settlements located on the mainland of Greece date back to about 1600 BCE. Graves from this period preserve a large number of golden objects as well as weapons of various sorts. Heinrich Schliemann, the nineteenth-century excavator of Mycenae, found golden masks, drinking vessels, and other treasure that convinced him he had found material related to the Trojan War. In fact, his finds predate the era of the Homeric tales by four centuries.

Mycenae reached its period of greatness after about 1450 BCE, perhaps invigorated by contact with the more sophisticated Minoan culture. In contrast to the seemingly undefended complex at Knossos, the citadel at Mycenae was built with a strong concern for defense. The city is situated on high ground, protected by mountains on the north and south and flanked by two ravines, allowing surveillance of a wide area down to the coast (Figs. 2.5–2.7). Fortifications erected in the fourteenth century BCE were expanded in about 1300 BCE to enclose the palace compound and an earlier grave circle. These walls are eighteen to twenty-four feet thick and up to forty feet high, constructed of boulders set in position with minimal shaping and no mortar, except for the sections immediately adjacent to the gates, where the stone has been cut into large blocks. The later Greeks thought this impressively scaled masonry to be the work of giants, the Cyclopes, hence the adjective **cyclopean** to describe its construction.

Principal entrance to Mycenae was made through the Lion Gate, which was added when the citadel was enlarged (Fig. 2.8). It was positioned so that the approaching visitor had to pass along an increasingly narrow passageway parallel to the enclosing wall, allowing defenders inside the settlement ample opportunity to attack hostile forces. The gateway is of considerable artistic interest. Single upright

**2.5** Ruins of Mycenae, ca. 1600–1250 BCE.

This fabled city was strategically situated to control major transportation routes in the vicinity. The enclosing wall is composed of roughly shaped boulders. Ruins of the palace can be seen at the high point of the site.

**2.6** Site plan of Mycenae, ca. 1600–1250 BCE.

This incomplete plan shows areas that have been excavated. Notice how the fortifications' walls extend to provide additional protection at the Lion Gate and the secondary gate on the north side. The palace megaron, one of the largest rooms in the city, is located at the center.

**2.7** Plan of Tiryns, ca. 1300 BCE.

The palace section is located on the southern end, where two megarons can be seen, and the northern extension enclosed the lower citadel. The entrance ramp along the eastern side passed through two fortified gates and between high walls that served as fighting platforms.

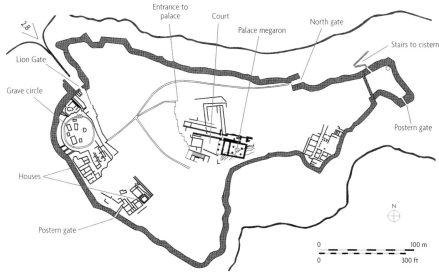

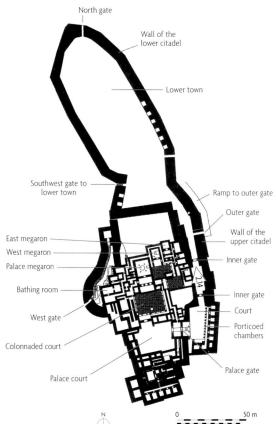

stones support a fourteen-ton lintel across the opening, above which is a corbeled arch. The space of the arch is filled by a triangular stone with relief sculpture of two lions with their forefeet on an altar bearing a column of the tree cult. (Mesopotamia had a tradition of venerating trees.) The lions' heads are missing; they were carved separately and attached with dowels, the holes for which are still visible. Even in its damaged state, however, the Lion Gate verifies contact by its creators with the Minoan world, for the column of the tree cult is unmistakably the same as the columns used at Knossos. To the north stands a second, smaller gate of the same age as the Lion Gate but without sculpture. There are also inconspicuous back entrances or postern gates built to provide access to a cistern and to provide outlets in case of emergency.

Beyond the Lion Gate are the remains of shaft graves where Schliemann uncovered so much golden treasure. Originally these lay outside the citadel walls, but when the fortress was enlarged the grave circle was carefully incorporated into the fortified area. The administrative and ceremonial spaces that lay beyond exist only as ruins, but from remaining foundations it appears that the palace at

Notice that the carved lion figures flank a column of the tapered type seen at Knossos. The use of guardian beasts associated with royalty links Mycenae with both Hittite and Egyptian traditions.

the highest elevation of the hill had many features derived from Crete, including a megaron as the major ceremonial space. Homer used this term to describe a large palace hall (hence Evans's use of the term at Knossos for the Queen's Megaron). In architectural usage, the word "megaron" is generally reserved to describe a simple rectangular space (**domos**) having solid long walls without openings and an entrance in the center of one short side, generally with an attached anteroom (**prodomos**) preceded by a court (see Fig. 2.12). It is an elementary house form still employed in Mediterranean countries, and the precursor of the classical temple and it has even been used by twentieth-century architects including Le Corbusier in his Citrohan houses (see Fig. 15.50). At Mycenae, the palace megaron is the largest room, roughly forty feet square. Bases for the four columns that supported the roof are still visible, as is the central hearth. This part of the palace was built in part on fill, supported by a retaining wall, and there is still a splendid view out over the valley from the court in front of the megaron. To the north, a smaller room with a stuccoed pool has been identified as a bathing room which legend associates with the murder of Agamemnon on his triumphal return from Troy.

The citadel at Mycenae was surrounded by smaller settlements, perhaps comprised of extended family groups who lived in houses closely associated with the tombs of their ancestors. Nine of these tombs in circular form (tholoi) have been found in the neighborhood of

Mycenae: of these, the largest and best preserved is the **tholos** or beehive tomb commonly called the Treasury of Atreus (ca. 1330 BCE) (Figs. 2.9–2.11). It is a corbeled stone chamber rising forty-four feet in thirty-three horizontal courses from a circular plan forty-eight feet in

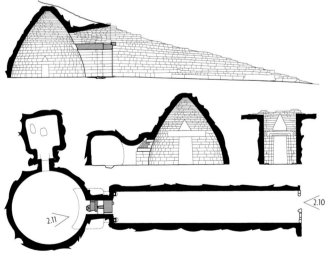

**2.9** Plan of and sections through the Treasury of Atreus, Mycenae, ca. 1330 BCE.

This corbeled tomb assumes the shape of a beehive. Its construction may be compared to the tomb at Er-Mané and the passage grave at Newgrange (see Figs. 1.2–1.3). The function of the side chamber is unknown, but it may have been used for burials.

2.10 Façade and dromos of the Treasury of Atreus, Mycenae, ca. 1330 BCE.

This axial view shows the stone-walled dromos and the triangular corbeled relieving arch that diverts weight away from the massive lintel stone. Ornamentation and paint that originally decorated the exterior have disappeared.

2.11 Interior of the Treasury of Atreus, Mycenae, ca. 1330 BCE.

Although the interior space is relatively large, it is also dark, deriving its light only from the open doorway and triangular transom of the corbeled arch above it. The even courses of ashlar, or shaped, stones can be compared to the irregular cyclopean stones used elsewhere at Mycenae.

diameter, with a small chamber to the right of the entrance. All the stonework, except for the stone-walled dromos, or entrance way, is covered by an earthen mound, whose weight adds stability to the dry masonry. The corbeled construction employed here is the same technique used by prehistoric megalith builders in northern Europe and by Egyptian masons as early as the Fourth Dynasty. Originally the entrance doorway was elaborately decorated, and there is evidence that the interior was embellished with bronze plates. Whatever the tholos contained in the way of burials or goods for the afterlife disappeared long ago.

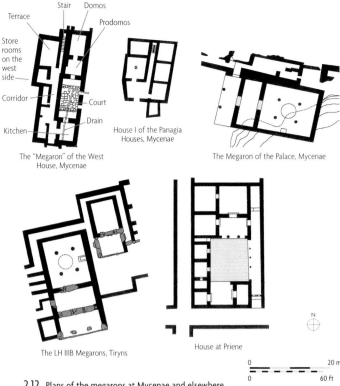

The "Megaron" of the West House, Mycenae

House I of the Panagia Houses, Mycenae

The Megaron of the Palace, Mycenae

The LH IIIB Megarons, Tiryns

House at Priene

0   20 m
0   60 ft

**2.12**   Plans of the megarons at Mycenae and elsewhere.

The West House, located just outside the walls at Mycenae, combines a courtyard porch, antechamber, and megaron. The palace megarons at Mycenae and Tiryns are considerably larger, both with remains of the four column bases that supported the roof around a central hearth.

Some of the houses outside the citadel have been excavated, and their remains provide an indication of what the dwellings of this period were like. Near to the Treasury of Atreus are the foundations of four closely grouped residences, of which the West House provides the easiest plan to interpret, as its main floor (rather than the basement) is preserved (Fig. 2.12). Entrance was made into a court, probably open to the sky, off which there is the three-room megaron sequence of porch, **vestibule**, and domos as the major spaces of the house. Off a corridor extending along the west side are a series of small rooms and a larger terrace that was probably unroofed. Stairs at the end of the corridor led to an upper floor whose layout cannot be determined, as the house was destroyed in antiquity by fire. The roof was probably flat, and both it and the upper story were framed in wood, which accounts for the survival of only the rubble stone foundations. Except for the court area, which was paved with stone, all the floors were of clay. A large drain extends across the court and exits under the foundation of the east wall, while a lesser drain is located in the megaron's domos. The use of the small rooms off the corridor has been determined from pottery and clay tablets found in them: all were storerooms, except for the chamber directly off the court, which had both a hearth and drain and was probably the kitchen. It is surmised that the house belonged to wealthier persons engaged in the manufacture of scented oils, for which Mycenae was famous. While not all Mycenaean houses had megaron layouts, the form is commonly enough

encountered for the West House to be considered a typical design.

A megaron layout on a grand scale is found in the palace at Tiryns, where the citadel sits atop a limestone ridge protected by a massive wall of cyclopean masonry that dates to the fourteenth century BCE (see Fig. 2.7). After a fire destroyed the citadel in ca. 1300 BCE, the whole was rebuilt to its present outline, including enclosure of the lower citadel with a twenty-five-foot-thick wall. An earthquake and fire in the mid-thirteenth century BCE damaged the complex, leading to the construction of the buildings whose remains are visible today. The surviving walls around the upper citadel vary from sixteen to fifty-seven feet in thickness. Like Mycenae, the citadel at Tiryns had several postern gates through which people inside could slip out unobtrusively. Corbeled galleries built into the thickness of the walls on the southeast side are handsome examples of such masonry construction (Fig. 2.13).

**2.13**   Corbeled gallery, Tiryns, ca. 1300 BCE.

These passages, built within the thickness of the fortified perimeter walls, provided access to guard chambers or postern exits for emergency use.

**2.14** Inner gate at Tiryns, ca. 1300 BCE.
This view shows the imposts of one gateway. Although the portal's gates are now gone, their positions can be seen in the cyclopean masonry. Attackers who made it this far would have been at the mercy of Mycenaean soldiers above and on both sides of them.

The approach to Tiryns has a more strongly defensive design than the entrance to Mycenae. An almost single-file passage beside and then between the walls made would-be attackers vulnerable well before they reached the first of two inner gates (for which the portals are gone) (Fig. 2.14). Beyond the second gate was a court bounded by porticoed chambers corbeled into the mass of the wall. These face the relatively narrow palace gate that opens into a palace court which connects on the north to a colonnaded court then to the palace megaron of porch, antechamber, and domos (see Fig. 2.12). As at Mycenae, four column bases surround the substantial central hearth, indicating the location of the roof and its opening to let out smoke. Fragments of wall paintings depicting processions of women and the hunting of boars were found in the excavations. A smaller megaron located to the east has an outer and inner court preceding the domos. Tiryns was again devastated by an earthquake in about 1200 BCE.

Between 1200 and 1100 BCE, Mycenaean settlements declined, perhaps in the face of invasions by nomadic peoples from the east, the Dorians and the Ionians, pushing down into the peninsula of Greece. The invaders used mounted cavalry with iron weapons that may have enabled them to defeat the Mycenaeans who had only bronze armory. Several centuries of cultural obscurity followed, during which the invading tribes settled down, mastered the art of writing, and assimilated certain aspects of Mycenaean culture and mythology as their own. Out of the confusion of this "dark age" rose the brilliance of Classical Greece.

## GREECE: THE ARCHAIC PERIOD

During the "dark age," population on the Greek peninsula began to exceed the land's limited agricultural possibilities, where only relatively narrow strips along the coast and in the river valleys could be productively farmed. Seeking additional farmland, as well as looking for metal ores and new trading opportunities, the city-states began a program of colonization, establishing new towns around the eastern Mediterranean in Asia Minor, Sicily, southern Italy, and North Africa. These colonial settlements were laid out in an orderly fashion, generally in elongated rectangular blocks grouped around the market and temples at the center of the city. There were public facilities for recreation and entertainment, and a protective wall surrounded the whole colony.

In addition to grid-plan towns, the major contribution to architectural history made by Greek architects and builders during the Archaic period (ca. 700–500 BCE) was the temple, which originated as a home for the gods and was based on the design of the Mycenaean megaron so that its plan consists of a rear room, or **opisthodomos**, then a **naos**, or **cella**, then a front porch, or **pronaos**. Judging from small surviving clay models, the early temples were simple one-room structures, built to accommodate a statue of the deity. They had a covered portico or porch at the entrance; walls were made of mud-brick, and the sloping roof was made of thatch. In the eighth century BCE, the small Temple of Artemis at Ephesus was constructed with wooden columns surrounding the temple chamber (**peripteral columns**), giving it additional distinction and a strong sculptural quality. The Temple of Hera at Olympia (ca. 600–590 BCE) continues this same idea at a larger scale (Fig. 2.15). Here the original wooden columns were replaced with stone, perhaps to provide better support for fired-clay roof tiles that were significantly heavier than thatch. The transition to stone construction appears to have been a gradual process, doubtless influenced by Egyptian precedent and technology. Stone column **shafts** in Greek architecture are characteristically fluted (incised vertically with concave grooves) in a manner similar to Hatshepsut's mortuary temple at

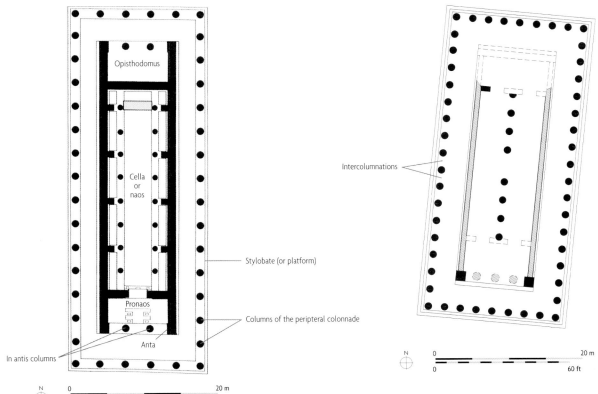

**2.15** Plan of the Temple of Hera, Olympia, ca. 600–590 BCE.

The original wooden columns of this early Greek temple were rebuilt in stone, perhaps to provide better support for heavier roof tiles that replaced thatch.

**2.16** Plan of the Temple of Hera, Paestum, ca. 550 BCE.

This temple presents one of the earliest examples of the Doric order. It is unusual in having an odd number of columns across the short side, placing a column in the center where one would expect an intercolumnar space for central, axial entry.

**2.17** Plan of the Temple of Apollo Epicurius, Bassai, ca. 430 BCE.

All three of the Greek orders were used here. Doric columns formed the external colonnade; Ionic columns were partially attached to the cella wall; and a single Corinthian column was placed on the central longitudinal axis. Light shone on the cult statue from an opening in the east wall.

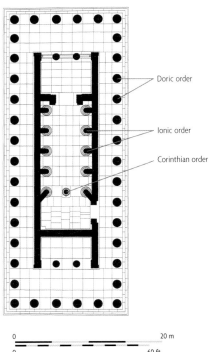

Deir-el-Bahari. The arrangement at the Temple of Hera includes two **in antis columns**, or columns in the plane of the front and rear walls and between **antae**, or wall thickenings, at the front and rear, and peripteral columns. The Greeks also developed a highly stylized treatment for **bases**, capitals, and the supported members, the **entablature**. In the sixteenth century CE these assemblies were termed the **orders** of architecture, the term by which we know them today, and became the basis for the **classical language of architecture**. Vitruvius, the Roman architect whose first-century BCE treatise was based in part on earlier now-lost Greek texts, names three such orders: the Doric, the sturdiest, was based on the proportions of a man (Fig. 2.16); the **Ionic** was lighter in character to reflect the proportions of a woman; and the **Corinthian**, slenderest of all, had a highly decorated capital to suggest the form and proportions of a young maiden. The Doric originated on the mainland of Greece, while the Ionic developed on the islands of the Aegean and the coast of Asia Minor. The Corinthian order only appeared later (Fig. 2.17).

Each order has its own particular combination of elements. The Doric column has no base and has the simplest capital atop the fluted shaft; its entablature consists of a plain **architrave** and alternating **metopes** and **triglyphs** in the frieze, which is crowned with a **cornice** (Fig. 2.18).

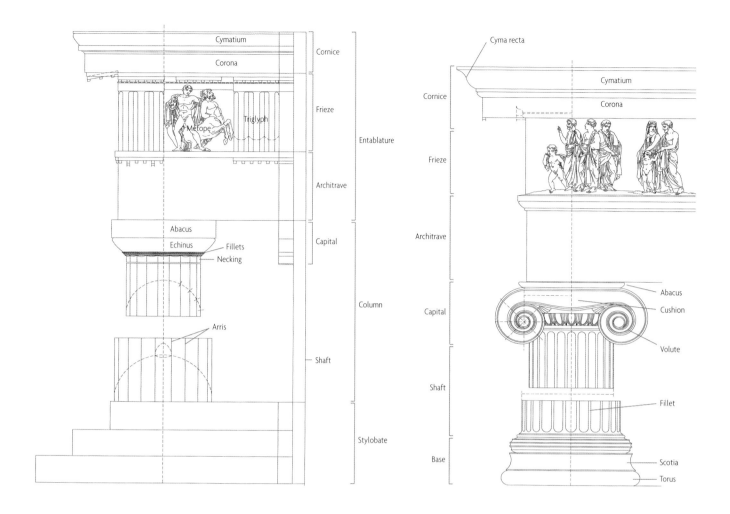

**2.18** The Doric order as found on the Parthenon, Athens.

The Doric's clear articulation of elements catches sunlight in an ever-changing play of shade and shadow across the carved surfaces. This may be one reason it has endured even to the present as an expressive part of Western architecture.

**2.19** The Ionic order as found on the north porch of the Erechtheion, Athens.

The Ionic's decorative flourishes may reflect influence from oriental sources. Although the entablature is simpler than the Doric's, its capitals and bases are subject to considerable artistic invention.

The Ionic has a base supporting its fluted column shaft and a capital with **volutes** (scrolls). Its entablature is also composed of an architrave and frieze. There is regional variation in the Ionic: along the coast of Asia Minor, the frieze is usually treated as three stepped bands of masonry, while on the mainland of Greece the frieze often features continuous sculpted relief (Fig. 2.19). A cornice, often with **dentils**, concludes the order. There were also general conventions regulating the proportions of the parts, the overall height, and the column spacing, which the ancient Greeks adjusted according to particular circumstances. Italian architects of the Renaissance 2000 years later codified the practice into a set of mathematical ratios based on the column's diameter at the base, but measurements of surviving temples provide no evidence that the Greeks ever reduced temple design to a single formula. The orders of architecture were thus at once specific and flexible, not a restriction for designers but an expressive medium that could be adapted to specific circumstances.

The origins of the architectural orders remain obscure. Vitruvius maintains that the orders were derived from earlier architecture in wood, a material that we know was once used for temples. In Doric temples, for example, triglyphs have been seen as echoing the protective panels applied to the ends of wooden roof beams, and metopes the infill panels between them. In its stone incarnation, the wooden end grain of the beams was stylized into vertical grooves, and the blank metope panel became a place for sculpture. Recent scholarship questions this derivation, proposing instead that the orders developed from a monumental decorative style using molded terracotta details, with no particular reference to structural features in wood. Even after the walls and columns were built in stone, wooden beams continued to be used for framing the roof, but these have not survived.

Builders of the early Doric temples made use of locally available material, most often limestone. This imposed structural limitations on the length of spans for lintels and the diameter of columns needed to support the heavy tile roof. Ionic temples used marble, a superior stone, and thus had a more slender profile. At Paestum in southern Italy, the Temple of Hera in the former colonial city of

**2.20** Temple of Hera at Paestum, ca. 550 BCE.

The end elevation consists of nine sturdy columns with entasis, capitals with flattened echinus profiles, and substantial abacus blocks, all supporting an entablature. Notice how shadows cast by fluting on the column shafts enhance the sense of volume.

short side of the temple, one of few times the Greeks would plan a temple with an odd number of columns on the entrance end. An even number places the central inter-columnar space at the central longitudinal entrance axis.

## GREECE: THE CLASSICAL PERIOD

During the Archaic period, the Persian Empire flourished in Mesopotamia, and Persian forces under Darius and Xerxes attacked Greek cities, both on the peninsula and around the Mediterranean. Ionian cities of Asia Minor had been under Persian domination from the middle of the sixth century. They revolted and were reconquered, and Darius attempted an invasion of the mainland, where his army was defeated in 490 BCE by the combined legions of Greek city-states at the battle of Marathon. In 480 the Persians attacked again, devastating the region around Athens and sacking the city itself, but the Greek navy scored a decisive victory over the Persian fleet near Salamis. In 479 the Persians were defeated on land and at sea, effectively ending the invasion threat to the peninsula.

A period of relative peace followed, and Athens emerged as the leading city on the mainland. To prevent further incursions by the Persians, it united with Ionian cities to form the Delian League. By 454 the League's trea-sury had been transferred from Delos to Athens, and a considerable portion of the money was controversially spent on rebuilding the ravaged Athenian Acropolis, which had been a military, political, and religious sanctu-ary since Mycenaean times (Figs. 2.21–2.23). The four buildings erected there after 479 ushered in the mature phase of Greek architecture known as the Classical period (479–323 BCE).

### THE PARTHENON, ATHENS

Largest and most famous of these temples was the Parthenon (448–432 BCE), dedicated to Athena Polias, patron goddess of the city (Fig. 2.24). An earlier temple, known as the Older Parthenon, had been begun in the general euphoria that followed the victory at Marathon in 490, but was still incomplete when the Persians destroyed it in 480. The new, peripteral temple, designed by the architects Iktinos and Kallikrates and built of the finest marble from Mount Pentelikos (Pentelic marble), was erected on the same site, with enlargements, and probably made use of column **drums** and metopes carved for the older temple. It is a Doric temple, eight columns wide by seventeen deep, but it incorporates Ionic attributes, including slender column proportions, a continuous frieze around the exterior of the cella wall, and actual use of the Ionic order in the western opisthodomos (back room) that housed the Delian League treasury, where four Ionic columns support the roof. The use of eight columns across the **gable** end, unusual in the Doric, has connec-

Poseidonia is one of the most substantial of surviving Archaic temples (Fig. 2.20). Built in about 550 BCE, it has sturdy Doric columns. The column shafts swell, then diminish, as they rise to the bulbous **echinus** molding that forms the capital. This change in column diameter is called **entasis**, and it was thought to be comparable to the muscular strength of an arm or leg, expressing visually the physical load sustained by the shaft. Each flute in the column has a precise edge, an **arris**, where the curved sec-tions of adjacent flutes intersect, and these arrises run absolutely straight up the shaft on every column. Above the echinus is a flat square block, the abacus, which pro-vides the transition from the cylindrical form of the column to the rectangular and linear architrave above. The logic of the Doric order is that alternate triglyphs are placed above columns, with metopes in between. This works well except at corners, where the established rhythm would make two half-metopes intersect. To avoid this problem, the final complete metope before the corner is generally elongated to allow the end triglyphs from both sides to meet at the corner. Columns near the corners may also be placed closer together—look at the rhythm of the frieze to see if this is the case. Joints between limestone blocks are easily seen at Paestum, and the limited span-ning capability of the stone is reflected in the close column spacing. On the interior, the central span across the sanctuary required additional support, so a line of columns extends through the middle of the cella. This cor-responds on the exterior to the nine columns across the

**2.21** The Acropolis, Athens, ca. 479 BCE, from the entrance side.

The remains of the Propylaea to the left and the tiny temple of Athena Nike in the center stand out in the foreground, with the gable end of the Parthenon visible on the right.

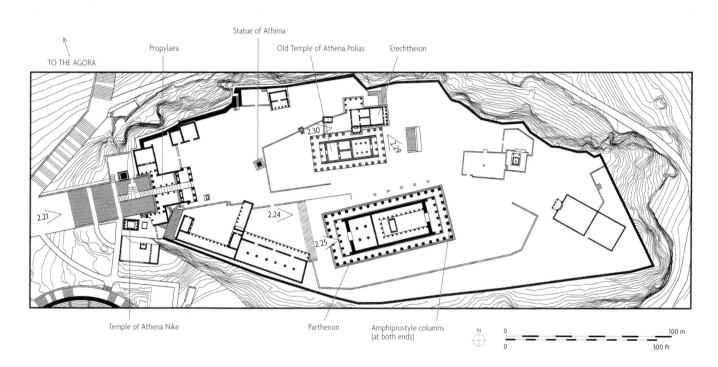

Statue of Athena
Propylaea
Old Temple of Athena Polias
Erechtheion
TO THE AGORA
2.30
2.29
2.21
2.24
2.25
Temple of Athena Nike
Parthenon
Amphiprostyle columns
(at both ends)

N

0           100 m
0           300 ft

**2.22** (above) site plan of the Acropolis, Athens, ca. 479 BCE.

The shaded temple plan in the center represents the foundations of an earlier temple to Athena Polias that was destroyed by the Persians. The Erechtheion's porch, with the Caryatid maidens, encroaches on these foundations, in a perpetual reminder of the destruction of the Persian War.

**2.23** View from below of the Acropolis, Athens, ca. 479 BCE.

The Parthenon temple sits on the highest ground and still dominates the modern city. Part of the Erechtheion is visible at the extreme left, while the Temple of Athena Nike stands at the far right side. In the right foreground remain the ruins of the ramps and stairs that led to the Propylaea. Notice in Fig. 2.22 how a viewer moving along the longitudinal axis of the Propylaea eventually sees the Parthenon at an angle and through a screen of columns.

tions to earlier Ionic temples (Fig. 2.25). Behind them at each end stand six **prostyle** columns, or columns in front of the east and west walls. Entasis, which was rather heavy-handed in the Temple of Hera at Paestum, was used subtly here to create a sense of repose. Minute adjustments in the horizontal and vertical lines of the structure enhance the perception of orthogonal geometry: the **stylobate** (the platform from which the columns rise) is actually convex upward; the columns incline imperceptibly away from the viewer; and the central axes of the columns are not vertical but lie along radii emanating from a point over 6800 feet above the ground. The columns are not the same diameter—the end ones are larger—nor are they equidistantly spaced: the corner ones are closer together. The architects made these slight variations in the column spacing and other details to avoid strict geometrical perfection and so to breathe life into their stone composition.

Sculpted figures adorned both the outside and the inside of the Parthenon. The two end **pediments** were filled with over-lifesize figures representing, on the east, the birth of Athena witnessed by the gods, and on the west, the contest between Athena and Poseidon for control of Athens. The metopes contained relief sculptures depicting struggles between Greeks and Amazons, Greeks and Trojans, gods and giants, and Lapiths (the people of Thessalonia) and centaurs (creatures combining the upper torsos of men with the bodies of horses), all commemorating the triumph of Greek civilization over barbarism.

**2.24** The Parthenon, Athens, 448–432 BCE.

This is how the Parthenon appears to someone leaving the Propylaea and looking southeast. As is the case with many Greek temples, the building is set so that the viewer looks up to it and sees two sides at once.

**2.25** The Parthenon, Athens, 448–432 BCE, seen from the west.

The Doric order used here is elongated to an almost Ionic slenderness. Not all optical refinements are readily discernible, but note the widening of the central intercolumnation relative to the slightly closer spacing of the end columns.

A continuous frieze ran around the outside of the cella walls behind the colonnade, portraying a sacred procession of Athenians bringing gifts to Athena, possibly as a thank offering for victory over the Persians or as a representation of the Panathenaic Festival held every four years. The procession shown on the frieze begins at the southwest corner and moves in both directions to meet again in the center of the east side, where Athena and other enthroned gods receive the offerings.

The sculptor Phidias served as artistic coordinator for the rebuilding of all monuments on the Acropolis, and he was responsible for the sculptural detail on the Parthenon, including the large cult statue of Athena housed in the cella. The latter was portrayed standing, with a Nike (goddess of victory) in her right hand and a shield resting at her left. The statue had a wooden armature finished with highly valued materials. Ivory was used for all exposed parts of Athena's body; her drapery, armor, and helmet were represented in gold; and precious stones were used for her eyes and for decorating her robes and armor.

The cella of the Parthenon was one of the largest interiors built in Classical Greece. It was intended to provide a proper setting for the enormous cult statue, which was the grandest of its time. Scholars differ as to whether the cella was completely roofed, as spanning the forty-foot width between the internal colonnades posed constructional challenges. Some speculate that the cella was open to the sky. A normally relatively dark interior would have been an appropriate location for the dramatic image of Athena, for the Parthenon was oriented so that the sun would penetrate the cella interior on the morning of Athena's birthday to shine on the great chryselephantine (gold and ivory) statue.

Time and circumstance have not been kind to the Parthenon. The statue of Athena had been broken up by the second century CE, probably for the value of its materials, and various adaptive reuses of the temple did little to preserve its best features. It became a Christian church, and then a **mosque** after the Turks occupied Greece. By 1687 it was being used for munitions storage, at which time it was bombarded by the Venetians. A direct hit caused an explosion that ripped out the cella wall and dislodged many sculptures. The victorious Venetians carried some off as trophies. Lord Elgin, the British ambassador to the Turkish Ottoman Empire from 1799 to 1803, negotiated for the remaining sculptures, which he had removed from the temple and shipped to England; his son later sold them to the British government. Known as the Elgin Marbles, they are now housed in London's British Museum, but the Greek government is eager to have them returned to a new building that has been constructed for them in Athens. Industrial air pollution from the Greek capital is now the biggest threat to the surviving bits of the Parthenon. A major restoration project on the Acropolis took place as part of the preparations for the 2004 Olympics in Athens.

## OTHER BUILDINGS ON THE ACROPOLIS

The remaining buildings on the Athenian Acropolis are disposed in a manner that at first seems almost random yet is actually carefully planned to respond to particular qualities of the site. The Acropolis is a plateau rising abruptly above the plain of the city. From the earliest times, the route of the Panathenaic Way from the civic and commercial center (the **Agora**) to the Acropolis traversed a

**2.26** Plans of the Propylaea (437 BCE) and Temple of Athena Nike (ca. 425 BCE), Athens.

The Propylaea defined the entrance to the Acropolis, while the small Temple of Athena Nike stood on the forward projection, visible at an angle to those entering the Acropolis. See Fig. 2.22 for a reconstruction view of this ensemble. Evolved from earlier fortified gateways, the Propylaea had become an architectural device for marking the transition from profane to sacred space and for controlling views toward the Erectheion and Parthenon.

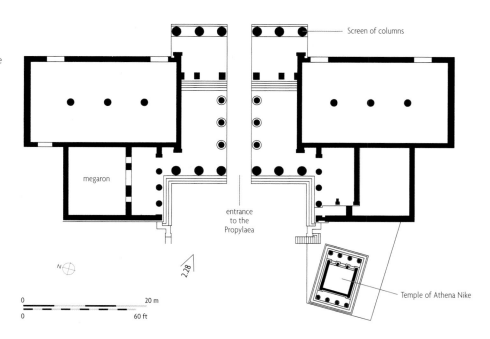

Screen of columns

megaron

entrance
to the
Propylaea

N

2.28

0        20 m
0        60 ft

Temple of Athena Nike

# CELEBRATING ATHENA'S BIRTHDAY

by David Lewis

his account of the Great Panathenaic procession (Fig. 2.27) is an excerpt from the fictional journal of an aristocratic Athenian woman. It is a description of the eighth and final day of the Great Panathenaic Festival in 424 BCE celebrating the birthday of Athena.

**2.27** Horsemen, Panathenaic Festival, Parthenon north frieze, Athens, 424 BCE. British Museum, London.

*28 Hekatombaion—the first month and our goddess Athena's birthday. The sea's wind blew warm even before the sun rose on this midsummer's day. Thousands gathered outside the city's walls. We wives and maidens dressed in purple robes and carried kannephoroi, bronze and silver trays filled with cakes, honeycombs and oak branches. Armed infantrymen, the victorious athletes, and the four men bearing the prize amphora were inside the Pompeion, while the young men who escort the 100 sacrificial cows, the equestrians (Fig. 2.27) and warriors on chariots, were next to the Dipylon Gate.*

*At the head of our procession were two maidens proudly bearing the sail-peplos of Athena, its breadth extending the whole width of the Sacred Way and facing the cavalcade, and the champion athlete with the ceremonial torch. The peplos's saffron and sea-purple linen threads glistened in the morning sun and torchlight while its silhouetted figures of Athena, Zeus, and other gods did battle with the giants. [Sail-peploi were commissioned every fourth year for the Great Panathenaic Festival and produced by professional male weavers. For the other three years, young daughters, arrephoroi, and wives of aristocratic citizens would spend months in the workshop, or*

*arrephorion, on the Acropolis, producing a human-sized robe.]*

*As we walked fifteen abreast on the Sacred Way through the cramped Kerameikos, the potters, who lived there, cheered proudly as the prize amphorai filled with sacred oils passed by. These men spent the last year sculpting and painting elaborate scenes on the 1400 trophies. Even from this outer precinct we could discern the Parthenon atop the Acropolis.*

*Continuing downhill, we entered the Agora at the Eridanos river bridge alongside the Poikile Stoa, with its jugglers and street musicians, and the Royal Stoa. We continued diagonally through the Agora, passing the Orchestra, where athletic events took place this week. As we approached the South Stoa, we began our ascent to the Acropolis, winding around its western rock face.*

*At the base of the ramp, we turned to face the Acropolis. Resplendently will it embrace our procession. Delicate Athena Nike to the south perched on her own askew promontory temenos [sacred precinct] while the Propylaea meets us head on. We marched up the ramp, for all of the polis to view. We stopped at the*

*Propylaea's blue step, allowing us to see to the north the Agora below, over our right shoulder the same battle between the gods and giants on the Athena Nike's east pediment, and ahead glimpses of the grand Athena Promachos statue beyond the Propylaea's doors. We sift through the gateway, animals and chariots led by the peplos through the central walkway, while those of us on foot walk to the outside of the Ionic columns and through the smaller doors.*

*Stepping over the east threshold and between the monumental Doric columns, we entered the temenos as the sun appeared over the mountains; Athena and Pericles's glorious pentelic temples glimmered. As we marched eastward on the Sacred Way along the north face of the Parthenon, the morning sun illuminated the cella frieze. As we proceeded to the east, so did the brightly colored figures as if telling us how and where to proceed. Like the frieze, our procession broke off into two groups; the men ushering the cows, and maidens bearing the kannephoroi walked to the Great Altar, while the remainder went to the open area to the east of the Parthenon.*

*As the two maidens, led by the high priestess, carried the peplos into the cella, we heard "IOIOIOIOIO," cries signaling the sacrifice of the first cow.*

**2.28** Hypothetical reconstruction of the entrance to the Acropolis, Athens.

Note the wide intercolumnation in the center of the Propylaea. A large exterior statue of Athena Promachos (no longer extant) dominated the view, balancing the Parthenon on the right (read about the statue's role in the Panathenaic procession in the essay on the previous page).

**2.29** The Erechtheion, Athens, ca. 421–407 BCE.

This view from the southeast shows the Ionic columns of the entry to Athena's shrine (right) and the porch displaying the Caryatid maidens (left). In the left foreground are the remains of the old temple of Athena Polias, destroyed by the Persians, on which the Caryatids gaze in perpetuity.

winding, stepped path up the western escarpment. (As most Greek temples face the east, this means the initial view one has is of the back sides of buildings.) In about 437 BCE construction began on an appropriately scaled entrance gateway, the Propylaea, designed by the architect Mnesikles. In a highly original design, Mnesikles created a dignified symmetrical entranceway amid asymmetries, accommodating a fragment of the original Mycenaean fortification wall and a gradient change through the depth of the building. His building marks the transition from the secular, or profane, world.

The Propylaea is essentially a Doric portico flanked by projecting wings (Figs. 2.26, 2.28). The central **intercolumniation** is wider than the rest, accommodating the processional way that passed through the axial colonnaded space into the sacred precinct of the Acropolis. This required two (rather than the usual one) unsupported triglyphs over the central space, as the architect had to take liberties with the exacting Doric. Three pairs of Ionic columns line the passageway, because the rising ground level and scale of the space dictated the choice of a more slender order. A second Doric portico terminated the Propylaea's central section. Its northern wing was a megaron, perhaps used as a picture gallery or banqueting hall, while on the south side there was a porch preceding the freestanding Temple of Athena Nike.

The overall layout of the Acropolis was designed to enhance the sense of procession as described in this chapter's essay. A visitor would first emerge from the eastern portico of the Propylaea to see the great statue of Athena Promachos close by, just left of center, balancing

**2.30** View from the south of the Erechtheion, Athens, ca. 421–407 BCE.

The entrance to Poseidon's shrine is made through the portico on the left. The height of its Ionic order (see drawn in Fig. 2.19) resulted from changes here in the site's terrain. This variation of the Ionic order became much admired by eighteenth-century neo-classical architects.

the majestic Parthenon, which rose farther back on the right-hand side. Even though the entrance to Greek temples is placed axially, it was the intention of the architects of the Acropolis that visitors should first view the Parthenon from below, at an angle where the west pediment and long north colonnade presented the essence of the temple's volume at a single glance. One reached the sanctuary entrance by traversing a rising pathway running the length of the Parthenon's north side, passing the exposed foundations of the old Temple of Athena Polias (destroyed by the Persians) on the left and turning south around the corner to ascend the steps into the eastern portico. Only after experiencing the totality of the temple exterior would the drama of the interior be unfolded (Fig. 2.28).

There are two other important temples on the Acropolis. The small Temple of Athena Nike (Athena Victorious) perches on rocks that were once the site of an ancient bastion (projecting fortification) on the edge of the hilltop forward of the Propylaea. Possibly designed as early as 448 BCE by Kallikrates but not constructed until the 420s, it is a simple sanctuary that housed a wooden image of Athena holding her helmet and a pomegranate, a symbol of fertility. Four Ionic columns create a portico before the eastern entrance, and an identical set is placed at the western (rear) side, which is the elevation seen clearly from below the Acropolis. Its refined detailing and small size made it a model for garden temples in the eighteenth century.

Across from the northern side of the Parthenon stands the more complex form of the Erechtheion, begun in ca. 421 and completed in 407 BCE to the designs of an unknown architect, on the site of the Mycenaean palace that was also regarded as the location of the contest between Athena and Poseidon (Figs. 2.29–2.30). Myth has it that in a competition to decide who should be named as patron of the city, Poseidon struck his trident, or three-pronged spear, on a rock and created a spring, while Athena brought forth an olive tree. The contest was judged in favor of Athena by Kekrops, the first legendary king of Athens, whose tomb is also commemorated here. Under the temple is the Sea of Erechtheus, a salt-water spring that made the sound of the sea and had a rock bearing the mark of Poseidon's trident. The Erechtheion knits together these assorted strands of site-specific history while deferring to the dominance of the Parthenon. The Ionic was chosen as the most suitable order for a temple built on two different levels to accommodate the uneven site. The eastern portico, distinguished by its slender Ionic columns, led to Athena's sanctuary, where an ancient wooden image of the goddess was housed, while the north porch, its stylobate ten feet lower, gave access to Poseidon's shrine through an even more elongated Ionic portico. Four Ionic columns, partially engaged in the wall, extend across the west façade to the south, where the roof of the splendid porch facing the Parthenon is supported by the six **Caryatid** maidens. Their pose is graceful, with one knee bent slightly and drapery revealing the form beneath. The base of the caryatid porch is the north foundation wall of the destroyed old Temple of Athena Polias, and the caryatids look out to the Parthenon across the ruins of the former temple, which were deliberately left exposed as an eternal reminder of the devastation wrought by the Persians. Although female figures had been used as columns (caryatids) before, the Roman architect Vitruvius explained their origins as follows:

*Caryae, a state in Peloponnesus, sided with the Persian enemies against Greece [Athens]; later the Greeks, having gloriously won their freedom by victory in the war, made common cause and declared war against the people of Caryae. They took the town, killed the men, abandoned the State to desolation, and carried off their wives into slavery, without permitting them, however, to lay aside the long robes and other marks of their rank as married women, so that they might be obliged not only to march in the triumph but to appear forever after as a type of slavery, burdened with the weight of their shame and so making atonement for their State. Hence, the architects of the time designed for public buildings statues of these women, placed so as to carry a load, in order that the sin and the punishment of the people of Caryae might be known and handed down even to posterity.*

We may find this punishment unjustified, given that it was the men of Caryae, not the women, who committed treachery, but it reminds us that even under Athenian democratic rule, women were no better than slaves when it came to legal and political rights.

As an example of the Ionic order, the elaborate detail of the Erechtheion has no equal in later Greek works, and the multiple complexities and scales that have been united here in a single temple are also exceptional in classical architecture. The exquisite decorative detail may well have influenced the later Corinthian order.

In all four of the Acropolis temples, one sees the architects fusing new constructions with elements from the site's history, be it the Persian Wars or the Mycenaean period. Evidence of Persian destruction was deliberately preserved in the ruins of the old Temple of Athena Polias, while historical references to the origins of the city are the very essence of the Erechtheion's design. Mycenaean fortifications were incorporated into one wall of the Propylaea, and the older Parthenon's base and architectural elements were reused for the existing building. The architects also sought to integrate the Doric architecture characteristic of Attica (the region around Athens) with Ionic elements (from Asia Minor) in an attempt to express the unity of the Delian League and Athens's ascendancy among the city-states of Greece.

When discussing the buildings of ancient Greece, it is important not only to imagine them complete, but also to remember that the Greeks never saw them as the bare stone structures we see today. Architectural and sculptural detail was generally painted in vibrant colors, perhaps with gilding, and plain walls may well have had murals. Traces of the original paint remain in protected crevices to confirm written accounts of the buildings' original appearances. If they were restored and repainted in authentic hues today, Greek temples might well appear surprising to our eyes.

## GREECE: THE HELLENISTIC PERIOD

Athens's moment of architectural glory, epitomized by the buildings on the Acropolis, came to an end in 431–404 BCE with the protracted and ultimately disastrous Peloponnesian War. Rival city-states quarreled with one another, weakening themselves in the process and opening the entire peninsula to opportunistic external powers. The eventual conqueror, Philip of Macedon, came from the north and effectively annexed all of Greece in 338 BCE. The close of the Classical age in Greece is generally associated with the reign of his son, known as Alexander the Great, but the influence of Greek culture continued to spread east owing to Alexander's conquests. From 336 to 323 BCE, his armies swept through much of the civilized world, including Asia Minor, Egypt, Mesopotamia, Persia, and parts of what today are Afghanistan, Pakistan, and northern India. Alexander died at the age of thirty-three, unable to consolidate his vast territories, but his enthusiasm for Greek heritage and his adoption of oriental aspects of the Persian court accelerated the assimilation and adaptation of Greek culture far beyond the Aegean. The term "Hellenistic" is applied to the art and architecture associated with the extended empire of Alexander and his successors, including the Seleucids, who ruled the area stretching from Anatolia to the Indus River, and the Ptolomies, who ruled in Egypt.

Hellenistic architecture differs from that of the Classical period by shifting away from staid traditions associated clearly with the region around Athens in favor of showier and freer interpretations as found along the western coast of Asia Minor. As the Doric order was intimately connected with the mainland of Greece, its use diminished in

**2.31** Temple of Apollo Epicurius, Bassai, ca. 450–425 BCE.

This is one of the few Greek temples on which one can look down, perhaps a function of the site conditions, perhaps a result of greater artistic freedom in the Hellenistic period.

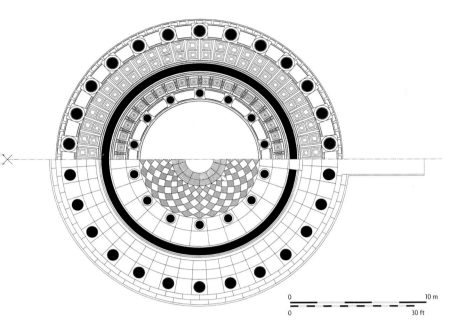

**2.33** Corinthian capital, tholos, Epidauros, ca. 360–330 BCE.

Lavish Corinthian capitals like this one combined Ionic volutes with the leaves of the acanthus plant, which is still commonly found in the Mediterranean area. Only Pentelic marble or another stone with so fine a grain allows for the carving of such fine detail.

**2.32** Floor plan (lower half) and reflected ceiling plan (upper half), tholos, Epidauros, ca. 360–330 BCE.

Parts of the beautifully detailed ceiling coffers have survived as indications of the exquisite Hellenistic detailing.

favor of the more ornate Ionic order, which reflected an oriental exuberance typical of the Ionian colonies. The meticulous sculptural ornamentation and coordination of column spacing required by the Doric were not part of either the Ionic or Corinthian orders, which overcame the Doric's limitations by eliminating the troublesome features. Their column flutes are jointed by flat **fillets** to simplify the carving, and the frieze runs continuously without metopes or triglyphs.

Even in the Classical period, the use of a particular order on the exterior of a building did not preclude the use of others within, as has already been seen in the Parthenon and the Propylaea. The Temple of Apollo Epicurius at Bassai (ca. 450–425 BCE) (Fig. 2.31), designed by Iktinos, employs all three orders: the Doric for the external colonnade, the Ionic for the cella side columns (which are connected to the cella wall by extended buttress-shaped piers), and the Corinthian for the single axial column placed at the end of the cella. A statue of Apollo was set adjacent to this column so that it faced to the east through an opening in the cella wall. Among Greek temples, this one is unusual for its orientation; the main entrance faces north, rather than east. The temple at Bassai is the first known use of the Corinthian order, and also marks the first time the Ionic was used for a cella interior. These forward-looking features are counterbalanced by some seemingly old-fashioned ones which must have been included for positive reasons, for the architect was thoroughly familiar with what was being built contemporaneously on the Athenian Acropolis. The temple's elongated plan and narrow cella have been explained as deliberate references to history (the cult of Apollo had long existed on the site, and there had been three predecessor temples here), and the earlier temples may also be the source of

the spur walls connected to the Ionic columns. It has been proposed that the single Corinthian column likewise made reference to the distant past, when wooden columns were sacred symbols of the gods. The temple may thus be interpreted as a fusion of historical references with innovative design.

The Corinthian order was employed on a substantial scale in the tholos at the Sanctuary of Asklepios at Epidauros (ca. 360–330 BCE), a circular building approximately seventy-two feet in diameter, known now from its foundations and reassembled fragments preserved on the site (Fig. 2.32). Epidauros was dedicated to the god Asklepios, the son of Apollo, and both gods were venerated here in a large complex dedicated to healing through exercise, diet, and medical care. The tholos is but a small part of a site that included a stadium, gymnasia, a theatre, altars, fountains and baths, temples, and accommodation for patients. Its external colonnade was composed of twenty-six Doric columns, and there were fourteen freestanding Corinthian columns in the inner circular colonnade fitted into a black-and-white rhomboidal flooring pattern. The ceiling had ornate coffers with floral decorations. An unused Corinthian capital found buried at the site shows the delicacy and grace achieved by Polykleitos, architect of the tholos (Fig. 2.33). The corner volutes, derived from Ionic models, are small, and their scroll form is complemented by the stylized curls of **acanthus** leaves that enrich the bell of the capital. How exactly this building was used is unknown. It has been suggested that its form at the upper story matches that of a shelter for a tomb (a **baldachin**) and that the circular corridors evident from the foundation remains were evocative of passages through the underworld to the tomb of Asklepios.

In a better state of preservation is the Choragic Monument of Lysikrates (ca. 335 BCE) in Athens (Fig. 2.34). This small cylindrical structure was erected to display the prize awarded to Lysikrates for the entry he sponsored in a

**2.34** Elevation of the Choragic Monument of Lysikrates, Athens, ca. 335 BCE.

Engaged Corinthian columns ornament this small structure. William Strickland, a nineteenth-century Greek Revival architect in America, used this monument in his design for the Tennessee State Capitol.

**2.35** Reconstruction view of the Sanctuary of Asklepios, Kos, ca. 300–150 BCE.

Compare the axial, hierarchical organization of this Hellenistic shrine with the angular, non-hierarchical, Hellenic distribution of buildings on the Athenian Acropolis, as seen in Fig. 2.22. While the results are dramatically different, the means for achieving them were much the same: column files, cella walls, and strategic topographic change.

thespian contest honoring the god Dionysos. Here the Corinthian order is used on the exterior of a building, with six columns being built into the cylinder so that they appear as half-columns. (Recall that the Erechtheion likewise had engaged columns on its western elevation. The decorative possibilities of the orders as wall articulation were exploited in Hellenistic and later Roman work.) The frieze they support illustrates the mythological story of Dionysos and the pirates of the Tyrrhenian Sea. There is no accessible interior space. Nineteenth-century American architects adapted the form of the Choragic Monument for quite varied purposes. It inspired the form of the Philadelphia Exchange and the **cupola** atop the Tennessee State Capitol in Nashville, both by William Strickland.

The introduction of multiple-building ensembles like the Sanctuary of Asklepios (ca.300–150 BCE), arranged on the sloping ground of the Aegean Island of Kos (Fig. 2.35), illustrates the change in design attitudes among Hellenistic architects. With its ascending terraces and files of columns, Kos's layout brings to mind the Egyptian mortuary complexes of Queen Hatshepsut (see Fig. 1.29) and Mentuhotep (see Fig. 1.27). At Kos, however, there is something new: a conscious definition of exterior space using **stoas** bent at right angles to become enveloping arms. Within these envelopments, temple buildings were then embedded (as at the lower-level entry), set in axial relationships with one another (as on the middle level), and treated as freestanding objects within an architectural precinct (as on the upper level). A single, central axis of movement runs through the embedded portico and up consciously aligned stairs to terminate at the freestanding Temple of Asklepios on the highest ground. Some scholars have associated the hierarchical rigidity of this type of planning with the change from Classical democracy to the autocracy of Alexander's empire.

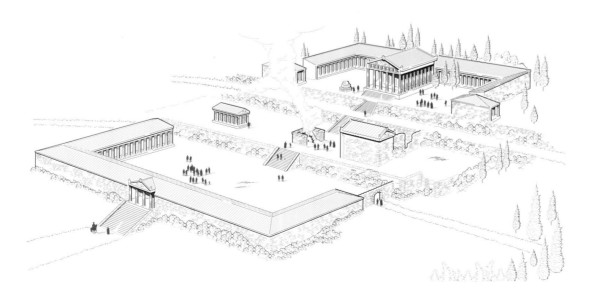

**2.36** Theater, Epidauros, 350–2nd century BCE.

This shows the rows of seating. The original skene or backdrop building shown in the plan is no longer extant.

During the Hellenistic period, permanent buildings for theatrical performances were constructed in many of the outlying cities. Many of these elegant designs postdate the plays by Euripides, Sophocles, and Aristophanes that were originally presented from carts to audiences grouped on wooden benches in public open areas. Fifth-century Athenians constructed the Theater of Dionysos on the south side of the Acropolis hill, using the rising embankment to provide support for a concentric seating focused on the circular **orchestra**, a flat area for dancing. Behind the orchestra was a backdrop structure, the **skene**, and the area directly in front, the **proskenion**, was a raised platform from which actors declaimed their lines. (Note how this terminology continues to be used today: the framing arch over the stage of today's theaters is known as the proscenium, while orchestra seats are those placed directly in

front of the stage.) Several doors set in the skene served as entrances and exits as needed in the drama, and actors spoke lines from the gods from the roof of the building.

Although the theater in Athens has been modified, surviving auditoria at Delphi, Dodona, Ephesus, Epidauros, Megalopolis, Pergamon, and Priene give a clear image of what Greek theaters originally looked like. The theater at Epidauros is exceptionally well preserved and beautifully sited in the landscape, looking out to distant hills (Figs. 2.36–2.37). Tradition assigns its design to Polykleitos, architect of the tholos, but not all scholars agree with this attribution. The theater was built in two stages, the lower 5000 seats in thirty-four tiers dating from 350 BCE, with the upper twenty-one tiers being added in the second

**2.37** Plan of the theater, Epidauros, 350–2nd century BCE.

Virtually every Greek city had its own theater that could accommodate a good portion of the population, as attending dramatic performances was encouraged to promote civic values.

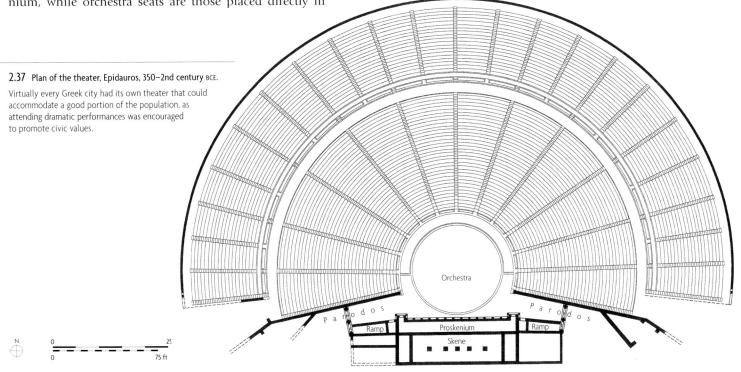

century BCE, extending the total capacity to about 14,000 seats. The ring of seats closest to the orchestra were provided with backs and used by dignitaries, while everyone else sat on continuous benches raised slightly above the row in front of them. An efficient system of radial and cross aisles provided circulation from entrances at multiple levels. Most remarkably, the acoustical design worked so well that words spoken in a normal voice from the orchestra projected intelligibly to all seats. The theater is still used for performances.

## GREEK CITY PLANNING
### THE ATHENIAN AGORA

We have seen how the spatial experience of buildings on the Acropolis in Athens affected the placement and design of temples on the site, so that what appears on plan to be a haphazard arrangement unfolds before the visitor as a logical sequence in an ordered and balanced universe. The static poise of a colonnaded temple is enhanced by the subtle arts of the site planner, who has used surprise and a changing perspective to reveal the full drama of the architectural forms. A similar spatial approach was taken in the layout of the Athenian Agora, the civic and commercial heart of the city, which developed around the ancient track of the Panathenaic Way entering the city from the northwest and leading to the Acropolis (Fig. 2.38). Development of the public structures in the Agora began in about 600 BCE, and by the end of the Archaic period its boundaries were defined. A group of civic buildings, including temples, a shrine to Zeus, and a senate house (**bouleterion**), had been built on the western side at the base of the Agora Hill (Kolonos Agoraios). The bouleterion was an ambitious project, built on a nearly square plan to accommodate the 500 senators who comprised the elected government of Athens. A columned porch led directly to the senate chamber, with seats in rows along three sides of the rectangular space. The roof was supported on the exterior walls and four intermediate columns. Another government building was the Royal Stoa, erected on the northwest corner beside the Panathenaic Way for the city's chief religious magistrate, who was responsible for official sacrifices, administration of the city's festivals, and adjudication of priestly disputes. The Royal Stoa was a small rectangular building with a colonnade and steps along the long side facing the Agora, the first of a type that would be constructed on a larger scale for various purposes in the Classical and later eras.

After the Persian Wars, when the Acropolis was being reconstructed with its famous temples, new works were undertaken as well in the Agora. On top of the hill to the west, the Hephaisteion, a temple to Hephaistos (god of the forge) and Athena (goddess of the arts), was constructed in about 449–444 BCE. This Doric temple, still remarkably intact, was enriched with relief sculpture and an elaborate ceiling of stone coffers. A gap in the buildings at the base of the hill allowed for the extension of the eastern axis of the temple across the Agora to the Stoa of Attalos. Within the Agora, war damage to the Royal Stoa was repaired and the building slightly enlarged, while new stoas were built. The Painted Stoa (so named because it displayed paintings of military triumphs, mythical and real, of the Athenians) had an external Doric colonnade and Ionic columns within. It was used for informal meetings (the Stoic philosophers were fond of meeting there and eventually took their name from it) as well as jury trials. The Stoa of Zeus replaced the earlier shrine and was used as an informal meeting place. The first South Stoa, whose small rooms behind a double colonnade were used for commercial activities and perhaps also for dining, was constructed adjacent to the Heliaia, which was probably the main law court. A new bouleterion was constructed ca. 415–406 BCE directly behind the existing building (which was renamed the Metroon to honor Rhea, mother of the gods of Olympus, and used for city archives). Its internal arrangements are not clear from the excavations, but archaeologists believe it had a curved configuration of seats like a theater. Adjacent was a circular building, the tholos, that was used for meals served to the fifty senators who happened to be on duty. The open spaces of the Agora were used both as a racetrack and as a setting for dramatic performances and dancing.

Building in the Athenian Agora continued after the conquests of Alexander the Great. In the Hellenistic period, some Classical buildings were modified, and new ones were constructed to create a more complete sense of spatial order and closure. The dominant Temple of Hephaistos and its axial approach remained. The old Metroon was replaced by a more elaborate building serving the same functions, with an external colonnade fronting onto the open civic space. The South Stoa was rebuilt on a shifted orientation, with an additional Middle Stoa extending parallel to it on what had originally been open land. Across the Panathenaic Way, which remained unchanged, the Stoa of Attalos (Fig. 2.39) was erected at right angles to the Middle Stoa, and its southern end worked with the eastern terminus of the Middle Stoa to establish a narrow point of entry, in contrast to the openness of the Agora beyond. In the colonnaded walkways of the stoas, one had a sense of shelter while at the same time being connected to the larger open space. The stoas were thoroughly urban buildings, providing space for merchants to trade in and inviting citizens to participate in the public life of the city, an important aspect of Greek society. The concept of a colonnaded or arcaded space containing shops and facing major public open spaces will reappear in later urban designs.

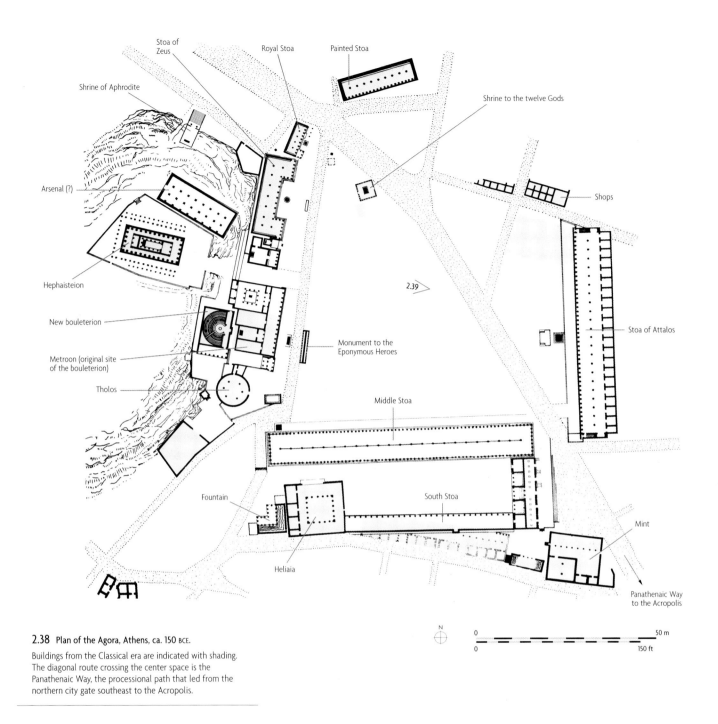

**2.38** Plan of the Agora, Athens, ca. 150 BCE.

Buildings from the Classical era are indicated with shading.
The diagonal route crossing the center space is the
Panathenaic Way, the processional path that led from the
northern city gate southeast to the Acropolis.

## HELLENISTIC CITIES

Greek city planning was not always as asymmetrical and
evolutionary in form as the Agora in Athens. The Greeks
were perfectly capable of producing regular, orthogonal
town plans and frequently employed them for colonial
cities, as may be seen at Paestum (Poseidonia), which had
a street pattern from the mid-seventh century BCE that
produced huge, elongated, rectangular blocks (Fig. 2.40).
While many cities grew organically over time, others were
rebuilt, often after suffering war damage, according to the
new, more regular town-planning principles. Such was the
case in the fifth and fourth centuries BCE, when a number
of towns were provided with grid blocks and carefully considered open spaces according to the theories of a fifth-
century pupil of Pythagoras, Hippodamus of Miletus, who
is often regarded as the father of city planning. This label
is misapplied if taken to mean that he "invented" the grid
plan, for orthogonal plans existed long before Hippodamus. More properly viewed, his contribution seems to
have involved consolidating and articulating the religious,
social, and commercial elements of the city center with
regular blocks of houses adjusted to fit the particular circumstances of the topography. Hippodamus's birthplace,
Miletus, a harbor town on the coast of Asia Minor, was in
its day the leading city of Ionia. After its destruction by the
Persians in 494 BCE, the city was rebuilt in the period following 479 BCE with a plan of rectangular residential
blocks and an orthogonal agora. Hippodamus's design

**2.39** Stoa of Attalos, Athens, 159–132 BCE (reconstructed 1952–56).

This building was contributed to the city by Attalos of Pergamon. In its reconstructed form, it and the Hephasteion are the only structures from antiquity remaining in the Athenian Agora. The column-file organization of the stoa form can be traced back to Egyptian complexes such as the temples of Queen Hatshepsut and Mentuhotep.

went beyond specifying the location of civic buildings, the layout of streets, and the positioning of open spaces, to encompass design of typical single-family houses for an estimated population of 15,000 to 20,000. Houses were consistently oriented with their major rooms opening to the south, and the megaron form already familiar from Mycenaean times was used again as the basic living unit of the house.

During the Hellenistic period, both architecture and city planning became more elaborate and theatrical, as can be seen in the design of Pergamon, another city in Asia

Minor that between 282 and 133 BCE aspired to imitate the glory that once emanated from Athens. It became the capital of the Attalid Dynasty, whose leaders took the title of king in part to celebrate their military victories over the Galatians (Celtic tribes). Originating as a hilltop fortress, Pergamon grew in terraced steps down from the summit, with level sites for buildings supported on well-engineered retaining walls and linked by monumental stairs. On such a precipitous site, a grid plan was out of the question; the road has switchbacks to minimize the slope. On the acropolis were temples, a distinguished library, the Sanctuary of Athena, and palaces, above a banked theater carved into the hillside that could seat 10,000 people. One of the most celebrated buildings at Pergamon was the Great Altar (ca. 181–159 BCE), dedicated to Zeus and Athena. The high

**2.40** Plan of Paestum (Poseidonia), 7th century BCE.

This Greek colonial city was laid out with elongated blocks on the orthogonal pattern. Across the center was the public sector, with commercial structures, government buildings, and temples, including the Temple of Hera (identifiable by its row of central columns in the lower right). The site was submerged by the sea during the Middle Ages, but is located again on dry land today.

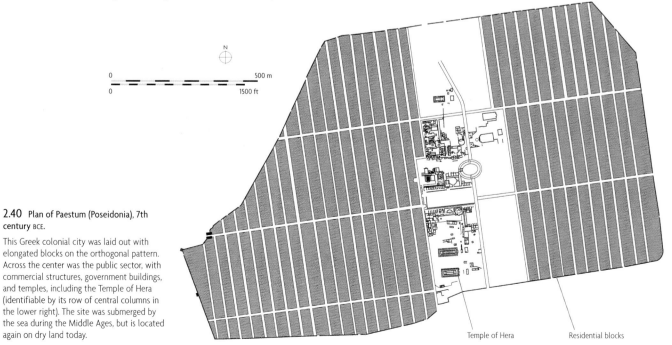

Temple of Hera          Residential blocks

**2.41** Great Altar of Zeus, Pergamon, ca. 181–159 BCE.

This has now been reconstructed in the Pergamon Museum in Berlin. This impressive shrine, originally set on a hillside above the city, features a dramatic frieze of large sculpted figures that contrasts with the serenity of the colonnade above.

plinth on which the altar stood became the location for a frieze over 300 feet in length and sculpted with scenes of battles between gods and giants, an obvious allusion to recent battles with the Celts (Fig. 2.41). Intertwined wings, arms, and writhing snake bodies create a dynamic composition: even the hair on the gods' heads and beards falls in animated coils. The highly dramatic frieze contrasts with the elegant colonnaded building above, and it also complements the equally dramatic site, an architectural tour de force that has little of the restraint and sublimated feeling that governed the design of the Athenian Acropolis.

## CONCLUSIONS ABOUT ARCHITECTURAL IDEAS

While archaeology on Minoan sites in Crete has not yet established a satisfactory picture of Minoan design thinking, evidence does suggest some kind of experientially based planning, or perceptual thinking, as opposed to abstract, geometric ordering, or conception thinking. The mainland Mycenaeans invented the megaron, with its two-spatial-unit plan of prodomos and domos. The megaron anticipated the Classical Greek temple plan, with its three spatial units: pronaos, naos or cella, and

opisthodomos. To these spaces, the later Greeks added various column configurations: in antis, prostyle and amphiprostyle, and peripteral, using them in isolation but more often in combination.

The impressive masonry of the Mycenaeans was succeeded by the exquisite stone craftsmanship of the ancient Greeks, and Pentelic marble made it possible for them to carve the fine detail required by the orders (Doric, Ionic, and Corinthian) that form the basis of the classical language of architecture. At the core of this language lies the ancient Greek system of arithmetic proportions. Encoded with societal values, temples like the Parthenon were meant to be "read," not just seen, as their sculptural programs explained the Athenian position in the world.

The approach to the Parthenon was, of course, along a route with constantly changing orientations, culminating in an oblique view of the freestanding temple through the column screen of the Propylaea. Such a fluid system of movement, comparable to Minoan designs, gave way in the Hellenistic period to geometric regularity, axiality, and rigorously organized building ensembles and environments, and this new type of planning would be appropriated by Republican Rome. In the nineteenth century, the classical language of ancient Greek architecture would reappear throughout Europe in the form of the Greek Revival, as discussed in Chapter 14.

# CHAPTER 3

# THE ARCHITECTURE OF ANCIENT INDIA AND SOUTHEAST ASIA

The prehistory of India is largely an account of settlements along the Indus Valley and its associated coastal plain, now part of the modern countries of Pakistan and Afghanistan, where various regional cultures flourished from ca. 3000 BCE. Its mature phase lasted about 1000 years, starting in about 2700 BCE, when Harappa (in the northeast portion of the valley) and Mohenjo-Daro (on the Indus, nearly 400 miles to the southwest) seem to have functioned as the leading cities of an extensive region. Many details about the culture remain sketchy, for there is no agreement among scholars concerning the decipherment of the Harappan script, which has over 400 characters; in any case, much of the surviving writing is found on personal seals, which hold little promise of revealing much about the civilization. The basis of the economy was agriculture, facilitated by irrigation and periodic flooding of the rivers. There was also commerce, both internal and with settlements in southern Arabia and Mesopotamia, as a result of which some external cultural influences were adopted. Literate civilization in the Indus Valley was later in developing and of shorter duration than in Mesopotamia or Egypt, but the region over which it exercised control was larger. Over 1000 Harappan sites have been identified across an area of nearly 500,000 square miles.

Archaeology reveals that Harappan settlements were laid out according to an orderly grid oriented to the cardinal directions. Orthogonal town plans are generally an indication of a high level of central governmental control, and that seems to have been the case in Harappan culture. Buildings were durable, being constructed of fired bricks of uniform size throughout the region, and houses were provided with underground drains connected to a well-planned sewer system. As the cities were built on plains beside the river, flooding seems to have been a constant menace. Mohenjo-Daro (Figs. 3.1–3.2) was repaired at least nine times after damaging floods. Cities accordingly featured a walled, terraced citadel on high ground, provided with ceremonial buildings, large public storehouses for grain, and mills which could be used in time of peril to

shelter and feed the population. Rising forty feet above the plain, Mohenjo-Daro's citadel also had a great stepped bath measuring thirty by forty feet that is thought to have served some ritual function. However, there are no clearly identified large shrines or temples like those found in Egypt or Mesopotamia. Small figurines suggest a reverence for trees and animals, a mother goddess cult, and a male god that may be the precursor of the later Hindu deity Shiva. Water and fire may have been associated with rituals that are still not understood.

In contrast to both Mesopotamia and Egypt, the Indus settlements seem to have been relatively egalitarian societies. There are neither palaces nor royal tombs, and no great temple complexes to indicate a concentration of power and wealth. Excavated residential areas of Mohenjo-Daro, the best-preserved and most extensive city, estimated to have had a population of 40,000, show tightly packed houses organized around internal courtyards that were open to the sky for light and air. The plans vary, but all houses presented virtually blank façades to the street, as external openings were set high in the perimeter walls. Rooms were small, perhaps because there was a scarcity of wood to serve as beams for second floors and roof framing. While the buildings themselves do not seem elegant in terms of architectural refinement, the clear urban layout, careful provision of a water supply through wells, and drainage and sewer systems are without parallel at the time and are marks of an efficient, highly organized society.

Reasons for the rapid decline of Harappan culture by about 1700 BCE are disputed, but natural factors (changes in river courses, failure of irrigation systems, earthquakes) and incursions by northern ethnic groups appear to have

Kandariya Mahadeva Temple, Khajuraho, 1025–50.

This view shows the plinth and entrance terrace in the foreground. From this angle, the orderly progression of roof masses simulates a mountain range.

## Chronology

| | |
|---|---|
| beginning of cultures in the Indus Valley | 3000 BCE |
| occupation of Mohenjo-Daro | 2400–2000 BCE |
| composition of the Vedas | 1500–900 BCE |
| life of Siddhartha Gautama (Buddha) | 563–483 BCE |
| Alexander the Great in the Indus Valley | 326 BCE |
| construction of the Great Stupa, Sanchi | begun 250 BCE |
| sculpting of the Great Buddha, Bamiyan | 7th century CE |
| construction of Ankhor Wat | begun ca. 1120 CE |

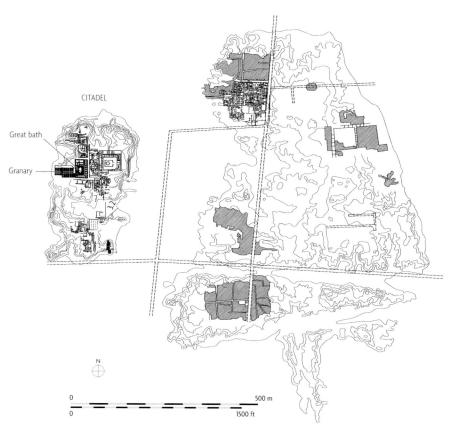

**3.1 Plan of Mohenjo-Daro, Indus Valley, ca. 2400–2000 BCE.**

The city was located on a plain beside the river, with a higher citadel section (left) that featured granaries and a large stepped bath. Shaded areas represent residential quarters that have been excavated, with one section (top center), showing orthogonal outlines of the foundations. As the valley was subject to flooding, storage of foodstuffs on a high point was a sensible precaution.

**3.2 View of the remains of Mohenjo-Daro, Indus Valley, ca. 2400–2000 BCE.**

Excavations of Mohenjo-Daro began in the 1920s, when archaeologists uncovered remains of the citadel and portions of the lower-lying residential area. Bricks made to a uniform size are the major construction materials used.

CITADEL

Great bath

Granary

N

0                          500 m

0                         1500 ft

played a part. Harappan cities ceased to be inhabited, and over the next two centuries the countryside was raided by nomads from the north. In about 1500 BCE migrations by Aryan tribes from eastern Iran began, and the Aryans eventually spread over the Indian subcontinent, displacing indigenous settlements. By 500 BCE their Indo-European language, the original root of many of the languages of Europe as well as Sanskrit in India, had displaced native tongues, a sign of cultural dominance. There was an ethnic factor here too: the invading Aryans were light-skinned in comparison to the darker-skinned native Indian populations. The distinction between conqueror and conquered became the earliest basis for the caste system that still operates in Indian society today.

Out of the confusion attending the migrations arose numerous small principalities. At about the time Alexander the Great was leading his army to the Indus (326 BCE), a young member of the Maurya tribe, Chandragupta, succeeded in bringing much of northern India under his command, eventually controlling most of what today is Pakistan and the eastern sections of Afghanistan as well. The empire continued to expand into southern India under his son and then grandson, Asoka (reigned 272–232 BCE), perhaps the greatest prince of the Maurya line and, as far as architecture is concerned, the first ruler of consequence. Asoka advanced the art of building in stone, bringing masons and stonecutters from Persia to construct monumental freestanding pillars, excavate caves for religious hermitages, and improve Buddhist shrines. His works have survived, and they will be considered below in the discussion of early Buddhist architecture.

A study of the ancient architecture in India and Southeast Asia is to a very large extent an examination of the development of temple architecture, for there are few structures not erected for religious purposes that have survived the passage of time. Temples were the primary buildings erected in durable materials, stone and brick, while houses and even palaces were constructed of less permanent wood, thatch, or stuccoed rubble and are therefore preserved only incidentally as, for example, in the backgrounds of scenes carved on temples. Princes, kings, and occasionally wealthy merchants were the major patrons of masonry temples, and thus architectural developments and religious preferences are closely related to political dynasties. In the period under consideration (up until about 1000 CE), the Indian subcontinent was not a unified country, although a certain level of cultural continuity was afforded by religious ties. A closer examination of Indian architecture would recognize the development of regional styles and the influences of powerful dynasties, but these will be given less emphasis here in the interests of creating a broad overview.

## RELIGIONS OF INDIA

Since religious buildings assume such a prominent position in Indian architecture, it is necessary to understand the rudiments of the faiths that inspired their construction. During the sixth century BCE, the Indian subcontinent witnessed the development of three major religions that all shared a general belief in the transmigration of souls. This doctrine, which was as pervasive in India as the belief in life after death was in ancient Egypt, held that living souls passed through an endless cycle of rebirth and suffering. In somewhat differing ways, Hinduism, Buddhism, and Jainism proposed means by which people could transcend the sorrow of temporal existence.

> *Never the spirit was born; the spirit shall cease to be never;*
> *Never was time it was not; End and Beginning are dreams!*
> *Birthless and deathless and changeless remaineth the spirit*
> *    for ever;*
> *Death hath not touched it at all, dead though the house of it*
> *    seems!*
> *Who knoweth it exhaustless, self-sustained,*
> *Immortal, indestructible,—shall such say, "I have killed a*
> *    man, or caused to kill?"*
> *Nay, but as when one layeth his worn-out robes away,*
> *And, taking new ones, sayeth, "These will I wear to-day!"*
> *So putteth by the spirit lightly its garb of flesh,*
> *And passeth to inherit a residence afresh.*
>           Bhagavad Gita (translated by Sir Edwin Arnold)

The common background for all three religions was a synthesis of traditional beliefs indigenous to the Indian peninsula and sacrificial cults brought by Aryans from the north. The oldest sacred writings, the Vedas, date from 1500 to 900 BCE. They contain hymns and prescribe rituals for worship of a pantheon of gods identified with the natural elements. From an early date, there was also a cosmology that invoked the joining of male and female as a metaphor for the union of the individual with the Universal. Simple shrines gave physical expression to this idea through a **linga**, or upright stone emblematic of the male element, surrounded at the base by a **yoni**, or concentric circles representing the female principle. Observation of religious rites and sacrifices required to maintain proper relationships between people and the gods was entrusted to a group of priests or Brahmins, who came to hold considerable power within society. Ascetic cults that developed during this period promoted the view that the physical world is but a small part of a much greater cycle of birth, death, and rebirth, and they offered their followers guidance for escaping repeated reincarnations.

Partly in reaction to the dominance of the Brahmin priests and their elaborate rituals, a number of individuals sought simpler means to religious understanding and ethical living. Two lasting religious movements—Jainism, which is still practiced by about two million Indians, and

Buddhism, one of the world's major religions, which is now virtually extinct in India but flourishes elsewhere—were founded by identifiable historical figures. Jainism was inspired by the life of Vardhamana, also known as Mahavira (great hero) and Jina (the victor). In 546 BCE Vardhamana found his version of the path to salvation in a complete rejection of the complex formulations of the Brahmins. He taught that escape from the world's unhappiness was attainable only through rigorous asceticism to purify the soul and by maintaining reverence for all living creatures. His followers, mostly merchants and bankers whose livelihoods enabled them to avoid all forms of violence against animals, established Jainism (literally, religion of Jina), in which participants seek to acquire spiritual merit through charity, good works, and, whenever possible, monastic retreats. In architectural terms, Jaini temples never developed a distinctive style, borrowing elements instead from other religious groups.

In contrast, the religion founded by Siddhartha Gautama (ca. 563–ca. 483 BCE) was destined to become a major influence on architecture, not only in India, but also in Sri Lanka, China, Tibet, and southeast Asia. Born into a wealthy family, Gautama left his wife and fortune to travel as a beggar and seek an understanding of the causes of suffering. After six years of ascetic mortification and contemplation, he achieved enlightenment while sitting under the bodhi tree. Gautama's Four Noble Truths proclaimed that the world was worthless, that ignorance must be overcome, that vain craving could be renounced through yoga, and that the true path to salvation lay in the middle way between self-indulgence and self-mortification. These Truths, in conjunction with the Eight-fold Way (right views, resolve, speech, conduct, livelihood, effort, recollection, and meditation), formed the basis of his teachings, which were intended to enable his disciples to overcome worldly suffering caused by human desires and thus to achieve *nirvana* or liberation from the eternal cycle of birth and rebirth. Buddhism, the religion he inspired, took its name from the word "Buddha," the Enlightened One, the name given to Gautama after his conversion. As initially expounded, the religion required neither complex worship rituals nor a specific architectural context.

The religion of the Brahmins, which evolved into Hinduism, responded to Jainism and Buddhism by incorporating popular devotional images of gods and spirits into its rituals of worship and making these rituals relate more closely to people's daily lives. Hinduism, which remains the major religion in India today, had no single founder, and it still has no clearly defined religious hierarchy. Essential to its beliefs are acceptance of the Vedas as sacred texts, and maintenance of the caste structure, whereby society is organized immutably into four classes (priests, warriors, merchants/craftsmen, and laborers). Hindus hold that each individual accumulates the consequences of both good and bad actions through a series of lifetimes and pursues freedom from the cycle of rebirth through reverence to the gods and the elimination of passions. Of the innumerable Hindu deities, many with multiple and sharply differing aspects, there are three supreme gods: Shiva, Vishnu, and Brahma. Shiva, the great lord whose essential characteristic is procreative energy, but who can also be the great destroyer, has as his consort Devi, the mother goddess, whose alternate form includes Kali the destroyer. Shiva's mount is the bull Nandi. Vishnu is the creator who embodies mercy and goodness, sometimes youthful romance, but who also has powers of destruction. His consort, Lakshmi, is the goddess of wealth, and his mount is the eagle Garuda. Brahma, the creator who is reborn periodically from a lotus growing in the navel of the sleeping Vishnu, has as his consort Sarasvati, patroness of learning and music.

## EARLY BUDDHIST SHRINES

The Buddha had not prescribed any particular architectural setting for worship, but his disciples established shrines to give permanent form to their religion. The first shrines were created after the death of the Buddha, when his cremated remains were divided by his followers and placed in ten locations associated with his life and teaching. To mark these places, a simple mound of rubble and earth known as a **stupa** was erected over the relics, in a manner comparable to traditional **chaityas**, or village memorials, where the ashes of deceased leaders were placed in a mound, often located on the outskirts of their settlement. It was this traditional form and placement that served as the genesis of later Buddhist architecture. In time, Buddhist monks settled in the vicinity of stupas to form **viharas**, or small **monasteries** of individual cells organized around open courts. Their rituals included walking around (circumambulating) the stupa while chanting verses from scripture. A processional path, generally followed in a clockwise direction, remains central to Buddhist temple design.

**3.3** Diagram illustrating the origin of the stupa.

The traditional practice of placing stones and earth over the graves of distinguished people evolved into the construction of a hemispherical form that incorporated the cosmological associations of a circle (in plan), the world mountain and dome of the heavens, and the vertical world axis.

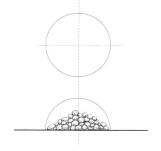

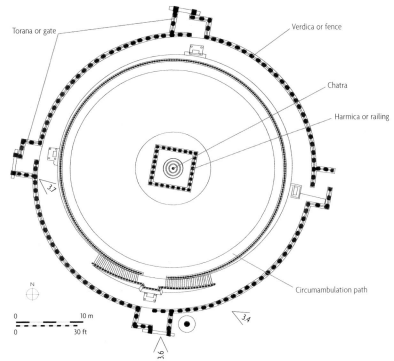

**3.4  Great Stupa, Sanchi, ca. 250 BCE–250 CE.**

The elevation-like view shows a *torana* (gate), a portion of the *verdica* (fence), and, on top of the mound, the *chatra* (stylized bodhi tree), which symbolizes the tree under which the Buddha received enlightenment.

**3.5  Plan of the Great Stupa, Sanchi, ca. 250 BCE–250 CE.**

This plan shows the four gates and their bent-axis entry design that creates a swastika, perhaps linked to ancient sun symbols. Openings correspond to the cardinal directions. Stairs on the south side lead to the elevated circumambulation path used by priests.

Torana or gate

Verdica or fence

Chatra

Harmica or railing

Circumambulation path

N

0        10 m

0        30 ft

The oldest surviving Buddhist stupas were enlarged with successive coverings or constructed anew during the reign of Asoka, the early Indian emperor who was converted to Buddhism. Through his contacts with Persian architecture and the Hellenistic world, Asoka brought to India builders proficient in the art of stonework, which until this time had not been used in construction. He also caused the roads leading to Buddhist shrines to be marked with tall columns inscribed with Buddhist teachings, known afterward as Asoka columns. These featured ornamental carving clearly modeled on Persian originals (see Fig. 1.17). Whereas the columns in Persian architecture supported a roof, in India they were freestanding elements used as commemorative markers in the landscape.

Under Asoka's patronage, the original simple stupas were enlarged and new shrines were created. All were regularized into hemispherical forms, reflecting the simplicity of the circle in plan, section, and elevation and creating a symbolic link to the cyclical nature of existence (Fig. 3.3). To provide for greater permanence, the stupas were faced with brick or stone. To indicate their sacred character, they were protected by a **verdica**, or enclosing fence, that delimited the path for circumambulation. And to mark their special association with the Buddha, they were crowned with a **harmica**, or square railing, and a **chatra**, or three-tiered umbrella form, stylized stone versions of the sacred enclosure fence and famous bodhi tree under

which the Buddha received enlightenment. The triple parasol was emblematic of royalty, and its supporting stalk symbolized the axis of the world passing through the precise center of the hemispherical form of the stupa, symbol of the heavenly dome.

The monastery at Sanchi, founded by Asoka and enlarged over the next 500 years, illustrates the fundamental elements of Buddhist shrines in India. The Great Stupa, originally constructed as a mound about seventy feet in diameter, grew to become a dome that was almost 120 feet in diameter and fifty-four feet in height (Figs. 3.4–3.5). At its top, the stupa is crowned by a chatra set inside a harmica. Its base is encircled by a two-tiered ambulatory: the upper level is reserved for priests, leaving

materials employed for the shrines, viharas were constructed of wood, and only their masonry foundations survive to indicate their layouts, which in many respects are an enlargement of the courtyard house already familiar from the early Indus Valley constructions and also used throughout Mediterranean civilizations. Buddhist monks lived in simple cells that were grouped around a square or rectangular open court containing community facilities, including the water supply. Sanchi also featured several enclosed chaitya halls, buildings permitting year-round devotions by enclosing a small stupa at the end of a rectangular hall. The end of the hall embracing the stupa was curved to reflect the shape contained within, and thus created an architectural form that could be erected as a free-standing structure raised on a base, or plinth, as in the so-called Temple 18 at Sanchi, or excavated from solid rock, as in the temples cut into cliffs at Ajanta, Ellora, and Karli.

**3.7** The verdica and torana, Sanchi, ca. 250 BCE–250 CE.

As seen from the inside, the space for circumambulation is effectively screened from the outside world by the stone rails of the fence.

**3.6** The torana (gate) and verdica (fence), Sanchi, ca. 250 BCE–250 CE.

The verdica is composed of massive stones, treated in a manner analogous to wooden construction, while the toranas are richly carved.

the ground level path for pilgrim use. Enclosing the stupa is a massive stone verdica (Fig. 3.6), nine feet in height, with four carved gates at the cardinal points of the compass. The construction of this fence shows how early masons were influenced by wooden construction. Octagonal upright posts and rounded horizontal rails replicate forms already familiar in wood, reinterpreted here on a much larger scale. The elaborate **toranas**, or entrance gates (Fig. 3.7), added in about 25 BCE, reflect bamboo prototypes. When built in stone, however, the size increased and it became possible, as here, to embellish the work with carved figures representing Buddhist legends, symbolism that may have been inspired by similar work on Asoka columns. The relative lack of modeling on the figures makes these gates seem more the work of wood carvers than masonry sculptors. All four gates are set in front of the encircling fence, and they are part of a staggered, or bent-axis, approach designed to reduce distractions outside the sacred enclosure from disturbing the meditations of pilgrims circumambulating the stupa.

The shrine at Sanchi is an accumulation of buildings constructed over time, including three stupas and viharas for the monks (Fig. 3.8). In contrast to the permanent

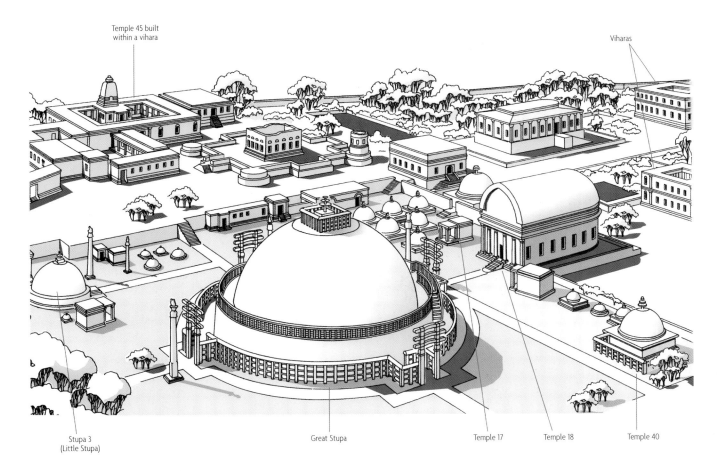

3.8 Reconstruction view of the temple complex, Sanchi.

In the center is the Great Stupa, and to the right is the so-called Temple 40, an early chaitya hall. The rectangular plan building at the upper left is a vihara, a residence for monks, of which only the foundations remain.

3.9 Plan of and section through the cave temple, Karli, ca. 100 BCE.

Excavated in a rock cliff, this temple consists of a chaitya hall with an ambulatory around the stupa shrine at the rear. Two freestanding columns (one now gone) flanked the entrance, while stone and teakwood carvings screened the opening to the cave.

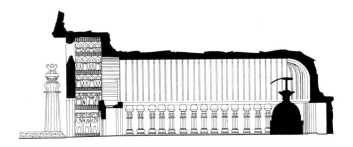

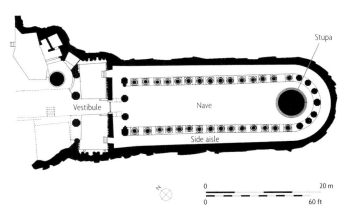

Construction of these cave-temples coincided with a period when the rulers of India's principalities favored Brahmin practices, and Buddhism was the religion primarily of wealthy merchants. Even though Buddhist shrines were thus financed by substantial donations, the monks increasingly sought remote sites for construction to avoid conflicts with Brahmins. Rock cliffs and gorges provided isolated locations, and the living rock contained durable material for masons to carve without their having to enclose space with stone beams. At the great cave-temple of Karli (Fig. 3.9), which dates from the first century BCE, the chaitya hall faithfully replicates the form and details of wooden architecture that provided its prototype, including the semicircular arched ceiling patterned after flexible bamboo structures. Karli's dimensions, however, exceed those of wooden buildings of the period: the hall is forty-five feet wide, a difficult span to achieve in timber, but one that presented no problem to the excavators. Starting from the cliff face, which was smoothed and shaped to resemble the façade of a chaitya hall, workers drove two tunnels 150 feet into the cliff to establish the length of the temple, then enlarged the excavation to create a barrel-shaped ceiling with arched "ribs." Rock on

# BAMIYAN AND THE COLOSSAL BUDDHA

by C. Murray Smart

Traders transported Indian design and iconography east by sea to Southeast Asia and Indonesia and west through the mountain passes to Central Asia by Silk Road caravans. The main text here deals with the most spectacular examples of Indian architecture in Southeast Asia—the great works at Borobudur and Angkor. Equally important, however, is the great Buddhist pilgrimage complex of Bamiyan in what is today Afghanistan; it was here that the colossal image of the Buddha first appeared. Bamiyan was the western terminus of three of the trade routes that connected China, India, the Near East, and the Western world. At Bamiyan, a great monastic complex more than a mile long was carved into a sandstone cliff overlooking a fertile valley between the Hindu Kush to the east and the Koh-i-Baba mountain range to the northwest. The site was visited in the seventh century by the Chinese pilgrim Xuanzang who described it in glowing terms. Another famous visitor, Genghis Khan, apparently found less to admire: legend has it that he massacred the entire population, turning Bamiyan into the deserted complex of today.

The monastery is terminated at each end by a colossal Buddha statue (Fig. 3.10). The figure at the eastern end, designated "Sakyamuni" by Hsüan-tsang, is 120 feet tall; the more spectacular figure at the western end, which Hsüan-tsang simply called "the Buddha," is 171 feet tall. It is the larger figure that is of greater importance, not only because of its size, but also because its iconography and style were replicated in small souvenir statues and exported to the home countries of visiting pilgrims. A comparison of the Bamiyan figures with those of the Dun Huang caves in China reveals that the Buddhist

iconography of China was influenced directly by the figures at Bamiyan.

The two Buddhas illustrate the cosmopolitan nature of the Buddhist art at Bamiyan. They are quite different in style. In every respect except its size, the smaller figure is a typical Gandharan Buddha figure of the second or third century CE. Its construction is interesting. Only the basic armature of the body was carved; over the rough stone body and head, facial features and voluminous drapery folds were modeled in plaster made of mud and straw. The figure was finished with a coating of lime-plaster which was painted and gilded. At the time of

**3.10** Great Buddha, Bamiyan, Afghanistan, late Gandhara school, 7th century. Height 171ft (52m).

Hsüan-tsang's visit, the statue was completely covered with gold leaf and metal ornaments, leading him to the erroneous conclusion that it was made of metal.

As interesting as the statue are the fragments of fresco that remain. Originally, the niche in which the figure stands was completely covered with paintings symbolizing the vault of

heaven. The central image of the fresco above the Buddha's head is a sun god driving a chariot drawn by horses and attended by winged angels. It could be Apollo, or Surya, the Hindu sun god, or perhaps Mithra, the Persian sun god. Two of the four flanking angels have human form and are inspired by Persian and Mediterranean prototypes; the other two are derived from Greek harpies and have birds' feet.

The drapery of the larger Buddha was modeled on ropes attached to wooden dowels driven into the stone armature. The result was an enormous replica of a late Gandharan Buddha type in which the robe was reduced to a series of lines that clung to and revealed the body form beneath. This statue is two centuries or more later in origin than the smaller figure; it probably dates from the fifth century CE. It stands in a trefoil niche that creates a double halo about the body and head; this double halo was much copied in both China and Japan.

These two figures are the first of many colossal images of the Buddha that would appear throughout the Buddhist world. Both Greece and Rome produced colossal figures that served as prototypes. And just as the colossal portrait sculptures of Roman emperors were intended to portray them as divine rulers of the world, the Bamiyan figures portray the Buddha as cosmic man, the source and substance of the universe.

Unfortunately, since this essay was written, the fundamentalist Muslim sect formerly in power in Afghanistan, the Taliban, destroyed both of these two colossal Buddha figures in 2001. Since the overthrow of the Taliban, there has been talk internationally of restoring the statues, but no plans have yet been announced.

the chamber floor was cut away and columns carved as workers completed excavating the entire interior space. Rubble extracted from the cliff became material for construction of a platform extending to the cave's entrance, a recessed, arched porch marked by paired freestanding columns supporting lion sculptures. This porch was adorned by relief carvings and (originally) painted scenes from the life of the Buddha. Inside the chaitya hall, the relatively dim light penetrating through high grilles in the windows allows the pilgrim to discern slowly the enormity of the space, measured by the stately rhythm of colonnades and dominated at the far recess by a stupa carved with the image of the Buddha. The architects of the temple at Karli achieved that elusive synthesis of space, light, and detail that characterizes the finest buildings of any era.

## HINDU TEMPLES
### EARLY BUILDINGS

Buddhist and Hindu traditions have a long history of coexistence on the Indian subcontinent, and among followers of various sects there has been a certain commingling of beliefs as well as temple forms. Although Hinduism draws strongly on some of the most ancient indigenous beliefs, it only developed a particular architectural expression for itself later. Buddhists built the earliest surviving shrines and thereby established the model on which early Hindu architecture was based, but from the fifth century CE onward, Hinduism became the dominant religion in India. Today few Buddhist sects remain there.

As in Buddhist practice, the Hindu temple creates a link between the gods and the worshiper. However, unlike the Buddhists, who focus on the life and teachings of one leader, Hindus venerate a multitude of deities including Vishnu, a solar deity. Their temples are simultaneously dwellings of the god, places for worship, and objects of worship in themselves. Aspects of the cosmos (and thus of the gods) are incorporated into the temple by the use of specific forms, sacred geometry, careful orientation, and axial alignments. Most Hindu temple designs include forms that are symbolic of the holy mountain, the sacred cave, and the cosmic axis (Fig. 3.11). Geometry derived from a subdivided square or **mandala** is commonly used, together with a single unit that sets all proportions. Numbers associated with the gods are important in constructing and interpreting the mandala, which provides links to divine proportions, hence harmony with the cosmos. Temple complexes are usually aligned on the cardinal points, representing the four corners of the earth, with the major entrances facing east. Priests perform sacred rites at regular times for the benefit of the entire community, and private devotions may be offered at any time. Since there is no congregational worship, there is no corresponding need for a large enclosed space. Rather, the temple as a three-dimensional form in the landscape becomes a focal point for community life, much as a Christian church might serve social and artistic purposes as well as religious functions.

Some of the earliest surviving Hindu shrines are found in the rock-cut temples of Udaigiri, near Sanchi, and these show clear influence from Buddhist work. Temple 17 at Sanchi, dating from the early fifth century CE, is modeled on the rock-cut temples at Udaigiri, set on a plinth and featuring a square sanctuary preceded by a pillared porch. This two-chambered temple form is amplified and embellished in virtually all later developments. The sanctuary is typically quite small. Known as the **garbhagriha**, or womb-chamber, it contains a sacred image or element as a symbol of the god's presence. If proper rituals are not observed, the god may choose to inhabit another place, so worship involves priestly ceremonies that welcome, entertain, and honor the deity with music, food, dancing, the recital of religious texts, and the singing of hymns. The covered porch provides a transition between the outside world and the sanctuary, and on its pillars and the exterior walls of the temple the visitor can generally find sculpted panels and images that complement the image of the deity within.

Hindu gods are believed to have a particular affinity for mountains and caves. As builders became more skillful in working in stone (or occasionally brick), they gave increasingly elaborate formal expression to the vertical mound

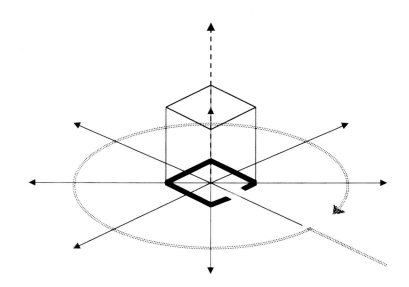

**3.11** Diagram illustrating the basis for most Hindu temples.

This axonometric view shows a womb-chamber (garbhagriha) that radiates energy to the cardinal and ordinal directions; a passage for circumambulation in a clockwise direction; and the sacred mountain defining a central vertical axis that towers over the garbhagriha.

**3.12** Ladkhan Temple, Aihole, 7th century CE.
Notice that a columned porch precedes the pillared main hall of the temple, translating into stone architectural forms previously built in wood as village assembly halls.

(mountain) arising over the sanctuary (cave). As an example of this process, consider the Ladkhan Temple (Fig. 3.12), built in the seventh century CE at Aihole, which preserves in its stonework the traces of a wooden village assembly hall that served as its model. The masons resolved questions of overall form and building details as a carpenter would. When translated into stone, however, the light and pliant wooden structure became overscaled and heavy.

## LATER TEMPLES

Later Hindu temples rise more dramatically, as builders exploited architectural form as the basis for sculptural embellishment, sweeping masses upward in imitation of entire mountain ranges. At Bhitargaon, the brick Vishnu Temple, dating perhaps to the first half of the fifth century, presents an early example of a more prominent super-structure erected over the sanctuary (Fig. 3.13). Even in its somewhat ruined state, the temple's profile shows an unmistakable allusion to mountain forms. The passage connecting the sanctuary and the porch is unusual for incorporating **true-arch** construction. Most Indian temples are built using post-and-lintel or corbeling techniques, but this temple demonstrates that builders had knowledge of the arch even though it was seldom employed. The source of the characteristic **shikhara**, or mountain-peak roof, of mature Indian temples has been traced to lightweight thatched bamboo structures with curving sides rising from

**3.13** Vishnu Temple, Bhitargaon, 5th century CE.
Constructed in brick, this is one of the earliest Hindu temples to have a towering mass constructed over the garbhagriha.

**3.14** Temple, Khajuraho, 10th century.

Dominant here is the shikhara roof commonly found over the garbhagriha of many Hindu temples. Its towering form creates a symbolic holy mountain over the sacred cave.

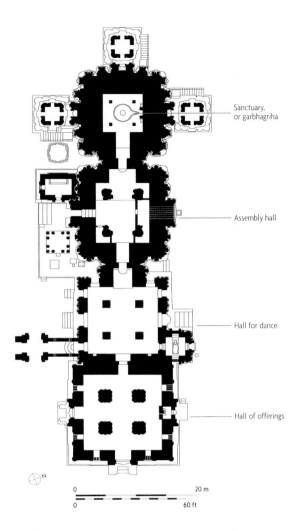

Sanctuary, or garbhagriha

Assembly hall

Hall for dance

Hall of offerings

N

| 0 | | 20 m |
| 0 | | 60 ft |

**3.15** Plan of the Lingaraja Temple, Bhubaneshwar, ca. 1050–1150.

More elaborate than some, this temple plan has three separate halls preceding the garbhagriha at the end of the processional axis. Each hall is provided with a distinctive roof profile so that the composition builds to the high shikhara.

a square base. No matter how elaborate the masonry temple forms became, with their exteriors covered with carved ornament and walls adorned with sculpture, the essence of a square sanctuary housed under the curving shikhara roof, preceded by one or more columnar halls or porches in axial alignment, remains the distinctive design paradigm for the Hindu temple (Fig. 3.14). The enormously thick masonry walls required to sustain the towering roof amplified the womb-like seclusion of the central shrine room, enveloping the chamber within the sacred mountain.

Two temple groups dating from the eighth to thirteenth centuries illustrate the prolific magnificence of northern Hindu architecture. Bhubaneshwar, in the state of Orissa, has over a hundred temples constructed across a period of five centuries. The plan of the celebrated Lingaraja Temple (mid-eleventh to mid-twelfth century) is an elaboration of the two-celled form, with three pillared halls on axis preceding the sanctuary. From east to west, these comprise a hall of offerings, a hall of dance, an assembly hall, and finally the sanctuary proper (Fig. 3.15). Pyramidal roofs over the halls resemble foothills, contrasting with the massive central shikhara over the sanctuary, whose form is echoed on a smaller scale by the subsidiary shrines erected inside the walled rectangular temple precinct. Within the worshiper's field of vision, there are sculpted figures carved with a high degree of detail as well as sensuous beauty to enrich the wall surfaces. Unlike a number of other historic temples, this massive shrine remains in active use.

At Khajuraho, royal city of the Chandella Dynasty, there were at least twenty-five temples constructed over a 200-year period, with sculptural programs reflecting lavish artistic patronage as well as devotion to mystic Tantric rites. Among the best-preserved is the Lakshmana Temple (ca. 950) (Fig. 3.16), raised on a rectangular platform anchored by four small shrines at the corners. The axial approach from the east brings the visitor up several flights of steps, whose ascent is repeated in the successively rising roof forms over an initial open porch, a second porch, a great pillared hall, and finally the internal sanctuary. The devotee may circumambulate the sanctuary by following an enclosed passage surrounding the shrine room. Light

**3.16** Lakshmana Temple, Khajuraho, ca. 950.

The temple stands on a platform, or plinth, a stylobate in ancient Greek architecture. Shrines at the corners reflect the main shrine at a diminished scale.

for the ambulatory is provided by openings placed above eye level so that the elaborate interior wall sculpture may be seen without admitting distractions from the external world. Images represented here include many animated scenes of loving couples, generally interpreted as both a literal representation of Tantric practices (which included sexual intercourse) and a symbol of the rapturous union of the human with the divine that was a goal of Hindu theology (Figs. 3.17–3.18).

All the Hindu temples considered thus far are products of dynasties who ruled primarily in the north and central sections of India. In the south, a distinctive regional style developed that featured roofs with rounded finials, walls with engaged columns or pilasters for articulation, multi-columned halls, and temple complexes that had sets of concentric walls with massive gateway entrances. As with architecture in northern India, the origin of this style can be traced to the early seventh-century rock-cut temples that generally featured a pillared hall as a prelude to a sanctuary set deep in the interior. In cave architecture, the pillared hall functioned much like a portico or porch, a transition between the outside world and the shrine. (The

**3.17** (above) Kandariya Mahadeva Temple, Khajuraho, ca. 1025–50.

Upper levels of the roof are carved with geometric ornament, which has the effect of making the massive form seem lighter while accentuating its contours. Sculpted figures populate the lower, frieze-like bands.

**3.18** Kandariya Mahadeva Temple, Khajuraho, ca. 1025–50.

In its lower registers, where figures are close enough to be seen by visitors, figural sculpture features prominently. Notice the figures' swaying, s-shaped postures.

**3.19** Dharmaraja Ratha, Bhima Ratha, and Arjuna Ratha, Mahabalipuram, 7th century.

These three monolithic temples, cut from granite outcroppings, replicate in stone an earlier temple architecture in wood. Note the chaitya-like roof on the Bhima Ratha that resembles thatch. Repetition of selected forms unites all three temples.

early temple of Ladkhan at Aihole may well have served as a model for the scheme.) The same stone-cutting skills that were used to excavate cave temples were put to more sculptural use in about 650, when a remarkable set of diminutive temples was carved out of a granite ridge at Mahabalipuram. The Dharmaraja, Bhima, and Arjuna temples seen in Figure 3.19, known as **rathas** (wheeled carts or chariots), are similar to large-scale architectural models, and each one is different. Some are obviously derived from the barrel-vaulted roofs of chaitya halls, while others are based on simple wooden shrines or elaborations of centralized designs. All are set on a raised base and make use of engaged columns or pilasters for wall articulation. Images of deities, mythological beings, and the royal family (the Pallavas) who commissioned the work are set in recesses defined by the pilasters. Multiple roofs in layers add verticality to the forms. When one realizes how much of the hard granite was cut away to create these diminutive masterpieces, it is apparent that the art of

working stone had reached a high level of sophistication and taste.

What began at small scale was continued at much greater size in the eleventh-century Brihadeshvara Temple at Tanjore (Figs. 3.20–3.21). Here the builders succeeded in erecting a tower over the garbhagriha that was three times the height (200 feet) of anything else that had been attempted prior to that time. The base is substantial, an eighty-two-foot square in plan, but there is a processional space around the central shrine included in the lower story, so it is not a solid mass. Half-columns and niches define a two-story elevation rising above the base, while uncounted roof levels recede as they ascend in the towering pyramid roof, which is capped by a monolith weighing over eighty tons that forms a dome-like finial. As one might expect, the temple complex is axially arranged, with a porch and two multi-columned halls preceding the shrine proper. A separate pillared shrine honoring Nandi the sacred bull is placed on axis between the temple and the great entrance gate. The enclosing wall is composed of a continuous double colonnade, and several lesser temples occupy corners of the courtyard.

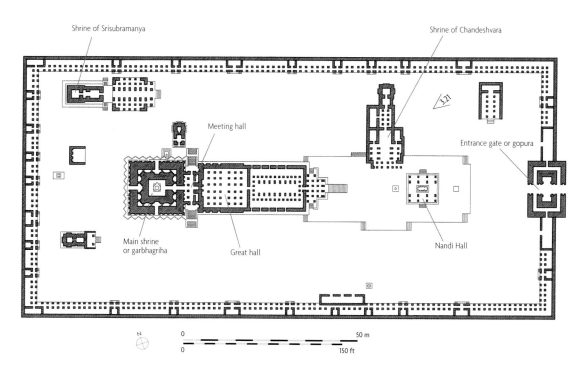

Shrine of Srisubramanya

Shrine of Chandeshvara

Meeting hall

Entrance gate or gopura

Main shrine
or garbhagriha

Great hall

Nandi Hall

N

0             50 m

0             150 ft

**3.20** (above) **Plan of Brihadeshvara Temple, Tanjore, 11th century.**

Compare this plan to that of the Lakshmana Temple at Khajuraho to see how all elements of the temple have been greatly increased in size. The central axis is defined by a gopura or towering entrance gate on the east side.

**3.21** (below) **Brihadeshvara Temple, Tanjore, 11th century.**

Seen beyond the Shrine of Chandeshvara, the pyramidal shikhara roof over the main shrine rises from a square base, towering over 200 feet to dominate the extensive temple. Its domed top is cut from a single piece of granite in a form that resembles a Buddhist stupa.

## ANGKOR WAT

Hinduism spread to other regions in Southeast Asia through the activity of Indian merchants, just as was the case with Buddhism, and the religion remains a force in those regions today. Among the numerous monuments of Hindu art outside the Indian subcontinent, one of the most impressive is the vast temple of Angkor Wat in Cambodia, which represents a fusion of Indian religion and native Khmer tradition (Fig. 3.22). The scale of the project makes it one of the largest religious structures ever built, with a rectangular perimeter wall measuring 4275 by 4920

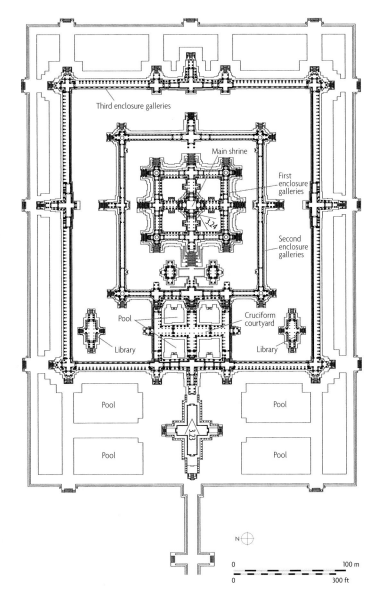

**3.22** Plan of Angkor Wat, begun ca. 1120.

The clarity of this design is remarkable. Nested sets of galleries focus on the main shrine, the symbolic representation of Mount Mehru, home of the gods.

feet. Visitors wishing to make a complete pilgrimage according to Hindu practice would walk about thirteen miles to visit all the galleries within the complex. Begun in ca. 1120 as a temple to Vishnu, Angkor Wat was finished as the royal shrine of the Khmer Dynasty that ruled Cambodia at that time before being converted to Buddhist worship.

Earlier Khmer temples consisted of a tower sanctuary within a walled enclosure. The tower again represented the sacred mountain, while the garbhagriha inside evoked the holy cave at the center of the cosmos. This theme was elaborated in later temples that featured multiple tower sanctuaries on a terrace. Later still, forms resembling step pyramids gave more vivid expression to the concept of the cosmic mountain. Until the construction of Angkor Wat, the most extensive interpretation of these themes in Khmer architecture came in temples that placed the tower sanctuary at the summit of a stepped pyramid, with open galleries for circumambulation extending around all four sides. Angkor takes this organization as the point of departure for an even more magnificent articulation, adding multiple towers, extended cruciform galleries, corner **pavilions**, and elaborate entrance gates to the central tower and elevated platform (Fig. 3.23). At the heart of the composition is a 215-foot-tall central tower over the main shrine (Fig. 3.24), built on a pyramid base whose corners are marked by four stepped towers that collectively are meant to symbolize Mount Mehru, the home of the gods. Two additional sets of square concentric galleries surround this core, punctuated by entrance gates in the centers of the four sides to reinforce the cardinal directions. The main axial approach passes through a square courtyard featuring artificial ponds before entering the second gallery and ascending the steep stairs to the innermost platform sanctuary. A moat nearly two-and-a-half miles in length encircles the entire site, symbolizing the oceans out of which the mountain rises.

Angkor Wat is built entirely in stone, and since it does not employ arched construction, only corbeling, there are no large interior spaces. Once laid, the stone became the domain of sculptors, who adorned walls and even roofs with ornament and shallow relief carvings. Some of the subjects are drawn from epics familiar within Hindu tradition, but these are blended with references to Khmer cosmology, and the whole serves as a mortuary shrine for Suryavarman II, the king who commissioned the work. In India, Hinduism never involved the concept of a god-king or ancestor worship, but these aspects are part of the Cambodian tradition and inform the design of Angkor Wat. Overall, the form captures the qualities both of horizontal expanse and vertical expression in a single composition. The architecture is symmetrical, balanced, and grand, the culminating expression of religious concepts begun centuries earlier in India.

**3.23** Angkor Wat, begun ca. 1120.

This view from the east shows how the plan is translated into a three-dimensional form through the interplay of horizontal and vertical elements.

## CONCLUSIONS ABOUT ARCHITECTURAL IDEAS

Chapters 1 and 2 drew some attention to what were termed constituent facts, facts that seem to have relevance in multiple eras and for multiple designers, and in the current chapter a consideration of some constituent facts of architectural ordering is again worthwhile. For example, as with the architecture of Egypt and Mesopotamia, Indian and Southeast Asian architecture long made dramatic use of the vertical (Khajuraho), the horizontal and multiple horizontal datum lines (Ladkhan and Kandariya Mahadeva temples), the richness of a building's silhouette as seen against the sky (Lakshmana Temple), central plans (Sanchi), orthogonal plans (Brihadeshvara Temple and Angkor Wat), and spatial sequence (Lingaraja Temple). And certainly all of this work displays a universal concern for proportional relationships in the careful balancing of horizontals and verticals.

Yet, we must admit that at least superficially the Indian, Cambodian, and Javanese results appear to be quite different. In the service of directing human energies toward a release from the cycle of existences, Hindu designers of religious structures chose to emphasize, even to exaggerate certain features and to intensify their application of certain design principles. The most obvious contrast between what we have seen previously and what appears in this chapter is the profusion within the latter of a sensual phantasma of ornamentation held within repetitive broken-frieze-like assemblies (not unlike what we will see in Chapter 9's presentation of the Gothic cathedrals in France and Chapter 10's presentation of temples in Pre-Columbian Central America). If we apply a metaphorical description, we might say that the systematic application of ornament in Indian and Southeast Asian work sometimes reaches such a level of richness, as at the Lakshmana Temple, that the building evokes the image of an exotic fruit or seed pod that has matured and burst, revealing the profundity of its inner, organic contents.

**3.24** Central tower of the main shrine, Angkor Wat, begun ca. 1120.

This tower was constructed over a garbhagriha or womb-chamber that is the core of every Hindu temple.

Metaphor is also useful as we look deeper, beneath the surface ornamentation to the underlying ordering principles. Consider the giant stupa at Borobudur and the palace at Angkor Wat. Both have plans that amplify gridded geometries to the level of tapestry-like woven-ness, such that the larger application of a systematic weft and warp is comparable to the detailed application of ornament, as if there were a single organic directive.

In the end, we can learn much about design intentions and design principles by viewing this Eastern work, both as an intrinsic part of the culture that produced it and as a universal result of human longings and aspirations and perceptions of the physical world and efforts to organize it. And this duality of viewpoint will be equally informative in the chapter that follows on the architecture of China and Japan.

# CHAPTER 4

# THE TRADITIONAL ARCHITECTURE OF CHINA AND JAPAN

China is vast in size and has the largest population of any country on earth. We tend to regard it as an ancient culture because, even though historic civilization developed there slightly later than in Mesopotamia or Egypt, China holds the distinction among civilizations of having maintained the highest degree of cultural continuity across the 4000 years of its existence. China's nearly ten million square miles contain varied geographical conditions and over fifty ethnic groups, but its society has generally been defined by the Han Chinese. Unified government under strong emperors encouraged uniformity in many societal structures, including city design and building practices, and Chinese architectural traditions were remarkably stable over the centuries until the forcible intrusion of Western culture in the nineteenth century and the toppling of the last emperor in 1911.

For buildings from the period before about 2000 BCE, there is little information because so many of the sites are still occupied and thus excavations necessary to understand early architecture have not yet been made. Archaeologists have found remains of farming and craft villages in the Yellow River Valley, most notably at Banpo, where small houses with both circular and rectangular plans have been reconstructed based on foundation remains (Fig. 4.1). The rectangular houses were sunk a half-story into the ground and had truncated, pyramidal roofs (no walls) of lightweight wooden members lashed together at the top. Earth-sheltering helped to stabilize the interior temperature in both summer and winter. Smoke from the central hearth escaped through a gap at the apex of the overriding, thatch-covered gable roof, and the sloping entranceway was protected by another gable roof. The circular huts had side walls of wattle covered inside and out by a thick layer of clay for insulation, and the same treatment was given to the truncated, conical roof, with an opening left at the peak for ventilation and covered by a gable roof, just as was the case with the rectangular houses. The doorway was recessed, and some houses seem to have had internal partitions or screens. Painted pottery remains suggest that skilled ceramists were working in these villages, and there are indications of weaving, although the textiles themselves have long since vanished. The next millennium saw the development of larger houses that still fall within the same architectural vocabulary of timber frame, earthen plastering, and thatch.

From these humble prehistoric origins came the legendary beginning of Chinese history with the Shang Dynasty, which emerged in about 1766 BCE to dominate the Yellow River Valley and extend its control as far south as the Yangtze Kiang. Shang technology included skill in bronze casting and pictograph writing preserved on oracle bones (the shoulder blades of sheep). With the Shang begins the series of dynastic successions—Zhou, Han, Tang, Song, Yuan, Ming, and Qing, to name the major ones—that dominated Chinese history until the early twentieth century.

In China, the primary impetus for building came from the government (the imperial court and the state) rather than from religious organizations or private patrons. The most obvious manifestation of this pattern of investment is the Great Wall, begun in pieces by feudal lords, unified by the first Qin emperor in 221 BCE, and largely rebuilt and extended during the Ming Dynasty (1368–1644 CE) (see page 80). It is an astonishing piece of construction, almost 4000 miles long, ranging from the coast through varied terrain to its terminus in the Gobi Desert. Originally it was largely made with rammed earth, but during the Ming Dynasty the height of most of the wall was raised and given its present casing of brick or stone. As it exists

Great Wall of China, 221 BCE–1368 CE.

Watchtowers and wall sections with battlements snake across the rugged terrain. The crenellations provide protection on the north side while on the south side (toward China) the parapet is lower and unfortified.

## Chronology

| | |
|---|---|
| beginning of cultures in the Indus Valley | 3000 BCE |
| Shang Dynasty | 1766 BCE–1123 BCE |
| Han Dynasty | 202 BCE–221 CE |
| construction of the Great Wall | 221 BCE–1368 CE |
| life of Confucius | 551–479 BCE |
| composition of the Kao Gong Ji | 5th century CE |
| Tang Dynasty | 618–906 CE |
| construction of the Ise Shrine | begun 690 |
| Song Dynasty | 960–1279 |
| composition of the Yingzao-fashi | 1103 |
| Yuan Dynasty | 1280–1368 |
| Ming Dynasty | 1368–1644 |
| construction of Imperial and Forbidden cities at Beijing | 15th century |

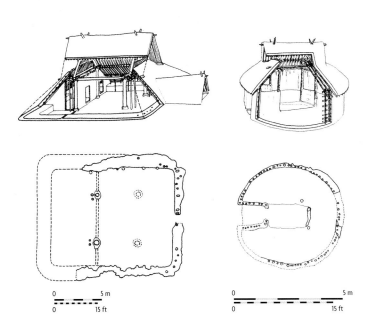

**4.1** Reconstructions of Neolithic houses, Banpo, ca. 2000 BCE.

These reconstructions show rectangular and circular designs. As was the case with prehistoric houses in western Europe, these dwellings used readily available materials—wood, thatch, and earth—to provide shelter. A central hearth is also part of many houses at Banpo.

**4.2** Pagoda, Dazu, Sichuan province, 12th century.

The pagoda's tiered organization is ultimately based on the chatra or stylized bodhi tree set atop Indian stupas. Its parabolic profile may also owe something to the shikhara roofs of Hindu temples.

today, the Great Wall varies from nineteen to thirty-nine feet in height, with an average width at the top of sixteen feet. The north-facing side is capped by crenellated battlements, with watchtowers at intervals connected by a road extending along the top. In the event of attack, beacons could be used to summon reinforcements from garrison camps that were strategically located on the southern side. Only a highly organized, powerful state could command the resources required to construct and maintain an engineering work on this scale. One should not be surprised to find the Chinese achieving similarly consistent building standards in more modest projects.

Indigenous Chinese religious traditions were based on a belief in life after death, ancestor worship, and animism (a reverence for natural features such as trees, rocks, and hills, as well as cosmic elements including the sky, sun, and moon). From early times, indigenous religions had included the concept already mentioned in the chapter on Indian architecture of the complementary duality of female and male, or *yin* and *yang*, which carries over as an artistic principle into architecture and landscape design. Chinese philosophy received its clearest articulation in the fifth century BCE through the lives and writings of two sages, Laotzu and Confucius. Laotzu's philosophy, Daoism, was mystical in approach, seeking harmony of human action and the world through the study of nature. Daoist philosophy is largely anti-rational and anti-authoritarian, as may be seen in the *I Ching*, or *Book of Changes*, an oracle text consulted in conjunction with the casting of coins to determine what part should be read for guidance in finding answers to perplexing questions. Aspects of Daoism may be found particularly in the Chinese approach to garden design, where carefully contrived

views and experiences are based on the model provided by nature itself. In contrast, the philosophy expounded by Confucius relied on respect for authority as established by the state. Its innately conservative tenets have dominated Chinese social and political structures throughout history. Those in power are to act benevolently on behalf of their subjects, and ordinary people are to show proper deference to the superior wisdom and understanding of their revered leaders. Ancestor worship and respect for one's elders in the family, hallmarks of a well-ordered Confucian family, had exact parallels in the veneration that society in general owed to the reigning emperor, regarded as a virtual deity whose welfare was crucial for the stability of the state. Chinese city planning and traditional house design embodied Confucian principles in their layouts and axial alignments of buildings.

While Confucianism and Daoism are not religions in the Western sense of the term, they are philosophies that have influenced the way many people think. Buddhism would become the most widespread organized religion in China, transmitted to the country during the first or second centuries CE by merchant caravans moving along

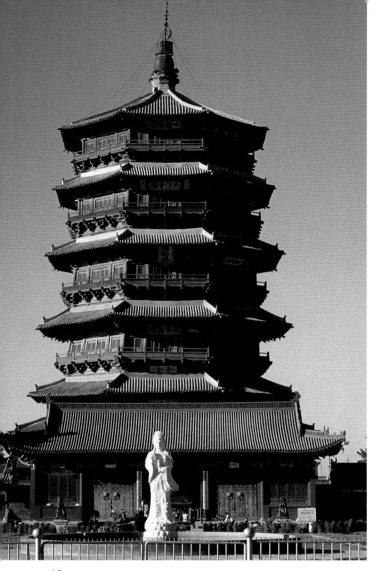

**4.3** Pagoda, Fogong Monastery, Shanxi province, 1056.
Like the pagoda at Dazu, this pagoda's organization is based on the stacking up of smaller, often repetitive elements.

**4.4** Pagoda, Fogong Monastery, Shanxi province, 1056.
This view of the massive pagoda reveals the construction of alternating layers of wood frame and horizontal logs with cantilevers creating five roof-and-gallery levels.

the Silk Roads across Central Asia, connecting China, Persia, and India. Architectural ideas accompanied Buddhist teachings, resulting in Chinese buildings that have roots in Indian practice. For example, the northern Indian cave temples around Gandhara, furnished with towering images of the Buddha, inspired similar cave temples with gigantic statues built in China as early as the fourth century CE. At Yungang (near Datong), over twenty large caves were cut into the steep sandstone cliffs during the fifth and sixth centuries. In their carved images and detailing, they exhibit artistic influences from India—elephants, lotus plants, scrolling vines—as well as dwindled aspects of Hellenistic art, such as acanthus leaf foliage. Modern photographs cannot do justice to the original conception of these cave façades, as their appearance has been damaged by erosion over the centuries.

More widespread than the creation of cave temples was the practice of building Buddhist temple complexes with a hall for venerating images of the Buddha and a separate **pagoda**, or tower, erected over relics symbolic of the Buddha's presence. The pagoda was inspired by the parasol-like finials atop northern Indian stupas and by

multi-storied watchtowers from Chinese military construction. As a religious structure, the pagoda became a graceful multi-story building with layered roofs. Early versions can be found as carved pillars inside cave temples. The pagoda's original purpose, to house relics and sacred writings, was expanded to make the structure into a vertical marker in the landscape (Fig. 4.2). Among the earliest freestanding examples is the 130-foot-tall Songyue Pagoda at Dengfeng, built in 523, the oldest surviving brick structure in the country. This is a tapering, twelve-sided, parabolic cylinder, hollow through the center, with fifteen tiers of roofs but without means of access to the top. The parabolic shape may have been inspired by shikhara roofs on Hindu temples, and the rounded finial shows close affinity to Indian stupa designs. The Longhua Pagoda in Shanghai (977) has a brick core and wooden perimeter galleries for viewing the landscape. The ends of the roof tiers cantilever outward and upward in a graceful fashion that was to become characteristic of Chinese roof profiles. The pagoda at the Fogong Monastery in Shanxi province (1056) is the oldest surviving pagoda constructed entirely in wood and one of the tallest wooden constructions in the world (Figs. 4.3–4.4). The 220-foot-tall octagonal building rises five levels in ten structural tiers, alternating upright posts with cantilevered roofs and balconies. On the exterior, these levels are expressed as intricately bracketed overhanging roofs and galleries that contrast with trabeated wall sections. The entire structure tapers slightly to the center, which contributes to stability and also gives the impression of greater height.

## CHINESE ARCHITECTURAL PRINCIPLES

Although the earliest surviving Chinese buildings date only from the sixth century CE, there is archaeological and written evidence of older practices. Ceramic objects found in Han-Dynasty burials were cast in the form of houses or watchtowers, preserving some indication of long-vanished timber structures. Wood was the primary material of early Chinese architecture, and it was used most often in post-and-beam construction. Roof structures were based on a series of beams set in parallel tiers, augmented over time by intricate bracketing for beam–column junctions and cantilevered overhangs. A modular unit called the **jian** (with variable dimensions) was defined as the basic measure in construction (Fig. 4.5). More elaborate buildings contained additional jian, usually in odd numbers so that the distinction of a central bay was preserved, much as the even number of columns on Greek temples emphasized a space between the central pair. Since the structure was separate from the system of enclosure, Chinese buildings have a certain interior freedom in plan, as lightweight, non-load-bearing walls can be located in response to internal needs.

Except for the humblest single-jian houses, Chinese buildings tend to occur in ensembles organized around courtyards. Different functions are generally located in separate structures linked through connecting corridors or set in careful relation to common open spaces, rather than being contained under a common roof. From the exterior, there is little to distinguish buildings with different functions. Chinese architecture relies on axial arrange-

**4.5** Diagram of a typical Chinese house.

The jian serves as the basic unit for wooden construction. Houses tend to be built with separate pavilions for different functions. This diagram shows the modular basis of the house presented in Fig. 4.17.

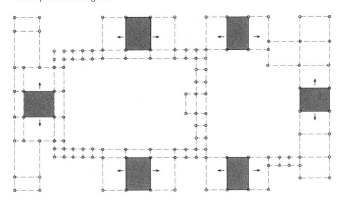

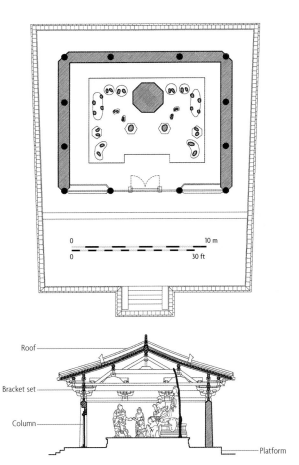

**4.6a** Longitudinal section through and plan of the main hall, Nanchan Monastery, Shanxi province, 782.

Among the oldest surviving buildings in China, the main hall of the temple is set on an axis in the position of greatest importance, preceded by two courtyards and level changes.

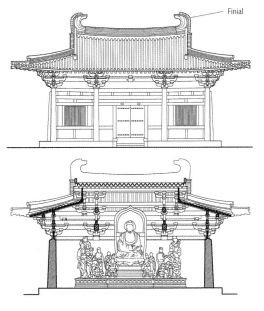

**4.6b** Elevation of and transverse section through the main hall, Nanchan Monastery, Shanxi province, 782.

These orthographic views show details of the roof bracketing system. Note also the slight curvature given to the roof ridge and the wider spacing applied to the central intercolumniation, both of which give the structure grace and liveliness.

ment, formal cues, and sequencing to establish dominance, for few buildings (aside from watchtowers and pagodas) are over one story tall.

Chinese builders developed sophisticated systems of timber construction by the time of the Sui and Tang Dynasties, and during the Song Dynasty functionaries codified related practices in the *Yingzao-fashi*, a book of building standards. As described in this text, a timber hall such as that at the Nanchan Monastery (see Figs. 4.6a, b) was to have four parts, beginning with a raised platform, like the ancient Greek stylobate, that announced the building's importance. Columns rose from this platform to **bracket sets**, interlocking supports that both allowed the roof to overhang for protection of the wooden construction from the weather and exhibited the sophisticated Chinese joinery that transcended construction and even decoration to become art. The bracket sets began with dou or wooden blocks that sat atop the columns, not unlike a capital in Classical architecture. The dou supported pairs of gong or brackets, the first one cantilevered parallel to the hall's longitudinal axis and the second cantilevered parallel to the hall's transverse axis. This sequence could then be repeated, beginning with a second dou, with the bracket set overhanging farther each time. In some cases, ang, or downward-sloping arms, further enlivened the brackets.

The completed bracket sets supported beams and purlins that, in turn, supported the fourth building part: the roof and its covering of glazed tiles in a variety of colors. The ridge and the often curving hips where the roof planes intersected were covered with special tiles and embellished with animal sculptures and with curving finials, comparable to the **acroteria** on ancient Greek temples. Ornament also appeared on ceilings and around

**4.7** East Hall, Foguang Monastery, Shanxi Province, 857.

Here the landscape has been terraced to create a higher platform for the main hall, which as one might expect is set on axis in the position of greatest importance.

windows and on doors as paneling or lattice-work in the form of squares, diamonds, and parallelograms.

The *Yingzao-fashi* also prescribed color schemes and the character of ornamental painting, with most remaining examples dating from the Qing Dynasty. The three Qing painting styles are *hexi*, *xuanzi*, and *Suzhou*. In the *hexi* style, golden dragons in various stylized postures represented the highest level of nobility. Other motifs include a chevron-like 'W' pattern, phoenixes, grass, and painted elevations of bracket sets. Artists used "powder dribbling" to make raised lines that received gold leaf. Paint colors became vivid and included the well-known Chinese red, dark blue, and leaf green. *Xuanzi* painting features so-called "whirling flowers" as well as dragons and brocades and a hierarchical ordering of color from gold and jade-like blue-green down to blue, green, black, and white. *Suzhou* painting is less stylized, featuring images of houses, pavilions, garden buildings, and linear spaces as well as fruits and flowers, animals, insects, and celestial beings. Colors again descend in importance down from gold, the most prestigious.

Both Confucian and Daoist principles are evident in Chinese attention to building placement. Orientation to the cardinal directions is common, with principal buildings tending to face south to take maximum advantage of the sun and prevailing winds. Buildings of secondary importance face east or west, shielded wherever possible by generous overhangs or vegetation. The approach axis extends from south to north, and a southern courtyard ensures that the most important rooms have ample exposure to light and air. This rather predictable arrangement gives physical expression to Confucian ideals of hierarchy while also incorporating Daoist teachings regarding harmonious living with respect to natural forces. **Feng shui**, the Chinese art of adjusting the building to particular features of the individual site and its microclimate, is but a further elaboration of the Daoist principle that human actions should be in accord with the cosmos.

The earliest extant examples of wooden buildings are Buddhist temple halls on Wutai mountain in Shanxi province. The main hall of the Nanchan Monastery, dated to 782, is a relatively modest structure of three bays, about thirty-eight by thirty-two feet overall, set in a south-facing courtyard with flanking structures (Figs. 4.6a,b). When the hall's doors are opened, the courtyard provides a space for worshipers to view from outside the statues housed inside the hall. Monks circumambulate the altar and place offerings on the platform. The hall's central bay has extra width to emphasize its axial placement, and its roof has wide, flaring eaves, crowned by a ridge with curving, hooked ends. Essentially horizontal eave and ridge lines have been transformed into a subtle upward curve by the addition of extra eave rafters and layered bracketing, thereby creating a feeling of delicacy and lightness. The end columns are even slightly inclined to the center of the hall. The tendency to build curves rather than perfectly straight ele-

**4.8** East Hall, Foguang Monastery, Shanxi province, 857. The broad eaves present an opportunity for the extensive brackets supporting the roof structure to be displayed.

ments is part of the optical refinement found in all Chinese building. It might appropriately be compared to the use of entasis and optical corrections on Greek temples. Similar refinements are seen at the east hall of the Foguang Monastery, constructed in 857 (Figs. 4.7–4.8). Its hillside site required terracing of the complex, so the main hall is elevated above the approaching courtyards. The front elevation is seven bays wide, with exceptionally deep overhanging eaves that cantilever over thirteen feet from the supporting column face.

Jinci, which includes the Hall of the Sacred Mother, is a temple complex at Taiyuan, erected in 1023–32 to honor ancestors in the Confucian tradition (Fig. 4.9). The site is hilly, with a running stream that encouraged the designers to integrate water features with numerous pavilions surrounding the main hall. Even within an irregular landscape, however, the idea of a processional axis is carefully maintained as a unifying idea. The visitor first passes a stage for performances, crosses a stone bridge and terrace, enters a hall for offerings, and finally crosses a four-way bridge over a square pool before encountering the Hall of the Sacred Mother (Fig. 4.10). Here the architects have supported the temple roof on an elaborate system of **transfer beams**, so that no interior columns interrupt the space for the large statues of the Sacred Mother flanked by her courtly attendants.

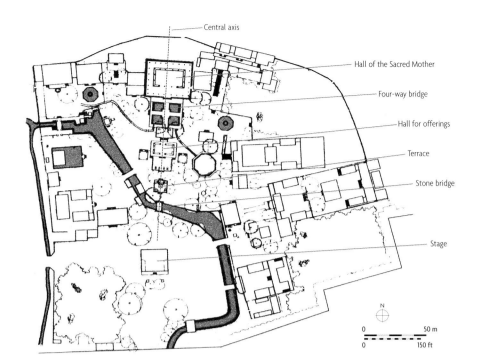

Central axis
Hall of the Sacred Mother
Four-way bridge
Hall for offerings
Terrace
Stone bridge
Stage

0       50 m
0       150 ft

**4.9** Site plan of the Jinci temple complex, Taiyuan, Shanxi province, 1023–32.

The central axis in the center of the plan organizes the pavilions and bridge that precede the Hall of the Sacred Mother (top center). Water features are shaded on this plan.

**4.10** Hall of the Sacred Mother, Jinci temple complex, Taiyuan, Shanxi province, 1023–32.

Carved dragons coil around the wooden columns. The double-roof structure indicates the hall's importance.

## PRINCIPLES OF CITY PLANNING

Among the earliest manuscripts to have survived in China is a treatise on city planning. Known as the *Kao Gong Ji*, or *The Artificer's Record*, it was composed in the fifth century CE as a guide for establishing a city based on Confucian teachings. According to the book, a capital city should be oriented to the cardinal directions and have a square plan roughly 4000 feet on each side. In the wall that surrounds the city, there should be three gates in each side, and roads projecting out from these establish the grid of the city's plan (Fig. 4.11). The central road on the south is the entrance for the major thoroughfare, nine cart lanes wide, which runs north to the palace complex. The palace itself is walled off from the rest of the city, preceded by an impressive courtyard and flanked by places of worship: the ancestral temple (to the east), and an altar to the earth (to the west). The city's marketplace is to the north of the palace compound. Otherwise, there are no public open spaces. Walls and a moat around the city provide protection from enemies without, while walls around the palace and residential blocks establish barriers that clarify the social hierarchy. (Unsurprisingly, the Chinese use the same word for city and wall.)

For an application of these principles, one may examine the plans of Chang'an (modern Xian), constructed in the sixth century as the capital of the mighty Tang Dynasty (Fig. 4.12). In its day it was among the richest and grandest cities in the world, with the urban area covering some thirty square miles. Its plan conforms in almost every respect with the principles articulated in the *Kao Gong Ji*: square layout, grid streets, three entrances in each side, and a 150-foot-wide tree-lined central artery leading from the center of the south wall to the palace along the northern side of the city. The administrative

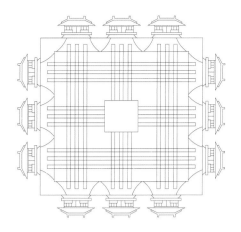

**4.11** Diagram of an ancient Chinese city.

This idealized schematic plan has three gates in each of the sides of the square forming the city walls. Straight streets leading from the gates establish a regular grid that divides the city into blocks.

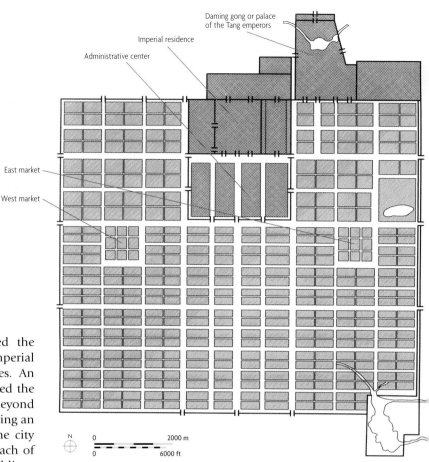

center housed government offices and reinforced the north–south axis. Behind it to the north were the imperial residence of the crown prince and support spaces. An extension on the northeast side of the city contained the Daming Gong, the palace of the Tang emperors. Beyond this palace to the north was the Imperial Park, covering an area larger than that of the city proper. Within the city walls, the plan comprised 108 residential blocks, each of which had boundary walls formed by the buildings within. Market areas were provided on both the east and the west side of town.

Although much of Tang Chang'an is known only from archaeology, Beijing preserves to this day plan features that stem from the design of Chang'an (Fig. 4.13). Beijing's site has been occupied since about 2400 BCE, and it has served intermittently as a northern capital since the third and fourth centuries BCE. From 1153 to 1215 CE it was the capital of the Golden Horde, the Mongols who breached the Great Wall, overthrew the Song Dynasty, and ruled as the Yuan Dynasty. In 1368, the Ming emperors drove out the Mongols, then reestablished Beijing as their capital city in 1403. They contracted the northern boundary, slightly enlarged the area to the south, and built a new set of perimeter walls, twelve-and-a-half miles in extent. A

**4.12** (above right) Plan of Chang'an, 6th century.

The basic features of the ancient Chinese capital conform to the diagram in Fig. 4.11, with the major exception that the palace complex is set in the middle of the north side, terminating the north-south axis. The Confucian ideal of hierarchy is clearly embodied in this plan.

**4.13** Plan of Beijing, 15th century.

The processional axis begins on the south side at the Yung Ting Men Gate and continues for over three miles to the imperial audience hall in the center of the palace, or Forbidden City. Although no one outside of the court would walk the remaining route to the north, the axis continues through the private palaces of the emperor and empress, across Coal Hill, and finally to the Drum Tower outside the Imperial City.

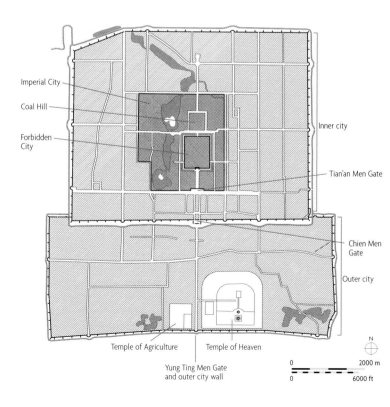

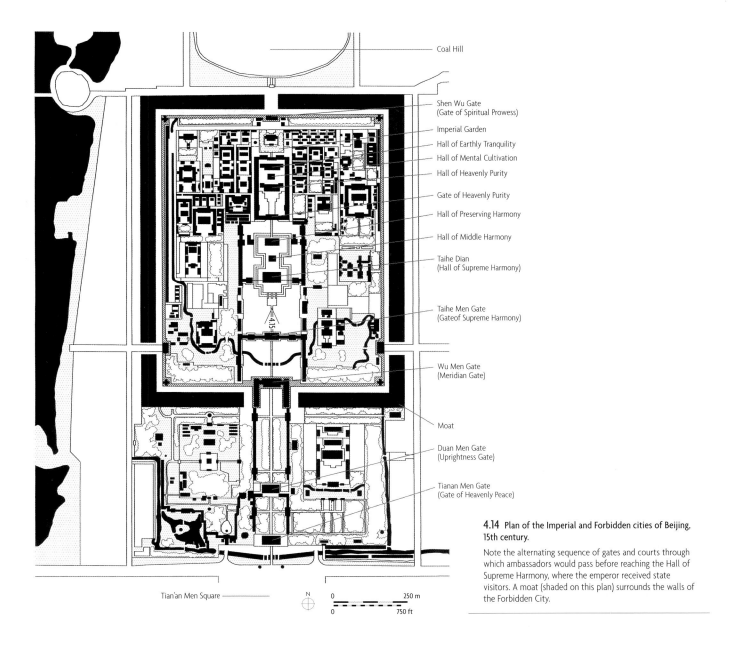

Coal Hill

Shen Wu Gate
(Gate of Spiritual Prowess)

Imperial Garden
Hall of Earthly Tranquility
Hall of Mental Cultivation
Hall of Heavenly Purity

Gate of Heavenly Purity

Hall of Preserving Harmony

Hall of Middle Harmony

Taihe Dian
(Hall of Supreme Harmony)

Taihe Men Gate
(Gateof Supreme Harmony)

Wu Men Gate
(Meridian Gate)

Moat

Duan Men Gate
(Uprightness Gate)

Tianan Men Gate
(Gate of Heavenly Peace)

**4.14** Plan of the Imperial and Forbidden cities of Beijing, 15th century.

Note the alternating sequence of gates and courts through which ambassadors would pass before reaching the Hall of Supreme Harmony, where the emperor received state visitors. A moat (shaded on this plan) surrounds the walls of the Forbidden City.

Tian'an Men Square

N

0          250 m

0          750 ft

new ceremonial axis line was created to focus on Coal Hill (Prospect Hill), an artificial mound that rises above the surrounding landscape and has five pavilions for viewing the city. In 1552, to accommodate the growing population, construction on a new nine-mile-long wall to enclose the southern suburbs (the so-called outer city) was completed. Even though much of existing Beijing is not particularly ancient by Chinese standards, almost all of it was executed in keeping with older traditions, so the city is an excellent three-dimensional realization of classical Chinese city-planning principles.

Visitors arriving in Beijing for an audience with the imperial court passed through four separate walled areas in traversing the ceremonial axis road. First came the Outer City wall, then the gates to the Inner City and the Imperial City (Fig. 4.14), before the palace, or Forbidden City, was reached. (The palace was termed "forbidden" because it was off-limits to the common people.) Moats further augmented the feeling of separation and protec-

tion engendered by the sequence of walls to the Outer City, the Inner City, the Imperial City, and finally the Forbidden City.

The gate to the Imperial City is known as the Tianan Men; the square directly in front of it has been greatly enlarged since imperial times to create a space for mass spectacles. Beyond it is an enclosed courtyard with trees, through which visitors pass to reach the Duan Men Gate, which leads to an elongated rectangular court. In the original scheme, there were temples in the large areas to the left and right: on the west were the Altars of Agriculture, and on the east was the temple to the imperial ancestors. (The latter has now been replaced by the People's Palace of Culture.) At the end of the court is the imposing Wu Men Gate, guarded by towers and flanking walls built over the moat that surrounds the Forbidden City. Once through its portals, visitors traverse a paved courtyard with a curved stream crossed by five bridges to reach the Taihe Men Gate, antechamber to the imperial audience hall, or Hall of

**4.15** Hall of Supreme Harmony, Forbidden City, Beijing, 15th century.

The axial stairway with a carved central section was reserved for the emperor, whose throne raised on a dais stood at the center of the hall.

Supreme Harmony (Taihe Dian) (Fig. 4.15). As befitted the status of the emperor, this hall is large and richly adorned, flanked by lesser structures creating a cross-axis, and elevated on a triple podium made accessible by stairs and a carved ramp over which the emperor was carried by his retinue. Although all the buildings to the north of the Hall of Supreme Harmony were private, for use by the imperial family and courtiers, the axis continues through two smaller halls used to prepare the emperor for audiences, then through gates to a walled triple-hall compound containing personal palaces of the emperor and empress before reaching the moat and northern wall of the Forbidden City. Directly behind rises Coal Hill.

There are of course many additional structures within the Forbidden City—over 9000 by one count, making it the largest ensemble of historic buildings in the country. The most skilled craftsmen and richest materials were employed in their construction, a fact that China's socialist government regards with both pride and regret, realizing that those who labored here did so "to cater for the decadent living of the ruling classes." Nevertheless, the Forbidden City has been carefully preserved as a museum.

At the point where visitors enter into the imperial presence in the Taihe Dian, they have traversed a distance of just over three miles from the Outer City gate. This whole axial approach was consciously designed to provide a suitably impressive setting for emperors who considered themselves the mightiest rulers on earth. At no point can one see the entire route or the final destination. The axis unfolds instead as a staged series of spaces, progressing logically from one to the next, and it is the cumulative experience of the sequence that gives it measured dignity and power. It may also be interpreted as a supreme expression of Confucian teachings regarding hierarchy and deference to authority.

## HOUSES AND GARDENS

The emperor's halls in the Forbidden City have a great deal in common with the houses inhabited by his more humble subjects, for the ordinary house in Beijing was also constructed of wood and set within a walled compound reached by a gate from the street (Fig. 4.17). Halls serving the various needs of an extended family were organized around one or more courtyards. On axis, and in the largest hall, were living quarters for the patriarch, flanked by side halls for use as residences of his sons and their families. (A married daughter joined her husband's family.) Courtyards provided adjunct spaces for living, being used in good weather for dining or other group activities. When possible, the whole compound faced to the south, just as does the Forbidden City. Commoners' houses would, of course, have been much smaller, simpler in construction, and much more reserved in their decoration, but the architectural principles governing house design applied to the palace as well.

Traditional Chinese house design placed great emphasis on family privacy. Residential streets were typically lined by high walls enclosing each house, relieved only by entrance gates, which were often identified by family crests and perhaps a touch of colorful decoration. Rarely was this entrance set on axis, for to have done so would have exposed the entire front courtyard area to public view when the gate was open. Access was more commonly to the side, facing a screen wall. In larger households, a servant would control the entrance of visitors at the gate,

# ELDER BROTHER ROCK

by Robert M. Craig

In the early twelfth century CE (Southern Song Dynasty), the scholar poet Mi Fu (1051–1107) was appointed magistrate of the Wu Wei district of China and was invited to greet his fellow officials and their guests prior to taking up his post. He entered the official precincts but was immediately distracted by a magnificent rock which ornamented the garden. Ignoring all around him, Mi Fu bowed low in front of the great stone, paying homage to nature rather than to man, and addressed the stone respectfully as "Shixiong," or "Elder Brother Rock." (Fig. 4.16)

The (perhaps apocryphal) story of Mi Fu inspired Chinese literati, painters, poets, and garden architects, whose themes and designs universalized the central role of nature in Chinese thought. Chinese and Japanese gardens, and the architecture they contain, are marked by continuity and a commitment to tradition, rather than by the changing historic styles characteristic of the West. The Chinese term for landscape, *shan shui*, means "mountains and water," and the traditional Chinese garden, of which the best are to be found in Suzhou, is essentially a "hill and water garden." On the simplest level, this is created by the excavation of a pond and the piling up of the excavated earth to form an adjacent artificial hill. As Ji Cheng, author of the seventeenth-century treatise *Yuan Ye*, or *Craft of Gardens*, wrote: "to have mountains situated beside a pool is the finest sight in a garden . . . Never say there are no Immortals on earth." These hills and mountains often took the form of rockeries (elaborate compositions of piled-up stones creating an artificial craggy hillock), and the most renowned garden of rockeries is the so-called Lion Grove, the garden in Suzhou once owned by the family of

the famed Chinese-American architect, I.M. Pei. When Pei built the Fragrant Hills Hotel in Beijing (1979–80), he incorporated such garden devices as *lou chuang*, traditional decorative windows marked by patterned grills. But it was not *lou chuang* but Elder Brother Rock that inhabited Pei's

**4.16** Chinese garden with pavilion and Taihu rock, Suzhou, 1522–1666.

family garden in Suzhou, the Lion Grove. Many imagined they saw in the Taihu (water-washed) stones forms reminiscent of lion shapes: cubs cavorting and lion manes in profile. The Lion Grove was planned by the fourteenth-century painter Ni Tsan (Zan) and was developed and repeatedly rebuilt over the centuries of the Ming and Qing Dynasties. Retaining its traditional features, it survives today as the garden par excellence for Taihu stonework.

In his treatise on garden design, Ji Cheng noted that the Chinese had been collecting rocks since ancient times and prized especially the grotesque, eroded stones from Lake Tai. Private individuals placed Taihu

rocks in their Suzhou and Wuxi gardens, and imperial emissaries sometimes transported huge rocks via the Grand Canal from southeastern China to as far north as Beijing, where they may still be seen in the imperial garden of the Forbidden City, in nearby Baihai park, and even in the nineteenth-century Summer Palace of the Qing-Dynasty empress dowager.

A Taihu rock might be sited in a garden pond not so much as an ornament as a symbolic representation of the islands of the Eastern Sea where the immortals dwelt. In Chinese mythology, it is on these islands that the gods distilled the *elixir vitae*, or "life force," what the Chinese called *Qi*. As natural as breath itself, *Qi* is embodied in all the universe: heaven, earth, mountains, and water. The garden becomes both a representation of the cosmos and a metaphoric and quintessential embodiment of Daoist concepts of natural order. Taihu rocks were shaped by water and wind over the centuries; contorted and grotesque, they were admired for their perforations and holes, their textures and marks evidencing geologic time. The amorphous shapes, both animate and inanimate, transform inert rock to organic nature. Elder Brother Rock was an embodiment of *Qi*. The world created by Chinese garden designers was a microcosm of the cosmic universe of matter and spirit, heaven and earth, male and female, yin and yang—one becoming the other in an eternal oscillation as natural as the tides or the diurnal movement of day becoming night.

Inspired by such Daoist concepts, Frank Lloyd Wright perceived building in stone to be organic, an architecture at one with nature. He was, like Mi Fu before him, bowing in homage to Elder Brother Rock.

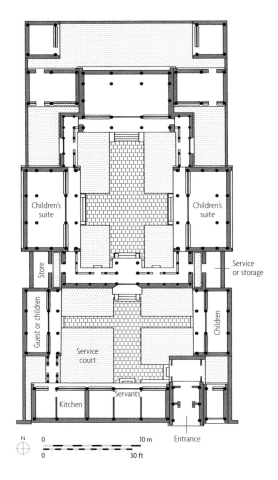

**4.17** Plan of a typical house, Beijing, 15th century.

This extended plan shows how the independent pavilions are organized around courts. Note that the entrance from the street is off axis, thus preventing those who called at the gate from intruding on family privacy.

garden within the walled compound. In landscape design, the Confucian precepts of hierarchy and dominance gave way to Daoist principles, as the irregular and picturesque were deliberately cultivated in the quest for a relaxing setting that would foster the free exploration of thoughts and feelings in a state of meditation upon nature (Figs. 4.18–4.19). The formality that governed virtually all building design was never applied to landscape design, and the principles of yin and yang are extended to all elements. Yin encompassed not only the feminine, but also such items as the moon, night, earth, water, moisture, darkness, shadows, and plant materials that reflected these properties. Yang, by contrast, stood for items interpreted as having masculine traits: sunshine, fire, heat, brightness, solidity, and landscape materials with these properties. While some gardens, such as the famous ones in Suzhou, cover extensive tracts, even the smallest space could be

**4.18** Plan of the garden of the Master of the Fishing Nets, Suzhou, 18th century.

The buildings are simple rectangular elements, while other features are scattered in a manner that suggests complete naturalism, as if in denial of the enormous care that has been taken in their design and placement.

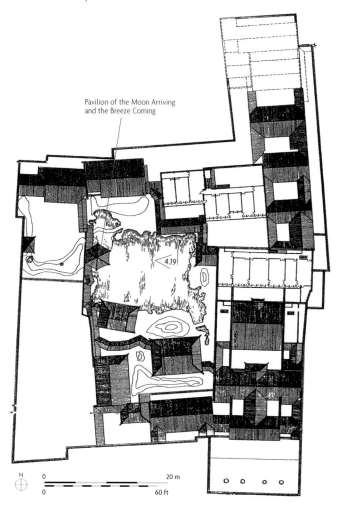

Pavilion of the Moon Arriving and the Breeze Coming

and a servants' hall might be constructed against the street-facing wall. The precise use of any of the assorted halls comprising the house varied according to the number of occupants and their activities. The regular module of wood frame construction used throughout permitted ready subdivision of interior spaces, for the walls, even those on the exterior, were constructed of thin wooden panels with solid and open sections. Windows were made of heavy paper that could be stored away during the summer months to encourage the free circulation of air. Broad overhanging eaves sheltered verandas that extended internal space to the exterior. In winter, however, the houses must have been both cold and drafty, for few had reliable means for being heated. Instead, people wore layers of quilted and fur-lined garments to keep warm both indoors and out. In rural areas, where brick or **adobe** was employed for construction, houses often had underfloor flues to provide heat during the cold months, but this arrangement was not suitable for buildings of timber construction.

The houses of more well-to-do or extended families grew by the addition of courtyards of varying size. Some might be paved and others planted with a carefully selected tree. Those who could afford it might have a

**4.19** Pavilion of the Moon Arriving and the Breeze Coming, the garden of the Master of the Fishing Nets, Suzhou, 18th century.

The irregular and picturesque have been carefully cultivated to create contrast, with rocks, water, and plants selected on Daoist principles.

made into a garden by the placement of unusually shaped rocks, a tree, sand, perhaps a water feature, and a few selected plants. Garden design became an art form rooted in the imitation of the scenic values of natural forms, exploiting properties inherent in the site. In larger gardens, the experience of the visitor was carefully sequenced and controlled through attention to paving textures, viewing points, framing devices (gates) for controlling vistas, and the like. Even though the whole garden was consciously designed, the aim was to have it appear as if it had grown wholly out of nature. Designing the landscape was considered a far more intellectual exercise than architectural design, so making gardens became a suitable pursuit for poets, philosophers, and men who had risen high in the civil service. Such wealthy and cultured individuals were responsible for the masterpiece at Suzhou.

In the eighteenth-century landscape of rural Fujian province, located in mountainous southeast China, the rural population built tulou, courtyard houses made of rammed earth. These distinctive structures were built to house multiple families brought together for their common defense. Some have square plans, some circular, with walls up to eight feet thick. Remaining examples of the circular type (Fig. 4.20) vary in size and number of stories, with the largest exceeding 200 feet in diameter and being subdivided into more than seventy rooms. Continuous porches face the courtyard, which is still used today for communal cooking and washing and agricultural processing.

**4.20** Tulou houses, Hajing county, Fujian province.

Houses like these remind us that there are certain architectural constants, such as the courtyard, which have appeared repeatedly across cultures and time. They also demonstrate the never-ending inventiveness of the human mind in organizing the activities of daily life.

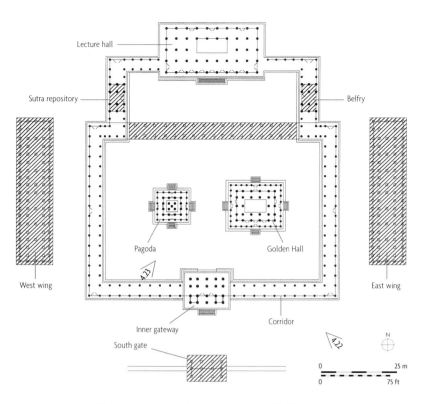

**4.21** Plan of Horyuji temple complex, near Nara, 670–714.

Note that the composition does not follow strict symmetry, using instead a balanced asymmetry in which the verticality of the pagoda counters the lower and more massive Golden Hall. The colonnades defining the perimeter wall were added later, and they incorporate previously freestanding pavilions for bells and sacred texts.

**4.22** Horjuyi temple complex, near Nara, 670–714.

This bird's-eye view shows the complex roof structure and eave brackets that were based on Chinese temple designs.

## JAPANESE TEMPLE ARCHITECTURE

Japan occupies an archipelago off the coast of Korea and China. It comprises four main islands and a thousand smaller ones scattered over nearly 800 miles. In prehistoric times, it was joined to the mainland by land bridges at various locations. Volcanic eruptions raised a chain of mountains, of which Mount Fuji is the most celebrated, that forms the spine of most of the islands; volcanoes and earthquakes associated with underlying plate tectonics have been and continue to be sources of disturbances and at times disasters. Although archaeologists have identified four ethnic groups among the earliest settlers in the archipelago, these have long since merged to produce a relatively homogeneous population that, like China, enjoyed lengthy governmental autonomy and minimal contact with other cultures until the mid-nineteenth century. In matters of architecture, there was early influence from China, particularly associated with the importation of Buddhism, and there are also elements in common with Korea, which functioned as an intermediary between China and Japan during the early centuries CE.

Japan's native religion is Shinto (the way of the gods), which reveres natural forces essential to agriculture through rituals and celebrations at shrines. Although the religion was already well established when its oral traditions were first recorded early in the eighth century CE, there is evidence that its myths and practices were used to help forge previously disparate farming and fishing settlements into a united people; with the rise of a powerful central government modeled on that of Tang China, the ruling priest-king styled himself as emperor and claimed direct lineal descent from the sun goddess, Amaterasu. (As part of the settlement of World War II, this claim was renounced by Japan's emperor in 1945.) But, while Shinto was the official state religion, from the sixth century CE onward it was colored by Buddhism, and in practice the two religions grew to overlap considerably in the ensuing centuries.

### BUDDHIST TEMPLES

The geographic spread of Japan's islands ensures that there is considerable diversity in their climates, from northern Hokkaido where snow and cold are features of long winters, to humid subtropical conditions on the southern islands. Wood has always been the primary building material, both because it was readily available and easy to work, and also because flexible wooden structures as built in Japan without significant diagonal bracing are more stable than masonry under earthquake conditions. Fire and natural deterioration have left few buildings extant from earlier than the eighth century, when the major architectural influence was that of China. Post-and-lintel building systems based on elaborately bracketed construction were used in the earliest surviving Buddhist temple

**4.23** Pagoda, Horyuji temple complex, near Nara, 670–714.

The slight upward curves of the eaves accentuate the gracefulness of the apparently hovering roof forms. A single wooden support extends from the base to the finial of the building.

complex, that of Horyuji near Nara (670–714) (Figs. 4.21–4.22). The temple buildings are set within a court-yard defined by a covered perimeter corridor and made accessible through an inner gateway (chumon). Although the axiality one would expect from Chinese influence is there, the symmetry gives way to balanced asymmetry: a five-story pagoda on the left counters the so-called Golden Hall (kondo), which is larger in plan but not as tall as the pagoda. Beyond these freestanding structures is the centrally placed assembly or lecture hall (**kodo**), used for instructing monks associated with the temple. Small pavilions for housing the sutras, or sacred texts, and a bell, now incorporated into the corridor enclosure, were originally freestanding, as was the lecture hall, so the monastery as initially constructed had a simple rectangular enclosure wall. As in Chinese practice, the pagoda contained symbolic relics of the Buddha, while the Golden Hall was the repository for religious images. Horyuji's pagoda is constructed around a single wooden support that rises the full interior height of the building (Fig. 4.23), and the pagoda's gracefully flaring eaves are supported by cantilevered cloud-pattern bracket arms. There is no means for ascending to the upper levels, so the pagoda's architectural function is strictly that of a vertical element in the overall composition.

A larger-scale elaboration of this scheme may be seen at the monastery of Todaiji, begun in 760 at Nara as part of a state-encouraged program to construct Buddhist monasteries in every province of the country, with this being the major temple in the capital. The monastery included two symmetrically placed, seven-story pagodas forward of the inner courtyard enclosing the Golden or Great Buddha Hall (Daibutsuden) and kodo, all three set on axis. Smaller structures for the monks' living quarters and dining hall flanked the kodo on three sides. The vast Great Buddha Hall housed a monumental gilt bronze statue, fifty-three feet high, of Vairocana, the Buddha of the Ideal World. The hall that survives today is a reconstruction from about

**4.24** Great South Gate, Todaiji Monastery, Nara, ca. 1200.

The roof structure of this building reflects influences from contemporary work in Song-Dynasty China. Eight layers of cantilevered brackets support the projecting eave of the lower roof, and another seven layers support the upper eave. Bracket ends have a distinctive reverse-curve profile typical of the Great Buddha style.

**4.25** Interior of the Phoenix Hall, Uji, 1053.

This view from below shows the Buddha sitting on a lotus flower in the lake of paradise. The sumptuous materials and intricate details of carved and gilded figures were employed in pious anticipation of a better world to come.

1700 at only two-thirds the size of the original, yet it is still counted among the largest wooden buildings in the world. In overall design and detail, the influence of Chinese temple design is evident. Todaiji was destroyed in 1180 and rebuilt in a manner paralleling that of Song-Dynasty China, which in Japan became known as the Great Buddha style, best exemplified in the Great South Gate completed in 1199 (Fig. 4.24). Here the eave brackets are directly set into the supporting columns that, in turn, are linked to each other by a succession of tie beams extending as tenons through the centers of the posts. Inside, there is no dropped ceiling and thus the entire roof structure is visible from below, including short rafters that radiate at the corners to create the cantilevered overhang. Main posts rise to the full height of the structure where, at the peak, a series of so-called rainbow beams with frog-leg struts are stacked to support the ridge.

Pure Land Buddhism arose during the tenth century from an esoteric sect that sought an ideal world (the Pure Land) through devotion to Amida Buddha, the Lord of the Western Paradise. The movement attracted pious and wealthy nobles, who erected halls on their estates to house an image of Amida, and increasingly the designers of these halls sought to capture the magnificence of paradise through elaborate and richly finished architecture. Such was the case with the Phoenix Hall (Hoodo) of the Byodoin, located at Uji (just south of Kyoto), constructed in 1053 by the Fujiwara family as part of the transformation of an existing villa into a family temple. The plan and massing of the building were inspired by the phoenix, a mythical bird that rises from the ashes of destruction. This

was an apt image, for many believed that the year 1052 had marked the beginning of an era of spiritual decline, when hope for escape from the cycle of birth and rebirth was lost. Only Amida was thought to have powers sufficient to save humanity, so this period was a particularly fruitful one for constructing Amida halls.

The Phoenix Hall's plan is symmetrical, consisting of a central hall with open L-shaped wings stretching from either side and a covered corridor attached to the rear like a tail. In elevation, the roof planes and bracketing system create the feeling of upward lift, as if to capture the sensation of flight. The central hall appears to be two stories tall because of its double roof layers, but in fact it is a single high space designed to provide an impressive setting for a gilded wooden statue of Amida, over nine feet tall, seated on a lotus throne in front of a golden mandorla frame and under an elaborately carved wooden canopy (Fig. 4.25). The wooden structure is painted red with golden accents, set off by white infill panels, a color scheme that parallels Chinese practice. The side wings rise up two stories, terminating in gable-roof pavilions and capped by turrets at the corners of the L shape. Viewed across the reflecting pond onto which the hall fronts, the golden image set amid this graceful and delicate architecture conveys the feeling of rising to that perfect paradise to which its patrons aspired.

## SHINTO SHRINES

In contrast to the elaborate Chinese-inspired Buddhist temple designs stand the Shinto shrines, typically small in scale and modest in architectural character. The most celebrated is the Ise Shrine at Uji-Yamada, which has been precisely rebuilt at twenty-year intervals since its founding in 690 CE, thus preserving its earliest form with reasonable exactitude, although scholars concede there have been some minor changes over time. Ise actually consists of two shrines set about four miles apart: the Outer Shrine (Geku) dedicated to Toyouke, goddess of agriculture and the earth, and the Inner Shrine (Naiku) dedicated to Amaterasu, goddess of the sun (Figs. 4.26–4.28). As both

the sun and the earth were necessary for agricultural prosperity, this union of opposites was in keeping with concepts of harmony and balance. The layout for each shrine is similar: four concentric sets of fences surround the shrine, each entered through a gateway (**torii**), and the buildings are symmetrically disposed to each side of a central axis. At the center is the main sanctuary, flanked by east and west treasure houses. Subsidiary buildings contain a kitchen and hall of offerings, used by the priests to prepare the daily offering of food for presentation to the deity. White stones cover the courtyard in which the shrine buildings are set, and the tranquility and emptiness of the site are not disturbed by visitors, who remain outside the fenced enclosure. Immediately adjacent to the

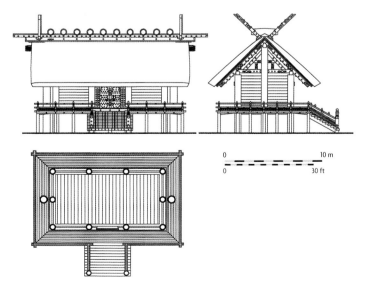

**4.26** Inner Precinct, Ise Shrine, Uji-Yamada, 690 CE–present.

In this view of the fence and treasure-house roofs, archaic forms of wooden construction are visible in all of the buildings. The shrine is part of a large complex beside the Isuzu River containing accommodations for pilgrims and priests. It is constructed anew every twenty years on adjacent rectangular sites, where the central post under the main building is retained from the previous rebuilding.

**4.27** (left) Elevations and plans of Main Sanctuary, Ise Shrine, Uji-Yamada, 690 CE–present.

The simple elegance of the proportions and materials used for these buildings has come to represent the quintessence of Japanese architecture.

**4.28** Main Sanctuary, Ise Shrine, Uji-Yamada, 690 CE–present.

Here you can see the chigi, or crossed-gable end rafters, and katsuogi, the short horizontal tapered wooden logs set on top of the ridge.

shrine is a cleared area, identical in size, which is the site for the next rebuilding.

Many historians see in the Ise shrine buildings the very essence of Japanese architecture. Here, building traditions were preserved and ideas were germinated that would be explored elsewhere in later periods. The architecture probably evolved from vernacular designs for granaries, utilitarian buildings that were raised on posts to protect their contents from damp and vermin. In agricultural cultures, it is not uncommon to find more care lavished on the construction of granaries than houses, for the community's survival depends on stored grain and sufficient seed to plant the fields in the following year. Raised-floor structures were also characteristic of early imperial palaces, another association that was appropriate to a shrine honoring the imperial ancestor. Ise refines this building type to a high art form, creating serene gabled-roof structures with elegant yet simple detailing.

At the Inner Precinct, the main sanctuary or shoden is raised over a central post that supports the heart of the shrine: a boat-shaped chest containing a mirror emblematic of the sun goddess and of the imperial family, who claimed descent from her. (This central post is all that remains on the site when the shrine is rebuilt on the adjacent plot of land. Covered and protected by a diminutive roof, it awaits the next cycle of construction, when it will again be the center of the sanctuary.) Only the emperor is allowed to enter the innermost shrine building. The cypress wood of which the shrine is constructed is left unpainted, although the exposed surfaces are finished with a great deal of refinement. Metal ornaments applied on the exterior reflect influence from Tang-Dynasty China. The weight of the roof rests on the shrine's exterior board walls, which over the years will settle and contract so that the posts and beams touch and thus assume a share of the structural load. Rafter extensions (**chigi**) at the gable ends recall the form of earlier bamboo structures, where rafter ends would cross after being lashed together. Horizontal tapered logs (**katsuogi**) originally set atop the ridge as weights to keep the thatch roof from blowing off in storms became decorative elements whose number signaled the importance of the building. Thus features that originated as practical reflections of construction necessities became highly refined expressions of simplicity, with enormous care being taken over even the smallest detail. This characteristic continues in most traditional Japanese architecture. Through ritual dismantling and re-creation, Ise represents continuity yet remains ever new.

## JAPANESE HOUSES AND CASTLES

Houses within the capital and other Japanese cities were built of impermanent materials. As a result of frequent fires and natural decay, none has survived to the present. Contemporary scroll paintings capture images of urban

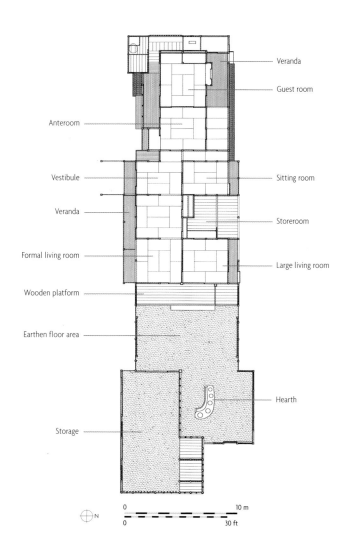

**4.29** Plan of the Yoshimura House, near Osaka ca. 1620. Minka were divided into two parts, an earth-floored section (shaded in this drawing) where animals were kept and cooking was done, and the raised-floor living area, covered in modular tatami.

life that show streets lined with one-story row houses, often with shops along the street frontage, as commerce was an important adjunct to governmental activity. The construction is simple, with wooden posts resting on foundation stones supporting a plank-covered gabled roof. Floors were of earth, although most houses may have had a raised wooden floor in at least one room. Enclosing walls were of wattle and daub or other lightweight screening, with curtains hanging over entrance doors to provide a sense of privacy. Windows facing the street were set above eye level to admit light but prohibit people from looking inside. A small garden might have been located behind the house.

Mansions of the wealthy had much in common with Chinese houses. Commonly occupying an entire city block, they were oriented to the south, with an axial main hall (shinden) facing a courtyard and flanked by side halls, although conditions particular to each site most often did not permit absolute symmetry of all parts. Perimeter walls

**4.30** Interior of a traditional house, Japan, 19th century.
This view shows sliding walls and the raised-floor section covered with tatami. Shelves and storage units hold household equipment, and furniture is minimal by Western standards.

**4.31** Traditional house (minka), Japan, probably 19th century.

This minka has a thatched gable roof with a large monitor rising above the ridge to provide additional light and air for the interior. Such roofs are characteristic of minka found in Yamanashi Prefecture, to the west of Tokyo.

ensured privacy from the street, and the buildings were often complemented by a pond and extensive landscaping.

Traditional building techniques and materials that have long since vanished from urban locations have survived in houses in the countryside. Japan has an unusually rich array of **minka** (wooden folk houses) that collectively illustrate regional diversity as well as the pre-modern living conditions of ordinary people (Figs. 4.29–4.31). In many cases, minka sheltered animals as well as people, with barn or stabling areas connected to the living quarters. In its simplest form, the living space consisted of two areas, an earth-floor section around a central hearth, the chief source of heat and the center of food preparation, and a living section with raised wooden flooring to protect

from ground damp. High roofs of thatch, bark, split bamboo, or wooden shingles were desirable to cast off rain and handle snow (in the north), and gable peak vents permitted smoke from the hearth to escape. Minka are generally modular, and the dimensions of **tatami** (rice-straw woven floor mats roughly three by six feet) determined room proportions and sizes. Elaborations of the basic scheme introduced secondary living/dining areas, guest rooms, and sleeping rooms that could be partitioned by lightweight screens. Although minka seldom have the formal symmetry that characterizes Chinese houses, they have the same flexibility in plan. The typical Japanese house had little furniture. Floor cushions were used for seating, and mattresses for sleeping were rolled out of the

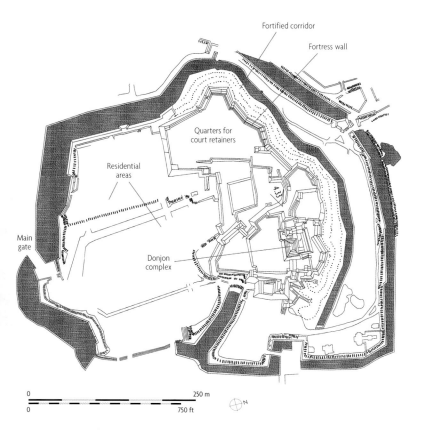

**4.32** Plan of Egret's Catle, Himeji, 1609.

This is one of the great surviving medieval castles. Its defenses include a moat (shown darkened) and massive stone foundations, but the superstructure is wood covered with thick layers of plaster.

**4.33** View up to the donjon complex at Egret's Catle, Himeji, 1609.

Stone foundations support wooden upper stories of this castle, built on a high point in the landscape. The approach route is protected by battered stone walls and defensive positions with square openings for cannons.

way during the day, so rooms could be adapted easily to serve multiple functions. The beauty of these houses lies in their simplicity, careful attention to detail, and the artistry that appears when a feature is made of the natural irregularities of the building materials. It is no wonder that Western architects as diverse as Frank Lloyd Wright and Mies van der Rohe have found inspiration in the forms and details of traditional Japanese architecture.

Japanese architecture and art often reflect qualities of composure and repose, terms that do not really describe medieval Japanese history. As the imperial family was relatively weak in the thirteenth through seventeenth centuries, feudal warlords competed for control over the country, and the incessant warfare contributed to the construction of a remarkable series of castles, twelve of which survive from the late sixteenth and seventeenth centuries. Based on earlier fortifications that are no longer extant, these castles are unusual in that they were built to accommodate and resist firearms that had been introduced by Portuguese traders in the course of the sixteenth century. The castle at Himeji (1609) is the most spectacular (Figs. 4.32–4.33). Dubbed the Egret's Castle, it shared a number of defensive features with medieval masonry castles in Europe: a strategic location on a promontory, massive

foundations for the central donjon, heavily fortified gateways, and walled enclosures protected by moats. What set Japanese castles apart from fortifications elsewhere was their reliance on timber as the primary structural material. Foundations and the lower courses of walls were stone, but the bulk of the superstructure was wood. In all cases, the wooden structure was made more fire-resistant with sand and pebbles before receiving a thick layer of plaster.

The castle at Himeji is composed of concentric layers of walls and moats, enclosing residential areas in the outer layer, quarters for court retainers in the second ring, and the donjon complex with its four towers at the center. Within this central section, a maze of passages connects the strongholds to confuse intruders. At intervals, there are overhanging galleries from which rocks or other materials could be dropped on those below. Walls are supplied with archer's slits and loopholes for firing weapons, and projecting turrets were used for surveillance. The donjon itself is framed into two massive staves that extend from basement to the roof six floors above. An internal courtyard provides light and air to rooms that would otherwise be dismal, for openings to the outside are minimal. The openings become larger in the upper stories, and there is a residential aspect to the fortress interior that is somewhat unexpected in a structure designed to resist siege. The castle's exterior presents an impressive aspect, with stacked roofs, multiple dormers, and superimposed gables. Like its European counterparts, the Egret's Castle was meant to dominate the surrounding countryside for which it served as the administrative center.

## ZEN BUDDHIST ARCHITECTURE AND ITS DERIVATIVES

Zen Buddhism, which developed in China and spread to Japan in the twelfth century, gave its name to a style of Japanese architecture that was based on examples from Song-Dynasty China. The essence of Zen is enlightenment through meditation, achieved by discarding conventional modes of thought through methods that can approach the irrational. In medieval Japan, Zen grew in popularity to become the form of Buddhism most practiced by the upper classes, and as such it came to influence all aspects of cultured life, including architecture. The Jizodo of Shofukuji (1404) is the oldest dated Zen temple in Japan, and may be used to illustrate architectural features typical of the style. As with the Great Buddha style, the wooden columns are pierced by horizontal tie beams, but the roof construction differs considerably in that it uses a double or "hidden" structure that presents one pitch and profile on the interior and eave overhang, and a different, steeper one on the exterior where outer-roof supports are concealed. The gentler pitch of the eaves contributes a sense of horizontality to the building. This form of roof construction is distinctively Japanese, having no parallel in China. The layout of Zen monasteries also came to have distinctive characteristics: their bilateral symmetry and predictable placement of structures for different functions reflected in physical form the mental discipline expected of the monks.

For many later Buddhist structures, little distinction was made between sacred and secular architecture. The Katsura Imperial Villa in Kyoto provides a splendid example of a country retreat built in the Shoin style that was based on elements from older mansions of the nobility and that also embodies concepts from the Zen tradition (Fig. 4.34). Built in stages from about 1616 to 1660 by three generations of the princely Hachijonomiya family, the villa was intended for occasional occupancy as a place for reflection, relaxation, creative works, and contemplation of nature. Katsura's plan is irregular, even sprawling, but all interior spaces are governed by the tatami module (Fig. 4.35). Japanese cedar wood (*hinoki*) is employed for the structural frame, with wooden doors or white paper-covered partitions forming the exterior walls. As at the Ise Shrine, the wood is left unfinished, and it has

**4.34** Katsura Imperial Villa, Kyoto, ca. 1616–60.

Built as a retreat for contemplation rather than as a permanent residence, this villa presents a series of spaces that can change as partitions are opened or closed, often blurring the distinction between inside and outside.

weathered to a dark chestnut to gray color, depending on exposure to light and weather. The rather somber architecture of the villa itself is complemented by the artistic layout of extensive gardens around a meandering lake. Sliding partitions and doors permit rooms to change dimensions and open up to the natural world in varying ways (Fig. 4.36). Exterior decks become extensions of the interior and frame views of the landscape; one serves as a platform for viewing the moon over the lake.

Nestled in the grounds are five tea houses, separate pavilions for practicing the Japanese art of the tea ceremony. Tea as a beverage originated in China, but a succession of Japanese tea masters, including Sen-no-Rikyu (1521–91), transformed informal tea-taking into a spiritual ritual symbolizing detached perfection in the Zen tradition. The ceremony involved with the making and drinking of tea, at once complex and simple, was performed in small structures that are seldom symmetrical or even regular but that were constructed expressly to incorporate the qualities of harmony, reverence, purity, and silence that are the very essence of the ritual. Tea houses are usually set, as at Katsura, in isolation from other buildings, and are approached by a path that enables the visitor to view the pavilion only at the last possible moment (Fig. 4.37). Rustic elements, such as wooden supports with the bark still attached or a wooden element of irregular shape, can be incorporated into the tea house as an extension of the natural world, for the tea ceremony aims at fusing the spiritual and the natural. Terms such as reticent, eloquent, and restrained have been used to describe these buildings.

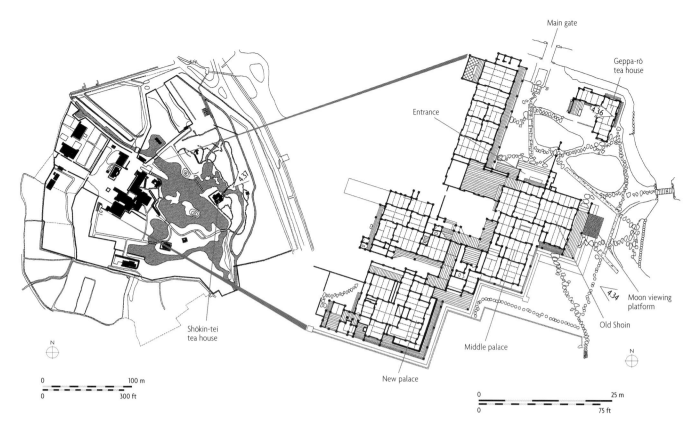

Main gate

Geppa-rō
tea house

Entrance

4.36

Moon viewing
platform

4.34

Old Shoin

Middle palace

New palace

Shōkin-tei
tea house

4.37

0 ____ 100 m
0 ____ 300 ft

N

0 ____ 25 m
0 ____ 75 ft

N

**4.35** Plan of the Katsura Imperial
Villa, Kyoto, ca. 1616–60.

The ordering of the pinwheel-like plan
is governed throughout by the
dimensions of tatami. Terraces and
open porches provide opportunities to
view the landscape, and link interior
spaces with the outside world.

**4.36** Interior of the Geppa-rō tea
house, Katsura Imperial Villa, Kyoto,
ca. 1616–60.

Sliding partitions and rice-paper panels
have been opened to reveal views to
the villa's garden.

**4.37** Shōkin-tei tea house, Katsura Imperial Villa, Kyoto, ca. 1616–60.

The tea house is set in a Zen-inspired landscape visually isolated from the villa itself. The tea house design emphasizes natural materials and controlled views within and without of the structure.

Entrance to the tea house may come through an exceptionally low door, deliberately designed so that one must almost crawl to get in. Shoes are left outside; participants sit on thick tatami and drink from exquisitely shaped vessels obviously crafted by hand. Views are carefully calculated. Windows are at eye level when one is seated, and artfully selected treasures are displayed in an alcove (**tokonoma**) with a raised floor. As the tea master serves the guests, there is time to contemplate the subtle juxtapositions of texture, material, and surface that comprise the room's interior, for the designers have imparted their reverence for materials and spatial harmony, which are intended to promote reflection that will achieve inward simplicity and tranquility of mind. The refinements of tea-house architecture encapsulate the essence of Japanese traditional design, in which architectural principles seen in the early Shinto shrines are merged with the esthetics and philosophy of Zen Buddhism.

The grounds of the Katsura Imperial Villa also include a Zen stone garden intended as both religious art and another setting for contemplation. At the renowned Kyoan-ji garden, also in Kyoto and north of Katsura, isolated, provocatively shaped rocks set in carefully manicured sand represent a serene world of mountains and seas that evoke the Buddhist universe.

## CONCLUSIONS ABOUT ARCHITECTURAL IDEAS

In China, a country dominated for millennia by hierarchical social and governmental systems and one where the government carried out most of the large-scale construction, the principles of architectural ordering were codified and rigidly applied at every scale from city plans to buildings to building components. At the urban scale, Beijing and its embedded palace complex, or Forbidden City, offers the most extreme example. It was laid out according to Confucian principles adopted in the city planning treatise called the *Kao Gong Ji* to have an intense orthogonal geometry and a primary, central, north–south axis along which the palace structures are arranged in relentless hierarchical order, culminating with the imperial audience hall. This organizational formula remained the same for Beijing's housing outside the Forbidden City, as it was based on a variable but repetitive module and laid out to have a central axis leading through courtyards to the living quarters of the family patriarch, which was flanked by the subordinate quarters of his sons and their families.

The Chinese building standards for temples were likewise codified in the *Yingzao-fashi*, which established four-part compositions of platform, columns, bracket sets, and roof, with the composition of the repetitive bracket sets specified in detail. And these specifications extended to formulaic color schemes. Chinese gardens, with their calculated irregularity, established a foil for the architecture's geometrical rigidity.

As Buddhism spread from China to Japan, Chinese Buddhist architecture did so as well. However, building ensembles such as the Horyuji temple complex exhibit a condition of stasis or equilibrium that exchanges Chinese hierarchical tension for serenity and calm. The epitome of this Japanese architectural achievement must be the Shinto Ise Shrine, where peasant buildings have been transformed to become a literally unreachable precinct fit only for the gods.

When the Japanese planned new towns like Kyoto, they employed the repetitive grid and axial thoroughfares as did the Chinese, and the traditional Japanese house was likewise modular, based on the rice-straw mat. This residential planning reached something of an apogee at Kyoto's Katsura Imperial Villa, where translucent sliding partitions enable a visitor to perceive buildings together with gardens in a unified, organic experience.

# CHAPTER 5

# THE ROMAN WORLD

During the first millennium BCE, while Greek civilization originated and flourished on the mainland and around the eastern Mediterranean, an enigmatic people, the Etruscans, were settling and developing their own culture in the area of north-central Italy now known as Tuscany. The origins of the Etruscans are not precisely understood; they are thought to have migrated onto the Italian peninsula from Asia Minor ca. 1200 BCE, after the collapse of Hittite power. From surviving inscriptions, art, artifacts, and architecture, it seems that the Etruscans drew on diverse roots. Greece during its early and Classical eras was a particularly strong influence, but there were other cultural connections as well. The Etruscans' language contained both Indo-European and non-Indo-European elements and was written in a script derived directly from Greek; their religion, which placed great emphasis on providing worldly goods for the afterlife, had much in common with that of Egypt. With that of the Hittites their art shares relief carvings of protective beasts at tomb entrances, and with the art of the Minoans and Mycenaeans naturalistic decorations depicting birds and dolphins. The Etruscan practice of reading omens from the entrails of animals follows that of Babylonia and Assyria, and their use of the arch and vault in monumental gateways indicates links with the architecture of Asia Minor. Even though they assimilated much from their neighbors, the Etruscans were an original people whose accomplishments left distinctive imprints on Roman civilization.

## ETRUSCAN IMPRINTS

Our understanding of the Etruscans is limited by the dearth of textual records. Funerary inscriptions comprise the bulk of surviving written documentation, and although these can be deciphered with reasonable accuracy, they tell us little about the language or Etruscan society and how it functioned. Etruscan settlements appear to have been loosely organized into autonomous city-states rather like those in Mesopotamia and Greece, and the Etruscan economy was based on agriculture and international trade, especially in metals: tin was imported from Britain, silver from Spain, and iron and copper were widely available. Etruscan culture was well established by the eighth century BCE and grew in influence for the next 200 years to encompass the area from the river Po in northern Italy to the region around Pompeii, south of Rome. One of their cities, Marzabotto near Bologna, had a grid plan, with the main streets running perpendicular to one another and intersecting in the center of town (Fig. 5.1). The Romans, who would use similar plans for their military camps (**castra**), labeled the main north–south street the **cardo** and the east–west route the **decumanus**. The orthogonal plan may have owed something to colonial Greek cities, known through trade.

It seems clear that the Etruscans borrowed the orders of architecture and the temple form from Greece, modifying both to suit their own purposes. Greek temples generally had a continuous colonnade surrounding the sanctuary at the center, with entrances on both gabled ends. In contrast, Etruscan temples typically contained a tripartite, or three-part, cella oriented in only one direction, generally to the south (Fig. 5.2). The temple was set on a high podium,

## Chronology

| | |
|---|---|
| beginning of cultures in the Indus Valley | 3000 BCE |
| height of power of the Etruscan civilization | 550 BCE |
| The Roman Republic | 509–27 BCE |
| dictatorship of Julius Caesar | 46–44 BCE |
| reign of Caesar Augustus and beginning of the Roman Empire | 27 BCE–14 CE |
| Vitruvius writes *De architectura* | ca. 27 BCE |
| reign of Nero | 54–68 CE |
| reign of Vespasian | 69–79 |
| construction of the Colosseum | completed 80 |
| reign of Domitian | 81–96 |
| reign of Trajan | 98–117 |
| reign of Hadrian | 117–138 |
| construction of the Pantheon | ca. 125 |
| reign of Septimus Severus | 193–211 |
| reign of Diocletian | 284–305 |
| reign of Constantine | 310–337 |

Pont du Gard, Nîmes, 20–16 BCE.

The water channel (aqueduct) runs along the uppermost level, which maintains a constant incline to carry the water, through the pull of gravity, from nearby mountains into the city of Nîmes. Aqueducts ran along the contours of the land whenever possible, but when a valley had to be crossed, as here, Roman engineers used arches to span the gap. Projecting stones and inset holes were used for bracing the wooden centering, or scaffolds, needed to erect the arches, and they were left in the finished work in case repairs were ever required. This aqueduct has long been severed, so the Pont du Gard no longer carries water.

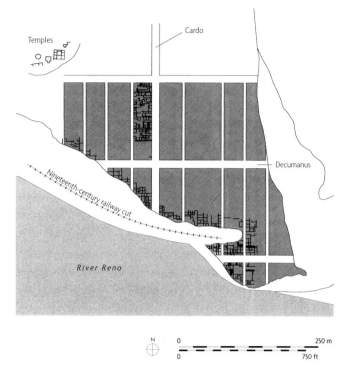

Cardo

Decumanus

*Nineteenth-century railway cut*

*River Reno*

N
0                    250 m
0                    750 ft

**5.1** Plan of Marzabotto, ca. 2nd century.

This plan shows a grid of blocks. Excavations of building foundations are shown in the same areas. The acropolis lies on the northwestern corner of the site, while the River Reno runs along the southern edge. The cardo is the Roman name for the primary north–south street and decumanus for the primary east–west street.

**5.2** Drawing of an Etruscan temple, based on descriptions by Vitruvius.

Compare this plan to those of Greek temples (see Figs. 2.15–2.17). Note that the colonnades extend only across the front to create a portico, while the cella has been expanded to several chambers set the full width of the temple. The highly sculptural building of the Greeks, meant in Classical times to be viewed at an angle, has been transformed into one dominated by a central axis and meant to be seen frontally.

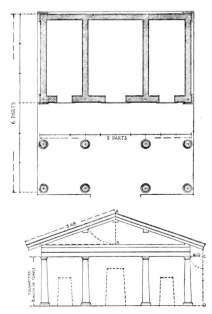

covered with a gable roof, and approached through a double row of columns set at the top of a single flight of stairs. The intricate refinement of the Doric and Ionic was forsaken for a greatly simplified original order, the **Tuscan**, which had the basic characteristics of the Doric but no fluting on the column shafts or sculpture on the frieze. Intercolumnar spacing on Etruscan temples was markedly wider, the roof pitch considerably lower, and the eave overhang greater than on Greek temples, creating a broadly horizontal emphasis. Both the columns and roof structure were built of wood, while the walls were laid up with unbaked brick. More durable terracotta was employed for roofing tiles, pediment ornamentation, and sculpture.

Because of the impermanence of their materials, no Etruscan temples survive, although literary and archaeological sources provide adequate evidence of their form and terracotta elements preserve decorative features. Architectural remains are scarce, and much of what is known about residential designs has been deduced from tomb architecture and funerary urns made in the shape of miniature dwellings. Tomb excavations at Cerveteri provide clues about upper-class housing. The rooms, hollowed out of easily carved volcanic rock (tufa), are entered through a vestibule and grouped around an inner court, which suggests an **atrium**. In some tombs, the architectural features of doors, roof beams, and moldings have been reproduced, and furnishings, such as chairs, cooking utensils, and other household items, are likewise carved in stone.

At Perugia, which was the Etruscan city of Perusia, there still exists a monumental gateway (the so-called Arch of Augustus) displaying Etruscan influence, although it dates from after the fall of Perugia to the Romans in 310 BCE (Fig. 5.3). Above the double row of voussoirs, or wedge-shaped stones, forming the gateway arch is a decorative motif consisting of metopes and triglyphs similar to a Doric frieze. Circular shields fill the spaces of the metopes, and the triglyphs are actually short fluted pilasters with volutes at the top. A relieving arch flanked by Ionic pilasters is set atop the band of Doric-inspired ornament. In borrowing here from the Greeks, the Etruscans used elements of the orders with originality, if not with understanding. Later the Romans would forge a coherent and powerful architectural style of their own by employing the arch and vault for structure and using the orders largely as decoration.

The Etruscans, together with native Italian peoples, the Latins and the Sabines, inhabited the hills that rose above the marshlands on either side of the river Tiber. Etruscan builders began to drain the marshes by digging the trench that later became the Cloaca Maxima, the major sewer of ancient Rome. According to legend, the city of Rome was founded on these hills in 753 BCE by Romulus and Remus, and it was ruled from 616 to 510 BCE by members of the Etruscan royal house, the Tarquins. In about 500 BCE, the Latins overthrew the Tarquins and established the Roman Republic. The expulsion of Etruscan rulers

**5.3** Semi-circular "Arch of Augustus," Perugia, after 310 BCE.

The lower portions were constructed by the Etruscans. The Romans later exploited the structural possibilities of the semicircular arch in their buildings.

from Rome did not signal their complete disappearance from Italy, however; other Etruscan city-states to the north continued to thrive even as Roman authority was growing. From 396 to 88 BCE Roman forces gradually incorporated these northern settlements, but not before many aspects of their culture had merged into Roman life. Etruscan art and architecture influenced Roman work, and Etruscan customs, such as chariot racing and bloody gladiatorial contests, were also popular in Roman society.

## THE ROMANS

The beginning of Roman civilization was contemporary with that of the Greeks, the Etruscans, and the later Egyptian dynasties. Unlike all of these other cultures, however, Rome continued to grow in importance as the first millennium BCE waned, reaching its apogee in the first and second centuries CE. In time Rome absorbed the Etruscans, Greeks, Egyptians, and many lesser peoples and

formed an empire with a remarkably homogeneous architectural style. Roman building practices, like Roman culture, were derived from many sources, especially Etruscan and Greek, but the forms of their architecture were in many respects original.

The ancient Romans were certainly materialistic, but also very practical. Their society is often depicted in popular culture as excessively brutal, particularly regarding its fixation with the slaughter of animals and people in the Colosseum and lesser amphitheaters and its use of crucifixion as a means of capital punishment. The Romans, however, must be judged within the context of their age and locale, one when and where slave holding, the wholesale slaughter of civilians by invading armies, and savage punishment, including crucifixion, meted out by the prevailing justice systems, were common in adjacent cultures as well. As a counterpoint, the Romans were strongly devoted to family life, astute lawmakers, gifted administrators, and, most importantly for us, highly competent and innovative builders.

Their architecture changed significantly, however, as their political system changed. Founded according to myth in the eighth century BCE by the brothers Romulus and Remus, the city of Rome became the seat of a republic governed by a senate with members drawn from notable families and by elected magistrates or consuls. As the Roman armies conquered more and more of Italy and beyond, the populace struggled to maintain a governmental system that could administer efficiently and that could satisfy both the landed aristocracy (patricians) and the general class of free citizens (plebs). A crisis eventually arose in the first century BCE that resulted in the assumption of dictatorial power by the military leader Julius Caesar. Although he was assassinated, his rule ushered in the Roman Empire and a succession of emperors beginning with Augustus Caesar in 27 BCE. The breadth and complexity of the Empire demanded new construction practices capable of producing very large buildings relatively quickly and economically. It is the architecture of the Empire on which this chapter will concentrate.

We are aided (and sometimes slightly amused or bewildered) in our understanding of Roman construction during the time of the Republic by a contemporary work, *The Ten Books of Architecture,* composed in the late first century BCE by Marcus Vitruvius Pollio, commonly known as Vitruvius, who dedicated his book to Emperor Augustus. As literature, his book is not a masterpiece. Like many architects since, Vitruvius was not particularly skilled as an author, and the precise meaning of some of his writing is difficult to deduce. Based in part on Greek precursors, his text was doubtless not the only one of its kind, but it is the only intact treatise on architecture to have survived from antiquity, and as such it has been consulted carefully by architects from the Renaissance to the present seeking to understand the principles of Roman architecture. Among the topics Vitruvius covers are building design, city planning, military engineering, and the design of machines, which indicates that architects dealt with a much wider array of problems in design and construction then than they do now. His opening comments on the education of the architect are enlightening:

*The architect should be equipped with knowledge of many branches of study and varied kinds of learning, for it is by his judgment that all work done by the other arts is put to the test. This knowledge is the child of practice and theory. Practice is the continuous and regular exercise of employment where manual work is done with any necessary material according to the design of a drawing. Theory, on the other hand, is the ability to demonstrate and explain the productions of dexterity on the principles of proportion. It follows, therefore, that architects who have aimed at acquiring manual skill without scholarship have never been able to reach a position of authority to correspond with their pains, while those who relied only upon theories and*

*scholarship were obviously hunting the shadow, not the substance. But those who have a thorough knowledge of both, like men armed at all points, have sooner attained their object and carried authority with them.*

## BUILDING TECHNIQUES AND MATERIALS

The Romans compartmentalized their activities and were able to build large interior as well as exterior spaces to hold them. The imposing quality and size of their construction is a result of their application of engineering skills to the problems they encountered in everyday life. Roman construction exploited structural elements that acted in compression: the arch, the vault, and the dome, elements developed by earlier civilizations but used in a very limited fashion (see Fig. 9.44). In Roman hands these elements became the basis for structural systems on a scale unimaginable with post-and-lintel construction.

A true arch consists of voussoirs set in a curved shape, often a semicircle. Building one requires a temporary timber formwork, or centering, to support the voussoirs as they are laid, for the arch will not stand on its own until all the voussoirs, including the central **keystone**, are set in place. (Contrast this true-arch construction to the technique of corbeling, where each course rests on and overhangs the preceding one (see Fig. 2.9). No centering is required, for the construction is always stable, but the form produced is not a true arch.) If the arch is continued along its longitudinal axis, it produces a vault; if an arch is rotated on its center, it produces a dome. By using arches, vaults, and domes, the Romans could enclose large areas with modestly sized stones cut carefully to shape. The space between supports, necessarily severely limited when stone lintels are used because stone in tension tends to crack over wide spans, could now be made much larger because vaulted construction carries the structural load almost completely in compression, for which stone is well suited. There is a price for this stability. The weight of the masonry in vaulted construction pushes not only downward but also outward on the supports on which it rests, and this outward thrust must be countered by dead weight. So vaulted construction requires walls or piers that are much thicker than those used in post-and-lintel buildings.

The earliest Roman vaults were built for utilitarian structures. Mention has already been made of the Cloaca Maxima, the trench begun by the Etruscans to drain the Roman marshes. By the mid-first century BCE, it was vaulted with stone, and the construction still functions as one of the main sewers of Rome. Discharging wastes into the Tiber, however, made the river water unfit for human consumption, so clean water was brought from rivers or springs in the Sabine Hills above Rome, piped in a gravity-fed system of **aqueducts** to city reservoirs, then distributed

**5.4** Axonometric drawing of the Sanctuary of Fortuna Primigenia, Palestrina, ca. 80 BCE.

Compare this multi-level architectural ensemble to the Greek Hellenistic Sanctuary of Asklepios on the island of Kos, as seen in Fig. 2.35. The ancient Greeks had, in turn, been influenced by such Middle Kingdom Egyptian site developments as the Temple of Queen Hatshepsut, seen in Figs. 1.29 and 1.30.

design is remarkably straightforward: the two lowest arch levels are identical rows of semicircular arches, sixty feet in diameter except for the span across the river, which is eighty feet. The uppermost tier has arches set on twenty-foot centers, so that a unifying rhythm ties all three levels together. Projecting stones used for support of the centering and scaffolding add surface texture, and they were retained in case repairs were ever needed. Enclosed above the highest arches is the water channel, about six feet square in cross-section, lined with mortar to prevent leaks. A roadway is carried above the lowest row of arches.

A dramatic example of Roman construction from the time of Vitruvius's childhood and one strongly influenced by Hellenistic Greek practices is the upper portion of the Sanctuary of Fortuna Primigenia (ca. 80 BCE) in Praeneste (modern-day Palestrina) near Rome (Fig. 5.4). In order to appreciate its organization, we must remember that the Hellenistic Greeks used stoas, bent and folded stoas, gateways, terraces, and stairs (see Kos, Fig. 2.35) to create architectural environments into which they inserted free-standing buildings. The Romans adopted this design strategy at Praeneste and elsewhere during the time of the Republic.

The complex is built into a steep hillside and culminates at the top with a small, circular, Corinthian temple housing the statue of Fortuna Primigenia. From the town below, ancient Roman visitors to the sanctuary would have proceeded up one of the longitudinally oriented stairs located to each side, moving, in effect, through an **opus incertum** retaining wall and toward colonnades shielding wells. At the top of these stairs, they would have turned 90 degrees left or right and moved toward the center by way of long, roofed-over ramps. At the top of the ramps and now on the centerline of the complex, they would again have moved longitudinally up a stair flanked by stoa-like files of attached Ionic columns and two Ionic **hemicycles** that concealed **barrel-vaulted** compartments housing shops and acting together as a retaining wall. Atop the roof of these trabeated-arcuated shops, they would again have climbed a central, longitudinal stair flanked by more applied trabeation concealing more vaulted, retaining-wall, shop compartments and ascended to a rectangular **forum** surrounded on three sides by a folded Corinthian stoa. Here they would have seen in front of them arches with applied trabeation astride another centrally located stair, this one leading up to a theater surrounded by yet another stoa, this one bent into a semicircle and serving as a final transitional experience to the circular temple. The sanctuary is in all respects a unified creation, whether seen from below along its central, longitudinal axis or experienced through time as a number of separate but related architectural incidents. While much of the original applied trabeation has been lost and the theater level has been enclosed to include flanking buildings, a visitor to Palestrina can still grasp the intended effects of this Romano-Hellenistic building ensemble.

to fountains or other uses around the city. As much as possible, the water channel or aqueduct followed the contour of the land, but where it had to cross valleys, it became necessary to elevate the conduit in order to preserve the constant slope of the supply line. The Romans erected handsome arched structures for this purpose. They completed the Aqua Appia in 312 BCE and constructed three more aqueducts in the second half of the second century BCE to provide water for the growing population of Rome. They added the impressive Aqua Claudia in 38 CE to bring water from Tivoli, some forty-five miles away. This aqueduct's great masonry arches, some more than 100 feet high, extended over the countryside for much of that distance.

Perhaps the most spectacular surviving aqueduct span is the Pont du Gard (20–16 BCE) outside Nîmes in southern France (page 104). Made of unmortared masonry (**opus quadratum**), the aqueduct strides 882 feet over the valley of the river Gard on three tiers of arches, carrying the water channel 160 feet above the level of the river. Its

In Nîmes itself, the so-called Temple of Diana (ca. 80 CE) uses a distinctive barrel vault of ashlar, or cut-stone, masonry to create its principal interior space (Fig. 5.5). This masonry is unusual, however, for the technique was costly and required highly skilled stonecarvers. The efficient Romans developed a more expedient building method by using a new material, hydraulic **cement**, derived from volcanic deposits first discovered around Puteoli (today's Pozzuoli) and named **pozzolana**. Vitruvius described it as "a kind of natural powder which from natural causes produces astonishing results." What the Romans discovered was that when pozzolana was mixed with lime, rubble, and water, the mixture reacts chemically and hardens to a stone-like consistency, even if under water. The simple lime mortars known to the ancients had some bonding strength, but they were ineffective for the bridge and harbor foundations where Roman builders first exploited the superior strength of pozzolana.

The Romans also found uses for this artificial stone away from the water, and during the third century BCE they gained experience in building with it. They placed a liquid mass composed of pozzolana, sand, water, and lime in horizontal courses over rough-laid rubble, which served both as aggregate in the wall and as an enclosure or formwork for the concrete. The mixture solidified into a monolithic material that behaved like solid masonry. Curves and irregular shapes were of course much easier to achieve in concrete than in cut-stone work, but the resulting walls were generally not handsome, so the Romans became adept at nonstructural wall finishes such as stucco, mosaic, and marble veneer.

Because most Roman buildings have lost their finish surfaces, one can see the underlying wall construction today in a way that Roman builders never intended. Early concrete walls were composed of rough stones surrounding a concrete core (opus incertum) (see Fig. 5.31), a technique later refined to pyramidal stones (**opus reticulatum**) (Fig. 5.6 and see Fig. 5.8) with square faces and their points embedded in the wall, which gave a more orderly exterior appearance. In imperial times (after 37 BCE) the Romans increasingly used triangular bricks as the concrete facing (**opus testaceum**) (see Figs. 5.33 and 5.34), laying their thin triangular shapes to present a smooth exterior and an

**5.5** "Temple of Diana," Nîmes, ca. 80 CE.

This is a fine example of barrel-vaulted masonry construction used to enclose space. Note the ribs of the vault and the use of alternating triangular and segmental arched pediments above blind windows to articulate the wall.

**5.6** Ancient Roman concrete wall construction.

By the time the Emperor Hadrian built his sprawling villa, Roman engineers had perfected the masonry-wall-construction process, using "formwork" made from two faces of stone or tiles, with the cavity between them filled with concrete. From left to right, this facing changes from uncoursed rubble masonry, to pyramid-shaped stones, to pie-shaped tiles that appear as elongated brick in the laid up walls in Fig. 5.38 above.

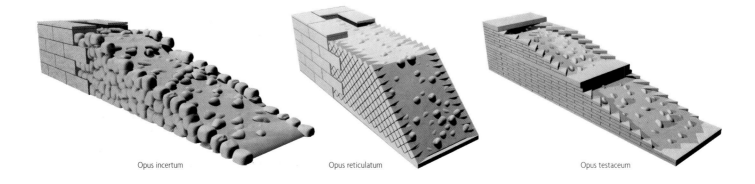

Opus incertum          Opus reticulatum          Opus testaceum

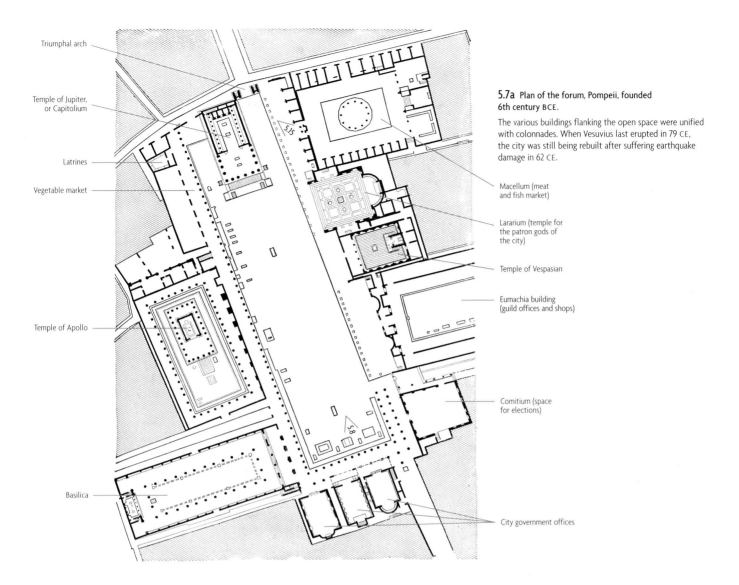

Triumphal arch

Temple of Jupiter,
or Capitolium

Latrines

Vegetable market

Temple of Apollo

Basilica

5.15

5.8

**5.7a** Plan of the forum, Pompeii, founded 6th century BCE.

The various buildings flanking the open space were unified with colonnades. When Vesuvius last erupted in 79 CE, the city was still being rebuilt after suffering earthquake damage in 62 CE.

Macellum (meat and fish market)

Lararium (temple for the patron gods of the city)

Temple of Vespasian

Eumachia building (guild offices and shops)

Comitium (space for elections)

City government offices

irregular inner face for maximum bonding surface with the soupy cement mixture. (Stamps impressed on the wet bricks in the factory have enabled archaeologists to date many Roman structures with reasonable precision.) After the second century CE concrete walls with stone rubble striped by horizontal courses of brick bonding every three or four feet (**opus listatum**) became common, the brick courses also serving as a leveling device to keep the work plumb and true. The strength, durability, and economy of concrete construction gave the Romans a versatile material for large-scale building, and by the middle of the first century CE they were using it with rapidly increasing architectural sophistication.

## CITY PLANNING

City planning practices in ancient Greece and in Rome had striking parallels. Both Athens and Rome, the cultural centers, grew without preconceived overall plans, while the colonial cities established by each were generally provided with orthogonal plans. Greek foundations might become Roman settlements later, as was the case with

Pompeii, one of the best-preserved examples of a Roman provincial town owing to its burial in the eruption of Mount Vesuvius in 79 CE. The fabric of the city, already shaken by an earthquake in 62 CE, was engulfed by ash, lava, and mud that preserved it until excavations begun in 1748 brought the remains to light.

Pompeii was founded by the Greeks in the sixth century BCE, and it was briefly inhabited by the Etruscans and Samnites before becoming a Roman city. At the time of its destruction, it had a population of about 20,000, including great patrician families, middle-class merchants, retired persons, and slaves. Its irregular grid plan covered about 160 acres within roughly oval town walls (Fig. 5.7b). The Roman civic center or forum was located in the southwest quarter, near the Marine Gate entrance (Fig. 5.7b). The earlier Greek center was two blocks to the east, on an acropolis with a Doric temple and a columned portico dating from the second or third century BCE. Streets ran approximately parallel and perpendicular to the forum, their pattern being adjusted to the varying topography.

Public facilities were dispersed around the town. Within the town walls, there were three baths, a large exercise facility (the **palaestra**) with a swimming pool, covered

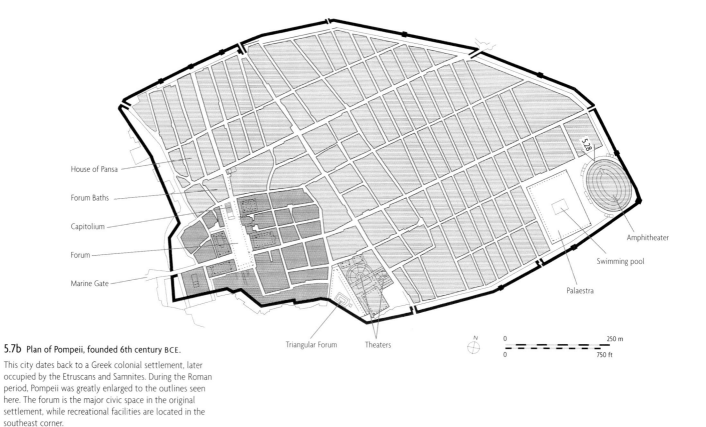

House of Pansa

Forum Baths

Capitolium

Forum

Marine Gate

5.28

Amphitheater

Swimming pool

Palaestra

Triangular Forum

Theaters

N

0                                250 m

0                                750 ft

**5.7b** Plan of Pompeii, founded 6th century BCE.

This city dates back to a Greek colonial settlement, later occupied by the Etruscans and Samnites. During the Roman period, Pompeii was greatly enlarged to the outlines seen here. The forum is the major civic space in the original settlement, while recreational facilities are located in the southeast corner.

and open-air theaters, and an **amphitheater** capable of seating the entire population. Nine temples dedicated to various gods—Greek divinities, Roman deities, deceased Roman emperors, patrons of the city, and the oriental mystery cults of Isis and Bacchus—indicate the diversity of religious beliefs in Pompeii. Cemeteries were located outside the town gates.

The forum in Pompeii was the focus of public life (Fig. 5.8). A two-story colonnade surrounded its rectangular form, 510 by 125 feet, on three sides, the open fourth (north) side being occupied by the Capitolium, the center for state-sponsored religious observances. A **triumphal arch** marked the north entrance and prevented wheeled

vehicles from intruding on the pedestrian domain. Buildings of various designs and uses flanked the forum. On the east side were the macellum, the meat and fish market; the lararium, a temple for the patron gods of the city; the eumachia building, containing guild offices and shops of the cloth workers and dyers; and the comitium, an open area where elections were held. The short southern side contained three halls used for government: offices for judges, public works officials, and the council chamber. On the west side, bordered by the road from the Marine Gate, was the large **basilica** where public assemblies for legal, commercial, and social purposes were held. It functioned much as did the stoa in the Athenian Agora, yet the

**5.8** The forum looking north, Pompeii, founded 6th century BCE.

Reconstructed remains of the colonnades can be seen to both sides. At the far end of the forum, the column stumps of the Capitolium rise up, and to their right is the city's triumphal arch. The square ends of opus reticulatum units appear on the face of the masonry mass in the foreground.

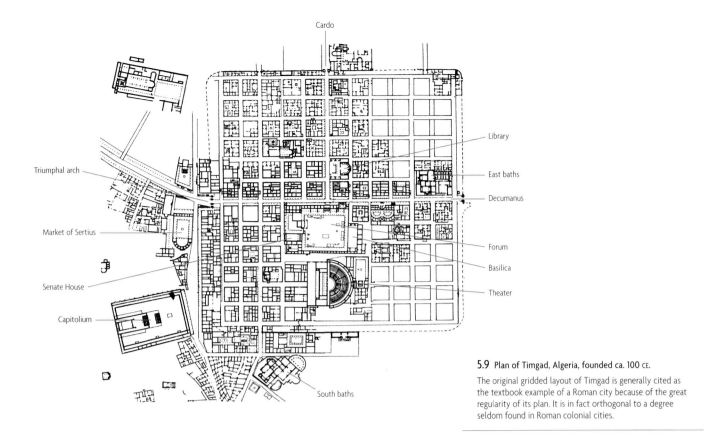

Cardo

Triumphal arch

Market of Sertius

Senate House

Capitolium

South baths

Library

East baths

Decumanus

Forum

Basilica

Theater

**5.9** Plan of Timgad, Algeria, founded ca. 100 CE.

The original gridded layout of Timgad is generally cited as the textbook example of a Roman city because of the great regularity of its plan. It is in fact orthogonal to a degree seldom found in Roman colonial cities.

space here was enclosed and introverted. Beyond the basilica were the Temple of Apollo, which dated from the earliest period of Pompeii; the vegetable market, one of the last buildings constructed on the forum; and public latrines. Colonnades linking most of the buildings gave the forum architectural consistency (see Figs. 5.7a and 5.15). Conveying unity within such a diverse grouping of buildings constructed over three or more centuries is no insignificant accomplishment, and it indicates the high quality of Roman civic design attained even in provincial centers.

Some Roman cities began as military garrisons (castra) located in unsettled areas as a means of defense and of bringing civilization to new territories. For these, and for many colonial cities as well, the Romans had a standard plan, perhaps derived from the Etruscans and applied with consistency throughout their empire, from Britain to North Africa, Italy, and the eastern Mediterranean. It was rectangular or square, with two main roads, the cardo and the decumanus, crossing at right angles in the center of town. A wall surrounded it, and the public spaces—the forum and military headquarters—were usually located at the principal intersection in the center of town. Residential sectors were laid out in square or rectangular blocks, with land reserved for neighborhood markets and recreational facilities as the town grew. Streets could be numbered sequentially so that a stranger in town could find any given address easily. Large public buildings, such as baths and theaters, served the whole community and were located according to topography.

This standard Roman plan underlies many present-day European cities, including Florence and Bologna in Italy, Cirencester in England, and Trier in Germany. Timgad in

Algeria is an original example that has not been overbuilt by a modern city, so its major features can be seen even though it is now a ruin (Fig. 5.9). Timgad was founded by the Emperor Trajan in 100 CE for veterans of the Roman legions and became a thriving regional center until it was destroyed by native tribes in the seventh century. The city walls enclosed a square, with the cardo and decumanus intersecting in the center of town. The forum is to the south, and a large theater was set just south of the forum. (Because of the theater's placement, the cardo did not continue through to the south.) Entrances into the city were framed by triumphal arches, and continuous colonnades lined the major streets to lend dignity and shelter to the sidewalks. Timgad had a population of perhaps 15,000 within a century of its founding, and in the third century CE it began to accumulate suburban developments along the approach roads to the north, west, and south. Large baths were built north and south of the walls, and markets and temples further served the expanding population outside the walls. None of the extramural growth conformed to the grid plan of the city proper.

Trajan is also remembered for the substantial contributions he made to the urban fabric of Rome itself. Civic life in Rome focused on the Forum Romanum at the base of the Capitoline Hill in an area drained by the Cloaca Maxima (Fig. 5.10). Here the functions of commerce, government, law, and religion mingled, and with the growth of the city, the space became increasingly congested. From the middle of the first century BCE onward, the development expanded as new colonnaded fora were constructed adjacent to the original Forum Romanum (Fig. 5.11). Julius Caesar laid out a forum containing a temple and governmental chambers; Augustus constructed a forum at

**5.10** View of the Forum Romanum, Rome.

This forum was largely transformed during the reign of
Augustus (37 BCE–14 CE) to become a splendid civic center
for Rome. Visible here (left to right) are three columns from
the Temple of Vespasian, the Arch of Septimus Severus
(203 CE), columns from the Temple of Saturn, and rows of
column stumps from the Basilica Julia.

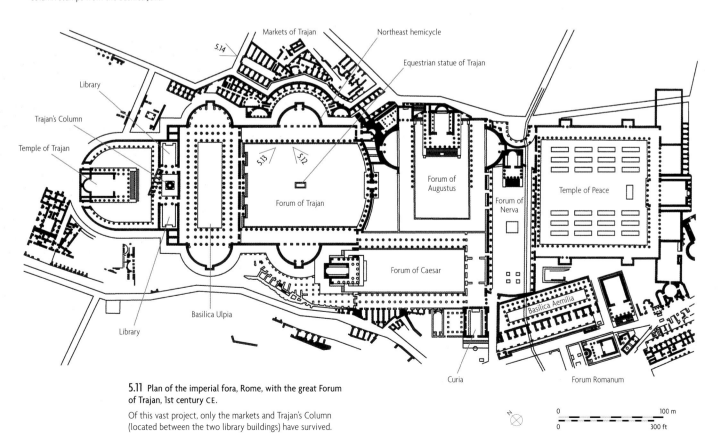

**5.11** Plan of the imperial fora, Rome, with the great Forum
of Trajan, 1st century CE.

Of this vast project, only the markets and Trajan's Column
(located between the two library buildings) have survived.

right angles to the Forum of Caesar to surround the Temple of Mars Ultor; and Vespasian built a forum around a library. The culmination of these constructions was the Forum of Trajan (ca. 100–14 CE), equal in size to all the others put together and built to the designs of Apollodorus of Damascus, who had served with distinction as a military engineer. The site was located north of the Forum of Augustus, where a ridge connecting the Capitoline and Quirinale hills was removed to provide a level area and improve access to all the fora from the north. Trajan's forum was symmetrically planned, with a monumental entranceway from the Forum of Augustus leading into the forum proper, a court 330 by 375 feet defined by double colonnades and semicircular elements (hemicycles) set on a cross-axis. Dominating the center of the court was a large equestrian statue of Trajan. Opposite the entrance was the Basilica Ulpia, a magnificent judicial building with entrances placed on its long side. Beyond the basilica was Trajan's Column, a marble shaft nearly 100 feet high set on a fifteen-foot-high base and carved with a spiraling narrative relief illustrating Trajan's victories in the Dacian Wars. Spoils from the Dacian campaign (in the region of present-day Romania) were used to finance the forum's construction. Trajan's Column, the sole surviving structure in this part of the forum, was flanked by two library buildings, one for Greek and one for Latin texts; the column's continuous frieze would have been readable from these neighboring buildings. At the terminus of the axis, in the center of a curving colonnaded courtyard, was a temple dedicated to Trajan and his wife by the later emperor Hadrian. Like those of Julius Caesar and Augustus, and like Etruscan temples, it has a deep porch with columns defining an entry space.

Needed commercial space adjacent to the forum was carved out of the Quirinale hillside behind the northeast hemicycle. Trajan's markets, a good part of which are extant, were set in a multi-story semicircle with adjoining, tiered buildings, reflecting the hemicycle of the forum below and becoming an arcaded complement to it (Figs. 5.12–5.13). The markets contained over 150 shops, offices, and a **groin-vaulted** market hall (Fig. 5.14), all of which could be reached from the forum and from streets on two higher levels. They were built of brick-faced concrete, a contrast to the marble and elaborate ornament of the forum. Durable barrel vaults provided the basic structural module both for the individual shops and for enclosed walkways between them. In the two-story market hall (Fig. 5.13), piers rising from the walls between the shops to each side of the central space support six groin vaults given lateral support by **flying buttresses**.

We have noted the presence of triumphal arches in both Pompeii (Fig. 5.15) and Timgad. These freestanding monuments were generally built to commemorate a military victory, and they added grandeur to the public realm by serving as reminders of civic greatness. (The Arc du Triomphe in Paris, erected in the nineteenth century, was

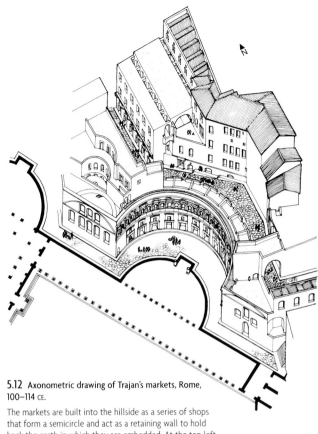

**5.12** Axonometric drawing of Trajan's markets, Rome, 100–114 CE.

The markets are built into the hillside as a series of shops that form a semicircle and act as a retaining wall to hold back the earth in which they are embedded. At the top left, the vaulted market hall lies further up the hill.

**5.13** Trajan's markets, Rome, 100–114 CE.

This view of the shops shows the great semicircle that completed one side of the principal cross-axis of the forum.

**5.14** Covered market hall build by Trajan, Rome, ca. 100 CE.

Constructed in concrete, this is an early example of a groin-vaulted space with clerestory lighting and flying buttresses (one of which is visible through the near-left-end bay at the upper level). It shows the care extended by Roman builders to civic structures accommodating such mundane activities as a fruit and vegetable market.

**5.15** Triumphal arch, Pompeii, before 79 CE.

Monuments such as these were the pride of the city, reflecting civic virtues and boldly marking entrances to important sites. In this case, the arch also restricted access of wheeled vehicles into the forum.

constructed in this same tradition, but on a scale greater than that of comparable Roman works.) Of surviving arches, those in Rome are the most elaborate. The Arch of Septimus Severus (203 CE) still stands in the Forum Romanum, while the larger Arch of Constantine (finished 315 CE) (Fig. 5.16) stands near the Colosseum. Both are triple-arched structures, the central arch being larger than the side arches, and the **attic** story (above the arch) is embellished with carved relief panels depicting the particular military victory for which the arch was constructed. Constantine's Arch incorporates panels from earlier monuments. As an architectural motif, the triumphal arch will have a long afterlife, being revived in **Carolingian**, Romanesque, Renaissance, and later works.

**5.16** The Arch of Constantine, Rome, 315 CE.

This triple-arched form became an architectural motif adapted to later buildings. Compare the abbey gatehouse at Lorsch (see Fig. 8.4) and the west front of S. Andrea in Mantua (see Fig. 11.16) for examples of later works inspired by this design.

# THE ENGINEERING MIGHT OF THE ROMANS

by Dan MacGilvray

*It now remains for us to speak of stones, or, in other words, the leading folly of the day . . . as to the mountains, nature has made those for herself, as a kind of bulwark for keeping together the bowels of the earth; as also for the purpose of curbing the violence of the rivers, of breaking the waves of the sea, and so, by opposing to them the very hardest of her materials, putting a check upon those elements which are never at rest. And yet we must hew down these mountains and carry them off . . . for no other reason than to gratify our luxurious inclinations. . . .*

*These very mountains are cut asunder to yield us a thousand different marbles, promontories are thrown open to the sea, and the face of nature is being everywhere reduced. . . . We now carry away the barriers that were destined for the separation of one nation from another; we construct ships for the transport of our marbles; and amid the waves . . . we convey the summits of the mountains to and fro: a thing, however, that is even less unpardonable than to . . . search amid the regions of the clouds for vessels with which to cool our draughts, and to excavate rocks, towering to the very heavens, in order that we may have the satisfaction of drinking from ice!*[1]

**5.17** Altar from Claudian period, 1st century CE. Villa Medici, Rome.

In these two paragraphs from his *Natural History*, Pliny neatly exposes both the arrogance and the capabilities of the Roman civilization. As opposed to the esthetically sensitive Greeks, the Romans were the mighty engineers of the ancient world, conquering not only all the peoples and nations of the Mediterranean, but subduing the sea itself and even the mountains that surround it.

Not since the Egyptians had architects and constructors had the routine capability of choosing building materials for their projects that came from great distances. Ancient buildings had always reflected the local geology: the sun-dried brick walls and vaults of Babylon were built of mud scooped from the Euphrates flood plain, the gleaming white Parthenon was constructed of marble from nearby Mount Pentelikos. Even the proud Egyptians were limited to materials found within the 600-mile-long watershed of the Nile below the first cataract—limestone for the pyramids came from the Giza plateau or Tura, across the river; sandstone for the temples at Luxor and Karnak was quarried at Silsileh, a few miles conveniently upstream. Only when they required the toughest of all stones, granite, for a 100-foot obelisk or to line the pharaoh's chamber in the Great Pyramid, were the Egyptians called upon to move their stones great distances.

In contrast, Roman architects routinely constructed concrete walls and vaults using pozzolana, a natural cement mined near Naples, and the emperors adorned their temples, palaces, and baths with a polychrome profusion of thin marble veneers and graceful columns: pure white from Carrara overlooking the Lingurian Sea above Pisa, or the island of Proconeseus in the Sea of Marmara; *giallo antico* (antique yellow) from Tunisia; *verde antico* (green) from Greece; onion-skinned *cipolino* from the Aegean isles; purple porphyry, rose and gray granite from Egypt. Romans outdid Egyptians by pulling down the great obelisks from their temple fronts, moving them on specially constructed ships over 1500 miles across the Mediterranean, and re-erecting them in the circuses, villas, and gardens of Rome (Fig. 5.17). In the process they seem to have offended not only the Egyptian gods but also Pliny, who comments on Roman "folly" and environmental arrogance.

Just as the ancient Romans indelibly marked the mountains with their quarries, Rome today still displays some of its ancient arrogance (and capabilities) as granite obelisks, marble veneers, and slender columns have been relocated to adorn the temples of the Catholic Church.

---

1 Plinius Secundus, C. (the Elder Pliny), *The Natural History of Pliny, Vol. VI*, translated by John Bostock and H.T. Riley (London: Henry G. Bohn, 1862), p. 305. Pliny is referring to quartz as the material that gives the "satisfaction of drinking from ice."

## TEMPLES

Discussion of the Roman fora has indicated the locations of temples, which the Romans built largely on the basis of Greek and Etruscan precedents. Generally speaking, the Romans did not build temples as isolated structures as had the Classical Greeks, but as axially approached buildings in an urban setting, like the temples of the Hellenistic period or the temples of the Etruscans. The placement of the Capitolium in the forum at Pompeii and the Temple of Mars Ultor in the Forum of Augustus in Rome was essentially the same, and the temple designs were similar. Both were raised on podiums, so that a flight of steps led up to the colonnaded portico of the cella space.

As the Capitolium and the Temple of Mars Ultor are largely destroyed, smaller Roman temples that have survived more completely provide us with a better image of temple architecture. In Rome the second-century BCE Temple of Fortuna Virilis (Fig. 5.18) superficially resembles an Ionic Greek temple. However, a closer look at the side and rear elevations reveals that the columns are engaged with the cella wall and not freestanding. Expanding the cella to the limits of the surrounding colonnade provides a larger interior space and reinforces the axiality of the whole.

Not all Roman temples were rectangular. The Greeks had built circular tholoi, and the Romans applied the circular ground plan to temples. One of the most striking is the Temple of the Sibyl (ca. 25 BCE) in Tivoli. Set on a promontory, it seems to reflect Greek precedent in both its design and siting. It is, however, distinctly Roman. The approach is axial, via a flight of stairs; the cella wall is constructed of concrete instead of marble blocks; and the ornamental frieze of the Corinthian order has Roman swags and ox skulls. Near the Temple of Fortuna Virilis in Rome is the so-called Temple of Vesta (a temple dedicated to Hercules), a circular-plan temple of the first century BCE that is similar to but slightly larger than the Tivoli example. Later modifications have changed the roof and destroyed the original entablature.

The greatest circular-plan Roman temple is the Pantheon in Rome (118–28 CE), considered by many to be the most influential building in Western architectural history (Fig. 5.19). Its size, the boldness of its design, and the technical accomplishment of its construction combine to make it a memorable work. Dedicated to seven planetary deities, the Pantheon was constructed in the reign of the emperor Hadrian, who is reputed to have been its architect. The entrance is an enormous portico with twenty Corinthian columns that originally supported roof trusses (their bronze covering long since removed). This portico is rather awkwardly joined to the circular cella, a space 142 feet and six inches in diameter and 142 feet high. The bottom half of the cella is a cylinder on which rests a hemispherical dome, with a circular opening or **oculus**, twenty-seven feet in diameter, at the top to let in light and air (Fig. 5.20). The contrast of the

**5.18** Temple of Fortuna Virilis, Rome, 2nd century BCE.

An early example of a Roman temple, which uses the orders (here, the Ionic) as one might expect from the Greek example, but the building was oriented to an axis in the manner of the Etruscans.

interior to the exterior is breathtaking, even to modern senses, and it has inspired visitors ever since it was completed. Unlike other pagan temples in Rome, the Pantheon was converted to Christian use and never pillaged for its marble facings, so it remains the Roman building closest to its original state.

The cylindrical cella wall is visually divided into two stories, a ground-level Corinthian order of fluted columns and pilasters supporting an attic story with rectangular openings resembling windows set in a patterned marble wall. The lower story is varied by niches, alternately semicircular and rectangular, set at quarter and eighth points around the circumference. Articulation in the dome is accomplished by five tiers of diminishing square coffers, designed with exaggerated perspective to enhance the sense of depth. The light pouring in from the oculus emphasizes the three-dimensionality of both the ceiling coffers and the eight niches below. As one stands in the center of the Pantheon, the building creates the feeling that the space extends beyond the cylindrical drum and that the dome is much higher than its actual dimension.

The conceptual simplicity of the Pantheon's dome-on-drum design should not be mistaken for constructional simplicity (Fig. 5.21). What looks like trabeated construction is in fact a structure based on arches and vaults. Behind the orderly interior columns, veneers, and coffers lies a technical masterpiece, a testament to Roman skill in building with concrete. The immense structural load of the dome is distributed to concrete foundations fifteen feet thick and thirty-four feet wide through drum walls that are

**5.19** Pantheon, Rome, ca. 125 CE.

The greatest of Hadrianic architectural projects has become one of the most influential works in Western architectural history, the inspiration for virtually every subsequent domed building. The exterior is imposing, while the interior is overwhelming.

**5.20** Giovanni Paolo Panini, *The Interior of the Pantheon*, ca. 1740. Oil on canvas, 4 ft. 2½ in. × 3 ft. 3 in. (1.28 × .99 m.). National Gallery of Art, Washington, DC.

A sphere 142 feet 6 inches in diameter conceptually determines the interior volume of the great dome, which constitutes half of the sphere. Columns in the wall belie the principal structure of arches and vaults that sustain the great dome. Concrete is the primary structural material, faced with marble veneers below and left exposed in the coffering above.

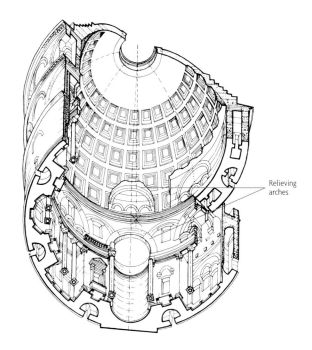

Relieving arches

**5.21** Axonometric section of the Pantheon, Rome, 118–128 CE.

This worm's-eye view shows part of the plan and the arched construction behind the internal marble veneers and inside the dome. Although none of this arcuated construction is visible from the interior, relieving arches can be seen on the exterior as in Fig. 5.19.

up to twenty feet deep. Most of the constructional complexity is not visible on the interior. The first two rings of coffering conceal eight great relieving arches that work with a second set, likewise hidden, to concentrate loads on the wall sections between the niches of the ground story. Even these sections are not solid, but are hollowed by chambers, accessible from the exterior, to equalize contraction of the concrete as it hardened and lessen the dead load transferred to the foundations, all this without compromising the stability of the whole. Aggregate in the concrete mix is progressively lightened, from heavy basalt in the foundations to sponge-like volcanic rock (tufa) in the oculus ring.

Virtually every domed building constructed since Roman times makes reference to the Pantheon. Sometimes its influence is very obvious, as in Jefferson's design for the Library at the University of Virginia (see Fig. 14.16), and at other times the connection is less apparent, as in Brunelleschi's dome for Florence Cathedral (see Fig. 11.3). Literally hundreds of domed museums, universities, banks, churches, and railroad stations, to mention only some of the building types, may be found that are ultimately connected to this masterpiece from the time of Hadrian.

## PUBLIC BUILDINGS

The Romans developed a number of public building types for specialized functions: the basilica, a large assembly hall used for law courts; the baths, a many-chambered building containing bathing and recreational facilities; and the theater, which was based on the Greek prototype but made into a freestanding structure and sometimes enlarged to become an amphitheater for spectacular entertainment. Each of these building types posed spatial and constructional challenges, and each left its imprint on subsequent architectural developments.

### BASILICAS

The basilica on the southwest corner of the forum at Pompeii has already been noted. Dated to ca. 100 BCE, it is the oldest known Roman basilica, though it was probably not the first. While it principally housed legal activities, it doubtless also served as a gathering place for social and commercial functions, as did the colonnades of the Greek stoas. In Greek, the word *basilica* literally means "king's hall." Rather than surrounding the exterior as in a stoa, the basilica's colonnades define the longitudinal central space. Entrance to the basilica at Pompeii was made primarily from the short side adjacent to the city governmental offices, but there were lesser entrances on both long sides. Set in a rectangular area in front of the end wall opposite the primary entrance was the tribunal seat of honor, terminating the longitudinal axis estab-

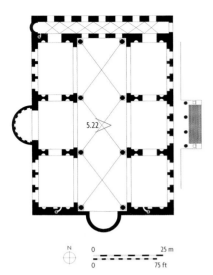

**5.22** Plan of the Basilica Nova (Basilica of Maxentius and Constantine), Rome, 307–15 CE.

This large vaulted building had groin vaults flanked by barrel vaults. Illumination was provided by large clerestory windows.

**5.23** Basilica Nova, Rome, 307–15 CE.

Although the groin vaults have collapsed, one set of barrel vaults remains. Astride each bay, the haunches of the groin vaults rise above the parapet. The columns that stood below them were only ornamental.

lished by the colonnades. The building was covered by a wooden gabled roof.

Trajan's Forum in Rome contained the more extensive Basilica Ulpia, which measured 200 by 400 feet excluding the curved end sections (**apses**). Here the entrances were placed in the building's long façades because the basilica completes one side of the forum. On the interior, double colonnades defined the long, narrow central space, and there were triple colonnades across the short sides in front of the semicircular apses. Architectural restoration drawings show the interior with second-floor galleries above the columns on both long sides and clerestory windows illuminating the central space. As at Pompeii, a gabled timber roof covered the building. Luxurious materials, financed by tribute money from Dacia, were employed in the construction: marble on floors and walls, bronze gilding suspended from the roof trusses on the coffered ceiling, and Egyptian granite for the columns. Impressive size, rich finishes, and dramatic lighting combined here to create a setting fit for the dispensation of imperial justice. Of all this magnificence only rude fragments remain, but the basilica form would become the basis for Early Christian church designs.

Not all basilicas had files of columns or were timber-roofed. The Basilica Nova (also known as the Basilica of Maxentius and Constantine) in Rome, dated 307–15 CE, had three great groin vaults over its central space, with three barrel-vaulted **bays** to each side (Figs. 5.22–5.23). Structurally, this organization allowed the semi-circular barrel vaults and their support walls, all at right angles to the principal axis of the central space, to provide lateral stability for the groin vaults. Finally, the two apses terminated longitudinal and transverse axes.

## PUBLIC BATHS

The interior of the Basilica Nova owed much to the greatest vaulted Roman buildings, the baths. As the name implies, Roman baths (**thermae**) were primarily hygienic facilities, but they also provided for exercise, relaxation, and informal socializing, activities more commonly associated with modern spas or health clubs than with bathrooms. The Romans actually cleaned their bodies without soap by first anointing with oil and then scraping the skin with spoon-like implements. Bathers induced perspiration in hot steam rooms (rather like Finnish saunas) and then cooled down and relaxed in a sequence of temperate and cool plunges. They might extend their time at the baths by swimming, taking walks, enjoying conversation, or reading in the baths' library.

Such an array of activities required an array of spaces: changing rooms, latrines, rooms for hot, warm, and cold bathing; exercise facilities, relaxing areas, and gardens if possible. Adequate water supplies were essential. The

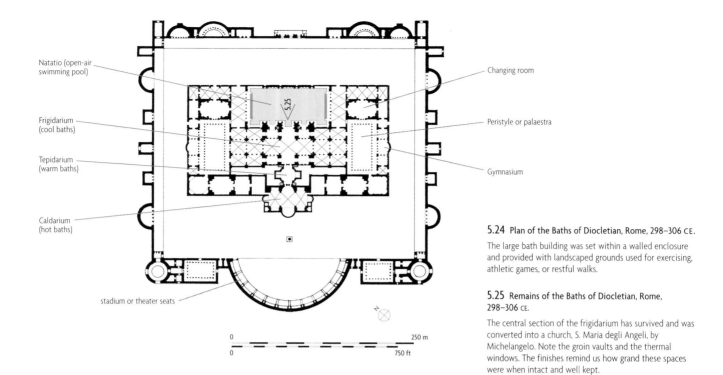

Natatio (open-air swimming pool)

Frigidarium (cool baths)

Tepidarium (warm baths)

Caldarium (hot baths)

Changing room

Peristyle or palaestra

Gymnasium

stadium or theater seats

0        250 m
0              750 ft

**5.24** Plan of the Baths of Diocletian, Rome, 298–306 CE.

The large bath building was set within a walled enclosure and provided with landscaped grounds used for exercising, athletic games, or restful walks.

**5.25** Remains of the Baths of Diocletian, Rome, 298–306 CE.

The central section of the frigidarium has survived and was converted into a church, S. Maria degli Angeli, by Michelangelo. Note the groin vaults and the thermal windows. The finishes remind us how grand these spaces were when intact and well kept.

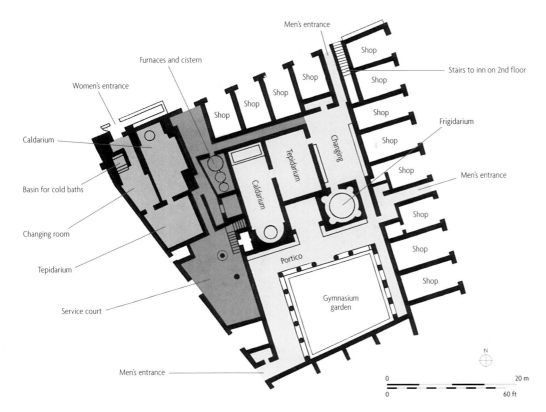

Men's entrance

Furnaces and cistern

Women's entrance

Shop
Shop
Shop
Shop
Shop

Stairs to inn on 2nd floor

Shop

Shop

Frigidarium

Caldarium

Shop

Basin for cold baths

Shop

Tepidarium

Changing

Men's entrance

Caldarium

Changing room

Shop

Tepidarium

Shop

Service court

Portico

Shop

Gymnasium
garden

Shop

Men's entrance

N

0                    20 m

0                         60 ft

**5.26** Forum Baths, Pompeii, ca. 80 BCE.

This is a small facility with separate but unequal sections for men and women. A common service area (dark shading) was used for heating water. Shops occupy most of the street frontage, since there was no need for an impressive street presence. See Fig. 5.7b for location within the city.

Romans used mineral springs when available (Bath in England was one such Roman establishment) and heated the water if the supply was not naturally warm. Because bathing was a healthful diversion for the large urban population, the later emperors vied with one another to build ever more elaborate complexes in Rome.

The Baths of Diocletian (298–306 CE) were the largest such complex in ancient Rome, covering about fifty acres of land, and were said to have the capacity for 3000 people (Fig. 5.24). The entire complex was symmetrically designed, with the principal sequence of rooms within the bath building placed on the central axis. From the center of the southwest façade, these included the groin-vaulted hot baths (**caldarium**), domed warm baths (**tepidarium**), cruciform cool baths (**frigidarium**), and open-air swimming pool (natatio). On either side of this central suite of spaces were oval-plan changing rooms and an unroofed rectangular **peristyle** or palaestra for exercising surrounded by ancillary service rooms, the use of which cannot be completely identified. **En suite**, or adjacent, rooms on the south side may have been steam rooms leading up to the caldarium. Interiors were finished with sumptuous materials, marble veneers and mosaics; statues were placed both inside and out; and the grounds were landscaped with trees and gardens to create a congenial environment for exercise, conversation, and relaxation. A large **exedra** in the southwest exterior wall was fitted with

tiered seats for use as a theater or stadium. Rectangular rooms to either side may have contained libraries. Of this vast structure, only parts survive. In 1561, Michelangelo converted the frigidarium into the Church of S. Maria degli Angeli (Fig. 5.25), where the interior reflects the scale and some of the splendor of the Roman original. One corner rotunda has been transformed into the Church of S. Bernardo, and a trace of the great southern exedra has been preserved in the nineteenth-century Piazza dell'Esedra near the present railroad station.

The Baths of Diocletian were exceptionally large, even by the standards of imperial times. Of ancient Rome's over 950 baths listed in a mid-fourth-century inventory, only a handful were this grand. One can appreciate the more common baths designs by looking at buildings that remain in provincial cities, such as the Forum Baths at Pompeii (Fig. 5.26), Paris (where the Cluny Museum incorporates part of a third-century CE baths), or Leptis Magna on the North African coast, where the so-called Hunting Baths (late second or early third century CE) are exceptionally well preserved.

## THEATERS AND AMPHITHEATERS

Athletic competitions and dramatic performances were part of the culture of ancient Greece. The Romans, who inherited these traditions and added to them the gladiatorial combats of the Etruscans, needed theaters and

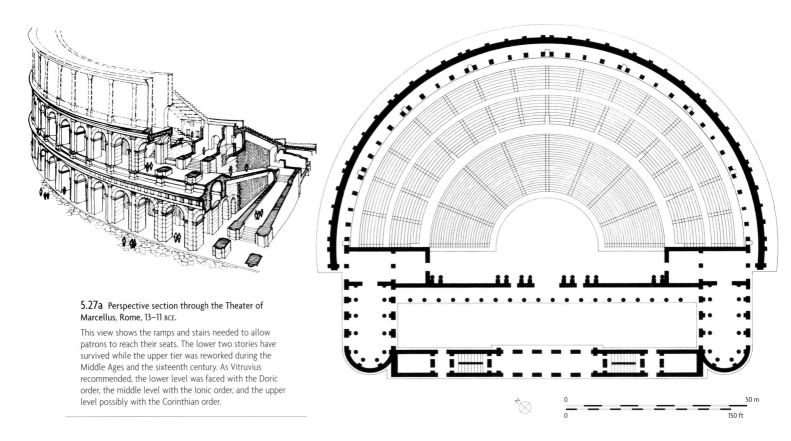

**5.27a** Perspective section through the Theater of Marcellus, Rome, 13–11 BCE.

This view shows the ramps and stairs needed to allow patrons to reach their seats. The lower two stories have survived while the upper tier was reworked during the Middle Ages and the sixteenth century. As Vitruvius recommended, the lower level was faced with the Doric order, the middle level with the Ionic order, and the upper level possibly with the Corinthian order.

**5.27b** Plan of the Theater of Marcellus, Rome, 13–11 BCE.

Roman theaters were based on designs already perfected by the Greeks. The difference here is that support for the seats depends not on a convenient hillside but rather on a vaulted structure of cut stone and concrete.

**5.28** The amphitheater, Pompeii, ca. 80 BCE.

This oval-shaped arena was used for the gladiatorial contests of which the Romans were exceedingly fond. Part of its seating is supported on arched construction and part is built into rising ground.

stadiums in which to stage these events. Greek building practice was to carve the shape of theaters or stadiums out of hillsides, thus adapting the sloping natural setting to tiered seating, but the Romans chose to construct their facilities whether the terrain was favorable or not, so they developed great vaulted structures to create the slope needed for spectator viewing. An early result of this process was the Theater of Marcellus (completed 13–11 BCE) in Rome (Figs. 5.27a,b), where a great semicircle of 11,000 seats rising in three tiers focused on a rectangular stage building that formed the backdrop for the drama. (This theater had the same capacity as the Greek theater at Epidauros.) Enough of the original construction has survived reuse, first as a medieval fortress and then as a Renaissance palace, to permit reasonable understanding of the structural ingenuity underlying the plan. Stacked radial barrel vaults accommodating ingress and egress, and ramps and stairs made of cut stone and concrete, were intersected by concentric rings of barrel vaults accommodating internal circulation. Fragmentary remains of the exterior veneer frame the arched terminations of the radial barrel vaults in the form of engaged half-columns and entablatures of the Doric and Ionic orders on the ground and second levels, respectively.

The design of theaters doubtless inspired that of amphitheaters ("amphi," meaning "both sides," so a theater on both sides), which were circular or oval in plan, with raked seating on all sides. The amphitheater at Pompeii, dating from about 80 BCE and the oldest surviving example, was sited so that seats at one end of the oval could be supported on rising ground (Fig. 5.28). Later amphitheaters built in southern France at Arles and Nîmes were constructed almost entirely above ground level.

**5.29** The Colosseum (Flavian Amphitheater), Rome, completed 80 CE.

Grandest of all the Roman arenas, the Colosseum's exterior was clad in travertine. This view shows sections where the veneer has been stripped away revealing the structural arches.

Greatest of all was the Flavian Amphitheater in Rome, more commonly known as the Colosseum, completed in 80 CE (Fig. 5.29). Although the building's plan is the familiar oval and its structure is modeled on that of the Theater of Marcellus, the novel element here is size. The outside dimension of the oval measures 510 by 615 feet, encompassing seats for an estimated 50,000 people in a continuously rising tier with an additional seating band above. Except for this top level of seats, which rested on wooden supports, the entire building was masonry, a combination of cut stone and concrete resting on carefully laid foundations. Under the seating was an intricate network of structural supports, horizontal passageways, ramps, and stairs to accommodate the attending throngs. The exterior walls were clad in travertine, usually a cream-colored marble. Stacked half-columns in the Roman Doric, Ionic, and Corinthian orders combined with arches of the supporting barrel vaults to create three stories of the façade. A fourth level of Corinthian pilasters without arches completed the elevation around two upper galleries (reserved for women and slaves). Attached to this level were brackets for the poles that some historians believe to have been supports for a canvas cover (velarium) providing shade for spectators. The area under the arena floor, an oval measuring 175 by 280 feet, was a labyrinth of passageways and chambers for gladiators, beasts, and hoisting machinery to service the spectacles staged above. The Colosseum is inextricably linked with savage and cruel entertainment, including fights to the death by gladiators and the perse-

cution of Roman Christians. During later eras the fine marble work was removed as the building became a source for ready-cut stone. It remains today as a partial ruin, but even in its crumbled condition the Colosseum testifies to Roman construction skill.

## RESIDENCES

To study Roman housing, we once again return to Pompeii, for the collection of ordinary dwellings, elaborate town residences, country villas, and farmhouses preserved there provides the most complete record we have of the types of buildings in which people lived. The earliest houses have atrium plans, an indigenous Italian type in which the principal rooms of the house directly adjoin an open courtyard for access and for light and circulation of air. Such a house presents a blank wall to the street on which it fronts without setback from the sidewalk.

### URBAN HOUSING

The House of the Surgeon is the most ancient dwelling found in Pompeii, and an examination of its plan reveals the typical features of atrium houses (Fig. 5.30a). It is an irregular quadrilateral because it exactly fills the plot of land on which it was built. On the street side it has three doors, two of which provide access to shops, one connected to the dwelling and the other forming part of a self-contained environment with living quarters upstairs. The center doorway, dignified by two entrance steps, was the principal entry to the house, and its location defines the axis of symmetry for the house proper. Passing through a vestibule, a visitor would next encounter the atrium, where a roof provided covering and shade except for a relatively small central area that was left open to the sky. Water running off the roof would fall in a basin (**impluvium**) in the center of the atrium. On either side of the atrium were chambers generally used as bedrooms; straight ahead on axis was the main reception room (**tablinum**), flanked by a dining room (**triclinium**). Beyond was a portico that opened onto the rear walled garden. Service spaces, including chambers for servants and the kitchen, were set in the wing beside the dining room. All the internal spaces depended on the unroofed atrium or the garden for light, as the exterior walls were without openings. Only the tablinum, the most distinguished room in the house, had direct access to both sources (and thus to the cooling breezes that would pass through); most of the remaining rooms must have been rather dim, even during the day.

The atrium plan had formal dignity and practicality too. The owner could rent the frontage shop with second-floor living quarters to a tradesman or artisan and use the shop connected to the interior of the house as his own place of business. The functioning of either shop was independent of domestic activity, which was in turn isolated from street noise. The scale was ample. The private quarters in the House of the Surgeon covered about 5500 square feet, including the garden. Nevertheless, in the second century BCE wealthier citizens were constructing expanded atrium houses. These newer houses might have more than one atrium, and the garden was greatly enlarged and surrounded by a colonnade to become a peristyle (Figs. 5.31–5.32).

The House of Pansa at Pompeii is an example of the atrium-peristyle house that has been dated to the mid-second century BCE (Fig. 5.30b). It occupies virtually one entire city block (approximately 27,000 square feet, over half an acre) and thus might have had windows on any of its four sides, but it has none, relying instead on an atrium, peristyle court, and a large walled garden for light and air. The entrance establishes an axial disposition of spaces similar to that at the House of the Surgeon. The small rooms around the atrium were used as bedrooms, with the dining rooms set adjacent to the peristyle. Beyond the peristyle, the axis passes through another reception room and portico to the walled garden, which occupied about a third of the site. Such a large house was uncommon in Pompeii. Examples of three smaller houses can be seen along the side street of the House of Pansa, where they were created out of the main house in a later remodeling. Lacking an atrium or internal court, these houses had windows for light and air, but they opened to the street, thus sharing the dust, noise, and smells of the public way. The two remaining sides of the House of Pansa contained shops. One can see the masonry mass surrounding the oven of a bakery on the plan.

Inward-looking houses such as those at Pompeii present a virtual wall to the street, an effect completely

**5.30a** Plan of the House of the Surgeon, Pompeii, 2nd century BCE.

This plan is organized around a central open space or atrium that admitted fresh air and light to surrounding rooms. A portico or porch at the rear opened into a small garden. Positioned between these two elements was the tablinum or main reception room.

**5.30b** Plan of the House of Pansa, Pompeii, 2nd century.

This house is so extensive that it occupies virtually an entire block and includes a spacious walled garden at the rear. Fresco paintings decorated its walls and mosaic tiles many of its floors.

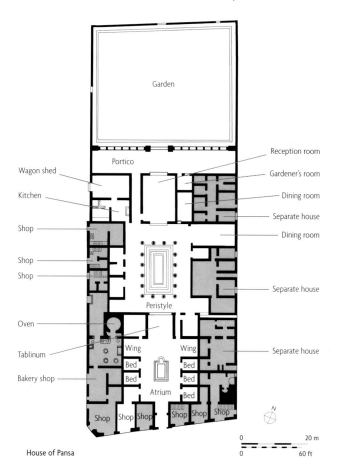

**5.31** Atrium of the House of Venus in the Shell, Pompeii, 2nd century.

The roof has been restored to give an idea of the original space and light quality. Water running off the roof collected in the impluvium at the center of the atrium. Fresco painting can be seen at the left. The opening in the center led to the garden peristyle. Notice the opus incertum stonework facing of the walls.

**5.32** Peristyle of the House of Venus in the Shell, Pompeii, 2nd century.

The house takes its name from a fresco found on the peristyle wall (to the left, not visible in the photograph). Fragments of other wall frescoes are evident to the rear. The dining room opened on the garden.

unlike the residential districts of American cities but not so dissimilar to the modern towns in Mediterranean countries. The streets in Pompeii were usually narrow, ranging from under eight to just over twenty-two feet. Major streets had raised walks on either side, and raised stepping stones at intersections enabled pedestrians to cross the street without sinking into the muck that often filled the roadway (Fig. 5.33). These crossing stones also permitted wheeled carts to pass, carefully, and thus controlled traffic speed. The walls in most sections of town were covered with graffiti. Election slogans, public notices, advertisements for commercial establishments and public

**5.33** Street in Pompeii, 2nd century.

Shop fronts predominated along the street, with the entrances to houses being rather modest openings. Carts could pass between the raised stepping stones and sidewalks. Notice the opus testaceum stonework facing of the walls here and in Fig. 5.34.

**5.34** Insula (tenement building), Ostia, 2nd century.

Much of the urban population in Rome lived in accommodations similar to this building. Cooking facilities for all units were located on the roof to minimize odors and the danger of fire, and water had to be carried from the public supply.

entertainments, and obscene remarks have all been found in the excavations of the city. On streets where tradesmen had shops, the walls sometimes contained murals illustrating the particular trade or product available within. Shop fronts opened directly to the street for the display of goods and were secured at night by wooden roller shutters.

Interior finishes in the houses at Pompeii have proven almost as interesting as the architecture. Art historians have identified four styles of wall paintings at Pompeii. One of these, in which imaginary scenes were painted as viewed from high or low vantage points, anticipates the elaborate Baroque creations that were used in the seventeenth century to expand optically the physical boundaries of walls and ceilings.

Stone and brick were the primary materials used in the construction of houses, although a surprising amount of timber was also employed, particularly for roof beams. In less affluent situations, walls were often provided by a wooden structural frame filled with rubble or brick, rather like the **half-timbering** construction of medieval Europe. Dwellings were originally one story, but as a city grew and urban land became more valuable, construction inevitably became multi-story, and older houses were converted to apartments. By the time of Pompeii's destruction, in fact, many of the atrium-peristyle houses had been divided into multi-family dwellings, as the wealthier citizens had moved to more spacious residences on estates outside the city.

For city residents, the dominant housing type after the fire that destroyed much of Rome in 64 CE came to be the apartment block or **insula**. An inventory made in the fourth century of buildings in Rome counted 46,000 insulae, while there were fewer than 1800 single-family houses. The best surviving insulae are in the port city of Ostia (Fig. 5.34). These apartment buildings, ranging up to six floors in height, occupied substantial plots of land and were designed around a central courtyard. Shops or commercial ventures were located on the ground-floor street frontages. Unlike the atrium houses, however, the upper-floor walls of insulae had windows opening to the street, so that rooms could draw on both the courtyard and street for light and air.

## RURAL VILLAS AND URBAN PALACES

Residences outside cities were called **villas**, and at Pompeii, a fine example is preserved just beyond the city wall. Known as the Villa of the Mysteries (Fig. 5.35) because of the wall paintings in one room that relate to the mystical cult of Bacchus, it grew gradually over a period of 300 years from a simple house to a complex of sixty rooms. Elements from atrium houses remain in its plan, including the preference for axial symmetry, but the ordering of rooms differs. The entrance led into the peristyle, followed by the atrium and finally the tablinum, while extensive terraced gardens surrounded the villa on the three non-entrance sides. Based upon the original inward-focused house, the architectural developments at the Villa of the Mysteries seem to suggest a building in

**5.35** Plan of the Villa of the Mysteries, Pompeii, ca. 120–80 BCE.

This plan resulted from some 300 years of development and enlargement. The germ of the plan is still the atrium/peristyle combination seen in urban residences, but the house also opens out to the landscape through numerous porticos.

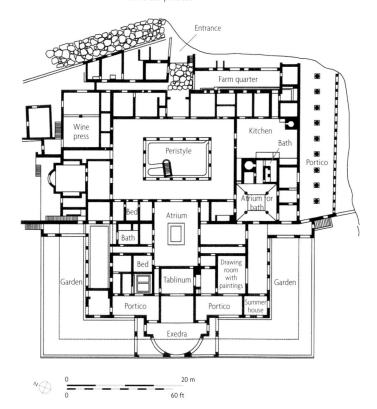

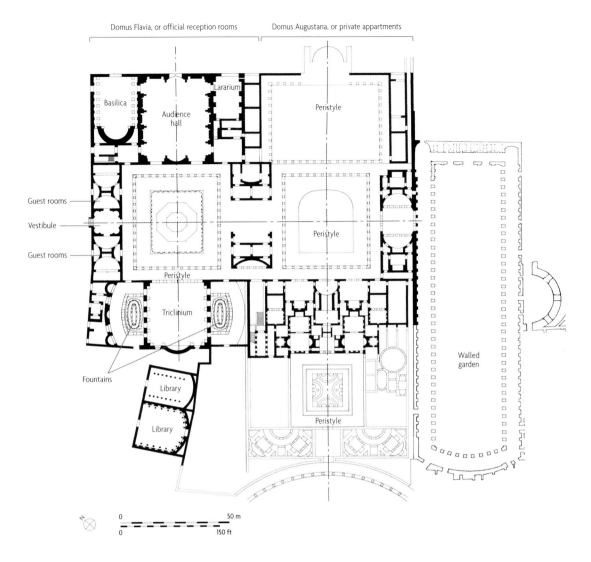

Domus Flavia, or official reception rooms     Domus Augustana, or private appartments

Basilica

Lararium

Audience hall

Peristyle

Guest rooms

Vestibule

Guest rooms

Peristyle

Peristyle

Triclinium

Walled garden

Fountains

Library

Library

Peristyle

N

0       50 m

0       150 ft

**5.36** Plan of the Palace of Domitian, Rome, completed 92 CE.

The extensive residence for the emperor has a suite of official reception rooms (left) and a set of more intimately scaled private apartments (right). At the extreme right is a walled garden in the shape of a stadium.

which the exterior elevations and their connection with the surrounding countryside were becoming more important.

The ruins of the Palace of Domitian, built to the design of the architect Rabirius for the emperor Domitian (finished in 92 CE) on the Palatine Hill (Fig. 5.36), suggest the complexity of elements incorporated into an imperial residence. The northwestern section contained a suite of official rooms, arranged along cross-axes, with a grand audience hall, peristyle with fountain, and a large vaulted triclinium with an exedra at the end to mark the emperor's seat. The more private residence section to the southeast was also organized cross-axially, and its more intimately scaled rooms on two levels present a virtuoso display of architectural ingenuity, incorporating varied room shapes, colonnaded gardens with fountains, and ornamental sculpture.

Interest in exploring such complex arrangements continued at the imperial villa erected by the Emperor

Hadrian outside Tivoli (Fig. 5.37). Constructed between 117 and 138 CE, it is a vast, sprawling accumulation of geometrically controlled building groups sited to follow the topography and linked to one another by a shifting set of axes and cross-axes. Passionate about architecture and widely traveled, Hadrian may have intended his villa to evoke architectural forms from all parts of the world, but there are no Disneyland-like copies of foreign buildings. Rather, it is the sheer variety of interior volumes and exterior vistas, as if the designers were experimenting with imaginative and untried forms, that make this a treasury of sequential spatial experiences without precedent.

The most recent scholarship on the villa has stripped away sometimes fanciful names traditionally associated with features found here in preference for descriptive terms, as the old names (given here in parentheses) were assigned by romantically inclined amateurs and not Hadrian himself. An enclosed garden around a rectangular fish

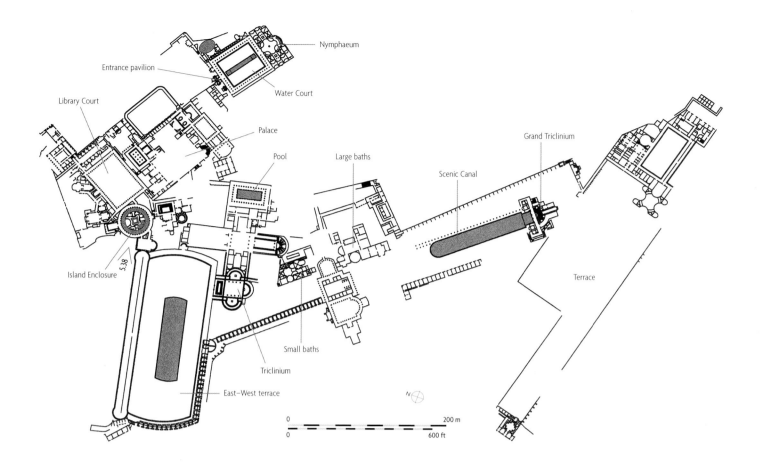

**5.37** Plan of Hadrian's Villa, Tivoli, 117–38 CE.

It is hard to convey in a single drawing the complexity of this sprawling collection of buildings that covers twice as much area as the city of Pompeii. Hadrian's architects exploited the structural possibilities of concrete to build unprecedented forms and compositions around water features.

Labels on plan: Nymphaeum, Entrance pavilion, Water Court, Library Court, Palace, Pool, Large baths, Grand Triclinium, Scenic Canal, Island Enclosure, 5.38, Small baths, Triclinium, East–West terrace, Terrace, N

0    200 m
0    600 ft

pond forms the East–West Terrace (the Poikele), the largest single element in the villa. Below the western end of the terrace are tiers of rooms where as many as 700 villa staff and servants were housed out of sight but close at hand.

To the east was the Island Enclosure (Maritime Theater), a circular, enclosed colonnaded area surrounded by a moat that provided a retreat for meditation or intimate meetings (Fig. 5.38). Water is also the central feature of the Scenic Canal (Canopus), a long colonnaded pool that was lined with statuary and focused at its southern end on a grand triclinium (the Serapeum), or banqueting hall, that became a grotto.

To the north of the Island Enclosure was the residential area, which included parts of an earlier family villa on the site, grouped around a rectangular court. Of greater interest from the standpoint of design sophistication is the Water Court (Piazza d'Oro or Golden Court), built on the northeast edge of the villa. The central axis of the composition was defined by an octagonal domed entrance pavilion that sat opposite the celebrated reverse-curve **Nymphaeum** or water pavilion.

## CONCLUSIONS ABOUT ARCHITECTURAL IDEAS

The Romans were the first ancient people to build large interior spaces. They did so by mastering the art of masonry vaulting, using brick and stone throughout the Empire and concrete within the Italian peninsula, where the raw ingredient pozzolana was available. In the end, it is impossible to understand the spatial arrangement of spaces at such sites as the Palace of Domitian or Hadrian's Villa without understanding the structural principles at work. In fact, from ancient Roman times to the second half of the twentieth century, it will be the supporting of the ceiling plane, most commonly with masonry vaulting, on which architects will lavish the most time and expense.

While the work of the Republic was largely trabeated and benefited from the planning experiments carried out by the Hellenistic Greeks, the architectural work of the Empire utilized elements of the classical language, particularly the orders, primarily as an exterior and interior veneer or as screens, giving elegance and proportion to the huge piles of compressive masonry that did most of the real work of spatial enclosure. The Colosseum, with its intersecting stacks of radial and concentric barrel vaults

**5.38** Island Enclosure (Maritime Theater), Hadrian's Villa, Tivoli, 117–38 CE.

Inside a circular colonnaded walkway, the moat surrounded a circular building that contained a library, dining area, and baths. For scale reference, the diameter of this complex is about the same at that of the Pantheon.

that provide access tunnels and support the seating and with its superimposed Doric-Ionic-Corinthian orders around the outer perimeter wall, provides a famous example as does the Pantheon, with its system of relieving arches and its coffered dome, still the standard by which domed spaces are measured.

A complex such as the Forum of Trajan illustrates the continuity of Hellenistic planning for official or corporate spaces and the introduction of vaults for utilitarian ones. Within the forum, stoa-like files of columns are folded and bent to capture exterior spaces that become the precincts for a temple, a triumphal column, and an equestrian statue, and the intervening basilica is also completely trabeated. The Markets of Trajan that hold back the earth to the northeast employ barrel vaults throughout and groin vaults with flying buttresses in the great hall, while the classical language is largely absent. Much the same can be said of the public baths and the Basilica of Constantine, where their ruined state allows us to appreciate their arcu-

ated and domed construction, without the veneer of frescoes, mosaics, and applied orders that have largely fallen away.

Like the builders of Egypt, Mesopotamia, and Greece, the Romans built houses around interior courts, either the paved atrium or garden-like peristyle. However, their most distinctive housing type was the tenement or insula, with its lower-story shops facing the street. While Rome itself grew over time in an often haphazard way, it was not considered the ideal. When given the opportunity to plan new towns, the Romans employed grid layouts into which they inserted public spaces, temples, baths, theaters, and amphitheaters, as at Timgad (see Fig. 5.9).

In Western Europe, all of this Roman architecture would lie fallow for centuries after the fall of the Empire, only to be reborn in the fifteenth century as a result of investigations and experiments, first made by Italians, then by others through Europe and England, as will be discussed in Chapter 11.

# CHAPTER 6

# EARLY CHRISTIAN AND BYZANTINE ARCHITECTURE

Christianity, the religion developed by followers of Jesus of Nazareth, began as a reforming sect of Judaism whose members regarded Jesus as the promised messiah. Over three centuries after Jesus' death, the religion developed into an organized Church with a hierarchy of bishops and clergy. The earliest expression of its beliefs is found in the Nicene Creed (325 CE with later revisions), still used by the Eastern Orthodox Church, the Roman Catholic Church, and some Protestant denominations:

> I believe in one God the Father Almighty, Maker of heaven and earth, and of all things visible and invisible; and in one Lord Jesus Christ, the only-begotten Son of God, begotten of His Father before all worlds; God of God, Light of Light; Very God of Very God; Begotten, not made; Being of one substance with the Father, by whom all things were made; Who for us men, and for our salvation, came down from heaven; And was incarnate by the Holy Ghost of the Virgin Mary, and was made man; And was crucified also for us under Pontius Pilate. He suffered death and was buried; And on the third day He rose again according to the Scriptures; And ascended into heaven; And sitteth on the right hand of the Father. And He shall come again with glory to judge both the quick and the dead; Whose kingdom shall have no end. And I believe in the Holy Ghost; The Lord and Giver of Life; Who proceedeth from the Father and the Son; Who with the Father and Son together is worshiped and glorified; Who spake by the prophets. And I believe in one Holy Catholic and Apostolic Church. I acknowledge one Baptism for the remission of sins. And I look for the Resurrection of the dead; And the Life of the world to come.

In the context of the late Roman Empire, Christianity was one of a number of religions troublesome to governmental authorities because its followers refused to acknowledge the state-sponsored deities, so the early history of Christianity is one of underground meetings and official persecution. Not until the emperor Constantine proclaimed toleration for all religions of the Roman Empire in the Edict of Milan in 313 did Christians have authority to construct buildings for public worship. Prior to that time services were held in private homes, where common domestic rooms, most often the triclinium (dining room), sufficed for worship. Christians developed congregational worship with a liturgy that focused on the celebration of the Eucharist (also known as communion), symbolic of the Last Supper of Jesus with his disciples and by extension of his sacrifice for humanity. One table was used for the Eucharist and another for offerings, with participants in the service sitting on the remaining furnishings or standing.

As the liturgy became more elaborate and the congregation grew, larger and more extensive sets of rooms were needed. In many cities Christians established community houses with a hall for worship, a **baptistery**, and rooms for the distribution of alms to the needy. They also organized separate cemeteries to distance their burials from those of other religions. Christians disapproved of cremation, and if suitable land for a graveyard was not available, the community developed underground cemeteries, generally begun in abandoned quarries, which became known as catacombs. Portions of the catacombs in Rome are among the oldest surviving Christian spaces, providing a glimpse of early religious decorative art.

Christian architecture after 313 derived in large measure from Roman precedent, and Early Christian and Byzantine buildings continue certain aspects of Classical antiquity. When, for reasons of security, Constantine relocated his capital from Rome to the town of Byzantium (on the western shore of the Bosporus Strait) and renamed it Constantinople (modern Istanbul), he began the bifurcation of the Empire, with modern-day Greece and Turkey at

S. Marco interior, Venice, rebuilt 1063–89.

This late Byzantine church, modeled on Justinian's Church of the Holy Apostles in Constantinople, is finished inside with elaborate mosaic figures on a golden background.

## Chronology

| | |
|---|---|
| reign of Caesar Augustus | 27 BCE–14 CE |
| life of Jesus | ca. 8–4 BCE–29 CE |
| reign of Constantine | 310–337 |
| Constantine legalizes Christianity | 313 |
| construction of Old St. Peter's | 318–22 |
| founding of Constantinople | 324 |
| end of the Roman Empire in the West | 476 |
| reign of the Emperor Justinian | 527–65 |
| construction of Hagia Sophia | 532–37 |
| fall of Constantinople to the Ottomans | 1453 |

the heart of the eastern portion and Italy in the western part. At the same time, stylistic developments in this period contributed to later buildings in the medieval period, thus creating a transition between the classical past and the medieval era in western Europe.

## EARLY CHRISTIAN BASILICAS

In giving official sanction to Christianity, Constantine became the sponsor of some of its early church-building efforts, most of which were based on the Roman basilica. Pagan associations rendered Roman temples unsuitable models for Christian worship, but the connotations of assembly hall and court of justice pertaining to basilicas suited the new religion much better. Basilicas could accommodate large crowds, an important consideration for a religion attracting increasing numbers of converts, and their layout created processional space that was part of worship services. With relatively minor modifications, the Roman basilica form was adapted to Christian ritual. The altar was placed in the apse where the magistrate's seat had formerly been, entrances were set in the opposite short wall, and an atrium set in front of the entrances accommodated gatherings before services and enabled the unbaptized to hear but not participate in the Mass. The longitudinal arrangement of atrium, **nave**, and apse formed an impressive axis for processions that terminated at the altar (see Figs. 6.3a,b).

**6.1** S. Apollinare Nuovo, Ravenna, ca. 490.

The tall nave of this early basilica has changed relatively little since its construction, preserving the very plain brick exterior that was common in many Early Christian churches. The vaulted arcade across the front is a 16th century addition.

**6.2** S. Apollinare Nuovo interior, Ravenna, ca. 490.

Grained marble columns define the aisles and nave. The nave walls are finished with mosaics and above them light enters through clerestory windows.

Constantine gave the Lateran Palace in Rome to the early church to serve as a residence for the bishop, and one of the earliest basilicas was built adjacent to the palace in about 313. Much rebuilt and extended, it stands today as St. John Lateran and is still the cathedral of Rome. (**Cathedral** is the designation given to a church that contains the seat or cathedra of a bishop. While cathedrals are often larger or more elaborate than ordinary churches, this is not necessarily the case, nor is every large church a cathedral.) The original building had paired **aisles** on either side of a lofty nave, which was concluded by an apse containing the cathedra and seats for the priests. Clerestory windows high in the nave wall illuminated the central space, while smaller windows in the outermost aisle and above the first aisle colonnade provided light for the ancillary spaces. Open wooden trusses spanned the nave and aisles, supported on brick-faced concrete walls and marble columns salvaged from earlier Roman buildings.

A more formulaic example of an Early Christian basilica is found at Ravenna in the church of S. Apollinare Nuovo, constructed about 500 as the palace church for the Ostrogoth King Theoderic and given its present name centuries later (Figs. 6.1–6.3a). Constructed of brick with single aisles flanking the nave, the church interior focuses on the semicircular apse (not the original). The walls above the nave **arcade** are finished with mosaics arranged in three horizontal layers. The lowest tier depicts stately processions of female saints (north side) and male martyrs (south side) advancing toward the altar. (This mosaic tier was installed in the ninth century, replacing original work whose subject we do not know.) Between the clerestory windows are single figures that may represent Old Testament prophets and New Testament evangelists and apostles. In the highest sections of the nave wall are scenes representing the Passion story (south side) and the miracles of Christ (north side). This elaborate interior decoration not only communicated Christian teachings to a largely illiterate public, but also symbolized the richness of the kingdom of God to which the soul could aspire. The sober exterior brickwork gives little indication of the shimmering golden mosaic work contained within.

## MARTYRIA, BAPTISTERIES, AND MAUSOLEA

Basilicas were not the only religious buildings erected by early Christians. Among the structures raised to serve Christian purposes were **martyria**, buildings erected as memorials to commemorate saints or sites of special importance to the Christian faith. Celebrated martyria might attract large crowds for services and thus need to function as churches, but major importance was always attached to the tomb or shrine around which they were built. Old St. Peter's in Rome (318–22), predecessor of the present Basilica of St. Peter, began as a martyrium marking the tomb of St. Peter and seems to have been used for several centuries as a place of burial for other Christians as well (Figs. 6.3a, 6.4). Its basilican plan has double aisles on each side of the nave and a transverse element or **transept** projecting beyond the side walls and extending across the nave in front of the apse. Placed at the junction of transept and apse was the tomb of St. Peter, surrounded by a railing and marked by a canopy rising on twisted spiral columns that reputedly came from the Temple of Solomon in Jerusalem. The transept spaces accommodated those coming to venerate the shrine, while the enormous nave (300 by 64 feet) and aisles functioned as a covered cemetery with space for burials and commemorative funeral meals. During the procession-dominated services, the nave accommodated only the clergy, with the laity relegated to the aisles. A spacious atrium preceded the martyrium, and the whole scheme provided the model for a number of churches built later, both in Rome and elsewhere.

A similar program influenced the design of the Church of the Nativity in Bethlehem, constructed under the patronage of Constantine in about 333 over the grotto that tradition identified as the birthplace of Jesus (Fig. 6.3b). As at St. Peter's, this building was a basilica preceded by an atrium, but rather than transepts and an apse, the Church of the Nativity had an octagon at the head of the nave. A passage around the octagon allowed pilgrims to circulate and view the grotto below through an opening in the floor, and there may also have been stairs going down to the actual level of the shrine. The junction of a basilica with an octagon shows Early Christian willingness to explore new forms in the course of seeking appropriate and functional religious buildings.

Baptism is an important Christian rite, and in the Early Christian period special buildings were often erected for this sacrament alone. Most were centrally planned around the baptismal pool, for at the time baptism was by complete immersion, and baptistery plans were frequently octagonal to encode the number eight, which symbolized regeneration or the Resurrection, since Jesus was said to have risen from the dead on the eighth day after his entry into Jerusalem. The Baptistery of the Orthodox in Ravenna (ca. 458) is a domed octagonal volume surrounding the octagonal marble font (Fig. 6.5). The central scene in the ceiling mosaic depicts Christ's baptism in the river Jordan, encircled by the twelve apostles and an outer ring illustrating altars in semicircular niches and empty thrones (Fig. 6.6). As was the case with S. Apollinare Nuovo, the plain brick exterior, articulated primarily by eight arched windows and corbeled arches with pilaster strips, gives no hint of the sumptuous finishes inside.

**Mausolea**, buildings erected to contain the tombs of important people, were also in the repertory of Early Christian architecture. Following Roman practice, these were often centrally planned, and they served as models for later domed churches. In Rome the mausoleum of

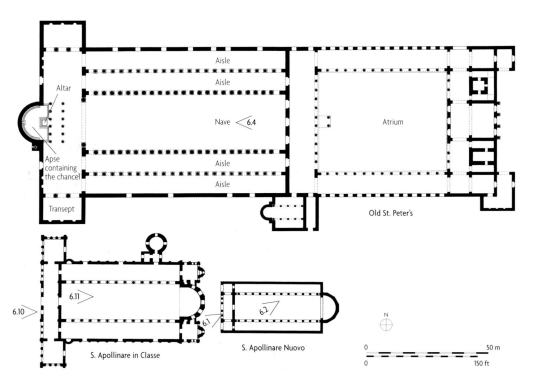

**6.3a** Plans of Old St. Peter's Rome, 318–22; S. Apollinare in Classe, Ravenna, 532–49; and S. Apollinare Nuovo, Ravenna, ca. 490.

The fundamental elements of basilican church plans are evident here: a longitudinal axis leads from the entrance (through an atrium and/or narthex) through the nave to the terminating apse, where the altar is located. High (clerestory) windows illuminate the nave. Triumphal-arch-like elements appear at both the entry into the atrium and that from the nave to the altar area, symbolizing the entry into more sacred territory.

Aisle
Aisle
Nave 6.4
Aisle
Aisle
Altar
Apse containing the chancel
Transept
Atrium
Old St. Peter's

6.11
6.10
6.1
6.2
S. Apollinare in Classe
S. Apollinare Nuovo

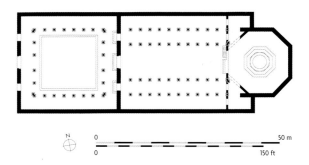

**6.3b** Plan of the Church of the Nativity, Bethlehem, ca. 333.

This innovative building combines the form of a double-aisle basilica with an atrium forecourt and an octagonal rotunda over the traditional site of Jesus' birth. The design thus accommodates the functions of worship while providing circulation space required for pilgrims visiting the holy site.

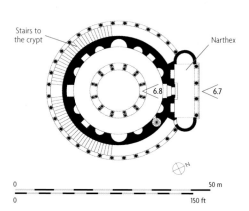

Stairs to the crypt
Narthex
6.8
6.7

**6.3c** Plan of S. Costanza, Rome, ca. 350.

This plan shows the original narthex and the stairs descending to the crypt. Paired columns support the drum and dome.

Constantine's daughter Constantia was built around 350 as a circular monument with a cross-section paralleling that of the basilica, having lower aisle spaces flanking the higher nave lit by clerestory windows (Figs. 6.3c, 6.7–6.8). In Constantia's mausoleum, now known as the church of S. Costanza, the basilican cross-section was rotated about the center axis to create a circular building, rather than being extended longitudinally to form a basilica. Originally the resulting dome with encircling **ambulatory** focused the visitor's attention on the sarcophagus placed in the center. Twelve paired sets of columns support the

**6.4** Section perspective of Old St. Peter's, Rome, ca. 318–22.

This building began as a martyrium, a cemetery developed around the grave of the apostle Peter. Notice how the lower aisle roofs permit direct light to enter the nave through high clerestory windows.

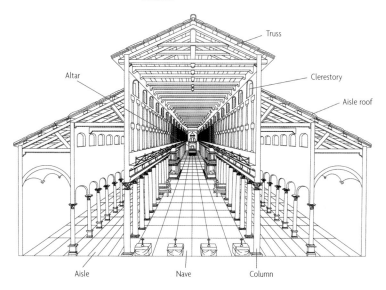

Truss
Clerestory
Aisle roof
Altar
Aisle
Nave
Column

**6.5** (above) Baptistery of the Orthodox, Ravenna, ca. 458.

This view shows the brickwork embellished primarily by pilaster strips and shallow arches near the eaves. These decorative elements are known as Lombard bands because they were developed by the highly renowned Lombard masons.

**6.6** (right) Baptistery of the Orthodox, ceiling mosaic, Ravenna, ca. 458.

Directly over the baptismal font in the center of the building is an image of the baptism of Jesus by John the Baptist. The dove of the Holy Spirit hovers above Jesus, while an old man, a personification of the River Jordan, stands in the water on the right side.

**6.7** (below) S. Costanza, Rome, ca. 350.

Erected as a mausoleum for the emperor Constantine's daughter, this central-plan building was converted into a church. Note the plain brickwork of the exterior, with two layers of voussoirs placed over the clerestory windows.

**6.8** (below right) S. Constanza interior, Rome, ca. 350.

A section through the building resembles that of a basilica, but rather than being extended longitudinally, the section is rotated about the central vertical axis to generate a central plan building.

# EUSEBIUS AND CONSTANTINE

by Lynn K. Barker

**6.9** Anon, Eusebius of Caesarea. Engraving.

Around 315, a visiting bishop rose to address the congregation gathered for the rededication of the new cathedral in the Levantine city of Tyre. He turned and both dedicated and addressed his "Festival oration on the building of churches" to his friend, the inspiration behind the cathedral's construction and its bishop, Paulinus. The speaker was Eusebius (Fig. 6.9), himself bishop of the nearby coastal see of Caesarea. He was famous both as the "father of Church history" and as Constantine's biographer and eulogist.

The adage "history is written by the winners" is nowhere more strikingly illustrated than in the generation of Eusebius and his contemporary, Lactantius, whose work *On the Deaths of the Persecutors* recounts the grisly deaths, divinely sanctioned as retribution, of the church's enemies at the turn of the fourth century. In his own *Historia Ecclesiastica*, Eusebius describes with eyewitness authority the sufferings of Palestinian martyrs under Galerius and Maximinius.

When Eusebius came to describe the world that he thought had been transformed by Constantine's practice of toleration of all religions, he thought of no better way to depict the new order than by inserting, at the beginning of Book X of his *Historia Ecclesiastica* a full transcription of his address that day in Tyre.

Soon after peace came building: "The next state was the spectacle prayed and longed for by us all—dedication festivals in the cities and consecrations of the newly built places of worship, convocations of bishops . . . unification . . . harmony . . . There came together bone to bone and joint to joint."

The fine new basilica at Tyre was the inspiration of the bishop, standing second only to Christ. Eusebius eulogizes his friend Constantine as "a new Bezalel" (Exod. 35:30); the "Solomon . . . of a new and far nobler Jerusalem;" "a new Zerubbabel," restoring the Temple to a "glory far greater than the old."

For all its spendor, however, this earthly building pales beside the more sublime truths of the archetypes behind it. The soul is a building, whose fall into sin Eusebius likens to the destruction of church properties at pagan hands. The "divine spiritual edifice in our souls" (what we call the image of God) fell to the battering rams of sin, "till not one stone of virtue was left." The work of Christ was directed to rebuilding the human soul. But while the bishop rebuilds his material church more splendidly than before, the true building project is God's work in history: raising up the edifice of the universal Church, in which God sets the people themselves as "living, securely-laid, and unshakeable stones." Even what Augustine of Hippo would one day call the city of man is a building, composed of most men in the world—"bad builders of bad buildings."

Modern historians have caught Eusebius out in promoting his vision of unity in harmony at the expense of a messier reality called historical truth; Constantine's Church was neither unified nor harmonious. Little wonder, then, that Eusebius' vision of God's edifice would nourish the architects—actual and metaphorical—of a Christian empire for a millennium to come.

drum wall from which the dome rises, lit by twelve clerestory windows. The aisle vaults are finished with mosaic, and the columns are of polished marble.

## BYZANTINE BASILICAS AND DOMED BASILICAS

The division between the Early Christian and Byzantine eras is generally made at the reign of Justinian (527–65), who, as emperor based in Constantinople, put an end to factional disputes, reasserted imperial influence in portions of North Africa and Italy that had fallen to heretical rulers, and engaged in a vigorous program of church-building. People living at the time probably did not perceive the change. As historians look back on the period, however, Justinian's reign serves as a convenient marker to differentiate increasingly separate developments in western and eastern sections of what had been the Roman Empire. Work tied by patronage or tradition to Constantinople is termed Byzantine. One characteristic of much Byzantine architecture is a clear preference for domes on both basilican and centrally planned churches. Like the Romans, the Byzantines saw the dome as symbolic of the

heavenly sphere, complementary to the earthly realm of floor and walls below.

Early Christian traditions were not entirely discarded, however. Basilicas were the most common church plan constructed in the sixth century, although none of the examples built in Constantinople survives. We turn instead to the church of S. Apollinare in Classe near Ravenna, constructed under Justinian's patronage from 532 to 549, for an example of a wooden-roofed basilica without transepts (Figs. 6.3a, 6.10–6.11). Its splendid apse mosaics are the glory of the interior, where St. Apollinaris, the first bishop of Ravenna, guards a flock of twelve sheep (representing the disciples by number and the people of Ravenna by extension) grazing in a lush meadow. Overhead is a golden cross with the image of Christ in the center, set in a starry blue sky, and figures of four early bishops of Ravenna are installed between the windows. Rich marble columns form the nave arcade, with portraits of saints set in **roundel** frames above the arches. In character and design the church is similar to the earlier S. Apollinare Nuovo, but its scale is considerably larger. In the century after its construction, the apse floor was raised to permit access to the crypt tomb of Apollinaris.

The innovative domes seen in Justinian's churches are notable contributions to architectural history. In Constantinople, two domed basilicas rose simultaneously and survive as models for the type. The smaller, S. Irene (begun in 532 and remodeled in 564), has a rectangular plan

**6.10** S. Apollinare in Classe, Ravenna, ca. 532–49.

Many Byzantine buildings continued the tradition of sober exteriors and rich interiors already seen in Early Christian times. The tall volume of the basilica and its lower narthex porch read clearly. The campanile rises to the rear.

**6.11** S. Apollinare in Classe interior, Ravenna, 532–49.

Windows glazed in thin sheets of alabaster reduced the intense Italian sun and provided soft light suitable for appreciating mosaic work and marbled columns. Note the absence of seating: congregations stood or knelt during services at this period.

**6.12** S. Irene interior, Constantinople, 532–64.

Lower sections of one pendentive supporting the dome are visible. Galleries (seen to the left) erected over the aisles braced the structure and were used by women during services. One needs to imagine the mosaics that were intended for this almost bare interior.

divided into nave and aisles with a projecting semicircular apse (Fig. 6.12). (The church seen today is largely a rebuilding after an earthquake in 740.) Two domes cover the nave, and their thrust is countered by massive rectangular piers, pierced by openings, and effectively strengthened by barrel-vaulted **galleries** over the aisles. The outlines of the aisle vaults articulate the exterior side walls, where tiers of arched windows admit light to the aisles and galleries. More windows are placed at the base of the dome and around the apse. S. Irene thus represents a new interpretation of the basilica, combining the liturgical logic of the longitudinal plan with the centralizing or heavenly qualities of domed construction. This same idea, on a much larger scale, was carried out at a contemporary church in Constantinople, Hagia Sophia, the Church of the Holy Wisdom.

Hagia Sophia (532–37) is one of the great buildings of the world and is without question the masterpiece of Byzantine architecture (Figs. 6.13a, 6.14–6.16). We know the names and backgrounds of its architects, Anthemius of Tralles and Isidorus of Miletus. Both were mathematicians and scientists skilled in mechanics, geometry, and engineering. These talents were all needed to design and supervise the construction of the exceptionally large Hagia Sophia. In plan it is a basilica with a central dome, complemented by pairs of semidomes at the front and rear. This configuration is at once linear, with a dominant

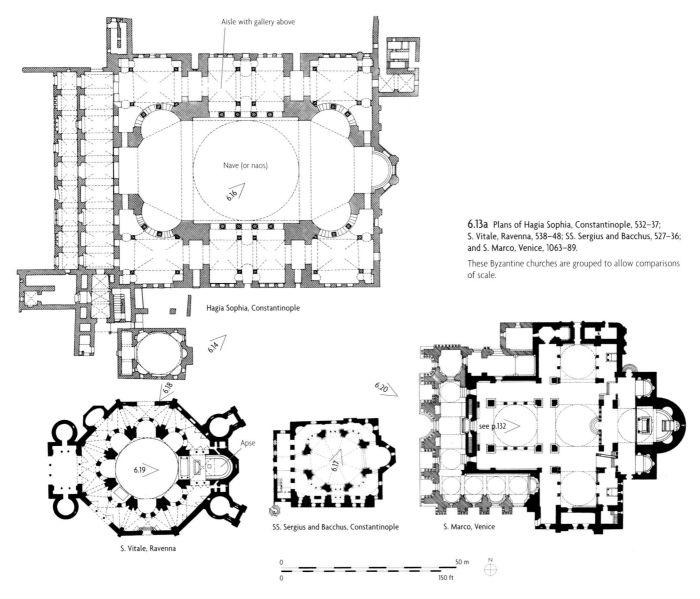

Aisle with gallery above

Nave (or naos)

Hagia Sophia, Constantinople

Apse

S. Vitale, Ravenna

SS. Sergius and Bacchus, Constantinople

see p.132

S. Marco, Venice

**6.13a** Plans of Hagia Sophia, Constantinople, 532–37; S. Vitale, Ravenna, 538–48; SS. Sergius and Bacchus, 527–36; and S. Marco, Venice, 1063–89.

These Byzantine churches are grouped to allow comparisons of scale.

0     50 m
0     150 ft

N

longitudinal axis, and centralized, with a dome on piers at its core. Its 107-foot-diameter central dome, supported on pendentives, rises 180 feet above the floor and is flanked by two lower **semidomes** of the same diameter, a clear span of nearly 250 feet. In the description of the church written by Justinian's court historian, Procopius of Caesarea, the dome was seen to hover over the interior.

> [It] seems not to rest upon solid masonry, but to cover the space with its golden dome suspended from Heaven. All these details, fitted together with incredible skill in mid-air and floating off from each other and resting only on the parts next to them, produce a single and most extraordinary harmony in the work, and yet do not permit the spectator to linger much over the study of any one of them, but each detail attracts the eye and draws it on irresistibly to itself.

Aisles with galleries above range on either side, while a colonnaded atrium (no longer extant) and groin-vaulted double **narthex** precede the church proper.

**6.13b** Plan of monastery churches, Hosios Lukas, ca. 980–1025.

There are two churches shown here, the Theotokos (*above*) and the Katholikon (*below*). The Theotokos church is a quincunx design, while the Katholikon has a single large dome buttressed by galleries.

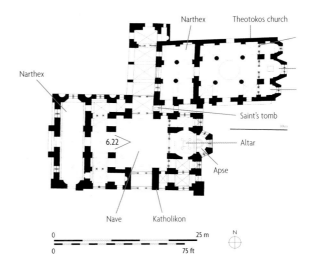

Narthex

Theotokos church

Narthex

Saint's tomb

Altar

Apse

Nave

Katholikon

0     25 m
0     75 ft

N

**6.14** Hagia Sophia, Constantinople, 532–37 and later.

This audacious building contains the greatest dome of its age, only slightly smaller than that of the Pantheon. This exterior view shows buttresses around the base of the dome added after earthquake damage. Four minarets were added when the church was converted into a mosque.

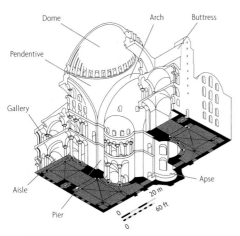

**6.15** Worm's-eye-view axonometric section through Hagia Sophia, Constantinople, 532–37 and later.

This view from below shows the massive arches that support the great dome. The dome is built of brick, which accounts for its relative thinness, and pendentives transform the square bay defined by the piers into a circle from which the dome springs.

**6.16** Hagia Sophia interior, Constantinople, 532–37 and later.

This view of the central space shows the multiple levels of windows that illuminate the interior. Windows set between the dome's ribs create the illusion that the dome floats unsupported. Hagia Sophia's architects intended to create a building that would rival the Pantheon, and their work has both inspired and challenged later builders who sought to emulate its space and structural daring.

The structural problems posed by such an audacious design were many, yet the necessary supports do not intrude on the internal space, creating the feeling that the dome floats effortlessly above the billowing interior volumes. Nothing could be farther from the actual case. While the brick used does constitute a relatively light construction material and the vaults are amazingly thin to minimize both thrust and weight, the size of the building means that the gravity forces are large. The forty windows at the base of the dome are set between buttresses that stabilize the junction of dome and **pendentives**. From this point the load is transferred to four great stone piers, which are further buttressed by being extended above the gallery vaults to join in great barrel vaults along the sides of the church (Fig 6.14). The semidomes, which appear to brace the narthex and apse ends, probably contribute little to the structure's integrity, however satisfying they are visually. The masonry mass of the four piers is more obvious on the outside than internally. Anthemius and Isidorus's structural daring overstepped the physical limits of their materials, and the first great dome collapsed in 558. It was reconstructed with a steeper pitch and ribbed construction in 563, but the western half of the rebuilt dome fell again in 989. Following repairs, the eastern half collapsed in 1346; the replacement dome is the one on the building today.

Structural problems aside, the effect of the arches, vaults, exedrae, semidomes, and domes is ethereal. Light pours in from windows at many levels, playing over surfaces enriched by polished marbles and mosaic. From a position at the center of the nave, the repetition of curved forms reflects the great dome overhead and creates a pervasive harmony that is constantly varied. From the aisles and galleries, the view into the nave is dramatic, providing a partial perspective of the interconnecting layered spaces surrounding the interior volume. In the church ritual for which Hagia Sophia was built, the major space was reserved for two groups, the ecclesiastics and the retinue of the emperor. The clergy claimed the sanctuary space before the apse, while the imperial court occupied the region at the narthex, or entry, end. The meeting of patriarch and emperor and celebration of the Mass under the great dome marked a high point of the religious ritual. Ordinary people were relegated to the aisles and galleries, women on one side and men on the other, where they could observe the impressive ceremonial processions and symbolic joining of Church and state in this magnificent setting.

## CENTRALLY PLANNED BYZANTINE CHURCHES

Roman temples such as the Pantheon and Early Christian baptisteries and mausolea had featured centralized plans. Not surprisingly, these precedents combined well with the Byzantine fondness for dome-building and contributed to

**6.17** SS. Sergius and Bacchus interior, Constantinople, 527–36.

This central-plan church features a "pumpkin vault" in its dome, a form that had been used in Roman times and that reappears in the Baroque era.

the development of the most characteristic Byzantine churches, which had circular or **Greek-cross plans**. Justinian's churches again provide the dominant models for later centuries.

SS. Sergius and Bacchus (527–36) in Constantinople and S. Vitale (538–48) in Ravenna illustrate two variations on the theme of central plans. SS. Sergius and Bacchus (Figs. 6.13a, 6.17) is essentially a domed octagon surrounded by aisles and galleries encased in a square, whereas S. Vitale's octagonal dome is echoed by octagonal galleries and aisles. The strong centralizing tendencies of both churches are countered somewhat by apsidal projections opposite the narthex side, and the interior space is more fluid than that seen in Early Christian S. Costanza, where a similar organizational idea is carried out in circular form. In SS. Sergius and Bacchus, the eight piers supporting the dome are interspersed with pairs of columns, set alternately beneath curving and straight arches, so that the domed area penetrates the surrounding corner spaces. The sixteen-sided "pumpkin vault" dome reflects the configuration below in alternate straight- and curved-profile sections above its rather low drum.

**6.18** S. Vitale, Ravenna, 538–48.
Another of the exceptional churches built under imperial patronage, S. Vitale is based in plan on an octagon. Using local Ostrogoth technology, its dome is constructed of hollow clay pots to create strength while minimizing weight.

**6.19** S. Vitale interior, Ravenna, 538–48.
This view looking toward the apse shows the rich array of book-matched marbles and mosaic work.

Although the dome at S. Vitale (Figs. 6.13a, 6.18–6.19) is smaller, the church design is more sophisticated, with a higher drum and greater internal cohesiveness than at SS. Sergius and Bacchus. Clerestory windows illuminate the nave directly, and between the piers of the octagon all the niches are semicircular, carving into aisles and galleries to borrow additional light from windows in the exterior wall. Semidomes over each of the niches complement the dome that rises over the nave. The proportions of the exterior are equally fine. Red-tile roofs in direct volumetric expression of the internal space cap simple arched windows set in brick walls articulated by pilasters. SS. Sergius and Bacchus has lost most of its original interior mosaic, but S. Vitale displays the beautiful products of imperial workshops in both marble and mosaic. Carved capitals complete richly veined marble column shafts, **book-matched** marbles face the lower wall surfaces, and both geometric and figural mosaics complete arch soffits, upper walls, apse, and floors. Mosaic donor panels set on the sides of the apse portray Justinian and his court across from the empress Theodora and her attendants. The apse semidome shows Christ flanked by angels, with St. Vitalis to Christ's right and Bishop Ecclesius to the left. The bishop holds a model of the church, and Christ passes a crown to St. Vitalis. The splendor of Byzantium glows throughout this handsome church.

For the Justinian prototype of centralized churches on a Greek-cross plan, we must rely on fragmentary evidence provided by the now-vanished Church of the Holy Apostles in Constantinople. Erected by Constantine as his own mausoleum and rebuilt by Justinian from 536 to 550, it was demolished in 1469 to provide the site for a mosque. A standing church built on the model of Justinian's Church of the Holy Apostles is S. Marco in Venice, begun in 830 and rebuilt in 1063–89 (page 132 and Figs. 6.20–6.21). Hemispherical internal domes cover each arm of the Greek-cross plan, and a central one crowns the **crossing**. All are set on pendentives, with barrel vaults connecting the large pierced piers that sustain the downward thrust of the domes. Windows at the base of some domes illuminate the upper regions of the church and allow light to sparkle across the gold-ground mosaics of the interior. While the basic design concept for S. Marco stems from Byzantium, much there reflects other architectural traditions. For example, the present exterior portal hoods date from the fifteenth century, and the external dome profiles, raised on a timber framework above the masonry work, reflect the shape of Eastern domes. Nevertheless, S. Marco is substantially Byzantine. It became the model for Romanesque churches in the south of France shortly after its completion.

In addition to the domed Greek-cross plan used at S. Marco, Byzantine churches built in the centuries after Justinian also followed two other general plan types, the **cross-in-square** and a single dome placed on a longitudinal base. The cross-in-square or **quincunx** plan has nine

**6.20** S. Marco, Venice, rebuilt 1063–89.

With a Greek-cross plan based on Justinian's Church of the Holy Apostles in Constantinople, S. Marco has five domes, of which the central one is highest. The west front and raised external dome roofs were added later.

**6.21** Longitudinal section through S. Marco, Venice, rebuilt 1063–89.

This view shows the original dome profile and the taller shells erected in the fifteenth century to dramatize the exterior effect. Note particularly the turrets atop the domes, which resemble the characteristic onion domes of Russian churches.

bays, with the central one domed, and diminutive domes over the corner bays. All other sections are barrel-vaulted. In cross-domed plans, the arms of the Greek cross are reduced and covered with barrel vaults that surround the crossing dome. Aisles and galleries enclose the church on three sides, and three apses complete the fourth side. Many of these churches were erected on a rather modest scale, so the vaulting did not pose undue constructional complications.

We can see both these plan types at the monastery of Hosios Lukas, located at Phocis northwest of Athens, where two churches were built adjacent to the shrine erected over the tomb of St. Luke, a local hermit who died in 953 (not to be confused with the evangelist of the same name). The smaller of the churches, designed on a cross-in-square plan with three apses, was dedicated in about 1000 to the Theotokos, the Greek term for the Mother of

God (Fig. 6.13b). Built of squared stones surrounded by brick, the Theotokos church has a central dome raised on a drum. Groin vaults rather than domes were built over the corner bays, perhaps because the scale is so small: the central dome is eleven feet in diameter. Although the interior today is devoid of fresco, mosaic, or marble facing, it was probably once richly finished to accord with the carved screen separating the nave from the chancel that is still in place.

The larger Katholikon was constructed in the following twenty years immediately to the south of the Theotokos church, thereby sharing proximity to the saint's shrine and allowing pilgrims to circulate on all sides of the tomb. Its plan is in some respects similar to S. Irene in Constantinople, with a large dome set over the nave, braced on three sides by a second level gallery. **Squinches** transform the square central bay into an octagon that supports a drum and dome thirty feet in diameter (Fig. 6.22). The interior was sumptuously finished, with marble facing on the walls and mosaics on the vaults and dome. The dome mosaics, destroyed in an earthquake in 1593, were replaced by frescoes of the original subjects. On the apse semidome, in a field of gold mosaic, is a majestic Mary holding the infant Christ.

## CHURCHES IN RUSSIA

Many of the features of later Byzantine architecture are reflected in Russian church designs, for that country's architecture is inextricably identified with the legacy of Byzantium. In the period under consideration here, roughly from 990 to 1725, Russia included what today are the independent states of Belarus, Georgia, and the Ukraine. Much of the territory west of the Urals is rolling countryside, covered with extensive grasslands, vast forests, lakes, and marshes. Its rivers were the first tracks through the wilderness, and by the ninth century Viking explorers had settled along water routes requiring minimal portages to travel from the Baltic to the Black Sea, where they traded with the Byzantines. Aside from the rivers, the Urals, and the Carpathian mountains, there are few natural boundaries, so the area has long been open to nomadic incursions. Russian history begins with the legendary Rurik, a Viking who was invited to Novgorod in about 856 to bring order to the scattered trading settlements along the trade route to Constantinople. Although Rurik's descendants ruled the country until the sixteenth century, the history of Russia was severely interrupted for the period from 1239 to the fifteenth century, when the region was effectively a surrogate state of the Mongol khans of Central Asia. For a variety of historical reasons, Russia became isolated from western Europe, so the chronologies and stylistic periods defined for France, Italy, England, or Germany do not apply here. Byzantine work influenced church architecture in Russia for centuries after

**6.22** Interior of the Katholikon, Monastery of Hosios Lukas, 1020.

This interior space repeats at a greatly reduced scale some of the dramatic lighting and rich interior of Hagia Sophia (see Fig. 6.16). Frescoes in the dome replace the original mosaic work that fell during an earthquake in 1593.

**6.23** Church of the Raising of Lazarus, Muromansky monastery, now at Kizhi, ca. 1391.

Reputedly the oldest wooden church surviving in Russia, it has three different roof pitches and two different forms of wall construction. The diminutive dome on a stalk marks it as a church rather than a simple log house. (Church of the Transfiguration in the background; see Fig. 6.28.)

the fall of Constantinople in 1453. Difficulties in maintaining contact with Church authorities in Constantinople and growing differences within the Russian Church led to the proclamation in 1443 of a Russian Orthodox Church, having its own primate or metropolitan independent of the patriarch in Constantinople.

Masonry construction records only part of the story of Russian architecture. Until the twentieth century, wood was the dominant building material in Russia. It was readily available, easily worked, and its insulating qualities were superior to masonry for comfort during the long winter. Horizontal log construction, employing notched corner joints similar to those seen in American log cabins, was used for houses, fortifications, and churches. (A major difference between Russian, indeed European, log construction and that usually seen in the United States is the sturdiness of the former and the relative impermanence of the latter. European log buildings were meant to last for centuries, whereas most American examples were hastily erected then abandoned as soon as something better could be built.) Foreign visitors remarked repeatedly on

the fact that Russian cities seemed to be composed entirely of wooden buildings. Wood of course is subject to both decay and fire, and these destructive forces have greatly reduced the number of old buildings available for study.

Both legend and physical evidence suggest that the oldest surviving Russian wooden building is the small Church of the Raising of Lazarus (ca. 1391) from the Muromansky monastery, now relocated to the open-air museum at Kizhi (Figs. 6.23–6.24). It is a simple, three-celled structure, composed of a vestibule, nave, and chancel, each covered by its own gable roof and each roof having a slightly different pitch. The oldest sections are the nave and chancel, constructed in horizontal log work, while the vestibule has wooden planks inserted into upright wooden members. A small shingle-covered dome on a stalk-like drum rises over the nave. Aside from the dome and the slight outward flare to the upper wall sections, there is little about this building that is different from what might be built for a house, but from these humble beginnings, far more elaborate designs would develop. Larger churches with higher gable roofs were built to stand out more prominently in the countryside, and their floor levels were raised a story off the ground to keep the entrance above winter snow levels. Covered access stairs and enclosing galleries were added to provide a protected place for those who may have traveled considerable distances to attend services.

These elements may be seen in the Church of the

**6.24** Elevation and plan of the Church of the Raising of Lazarus, Kizhi, ca. 1391.

The three sections are an entrance porch, nave, and sanctuary.

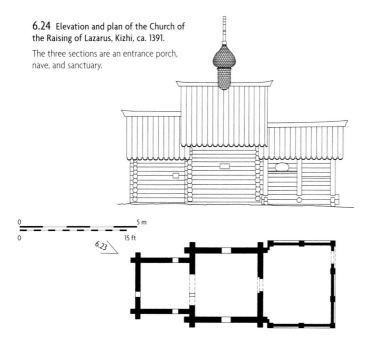

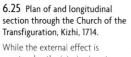

**6.25** Plan of and longitudinal section through the Church of the Transfiguration, Kizhi, 1714.

While the external effect is spectacular, the interior is not particularly exceptional and the iconostasis cuts abruptly into the nave. The same three-part division in plan seen in the small Lazarus church is repeated here.

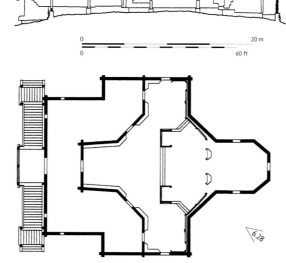

**6.26** Church of the Nativity of the Virgin, Peredki, now at Novgorod, 1593.

This building is clearly more elaborate than the Lazarus church, having a Greek-cross plan and a shatyor roof over the crossing to increase the sense of verticality.

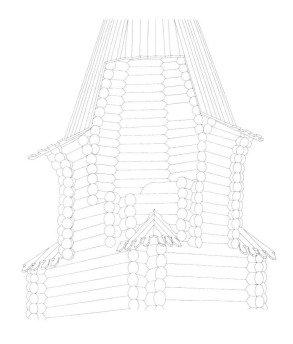

**6.27** Diagram of the construction of a shatyor roof.

Logs of diminishing length are laid in an octagonal plan to create a tent-like shatyor roof. The weatherproof cap is made of long wooden boards with angled terminations to cast water away from the building.

**6.28** Church of the Transfiguration, Kizhi, 1714.

This masterpiece church of 22 domes rises from a Greek-cross plan. Aspen used for shingles on the domes and bochki (reverse-curve gables) weathers to a silver gray that gleams like polished metal. To the left is the companion Church of the Intercession, built for use in winter and provided with a stove.

Nativity of the Virgin (1593), originally in the village of Peredki and now preserved at Novgorod (Fig. 6.26). The church has a Greek-cross plan, with an octagonal tower over the crossing that is capped by a tent roof (**shatyor**) to create a strong vertical landmark. Logs in diminishing lengths are well suited to support such a roof, and shatyor roofs became common not only for churches but also for fortress towers (Fig. 6.27). The church also has a great external gallery that wraps around three sides of the building, supported on stacked cantilevers (**pomochi**) extending from the wall underneath. One gets a clear idea of the depth of winter snow from the height of this gallery! Russian builders understood the properties of different woods and how to use them effectively. Larch logs that resist rot well are used for the lowest log rounds, while pine is the usual material for the upper sections. Wall logs are cut away on the bottom edge to match the rounded

profile of the log below, thus ensuring a tight joint and providing no place for water to collect. Birch bark is used for flashing where roofs intersect walls. Aspen wood was employed for shingles because it weathers to a smooth silvery color. Shingles were split or rived along the grain and then cut to create an interesting pattern and texture when installed. Boards used for the roof have pointed ends to encourage water to drip quickly at the edges. Roof pitches on the towers change near the base to cast run-off clear of the supporting walls. Not everything is so strictly functional, however, for there is also poetry. Folk symbols that date to pre-Christian times are seen in the sun signs on barge boards (decorative trim at the gable ends), and a carved bird may grace the ridge to bring good fortune.

Both practical concerns and symbolic elements are turned to stunning advantage in the masterpiece Church of the Transfiguration (1714) at Kizhi (Fig. 6.28), the only survivor of what were at least three churches with multiple domes constructed under the patronage of Peter the Great. Its plan is based on a Greek cross with the crossing transformed into an octagon (Fig. 6.25). What at Peredki was treated as a tent roof here becomes the entire external composition, a central tower that steps back in two stages

**6.29** Church of the Transfiguration detail, Kizhi.

This view shows the elaborate shingle work and framing of bochki. Note the stepped shapes of shingle ends, cut not only for decorative effect but also to promote water run-off and minimize capillary attraction.

with reverse-curve gables (**bochki**) and domes (Fig. 6.29). The church in fact has twenty-two domes on slender drums, creating a pyramidal composition. Counting from the top, there is a large single dome at the summit, four domes on the middle stage of the octagon, and eight on the lower octagonal story. Two more sets of four domes each are stacked at the bochki gables over the arms of the Greek cross, and the lowest single dome is placed over the sanctuary. This church continues the tradition begun nearly 700 years earlier at St. Sophia in Kiev: an elaborately domed exterior and an interior of smaller compartmentalized spaces not necessarily reflected in the overall massing. At Kizhi, there is a suspended ceiling across the octagonal tower, so the interior does not share the soaring volume suggested by the tower of domes. Furthermore, the internal space division in plan is not what one might expect from the outside. The vestibule wraps around the Greek cross, obscuring the actual shape of the nave, and the **iconostasis** projects into the center of the octagon, resulting in an irregular shape for the congregation. Kizhi is dramatic in the expansive northern landscape. On the inside, it is the icons that capture one's attention rather than the volume of the space.

The widespread destruction and economic upheaval that accompanied the invasion by the Mongols or Tartars in 1238–40 brought an end to the dominance of Kiev as a center of Russian government. Russian cities paid annual tribute to the khans of the Golden Horde, leaving little for investment in major buildings at home, so there was a corresponding decline in construction skills. Over the course of the fourteenth and fifteenth centuries, Moscow gradually established itself as the leading Russian city and became the seat of the metropolitan of the Russian Orthodox Church. Church and state combined efforts to overthrow the domination of the khans. Moscow's central fortress, the Kremlin, was gradually reconstructed in stone from the original wood, and new churches were erected there under patronage of the princes of Moscow, who now styled themselves as tsars (from the Latin *caesar*).

Motifs from wooden architecture found their way into masonry building, particularly the tent roof already seen in the church from Peredki, which came to be used for votive churches (as opposed to churches needing to accommodate a congregation) built in Moscow during the sixteenth century. The most famous of these is Moscow's Cathedral of the Intercession on the Moat, more usually known as St. Basil the Blessed (1555–60) (Fig. 6.30), erected on Red Square just outside the Kremlin walls to commemorate Ivan IV's victory over the Horde at the battle of Kazan in 1552. The architects were Barma and Posnik, who came from Pskov. Their design is fundamentally a central sanctuary surrounded by four large octagonal chapels and four smaller chapels that are square in plan. Eight of the chapels are dedicated to saints whose days coincided with key dates in the siege of Kazan, and the ninth is dedicated to the Entry into Jerusalem, so in some respects this building is really nine chapels sharing a common foundation. The central sanctuary is covered by a tall shatyor roof, while the eight subsidiary chapels receive individual vertical expression as domed towers. It is a tribute to the architects that this diverse array of elements, including also the covered entrance galleries and stairs, reads not as a random collection of parts but as a complex, intriguing whole, interesting from whatever angle it is approached. A close look at the exterior reveals decorative elements including layers of semicircular and triangular gables, pilasters, and diamond-shaped motifs, along with the expected onion domes, which are actually seventeenth-century replacements for helmet domes of the original design. These replacement roofs are a riot of glazed tiles in faceted, zigzag, spiraling, and striped designs that contribute additional color to the already elaborate red-brick and white-stone trim of the exterior. Interior space is highly compartmentalized. Since the volume under each tower is open to the chapel below, processing through the church is like traveling along a passage connecting a series of discrete chambers, each the size of a domestic room in plan but having an enormously tall ceiling.

**6.30** St. Basil the Blessed, Moscow, 1555–60.
Barma and Posnik utilized forms from wooden churches to create an extraordinary design in masonry. The riot of forms and colors on the exterior is more memorable than the interior, which is extremely compartmentalized.

St. Basil's is a reasonable place to conclude this consideration of the Byzantine architecture of Russia. Even though its construction coincides chronologically with buildings of the late Renaissance in Italy, St. Basil's is still rooted in traditions begun a millennium earlier in the eastern empire centered in Constantinople. Byzantium's lasting impact would continue in Russia as foreign architects came to build Baroque churches during the seventeenth and eighteenth centuries. Under Peter the Great, who avidly sought to end Russia's cultural isolation and overcome its perceived backward ways, secular Russian architecture came to resemble contemporary European architectural movements more than honoring its own historical past.

## CONCLUSIONS ABOUT ARCHITECTURAL IDEAS

Early Christian and Byzantine architecture affords an opportunity for the didactic comparison of longitudinal versus central planning. Driven by the liturgical importance of the processional, designers of western (what became Roman Catholic) churches most frequently based their layouts on the ancient Roman basilica, with its long, tall, clerestory-lit central space flanked by lower, narrower aisles and terminated by an apse. They sometimes projected twin wings, or transepts, from the chancel area, producing a Latin-cross plan: one with three short arms and one longer arm in the form of the nave and aisles. These Early Christ-

ian designers also commonly used central, often circular plans for smaller martyria, baptisteries, and mausolea.

In the Byzantine east, what we know today as Greek Orthodox churches took on central plans that emphasized not the processional but the Mass. The simplest of these plan types was the quincunx or nine-part grid with perimeter bearing walls and a columned core. The most complex was the great, unique Hagia Sophia, with its interlocking system of piers, walls, vaults, domes, and buttresses.

Both longitudinal and central schemes solved myriad liturgical, esthetic, and constructional problems. The Early Christian basilican plans allowed for a separation of the uninitiated from the initiated and from the clergy and frequently promoted the viewing of relics. The Byzantine central plans took on numerous forms, from octagons to Greek crosses (four equal arms) to the complex merging of a powerful longitudinal axis with a central nave or naos at Hagia Sophia. In both east and west, but particularly in the east, light interacting with faceted mosaic surfaces yielded overtly spiritual environments epitomized by Hagia Sophia's, one of almost palpable luminosity that still moves visitors today and must have stunned those who experienced it in the sixth century.

As an exotic coda, the churches of Russia offer regional interpretations of Byzantine models, many of them built of masonry but some constructed of plentifully available wood. They are so distinctive that the image of such a structure as Saint Basil's in Moscow has remained a consistent popular image even through the anti-religious period of the U.S.S.R.

# CHAPTER 7

# ISLAMIC ARCHITECTURE

As we have seen, the Early Christians went through an extensive process to develop architectural forms suitable for and expressive of their religion. Followers of the religion founded by the prophet Mohammed experienced a similar evolutionary process, but one that led to quite different results as they created buildings to serve and symbolize Islam.

Islam originated in Arabia. In 610 the angel Gabriel is said to have appeared to Mohammed in Mecca and over time expounded the revelation of God, or Allah ('Al-lah' meaning 'the God'). These revelations were collected into a holy book, the Qur'an (or Koran), which expressed in Arabic the message of Islam, a word signifying submission to the will of Allah. Each Muslim accepted five basic truths or duties: to believe in the oneness of God, and that Mohammed was the messenger of God; to pray five times daily; to fast from sunrise to sunset during the month of Ramadan; to give alms to the poor; and to make at least one pilgrimage to the holy city of Mecca, wealth and health permitting.

Conversion of the tribes to Islam was accompanied by an intense awakening of Arab fervor, and the courage and fighting skill of Arabic tribes, previously exploited by the Sassanian and Byzantine empires, was turned against these masters in a fury of rapid conquests, frequently aided by local contempt for the corruption associated with Byzantine rule. By 661 Islamic armies had swept through what is today Iran, Iraq, Israel, Syria, and Egypt, and they then moved across the North African coast to enter Spain in 711. From Spain they pushed northward into France, where forces led by Charles Martel stopped their European expansion in 732 at the battle of Tours. Islamic settlers remained in central and southern Spain until 1492, however, and their armies continued to batter the southern borders of the Byzantine Empire until, under the Ottoman Turks, they finally conquered Constantinople in 1453. Through trade, Islamic dynasties made contact with China and India, where their religion would eventually take root, and strong Islamic influence made a leap as far east as modern-day Malaysia and Indonesia. With military conquest came economic, social, and cultural dominance as Islamic customs and the Arabic language replaced surviving practices in the old Roman Empire. Islamic policy toward conquered populations was generally one of accommodation. Islamic rule was often preferred by the natives of occupied lands to that of harsh Byzantine governors, and the multi-cultural society the invaders fostered provided a model of respectful interaction that the modern world might do well to rediscover. The heady mix of learned men from Islamic and Jewish traditions, sometimes joined by Christian theologians, contributed to a highly productive era in the arts and sciences from the ninth through sixteenth centuries.

Today, Muslims represent a majority of the population in the Middle East, North Africa, parts of Central and South Asia, the Malaysian peninsula, and the Indonesian archipelago, but sizeable minorities also live in Europe and the United States. Islamic worship requires prayer five times a day, and this prayer is practiced at four levels of participation: 1) the individual or small group, 2) the neighborhood congregation, 3) the entire populace of a small city, and 4) the whole Muslim world, and discrete structures are built for the first three levels of worship. For daily prayer (except on Fridays), small numbers of worshipers use the modestly sized **masjid**, containing a prayer niche, but no facilities for preaching. For universal corporate worship, a Muslim town requires an idgab, a very large, unroofed open space with a long prayer wall on one side. The residents of a neighborhood attend the most well-known Islamic religious structure: the congregational or Friday mosque, where the principal or weekly service is held, hence its naming for a day of the week. It is in the covered prayer hall of such a Friday mosque that mass prayer takes place. Worshipers assemble in tightly packed

## Chronology

| | |
|---|---|
| appearance of the Angel Gabriel to Mohammed | 610 |
| revelation of the Qur'an to Mohammed | 610–633 |
| spread of Islam throughout the Middle East | 7th century |
| construction of the Dome of the Rock | 687–91 |
| spread of Islam across North Africa | early 8th century |
| defeat of Islamic forces at Tours by Charles Martel | 732 |
| construction of the Great Mosque, Cordoba | 833–988 |
| spread of Islam to India, Malaysia, and Indonesia | 12th–13th centuries |
| conquest of Constantinople by the Ottomans | 1453 |
| construction of the Mosque of Süleyman the Magnificent | 1550–57 |
| construction of the Taj Mahal | 1631–4 |

Qibla iwan of the Friday mosque, Isfahan, 12th century.

What began in the ninth century as a columnar hall mosque was transformed over time into a more elaborate plan, culminating with a large four-iwan courtyard. Note the iwan's muqarnas vaults.

**7.1** Muslims at prayer in the Mosque of the Prophet, Mecca.

This dramatic photograph illustrates a consistent patterning of highly ordered worshipers at prayer, the repeated orthogonal structural bays, and polychromatic masonry. All the worshipers are facing the prayer wall.

ranks and files, placing themselves as close as possible to the prayer wall, which explains the square or wide-rectangle shapes of such halls as opposed to the long, narrow plans of Christian churches or the central plans of Byzantine ones. Prayer is directional, oriented toward Mecca, and requires that worshipers, after ritual purification, proceed through a series of bowings, prostrations, and recitations from the Qur'an (Fig. 7.1).

Islam prescribes that ornamentation be **aniconic**, meaning symbolic or suggestive rather than literally representational. This ornament is sometimes executed in stone, but more frequently in glazed brick or tile, gypsum stucco, glass, or even wood. The exterior envelopes of Islamic religious buildings are treated like a skin that can receive universally applied decoration. The ordering of this decoration, though apparently complex, is typically controlled by primary and secondary grids and makes extensive use of repetition, symmetry, and patterning. This ordering can be subdivided according to four design strategies: 1) the repetition of an architectural element like an arch, 2) geometric manipulations like rotated and interlocking polygons, 3) organic growth in the form of plant-like foliation, and 4) calligraphy. Architectural elements can be two- or three-dimensional and appear most commonly as window or door openings. Geometric motifs allow for almost endless creativity and include the

ribbing of vaults. Two- and three-dimensional organic compositions can be highly stylized or approach naturalism, and as they become linear and seemingly endless produce a so-called arabesque, or intricate pattern of interlaced lines. Calligraphy is the most important of the four strategies because it records the word of Allah. It can be flowing, or cursive, as well as angular. Some ornamental conditions exploit light, such as glass or translucent screens that filter illumination, and **muqarnas** vaults that both reflect and refract it.

## EARLY SHRINES AND PALACES

For their earliest buildings, the largely nomadic Islamic Arabs assimilated techniques and forms from the civilizations they encountered. Syrian and Christian influences are clear in one of the most prominent early shrines, the Dome of the Rock (687–91) in Jerusalem (Figs. 7.2–7.4). Its location on Mount Moriah was sacred to the Jews, both as the site on which Abraham had offered his son Isaac as a sacrifice to the Lord and as the location of Solomon's Temple. Muslims honored it for Abraham's presence, but also venerated it as the place from which Mohammed ascended in his night journey to paradise. At the center of the Dome of the Rock is a rock, under which lies a small cave with a single opening. The shrine is carefully positioned around this rock, the domed central portion enclosing the rock and a concentric aisle permitting circumambulation. The building's form was probably derived from Christian precedent. Constantine's Church

**7.2** Dome of the Rock, Jerusalem, 687–91.

One of the earliest Islamic shrines, this octagonal domed building has a double ambulatory surrounding the rock from which Mohammed ascended on his journey to paradise.

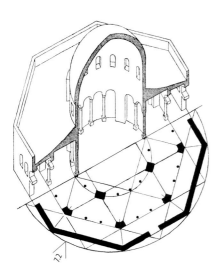

**7.3** Axonometric section of the Dome of the Rock, Jerusalem, 687–91.

This section shows the sophisticated geometry involved in the Dome of the Rock's design, a characteristic shared by a number of fourth- and fifth-century Syrian churches.

**7.4** The Dome of the Rock interior, Jerusalem, 687–91.

This celebration of a holy site through the erection of a dome, in this case over a rock above a cave and by Jews and Muslims in Jerusalem, can be compared to the building of the dome of St. Peter's by Christians in Rome (see chapter 11) over the spot where the apostle Peter is believed to have been buried.

**7.5** Muslims circumambulating the Ka'ba during the Haj, Mecca.

The idea of pilgrimage is one shared by Christians and Muslims. In this scene in Mecca, throngs of pilgrims surround the Ka'ba. In chapter 8, you will find Romanesque churches along the pilgrimage roads in France and Spain that lead to the city of Compostela and the highly venerated tomb of the apostle James son of Zebedee.

of the Holy Sepulcher in Jerusalem had featured a similar rotunda, and there were many centrally planned domed churches throughout the Byzantine world. Unlike most Byzantine domes, however, the structure here is of wood. (There is evidence that early Christian shrines also had wooden domes, although none has survived to the present day.) The dome of the Jerusalem sanctuary, sixty-seven feet in diameter, is constructed of a double shell, each shell having thirty-two converging wooden **ribs**, and the whole rests on a cornice atop a masonry drum. The inner ribs are plastered and adorned with painted and gilded designs (fourteenth-century reconstructions), while the exterior is sheathed with boards and finished with lead and gold leaf.

The general scheme employed at the Dome of the Rock, that of a central shrine around which the faithful could circulate, was used earlier at Mecca in rebuilding the Ka'ba, the goal of Islamic pilgrimage (Fig. 7.5). This cloth-draped cubical shrine contains the Black Stone, believed to have been given to Abraham by the angel Gabriel. The stone was venerated in pre-Muslim times. Mohammed destroyed the idols placed around it, and his successors cleared neighboring buildings in order to provide clear circulation space around the stone. At the Haj, or annual pilgrimage, the devout process seven times around the Ka'ba, following the sets of concentric rings set in the pavement encircling the shrine.

## CONCEPTION OF THE MOSQUE

The building type most closely associated with Islam is the mosque, the primary place of worship, which evolved from several sources. These included the House of the Prophet at Medina (ca. 622), Christian churches, and perhaps the audience halls of Persian kings.

Beside Mohammed's house stood a square enclosure, with small chambers set in the southeast corner for his living quarters (Fig. 7.6). The remainder of the space was a partially open central court. Although constructed originally for domestic purposes, it also served as a gathering place for his followers to hear sermons and prayers, and after Mohammed's death its form was imitated in simple worship facilities built in other settlements.

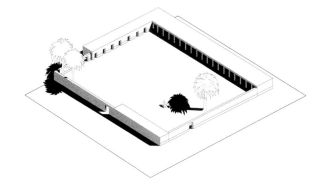

**7.6** Reconstruction of the House of the Prophet, Medina, ca. 622.

This building became a prototype for the mosque. Followers of Mohammed assembled in the open courtyard to hear sermons and participate in group prayer, functions that had to be accommodated into mosque design.

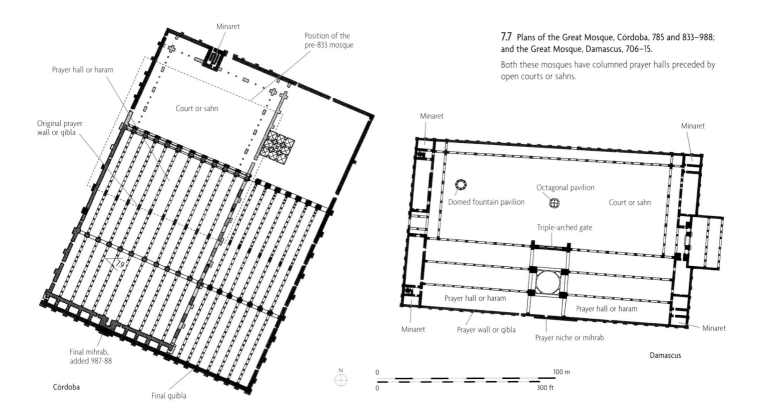

Minaret

Position of the
pre-833 mosque

Prayer hall or haram

Court or sahn

Original prayer
wall or qibla

7.9

Final mihrab,
added 987-88

Córdoba

Final quibla

7.7 Plans of the Great Mosque, Córdoba, 785 and 833–988; and the Great Mosque, Damascus, 706–15.

Both these mosques have columned prayer halls preceded by open courts or sahns.

Minaret

Minaret

Domed fountain pavilion

Octagonal pavilion

Court or sahn

Triple-arched gate

Prayer hall or haram

Prayer hall or haram

Minaret

Prayer wall or qibla

Prayer niche or mihrab

Minaret

Damascus

N

0                                            100 m
0                                            300 ft

The Great Mosque at Damascus (706–15, with later rebuildings) is the oldest extant mosque and illustrates a process through which the form developed (Fig. 7.7). The site is an ancient one on which had stood a Roman temple dedicated to Jupiter and a fourth-century Christian church dedicated to St. John the Baptist. For a time after the Islamic conquest of the city in 635, both Christians and Muslims worshiped on the site, but in 706 the church was pulled down and an impressive mosque, based in part on tripartite aisle-and-nave basilican church plans, was constructed under the caliphate of al-Walid I. The mosque's outline was determined by the shape of the Roman shrine that was entered through a gateway in the center of the shorter, east side. Four towers, or **minarets**, provided elevated platforms at the corners of the site from which a caller (muezzin) could summon the faithful to prayer. The general design of these towers may have been based on earlier fortification towers or lighthouses, but, with their incorporation at Damascus, minarets became standard features of subsequent Friday mosques. Just as belltowers or raised domes do for churches, minarets serve to identify the mosque in the landscape. Much later, particularly important mosques were sometimes given multiple minarets, but one generally sufficed.

Over half of the inner space is given over to an open arcaded court, or **sahn**, containing a domed fountain pavilion for ritual ablutions and an octagonal pavilion originally used for the public treasury. The covered prayer hall, or **haram**, extends along the entire long south wall. Two parallel rows of columns divide this hall longitudinally into thirds, near the center of which the arcades are interrupted by a broad transverse element similar to a nave, with a wooden dome over its central bay. This

element develops in later designs into the **maqsura**, a special processional area reserved for the retinue of the caliph, thereby justifying its dome as a special architectural accent. The south wall being the prayer wall, or **qibla**, there are three niches, or **mihrabs**, set into it to indicate the direction of Mecca. A raised pulpit, or **minbar** (not indicated on the plan), from which Qur'anic readings, sermons, or official proclamations and addresses are given, is located to the right of the central mihrab.

## REGIONAL VARIATIONS IN MOSQUE DESIGN

Because mosques have been built throughout so much of the world, it will not be possible to represent their full diversity in this short chapter. The discussion that follows concentrates on 1) columnar or hypostyle mosques favored in Arabia, North Africa, and Spain, 2) **iwan** mosques popular in Iran and Central Asia, which consist of a rectangular court flanked by large, often vaulted spaces, or iwans, and 3) large, centrally organized, domed-space mosques found in Turkey.

### COLUMNED HALL OR HYPOSTYLE MOSQUES

The Great Mosque of al-Mutawakkil at Samarra, Iraq (848/49–52) has both a columned hall and a single, extraordinary minaret. Enormous in size, the mosque consists of a rectangular burned-brick-wall enclosure more than 800 feet by more than 500 feet, with attached semi-circular towers. To the north along the enclosure's central, longitudinal axis rises the brick minaret (Fig. 7.8), its spiral

**7.8** The Great Mosque of al-Mutawakkil, Samarra, 848/849–52.

This prominent minaret in the form of a tall spiral has a lineage traceable as far back as the Mesopotamian ziggurats. Note how the long, horizontal outer wall serves as a foil for the minaret's rich, strongly vertical silhouette.

form associated by some with the ziggurats of Ancient Mesopotamia. Inside the mosque's walls, a forest of square columns once surrounded a rectangular sahn, with the qibla adjacent to the deepest accumulation of column bays, altogether a highly ordered, even profound composition.

The Great Mosque begun in around 785 in Córdoba, Spain (Fig. 7.7), evolved to have a much more complex columnar hall form than that at Samarra. In the first construction period, the mosque occupied a nearly square plan, half comprising the sahn and the other half the haram, which contained ten rows of eleven columns to create an eleven-aisled sanctuary. In the haram, superimposed arches connect the columns, the lower arch being horseshoe-shaped and the upper one not quite semicircular (Fig. 7.9). The effect of this work is light and delicate, and although both the tiered arcades of the Damascus mosque and the stacked arches of Roman aqueducts have been suggested as the inspiration for the superimposed arches, their treatment here is entirely original. Both arch levels are polychrome, composed of white stone voussoirs set alternately against red brick ones.

Beginning in 833, this mosque was enlarged three times. In the first renovation campaign (833–48), the prayer hall was extended to the southwest by the addition of eight new bays that maintained the alignment and rhythm of the original mosque but necessitated reconstruction of the qibla and mihrab. In 951, the sahn was extended to the northeast and a new minaret erected. The haram was again expanded to the southwest beginning in 962, when another twelve bays were added along with a new qibla and mihrab. The new mihrab was a richly ornamented niche, given prominence on the interior by a virtual forest of lobed and cusped arches, covered by a dome formed by boldly interlacing arches (Figs. 7.10–7.11), flanked by smaller domes also composed of interlaced arches in the bays to either side. So far as we know, these exceptional domes are an original invention here, and they are the possible inspiration for similar domes built in the Baroque by Guarini (see Fig. 12.25). The final extension of the mosque took place in 987–88 along the southeastern side, adding another eight aisles running the full length of the existing haram, and enlarging the sahn as well to create the largest mosque in Spain. In the sixteenth century, after the Moors were expelled from Spain, the cathedral of Córdoba (Fig. 7.12) was inserted inside the mosque, disrupting the colonnaded expanse of the haram but perhaps inadvertently preserving a good portion of the Islamic fabric through the mosque's conversion to a place of Christian worship.

**7.9** The Great Mosque interior, Córdoba, 833–988.

This view of the prayer hall shows the horseshoe-shaped polychrome stacked arches that dominate the interior. Eventually 610 columns defined the immense space.

**7.10** The Great Mosque vault above the maqsura, Córdoba, 833–988.

Note the use of lobed arches, polychromy, and the interlaced-arch structure of the dome.

**7.11** The Great Mosque vault above the mihrab bay, Córdoba, 833–988.

This vault also employs interlaced arches in its construction.

**7.12** The Great Mosque from the minaret, Córdoba, 833–988.

Parallel rows of ridge-and-valley roofs cover the prayer hall, and the foreground trees are growing in the sahn. One regrets the intrusion of a later Christian church in this splendid Islamic building.

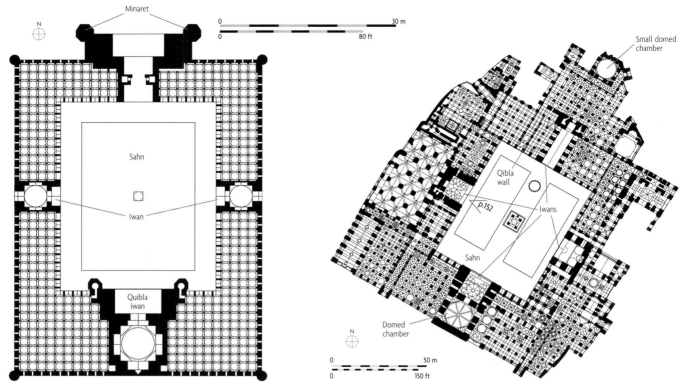

**7.13** Plan of the Bibi Kanum Mosque, Samarkand, begun 1399.

Compare this modular mosque plan with the equally regimented ranks and files of Muslim worshipers in Fig. 7.1 and remember that they are called to prayer five times daily. This rigorous prayer regime is mirrored in the rigorous planning of the mosque.

**7.14a** Plan of the Friday mosque, Isfahan, 8th–17th centuries.

This mosque is interesting for its early incorporation of substantial domes within a multi-columned prayer hall. In its final form, the mosque evolved into a four-iwan type, having a large central courtyard bisected by cross-axes established by the iwans.

**7.14b** Plan of and section looking southeast through Masjid-i-shah, Isfahan, 1611–ca. 1630.

The mosque sits at the top of the public square. Entrance to it is centered in the arcades defining the square, but the axis turns to bring the mosque into alignment with Mecca. Madrasas, or theological schools, are located beside the mosque.

## IWAN MOSQUES

To the east, in Central Asian lands now part of Iran, Uzbekistan, Turkmenistan, and Afghanistan, mosque designs developed initially from multi-columned halls. The Bibi Khanum Mosque at Samarkand, Uzbekistan, begun in 1399 by the military and political leader Timur, who founded a dynasty at the end of the fourteenth century, presents the essentials of the multi-columned iwan mosque form. Its constituent element, the iwan, is a vaulted or domed volume, walled on three sides and open on the other. At Samarkand, the plan (Fig. 7.13) is comparable to that at Samarra, with a sahn inside ranks of columns forming four L-shaped halls, all bounded by a rectangular perimeter wall. Here, however, an entry portal, with stumps of flanking minarets remaining, opens into one short side of the sahn, and iwans appear at the center of the other three sides, becoming porch-like extensions of the central open space. The iwan facing the entry and terminating its axis is the qibla iwan and is domed and flanked by additional minarets.

**7.15** Masjid-i-Shah, Isfahan, 1611–ca. 1630.

In order to respect the direction of Mecca, the mosque is turned forty-five degrees to the axis of the public square (left side of the photograph) laid out by Shah Abbas.

**7.16** Iwan, Masjid-i-Shah, Isfahan, 1611–ca. 1630.

Two-story arcades flank the central arch, which is finished with elaborate tile decoration and a muqarnas vault. In the background is the rear of the entrance iwan on the public square.

The earliest mosque about which we have reliable archaeological information is the Friday mosque in Isfahan (Fig. 7.14a), begun in the eighth century, finally achieving a form not unlike that at Samarkand and reworked repeatedly until the seventeenth century. The original form seems to have been a rectangular multi-columned hall covered with a wooden roof, with a large sahn at its core. In 1086–87 a domed chamber was introduced at the southwest end of the existing building, probably to serve as a maqsura. It differed significantly in scale from the domes already seen as part of the maqsuras at

Damascus and Córdoba: rather than covering one bay of the columnar hall, the southern dome covered twenty bays. In 1088, a slightly smaller dome was added in an axial line to the north. It is not clear what function it served initially, for it was outside the building at the time of its construction but was soon incorporated into arcades.

At some later date, Isfahan's Friday mosque was modified again to include four iwans set in the center of each side of the sahn. Their boldly scaled arched openings provided builders with an opportunity to exercise their skills in geometric ornamentation, including the application of glazed tiles in shades of blue, turquoise, white, and yellow, and stalactite-like muqarnas vaults, the ornamental treatment of curved wall surfaces with corbeled concave elements that has the overall effect of dissolving the material presence of the wall into facets that seem to hover in

**7.17** Masjid-I-shah, entrance to prayer hall, Isfahan, 1611–ca. 1630.

This view shows the elaborate blue-glazed tile work and muqarnas vault. Sometimes compared to a honeycomb, these cellular vaults are formed by corbeling.

space. The mosque is also renowned for its intricate brick-work patterns in the domes.

During the reign of Shah Abbas I, the core of Isfahan was greatly expanded, as a whole new market area was developed at some distance from the older settlement around the Friday mosque. Included in the new construction was a congregational mosque, the Masjid-i-Shah (1611–ca. 1630), built to designs of Badi' al-Zaman Tuni and Ali Akbar al-Isfahani (Figs. 7.14b, 7.15–7.17). Entrance into it is made through the center of the southern side of the market, so as to provide a monumental portal to the public area and match the gateway to the **bazaar** at the opposite end of the square, but the mosque itself is turned forty-five degrees so as to be correctly aligned with Mecca. The skill with which the designers accommodated the change in axis is one of the most admired aspects of the plan. From the entranceway, one

can see the iwan constructed in front of the qibla, but the circulation path leads first laterally to either side of the initial iwan, then toward the sahn, thereby accomplishing the axial shift with finesse. Apart from the transitional elements at the entrance, symmetry governs the entire design. A still pool at the center of the sahn reflects the blue-background glazed tilework covering the four iwans and the great dome of the haram. Among the decorative elements portrayed in the tiles are peacocks, reflecting the builders' willingness in this case to depict animals in art rather than confining ornament to recursive geometric elements and calligraphy. The domed prayer hall is augmented by rooms on either side, also covered by a succession of small domes, that served as a winter mosque, and it is further complemented by two religious schools (**madrasas**), thus continuing an established tradition of incorporating education with worship. (The study of law and religion are inseparable aspects of Islamic higher education.)

Islam came to India in successive waves of military invasions in the eleventh through thirteenth centuries, challenging the established religions of Hinduism and Buddhism with its fundamentally different religious perspective. India's cave-like temples with interiors used only by priests and covered inside and out with intricately wrought sculpted figures were totally alien to the Islamic idea of the mosque with accessible open courtyards, spacious prayer halls, and scrupulous avoidance of the human figure in representational art. Hindu and Buddhist temples were replaced with mosques initially based on multi-columned hall designs. Beginning with the ascendancy of the Mughal Dynasty (mid-sixteenth to eighteenth centuries), however, one sees a distinctly Indo-Islamic style come into being, spurred on in large measure by the arrival of foreign craftsmen from Central Asia. Some of

**7.18** Plan of the Friday mosque, Fatehpur Sikri, ca. 1568–71.

The monumental gate is on the southern side of the mosque, preceded by a wide stairway, while the haram is set to the west.

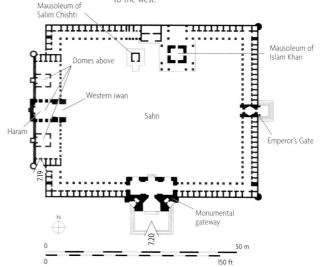

**7.19** Friday mosque interior, Fatehpur Sikri, ca. 1568–71.

This view shows the distinctive detail developed by Akbar's architects as they fused Islamic forms (the pointed arch, for example) with elements from Hindu and Buddhist traditions already well established in India.

**7.20** Friday mosque gateway, Fatehpur Sikri, ca. 1568–71.

As Akbar's city was set on a plateau above the surrounding terrain, a monumental flight of steps is required to gain entrance to the mosque from the southern side. It serves as a plinth for an impressive arched gateway.

these individuals were descendants of Indian craftsmen taken captive by the Mongol conqueror Timur in 1398. Their return in the sixteenth century brought skilled builders familiar with the Islamic architecture of Persia to India, and the resulting works done for the Mughal rulers are some of the most magnificent to be found in the Islamic world.

Jalil al-Din Akbar, the third Mughal emperor, who ruled 1556–1605, was responsible for constructing an entirely new capital at Fatehpur Sikri (1569–ca. 1580), a site abandoned after his death and preserved now as a national monument in India. The monumental palace buildings are all that remain, but sixteenth-century accounts describe it as a city larger than London at the same period, which explains in part the grand scale employed for its Friday mosque (ca. 1568–71) (Figs. 7.18–7.20). Constructed in red sandstone, the mosque has an immense sahn, 312 by 387 feet, entered from the south through a monumental gate enlarged in 1596. From the palace, entrance was made through the Emperor's gate, placing it on axis with the haram on the western side. Behind the western iwan is the major dome of the haram, flanked by two smaller domes, setting a pattern for Indian mosques that would often be repeated. In its architecture, the building reflects arched and domed forms familiar from examples in Iran, but some of the detail also borrows elements from the Hindu and Buddhist architecture of India, a blend that contributes a distinctive quality to Islamic buildings on the subcontinent. The mosque's sahn contains the exquisitely detailed marble tomb of Salim Chishti (d. 1572), a holy man who had predicted that the childless Akbar would have three sons. Fatehpur Sikri was built in celebration of the birth of Akbar's son Jahangir in 1569, and the east–west axis through the Friday mosque aligns with Chishti's hermitage, which was already on the site.

**7.21** Shezade Mosque, Istanbul, 1545–48.

Sinan's first major mosque, this building is notable for its clearly articulated geometry of squares. One square comprises the sahn, while the second defines the domed haram. Minarets are incorporated into the corners where the squares join.

## MULTI-DOMED MOSQUES

In Asiatic Turkey, or Anatolia, the spread of Islam came at the expense of the Byzantine Empire, which was gradually reduced in size until the fall of Constantinople in 1453 brought an end to a civilization over 1000 years old. The victors were the Ottoman Turks, led by Sultan Mehmet II, who thus completed the Islamic conquest of the Balkans. Hagia Sophia, the most impressive church in the eastern Mediterranean, was converted into the city's congregational mosque; minarets were eventually added. Ottoman architects, who already had experience in building domed structures set on cubical masses, received new inspiration from the city's great Byzantine churches, which now stood before them as models, and in succeeding centuries they constructed a number of mosques that in structure and architectural detail rank with the best religious buildings that Byzantium produced.

Among these one must count the works of Koca Sinan (ca. 1490–1588), a distinguished engineer and architect who has been compared with his Italian contemporary Michelangelo. Born to a peasant family of non-Muslim background, Sinan was recruited for governmental service as a youth and trained in the corps of Janissaries, elite infantry units of the Ottoman army composed of non-Muslims abducted as children and forced to convert to

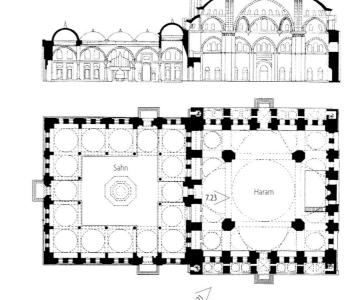

**7.22** Longitudinal section and plan of Shezade Mosque, Istanbul, 1545–48.

These drawings show how Sinan took Hagia Sophia's theme of the central dome with flanking semidomes and expanded it into a completely centralized design. The square plan of the sahn matches the square enclosed space of the haram.

**7.23** Shezade Mosque interior, Istanbul, 1545–48.
This view shows the piers supporting the great dome and the flanking semidomes.

Islam. After participating in military campaigns in Austria, Greece, and Mesopotamia, he served as court architect in Constantinople for fifty years, during which time he designed and supervised construction of a large number of projects, including waterworks, bridges, fortifications, and buildings. Sinan's career coincided with the reigns of generous sultans, and he was undoubtedly fortunate to have the vast Ottoman building corps of skilled workmen at his command. Without both liberal patrons to finance them and capable assistants to carry them out, major projects could not have been realized, no matter how brilliantly designed.

Sinan's first major architectural commission in Constantinople was the Shezade mosque complex (1545–48), commissioned by Sultan Süleyman in memory of his son, who had died as a young man. Constructed on the site of Justinian's Church of the Holy Apostles, the mosque is composed of two joined squares (Figs. 7.21–7.23). One square contains the sahn, which has a central fountain and is surrounded by domed bays behind arcades. The second square is the enclosed haram, where the central dome is complemented by four semidomes set at the sides, with smaller domes and semidomes filling the remaining spaces. The elegantly symmetrical geometry of the plan is matched by the balanced volumes of the interior space and the exterior massing, punctuated by paired minarets at the corners where the two squares adjoin.

Sinan has handled the great piers and necessary buttressing so as to minimize the apparent bulk of the masonry. As a result, window openings are larger and the volumetric massing on the exterior presents a harmonious composition of successive layering of domes and semidomes. Associated with the mosque are the tomb of Shezade Mehmet, a madrasa, a hospice for the infirm, a school, and a **caravanserai** (accommodation and markets for foreign merchants who sold at wholesale prices), reminders that even in a well-established city, mosques provided space for both civic and sacred functions. It was Ottoman practice to provide separate buildings dedicated to different particular needs.

A similar quality marks Sinan's celebrated mosque of Süleyman the Magnificent (1550–57), within a vast complex, or **Külliye**, containing the mosque and cemetery at the center, with four madrasas, a primary school, a medical school, a caravanserai, a hospital, a community kitchen to feed the poor, a hospice, public baths, and even a house for Sinan (Figs. 7.24–7.25). It was sited on the sloping side of a hill fronting on the Golden Horn (harbor of Constantinople), and Sinan located the complex so as to exploit the dramatic possibilities of the terrain, which required that the layout be asymmetrical. Marked by four slender minarets, the mosque dominates the ensemble of buildings. Its plan is familiar: an arcaded sahn, a domed haram, and a walled cemetery set on a linear axis. The

**7.24** Mosque of Süleyman the Magnificent, Istanbul, 1550–57.

Constructed as the centerpiece of a larger complex of schools, shops, and community facilities, the mass of this mosque is balanced by the slender vertical accents of its four minarets.

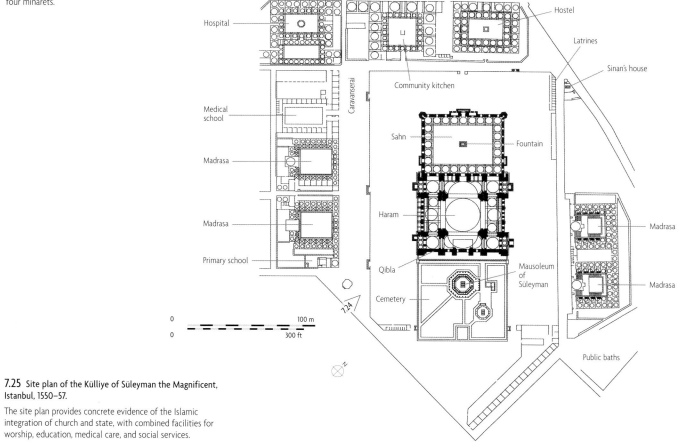

Hospital

Hostel

Latrines

Sinan's house

Community kitchen

Caravanserai

Medical school

Sahn

Fountain

Madrasa

Haram

Madrasa

Madrasa

Primary school

Qibla

Mausoleum of Süleyman

Cemetery

Public baths

0          100 m
0          300 ft

7.24

**7.25** Site plan of the Külliye of Süleyman the Magnificent, Istanbul, 1550–57.

The site plan provides concrete evidence of the Islamic integration of church and state, with combined facilities for worship, education, medical care, and social services.

**7.26** Selimiye Mosque, Edirne, 1568–75.

Generally held to be Sinan's masterpiece, this mosque is essentially a single dome supported on eight great piers and braced by external buttresses. The minarets are exceptionally tall and provided with internal spiraling staircases of considerable geometric complexity.

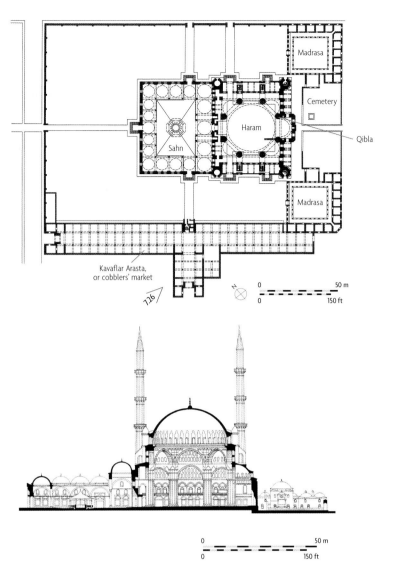

**7.27** Plan of and section through the Selimiye Mosque complex, Edirne, 1568–75.

Sinan attempted here to equal the dome of Hagia Sophia and exceed its integration of interior space.

haram is a variant of that at Hagia Sophia, having a central dome flanked by two semidomes, but here the aisles, also domed, are so configured as to allow the entire building to exist within a square. Spatially, the interior functions as a single volume, with aisles and nave available for prayer. (There is no second-level gallery as at Hagia Sophia.) The whole presents a more consistent articulation, both inside and out, than was achieved in the Byzantine building. Buttressing elements, arches, vaults, and domes work together structurally and visually to create a satisfying architectural composition. The octagonal mausoleum of Süleyman (d. 1566), placed in the center of the cemetery behind the qibla wall, has a plan inspired by the Dome of the Rock, although this is not evident from the exterior treatment.

Sinan's final major work was the Selimiye Mosque in Edirne, built in 1568–75 for Selim II, successor to Süleyman (Figs. 7.26–7.27). The complex contains the usual madrasas and commercial buildings (whose revenues helped to offset the running costs of the mosque and its related educational and charitable facilities), but it is the domed haram that commands particular attention. Sinan boasted that here he had built a dome both wider and taller than Hagia Sophia, which is not quite the case, but his method of conceiving the space transcends that of the Byzantine original. There are no semidomes. The dome is set directly on eight piers, six freestanding and two engaged in the qibla wall. Arches connecting these piers support the dome, which rises above ranks of windows pierced in the exterior wall. Buttressing necessary to brace the dome's lateral thrust is placed within the walls and seen more clearly on the exterior. As daring as is the dome, one must also marvel at the four slender minarets that mark the corners of the haram. Of exceptional height (232 feet), they are grooved to accentuate their verticality. Inside two of the minarets are separate staircases leading to each of the three balconies, a complex exercise in spiraling geometry and a structural challenge that Sinan boasted proudly that he had met successfully.

**7.28** Tomb of Ismail the Samanid, Bukhara, ca. 900.

In places where constant, bright sunlight is the norm, architects of various cultures have used cast shadows to great advantage. Here smooth wall-surfaces have disappeared in favor of advancing and receding masonry units that create a rich patterning of light and dark.

**7.29** Section and plan of the Tomb of Ismail the Samanid, Bukhara, ca. 900.

Note how the reentrant, or notched-out, corners are filled with circular columns that decorate the joining of the tomb's faces. The arched openings in each façade are splayed so that the arches become wider as they advance outward. The same device was frequently used in the medieval churches of Europe.

Squinch arch above

## TOMBS

It is common for a mosque to include the tomb of a founder or holy man. Freestanding monumental tombs, usually with domes, also became popular by the tenth century. The Tomb of Ismail the Samanid in Bukhara, Uzbekistan, dates from ca. 900 or even earlier. A cube-like mass with inset cylindrical corners houses a single domed chamber supported by four squinch arches and ringed by an upper-level ambulatory (Figs. 7.28–7.29). Most distinctive is its highly textured brickwork laid in forceful geometric patterns that contrast solids and voids.

Returning to Samarkand, location of the previously discussed Bibi Khanum Mosque, we find the Gur-i-Amir, built as the resting place of Timur's grandson, who died in battle. It consists of a Greek-cross-plan interior space, with its four arms crowned by **muqarna** vaults inside an octagonal mass that is surmounted by a tall cylindrical drum on squinch arches and tall, bulbous dome (Fig. 7.30). The interior ornamentation is lavish, including hexagonal alabaster panels, jasper, and even painted, molded paper.

With the construction in Delhi of the tomb of Humayun, father of Jalil al-Din Akbar, the idea of the domed-chamber tomb arrived in India. The most famous of these domed tombs is the Taj Mahal in Agra (1631–47) (Figs. 7.31–7.32). Its builder was Jahangir's son, Shah Jahan, who ruled from 1628 to 1658 and is remembered as a prolific Mughal patron of building. Aided by a well-trained group of architects attached to his court, Shah Jahan promoted a style that included an emphasis on bilateral

**7.30** Gur-i-Amir, Samarkand, early 15th century.

The bulbous dome, a dome that grows wider above its drum before curving inward, is a distinctive Muslim device and one comparable in profile to the Muslim horseshoe arches seen in Fig. 7.9.

**7.31** Taj Mahal, Agra, 1631–47.

This tomb is one of the world's most famous buildings. Its serenity derives in part from its sheer elegance and its placement in a totally designed landscape of plants, water, and paving.

symmetry, the use of cusped arches, and white marble or stucco facing instead of red sandstone for exterior finishes.

Because of its great size, elegant massing, refinement of detail and ornamentation, and general countenance of serenity, the Taj Mahal is unquestionably one of Islam's and indeed the world's most celebrated buildings. It was built as a tomb for Shah Jahan's beloved wife, Mumtaz Mahal, by a trio of architects: Ahmad Lahawri, along with 'Abd al-Karim Ma'mur Khan and Makramat Khan, all three assisted by craftsmen from Persia, Central Asia, and India. The site adjoins the Jumna River to the north, and the tomb is placed next to it, rather than being in the center of the layout as was Humayun's. Entrance is made from the south, through a main gateway set on axis with the tomb. In between the two lies a square garden, with canals dividing the square into quadrants defining the central and cross-axes. Flowering trees, cypresses, and blooming plants originally grew in the garden areas as symbols of rebirth and immortality. The tomb itself is symmetrical, crowned with a large bulbous dome raised on a drum and graced by smaller octagonal pavilions with domical roofs set at the corners. Highly polished and inlaid marble adorns the exterior, so that the building appears to glisten in the sun. The whole structure is raised on a square platform, the corners of which are marked by minarets. Flanking the tomb are symmetrically placed red sandstone buildings, to the west a mosque and to the east a guest house, whose color contrasts deliberately with the shimmering white marble. Against a verdant foreground of plant material, accentuated by reflecting water channels, the Taj Mahal seems ethereal, its proportion and detail so finely wrought as to capture the beautiful memory of the woman whose untimely death prompted its construction.

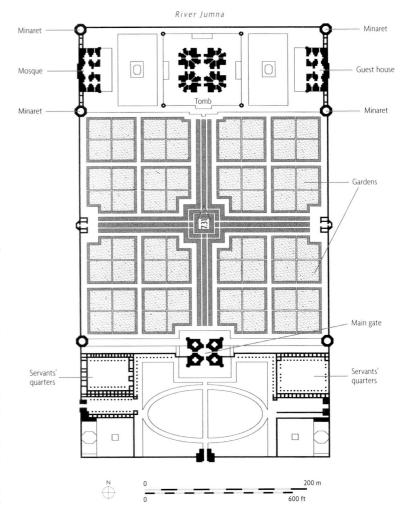

**7.32** Site plan of the Taj Mahal, Agra, 1631–47.

In this orthogonal scheme, the tomb (top) is set in a larger landscape of square courts divided into quadrants by watercourses, creating a nested hierarchy of axes and cross-axes that allude to the garden of paradise.

## HOUSES AND URBAN PATTERNS

Across the broad geographic area that comprises the Islamic world, there is obviously considerable diversity in climate, traditional house forms, and construction materials, making it impossible to propose a single definition for an Islamic house. From the Qur'an and related texts comprising traditions and laws, however, there developed certain principles governing both private and public life that also regulated aspects of house forms and city planning. Islam recognizes the fundamental right of privacy for the family within its own house, hence in many places houses present plain exterior walls to the street. In hot, arid climates, residences tend to be designed around courtyards that preserve privacy and also modify the microclimate advantageously (Figure 7.33). Doorways of houses on opposite sides of the street must be located so that one cannot look from one dwelling into the other when both doors are open, and ground-level windows are set so high that those passing by cannot look in. Windows above the ground floor may be larger, but they may not be placed so as to overlook courtyards or rooftop areas of other houses and thus invade the privacy of those occupying them. These upper-floor windows may project beyond the plane of the wall, and they are frequently provided with elaborately carved screens to restrict the view from the outside. Within the family, women and children are segregated from men and visitors, so the family living area (haram: note that the same word describes a mosque's prayer hall; in both cases they are spaces "set apart") is separated from reception facilities provided for male guests, and from the entrance to the house one cannot see directly into living areas. Privacy and seclusion are often achieved by the use of separate doors and carved screens or grilles, which admit light and air while also allowing those behind to look out without being seen.

Islam has a lengthy urban tradition, and aspects of the Prophet's teachings were applied to the problems inherent in establishing rights when living in larger communities. Pre-modern Islamic society made no distinction between the sacred and secular realms. In many traditional settlements located from North Africa to the Middle East, the essential features of an urban area were a Friday mosque large enough to serve the community and surrounding settlements, a governor who exercised control over the territory, and a bazaar or market with covered stalls for the city and surrounding countryside. The Friday mosque and the bazaar were inseparable. Market stalls were grouped by trade or type of merchandise, with those of highest status (perfume, books) located closest to the mosque entrance, and those associated with noise or noxious odors (coppersmiths, leatherworkers) farthest away. Interspersed with the public areas might be fountains, cafés, caravanserais, public baths, and madrasas. This whole public area was the domain of men, and its plan tended to be irregular, built up over time. The city's neighborhoods

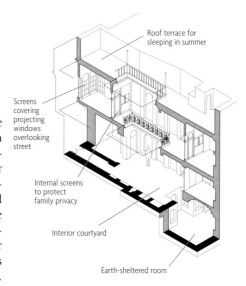

**7.33** Axonometric section through a traditional house, Baghdad.

This house incorporates many characteristics of Islamic urban dwellings in hot, dry climates. Under the courtyard floor is an earth-sheltered room that provides cooling air during the day. Screened rooftop areas are used for sleeping in hot weather. Grilled windows at upper levels can be opened for air circulation while preserving privacy.

**7.34** Plan of the Maidan-i-Shah (public square) and related developments, Isfahan, 1590–1602.

Shah Abbas had an ambitious new city center laid out around the Maidan-i-Shah, a twenty-acre urban square. The Masjid-i-Shah (Shah's Mosque) was built at the south end to draw the faithful from the older Friday mosque.

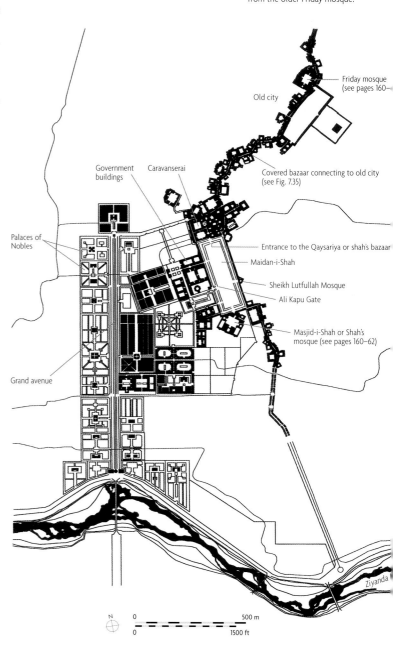

**7.35** View of the bazaar at Isfahan.

The bazaar is composed of a street linking merchants' stalls and small shops, interspersed with baths, workshops, and theological schools. Vaults over the street provide relief from the intense sun, while skylights admit necessary daylight and fresh air.

or residential quarters began as homogeneous groupings of families affiliated by a common trade or religious and ethnic connections. At one time, many quarters had a gate or door that could be used to close off the area when desired. Within the neighborhood, families shared a mosque, fountains, public baths, communal ovens, and shops. The distinctive organization of residential quarters helps to explain why the street plans of traditional Islamic cities such as Tunis or Isfahan have few through roads, on which are found the major public places and markets; a limited number of secondary streets; and hundreds of cul-de-sacs, along which most houses stand. The street pattern resembles a maze with many dead ends, far more than in the grid layouts more common in Europe.

The Iranian city of Isfahan provides perhaps the most handsome example of the application of Islamic principles of city planning, although one must admit from the start that its royal quarter and new section as laid out by Shah Abbas I (1587–1629) are not typical of the growth by accretion associated with traditional Islamic urbanism (Fig. 7.34). In the older part of town, around the Friday mosque, one finds the traditional network of streets and cul-de-sacs. The historic trade route extending south toward the Ziyanda River grew into a linear covered bazaar (Fig. 7.35) of small shops that meandered past entrances to other facilities that lay behind the merchants' stalls: caravanserais, madrasas, mosques, baths, fountains, and craft workshops. Shah Abbas, determined to bring greater glory to his capital city, undertook redevelopment of the public square established just outside the traditional area and defined it as a formal rectangular square, the Maidan-i-Shah, lined with shops and punctuated by major monuments: two mosques, the Ali Kapu gate (the imperial porch, which served as a viewing stand), and the entrance to the Qaysariya, the shah's bazaar. The center of the open space was normally available for small vendors to sell their wares in, but it could also be cleared and used for military or athletic events, the two-story arcades around the edges providing a good base for observation.

The Shah's contributions to this grand urban scheme included construction of a complex of governmental buildings on the western side of the square behind the Ali Kapu gate. Directly opposite the gate was the imposing entrance to the small Sheikh Lutfullah Mosque (1602) that has a bent-axis entry around two sides of the square haram to bring the faithful into the mosque on the axis aligned with Mecca. The Masjid-i-Shah, or Shah's mosque (see pages 160–62), occupies the short southern end of the square, set opposite the grand entrance to the shah's bazaar on the northern side. This formally conceived space comes as a surprise after the more organic city core, but its layout is not out of character, for it displays at a large scale what many of the older buildings, including the Friday mosque, had become over a longer period of time: spaces with biaxial symmetry and uniform perimeter articulation, whether in arcades or colonnades. Shah Abbas's ambition was to link the Maidan-i-Shah, by means of a grand new avenue lined with palaces of nobles, to the river and a new bridge, making accessible gardens and the commercially important Armenian settlement beyond, but not all of his program came to fruition.

## THE PALACE AND THE GARDEN

Some of the formal concepts that characterized the planning of Isfahan are also seen in the fortress-palace of the Alhambra, a royal citadel erected above the city of Granada (Fig. 7.36). Built in the thirteenth and fourteenth centuries, the Alhambra was the work of the Nasrid Dynasty, which governed the dwindling Islamic territories of southern Spain until expulsion in 1492 by Ferdinand and Isabella, the monarchs who also financed Columbus's expedition to the Indies in the same year. Some parts of the Alhambra are now ruined, and the center of its site on a ridge overlooking the city is crowded by the later palace of Charles V. The red-brick exterior wall bristles with towers capped by crenellated battlements. It originally enclosed an entire palace city, including common dwelling houses, craft workshops, the royal mint, several mosques, public baths, and a military garrison, in addition to seven palace buildings. Archaeological work on the surviving buildings is ongoing as historians try to understand the site's construction history.

Of the surviving palace chambers, the two most impressive are grouped around rectangular courts: one known as the Patio of Arrayanes or Myrtle Trees, which provided access to the Hall of the Ambassadors; and the other called the Patio of Leones or Lions, so named for the fountain at its center. The Patio of Myrtle Trees has a central rectangular pool fed by gently overflowing fountain basins at opposite ends (Fig. 7.37). Arcaded galleries are set across the short sides, and rows of myrtles parallel to the pool on the long sides are reflected in its smooth surface. At the north end is the Comares Tower, which contained the square-plan Hall of the Ambassadors, thirty-six feet on a side, with a soaring sixty-foot height (Fig. 7.38). This was the throne room of the sultan, and its domed ceiling, composed of over 8000 wooden sections, captures the effect of thousands of stars in the seven levels of heaven as described by Islamic theology.

The Patio of Lions (Fig. 7.39) includes arcades resting on slender columns, and is divided into four parts by shallow watercourses emanating from the lion fountain at the center. As with the Tomb of Humayun and the Taj Mahal, this layout is thought to symbolize the Qur'anic vision of paradise—a garden below which four rivers flow with water, wine, honey, and milk—and the courtyard was originally planted. Square pavilions on the short sides project into the court and have clustered columns supporting intricately carved arcades. There has been considerable scholarly discussion about the dates and origins of the fountain's twelve lions, which as figurative representations of animals would seem to have no place in Islamic art. The basin is clearly Islamic, as attested by its fourteenth-century inscription, but it does not match the animals in style. It has been speculated that the lions originated in a Jewish palace formerly on the hilltop, where they may have replicated the animals supporting the great bronze basin that was found in the courtyard of the Temple of Solomon. Opening off the long sides of their court are two chambers, each of which is a jewel of ornamental vaulting. To the south, the Hall of the Abencerrajes is covered with a splendid muqarnas vault in the shape of an eight-pointed star. The northern room, the Sala de las Dos Hermanas (Hall of

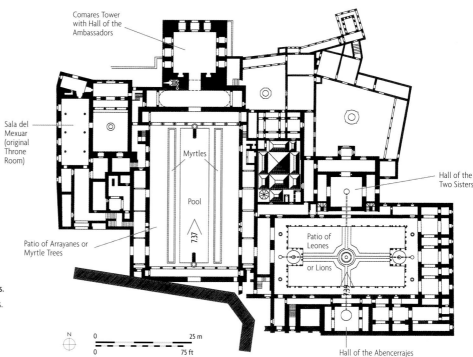

**7.36** Plan of the Alhambra, Granada, 13th–14th centuries.

This plan shows what were originally two separate palaces. In the center are the Patio of Myrtle Trees and the associated Hall of the Ambassadors, constructed on the foundations of a military tower. To the right is the Patio of Lions.

**7.37** Patio of Myrtle Trees, Alhambra, Granada, 13th–14th centuries.

This view shows the reflecting pool and the Comares Tower in the background. The delicacy and grace of late Islamic architecture in Spain is evident in the arcade.

**7.38** Ceiling and upper wall, Hall of the Ambassadors, Alhambra, Granada, 13th–14th centuries.

Thousands of small wooden pieces are suspended from the roof timbers to transform this ceiling into the seven layers of heaven surrounding a small dome at the center representing the heavenly throne. Pierced grilles filter sunlight.

**7.39** Patio of Lions. Alhambra, Granada, 13th–14th centuries.

This view shows the central fountain and the water channels dividing the court into four quadrants. In the background is the roof of the Hall of the Two Sisters.

**7.40** Hall of the Two Sisters, Alhambra, Granada, 13th–14th centuries.

The Muslim fascination with patterning takes on three-dimensional form in muqarna vaults like this one. While much more elaborate than the results produced by civilizations such as the Mycenaeans (see Figs. 2.8 and 2.9), the vault in the Hall of the Two Sisters still relies on the elementary structural device of corbeling.

the Two Sisters), has an octagonal drum supporting what appears to be a star-shaped muqarnas vault that is actually suspended from wooden trusses (Fig. 7.40).

In contrast to its simple exteriors, the Alhambra's interiors are enriched by a profusion of decorative detail that covers all surfaces, conveying splendor, ineffable lightness, and the ethereal quality of a dream world. Marbles, colored ceramic tiles, and carved and gilded wood or stucco screens create changing patterns of shadow as light reflects on water and polished surfaces, or flickers through pierced walls and ceilings. Pattern and texture abound in both geometric arabesques and stylized plant forms embellished with flowing Arabic inscriptions; arches are lobed and cusped; windows have elaborate grilles; and ceilings feature stalactites of carved wood or plaster. Behind the ornament, the underlying rubble masonry construction is not of the highest quality—it was the effect of magnificence that was desired rather than its actual substance. Even without its interior furnishings and original courtyard plantings, however, the Alhambra's sumptuous character can still be appreciated today.

By 1492, when the Moors were expelled from Spain, many aspects of Islamic architecture had long since found their way into buildings in western Europe. During the medieval period, interactions among learned men from Islamic, Hebraic, and Christian traditions had generally been amicable, undermined primarily by intolerance for non-Christian religions on the part of the Catholic Church. Elements that became important features in Western architecture, among them **polychromy**, the pointed arch, and domes with interlacing ribs, originated in mosque designs, and the gracious elegance of palaces integrating landscape and architecture, such as the Alhambra, were unmatched in northern Europe.

## CONCLUSIONS ABOUT ARCHITECTURAL IDEAS

While the basic forms of Islamic architecture, including those of the mosque—the building type emphasized in this chapter—can seem bewilderingly unfamiliar to Western eyes, they are actually remarkably limited but extremely versatile. As evidence of this condition, consider the abambars, or urban cisterns, found in Iran. Their function is, of course, simply to store water in a cool, fresh condition, and they must be easily and regularly cleaned. At the heart of

the abambar is the storage reservoir, which is covered with a dome, a quintessential element of Iranian mosques. The ventilation device for this reservoir is a minaret-like wind-catcher that directs air down to the storage level. Entry into the reservoir is made by way of a stair that descends to an iwan-like porch, sometimes including muqarna vaults. Altogether, the abambar can be interpreted as a domed iwan mosque disassembled and its constituent parts reassembled as a utilitarian structure. This repetitive use of certain architectural, as well as ornamental, forms has, in fact, been a principal theme in this chapter.

When initially faced with the production of religious structures, Islamic designers assimilated and reinterpreted the buildings left around them by the ancient Romans, Sassanians, and others. They derived their conception of the mosque from the form of Mohammed's own house in Medina. Based upon his teachings, they quickly established the sahn (court), haram (prayer hall), qibla (prayer wall), and mihrab (prayer niche) as essential elements. After an initial period of experimentation and depending on the location, they settled on several, regional, mosque-design variations. The columnar or hypostyle mosque, most popular in Arabia and across North Africa, includes numerous ranks and files of columns surrounding a court, with a prayer hall at one end. The iwan mosque, preferred in Iran and farther east, includes a court, possibly with surrounding columns, expanded on three sides by vaulted or domical porches, with one of these porches lying opposite the entry. The domed, central-plan mosques of Turkey begin with a court surrounded by domed bays and conclude with a domed worship space surrounded by more domed bays. Large Islamic tombs also frequently have central plans, sometimes expanded by porch-like arms.

Gardens for enjoyment as well as the evocation of paradise were sometimes integrated with funerary architecture and with palaces, which is exemplified nowhere better than at the Alhambra, where landscaped courts with water features reflect highly ornamented wall surfaces. Islamic ornamentation is generally prolific, over not only exterior walls but interior ones as well and even across ceilings, where it is integrated with exposed structural elements. Ranging from puzzle-like fields of geometric figures to plant-inspired arabesques to organic or angular calligraphy, this abstracted ornamentation reached a level of invention and sophistication arguably unexcelled by any designers and craftsmen at any other time and in any other place.

# CHAPTER 8

# EARLY MEDIEVAL AND ROMANESQUE ARCHITECTURE

While Byzantine and Islamic cultures were flourishing in eastern Europe and around the southern rim of the Mediterranean, those portions of western Europe that had been part of the Roman Empire entered a sustained period of decline. From the first centuries of the Christian era, outposts of the Empire had been repeatedly besieged by waves of nomadic peoples migrating from Central Asia. These tribes, called barbarians by the civilized Romans, eventually overran the frontiers established by Rome and occupied the city of Rome itself by 476. Many place names across Europe preserve the memory of these nomadic tribes. The Franks settled in what eventually became France. The Burgundians in east-central France and the Lombards in northern Italy gave their names to Burgundy and Lombardy, respectively. The Goths and the Visigoths were memorialized in the architectural style called Gothic, and the behavior of the Vandals, who went everywhere and often wreaked havoc, is remembered in the word "vandalism." Gradually the nomads settled down, became converts to Christianity, and attempted to continue Roman governmental traditions, which they greatly admired although they lacked the necessary administrative expertise. The period in western European history extending from the decline of Roman authority until the beginning of the Renaissance (approximately 400 to 1400) is known as the medieval period or the Middle Ages, because historians saw it as a middle era separating antiquity from modern times.

Roman culture was based on city life and depended on a strong central government. In the chaos that accompanied the barbarian invasions, the basic skills required to maintain governmental authority, such as literacy, virtually disappeared. Urban settlements and the money economy that sustained them were replaced by small agricultural units organized by local strongmen, who lived in fortified dwellings and controlled the surrounding land by force of arms. Peasants tilled the land in exchange for meager sustenance and the physical protection afforded them by the strongman's military might. Over the centuries this arrangement of mutual service and protection developed into the feudal system, embracing all levels of society from peasant to king in an intricate social, political, and economic order.

Because feudalism meant a geo-politically fragmented Europe, architectural styles were necessarily regional and even local in character. But this fragmentation did not mean universal architectural parochialism. The popes resided in Rome (with part of the fourteenth century spent in Avignon, France), and the papacy controlled or at least strongly influenced a considerable portion of central Italy. Widespread monastic communities thrived and frequently became centers for architectural innovations, as well as agriculture, education, and religion. From its capital in Constantinople, the Byzantine Court ruled over an ebbing and flowing empire that stretched as far west as Ravenna and exercised influence even more widely through political alliances and dynastic marriages. For Islam, it was a time of geographical expansion, as cultural influences as well as armies from the Middle East swept across Africa and up into Spain, and Islamic incursions constantly threatened Byzantium. In a counter-current, European Crusaders eventually carved out Christian kingdoms in the Holy Land and so established and maintained transportation routes from west to east. In Italy and southern France, ancient Roman classicism remained highly visible in the form of abandoned and often reoccupied buildings and sites. Most importantly for architectural development, throughout Europe and beginning modestly, even crudely, there arose an almost universal impetus toward fireproof, masonry-vaulted construction for churches and monasteries. Eventually, migrating medieval stonemasons, one of the few groups of individuals within the feudal system allowed to move about fairly freely, made the Middle Ages a period of extensive and extraordinary building construction.

## Chronology

| | |
|---|---|
| reign of Caesar Augustus | 27 BCE–14 CE |
| end of Roman Empire in the West | 476 |
| defeat of Islamic forces at Tours by Charles Martel | 732 |
| reign of Charlemagne | 768–814 |
| construction of the Palatine Chapel at Aachen | 792–805 |
| Charlemagne crowned Holy Roman Emperor | 800 |
| development of the plan of St. Gall | 817 |
| rise of Santiago de Compostela as a pilgrimage site | ca. 900 |
| founding of the monastery at Cluny | 910 |
| Battle of Hastings | 1066 |
| construction of Durham Cathedral | 1093–1113 |

**Interior of the Nave, Vézelay, France.**

This barrel-vaulted nave is divided into bays by transverse arches constructed of polychromatic masonry. Each arch springs from two colonettes attached to the nave wall. Between the colonettes are arched openings connecting the nave to the side aisles.

## CAROLINGIAN ARCHITECTURE

Outside the Italian peninsula and the Mediterranean coast, where Early Christian traditions were maintained in a number of masonry basilicas and baptisteries, very little architecture in western Europe has survived from the period 400–800. Caught in the chaos created by barbarian invasions, most of northern Europe experienced several centuries of unsettled life, during which the stability needed to allow the design and construction of durable buildings was lacking. From the many strongmen who were leaders in the developing feudal system emerged one whose strength and military might enabled him to dominate his rivals. Known as Charles the Great, or Charlemagne, he was the grandson of Charles Martel, the Frank who had led assembled forces to victory over the Islamic army at the battle of Tours in France in 732. During his reign (768–814), Charlemagne unified a large portion of present-day France, the Low Countries, and Germany through a series of successful military campaigns. Charlemagne's influence extended even to Rome where, on Christmas Day in the year 800, Pope Leo III crowned him Holy Roman Emperor. This illiterate descendant of barbarian chieftains had become the spiritual heir of the Roman Empire, the temporal equivalent of the pope.

### THE REVIVAL OF MASONRY CONSTRUCTION

Charlemagne aspired to a renaissance of Roman achievements, including the excellence Rome had exhibited in government, literature, and the arts. He summoned the greatest minds to his court, established schools for the training of governmental administrators, had his scribes assemble and copy ancient manuscripts, and encouraged architecture by donating lands and money for the construction of churches and monasteries. The resulting buildings, termed Carolingian (from *Carolus*, the Latin name for Charles), are in many cases based on the Early Christian and Byzantine buildings Charlemagne visited during his travels in Italy. Such was the case with the palace complex built at Aachen (Fig. 8.1). The overall plan is modeled on the Lateran Palace in Rome, with the chapel derived from S. Vitale at Ravenna and the audience hall being a Roman basilica. In keeping with Roman tradition, the whole complex was laid out on a square grid. What survives today is the buildings (or foundations) that were constructed in stone, but there were doubtless wooden buildings that contained living accommodation. Much as Charlemagne and his architects admired Roman buildings, they lacked the construction skills necessary to duplicate them, so in comparison to their Roman prototypes Carolingian buildings may seem somewhat unrefined. We should not judge these works too severely, however, for Charlemagne was effectively reviving monumental masonry construction in a region that had not built in this way for about half a millennium.

The Palatine Chapel at Aachen (792–805) was designed by Odo of Metz and probably built by Lombard masons using stone salvaged from nearby Roman structures (Figs. 8.2–8.3). A sixteen-sided aisle with a gallery overhead surrounded its central domed octagon. The construction, including barrel- and groin-vaults and an octagonal **cloister vault** in the dome, reflects late Roman practice rather than the Byzantine techniques employed at S. Vitale, and its plan simplifies the complex geometry of the Ravenna building. The main entrance is dominated by a **westwerk**, that is, the western façade including the entrance vestibule, rooms at one or more levels above, and one or more towers. The addition of a westwerk to churches is one of the Carolingian contributions to the

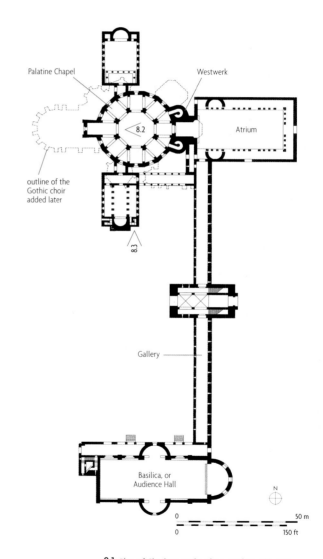

**8.1** Plan of Charlemagne's palace, Aachen, 792–814.

The sixteen-sided building is the Palatine Chapel, connected by a passageway to a basilican audience hall. Note that the chapel was preceded by a forecourt or atrium. From a loggia at the second level of the chapel, Charlemagne could address an audience assembled there. Only the chapel remains from this ambitious complex.

**8.2** Palatine Chapel interior, Aachen, 792–805.

S. Vitale at Ravenna served as a model for this building, but the chapel also contains original features. The second level was used by Charlemagne and his court to observe services without interfering with those celebrating holy offices. This view includes the choir section added in the Gothic period.

**8.3** Palatine Chapel, Aachen, 792–805.

The Carolingian building in the center has been modified by the addition of a higher roof over the dome and a Gothic choir and chapels to the left and in the foreground and the westwerk tower to the right. Only the lower wall sections of the central part are authentic from the time of Charlemagne.

**8.4** Abbey gatehouse, Lorsch, ca. 800.

Influences from Roman architecture can be seen in the overall form, derived from the triumphal arch, and the arch-and-column motif used on the ground level.

Western architectural tradition. Early Christian churches featured freestanding **campaniles**, or **belfries**, if they had towers at all, but during the Carolingian period towers were often incorporated as integral components of the church.

The interior of the Palatine Chapel has a heavy effect, particularly the eight great piers that support the dome, but the proportions of the arched openings at the ground and gallery levels are well chosen. Polychrome masonry is used in the semicircular arches of the main floor, while sixteen polished marble columns from the Palace of the Exarchs in Ravenna were hauled over the Alps to be reused in the arcade of the gallery. Locally cast bronze balustrades at the gallery level and mosaics in the dome contributed to the richness of the interior. Charlemagne's throne was set on the gallery level on axis with the altar. As the first domed

building north of the Alps since the decline of the Roman Empire, the Palatine Chapel is comparable in scale, if not in elegance, to S. Vitale, and it reflects Charlemagne's intense desire to revive classical ideals in architecture.

Of the abbey at Lorsch, which was endowed by Charlemagne, only a small freestanding gatehouse now remains (Fig. 8.4). Its architectural precedents can be found in Roman triumphal arches, such as the Arch of Constantine in Rome (see Fig. 5.16), and also at Old St. Peter's in Rome, where a triple-arched pavilion marked the entrance to the atrium. Arches supported with Corinthian columns articulate the gatehouse at Lorsch, and triangular frames in a decorative pattern derived from late Roman sarcophagi surround the second-floor windows. One could never confuse the gatehouse with an actual Roman building, however, for it features such non-classical elements as a steeply pitched roof and decorative red and white tiling. The roof pitch was dictated by the potential snow loads of the northern European climate, while the tiled designs seem to have been devised by local masons, perhaps influenced by Islamic polychromy or Roman opus reticulatum.

Another small building surviving from Carolingian times is the oratory at Germigny-des-Prés (806–10), which was built for Theodulf, Bishop of Orleans, Abbot of Fleury, and close advisor to Charlemagne (Figs. 8.5–8.7). Conceived as a private chapel for quiet reflection and prayer, the oratory was designed with a Greek-cross plan and a

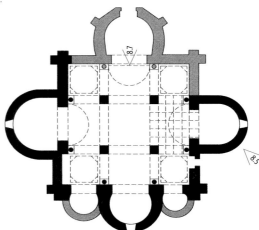

**8.5** Oratory, Germigny-des-Prés, 806–10.

This small, centrally planned building combines elements from Byzantium (the central plan and an apse mosaic) with horseshoe arches found in Islamic work in Spain and the semicircular arch of Roman work.

**8.6** (right) Plan of the Oratory, Germigny-des-Prés, 806–10.

This plan, comparable to the Byzantine quincunx, reflects connections between the Carolingian court and Constantinople.

**8.7** (below) 7Interior of the Oratory, Germigny-des-Prés, 806–10.

This view of the crossing and apse shows that the horseshoe shape is used both in elevation and plan.

square central tower. (Compare this plan to that of a Russian cross-in-square scheme as shown in Fig. 6.13b.) Horseshoe arches are found in both plan and elevation. Together with the centralized plan, these suggest influence from Mozarabic churches (those in which art and architecture was produced by Christians under Islamic rule) in Muslim-dominated Spain. This assumption is made more plausible by the fact that Theodulf was from Septimania, the area between present-day France and Spain along the Mediterranean coast. Rather surprisingly, the oratory also has a magnificent mosaic depicting the Ark of the Covenant in the eastern apse, the technique and style of which both indicate artistic contributions from Byzantium. In these few surviving Carolingian buildings, one can thus trace elements from Roman, Early Christian, Byzantine, Islamic, and northern European civilizations, combined in what must be seen as the beginnings of an architecture unique to western Europe.

## MONASTERIES

Charlemagne's unifying work did not long survive him. In 843, on the death of his son and heir, Louis the Pious, the Carolingian Empire was divided among Charlemagne's three grandsons. Governmental power in western Europe gradually reverted to the hands of local or regional lords. The one cohesive social institution that transcended regional groups was the Church, which organized medieval Europe into ecclesiastical dioceses, each administered by a bishop. The seat of episcopal authority was frequently a town that had been a Roman provincial center, and there was much of Roman governmental structure preserved in the organization of the Church.

Complementary to the town-based diocesan units were the largely rural monasteries that grew and flourished widely during the medieval period. Charlemagne had encouraged their establishment as a matter of practical policy for the settlement of conquered territories, in addition to their spiritual and educational contributions. Few institutions had as extensive an impact on the architecture of the medieval period as monasticism. Indeed, it would be difficult to discuss almost any aspect of medieval history and culture without considering the role played by monks of the various orders. Medieval society was divided broadly into three classes: those who fought (the landowning lords and knights); those who labored (the peasants); and those who prayed (the priests and monks). The work of each was considered essential to the well-being of all. Prayers of the monks were particularly necessary, it was thought, to provide a never-ending flow of praise to propitiate a God who was justifiably wrathful about humanity's errant ways. Medieval Christians considered their heavenly Lord to be as susceptible to flattery as his earthly counterpart.

The concept of monasticism, the withdrawal from the corruption of everyday life in order to contemplate things spiritual, originated in fourth-century Egypt, where Christian hermits led solitary lives in the desert wilderness. At about the same time, the idea developed that groups of monks might live together communally, and both the hermitic and communal forms of monasticism spread rapidly from Egypt to the edges of the Christian world. Irish monks were active from 432 until 793, when Viking raiders destroyed their settlements. Communal forms of monasticism became the dominant models for the organization of Western monasticism, while hermits continued to be common in the Eastern Church. In most cases, twelve monks and an abbot were sufficient to found a monastery, and the monks often selected remote sites for building. Their major requirement was a reliable water supply. During the Middle Ages, new monastic foundations eventually numbered in the thousands. Monastery schools brought learning to every part of Europe, and monastic building and farming enterprises preserved and advanced the best in architecture, the arts, and agriculture. Medieval civilization throughout western Europe was achieved in no small measure through the work of the monks.

Charlemagne's interest in centralizing and standardizing administration extended to religious institutions. After examining several models of monastic organization, he required that all monasteries within his realm should follow the Rule of St. Benedict, a flexible but rather specific set of regulations formulated by Benedict of Nursia in around 535 for monks living communally under the direction of an abbot. (St. Benedict's precepts relating to the organization and management of a monastery were called a "Rule" because they regulated the lives of those who followed them.) The monastic life of prayer, contemplation, and mental and manual work, marked by poverty, chastity, and obedience, was intended to emulate the example of Christ. In 817 abbots from leading Carolingian monasteries held a conference to resolve differences in interpretation of the Benedictine Rule. Out of its discussions came a document detailing a model layout for a Benedictine **abbey**. We know of this drawing through a copy sent to the abbot of the monastery of St. Gall, where the plan remained in the abbey's library until rediscovered in the eighteenth century (Fig. 8.8). Known now as the Plan of St. Gall, this manuscript is the oldest surviving architectural drawing from the medieval period, and from it modern scholars Walter Horn and Ernest Born have deduced much about monastic life and building practices in the Carolingian age.

The Plan of St. Gall clearly sets forth the major components of a self-sufficient religious community. The largest building was the church, a double-ended basilica in plan, with a western hemicycle flanked by twin cylindrical towers. Inside the masonry-walled and timber truss-roofed church was the worship space for the monks. Altars were located throughout the nave, transepts, and apse, as medieval religious practice, which placed growing importance on the veneration of relics, required multiple altars

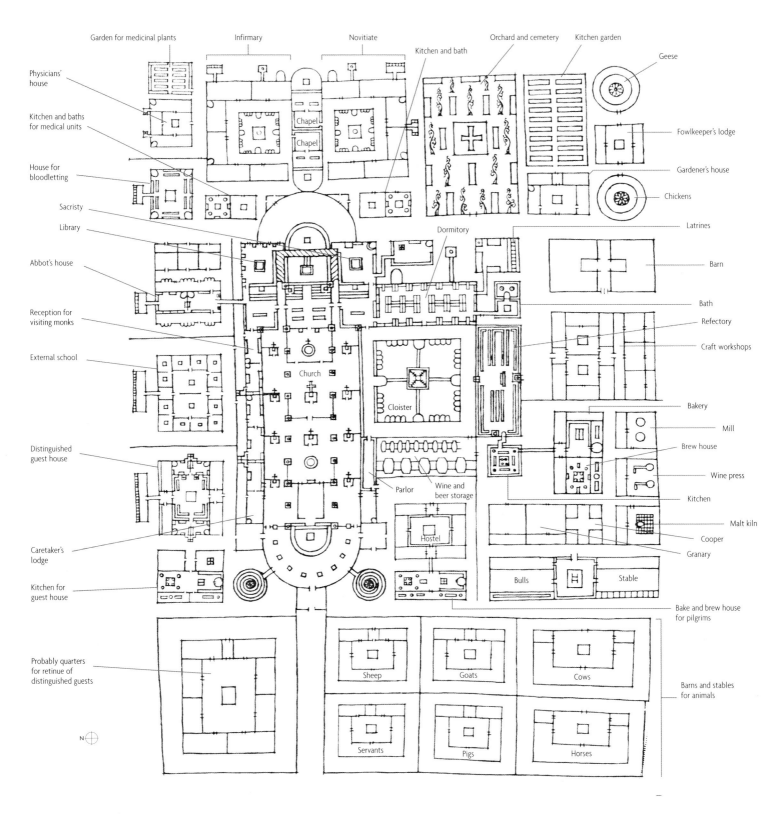

Garden for medicinal plants — Infirmary — Novitiate — Orchard and cemetery — Kitchen garden

Physicians' house

Kitchen and bath

Geese

Kitchen and baths for medical units

Chapel

Chapel

Fowlkeeper's lodge

House for bloodletting

Gardener's house

Sacristy

Chickens

Library

Dormitory

Latrines

Abbot's house

Barn

Reception for visiting monks

Bath

External school

Church

Refectory

Craft workshops

Cloister

Bakery

Distinguished guest house

Mill

Brew house

Wine press

Parlor

Wine and beer storage

Kitchen

Caretaker's lodge

Hostel

Malt kiln

Cooper

Kitchen for guest house

Granary

Bulls — Stable

Bake and brew house for pilgrims

Probably quarters for retinue of distinguished guests

Sheep — Goats — Cows

Barns and stables for animals

N

Servants — Pigs — Horses

**8.8** Plan of St. Gall, ca. 817.

This drawing sets forth the major elements of a Benedictine monastery, establishing a model that would be used for the next 400 or more years as the basis for monastic design.

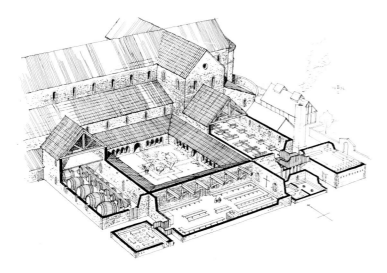

**8.9** Cutaway axonometric view showing the cloister, St. Gall, ca. 817.

Visible around the cloister are the monks' beds in the dormitory to the east (right), the tables in the refectory to the south (bottom), and the casks of wine or beer in the room to the west (left), with the south side of the church in the background.

to honor individual saints. On the south side of the church was the **cloister**, 100 feet square, surrounded by a covered, arcaded walk connecting the major buildings on its sides: the **chapter house**, workroom, and warming room below the dormitory on the east; the refectory (dining hall) on the south; and the cellar or storeroom on the west (Fig. 8.9). A stairway connected the dormitory with the south transept since the monks arose at 2 a.m. for Matins, returning to sleep until Lauds at daybreak. Six more services—Prime, Terce, Sext, None, Vespers, and Compline—completed the daily cycle.

By counting the beds drawn on the plan, Horn and Born have concluded that the monastery was designed for approximately 110 monks. Service buildings were grouped outside the cloister and staffed by an additional 130 to 150 workmen and servants necessary to provide for the monastery's sustenance. A bake and brew house, artisan craft workshops, and a complete working farm, with pens or barns for goats, geese, pigs, horses, and cows, are indicated on the plan to the south and west of the cloister, although their actual arrangement on the land would doubtless have been adjusted to the location of fields and pasture. They are grouped here to have all the buildings fit on the parchment. To the east of the church, the plan indicates a miniature double cloister to house the novitiate and the infirmary, together with a house for two physicians, a medicinal herb garden, and the cemetery. On the north side of the church was the abbot's house, connected to the transept by a passage. As the administrator and spiritual leader of the monastery, the abbot was responsible

for the management of the monastery's life, and as its representative to the outside world he was charged with public relations and with providing hospitality for distinguished guests. Adjacent to the abbot's house were the external school, required by Charlemagne's decree to provide education for young men not intending to become monks, and the guesthouse and stables for high-ranking visitors. The more common sort of traveler would be cared for by the almoner at the cloister gate to the south of the church entrance.

Through its clear ordering of the practical requirements for a monastic community, the Plan of St. Gall encapsulates the high quality of functional planning achieved by Carolingian architects. While no monastery ever built followed the Plan of St. Gall precisely, its general disposition of monastic buildings was employed in Benedictine abbeys throughout the medieval period.

## VIKING ARCHITECTURE

The Vikings, also known as Danes or Norsemen, both terrorized western Europe and served as intrepid explorers and traders, maintaining contacts with places as remote as Constantinople. (Recall that one of their number, Rurik, was invited in 856 to become the founder of the ruling family in Russia, and that Leif Ericsson led an expedition that reached the North American continent in about 1003.) In Britain, they harried the Anglo-Saxon kingdoms, occupying the whole of East Anglia and land as far north as York, which became a Viking city. The Danes extracted annual payments (the danegeld) from territories under their control, while also profiting from organized piracy on the cities of Europe. When shallow-draft, swift Viking ships sailed or rowed up the navigable rivers along which medieval settlements clustered, the burning, looting, and massacre visited on these communities only added to the instability of the time.

The artistic legacy of the Vikings is best seen in smaller objects, including jewelry, ceremonial and household objects, and military regalia, which are adorned with intricate interlaced ornament based on stylized plant and animal forms (hence its name, the Animal Style), an artistic tradition that has links to the fierce Scythians who came from the steppes of Central Asia. Interlace ornament finds its way into Romanesque architectural decoration.

Scandinavia itself remained outside the Christian sphere until the middle of the eleventh century, when Anglo-Saxon missionaries who returned with Viking raiders from England succeeded in converting the vigorous pagans of Norway. The missionaries brought knowledge of Anglo-Saxon church architecture with them, so the simple plans of parish churches in Britain, themselves based on Early Christian precedent, became the models for equally small Norwegian churches. The combination of these simple plans with native building traditions created a

**8.10** Stave church, Urnes, Norway, ca. 1125–40.
Building volumes reflect plain elements: the tall nave with lower aisles, the rear choir, and apse extension each have a separate expression.

unique and distinctive architecture, the **stave** church, or narrow-board church.

The church at Urnes, Norway, the oldest extant stave church, dates from about 1125–40, and its design illustrates the type (Figs. 8.10–8.14). The staves are upright poles, usually pine trees from which the bark has been removed, that form the basic structure for the building. They are supported on four crossed horizontal sills forming a rectangular chassis. The chassis is raised off the ground by large flat stones at the intersections of the sill planks because excavated foundations would have been subject to heaving as the ground froze and thawed. These corner stones also protect the timber structure by isolating it from ground moisture. Low exterior walls, made of vertical boarding anchored by rounded corner posts, rest on an outer chassis sill supported on the short cantilevered ends of the main chassis, while the upper wall, braced above head height by one or more clamping beams that encircle the staves, follows the vertical line of the stave frame up to the roof rafters. A cupola completes the roof ridge visually, although it has no connection to the interior space. The major structural elements, the staves, are kept dry by shorter exterior boards that are renewed from time to time as required. Urnes and other stave churches are very dark inside, for the original design had no windows, depending instead for light and ventilation on small circular openings (wind-eyes) located high in the walls. Scandinavia and Anglo-Saxon Britain are the major places where one finds wooden buildings constructed of upright staves rather than horizontal logs. It is interesting

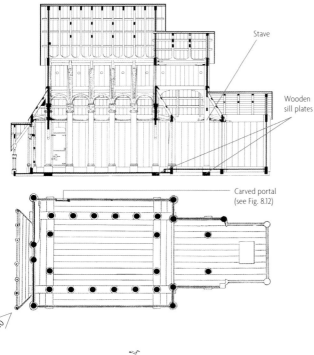

Stave

Wooden sill plates

Carved portal (see Fig. 8.12)

8.10

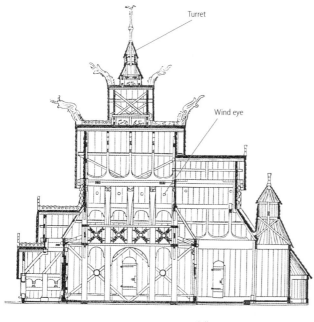

Turret

Wind eye

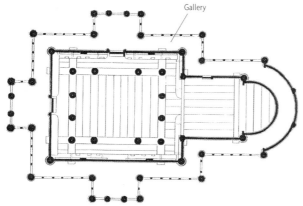

Gallery

**8.11a** (left) Plan (north to the top) of section through the stave church, Urnes, Norway, ca. 1125–40.

The foundation of the building is a rectangular grid of wooden sill plates laid on foundation stones resting on the ground. On this chassis rest the ends of upright poles or staves that form the vertical structure of the church. The tower shown in Fig. 8.10 is not included in the section.

**8.11b** (bottom left) Plan of and section through the stave church, Borgund, Norway, ca. 1125–40.

Like Urnes, the Borgund church relies on small openings, or wind-eyes, high in the wall to admit light and air, and to relieve wind pressure against the sides of the structure.

**8.12** (below) Carved portal from an earlier church at Urnes, ca. 1015.

This portal is now preserved on the north wall of the present church. The intertwined snakes and dragons represent the end of the world according to the Norse legend of Ragnarok. Christian missionaries substituted this local imagery for the Last Judgment as a way of making Christian teaching more accessible.

**8.13** Stave church, Borgund, Norway, ca. 1125–40.

While this church looks considerably more elaborate than that at Urnes, it is fundamentally the same in structure, but with additional roof turrets and an external gallery at the base.

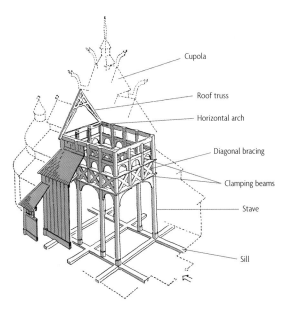

**8.14** Diagram showing the construction of a stave church.

The church illustrated here comes from Gol, one of a number of stave churches that were restored in the twentieth century according to features seen in the church at Borgund.

to note that the stave church at Greensted was associated with a Viking settlement.

Urnes also possesses a remarkable carved portal, now located on the north wall of the church, which probably belonged to a previous church of about 1015 built on the same site (Fig. 8.12). Bands of boldly undercut figures, carved from single planks of wood, represent four-legged beasts and serpent-like animals intertwined in intricate patterns with a scrolling vine. The similarity of this work to Animal Style ornament is immediately apparent. What is less clear at first glance is why such carving should be found as ornament around a church doorway. Although no documents provide absolute proof, scholars believe that these figures represent a carry-over from the pagan past applied to the fresh purposes of the Christian faith. In Norse mythology, the end of the world was to come when snakes and dragons, representing the forces of evil, were locked in mortal combat. Known as Ragnarok, this struggle was the Norse equivalent of the Christian Last Judgment, which became established as a subject for sculpture on the doorways of churches in other parts of Europe. The best explanation for the snakes and dragons on stave

churches seems to be that in Norway, as elsewhere, early missionaries found it convenient to adapt established traditions to the causes of the Christian Church.

Stave churches were widely constructed in the sparsely populated and isolated valley communities along the fjords of Norway. As late as the nineteenth century, 322 such buildings could be documented through remains or textual references, but today only thirty-two survive. The church at Borgund, dated to about 1150, probably represents the most authentic mature stave church, and aspects of its form and detail have served as models for the restoration of other stave churches that were not so fortunate in preserving their original character across the centuries (Figs. 8.11b, 8.13–8.14). Borgund began much as Urnes did, but in the thirteenth century it was embellished with an external gallery and elaborate turret that give it a more complex profile. Crosses and dragons were placed on the ends of the roof gables to protect the church from the powers of darkness as pagan forces, though banished by Christianity to remote areas, still remained a potential menace to be countered by these prominently displayed symbols.

## EARLY ROMANESQUE ARCHITECTURE

The monastery of St. Martin at Canigou (1001–26) in southwestern France survives as an example of the process by which monasticism spread, and its buildings illustrate architectural accomplishments of the early Romanesque period (Figs. 8.15–8.16). Its patron, the Count of Cerdagne, landlord of this mountainous territory in the Pyrenees, endowed the monastery on a rocky outcrop to expiate his sins. Although it never housed more than about thirty monks, its place in the history of architecture is assured because it has survived, with the aid of an entirely sympathetic twentieth-century restoration, as one of the earliest completely vaulted Romanesque churches. In plan the church is a basilica without transepts but with semicircular apses terminating the aisles and nave. The barrel vaults of the nave and aisles rest on ten supports— eight stubby columns and two grouped piers—and the solid exterior walls (Fig. 8.17). The only natural light enters through small windows at the east and west ends, resulting in a very dark interior. On the exterior, the entire monastery forms a harmonious composition. A square-plan tower abuts the side of the church, guarding the entrance to the abbey, while the cloister and its related buildings form an irregular quadrangle on the limited building site rather than the neat square indicated on the Plan of St. Gall. The stone construction is simple, articulated primarily by semicircular arches used over windows and also set as surface relief in horizontal bands. The stepped crenellations atop the tower recall Islamic fortifications found in neighboring Spain.

St. Martin at Canigou exemplifies the early Romanesque style. As the name implies, Romanesque buildings have a certain affinity with Roman architecture, primarily because they tend to employ the semicircular or Roman arch. Beyond this simple generalization (which itself is not always true), it is difficult to characterize Romanesque buildings with great precision. The style flourished from around 1000 to 1250. Romanesque buildings tend to be massive and heavy. The construction problem that Romanesque builders set for themselves, that of efficiently supporting a ceiling made entirely of small stones, posed a real challenge and encouraged varied approaches according to the materials available, the experience of the builder, and the ambitions of the patron. It is perhaps easiest to understand the Romanesque as a great series of experiments directed toward enclosing and illuminating interior space, using incombustible masonry construction to reduce the chances of fire and thus protect the valuable relics held in churches.

Most Romanesque buildings rely on the mass of continuous walls to sustain the weight of the vaulting overhead. Medieval builders could not make structural calculations as we can today. (Indeed, the systematic study of materials and structural theory was not sufficiently advanced to be applied to ordinary buildings until about

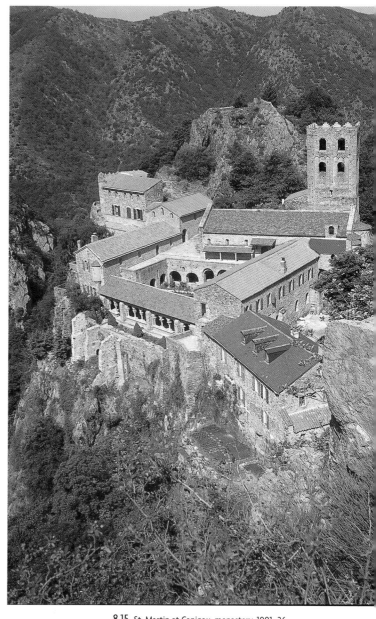

**8.15** St. Martin at Canigou, monastery, 1001–26.

Founded as a pious act by the Count of Cerdagne, this monastery sits on a mountainous site that is difficult to reach even today. The presence of a freely running spring made habitation possible here, and a small monastic community continues to occupy the buildings.

1850.) Trial and error based on previous projects formed the basis of building practice. Yet within the span of 150 years the structural experiments of hundreds of Romanesque builders led to the refined masonry techniques that made Gothic architecture possible. It was a long process, however, for the semicircular arch is not a particularly efficient structural element. The Romans had employed it extensively for its esthetic qualities and ease of construction (the arch scaffolding or centering is relatively

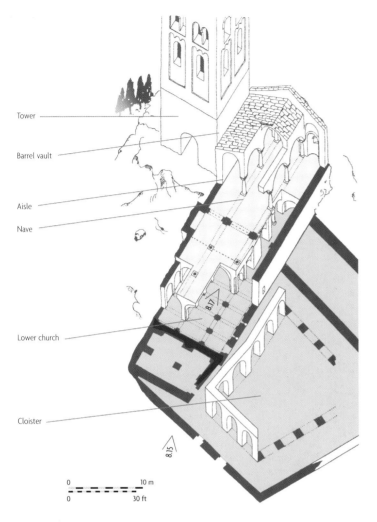

Tower

Barrel vault

Aisle

Nave

Lower church

Cloister

8.17

8.15

```
0          10 m
0          30 ft
```

uncomplicated to build), qualities that doubtless recommended it to Romanesque architects as well, even though the outward, overturning thrust it generated caused problems, which were commonly resolved by building massive supporting walls. Since openings could weaken the supporting wall, Romanesque builders used windows very sparingly to avoid challenging the structure's integrity. The semicircular arch, the barrel vault, and the groin vault (two barrel vaults intersecting at right angles—see Fig. 9.44) also imposed geometric constraints. Square or rectangular bays could be handled easily, while irregular or circular sections posed esthetic and structural difficulties.

**8.16** Cutaway axonometric view of the church and cloister, St. Martin at Canigou, 1001–26.

The church has two levels, both vaulted. Romanesque architects had to rediscover building techniques used by the Romans, and here one gets a sense of their struggle to produce durable and fireproof construction.

**8.17** St. Martin at Canigou interior, 1001–26.

Windows are minimal, for every opening cut into the wall weakened the structure. Since the monks knew the services by heart, dim light levels inside the church were not a problem.

## ROMANESQUE ARCHITECTURE OF THE HOLY ROMAN EMPIRE

The middle portion of Charlemagne's empire, corresponding roughly to modern Germany and northern Italy, eventually came under the control of the vigorous House of Saxony, whose three successive heads each named Otto gained the title of Holy Roman Emperor in the course of their capable leadership. Their rule, termed Ottonian, extended from 936 to 1002, but its effects lasted nearly a century longer.

Ottonian architecture is in many respects an extension of Carolingian traditions: it is the German expression of Romanesque. An outstanding example is the Ottonian church of St. Michael at Hildesheim (1010–33), which is a double-ended basilica with entrances along the side aisles as in many original Roman basilicas (Fig. 8.18). Its two apses also recall the general church layout indicated on the Plan of St. Gall. On the interior (Fig. 8.19), the eastern apse contains the altar, and the western apse contains a raised platform for seating the emperor and his court. Illumination is provided by clerestories, simple punched openings in the unarticulated nave wall, while the supporting nave arcade has a subtle A-B-B-A rhythm established by piers alternating with two columns. Polychrome arches, boldly carved column capitals suggestive of Italian examples, and an elaborately painted wooden ceiling enrich the interior.

Slightly later than St. Michael at Hildesheim is the spacious imperial cathedral at Speyer, built about 1030 and revised in three successive building campaigns until 1082 (Figs. 8.18, 8.20–8.21). It is a massive and majestic construction, extending over 425 feet from the thick walls of its imposing westwerk to the semicircular apse flanked by a pair of square-plan towers. The nave is wide, long, and tall, framed by semicircular arches surrounding each wall bay. Covered at first by a flat wooden ceiling, the nave received groin vaults set over paired bays and separated by **transverse arch** bands in the course of building activity from 1082 to 1137. At 107 feet above the floor, these vaults rank as the highest built in the Romanesque period and approach the accomplishments of Roman construction. The piers become compound assemblies of projecting pilasters and colonettes between sometimes-recessed arched openings. Interior decoration is restrained, even severe, with the variegated warm yellow-to-pink hues of the stone enlivening the surfaces of walls and piers. Influences from Lombardy are seen in the cubiform capitals of the crypt and the **Lombard bands** (corbel arch tables and pilaster strips) of the exterior wall.

In the southern regions of the Holy Roman Empire, the classical heritage of Rome heavily influenced Romanesque architecture. Italian cities developed their own versions of Romanesque architecture, retaining a strong reliance on the classical past with little influence from northern

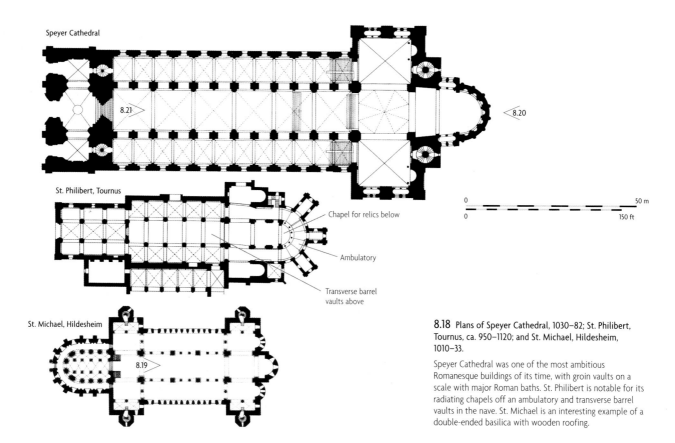

Speyer Cathedral

St. Philibert, Tournus

Chapel for relics below

Ambulatory

Transverse barrel vaults above

St. Michael, Hildesheim

**8.18** Plans of Speyer Cathedral, 1030–82; St. Philibert, Tournus, ca. 950–1120; and St. Michael, Hildesheim, 1010–33.

Speyer Cathedral was one of the most ambitious Romanesque buildings of its time, with groin vaults on a scale with major Roman baths. St. Philibert is notable for its radiating chapels off an ambulatory and transverse barrel vaults in the nave. St. Michael is an interesting example of a double-ended basilica with wooden roofing.

**8.19** (above left) St. Michael interior, Hildesheim, 1010–33.

The square module that governs much of the plan is defined by the piers and the bay under the eastern tower, outlined by bold polychrome arches.

**8.20** (below left) Speyer Cathedral east end, ca. 1030–82.

Speyer is distinguished by its large scale and multiple towers. The two seen here are set at the junction of choir and transepts, and they are taller than the dome over the crossing. Note the use of Lombard bands.

**8.21** (below right) Speyer Cathedral nave, interior looking east, ca. 1030–82.

The groin vaults were erected in 1082–1137, making this one of the highest vaulted churches of its time.

**8.22** S. Miniato al Monte west front, Florence, 1062–90.

This façade would not have seemed strange to the ancient Romans, for it continues the use of marble veneers in geometric patterns combined with arch-and-column motifs familiar from the Classical past.

**8.23** (below) Plans of S. Ambrogio, Milan, 1080–1140; S. Miniato al Monte, Florence, 1062–90; and Pisa Cathedral, 1063.

S. Miniato preserves the plan of simple Early Christian basilicas. S. Ambrogio includes an atrium and two separate campaniles, while the cathedral at Pisa has a cruciform plan, with transepts that are treated as smaller basilicas. Pisa's oval crossing dome provided the impetus for Florence to attempt an even more ambitious dome for its cathedral.

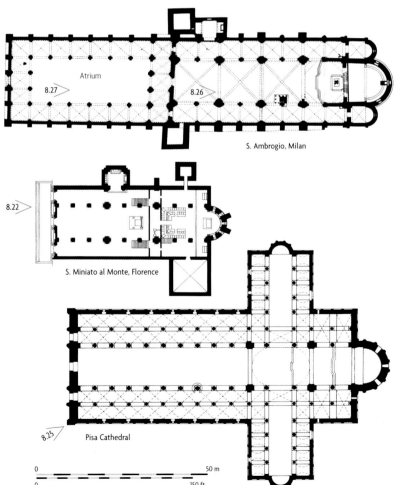

S. Ambrogio, Milan

S. Miniato al Monte, Florence

Pisa Cathedral

0 — 50 m
0 — 150 ft

Europe. In general, the Early Christian basilica remained the standard church form, seldom having a westwerk or attached towers as in Ottonian or Carolingian architecture. The church of S. Miniato al Monte in Florence (1062–90 and later) is typical (Figs. 8.22–8.24). A single pair of aisles flanks the transeptless nave, which is terminated by a simple semicircular apse. Alternate bays of the nave are grouped by diaphragm arches (where a wall is built to create a level, horizontal top), above which wooden trusses support the roof. Its façade is articulated on the ground level by five arches supported by Corinthian half-columns, with Corinthian pilasters and a gable defining the roof of the nave. Geometric patterns set in marble veneers enliven the essentially flat wall plane, and the entire elevation clearly follows the profile of the basilican space behind it.

The freestanding cathedral at Pisa (begun in 1063 and finished 1089–1272) is more elaborate, although still close to Early Christian tradition (Figs. 8.23, 8.25). In plan the cruciform basilica has double aisles and galleries flanking the nave, and single aisles and galleries flanking the transepts. At the crossing, an oval dome is raised on squinches and shallow pendentives, recalling the centralized church plans of Byzantium, while wooden trusses roof the remainder of the church. The exterior is articulated with marble arcades, stacked row on row across the western façade and continuing around the church. The interior is marked by polychromy, in this case alternate courses of dark and light marble set in horizontal bands, and there are Byzantine mosaics in the apse. The cathedral is complemented by two adjacent structures, a circular

**8.24** S. Miniato al Monte interior, Florence, 1062–90 and later.

During the Romanesque period Italian churches frequently had wooden roofs like this one. Like the façade, the interior walls depend for their effect on a veneer of polychromatic marble that allows for the creation of complex geometric patterning.

**8.25** Pisa Cathedral west front, 1063; 1089–1272.

Marble arches and columns march around the building, which is further enriched with alternating bands of dark- and light-colored marble. The campanile is better known as the Leaning Tower of Pisa, a building that has never been vertical because of difficult foundation conditions.

baptistery and a cylindrical campanile, the famous Leaning Tower of Pisa, now over thirteen feet out of plumb.

In the northern Italian region known as Lombardy, the outstanding Romanesque building is the abbey church of S. Ambrogio in Milan (Figs. 8.23, 8.26–8.27). The dates of this important monument are still a matter of scholarly debate. Research indicates that work on the present brick structure began in around 1080, and the nave was begun after 1128. The **rib vaults** of the nave were probably built in about 1140. In plan S. Ambrogio continues Early Christian practice. An arcaded atrium precedes the church proper, and a semicircular apse and smaller semicircular chapels at the ends of the groin-vaulted aisles terminate the transeptless basilica. Galleries over the aisles help buttress the thrust of the nave vaults, but they preclude the possibility of clerestory lighting.

## PILGRIMAGE ROAD CHURCHES

In addition to monasticism, the medieval period was marked by another important religious institution: pilgrimage. To atone for sins, seek a cure, or assure salvation, medieval men and women traveled as pilgrims to shrines containing the relics of saints. All churches established since Carolingian times were required to possess relics for each altar, providing local, regional, or international opportunities for pilgrimages. Jerusalem and Rome were the most celebrated centers, but they were also the most expensive and hazardous for northern Europeans to visit.

Around the year 900 a new center for pilgrimage arose to rival the popularity of Rome and Jerusalem, the shrine of the apostle James (Sant' Iago in Spanish), located at Compostela in northwestern Spain. With considerable assistance from the Church, Compostela became the goal for thousands of pilgrims as stories of miracles wrought by St. James encouraged people from all parts of Europe to visit his tomb and pray for his assistance. Gradually an entire network of roads and hospices developed to support the growing tide of pilgrims traveling to Compostela. Monasteries, the traditional centers of hospitality for travelers, found the increasing numbers of visitors disruptive to their prescribed cycle of services. The monks accommodated these pilgrims by modifying the basilican church plan to include an ambulatory, like that found at St. Philibert at Tournus, which worked as an extension of the aisles to provide a continuous passageway around the entire church. At the east end, radiating chapels opened off

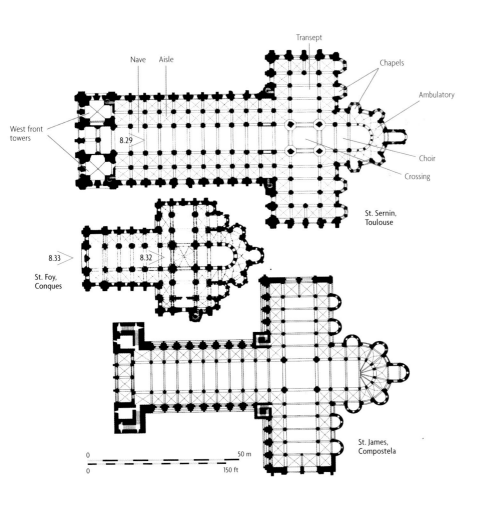

8.28 Plans of St. Sernin, Toulouse, ca. 1077–1119; St. Foy, Conques, ca. 1050–1130; and St. James, Compostela, ca. 1075–1211.

All three of these churches are located along the pilgrimage routes to Santiago de Compostela, and they share common traits, including aisles linking to an ambulatory and so providing a continuous path for pilgrims to access relics in the chapels.

8.29 St. Sernin interior, Toulouse, ca. 1077–1119.

The colonnettes, or attenuated columns attached to the nave piers, rise to support the transverse arches. The resulting ensemble is extremely dramatic when seen in perspective.

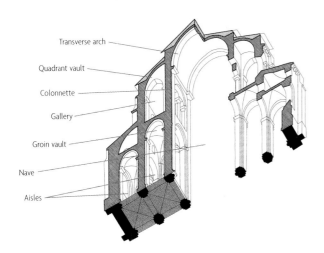

8.30 Worm's-eye axonometric view of St. Sernin, Toulouse.

The paired aisle vaults work together with the gallery vaults over the inmost aisle to brace the thrust from the high barrel vaults with transverse arches in the nave and choir.

the ambulatory, and there were sometimes additional chapels located on the east side of the transepts for use by monks who were also ordained clergy. These chapel altars could also be visited by pilgrims without interrupting monastic services being sung in the **choir**.

Churches built in response to the pilgrimage are common on the major roads to Compostela. Five of the largest are so similar in plan, scale, and architectural detail that they illustrate strikingly the transmission of artistic ideas up and down the roads. The oldest of the five was St. Martin at Tours (now destroyed), where a rebuilding of the apse as early as 918 introduced the scheme of radiating chapels and ambulatory attached to a large nave and spacious transepts. By the middle of the eleventh century, this theme had been picked up by the churches of St. Martial at Limoges (now also demolished), St. Foy at Conques, St. Sernin at Toulouse, and St. James at Compostela, producing a series of buildings with an unmistakable family resemblance (Fig. 8.28).

The church of St. Sernin at Toulouse clearly illustrates the group (Fig. 8.29). St. Sernin remains a major monument of the Romanesque even though its west front was never finished and its crossing tower was greatly enlarged

**8.31** St. Foy, Conques, ca. 1050–1130.

Set in a remote mountain valley, this is the smallest of the great pilgrimage road churches. Site restrictions limited the length of the building.

**8.32** St. Foy crossing, Conques, ca. 1050–1130.

This view shows the gallery over the aisle and the squinches supporting the crossing lantern. Placement of the altar at the crossing is modern; the medieval altar was set in the choir.

in the Gothic period. Begun in about 1077, the choir was consecrated in 1096, and the transepts and nave were probably complete, except for the vaulting, by 1119. In plan the church has paired aisles on each side of the nave, four chapels on the east of the large transept, and five radiating chapels around the apse. At nearly 360 feet it is a long building, with a width of nave and aisles totaling about 100 feet, spaciousness that may have been inspired by Old St. Peter's in Rome. The barrel vaults, with transverse arches supported by colonnettes, or columns conceptually captive in the wall, rise about sixty-five feet and are braced by second-floor galleries over the inner pair of aisles (Fig. 8.30). This organization gives the church a triangular cross-section, but precludes the insertion of clerestory windows to light the nave directly. Windows at the east end and light from the windows in the crossing tower provide relative brilliance near the altar in contrast to the dim light of the

nave. The exterior arrangement of chapels, ambulatory, and choir rising to the great crossing tower is harmoniously composed, and the ensemble is enhanced by its construction materials, red brick trimmed with stone.

St. Foy at Conques in a remote region of central France is the smallest of the pilgrimage-road churches (Figs. 8.31–8.32). In plan it has only a single pair of aisles and galleries flanking the nave, but its structural scheme is identical to that at St. Sernin. Over the crossing is an octagonal **lantern** built on a squinch, a series of corbeled arches that makes the transition from a square bay to an octagon. (Pendentives as seen at Hagia Sophia do the same thing in a different geometric configuration, but the squinch is more commonly found in Western buildings.) St. Foy preserves on its **tympanum** (the semicircular panel created under the arch of a doorway) a magnificent sculpture (ca. 1140) of the Last Judgment (Figs. 8.33–8.34), including

**8.33** St. Foy west front, Conques, ca. 1050–1130.

This view shows the large tympanum depicting the Last Judgment set over the doors. Church authorities used sculptures such as this one to communicate Christian teachings to a largely illiterate public.

**8.34** St. Foy tympanum, Conques, ca. 1140.

Here we see Christ as the large central figure. Heaven is depicted at the lower left, while the varied torments of hell occupy the corresponding position on the right. Persons awaiting judgment line up on Christ's right hand.

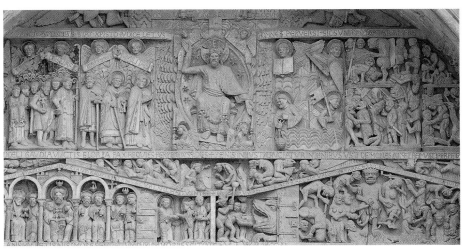

visions of heaven and hell. Christ the judge sits at the center, the largest figure because he is the most important. On his right (your left) is a line of people appearing at Judgment Day, led by Mary, St. Peter (carrying the key), and Church personages escorting Charlemagne and his family, who are remembered because they gave money to build earlier churches on the site. Under Christ's feet is the weighing of souls, and on the lintel at the left is the serenity of heaven, where the architecture, fittingly, is Romanesque. On the right lintel is a more active scene of hell, entered through the mouth of the monster Leviathan. Presiding over various punishments is the devil, identifiable by his spiked hairstyle, and assisted by reptilian minions. Close observation reveals that the Seven Deadly Sins, among other transgressions, are rewarded by appropriate punishments, graphically illustrating the concept that Dante would use centuries later in the *Divine Comedy*. Those enter-

ing the church could not fail to understand the connection between their actions and their fates in the world hereafter. This tympanum, like most Romanesque sculpture, had a strong didactic purpose in addition to its decorative role.

At Compostela, the church of St. James still functions as a major pilgrim shrine. It was planned with a full complement of nine towers: one at the crossing, pairs at the entrances (west front, south and north transepts), and two more flanking the intersection of nave and transepts (Fig. 8.28). At the east end is an axial chapel with a door to the plaza outside that is opened on jubilee years (those years when St. James's Day, July 25, falls on a Sunday or other years as declared by the Church) so that the faithful may enter directly from the east. All three of these churches—St. Sernin, St. Foy, and St. James—reflect the religious devotion that for centuries has motivated pilgrims to travel great distances in search of the holy.

## THE ORDER OF CLUNY

In 910, Duke William of Aquitaine, desiring to atone for his less than saintly life and seek divine favor, endowed a monastery on his lands at Cluny, where there was a Gallo-Roman villa or farm. Through an unusual provision in its charter, the new monastery was exempted from the jurisdiction of the local bishop and made directly responsible to the pope. Twelve monks, led by Abbot Berno, came to Cluny seeking a stricter observance of the Benedictine Rule, and their monastery prospered. The exemplary life of its monks attracted more converts and bequests; its position in Burgundy on the route from Paris to Rome and its virtual independence from local religious authorities allowed it to grow into an influential organization, with 1450 abbeys and priories all over Europe; and the exceptional leadership and longevity of its early abbots brought distinction to the Congregation and Order of Cluny. By 1088, the church and monastic complex (known as Cluny II), built after the original villa has been outgrown, had also become too small, and a new church (known to historians as Cluny III) was begun to accommodate the ever-increasing number of monks.

The church of Cluny III (Figs. 8.35–8.37) had the features of mature Romanesque architecture, for it was appropriate to the monastery's importance that its major church should be the largest and most splendid in Christendom. Based on the basilican plan, the church was enriched by a double set of transepts and further augmented by a series of radiating chapels around the apse and eastern walls of the transepts. The nave, 100 feet high and 496 feet long, was large enough to accommodate impressive processions and was flanked by two aisles on each side, the innermost

pair of which continued around the choir as an ambulatory, linking the five radiating chapels of the east end. On the exterior, each of the plan elements was clearly expressed as an individual volume, but all were beautifully integrated into a coherent whole. Towers provided vertical emphasis: a pair at the western entrance, one over each arm of the major transept, the highest tower at the intersection of the major transept and nave, and a shorter tower over the crossing of the minor transept. Viewed from the east, the church appeared as a triangular mass, with roofs ascending from the chapels to the ambulatory, the apse semidome, the minor crossing tower, and finally the major crossing tower. Inside, the effect was even more wonderful, for the sanctuary was filled with light from the many windows in the chapels and clerestories. Images of how this may have appeared come largely from the research of Kenneth John Conant, since the actual church of Cluny III was dismantled for its stone after the French Revolution. Only the south arm of the major transept remains (Fig. 8.38).

Considered from the standpoint of structure, Cluny III shows the great progress made in building art since the completion of St. Martin at Canigou. The paired aisles, which stepped down in height, buttressed the high vaults of the nave. The vault itself was not a continuous barrel vault as at St. Sernin, but a broken barrel vault, banded with transverse arches in each bay for visual articulation and structural reinforcement. Whether by accident or deduction, the monks who served as the architects of Cluny III, the musician Gunzo and the mathematician Hézelon, found that vaults constructed on the profile of a pointed arch exert less outward thrust than the Roman arch, and they exploited this discovery in the vaulting of

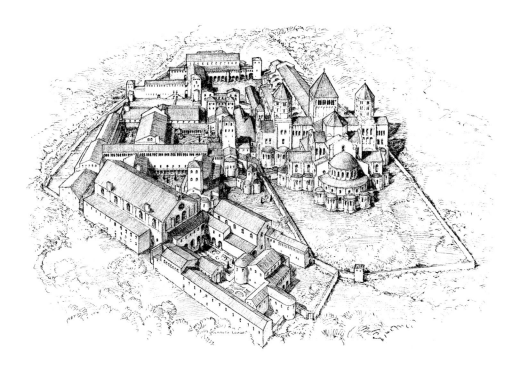

**8.35** Reconstruction view of the monastery of Cluny III, seen from the east, 11th century.

This was the largest church in western Christendom at the time of its construction. In the foreground to the left stand the infirmary and the abbot's palace.

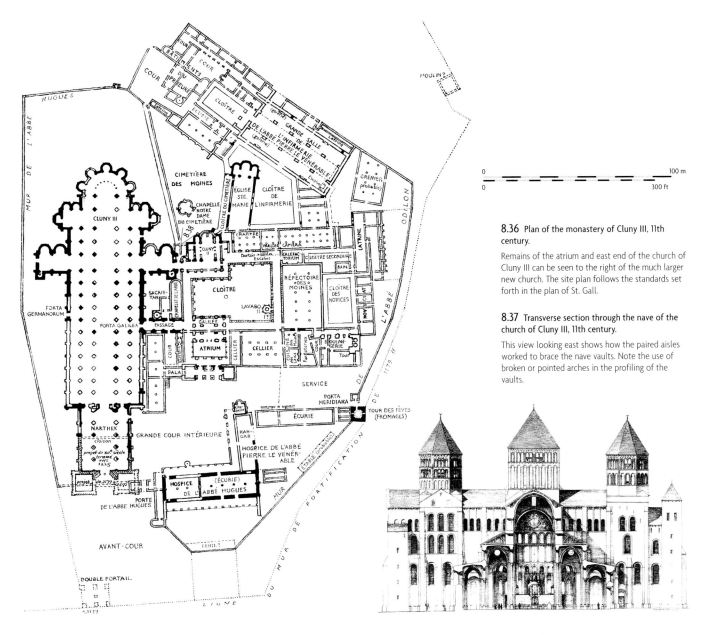

**8.36** Plan of the monastery of Cluny III, 11th century.

Remains of the atrium and east end of the church of Cluny III can be seen to the right of the much larger new church. The site plan follows the standards set forth in the plan of St. Gall.

**8.37** Transverse section through the nave of the church of Cluny III, 11th century.

This view looking east shows how the paired aisles worked to brace the nave vaults. Note the use of broken or pointed arches in the profiling of the vaults.

**8.39** Cluny III capital from the choir, 11th century.

This column detail depicts one of the tones of the musical scale shown as a figure playing an instrument similar to a lute. The monks of Cluny were great patrons of the arts, as they believed beautiful surroundings, including lovely music, helped the mind to contemplate spiritual values.

**8.38** (left) Cluny III south transept, 11th century.

This is all that remains of the once-grand monastic church.

# THE MYSTIC MILL FROM VÉZELAY

by Marian Moffett

**8.40** Ste. Madeleine south aisle capital, the "Mystic Mill," Vézelay, France, 1120–38.

Romanesque artists undertook the task of adapting their work to fit architectural frames. Doorways and columns became the domain of sculptors, while wall surfaces were taken over by mural painters. The artists worked not only to ornament architecture but also to make church buildings a visual extension of Christian teachings by using images that could be understood by the largely illiterate population. Within the limitations imposed by functional parts of the building, these artists created memorable scenes that illustrate principles of medieval theology.

One particularly fine example of their efforts is the Mystic Mill capital from the nave of the abbey church at Vézelay (Fig. 8.40). Its subject, the grinding of grain to produce flour, depicts a common activity in the Middle Ages, a necessary first step in the production of bread. Grain as harvested from the fields cannot be consumed by people until the hard outer coating (the bran) is broken and the nutritious kernel inside is pulverized, actions accomplished by milling either in hand querns or between the large millstones of a water-powered mill.

For medieval pilgrims, this scene depicts a theological allegory, for this is no ordinary mill, and the figures operating it are not local people. The man pouring the grain on the left is Moses, and the figure bagging the flour is the apostle Paul, while the mill itself represents Christ. Note the cross-shaped brace of the mill's toothed wheel. The two figures, one from the Old Testament and one from the New, are brought together by Christ. The scene thus represents the transformation of promises and prophecies of the Old Testament (the grain) into the teachings and blessings of the New Testament (the flour) through the action of Jesus Christ (the mill). Reconciliation of the Old and New Testaments was a key concern of medieval theologians, and in this one image the artist has captured this abstruse concept through analogy to a process familiar to all. By extension, flour from the mill represents communion bread, the body of Christ. The transformation of grain into flour also implied the conversion of the Jews to Christianity, an event medieval people believed prefigured the Second Coming of Christ.

This scene also embodies a yet deeper meaning that would have been understood by the more learned monks. Just as the bran protects the nutrients of the wheat kernel, the true meaning of scripture is concealed from unbelievers. Through the study of biblical texts and guidance from sacred commentaries, symbolized by the figures of Moses and Paul, those seeking a fuller insight into religious truths could eventually crack the outer shell of appearance and gain spiritual nourishment from the truths revealed only to those who attained the highest levels of religious learning. While not all the capitals at Vézelay are this rich in meaning, they remind us that medieval art existed for more reasons than to delight the eye. Art worked with architecture to advance Christian teachings.

the nave and aisles. Even so, a portion of the nave vault collapsed in 1125, but it was repaired before the general dedication of the church on October 25, 1130. Light for the nave was provided directly by rather small clerestory windows located just under the vaulting, since the great loads sustained by the walls severely restricted the possibilities for larger openings.

The great vaulted spaces of the church created excellent acoustics for the exceptionally beautiful and elaborate services sung by the monks. The rich splendor of the heavenly kingdom was further reflected in the artistic embellishments, particularly sculpture, lavished on the building. Some of this sculpture survived post-revolutionary destruction, although in considerably damaged condition (Fig. 8.39). To assess the artistic impact of Cluny, therefore, it is necessary to see the better-preserved work at its

affiliated foundations, for where the religious influence of Cluny traveled, so did its policy of artistic patronage. At Ste. Madeleine, Vézelay, the abbey was enlarged during a period of Cluniac reform, and the church nave preserves its stately Romanesque dignity (Fig. 8.41). (The choir was rebuilt during the Gothic period.) Polychrome, transverse, semicircular arches divide the nave vault into bays, each of which is groin-vaulted. Splendid sculptural work on column capitals and the narthex portals remains. Nave capitals depict a range of subjects, from Old Testament events to the lives of the saints and allegories illustrating teachings of the Church. The tympanum over the door from the narthex to the nave (dated 1120–32) represents the descent of the Holy Spirit at Pentecost, in which Christ sends the apostles to the corners of the earth to preach, teach, and heal the sick (Fig. 8.42). The sculptor here has

**8.41** Ste. Madeleine nave, Vézelay, 1120–38.

The nave was constructed while the abbey was part of the Cluniac order. Even though the building does not resemble Cluny architecturally, the tradition of creating a handsomely embellished environment for worship continues here.

**8.42** Ste. Madeleine narthex portal, Vézelay, 1120–38.

The portal shows the descent of the Holy Spirit at Pentecost. The apostles look startled, reflecting the surprise at encountering the risen Christ. Faces on many of them were damaged during the turmoil of the French Revolution.

**8.43** (above) St. Lazare, Last Judgment, west-front tympanum, Autun, 1120–32.

The subject is the same as that at Conques, although the placement of particular scenes is different. This work was signed by its sculptor, Gislebertus, in the band under the feet of Christ.

**8.44** St. Lazare capital (formerly in the choir), Autun, 1120–32.

This work shows the Flight into Egypt, with Mary and Jesus riding a donkey led by Joseph. Note the nimbus or halo behind the heads of Mary and Jesus. Romanesque sculpture often exaggerates the sizes of heads and hands, as these are the most expressive parts of the body.

bordered the central scene with signs of the zodiac, illustrations of the months of the year shown through agricultural labors, and imaginative depictions of diverse peoples of the world, including Scythians with collapsible, elephant-sized ears, Ethiopians with pig snouts, and pygmies with ladders. As a totality, the tympanum expresses the assertion that Christ and his teachings are present at all times, in all places, to all people.

There is a more austere tympanum at the nearby Cluniac church of St. Lazare at Autun (Fig. 8.43). Here the subject is the Last Judgment, replete with hideous demons and risen souls summoned to the final reckoning. An impassive and enormous figure of Christ occupies the center of the panel, with heaven on his right and the weighing of souls on his left, next to the miseries of hell. (Notice that, as at Conques, the devil's agent in the weighing of souls cheats by placing his hand in the balance pan!) The interior of the church repeats many of the architectural features of Cluny III at a reduced scale, while the beautifully carved capitals of the nave and choir present a range of biblical stories, including a Nativity cycle (Fig. 8.44), as well as fanciful beasts and foliage.

## AQUITAINE AND PROVENCE

As one would expect from a period when the means of communication were limited and political control was dispersed, a number of regional variants of the Romanesque developed in France. All share the common heritage of Romanesque influences, but they differ according to the materials, culture, and artistic interests of the individual locales. The major portion of France south of the Loire comprised Aquitaine, an important region that was successively independent, allied with the king of France, and a possession of the king of England. Seat of a flourishing culture, its architecture was perhaps the most open to varied influences from other parts of Europe, especially from eastern Christendom. Aquitaine has a series of some seventy churches with domes, an atypical feature in Western medieval architecture. That they reflect Byzantine influence is strongly implied by their use of pendentives, a characteristically Eastern device.

The church of St. Front at Périgueux, built largely after 1120, provides an interesting parallel with S. Marco in Venice (Fig. 8.45). S. Marco, itself modeled on the Greek-cross plan of the now-vanished Church of the Holy Apostles in Constantinople, was rebuilt after a fire, with the work being completed about 1089. Nearly thirty years later, the existing church of St. Front at Périgueux was greatly enlarged into a Greek-cross plan remarkably similar to S. Marco. Five domes on pendentives rise from massive pierced piers to cover the arms and crossing of the church. The stone cutting, or **stereotomy**, is exquisite. At Périgueux, the work lacks both the typical Byzantine mosaic decoration inside and the exterior profile of later Byzantine domes (Fig. 8.46). Instead the detailing is based on classical architecture, including closely spaced classical columns on the lantern turrets above the conical roofs over each dome.

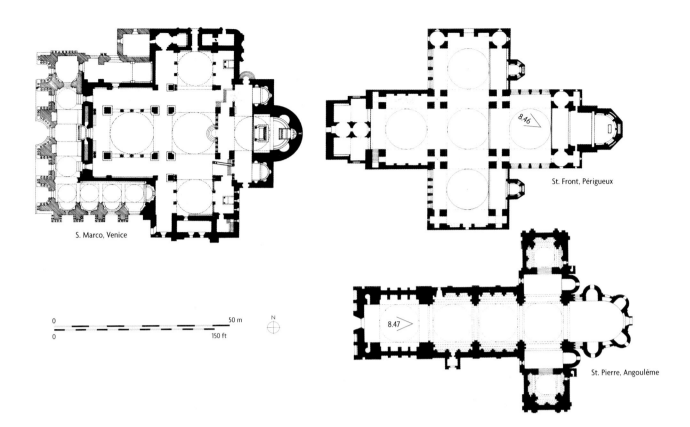

S. Marco, Venice

St. Front, Périgueux

St. Pierre, Angoulême

**8.45** (above) Plan of S. Marco, Venice, 1063–89; St. Front, Périgueux, ca. 1120; and St. Pierre, Angoulême, 1105–28.

St. Front's design seems derived from that of S. Marco in Venice, while the cathedral at Angoulême has domes on the scale of those at Périgueux.

**8.46** St. Front interior, Périgueux, ca. 1120

In the south of France, it is unexpected to find a centrally planned church having domes on pendentives. (Compare this interior to that of S. Marco on p. 132).

Périgueux is somewhat exceptional even among the unusual churches of Aquitaine. The other domed churches there, such as the cathedral of St. Pierre at Angoulême (1105–28 and later), are aisleless basilicas with domes replacing the customary vaulting in the nave (Figs. 8.45, 8.47). Major structural loads in each bay are concentrated by pendentives to four piers set in the wall, allowing a reasonable area to be opened for windows, thereby providing direct illumination to the nave. The sequence of pointed arches framing each bay provides a stately processional space. On the west front is an inaccurately restored sculpture depicting a vision of the Second Coming of Christ.

The region of Provence, along the Mediterranean coast close to Italy, remained most faithful to the classical architecture of ancient Rome. Provence had been a major Roman colony, and well-preserved Roman buildings still exist at Nîmes and other cities. Not surprisingly, therefore, Romanesque architecture there exhibits strong Roman influence in its composition, proportions, and details. The Cluniac priory church of St. Gilles-du-Gard (ca. 1140–70)

**8.47** Cathedral of St Pierre interior, Angoulême, 1105–28.

This view shows the nave with domes on pendentives. Note the pointed arch used to define each bay. The domes permit direct light into this aisleless church.

**8.48** St. Gilles-du-Gard west front portals, ca. 1140–70.

The sculpture has a Classical character, and the overall design recalls a triple-arched Roman triumphal arch.

**8.49** St. Trophime west front, Arles, ca. 1140–70.

As with St. Gilles, this church façade is based on a triumphal arch and the sculpture recalls Roman models. Provence was relatively close to Italy, and it had a substantial store of authentic Roman works.

(Fig. 8.48) has a triple-arched west façade based on the model of a Roman triumphal arch. Accurately proportioned Corinthian columns, some of which were actually recycled from Roman buildings, are incorporated in the work. Aside from the façade, little remains of the original church, which was an important regional center of pilgrimage. The contemporary façade of the former cathedral of St. Trophime at Arles also recalls Roman construction in its dignified setting of sculpture in classical surroundings (Fig. 8.49).

## CISTERCIAN MONASTERIES

The eleventh century witnessed the establishment of several new monastic groups, including the Order of Cîteaux, known as the Cistercians. Like the Cluniacs, the Cistercians originated in Burgundy, but in terms of artistic and religious development they were in many respects the antithesis of Cluny. The Cistercians were founded in 1098 by a group of twenty-two monks from Molesme who desired to follow a stricter observance of the Benedictine Rule, and their name came from that of their first monastery, at Cîteaux, in a wooded swamp donated by the Viscount of Beaune. The first years were difficult, but the new monastery gained an important convert in 1112,

when a young nobleman named Bernard joined the order. His religious zeal and organizational skill shaped the Cistercians into a uniform, highly regulated ascetic community. (Other members of his family also eventually joined the order, and their financial contributions doubtless helped as well.) In 1115 Bernard founded the third daughter house at Clairvaux, from which he was to continue to act as the guiding spiritual force for all Cistercian houses until his death in 1153.

In time the Cistercians rivaled the Cluniacs in influence. Although their affiliated monasteries totaled only about half the number of Cluniac houses, they spread throughout western Christendom. The Cistercian Order required a great measure of conformity from its dependent monasteries, and this uniformity extended to architecture. As was appropriate to the austere life laid out for their monks, Cistercian abbeys were of the simplest possible construction consistent with durable masonry building. In sharp contrast to the Cluniacs, the Cistercians initially did not allow luxurious features like towers, stained-glass windows, or paved floors. They shunned expensive materials and discouraged sculptural ornament. Cistercian monasteries had straightforward, orderly plans based on a square module, devoid of the elaborate articulation of many Cluniac designs. Thus the Cistercians produced an international set of buildings with unmistakable common features.

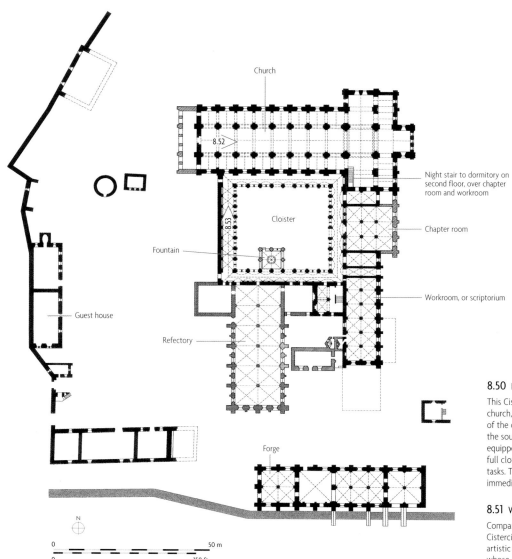

Church

8.52

Cloister

Fountain

8.53

Night stair to dormitory on second floor, over chapter room and workroom

Chapter room

Workroom, or scriptorium

Guest house

Refectory

Forge

N

0                 50 m

0                 150 ft

**8.50** Plan of the abbey, Fontenay, 1139–47.

This Cistercian plan recalls the Plan of St. Gall, with church, dormitory, and refectory defining three sides of the cloister. The original refectory is missing. On the south side is the forge, a utilitarian building equipped with water-powered machinery that could full cloth, forge iron, or accomplish other heavy tasks. The monastery's vegetable garden was located immediately to the east.

**8.51** West front, Abbey Church, Fontenay, 1139–47.

Compared to the embellished buildings of Cluny, this Cistercian church seems rather severe, observing the artistic strictures established by St. Bernard, under whose direction this monastery was founded.

Cistercian houses were founded at least twenty miles from any existing settlement, preferably at the end of a narrow valley that had a reliable water supply. While the monks did not shun their obligation to extend hospitality to visitors, they did not locate their buildings so as to encourage pilgrim traffic. Persons able to endow monasteries through gifts of land soon learned that even the most unpromising sites became productive in the hands of the Cistercians, and the example of their superior agricultural management spread to surrounding areas. Whatever long-term spiritual benefits attended the initial donation were generally compounded by very tangible increases in rents and revenues. In the early years the monks provided for all their own needs, supplying their vegetarian diet from garden plots adjacent to the monastery, but soon the care of crops and animals required more time than monks could spare from their religious duties, so lay brothers assumed most of the manual labor, leaving the monks to prayer and the copying of manuscripts. As with many medieval monastic movements, success spoiled the Cistercians. They became wealthy and relaxed the rigors of their religious observances, behaving more like other monastic groups, and when religious institutions came under attack in the post-medieval period, Cistercian abbeys were particularly targeted for their luxury. While their original ideals remained intact, however, they were a powerful religious and architectural presence, contributing much to the spread of learning, progressive agricultural practices, and sound building techniques across western Europe.

The abbey of Fontenay in Burgundy is today among the best preserved of early Cistercian monasteries. Built from 1139 to 1147, with some portions reconstructed in the thirteenth and sixteenth centuries, it is a clear illustration of Bernard of Clairvaux's architectural ideals. The monastery is closely modeled on the layout of the Plan of St. Gall, having a modular unit established by the square bay of the church aisle (Fig. 8.50). Two of these units determine the width of the nave; four, the area of the crossing; and one for each of the four chapels on the east wall of the transept. The module continues as the standard unit for the cloister walk, and it is repeated in the chapter house, workroom, and forge building. (The non-modular refectory is a sixteenth-century structure.)

The same simplicity distinguishes the three-dimensional reality of the buildings (Fig. 8.51). The nave, modest in height, is covered by a broken banded barrel vault, while the aisles have transverse broken barrel vaults over each bay (Fig. 8.52), reminiscent of the nave vaults at St. Philibert at Tournus. Light for the church comes from windows in the aisles and at the east and west end walls, as there are no clerestories. The church floor is of compacted earth, with only the raised choir section being paved in stone. The harmonious proportions relieve the utter plainness of the construction. The cloister walk, with its semicircular arcading, reflects sunlight softly and creates an appropriately human scale (Fig. 8.53).

**8.52** Fontenay Church interior looking west, 1139–47.

Note the pointed transverse arches and the absence of clerestory windows. The church is not tall, and its architectural detail is austere.

**8.53** Cloister walk, Fontenay, 1139–47.

The cloister connected major monastic buildings and served as a covered passage for meditation or exercise. In good weather, monks sat on the ledges under arches to read. Modular proportions and restrained architectural detail create a sense of repose.

The Cistercians built well. Their standardized designs did much to spread sound building practices and the progressive Romanesque style preferred by Bernard across most of Europe. After Bernard's death, many Cistercian houses expanded and built more elaborate structures than those at Fontenay. Choirs in particular were enlarged, as in the plan of Cîteaux, where the original square-ended chapels were replaced with a radial layout, producing a design copied later at many daughter houses. Although minor regional variants are reflected in Cistercian work, monasteries as distant from one another as Fossanova in Italy, Sénanque in Provence, Poblet in Spain, Maulbronn in Germany, and Fountains in England all share the fundamentally straightforward and unadorned character of Cistercian architecture, the first international style of the medieval period.

## NORMAN ARCHITECTURE

We have already noted how the Vikings in Norway became converts to Christianity and built stave churches there. Other Vikings became permanent residents outside of Scandinavia: in 911 a group led by Rollo was granted territory in western France in exchange for a cessation of its raids on settlements within the Frankish kingdom. The settlers became known as Normans, their land as Normandy, and their ruler as the duke of Normandy. Within the span of a century they developed into capable builders in stone, and, like Charlemagne, they encouraged the construction of monasteries.

In 1068 work began on the abbey church of St. Etienne at Caen, also known as the Abbaye-aux-Hommes (1068–1120), founded by William, Duke of Normandy, to expiate his consanguineous marriage (Fig. 8.54). Initially the church had a long nave with two western towers. Aisles flanked the wooden-roofed nave, and groin vaults supported the galleries above. Between 1115 and 1120 the wooden roof was removed, and the upper stage of the nave wall was rebuilt to incorporate ribs of sexpartite vaulting constructed across the nave. These vaults, encompassing two bays of the nave for each unit, engage existing major and minor supports in the alternate grouped and single wall shafts so as to continue the line of the vaulting rib down to the floor.

Duke William is remembered in history for more than his endowment of St. Etienne. In 1066 he led an army of Normans across the Channel, defeated the assembled Anglo-Saxon forces at the battle of Hastings, and extended Norman rule to England. Henceforth he was known as William the Conqueror, and his military triumph was to have lasting consequences for English history and architecture. Compared with contemporary Norman work, Britain's Anglo-Saxon buildings were small and poorly built. William reorganized the English Church and began a major campaign of church- and castle-building. He

**8.54** St. Etienne west front, Caen, 1068–1120.

Its façade is austere, with a straightforward ordering of doorways, windows, and wall buttresses. The more florid upper stages of the towers are later additions.

encouraged monasteries, and great cathedrals arose at Canterbury, Durham, Lincoln, Winchester, Gloucester, Norwich, Ely, and other sites.

At Durham, the cathedral of St. Cuthbert (Fig. 8.55) was constructed from 1093 to 1133 under the leadership of Norman bishops as a replacement for an earlier monastic church containing the relics of St. Cuthbert. It remains one of the best-preserved major Norman churches in England, interesting for its impressive massing and early use of rib vaulting throughout the church and creation of

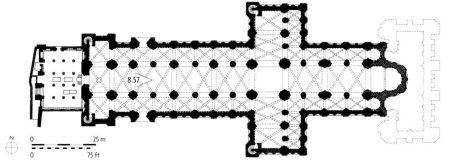

8.55 Plan of and section through the cathedral of St. Cuthbert, Durham, 1093–1133.

The original semicircular apse was rebuilt in the thirteenth century as a transept with nine altars to house St. Cuthbert's shrine. The builders reduced the height of the gallery over the aisle to leave room for a clerestory window tucked between the folds of the rib vaulting. Compare this section to that of St. Sernin, which uses a similar technique.

striking geometric patterns on its piers, arches, and ribs. Two west-front towers and a square crossing tower announce the cathedral's presence on the hilltop above the river Wear. The original plan was an aisled basilica with transepts, with the choir terminating in a semicircular apse and the aisles concluded by chapels. (The apse was rebuilt to its present transept design in the Gothic

period.) Evidence suggests that only the choir was initially planned for vaulting, but eventually vaulting was undertaken throughout the church. In the choir aisle vaults, built in about 1096, the ribs were built integrally with the vault cells. When rib vaults were begun over the nave, in about 1128–33, masons used the ribs as a framework from which to construct vault infill that was significantly thinner than corresponding work in the choir, indicating that they understood rib vaulting's constructional advantages (Fig. 8.56).

Durham's high vaults lack the vertical continuity from **diagonal** ribs to wall shaft that characterize the interior of

**8.56** Nave vaults, St. Cuthbert, Durham, 1093–1133.

Here Norman builders used septpartite, or seven-part, vaults between pointed, transverse arches. Notice how the ribs spring from the corbels above the triforium.

**8.57** Nave looking east, St. Cuthbert, Durham, 1093–1133.

The nave features compound piers alternating with magnificently bold cylindrical columns, each having an incised design. The continuous ridge line produces spatial unity among the vault bays.

constructional advantages of rib vaults and the structural efficiency of pointed arches, masons reduced the material (and thus the weight and cost) required to vault a building. The square bays and diagonal groin vaults from Roman times were transformed into rectangular bays having continuity of line from wall shaft to vaulting rib. Uninterrupted walls that were so important to structural stability in early Romanesque vaulted buildings were abandoned in favor of a skeletal system with loads concentrated at particular points, and a new esthetic of spaciousness and light came into being in the style we term Gothic.

## CONCLUSIONS ABOUT ARCHITECTURAL IDEAS

Charlemagne's ninth-century attempt to associate himself with the ancient Roman Empire produced a false spring of classical revivalism. While his scribes aggressively assembled and copied ancient manuscripts, thereby assuring their preservation until the present day, Charlemagne was unable to reconstitute the classical way of thinking, and Carolingian builders were equally unable to recapture the essence of classical architecture. Charlemagne drew upon what he had seen in Italy, particularly the church of S. Vitale in Ravenna, and the knowledge of Lombard builders whom he enticed to come north, and fused the accumulated models and technologies with Germanic building traditions. This fusion produced his Palatine Chapel at Aachen and, speaking a related architectural language, the Oratory at Germigny-des-Prés, which sits atop a nine-part, or quincunx, plan that came from Anatolian Byzantium. Charlemagne used monasteries as instruments of settlement and control of the countryside. The document known as the Plan of St. Gall illustrates that his planners conceived a universal monastic ideal that could be adapted to local conditions, as, for instance, was the case at Cluny.

Anglo-Saxon and Viking builders exploited wood in the form of logs and staves. Inventiveness reached apogees of ornamentation and vertical ascent in Norway with richly energetic woodcarving and telescoping building masses covered by multiple, steep gables. But it was massive, fireproof, stone masonry that most appealed to Romanesque builders, and they gradually explored structural capabilities and visual effects inherent in round-arch-penetrated, mostly stone bearing walls supporting barrel vaults and sometimes groin vaults and even domes.

Designers for Ottonian rulers who followed Charlemagne in the northern reaches of the Holy Roman Empire loved multiple towers, including the Carolingian westwerk tower, and built in local, often polychromatic stone. Lombard masons contributed such features as corbel-arch tables, or Lombard bands. Nave walls in churches eventually took on three-dimensionality in the form of advanc-

St. Etienne at Caen. Although the nave and choir are composed of double bays comprised of compound piers alternating with distinctive cylindrical columns (Fig. 8.57), the vaults are septpartite, and their diagonal ribs spring from corbeled heads high on the gallery wall rather than connecting with wall shafts. Pointed, transverse arches define the double bays by connecting compound piers across the nave. The heavy quality of construction is increased by the relative absence of figural ornament. Striking geometric designs of chevrons, spirals, and diaper patterns are incised on the cylindrical columns, almost like the abstractions of Viking interlace work, while the arch moldings in the **Galilee** Chapel attached to the western end of the cathedral in about 1170–75 have zigzag patterning.

Vaulting strategies that Norman builders explored at Caen and Durham led to structural changes that are associated with the Gothic style. By finding ways to exploit the

ing layers of pilasters and colonnettes, the latter appearing as columns conceptually captive in the wall, and some-times-receding layers of round-arched openings. The great, fully vaulted nave of Cluny in Burgundy spoke much the same architectural language, as do the remaining, related churches along the pilgrimage roads to Santiago de Compostela. Rigorous in their planning as a result of repetitive bays of barrel and groin vaults in naves and aisles and repetitive, projecting chapels (as at Cluny), such buildings as St. Sernin and St. Foy include transverse nave arches that continue visually down to the floor in the form of colonnettes between which recessed arches open up at the nave and gallery levels. In Aquitaine in southwest France, vaults gave way to repetitive domed bays, producing interiors where the French skill in stonecutting, or stereotomy, produced a zenith of spatial lucidity.

Builders in Normandy on the northern French coast exported their regional style across the channel to England by following the armies of William the Conqueror. While England's Durham Cathedral was eventually fully vaulted, perhaps its most distinctive characteristic is the intensity of its carved-stone textures, from chevron-incised piers to zigzag patterning on arches and vault ribs. Ribs also appeared early in Lombardy in northern Italy. At the brick church of S. Ambrogio, Lombard construction signatures, such as the repetitive corbeled arches named for them, also appear, as do mutant classical orders and uncomfortably attenuated external colonnettes.

In central Italy, the heavy northern Romanesque style never pushed aside the classical tradition, meaning the maintenance of basilican plans and the appearance of few attached towers. The availability of marble in various colors encouraged the subdivision of façades according to geometric patterning; the use of repetitive, polychromatic, horizontal banding; and the repetitive stacking up of carefully carved quasi-classical motifs. Classical reinterpretations also continued unabated along the southern French coast in Provence, where many ancient monuments remained intact to serve as models.

While the subsequent, more extravagantly vertical and dramatically lit Gothic architecture of the Ile de France around Paris, covered in the next chapter, emerged from Romanesque stock, this extraordinary change does not in any way suggest that heavier, darker Romanesque work was inferior or immature. Rather, Romanesque builders north of Italy and southern France unashamedly exploited the weighty, shadowy massiveness of stone masonry and reveled in this exploitation.

# CHAPTER 9

# GOTHIC ARCHITECTURE

As we consider the Gothic, the final phase of medieval architecture, we are faced with defining the style. The term "Gothic" was first applied in the seventeenth century to denote designs not based on precedent from classical antiquity, and the label was applied with derision. By the nineteenth century, pejorative connotations had largely been overcome, but historians have struggled since to clarify what exactly constitutes the Gothic style. The most obvious definition involves key elements employed in many Gothic buildings—the pointed arch and the rib vault—although, as we have seen, these were also found in some Romanesque work. There are, however, elements original to Gothic buildings, including flying buttresses, windows with tracery, and piers composed of colonnettes or shafts bundled around a core, that serve as hallmarks of the style (Fig. 9.1).

Another common definition relies on the way these elements were brought together in the structure of large-scale churches and cathedrals, particularly those built in the region around Paris during the period from 1140 to 1220. Unlike Romanesque buildings, in which a continuous mass of wall is necessary to sustain the load, the Gothic structure is a skeletal system that transfers roof loads down to the ground at discrete points, thereby freeing large expanses of wall to be opened for windows. Secular buildings seldom have this wall section, however, so a purely structural concept is insufficient by itself to define the Gothic. One can define Gothic buildings by their spatial characteristics, which tend to emphasize the vertical, consist of articulated but unified cells of space, and have a sense of openness afforded by the construction system. Lastly the style can be seen as a reflection of the historical era and religious imagery of the period in which it was built, connected both to the growth of urban society and to theological analogies to Old Testament tabernacles and temples and concepts of the New Jerusalem. We need to keep all these definitional perspectives in mind as we seek to understand Gothic architecture.

Let us look more closely at the key elements associated with Gothic structure—pointed arches, rib vaults, and flying buttresses. Pointed arches are better approximations of catenary curves that represent the line of compressive force acting in any arch, and thus they exert less outward or overturning thrust. They also present considerable design flexibility, as one can vary to some extent the angle of the arch. By contrast, the dimensions of a semicircular arch are established by the width of the span. Pointed arches are probably a contribution from Islamic architecture, having been used in Syria and North Africa before their earliest application in northern Europe. They were used in a number of major Romanesque buildings, including the great church of Cluny III and St. Pierre Cathedral at Angoulême. Rib vaults can also be found in late Romanesque architecture, those constructed at St. Etienne at Caen and Durham Cathedral being generally thought to be among the earliest examples. Ribbing a groin vault had the virtue of visually "tidying up" the sometimes awkward arris created at the fold of the groin vault, but builders soon discovered that there were constructional advantages to be gained from laying up the ribs first, then using them as in-situ scaffold for erecting the thinner web sections of the vault. Builders also found they could lighten the webbing, thereby reducing the material weight of groin vaults. As the dead load on the vaulting was created primarily by the weight of the stone, reducing this weight not only economized on materials but also eventually facilitated greater building heights. The third element, the flying buttress, was probably first used at Sens Cathedral in about 1160, but it can be seen in embryonic form in the quadrant vaults over galleries of the pilgrimage road churches. Since Gothic construction concentrates loads at piers rather than distributing it continuously along the wall, the need for reinforcement at specific points is great. Gothic architects soon developed external buttressing, set at right angles to the wall and connected to it at strategic junctions by arches, which appear to "fly" or leap as they reach out to strengthen the upper sections of the skeleton

## Chronology

| | |
|---|---|
| Battle of Hastings | 1066 |
| beginning of the crusades | 1096 |
| construction of the choir at St. Denis | 1140–44 |
| construction of Notre-Dame Cathedral, Paris | 1163–ca. 1250 |
| construction of St. Etienne Cathedral, Bourges | 1195–1250 |
| construction of Salisbury Cathedral | 1220–58 |
| notebooks of Villard de Honnecourt | ca. 1225–50 |
| collapse of the choir vaults at Beauvais Cathedral | 1284 |
| completion of Milan Cathedral | 1572 |

Notre-Dame Cathedral interior, Chartres, 1194–1230.

Chartres has an exceptionally wide nave because of the dimensions of the earlier Romanesque basilica.

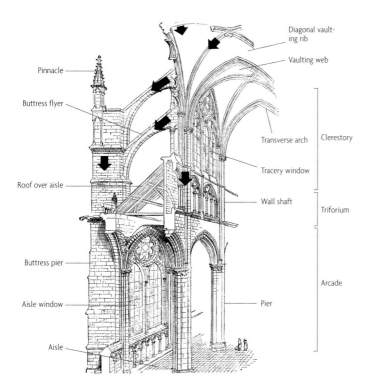

Pinnacle

Buttress flyer

Roof over aisle

Buttress pier

Aisle window

Aisle

Diagonal vault-
ing rib

Vaulting web

Transverse arch

Clerestory

Tracery window

Wall shaft

Triforium

Pier

Arcade

**9.1** Section perspective showing the Gothic structure of a major church.

Arrows indicate how dead loads from the vaults are transferred to the piers of the arcade and, through the lower flyer, to the buttress piers outside the building. The upper flyer helps to resist lateral or side loads caused by the wind blowing against the building.

frame. (Gothic openness can be achieved without flying buttresses, particularly in smaller structures where wall buttresses suffice to handle the structural loads. In Italy, builders developed alternate structural solutions to obviate the need for flying buttresses, as we shall see.)

Gothic architecture is more than a collection of structural techniques, however, for it embraces an integrated esthetic system. The flexibility of the pointed arch allowed irregular areas to be vaulted while maintaining a common ceiling height. Elements of the church plans that in Romanesque had been expressed as separate volumes (nave, aisle, chapel) could be combined into a unified, ordered composition, thanks to the geometric freedom offered by the combination of rib vaults and pointed arches. Gothic builders learned to integrate vaulting ribs with wall shafts, thus visually anchoring the floating overhead canopy to the ground. With the reinforcement provided by external buttresses, entire wall sections could be devoted to windows, particularly in the clerestory, where increased window height and width contributed to a diaphanous interior effect. Window **tracery**, the decorative intersecting stonework in the upper sections of windows, was introduced and became increasingly slender, evolving from plate tracery (punched openings in a solid field) to bar tracery (thin lines of cut stone set in geometric patterns). As the Gothic style developed, one can sense the desire to reduce solid building mass and to enhance the

quality of space and light, for both metaphysical and practical reasons, thus stimulating technical and artistic innovations.

## EARLY GOTHIC

### THE ABBEY CHURCH OF ST. DENIS

The Gothic style originated in northern France, in the region around Paris known as the Ile-de-France. This area had relatively little Romanesque building, so perhaps it was more open to developments from other places. It also was the home of one of the period's most energetic, informed, and innovative patrons of the arts, Abbot Suger, who rose from humble origins to become one of the most powerful Church figures of his age. Suger's parents had donated him to the abbey of St. Denis when he was three years old, and he was raised in the monastery school to become a monk. Among his young companions in the school was the future King Louis VII of France. Suger's diplomatic and administrative skills were soon noticed, and he rose rapidly in the Church hierarchy. In 1122, at the age of thirty-six, he was elected abbot of St. Denis.

Located about six miles north of Paris, St. Denis was the French royal monastery. It was the burial place of Denis, the first bishop of Paris, who was martyred by the Romans in the third century and later designated the patron saint of France. The kings of France were buried at the abbey, and the royal banner, the Oriflamme, was kept there between military campaigns. For all its prestige, the abbey was overcrowded and somewhat decayed when Suger became abbot. The existing building, consecrated in 775, was a Carolingian basilica that had received an enlarged eastern chapel in 832. Suger wanted to rebuild the church for the greater glory of God and France, but first he had to set the abbey's financial affairs in order and respond to criticism from Bernard of Clairvaux by reforming the religious practices of its monks. While he worked toward these goals, Suger developed images of what he wished the new church to be. He studied biblical descriptions of the Temple of Solomon, a design specified by God; he examined writings attributed (incorrectly) to St. Denis, in which there was much discussion of the mystical and metaphysical properties of visually manifested spiritual images, especially phenomena associated with light; and he inquired of travelers from Constantinople for descriptions of Hagia Sophia (see Fig. 6.16), widely regarded as the most splendid church building in Christendom, which Suger was determined to exceed.

By 1137 Suger was ready to build. To enlarge the church he constructed a new west front and narthex forward of the existing structure, probably to the designs of a Norman architect capable of translating Suger's ideas into reality (Fig. 9.2). This work, consecrated in 1140, incorporated both the twin-towered west façade of Norman churches and the tradition of sculptured portals

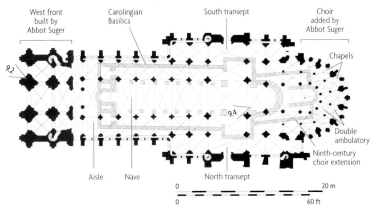

**9.2** St. Denis, west front, 1137–40.

Generally recognized as the first Gothic building, this church has lost its northern tower.

**9.3a** Plan of St. Denis, 1137–40.

This plan shows in hatched outline the basilica of 775 enlarged in 832. Suger built his new west front well forward of the existing building and had the choir positioned to incorporate foundations of the older building.

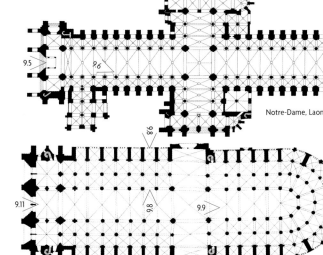

**9.3b** Plans of Notre-Dame, Laon, 1155–ca. 1205, and Notre-Dame, Paris, 1163–ca. 1250.

Notice that Laon has a pronounced cruciform plan, whereas Paris has transepts that scarcely project beyond the line of the buttress piers. The initial design for Paris had no radiating chapels off its double ambulatory, but chapels (shown here) were subsequently inserted between all the buttress piers.

developed in the south of France. The three doorways had carved tympana and jamb statues, while the articulation of windows, including a circular or rose window, went beyond the linear façade compositions of Normandy. On the interior, rib vaults in the narthex sprang from grouped piers, thus exploiting the potential for continuity of line.

So enthusiastic was the reception for this new work that construction began almost at once on an enlargement of the east end (Fig. 9.3a). Less than four years later (1144) the new choir was dedicated in elaborate ceremonies involving distinguished churchmen and royalty. Suger's preoccupation with colored light is clearly manifested in the seven shallow radiating chapels of the choir, each with two large stained-glass windows (Fig 9.4). The irregular bays of this complex plan are consistently covered by rib vaults rising to a uniform crown height, while slender buttresses, set in the angles between the chapels, reinforce the upper wall. The ensemble creates an airy, luminous, rich interior that glows like jewels, precisely the effect desired by Suger: "a circular string of chapels, by virtue of which the whole church would shine with the wonderful and uninterrupted light of most sacred windows, pervading the interior beauty."

**9.4** Abbey Church ambulatory and choir, St. Denis, 1140–44 and later.

The ambulatory (left) dates from Suger's abbacy, while the triforium and clerestory are a century later, constructed anew when the nave of the church was completed. The skeletal nature of Gothic construction facilitated the installation of large windows in the shallow chapels surrounding the apse, creating the wondrous luminosity desired by Suger.

Planned next for construction was a nave to link the new narthex and choir, but Suger did not live to see the completion of his ambitious dream. Louis VII departed for the Second Crusade in 1147, leaving Suger in charge as regent of France, with neither time nor money for building. He died shortly after Louis returned from the Holy Land in 1151. The present nave at St. Denis was completed nearly a century later, when the upper stories of Suger's choir were rebuilt to match the height of the new nave vaults.

The wondrous quality of light and space created by the new choir at St. Denis was not lost on the Church authorities and lay people who visited the abbey. Within two decades of its dedication, Gothic churches were under construction at several sites in the Ile-de-France, both for monasteries and increasingly for cathedral churches in the growing towns. The style seemed to flourish particularly within the orbit of the king of France's political influence. In regions such as the south of France, where royal control was weak and religious interest in the theology of divine manifestations was not strong, the mature Romanesque style continued to be used for at least a century after the Gothic had been developed.

## EARLY GOTHIC CATHEDRALS

Gothic architecture also coincided with an increase in the veneration of the Virgin Mary. As a mother who had suffered great sorrow, she had enormous popular appeal and became an important intercessor figure, standing before Christ the judge and pleading for leniency for erring humanity. Many of the great cathedrals were dedicated to her—she is "Notre Dame" in French, "Our Lady" in English—and sculpture and stained glass featured her far more often than was the case in Romanesque work. One index of this change is the way in which the Last Judgment was depicted on west-front portals. In Gothic work the scene is more life-like, appealing to the viewer's empathetic identification with theological verities rather than impressing with abstractly conceptual representations of the same spiritual issues.

Two early Gothic cathedrals in northern France are of particular interest. The cathedral of Notre-Dame at Laon was begun in about 1155 to replace an older structure that had become too small for the needs of the prosperous town and the growing cathedral school (Figs. 9.3b, 9.5–9.6). The choir and transepts were finished within twenty years, and the nave, west front, and crossing tower

**9.5** Notre-Dame Cathedral west front, Laon, 1155–ca. 1205.

This façade has a greater feeling of depth and openness than was seen at St. Denis. Deep hoods protect the entrance portals, and the upper stages of the twin towers change to octagonal plans.

**9.6** Notre-Dame Cathedral nave, Laon, 1155–ca. 1205.

The nave has a four-story elevation: aisle arcade, gallery, triforium (corresponding to the section where the roof over the aisle abuts the exterior wall), and clerestory. Bundled wall shafts correspond to ribs of the sexpartite vaults overhead.

were completed by about 1205. To provide more space for the cathedral's canons, the original semicircular Gothic apse was replaced early in the thirteenth century by the present elongated choir with its rectangular east end. The flying buttresses may not be original to the church, because the galleries and their roofs over the aisles stabilize the vaults. Some scholars believe they were added in the thirteenth century to provide additional bracing against lateral wind forces.

At Laon one can see how cautious architects and builders were in experimenting with new Gothic techniques. In its pre-1205 state, Laon retained elements from Romanesque works, including the long nave, **sexpartite rib vaults**, lantern crossing tower, galleries, semicircular apse, and western towers that could be found in Norman churches. The critical difference on the interior is the incorporation of the pointed arch into the profile of the diagonal ribs of the sexpartite vaults. Ribs from the vaults and moldings around the clerestory windows continue as clustered wall shafts to the capitals of cylindrical piers in the nave arcade, thus emphasizing verticality. The three-dimensional, sculptural quality of the west front, built in 1190–1205, also departs from Romanesque precedent, for even Caen or the most ambitious of Cluniac churches were never conceived this boldly. Protective porch hoods over the three portals project from the plane of the façade,

creating a sense of depth that is repeated in the arched windows flanking the rose window in the story above. The western towers begin on square plans and are transformed into octagons in the upper stages. Stone oxen peer down from the towers' heights, silent tributes to the patient animals that hauled the construction materials up to the ridge on which the cathedral sits. In the early thirteenth century, Villard de Honnecourt, whose sketchbook has survived to modern times, drew the towers of Laon and noted, "I have traveled in many lands, but in no place have I seen such a tower as the one at Laon." Even with its later modifications, Laon stands as the purest example of the Early Gothic.

In about 1150–55, the bishop of Paris began construction on the new cathedral of Notre-Dame to replace a sixth-century basilica, clearing a site on the Ile de la Cité and laying substantial foundations for the church (Fig. 9.3b). Work began on the choir, progressing to the nave by 1178–1200. The west front was completed between 1200 and 1250. During the course of construction, however, modifications were made to the fabric of the church, so that what one sees today is an altered version of the original twelfth-century design. Notre-Dame is a tall church, 110 feet from the floor to the crown of its vaults, and the direct light admitted into the nave by the original clerestories proved insufficient for the height of the space. To

**9.7** Notre-Dame Cathedral south side, Paris, 1163–ca. 1250.

Note the large transept rose window. Thanks to Victor Hugo's *The Hunchback of Notre-Dame* (1831), this building was restored after decades of neglect. It is important both as an early Gothic monument and as a nineteenth-century example of historic preservation.

bring in more light, the clerestories all around the cathedral were enlarged in about 1225, flying buttresses were added to the choir to stabilize the great hemicycle, and the original nave buttresses were rebuilt (Fig. 9.7). The transepts with their enormous rose windows are another addition. The north transept was built from 1246 to 1257 to the designs of Jean de Chelles, and the south transept was constructed in 1258–61 by Jean de Chelles and Pierre de Montreuil. In the course of the late thirteenth century, chapels were inserted between all the buttresses around the choir and nave. Finally, in the nineteenth century, Eugene Emmanuel Viollet-le-Duc restored the cathedral, rebuilding all the flying buttresses, returning the bays at the crossing to their original design, and repairing the sculpture on the exterior (Fig. 9.8).

Despite all these modifications, the Early Gothic qualities of Notre-Dame in Paris are remarkably well preserved on the interior (Figs. 9.9–9.10). Although less pure than Laon, the cathedral remains an important monument of the period. Its original plan was innovative and ambitious. A long church, completely surrounded by a double ambulatory, it was the first Gothic building to exceed the height (but not the length) of Cluny III.

The west front, a splendid study in proportions, has a solid, almost military quality, in contrast to the more open character of Laon (Fig. 9.11). At Paris it is the strength of

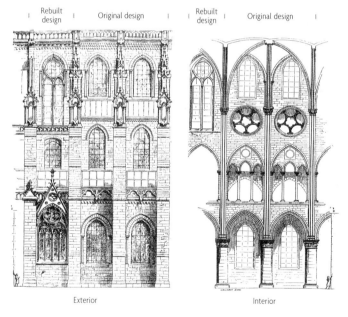

Exterior    Interior

**9.8** Exterior and interior nave elevations of Notre-Dame Cathedral, Paris, 1150–55–ca. 1250.

This view shows the original form (right side of each drawing) which included a roundel opening in the triforium. When flying buttresses were added in about 1175–80, the clerestory was enlarged.

the wall that commands attention. Triple portals, each slightly different in size and shape, are surmounted by the horizontal Gallery of Kings, representing twenty-eight kings of the Old Testament. A radiant rose window, flanked by paired lancet windows, forms a halo backdrop

for a sculpture of the Virgin and Child with two angels. Below the twin towers is a second arcaded horizontal gallery that lightens the upper wall while completing the basically square configuration of the lower façade. This elevation rewards close study, for the more one looks, the more visually delightful detail one finds. From a distance the basically symmetrical disposition of features within the overall composition is obvious, while the slight irregularities in individual elements become noticeable (and endearing) upon examination. None of the three portals is the same size or shape, and the great towers are unequal in width. The sculptural programs of the three portals extend Christian teachings to those who could not read, just as Romanesque work did. On climbing the stairs to the upper levels, one gets an intimate view of the individually designed **crockets** projecting from the stones at the corners of the towers and of the fanciful sculpture (generally of the nineteenth century) perched high up on the parapets.

**9.11** Notre-Dame Cathedral west front, Paris, ca. 1250.

What seems at first glance to be an obvious symmetrical composition turns out on closer examination to be not entirely so. These small variations and details make this a highly individual building.

**9.9** Notre-Dame Cathedral nave and choir, Paris, 1163–ca. 1250.

Compare this photograph with the drawings in Fig. 9.8 to see the revised interior elevation built when the clerestory windows were enlarged. Later Gothic cathedrals featured much larger windows.

**9.10** Notre-Dame Cathedral nave vaults, Paris, 1163–ca. 1250.

These are sexpartite vaults constructed over two bays. Notice how there is continuity of line from the vaulting ribs to the wall shafts, giving the interior a vertical sweep.

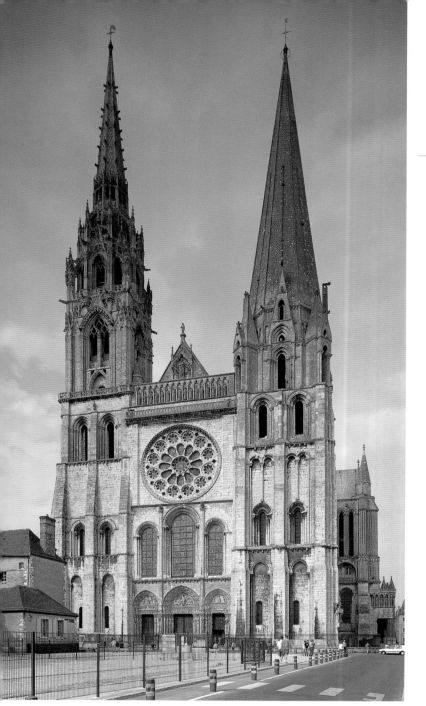

**9.12** Notre-Dame Cathedral west front, Chartres, 1194–1230.

The triple doorways, lancet windows, and tower bases were built ca. 1150 as a new façade for a predecessor church. The horizontal string course just below the rose window marks the seam between Romanesque and Gothic work. The north tower was finished in 1513.

**triforium** passage, and the clerestory windows. In the process, the clerestory windows increased markedly in size, and vaulting shifted from sexpartite (over two bays) to **quadripartite** (over one bay).

Chartres Cathedral has an even more complicated chronology than the cathedral of Paris. The site had long been sacred to the Virgin Mary, and the cathedral treasure contained, among other valuable relics, a tunic believed to have been worn by Mary. Chartres became a center of pilgrimage, and from 1020 to 1037 a Romanesque basilica with three deep radiating chapels was constructed to replace an earlier church destroyed by fire. By the twelfth century, this church had itself been enlarged, and a fire in 1134 had damaged the westwerk. Work began that same year to build a new west front and narthex in much the same manner that Abbot Suger was to extend St. Denis. Sculptors from the workshops at St. Denis came to Chartres in 1145–50 to carve the three portals of the new west façade, and the three lancet windows overhead were filled with stained glass depicting themes pioneered at Suger's church: the infancy of Christ, the Passion story, and the Tree of Jesse or the genealogy of Christ.

On the night of June 10, 1194, fire again struck the cathedral and town, destroying the wooden-roofed basilica and eighty per cent of the city. Even though the new west front survived without major damage, the people of Chartres interpreted the fire as a sign of divine displeasure. Sensing the general feeling of hopelessness, the visiting bishop of Pisa called a town meeting, during which the sacred tunic was carried out, miraculously unharmed, from the ruins of the crypt. The mood quickly changed from sorrow to jubilation as the townspeople decided that the fire was a sign that Mary desired a larger church. Building funds were raised with remarkable speed and construction commenced. The Gothic cathedral at Chartres was built in the span of twenty-six years, from 1194 to 1220, and the sculpted north and south transept porches were finished between 1224 and 1250. However, the north tower on the west front was completed only in 1513, giving the west front at last a balanced asymmetry of form and style.

In rebuilding the cathedral, the master masons reused the foundations and crypt and incorporated the surviving west front. On the exterior one can still see the seam where the new work was joined to the old, a horizontal string course immediately below the western rose (which itself is slightly off center). The Romanesque apse was transformed into a Gothic choir by the insertion of four shallow chapels between the three existing deep chapels of the crypt, thus creating seven shallow chapels with a double ambulatory on the main level. The builders also added a transept to the original Romanesque basilica plan

## HIGH GOTHIC

The incorporation of flying buttresses at Notre-Dame in Paris integrated the three major structural components of Gothic, and redundant features from the Romanesque could be deleted from subsequent Gothic building. The period of tentative exploration was over, and the mature or High Gothic that followed saw the erection of churches with increasingly refined artistic and structural features.

### CHARTRES AND BOURGES

The first monument of the High Gothic was the cathedral of Notre-Dame at Chartres, where flying buttresses were planned from the start so that the galleries were unnecessary (Figs. 9.12, 9.13, and 9.15). This simplified the interior elevations to three divisions: the nave arcade, the

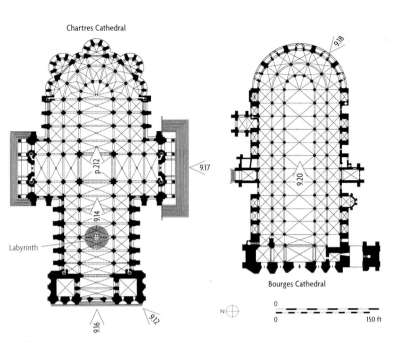

Chartres Cathedral

Labyrinth

Bourges Cathedral

0 ___ 150 ft

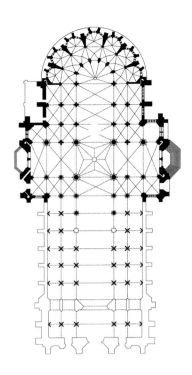

**9.13** Plans of Chartres Cathedral, 1194–1230, and Bourges Cathedral, 1195–1250.

These buildings, begun within two years of one another, show different approaches to Gothic design. Chartres continues the tradition of pronounced transepts seen at Laon, while Bourges has a double ambulatory rather like Paris.

**9.14** Projected plan of Beauvais Cathedral, ca. 1225–1573.

Built in discontinuous campaigns, the choir, transepts, and one bay of the nave (shown here in black) were all that was completed. After the nave vaults collapsed in 1284, pairs of additional piers were inserted in each of the three choir bays to create sexpartite vaults.

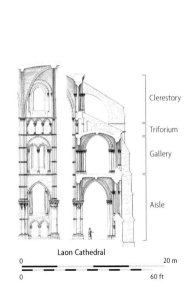

Clerestory

Triforium

Gallery

Aisle

Laon Cathedral

0 ___ 20 m
0 ___ 60 ft

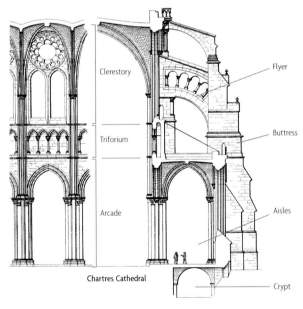

Clerestory

Triforium

Arcade

Chartres Cathedral

Flyer

Buttress

Aisles

Crypt

**9.15** Elevations and sections of Laon Cathedral nave and Chartres Cathedral nave.

These have been drawn to the same scale. Notice the changes from Early to High Gothic, as well as the greatly increased width and height of the arcade and clerestory at Chartres. Neither drawing includes the wooden roof trusses.

and, after construction was underway, decided to include three sculpted portals on each transept arm, giving Chartres a total of nine entrances.

The completed cathedral glows inside with a wonderful luminosity, in part because the clerestory window height has increased to equal the height of the arcade, while clerestory width has expanded to consume virtually all of the wall area between the wall shafts. Compare the interior nave elevations of Laon and Chartres (Fig. 9.15) to appreciate how substantially the proportions of window to wall have changed in the shift from Early to

High Gothic work. Note also the development at Chartres of plate tracery in the rose windows above the paired lancets of the clerestory. At Chartres, visible structural elements, including the vaulting ribs and wall shafts in particular, are slender and deeply undercut so that they appear to float free of the surfaces to which they are connected. Alternate nave piers have cylindrical and octagonal cores, with wall shafts that are either faceted or cylindrical, respectively. Even the buttresses, particularly the flyers around the choir, have a sense of lightness. Of all Gothic cathedrals, Chartres alone has preserved about two-thirds

**9.16** Jamb figures from the central portal of Chartres Cathedral, west front, ca. 1150.

These elongated crowned figures, representing Jewish kings and queens from the Old Testament, have timeless staring faces and stylized drapery suggesting Byzantine influence. They are probably the work of the sculptors from St. Denis, who came to work at Chartres when Suger's west front was completed.

**9.17** Jamb figures at Chartres Cathedral south porch, ca. 1250.

The transept sculptures demonstrate the increasing naturalism of later Gothic work. These apostles inhabit bodies that are closer to actual human proportions, and their poses are more animated. From left to right are Saints Matthew, Thomas, Philip, Andrew, and Peter.

of its original stained glass. Bold figures of the holy family and the saints dominate the high clerestory windows, while more intricately detailed illustrations of biblical stories and saints' legends predominate in the windows of the aisles and ambulatory. Old Testament subjects are shown in the glass of the north transept, balanced by New Testament themes in the south-transept rose and lancet windows. On the west front, the twelfth-century lancets relating the genealogy and life of Christ were retained from the pre-Gothic church. Suger's ideal of pervasive interior beauty is nowhere more evident than at Chartres.

The west-front doorways, known as the Royal Portals because of the crowned figures in the jambs, provide a splendid image of the theology of salvation as it was visualized in 1150 (Fig. 9.16). The influence of Suger's façade at St. Denis can be seen in the stately, elongated jamb figures, while the tympana subjects reflect the teachings of the School of Chartres, a prominent medieval center of learning associated with the cathedral. The portals carved

a century later on the north and south transepts provide a measure of increased naturalism that occurred in Gothic sculpture (Fig. 9.17). Some of the subjects shown are repeated from the Royal Portals, but their treatment is far more life-like.

The cathedral of St. Etienne at Bourges (1195–1250) presents a conceptual contrast to Chartres (Figs. 9.13, 9.18–9.20). Its plan shares features with Notre-Dame in Paris. Double aisles flank the nave and continue in uninterrupted arcs around the choir and sexpartite vaults are used in the nave and choir. A glance at the interior, however, indicates immediately that Bourges is no copy of Paris, but an original adaptation of High Gothic vocabulary. The paired aisles increase in height to help brace the high vaults of the nave and choir, recalling the triangular cross section of Cluny III, with the addition here of flying buttresses that follow the slope of the roofs. At Bourges, choir and nave vaults spring from alternating major and minor piers set on a square module plan. The spatial effect

**9.18** St. Etienne Cathedral from the east, Bourges, 1195–1250.

This view shows the buttresses that provide bracing for the high vaults. Notice how much smaller the clerestory windows are than those at Chartres.

is one of breadth and expansiveness, but the layered aisle vaults and roofs preclude clerestory windows as tall as those of Chartres, although here too they fill virtually the entire wall area between wall shafts. On the west front, the five major interior volumes are reflected in five portals, completed in about 1285.

Robert Mark, an engineer who has researched the structural behavior of historic buildings, documented the structural logic of Bourges, which achieves a comparable interior height and area to Chartres, yet requires significantly less stone. Despite its cost-effectiveness (for stone was a major expense in building construction), the double-aisle design of Bourges was seldom used thereafter, while the more costly and inherently less stable model of Chartres was adopted for the tallest cathedrals—Reims, Amiens, and Beauvais (Fig. 9.14)—of the Gothic era. One suspects that building patrons, in northern France at least,

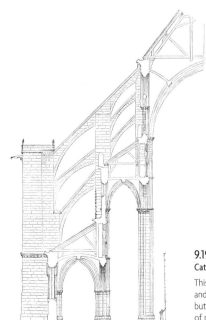

**9.19** Section through Bourges Cathedral, 1195–1250.

This view shows how the inner and outer aisles function with the buttresses to brace the high vaults of nave and choir.

**9.20** Bourges Cathedral nave, 1195–1250.

Because of the distinctive cross section (see Fig. 9.19) Bourges Cathedral has not only relatively small clerestory windows in the nave but also exceptionally tall nave piers. Note also the use of sexpartite vaulting that replaced original quadripartite vaulting.

preferred the dramatic luminosity afforded by the tall clerestory windows of the single-aisle design more than structural efficiency, since Gothic was not primarily an expression of technique but an architectural embodiment of religious and cultural ideals. Cathedrals built on the model of Bourges are found in Spain and Italy, where bright skies prevail. The Cathedral of Milan, a late Gothic building, uses a cross section similar to Bourges Cathedral to attain a nave vault height equivalent to that of Beauvais.

## THE SAINTE-CHAPELLE

Even as the great French cathedrals were being built, there were also smaller Gothic projects under way. One particularly lovely example is the Sainte-Chapelle (1243–48), added by Louis IX to the royal palace in Paris as a repository for relics he had acquired from Constantinople, including the Crown of Thorns and a piece of the True Cross (Figs. 9.21–9.23). The relics cost twice as much as the building. The Sainte-Chapelle has two levels, a ground-floor chapel for use by the household servants and an upper chapel, surrounded by stained-glass windows with bar tracery in the new **rayonnant** style, for use by the royal family. This upper chapel is filled with jewel-like color by walls diminished to slender piers set between

**9.21** Upper chapel interior, Sainte-Chapelle, Paris, 1243–48.

In great expanses of stained glass, most of it original, these windows illustrate stories from both the Old and New Testaments in chronological sequence from the entrance door to the apse.

**9.22** Sainte-Chapelle, Paris, 1243–48.

Built as a palace chapel by King Louis IX to house relics he had acquired from Constantinople, this small jewel of High Gothic design is a virtual glass-walled structure, with stone cross sections reduced to a minimum. The relatively small scale and internal metal tie-rods make flying buttresses unnecessary.

**9.23** Transverse section through Sainte-Chapelle, Paris, 1243–48.

The low-ceilinged room below is the chapel for household servants, while the spacious upper chapel was the domain of the royal family.

great expanses of largely original stained glass. Wall buttresses are linked together horizontally by iron tie-rods that encircle the building concealed in the masonry, passing across the windows as part of the framework supporting the glass. As a miniature statement of the dematerialization of masonry walls and the wondrous properties of colored light sought by Abbot Suger, the Sainte-Chapelle has no equal.

## ENGLISH GOTHIC

Although the Gothic style originated in France, it spread to other parts of Europe, particularly England, Germany, and Italy, and became the predominant style of northern Europe until the fifteenth century. English builders soon formed their own Gothic esthetic, and within a century had created Gothic churches that differed considerably from those built in France.

Nineteenth-century historians who first studied the Gothic buildings of England categorized the work in three overlapping phases, which are still useful for describing the progressive development of English medieval architecture (Fig. 9.24). **Early English**, built from 1175 to 1265, corresponds roughly to High Gothic work in France. Vaulting is straightforward, usually quadripartite, and windows have lancet-shaped heads. The **Decorated** period, extending from about 1250 until about 1370, uses vaulting elaborated with extra ribs, called **tierceron** and **lierne**, or

decorative, ribs (meaning those that neither rise from a pier colonnette nor are ridge ribs), and window tracery worked into **trefoil** (three-part) or **quatrefoil** (four-part) cusped shapes, intersecting lines, or flowing curvilinear shapes. The final phase, the **Perpendicular**, is the most distinctly English. In fashion from about 1330 until 1540, it is distinguished by panel tracery and vaulting in elaborate conical fan shapes. Despite their visual magnificence, **fan vaults** (Fig. 9.36) represent no structural advance; in fact, they are best suited to smaller churches where great heights and spans are not required. It is not possible to examine English cathedrals in strict chronological order, as portions of all three medieval periods are represented in the fabric of many of them. Discussions here will present the buildings as a whole.

### EARLY ENGLISH

Canterbury Cathedral was rebuilt in a Gothic style after the Norman church, begun in 1070, was devastated by fire in 1174 (Figs. 9.26a–9.27). Leading master masons of England and France were summoned to give their advice about rebuilding the ruined site, and William of Sens was selected to direct the work. He convinced the monks to demolish the remaining sections of the choir because the fire's heat had damaged the stonework beyond repair, but he confidently retained the fine Norman crypt and aisle walls. Between 1175 and 1184 the choir was rebuilt to a Gothic design based on the French cathedral of Sens (Fig.

Early English

Decorated

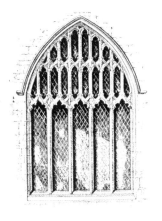

Perpendicular

**9.24** Examples of English Gothic window tracery.

As many English churches were built over extended periods, variations in window tracery provide one clue to the construction sequence.

**9.25** Sens Cathedral choir, ca.. 1135–1180.

Sens was a French Early Gothic cathedral that served as the model for Canterbury Cathedral. Compare this image to the choir of Canterbury (see Fig. 9.27).

9.25). During this time, William was severely injured in a fall from the scaffolding, and he returned to France in 1179, leaving his assistant, William the Englishman, to complete the work.

The choir at Canterbury was designed to house England's most popular shrine, that of St. Thomas à Becket, Archbishop of Canterbury and advisor to King Henry II, who in 1170 was murdered in the northwest transept by four of Henry's knights. Pilgrims from all over Europe soon flocked to Canterbury to partake of the miracles performed at the tomb of St. Thomas, and the monks, enriched by pilgrims' offerings, needed suitable accommodations both for the steady stream of visitors and their own services. (Recall that the destination of Chaucer's pilgrims was Canterbury.) As was the case in earlier pilgrimage churches, a satisfactory arrangement involved an aisle and ambulatory, which linked the site of Thomas's martyrdom with his shrine in the Trinity Chapel.

Canterbury's somewhat rambling plan can be explained by the reuse of the Norman crypt and the pilgrim traffic to Becket's shrine. The Norman church had both east and west transepts and two apsidal chapels set at angles to the main axis rather than radiating from it. Beyond these spaces to the east, William the Englishman built the Trinity Chapel and its single axial chapel, the Corona, which terminates the church on the east. A second, smaller transept was constructed to the west of the choir; and the wider, majestic nave was built early in the Perpendicular period, 1377–1405, possibly to the designs of Thomas of Hoo. The crowning element in the cathedral is the 235-foot-high crossing tower named Bell Harry after the bell hung there, which was erected in the mature Perpendicular period (1491–98) to the designs of John Wastell. The fan vaults of the tower are forerunners of those Wastell would erect later at King's College Chapel in Cambridge.

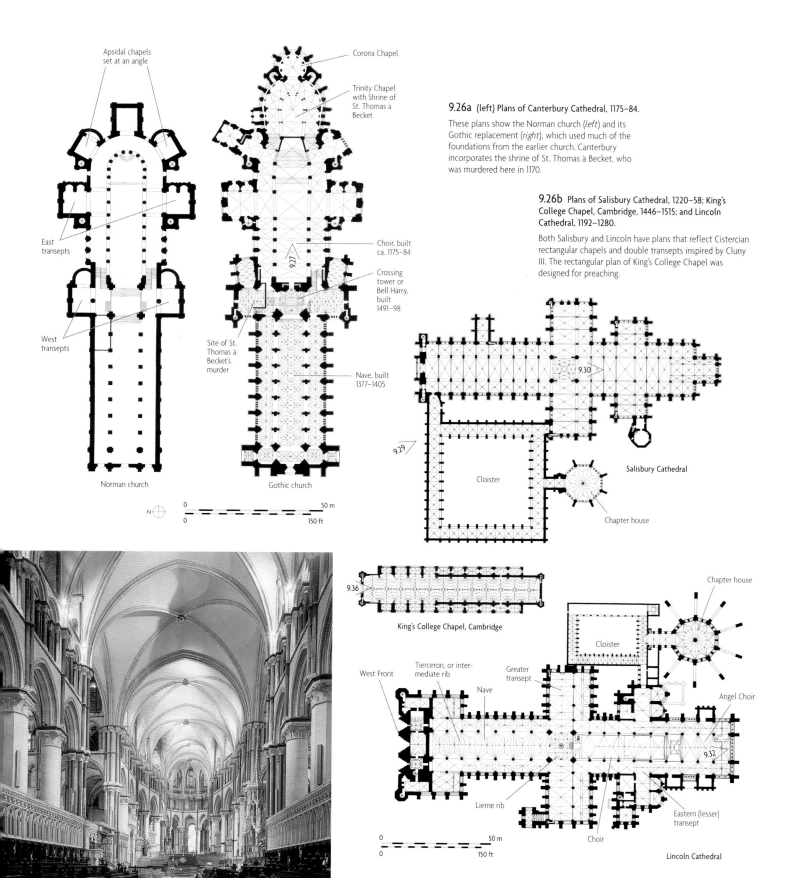

**Apsidal chapels set at an angle**

**East transepts**

**West transepts**

**Norman church**

**Corona Chapel**

**Trinity Chapel with Shrine of St. Thomas à Becket**

**Choir, built ca. 1175–84**

**Crossing tower or Bell Harry, built 1491–98**

**Site of St. Thomas à Becket's murder**

**Nave, built 1377–1405**

**Gothic church**

N

0 _ _ _ _ _ _ _ 50 m
0 _ _ _ _ _ _ _ 150 ft

**9.26a** (left) Plans of Canterbury Cathedral, 1175–84.

These plans show the Norman church (*left*) and its Gothic replacement (*right*), which used much of the foundations from the earlier church. Canterbury incorporates the shrine of St. Thomas à Becket, who was murdered here in 1170.

**9.26b** Plans of Salisbury Cathedral, 1220–58; King's College Chapel, Cambridge, 1446–1515; and Lincoln Cathedral, 1192–1280.

Both Salisbury and Lincoln have plans that reflect Cistercian rectangular chapels and double transepts inspired by Cluny III. The rectangular plan of King's College Chapel was designed for preaching.

**Cloister**

**Salisbury Cathedral**

**Chapter house**

**King's College Chapel, Cambridge**

**Chapter house**

**Cloister**

**West Front**

**Tierceron, or intermediate rib**

**Nave**

**Greater transept**

**Angel Choir**

**Lierne rib**

**Choir**

**Eastern (lesser) transept**

0 _ _ _ _ _ _ _ 50 m
0 _ _ _ _ _ _ _ 150 ft

**Lincoln Cathedral**

**9.27** Canterbury Cathedral choir, 1175–84.

The choir was built to the designs of William of Sens and William the Englishman. Although many features superficially resemble Sens Cathedral, there are characteristic English elements here, most notably the darker Purbeck marble trim that is used to emphasize horizontal lines.

# A WOOL CHURCH

by Marian Moffett

Across Europe are legions of parish churches that originated in the medieval period—England alone has about 8000 surviving examples that collectively constitute a national treasure. More than the great abbeys and cathedrals that attract the attention of scholars (and tourists), these modest churches give us an indication of how medieval architecture was experienced by ordinary people of the time.

Parish churches were built in an era when all Christians in a given community worshiped in the same church and regular attendance (not to mention compulsory financial support in the form of tithes) was the norm. When the local economy was strong, well-to-do individuals tended to invest in building churches as a means both of ensuring divine favor and displaying their wealth, which in the late medieval period in England came largely from trade in wool and woollen cloth. St. Agnes's at Cawston in Norfolk (Fig. 9.28) is known as a "wool church" because its fifteenth-century nave and western tower were largely

financed by Michael de la Pole, Earl of Suffolk, whose fortune derived from the wool trade. (The fourteenth-century chancel from an earlier church was retained.) St. Agnes's size is clearly in excess of what was required by Cawston's medieval population, so we must understand the building as a demonstration of the earl's piety and pride. His family crest is carved above the entrance. Stone imported from France was used for the tower and nave arcade, rather than the cheaper local knapped flint. As is common in English parish churches, the nave and aisles were covered by timber roofs rather than vaulting. Even here, however, the earl's munificence is evident: Cawston's nave has a spectacular hammerbeam roof, adorned with standing angels at the ends of the beams, with three more angels hovering on outstretched wings above each clerestory window.

Not all the medieval work on the interior survives. When Henry VIII broke with the Church in Rome, he set in motion more than a century of religious unrest, during which English churches were stripped of images—altars, sculpture, paintings, and stained glass—that were regarded as being "popish." Traces of a mural over the chancel arch remind us that these walls were originally painted, and remnants of stained glass now set in the south-aisle windows hint at what colored splendor once filled the windows. The wooden screen separating nave and chancel originally supported a gallery on which stood the rood, sculptures of the crucified Christ flanked by Mary and St. John. Its lowest tier still retains sixteen panels painted with figures of the saints, including St. Simon, who most anachronistically is wearing eyeglasses. It's a naïve yet touching detail, like the dragons and wild men carved in unexpected places, reminding us of the fundamental humanity of the artists who created these churches.

**9.28** Interior of the church of St. Agnes at Cawston, Norfolk, 14th–15th century.

Salisbury Cathedral presents the rare example of an English Gothic cathedral built almost entirely in a homogeneous style, Early English (Figs. 9.26b, 9.29–9.30). It was begun in 1220 on an entirely new site, the cathedral and town having been relocated from Old Sarum to be near more reliable water sources. Construction of the majority of the church progressed with remarkable rapidity and was completed by 1258, leaving only the soaring crossing tower and spire to be built from 1334 to 1380. Salisbury incorporates features from monastic plans, including the double transepts of Cluny III and the square east end of the Cistercians, in a long, orthogonal building that is unmistakably English. On the interior, quadripartite vaults rise from three-story nave elevations, yet the continuous vertical line exploited by the French has been replaced by a horizontal emphasis created by a string course under the triforium and another under the clerestory windows. Even the ribs of the vaults do not

extend down the wall but spring instead from wall corbels at the base of the clerestory. Surfaces are articulated by shafts and trim in black Purbeck marble, an English stone that is not actually marble but takes a highly polished finish. The exterior receives the same horizontal emphasis as the interior. Flying buttresses do not have a strong vertical character, and the walls are coursed in horizontal bands that extend across the west front. With all this horizontality, the 404-foot tower and spire provide the necessary vertical counterpoint, and their great weight has noticeably deformed the piers at the crossing. The cloisters (completed 1284) are fine examples of early Decorated

**9.29** Salisbury Cathedral, 1220–58; tower 1334–80.

A cathedral built almost entirely in Early English Gothic. Note the lancet windows of the west front and clerestory and the horizontal lines that carry across the exterior.

**9.30** Salisbury Cathedral nave, 1220–58.

This view shows how horizontality prevails on the interior as well as exterior. Notice how vaulting ribs do not extend as wall ribs down grouped piers, but spring instead from corbels set between the clerestory windows. Horizontal string courses along the triforium direct the eye down the length of the nave.

tracery, and off the east range one finds a lovely octagonal chapter house (begun 1263). Salisbury, like many English cathedrals, was both an abbey and a cathedral. Accommodations were accordingly needed for the brothers to meet daily to hear a chapter from the Rule of St. Benedict read and elaborated; hence the polygonal chapter house. In Romanesque monasteries, this was generally a square or rectangular room off the cloister, but in English cathedrals it becomes an occasion for elegance in vaulting an octagonal space of considerable size.

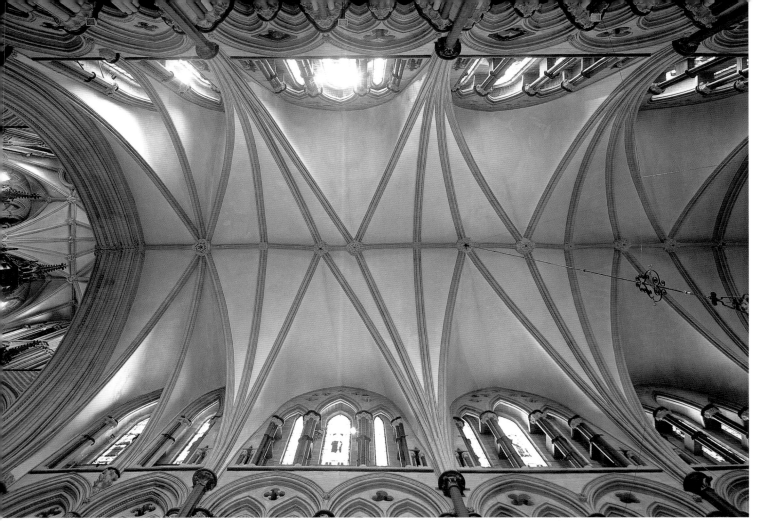

**9.31** Lincoln Cathedral choir vaults, 1192–1280.

Lincoln provides a wonderful sampler of vaulting. The transepts are sexpartite, while the nave features tierceron and lierne vaults of the Decorated period. Most unusual of all are the choir vaults, known as "crazy" vaults because their rib pattern is asymmetrical.

**9.32** Lincoln Cathedral, Angel Choir, 1192–1280.

The Angel Choir is the easternmost extension of the church, concluded with an enormous wall of stained glass.

## DECORATED AND PERPENDICULAR

At Lincoln Cathedral, a more complicated building history has resulted in a splendid combination of English Gothic periods (Figs. 9.26b, 9.31–9.32). The Norman church, damaged by an earthquake in 1185, survives today only in the lower portions of the west front. Rebuilding work, started in 1192, continued harmoniously through 1280. Construction began with the choir and eastern (lesser) transept, followed by the western (greater) transept, chapter house, nave, and west-front upper portions. The retrochoir (meaning "behind the choir" and here known as the Angel Choir) was begun in 1256. Concluded by an enormous eastern window, it was finished in 1280.

Lincoln offers several novel architectural features. Most obvious on the interior are the varied vaulting systems, including the tierceron vaults of the nave which link with an ornamented ridge rib. The "crazy" vaults of the choir are an asymmetrical experiment showing an original and free interpretation of established Gothic conventions. Throughout the cathedral, but above all in the Angel

**9.33** Ely Cathedral west front, begun 1081; lantern built 1322–36.

Most of the façade dates from the Norman period. The west front was originally symmetrical: a tower to balance the one on the right side no longer exists.

Choir, there is a wealth of elaborate trim in the form of Purbeck marble shafts, stiff-leaf capitals, and the sculpted angels that give the retrochoir its name. The Angel Choir clerestories and east-end window have tracery of the Decorated period. On the west front, a broad screen wall extends from the Norman work to increase the apparent width of the façade, obscuring the bases of the west-front towers, which define the actual width of the church.

Finally, the ten-sided chapter house with its bold flying buttresses is a departure from the usual octagonal form.

Ely Cathedral illustrates another aspect of medieval architecture in England, large-scale construction in timber (Figs. 9.33–9.34). Norman work predominates in the nave, which is covered by a timber roof; on the west front, a late Norman project designed with transepts but never finished; and in the transepts east of the nave. The original Norman choir was enlarged (1230–50) by an eastern extension of six additional bays, based on the Early English nave of Lincoln. The collapse of Ely's Norman crossing tower in 1322 provoked the most extraordinary

**9.34** Ely Cathedral lantern, 1322–36.

Notice how the octagon is turned 22.5 degrees to the axis of the nave. Wooden ceilings are treated on the interior as if they were stone vaults. The painted wooden ceiling of the Norman nave extends to the left side.

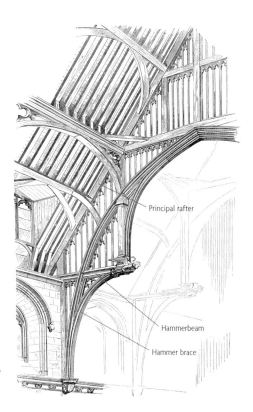

**9.35** Hammerbeam truss, Westminster Hall, London, 1394–1402.

A hammerbeam is a short, horizontal member attached to the foot of a principal rafter. Notice how the wooden assembly comes to rest on the masonry wall, with the hammerbeam partially supported by the hammer brace.

construction. The church foundations were judged insufficient to support a masonry reconstruction, so the tower was replaced by a lantern in wood, the design of which also increased the light and usable space at the crossing. The designer of this masterpiece of medieval engineering was William Hurley, the King's Carpenter. He used eight giant oak posts—sixty-three feet long, forty inches thick, and thirty-two inches wide—for the vertical members of the octagonal tower, which has a diameter of sixty-nine feet. These are supported on **hammerbeams** (Fig. 9.35) tied to the masonry crossing piers. The octagon itself is set at 22.5 degrees to the axis of the nave, providing a spatial contrast at the crossing. Most of the vaulting of the octagon is wood made to look like stone; the actual structural members are visible only if one climbs into the lantern via the access stair.

Ely's exceptional crossing tower is not the only example of English monumental timber construction. A number of late medieval hammerbeam roofs survive, the grandest being Westminster Hall in London (now incorporated into the Houses of Parliament, a nineteenth-century building). The hall itself dates back to the early 1100s, when it was constructed as an aisled space for royal banquets. By the late Middle Ages, a covering not requiring intermediate supports was desired, so in 1394–1402 the hall was roofed, using hammerbeams that are supported on the older walls (Fig. 9.34). Hammerbeam construction is actually a series of successive short cantilevers that enable builders to roof a span wider than the length of available timbers. The craftsmanship behind the hammerbeam roofs, with their interlocking pegged joints and elegantly carved finials and angels, is a testimonial to the technical skills and artistry of medieval carpenters.

As an example of Late Gothic masonry construction in England, the chapel at King's College, Cambridge, deserves attention for its exceptional fan vaults designed by John Wastell (Figs. 9.26b, 9.36). Begun in 1446 with donations by Henry VI and completed by 1515 with contributions from Henry VIII, the chapel was designed for use in an era when the sermon had become an important aspect of worship services, so it was built with a simpler plan and smaller area to reduce reverberation so that speech could be better understood. Medieval monastic chant is enhanced by long reverberation times, but the spoken

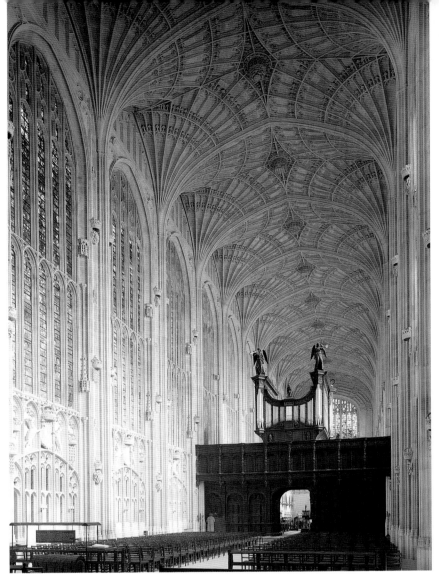

**9.36** King's College Chapel interior, Cambridge, 1446–1515.

The fan vaults make this glass box a masterpiece of late medieval architecture. As in the Sainte-Chapelle, the walls have been reduced to glass screens set in a skeletal stone frame.

**9.37** St. George Church nave and aisle, Nördlingen, 1427–ca. 1500.

This is a hall church, where the nave and aisle vaults are virtually the same height. Grey stone ribs form intricate geometric patterns on the plastered surface of the vaults.

word is virtually incomprehensible in the same space. Medieval churches still in use for church services employ electronic amplification systems that help cancel out reverberation. King's College Chapel is basically rectangular in plan, with Perpendicular tracery in the large windows and majestic fan vaults overhead. The ornate organ loft atop the choir screen divides the space into two parts, one for townspeople and the other for students. The chapel is contemporary with the High Renaissance in Italy, and the woodwork of the choir screen contains classical detail in what is otherwise a late medieval building.

## GERMAN, CZECH, AND ITALIAN GOTHIC
### HALL CHURCHES

Just as the Romanesque developed regional variants as it responded to local traditions and preferences, so too did the Gothic. German builders initially used French cathedrals as models, occasionally importing master masons, but they were soon creating their own versions of the Gothic style. Particularly characteristic of German Gothic is the **hall church**, a type where the vaults of both the nave and aisles are essentially the same height. (Recall that St. Savin-sur-Gartempe has been presented as a Romanesque hall church.) This is the design used at St. George in Nördlingen (1427–ca. 1500), a church without transepts but which has aisles on either side of the six bays of the nave that continue up the five bays of the choir to a chapel at the eastern polygonal end (Figs. 9.37–9.38). A massive tower on axis anchors the western front. On the interior, the structure is clearly expressed: gray stone cylindrical columns with attached shaft moldings support a vaulted ceiling where ribs describe intricate patterns. Aisle windows, set between the buttress piers, are treated as punched openings, but they are tall and without colored glass, so they provide ample illumination. Mies van der Rohe, the twentieth-century German-American architect who advocated "skin-and-bones" buildings in glass and steel, found much to admire in such German Gothic hall churches.

**9.38** St. George Church vaults, Nördlingen, 1427–ca. 1500.

This view shows the pattern created by the ribs.

St. Barbara at Kutná Hora in the Czech Republic is an extraordinary example of Late Gothic with a complex history and form. The town's economy was fueled by silver mines and the king of Bohemia's royal mint. Construction began in 1388 on the model of a French Gothic cathedral with eight radiating chapels, perhaps designed by Johann Parler, but work stopped in about 1400 and was not resumed until 1481, after the turmoil of the Hussite Wars had subsided. In 1489, Matej Rejsek completed the choir more or less according to the original design. A new master, the royal architect Benedikt Ried, assumed direction of the work in 1512, and in building the nave, he departed from the basilican scheme by building the nave piers as freestanding elements to support the vault of a hall church, with well-lit galleries over the side aisles. Intricate net vaulting in the choir was joined in the nave by flowing ribs that emerge near the piers to swirl into six-petal forms (Fig. 9.39). Whereas the vaulting ribs at Nördlingen were defined within each bay, the pattern on the thin shell vault here exists almost independently of a bay structure and creates an extraordinary sense of weightlessness. The exterior wall with its flying buttresses gives little hint of the spatial surprises within, although the three tent-like tetrahedrons that comprise the roof are unexpected. Ried probably used these more to reduce wind loads and economize on construction material than for exotic effect, but their profile against the sky is unforgettable. Funding ran out once the nave vaults were complete in about 1557, leaving the west front to be finished in the nineteenth century.

**9.39** St. Barbara Church nave vaults, Kutná Hora, 1388–1512.

The supporting piers rise as unbraced shafts above the inner aisles to vaults that match the height of the nave. Large gallery windows flood the interior with light, illuminating the flower-like ribs that flow gracefully across the vaulting shell.

## ITALIAN GOTHIC VARIATIONS

Italian designers modified the Gothic style to fit local conditions, and the differences one observes from northern European versions of the style should be understood as adaptations that demonstrate the flexibility of the Gothic to accommodate varying interpretations. Given Italy's bright skies, large windows were not necessary to provide illumination inside buildings. Italian Romanesque builders were proficient in **domical vault** construction that reduced lateral thrust and thus required less in the way of buttressing. Cultural esthetics predisposed Italians to prefer internal tie-rods instead of visible external buttressing, so flying buttresses appear only rarely. (Tension ties also make sense in earthquake-prone areas.) Many of the religious orders desired churches that maintained a sense of openness and visibility, qualities that could be achieved using the Gothic.

Gothic architecture first came to Italy with Cistercian monks, who had slipped easily into the style after absorbing the architectural sensibilities of Bernard of Clairvaux. Other monastic orders, particularly the mendicant Dominicans and Franciscans who came to minister to growing urban populations, also tended to build in Gothic. Among the earliest of their buildings was the great Dominican church of S. Maria Novella in Florence (1279–ca. 1310), built to a plan that would seem familiar to a Cistercian (Fig. 9.40a). The nave consists of nearly square bays and a square crossing and chancel. Four square chapels opening off the transept give the church structural clarity. Plain wall surfaces contrast with polychrome stonework outlining arches of the arcade, transverse nave arches, and vaulting ribs in the nave and aisles (Fig. 9.41).

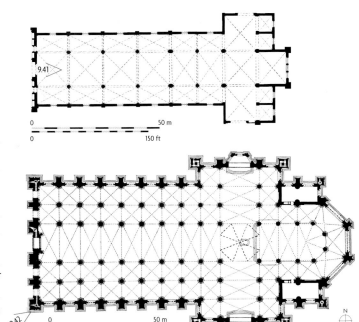

**9.40a** Plan of S. Maria Novella, Florence, 1279–ca. 1310.

There is a Cistercian-like simplicity to this plan, which was built for the Dominican Order. Its ribbed domical vaults are braced by buttresses concealed under aisle roofs, thereby avoiding the need for flying buttresses.

**9.40b** Plan of Milan Cathedral, 1387–ca. 1572.

This is the largest Gothic church in Italy, and its structure is based on the cross section of Bourges Cathedral, where pairs of aisles help to brace the high nave vaults. Master builders from France, Germany, and Italy were consulted concerning its design and construction.

**9.41** S. Maria Novella interior, Florence, 1279–ca. 1310.

This view shows the polychrome ribs of the vaults. Notice the small roundels in the clerestory.

**9.42** Milan Cathedral buttresses and pinnacles, 1387–1572; 19th century.

The west front blends classical and Gothic motifs. Flying buttresses were added in the nineteenth century as the exterior was completed.

By constructing ribbed domical vaults in the nave, the builders minimized lateral thrust to the point where support from the high aisle vaults and buttresses concealed under the aisle roofs was sufficient to brace the structure. A connection to the classical orders is evident in the half-columns engaged in the slender piers of the arcade. Aisle windows are small, and the clerestory consists of modest circular openings punched near the top of each bay. A large triple window in the chancel wall provides the strongest direct light. The internal effect is open and clear, well suited to a church for preaching to a congregation. We will encounter S. Maria Novella again in the Renaissance chapter, when its façade is completed.

At Todi, the Franciscans built S. Fortunato (1292–early 1400s) to a hall church design. Here the highest point (crown) of the vaults is uniform across the church, unlike the billowing ceiling compartments created by domical vaults and transverse arches in S. Maria Novella. Without lower aisles to counter the vaulting thrust, the builders here constructed braces from the exterior wall to the nave piers in order to stabilize the building. As at S. Maria Novella, the nave bays are essentially square. Slender half-column shafts on the piers align with graceful vaulting ribs, giving a sense of considerable spaciousness to the interior. On both sides of the nave, chapels for use by the brothers are set between transverse buttressing walls. Tall windows above the chapels light the interior, complemented by illumination from five windows in the polygonal choir.

Italy's largest and most ambitious Gothic church is Milan Cathedral, begun in 1387 and not finished until 1858, although it was essentially complete by 1572. Its plan features a broad nave with double aisles, an aisled transept, and a polygonal apse with ambulatory (Fig. 9.40b). The aisle bays are square in plan, while the nave bays are rectangular. The structure follows the model of Bourges Cathedral, where the aisles rise in a roughly triangular

section to brace the nave vault, and the height of the nave, at 157 feet, is virtually equal to that of Beauvais Cathedral. Remarkably, it was constructed without flying buttresses, the ones on the cathedral today having been added in the nineteenth century.

Less than two years after construction began, decisions of the master builder Simone da Orsenigo were being second-guessed by consultants engaged by the client. Italian master builders, artists, and mathematicians gave opinions regarding theory, design, and technology, and building experts from France and Germany were summoned to give their views as well. Because some of the debate that ensued was transcribed (albeit by persons who did not fully understand what was being discussed) and these written records still exist, documents relating to Milan Cathedral provide an extraordinary insight into the variety of Late Gothic theory and practice, and the contrasting approaches to art and science. Opinions held by these experienced builders and theoreticians reflect differences in regional traditions and esthetics: the Italians favored broad proportions, the French argued for the particular vaulting techniques that they employed, and the Germans advocated soaring verticality. Consultations continued for more than a decade as the work was assigned first to one and then another master. In the end, proportions advocated by the Italian mathematician Gabrielle Stornoloco were used: the cathedral's section, based on an equilateral triangle, establishes the height of the nave at three times the height of the outermost aisle and one-and-a-half times the height of the inner aisle. Italian masons, accustomed to building within the load requirements of domical vaults, used them in the aisles and in a modified form in the nave, reinforcing the vaults with strong iron tie-rods. This approach was foreign to the French and German masters, but it worked.

The resulting building is unlike most other Italian Gothic churches, lacking a sense of spatial openness

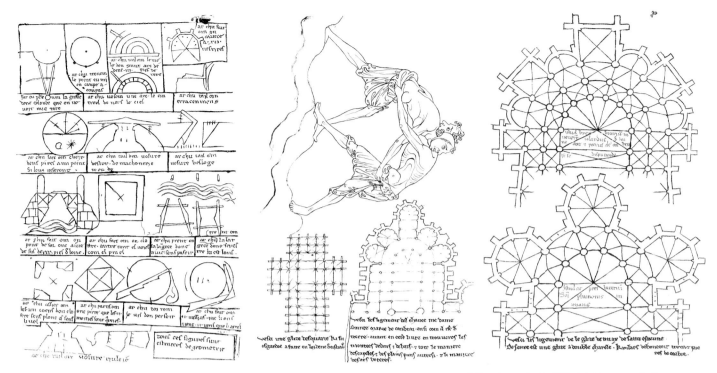

**9.43a**  The notebook of Villard de Honnecourt (left), ca. 1225–50.

Villard collected drawings from various places, intending to pass his work on to others. This page shows methods for obtaining the solution to geometric problems, important skills for medieval builders.

**9.43b**  The notebook of Villard de Honnecourt (center), ca. 1225–50.

This sketch combines wrestling men with the scheme for a Cistercian church and the plans for the choir at Reims Cathedral. Villard's drawings are the earliest record we have of a medieval builder's graphic representation of buildings.

**9.43c**  The notebook of Villard de Honnecourt (right), ca. 1225–50.

Here Villard drew two Cistercian church choirs. Some scholars think that he was involved in rebuilding the choirs of Cistercian churches to more elaborate designs. Notice that these plans show wall thickness and vaulting ribs.

because of the bulk and close spacing of its piers. The volume is enormous, and as the small clerestory windows are filled with stained glass, even in full Italian sunshine little light enters the nave. Windows in the choir provide brilliance, however, drawing the visitor to the liturgical center of the church. Much of the exterior is post-medieval, but the work was carried out to the very end within the Gothic esthetic (Fig. 9.42). The exterior of Milan Cathedral is a veritable forest of carved marble and spiky pinnacles from the vantage point of the roof level, which is accessible.

## MEDIEVAL CONSTRUCTION

Milan Cathedral is exceptional in having preserved documents relating to its design and construction. For most of the great medieval building campaigns, the absence of written or graphic material limits our ability to make definitive statements about the nature of medieval architectural practice or construction procedures. Nevertheless, historians have analyzed the materials that are available—a few sketchbooks, isolated drawings and preserved tracing floors, works accounts, monastic chronicles, and the evidence provided by the buildings themselves—to piece together some understanding of building in the medieval world.

A building designer in the Middle Ages was usually called a master builder, the title of architect not being used until late in the period. The master builder's training would have included the acquisition of language and mathematical skills in a grammar school run by the local priest or monastery, followed by apprenticeship in one of the building trades (carpentry or masonry) at about age thirteen. The apprentice would be taught all aspects of the craft, including theoretical matters and practical applications, especially the construction of arches and vaults using centering (Fig. 9.44). After three to seven years thus spent under the direction of a master craftsman, the apprentice would be certified as a journeyman, a worker qualified to hire himself out for a daily wage. For several years, he would work on different building sites, traveling about and keeping a sketchbook while gaining practical experience. To advance to the level of master he would be required to present a masterpiece—either an actual building or a finely executed model—to the masters of his craft guild, who would evaluate his fitness to direct journeymen and teach apprentices. Only the most capable and experienced master craftsmen would acquire the title of master builder.

A collection of drawings made by Villard de Honnecourt, who was active ca. 1225–50, constitutes the earliest surviving documentation from the medieval period (Figs. 9.43a,b,c). His notebook includes a wide range of observations and sketches: geometry problems and their solutions; timber roof trusses; sculpture and carved ornament; nature sketches; church plans; sketches of details

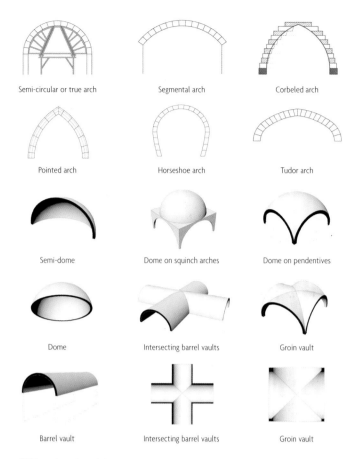

Semi-circular or true arch　　Segmental arch　　Corbeled arch

Pointed arch　　Horseshoe arch　　Tudor arch

Semi-dome　　Dome on squinch arches　　Dome on pendentives

Dome　　Intersecting barrel vaults　　Groin vault

Barrel vault　　Intersecting barrel vaults　　Groin vault

**9.44** Arch, vault, and dome types.

Understanding masonry vaulting is crucial to understanding most permanent construction from the time of ancient Rome to the development of iron, steel, and reinforced concrete in the nineteenth century.

from cathedrals at Laon, Chartres, and Reims; machines and devices; and such esoteric information as how to tame a lion. Other than what is contained in his notebook, little is known of Villard or his works. He claims to have traveled from the Low Countries to Hungary and back, and some historians surmise that he may have been employed by the Cistercians, perhaps in rebuilding **chancels** in the more elaborate Gothic style employed after the death of Bernard of Chairvaux. Others believe that he was merely a collector of drawings with a particular interest in details. From an inscription on the opening pages of the book, it is obvious that Villard intended his collection to be used by others. He identifies geometry as the basis of drawing, claims to present advice on masonry and carpentry, and asks that readers remember him and pray for his soul. His drawings show the earliest known representations of interior and exterior elevations (for Reims Cathedral) and also contain architectural plans with wall thicknesses specified, unlike the single-line walls marked on the Plan of St. Gall. Whatever his role in the building trades, Villard's drawings show that architectural ideas traveled as workers moved from site to site and also through the exchange of sketches and notations.

Geometry was indeed the theoretical core of medieval architecture. Following Roman practice, the master established basic building dimensions by a module and derived all other measurements from this standard through the manipulation of compass and straightedge. (Medieval people used Roman numerals that were uncongenial for all but the simplest arithmetical calculations.) The "secrets" of the masons were primarily principles of plane and solid geometry and knowledge of how to use triangles, squares, pentagons, and other figures to generate proportional lines, most of which have dimensions represented by irrational numbers. Just as beauty in medieval chant was defined by proper relationships in the intervals between musical tones, so beauty in architecture was assured if the proportions of major elements and minor details were in geometric harmony.

Building a church of any size required money to pay skilled craftsmen. Masters and their workshops moved around according to the availability of construction funds, so it is sometimes possible to trace specific crews from project to project. The idea that churches were built either by monks or by volunteer laymen is a misconception. The overall size of the church and its major features would be determined by the master builder in consultation with church officials, and then professional quarrymen, masons, carpenters, sculptors, glaziers, and tilers would be employed to execute the work. Depending on the wealth of the client, a major cathedral could be built in as little as thirty years, as was the case at Chartres, or construction could drag on in discontinuous campaigns stretching over centuries.

## MEDIEVAL HOUSES AND CASTLES

Our consideration of Romanesque and Gothic architecture has necessarily concentrated on the design of religious buildings, primarily because the Church commanded the best design talent and greatest financial resources. Medieval buildings remaining for study are from 400 to 1100 years old now, and only the best-constructed architecture can be expected to last that long. In the Middle Ages, churches formed the main group of buildings erected with great care, so inevitably they comprise the bulk of medieval architectural history.

### HOUSING

Enough secular structures survive from the Middle Ages to give a general idea of the buildings in which ordinary people lived, and archaeological investigation is providing more information all the time. Rural houses of peasant families were simple, providing minimal shelter for cooking and sleeping. These buildings used local materials, mostly earth, wood, and thatch, and basic construction techniques, as they were probably built by the families that inhabited them. The combined house-barn or longhouse is a type that was widely used throughout the medieval period (Fig. 9.45). It was built on a rectangular plan entered through doorways placed opposite one

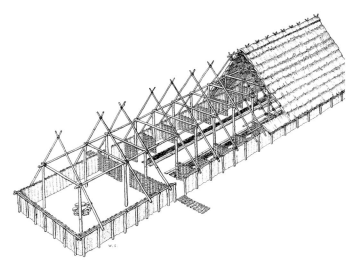

**9.45** Reconstruction view of an early medieval longhouse, Bremerhaven, Germany.

Entrances set on opposite sides of the long walls divide the building into two parts, one with a hearth for cooking and warmth, and the other with stalls for animals.

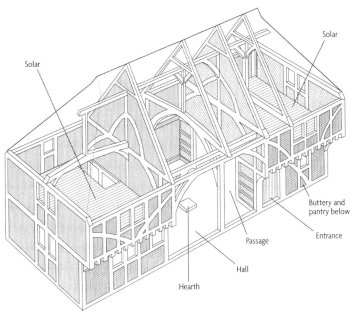

**9.46** A medieval manor house.

The hall was the main living space, provided with a central hearth for warmth. Meals would be taken here in common with household servants and retainers.

another on the long sides, thus providing cross-ventilation and dividing the building into two sections. One end focused on an open hearth, around which the family gathered, and sometimes there was a second chamber partitioned off for sleeping or storage. The remaining section housed livestock, whose body heat helped warm the interior. As the building lacked a chimney, smoke would filter into the high volume overhead, where it could exit through gaps left in the gable ends without igniting the thatch of the roof. Peter Brueghel the Elder depicts just such a house in the background of *The Birdnester*, painted in 1568, which indicates that these rural structures were even then common sights in the countryside.

Land-owning families who were several steps further up the social ladder might inhabit a house (without animals) divided into a hall and solar, a private room on an upper floor. The hall was the major gathering and entertaining space (Fig. 9.46), warmed by a fire or central hearth, and the solar was a more private space reserved for the family. By the late Middle Ages, these basic rooms were usually improved by the addition of a buttery (for storage of drinks and other foods to be kept cool), a pantry (for storage of dry foodstuffs), and a passage screening circulation space to these storage rooms and the kitchen, which was a separate structure. The solar might move to an upper story and have its own stair for greater privacy. Since the nobleman fed his guests and retinue of servants in the hall, meals were important occasions for displaying hospitality and wealth. (It is ironic that the hall in modern houses has dwindled to an entryway or connecting passage, when once it was the major living space.)

Houses built in towns were more compact, often including several floors to conserve available land. The structure would again be wood, the roof would be thatch, and the entire building would accordingly be very combustible. Devastating fires are frequent events in the chronicles of medieval cities. Larger towns eventually regulated building by insisting on masonry construction and tile or slate roofs to reduce the spread of fire. Nevertheless,

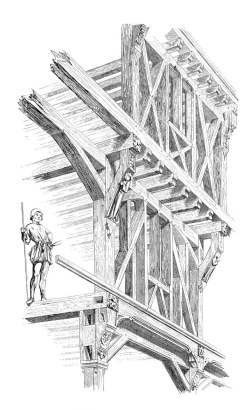

**9.47** Brace heavy timber frames (half-timbering) used in medieval construction.

Notice the slight cantilevers or jetties that extend the floor space on the upper levels. Along narrow medieval streets, these overhangs would reduce available light.

some wooden dwellings survive in England and on the European continent to illustrate half-timber construction (Fig. 9.47). Buildings so designated have a heavy timber frame, exposed on the exterior, which is completed by non-structural wattle and daub, plaster, brick, or other

**9.48** Medieval house, Cluny, 12th century.

This townhouse is typical of many medieval urban residences, combining workshop or commercial space on the ground floor with the owner's living quarters on the floor above.

**9.49** Tower houses, S. Gimignano, 13th–14th centuries.

In many northern Italian towns medieval families constructed towers on masonry houses out of a sense of competition or perhaps for defense. In S. Gimignano, they were apparently also used to hang lengths of dyed cloth.

infill. Whether of masonry or timber, town houses would typically have a shop on the ground floor and the dwelling apartments on the floors above (Fig. 9.48). The kitchen would be on the ground floor separated by a small light court from the rear of the shop to keep its odors and fire hazards away from the main part of the house. Italian cities tended to have houses built in brick or stone, with tile roofs, and a number of Italian towns preserve substantial numbers of medieval masonry houses. S. Gimignano is particularly notable for the towers that survive on some houses (Fig. 9.49). While tower houses elsewhere may well have been constructed for defense, their likely function was drying lengths of fabric away from sunlight, a necessary process to fix the yellow dye used here.

## CASTLES

Fortified residences or castles were homes of the nobility, although they probably offered little more in the way of creature comforts than the homes of the more modest folk. Castles were constructed for defense, guarding strategic roads or rivers, and they also served as administrative centers for the surrounding territory. The earliest such fortifications were wooden, and only post-holes survive for archaeologists to base their conjectural restorations on. More easily visible are the earthworks that accompanied the early wooden castles, **motte and bailey** (mound and yard) being the most common form for these (Fig. 9.50). For a better command of the surrounding countryside, castles were constructed atop a mound (the motte), based whenever possible on an existing hillock and enlarged by fill from a ditch, or **moat**, dug around the base. Between the ditch and the motte was an open area (the bailey) that provided room for the more temporary accommodation of castle retainers—servants, craftsmen, soldiers, horses, and the like. Enclosures of wooden palings, similar to the palisades erected in American frontier forts in the eigh-

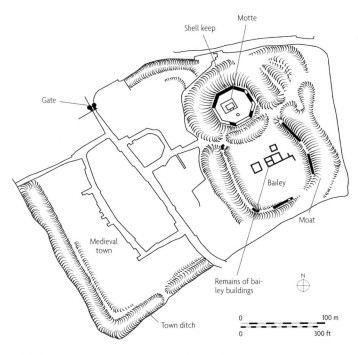

9.50 Plan and section through a motte-and-bailey castle, Castle Acre, Norfolk, 12th century.

The castle buildings are long gone, but the earthworks survive to show the motte or mound and the moat that surrounded the bailey or courtyard associated with the mound.

9.51 The White Tower (Tower of London), London, 1078–80.

Its three floors are vaulted to make them fireproof, and the roof served as a fighting platform. A Norman chapel occupies the rounded section on the third level.

teenth and nineteenth centuries, were built around the bailey, and a watchtower might protect the sole gateway. Hundreds of motte-and-bailey sites are detectable today, the outlines of their mounds and surrounding ditches still visible in aerial photographs.

The pace of castle construction in England increased markedly after the Norman invasion of 1066. William the Conqueror may have brought pre-cut wooden timbers on his ships to build a castle on the coast at Hastings, for his fortification there was completed in the very short time-span of two weeks. The Bayeaux Tapestry depicts peasants digging the ditch and piling dirt for the motte. (The site of the castle at Hastings has since been claimed by the sea.) When William came to London, however, he desired something more permanent to signify his jurisdiction over the most important city in the country, and he was granted a site on the eastern edge of the Roman wall surrounding the City of London, where he constructed the White Tower (Figs. 9.51–9.52), now better known as the Tower of London (1078–80). It is a three-story masonry **keep**, or stronghold, basically rectangular in plan, with a semicircular projection reflecting the apse of a chapel constructed within at the third level. In the years since its construction, turret roofs of the corner towers have changed its profile, and layers of enclosing walls and ancillary buildings have been added around William's castle, but the massive strength of the original Norman keep remains.

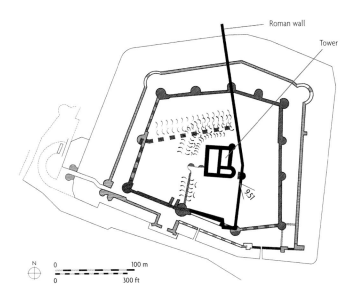

9.52 Plan of the Tower of London, 1078–80.

This view shows the ancillary walls and moat constructed since William's day. When first built, the Tower sat just inside the Roman wall around London.

**9.53** Carcassonne, built 800–1300.

Carcassonne is a medieval French city with fortifications dating back to the seventh century. These early fortifications were extensively repaired and provided with a second set of walls from 1248 to 1290.

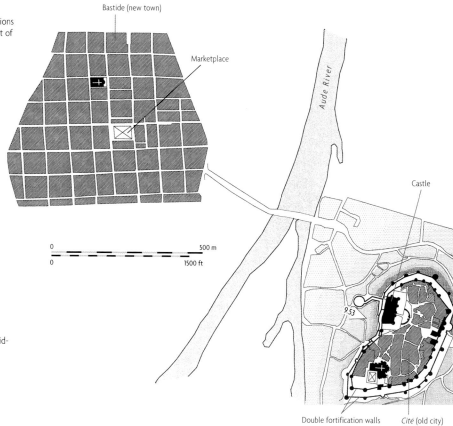

**9.54** Plan of Carcassonne, built 800–1300.

This plan shows the fortified *cité* (*lower right*) and the grid-plan bastide that was established in 1248 across the river Aude. When the second set of walls was planned for the *cité*, the hilltop became essentially a military camp.

## MEDIEVAL CITIES

There is an obvious connection between medieval castles and cities, for both relied on well-built fortifications to withstand attack, and they are frequently found together. Most medieval cities were provided with a solidly constructed wall with lockable gates that in ordinary times enabled the municipality to collect taxes from merchants entering the city. As the innumerable armed struggles characteristic of the Middle Ages usually had the capture of towns as their objective, the town walls served important defensive purposes as well. Fortunately for cities, medieval warfare was seldom a sustained event with large armies, and weapons before the introduction of gunpowder and metal cannonballs in about 1400 were rather primitive: battering rams, catapults, siege ladders or towers, and bows and arrows. Fire and pestilence could also be used for strategic advantage. A well-built fortification, punctu-

ated by towers, provided defenders with a platform from which to return catapult and arrow fire and to dump stones or boiling liquids on persons trying to undermine or scale the wall. The most common form of attack was the siege, in which attackers tried to cut off supplies to the town and thereby force the inhabitants into surrender.

Experience gained over time suggested that the most defensible wall was one protected by projecting towers of cylindrical rather than rectangular shape, equipped with archer slits that would allow defenders to shoot almost parallel to the section of wall between towers. **Moats** or ditches provided useful protection, and a double set of walls made attack that much more difficult. Most of these innovations can be seen at Carcassonne, a strategic site that had been fortified successively by the Gallo-Romans, the Visigoths, and local counts before Louis IX of France gained control of the site in 1248 (Figs. 9.53–9.54). Louis's intention was to make the city an impregnable

**9.55** Carcassonne walls, 1248–90.

Notice the square holes left near the tops of towers for the construction of timber hourds, projecting galleries that could be quickly erected for defense.

**9.56** Plans of four bastide towns, southern France, 1220–1375.

Note the tendency to provide a square arcaded marketplace at the center of town. In most cases, the church is set away from the square, where commerce was most important.

stronghold as he sought to bring the south of France under royal control. In addition to repairing and strengthening existing work in the old fortified town (the *cité*), he constructed a second ring of towers and walls (Fig. 9.55). The resulting fortifications were so formidable that the city was never seriously attacked thereafter. Carcassonne's strategic importance waned with the medieval period, but when there was a proposal to pull the crumbling walls down in the nineteenth century, preservationists intervened and restored the battlements and tower roofs to the condition seen today. It is one of relatively few French cities to have its medieval defenses intact.

To encourage commerce and trade without overcrowding the *cité*, which had essentially become a military garrison, Louis IX developed a new town in the valley below Carcassonne. Its regular grid plan organized around a central marketplace contrasts sharply with the irregular layout of the hilltop city, which like many medieval towns grew without regulation or advance planning. This lower town is in fact one of about 500 new town foundations known as **bastides** that were made in the south of France in the period between 1220 and about 1370. The motive behind establishing new cities was primarily economic: the bitter campaign against the Albigensian heresy had devastated the countryside, and as several parties—the kings of France and England, along with local counts—had claims to the territory, they sought to encourage settlement through the granting of freedoms and economic privileges associated with town residence. Not all bastides were built to the same plan, but many share certain characteristics: an orthogonal street layout, a central market square (often surrounded by arcaded buildings) and town hall, and uniform lot sizes for houses. The church is usually relegated to a side location. Monpazier, founded by Edward I in 1284, is often cited as the "typical" bastide, but its actual layout is not so regular as the idealized plan would suggest. The plans of Revel, Mirande, and Villefranche-de-Rouergue illustrate some of the variations found in bastide layouts (Fig. 9.56). While the architecture of bastide towns is usually not extraordinary, the clarity conferred by the plan creates a unifying harmony that

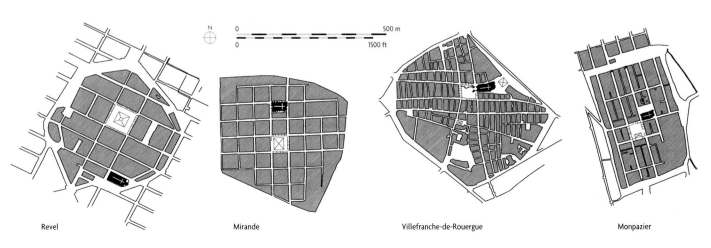

Revel          Mirande          Villefranche-de-Rouergue          Monpazier

N    0 ———————— 500 m
     0 ———————— 1500 ft

**9.57** Monpazier market square, ca. 1300.

The architecture here, as in many bastides, is not exceptional, but the clear urban pattern and use of arcades around the square gives these cities a strong sense of urbanism.

makes many bastides small gems of urban design (Fig. 9.57).

A similar colonizing intent in central Europe resulted in the founding of hundreds of regularly planned towns under German influence in Poland, Slovakia, and Hungary. Trade was the prime objective, because the founder collected sales taxes from commerce, so the cities encouraged settlement with charters based on the Law of Magdeburg that guaranteed citizens freedoms of the market. One particularly handsome example of a deliberate foundation under Magdeburg customs may be seen in Kraków, the historic capital of Poland, where an old castle and related settlement predated the new foundation created with the granting of a Great Charter in 1257 (Figs. 9.58–9.59). An area immediately north of the built area was laid out around a major market square, 600 feet on a side, with uniform building plots marked on the surrounding square blocks. The only exceptions to the grid were two existing churches, which remained where they were. In time, a substantial cloth hall, large and small weigh houses, market stalls, and the city hall were built in the market square. Fortifications added in the fourteenth century linked the town and castle. Although few medieval houses survive, the original street layout and plot divisions continue to govern the fabric of the historic core.

Italian towns and cities experienced a slightly different situation during the medieval period. There, the commercial activity on which all urban life depends never completely ceased in the period following the decline of Rome, although urban services, most notably the public water supply, tended to fall below standards established under Roman jurisdiction. Medieval Italian communes participated vigorously in the revival of long-distance trade that

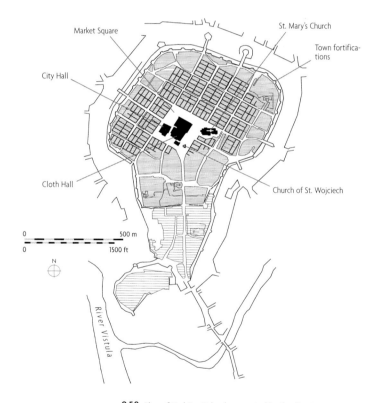

**9.58** Plan of Kraków, Poland, generated by the Great Charter of 1257.

The orderly town plan (shown hatched) includes a large market square. Building lots were laid out to maximize frontage on important streets and around the square.

characterized the later Middle Ages. Larger city-republics functioned as independent states, controlling smaller communities in the region and squabbling with other city-states for rights to border areas. At Siena, a medieval town formed by combining three separate ridgetop settlements, citizens celebrated the merger by building a new urban

**9.59** Kraków market square, showing St. Mary's Church (*left*) and the Cloth Hall.

Textile merchants were very important, and their trading hall had stalls on the ground floor and rooms for the cloth guild upstairs.

**9.60** Palazzo Pubblico, Siena, 1298.

The slender brick belltower, one of the tallest in all Italy, serves as a vertical marker for the town hall.

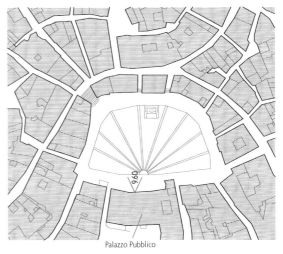

Palazzo Pubblico

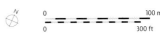

**9.61** Plan of the Campo, Siena, 1298.

The fan-shaped piazza slopes down to the Palazzo Pubblico, set at the lowest part of the site. While this is often not the best location for a prominent building, the citizens of Siena made sure that all buildings fronting on the Campo were compatible with the town hall.

**9.62** Doge's Palace, Venice, 1309–1424.

This is a splendid example of the Gothic style adapted in Venice. Mixed with exotic influences from the East, the Gothic in Venetian hands becomes a lacy filigree to adorn buildings adjacent to the water.

**9.63** Ca' D'Oro, Venice, begun 1421.

This is an exceptionally fine merchant's house facing onto the Grand Canal. Its name, House of Gold, came from the gilding that was once applied to the exterior detail. Even without the gold, its lace-like arch tracery and marble walls shimmer in the light reflected off the Grand Canal.

center on a marshy field (campo) where the ridges joined (Figs. 9.60–9.61). The town hall or Palazzo Pubblico (1298) dominates the bowl-shaped open area, which is an irregular fan-shaped **piazza**. Even though it has no regular geometry, the Campo was deliberately shaped and governed by municipal regulations that required façades of surrounding structures to harmonize with the town hall. The Palazzo Pubblico is nominally Gothic in style, but elements of the style have been used more for surface articulation than for structure. Crenellations and **machicolations** atop the building and its slender belltower are likewise ornaments in the modern style rather than serious attempts at fortification.

In Venice, a maritime republic that dominated trade between Europe and the Byzantine Empire, a decorative variant of the Gothic developed in which northern European features were blended with exotic influences from the East. The result is an airy, delicate architecture animated by the shimmering light reflected by the city's canals. The Doge's Palace is perhaps the most famous example of Venetian Gothic (Fig. 9.62). A blocky structure with an open courtyard, it has a solid exterior wall resting on two stories of open arcades. Pink and white diaper patterns enliven and lighten the visual impact of solid wall, so that it does not appear to overload the delicate filigree of the arcades below. The Ca' d'Oro illustrates Venetian Gothic applied to the traditional merchant's house, with its central section of large arcaded windows that open onto the **grand salon**, the major living space that extends the full depth of the house (Fig. 9.63).

In general, however, the Gothic was strongly identified with northern Europe and never attained great significance in Italy. By the fifteenth century a new artistic movement, based on the ideals of classical antiquity, was developing in the urban centers in the north of the country. In the following centuries this new style, the Renaissance, would spread to the rest of Europe. In isolated communities, however, medieval building traditions continued with little change until the nineteenth century, and medieval house forms are reflected in the earliest American architecture, particularly in New England and Virginia. There is even an American church built in 1682, St. Luke's in Isle of Wight County, Virginia, that is considered part of the Gothic survival. In the nineteenth century, the Gothic Revival originated with reform-minded Victorians as a second flowering of medieval art and architecture.

## CONCLUSIONS ABOUT ARCHITECTURAL IDEAS

It is useful to speak of the Gothic architecture conceived in the Ile-de-France as a "system" in which pointed arches, ribbed vaults, and flying buttresses, their effects enhanced by stained glass, were made to interact structurally and esthetically. Obsessed with what he believed to be the mystical quality of light, Abbot Suger at St. Denis near Paris called upon his builders to erect a sunlight-filled masonry-defined space for the new choir of his church. Their experiments set in motion an inquiry into the nature of stone as a medium for erecting a framework of slender vertical supports, arching lateral stabilizers, and thin-webbed, ribbed ceilings as an alternative to the thick, continuous walls and heavy barrel and groin vaults of the

Romanesque. Within the development of Western architecture, there has been no more dramatic change in the conception of form and space.

Experiments proceeded along various lines. At Notre-Dame Cathedral in Paris, masons erected six-part nave vaults atop walls rising in four stories: nave arcade, gallery, triforium, and clerestory. At not-too-distant Notre-Dame Cathedral in Chartres, builders changed to four-part nave vaults and a three-story elevation of arcade, triforium, and a much taller clerestory. It was this larger-windowed system that carried the day in northern France. Proving that decisions were being made on the basis of appearance as much as, if not more than, structural logic, St. Etienne Cathedral in Bourges received a triangular cross section that was more efficient, therefore more economically built, than either Paris's or Chartres's, but its model was largely ignored. French churchmen continued to push builders toward the construction of ever-wider, ever-taller vaults until the collapse of the choir at Beauvais defined the limits of thirteenth-century masonry technology. The much smaller Sainte-Chapelle in Paris—its upper level akin to a cathedral shorn of all but its nave core—became a jewel box of stained-glass-tinted light admitted through virtually floor-to-ceiling windows with rayonnant tracery.

In fog-shrouded England, builders never considered light to be the essence of their chauvinistic interpretation of the Gothic. Here, churches have typically been categorized as Early English, Decorated, and Perpendicular. While most English cathedrals are agglomerations from more than one of these periods, Salisbury presents itself as pure Early English. Orthogonal in plan, including the choir, as was the English (by way of Cistercian) preference, it has four-part ribbed vaults, though the ribs do not extend visually down to the floor in the form of colonnettes, as in the French system, meaning a much lessened sense of verticality. Dominant instead are receding layers of arched openings at the nave, triforium, and low-clerestory levels that feature a rich patterning of severely molded arches springing from their own colonnettes. Traceable as far back as the nave at Durham, this English fascination for textured surfaces is also vividly displayed on Salisbury's west façade.

No cathedral in the Decorated style is nearly so pure as Salisbury. This style represented an extension of French rayonnant taste, and is characterized by ornamental richness and the appearance of new rib types. Lincoln Cathedral includes Decorated tracery in its Angel Choir and tierceron, or secondary, ribs in the nave that produce "crazy" vaults, so called for their asymmetry. King's College Chapel at Cambridge exemplifies the Perpendicular style, somewhat confusingly named, as it is really characterized by strong verticals, as seen in the mullions of the chapel's lateral windows. In the ceiling, the ribs become filigree defining fan vaults making the ceiling texture as insistent as that of the sidewalls.

While the German Gothic produced some monuments dependent on French models, German masons, especially those in Bohemia, emancipated themselves from French inclinations by pushing ribs to ornamental extremes. They made them flow and swirl in organic, florid compositions, something like stone icing piped on the vault web with a giant pastry tube. In extreme examples, ribs detach themselves from the web, and "fly," in apparent defiance of structural logic.

The Gothic remained something of an interloper in sun-drenched, classically disposed Italy. The Cistercians brought the style south, but no structural innovations were made there. Producing Milan Cathedral's spiky countenance involved almost endless consultations about proportioning systems rather than the esthetics of light or the techniques of stone, a far cry from Abbot Suger's initial intentions.

During the Middle Ages, building experts were stonemasons, and the most skilled of these men became masters capable of supervising and coordinating the construction of cathedrals. In addition to their expertise in the physical laying of stone and their empirical knowledge gained through experience, they possessed certain "secrets," which turned out to be geometric manipulations needed to determine proper dimensions and shapes.

Smaller medieval buildings, including residences, were often constructed using half-timbering, or heavy-timber framing, infilled with masonry. The results were extremely impressive and required great carpentry skills to accomplish them, but the manner of building was not a very efficient one. Some houses, especially urban examples, were constructed of stone and given Romanesque and Gothic features. In the case of S. Gimignano in Italy, houses sprouted tall towers that could be used as strongholds, or as indicators of family prestige, or for drying long lengths of fabric.

Medieval castles, in a time before gunpowder-charged cannons, were constructed of heavy masonry. British versions included a keep, or stronghold, in a central tower; then a surrounding yard; then the perimeter walls, often fortified with towers of their own; and finally a moat. These castles developed in isolation or as part of cities that grew around or adjacent to them. Medieval city plans were either modular and orthogonal like the bastide, or planned new town, at Carcassonne, or organic, like Carcassonne's old town, with its double layer of towered, masonry walls. In such cities, open spaces were typically located adjacent to castles, churches, and city halls, with the most active being the central marketplace, where a municipal fountain could provide public water.

While aberrant in its substitution of canals for streets and its extremely eclectic building styles as a result of far-ranging international trade, Venice provides a fitting conclusion to this overview of the Gothic style. Gothic buildings in Venice have an exotic quality, and, likewise, the local Renaissance style, discussed in Chapter 11, exhibits a sensuality and suppleness unique to the Veneto, or Venetian region.

# CHAPTER 10

# INDIGENOUS ARCHITECTURE IN THE AMERICAS AND AFRICA

n 1964, polymath architect-engineer-historian Bernard Rudofsky organized a then surprising and ultimately extremely influential exhibition at the Museum of Modern Art in New York City titled *Architecture without Architects* and accompanied it with a book of the same title. The exhibition created something of a sensation, appearing as it did at a time of general cultural upheaval in the United States, and its subtitle—*A Short Introduction to Non-Pedigreed Architecture*—suggests why it was so sensational or perhaps more accurately, so iconoclastic. Illustrating, with obvious personal admiration, what he called "vernacular, anonymous, spontaneous, indigenous, rural" architecture, Rudofsky argued for a much more chronologically and geographically inclusive study of the built environment and one that did not cater exclusively to constructions for the wealthy and powerful and did not result exclusively from the efforts of what we might today call academically trained designers.

Reading this chapter on indigenous American and African architecture, as reading Rudofsky's book, you will be directed away from matters of fashion and even style, in favor of "anonymous" but distinctive, even archetypal, forms, and you may come away with a deeper understanding of human responses to particularized environments, to specific local building materials, to elementary but expressively logical structural systems, and to nuanced social conditions.

## NORTH AMERICA

As in Europe and Asia, indigenous architecture in North America responded to complex social, economic, political, and environmental forces. However, its salient characteristics were a directness of construction and an honest use of materials. To some extent, such directness and honesty were inevitable, as most native cultures did not build road systems or construct large ships, and, while there was extensive trade between different peoples, it mostly involved smaller objects. This meant, with a few notable exceptions, that construction materials were drawn from local sources. Yet a feeling remains among many that the indigenous cultures of the Americas maintained a connectedness to place,

a reverence for nature, and a noble forthrightness in their building that has been all but lost in today's society. Figure 10.1 shows the geographical distribution of the North American tribes.

### TRIBES OF THE GREAT PLAINS AND THE GREAT LAKES

Tribes like the Lakota Sioux, hunting bison on horseback and led by their famous chief Sitting Bull in his eagle-feather headdress, have come to represent the Native American in the modern imagination. At their peak, some sixty million bison roamed the Great Plains, and Plains tribes based their cultures on these huge but skittish animals, using their meat for food, their hides for clothing and housing, and their bones for tools. In the seventeenth century, the Spanish introduced horses into New Mexico. Native Americans quickly recognized their value, and horses soon became available in the Great Plains, where they made it possible for nomadic peoples to accumulate wealth, carrying large quantities of valuable possessions with them in the form of food, housing, clothing, and other amenities. With this rise in the standard of living

## Chronology

| | |
|---|---|
| earthen pyramids built in Peru | ca. 3000 BCE |
| rise of the Olmecs | 1300 BCE |
| castillo built at Chavín de Huántar | 900 BCE |
| occupation of Teotihuacan and the Classic period in Pre-Columbian Mexico | 200–1000 CE |
| Maya culture in Central America | ca. 300–1450 |
| Chimor Empire begun at Chan Chan | ca. 1000 |
| occupation of Mesa Verde | 1100–1275 |
| occupation begins at Poverty Point site in Louisiana | 1200 |
| construction of fortress complex of the Great Zimbabwe | 1200–1300 CE |
| building of Great Mosque in Djenne | 1200–1300 CE |
| construction of St. George's Church, Lalibela | 1200–1300 CE |
| founding of Tenochtitlán | 1325 |
| construction of the palace at Gedi | 1400s and later |
| founding of the Inca Empire | 1438 |
| first voyage of Christopher Columbus | 1492 |
| Spanish conquest of the Aztecs | 1519 |
| Spanish conquest of the Inca | 1532 |
| construction of Bobo-Dioulasso Mosque | late 19th century |

Machu Picchu, Peru, ca. 1450.

One could hardly imagine a more dramatic site. However, its exact function—ritual center, military outpost, or something else—remains unclear.

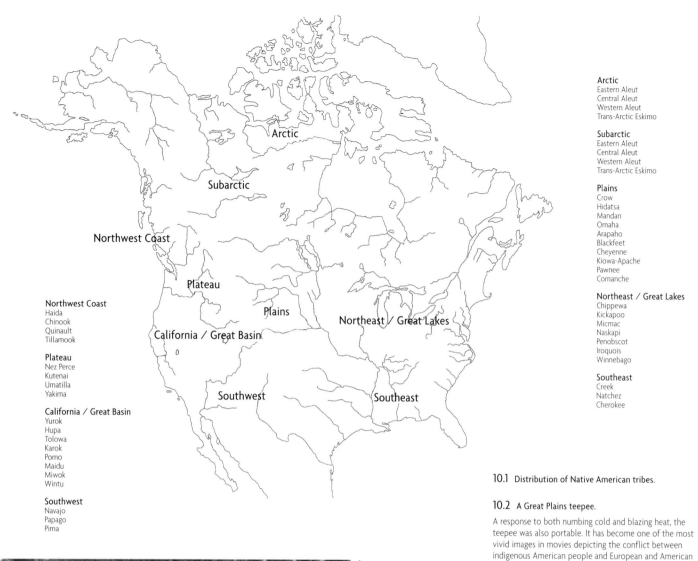

Arctic
Eastern Aleut
Central Aleut
Western Aleut
Trans-Arctic Eskimo

Subarctic
Eastern Aleut
Central Aleut
Western Aleut
Trans-Arctic Eskimo

Plains
Crow
Hidatsa
Mandan
Omaha
Arapaho
Blackfeet
Cheyenne
Kiowa-Apache
Pawnee
Comanche

Northeast / Great Lakes
Chippewa
Kickapoo
Micmac
Naskapi
Penobscot
Iroquois
Winnebago

Southeast
Creek
Natchez
Cherokee

Northwest Coast
Haida
Chinook
Quinault
Tillamook

Plateau
Nez Perce
Kutenai
Umatilla
Yakima

California / Great Basin
Yurok
Hupa
Tolowa
Karok
Pomo
Maidu
Miwok
Wintu

Southwest
Navajo
Papago
Pima

**10.1** Distribution of Native American tribes.

**10.2** A Great Plains teepee.

A response to both numbing cold and blazing heat, the teepee was also portable. It has become one of the most vivid images in movies depicting the conflict between indigenous American people and European and American settlers.

came a dramatic growth in population. These conditions, in turn, increased warfare between tribes over the best grazing lands.

Because tribes moved about frequently, or at least had separate summer and winter dwellings, their architecture was necessarily temporary, rapidly constructed, mobile, and reusable. The best known of such nomadic structures is the teepee, a conical skeleton of poles covered with bison hides (Fig. 10.2). It was preferred by such tribes as the Arapaho, Blackfeet, Cheyenne, Comanche, and Crow, all names made familiar to movie-goers during the heyday of so-called "westerns." Most often depicted in this medium only as savage obstructionists bent on thwarting white settlement, these Plains-dwellers were in fact able designers who developed the teepee as a flexible solution to the contradictory problems of raging winds, numbing cold, internal fires and smoke, and blazing heat. Accordingly, the teepee had its vertical axis tilted and its plan distorted to an egg shape in order to combat prevailing winter winds, while its covering could be opened up for hot-weather ventilation. This covering also provided a

**10.3** A Midwest wigwam.

This domical structure is covered with mats. The mats overlap like shingles to prevent the entry of moisture.

mural surface for painted images, which typically depicted sacred symbols and the significant events of inter-tribal warfare. The teepee achieved its great size, requiring a covering of thirty or more bison hides, only after the horse became available to drag it on a travois of two poles joined by a frame.

Other tribes produced temporary buildings in different forms and using different materials. The Kiowa-Apache of the northwestern Plains constructed the wikiup as well as the teepee. To build it, they bent saplings into arch-shaped profiles, collectively forming a domical skeleton that they covered with smaller saplings and finally thatch. Tribes of the southern Plains assembled their similar grass houses by bending saplings like ribs over a ring of wooden posts, then covering the saplings with overlapping bundles of thatch.

Various Plains tribes, including the Mandan and Hidatsa, built earth lodges. They began by constructing a post-and-lintel rhombus of logs; next they leaned poles against it in a conical configuration; finally they covered the poles with earth to produce a cone- or dome-like enclosure. The Mandan and Hidatsa founded agricultural towns along rivers in Missouri, making some of them into market centers. Nomadic groups from the north and west brought exotic and precious items like dentalium, a type of mollusk shell, to trade for the local surplus of maize.

## TRIBES OF THE NORTHEAST

In the northeast, hunting tribes such as the Penobscot, Micmac, and Naskapi constructed their versions of the teepee and covered them with bark. Various others, including the Great Lakes Chippewa, moved the teepee cone along a horizontal axis to form an extended version that was used as a multi-family dwelling.

Similar to the teepee and wikiup was the wigwam (Fig. 10.3), which was made by bending enough saplings into arch-shaped cross sections to form a vault- or dome-like volume, then covering it with mats or bark. In the northeast, various Algonquin tribes, including the Chippewa, Kickapoo, and Winnebago, favored the wigwam. When the first English settlers arrived to found the Massachusetts Bay Colony, they also lived in wigwams until they could erect larger structures like the ones they were accustomed to in England.

In what is today upstate New York, tribes of the Iroquois Confederation erected longhouses, vault-like wigwams extended along their primary axes, sometimes to a length of more than 300 feet. The Iroquois used these large buildings as community halls for holding religious rituals. They practiced agriculture, growing maize, beans, and squash, and trapped animals for their pelts. They established a fur trade with Europeans in the early seventeenth century, competing with and eventually dominating their Algonquin neighbors. By the late eighteenth century, the English and the French were themselves competing for furs, and the Iroquois threw in their lot with the English. Though the Iroquois attempted to remain neutral during the Revolutionary War, they soon found themselves fighting a losing battle with the settlers and retreated to reservations, as would many other Native Americans as the new arrivals spread across the continent.

## TRIBES OF THE MISSISSIPPI RIVER BASIN

Tribes of the Ohio River Valley and the southeast were distinguished by their construction of earth mounds. The Adena culture (ca. 800 BCE–400 CE), in what is today Ohio, is admired for its earthwork depictions of animals. Perhaps the best known of these, the so-called Serpent

# THE BIRTHPLACE OF THE CHOCTAWS

By Jack D. Elliott

*The reality of things, it appears, cannot be fully understood in terms of the world and its time; for the things are circumfused by an ambience of mystery that can be understood only in terms of the myth.* Eric Voegelin

**10.4** Nanih Waiya mound, rural Mississippi, ca. 100 CE.

The landscape is suffused with symbolism. Even for information-obsessed moderns who fancy themselves to be detached and objective observers, it still has evocative associations. Like most peoples, early Native Americans lived in landscapes replete with mythological symbols. In particular, mounds, relic landscape features built by earlier settlers who were forgotten by their successors, often took on mythical associations.

Nanih Waiya (Choctaw—"bending hill") is an earthen mound that stands in rural central Mississippi (Fig. 10.4). Today it is approximately twenty-five feet high and covers about seven-tenths of an acre at its base. Early accounts indicate that the site also once possessed a smaller burial mound and a surrounding earthen breastwork. These features have been destroyed as the result of agricultural practices during the nineteenth and twentieth centuries. Recent research conducted by Ken Carleton, archaeologist for the Choctaw tribe in Mississippi, suggests that the mound

dates to the Middle Woodland period, that is, about 2000 years ago, almost certainly predating by centuries the emergence of the Choctaw tribe.

The mysterious mound came to be regarded by the historic Choctaw tribe as sacred through linkage to their origin myths; it was the "ishki chito," "the great mother." Two basic themes are to be found. According to the more prevalent story, the Great Spirit created the first Choctaws in the interior of the mound, whence they crawled forth wet and moist through a cave or hole into the daylight and lay out in the sun to dry. During the early nineteenth century there was a "large and deep" hole in the top of the mound. The Choctaws' regard for the great mother mound was such that if they were hunting in the vicinity, they would bring a portion of their kill and throw it into the hole, feeding their mother, as they saw it.

The second story was the migration legend, in which the ancestors of the Choctaws moved from the west led by prophets, who envisioned a land with

fertile soil and abundant game, carrying a pole. They traveled eastward, and at the end of each day they camped and planted the end of the pole in the ground so that it stood vertically. In the morning they would find that the pole had tilted, and their journey would resume in the direction in which it had tilted. The journey continued for months until one evening they arrived at Nanih Waiya and planted the pole; the next morning they found it still standing erect. This was interpreted as an oracle indicating that they had arrived at their new home.

We often smile today at the mythologies of the past; the details, for the most part, are not factually true. Yet there is more to our appreciation of these stories than whether they contain strict historical fact or not; the linkage between mythic story and place makes us see places as we might not otherwise see them. They evoke in us a sense of wonder at things that we have all too often lost in a world where the mystery of Being is often ignored.

**10.5** Earth mound, Moundville, Alabama, 1200–1500.

This earth mound at Moundville in west-central Alabama was constructed as a base for a temple or residence of an important person. Unlike the pyramids in Mexico, it was never encased in a stone veneer.

Mound, meanders some 600 feet in an oscillating curve. The Adena people also constructed conical mounds, some more than sixty feet tall, covering log structures used for burials or as depositories for cremated remains. A full explanation of the motivations that so inspired these ancient builders has not yet been developed; some mounds were obviously effigies and some were funerary, others apparently defined ritual spaces, and others still may have been built to provide relief from periodic flooding.

Tribes throughout the Mississippi Basin found abundant wildlife and other natural resources around them and cultivated maize, beans, and squash like their neighbors to the northeast. They also established long-distance trade routes. Excavations in Cahokia, Illinois have unearthed copper objects from the Great Lakes, mica from the southern Appalachians, and seashell ornaments from the Atlantic coast. In around 1000 CE, Cahokia was the largest city north of Mexico, covering five square miles and having a population of some 30,000 inhabitants. Among Cahokia's platform mounds is the so-called Monk's Mound, built entirely of earth, which is half the size of the enormous Temple of the Sun (see Fig. 10.15) at Teotihuacán near modern-day Mexico City. This pyramidal structure is situated at the head of a great plaza and large posts in the ground nearby probably once facilitated astronomical observations.

Development of the vast Poverty Point site, in what is today northeast Louisiana, is believed to have begun in about 1200 BCE. Some have argued that it was a regional trading center established by the Olmecs of eastern Mexico. Poverty Point consists of concentric semicircular, ridge-like mounds enclosing a plaza 1800 feet across. In order to shape such a landscape, the amount of earth that had to be moved was prodigious. Light wooden houses, long since gone, once stood atop the ridges. Mound-building was still being practiced by the Natchez tribe on nearby sites in the early eighteenth century when the phenomenon was observed and commented on by French explorers.

To the east, Native Americans also constructed mounds, such as those in Moundville, Alabama (Fig. 10.5), which are situated on a high bluff above the Black Warrior river. On a site covering 300 acres, there are twenty mounds, most with their ramps still visible, surrounding a large plaza. Dwellings once ringed the mound complex and were protected by a wooden palisade. Atop the mounds stood timber-frame structures with walls covered in plaster on lath formed of smaller limbs and twigs and with roofs covered in bark.

At Moundville, a museum was opened in the 1930s which allowed visitors to look at skeletal remains in an excavated burial site. While this display seemed reasonable at the time, the modern view is that such exhibitions, made without the permission of associated parties, represent inappropriate intrusions upon the most personal kind of human settings. Consequently the excavation has now been sealed off from public view. Likewise, museums throughout the country have returned for reinterment Native American remains removed unilaterally by archaeologists in years past.

While mound-building has received the most attention, more modest Native American constructions in the southeast are equally interesting. The Creeks of Alabama and Mississippi erected buildings with mud-over-timber-frame walls, which they arranged around square courts, as well as octagonal townhouses and, as communal centers, buildings on round or polygonal plans with conical roofs. They sealed their walls using a whitewash made of ground oyster shells and covered their roofs with a variety of materials including thatch and bark. Farther south, the lower Creeks built the chickee, a raised platform protected by an openwork wood frame supporting a thatched gable or **hipped roof**.

## ARCTIC AND SUBARCTIC TRIBES

The Aleuts of the Aleutian Islands in Alaska favored whale meat for food, but made use of the entire animal, from its intestines to its bladder and tongue. They hunted whales in boats called baidarkas, constructed, appropriately, with whalebone frames. These boats seated as many as forty men, though a typical hunting party usually had only ten or so. They also plied the waters in kayaks in search of smaller game such as sea lions, seals, and porpoises. On land, they used sleds, but still had no dogs as late as 1000 CE. The Aleuts called their semi-subterranean sod-covered house a barabara, and entered it through a roof hatch. Underground buildings took advantage of soil mass to moderate temperatures. In the Arctic, the Canadian Inuit (Eskimos) also lived in subterranean houses, which they built of stone, wood, and almost any other available material. Traditionally, Inuits have hunted sea mammals and caribou, living in villages in winter and then separating and moving inland in the summer. To this

**10.6** Inuit iglu.
While the iglu is shaped like a dome, it is actually made of spiraling courses, with the bed of each block sloping inward. The blocks are cut from packed snow, meaning ice crystals rather than solid ice, so that trapped air provides insulation.

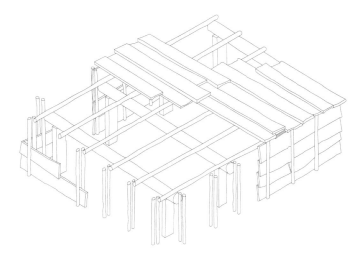

**10.7** Bird's-eye view of a northwestern shed house.
Shed houses could be quite large, with eaves rising to twenty feet and main rooms stretching up to 100 feet across. The production of individual planks by splitting and finishing them with an adze was a technological challenge in a culture that had no power-drive saws.

day, they continue to construct the well-known iglu (Fig. 10.6), a structure made of snow blocks. They cant blocks inward to create a stable domical profile, but rather than laying them in courses, spiral them upward. They enter the completed iglu through a small barrel-vaulted porch.

The teepee form was adaptable even for the subarctic region. Here, tribes built the tupik, a teepee-like structure that they covered with animal skins. During the summer months, Arctic Inuit constructed a tupik that appears at first glance to have been a type of extended teepee, but was actually a tent made of poles covered with skins that mimicked the form of their winter iglu, even to the inclusion of a tunnel-like entry.

## TRIBES OF THE NORTHWEST AND NORTHERN CALIFORNIA

Native American cultural patterns were similar along the Pacific coast from Alaska to Baja California. Diet was diverse, including plentiful fish and sea mammals and a variety of indigenous plants. The Quinault tribe of Washington state is famous for its potlatches, enormous feasts celebrating a child's coming of age, a death and subsequent memorialization, or the annual salmon run.

Along the northwest Pacific coast, the Quinault, as well as the Chinook and Tillamook, built **shed houses** (Fig. 10.7), log frames sheathed in cedar planks and covered with single-sloping or gable roofs. Such constructions were long on a locally abundant building material but short on technology, using inefficient structural cross sec-

tions such as circular beams and joists and simple fasteners such as cedar-bark ties. Farther north, tribes such as the Haida built **plank houses** and also erected **totem poles**, carving them with images of stylized animals. Some scholars argue that such carving could have been done with bone and shell tools; others see it as a later development dependent on the appearance of metal. The tribes of the northwest also applied similar painted images to the exterior walls of their chiefs' houses.

The Nez Perce, famous for their hospitality to the Lewis and Clark expedition in 1805, wintered in small villages along the Columbia river in carefully chosen, sheltered locations. They lived off salmon, root vegetables, and bulbs, which they preserved by drying them on racks or in earthen ovens. They then stored the processed items in baskets lined with salmon skins, and finally placed them in specially designed storage houses or stone- or bark-lined pits. They also hunted game and, having horses, bison as well. The Nez Perce and Yakima occupied **pit houses** (Fig. 10.8), timber frames set above three to four-foot-deep pits and covered with pine needles, reed or grass mats, and earth. They erected these timber frames in a configuration akin to conventional post-and-lintel and hipped-roof framing.

Northern California is a land of rugged topography and dense forests. The preservable carbohydrate that Native Americans here favored was flour made from acorns and buckeyes, and their preeminent craft was basketry. The Yurok, Karok, Hupa, and Tolowa tribes built gable-roofed frames above pits but covered them with

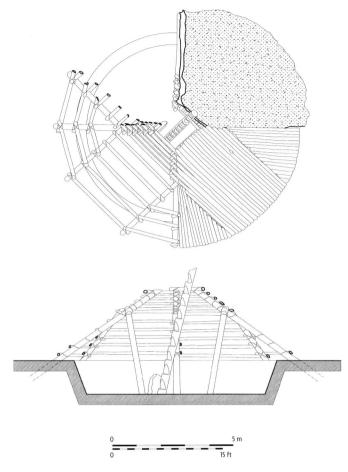

**10.8** Overhead view and cross section of a northwestern pit house.

Such domestic environments took advantage of the insulating qualities of surrounding rather than covering earth. While rarely seen in Europe, the entry from above was not uncommon in North America.

planks from locally available redwoods. In central California, the Maidu and Miwok tribes constructed oval and octagonal pit houses using radiating poles set atop polygonal frames. Over the poles, they layered sticks, then grass or tule mats, and finally a coating of earth.

### TRIBES OF THE SOUTHWEST

In the southwest, members of the Pima and Papago tribes lived in **ki** or **ramada** depending on the season. A ki began as a shallow pit surrounded by a low wall made from the excavated spoil. This walled pit was then roofed with a domical structure made by covering sapling frames with brush, then mud. Working together, the two systems lessened the effects of both heat and cold. Both tribes made a warm-weather ramada by planting upright posts in the ground to support a brush-covered roof. Family groups lived in rancherías, communities of farmsteads located near water sources.

Unique conditions in the southwest also led to a permanent indigenous architecture. Three cultures contributed: the Mogollan—named for the Mogollan mountains in southwestern New Mexico; the Hohokam—

their name taken from a Pima word meaning "those who have vanished"; and the Ancestral Pueblo, long called the Anasazi, which has often been translated as "Ancient Ones." By 300 BCE the Mogollan culture of central Arizona and southwestern New Mexico had established villages atop mesas, or steep-walled plateaus. They built pit houses enclosed by timber frames covered with brush and earth and entered down a ramp or ladder. Along the Gila and Salt rivers, the Hohokam people developed sophisticated systems of irrigation and built castle-like structures with adobe walls as much as five feet thick.

The Ancestral Pueblo began their culture in what is today Utah, then gradually migrated into southwestern Colorado, eastern Arizona, and western New Mexico. They developed a distinctive form of black-and-white pottery, as well as methods for conserving and managing precious water for irrigation. Their building of compact, permanent settlements reached a zenith in 1100–1300 near the Four Corners region at Mesa Verde and Chaco Canyon, and consisted respectively of extensive alcove dwellings beneath protective mesas (Fig. 10.9) and agricultural and trading townships.

Ancestral Pueblo architecture began as pit houses entered from above, with excavated floors covered with timbers and then earth. In around 700 the Ancestral Pueblo modified their construction practices, erecting their houses for use during the summer months at ground level, using sandstone masonry for walls and adobe over small timbers for roofs. They combined these houses in a party-wall fashion, arranged them around irregular plazas, and continued to provide entry into them only from above. In around 1000, they began to transform their

**10.9** Mesa Verde, southwest Colorado, 1100–1275.

The Mesa Verde site was chosen for habitation for practical reasons rather than for its dramatic landscape: it offered protection from winter winds out of the north and security against potential invaders.

**10.10** Pueblo Bonito, Chaco Canyon, New Mexico, 900–1120.

This view gives a sense of the expanse of the site. Its semicircular arrangements of terraces, now in ruin, responded to the path and inclination of the sun. A disadvantage of this kind of tiered arrangement was that it created a high percentage of unlit interior rooms.

remaining pit houses into sunken, circular **kivas**, sacred and social spaces that celebrated their clan-oriented society. Each kiva contained a **sipapu**, or ceremonial opening, to the world below. Around a kiva, the Ancestral Pueblo distributed several suites of living spaces. As their population increased, they added second and third stories to their already-dense housing complexes, called **pueblos**, probably relegating the largely unlit lower-level rooms to use for food storage. The vast Ancestral Pueblo alcove dwelling or Cliff Palace at Mesa Verde contains some 200 rooms and twenty-three kivas. While Mesa Verde's stone masonry is today much admired for its intricate workmanship, it was originally covered with adobe plaster to protect it from the elements.

The Ancestral Pueblo developed numerous settlements, typically in compact, naturally sheltered locations like Mesa Verde, which enabled them to combat invaders, mitigate the effects of harsh climate, and orient structures to important celestial events. For example, at Fajda Butte in Chaco Canyon, during solstices and equinoxes, upright stones still allow the passage of thin bands of light between them that frame a spiral petroglyph. Atop the mesas at Mesa Verde, they developed terraced gardens like those of the Incas and constructed reservoirs for agricultural- and drinking-water retention.

At Pueblo Bonito in Chaco Canyon, the Ancestral Pueblo built an intricate irrigation system that included dams, ditches, and flood gates. They erected a great five-story, tiered, semicircular megastructure with some 800 rooms and at least thirty-seven kivas facing the arc of the sun as it traversed the southern sky; only ruins remain today (Fig. 10.10). They built walls from bonded wythes of stone set in thin beds of clay mortar and applied a veneer of coursed ashlar covered with adobe plaster. As at their other sites, they arranged for entry into rooms only from above via ladders. They also developed an extensive system of roads, many of them still apparent in aerial photography. Based upon the exotic artifacts found here, such as seashells and parrot feathers, it seems clear that Pueblo Bonita was the major trading center in the Ancestral Pueblo southwest.

The Ancestral Pueblo culture declined rapidly after 1300 for reasons that are not yet adequately understood. The most likely cause was an extended drought resulting from changing weather patterns. Their descendants, including the Zuni, the Hopi, and the Navajo, still dominate in the region. The Navajo nation, in what is today northeastern Arizona and northwestern New Mexico, represents the largest tribe in the United States, some quarter of a million strong, and occupies some nine million acres of reservation land. Traditionally, the Navajo lived in hogans (Fig. 10.11), which consisted of various configurations of log frames covered with earth. Some of these log frames were conical; some began as post-and-lintel squares against which smaller logs were then leaned; and some had notched log walls and corbeled log roofs. The Navajo are particularly noted for their silver work and their blankets. They also made sand paintings by sprinkling colored sand and maize meal over flat surfaces.

**10.11** A southwestern hogan.

To build a hogan, a log frame was covered with earth, producing a living environment compatible with climatic extremes. Wood provided the structural integrity, while the earth covering provided the insulation.

## MEXICO AND CENTRAL AMERICA

The following discussion of Pre-Columbian Mexico and Central America covers multiple cultures and sites, from the Olmecs at La Venta to the Aztecs at Tenochtitlán.

### THE OLMECS OF THE EASTERN MEXICAN COAST

Men and women migrated east across the Bering Straits more than 30,000 years ago. They settled all along the way, traveling down through North, Central, and South America. The earliest evidence (ca. 1500 BCE) of a sophisticated culture in Mexico comes from the Gulf Coast in the northern portion of the state of Tabasco and southern portion of the state of Vera Cruz. This was the land of the Olmecs, best known for their jaguar motifs and great bodyless stone heads (Fig. 10.12) with seemingly oriental features. Olmec sculptors carved these heads from six- to eight-foot-tall basalt blocks weighing up to thirty tons that had to be imported from quarries located in the Tuxtla mountains some distance away. They are probably depictions of real rulers, but this has not been proven.

While knowledge of the Olmecs is limited, their position as progenitors of Mesoamerican culture in Mexico and Central America is well established. They invented a calendar, a numbering system, and hieroglyphic writing and made astronomical observations. They began the worship of the region's principal gods. They invented the ball court that became a widespread device for public rituals. They established a hierarchical society with a nobility and perhaps kings. Finally, the Olmecs created the first Mesoamerican artistic style that united an ethnic group, and they may have created an empire of city-states.

The most impressive Olmec ceremonial center is La Venta (Fig. 10.13), where the oldest known earthen pyramid in Mexico, almost 100 feet tall, served as one terminus for an axis defined by an orthogonal arrangement of earthen platforms surrounding a ceremonial plaza lined with basalt columns. The basic elements of this composition would be repeated again and again throughout the region.

### TEOTIHUACÁN IN THE VALLEY OF MEXICO

During the Classic period of Pre-Columbian Mexican culture (ca. 200 BCE–900 CE), a vast, planned urban development was created at Teotihuacán (Fig. 10.14), meaning "place of the gods," in the Valley of Mexico, by a people whose name we do not know. It arose northwest of the Olmec sites subsequent to the Olmec decline, covers some thirteen square miles, and once served a population as large as 200,000 people. In the city's ritual center, designers laid out a great north–south causeway, terminated on the north by the stepped Pyramid of the Moon. Alongside the causeway, they placed a series of earthen terraces with battered walls faced with stone veneer; a great stepped pyramid—the Pyramid of the Sun (Fig. 10.15); and walled enclosures, some sunken and some defined by trabeated construction covered with low-relief sculpture.

The horizontal plane dominates here, perhaps inspired by the sprawl of the valley floor. This horizontality is celebrated by means of two distinctive ordering devices. The battered walls of the terraces and pyramids display the **talud** and **tablero** motifs that would be repeated with many variations throughout Mesoamerica. The talud is a sloping plane and the tablero a frieze of random stones framed by plain moldings (see Fig. 10.15).

Exquisitely carved columns in the so-called Palace of the Quetzalbutterfly, located on the west side of the plaza

**10.12** Olmec stone head, before 900 BCE.

This artifact, relocated from its original site, displays the distinctive Olmec facial features and ceremonial headdress.

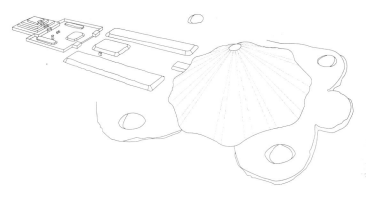

**10.13** Diagram of La Venta, Tabasco, Mexico, 1100–400 BCE.

The conical earth mound and stepped pyramid stand at the opposite ends of an axis defined by earthen platforms and walled enclosures. Such a sequential organization of space and mass can be compared to Egyptian pyramid complexes and Mesopotamian ziggurats and their compounds.

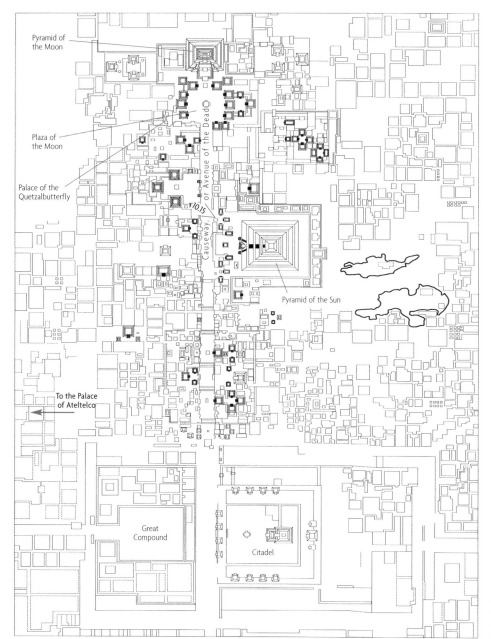

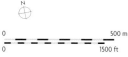

**10.14** Plan of Teotihuacán, Valley of Mexico, Mexico, ca. 200 BCE–900 CE.

As at La Venta, the principal forms are pyramids and platforms, here stretched out beside a long causeway.

**10.15** Pyramid of the Sun, Teotihuacán, begun ca. 100 BCE.

Made of earth with a stone-veneer covering, the Pyramid of the Sun has a profile of ascending, sloping taluds. The platforms in the foreground, which once supported temples, have more complex talud–tablero arrangements. The variations on a basic theme offered by these companion motifs provide unity among diversity at the many Pre-Columbian sites in Mexico and Central America. Various talud–tablero combinations appear as pyramid tiers, building walls, and even roofs.

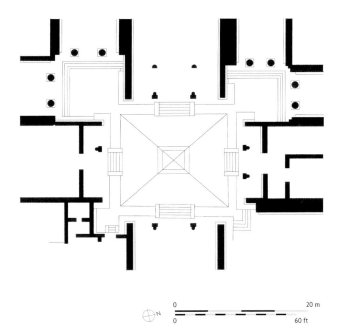

**10.16** Plan of the Palace of Ateltelco, Teotihuacán, ca. 200 BCE–900 CE.

This pattern of interlocking orthogonal geometries attests to the sophisticated design ideas of the people of Teotihuacán. Notable are the cross-axial organization, the column screens, and the resulting rich sequence of spaces.

**10.17** (above) Monte Albán, Oaxaca, Mexico, 600 BCE–1000 CE.

Unlike Teotihuacán's axial organization, Monte Albán's is spatial and centrally planned. Platforms once capped by temples define a plaza in which the Zapotecs placed two structures, one certainly an observatory that was canted in plan to align it with significant stars or planets.

**10.18** (right) Ball court, Copán, Honduras, before 800.

This ball court, like that at Monte Albán, has sloping talud walls resembling modern stadium seating. However, these slopes were a part of the play field, with onlookers standing on the platforms above.

and in front of the Temple of the Moon, document the appreciation among Teotihuacán's inhabitants of the hard-edged quality of stone. The plan of the Palace of Ateltelco (Fig. 10.16), located well west of the causeway and just north of the so-called Citadel, demonstrates—in its complex geometry of interlocking squares, its many level changes, its proportioning systems, and its layering of columns, piers, and walls—a sophisticated understanding of geometric ordering and spatial sequence.

## THE ZAPOTECS AND MIXTECS AT MONTE ALBÁN, OAXACA

In Oaxaca, south of the Central Plateau of Mexico, the Zapotecs also rose in prominence after the decline of the Olmecs. They transformed their local culture into a territorial one, with the populace scattered throughout the Oaxaca Valley. At Monte Albán (600 BCE–1000 CE), they organized their great ritual center quite differently from that at Teotihuacán. By leveling the top of a mountain some 1300 feet above sea level, they developed an earthen platform on which they built a series of stepped pyramids as bases for their temples (Fig. 10.17).

The Zapotecs arranged these pyramids around the perimeter of their site, creating a great plaza, 1000 feet long and almost 500 feet wide, and, within this plaza, they placed two additional pyramids, making them built objects inside a larger built environment; such ideas can be compared conceptually to those of Hellenistic Greece in the fourth to second centuries BCE. Equally spatial is the ball court at the southwest corner of the site. This form type appeared throughout Mesoamerica where its misleadingly serene composition of talud-and-tablero-like battered walls and platforms provided a setting for ritual games played with a small resilient ball, games in which the consequence of losing was death (Fig. 10.18).

The Zapotecs built their pyramids using talud–tablero motifs but emphasized wide stairs often bracketed by sloping cheekwalls. Their interpretation of the

talud–tablero was strongly linear, with corbeled layers configured as if overlapping and turned down at their extremities. Atop their pyramids, the Zapotecs placed temples with notable plan configurations. Each temple was one or two spaces deep (like an ancient Greek cella and porch) with frontal columns in antis or prostyle. Particularly interesting is the sunken court at the southern end of the site which is comparable in its plan to the Palace of Ateltelco. A square with four smaller, overlapping squares at its corners, it was approached by means of a wide stair, then through a portico with a double file of square columns. Such an exploitation of ranks and files of columns was rare in Pre-Columbian America, but would appear again among the Toltecs in both northern Mexico and Central America. Excavations at Monte Albán have unearthed the tombs of the Zapotec nobility and the largest cache of jewelry found in North America.

The Mixtecs followed the Zapotecs in Oaxaca (ca. 800). Their sacred city of Mitla includes the Palace of the Columns. Here the tablero motif took on a much more intricate character than any seen before. A plain talud serves as the base from which rise tiers of tablero elements framed by corbeled bands. The tablero is formed of inlaid panels of geometric ornamentation in both orthogonal and diagonal patterns (Fig. 10.19).

## THE MAYA

East of Oaxaca, in what today is Guatemala, Honduras, the Mexican state of Chiapas, and the Yucatán Peninsula, another great Pre-Columbian culture developed, that of the Maya. At its height, the Maya civilization included some fifty independent states and more cities than anywhere else in the Pre-Columbian Americas. The Maya developed irrigation systems and cultivated a wide variety of crops, particularly maize, which they made into tortilla-like pancakes. Maya society was rigidly stratified, with peasant farmers at the base and the priest class, merchants, and warriors above. At the top was a hereditary king, who was both a civil ruler and a priest.

The Maya were unique in the Americas in developing a system of writing, recording their history and ritual practices on paper. While their libraries were destroyed by the Spanish, many of their hieroglyphic texts survive, carved in stone, modeled in stucco, and painted on pottery or in murals. Their glyphs, long a subject of intense study, have only recently been deciphered. They include signs that represent both individual sounds and whole words. Unfortunately, because the only extant texts are displayed on public architecture, they represent the official government interpretation of events and do not allow for alternative points of view. Still, they offer rich insights into such matters as the Maya concept of time and their world view.

The Maya saw their world as made up of three distinct regions: the starry realm of the heavens above, the middle realm of the earth, and the dark nether realm below.

**10.19** Talud–tablero wall, Mitla, Oaxaca, Mexico, ca. 800.

The contrast between the geometric ornament here at Mitla and the organic Maya ornament farther south (see Fig. 10.26) is striking. Perhaps it has to do with the differing contexts in Oaxaca and the Yucatán.

Building on concepts developed by the Olmecs, and perhaps the Teotihuacános, the Maya created a world-view in which religious rituals codified a shared reality. Some of these rituals involved the introduction of trance-like states, including as a principal device the act of bloodletting—particularly from the tongue and penis, which in their most exalted form, the Maya believed, allowed their kings to make contact with the other regions. Their creation myths included sacred twins, who played a sacred ball-game, died through decapitation, were resurrected, and eventually outwitted the gods. Within this mythic structure, the Maya ball court was a place of confrontation and communication. While ballgames could be played among friends in an ordinary setting, in their most elevated form they symbolized the twins' life-and-death battle. From this myth, the Maya arrived at beliefs in triumph over death through ritual, victory over enemies through outwitting them, and resurrection and rebirth through sacrifice.

The Maya developed a complex set of interlocking calendars, which were of extreme importance because they believed that history was cyclical. Their solar calendar included 365 days broken down into eighteen months of twenty days each, with five residual days, and it was the most accurate anywhere in the ancient world. A separate religious calendar had 260 days, and the two calendars coincided every fifty-two years. This interval was viewed as a birth–death–rebirth cycle and was celebrated with lavish rituals. The rebirth was accompanied by the igniting of a ritual flame and by the reconstruction of significant temples and pyramids.

Maya astronomers meticulously plotted celestial movements, including those of the planet Venus, and predicted events such as lunar eclipses. They developed a bar-and-dot system with which they could carry out mathematical calculations and either invented zero or inherited its use

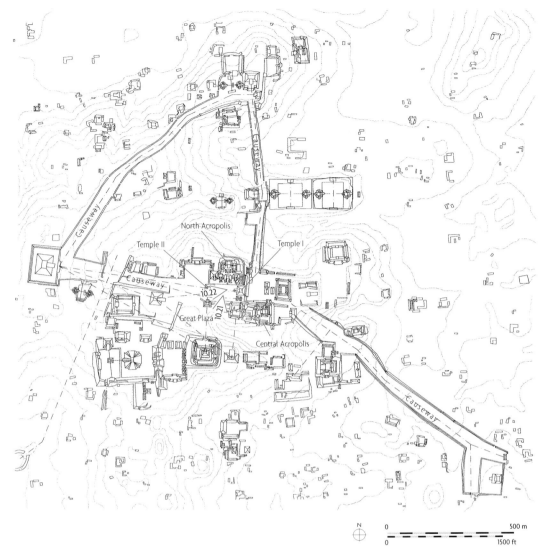

**10.20** Plan of Tikal, Guatemala, 600 BCE–ca. 900 CE.

This site contains thousands of structures and stone monuments, with the most extensively excavated areas located around the North Acropolis at the junction of the three causeways. Archaeologists must uncover such ruins advisedly, as they then become vulnerable to the effects of wind, sun, and rain, and must somehow be protected from the encroaching jungle vegetation.

from the Olmecs—only the Sumerians and Hindus did so elsewhere. After 800 CE, some catastrophic event or combination of them led to the complete collapse of Maya civilization. Scholars have reached no definitive conclusions about how the Maya downfall came to pass, but recent theories suggest that a shift in weather patterns leading to prolonged drought and subsequent famine may have played a key role in the disaster.

## TIKAL

Perhaps the most impressive Maya city is Tikal, set within the lowland jungles of the department of El Petén in Guatemala. The city was not only a ceremonial site, but also a true urban center with a permanent population of some 45,000 inhabitants. The site plan (Fig. 10.20) is

organized by means of causeways laid out in a rough triangle and linking major building complexes. At the southeast corner of this triangle stands the so-called North Acropolis, a closely packed cluster of pyramids facing a great plaza to the south. This plaza is defined on its eastern and western extremities by large pyramids and bristles with **stelae**, upright slabs with inscriptions. The units of pyramid composition are again the talud and tablero. Talud elements, in the form of sloping embankments, define platforms. Atop these platforms sit stepped pyramids formed of largely unarticulated sloping talud and equally plain vertical tablero motifs relieved only by horizontal returns and recessed panels, both of which cast sharply defined shadows (Fig. 10.21). Tikal's pyramids are its most distinctive built forms with their steep but plain tablero and talud walls and surmounting temples (Fig.

**10.21** North Acropolis, Tikal, ca. 700.

The portion of the city seen here includes the great plaza in the foreground, with stelae and the pyramid bases of the North Acropolis beyond. The Maya used temples and their bases to shape outdoor spaces intended for ritual spectacle.

**10.22** (below) Pyramid, Tikal, ca. 650.

Most striking about Tikal's pyramids is their verticality. However, they were once part of a densely developed urban fabric rather than being isolated towers amid a dense jungle canopy as they are today.

10.22). Atop the talud-like roofs sprout flamboyant, richly carved roof combs, repetitive talud-like elements that rest on the temples' corbel vaults. Steep stairs rise up one side of each pyramid and lead to the temple doorways. The original stucco reliefs have now almost completely vanished. Inside, modest spaces were created by the Maya's use of the corbeled vault, a structural device not seen at Teotihuacán or in Oaxaca. The complete ensemble of pyramids is extraordinary for its verticality, all the more so when the multiple pyramids are viewed as an urban unit; today they rise like great stalagmites from the jungle floor in so dramatic a fashion that George Lucas chose an aerial view of them to represent a moon of the rebel planet in the first *Star Wars* movie. Together with ball courts, a rain-storage reservoir, and the low-rise market structures, also composed using talud and tablero elements, the ritual pyramids at Tikal define a series of linked acropolises, open markets, and plazas.

Mural paintings have been discovered at Tikal in which artists drew black lines over a red-painted background. The most famous Maya murals are those at the modest site on the Usamacinta River, dubbed Bonampak (Maya for "painted walls") by archaeologists. Here the images are unusual for their realistic depiction of scenes from everyday life.

### COPÁN AND PALENQUE

Copán lies southeast of Tikal and was famous for its periodic gathering of astronomical experts. The ceremonial center is roughly rectangular, with a great plaza to the north and acropolis to the south and the ball court seen in Figure 10.18 between them. Perhaps its most distinctive feature is the many stelae: in this case, vertical, carved

10.23 Stelae, Copán, Honduras, 600–800.

Upright stone objects have appeared in cultures around the world, the most obvious type in the West being the tombstone or grave-marker. The Maya erected them for various purposes, including the commemoration of significant events.

10.24 Temple of the Inscriptions, Palenque, Chiapas, Mexico, completed by 683.

This stepped pyramid is embedded in the mountain behind it. A vaulted stair descends from the temple to the tomb chamber at the level of the pyramid's first stage.

10.25 Tomb chamber, Temple of the Inscriptions, Palenque, completed by 683.

Stone lintels complement the corbel vault in this space. The incised images on the sarcophagus lid depict King Pacal descending the trunk of the world-tree to the otherworld from which he was to arise like the hero twins.

monoliths, conceptually not unlike Aluit totem poles (Fig. 10.23). The style of carving has been characterized as "baroque" and "oriental" because of its organic complexity, but was perhaps derived from the lush jungle environment in which it was created. The Maya called these stelae "tree-stones" and carved them with images of kings, so that plazas filled with them both recounted the sequence of rulers and symbolized the tropical forest.

At Palenque in Chiapas, similar elements appear but with distinctive adaptations: earthen platforms; stepped pyramids, sometimes with wide stairs; and temples, often with elongated plans. The Temple of the Inscriptions is unusual for having within it a tomb built contemporaneously with the pyramid and reached by a series of subter-

ranean passages that were long ago sealed off. The burial chamber is twenty-three feet long, twenty-three feet high, and about twelve feet wide. Within it resides a huge sarcophagus carved from a single block of stone and covered with a richly ornamented slab. A skeleton draped with jade jewelry was found inside (Figs. 10.24–10.25). Many façades and some interior walls of Palenque's temples were once covered with stucco, ornately modeled in low relief and painted, and their roofs are crowned by lattice-like roof combs.

**10.26** Nunnery masks, Uxmal, Yucatán, Mexico, ca. 900.

Here, the ornament is both highly geometric and highly organic, the latter reflecting the Puuc style developed in northwest Yucatán. While the individual stones are modular, the images, dominated by the nose piece of the rain god Chac, are boldly sculpted.

**10.27** Governor's Palace, Uxmal, ca. 900.

This building has a three-part composition, with a dominant central mass separated from smaller masses to each side by a setback, or recessed strip. This composition is comparable to the schemes developed by celebrated sixteenth-century Italian architect Andrea Palladio for his villas.

## UXMAL AND CHICHÉN-ITZÁ

At Uxmal in the Puuc region, the Maya laid out their ceremonial center as objects on raised platforms, several of them taking the form of quadrangles, freely distributed in space. The geometric ornamentation here is reminiscent of Mixtec work, while the contrasting organic ornament reaches its highest level of elaboration in the interlocking masks of the rain god Chac (Fig. 10.26).

Two of Uxmal's most distinctive buildings are the so-called Governor's Palace and Nunnery (Figs. 10.27–10.28). The Governor's Palace is a single, elongated rectangle in plan, some 328 feet long, while the Nunnery consists of four smaller such rectangles defining a quadrangle. The Governor's Palace is divided into three parts by inset bays with corbeled vaults, making for a five-part composition. On the interior, some twenty rooms of various sizes are covered with corbeled vaults. At their lower levels, both buildings display large areas of mural wall surface and windows with recessed frames. In the frieze above, sculptors at the Governor's Palace combined orthogonal and diagonal geometries with multiple Chac masks. At the Nunnery, stunted columns appear on the north side, supporting a frieze similar to that at the Governor's Palace. Around the perimeter and inside the quadrangle, the frieze is alternately aggressively geometric and organic, with Chac-mask compositions above some openings and projecting dramatically at corners.

**10.28** Nunnery, Uxmal, ca. 900.

The ornamentation of this tablero can be compared to the frieze of the classical Greek or Roman temple. Here, however, the effect is created not by large panels but by many small geometric units that interlock.

Chichén-Itzá, in Yucatán at the delta of the Usumacinta and Grijalva rivers, is a Maya site that combines native elements of the Putún culture with those of Toltec raiders. The Putún, who were merchant seafarers in control of the ocean trade routes around Yucatán, were called Itzá in that area. In around 900 they conquered new lands, including Chichén, hence the name of the Chichén-Itzá site. By the eleventh or twelfth century, the city was controlled by the Toltecs.

The most notable buildings here are the so-called Caracol (Fig. 10.29), Castillo, and the Temple of the Warriors. Located to the south of the central section of the city and, some have argued, used as an astronomical observatory, the Caracol, meaning "snail," is unusual in Maya architecture for its circular-plan tower. It is ornamented with Maya masks of Chac but also with elements brought here by the Toltecs: images of the plumed serpent and heads of Toltec warriors. Inside the Caracol's central cylinder, a series of openings made possible specific observations of the planets and the stars. The Castillo, or Temple of Kulkulkán, is equally distinctive, a pyramid with stairways leading up each of its four sides. This configuration is explained by its location inside a colonnaded plaza; it is an architectural object placed within an urban space, making Chichén-Itzá comparable in its spatial conception to Monte Albán. The Castillo's form may also have cosmological symbolism, as each stair has ninety-one risers, making a total of 364 in all. If one adds the base on which the pyramid sits, the total becomes 365 or the number of days in the Maya year. Furthermore, a plumed serpent at the base casts a shadow across the stair at an equinox or solstice. Standing east of the Castillo and overlooking the plaza is the Temple of the Warriors, which bears a striking resemblance to the pyramid complex at Tula, both in its planning and execution. Here, finely carved ranks and files of columns flank two sides of the pyramid, as densely placed as the columns in an Egyptian hypostyle hall. The carving includes eagles and jaguars devouring human hearts, plumed serpents, and Toltec warriors.

## THE TOLTECS IN THE VALLEY OF MEXICO

In around 900, the warlike Toltecs from the north of Mexico settled in the Valley of Mexico, at a time when the culture of Teotihuacán was in decline, and eventually continued south to interact with the Maya. From among the Toltecs sprang the myth of Quetzalcóatl, the plumed serpent, who, they believed, set out on a journey to the east, promising one day to return. Subsequently, this prophecy would have profound implications for the Aztecs.

The greatest Toltec city was Tula (Fig. 10.30) in the state of Hidalgo. Its ritual center includes the remains of a multi-columned palace and a pyramid supporting huge carved male warrior figures, once inside a temple but now exposed. The most striking features of the complex are the

**10.30** Temple-palace, Tula, Valley of Mexico, Mexico, after 900.

In its ruined state, this building at Tula makes clear the Toltec's dramatic use of the column, their square stumps seen in the foreground. As much symbols of militancy as structural elements, the ranks and files capture the warlike nature of the culture that created them.

two- and three-deep files of stuccoed columns that define one end of the ceremonial plaza and continue around the west and south façades of the palace. Ranks and files of columns are repeated inside the palace, where three great rooms, once roofed except for central openings, stand side by side.

On the north side of the pyramid, portions of talud and tablero motifs remain. On its other three sides, its talud-like stepped layers have only individual projecting stones as shadow-casting ornamentation. In this Toltec interpretation of the decorative form, a plain talud supports a two-tiered tablero, its upper levels stepped back, that serves as a frieze displaying images of coyotes, jaguars, eagles devouring human hearts, and effigies of gods. On both flanks and the rear, a so-called serpent wall once enclosed the pyramid and was crowned by seashell-shaped symbols of Quetzalcóatl.

## THE AZTECS AT TENOCHTITLÁN

The sun-worshiping Aztecs arrived in the Valley of Mexico in the thirteenth century and proceeded to assemble a large military and economic empire. Legend held that their capital and chief ceremonial center of Tenochtitlán (Fig. 10.31), the remains of which lie beneath modern-day Mexico City, had been identified to the Aztecs through the sighting of an eagle grasping a snake while perched on a prickly pear or tenochtli. By the time of the Spanish conquest in 1519, Tenochtitlán had a population of some 200,000 people and some eighty ritual-related structures, and the Aztec Empire extended from northern Mexico as far south as present-day Guatemala and El Salvador.

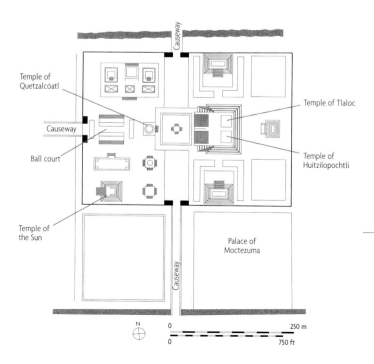

Temple of Quetzalcóatl

Causeway

Ball court

Temple of the Sun

Causeway

Causeway

Temple of Tlaloc

Temple of Huitzilopochtli

Palace of Moctezuma

N

0                 250 m

0                 750 ft

Tenochtitlán was established on a series of small islands. The Aztecs filled in earth among them to produce a unified setting which, ironically, dazzled their Spanish conquerors. They constructed four long causeways that divided the city into quadrants, each with its own neighborhoods, shrines, and administration buildings. In the center, they laid out a great ceremonial center and built the by-now-requisite platforms, pyramids, ball courts, and temples, including the central ritual complex, or Templo Mayor, once again using the talud and tablero as their basic ordering forms. A centerpiece of this architectural ensemble was the skull rack displaying the heads of sacrificial victims.

The Aztecs imagined Tenochtitlán to be at the center of the world and the city itself to be the cosmos in miniature, with its causeways oriented to the cardinal points. They believed the causeways' central intersection to be the point through which a vertical axis ran upward through thirteen levels and downward through nine more and believed souls, once released from their physical bodies, made a quest for eternal peace, beginning at the lowest level and assisted by magic charms interred with their physical remains. The Aztecs further believed that their empire and the cosmos depended on one another for existence and that the Aztec state was obliged to express this reciprocal relationship through ritual, including the practice of human sacrifice, most often by cutting out the hearts of their victims using obsidian knives.

The Templo Mayor included two subsidiary temples, one dedicated to the rain, water, and agriculture god Tlaloc and the other to Huitzilopochtli, the god of the sun, war, conquest, tribute, and dominion (Fig. 10.32). The Aztecs' religion required that they perform human sacrifices to Huitzilopochtli, their patron deity, in order to ensure that the sun rose each day and that they remained in the god's favor. The religious demands for human sacrifice were reinforced by military, political, and economic factors. The Aztecs fought wars not only to control territory but also to exact tribute. Once conquered, however, tribes constantly sought to disengage themselves from the empire, and tensions were understandably exacerbated by the Aztecs' never-ending demands for more sacrificial captives. Additionally, long-distance trade made luxury goods available to the Aztec elite, who then had to rely on military conquest and expansion both to maintain access to these goods and to obtain wealth through tribute. Thus, Aztec religious practice reinforced expansionist materialism of a warrior state.

**10.31** Plan of Tenochtitlán, location of present-day Mexico City, Mexico, after 900.

Focused on the skull rack at its center, this orthogonal layout makes use of the same platform and pyramid types seen centuries earlier at nearby Teotihuacán. What set this city apart and what first amazed Spanish explorers was its dramatic location at the center of a lake. The lake has long since disappeared, as have the remains of Tenochtitlán beneath the modern-day city.

**10.32** Excavated ruins of the Templo Mayor, Tenochtitlán, Mexico City, Mexico, after 900.

The ceremonial center of Tenochtitlán lies beneath modern-day Mexico City, so that only rarely are its excavated remains made visible. Likewise, it has been impossible to excavate more than a fraction of the city's ritual burial sites, so that information about Aztec sacrificial practices must come from other locations.

When the conquistador Hernán Cortés appeared with his small army, some of the Aztecs may have believed him to be the god Quetzalcóatl returned from a mythical journey, which, in turn, may have caused their king Moctezuma to act indecisively in the face of the Spanish threat. Whatever the case, allied with other tribes eager to end Aztec domination, in possession of more advanced weapons, and unwittingly assisted by the devastating spread of European diseases among the native population, the Spanish were able to conquer the vast Aztec Empire relatively quickly, decisively altering the course of Mesoamerican history.

## SOUTH AMERICA: THE ANDEAN WORLD

The Andes mountain chain runs the length of South America's Pacific coastline. It is in this region, particularly in what is now Peru and Bolivia, that a number of advanced Pre-Columbian civilizations flourished. Several "commodities" stand out as critical determinants of architectural development in the Andes: earth, stone, and water. As for earth and stone, these were basic construction materials: adobe for building walls near the coast and rubble and ashlar stone for laying up walls in the mountains. Water was manipulated everywhere and on an enormous scale for agricultural irrigation and occasionally and much more modestly, but extremely dramatically, for ritual purposes. Other factors such as altitude and weather, specifically drenching rains and parching droughts resulting from the appearance and disappearance of El Niño ocean currents, played important roles, too. Altitude, stemming from the precipitous rise of the Andes from the Pacific Ocean to a spine of peaks over 20,000 feet, greatly influenced the culture of Andean civilization. The highland peoples to the east and the river-valley cultures nearer to the coast were confronted with very different environments and, therefore, presented with various options for food production, principally systematic agriculture, fishing, and animal husbandry. As for the weather, fluctuations in El Niño events could lead to dramatic shifts in meteorological conditions, sometimes lasting longer than a year.

Remains of agricultural canals, lakes, and terraces, as well as ritual settings and urban developments, built by the Pre-Columbian peoples of South America's Pacific coast and highlands are so vast that they now represent the largest archeological "site" in the western hemisphere. Caral, near the modern city of Lima, Peru, is the oldest known, large-scale, urban ceremonial complex, perhaps the oldest major settlement, in the Americas. Covering some 165 acres, it includes earthen pyramids built almost 5000 years ago (at a time when Old Kingdom Egyptians were only building mastabas), and between the time of Caral's occupation and the rise of the Inca in the fifteenth century, numerous cultures and hundreds of cities and ritual centers were occupied, developed, and abandoned. The discussion that follows can only introduce a few of the sites of greatest architectural interest.

## EARLY CITIES ON THE NORTH COAST OF PERU

More than 1500 years after Caral's development, Sechín Alto, located on the Sechín branch of the Casma Valley, rose to become what was then the largest architectural complex in the Americas (Fig. 10.33). The ceremonial center's U-shaped plan consists of a granite-veneered stepped pyramid, 300 feet on its long sides, facing a sunken court flanked by low buildings and establishing an axis uniting a series of terraces. This was a precocious design, and its U-shaped planning pattern would be much emulated in later South American architecture.

Further to the north and contemporary with Sechín Alto, the ceremonial center of **Huaca** de los Reyes at Caballo Muerto displays the same U-shaped plan, but with a much greater degree of building articulation and with U-shaped structures repeated at various scales (Fig. 10.34). Here, a principal axis extending out over descending terraces is countered by cross axes terminated by flanking files of rooms, some fronted by in antis columns. In addition, there are a sunken court, embedded stairways, and colonnades with double and triple ranks of square columns. As construction began here circa 1500 BCE, Middle Kingdom Egyptians were building the similarly organized Temple of Queen Hatshepsut.

## EARLY DEVELOPMENT IN THE NORTHERN PERUVIAN ANDES

About 900 BCE, as Sechín Alto and Huaca de los Reyes were in decline, a new location rose to prominence as a cult center in the north-central highlands. Here, at Chavín de Huántar, coastal organizational principles were united with the skillful working and laying of stone, including monumental incised panels and freestanding sculpture. The site lies at almost 10,000 feet in the Andes but in a dramatic valley at the confluence of two rivers such that surrounding mountains still tower above it. The largest construction is the castillo, or castle, built in two stages

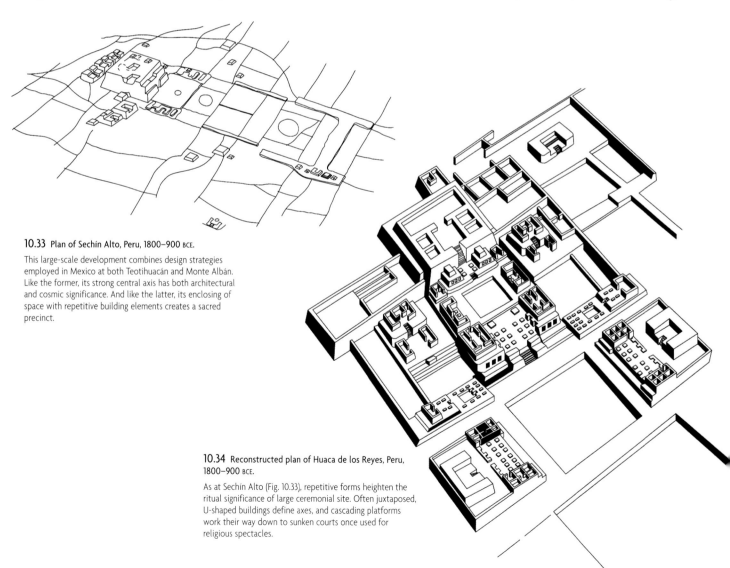

**10.33** Plan of Sechín Alto, Peru, 1800–900 BCE.

This large-scale development combines design strategies employed in Mexico at both Teotihuacán and Monte Albán. Like the former, its strong central axis has both architectural and cosmic significance. And like the latter, its enclosing of space with repetitive building elements creates a sacred precinct.

**10.34** Reconstructed plan of Huaca de los Reyes, Peru, 1800–900 BCE.

As at Sechín Alto (Fig. 10.33), repetitive forms heighten the ritual significance of large ceremonial site. Often juxtaposed, U-shaped buildings define axes, and cascading platforms work their way down to sunken courts once used for religious spectacles.

**10.35** Eastern façade of the New Temple, Chavín de Huántar, Peru, after 900 BCE.

The Inca are widely celebrated for their ability to carve stone. However, pre-Inca sites like this one show that skilled stonemasons had been at work in Peru for centuries before the Inca assembled their vast empire.

and faced with polished sandstone, limestone, and granite, with its U-shaped plan enveloping a sunken, circular court (Fig. 10.35). Evidence suggests that designers manipulated river water here for ritual purposes, possibly even creating dramatic sound effects by rushing it unseen through channels left within the stone construction. A larger labyrinth of corridors in the castillo connects to a chamber holding the Lanzón, a carved effigy of the principal god. The religious experience in this provocative physical and acoustical environment was apparently enhanced by the ingesting of hallucinogenic substances.

On the north coast of Peru, the Moche culture thrived from the first to the eighth centuries CE. Moche craftsmen fashioned exquisite metalwork, particularly in hammered gold, and the Moche power structure became the first in

Peru to unite coastal populations into a regional development, which included the Moche River Valley and the parallel Chicama Valley. At the coastal capital of Cerro Blanco, located just south of the Moche River's entry into the Pacific Ocean, workers built two great, adobe-brick structures (Fig. 10.36) by 100 CE: the Huaca del Sol (Pyramid of the Sun), 1130 feet by 525 feet on its sides and 130 feet tall, and the smaller Huaca de la Luna (Pyramid of the Moon), both now much deteriorated due to erosion. What were

---

**10.36** Huaca del Sol, Peru, before 100 CE.

Temple mounds, of which this is a very large South American example, appeared all the way from what is today the state of Missouri to Bolivia. This one measures more than 1100 feet on a side, making it much larger than the largest Egyptian pyramid, that of Khufu or Cheops (Fig. 1.24).

**10.37** Gateway of the Sun, Tiwanaku, Bolivia, after 200 CE.
Of all pre-Inca stonework, this monolithic gateway must be the most impressive. The incised frieze includes an effigy of the weather and sky god Thunupa standing atop a stepped platform.

Tiwanaku thrived for some 800 years, with occupancy beginning by 200 CE. The city had a population of at least 20,000, possibly as many as 40,000, and an economy based on llama and alpaca herding and agriculture. It was not an isolated urban settlement but one among many centers united by a road system that helped consolidate the region into South America's first, and longest lasting, empire. Tiwanaku's ceremonial-center monuments are most impressive for their exquisitely hewn, monumentally scaled, ashlar sandstone and feldspar masonry that anticipates the celebrated stonework of the later Inca. The city's largest structure is the Akapana temple, a sandstone-faced, stepped pyramid with an earthen core, some 650 feet on a side, with a sunken court atop it. As at Chavín de Huántar, water was probably manipulated here as a part of religious rituals. There are also numerous stelae, one 24 feet tall, and gateways, including the Gateway of the Sun (Fig. 10.37), made from a single stone block and ornamented with an incised frieze and projecting image of a deity.

## THE CHIMOR KINGDOM

While Tiwanaku was part of an impressive regional development, the Chimor Kingdom was even larger, exceeding in size all South American empires except that of the Inca. It eventually combined coastal and Andean cultures and was governed from the Pacific-coast capital city of Chan Chan founded about 1000 CE. The city's most distinctive architectural features are ciudadelas, or large palace compounds (Fig. 10.38), roughly rectangular in plan and most often divided into three sequential precincts: a large, northern entry court with smaller adjacent courts, U-shaped audiencias, or offices, and files of small storage rooms; a burial platform adjacent to family living quarters and more multipurpose rooms; and a smaller area reserved for a well and probably quarters for servants. Throughout the remainder of the city, with its orthogonal streets, lie the remains of neighborhoods with cane-walled residences, two large plazas, cemeteries, sunken gardens, reservoirs, and ceremonial mounds.

## THE INCA

The Chimor Empire and others in the Andean world were eventually conquered by the Inca, and no culture in the Pre-Columbian Americas occupied an environment more dramatic than theirs. A militaristic and intensely socially stratified people, they organized the precipitous terrain of the Andes by terracing the rugged mountainsides and by providing sophisticated irrigation systems for agriculture. The Incas eventually controlled an area stretching some 2500 miles throughout much of modern-day Colombia, Ecuador, Peru, and Bolivia; their greatest era of empire-building was 1438–1532, only a short time before the appearance of Francisco Pizarro and the beginning of the Spanish conquest.

actually irregularly shaped, stepped adobe platforms now face one another across only the remains of residences and workshops. Moche artisans depicted one local deity, known as the decapitator, as an anthropomorphic spider with a fanged mouth. The prominent image of another fanged god, this one half human, was frequently shown holding a ceremonial crescent-shaped knife, suggesting that the platforms were at times the setting for human sacrifice. Rather than being practiced continuously, as among the Aztecs, these sacrifices may have taken place only during El Niño years, when the Moche sought divine intervention to end the destructive rains. By 600 CE, such a rain event and the floods it triggered so ravaged the irrigation system of the Cerro Blanco site that occupants began to abandon it.

## THE NAZCA ON THE PERUVIAN SOUTH COAST

At the same time the Moche occupied Cerro Blanco, the Nazca to the south were renowned for their ceramics and textiles, their engineering of underground conduits and reservoirs, and their construction of enormous glyphs laid out across the hillsides above the Pacific. By removing the upper desert strata of rusted metallic particles, Nazca glyph-makers exposed the lighter-colored sediment beneath. Some giant glyphs depict humans, llamas, and even a monkey and a spider. On flat terrain, the glyph's lines appear to have been used as ritual pathways, with lines running for distances greater than ten miles and defining such geometric forms as triangles, trapezoids, zigzags, and spirals.

## AN EMPIRE IN THE WESTERN BOLIVIAN HIGHLANDS

Southeast of the Nazca region, inland from the coast, near Lake Titicaca, at more than 13,000 feet above sea level are the northern Bolivian highlands. Here, the city of

**10.38** Aerial view of Chan Chan, Peru, after 1000 CE.

This Moche Valley city covered almost 5000 acres and housed a population estimated by some at 250,000. The wall construction is adobe brick, which was frequently carved in high relief, covered with plaster, and then painted.

While they had no written language, they kept numerical records using knotted cords. Their knowledge of medicine and surgery was highly developed, and included the practice of cutting circular openings in human skulls, perhaps to relieve internal pressure. They domesticated the alpaca and llama, and grew a wide variety of crops, from maize to sweet potatoes and tomatoes to peanuts, and even cotton from which they wove cloth. They built extensive road systems and suspension bridges, and formidable stone fortresses. No other contemporary culture in the western hemisphere was so skilled at fashioning and laying Cyclopean stone masonry.

The Incas located their capital at Cuzco, between the Huatanay and Tullumayo rivers. While the construction there does not exceed one story in height, the site is impressive for the rigor of its linear stone buildings grouped around quadrangles and for the great fortress of Saqsaywaman, where enormous stone blocks were exquisitely set without the use of mortar (Fig. 10.39). Among the city's temples is the Corichanca, which has a radial organization determined by forty-one celestial sight lines extended into space by means of freestanding pillars.

**10.39** Cyclopean masonry, Cuzco, Peru, ca. 1500.

In Inca stonework, each stone was dressed, then placed adjacent to its neighbors without the use of mortar. Masons then marked the outline of the new stone on those already in place, removed it, and pounded out a new profile to receive it. This process was repeated again and again until a tight fit was achieved.

Perhaps even more impressive is the dramatic royal estate developed at Machu Picchu by the Inca ruler Pachacuti (page 250), which is located at a height of 7600 feet in the Andes. The site includes 200 or so houses that could have sheltered only about 1000 persons, in a climate that can only be described as inhospitable other than in the summer months. Here, the Incas transformed a saddle of land into a cohesive ensemble of agricultural terraces, distinctive house types, meeting halls, and carefully defined plazas. The houses are notable for their stone construction, sometimes battered walls, tall endwall gables, trapezoidal openings, and distinctive plans, many of which have three closed sides and only a pier or piers on one long side. Their light wooden roof framing and covering of thatch have long since disappeared, leaving their isolated, tall gables to form the dramatic Machu Picchu skyline.

Pizarro, who had come to the New World as early as 1510, returned in 1530 with only 180 troops. Arriving in Peru, he found the Inca Empire recovering from civil war and two brothers, sons of the previous Inca emperor, vying for power. Pizarro captured one brother just after he had ordered the murder of his sibling. The Inca political system was so hierarchical that he was able to take complete control and ransack the culture. It was a sad end to an unfortunate period of Spanish-led cultural destabilization.

## AFRICA

Before we begin our exploration of the indigenous architecture of Africa, first some comments about African buildings and sites found elsewhere in this book. The ancient Romans occupied North Africa, and their city of Timgad (see Fig. 5.8) in Algeria is discussed in Chapter 5. Islamic invaders subsequently spread across North Africa, and Islamic influence percolated south and west into the African continent. Two Islamic mosques are discussed below because their construction methods are singularly African; other mosques, as well as a discussion of mosque planning, appear in Chapter 7. Various European powers colonized Africa from the late fifteenth through the twentieth centuries and generally brought their architecture with them. While this widespread work is not covered, one example of modern African architecture appears in Chapter 16 (see Fig. 16.95).

Second, a recognition that what follows is unfortunately brief, given that the African continent includes several dozen countries with widely varying climatic conditions, vegetation, and building materials, and that many of them have radically different cultures. In addition, Africans continue to suffer from more than their share of war, famine, and disease, and partly because of these problems, a comprehensive, in-depth history of African architecture has yet to be written.

Third, an explanation of this section's organization. There are three broad, geographical regions on the African continent: 1) the North Atlantic and Mediterranean coasts (including the coast of Egypt); 2) the Sahara Desert; and 3) the sub-Sahara. While the first two are represented here, the vast majority of the examples are drawn from the third: the sub-Sahara. This means that building types, rather than region or tribe as used above for the Americas, offer the most logical categories for organization, specifically: 1) portable fabric structures, 2) permanent dwellings, 3) urbanization and fortification, 4) palaces, and 5) churches and mosques. In all instances, sites are located according to modern country names, but peoples are identified according to traditional tribal names.

### PORTABLE FABRIC STRUCTURES

For the semi-nomadic people of the western Sahara, the tent is the only practical means of shelter, as it can be folded up and moved about on the back of a camel. In southern Morocco, herdsmen maintain both sheep and goats in a desert environment that includes plenty of scrub brush as well as occasional luxurious oases. Atop grass-mat flooring, families erect two poles, running longitudinally and forming a triangle, and stretch over them a pieced-together trapezoidal cloth, its wider side to the front and woven from animal hair, and lash it down using guy ropes attached to pegs driven in the ground (Fig. 10.40). They make the tent-cloth by sewing together woven strips running the full width of the piece, the width of each strip determined by the size of their loom. They insert short poles at the front and rear of their tent to lift the edges of the cloth, providing for access and ventilation, and they add skirts at both sides for closure. These tents are only tall enough for sitting or kneeling and sleeping inside.

Larger tents used by desert nomads farther east are supported by pairs of upright wooden poles spanned by a third horizontal pole and so forming a wicket-like frame. Using one of these frames in the center and one to each side, the nomadic builders raise up their tent structures to the height of conventional rooms.

In sub-Saharan, largely forested, central Zaire, the Kuba tribe uses mats of split palms tied to closely spaced reeds to enclose their gable-roofed houses (Fig. 10.41). They frame up walls using light poles and infill them with a lattice of smaller sticks, then attach the horizontal mat strips that they weave into elaborate geometric patterns. The Fulani people of Burkina Faso use woven mats to cover their sapling-frame domical structures, which can be compared to the Native American wigwams of the Midwest (see Fig. 10.3).

### PERMANENT DWELLINGS

Structures like those of the Fulani present only one example in the dizzying variety of small, round- and square-plan dwelling types developed in the sub-Saharan region. These may have (or have had) walls of upright

**10.40** (above left) Two-pole tent of nomadic Moroccans.

Compare these portable fabric structures with the Great Plains teepee developed by Native North Americans (Fig. 10.2). In both cases, nomadic people brought their dwellings to needed resources rather than bringing the resources to fixed habitations.

**10.41** (above) Gable-roofed Kuba house made of mats of split palms, Zaire.

Pervious, or permeable, surfaces like the palm mats seen here are ideal for enclosing space in southern African Zaire's hot and sunny climate. They allow both light and air to filter through them while they maintain privacy for occupants.

**10.42** (left) Conical adobe structure, Musgum, Chad.

On no other continent has the potential of adobe, or soil with clay content, been more thoroughly investigated as a construction material than in Africa. Among its assets are a receptivity to carving and sculpting as well as paint.

poles or bamboo, sapling lattice (or wattle) covered with clay (or daub), or of rubble stone or adobe or a combination of the two, with conical (often concave- or convex-profile) thatched roofs, or they may have no upright walls at all, but pointed-arch or triangular cross-sections and be built of adobe, sometimes dramatically textured (Fig. 10.42), or sapling frames covered with coarse grass.

Among these dwelling types are the cylindrical, adobe tower houses of the Botammariba tribe in northeast Togo, which have recently been added to the United Nations' list of World Heritage Sites (Fig. 10.43). In adjacent Benin, coastal fishing tribes build pole-frame houses on rectangular plans and cover them with thatched hipped or gabled roofs. They raise these houses above the water on multiple stilts that also form the vertical framework for submerged fish-farming pens. While these houses are raised in the air, African dwellings elsewhere consist of subterranean dugouts and even artificially enlarged caves.

The rectilinear houses in such places as Cameroon may have, via the Atlantic slave trade, influenced the development of architecture in the southeastern United States. The Tikar tribe of Cameroon still builds square- or rectangular- or sometimes round-plan houses on stone bases, with walls of vertical bamboo or bundled palm fronds chinked using mud and with tall, slender, wooden posts supporting gabled or hipped, thatched roofs and porches (Fig. 10.44). Some remaining slave dwellings in the Caribbean and the cotton-plantations of Mississippi and Louisiana have similar forms and the interconnections are still being studied.

The Ashanti (or Asante) people in Ghana have long built houses that display a common African residential

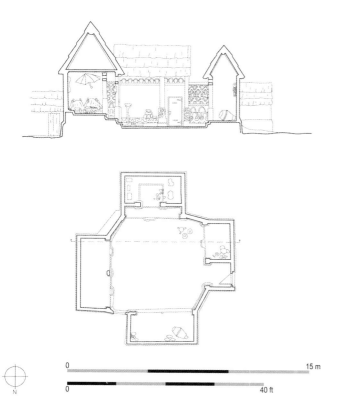

layout: a square or rectangular courtyard surrounded by four, wide, shallow, gable-roofed rooms (Fig. 10.45—plan and section). In their larger houses, they combine several of these courtyard-and-four-room units. They use adobe for walls on which they develop low-relief ornamentation in the form of stylized animals and geometric motifs.

In the nineteenth century, the militant Zulu tribe in what is today northeastern South Africa constructed domical structures (Fig. 10.46). After digging a circular trench, they inserted saplings or bundles of saplings into it and bent them into concentric arches, one set leaning back from the front door and another leaning forward from the rear. On top of this frame, they sometimes overlaid a similar set of concentric arched saplings increasing in arch size from left to right and right to left until meeting at the top, the four arching semi-domes together forming a single lattice. If necessary for stability, they erected post-and-beam frames of sapling poles inside the dome and attached the two systems. Atop their domes, they placed concentric grass mats, overlapping them from bottom to top like shingles, and tied them down with circumferential grass ropes. Zulu descendents continue to build some similar structures, but changing economic and social conditions have greatly diminished the number of such traditional buildings.

## URBANIZATION AND FORTIFICATION

As an urban vessel for their complex, polygamous, cattle-herding social organization, the Zulus arranged their circular dwellings to form circular villages. At the center and surrounded by a palisade, they laid out a parade ground for military maneuvers, which also served as an open pasture for the king's cattle. Outside the palisade, they distributed the individual houses, several structures deep, with their own cattle pens. And around the houses, they

**10.43** (top left) Adobe tower house of the Botammariba tribe, Koutammakou, Togo.

In the United States, significant historical buildings are listed on the National Register of Historic Places. The most significant of these become National Historic Landmarks. On the scale of the entire planet, the United Nations identifies World Heritage sites like this one.

**10.44** (above left) Thatch-roofed Tikar home, Bali, Cameroon.

The canny builders of these houses combined construction materials and methods to very good effect: stone at the bottom for the moisture-resistant sill, bamboo or palm fronds and a mud sealant for the protective walls, and thatch sloped to shed water for the roof.

**10.45** (left) Plan and section of Asante home, Ghana.

Within the pages of this book are found many examples of courtyard houses built by multiple cultures at multiple times. Notice here that access to the courtyard is made along its edges rather than toward its center, a non-axial and therefore less formal and hierarchical arrangement.

0               15 m
0               40 ft

raised up a second, taller palisade. Some of these tribal developments were huge, a mile or so in diameter, and accommodated several thousand inhabitants.

Members of the Fali tribe in northern Cameroon still lay out similar settlements. Beginning with generally cylindrical structures, having adobe walls and thatched roofs, they form walled compounds that include kitchens, sleeping quarters, and granaries. In some cases, they link these compounds together to form a larger, roughly circular farm enclosure in which there are granaries and pens for the head of the family's livestock (Fig. 10.47). In the complex, spatially-based cosmic symbolism of the Fali, the granaries are the most important buildings. Historian

of urbanism Enrico Guidoni says that "as places where edible seeds are stored, they represent the ark that descended from the sky in the mystic age and contained, among other things, all the vegetable species." Granaries like those of the Fali are so essential to village life that attention has invariably been lavished on their design and construction. Bernard Rudofsky celebrated such structures in areas as widely separated as Ivory Coast and Libya. In the former, miniature silos with thatched roofs are made of clay, some cylindrical, some cook-pot shaped with a curving bottom, both types raised on stubby, clay legs that serve to avoid dampness and lend a delightful anthropomorphic character to these inanimate objects. In the case of the example in Figure 10.48, white-wash handprints provide exuberant, personalized ornamentation. In

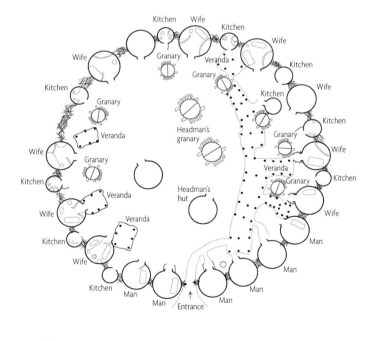

10.47 Plan of Fali tribe compound, Cameroon.

The expression "circling the wagons" is a familiar one in American Westerns, and it suggests forming a circle for purpose of security. Here the Fali tribesmen have applied the same strategy to a permanent settlement.

10.48 Cylindrical granary, Yenegandougou, Ivory Coast.

It would be difficult to imagine a more direct and personal way of marking a building than with handprints. Likewise, there could be a no more classic composition than this one, with its bottom, middle, and top comparable to the base, shaft, and capital of the classical column.

**10.49** Qasr (storage fortress), Kabao, Libya.

The extension of horizontal wooden members through adobe walls, as in this multi-story structure, is a device that has been widely used in arid climates. For instance, similar Spanish Colonial construction remains in the American Southwest and farther south in Africa at Djenne in Mali (see Fig. 10.56).

Kabao, Libya, individual family storehouses have been agglomerated as storage fortresses, or **qasr**. With walls made of rubble stone and adobe and an inner structure of wood that frequently penetrates to the outside to support balconies, they have been constructed over time as places of security for crops but also for families in times of danger (Fig. 10.49).

No African settlements are more provocative than those of the Dogon people, who live in the upper Niger River region of Mali, and none have more impressive art or more elaborate myths to explain a state of being. Because of their density and the absence of wheeled vehicles and, therefore, the need for any kind of grid or even short, straight streets, and because they are often raised up amid the detritus of fallen rocks beneath cliff faces, Dogon villages have a shockingly chaotic appearance to modern Western eyes (Fig. 10.50). Seen from the air, they look to be, Rudofsky wrote, no more than "debris." These villages and their structures are, in fact, laid out not according to principles of geometric regularity or caste hierarchy but according to a common cosmological view. A diagram of a Dogon village derived by anthropologist Marcel Griaule from his interviews with tribal elders is anthropomorphic, based upon a reclining male figure. Among other things, this diagram situates the meeting house at the head, altars at the feet, and male and female symbols (vertical phallic shaft and circular stone with a cavity) at the positions of the genitalia. The Dogon meeting house, or toguna, is usually rectangular, but sometimes round, is freestanding, oriented to the cardinal points, open on one side, and raised up on wooden uprights or stones, and the uprights are sometimes embellished with fetish images (Fig. 10.51).

Dogon houses are intended not only to serve the functional needs of the family but also to induce fertility. They have cruciform plans, with large central rooms surrounded by four, stubby projections. The central room accommodates sleeping and weaving, with a kitchen in the projection to the rear and storerooms to either side, and a porch at the entry. Like the village, the dwelling plan has anthropomorphic connotations, representing a female figure on her back prepared for sexual intercourse, with the door opening from the porch to the central room symbolizing genitalia. These houses rise up two stories but with very low ceilings. Their adobe walls are covered with thatched roofs shaped like slightly deformed cones.

It cannot be surprising that the inventive Dogon minds have created a fantastic, fanciful, and potent art. Dramatically painted figures of serpents, hyenas, and crocodiles appear to emerge from adobe walls. In an arid land, water spirits, or nommo, are sculpted in clay, wood, and iron, with raised arms producing elongated figural proportions. Decorations carved into wooden granary shutters connect owners to the totemic altars, or binus, of their kinship groups.

We have already examined Moroccan tents. In their country's southern valleys and Atlas Mountains, Moroccans have also built compact, fortified towns with both circular-concentric and orthogonal layouts. These towns include a repetitive building type, the kasbah (Fig. 10.52), a fortified multi-family house with a square plan anchored at its corners by square, projecting, battered towers. These

**10.50** Dogon cliff village, Bandiagara Escarpment, Mali.

The complexity of this low-rise but dense urban settlement seems disorienting from the air and to the untrained eye. However, the Dogon navigate its unpaved, winding paths as deftly as Venetians travel through their no-less-irregular city of canals and paved pedestrian walkways and piazzas.

**10.51** South side of a toguna, from the Dogon village of Madougou, Mali.

Dogon craftsmen are highly skilled in working with wood, as can be seen in the carved wood posts at the base of this toguna. The carvings represent Dogon fertility beliefs.

**10.52** Kasbah, Ait-Benhaddun, Morocco.

For some movie watchers, the word kasbah evokes images from films steeped in intrigue. In reality, a kasbah is no different from a fortified castle in medieval Europe.

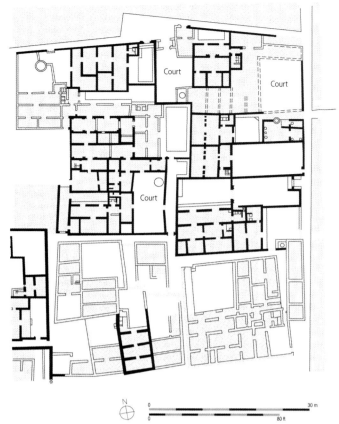

**10.53** Plan of Gedi, Kenya, 15th century and after.

Another courtyard house, this time part of a palace complex. One of the giants of twentieth-century architecture, Ludwig Mies van der Rohe (see chapter 15), spent considerable time exploring the design potential afforded by this residential type.

**10.54** Outer and inner walls of the main audience room, palace, Gedi, Kenya.

This view of the main audience hall gives an impression of the scale of the Gedi complex. While the architectural forms may appear European, the palace predates Portuguese incursions in the sixteenth century.

dwellings are constructed of stone, brick, and adobe and sometimes rise up ten or more stories. The upper reaches of the tower walls are ornamented with unframed windows and repetitive smaller openings and recesses—frequently involving corbeling, and are sometimes capped with crenellations, all of which produce a distinctive silhouette and a dramatic pattern of light and shadow in the brilliant desert sun.

No African fortress complex has been more celebrated than the Great Zimbabwe (for which the country is named), a cluster of stone structures laid up in coursed granite without mortar, with a fortified, terraced acropolis on an adjacent hill, all covering some 1800 acres. More ruins, including cattle pens, lie between the two sites. The perimeter wall of the main compound, more than ten feet thick and thirty feet high, runs along a circumference of more than 800 feet, with a smaller secondary compound inside it, anchored by the solid-stone so-called "elliptical tower," its base more than seventeen feet in diameter. Inside this secondary compound lie the remains of housing units: circular-plan structures surrounding central sunken courts that were entered by way of tunnels. Activity on the site dates back as far as 1000 CE, with most of the construction carried out in the thirteenth and fourteenth centuries at a time when the population may have reached 40,000 inhabitants. The Great Zimbabwe was gradually abandoned in the fifteenth century. Also impressive are

the fortresses in the Gondar region of Ethiopia, begun during the thirteenth-century reign of King Facilidas (Gondar's rock-cut churches are discussed below). Most notable in this group is the walled city of Fasil Ghebbi, built in the sixteenth century.

In Kenya on the Indian Ocean, a cosmopolitan population arose by the mid-thirteenth century as a result of extensive regional trade. The indigenous Swahili tribe, influenced by the spread of Islam, built cities along the coast and, in the case of Gedi, a few miles inland. This city flourished for some 200 years, went into decline, and was abandoned by the seventeenth century. Excavations have revealed a development covering almost fifty acres, with a palace and a mosque and courtyard houses. The one-story houses began as a wide, shallow principal room behind a street-front court, with secondary, more private rooms to the rear and to each side. Eventually, the builders added an inner court for cooking and enclosures for commercial use along the street (Fig. 10.53). A kind of annular arrangement of such courtyard houses can still be seen in Marrakech, Morocco.

## PALACES

The palace at Gedi, probably dating to the fifteenth century and later, is a larger version of the city's houses, with an entrance court opening off the town square and an audience court for public receptions, as well as other courts elsewhere, all adjacent to rectangular rooms. Like the houses of the wealthy, this palace was constructed of stone and, even in its ruined state, still displays sophisticated moldings, arches, and other finely worked features (Fig. 10.54). The audience court was also richly detailed and included pegs for hanging ornamental carpets. In Uganda, at the headwaters of the Nile in what was then the Kingdom of Buganda, the palace of the chiefs, or kabakas, was constructed in 1882 and transformed into a royal tomb in 1884. It sits on a hilltop, is circular in plan, and is constructed of wood and wattle and daub and covered with a thatched roof. The royal palaces of the Abomey in Benin, now converted to museums, contain celebrated bas reliefs dating from as early as ca. 1700.

## CHURCHES AND MOSQUES

Ancient Egyptian architecture influenced building styles to the south in Ethiopia and the Sudanese desert, resulting in the construction of temples, pyramids, and obelisks, including the giant shaft and the ruins of the palace at Aksum, both in place by the early fourth century. Christianity made its way into Ethiopia in the early years of the Church and was well established there by this time. Among the architectural results are a remarkable series of freestanding churches, each carved from a single mass of live rock. Constructed (or excavated) in the thirteenth century by the craftsmen of King Lalibela, they include St. George's Church, which has a cruciform plan extruded to form a cruciform mass (Fig. 10.55).

Mosques of distinctly African character can be found in Mali and Burkina Faso. The Great Mosque in Djenne, Mali is the third on the site and dates to 1906–07 in a city that was founded in the third century BCE. Oral histories and

**10.55** View from above St. George's Church, Lalibela, Ethiopia, 13th century.

It is unusual to find architectural space, like the interior of this church, carved out of live rock rather than enclosed by quarried stones. Other celebrated examples are the cave temples of India and the city of Petra in Jordan.

**10.56** Great Mosque, Djenne, Mali, 1906–07.

While adobe construction has been prominent in this chapter, nowhere has it been exploited to greater dramatic effect than in this mosque. Some controversy continues regarding possible French contributions to this building's design and construction.

**10.57** Mosque, Bobo-Dioulasso, Burkina Faso, late 19th century.

One might expect such an architectural phantasm to occur only within the "mysterious" continent of Africa. However, Dutch architects in Amsterdam in the early twentieth century produced brick-and-wood apartment buildings that display kindred forms.

surface archeology suggest that the second structure, dating from the thirteenth century, was constructed of adobe, and was almost 200 feet long and more than 100 feet wide and surrounded by a moat; its outer walls were apparently articulated with a relentless file of picket-like towers and sloping buttresses. The present Great Mosque (Fig. 10.56) is also constructed of adobe, with buttressing pickets, pinnacled towers, and prominently projecting, horizontal, wooden members that cast dramatic shadows and so are comparable to Spanish Colonial work in the American Southwest. The same type of handmade clay construction extends to the houses of Djenne and to those in Timbuktu, located to the northeast, and to those in other towns of Mali, Niger, Ivory Coast, and Burkina Faso. In the latter, the Bobo-Dioulasso Mosque (Fig. 10.57), which probably dates from the late nineteenth century, can only be described as fantastic, with its "ancestral pillars" shaped like attenuated pyramids and sprouting spiky, wooden projections and mottled with white and terracotta-colored pigments.

## CONCLUSIONS ABOUT ARCHITECTURAL IDEAS

In North America, indigenous peoples produced a wide variety of portable, or at least temporary, architecture. Where conditions allowed, or even demanded, they also produced impressive permanent structures: "frozen" ones in the far north; sandstone and adobe pueblos in the arid southwest; and monumental earthworks in the Ohio and Lower Mississippi valleys and the Southeast, especially in the form of pyramids and pyramid-like structures that dominated ceremonial centers here as well as throughout the remainder of the Americas from Mexico to Bolivia.

Sophisticated architectural ordering systems imposed on large complexes appeared very early on in both the Gulf Coast of Mexico and in Peru. In the former, during the second millennium BCE, the Olmecs at La Venta built an earth mound that terminated an axis defined by flanking plaza-defining buildings. The Teotihuacános in the Valley of Mexico, who adopted Olmec devices, articulated the faces of their stepped platforms and pyramids with sloping talud and frieze-like tablero elements. The axially organized city of Teotihuacán stands in stark contrast to spatially organized Monte Albán in Oaxaca, where stepped platforms, once crowned with temples, define a central space in which other platforms reside, including one canted at an angle, presumably for the purpose of celestial alignment.

The Maya of the Yucatán Peninsula and Central American lowlands developed astronomy to its ancient American apogee, including their invention of a highly accurate calendar. In their cities of Tikal, Copán, and Palenque, amid dense jungle foliage, they built tall pyramids and low-slung ball courts as part of large ceremonial centers or acropolises, constructed corbel-vaulted temples, and sculpted stelae in the form of tree-stones that celebrated the reigns of their kings. Their wall articulation using the talud and tablero explored variations on themes set forth earlier in the Valley of Mexico.

At the Yucatán city of Chichén Itzá, the Toltecs from the north merged their aggressive architectural style with the sometimes geometric, sometimes organic, even ornate stone assemblies preferred by the Maya. The most distinctive features of Toltec religious buildings in their capital city of Tula in Hidalgo are ranks and files of columns, which are seen as well in the hypostyle hall-like Temple of the Warriors at Chichen-Itzá.

Back in the Valley of Mexico by the thirteenth century, the Aztecs used the by now familiar stepped pyramids and platforms, plazas, and talud–tablero combinations to create the ceremonial center of their orthogonally planned capital of Tenochtitlán. The sophistication of their ordering systems reflects a design continuity in Mexico and Central America that dates back more than 2000 years to the Olmecs.

In South America the scope of development was comparable to that in Mexico and Central America. In the Andean world, ceremonial centers with stepped pyramids were impressive, but no more so than the vast irrigation systems and sprawling giant glyphs laid out on Peru's south-coast hillsides and plains. At such Peruvian sites as Sechín Alto and Huaca de los Reyes, pyramids dominated U-shaped complexes organized by means of axes and cross axes and carefully defined plazas. Stone masonry was already well developed at these ceremonial centers by the first millennium BCE, but became even more so at the Bolivian city of Tiwanaku, and yet more so again among the Inca, with their highland buildings, fortifications, and agricultural terraces. Despite the effects of erosion, the two great adobe-brick pyramids built by the Moche at Cerro Blanco are still impressive, as are the remaining "footprints" of palace compounds occupied by the Chimor kings at Chan Chan.

In the end, Pre-Columbian architecture and planning, from southern North America, through Mexico and Central America, and into South America can be seen as all of one piece, with certain design themes pursued across millennia and cross-culturally. In North America, where periodic or continual migrations were common, a diversity of architectural forms and construction methods were largely a response to building-material availability and the demands of climate. None of these constructions is a more elegant result of such constraints than the Great Plains teepee. Limited wood for frames and plentiful buffalo hides for coverings inspired a lightweight, conical structure that could be adjusted to accommodate both extreme heat and extreme cold.

The collapse of indigenous cultures in Mexico and farther south began with internal strife and environmental pressures, then was rapidly accelerated by the Spanish importation of Old World diseases, the overpowering effect of European weaponry, and blatant Spanish greed. In North America, the pattern was similar but took place over a much longer period of time, until virtually all Native American tribes had been forced onto reservations. Despite their mistreatment, the indigenous peoples of North America have not disappeared, be they the Mississippi Choctaw tribe; the Navajo descendants of the Ancestral Pueblo of the Southwest; or the Maya and Inca descendants who still populate Central America and Peru respectively. Vivid evidence of this continuum can be seen at the recently completed National Museum of the American Indian on the Mall in Washington, D.C. (with satellites in Maryland and New York City), where the "diversity of cultures and the continuity of cultural knowledge among indigenous peoples" is celebrated.

Reaching meaningful conclusions about indigenous architecture in Africa is difficult. Artificially configured and governed during the colonial period, then left largely adrift after the exit of European colonial powers, the vast African continent now offers up equal parts of beauty and mystery and of conflict and tragedy. Where its architecture has been closely studied, the work has most often been done by anthropologists and not architectural historians and so is probably most familiar to the public though the pages of such publications as *National Geographic Magazine*, and while African art became extremely influential in Europe and America in the early twentieth century, African architecture has not achieved such prominence, a condition exacerbated by the sheer difficulty and sometimes outright danger involved in visiting many of the important monuments and sites. In addition, the intuitive, highly symbolic, natural-world connectedness of so many African structures and landscapes (while appropriately compared to many Native American constructions) has made them seem remote and even incomprehensible to those conditioned by the Western architectural traditions.

As among Pre-Columbian Americans, African tribesmen have erected and continue to erect many types of portable structures using a wide variety of local materials. Available materials have also been the principal form-determining agents for their more permanent buildings, with some form of adobe being the most common medium for everything from modest shelters to the largest, most exotic mosques. African builders have also worked stone when they have found it available, producing sprawling complexes like the Great Zimbabwe and the fantastic, monolithic, rock-cut churches of Ethiopia.

In the end, the study and appreciation of African architecture must be viewed as a work in progress. Those who find fascination in the diversity of the built environment can only hope that all Africans will, sooner rather than later, achieve a state of peace and prosperity and that this, in turn, will make it possible for the rest of the world to appreciate better their rich building traditions.

# CHAPTER 11

# RENAISSANCE ARCHITECTURE

European mariners began their voyages of exploration first to Africa and then to the Americas in the fifteenth century, a time when architecture in Europe was undergoing a dramatic change from the Gothic of the late Middle Ages to that of the Renaissance. Chapter 9 on the Gothic period contained little discussion of buildings in Italy. Here, Romanesque churches were never completely purged of their classical elements, and monumental Gothic religious architecture never became completely at home in the one-time center of the Roman Empire, where vestiges of a grand classical past loomed about portentously.

Still, the fabric of most Italian cities, particularly that of the everyday residential buildings, was woven in the eleventh through fourteenth centuries. In such inland centers as Florence, these buildings were rather plain: heavy masonry blocks punctured with arched openings and sometimes provided with shady **loggias** or porches. Likewise, medieval governmental buildings anchored the civic cores of cities and caused to form around them the open spaces or piazzas that to this day speak the very language of urbanism. It was within this well established medieval context that Renaissance architects would make their radical proposals.

While both France and England were unified monarchies by the end of the Middle Ages, Italy remained an assemblage of fractious but vigorous city-states and fiefdoms. Trade flourished as a result of Italy's position between western Europe and Byzantium in the east, which was then the trade hub for products coming out of the Orient. Aggressive merchants exported luxury goods and organized textile industries. Civic life in the principal Italian city-states became dominated by families whose wealth arose not from the traditional source of inherited landholdings but from new mercantile profits. The economic stimulus prompted by the boom in trade led to urban and cultural revival in the leading Italian city-states.

Nowhere was this change more dramatic than in Florence, the city regarded as the birthplace of the Renaissance. Here the newly wealthy wool merchants and powerful bankers, including members of the Medici family, sought prestige and status through their patronage of arts and letters, and local artists and architects were up to the task. The spirit of their revolutionary painting, sculpture, and architecture arose from the new Renaissance world-view of humanism (and its accompanying condition of secularization), which celebrated rationality and individuality and mankind's ability to make and act upon empirical observations of the physical world. Humanist scholars and artists recovered Classical Greek and Roman texts, including Vitruvius's *De Architectura*, and aspired to create a modern world rivaling that of the ancients. Within their new intellectual construct, it was not only permissible, but even desirable, to achieve fame, meaning that, unlike the largely anonymous designers of the Middle Ages, Renaissance architects became celebrated as personalities such that their identities and even details of their personal lives have come all the way down to us today.

These architects, absorbing the writings of the Greek philosopher Plato, set out to create an architecture of mathematical perfection. In pursuit of this goal, they turned to whole-number ratios, such as 1:1, 1:2, 2:3, and 3:4, taken from the musical consonances discovered by the Greek mathematician Pythagoras, and concluded that

## Chronology

| | |
|---|---|
| life of Lorenzo de' Medici | 1449–92 |
| Brunelleschi constructs the dome of Florence Cathedral | 1404–18 |
| Masaccio paints the Trinity fresco | 1427–28 |
| Alberti writes *De re aedificatoria* | 1452 |
| French invasions of Italy and resulting return of Italian influence to France | 1494 and 1527 |
| Bramante constructs the Tempietto | 1502 |
| papacy of Pope Julius II | 1503–13 |
| Bramante's initial design for St. Peter's | 1505 |
| Raphael designs the Villa Madama | ca. 1516 |
| reign of Henry VII and arrival of initial Renaissance influence in England | 1485–1509 |
| Michelangelo begins work at St. Peter's | 1546 |
| Michelangelo designs the Sforza Chapel | 1564 |
| Palladio builds the Villa Rotonda | 1556–57 |
| Palladio publishes *I Quattro Libri dell' architettura* | 1570 |
| Inigo Jones travels to Italy | ca. 1601 and 1614 |

Filippo Brunelleschi, Pazzi Chapel, S. Croce, Florence, 1430–33.

Brunelleschi chose as his precedent for this façade the Roman triumphal arch. Here, rather than massive, as in ancient examples, it appears somewhat brittle. The shed roof above and the drum with conical roof and cupola were not part of Brunelleschi's design.

the innate harmony of these ratios would be impressed upon anyone experiencing spaces determined by them. Humanists were convinced that God's cosmic order could be expressed on earth through such mathematical proportions, which were inevitably related to the mensuration of the human body.

Renaissance architects maintained the interest in geometry that had so strongly influenced medieval architecture. Rather than using the complex, geometric transformations of medieval master masons, they held in particular reverence such "ideal" forms as the square and circle. In this context, the central-plan church came to represent the most perfect form, absolute, immutable, echoing celestial harmony. Artists made drawings of the human figure inscribed within a "perfect" geometric context and, thereby, "proved" that human proportions reflected divine ratios. Of these drawings, the most famous is the *Vitruvian Man* (Fig. 11.1) found in the notebooks of Leonardo da Vinci, which, like the other examples of its type, illustrates the precedent established by Vitruvius in his third book. Vitruvius wrote:

*For if a man be placed flat on his back, with his hands and feet extended, and a pair of compasses centered at his navel, the fingers and toes of his two hands and feet will touch the circumference of a circle described therefrom. And, just as the human body yields a circular outline, so too a square figure may be found from it. For if we measure the distance from the soles of the feet to the top of the head, and then apply that measure to the outstretched arms, the breadth will be found to be the same as the height, as in the case of plane surfaces which are perfectly square.*

## FILIPPO BRUNELLESCHI

From the beginning of the fifteenth century to 1494, when French armies overran the city, Florence flourished as the center of the early Renaissance, and the figure who ushered in this profoundly creative period for architecture was Filippo Brunelleschi (1377–1446). The son of a notary, Brunelleschi was trained as a goldsmith. In 1400 he entered the competition to design a new set of bronze doors for the baptistery of Florence Cathedral. His main competitor, and the man who won, was Lorenzo Ghiberti (1378–1455). Discouraged by his loss, Brunelleschi set off for Rome with his friend, the sculptor Donatello (1386–1466), and his subsequent career as an architect owed much to the extended visit he paid to the Eternal City and the observations he made there.

During his stay in Rome, and perhaps as a means to record more accurately what he saw, Brunelleschi codified the principles of geometrically accurate linear perspective, making possible the exact representation of a three-dimensional object on a two-dimensional surface. Various artists in Italy had struggled with the question of how best to depict spatial relationships in their paintings, but their solutions fell short of the precision achieved by Brunelleschi. In making careful drawings of such repetitive elements as the arches of aqueducts, he realized that parallel horizontal lines converge at a point on the horizon and that elements of like size diminish proportionally into the distance. His development of this new system of spatial representation had a profound effect on art, architecture, and civic design during and after the Renaissance.

Brunelleschi must have assisted his friend, the painter Masaccio (1401–1428), in the application of linear perspective to a fresco painting, *The Trinity* (1427–28) at S. Maria Novella in Florence (Fig. 11.2). It depicts God the Father standing on a large sarcophagus supporting the crucified Christ. Below are Mary and St. John with two kneeling donors. The holy figures are framed by modified Ionic columns supporting an arch that creates a coffered, barrel-vaulted chapel, accurately projected according to the rules of perspective. Masaccio, it would seem, was illustrating Brunelleschi's momentous discovery.

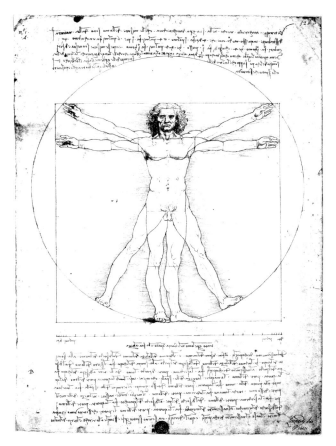

**11.1** Leonardo da Vinci, *Vitruvian Man*, ca. 1485.

Probably no image has been more frequently used than this one to convey the spirit of the Renaissance. Here, Leonardo has drawn the so-called *Vitruvian Man* to illustrate the era's belief that the human body was proportioned according to divine ratios.

**11.2** Masaccio, *The Trinity*, S. Maria Novella, Florence, 1427–28.

Brunelleschi first demonstrated his invention of mechanical perspective by displaying his painted view of the Florence Cathedral baptistery. He obviously showed the artist Masaccio his method, and Masaccio used it to create this illusion of a coffered barrel vault housing the crucified Christ.

## FLORENCE CATHEDRAL

By 1407 Brunelleschi was again living in Florence. In that year the directors of the cathedral works consulted distinguished engineers and architects from France, Spain, England, and Germany for advice on the cathedral's dome. The cathedral was begun in 1292 to the designs of Arnolfo di Cambio and continued by Francesco Talenti. It was always intended to have a dome exceeding the Romanesque cathedral of Pisa in size. Arnolfo and Talenti produced a building with some obvious Gothic characteristics such as pointed arches and ribbed vaults atop piers. Their work proceeded to the level of the octagonal drum, from which a dome reaching nearly 150 feet on the diagonal was to spring, but without anyone having a firm idea about how to achieve such a huge span. The outward thrust of such a dome, built using conventional techniques, without internal tension members, and unbraced by extensive buttresses, would have burst the drum. In addition, the scale of centering required to support the masonry while construction was in progress vastly exceeded anything attempted in the medieval period. This was the situation that Brunelleschi inherited when the works directors eventually turned to him (Fig. 11.3).

Brunelleschi drew upon his knowledge of ancient Roman construction as well as lingering Gothic traditions to produce an innovative synthesis (Fig. 11.4). In order to reduce the outward thrust, he employed a Gothic pointed-arch cross section instead of a semicircular one. In order to reduce the dead load, he created a double shell of radial and concentric ribs, a strategy traceable both to ancient monuments such as the Pantheon and to Florentine medieval work such as the nearby cathedral baptistery. In order to reduce the amount of temporary construction, he devised portable centering that supported concentric courses of masonry until they were completed as stable compression rings, and he used this rising masonry to support scaffolding which in turn supported more centering.

The cleverness of Brunelleschi's system of ribs is worthy of more detailed description. He devised as his principal structural members sandstone ribs rising from each of the eight corners of the octagonal drum. At the springing of the dome, they have a cross section of eleven by seven feet, and they taper upward to an apex ring beneath the cupola. Between each of these corner ribs, Brunelleschi placed a pair of intermediate ribs, making a total of twenty-four vertical ribs. To hold the inner and outer shells apart, he inserted five horizontal rings of sandstone, connected by tin-plated iron clamps: he had observed such imbedded metal fastenings in the ruins of Roman construction. Finally, near the base of the dome, he placed twenty-four chestnut timbers, each one foot square and twenty-three feet long, banded together with straps and bolts into a continuous wooden tension ring that resists the outward thrust of the dome. However, according to modern structural analysis, the action of this ring is negligible.

**11.3** Filippo Brunelleschi, Florence Cathedral, 1292 and later.

The body of Florence Cathedral was designed by Arnolfo di Cambio and Francesco Talenti, but the dome was only completed by Brunelleschi in the fifteenth century. The campanile, or belltower, was begun by the painter Giotto in the fourteenth century.

**11.4** Filippo Brunelleschi, Florence Cathedral transverse section, 1292 and later.

The pointed-arch profile of the Florence Cathedral dome reveals its medieval inspiration. However, internal construction techniques such as a double shell resulted from Brunelleschi's close observation of ancient Roman building methods.

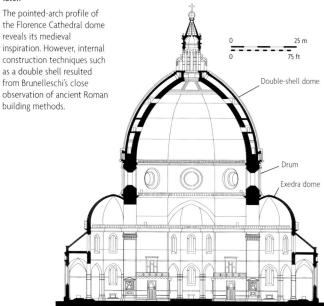

## OTHER FLORENTINE BUILDINGS

Work on the cathedral dome continued throughout Brunelleschi's lifetime; the cupola was completed after his death. Concurrently, he was able to build several smaller projects in which the ideals of Roman architecture could be expressed more directly than in the cathedral dome. In these commissions, which had fewer troublesome technical problems, Brunelleschi was able to express outwardly his empathy for ancient Rome. The earliest, the Ospedale degli Innocenti or Foundling Hospital, is often considered the first building of the Renaissance. Designed in 1419 and built from 1421 to 1444, it continues the link with classical tradition that had been maintained in Florence through such proto-Renaissance buildings as the Romanesque S. Miniato al Monte and the cathedral's baptistery. The Foundling Hospital has a continuous arcade,

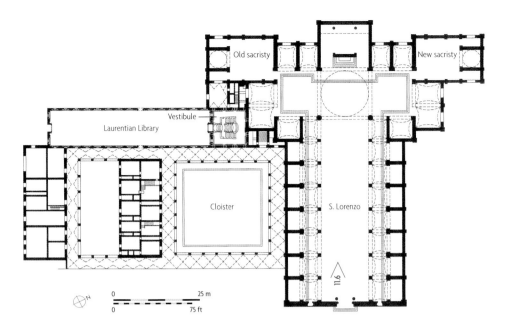

**11.5** Filippo Brunelleschi and Michelangelo Buonarroti, plan of S. Lorenzo, begun 1421.

The church of San Lorenzo is part of a larger monastic complex that includes chapels and the Laurentian Library by Michelangelo (see Fig. 11.36). The major spaces are organized around a square cloister that corresponds to the modular regularity of Brunelleschi's church plan.

**11.6** Filippo Brunelleschi, S. Lorenzo interior, Florence, begun 1421.

The nave and aisle configuration of S. Lorenzo is no different than that of Romanesque and Gothic churches in Florence. Brunelleschi simply substituted classical elements for medieval ones: Corinthian columns and an arcade as at the Foundling Hospital. His design innovation is the modular regularity in plan, visible here in the floor pattern.

carried on Corinthian columns across its main façade and around an internal courtyard that is comparable to the ground-floor arcading in marble veneer that adorns both S. Miniato and the baptistery; these Romanesque elements were ultimately based on Roman architecture. At the hospital, the arcading is three-dimensional, creating a loggia with domed vaults in each bay. Semicircular arches span the width of the loggia, from the freestanding columns with abaci to corbeled brackets on the opposite wall.

A similar columnar arcade is found in the aisles of the Latin-cross church of S. Lorenzo (Figs. 11.5–11.6), begun in 1421. Here, Brunelleschi defined each bay with arches that spring from columns of the nave arcade to pilasters set between side-aisle chapels. This configuration achieves a more balanced effect than the wall corbels at the hospital, yet Brunelleschi found an even more satisfactory resolution in his design for the church of S. Spirito (Fig. 11.7), begun as late as 1445, where he

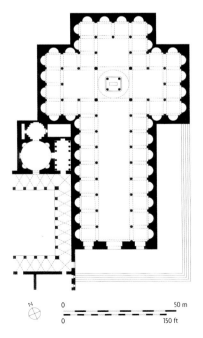

**11.7** Filippo Brunelleschi, Plan of S. Spirito, Florence, begun 1445.

Brunelleschi perfected his system of modular planning at S. Spirito. Perhaps he intended for the building's exterior perimeter to have a continuous series of projecting semicircular chapels. If so, these proved objectionable to his patrons as the walls were infilled to be externally flat.

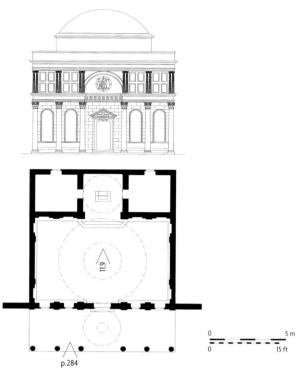

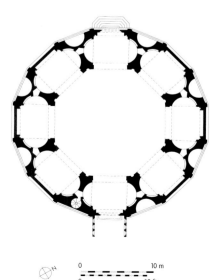

**11.8** Filippo Brunelleschi, plan and elevation reconstruction of the Pazzi Chapel, Florence, 1430–33.

Here is one possible reconstruction of Brunelleschi's dome. If it is accurate, it displays on the exterior the perfect circular form on which the plan was based.

**11.9** Filippo Brunelleschi, Pazzi Chapel interior, Florence, 1430–33.

As with the Florence Cathedral dome, Brunelleschi looked here to local traditions for design motifs, in this case the gray pietra serena stone used for the framing elements: pilasters, entablatures, and arches. New is the classical language and the geometry based upon squares, half-squares, semicircles, and circles—comparable to the squares and circles bounding Leonardo's *Vitruvian Man*.

attached half-columns to the wall in place of the pilasters he had used at S. Lorenzo. This may seem an undue emphasis on Brunelleschi's part on admittedly minor architectural details, but such attention to each element and to the relationship of all elements to one another characterizes the proper manipulation of the classical language of architecture.

In both S. Lorenzo and S. Spirito, Brunelleschi sought to accommodate the traditional practical requirements of his clients within a unifying system of mathematical proportions. At both churches, the square bay of the aisles defines a module that is repeated throughout. At S. Spirito, four modules form a double bay of the nave, and this larger square is repeated four times down the nave and then once for each transept, the crossing, and the choir. Equally carefully proportioned Roman elements such as the semicircular arch, Corinthian columns, and coffering impart a classical monumentality to the interiors of both churches.

Brunelleschi made prominent use of simple numerical ratios in three of his smaller commissions. For the church of S. Lorenzo, he erected the Old Sacristy (1421–28) in a corner of the south transept. The floor, walls, and pendentives are contained in a cube, capped by a hemispherical dome with an oculus. Pilasters, an entablature, and arches of gray **pietra serena**, a local stone much favored for architectural detail, are set against the white plaster of the walls, giving a linear definition to the interior. The thinness of the pilaster strips as they turn the corner and the isolated,

**11.10** Filippo Brunelleschi, Plan of S. Maria degli Angeli, Florence, begun ca. 1436.

Brunelleschi had observed the circular temples of antiquity. His proposal for a pure, central plan was the first of the Renaissance, but it was a theme that would be explored by almost every Renaissance designer thereafter.

undersized brackets "supporting" the entablature have been pointed to as signs of Brunelleschi's "uncertainty" in manipulating the still-new classical language.

Slightly larger than the Old Sacristy is the Pazzi Chapel (1430–33), erected off the major cloister at the monastery of S. Croce. While it is not certain what Brunelleschi intended the façade (page 284 and Fig. 11.8) to be like above the Corinthian columns that support a series of square panels flanking a central arch, the interior is entirely his (Fig. 11.9). The space is a carefully conceived but occasionally awkward essay based on numerical ratios, the classical language, and local building practices. The plan is generated by placing the circle of a dome above a square divided into three bays, and expanded one barrel-vaulted bay to each side and one domed square bay in depth. All these bays are defined by Corinthian pilasters supporting a continuous entablature with arches above, and all are delineated in gray pietra serena against white plaster.

Renaissance architects considered the central plan to be an ideal type. Brunelleschi's design for S. Maria degli Angeli (1434–37) was the first such structure of the fifteenth century (Fig. 11.10). While it was left unfinished at Brunelleschi's death and subsequently badly reconstructed and altered in the 1930s, engravings probably based upon the original drawings survive to indicate Brunelleschi's intentions. The church's plan and massing were to be Roman, with a domed octagon expanded by eight lozenge-shaped chapels. Piers composed of clustered pilasters provided support for the dome, and the overall spatial effect would have suggested that the chapels were carved from the solid exterior wall. Had the dome been constructed, its monolithic single shell would have been true to Roman prototypes.

## MICHELOZZO BARTOLOMEO AND THE PALAZZO MEDICI

Michelozzo Bartolomeo (1396–1472), a student of Brunelleschi, worked not only in Florence but also in other northern Italian cities. Although not so celebrated a designer as Brunelleschi, Michelozzo was a capable architect and was awarded several commissions by those archetypal Renaissance patrons, the Medici. Most noteworthy of these was the Palazzo Medici (Fig. 11.11) in Florence, begun in 1444 after an earlier design by Brunelleschi was

**11.11** Michelozzo Bartolomeo, Medici Palace, Florence, 1444.

The palazzo form of this urban house built by the Medici family can be added to the temple, stoa, and basilica as fundamental form types that have been repeated and reinterpreted down to the present day. The Medici intended its fortified quality to afford them protection in a Florence accustomed to political intrigue.

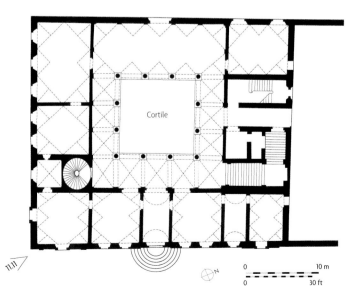

**11.12** Michelozzo Bartolomeo, Plan of the Medici Palace, Florence, 1444.

The fortified quality of the Medici Palace's exterior walls belies the delicate openness of the arcaded cortile or courtyard. It is as though Michelozzo had taken the external arcade used by his friend Brunelleschi at the Foundling Hospital and made it an internal element reflecting humanist preoccupations.

rejected as being too ostentatious. The client, Cosimo de' Medici, did not want to arouse feelings of envy among other important families in the city. Michelozzo's design reflects his awareness of traditional Florentine domestic buildings and his admiration for the Foundling Hospital arcade and its traditional Florentine courtyard plan. The **palazzo**'s square plan includes such a central courtyard, or cortile, serving as a circulation core for perimeter rooms that open to one another en suite, that is, without a continuous corridor (Fig. 11.12). Michelozzo made use of **rustication**, stone blocks with deeply recessed chamfered joints. He arranged the street elevation in three tiers of graduated textures, beginning with rock-faced stone at the street level and concluding with smooth ashlar at the third level below a ten-foot-high crowning cornice with **modillions**, **egg-and-dart moldings**, and a dentil course, the first such cornice since ancient Roman times. The cornice projects out eight feet from the building, supported by acanthus-leaf modillions or large brackets, and it combines with the string course between the floor levels to create a strong horizontal emphasis, even though the façade is eighty-three feet high.

The ground floor originally had three open arches along the street, the central one giving access to the courtyard and rooms serving the Medici banking business. From the courtyard a staircase led to the major family rooms on the second floor, or **piano nobile**. Deep shadows in the courtyard make the palazzo's core cool and quiet, and the upper-level galleries provide access to and shade for the individual rooms. Typical Romanesque windows with circular heads are used throughout. While without radical innovations, the Medici Palace reflects Michelozzo's connection to Renaissance circles through its symmetry, inclusion of classical elements, and careful use of mathematical proportions.

## LEON BATTISTA ALBERTI

In contrast to the pragmatic and technically skilled Brunelleschi, Leon Battista Alberti (1404–1472) was a classical theorist who saw architecture as a way to address societal order. The Renaissance architect, in Alberti's mind, was to be a universalist, an intellectual, a man of genius, and a consort of those in positions of power and authority. In his autobiography (written in the third person), he offered this description of himself:

> [He was] assiduous in science, and skilled in dealing with arms, horse, and musical instruments; as well as the pursuit of letters and the fine arts, he was devoted to the knowledge of the most strange and difficult things. His genius was so versatile that you might almost judge all the fine arts to be his. He played ball, hurled the javelin, ran, leapt, wrestled, and above all delighted in the steep ascent of mountains. He could leap over the shoulders of men and had almost no equal among those hurling the lance. . . . He was considered an expert among the leading musicians.

Alberti was not being immodest: an accomplished scholar from an exiled Florentine family, he became one of the most influential thinkers of his time. His education at the universities of Padua and Bologna included mathematics, music, Greek, Latin, philosophy, and Roman law.

On completing these studies, Alberti entered the Papal Chancery in Rome as secretary to the chancellor. Living in Rome provided him with many opportunities to meet artists visiting the monuments of antiquity, and his travels gave him the chance to observe the works of artists in many cities throughout northern Italy. Because Alberti searched the writings of Plato, Aristotle, Plutarch, and Pliny the Elder for references to the arts and carefully studied the collections of antique sculpture that were being assembled by patrons of the arts, his writings reveal a mixture of scholarly research and informed observations.

### WRITINGS

The manuscript of Alberti's *Della pittura*, or *On Painting*, completed in 1435, documents Brunelleschi's theories of perspective. It was dedicated to the five young artists of Florence whom Alberti most admired and who came closest to creating a personal style that reflected the art of ancient Rome. We now regard these five—Brunelleschi, the sculptor Ghiberti, the painter Masaccio, and the sculptors Donatello and Luca della Robbia (1399–1482)—as among the founders of the Renaissance.

Alberti's interest in architecture was probably first aroused when he came across the already well-known manuscript *De architectura libri decem*, Vitruvius's *The Ten Books on Architecture*. While there may have been many such treatises, it is the only one to have survived. Vitruvius was a mediocre writer at best, and owing to the uncertainty of his language, his text is often ambiguous; nevertheless, as an authentic book from Roman times, the work was greatly respected by Renaissance architects. In response to the obscurities in Vitruvius's text, in order to discuss principles of Roman buildings designed after the time of Vitruvius, and in order to argue that architects should be highly educated humanists, like himself, Alberti began writing his own treatise, modeled on the antique text and, like it, organized into ten books or chapters. He worked on his book, which he titled *De re aedificatoria*, or *On Building*, from the early 1440s until his death, completing a first version by 1452, which was circulated in manuscript form. The text as we know it was published posthumously in Florence in 1485. As the first architectural treatise of the Renaissance, it is important for cataloging the features and proportions of the orders of antiquity and establishing a theory of harmonious proportions to be observed in buildings. Alberti adapted proportioning systems expounded by Vitruvius because he believed that they should unify plans, elevations, and sections of a building. For example, church plans could be centralized, using a circle, hexagon, octagon, decagon, dodecagon, or based on a square, such as a square-and-a-half, square-and-a-third, or double square. Whatever the plan selected, the three-dimensional realization was to be derived from it. Furthermore, to assume their proper symbolic role in the cityscape, churches needed to be centrally located, isolated from other structures so that they could be seen from all sides, and raised above ground level on a plinth or base.

Although Alberti was concerned with the theoretical and esthetic implications of proportional systems, he was equally attentive to the practical aspects of architecture and city planning. Vitruvius had written of public health considerations in the siting of towns, and Alberti extended this approach to include other factors such as the purity of the water supply and the distribution of land uses. He suggested that arrangements should respond to both convenience and hygiene. He recommended that facilities for noxious trades, such as dyeworks and slaughterhouses, be positioned away from residential districts, and he studied the location of recreational facilities and the dimensioning of streets and open spaces with respect to the heights of buildings. He proposed individual house plans with consideration for the needs and ordinary uses of the inhabitants. As kitchens are noisy, he proposed that they should be away from quiet parts of the house and yet near enough to the dining room. Bedrooms should face east toward the rising sun, and the parents' rooms should be near the children's quarters. Old people should have rooms without drafts, and guests should have rooms near the entrance to enable them and their friends to enter and leave without disturbing the whole household. A country house could be more elaborate in design than a town house, where restrained ornamentation could add to the unity of the streetscape. He even described the quality of basic building materials in a manner not too different from the style used in modern specifications. Sand, he said, should be clean and free of impurities, lime should be well slaked, and timber should be straight, well seasoned, and free of knots and checks.

## THE PALAZZO RUCELLAI, FLORENCE

Some of this advice is reflected in Alberti's design for the façade of the Palazzo Rucellai in Florence (1446–51) (Fig. 11.13). To organize it, he applied **superimposed** Doric and Corinthian orders to demarcate the individual floors; this was the first use of the classical orders on a Renaissance domestic building. He raised the order of the ground floor on a high plinth scored into diamond shapes in imitation of Roman opus reticulatum, where diamond-shaped masonry units were used as formwork for concrete walls. Here, however, the subdivision serves only as a surface texture reflective of antique practices.

**11.13** Leon Battista Alberti, Palazzo Rucellai, Florence, 1446–51.

Alberti's palazzo proposal owes more to ancient models than Michelozzo's Medici Palace. Superimposed orders like those used at the Colosseum articulate the three floors, and diamond shapes at the base of the first floor mimic Roman *opus-reticulatum* masonry.

## CHURCHES IN RIMINI, FLORENCE, AND MANTUA

Alberti's four other major commissions were ecclesiastical. Sigismondo Malatesta was his client for the modernization of the thirteenth-century church of S. Francesco in Rimini (Fig. 11.14), begun in 1450 but never completed. Malatesta was a consummate Renaissance despot as defined by the Florentine political theorist Machiavelli in his influencial treatise *The Prince*. Alberti's wrapping of the existing medieval building with new walls is so thoroughly classical that the building is known to this day as the Tempio (Temple) Malatestiano.

Malatesta wished the structure to serve as a tomb for himself and his wife and for the scholars of his humanist court. For the sepulchers of the scholars, Alberti chose to subdivide the building's flanks using heavy round arches modeled on those of the Tomb of Theodoric (ca. 526) in nearby Ravenna. This composition inspired a series of subsequent buildings including McKim, Mead, and

**11.14** Leon Battista Alberti, S. Francesco, Rimini, begun 1450.

Alberti never saw this church completed, but he certainly visited the site, modeling the façade on the nearby ancient Roman Arch of Augustus. Arches along the right sidewall house sepulchers for humanist scholars.

**11.15** Leon Battista Alberti, S. Maria Novella, Florence, 1456–70.

Alberti's façade composition for this church became a prototype much reinterpreted by other Renaissance designers. Its two-story central bays capped by a pedimented temple-form conceal the gable-roofed nave of a basilican cross section, and the flanking scrolls mask the shed roofs over the aisles.

White's late-nineteenth-century Boston Public Library (see Fig. 14.31). At the front façade of S. Francesco, Alberti superimposed a temple front over a triumphal-arch form, like the ancient Roman Arch of Augustus a few blocks away, and proposed to place the tombs of Malatesta and his wife in the blind-arched portals flanking the central entry. Alberti's on-site assistant, Matteo de' Pasti, updated the Gothic interior of the church but never constructed the huge Pantheon-like dome that Alberti envisioned.

The task of adapting classical details to the façade of a church with a basilican cross section was a compositional problem for Renaissance architects. Alberti's work on S. Maria Novella in Florence (ca. 1456–70) produced the first completed design for a church façade in the Renaissance, but in some respects it is an extension of eleventh-century Florentine traditions with its geometric panels of white and green marble (Fig. 11.15). Alberti was obliged to preserve some Gothic aspects of the existing church, particularly the pointed arches of the lower level and the central rose window above. Rudolf Wittkower's analysis of Alberti's façade emphasizes the predominance of the square as a unit of composition. As at S. Francesco, Alberti attempted to unify the façade by linking lower aisle roofs to the pedimented higher nave with flanking scrolls, a solution that was much repeated throughout the Renaissance.

Farther north, in Mantua, Alberti worked for the Gonzaga family. Here he gave the church of S. Andrea (1472–94) an entrance portico based, like S. Francesco, on a temple front and triumphal arch, and he intended to extend this treatment to the east and west transepts (Fig. 11.16). The temple portion's order of Corinthian pilasters stands on pedestals; this order reappears on the interior, supporting the great barrel vault of the nave. A shorter Corinthian order supports the arch of the central portal and an entablature that disappears beneath the temple-front pilasters; it also reappears on the interior in the jambs of the barrel-vaulted chapels.

The church's plan (Fig. 11.17) is that of the ancient Roman Basilica of Constantine, with the transverse barrel vaults of the chapels and their bearing walls resisting the lateral thrust of the longitudinal barrel vault of the nave. It would serve as the pattern for many subsequent churches. The assemblage of classical elements on the interior presents the first Renaissance vision rivaling the monumentality of the interior spaces of such ancient Roman monuments as the basilicas and baths. Unfortunately, Alberti did not live to walk through his creation, as he died early in the construction process. (S. Andrea's choir and transepts cannot be positively attributed to Alberti. Its dome was added by Filippo Juvarra in the eighteenth century.)

S. Sebastiano (begun 1460), which stands not far away, was designed as a Greek cross with a hexastyle pilastered temple front. The central interior space is spanned by a groin vault, not a dome as one might expect; the stubby arms of the Greek cross are barrel-vaulted. In its present incomplete state, the church does not clearly reflect its designer's intentions, but it does illustrate Alberti's interest in the centrally planned church.

**11.16** Leon Battista Alberti, S. Andrea, Mantua, begun 1472.

Here Alberti built upon his experience in Rimini to produce a confident synthesis of the temple and triumphal-arch forms. The two are effectively interlaced by the entablature that disappears behind the Corinthian pilasters of the temple front.

**11.17** Leon Battista Alberti, Plan of and longitudinal section through S. Andrea, Mantua, begun 1472.

In contrast to Brunelleschi's S. Spirito and S. Lorenzo, S. Andrea has no internal files of nave columns. Rather, this church is based upon the Basilica of Constantine, itself derivative of the Roman baths. The chapel walls provide the buttressing necessary to resist the lateral thrust of the monumental barrel vault.

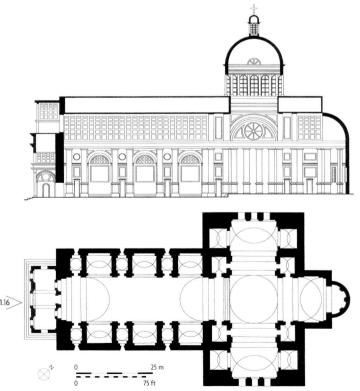

11.16 ▷

0       25 m
0       75 ft

## THE IDEAL CITY

Alberti's vision of the centrally planned temple was also represented in Perugino's fresco *Giving of the Keys to St. Peter* (1481–82), Raphael's painting *The Marriage of the Virgin* (1504), and the *cassone* panels (the sides of a wooden chest) in the Palazzo Ducale in Urbino. Each of these art works depicts the Albertian ideal of the temple of God in the center of a geometrically planned city. Alberti's design for S. Sebastiano, as well as his theoretical writings, emphasized the ideal-city form, in which a centrally planned church is set in a broad piazza in the middle of the town. The horizontal cornices of the buildings along the approach streets converge as lines of perspective at the focal point, the church. This ideal was less often realized by architects than painters, who were not restrained by the physical dimensions of actual cities and the costs associated with demolition and new construction. Renaissance planning contrasts with medieval practice, where the church commonly formed part of the piazza's edge, if there was a sizable open space at all. Ideal-city schemes drawn by various Renaissance architects often extended the centralized concept to include radial streets and a polygonal town wall with arrowhead-shaped bastions at the vertices. Such fortifications are also

# PIUS'S RESOLUTIONS

by Charles R. Mack

**11.18** Bernardo Rossellino, Cathedral (left) and Palazzo Piccolomini (right), Piazza Pio II, Pienza, 1459–64.

Although respect for the visible presence of the ancient past was not universal during the Italian Renaissance's first century, there is abundant evidence for a renewed interest in the remains of classical Italy and for a desire to record and preserve its monuments. This preservationist impetus is nicely seen in the actions of Pope Pius II (ruled 1458–64, the humanist Aeneas Silvius Piccolomini). It is true, of course, that Pope Pius did have marble transported from the Colosseum to rebuild the steps leading up to St. Peter's and despoiled the Portico of Octavia for columns to be used in the new Benediction Loggia that he ordered built across the front of the same basilica. But Pius also issued a papal bull (probably the first official document in the history of the historic preservation movement) on April 28, 1462 forbidding the destruction of antiquities in the Roman region. That the document accorded the Pope the privilege of violating his own injunction is interesting and demonstrates two aspects of the Early Renaissance's attitude

toward its antique heritage. It prohibited the unrestricted dismantling of Roman ruins by the lower classes, but it allowed the utilization of the surviving remnants of ancient glory in new campaigns of officially sponsored construction. The melding of the remains of pagan antiquity into the fabric of a reconstituted Christian Rome was typical of the age's attitude toward the past.

Curiously, the same Pope Pius, while still a cardinal in 1456, could criticize the title of Flavio Biondo's *Rome Restored* by complaining: "Even if all the forces of Europe were to unite, they could not restore Rome to its early form, for towns also have their end; the fallen ones cannot rise any more than the old can grow young." Perhaps the future pope was just expressing a momentary fatalism inherited from some ancient Etruscan forebear or was simply imitating the cyclical view of history found in the writings of Augustan Age Roman philosophers during the reign of Caesar Augustus (31 BCE–14 CE). In any case, the concept of

rebirth was very much on the mind of the confident new pope Pius II only a few years later. It formed a conscious part of his plans for the refurbishing of the Vatican and was very much evident when he set about reforming his very own rustic birthplace of Corsignano, renamed Pienza in his honor (Fig. 11.18). Pius must have recollected his earlier comments concerning the futility of attempting a Roman restoration when he visited his hometown in February of 1459. There he found both the companions of his youth and the community itself "bowed down with old age," but, instead of accepting the inevitable, that towns like people "also have their end," he determined upon a truly Renaissance course of action which led to an extensive reconstruction of the town, incorporating much of the classicizing vision he must have held for Papal Rome. Pienza exists today as the very model of the integrating spirit of Pope Pius's generation, a generation that adapted the vocabulary of ancient art and architecture to new, post-medieval circumstances.

**11.19** Palazzo Ducale cortile arcade, Urbino, 1450–ca. 1480s.

The cliff-like façade of the palace conceals this serene three-story arcade around the cortile. Its informed manipulation of the classical language includes pilasters above arcaded columns.

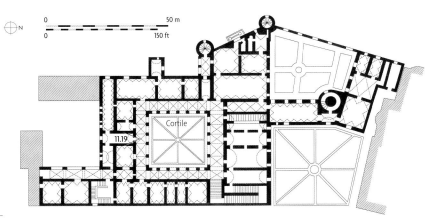

**11.20** Plan of the Palazzo Ducale, Urbino, 1450–ca. 1480s.

The irregularity of this plan reflects the need to fit it onto a precipitous but dramatic site. Once inside, one finds light, airy rooms that made it an island of Renaissance culture in a sea of medievalism.

a departure from the towers and turrets of medieval city walls. Changes in military technology, most notably the introduction of metal cannonballs and gunpowder after 1400, rendered high city walls vulnerable, as a well-aimed shot could shatter the masonry. Renaissance town walls became low and earth-sheltered, to absorb the impact of projectiles, and complex outerworks of ditches and moats set in the cleared area beyond the wall impeded an attacking army's advance. Cannons pivoted on the bastions could direct their fire over a range of more than 180 degrees, even firing in enfilade, or parallel to the town walls, if necessary.

## THE SPREAD OF THE RENAISSANCE

### URBINO

Not far from Sigismondo Malatesta's Rimini is Urbino, situated in hilly terrain about twenty miles from the east coast of Italy. Here the humanist and condottiere Federigo da Montefeltro held court, governing an area of about 3600 square miles that included 400 villages. Federigo was a loyal commander who served the dukes of Naples and Milan and three popes, and raised an army for Florence in 1448. His military accomplishments were balanced by his patronage of liberal learning. Humanists resided at his court, and dozens of scribes were employed to hand-copy ancient manuscripts.

Dalmatian-born architect Luciano Laurana expanded Federigo's Palazzo Ducale (1450–ca. 1480s) (Figs. 11.19–11.20) in 1464–72. Architect-engineer Francesco di Giorgio followed Laurana and continued the work until some time in the 1480s. The palace surrounds di Giorgio's **cortile** of ca. 1475 but is slightly more rambling in plan than a typical Florentine merchant's residence; its rooms are light, airy, and carefully proportioned. The walls of Federigo's small study are covered with exquisite variegated wood **intarsia** or inlay executed by Baccio Pontelli to designs by Botticelli. Cupboards apparently with doors ajar exhibit their contents. A spinet, a squirrel, and a basket of fruit on the ledge of a colonnaded opening are all rendered in varied types of wood on the two-dimensional surface. Even the distant landscape is shown beyond the simulated open window. Such a unified illusionistic extension of space beyond the actual walls of a room illustrates the complete assimilation of perspectival space in fifteenth-century art and anticipates the trompe-l'oeil effects of sixteenth-century design. In Urbino, what began as a fortress overlooking the Valbona river became a monument to humanist optimism. It celebrates man's ability to observe, to reason, to act effectively in the physical world, and to create civilized society.

## MILAN

For almost thirty years before being sacked in 1499 by the forces of Louis XII of France, Milan was a focal point of the Renaissance, attracting both Leonardo da Vinci (1452–1519) and Donato Bramante (1444–1514) in the early 1480s. Renaissance influence had come early to Milan when the local duke, Francesco Sforza, gave Cosimo de' Medici a palace for a branch of the Medici bank, which was vital to Florentine trade links with the north. Michelozzo's alterations to the two-story palace, which became the Banco Medico in the 1460s, paid homage to the applied brick-and-terracotta decorative traditions of Milan. The bank's elaborate central entrance, while composed of nominally classical elements, approaches northern Gothic flamboyance. On the piano-nobile level, Gothic cusped and pointed arches are set between classical roundels.

## LEONARDO DA VINCI

Leonardo prepared sketchbooks illustrating his inventions, observations, experiments, and discoveries in order to demonstrate his potential to prospective clients. Pages from these sketchbooks, which have been widely dispersed over the centuries, include anatomical drawings; studies of geological formations, air currents, and water movements; proposals for architecture and city planning; and a host of drawings, sketches, and studies related to his paintings and sculptures. Other drawings illustrate his inventiveness with such diverse devices as canal locks; underwater craft; parachutes; helicopters; wing attachments for flying; and tanks, guns, cannons, and other instruments of war. Leonardo's experiments and research brought him close to understanding blood circulation in the human body, to verifying that the earth was more than 5000 years old (as was believed at the time), and to proposals for magnifying glasses to observe the moon, all discoveries that would later be made independently by other men. In his sketchbooks, Leonardo noted various designs for centrally planned churches (Fig. 11.21).

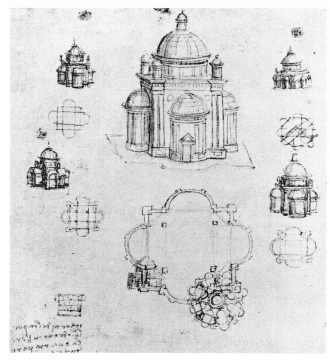

**11.21** Leonardo da Vinci, Sketches for centralized churches, ca. 1490.

The central-plan church interested Renaissance designers more than any other architectural problem. Even Leonardo carried out investigations, possibly as a result of his contact with Bramante.

S. Maria della Consolazione at Todi (begun in 1508) (Fig. 11.22) is so similar to some of Leonardo's sketches that its master mason, Cola da Caprarola, must have been influenced by them, perhaps through Bramante's works. The church at Todi is square in plan, with one semicircular and three polygonal apses. Projected into three dimensions, the square generates a cube, while the apses are capped by semidomes. Above the major interior space rises a dome set on a drum and pendentives.

At the Sforza court in Milan Leonardo designed costumes and masques for the marriage and entertainment of Ludovico and his wife Beatrice d'Este; he proposed a two-level city with pedestrian and vehicular separation; and, when the 1485 plague in Milan killed 5000 people, he suggested building ten satellite towns, each of 30,000 people, to reduce the likelihood of subsequent outbreaks. Between 1487 and 1490, he and Bramante worked on designs for the central crossing of Milan Cathedral; these were never built. The 1499 attack on Milan by French forces brought down the Sforza family, and Leonardo briefly sought employment as a military engineer to the infamous Cesare Borgia. Leonardo later returned to Milan to work for the French military governor, Charles d'Amboise, eventually becoming a painter and engineer for King Louis XII. In 1516 he moved to France under the patronage of Francis I and lived in comfort near Amboise until his death in 1519.

**11.22** Cola da Caprarola and Donato Bramante (?),
S. Maria della Consolazione, Todi, 1508.

Various architects, including Bramante, have been associated
with the design of this church. Compare its design to the
central-church plans by Leonardo in Fig. 11.21.

**11.23** Donato Bramante, Plan of and longitudinal section
through S. Maria delle Grazie, Milan, 1492–97.

Here Bramante grafted a central-plan crossing onto an
existing medieval nave. The union is awkward. The problem
was more satisfactorily solved by Andrea Palladio in the
Venetian church of Il Rendentore.

## DONATO BRAMANTE

In Milan from 1482 to 1499 Leonardo was a close associate of Donato Bramante, and he undoubtedly influenced two of the younger architect's commissions that emphasized the concept of central planning. The first was an addition to the wide Milanese church of S. Maria delle Grazie (Fig. 11.23), a medieval building consisting of a nave, aisles, and chapels. Between 1492 and 1497 Bramante added the centralized crossing, capped by a dome sixty-five feet in diameter and completed on either side by transept apses and a choir with apse. Although in harmony with the spirit of Leonardo's sketches of centrally planned churches and consistent with the spirit of Renaissance detail on the interior, Bramante's design is behind the times, its highly decorative exterior details falling into the Milanese tradition of brick-and-terracotta appliqué. The church's major interior feature, the hemispherical dome, is not even expressed on the exterior.

A far more original design is Bramante's earlier church, S. Maria presso S. Satiro (1482–92), a rebuilding that included part of the old ninth-century church and campanile of S. Satiro (Fig. 11.24). Bramante's design for the interior included a barrel-vaulted nave and transepts that intersect at a central crossing with a coffered dome on pendentives concluded by an oculus. An existing street restricted the site east of the crossing, preventing Bramante from adding a conventional choir. While the wall behind the altar is almost flush with the east wall of the transepts, Bramante created there a low relief that, when viewed on axis, has the convincing appearance of a barrel-vaulted choir (Fig. 11.25). Using the illusionistic potential of linear perspective, he simulated the space he wished to build in actuality, creating in the process what must be the ultimate use of this device in fifteenth-century architecture. Bramante's reworking of the quincunx plan of the ninth-century chapel, and his addition of an octagonal sacristy similar to Brunelleschi's sacristy at S. Spirito in Florence, both anticipate his more ambitious central-plan proposals in Rome, culminating with his designs for a new St. Peter's basilica.

**11.24** Donato Bramante, Plan of and longitudinal section through S. Maria presso S. Satiro, Milan, 1482–92.

The oddity of this plan, with its stunted nave, resulted from site conditions that prohibited Bramante from building a spacious chancel. His solution was to have painted on the slightly telescoping chancel walls a perspective image of a barrel vault.

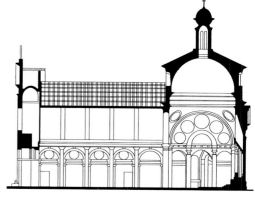

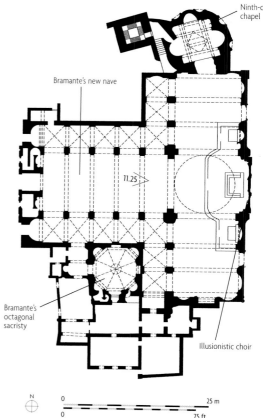

Ninth-century chapel

Bramante's new nave

11.25

Bramante's octagonal sacristy

Illusionistic choir

N

0                    25 m

0                    75 ft

**11.25** Donato Bramante, S. Maria presso S. Satiro interior, Milan, 1482–92.

Here is the visual effect of Bramante's clever illusionistic manipulation of the shallow chancel wall. The effect works perfectly, of course, only for someone standing along the center line of the nave.

## THE TEMPIETTO, ROME

Leaving Milan after its sack by the French in 1499, Bramante moved on to Rome where, like Brunelleschi and Alberti before him, he was able to study the ancient monuments first-hand; the effect on his design thinking was profound. In 1502 he was provided with an ideal opportunity to create a cerebral synthesis of humanist worldliness and Christian piety. The clients were conveniently remote: King Ferdinand and Queen Isabella of Spain, most famous for their support of the voyages of Christopher Columbus. The program called for the erection of a monument atop the spot where St. Peter was believed to have been martyred and adjacent to the recently completed church of S. Pietro in Montorio.

Bramante's site plan (Fig. 11.26), though never realized in this form, is critical to an understanding of his complete

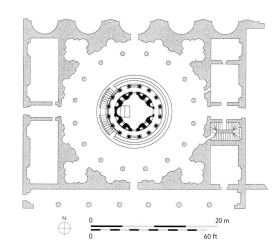

**11.26**  Donato Bramante, Plan of the Tempietto, Rome, begun 1502.

Bramante planned for his interpretation of the circular temple to be placed in this ideal environment. As was so often the case with such grand Renaissance plans, it was never fully realized.

**11.27**  Donato Bramante, Tempietto, Rome, begun 1502.

Bramante placed the principal door opposite the altar. However, the only absolutely logical way geometrically to enter the circular plan would have been in the center and from below.

vision. It called for the creation of a circular cloister, a perfect hermetic architectural environment, and the insertion into it of a circular temple. Bramante designed his building to embody both the Platonic preference for ideal form and Christian reverence for tradition, in this case reverence for the circular martyria of the early church. His command of form and detail approaches perfection.

Known as the Tempietto (Fig. 11.27) the completed building is a two-story cylinder capped by a hemispherical dome and surrounded by a one-story Doric colonnade with entablature and balustrade. The metope panels of the frieze display symbols connecting the current authority of the pope to the grandeur of antiquity, specifically keys, chalice, and paton (or plate for the eucharist), incense boat, and tabernacle—all symbols of St. Peter—and liturgical instruments of the Mass. Only the doorway is awkward in its random positioning within one of the sixteen repetitive column bays, its uniqueness celebrated only by a modest set of steps.

## ST. PETER'S, ROME

In 1505 Michelangelo was at work on a tomb for Pope Julius II. Because such a huge monument would not fit readily into the old and crumbling basilica, now almost 1200 years old, the Pope hired Bramante to help him explore his options. They first considered a centrally planned addition for the tomb at the western end of the existing church, similar to Bramante's addition to the church of S. Maria delle Grazie in Milan.

This was not the first Renaissance attempt to modify or add to St. Peter's. Pope Nicholas V had instructed Alberti to report on the condition of the building. Not surprisingly Alberti found the walls out of plumb and the aging fabric in such a dilapidated state that he considered repairs inadvisable. Nicholas accepted this recommendation and in 1451 appointed Bernardo Rossellino to design an apse as the first stage of an anticipated new St. Peter's. The deaths of Nicholas in 1455 and of Rossellino in 1464 terminated this project, even though Rossellino's choir was eventually built.

After this tentative beginning, the project to rebuild St. Peter's languished for another fifty years. Eventually Julius II decided that a completely new church was the only suitable accommodation for the tomb he envisioned for himself, and Bramante created an appropriately bold Greek-cross design in 1505 (Fig. 11.28). A medal cast in 1506 depicts Bramante's scheme, which represented a building on the scale of the Baths of Diocletian capped by a dome comparable to that of the Pantheon. This combination was carefully considered by Bramante. A drawing of the church in his notebooks shows it surrounded by gardens and a colonnade; on the reverse of the sheet is his drawing of the baths. Rather than merely continuing patterns of antiquity, Bramante was attempting to outdo Roman builders by proposing a domed structure more ambitious than any ancient edifice. The structural concept

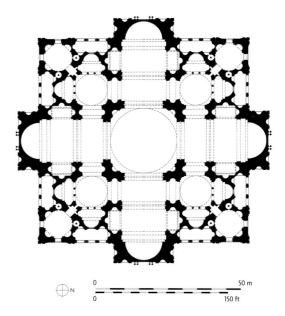

**11.28** Donato Bramante, Plan of St. Peter's, Rome, 1505.

The delicacy of the plan, almost like embroidery, foreshadows the problems Michelangelo would face when he replaced Bramante as architect at St. Peter's. The central piers proved to be insufficient to support the projected dome.

of a dome and drum supported on pendentives and semicircular arches actually had more in common with Byzantine work, which had itself developed from Roman models, than with any authentic Roman construction. Bramante's audacious design exceeded his structural understanding, however, for the piers he proposed would undoubtedly have been inadequate for the great loads imposed by the dome.

The cornerstone of this vast project was laid on April 18, 1506, as a labor force of 2500 began the foundations for the crossing piers. Bramante died in 1514, when they were scarcely above ground level. By the time the church was completed nearly 150 years later, almost every major architect of the sixteenth and seventeenth centuries had been engaged here at one time or another. Thus, the rebuilding of St. Peter's embraces work of several periods, from the High Renaissance to the Baroque.

High Renaissance buildings were generally more Roman and three-dimensional in spatial conception than the less massive Early Renaissance ones. Architects such as Bramante had reconciled the theoretical positions of Vitruvius, Alberti, and Leonardo with the realities of Roman construction practices and had developed the confidence to design buildings suitable to the requirements of their own age, while at the same time maintaining the spirit of antiquity. They handled matters of proportion, the manipulation of space, and correct detailing skillfully and subtly, so that in the span of less than a century the explorations of Brunelleschi had matured into the calm, self-assured style of the High Renaissance.

## THE BELVEDERE COURT AND THE HOUSE OF RAPHAEL, ROME

Pope Julius II also directed Bramante to organize the land north of the basilica into a great palace. Bramante inherited a modest irregular palace contiguous with Old St. Peter's and, some 900 feet away, a fortress-like **belvedere** used as a summer residence. Intent upon the creation of a complex rivaling the imperial villas of antiquity, he masked the irregularity of the existing structures by adding new façades: the one to the south eventually made into a semicircular theater, and the one to the north organized around a central hemicycle (Fig. 11.29). His strategy for connecting them produced the first great landscaped urban space of the Renaissance and involved the first use of monumental stairs since ancient times. It looked back, as was by now expected, to various inspirations from antiquity, including the villas described by Pliny the Younger. In order to tame the irregular topography, Bramante took inspiration from the Roman Sanctuary of Fortuna Primigenia at Praeneste (now Palestrina; see Fig. 5.4) near Rome, specifically its use of stairs and ramps as a means of organizing space within a view based upon a

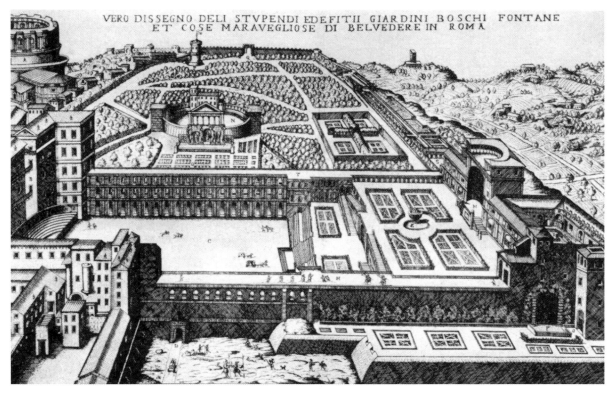

VERO DISSEGNO DELI STVPENDI EDEFITII GIARDINI BOSCHI FONTANE ET COSE MARAVEGLIOSE DI BELVEDERE IN ROMA

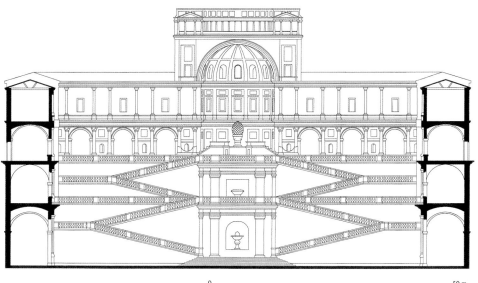

**11.29** Donato Bramante, Belvedere Court, Rome, begun 1505, engraving.

This great outdoor space adjacent to St. Peter's was intended by Pope Julius II to re-create the grandeur of ancient Rome. One can imagine him and Bramante walking through the ruins on the Palatine planning to recapture the site's former glory.

**11.30** Donato Bramante, Transverse section through the Belvedere Court, Rome, begun 1505.

This view (looking from left to right in Fig. 11.29) makes clear Bramante's use of the Roman Hellenistic Sanctuary of Fortuna Primigenia at Praeneste (now Palestrina) as one of his models. It also demonstrates the continuing Renaissance fascination with a single viewpoint—the station point, or position of the observer, in mechanical perspective.

0 ———— 50 m

0 ———— 150 ft

contrived perspective vista (Fig. 11.30). For the flanking east and west walls, he chose as his model the Colosseum, in effect turned inside out, articulating the three stories at the lower, south end of the site with first Doric, then Ionic, then Corinthian pilasters defining bays for arcades and windows, and articulating the one-story section to the north with arcaded openings flanked by Corinthian pilasters. The stairs, ramps, and punctured east and west walls provided vantage points for spectacles staged in the lower court. Many changes have been made to Bramante's scheme in the final built version, most notably Pope Sixtus V's insertion of a library which cuts across the court, eradicating the ramps and stairs and subdividing the space.

Bramante also built a house for himself in Rome (ca. 1512) (Fig. 11.31). It was purchased by the artist Raphael (1483–1520) after he had been summoned to Rome to decorate the papal apartments, and so became known as the House of Raphael; unfortunately, it has long since been demolished. Like many urban dwellings and following the model of the ancient Roman insula, it had shops at the street level, treated by Bramante as the rusticated base for pairs of engaged Doric columns articulating the piano nobile above. It was a distinct innovation in palace design because it produced a more three-dimensional façade, especially when compared with the flat modeling of the orders on Early Renaissance buildings such as the Rucellai Palace. It became one of the most influential models for façade designs in Western architecture, particularly in England and France in the eighteenth century.

## THE LATE RENAISSANCE AND MANNERISM

While the architects of the Early and High Renaissance saw the buildings of antiquity as models to be emulated, those of the Late Renaissance, often called Mannerists, sought to achieve a more personal artistic expression through the imaginative and individualistic manipulation of the classical language. Mannerism began in the 1520s and has sometimes been associated with the political destabilization surrounding the Sack of Rome by the army of Charles V, emperor of the Holy Roman Empire. While the High Renaissance designers were disciplined and resolute and attempted to produce integrated, harmonious buildings, Mannerists favored disharmony, discord, imbalance, tension, distortion, and unresolved conflicts. However, the difference in the two periods was not quite so simple.

The term "Mannerism" was derived from the Italian word *maniera*, which, in the sixteenth century, connoted virtuosity, refinement, and grace, but, by the seventeenth century, had come to mean self-indulgence, self-consciousness, and superficial artifice. Both definitions can reasonably be applied to Mannerist work, depending upon the talent of the practitioner and the attitude of the viewer.

Among the more inventive Mannerists were Raphael, Giorgio Vasari (1511–74), and Giulio Romano (ca. 1499–1546). The genius of Michelangelo Buonarroti (1475–1564), whose career was contemporary with these men and whose designs share some qualities with theirs, transcended any stylistic label. Likewise, Andrea Palladio (1508–80), at work during the same period, was inspired at one point by Giulio Romano but looked back more to the models of Bramante. In the end, Palladio produced a body of work that arguably has been the most written about in all of Western architecture.

**11.31** Donato Bramante, Elevation of the House of Raphael, Rome, ca. 1512.

This modest building has been as influential a prototype as any created by a Renaissance architect. Its rusticated, arcaded ground floor and columned piano nobile with entablature would reappear at various scales in France and England and eventually in America. Its own model was the ancient Roman insula or apartment house.

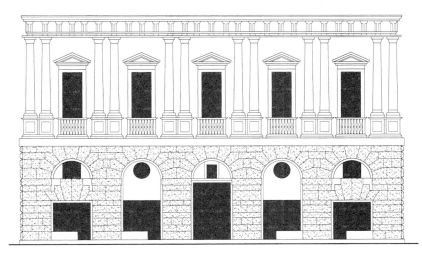

## THE VILLA MADAMA, ROME

A good place to begin is the Villa Madama, designed by Raphael for Cardinal Giulio de' Medici, who was later Pope Clement VII; intriguingly it was left half-completed (Figs. 11.32–11.33). The villa was to become a characteristic building type for Renaissance architects. In contrast to the urban dwelling or palace, it was a country retreat, ostensibly inspired by the Roman **villa rustica** or estate farm. The villa's essential architectural attribute was a loggia or open elevated porch, from which visitors could view carefully designed gardens and perhaps enjoy a distant vista. The wealthy owner of a villa would come there to escape the city's summer heat, to rest and relax, and to stroll about and talk with friends. At the Villa Madama, the building was set into the hillside on a south-facing slope of the Monte Mario, beyond the walls of

**11.32** Raphael, Villa Madama rotunda, Rome, begun ca. 1516.

As constructed, this villa represents only half of Raphael's plan. If completed, the central feature would have been an open rotunda, modeled perhaps on the Island Enclosure at Hadrian's Villa; but it was left incomplete as a semicircle.

**11.33** Raphael, Plan of and longitudinal section through the Villa Madama, Rome, begun ca. 1516.

The plan shows constructed and unconstructed portions of the villa. The section along the principal axis shows, left to right, the half-completed cortile, the short passage to a domed bay of the loggia, the loggia, and the parterres atop their arched terrace. Raphael and Giulio Romano painted the vaulted bays of the loggia with grotesques based on the wall paintings in the recently discovered Palatine wing of Nero's Golden House.

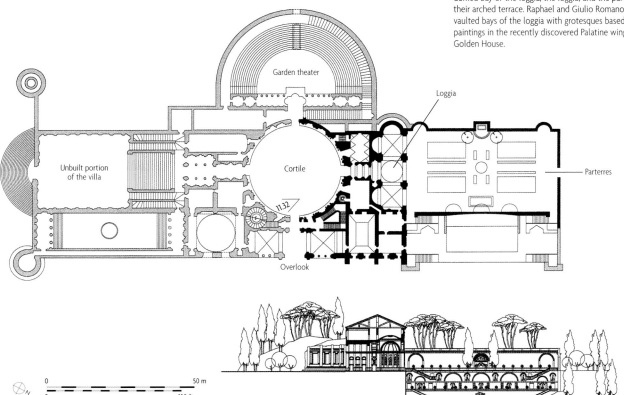

Garden theater

Loggia

Unbuilt portion of the villa

Cortile

Parterres

Overlook

0    50 m

0    150 ft

Rome, with a view over the city and the Tiber. The hillside, terraced into a number of levels, had formal gardens with fountains spouting and pouring water from level to level. Had its buildings been finished, the villa would have had a circular cortile with a design based, like the Belvedere Courtyard, on the superimposed orders of the Colosseum, off which loggias, a theater, and an overlook would have radiated. Only half the work was completed, however. Its major space consists of a loggia opening onto a **parterre**, inspired in part by the three partially extant groin-vaulted bays of the Basilica of Constantine, except that the middle space here is covered by a dome on pendentives. Pavements are set in mosaic tiles, and walls and ceilings are covered with frescoed festoons containing mythological, religious, and Medicean symbolism inspired by the excavations, then being directed by Raphael, going on at Nero's Golden House. Most of the paintings were completed after Raphael's death by his two major assistants,

Giovanni da Udine, who rediscovered the lost technique of Roman stucco, and Giulio Romano.

The building and its grounds posit new conditions and problems for sixteenth-century designers. Movement through the site offers choices and potential moments of indecision. The various areas—cortile, garden theater, and parterres—offer abrupt and dramatic contrasts. At the Villa Madama, the classical language reached a new level of sophistication, particularly in the frescoed loggia, but also documented the change from the self-assured countenance of the High Renaissance to the anxiety and ambiguity of Mannerism.

## THE UFFIZI, FLORENCE

Giorgio Vasari's design for the Uffizi in Florence (Fig. 11.34), begun in 1560, illustrates the Mannerist attitude toward urban design. The building, an office annex for

**11.34** Giorgio Vasari, Uffizi, Florence, begun 1560.

Vasari so composed his Uffizi complex that it framed this view of the medieval Palazzo Vecchio. Such urbanistic interaction of existing and new construction was a significant contribution of Manneristic planning.

the Palazzo Vecchio, consists of a long, narrow cortile flanked on its two long sides by multi-floor wings to which Vasari applied crisply modeled window surrounds and broken **belt courses** that move aggressively forward and back. One end of the cortile terminates at the Arno river with a series of three openings, the center one wider and arched, and the opposite open end discharges into Piazza della Signoria, with the tower of the Palazzo Vecchio standing off-center. While the river end of the cortile confronts a road and the spatial corridor of the Arno, a view in through the central arched opening captures the perspective diminution of the Uffizi cornices together with the Palazzo Vecchio's tower. Rather than creating a static, hermetic urban ensemble as Bramante had chosen to do with the Tempietto, Vasari created an open-ended interactive one in which he dexterously combined old and new and stressed the dynamics of motion and change over time.

## THE PALAZZO DEL TE, MANTUA

Unlike many artists of the High Renaissance working in Rome, Giulio Romano was actually born there, so his understanding of the buildings of antiquity came from his personal, intimate experience of the city rather than from study undertaken for professional reasons. Therefore, it is not surprising that, as one of the creators of Mannerism, Romano chose to represent the ruined condition of ancient monuments as his contribution to sixteenth-century architecture. This can be seen in one of his early paintings, *The Stoning of St. Stephen* (1523), in which Roman ruins in the background provide the setting. Giulio's architectural works feature the willful and amusing misuse of classical elements. In his own house at Mantua (1544), he built a Pantheon Salon, with an image of Julius Caesar, his namesake, carved over the fireplace.

His most important building is the Palazzo del Te (1525–34), designed for Federigo Gonzaga as a honeymoon villa on an island at the edge of Mantua. The Gonzaga family were horse-breeders, supplying steeds to the courts of Europe, and they were also extensively involved in political intrigue and military alliances. The palace was originally conceived as an enormous stable complex. It consists of a large square cortile, enclosed on all four sides by a series of rooms arranged en suite, with central entrances on the north and east sides. A loggia on the west side leads into a garden, at the end of which is a semicircular colonnade. The garden is laid out in geometric flowerbeds, and a moat used for staging miniature naval battles was dug adjacent to the villa, which is linked to the garden by a bridge. The loggia is barrel-vaulted and supported on alternate paired and single columns, while the north entrance has rusticated columns, deliberately made to appear unfinished. These columns support lintels with keystones, above which is an octagonally coffered ceiling as in the Basilica of Constantine. In the courtyard, heavy Doric columns support parts of the architrave and frieze with triglyphs dropped down out of place as if part of an ancient Roman ruin (Fig. 11.35). Together with the unframed niches and windows, pediments lacking a bottom cornice, and heavy rustication, these features create extreme contrasts and a sense of ambiguity and tension.

**11.35** Guilio Romano, Palazzo del Te cortile, Mantua, 1525–34.

It is unclear whether the effect was intended to shock or amuse, but Giulio Romano designed some of the stones of the entablature to be displaced downward as if part of a ruin.

The illusion of imbalance and the perverse use of classicism continue on the interior. The wall and ceiling surfaces of the rooms around the courtyard are filled with frescoes by Giulio Romano and his assistants, with additional enrichment provided by inlaid doors and mantels of oriental jasper, gold, and marble. Cracked brick lintels painted on the wall surfaces above doors create an uncomfortable feeling in visitors passing beneath them. Above the cracked lintels in the Sala dei Giganti is painted a scene of great destruction, with the weight of collapsing columns crushing the limbs and bodies of giant figures, one going cross-eyed as his head becomes trapped between two falling boulders. Walls merge into billowing clouds painted on the ceiling, the center of which carries a representation of a colonnaded drum supporting a hemispherical dome. Horses painted in the Sala dei Cavalli stand on cornices more than half the height of this large chamber, and behind them are landscapes seen through painted window surrounds between the pilasters and architectural detailing.

The Palazzo del Te was never finished, yet it remains a masterpiece of the Late Renaissance, designed by a sophisticated architect as a play on the conventions of revived classicism. Only those who shared Romano's understanding of Roman architecture could fully appreciate his accomplishment.

## MICHELANGELO

Michelangelo Buonarroti, widely regarded as one of the greatest geniuses of Western art, made important contributions to the fields of sculpture, painting, and architecture during the course of his long and productive life. The second son of a minor governmental official in Florence, he was apprenticed at the age of thirteen to the painter Domenico del Ghirlandaio, despite his father's reluctance to have his son become an artist. His training in sculpture began a year or so later when Michelangelo was invited to join the workshop sponsored by Lorenzo de' Medici as part of the Medici effort to revive the sculptural arts of antiquity. Until the death of Lorenzo in 1492, Michelangelo lived in the Medici Palace as a member of the household, gaining a humanist education from the eminent scholars, writers, and poets who gathered there under Lorenzo's patronage.

### S. LORENZO, FLORENCE

Under Pope Leo X, the younger son of Lorenzo de' Medici and successor to Pope Julius II, Michelangelo embarked on the first of three architectural commissions for the monastery of S. Lorenzo, Florence, in 1515. His design for the façade of the basilican church was a screen consisting of two equally developed stories divided by an attic, forming a backdrop for relief panels and sculptures set in niches. Nothing had come of this design by the time Leo died in 1521, and the church exists today without a façade, but Michelangelo's proposals established a second tradition in façade architecture, providing an alternative to Alberti's S. Maria Novella type.

Before the façade design was abandoned, the Medici asked Michelangelo to design a funerary chapel adjacent to the north transept for the burial of Lorenzo de' Medici and four of the lesser Medici (see Fig. 11.5). This New Sacristy, or Medici Chapel, was to complement Brunelleschi's Old Sacristy located off the north transept.

Michelangelo paid homage to Brunelleschi by employing a similar form, a hemispherical dome on pendentives, over the cubical main space, and using some of the same materials: white stucco walls trimmed with gray pietra serena. The tombs themselves are marble. The number of statues and Michelangelo's placement of them underwent a series of changes; his sketches show that he considered a central mausoleum, but he finally placed two sarcophagi on either side of the chapel. Each supports symbolic but unfinished sculptures of the Times of Day, with seated figures of the dukes Lorenzo and Giuliano placed above in niches set into the wall. The large symbolic figures of Day and Night, on Giuliano's tomb, and Dawn and Dusk, on Lorenzo's, recline precariously on top of the sarcophagi, their very weight seeming to cause them to slide off the curved lids. The ghoulish mask on Night suggests nightmares. These sculptures are in the lowest of three levels within the chapel, where a profusion of architectural elements—heavy blank tabernacles above the doors, tapering blank windows, and even pilasters without capitals—vie with one another. Above are **lunettes**, punctuated with tapering windows; and surmounting the whole ensemble is a coffered dome with oculus, capped by a cupola.

Pope Leo X's illegitimate cousin, elected to the papacy as Clement VII, wished to house the Medici library for use by scholars within the cloister of S. Lorenzo, the family parish church, perhaps to emphasize that the Medici were no longer mere merchants but members of intellectual and ecclesiastical society. Michelangelo therefore began work on the so-called Laurentian Library in 1524 (Figs. 11.5, 11.36). It was built above existing monastic quarters on the east range of the cloister, with an entrance from the upper level of the cloisters. Michelangelo wanted to use a skylight over the vestibule, but the Pope believed that this would leak, so clerestory windows were incorporated into the west wall overlooking the cloister instead. Thus the vestibule (Fig. 11.37) is shocking in its verticality, almost half as tall again as it is wide. Blank tapering windows, framed in pietra serena, surround the interior of the vestibule; these are separated by paired columns set into the wall. The normally illogical recessing of columns into a wall would seem to be a Mannerist invention, yet the column positions are actually necessitated by the location of the existing walls of the building beneath the library. The walls between columns are like a taut skin stretched

**11.36** Michelangelo Buonarroti, Plan of and longitudinal section through the Laurentian Library, Florence, begun 1524.

One should not forget that the sculptural drama of Michelangelo's entry vestibule is only a prelude to the principal space: the reading room for Greek and Latin texts. Here he abandoned his preferred tension and dynamics in favor of a modular serenity befitting the space's function.

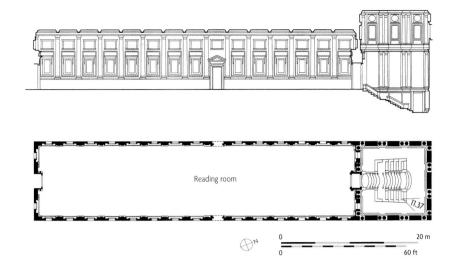

Reading room

**11.37** Michelangelo Buonarroti, Laurentian Library vestibule, Florence, begun 1524.

The vestibule stairs appear to cascade downward from the reading room doorway as though its treads and risers were once molten. The impacted columns astride this doorway create in architecture the same kind of tension expressed in the reclining figures at Michelangelo's Medici Chapel.

between the vertical supports. Michelangelo further emphasized the seeming instability of the whole by having the columns appear to be supported on **consoles**, so that weight seems to be carried on rather weak elements, and one cannot determine visually whether the columns or walls support the roof. The sense of ambiguity is increased further by the apparently unorthodox forms of the tabernacle windows, and all of the architectural elements have been compressed together, creating a sense of tension and constrained energy.

The tour de force of this restless space is the huge staircase leading up to the reading room. Michelangelo's original sketches for the library show the stair as divided flights placed against the wall. By 1558–59, when the present stair was designed, his proposal had grown into a piece of dynamic sculpture that appears to pour forth from the upper level like lava and compress the limited floor space of the vestibule. As it descends, the stair divides into three flights, the outer ones having no handrails. On the central flight, the convex treads vary in width, making the whole arrangement somewhat disquieting. By contrast the library's reading room is serene, quiet, and restful, entirely appropriate for research and study. In the manner of monastic libraries, it is a long room lit by evenly spaced windows set between pilasters in the side walls. Thus reading desks, arranged perpendicular to the side walls, were amply illuminated by natural light.

## THE CAMPIDOGLIO, ROME

In 1534, with both the Medici Chapel and the Laurentian Library still incomplete, Michelangelo left Florence for Rome, where he remained until his death in 1564. Only seven years before, in 1527, Rome had been sacked by Charles V. One of Michelangelo's first architectural commissions there came from the local government authority, which decided to reestablish the grandeur of Rome by developing the Campidoglio, the ancient seat of government on the Capitoline Hill occupied since the twelfth century by a communal palace. Shortly thereafter Pope Paul III had transferred the great equestrian bronze of Marcus Aurelius specifically for use as the centerpiece of the site. Thus Michelangelo was required to provide a setting for the statue and to bring order to an irregular hilltop already encumbered by two crumbling medieval buildings set at an acute angle to one another. Despite these conditions, it was in one sense a Renaissance architect's ideal commission, for it offered the opportunity to build a monumental civic plaza for a major city. Michelangelo produced a brilliant response to this awkward commission. He planned a trapezoidal piazza to regularize the difficult geometry established by the existing buildings, and intended to inset an oval paving pattern that would focus attention on the equestrian statue in the center (Fig. 11.38). Precedent for this general disposition of elements

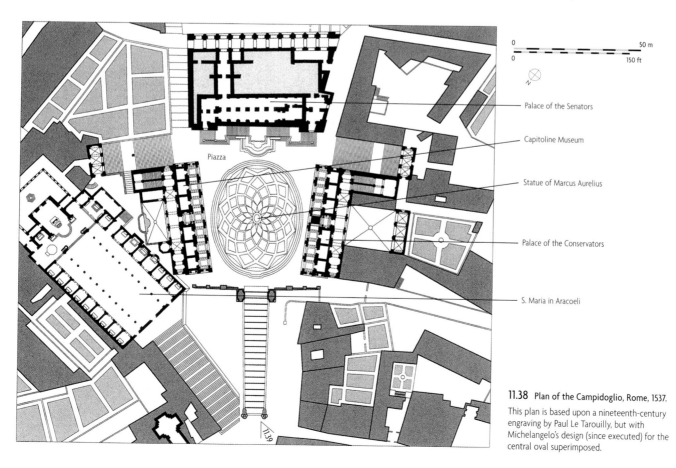

0                50 m
0              150 ft

Palace of the Senators

Capitoline Museum

Statue of Marcus Aurelius

Palace of the Conservators

S. Maria in Aracoeli

Piazza

**11.38** Plan of the Campidoglio, Rome, 1537.

This plan is based upon a nineteenth-century engraving by Paul Le Tarouilly, but with Michelangelo's design (since executed) for the central oval superimposed.

**11.39** Michelangelo Buonarroti, Campidoglio, Rome, begun 1537. Engraving by Le Tarouilly.

Le Tarouilly's view is deceptive. The absolute regularity gives no hint of the previous disorder of this formerly rutted hill with its hulks of medieval buildings disposed in an asymmetrical and non-orthogonal configuration. Michelangelo's genius was to unify the unrelated parts.

can be found in Rossellino's plan for the cathedral piazza at Pienza (1459–64; see page 296), although the scale and coherence of Michelangelo's design are much greater.

Axiality and symmetry govern all parts of the Capitoline Hill work. Michelangelo gave the medieval Palace of the Senators (Fig. 11.39), remodeled in ca. 1547 and later, a central campanile, a renovated façade, and a grand divided external staircase. He designed a new façade for the colonnaded Palace of the Conservators, with a giant order of Corinthian pilasters extending over two stories, and projected an identical structure, the Palazzo Nuovo (now the Capitoline Museum), for the opposite side of the piazza. On the narrow side of the trapezoidal plan, Michelangelo extended the central axis with a magnificent ramp-stair to link the hilltop with the city below. Work on the Capitoline Hill was incomplete when Michelangelo died, but his designs were carefully followed in subsequent centuries, down to the installation of the paving pattern in 1928.

**11.40** Antonio da Sangallo the Younger and Michelangelo Buonarroti, Palazzo Farnese, Rome, 1517–46.

This joint effort became the model for a variety of urban monuments in the late nineteenth and early twentieth centuries. Unlike the Florentine interpretation of this type, this palazzo has rustication only in the form of quoins at the corners and at the entry and has classically inspired window surrounds.

## THE PALAZZO FARNESE, ROME

In 1546 Pope Paul III employed Michelangelo to continue construction of the Palazzo Farnese (Fig. 11.40), his family residence, begun in 1517 by Antonio da Sangallo the Younger. At the main façade, Michelangelo added the cornice and the central window with coat of arms at the piano-nobile level. In the courtyard, he added the two upper floors, compressing the pilasters, attached columns, and windows in a manner not unlike the entry vestibule at the Laurentian Library. As an expression of the social position and wealth of the newly rich Farnese family, the palace commands the piazza on which it fronts, lending an impassive dignity to the space.

## ST. PETER'S, ROME

Pope Paul III had been in office five years before the Vatican had amassed adequate funds to resume the building of St. Peter's, begun in 1506 by Bramante. Plans had been submitted by Raphael, Giuliano da Sangallo, and

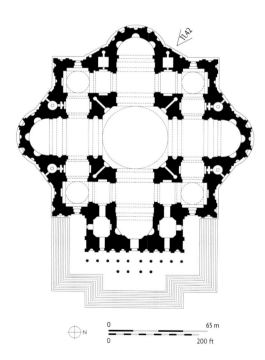

**11.41** Michelangelo Buonarroti, Plan of St. Peter's, Rome, begun 1546.

A comparison of this plan to Bramante's (see Fig. 11.28) reveals that the column screens have disappeared, the central piers have been enlarged, and an entry portico developed. If completed in this form, it would have represented the culmination of centrally planned church explorations during the Renaissance.

Baldassare Peruzzi, but the Sack of Rome by the army of Charles V in 1527 had emptied the Vatican coffers and prevented much actual construction being carried out. Antonio da Sangallo the Younger spent the amount required to build a small church in making a model to illustrate the ungainly agglomeration of underscaled classical orders he proposed for the north and south transept ambulatories. Even though these admitted only indirect light into the great central space, the southern transept was completed according to his designs in 1546, the year in which he died. Michelangelo's appointment as architect-in-charge provoked Vasari to write that Paul III was indeed fortunate that God had ordained that Michelangelo should live during his pontificate, saying: "How great are thy merits elevated by his art." Michelangelo, who considered himself primarily a sculptor, agreed to the assignment as a pious act for the glorification of God, and he accepted no more than a minimum

living wage for his architectural work on St. Peter's. He quickly saw the faults of Sangallo's unimaginative scheme and razed the exterior walls of the transept ambulatories, in part because they encroached on the Vatican Palace and would have necessitated the destruction of several buildings had they been completed around the church. They would also have provided dark internal passageways in which, Michelangelo said, vagrants could hide and attack pilgrims. Michelangelo made a small clay model of the church, from which a wooden model was then constructed; the design restored Bramante's initial conception of a Greek-cross plan, but in a reduced and simplified version (Fig. 11.41), and increased the size of Bramante's under-structured central piers, the foundations of which were already in the ground. Michelangelo corresponded with his nephew in Florence to learn the dimensions of Brunelleschi's cathedral dome there, a design he admired and wished to emulate. "I am going to make its sister bigger, yes, but not more beautiful," he wrote.

Although construction on the dome of St. Peter's was not begun in his lifetime, Michelangelo endowed its design with internal and external unity (Fig. 11.42). Brunelleschi's dome for the Florence Cathedral has a tall Gothic profile;

**11.42** Michelangelo Buonarroti, St. Peter's, Rome, begun 1546.

It takes a view such as this one to get a sense of the centrally planned massing intended by Bramante and Michelangelo. The dominant feature here is the great dome, which, at ground level, is no longer the case today as a result of the extension of the nave by Carlo Maderno.

**11.43** Michelangelo Buonarroti, Porta Pia, Rome, 1561–65.

This gateway still welcomes people approaching the city from the east. When first constructed, its unorthodox elements, ambiguous structural systems, and discordant textures must have shocked anyone seeing it for the first time.

Michelangelo chose instead a hemispherical form. He also increased the number of stone ribs expressed on the outside of the dome from eight to sixteen in order to eliminate the faceted octagonal massing of the Florence Cathedral dome. Had the dome been constructed as planned by Michelangelo, the outward thrust of the ribs would have been enormous, and it is doubtful whether a masonry drum could have withstood the accumulated forces. Giacomo della Porta, who constructed the dome after Michelangelo's death, employed a slightly taller profile in order to decrease the lateral thrust and used the lantern cupola to force the weight of the dome downward to the drum. He used columns, attached visually to the drum by a broken entablature, to act as buttresses that further force the loads downward to the arches and four great piers of the central crossing. Even so, tension chains were subsequently incorporated into the brickwork of this double-shelled dome, which is only five feet smaller in diameter than the Pantheon dome. The triangulated massing of the whole project rises to a height of 452 feet, enough to have strong visual presence had Michelangelo's façade been built as planned. Eventually, however, St. Peter's was completed early in the seventeenth century with a nave and entrance façade designed by Carlo Maderno (see Figs. 12.4–12.5) that diminished the presence of the dome.

## PORTA PIA, ROME

In his later designs Michelangelo anticipated the Baroque in several ways, as in his design of the Porta Pia (Fig. 11.43), a city gate built at the end of the Via Pia. Rather than a defensive gateway within a fortified city wall, it was and is a scenic backdrop terminating a vista. Stone architectural elements, many of them unusual, are isolated against a plane of brick: a broken pediment stuffed with an oversized swag and plaque, oddly draped-over roundels, and volute-topped crenellations. Michelangelo emphasized the central passageway by packing within it an array of redundant structural elements—arch, rusticated arch, and broken pediment above deeply grooved pilasters with **mutules** in their capitals; the concatenation of architectural details recalls Renaissance stage-set designs for the theater. Begun in 1561, the Porta Pia was almost complete, unlike so many of Michelangelo's other architectural commissions, at the time of his death.

## SFORZA CHAPEL, ROME

His most adventurous project spatially is the Sforza Chapel at S. Maria Maggiore in Rome (Fig. 11.44), built for the same family that had employed Leonardo da Vinci in Milan. Like the Laurentian Library, it is both dynamic and ambiguous. The chapel combines central and longitudinal planning and emphasizes not orthogonal but diagonal directionality, defined by four columns attached to rotated piers and supporting a groin vault that can be described as "billowing." The curving wall segments that cradle the lateral altars are the boundaries of an incomplete circle with the vaults above them equally incomplete and sail-like. The principal altar opposite the entrance, as at the Pazzi Chapel, resides in a subsidiary square. The Sforza Chapel offered a source of inspiration for a host of spatial experiments by designers for at least the next 150 years.

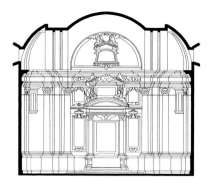

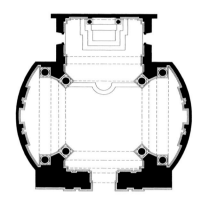

**11.44** Michelangelo Buonarroti, Plan of and longitudinal section through the Sforza Chapel, S. Maria Maggiore, Rome, 1564.

There was no more revolutionary Renaissance building than this one. Its column and vault configuration and resulting spatial dynamics and spatial interpenetrations inspired designers throughout Europe for more than a century afterward. While stone obviously cannot billow, this word does express the feeling that Michelangelo captured. The vault appears to be held down by the columns rather than resting heavily upon them.

## ANDREA PALLADIO

Andrea Palladio was born Andrea di Pietro della Gondola in 1508 and was trained as a stonemason. When he was about thirty, he was employed on a building site, where his talents attracted the attention of the humanist Count Giangiorgio Trissino. Trissino became his mentor, renaming him Palladio after a character in his epic poem *Italy Freed from the Goths*, and providing him with a humanist education. Along with several study trips to Rome, this gave Palladio an education in architecture. In particular, by measuring the buildings of ancient Rome, he collected accurate information on classical proportions, which he later used in designing his own buildings.

Palladio's profound influence on the development of Western architecture can be attributed to both his writings and his buildings. In 1570 he published his *I quattro libri dell'architettura* or *The Four Books of Architecture* (Fig.

11.45), in which he illustrated and discussed his own work as well as that of antiquity. Palladio wrote about the orders of architecture, domestic architecture, public buildings, town planning, and temples, "without which," he said, "no civilization is possible." Although he could measure and illustrate actual Roman temples, theaters, bridges, triumphal arches, and baths, Palladio had to speculate about the design of Roman houses, so he included ideal versions of his own buildings—often at odds with these designs as built—to demonstrate antique ideals. Numerals printed on the plans give the widths and lengths of rooms, and sections and the text sometimes have indications of heights. Making reference to his buildings and their dimensions, he published the Renaissance's most coherent system of proportions. He began with modules based on wall thicknesses, then determined all of his rooms' dimensions using ratios derived from the musical consonances, and arranged these rooms according to modulated grids.

**11.45** Frontispiece to the second book of Isaac Ware's English edition (1738) of Palladio's *I quattro libri dell' architettura*.

While various garbled editions of Palladio's book had appeared in England from the mid-seventeenth century, this was the most reliable and the first one approved of by the Neo-Palladians.

**11.46** Andrea Palladio, Basilica, Vicenza, 1549.

The roof is a nineteenth-century addition. Palladio's two levels of arches conceal the medieval vaults of the old basilica or town hall.

Here, as in all his architectural designs, he was concerned with practical convenience as an essential component of good design; firmness, commodity, and delight were to him the basic tenets of all architecture. Eventually many architects, beginning with Inigo Jones in England in the seventeenth century, used Palladio's publication as a guidebook and made close observation of his buildings their primary objective during travels through Italy.

### BUILDINGS IN VICENZA

Palladio's first public commission was a new skin for the medieval market and council hall, or basilica, at Vicenza; he added a two-story arcade of Doric and Ionic columns (Fig. 11.46). He submitted proposals for the project in 1546 at the request of the civic authorities, who accepted them with modifications in 1549. Construction was based on Roman brick groin-vaulting techniques, but the dominant element of the design is the repeated unit of three openings, the central one arched, supported on pairs of small columns, set off with a larger half-column between each bay. The end bays are smaller to give the appearance of strength to the corners, which have double columns. Although Bramante was the first Renaissance architect to use an arch flanked by square-headed openings, the unit is sometimes known as a **Serliana** because it was first illustrated in Sebastiano Serlio's publications. In using the Serliana here, Palladio was undoubtedly most directly influenced by the use of the motif at Jacopo Sansovino's Library of S. Marco (1537–53) in nearby Venice (see Fig. 11.57).

Some of Palladio's palazzo designs in Vicenza reflect his Roman experiences. The Palazzo Valmarana, for instance, includes the giant order used by Michelangelo at the Campidoglio. More original is his Palazzo Chiericati (1550–52), which was erected on a very shallow site with a long frontage onto a public open space (Fig. 11.47). Palladio treated the building like a Roman palace, two stories high, fronting onto a forum, with a ground-level Roman Doric colonnade intended to link with other colonnades (never constructed) on buildings around the remaining sides of the square. Like those of many Palladian houses, the palace's façade is divided into three parts, the central section being a pavilion or projecting bay accentuated by clustered columns that create an impression of strength. The second floor is composed in the Ionic order, with loggias flanking the main salon. Thus, by projecting the salon over the public colonnade below, Palladio gained additional space for the largest room in the house. The palace is open and airy. Because of the restricted site, the long axis of its entrance hall and the majority of its rooms run parallel to the street, rather than being perpendicular to it.

**11.47** Andrea Palladio, Palazzo Chiericati, Vicenza, 1550–52.

Palladio intended for the first-floor Doric colonnade to be continued around a forum-like piazza. The openness of the façade is surprising, particularly the cage-like corner spaces on the second floor.

## VILLA DESIGNS IN THE VENETO

Rather than his urban houses, it was Palladio's villa designs that gained him such a wide following among later architects. Unlike most Renaissance villas, his country estates were generally working farms owned by the younger sons of Venetian nobles. Their lands were located on the mainland north of Venice, the Veneto, to which capital generated by maritime commerce had been redirected as Venetian trading opportunities diminished. Although isolated from sophisticated Venetian society, these gentleman farmers maintained an elegant and cultured life in appropriately grand houses. Two of Palladio's early clients were Daniele Barbaro, a scholarly author and editor of a published version of Vitruvius, and his brother Marcantonio. Palladio designed the Villa Barbaro at Maser for them (1557–58) (Fig. 11.48). As with all his villas, the scheme is symmetrical, the central living block balanced by end pavilions connected by flanking arcades. The building is sited on a slight rise, so although it is strongly horizontal, it affords a view out into the landscape. The elegance of the composition belies the building's practicality. Following ancient Roman practices, Palladio combined the many functions of a large farm into a single structure, including storage for hay and equipment, provision for livestock, and spaces for threshing grain.

**11.48** Andrea Palladio, Villa Barbaro, Maser, 1557–58.

Palladio's combining of living and agricultural functions into a single, extended structure enabled him to make farm buildings monumental. He was the first Renaissance architect to use the temple front extensively on domestic buildings.

Inside the Villa Barbaro, the rooms are gracefully proportioned, well lit, and ingeniously ornamented with perspective frescoes by Paolo Veronese (ca. 1528–1588). Through the skillful application of pigment, walls merge into barrel-vaulted ceilings. In one room, balustraded balconies appear to support spiraled columns, behind which are painted openings where the mistress of the house can be seen emerging with a page boy, a domestic servant, a lapdog, and a parrot. Shadow projections increase the sense of depth in a series of rooms where actual architraves and pedimented doorways may be confused with those painted on flat wall surfaces. Huntsmen and children appear in open doorways, and sculptures stand in niches flanked by columns, all conjured into existence by the painter's brush. Landscapes lead the eye beyond columns and pilasters in the dining room into imaginary vistas inspired by scenes from antiquity.

With the Villa Barbaro, Palladio made a significant contribution to the development of residential design that continues to influence the architecture of our own time, even though he had no idea that he was being innovative: this was the application of the columns and pediment of a temple front to a house. He had interpreted Vitruvius as saying that Greek temples had evolved from houses, an observation that may refer to the similarity of the megaron and the cella of a temple. Having no knowledge of the megaron, Palladio assumed Vitruvius's remark to mean that Greek houses looked like Greek temples, which he knew to have columns and a pediment. Therefore, in using these elements on the façade of a house, Palladio believed that he was following Greek precedent, when in fact he was breaking new ground.

Palladio designed the Villa Foscari at Malcontenta (1559–60), located on the Brenta Canal outside Venice, on a single axis, with the intention that side courts would mask the end elevations, but the courts were never built (Figs. 11.49–11.50). Dog-leg stairs lead to a portico on axis at the piano-nobile level, and the entrance from the portico opens into a vaulted cruciform space extending the full depth of the building. One of the barrel vaults in the arms of the cross is expressed on the rusticated garden front. There is a consistent proportioning system used throughout the house, all rooms having ratios of 1:1, 2:3, 1:2, or 3:4. In plan the building's measurements of length to width conform to the Golden Section ratio of 5:8, while the height is the same as the width.

By far the most famous residence by Palladio is the Villa Americo-Capra, also known as the Villa Rotonda, located just outside Vicenza (1566–70) (Figs. 11.51–11.52). The client for this villa was a retired churchman, who used the house for elaborate entertainments as well as for agricultural processing. The Villa Rotonda is square in plan, with, as the name implies, a central two-storey rotunda. According to Palladio, "there are loggias made on all four fronts" so that "it enjoys from every part most

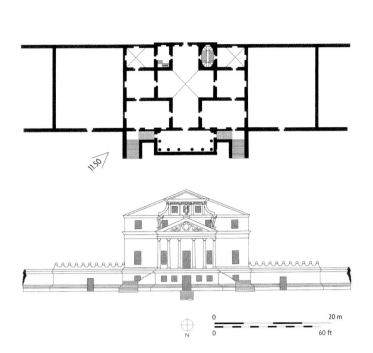

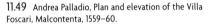

**11.49** Andrea Palladio, Plan and elevation of the Villa Foscari, Malcontenta, 1559–60.

Compare this elevation to the adjacent perspective view. The prominent roof disappears through foreshortening, while the portico becomes more dominant.

**11.50** Andrea Palladio, Villa Foscari, Malcontenta, 1559–60.

This perspective view reveals Palladio's genius for creating monumentally without relying on great size. He relied instead on large mural wall surfaces and careful proportioning and avoided scale-diminishing elements like handrails.

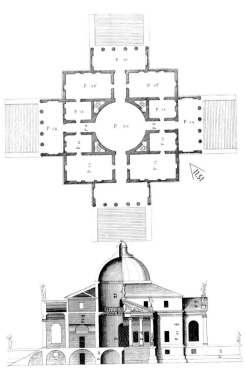

**11.51** Andrea Palladio, Villa Americo-Capra (Villa Rotonda), Vicenza, 1566–70.

Careful study of the bricks in the stairs has revealed significant changes since the villa's construction. Arched openings at the center of these stairs once allowed carts to carry grain into the basement.

**11.52** Andrea Palladio, Plan and elevation/section of the Villa Americo-Capra (Villa Rotonda), Vicenza, 1566–70.

These orthographic views show how Palladio illustrated his work with woodcuts in *I quattro libri*. He included the whole-number proportions of his rooms in the plan.

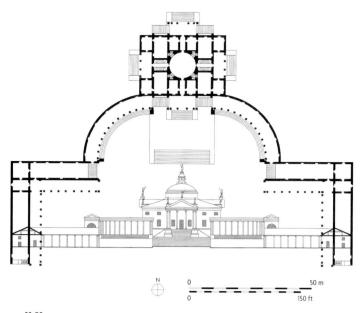

**11.53** Andrea Palladio, Plan and elevation of the Villa Trissino, Meledo, begun 1567.

While never completed, this villa design anticipated the sprawling Neo-Palladian compositions of early eighteenth-century England. The quadrant-shaped connectors between the central block and wings were to become a popular motif in eighteenth-century America.

beautiful views, some of which are limited, some extended, and others which terminate with the horizon." Internally the central domed space radiates out to the four porticoes and to the elegantly proportioned rooms in the corners. It is a simple yet powerful scheme, one that would be copied many times.

Palladio started from the same plan in his project for the Villa Trissino at Meledo (Fig. 11.53), an ambitious scheme of which only a tiny end fragment was ever built.

To the basic cube of the house, he added quadrant-shaped colonnades on either side of one porticoed entrance, widening it out to define a rectangular forecourt. Such colonnades would become a popular feature in gigantic Neo-Palladian country houses in England and in the smaller American Georgian houses of the eighteenth century. Comments made by the architect about the villa indicate that the ground floor was to be given over to domestic services, while the dependencies were to shelter farm activities.

## CHURCHES IN VENICE

Palladio's most significant church is S. Giorgio Maggiore in Venice (Fig. 11.54), which has a façade design derived from his earlier S. Francesca della Vigne, also in Venice. Both churches offered a new solution to the Renaissance problem of placing a classical façade in front of a basilican cross section. Palladio combined two temple fronts: a tall one, consisting of four Corinthian columns on pedestals that support a pediment at the end of the nave, superimposed over a wide one, with smaller Corinthian pilasters, that matches the sloping aisle roofs. Vitruvius had discussed a double arrangement of gables, and the idea of using double pediments on one façade was further legitimized by the example of the Pantheon, where an attic

**11.54** Andrea Palladio, S. Giorgio Maggiore, Venice, begun 1565.

Three scales of orders and three sizes of pediments give this façade clarity and richness. Palladio's use of overlapping temple forms would be much copied in America. Thermal windows are visible above the roof of the aisle.

**11.55** Andrea Palladio and Vincenzo Scamozzi, Teatro Olimpico interior, Vicenza, 1579–80.

This stage set by Scamozzi was not intended to be permanent. It represents the kind of ideal cityscape imagined by many Renaissance town planners. The buildings' façades are configured so as to create a false perspective. Not only do the cornices and belt courses converge in reality, but so also do the floor and ceiling planes.

level with cornice stands between the portico and the rotunda. At S. Giorgio, the Corinthian columns and pilasters on the front carry through to the interior arcading between nave and aisles, providing an Albertian unity in this ecclesiastical building. Palladio looked to the Roman thermae for a precedent in handling the interior. Barrel vaults are illuminated by the semicircular clerestory windows or thermal windows found in such baths as those of Diocletian, and the whole is painted white to reflect light and emphasize the church's volumetric clarity.

### THE TEATRO OLIMPICO

One of Palladio's last works was the Teatro Olimpico in Vicenza (1579–80), inspired by Roman theaters with a proscenium like the Theater of Marcellus, but roofed here with a ceiling painted to depict the sky. Steeply banked rows of seats are arranged in a semicircle facing the stage; to this day, the original stage set, designed by Vincenzo Scamozzi (1552–1616), remains as the scenery for all productions in the theater. Scamozzi's set shows an urban piazza, from which three streets extend back into the distance, their apparent length exaggerated by the false perspective of a sloped floor plane and artificially diminishing building heights (Fig. 11.55). When the actors leave the stage, they appear to recede along the street, even though their own height does not diminish according to the perspective of the set.

The continuing influence of Palladio on Western architecture is in no small measure due to the logical planning, careful proportioning, and conceptual clarity that characterize his designs. Indeed, the principles Palladio advocated have been found applicable to a variety of circumstances. Both his writings and buildings demonstrate the achievements of this stonemason turned architect who declared, "Vitruvius is my master, Rome is my mistress, and architecture is my life."

## PALLADIO'S VENICE

Palladio's Venice, located in Italy but with commercial connections to Constantinople and farther east, developed its own exotic form of Gothicism, which it overlaid with selected Renaissance ideas. Although Venice ultimately contained a considerable amount of Renaissance architecture, the style developed as a variant relying on local traditions, climate, and disposition. The Palazzo Vendramini-Calergi (1500–10) of Mauro Coducci (ca. 1440–1504) has Corinthian pilasters, columns, and cornices framing large round-headed windows that are also decorated with classical detailing. These windows catch the breezes coming off the lagoon and cool the loggia and central hall that replaced the cortile found in Florentine palaces. Martino Lombardo employed perspective relief panels, executed by Tullio Lombardo, at the ground level of the Scuola di S. Marco (1487–90). The scenes depict lions, the animal identified with St. Mark, peering out from an implied barrel-vaulted space behind the plane of the façade.

Perhaps most vivid in the mind of anyone who has visited this dowager-queen city of the Adriatic is the Piazza S. Marco (Fig. 11.56). Located at the point where the Grand Canal empties into the lagoon, it is one of the great civic spaces in Western urban design and offers a cross section of Venetian architectural developments in the fourteenth to sixteenth centuries. The piazza is L-shaped with a wide shaft of space extending from the water between the Doge's Palace and the Library of S. Marco to the campanile, around which it pivots to form a long trapezoid, which, though it evolved over a long period of time, appears as a perfect spatial response to the exotic cathedral of S. Marco that faces it.

The Doge's Palace (see Fig. 9.62) and S. Marco (see Figs. 6.20–6.21) have been discussed earlier. The campanile collapsed in the nineteenth century and was rebuilt. The

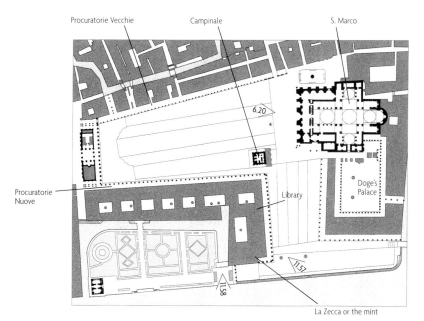

Procuratorie Vecchie    Campinale    S. Marco

Procuratorie
Nuove

6.20

Library

Doge's
Palace

11.57

11.58

La Zecca or the mint

**11.56** Plan of the Piazza S. Marco, Venice, 1487–90.

The space between the Procuratorie Vecchie and
Procuratorie Nuove, both housing offices for city officials,
was gradually hollowed out to produce the piazza's present
form. While Venice has many smaller piazzas, this one
symbolized the power of one of the West's greatest trading
cities in the tenth through the eighteenth centuries.

**11.57** Jacopo Sansovino, Library of S. Marco, Venice,
begun 1537, completed 1583–88.

The library's façade can be read as three layers: the arched
openings, the columns and entablatures, and the lavish
ornamentation. The resulting scenographic effect appealed
to the sensual nature of sixteenth-century Venetians.

**11.58** Jacopo Sansovino, La Zecca, Venice, begun 1536.

Heavy rustication conveys a sense of security in the building where Venetians minted their coins. Its massive, highly textured walls are particularly impressive when seen across the Venetian lagoon. The Library of S. Marco stands to its right.

**11.59** Michele Sanmichele, Palazzo Grimani, Venice, begun ca. 1556.

Venetian palazzi like this one became models for cast-iron façades applied to wood and masonry commercial buildings in nineteenth-century America. The repetitive columns, elaborate windows, and detailed cornices were ideal for mass production.

loggetta at its base and the adjacent library (begun 1537, completed 1583–88) (Fig. 11.57) were the creations of Jacopo Sansovino (1486–1570) and Vincenzo Scamozzi. Sansovino was a friend of the Venetian painter Titian, whose nudes and landscapes have a supple, luxurious, and slightly mysterious character. The library has the appearance of a Titian interpreted in stone. Its bays are defined by attached Doric and Ionic columns with open Serliana between them. The composition is capped by a balustrade and a deep frieze filled with a fecund array of swags, **putti**, and masks. The effect, often described as scenographic, is one of sensuality and vividly contrasts with the brittleness of Renaissance monuments in Florence and the gravity of those in Rome. Adjacent to the library and facing the lagoon is Sansovino's La Zecca, or mint building (begun 1536) (Fig. 11.58). Its complete rustication obviously reflects the influence of Giulio Romano, and its related massiveness is ideally suited to its function as a great vault. The third story is a later addition, meaning that the original building-façade composition corresponded to Bramante's House of Raphael.

The sculptural quality of these public buildings also carried over into Venetian palazzi. The Palazzo Grimani (begun ca. 1556) (Fig. 11.59) by Michele Sanmichele (1484–1559) has robust attached columns, in this case of the Corinthian order, and a heavy overhanging cornice.

## GARDEN DESIGN

The history of landscape architecture is in some respects more difficult to reconstruct accurately than the history of architecture, because without continual maintenance and replanting, the living materials that constitute the designer's work decay more rapidly, and change and vanish more completely than do most buildings. We know that the sacred enclosures and sanctuary precincts of Egypt, Mesopotamia, the Aegean, and Rome were landscaped, although the appearance of these gardens is known now only from reliefs, descriptions, or other representations of them. Better preserved are many Islamic works, such as the Alhambra, where the garden embodied the idea of paradise. The medieval gardens illustrated in manuscripts and described in literature tended to be functional, laid out in orderly beds and contained within a wall or hedge. Many of these were purposeful plantings for culinary or medicinal herbs as in the plan of St. Gall.

During the Renaissance the garden as an extension of architecture became important once again, with designs that originated as free adaptations of antique landscapes. Roman terraced gardens, for example, influenced both Bramante's design for the Belvedere Courtyard (see Figs. 11.29–11.30) and Raphael's designs for the Villa Madama (see Figs. 11.32–11.33). At the Villa Madama, geometric perimeters of miniature box hedges encircled colorful planting beds, and the taller backdrop of trees defined the limits of the garden. During the Renaissance, however, landscape architecture was raised to the level of a major art, providing a stage setting for the enactment of the splendor of the aristocracy and princes of the Church. Pope Julius III, who commissioned the Villa Giulia just outside Rome, made use of its loggias and courts for theatrical performances and leisurely promenading. Late Renaissance gardens were elaborate, using water, sculpture, and foliage in an architectural manner. A number also provided a foretaste of Baroque urban planning.

Renaissance gardens began modestly, as at the Medici Villa (1458–61) in Fiesole, north of Florence (Fig. 11.60). Designed by Michelozzo and intended as a retreat for the Medici family and their humanist associates, it includes two levels of parterres, a lemon garden, and an occasional fountain, whose quietly flowing waters once provided an environment for scholarly contemplation.

Larger and more dramatic is the Villa Lante at Bagnaia near Viterbo (begun 1566) (Fig. 11.61), probably designed by Vignola, which uses perspective as an organizing agent. While the gardens were originally entered from below, the mature vegetation now makes the most dramatic view one from above, where a square upper parterre is extended down the sloping site through a shaft of space or **allée** defined by a **bosco**, a dense planting of trees. The allée is reinforced by twin casinos that act almost like sighting mechanisms for the perspective view; stairs and ramps occupy the space between them. Water features appear at the various levels, beginning with the Fountain of the

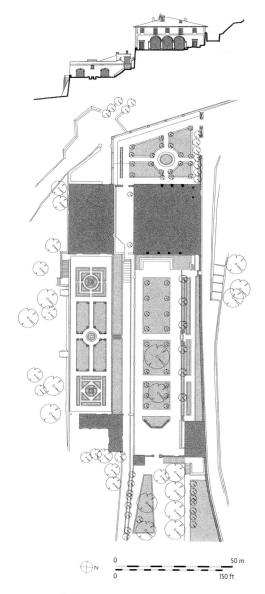

**11.60** Michelozzo di Bartolomeo, Plan of and section through the Medici Villa, Fiesole, 1458–61.

Florentine gardens of the Early Renaissance were quite small compared to the Roman gardens of the next century and the French gardens that appeared around seventeenth-century châteaux. Here the villa's loggia opens out onto a parterre, with another parterre one level below. The back side of the villa looks out over a smaller lemon garden.

Deluge at the top. Water then disappears and reappears at intervals down the central axis, sometimes as fountains, sometimes as a cascade, and finally as four placid pools in the center of the parterre on the lowest level.

The first major Mannerist garden was built at the Villa d'Este in Tivoli (Fig. 11.62) outside Rome, to the designs of Pirro Ligorio (ca. 1510–83). His client, Ippolito II Cardinal d'Este, owned a site that included both a north-facing

**11.61** Giacomo Barozzi da Vignola, Plan of and section through the Villa Lante, Bagnaia, begun 1566.

The Villa Lante's typically Roman organization includes stairs and water features and a parterre at the lowest level. The central axis in the form of an allée is defined by boscos or dense groves of trees.

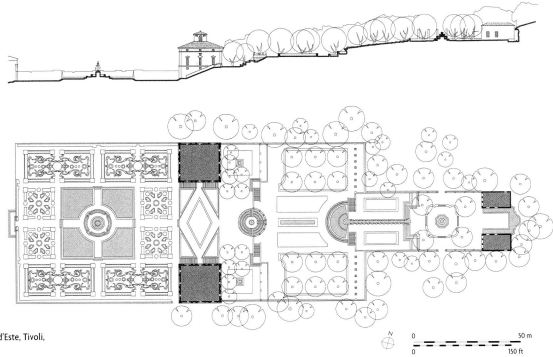

**11.62** Pirro Ligorio, gardens of the Villa d'Este, Tivoli, ca. 1565–72.

Most striking in the fully developed gardens are the myriad water features. In this view a waterfall stands behind fishponds.

slope and a large reliable water supply. Anyone visiting the gardens today during the hot summer months is struck by the marvelous microclimate—cool by virtue of shady trees and water everywhere. As designed by Ligorio, however, the gardens were intended as a setting for the Este family's sculpture collection, with plantings mostly in the form of low shrubs and hedges. Furthermore, while visitors enter today through the villa on the garden's high ground, the original entrance was from below. This lower access meant that the entire site could be taken in at a single glance rather than being experienced as a series of episodes along channels of large-scale greenery, as it is today.

Ligorio took as his principal theme the god Hercules, to whom the d'Este family traced their lineage mythologically. Hercules's strength and the magnitude of his labors were represented metaphorically by the efforts required in modeling the site, constructing aqueducts, and digging tunnels up to 3200 feet long. Ligorio's plan emphasized orthogonal and diagonal cross axes above; large rectangular fishponds and parterres below, with every manner and scale of water feature; architectural environments from an artificial cave to a huge water organ to a model of ancient Rome; and myriad pieces of sculpture, much of which now resides in the Capitoline Museum in Rome and elsewhere.

11.63 Château, Francis I wing, Blois, 1515–24.

The medieval-Renaissance style of Francis I resulted from the King's contacts with new architectural developments in Italy while on a military campaign. Though a hybrid, the château was much admired as a source for early twentieth-century residential designs in America.

## THE RENAISSANCE IN FRANCE

The extension of artistic developments from Renaissance Italy to France was hastened in part by French military interventions in the peninsula. In 1494 the armies of King Charles VIII invaded Italy in pursuit of his claims to the kingdom of Naples; in 1498 Louis XII attacked Milan, toppling the Sforza family from power (precipitating Bramante's departure for Rome), and Francis I campaigned in Italy until 1525, when his defeat at Pavia brought a halt to French pretensions in the region of Milan. Although these military excursions ultimately resulted in no permanent expansion of French territory, the reverse flow of Italian artistic ideas was to have lasting consequences for architecture in France. By the end of the fifteenth century, France was changing from a feudal society into a strong centralized state headed by the king. Unlike urban-centered Italy, where merchant princes eclipsed the landed nobility and commissioned works from the great Renaissance artists, the court was the dominant force in French society, and the king led the way in supporting design in the Italian style. As Milan was the center of French contacts in Italy, the early Renaissance buildings there, including the Certosa at Pavia, were the best known and most generally admired structures, perhaps because their combination of highly ornamented surfaces and classical details was not far removed from the Late Gothic style with which the French were most familiar. From the last

years of the fifteenth century, the French transported Italian art back to their own country, invited Italian artists and architects north to undertake commissions, and sent French artists to Italy to train in Renaissance workshops.

### CHÂTEAUX IN THE LOIRE VALLEY

The cultural center of France in the early sixteenth century was not Paris, but the valley of the Loire, where the king and his nobles maintained elaborate **châteaux** or castles for leisure, entertaining, and attending to the pleasures of the hunt. Within these châteaux are found some of the earliest French architectural manifestations of the Renaissance style. Blois in particular illustrates the transition from the Middle Ages to the Renaissance through the successive stages in its construction. The château was begun in the thirteenth century with the erection of a large medieval hall and associated rooms. Between 1498 and 1504, Louis XII added an east wing, incorporating an entrance gate to what would ultimately be a large courtyard. The construction, in red brick with

**11.64** Domenico da Cortona, Château, Chambord, 1519–47.

Chambord appears as a Renaissance trunk with medieval branches sprouting above it. The outbreak of steep roofs, dormers, and chimneys reflects an accommodation of the classical language to the northern climate.

light-colored stone trim at corners, doorways, and window surrounds, reflects the continuity of medieval traditions. Above the entrance way there is an equestrian statue of Louis set into a large niche with double-cusped pointed arches and other Gothic detailing in stone. Windows align one above the other, culminating in elaborate Gothic **dormers** in the steeply pitched roof; these dormers read as a series of vertical elements, even though string courses and the cornice establish horizontal lines. Between 1515 and 1524, Francis I embarked on extensive building operations at Blois, adding a north wing to the medieval hall to form the north side of the court, with the opposite side facing over the town. Francis demolished an old tower and upon its foundations built the famous open spiraling stair (Fig. 11.63). It features decorative carving of wreaths, porcupines, and salamanders, emblems of the royal family. Windows on the courtyard façade are regularly arranged, although once again their vertical emphasis clashes with horizontal elements. All rooms are placed en suite, an arrangement the French long preferred. On the town façade, the Francis I wing is like a cliff face, with two loggias and an open third story with freestanding columns, modeled on papal palaces at

the Vatican and at Pienza. Its mixture of classical columns and details also includes Gothic motifs.

In contrast to this town-based château, the château of Chambord (1519–47) was built in the countryside in the style of a fortified castle within a bailey or outer wall, thus neatly overlaying Renaissance symmetry and detailing on a fundamentally medieval building type (Fig. 11.64). Its Italian architect, Domenico da Cortona, employed simple cylindrical towers, which were to have been surrounded by open loggias; the latter were never built, however, since shade from intense sunlight was not as necessary in France as in Italy. The keep, or defensible core of the castle, has a suite of rooms in each corner, divided by a cruciform circulation pattern and a double staircase undoubtedly influenced by a sketch of Leonardo's. People ascending one set of risers in the double-helix staircase can do so without seeing people descending the other. A great lantern above the staircase is one of a whole cluster of cones, chimneys, and dormers on the roof, presenting an almost medieval profile against the sky. Surrounding this abundance of vertical roof features is a terrace from which the ladies of the court could view the progress of the hunt in the wooded countryside beyond the château. The contrast between the

**11.65** Philibert de l'Orme, Jean Bullant, and others, Château, Chenonceau, begun 1515.

There is no more picturesque château than this one. To the rear of the main block, the bridge was first added by Philibert de l'Orme. It then became a base for the grand dining hall designed by Jean Bullant.

ordered clarity of the walls and the wild exuberance of the rooftops reflects the partial assimilation of Renaissance architectural ideas into a firmly established medieval building tradition.

Not all the Loire châteaux were built for the king. Chenonceau (Fig. 11.65) is an example of a château constructed by a wealthy courtier and financier, Thomas Bohier. Begun in 1515, Chenonceau has a regularized plan, with all the major rooms opening off a central corridor, and a straight-run stair that illustrates Renaissance influence in its design, even as its moat, turreted corners, and chapel with rib vaults, pointed arches, and buttresses reflect medieval practices.

### SEBASTIANO SERLIO AND PHILIBERT DE L'ORME

A second phase of Renaissance development in France began around 1540 with the arrival of Sebastiano Serlio (1475–1554), an Italian architect who came north at the invitation of the king, and the return of Philibert de l'Orme (ca. 1510–70), a Frenchman who trained in Rome and settled in Paris to practice as an architect and engineer. Both men brought knowledge of High Renaissance work in Rome, especially that of Bramante, and their writings did much to explain Renaissance design principles and modify building practices in France. Little of Serlio's archi-

tecture survives, aside from the exteriors of the château of Ancy-le-Franc, a mediocre square-plan building with a central open courtyard. The design, with its corner pavilions, Doric pilasters, and rustication, is almost entirely north Italian in derivation, but the high pitched roof is typically French.

Of greater importance than his buildings were Serlio's writings on architecture, published in several installments from 1537 to 1551 and gathered together in 1584 as *Tutte l'opere d'architettura et prospettiva*, known today as *The Five Books of Architecture*. The first architectural treatises not composed in Latin, these books contained woodcut illustrations, and the text addressed the ordinary builder more than the architectural scholar. Book One explains geometry; Book Two covers the construction of perspective drawings; and Book Three illustrates antique Roman buildings and the High Renaissance works of Bramante and Raphael. Book Four outlines the five orders of architecture (Doric, Ionic Corinthian, Tuscan, and **Composite**), illustrates arched rusticated door and window surrounds appropriate for each order, and includes notes on construction materials. Book Five features centralized church designs. Three more volumes containing many of Serlio's own designs complete the opus.

Philibert de l'Orme's writings were also practical in nature. His first volume, published in 1561, was *Nouvelles*

**11.66** Pierre Lescot and Jacques Lemercier, Louvre, Paris, begun 1546.

A small portion of Pierre Lescot's sixteenth-century Louvre is still visible to the left. In the center, on Jacques Lemercier's seventeenth-century Pavilion de l'Horloge, the orders are used extensively but in a distinctively French manner of pairs surmounted by pavilion roofs. Lemercier's additions continue to the right.

*inventions pour bien bastir et petits frais* (*New Inventions for Building Well and Economically*). It considers the construction of vaults and roofs from an engineering standpoint. His major work, *Architecture*, was published in 1567. While it draws some content from the earlier treatises by Vitruvius and Alberti, it relies extensively on de l'Orme's personal experiences in building to offer architects guidance grounded in both theory and practice.

Of the many projects on which de l'Orme worked, only a few remain. One of the most celebrated is the addition he made to the château at Chenonceau, a bridge over the river Cher composed of five arches of varying span (see Fig. 11.65). The building atop the bridge was added later by Jean Bullant.

### THE LOUVRE AND THE PLACE ROYALE

After 1526, when the French capital became fixed in Paris, Francis I decided to update the medieval Louvre Palace, beginning with the removal of the cylindrical keep in the center of the square courtyard. Some years later, he decided to rebuild one wing of the enclosed court, with the possibility of extending the design around all four sides of the palace. Serlio proposed a design incorporating a series of courtyards, but the commission for rebuilding the Louvre wing went instead to the French architect Pierre Lescot (ca. 1500–78). Lescot's design (Fig. 11.66) dates from 1546, and while it is more correct in its use of the classical orders than most French buildings of the same period, it could never be confused with Italian work.

Lescot's façade emphasizes verticality rather than the horizontal line characteristic of the Italian Renaissance, even though it has cornice lines between floors. The courtyard façade is three stories high including the attic and is composed of Corinthian and Composite half-columns and pilasters, with elongated windows and pavilions at the extremities and in the center. The architecture is complemented by sculpture executed by Jean Goujon, one of the most talented artists of the period. It is possible that Lescot's façade was derived from Serlio's courtyard plan for the Louvre, although it seems that both miscalculated the interior implications of the courtyard's proportions. The great height of the building in relation to the width of the courtyard was such that, had the three additional façades been built to form the intended courtyard, the palace rooms would have received little direct sunlight. As events progressed, however, a later designer, Jacques Lemercier (1585–1654), enlarged the courtyard in 1624 to 400 feet square, more than four times the size proposed by either Serlio or Lescot.

For the last four decades of the sixteenth century, France was tormented by civil strife, the so-called Wars of Religion, which had economic and social causes as well as religious ones. Order was not restored until the arrival in 1594 of King Henry IV, whose policies brought an end to domestic and foreign turmoil. During the relative tranquility of his reign, France implemented Italian ideas of town planning that were to have an impact on later architecture in both Britain and colonial America. In an effort to unify the aristocracy and rebuild Paris, which was still

**11.67** Place Royale (Place des Vosges), Paris, 1605–12.

Around the Place Royale lie regularized residential façades, all connected by a continuous ground-level arcade. The taller pavilions were constructed by Henry IV, who promoted the project.

**11.68** Bird's-eye view of the Place Royale (Place des Vosges), Paris, 1605–12.

The French *place* is a paved residential square. It focuses inward, in contrast to the subsequent Baroque spaces linked by axial boulevards.

largely medieval, Henry IV sanctioned the construction of a number of residential squares, bounded by row houses with uniform façades. The Place Royale—now Place des Vosges—(Figs. 11.67–11.68) was the first of these urban squares used exclusively for residential purposes; it was laid out from 1605 to 1612. In addition to lending the enterprise his title, Henry supported the project by constructing two pavilions, one each in the center of both the north and south sides of the square. Thirty-eight plots surrounding the 460-foot-square court were then leased on condition that the row houses to be constructed there conformed to the overall design scheme: each house was to be four bays wide and three stories high, not including the dormered attic story, built of brick with stone trim and roofed with slate. The royal pavilions featured more elaborate details and higher rooflines than adjacent structures, although they shared the continuous ground-level arcade that linked the buildings, a feature derived from Renaissance squares in Italy, such as the Piazza S. Annunziata in Florence onto which Brunelleschi's Foundling Hospital fronts. Originally the central open space of the Place Royale was unplanted and its sand surface used for festivals and tournaments. An equestrian statue of the King later served as the focal monument in the center. The houses proved to be too small for the aristocrats whom Henry wished to attract to Paris, however, so the first residents of the Place Royale were minor nobility and wealthy Parisian merchants instead.

## THE RENAISSANCE IN ENGLAND

As was the case in France, Gothic architecture continued to be the predominant building style in England long after the Renaissance had originated and matured in Italy. Perpendicular Gothic, a particularly English variant, enjoyed favor well into the sixteenth century. The earliest expression of the Renaissance in Britain is found in sculpture and the decorative arts. In about 1511, King Henry VIII brought Pietro Torrigiani (1472–1528) and other artists directly from Italy to work on a number of royal commissions, the most important of which was a tomb for Henry's parents, Henry VII and his queen, in the Late Gothic chapel at Westminster Abbey in London. Cardinal Wolsey employed Italian sculptors, including Giovanni da Maiano, to make ten glazed terracotta roundels containing busts of Roman emperors. These roundels, which followed antique models and were thoroughly Renaissance in spirit,

**11.69** Robert Smythson, Wollaton Hall, Nottinghamshire, 1580–88.

While Robert Smythson was well aware of the work of the Italian Renaissance, including that of Andrea Palladio, his design decisions reflect a concern for the local context, most obviously in the provision of many windows, a response to the often overcast English climate.

were ultimately incorporated into the gateways of the Cardinal's medieval castellated palace at Hampton Court, begun in 1515. After Wolsey's fall from royal favor, Henry VIII confiscated the palace and enlarged Hampton Court to more than twice its original size. He added courts, galleries, a chapel, and a hall, but the building remained more medieval than Renaissance, including the hall with its splendid hammerbeam truss roof of 1531–36.

Another essentially Gothic building of the same era is King's College Chapel, Cambridge (see Fig. 9.36), begun in 1446 and completed in 1515. Inside, however, the wooden choir screen is a piece of early Renaissance design. It was erected in 1533–35, as a gift from Henry VIII, to separate collegians from townspeople and to support the organ. The artist is unknown, but his work represents the first truly Renaissance design in Britain, exhibiting a wide range of classical details with only a few pendants suggesting Gothic influence.

Henry broke with the Church of Rome in 1534, and numerous Italian artists of the Roman Catholic faith left Britain soon thereafter. Thus, the full flowering of the Renaissance in Britain was delayed until the beginning of

the seventeenth century. This does not mean that Italian ideals ceased to influence Britain, but that the direct inspiration from Italian artists resident in Britain stopped, while a more indirect influence continued to come from Italy via the Low Countries and France. The treatises of Scamozzi, Vignola, and Serlio were translated into English from the Dutch, not directly from the Italian, and numerous Dutch architectural books were exported to England. These illustrated strapwork, low-relief designs based on studded leather straps, that was arranged in geometrical and sometimes interlaced patterns. The strapwork decoration published by Flemish and Dutch architects, such as Hans Vredman de Vries, found its way into the works of the English architect Robert Smythson (1536–1614).

### ELIZABETHAN COUNTRY HOUSES

Renaissance influence from Italy continued to come into Britain via Flanders during the reign of Queen Elizabeth I. Her own architectural commissions were insignificant, but her courtiers and governmental officials built on a lavish scale for the Queen and her traveling entourage. Wollaton Hall in Nottinghamshire (1580–88) is an example of a great house built during the Elizabethan era (Figs. 11.69–11.70). Designed by Robert Smythson for the sheriff of Nottingham, the house draws on numerous sources. The building's symmetrical square plan with corner pavilions is taken from Serlio; in the center of the scheme, the great hall with ancillary accommodation is medieval; and the **long gallery** for the lodging of courtiers comes from

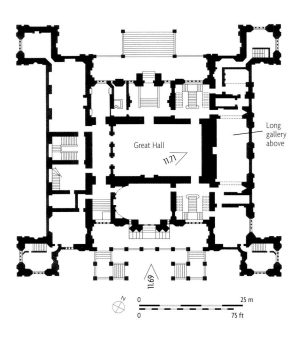

**11.70** Robert Smythson, Ground-floor plan of Wollaton Hall, Nottinghamshire, 1580–88.

This plan had its origins among the English castles of the Middle Ages. In the center is the great hall, and at the corners are the square-plan rooms that evolved from fortified towers.

**11.71** Robert Smythson, Great hall, Wollaton Hall, Nottinghamshire, 1580–88.

Renaissance influence is apparent in the Doric frieze of the wood paneling. The hall is dominated by medieval hammerbeam trusses that support the roof.

**11.72** Robert Smythson, Hardwick Hall, Derbyshire, 1590–97.

"Hardwick Hall more window than wall" went the popular refrain of the time. Above the many windows, the filigree-like gables reflect Dutch influence itself based on so-called strapwork—leather work derived from Italian Renaissance ornament in plaster.

France. Although Wollaton Hall is built of masonry, the huge expanse of windows is comparable to the fenestration found in timber construction. Renaissance pilasters and cornices punctuate the elevations, while the **parapets** are inspired by de Vries, and the upper clerestory levels of the great hall (Fig. 11.71) protrude above the roofline like a medieval keep with pepper-pot corner turrets.

Another great Elizabethan mansion, in all probability designed by Smythson, is Hardwick Hall in Derbyshire (1590–97) (Fig. 11.72). It shares many of Wollaton's characteristics in plan and elevation, but of greater importance here is the symmetrical arrangement of the main hall and its contiguous exterior colonnades, which reflect contemporary Italian design. Moreover, its plan appears as a Wollaton ripped open, less concerned with defense and more interested in light and warmth from the sun. Like all these grand and pretentious late sixteenth-century country residences, Hardwick helped advertise the wealth and social standing of its owner, the extremely wealthy Elizabeth of Shrewsbury, known as Bess of Hardwick. Her initials, E.S., are displayed in the house's decorative crowning balustrade.

## INIGO JONES

It is amazing how heterogeneous this second phase of the English Renaissance appears when compared to what was initiated under Henry VIII or what was to come during the reign of Elizabeth's successor, James VI of Scotland, who became James I of England. Inigo Jones (1573–1652), an architect of profound significance in English architecture, emerged during the reign of James I. Jones was born seven years before the death of Palladio, and his first building, the Queen's House at Greenwich, introduced Palladian ideals to England. With the appearance of Jones, English classical-revival architecture immediately mirrored that of late sixteenth-century Italy.

Unlike earlier English architects, Jones acquired his knowledge of Italian architecture first-hand. He was in Italy as early as 1601. Two years later he traveled to Denmark, and he made a second trip to Italy during 1613–14 in the entourage of the earl of Arundel. In his baggage Jones carried a copy of Palladio's *Four Books of Architecture*, which he annotated generously. He met Scamozzi and visited Vicenza, where Palladio's works profoundly influenced him. Upon returning to England, he designed stage sets for the court in which he was able to experiment with Renaissance forms.

His first building commission, the Queen's House (Fig. 11.73), begun in 1616 but still being extended in 1661, was situated astride the road from Deptford to Woolwich, which divided the building in two. A bridge spanned the road at the second-floor level and acted as a **porte-cochère**, or covered drive-through for vehicles, leading to

**11.73** Inigo Jones, Queen's House from the front, Greenwich, begun 1616.

The change in appearance from Hardwick Hall to the Queen's House is stunning. Its design reflects Inigo Jones's close study of Palladio's work while traveling in Italy.

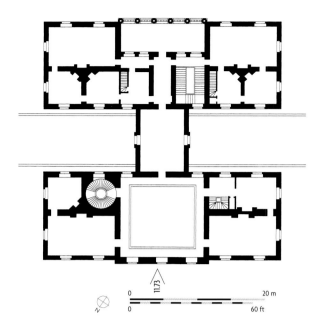

**11.74** Inigo Jones, Plan of the Queen's House, Greenwich, 1616.

The Queen's House plan reflects the same Renaissance rigor as the façades. Its two wings are connected by a bridge that once spanned a road passing through the site.

the entrance in the center of the building (Fig. 11.74). From the rather modest doorway, one is led directly into a room with the proportions of a cube. Access to the second floor is gained by a circular stair without a **newel**, or central post, a daring structural accomplishment in its day. A **balcony** across the cube room connects second-floor rooms, including the queen's bedroom, with the bridge. The garden façade of the house is based on Palladio's Palazzo Chiericati (see Fig. 11.47) at Vicenza; but, whereas the Palladian building has a two-story colonnade interrupted in the center of the second floor by a ballroom, the garden front of the Queen's House is a fenestrated wall

**11.75** Inigo Jones, Banqueting House, Whitehall, London, 1619–22.

Notable here is the English emphasis on the surface texture of the stone façade. It was a fixation of English designers at least as far back as the construction of Durham Cathedral, where many of the piers were carved with chevron patterns that defied their circular geometry.

with a central recessed loggia, well protected from the cool winds of Greenwich. Solid and void have been reversed in the exteriors of the two buildings.

Jones's most famous structure, the Banqueting House (1619–22) at Whitehall in London (Fig. 11.75), was built to replace an earlier building that had burned down. Its design, part of a much larger vision for an enormous Whitehall Palace complex, is an anglicized version of a Vitruvian basilica as interpreted by Palladio. The main interior space consists of a double-cube room with continuous balcony. In Jones's first project, he expressed this volumetric arrangement on the exterior as a two-story composition with a pedimented central pavilion at the principal façade. Jones eventually modified this elevation, articulating it in three parts according to the example of Palladio and omitting the pediment. He placed half-columns on the central three-bay pavilion to provide a contrast in depth with the flat pilasters of the two bays on either side. He arranged the windows to have alternate segmental and triangular pediments along the piano nobile, distinguishing it from

the heavily rusticated masonry of the base, where he employed flat lintels. He masked the roofline with a balustrade.

When Jones proposed a new design for the whole of Whitehall Palace in 1638, the Banqueting House was to be incorporated into half of one side of the central court. The enormous palace, based on Palladio's and Scamozzi's interpretations of a large Roman domus, here expanded to a gargantuan scale, would have replaced an area of rambling medieval structures. Although Jones's palace design was never built, the Banqueting House stood tall and monumental in its surroundings of earlier, domestically scaled medieval buildings, and its basic features were adapted in subsequent centuries for the ranks of over-scaled governmental buildings that form its present-day context.

On a site approximately halfway between the Banqueting House and the City of London to the east, the fourth Earl of Bedford employed Jones in 1630 to design a speculative development, called Covent Garden, in the

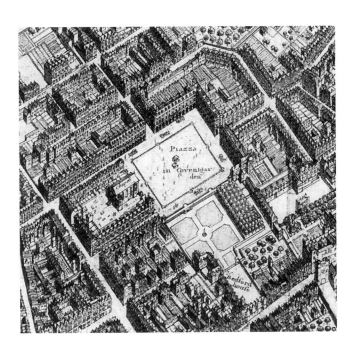

**11.76** Inigo Jones, Bird's-eye view of Covent Garden, London, 1658.

With residential units built up into large blocks, this scheme focused on a church (labeled "chapell"), making it the first such composition in Renaissance England. The purpose of the project was to turn the Earl of Bedford's agricultural land into a cash-producing real-estate development.

**11.77** Inigo Jones, St. Paul's, Covent Garden, London, 1631–35.

Referring to its use of the rustic Tuscan order, Jones called his church the "handsomest barn in England." It was rebuilt after a fire in 1795.

grounds of Bedford House. Jones collaborated with Isaac de Caux in this work, the first of several English residential squares based on the designs for the French king Henry IV's Place Royale in Paris. As in its French predecessor, the houses facing Covent Garden had continuous ground-level arcades, masking their individual entrances but providing a covered passageway around two sides of the square (Fig. 11.76). Five streets entered the square, which had Bedford House to its south and, to the west, the first completely new London church erected since the Reformation. Although rebuilt after a fire in 1795, the church of St. Paul (1631–35) (Fig. 11.77) still resembles Jones's original design, a simple box with a Tuscan-order portico, false door and altar at the east end, and the actual entrance at the west. The open space of the square soon became the site of a flourishing market, a use that continues to this day in permanent cast-iron halls constructed during the nineteenth century.

St. Paul's Cathedral in London was in poor repair at the beginning of the seventeenth century, and Jones was commissioned to restore it. He added a Corinthian portico to the west front, incorporating large scrolls to mask the aisle roofs, but the whole church was badly damaged in the fire of 1666, and both church and portico were demolished to make way for the later design of Christopher Wren. Wren's works belong to the seventeenth century and will be considered with those of other Baroque designers in Chapter 12.

## CONCLUSIONS ABOUT ARCHITECTURAL IDEAS

Central to the fifteenth-century Renaissance re-conception of architecture was the return to the classical language, which had a vocabulary of elements based on the orders, and a set of rules, or a syntax, establishing their proper arrangement and mutual relationships. With this vocabulary and within this syntax, structure, in the form of free-standing or applied columns and beams, was routinely and logically displayed. And within the new Renaissance way of design thinking, the mind of the designer was equally apparent, so much so that his personality could, and even should, show through in his finished work. Also within this new design system, each architectural element was both clearly discernible and subordinate to the whole. This condition can be observed in the Tempietto in Rome (see Figs. 11.26–11.27), which makes manifest the rebirth of purified classicism. The Tempietto is serene and measured, with its every element derived from antiquity, literally or by analogy, and systematically disposed. Additionally, its central plan represents the Renaissance ideal, even without the perfect circular environment planned for it by Bramante.

Brunelleschi set this new architecture in motion by traveling to Rome in search of the design and construction knowledge he believed to be embedded in the city's antique monuments, and legions of designers from across Europe would eventually follow him. His Florence Cathedral dome, made possible by his new understanding of ancient technologies, still had a Gothic pointed-arch profile. His Pazzi Chapel exhibits elements of the classical language both inside and out, but with some tentative and awkward moments. His associate Michelozzo arrived at a new form-type, the palazzo, by creating outwardly imposing domestic quarters for the rich and powerful, but apprehensive, Medici family. His friend Masaccio exploited Brunelleschi's invention of mechanical perspective by painting the Trinity Fresco inside the Church of S. Maria Novella. Its juxtaposition of biblical figures with contemporary ones within an illusionistic, classized-but-modern architectural space celebrated the reestablishment of the classical tradition, the piety as well as the status of the donors, and the new Renaissance way of seeing the world.

Alberti approached classicism not through practice but through theory. Expanding Brunelleschi's vision, he aspired, as evidenced by the vast, coffered, barrel-vaulted nave of S. Andrea in Mantua, to recreate the scale and splendor of the ancient Roman world, an idea appropriated by Bramante once he came to Rome to work for the papacy and closely studied the ruins there himself. We can imagine him in the company of Pope Julius II, wandering through the decrepit fabric of old St. Peter's and the adjacent scattered constructions of the Vatican, and imagining the return of the city to its former imperial grandeur.

While his centralized plan for new St. Peter's was structurally unsound, his vision—placing the Pantheon's dome atop a vaulted square equivalent in scale to the ancient Roman baths—was profound enough to satisfy even Michelangelo, who took over the project on Bramante's death. Striking out north from St. Peter's and the Vatican, Bramante created the Belvedere Court, an exterior space, rivaling in scale the Colosseum on which its inner stacked orders were based.

Bramante's self-confident, High Renaissance production was short-lived, as political, as well as artistic, turmoil brought on the insecurities and accompanying ambiguities of Mannerism. With the artistic accomplishments of antiquity now matched and even superseded, many sixteenth-century Italian architects grew impatient with the restraints placed on them by the perceived rigidity of High Renaissance esthetic thinking and so flouted the rules of classical ordering, some would say to troubling excess. At the Sforza Chapel, Michelangelo transcended compositional mischief and created a wholly new kind of plan and vaulting type that yielded a dynamic spatiality, one that pointed toward the Baroque style (presented in the next chapter) that would accompany the Catholic Counter Reformation. One sixteenth-century architect, Andrea Palladio, never yielded to the extremes of Mannerism, and in his body of work in the Veneto, particularly his villas, created a set of form-models that would be perhaps the most influential in all of Western architecture.

Palladio's buildings made a profound impression on the Englishman Inigo Jones, who came south (a copy of the *I Quattro Libri* in hand), made close observations of Palladian buildings, then carried Palladio's ideas in a pure form back to England, where they eventually superseded the raucous medieval-Renaissance hybrids that had arisen during the Elizabethan and Jacobean periods. Likewise, Renaissance architectural thinking was carried back to France when French armies returned home from their Italian incursions at the end of the fifteenth century. Here, like the initial Renaissance work in England, the early-sixteenth-century châteaux of the Loire Valley display Renaissance forms applied superficially and with little appreciation of underlying ordering principles. The results, while impure, are somehow both chaste and exuberant and reflect the optimism of a nation, long in a state of almost constant turmoil, enjoying a period of prosperity and influence. This condition encouraged French architects to visit Italy and Italian architects, like Sebastian Serlio, to move to France. Urban architecture of the period, most notably the Parisian Louvre Palace, demonstrates that French designers were searching for ways to make the newly imported Renaissance classicism their own, but without abandoning the spirit of the extraordinary Gothic architecture that was still highly regarded in the Ile-de-France. The mature products of their investigations, what some have termed French Baroque classicism, are discussed in the next chapter.

# CHAPTER 12

# BAROQUE ARCHITECTURE

Just as the bankers and merchants of Florence supported Early Renaissance artists and architects, so the Catholic Church was the primary patron of art and architecture around Rome in both the seventeenth and eighteenth centuries, and the works it commissioned gave rise to a new style, the Baroque.

By the end of the Renaissance, the Church had great temporal power, but its moral foundations had deteriorated. The office of cardinal was sold openly; high and low Church officials maintained mistresses and sought sinecures for their sons, who were euphemistically called "nephews"; and donations from the pious were spent on projects wholly lacking in spiritual purpose. The popes lived grandly, treating the Church's treasury as personal funds. To finance both sacred and secular projects, the Church instituted questionable fundraising practices, such as the sale of pardons and indulgences to save the payer or a relative from a stipulated number of days in Purgatory.

## THE REFORMATION AND COUNTER-REFORMATION

As might be expected, the corruption of the Church brought about calls for religious reform, some as early as the thirteenth century. The most dramatic and influential reaction came from the monk Martin Luther of the monastery at Wittenberg, Germany. In 1517 he nailed his ninety-five theses or propositions to the door of All Saints' Church, in the opening salvo of what would become known as the Protestant Reformation. Until this time the Church had always overcome challenges from deviants within its ranks, usually by declaring them heretics and destroying them by force. This time, however, the discontent was too widespread for inquisitional methods to work, although they were tried.

The Church's more reasoned response was the Catholic Counter-Reformation, a program that involved both reform within the Church and a sustained campaign to win people back to the beliefs of Catholicism. The Council of Trent convened in 1545 and decreed that art was an essential tool for spreading the prestige and teachings of the Church. All the arts were deployed in this public-relations effort, and the artistic style that developed to restate traditional Catholic teachings became known as the Baroque. The results were openly propagandistic, overtly emotional, and long on sensory appeal. Based on an elaboration of classical forms, already made highly individualistic by artists and architects in the early sixteenth century, the Baroque was a didactic, theatrical, dynamic, and dramatic style. Later critics have faulted its exaggerated gestures, excessive ornamentation, and unconcealed emotionalism. In context, however, Baroque ecclesiastical work should be seen as aiming to involve people directly with religious ideals. In general, Baroque architecture is characterized by spatial complexity and drama created by light from undisclosed sources. Its effects were achieved through the dynamic play of concave against convex curves; a preference for axial and centralized spaces that found particular expression in the ellipse or oval, at once axial and centralized; and the imaginative integration of painting, sculpture, and architecture to create illusions and dissolve physical boundaries.

## IL GESÙ, ROME

Among the new institutions of the reformed Catholic Church was the militant Order of the Society of Jesus, established by Ignatius Loyola in 1534 and commonly known as the Jesuits. Serving as missionaries and educators, particularly in remote areas, the Jesuits reached China by 1550 and accompanied Spanish conquistadors to the Americas. Their headquarters were in Rome, however, and it is fitting that one of the earliest Baroque architectural designs, Il Gesù (Figs. 12.1–12.2), was their principal

Johann Balthasar Neumann, Würzburg Residenz stair hall, 1720.

Tiepolo's painted ceiling looks down on this stair, which seems to float inside a great room of its own. The level of ornament and drama befits men in uniform and women in court dresses.

## Chronology

| | |
|---|---|
| Martin Luther presents his 95 theses | 1517 |
| Catholic Church establishes the Society of Jesus | 1534 |
| Council of Trent and the beginning of the Counter-Reformation | 1545 |
| Jesuits build the Gesù | 1568–76 |
| papacy of Pope Sixtus V | 1585–90 |
| English Civil War | 1625–49 |
| Bernini works at St. Peter's | 1629–80 |
| reign of Louis XIV in France | 1661–1715 |
| Peace of Westphalia and introduction of Renaissance influence into Germany | 1648 |
| Great Fire of London | 1666 |

**12.1** Giacomo Vignola and Giacomo della Porta, Il Gesù, Rome, 1568–76.

Innumerable church designs were based on this one, the mother church of the Jesuit order. The three-dimensionality and accumulation of detail in the central bay suggest a new kind of façade composition.

church, begun in 1568 to plans by Giacomo Vignola and completed in 1576 by Giacomo della Porta, who designed the façade as built and the dome.

Il Gesù resembles Alberti's S. Andrea at Mantua in plan, having transverse-barrel-vaulted chapels (in place of aisles with columns) flanking a longitudinal-barrel-vaulted nave. However, Vignola's motives for using such a plan were quite different from Alberti's. Alberti had sought to re-create ancient Roman grandeur and monumentality.

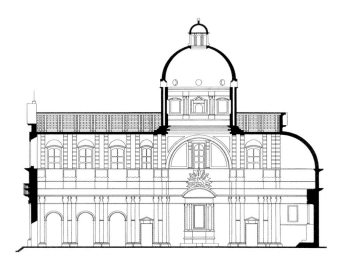

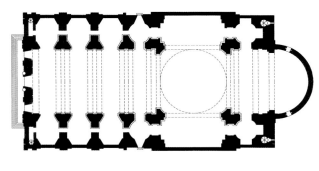

**12.2** Giacomo Vignola and Giacomo della Porta, Plan of and section through Il Gesù, Rome, 1568–76.

The stunted nave announces that this is a preaching church of the Counter-Reformation. The use of piers and lateral chapels provided an alternative to the column-and-side-aisle plan inherited by Brunelleschi from the Middle Ages.

By suppressing the transepts and shortening the nave, Vignola produced clear sightlines and acoustics that allowed for preaching to be heard clearly. The Gesù design was also forward-looking in its strong axial emphasis and in the three-dimensionality of elements on its west front. The composition of this façade is traceable to Alberti's S. Maria Novella in Florence, but with classical orders replacing the traditional Florentine subdivision based on geometric shapes. At Il Gesù, pairs of pilasters step out from forward-projecting planes until, on either side of the entrance, engaged columns support a triangular pediment, which in turn is framed by a segmental pediment supported by flanking pilasters. The original interior design was absolutely plain; the interior seen in the church today reflects a later decorative campaign that began in the late seventeenth century. Looking up at the nave ceiling, one is never sure where the architecture stops and the sculpture begins, or where the sculpture terminates and the fresco of the *Adoration of the Name of Jesus,* which was painted between 1675 and 1679 by Giovanni Battista Gaulli, begins. Clouds, draperies, and human bodies float in space, and one is swept up by this vision of heaven.

## POPE SIXTUS V AND THE REPLANNING OF ROME

Within a decade of the completion of Il Gesù, early Baroque influences could be seen in the modifications made to the urban pattern of Rome. Pope Sixtus V (1585–90) began radical changes, and his design program both guided the city's development for the next hundred years or more and influenced urban design throughout Europe and eventually in America.

Sixtus V was not the first pope to be concerned about the neglected physical appearance of Rome. His work can be seen as a vigorous elaboration and extension of initiatives taken in the 1450s by Nicholas V (1448–55), the first Renaissance pope to gain full control over the city following the long period of unrest when the popes resided instead in Avignon, France. Nicholas had undertaken fundamental repairs to ancient structures, such as the city walls, bridges, aqueducts, and roads on which Romans still relied, and he also had certain monuments modified to meet current needs, such as the conversion of Hadrian's Mausoleum into the Castel Sant'Angelo, a fortress for the papal court. Pope Sixtus IV (1471–84) had restored old churches and commissioned the building of others, and had attempted to improve circulation within the chaotic and densely populated medieval quarter by straightening the streets that led to the Ponte Sant'Angelo, the bridge over the Tiber that connected the bulk of Rome with St. Peter's. Julius II (1503–13) continued Sixtus IV's projects, as discussed in the last chapter in connection with Julius's patronage of Bramante and Michelangelo. In addition to those notable works around the Vatican and St. Peter's, Julius directed his energies toward civic improvements, including the creation of three straight streets (Strada Leonina, Strada del Corso, Strada del Babuino) radiating like spokes from the Porta del Popolo, the northern city gate. One of Julius's successors, Paul III (1534–50), commissioned Michelangelo's redesign of the Capitoline Hill. Pius IV (1559–65) laid out a straight avenue, the Strada Pia (1561–62), for which Michelangelo designed the Porta Pia (see Fig. 11.43) as the terminating portal.

These interventions in Rome were accelerated and intensified during the five years and four months of the pontificate of Sixtus V. Public works were undertaken, including the building of twenty-seven new fountains and the provision of a reliable water supply through the repair of ancient aqueducts and the construction of a new one, and law and order were restored to the city. The wool and silk industries were revived, further increasing employment opportunities. Had Sixtus lived another year, the Colosseum might have been refurbished into a wool-spinning establishment!

The people who most benefited from the changes wrought by Sixtus were pilgrims coming to see the major Christian shrines. Recognizing that these religious visitors were important to the city's economy, Sixtus planned to link Rome's seven Early Christian basilicas with direct processional routes, punctuated by vertical elements and fountains to mark major points along the way (Fig. 12.3). This was a much larger realization of ideas first developed in sixteenth-century gardens, such as the Boboli Gardens in Florence. Given the irregular topography of the city, it would be no easy task to superimpose a paper plan of straight roads on the terrain. The reworking of the city proposed by Sixtus was so convincing, however, that nearly all architects, planners, and civic authorities who have continued the work in the following centuries have done so in accordance with his scheme.

Sixtus began with the construction of a new street, the Strada Felice, which extended from S. Maria Maggiore to S. Croce in Gerusalemme in one direction and in the other direction to SS. Trinità dei Monti on the Esquiline Hill. The initial intention was to continue this street on to the Porta del Popolo, the major entry point for those arriving from the north, but the intervening hills prevented this idea being realized. As a related project, the Piazza del Popolo was later redesigned (see pages 352–53) to provide an appropriate entranceway for pilgrims. After passing through the gate, visitors entered a space that focused on a central obelisk. Radiating from this center were the three straight streets added by Julius II which provided direct access to major districts of the city. From the

Piazza del Popolo, the left radial street, the Strada del Babuino, led to a fountain at the base of the Esquiline Hill on which sits the church of the Trinitá dei Monti. Sixtus dedicated the church in 1585, and a stair linking the church and the fountain below was built over a century later (see pages 352–53).

## ST. PETER'S

The most important Christian monument in Rome was the Basilica of St. Peter, located across the Tiber from the older parts of the city. During Sixtus's reign, work was resumed on the construction of the dome after twenty-five years of relative inaction following the death of Michelangelo. Sixtus also turned his attention to the route linking St. Peter's to the rest of Rome. Pilgrims crossed the Tiber on the Ponte Sant'Angelo, at the end of which was the massive Castel Sant'Angelo. The route to St. Peter's continued to the west, but the direct link projected by Sixtus did not become a reality until the 1930s, when the Fascist dictator Benito Mussolini pushed through the Via della Con-

**12.3 Sixtus V's plan for Rome, 1585–90.**

With S. Maria Maggiore at the center, Pope Sixtus V developed axial connections to the city's seven principal churches. With this plan, the Renaissance concept of static, self-contained spaces gave way to the Baroque concept of dynamic axial connections between important urban points.

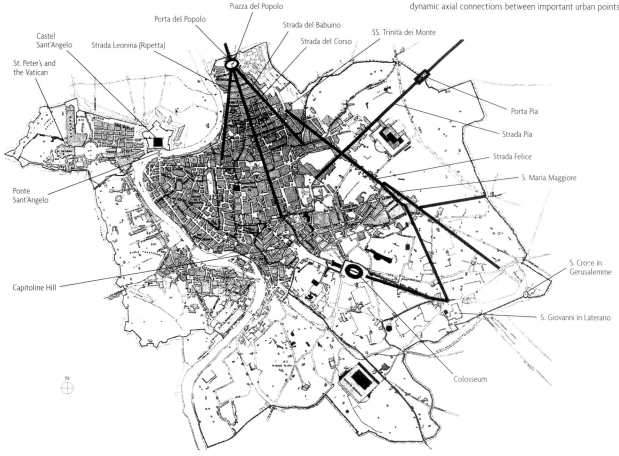

cilazione to provide a majestic axial approach to the great church. From a distance one can clearly see the dome of St. Peter's rising above the nave and wide façade, although Michelangelo's dome, designed for a naveless church, gradually recedes from view as one comes closer to the building.

In the center of what is now the Piazza of St. Peter's is Sixtus's contribution to the shaping of the space in the front of the basilica, the eighty-three-foot-tall Vatican Obelisk, which was installed there in 1586. Technical direction for this monumental feat of engineering was provided by Domenico Fontana, who later wrote a book describing and illustrating the entire process. The Vatican Obelisk was the largest intact specimen of the dozen Egyptian obelisks moved to Rome during the empire. How the ancient Romans maneuvered these monoliths into place is unknown, but the presence of several broken ones indicates that their methods were not always successful. Fontana's task was to lower the 681,221-pound obelisk from its position in the former Circus of Nero and move it about 260 yards to its new location in the Piazza of St. Peter's, all without damaging the shaft or its carvings. His solution to the problem involved encasing the obelisk in a protective timber framework, transferring it to a horizontal position by means of ropes and pulleys, which were controlled by the coordinated action of men and horses working thirty-eight windlasses, and then moving it over rollers to the new site. An elevation drop of approximately thirty feet between the old and new sites facilitated the horizontal transport. Once in the piazza, the obelisk was moved down an inclined plane and reerected using the same hoists and capstans employed to lower it. The whole operation was carefully planned and supervised by Fontana, who was empowered by the Pope to appropriate men, materials, and horses as necessary for the completion of the work. As the obelisk was raised in front of St. Peter's on April 29, 1586, the entire College of Cardinals along with the citizenry of Rome turned out to watch the spectacle. Barricades kept the curious at a safe distance, and absolute silence was enforced during the critical lifting stages so that the workmen could hear and respond correctly to Fontana's signals, given by a trumpet and a bell.

Following his successful removal of the Vatican Obelisk, Fontana was commissioned to relocate three smaller obelisks in Rome. Those standing today in the Piazza del Popolo, at S. Giovanni in Laterano, and at the apse of S. Maria Maggiore were all positioned by Fontana. The pyramidal points of these great shafts are prominent landmarks indicating the important surrounding monuments in the city. Sixtus V's work in Rome doubtless had a major influence on Pierre L'Enfant's late eighteenth-century plan for Washington, D.C., Baron Eugène Georges Haussmann's cutting-through of boulevards in Paris in the mid-nineteenth, and even on the twentieth-century city planner Edmund Bacon, who was responsible for major redevelopment work in Philadelphia in the 1950s and

'60s. Bacon's use of axial avenues to link major areas of the city and not obelisks but high-rise buildings to mark different areas shows the continuing impact of city planning in Baroque Rome.

## GIANLORENZO BERNINI
### THE COMPLETION OF ST. PETER'S

After the death of Sixtus V, work continued on St. Peter's; this project, so long in preparation by a series of architects whose abilities, styles, and philosophies varied considerably, was at last brought to completion during the Baroque period. The dome was finished in 1612 under the direction of architect Giacomo della Porta and engineer Domenico Fontana, and the nave addition, not envisioned by Michelangelo, was made by Carlo Maderno, who also designed the main façade (Figs. 12.4–12.6). The nave shifts orientation imperceptibly to align with the Vatican Obelisk, which Fontana had accidentally set off-center; Maderno considered it easier to turn the nave than to move the Egyptian needle. The largest church in Christendom was finally consecrated in 1626.

Urban VIII's favorite artist was Gianlorenzo Bernini (1598–1680), a man who might easily be compared with Michelangelo. Both were recognized as prodigies at an early age; both had long and productive lives; and both were immensely inventive sculptors who also did important work in architecture and city planning. Bernini was the son of a sculptor, and his artistic education had been directed in part by Urban VIII, a noted patron of the arts even before he was elected to papal office. The vigorous building programs of the Catholic Church in the seventeenth century were responsible for the development of the Baroque style, and for over fifty years Baroque work in Rome was dominated by Bernini.

Nowhere is his presence felt more strongly than at St. Peter's, where he served as official architect from 1629 until his death. Much of the present interior's character is the result of Bernini's genius. Either directly or through workshops under his supervision, Bernini was responsible for the flooring in the nave and narthex, for the decoration of the nave piers, and for the design of four sculptural groupings for altars and tombs. His designs for the crossing and main apse of the church, however, are the most substantial contributions he made to the interior. To reduce the scale of the vast space under Michelangelo's dome, Bernini designed the bronze Baldacchino (1624–33), a symbolic protective canopy over the high altar above the tomb of St. Peter. To match the scale of the rotunda, the Baldacchino is nearly ninety feet high; its twisted columns are not a Baroque invention, but a greatly enlarged version of marble columns from the Constantinian basilica, some of which are preserved as part of the reliquaries at the second-floor level of the crossing piers. It was believed that the original twisted columns were

**12.4** St. Peter's, Rome, 1546–64, 1606–12.

Maderno's façade stretches the full width of the church. The small cupolas were the work of Vignola. The dome was planned by Michelangelo and refined by Giacomo della Porta. Bernini added the colonnade that creates the trapezoidal and oval piazzas.

brought by Constantine from the Temple of Solomon in Jerusalem, so their continued use here links St. Peter's with the Holy Land. Material for the Baldacchino was obtained by melting down the Roman bronze supports of the Pantheon's portico, a reuse of historic material sanctioned by the Pope over popular opposition; there was even enough metal left over to cast eighty cannons for defense of the city. In the enormous space of the basilica, the Bal-

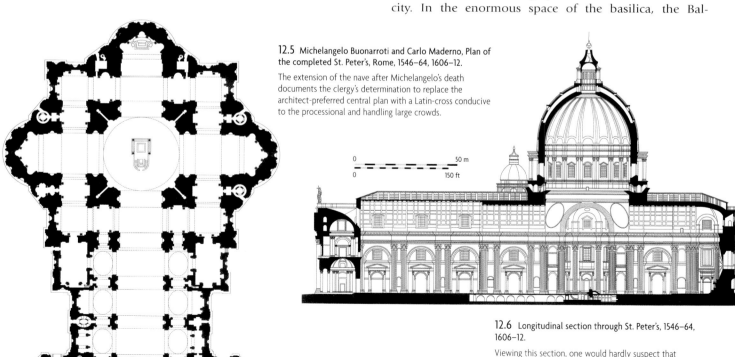

**12.5** Michelangelo Buonarroti and Carlo Maderno, Plan of the completed St. Peter's, Rome, 1546–64, 1606–12.

The extension of the nave after Michelangelo's death documents the clergy's determination to replace the architect-preferred central plan with a Latin-cross conducive to the processional and handling large crowds.

**12.6** Longitudinal section through St. Peter's, 1546–64, 1606–12.

Viewing this section, one would hardly suspect that Bramante and Michelangelo intended this church to be the greatest of the Renaissance central plans. However, the architects did succeed in re-creating the scale and grandeur of ancient Rome.

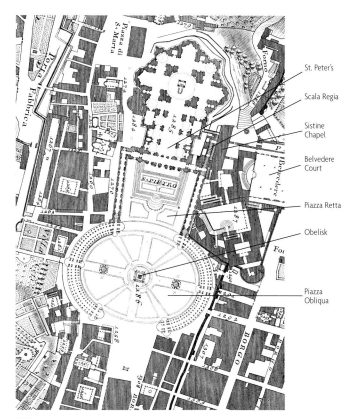

**12.7** Gianlorenzo Bernini, Site plan of St. Peter's complex and part of the Vatican, Rome, 1748.

In this site plan the southern extremity of Bramante's Belvedere Court is visible to the right. The final plan for the church still carries the imprint of its central-plan origins. The quarter east of the piazza (bottom of the site plan) is shown densely populated, as it was before Mussolini cleared it to provide open space all the way to the Tiber.

St. Peter's

Scala Regia

Sistine Chapel

Belvedere Court

Piazza Retta

Obelisk

Piazza Obliqua

unlike some Early Christian buildings, is not aligned with its apse to the east but rather to the west, so the rays of the afternoon sun pass through the window and merge with the golden radiance of the sculpture surrounding the chair. By incorporating a window behind the work to provide brilliance for the ensemble, Bernini's design admirably illustrates the theatricality of the Baroque.

As the greatest church in Western Christendom, St. Peter's required an appropriate approach and exterior setting, and Bernini was also commissioned to undertake this work. In 1637 he proposed that two belltowers be constructed at the ends of the narthex in order to counter the horizontal emphasis of Maderno's façade. Only the southernmost tower had been partially built when soil subsidence and subsequent cracking of the structure necessitated removal of the campanile in 1645, almost ending Bernini's architectural appointment in disgrace. In 1657, however, Bernini designed the Piazza of St. Peter's, one of the most famous urban spaces in the world (Fig. 12.7). Composed of two parts, the piazza has an oval section, the *piazza obliqua*, which focuses on the Vatican Obelisk, followed by a trapezoidal section, the *piazza retta*, directly in front of the church entrance. Both sections work together to provide a symbolic embrace for Christians who come to visit the tomb of St. Peter. The *piazza retta* attempts in two ways to ameliorate the proportions of the façade by increasing the apparent height of the church. Its trapezoidal shape, which is perceived as a rectangle, "squeezes" the façade to emphasize verticality, and the flanking colonnade diminishes in height as it extends toward the church, thereby providing a smaller unit to which the engaged Corinthian columns of the façade are compared. Although the converging sides of the *piazza retta* may suggest influence from Michelangelo's Piazza del Campidoglio, the form was probably generated by the oblique placement of the Vatican Palace relative to the narthex of the church.

The *piazza obliqua* is more characteristically Baroque, with curving arms that do not form a true oval but are actually two semicircles connected to a square. Two symmetrically placed fountains and the obelisk establish a cross axis to the approach to St. Peter's, thus introducing an element of tension into the design. The piazza's sides are formed by freestanding Tuscan-order colonnades, thirty-nine feet high and four columns deep, arranged in radial lines to provide a constantly shifting pattern of light and shadow as one moves around the edge. The colonnades generate a sense of enclosure without confinement; the space is defined without being cut off from the fabric of the city. Over 250,000 people can gather in the Piazza of St. Peter's to be blessed from the Benediction Loggia above the central entrance to the church or from a window in the papal apartments, at the right of the piazza. Through its dignified and all-encompassing design, the Piazza of St. Peter's extends the Church's welcome beyond the boundaries of the basilica itself.

dacchino distinctly marks the spiritual center of the church, which would otherwise appear insignificant. So large is the interior that the Baldacchino's height, equivalent to a nine-story building, is not overpowering from a distance.

In the angles of the crossing piers Bernini's design placed four dramatic statues of saints associated with the Passion of Christ, all more than twice lifesize. Of these, Bernini himself carved the statue of St. Longinus (1629–38), the Roman centurion who pierced Christ's side at the Crucifixion; Longinus is shown at the moment he realizes Christ's divinity. Beyond the Baldacchino, and framed on axis by its columns, is Bernini's culminating work in the basilica, the Cathedra Petri, or Chair of Peter (1657–66), an elaborate reliquary in bronze constructed around the reputed wooden seat of the first apostle. Lightly supported by four figures representing Doctors of the Church, those men who established the doctrine of the faith, the chair floats above the visitor's head against a glorious backdrop where golden rays emanate from a brightly illuminated stained-glass center on which rises the dove of the Holy Spirit. The church of St. Peter's,

Bernini also designed the small oval-plan church of S. Andrea al Quirinale (1658–70) as a quiet retreat for Jesuit novices (Figs. 12.8–12.9). The shape of the interior space is clearly expressed by the convex body of the church. To each side, countercurves turn into concave enveloping arms that connect the building to the street. Entry is made between giant-order Corinthian pilasters supporting a pediment; within this frame a thermal window allows light into the interior and, as though folded down from it, a convex curving portico is supported by Ionic columns. Around the exterior walls at the upper level, scroll-like buttresses stabilize the dome.

The entrance and altar lie opposite one another across the short axis of the oval plan. To maintain emphasis on the altar and establish the short axis as the dominant one, Bernini placed pilasters, not chapels, on the cross axis, forcing the visitor's attention back to the origin point of the dramatic action. The architectural space around and above provides the setting for what would today be called a multimedia experience, as Bernini combined painting, sculpture, stucco work, and lighting effects to dramatize the martyrdom and apotheosis of St. Andrew. First, a painted image of the future saint hangs above the altar, lit by a hidden, secondary dome with lantern. Around the painting, sculpted angels and putti, or figures of unclothed, chubby infants, levitate among gilded light rays. Above, a sculpted figure of St. Andrew rises through the broken pediment that defines the altar, accompanied around the base of the dome by more sculpted putti and fishermen representing the profession from which the saint was drawn. The coffered dome includes ten ribs, diminishing in width as they rise to visually support the base of the lantern. Here, an audience of still more putti awaits St. Andrew's admittance into heaven, represented by the glow from the principal lantern. All in all, it is a tour de force of Counter-Reformation theatricality.

## FRANCESCO BORROMINI

While the completion of the interiors of the basilica and construction of the Piazza of St. Peter's were to occupy a substantial portion of Bernini's time, these were not by any means the only projects undertaken by this enormously gifted and energetic artist. Nor did he accomplish the work on St. Peter's singlehandedly. He had assistants, some of whom became prominent designers in their own right. This was the case with Francesco Borromini (1599–1667), who began his career as a stonecutter in his uncle Carlo Maderno's shop and rose quickly to become a master mason and Bernini's collaborator on the St. Peter's Baldacchino. After a time these two men of strong personalities clashed; before 1630 Borromini had emerged as Bernini's rival. Of his many commissions around Rome, two are of particular interest as demonstrations of Borromini's strikingly original approach to design.

**12.8** Gianlorenzo Bernini, S. Andrea al Quirinale, Rome, 1658–70.

A reflection of Counter-Reformation policies, S. Andrea has flanking walls that reach out as if to embrace passers-by. Its huge frontispiece is an essay in semicircular geometries: thermal window, portico roof, and entry stairs.

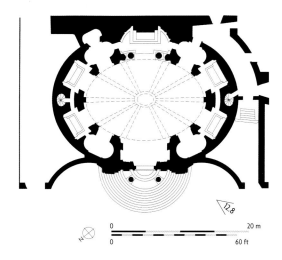

**12.9** Gianlorenzo Bernini, Plan of S. Andrea al Quirinale, Rome, 1658–70.

Bernini chose to place the altar along the short axis of the oval. He also chose to terminate the cross axis with pilasters rather than chapels. Both were unorthodox, tension-creating choices in the mid-seventeenth century.

**12.10** Francesco Borromini, S. Carlo alle Quattro Fontane, Rome, begun 1634.

The theme of the façade is set by the figure of St. Charles Borromeo above the doorway, his eyes uplifted and his hands positioned as if in prayer. This vertical motion extends to the attenuated, superimposed columns and even the oval plaque at the scalloped pediment.

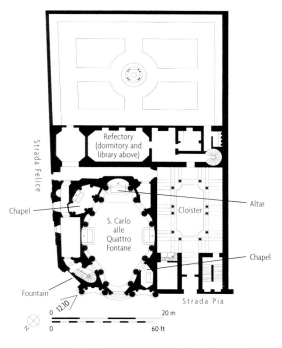

**12.11** Francesco Borromini, Plan of S. Carlo alle Quattro Fontane, Rome, begun 1634.

The intensity of Borromini's organizational skills can be read in the dual ordering of the church and the cloister. In each, the theme is sets of paired columns. In the cloister, six sets are freestanding; in the church eight sets are pressed into the undulating surrounding wall.

## S. CARLO ALLE QUATTRO FONTANE, ROME

Projects for the monastery and church of S. Carlo alle Quattro Fontane (dedicated to St. Charles Borromeo and also called S. Carlino or Little S. Carlo) involved Borromini on and off from 1634 until his death. He began with renovations to the monks' living quarters, including a new refectory and cloister (1634–38), a courtyard in which bulging panels above pairs of columns replaced the customary corners.

In 1638 he designed the diminutive but highly innovative church (Fig. 12.10) at the corner of the Strada Felice and the Via Pia (today known as the Via Quattro Fontane),

one of Sixtus V's grand routes linking districts of the city. He embellished the intersection with four fountains set diagonally across from each corner, hence the descriptive words "Quattro Fontane" appended to the name of the church. The church plan consists of an undulating oval, its long axis leading to the main altar (Fig. 12.11). The curving side walls swell outward on the short axis to form shallow side chapels in a counterpoint evoking the spirit of a stretched Greek-cross plan. Borromini's own drawings show that he conceived his complex plan by interlocking a series of geometric figures from circles to equilateral triangles, and he based his proportions in section on more

**12.12** Francesco Borromini, S. Carlo alle Quattro Fontane, Rome, begun 1634.

At the inside surface, or intrados, of the dome, Borromini introduced a pattern of octagons, hexagons, and trinitarian crosses. These figures diminish in size as they move upward, creating an exaggerated perspective.

**12.13** Francesco Borromini, S. Ivo della Sapienza, Rome, begun 1642.

The first two levels of the courtyard were planned by Pirro Ligorio and Giacomo della Porta. Borromini accepted the extant structure as the base for his unorthodox drum with its exotic cupola crowned by a spiral.

equilateral triangles. This reliance on geometry rather than Renaissance arithmetical ratios reflects Borromini's immersion in the more strongly Gothic design and construction practices around Milan where his father had been a builder. Columns at S. Carlo's lower level appear to have been pressed into the surrounding walls. Pendentives above the entablature reduce the undulating plan to an oval drum supporting an oval dome, elaborately coffered with octagons, hexagons, and Trinitarian crosses, diminishing to an oval oculus (Fig. 12.12).

The principal façade, constructed in 1665–67, mirrors the internal play of concave and convex, swinging in and out over its three-bay width with its two stories separated by an intermediate oscillating entablature. A figure of St. Charles Borromeo with praying hands and eyes uplifted sets the façade's vertical theme, and angels, their wings contorted to form a pediment, shelter the saint and anticipate the almost bizarre character of the interior. This verticality is terminated by a crowning balustrade broken by a large oval **medallion**. With consummate skill Borromini incorporated one fountain and its mitered corner into the façade design, so that all parts project the dynamism of the Baroque.

## S. IVO DELLA SAPIENZA

At S. Ivo della Sapienza (Fig. 12.13) Borromini created an archetypal masterpiece of the Baroque. The building consists of a chapel inserted behind the curved end of an existing two-story courtyard at the Archiginnasio, a college popularly known as La Sapienza and now part of the University of Rome. Giacomo della Porta had designed the façade inside the curve, which necessarily became the visual base for Borromini's dome when viewed from the

entry to the courtyard. Borromini proposed alterations to della Porta's façade, but none of them was carried out.

Pope Leo X donated the site, but the chapel was not begun until 1642 under the patronage of Urban VIII. Urban's coat of arms incorporates bees symbolic of his own family, the Barberini, and Urban was affectionately known as the "King of Bees." Therefore, it is not surprising that Borromini, who had waited ten years for the commission, flattered his patron by incorporating the shape of a flying bee into the form of the plan, which is geometrized as a hexagon (Fig. 12.14a) by the intersection of two equilateral triangles that also create a six-pointed star. The

**12.14a** Francesco Borromini, Plan with reflected ceiling plan of S. Ivo della Sapienza, Rome, 1642–50.

Borromini made use of two interlocking equilateral triangles as a conceptual structure for his complex plan. The reflected ceiling plan reveals the facets of his "pumpkin" vault, similar in spirit to those apparently used by the emperor Hadrian at his villa in Tivoli near Rome.

**12.14b** Francesco Borromini, Transverse section through S. Ivo della Sapienza, Rome, 1642–50.

This section reveals Borromini's unconventional layering. Atop the pilasters sits the faceted entablature. Springing from this entablature are the ribs, folded against one another and diminishing in width as they rise.

**12.15** Francesco Borromini, S. Ivo della Sapienza dome, Rome, 1642–50.

With obvious similarity to Gothic ribbed vaults, the dome contains symbols of the Barberini family, the building's patrons.

internal entablature between the lower level of the church and the dome does not separate the two areas in a conventional fashion. Rather, the concave–convex rhythms of the plan rise in planes through the bent and folded entablature into the ribs of the six-lobed dome (Figs. 12.14b, 12.15). Externally, the bulging walls and stepped cap of Borromini's dome support an exotic lantern tower that spirals upward in a form that allows multiple associations: that of the papal tiara, which contains bands of a triple crown, merged into a continuous spiral, symbolizing the pope's authority in priestly, royal, and imperial affairs; that of a conch shell, one species of which was generally known as the *corona papale* because of its resemblance to the papal tiara; and that of Divine Wisdom, which complemented the symbolism of an upwardly rising spiral. In fact, the iconography of the whole chapel expresses the idea that "all wisdom is from the Lord God" and that "fear of the Lord is the beginning of wisdom" (Ecclesiasticus 1:1).

## URBAN OPEN SPACES IN BAROQUE ROME

With a few notable exceptions, urban design is a shared undertaking, occurring across several generations. The bold strokes of Sixtus V's plan for Rome created opportunities for later architects to complete his grand scheme with designs for churches, fountains, and piazzas to enrich civic life. For example, Fontana's placement of the Vatican Obelisk preceded and was therefore not part of Bernini's overall design for the piazza, but its position in front of St. Peter's identified the area as one of major importance within the city and contributed to Bernini's specific spatial conception of it as realized in 1657. The collaboration of talented designers in Rome on various urban projects has endowed the city with many handsome public spaces; three particularly fine Baroque ones will be discussed here.

### THE PIAZZA NAVONA

Bernini and Borromini jointly created the urban design of the Piazza Navona, an unusually proportioned space (177 by 906 feet) that was once the Stadium of Domitian (Fig. 12.16). In the medieval period houses were built on the ruins of the grandstands, while the open center was used for informal games and a market. Pope Innocent X's palace faced the square, and on his election in 1644 he undertook the refurbishing of the piazza and its church, S. Agnese in Agone (Fig. 12.17). The church commission was first given to Girolamo and Carlo Rainaldi, but their designs displeased Innocent, and in 1653, with the foundations already in place, Borromini assumed control of the building process. He retained their Greek-cross plan but pulled back the flight of steps protruding into the narrow square and provided a new concave façade, above which rose a high drum, elongated dome, and slender cupola. After 1657 and the death of Innocent X, Carlo

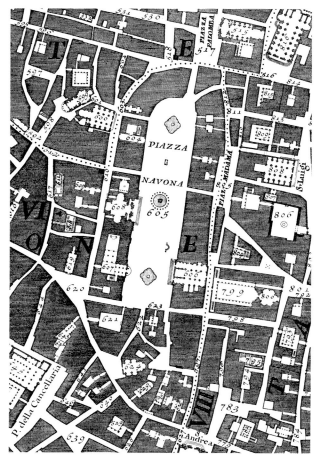

**12.16** Gianlorenzo Bernini and Francesco Borromini, Piazza Navona, Rome, begun 1644.

Piazza Navona's outline results from its origins as an ancient Roman circus or racetrack. Around it are the narrow irregular streets of Rome's medieval core. S. Agnese in Agone is #608; S. Maria della Pace is #599; and S. Ivo della Sapienza is #800.

Rainaldi returned to complete the work, adding the twin towers positioned on either side of the curved façade. In its massing S. Agnese represents the silhouette that St. Peter's might have had without the nave addition.

Bernini, temporarily out of favor for political reasons and because of the failure of the towers at St. Peter's, was not considered as a possible architect for S. Agnese, yet his proposal for the central fountain in Piazza Navona so pleased Innocent that the Pope set aside personal animosities and awarded Bernini the fountain commission. The Fountain of the Four Rivers (1648–51), located in the center of the piazza but off the main axis of S. Agnese so as not to compete with it, has symbolic figures set amid splashing water and representing the major rivers of the continents to which Catholicism had spread. The Ganges figure holds an oar because of that river's great navigable length; the Danube looks toward emblems of Innocent X; the Nile's face is obscured because its origin was then unknown; and the Rio della Plata figure is a highly imaginative evocation of a native South American, bald, bearded, and surrounded by coins to reflect the wealth of the New World. The figures support a central obelisk, crowned with a representation of the dove of the influential Pamphili family symbolizing the triumph of

**12.17** Carlo Rainaldi and Francesco Borromini, S. Agnese, Rome, begun 1644.

Borromini chose to place the dome close to the façade so it could be seen between flanking towers. It is the same scheme intended by Bernini at St. Peter's before his towers became unstable.

Christianity over paganism, and, by extension, Catholicism over Protestantism. Thus, in Baroque hands, even so secular an item as a public fountain became an allegory for the Roman Catholic Church. At either end of the piazza are additional fountains; all three provide visual delight while refreshing the air with cooling moisture.

Just behind Piazza Navona is one of Rome's smallest squares, in front of the church of S. Maria della Pace, which is the work of Pietro da Cortona (1596–1669). The main church building dates to the fifteenth century; Cortona gave it a new convex façade in 1656–58 (Fig. 12.18), its plasticity restrained by flanking Corinthian pilasters supporting a pediment. That pediment frames yet another pediment with a curved top cornice and a dropped lower one. Cortona improved access to the church by demolishing parts of surrounding buildings to

**12.18** Pietro da Cortona, S. Maria della Pace, Rome, 1656–58.

Cortona's façade appears to have been bent and expanded from within. The flanking walls are analogous to stage wings and connect the church to existing buildings.

create the tiny piazza. A semicircular portico with paired Tuscan columns protrudes into the square, and the portico's curve is answered by countercurving wing walls. The concave–convex interplay is subtle but effective in this diminutive Baroque stage setting.

## THE PIAZZA DEL POPOLO AND THE SPANISH STEPS

The next Baroque square to be considered is the Piazza del Popolo. Fontana's placement of an obelisk at the point where its three radial streets converge (see Fig. 12.3) gave the space a monumental focus. In the mid-seventeenth century, Roman planners wanted to regularize this important gateway to Rome by placing identical domed churches on the trapezoidal sites created by the three streets. This posed a geometric dilemma, however, for the sites were of unequal width. Carlo Rainaldi, assisted by Bernini, solved the problem by giving one church, S. Maria dei Miracoli (1675–79), a circular plan, and the other, S. Maria in Montesanto (1662–75), an oval plan to accommodate its narrower site. Viewed from the obelisk, the churches look identical because of their domes and porticoed façades, and their profiles enhance the dignity of the

**12.19** Carlo Rainaldi and Gianlorenzo Bernini, S. Maria dei Miracoli and S. Maria in Montesanto, 1662–79.

As at St. Peter's, Pope Sixtus V had anticipated the development of a great piazza here by placing an Egyptian obelisk in the then formless terrain first seen by pilgrims arriving in the Eternal City from the north. The so-called twin churches were designed by Carlo Rainaldi.

piazza (Fig. 12.19). In 1816–20, the architect Giuseppe Valadier carved out an oval volume for the piazza in imitation of Bernini's plan for the Piazza of St. Peter's and added a set of viewing terraces to the east leading up to the Borghese Gardens (Fig. 12.20). The terraces offer viewers the opportunity to appreciate the geometry of the oval plan from above.

Halfway down the Via del Babuino from the Piazza del Popolo is the point where the route to S. Maria Maggiore envisioned by Sixtus V sidesteps to connect with the Via Sistina at the top of the Pincio Hill (see Fig. 12.3). Topographic difficulties here required the route to make a steep ascent, which was imaginatively resolved by the Spanish Steps (1723–26), built by Francesco de Sanctis following designs made a decade earlier by Alessandro Specchi (Fig. 12.21). The project was underwritten by a wealthy Frenchman and constructed on land owned by the French church of the Trinità dei Monte; the steps were so named because the Spanish Embassy was nearby. From the fountain at its base, gentle curves and countercurves form a dramatic cascading stair that narrows and then divides before reaching an intermediate platform, beyond which the stairs again unite, only to split once more into opposing curves that ultimately ascend to the platform in front of the Trinità dei Monti, at the end of the Strada Felice. It is a popular and effective stage setting, inviting promenaders to be both actors and audience, and the design brings enjoyment to the mundane task of climbing or descending by encouraging the pedestrian to linger and look.

**12.20** Giuseppe Valadier, Piazza del Popolo from the Pinicio Hill, Rome, 1816–20.

While the former trapezoidal piazza can still be identified, it has been subsumed in Valadier's new oval, its long axis directed up the slope of the Pincio Hill. The steep hillside is made accessible by ramps and has been terraced into platforms serving as overlooks. The twin churches stand to the left in this view.

**12.21** Francesco de Sanctis and Alessandro Specchi, Spanish Steps, Rome, 1723–26.

If architecture can be "frozen music," as suggested in the Introduction to this text, then the Spanish Steps are an excellent example of the phenomenon. The principal elements are the steps with their landings, the obelisk, and the church of the Trinità dei Monte, built at separate times but deftly pulled together by Francesco de Sanctis and Alessandro Specchi in the eighteenth century.

# PIAZZA NAVONA—A SPACE FOR SPECTACLE

by Julia M. Smyth-Pinney

**12.22** Giovanni Paolo Pannini, *Piazza Navona Flooded*, 1756. Oil on canvas, 37 ½ × 54 in (95.5 × 137 cm). Landesgalerie, Hanover.

The year is 1756, and this is Piazza Navona, in the heart of Rome (Fig. 12.22). Already, the Baroque age is ending and the wonderful monuments of the piazza, created for the glorification of the Pamphili family's pope, Innocent X, are a hundred years old. Yet the setting designed by the greatest Roman Baroque architects at the height of their powers, reflected in the waters of the flooded square, re-creates the spirit of Innocent's High Baroque papacy.

Innocent's renovated family palace is in the foreground on the left-hand side of the piazza; from the balconies he and his retinue could participate in the dramatic pageantry occurring in the "royal front yard." Among the Pope's guests would have been visitors from many countries, diplomats representing the absolutist monarchs of expanding European nations, still competing for the Catholic Pope's favor despite his declining power.

Life in Piazza Navona thus offered itself as a permanent theatrical event, managed by increasingly stringent rules of etiquette, supported by New World wealth, and dominated by open enjoyment of artifice and unusual entertainments. Whether it was a festive secular event planned to honor a visiting dignitary, or a sacred cere-

monial occasion, sights and sounds, smells and tastes were organized to delight the senses and to sway hearts and minds. This silent and static painting captures the emotional excitement of the parade, and strives to suggest the shouts and splashes, the rich perfumes wafting along with the carriages, all continuously moving, animated by the bright sunlight striking silk and gilt and silver lamé, light refracting from the active surfaces of spouting, rippling water.

At nightfall, from the interiors of the palaces and churches, more solemn processions lit by tapers and torches flowed out into a Piazza Navona illuminated by bonfires and colored waxed paper lanterns. For ceremonies celebrating the election of Innocent to the papacy, the sober surface of the Renaissance church in the foreground on the right was the background for an enormous wooden, plaster, and canvas construction—Noah's ark on its mount—which later erupted with dazzling firework displays that delighted an audience of rich courtiers, pilgrims and paupers, shopkeepers and soldiers.

Events such as these proceeded with occasional hiatuses for the

harsher realities of the years around 1650: debt-ridden papal finances, serious famines, plague outbreaks, and the terrible battles, both physical and intellectual, among Protestants and Catholics, Christian forces and "non-believers." Statues could sometimes still spout wine, not water. Does all this recall the excesses of ancient Rome? Certainly one of the aims of Baroque rulers was to impress their rivals and subjects, and the underlying classicism evident in the Baroque age arises from explicitly revivalist dreams of an idyllic classical "Golden Age." It is not surprising, then, that Rome was the site of the style's initiation.

Yet fierce inner devotion often animated individual Baroque lives, activating the outward drama of the exuberant public events. Innocent himself, for example, was pious and moderate in his personal habits, and the great sculptor and architect Bernini regularly practiced St. Ignatius Loyola's prescribed spiritual exercises. Combining private piety and public devotion, secular power united itself with religious organizations to demand excesses of scale and emotional effect. Innocent and his architects created the lasting grandeur of Rome's Piazza Navona, and the space has served the city's inhabitants and visitors magnificently ever since.

# THE SPREAD OF BAROQUE ARCHITECTURE TO NORTHERN ITALY

## GUARINO GUARINI

Borromini's work, especially his design for S. Ivo della Sapienza, became the starting point for the work of Guarino Guarini (1624–83), an architect whose buildings in Turin represent the northern extension of Baroque Rome. Guarini was a member of the Theatine monastic order, and he served an eight-year novitiate in Rome from 1639–47. His early work in Modena for the Theatines does not survive; political difficulties led to his expulsion from the city in 1655, and he was to spend the following decade in various places, including France and possibly Spain. On his return to Turin in 1666, he worked on two central-plan churches.

The Cappella della SS. Sindone, or Chapel of the Holy Shroud (Figs. 12.23a,b), was added to the east end of the cathedral of Turin to house the important relic of the Holy Shroud. Guarini received the commission in 1667, after another architect had begun construction on a circular plan, which Guarini was obliged to retain. By inscribing an equilateral triangle in the circle and redesigning the access stairs and landing vestibules, Guarini brought mystery and dynamism to the unimaginative original scheme. The domed chapel pulsates with the counter-curves introduced by the vestibules and an axial niche, and three pendentives touch tangentially the circle of the dome above, which is not really a dome at all but an ascending hexagonal network of arches diminishing to an interlaced-arch oculus topped by a spiraling lantern. Light filters into the upper zone through small windows set within the arch network and pours in from six large windows at the base of the dome.

For his own order Guarini designed S. Lorenzo (1668–80), based on an octagon defined by convex Serliana surfaces bulging into the main space, all set within a square and completed by an elliptical choir (Figs. 12.24a,b). The geometric complexity here is astonishing. Squares, octagons, a Greek cross, ovals, and circles are involved. Again the dome is not a solid vault but an openwork structure with eight interlacing elliptical ribs. The church is illuminated by oval, pentagonal, and circular openings set between the ribs and by scattered chambers that capture and modulate the light. Over the choir is a lower, six-pointed ribbed-star vault, which, like the main vault, is reminiscent of Islamic ribbed domes at the Great Mosque of Córdoba (see Figs. 7.10–7.11); possibly the mosque was known to Guarini from his travels. S. Lorenzo's dome, drum, and cupola mirror the play of concave and convex forms seen on the interior (Fig. 12.25). Further examples of ribbed domes on unbuilt projects appear in Guarini's *Architettura civile*, published posthumously in 1737.

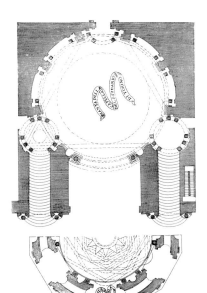

**12.23a** Guarino Guarini, Plan and partial reflected ceiling plan of the Sindone Chapel, Turin, begun 1667.

Guarini inherited the plan, but the reflected ceiling plan reveals his innovations: a telescoping, layered vault of rotated polygons.

**12.23b** Guarino Guarini, Section through the Sindone Chapel, Turin, begun 1667.

The drawing reveals the extraordinary organic quality of Guarini's dome construction. It is a dramatic change from the hemispherical domes of Brunelleschi.

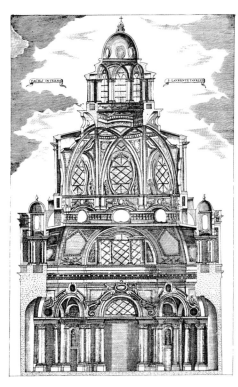

**12.24a** Guarino Guarini, Transverse section through S. Lorenzo, Turin, 1668–80.

Guarini used a cantilevered vault at the first level and interlocking elliptical ribs at the dome. Most interesting perhaps are the many light modulators that form the transition from the exterior to interior space.

**12.24b** Guarino Guarini, Plan of S. Lorenzo, Turin, 1668–80.

This plan, with reflected ceiling plan, reveals the complex patterns of Guarini's vaults. The four pairs of rotunda columns provide a richness through the layering of architectural elements. However, their small diameters indicate that they are false structure, with the loads above being carried by the cantilever.

**12.25** Guarino Guarini, Intrados of the Dome, S. Lorenzo, Turin, 1668–80.

The ribbed vaults of the Great Mosque at Córdoba, which Guarini may have seen during his travels, are often mentioned as his inspiration. The lantern appears to float above the ribs.

# THE BAROQUE IN CENTRAL EUROPE

While Guarini's influence continued in and around Turin, the artistic ideals of Baroque Italy were being spread to the north and east through Switzerland, Austria, southern Germany, and Bohemia. There Italian influences merged with local tastes and surviving craft-guild traditions to create a version of the Baroque distinctive to central Europe. As in Italy, the driving force was the Catholic Counter-Reformation, yet the style received support not only from Church officials, but also from princes and monarchs, who hoped to project a progressive image, and from the common people, for whom it reflected deeply held religious beliefs. In many respects Baroque churches in central Europe continued medieval themes, and architecture, sculpture, and painting advanced a single idea: the evocation of a heavenly realm. Number symbolism is prominent, as are the images of saints serving as intercessors between earth and heaven. Twin-towered west fronts are commonly found capped by bulbous domes rather than Gothic spires. The impression of lofty volume that is conveyed in the Gothic by soaring vaults is created in the central European Baroque by much lower plaster vaults on which paint and stucco have been expertly applied to create the illusion of an open sky filled with heavenly hosts. These Baroque churches are bright and airy; the windows are glazed with clear glass, and daylight is directed onto white interior surfaces embellished with gold and pastel hues.

The Baroque monuments of Italy were important sources for central Europe. Il Gesù in Rome was particularly influential because its design led to the development of the **Wandpfeiler** or **wall-pillar** that characterizes many central European Baroque churches. At Il Gesù the barrel-vaulted lateral chapels are separated from one another by cross walls faced at the nave with pilasters. North of the Alps, these cross walls became wall-pillars, which Baroque architects exploited for both structural stability and the shaping of internal space. Although the churches may retain side aisles, some even with galleries overhead, the wall-pillars were used as space-shaping elements to establish the concept of centrality within what were generally longitudinal plans. Thus, the interaction of axial and centralized plans, already seen in the oval designs of Borromini and Bernini, was continued in the Baroque of central Europe.

The life and work of Johann Bernhard Fischer von Erlach (1656–1723) exemplify one of the ways in which Italian ideas were transferred to central Europe. Fischer von Erlach came from an Austrian family of masons, and he was sent to Rome for training in the studio of Carlo Fontana. During the sixteen years he spent in Rome he became familiar with both ancient and contemporary works there, and these influences, combined with knowledge from travels across Europe, were later reflected in his own designs and in the illustrated *Entwurf einer historichen Architektur* (*Historic Architecture*), a precocious history of architecture which he published in 1721. Fischer von Erlach's architectural fortunes were tied to those of the Hapsburgs. He joined the imperial court at Vienna as architectural tutor to Joseph I in 1689, was raised to the nobility in 1696, and served as chief inspector of court buildings from 1705 until his death. During his lifetime, Austria experienced a surge of nationalistic pride after decisively repelling the Turkish attack on Vienna in 1683. Seeking to create an impressive international city that would rival Rome or Versailles, Viennese princes built Baroque palaces and raised new churches.

Fischer von Erlach's major contribution to Vienna was the Karlskirche (1716–25), a building that reflects his view that every work should be unique (Fig. 12.26). By borrowing from a wide range of historical sources, he created a highly original design that referred to many major buildings of the past. The church was dedicated to St. Charles Borromeo, the emperor's patron saint, and was built in fulfillment of a vow Charles VI made in 1713 during an outbreak of the plague. Its broad façade is dominated by a dome on a drum rising above a pedimented portico, flanked by columns in a manner recalling the front of S. Agnese in Agone, where the central dome is flanked by twin campaniles. Elements from historical buildings incorporated here include the columned portico from Roman temples such as the Pantheon; Trajan's Column from imperial Rome, repeated on both sides of the rotunda and adorned with scenes from the life of St. Charles Borromeo rather than reliefs of the Dacian Wars; the drum and dome from papal Rome; and an overall composition suggesting the dome and minarets of Hagia Sophia in Constantinople. The interior is impressive for its elongated oval nave (Figs. 12.27a,b), the ceiling of which is embellished with illusionistic frescoes depicting St. Charles Borromeo appealing to the Virgin Mary as intercessor for relief from the plague. Fischer von Erlach had seen the ceiling frescoes being installed at Il Gesù during his residence in Rome, so he used painting, rather than coffering or ribs as Bernini or Borromini would have done, to complete the dome's interior.

The rather severe and classical approach of Fischer von Erlach contrasts with the work of his contemporary, the Tyrolese architect Jacob Prandtauer (1660–1726), who was trained in Munich as a mason and practiced as an architect-sculptor. The works of Borromini and Guarini are reflected in his designs, but he was also influenced by Fischer von Erlach. A member of a religious brotherhood, Prandtauer was closely involved with his designs while they were under construction, and he is known primarily for monastic projects, including rebuilding the great abbey of Melk (1702–14), set dramatically atop a rocky ridge rising 200 feet above the Danube. The monastery's buildings are arranged in an elongated U shape, with the church placed inside the U, its compressed cloister interrupting one long range of rooms. From the river below

**12.26** Johann Bernhard Fischer von Erlach, Karlskirche, Vienna, 1716–25.

Fischer von Erlach possessed an early knowledge of classical architectural history, which he put to use here. The triumphal columns symbolically connect the Hapsburg Empire to Roman antiquity and the dome alludes to papal Rome.

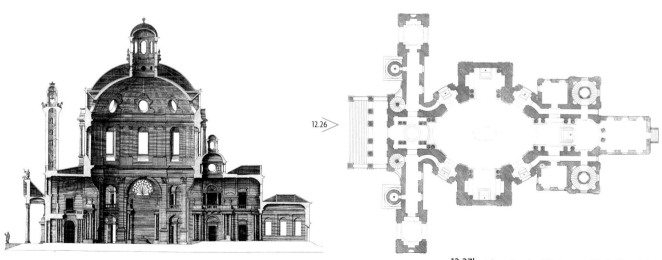

12.26 ▷

**12.27a** Johann Bernhard Fischer von Erlach, Section through the Karlskirche, Vienna, 1716–25.

Compared to the plan and elevation, the section is tame. Cut along the central axis, however, it gives no hint of the cowboy-storefront quality of the façade.

**12.27b** Johann Bernhard Fischer von Erlach, Plan of the Karlskirche, Vienna, 1716–25.

It is hard to imagine a more unusual plan than this one. The attitude of its designer, who borrowed from numerous sources, anticipates the tide of eclecticism that would reach a high point in the late nineteenth century.

**12.28** Jacob Prandtauer, Abbey church interior, Melk, 1702–14.

The oscillating walls and pillars create a dynamism in sharp contrast to the serene, modular interiors of a Renaissance building such as Brunelleschi's S. Lorenzo, Florence (see Fig. 11.6).

**12.29** Christoph Dientzenhofer, St. Nicholas on the Lesser Side interior, Prague, 1703–11.

One of six architect brothers, Christoph Dientzenhofer designed this church using wall-pillars. Setting these pillars on the diagonal, he was able to support syncopated, three-dimensionally curving transverse arches that meet tangentially at the centers of the bays, producing dual spatial readings.

and the small courtyard that precedes the west front, the twin towers of the main façade dominate, while the drum and dome over the crossing are best seen from the major courtyard at the east end of the church. This is a wall-pillar church with galleries above the oval chapels instead of aisles; a longitudinal emphasis was unavoidable because of site restrictions, and Prandtauer emphasized verticality through fluted pilasters and a dome on pendentives that soars above the clouds and the swirling drapery of the figures in the ceiling frescoes (Fig. 12.28). The undulating cornice of the nave supports recessed arches around clerestory windows, causing the whole ceiling to appear as a floating world. The painted illusion of heavenly figures spilling out from the vaults above provides a dramatic link between earthly matters and the spiritual world.

In Switzerland, Bavaria, and Bohemia (now the Czech Republic), Baroque design was generally the province of families of architects, sculptors, and painters, in which fathers, sons, uncles, and nephews collaborated on building projects. For example, five Dientzenhofer brothers—Georg, Christoph, Leonhard, Johann, and Wolfgang—were active in Bohemia and southern Germany just before and after 1700, where they combined the free-swinging curves found in the works of Borromini and Guarini with Slavic and Gothic motifs; Christoph's son, Kilian Ignaz,

also became an established designer. These families of master builders should not be thought of as rustics: a number of them were trained in major centers such as Turin, Vienna, and Prague, and they knew both the built and the unbuilt designs of leading Italian architects, even though they practiced architecture as guild members. Christoph Dientzenhofer (1655–1722) designed the church of St. Nicholas on the Lesser Side in Prague (1703–11) (Fig. 12.29) to have a longitudinal plan with deep wall-pillars set between chapels below and galleries above. The wall-pillars near the nave are splayed to support doubly curving arches. This configuration creates what has been called syncopation: a double reading of the spatial units as either a traditional bay system or a series of overlapping ovals.

## DIE WIES, BAVARIA

An alternative strategy of spatial dematerialization was employed by Dominikus Zimmerman (1685–1766) at the church of Die Wies, or The Fields (1746–54) (Fig. 12.30), located in a meadow beneath the Bavarian Alps. Fusing hall church and oval schemes and creating an outer bearing-wall layer and an inner trabeated layer of coupled columns, Zimmerman supported a nearly flat wood-and-

**12.30** Dominikus Zimmerman, Die Wies interior, near Munich, 1746–54.

The fairly plain exterior walls and steep draping roof of this small church give little indication of the dramatic, illusory effects waiting on the interior. Die Wies attracted pilgrims who came to see an image of the Scourged Christ said to weep real tears.

plaster vault on which his brother, Johann Baptist Zimmerman (1680–1758), could create an expansive illusionistic fresco of Christ at the Last Judgment. Applied to a background of white plaster dematerialized by brilliant light from large, surrounding windows, paintings, areas of pastel and gold colors, organic stucco ornament, and cut-outs in the vault supports produce an apparently weightless visual unity from this abundance of elements and effects.

**12.31** Johann Balthasar Neumann, Würzburg Residenz, begun 1720.

Here is the garden front of the palace, or Imperial hall, reached by one of the great stairs of the period (see page 338).

The collaboration of two other brothers can be seen in the abbey church of Einsiedeln (1719–35), where the design was begun by a lay brother of the monastery, Caspar Moosbrugger (1656–1723), and was finished after his death by his brother Johann Moosbrugger and others. Einsiedeln is still a major center of religious activity in Switzerland, and the monastery has an appropriately grand façade fronting a sloping plaza at the end of the town. In the center of the composition is the church, its great bowed front with twin towers projecting from the straight line of the flanking monastic buildings. This curved element directly reflects the principal feature of the interior, the shrine constructed on the site of the cell of St. Meinrad, who is venerated here. A great octagon completed by a dome surrounds the shrine, which thus occupies the first and largest bay of the nave. Wall-pillars pierced by aisles and galleries help define this space and form the transition to the smaller, circular domed bays of the nave.

The Asam brothers, painter Cosmas Damian (1686–1739) and sculptor Egid Quirin (1692–1750), were responsible for the wonderfully coordinated fresco and stucco work that graces the interior of the abbey church of Einsiedeln (1719–35). The narrower choir, built to the designs of Egid Quirin, is completed by an enormous altar and embellished with floating stucco figures that complement the ceiling frescoes above. The Asams tended to create

pictorial rather than architectural space. With paint and stucco they transformed what appear to be rather commonplace plans and sections into an extraordinary confection of light, color, and illusionistic space. The nave ceilings combine paint and plaster to create a joyous expression of the Nativity, with angels perched on high cornices and putti floating down to earth bearing the good news.

Not all central European Baroque buildings were churches. As in Italy and France, the nobility wanted to display their importance by building great palaces, and the theatricality of the Baroque was well suited to providing them with an appropriate setting. Of these princely abodes, the grandest was the Würzburg Residenz (Fig. 12.31), begun in 1720 for the prince-bishops of the Schönborn family. Its architect was Johann Balthasar Neumann (1687–1753), generally regarded as the greatest master of the German Baroque. Neumann was trained in mathematics, engineering, and architecture. He served the Schönborns as an artilleryman, civil engineer, and military engineer, before being encouraged to devote his designing talents and engineering dexterity to the creation of architectural spaces. The enormous Residenz was symmetrically

**12.32** Johann Balthasar Neumann, Plan of Vierzehnheilgen, near Bamberg, begun 1744.

This drawing shows the vaults above reflected onto the floor plan. Together, they illustrate how, within the cruciform plan, Neumann interlocked highly ornamental oval and circular bays by inserting spherical triangles at their intersections.

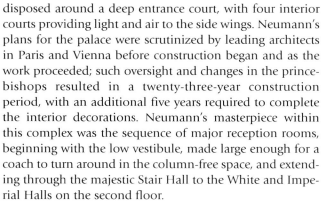

**12.33** Johann Balthasar Neumann, Vault detail Vierzehnheiligen, near Bamberg, begun 1744.

A spherical triangle is created by tracing a triangle onto a spherical surface. Here, craftsmen overlaid these curving surfaces with organic plaster ornamentation.

disposed around a deep entrance court, with four interior courts providing light and air to the side wings. Neumann's plans for the palace were scrutinized by leading architects in Paris and Vienna before construction began and as the work proceeded; such oversight and changes in the prince-bishops resulted in a twenty-three-year construction period, with an additional five years required to complete the interior decorations. Neumann's masterpiece within this complex was the sequence of major reception rooms, beginning with the low vestibule, made large enough for a coach to turn around in the column-free space, and extending through the majestic Stair Hall to the White and Imperial Halls on the second floor.

It is the lofty Stair Hall that most clearly exhibits the architect's technical skill (page 338). At nearly 100 by 60 feet, the hall is the largest single room in the palace, and it is roofed by a clear-span stone vault. The centrally placed

stair rises in a single flight to a landing, where it reverses direction and divides before extending to the upper floor—a so-called **imperial stair**. A balcony placed around the staircase allows onlookers a view of the processional space. The ceiling is enriched by the world's largest fresco, executed by Giovanni Battista Tiepolo and celebrating the sun god Apollo and the prince-bishops as patrons of the arts. Representations of the seasons, the zodiac, Europe, Asia, Africa, and America are assembled at the perimeter, the figures gazing into the clouds opening up in the heavens or staring down at those ascending the stair. Among the individuals depicted on the parapet are Tiepolo, the stucco artist Antonio Bossi, and Neumann himself, seated with his dog among items of artillery and taking a well-earned rest. Statues on the balustrades and stucco **cartouches**, swags, and putti above the door and window surrounds harmonize with the allegorical host overhead.

Further delights of stucco and fresco await in the subtle shades of the White Hall, which serves as a foil for the Imperial Hall, the most important room in the palace. Its elongated-octagon plan rises to a high oval, vaulted ceiling filled with Tiepolo's allegorical frescoes, alluding to historical scenes of the Holy Roman Empire and peopled with contemporary members of the Würzburg court.

Neumann was also a designer of churches, the most celebrated of which was the pilgrimage church of Vierzehnheiligen (begun 1744), outside Bamberg. Vierzehnheiligen commemorates the hilltop on which a shepherd boy in 1445 had an apparition of the Fourteen *Nothelfer* (a sort of heavenly witness, or guardian angel) for whom the church was named. A previous chapel on the site had become inadequate, and jurisdictional conflicts between the prince-bishop of Bamberg and the Cistercian abbot whose monastery was financing the work led to confusion over Neumann's appointment as architect. Construction was finally begun in 1744, but the foundations were laid too far to the east by the supervising architect, who also made design changes of which Neumann did not approve. Neumann redesigned the church, producing a scheme that is remarkable for the way its basically basilican ground plan is transformed into a composition of Baroque circles and ovals (Fig. 12.32). The freestanding altar of the fourteen saints occupies a central position in the nave, while the transepts become circles and the apse is defined as an oval. Neumann manipulated the interior space by arranging the aisle piers freely, both to support the oval vaults overhead and to form screens obscuring direct vision of windows in the side wall, thus combining the drama of light from unseen sources with swirling, curving forms (Fig. 12.33). He used delicate pastel colors, accented with gold, on marble piers and ceiling frescoes to emphasize the airy volumes of the interior. The warm sandstone exterior is grand but restrained, and the twin towers of the entrance front respond to the axis established by the Baroque abbey of Banz on a hill across the valley.

This discussion of major Baroque monuments should not obscure the fact that the Baroque became an almost vernacular style for churches in the countryside of southern Germany, Switzerland, Austria, the Czech Republic, and Poland, much as medieval styles characterize the French and English landscape. Existing churches were remodeled and new ones were built in the Baroque style; their distinctive reverse-curve domed towers still dot the rural districts. The Baroque even had an impact in Russia, where St. Petersburg was laid out early in the eighteenth century by French and Italian architects.

## THE BAROQUE IN FRANCE

The ideas of the Italian Baroque were transferred, although not without modifications, to France. By the mid-seventeenth century, as Louis XIV was coming into his majority, Renaissance-inspired classicism was sufficiently well established in France to mute the most elaborate excesses of the Roman Baroque. French official patronage of the period was more than ever centered on the royal court, and the propaganda of the Catholic Counter-Reformation was not an important issue. The official court style glorified the monarch, and the primary function of the state-run artistic establishment was to provide splendid settings, furnishings, and objects for the display of royal power. In pursuit of this objective, French architects built impressively elaborate works on a scale seldom seen, and the manners, costumes, and style of the French court became the model for other European capitals.

### THE LOUVRE, PARIS

Several building projects exemplify this process. In Paris the rebuilding of the Louvre, begun over a century earlier with the interior court wing by Lescot, was still not complete. First Lemercier and then Louis Le Vau (1612–70) worked on the interior elevations of the square court. During the 1660s a number of architects, including four Italians, were invited to submit designs for the east façade. Bernini, the leading European architect, sent a design proposing a central oval pavilion terminated by end pavilions, the whole composed of giant engaged columns and colonnades better suited to the bright sun of Italy than to the overcast skies of northern Europe. After hearing French objections to the scheme, Bernini sent a second proposal, this time with a concave plan, but Louis XIV and his ministers were still not satisfied. At the insistence of the King, Bernini came to Paris for six months in 1665 to consult directly on the Louvre design, in spite of opposition from French architects who hoped to receive the commission themselves. While in Paris, Bernini prepared a third proposal, not just for the east wing but for the entire palace. In this plan, the original square court was completely shielded by open loggias with blocky staircases protruding at the corners. The exterior façades were no longer curved but articulated by giant engaged columns on the central pavilion and pilasters on the end pavilions; the ground floor was treated as a rusticated base for the giant orders above.

Perhaps because Bernini failed to reflect French taste in his designs, Louis decided not to adopt any of these schemes. Instead he gave the commission to a trio consisting of the architect Le Vau, the painter Charles Lebrun (1619–90), and a doctor of medicine, Claude Perrault (1613–88). While the exact contributions of each remain unclear, these three men were responsible for the present-day east façade (1667–70), composed of a colonnade of paired Corinthian columns with central and end pavilions, all set atop a rusticated ground story (Fig. 12.34). This use of paired columns links the work to Baroque precedent, although the design is far more restrained than contemporary architecture in Italy. In contrast to earlier

**12.34** Louis Le Vau, Charles Lebrun, and Claude Perrault, East façade of the Louvre, Paris, 1667–70.

The paired columns symbolize the monarchy. The façade composition is distinctly French: end pavilions, central pedimented unit, and connecting stoa-like wings.

French Renaissance works, the roof of the east façade is hidden by a balustraded parapet, reinforcing the horizontal emphasis of the whole elevation.

The austerity of the east façade, with its central pediment, end pavilions, and paired columns carrying a continuous architrave, is often associated with Perrault's ideas about architecture. He edited a well-received French edition of Vitruvius in 1673, in which he illustrated the grave monumentality of the trabeated Roman work of the republic. In 1683, he produced a controversial treatise on the orders in which he argued that their proportions were not absolute but were best determined by a discerning eye. This attitude of relativism had profound implications for the development of subsequent architectural theory, including twentieth-century Modernism.

## FRANÇOIS MANSART

François Mansart (1598–1666) is as well known for his difficult disposition as for his design genius. Trained by his master-carpenter father, Mansart was "arrogant, touchy, and unpopular," and perhaps corrupt. His inclination to work and rework projects almost endlessly caused him to lose control over many of them before completion. While owing much to the continuing importation of both High Renaissance and Mannerist forms from Italy, he produced work that was chauvinistic in its emphasis on openwork structure, a continuation of French Gothic traditions, and on stereotomy—the art of precise stone masonry. Regarding the latter, his buildings exhibit a precision of detail and conviction of composition that give them a "severe richness" achieved by few others.

Mansart's Ste. Marie de la Visitation in Paris (1632), built for a group of nuns who served the sick and needy outside their convent, demonstrates his interpretation of the central-church scheme, a radical innovation in France

at the time. He took his plan (Fig. 12.35) through a number of iterations before settling on a rotunda ringed by column screens and apsidal and kidney-shaped chapels cut into the thick, surrounding wall, with one chapel leading to a nuns' choir. His section studies reveal a fascination with telescoping vertical spaces generated by a series of truncated low-slung domes, which were to become his trademark. The entrance façade (Fig. 12.36), with its huge Serliana-like composition capped by a convex pavilion roof, recalls the work of Salomon de Brosse, designer of the Luxembourg Palace.

Mansart began the Parisian church of the Val-de-Grâce in 1644; it was completed by Lemercier after 1646. Built with funds granted by Anne of Austria after she conceived Louis XIV, it gave Mansart an opportunity to explore the longitudinal church plan in a scheme not unlike Il Gesù in

**12.35** François Masart, Plan of Ste. Marie de la Visitation, Paris, 1632.

Mansart's central-rotunda plan was unique at the time in France. The column screens were motivated by the need to shield the nuns' choir from the public space of the church.

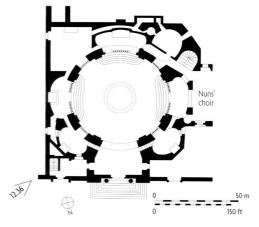

Nuns' choir

N

0   50 m
0   150 ft

**12.36** François Mansart, Ste. Marie de la Visitation, Paris, 1632.

Here Mansart combined an entry pavilion, based upon the gateway pavilions of earlier French châteaux, with a tall rotunda. While relatively small, the entry pavilion is impressive, illustrating the French preference and aptitude for monumentality.

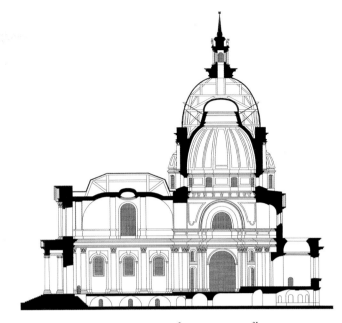

**12.37** François Mansart, Early section drawing for the church of Val-de-Grâce, Paris, 1644–46.

Low-slung vaults in the stunted nave and steep, telescoping domes at the crossing connect Mansart's work to spatial investigations in the work of Guarini and Vittone.

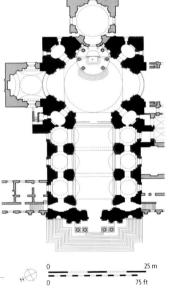

**12.38** François Mansart, Plan of the church of Val-de-Grâce, Paris, 1644–46.

Mansart simplified his early schemes for this church in order to make it economically viable. The hatched-in portions were added by Jacques Lemercier, who replaced Mansart during construction.

Rome. Several projects preceded the design as built. One early scheme included a great baldachin like that at St. Peter's, a truncated double dome at the crossing, and a distinctive combination of intersecting barrel vaults, semi-domes, and domes in the short nave (Fig. 12.37). As built (Fig. 12.38), the structure became much simpler, with a hemispherical dome at the crossing capped by a second, larger dome scaled to be seen above the façade, and a barrel-vaulted nave.

At Maisons-sur-Seine near Paris, Mansart built a château (1642–51) that has few equals in its confident composition and severe masonry treatment. His grand site plan, some of which has been lost, included an elaborate entry sequence with monumental gateways and tree-lined boulevards leading to a forecourt defined by stables and an intended **orangery**. Next comes a moat, an entry court, then the body of the house, the **corps-de-logis**, surrounded by garden parterres. Mansart arranged the building to have a U-shaped plan (Fig. 12.39) with end pavilions capped by truncated pyramidal roofs and a larger central pavilion with a three-story centerpiece of attached columns and a pediment. The masonry façades (Fig. 12.40), articulated using crisp pilasters, have the appearance of a skin stretched tightly over a structural skeleton beneath. The same sober, assured classicism can be seen on the interior, where the main vestibule appears as a thick-walled masonry box inside which Mansart inserted a set of eight columns, producing an apparently

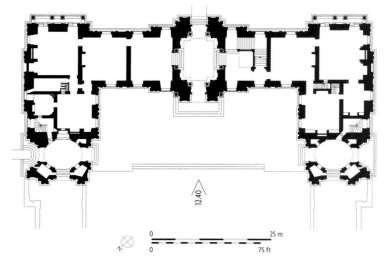

**12.39** François Mansart, Plan of the château, Maisons-sur-Seine, near Paris, 1642–51.

Of particular interest here is the central entry. Its cruciform plan is defined by massive walls inside which stand four pairs of columns. The plan also illustrates the French preference for dominant end pavilions.

**12.40** François Mansart, Château, Maisons-sur-Seine, near Paris, 1642–51.

Mansart's façade appears as a thin, taut skin stretched over a sharp-edged skeleton. It reveals the French reverence for stereotomy: the combined results of projective-geometry knowledge and skill in stone carving.

trabeated building inside an arcuated one. Space in the adjacent stair tower extends upward through low, truncated domes like those at Ste. Marie de la Visitation and his additions to the château at Blois (begun ca. 1635).

## THE CHÂTEAU OF VERSAILLES

The designers of other French country estates also enthusiastically adopted aspects of the Baroque style. In 1624 Louis XIII had built a hunting lodge with a C-shaped plan on swampy land at Versailles, some twenty miles southwest of Paris. When the future Louis XIV was a child, he spent relatively happy times in this twenty-room château,

and on becoming monarch he decided to make modifications to it. Being sentimental about the original lodge, he would allow none of it to be removed. So, in 1661 Louis Le Vau first added two freestanding service wings projecting to the east and extending the enclosure of the château's east-facing forecourt. Then, in 1669, Le Vau enveloped the north and south flanks of the original château with **enfilades** of rooms in front of courtyards and stairs.

From the first, Louis intended Versailles to be the permanent residence of the royal court, dismissing medieval Paris as an unfit setting for the Sun King. A site less suitable for major construction than Versailles would have been difficult to find. The marshy ground was fine for game, but it was incapable of supporting elaborate plant life, and there was no adequate water supply readily available to run fountains. Under the direction of André Le Nôtre (1617–1700), the army drained 37,000 acres of land and diverted an entire river thirty miles to supply water for the fountains, which eventually numbered 1400. Then Le

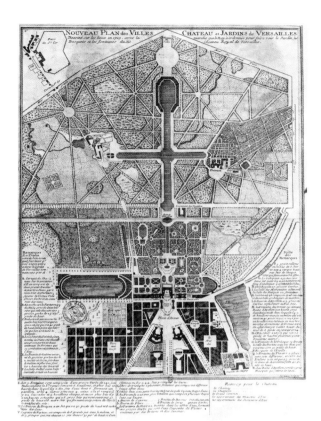

Nôtre planned vast gardens, with axial vistas, terraces, sculpture, formal flowerbeds, fountains, water basins, and paths integrated into a grand plan that focused on the King's bedroom in the center of the palace (Figs. 12.41–12.42).

In 1678, when the entire court took up residence at Versailles, the palace was again enlarged, this time under the direction of François Mansart's nephew, Jules-Hardouin Mansart (1646–1708), who continued to work there until his death thirty years later. At one point, in

**12.41** André Le Nôtre, Plan of the palace and gardens, Versailles, begun 1661.

The vast axial plan at Versailles is a fulfillment of the proposal put forward in the sixteenth century by Sixtus V in his replanning of Rome. The young Pierre L'Enfant lived at the palace and remembered his experience when he laid out the axes-over-grid plan for Washington, D.C.

**12.42** Pierre Patel, Bird's-eye view of Versailles from the east, 1668.

This view shows the old C-shaped château, or hunting lodge, at the center, with the addition of Le Vau's projecting service wings of 1661 and the surrounding gardens by Le Nôtre. Le Vau's 1669 north and south enveloping of the old château's flanks and J. H. Mansart's vast north- and south-wing extensions were yet to come but can be seen in Figure 12.41.

**12.43** Jules-Hardouin Mansart, St.-Louis-des-Invalides, Paris, 1670–1708.

J.-H. Mansart made use of drawings inherited from his uncle, François, in preparing his design of this church. His central plan can also be compared to Bramante's scheme for St. Peter's.

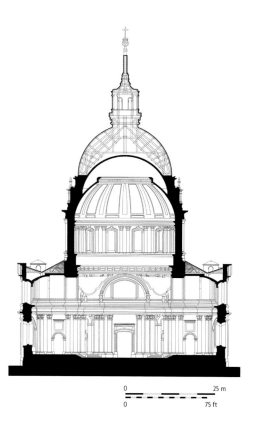

**12.44** Jules-Hardouin Mansart, Section through St.-Louis-des-Invalides, Paris, 1670–1708.

Mansart's triple-shell dome not only creates two scales, interior and exterior, but also pursues his uncle François Mansart's experiments with spatial layers resulting from dome truncations.

1685, 36,000 men and 6000 horses were involved in construction of the buildings and grounds. A town of about 20,000 people grew up adjacent to the palace to house the aristocracy, their soldiers and servants, and other minor courtiers. Like the gardens, the town was organized around radiating boulevards extending from the center of the palace—a device first seen in Rome, with the three streets extending south from the Piazza del Popolo. Mansart extended the palace symmetrically to the north and south by building long wings, continuing the 1669 elevation scheme established by Le Vau. Mansart also added the Galerie des Glaces, or Hall of Mirrors, and two adjacent salons of War and Peace behind the west façade of the central block, finally completing the envelopment of the original château. Le Vau's Staircase of the Ambassadors (begun 1671) divided to lead to both salons, so that any ambassador would know of Louis's intentions before these were actually announced to him in the appropriate setting. A large circular panel in the Salon of War depicted Louis as Mars triumphant over his enemies. The King's own suite of rooms included salons where

paintings depicted monarchs of antiquity with the attributes of the gods representing the seven known planets, including Mercury and wisdom; Venus and love; Mars and war. His throne room was the Salon of Apollo. The only vertical feature at Versailles is the chapel added by Mansart in 1698–1710 on the right side of the forecourt, a building of Gothic proportions and spatial conception expressed using the classical language.

All of the interior decoration at Versailles was carried out under the direction of Lebrun, and his ornamental work, furniture, tapestries, reliefs, and paintings were as elaborate as anything to be found in Baroque palaces of the period. However, while Versailles has much of the grandeur, it has little of the dynamism of seventeenth-century architecture in Italy.

### JULES-HARDOUIN MANSART

Jules-Hardouin Mansart also designed structures in Paris. He added the church of St.-Louis-des-Invalides (Fig. 12.43) to the hospital for disabled soldiers. Although the interior of Les Invalides, as it is known, was still incomplete at Mansart's death in 1708, it was essentially finished by 1691. Its plan is based on Bramante's design for St. Peter's, and the drum and dome are derived from Michelangelo's design for the same church, though Mansart gave his interpretation a strong vertical accent. The dome of Les Invalides is buttressed by pairs of Ionic columns protruding from the fenestrated surface of the drum. The dignity of the exterior is achieved by a system of three dome shells (Fig. 12.44). The innermost, truncated masonry dome relates to the scale of the interior space; the intermediate masonry dome caps the truncated one and supports the external timber-framed dome, which is covered with lead sheets and is scaled to the building's exterior silhouette, mass, and composition.

## CHRISTOPHER WREN AND THE BAROQUE IN ENGLAND

Mansart's design for Les Invalides was to have a direct impact on the most outstanding architect of the English Baroque, Christopher Wren (1632–1723). Wren came to national prominence as a result of the Great Fire, which began on September 2, 1666 and destroyed 373 of the 448 acres comprising the walled area of the City of London, including 13,200 houses, forty-four city companies, eighty-seven churches, the Royal Exchange, the Custom House, and St. Paul's Cathedral. Numerous prominent men made plans for rebuilding the burnt area. Wren produced a plan dated September 11; the diarist Sir John Evelyn, September 13; and Robert Hooke, Curator of Experiments at the Royal Society, September 19. Wren proposed a grid superimposed with axial routes connecting commercial, religious, and governmental centers within the city. Precedent for this plan organization can be found in the Baroque designs for Rome and Versailles. None of the plans submitted for the rebuilding of London was used in the actual work. Merchants wanted to reestablish their homes and businesses as rapidly as possible, in the same location within the city, without having to wait for radical planning changes to be approved and implemented.

Christopher Wren has been acclaimed as Britain's greatest architect. Trained as a mathematician, he was also well connected in the Church, his father having been Dean of Windsor. In 1661 Wren became Professor of Astronomy at Oxford University. While there, he designed the Sheldonian Theater (1662–63) for an alumnus, Archbishop Sheldon, basing it on the semicircular plan of the Theater of Marcellus in Rome (see Fig. 5.27b). Huge wooden roof trusses above the theater space support a canvas ceiling, which Wren had painted to resemble the open sky, complete with simulated ropes to hold the shading device taut. The entrance front is a pedimented pavilion with a raking cornice carried down to the perimeter walls. Arcades, half-columns, pilasters, oval dormers,

**12.45** Christopher Wren, St. Stephen Walbrook interior, London, 1672–87.

Striking in this view is the slenderness and wide spacing of the columns that support the entablature and, in turn, the dome. These proportions are possible because the vaults are not stone, but wood and plaster.

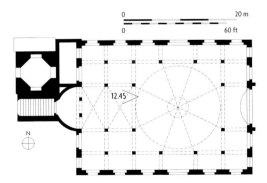

**12.46** Christopher Wren, Plan of St. Stephen Walbrook, London, 1672–87.

Wren organized St. Stephen Walbrook by means of a modulated grid—an orthogonal grid with the bay spacing varied. He removed four columns to produce the rotunda defined by an octagon of dome-supporting arches.

and a cupola complete the design. It was based on a plate in Serlio's *Five Books of Architecture*, as was the pilastered and pedimented design of the street façade of Wren's Pembroke College Chapel, Cambridge (1663–65), created for his uncle, Matthew Wren, Bishop of Ely. The chapel's ceiling is elaborate, and its woodwork was richly carved by the master woodcarver Grinling Gibbons.

Wren visited Paris from July 1665 through March 1666, probably to escape the plague that was sweeping Britain at the time. There he met Bernini and wrote, "I would have given my skin for . . . a few minutes' view" of Bernini's design for the Louvre.

## THE CITY CHURCHES

After the fire of 1666 Wren became one of the six commissioners who prepared the Act for Rebuilding the City of London (1667), specifying, among other things, the use of brick walls and slate roofs to reduce the spread of any future fires. Fifty-one (just over half) of the burnt parish churches of the city were rebuilt to designs done by Wren from 1670 to 1686, although much of the detail was probably left to the master carpenter or mason in charge of each individual church since Wren was preoccupied with his major lifework, the rebuilding of St. Paul's Cathedral. The towers and spires of his churches, perhaps influenced by what he had seen in Gothic France, created a distinctive silhouette on the skyline, rising above the lower brick buildings and contrasting with the domed profile being developed in the design of St. Paul's. Wren's parish church designs vary considerably as he had to accommodate many different site conditions; he sometimes provided a reinterpretation of the earlier church destroyed in the Great Fire, so not all the designs are classically derived. Several of the steeples are particularly memorable. The spire of St. Mary-le-Bow rises on a circular plan above a square-plan tower, while St. Bride's, Fleet Street has four diminishing octagons of arched openings in its upper stories. In contrast, the steeple of St. Dunstan-in-the-East was built in a simplified Gothic form that reflected the previous church.

Like many others of Wren's city churches, the church of St. Stephen Walbrook (1672–87) served him as a rapidly built experimental model during his on-going effort to design St. Paul's Cathedral. Except for its rather medieval tower capped by a Renaissance crown, the exterior of St. Stephen Walbrook is insignificant, but the interior is an extraordinary centrally planned space developed on a modulated grid, with a stubby nave and a coffered Pantheon-like dome (Figs. 12.45–12.46). That rests on eight arches supported by an octagonal arrangement of Corinthian columns atop high pedestals. Since the dome was a wooden construction, the supports could be slender and refined; for this reason it did not present any of the structural problems involved in the triple-shelled masonry dome of St. Paul's.

## ST. PAUL'S

Wren's design for St. Paul's Cathedral went through a number of changes. The so-called "Great Model" (Fig. 12.47), dating from 1673, consisted of a major dome on eight piers ringed with secondary domes forming a continuous ambulatory similar to Bramante's 1506 design for St. Peter's; but this design was too strongly linked with Roman Catholicism to be found acceptable by the cathedral's dean and chapter. A Latin-cross plan, similar to the previous Gothic building on the site, was requested, and that was what Wren provided in the "Warrant Design" of 1675. Even its silhouette was Gothic, consisting as it did of a minuscule drum and dome capped by a six-tiered cupola. Construction began on the basis of this design, which Wren modified slowly over the thirty-year building period. The structure completed in 1709 was refined and academic, incorporating elements from a wide variety of sources (Figs. 12.48–12.49). In plan the cathedral is a basilica, a form that Wren admired in the basilica at Fano as published by Vitruvius. Most of Wren's nave-and-aisle churches were based on the Roman basilica. At St. Paul's, the basilican structure is comprised of saucer domes in the nave and aisles, with buttresses above the aisle roofs (Fig. 12.50). To hide these buttresses and impart a classical character to the exterior, Wren raised the aisle walls to create screens articulated in a manner similar to those in Inigo Jones's Banqueting House (see Fig. 11.75), while the north and south transept porticos were a restatement of Cortona's façade of S. Maria della Pace (see Fig. 12.18) in Rome. The west front is based on Perrault's façade for the Louvre (see Fig. 12.34), with towers like S. Agnese in Agone in Piazza Navona in Rome (see Fig. 12.17). Wren greatly changed the dome, not begun until 1697, from that proposed in the "Warrant Design" of 1675, synthesizing Michelangelo's buttressing system for St. Peter's in Rome with Bramante's original design for the drum. Such a large dome required substantial supporting piers, necessitating the infill of the sides of the four diagonal arches of the central crossing to create segmental rather than hemispherical arches. The external massing of the dome had to be tall and dignified to dominate the London skyline, but this would have created an excessively vertical internal space. Thus Wren resorted to the triple-domed strategy employed by J.-H. Mansart at his church of St.-Louis-des-Invalides (see Fig. 12.44). The innermost dome is of masonry. Above this, a brick cone supports both the cupola and the wooden superstructure of the lead-covered exterior dome. Despite Wren's background as a mathematician, there is no evidence that he used his academic knowledge to make calculations predicting structural behavior.

The richness of St. Paul's relies equally on the architecture and the internal decoration, which includes work by woodcarver Grinling Gibbons (1648-1721) and master ironworker Jean Tijou. Gibbons was born in Rotterdam and discovered there by John Evelyn. He carved numerous

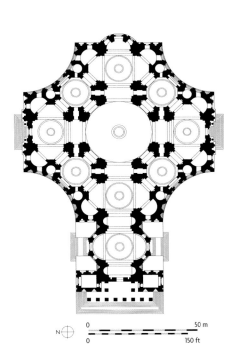

**12.47** Christopher Wren, "Great Model" plan for St. Paul's Cathedral, London, 1673.

Wren's so-called "Great Model" was unacceptable in England because it had strong Catholic overtones, derived from the churches of the Italian Baroque style in Rome.

**12.48** Christopher Wren, St. Paul's, London, 1675–1709.

Wren's façade composition looks back to such models as S. Agnese in Piazza Navona (see Fig. 12.17). His triple-shell dome includes the unique feature of a conical intermediate shell that supports both the lantern and the timber superstructure of the outer shell.

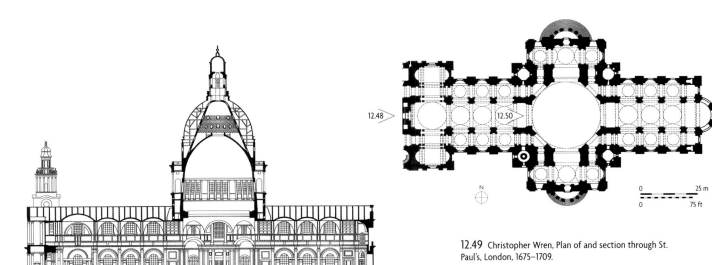

**12.49** Christopher Wren, Plan of and section through St. Paul's, London, 1675–1709.

Remnants of the "Great Model" can be found in the many domed units covering both nave and aisles. It is Wren's interpretation of an ancient Roman basilica.

**12.50** Christopher Wren, St. Paul's interior, London, 1675–1709.

In this view looking east, the saucer-domed bays of the nave lead to the octagonal rotunda. About it rises the triple-shell dome, comparable to the one J.H. Mansart designed for Les Invalides (see Fig. 12.44).

Wren interiors, including Trinity College Library in Cambridge and St. James's Piccadilly in London, but he excelled himself in the choir stalls and organ case of St. Paul's. Tijou, a French Huguenot, was patronized by the monarchs William and Mary. He worked mainly at Hampton Court and St. Paul's, where rosettes and embossed leaves distinguish his elaborate creations in wrought iron.

## HOUSING IN THE MANNER OF WREN

Wren was much too busy with royal commissions to design private houses. Often presented as a residential building in the manner of Wren is Coleshill, Berkshire (ca. 1650) by Roger Pratt (1620–84) (Fig. 12.51). The two-room-deep or double-pile plan included a transverse service corridor. Such a house can claim ancestry to many Georgian mansions that would appear in eighteenth-century America, although the later buildings would have longitudinal central halls. Uppark, Sussex (1695) (Fig. 12.52) by William Talman (1650–1719) has a façade anticipating many later American works. This house is blocky, with a central, projecting pedimented bay and an elaborate **frontispiece** but no use of the orders except

**12.51** Roger Pratt, Coleshill, Berkshire, ca. 1650.

While Wren designed no houses as modest as this one,
Coleshill seems to exhibit his form preferences. Its water
table, belt course, entry frontispiece, heavy cornice, dormers,
and rooftop balustrade all became standard features of the
English and American Georgian styles. The house was
destroyed by fire in the 1950s.

**12.52** William Talman, Uppark, Sussex, 1695.

Ironically, Georgian houses in America were more successful
than their English models such as this one. In America, designs
were often based upon drawings in English and American books,
which represented refinements of the built originals.

astride the doorway. Similar houses can be seen in such places as the cathedral close in Salisbury; the related American examples are often more refined and possessed of finer proportions because they were drawn from publications in which English experience had been codified.

## NICHOLAS HAWKSMOOR, SIR JOHN VANBRUGH, AND JAMES GIBBS

While working on St. Paul's, Wren employed a domestic clerk who eventually became his assistant. This man was Nicholas Hawksmoor (1661–1736), who added to St. Paul's the west-front towers that emphasize massing, in contrast to the linear façades and accurate detailing of Wren's design. Hawksmoor also collaborated with an equally famous contemporary, Sir John Vanbrugh (1664–1726), a gentleman-soldier and colorful character who at one time was imprisoned by the French on suspicion of spying and who on his return to England became a successful comic playwright. In 1699 the Earl of Carlisle chose him over William Talman to design a palace in Yorkshire called Castle Howard (Fig. 12.53). Work on this elaborate and extensive complex began in 1701, with the assistance of Hawksmoor, who contributed architectural know-how to Vanbrugh's theatrical daring. They proposed a symmetrical design anchored by a domed great hall from which the principal apartments would extend laterally. Curved colonnades flanking the great court maintain strict axiality while connecting the main block with subsidiary courts for kitchens and stables that were never built.

The most celebrated house of the Vanbrugh–Hawksmoor partnership is Blenheim Palace (Fig. 12.54), built by a grateful England for the Duke and Duchess of Marlborough in commemoration of the Duke's success at the battle of Blenheim in 1704. A large and pompous building following the themes established at Castle Howard, Blenheim is representative of this period of grandiose design and is one of the most monumental pieces of domestic architecture of any period in Britain. The exterior is dominated by giant Corinthian columns and massive corner pavilions. Entrance is made through the north portico which leads on axis from the great court into the hall and salon. Symmetrically disposed on either side of this central group are smaller rooms arranged around two internal courts; on the west front is a long gallery. Colonnades link the main block to the kitchen and stable courts, which balance each other on either side of the great court. Sarah, Duchess of Marlborough, objected to its impracticality as a home, because kitchen and dining room were a quarter-mile apart. The poet Alexander Pope observed, "'Tis very fine, But where d'ye sleep, or where d'ye dine?"

While Vanbrugh designed some ten grand country houses, Hawksmoor's major architectural works were the six churches he built in London; two were paid for under the Act for Building Fifty New Churches of 1711, for which he was appointed commissioner. Most of his basilican planning is derived from Wren, but the exuberance is all Hawksmoor's. At Christ Church, Spitalfields, London (1723–29), Hawksmoor's interest in the late Roman temples at Baalbek is reflected in his overscaled and

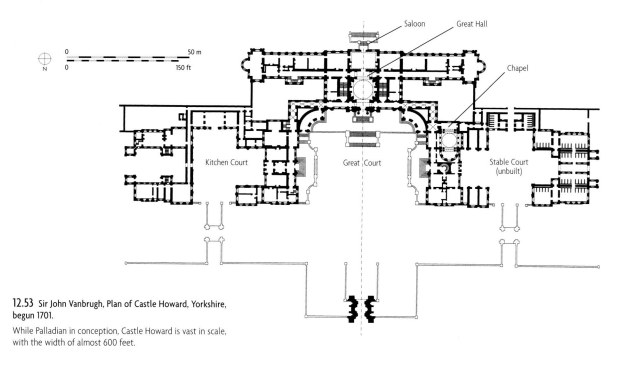

**12.53** Sir John Vanbrugh, Plan of Castle Howard, Yorkshire, begun 1701.

While Palladian in conception, Castle Howard is vast in scale, with the width of almost 600 feet.

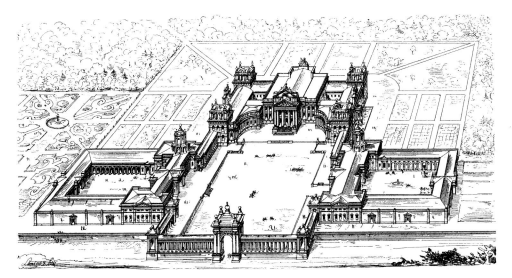

**12.54** Sir John Vanbrugh and Nicholas Hawksmoor, Blenheim Palace, Woodstock, Oxfordshire, 1705–24. Engraving.

This sprawling residence was financed by the British Crown as a means of rewarding the Duke of Marlborough for his military exploits at the battle of Blenheim.

**12.55** Nicholas Hawksmoor, Christ Church, Spitalfields, London, 1723–29.

For this façade, Hawksmoor fully exploited the well-worn Serliana or Palladian motif. A giant version appears as the entry porch, a smaller one as the base of the tower, and a third, still smaller one as the frame for the clock.

unusually detailed scheme. The nave is illuminated by clerestories above elliptical barrel vaults running parallel to the nave. Below these vaults, the nave arcade is composed of cylindrical columns with complete entablatures surmounting each one. The nave is not vaulted but is covered with a flat coffered ceiling, and the whole of the interior is bold. On the exterior, the porch is composed of a large Serliana, above which the tower rises, buttressed at front and back by screen walls containing windows arranged in another Serliana composition (Fig. 12.55). The styles of Vanbrugh and Hawksmoor are very personal and individualistic, forming a rich extension of the more academic work of Wren and thus presenting a distinctive part of the English tradition.

The church of St. Martin-in-the-Fields, London (1721–26) by James Gibbs (1682–1754), who was unusual in England for having studied in Rome, is an essay on the Corinthian order, employing giant columns and pilasters both inside and out (Fig. 12.56). A Wren-derived tower and steeple lie on the main axis; the entrance to the church is through their base and is protected by a dominating Corinthian portico. This church set a precedent for countless religious buildings, most notably in the American colonies both before and after the Revolution, mainly as a result of Gibbs's *A Book of Architecture*, published in 1729, which illustrates his numerous designs. For instance, Joseph Brown's Baptist church at Providence,

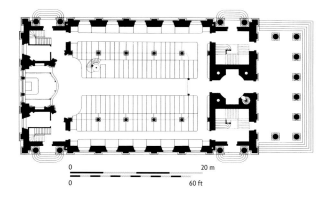

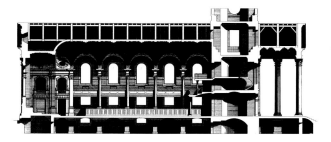

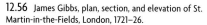

**12.56** James Gibbs, plan, section, and elevation of St. Martin-in-the-Fields, London, 1721–26.

Gibbs successfully united the temple front, Wren-like tower, and basilican nave to produce a prototype for churches in England and America. He tried out several variants before settling on this tower composition, which begins as a square in plan, moves through sets of octagons, and terminates with a faceted spire.

Rhode Island (1774–75), is based on St. Martin, as are St. Michael's in Charleston, South Carolina (begun 1752, possibly by Peter Harrison), and churches in Vermont and Connecticut by Lavius Fillmore.

Gibbs is an architect whose works establish a bridge between the most elaborate examples of the English Baroque and more restrained designs based on the serenity of Andrea Palladio. The designs in his publication illustrate both inspirations. By the middle of the eighteenth century, the return to purer interpretations of classical antiquity emerged as Neo-Classicism, an important movement to which Gibbs gave an impetus and which is discussed in the next chapter.

## CONCLUSIONS ABOUT ARCHITECTURAL IDEAS

During the Baroque period, architects retained the classical language, but often permitted themselves considerable license in its interpretation and made it only one part of a larger "multi-media" experience. At the Council of Trent in 1545, the Catholic hierarchy, while setting in motion the Counter-Reformation, concluded that art was to be exploited as an instrument of Church policy, captivating the currently faithful and enticing back the wayward. A decade earlier Ignatius Loyola had founded the evangelical

Society of Jesus (the Jesuits), and its missionary educators eventually took Catholic teachings worldwide. The order's mother church in Rome, Il Gesù, established a new direction for façade design and for interior spatial organization, being a modestly scaled, acoustically coherent preaching environment.

Il Gesù became one among many monuments made urbanistically prominent by the replanning of Rome continued under Pope Sixtus V. By cutting through long, straight streets that minimized travel distances, papal engineer Domenico Fontana connected the city's seven major churches, including St. Peter's, with S. Maria Maggiore at the center of the nexus. Architects responded by creating grand civic spaces within the dense antique-medieval fabric, including the Piazza del Popolo at the northern gate, the Spanish Steps beneath the church of the Trinità dei Monti, and the Piazza Navona within the boundaries of an ancient Roman circus. Streets and piazzas acted in concert, producing a dynamic new urbanism that would affect city planning for the next three hundred years.

The churches of S. Andrea al Quirinale and S. Carlo alle Quattro Fontane present two applications of Counter-Reformation theory. Bernini's S. Andrea is stage-like, a container for the reenactment of the martyrdom and ascension of Saint Andrew. In the service of this dramatic action, Bernini brought together painting, sculpture, and stucco-work within a dynamic oval-plan space. At S.

Carlino, Borromini employed almost exclusively architectonic means to produce drama through the manipulation of form, as for instance the elongated columns and sinuous curves of the façade and the internal paired columns "pressed" into the oscillating walls that define an elongated-Greek-cross plan.

Both structures had important progeny. Following Bernini's line of investigation, J.B. Fischer von Erlach, author of *Historic Architecture*, the first book on architectural history, designed the Karlskirche in Vienna as a carrier of Hapsburg symbolism to have a broad, billboard-like façade and oval, illusionistically painted, worship space. The Zimmerman brothers' Bavarian church of Die Wies, with its wood-and-plaster vaults, took illusory experience to an extreme of artistic fusion where stucco work, sculpture, painting, and architecture bathed in brilliant light became a unified vision.

Borromini, on the other hand, inspired the architect and engineer Guarino Guarini to experiment with new vaulting types, concealed structure, and dramatic light manipulation in such projects as S. Lorenzo, Turin. In Prague, in what was then called Bohemia, Christoph Dientzenhofer exploited the wall-pillar as a means for creating dual spatial readings and, as a result, a sense of spatial ambiguity and syncopated rhythms. Near Würzburg, at the pilgrimage church of Vierzehnheiligen, court architect Balthasar Neumann designed complex masonry vaults with double curvatures that required his engineer's knowledge of mathematics and the strength of materials, then a legion of craftsmen applied stucco, paint, and gilding—without detailed direction from the architect—in pursuit of a homogeneous spatial and dramatic experience appropriate for a church dedicated to the mystical vision of a local shepherd. Neumann enlisted the same strategies in producing the Würzburg Palace, where a monumental stairway (see page 338), inside a room painted illusionistically by Tiepolo, became a stage-set for the ascent and descent of men and women in exquisite court dress.

In France, surface effects never subsumed the techniques of building. Here François Mansart pursued spatial investigations like those of Borromini, but also remained loyal to the local Gothic vision of lofty interior space and to the French medieval emphasis on stereotomy. Working at the east façade of the Louvre, physician Claude Perrault, architect Louis Le Vau, and painter Charles Lebrun collaborated on a building expansion with Mansartian precision that was dominated by columns (in this case paired), a condition repeated throughout the remainder of the palace as constructed both before and after the mid-seventeenth century.

The English scientist Sir Christopher Wren traveled to France where he studied the Gothic cathedrals, becoming especially impressed by their towers, and met Bernini, who was there consulting on the Louvre extension. Wren returned in 1666 to a post-fire London that desperately needed dozens of neighborhood churches rebuilt to include easily seen and identified towers, as well as a new St. Paul's Cathedral. The production of Wren and his contemporaries Vanbrugh and Hawksmoor swung as far toward the Baroque as English work ever would, before taste moved back to a more gentle classicism. Designed by others than Wren, but following his lead, houses such as Coleshill and Uppark set the direction for the kind of English domestic design that would be imported to the American colonies as the Georgian style. James Gibbs, trained in Rome to appreciate the late Baroque, returned to London to build St. Martin-in-the-Fields in a form that would become the model for innumerable churches in America (through Gibbs's illustration of it in his 1729 *A Book of Architecture*) and that was compatible with the emerging Neo-Palladian taste discussed in the next chapter.

# CHAPTER 13

# THE EIGHTEENTH CENTURY

Eighteenth-century architectural developments were complex, encompassing divergent elements and themes, some old and some new. Especially in central Europe, Late Baroque work lingered, particularly in major commissions for the nobility or the Catholic Church. Vierzehnheiligen and the Würzburg Residenz in Germany as well as Blenheim Palace in England and the later stages of French construction at Versailles all date from the eighteenth century.

In some quarters, architects produced confections such as Françoise Cuvillés's Amalienburg Pavilion at Nymphenburg Castle near Munich (1734–39). Within this diminutive garden pavilion, which includes kennels almost as elaborate as the principal salon, Johann Baptist Zimmerman's stucco ornamentation breaks out in a riot of color and texture to accompany the **boiserie** or gilded woodwork. This late flowering of the Baroque during the first half of the eighteenth century is known as the Rococo. The name combines the words **rocaille**, describing the organic shapes of water-worn rocks, plants, and shells, and **coquille**, meaning "seashell." In France, the Rococo was primarily a style for interiors, typified by the work of J.A. Meissonier (1695–1750), and Neo-Classical architects there eventually reacted against its excesses.

In the work of others there were already harbingers of things to come. While created during the Rococo period, Germain Boffrand's (1667–1754) manner looks back to the conservative classicism of Le Vau, and so anticipates the Neo-Classicism that would dominate French architecture in the second half of the eighteenth century. Boffrand designed the Parisian Hôtel Amelot (1712) around an elliptical court with loggias. Its varied room shapes, modest room sizes, and attention to service functions make it a model of convenience and comfort in striking contrast to the megalomania that was Versailles.

Radical new ideas were put forward in other domains. The eighteenth century witnessed the birth of the Enlightenment, the movement in which scientists and mathematicians laid the foundations for modern achievements in their fields; philosophers proposed rational forms of government that were put into practice after the American and French revolutions; archaeologists and explorers probed past and distant civilizations for an understanding of other cultures; and first traditional mechanics, then modern engineers invented devices and machines that were to transform industry, commerce, and transportation. Enlightenment historians also began the first accurate chronology of world events, and with it came an understanding of the architectural accomplishments of the various Western civilizations. Foremost among these were ancient Greece and Rome, and artists and architects traveled south in droves to swarm over the classical ruins, studying and measuring; many published their findings. The result would be Neo-Classicism. Even broader changes were brought about by the beginning of the Industrial Revolution, for convenience dated here to about 1750. It is difficult to find any aspect of modern society that remains untouched—positively or negatively—by this sea change in the way Western society attempted to control the world. As for architecture, new materials, new technologies, and new systems of construction would radically alter traditional building forms and would make completely new building types possible. Finally, the forces of Neo-Classicism and the Industrial Revolution led to an equally forceful countercurrent: Romanticism. For many, Neo-Classicism was too precise, too predictable, and too emotionless. For others, the Industrial Revolution brought not progress, but ugliness, brutality, and numbing same-

## Chronology

| | |
|---|---|
| Jean-Baptiste Colbert founds the Académie Royale d'Architecture | 1671 |
| Colen Campbell publishes *Vitruvius Britannicus* | 1715–25 |
| Louis XV begins his regency | 1715 |
| regular design competitions offered by the academy | 1720 |
| J. B. Fischer von Erlach publishes *Historischen Architecture* | 1721 |
| beginning of the European Enlightenment | ca. 1750 |
| beginning of the Industrial Revolution | ca. 1750 |
| French *pensionnaires* begin to study in Rome | ca. 1750 |
| Piranesi publishes *Vedute di Roma* | 1750s and after |
| Abbé Marc-Antoine Laugier publishes *Essai sur l'architecture* | 1753 |
| Edmund Burke publishes *A Philosophical Inquiry into the Origins of Our Ideas on the Sublime and the Beautiful* | 1756 |
| J. F. Blondel publishes the *Cours d'architecture* | 1771–77 |

Horace Walpole, Strawberry Hill Long Gallery, Twickenham, begun 1748.

Antiquarian Horace Walpole was fascinated by the English Gothic. Rather than being academically correct, this interior is a highly personal architectural statement that expresses the emotion of Romanticism.

ness. Romanticism offered visual and perhaps emotional relief from these developing phenomena in the form of Picturesque esthetic theory and its application.

## THE ENGLISH NEO-PALLADIANS

Even as construction was being completed on the grandiose Blenheim Palace, some English architects were turning away from the style of Wren, Vanbrugh, and Hawksmoor in favor of the simpler approach that they found in the works of Andrea Palladio. The leaders of this Neo-Palladian movement included Colen Campbell (1676–1729), a Scottish architect and editor of the influential book *Vitruvius Britannicus*, which appeared in three volumes from 1715 to 1725; Richard Boyle, third Earl of Burlington (1694–1753), a wealthy nobleman who practiced as an architect in addition to fulfilling government duties; and William Kent (1685–1748), an Englishman who originally trained in Rome as a painter and branched out into architecture and landscape design under the patronage of Lord Burlington. All three men were Whigs and staunch supporters of the House of Hanover, which had replaced the Stuart line on the English throne. Both the first volumes of *Vitruvius Britannicus* (1715) and Giacomo Leoni's English translation of Palladio's *I quattro libri dell'architettura* (1716) were dedicated to King George I. Central to the movement they spawned was a great respect for Vitruvius, enthusiasm for the buildings of Palladio, and admiration for the works of Inigo Jones.

Colen Campbell may well have been responsible for converting Lord Burlington to the cause of Palladio. His illustrations of classical English buildings in *Vitruvius Britannicus*, including country houses influenced by Inigo Jones as well as his own designs, brought him to the atten-

tion of Lord Burlington, who commissioned him to undertake renovations to Burlington House in London (since further modified and enlarged into the Royal Academy). At Mereworth Castle (1723) in Kent, Campbell designed a near-replica of the Villa Rotonda (as Palladio illustrated it) at a slightly larger scale (Fig. 13.1). He attached four Ionic porticos to a simple cube and crowned it with a pyramidal roof and dome. Mereworth contains several practical and ingenious devices, such as the incorporation of fireplace flues in ribs of the dome, with the cupola used as the chimney exit.

Like many aristocrats of the period, Lord Burlington went on the Grand Tour of Europe, traveling from 1714 to 1715; in 1719 he returned to Italy specifically to study the buildings of Palladio. There he met William Kent, whose work so impressed him that they began a lifetime of friendly collaboration. With Kent's assistance in landscape design and interior detailing, Lord Burlington designed his own variation of the Villa Rotonda at Chiswick House (1725–29) on the outskirts of London (Figs. 13.2–13.3). Chiswick is a smaller version of the Palladian original, enlivened by a certain amount of creative borrowing from various sources. It has one portico instead of four, and its octagonal drum and dome perhaps owe more to Scamozzi than to Palladio. Obelisks placed at the edge of the roof contain the chimney flues in an antique disguise, derived perhaps from similar features on villas in the neighborhood of Vicenza, while the garden elevation is distinguished by three windows of original design, composed of Serliana inside recessed arches. The interior spaces follow Palladian proportions and incorporate elements from designs by Inigo Jones in their details. Lord Burlington used Chiswick to house his architectural library and to provide space for entertainments; he actually lived in an adjacent building that was attached to the new villa only at one corner.

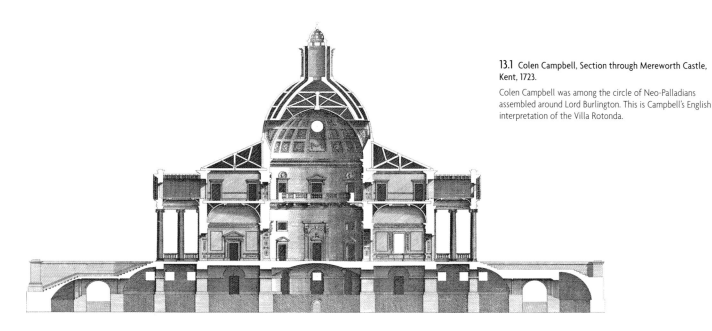

**13.1** Colen Campbell, Section through Mereworth Castle, Kent, 1723.

Colen Campbell was among the circle of Neo-Palladians assembled around Lord Burlington. This is Campbell's English interpretation of the Villa Rotonda.

**13.2** Lord Burlington (Richard Boyle), Chiswick House, London, 1725–29.

Lord Burlington was certainly thinking about the Villa Rotonda when he added this pavilion for entertaining to this estate. However, there are features not used by Palladio: the dominant twin stairs, the thermal windows placed in the octagonal drum, and the Pantheon-like dome.

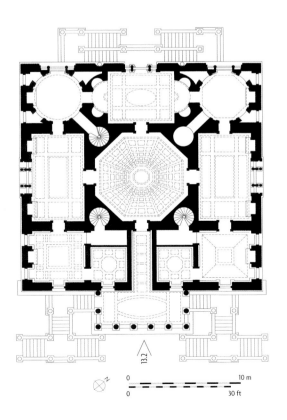

**13.3** Lord Burlington (Richard Boyle), Plan of Chiswick House, London, 1725–29.

The plan is even more unlike Palladio's work than the elevation. It is a nine-part grid of squares, rectangles, circles, and polygons.

0          10 m

0          30 ft

In addition to his work with Lord Burlington at Chiswick, Kent edited a two-volume collection published in 1727 as *Designs of Inigo Jones*. After about 1730 Kent began to practice architecture on his own, designing Holkham Hall in Norfolk in 1734 (Fig. 13.4). It is a grand country seat in the tradition of Vanbrugh and thus much larger than the villas of Palladio. Pavilions, pediments, Serliana, and a certain simplicity in the composition of multiple elements recapture the spirit of the sixteenth-century master in what could be termed a cluster of five Italian residences, consisting of a central reception block and four wings containing the kitchen, a chapel, a music gallery, and private rooms with associated accommodation spaces.

## THE RETURN TO ANTIQUITY

The Neo-Palladians in England were among the first, but far from the last, to undertake a thorough study and revival of architecture from the classical past. By the middle of the eighteenth century the artistic elite of Europe had developed a renewed interest in the buildings of antiquity. This had happened before. Carolingian architects had looked to Roman, Early Christian, and Byzantine buildings for inspiration, and the architects of the Italian Renaissance had made extensive studies of the ruins of Rome and the writings of Vitruvius. This eighteenth-century interest in antiquity, however, differed from previous "returns to Rome" in both its focus and its breadth of impact. Artists and architects of the Neo-Classical period sought an accurate understanding of ancient buildings and art works from the past, and historians placed these creative achievements in a proper context through their comprehensive studies of ancient civilizations. Popular curiosity about remote places and exotic cultures encouraged travel by dilettanti or gentleman amateurs as well as artists and architects.

During the eighteenth century, publications of measured drawings from ancient sites greatly expanded the available information relating to architectural history. Remains of the Greek colonial town of Paestum were closely examined, and the Roman cities of Herculaneum and Pompeii were discovered in the course of road construction in the kingdom of Naples. Excavations, begun at Herculaneum in 1735 and at Pompeii in 1748, eventually freed a wealth of buildings from the volcanic ash and mud that had buried both sites during the eruption of Mount Vesuvius in 79 CE. For the first time scholars and architects had abundant detailed evidence of imperial Roman architecture, decoration, and daily life. Thomas Major published *The Ruins of Paestum* in 1768, contributing measured examples of Archaic Greek temples to the growing knowledge of Greek architecture; in 1762, James Stuart and Nicholas Revett began publishing *Antiquities of Athens*, a series of four volumes completed by others in 1816. Roman settlements around the Mediterranean were also investigated. Robert Wood's *Ruins of Palmyra* (1753) and *Ruins of Baalbec* (1757) documented these important sites in the Middle East. The Frenchman Charles-Louis Clérisseau, later an adviser to Thomas Jefferson, published *Antiquities of Nîmes* in 1778.

This interest in antiquity was not confined to the classical civilizations of Greece and Rome. Napoleon's military expedition to Egypt in 1798 included a large group of archaeologists and engineers whose published reports, notably the *Voyage dans la basse et la haute Egypte pendant les campagnes du Général Bonaparte* (1807) and the twenty-volume *Descriptions de l'Egypte* (1809–22), by Baron Dominique Vivant Denon, encouraged popular enthusiasm for things Egyptian. Public interest in non-Western

# PIRANESI'S VIEW OF ROME

by Michael Fazio

Walking through Michelangelo's Campidoglio (see Figs. 11.38–11.39) and continuing south beyond the crest of the Capitoline Hill, an eighteenth-century visitor to Rome would have found this panoramic view over the ancient Roman Forum Romanum (Fig. 13.5) with the triumphal arch of the emperor Septimius Severus in the foreground and the Colosseum (see Fig. 5.29) in the background. Since Giovanni Battista Piranesi engraved this view, the scene has of course changed considerably as archaeologists and modernity have done their work. The valley between the Palatine and Esquiline hills has been cleaned up (of vegetation) and earth that had half-buried the monuments has been excavated. Fallen stones have been reassembled and inferior constructions removed.

In Piranesi's day, the panorama was incomplete, even mysterious, and the artist reveled in it. Raised in densely built-up Venice, surrounded by its tradition of dramatic urban-scene painting by artists such as Canaletto, and trained as an artist-engraver, Piranesi had come to Rome in 1740, where he supported himself by producing views of the city to be sold as souvenirs. Operating from his showroom on the Via Sistina atop the Spanish Steps (see Fig. 12.21), he became very successful, even a sought-after celebrity. But Piranesi was much more than a local entrepreneur. Fascinated by the grandeur that had once been ancient Rome, he participated in the radical questioning of the past that grew out of the Enlightenment.

In this view of the Forum Romanum, Piranesi ponders the effects of time and invites the viewer to imagine the scene centuries earlier when the Roman Empire was at its zenith. His moody, atmospheric depiction is enhanced by the eruption of erratic vegetation and an array of actor-like figures, all dwarfed by the ruins around them. This engraving and others like it appealed not only to the casual tourist but also to the

**13.5** Giovanni Battista Piranesi, *The Forum, or Campo Vaccino*, from *Vedute di Roma* (1745).

waves of pensionnaires, architectural students who came south from France and England to drink from the fountainhead of classicism.

Pensionnaires such as Marie-Joseph Peyre and Charles de Wailly, designers of the Comédie-Française in Paris (see Fig. 13.18), met Piranesi at the French Academy in Rome. The Englishman William Chambers knew him, and the great rusticated arches of Chambers' Somerset House in London (see Fig. 13.9) demonstrate Piranesi's lasting influence. Robert Adam, who became an inseparable companion of Piranesi in Rome, drew upon the engraver's often fanciful depictions of

ornamental motifs in developing a style of interior decoration in England that became fashionable enough to assume his name, the "Adamesque" (see Fig. 13.7b).

Piranesi's influence did not end with his reproductions of existing views or imaginative illustrations of the past. As his career evolved, he became more and more interested in architectural reconstructions and speculative archaeology. Experimenting with provocative evidence from the past, he sought to give architects a glimpse of architecture's inherent possibilities. Gradually his work became more and more eclectic, more and more fantastic, distasteful to some but ever more inspiring to others.

Piranesi's work illuminates the two major and competing currents in eighteenth-century art and architecture: Neo-Classicism and Romanticism. Firstly, the basis for his art lay with the remains of classical Roman antiquity. He packaged its images in a form that was desirable and portable. He also communicated with young designers studying in Rome. Piranesi's accurate rendition of the Roman monuments provided a ready source of information for these emerging Neo-Classicists. Secondly, his personal, perhaps idiosyncratic interpretation of what he saw matched the sensibilities of Romanticism and its manifestation in the buildings and landscapes of the Picturesque. Consequently, it is hard to imagine European Neo-Classicism or Romanticism without considering the work and ideas of Giovanni Battista Piranesi.

**13.6** Giovanni Piranesi, from *Carceri*, 1745. Engraving.

Piranesi's views of Rome inspired many architectural students. His depiction of moldering, half-buried monuments appealed to eighteenth-century Romantic sensibilities. The view of *carceri* (prisons) are his most imaginative spatial investigations, depicting as they do the interiors of fantastic, probably unbuildable, but profoundly evocative constructions.

civilizations had already been sparked by trading contacts and by Jesuit translations of the writings of Confucius and the Qur'an; soon architectural knowledge was extended still further by Thomas Daniell's *The Antiquities of India* (1800). Historical information documented through drawings of ancient buildings provided designers with a greater repertoire of artistic styles than ever before, and eighteenth-century publications made possible the freedom in design that subsequently led to nineteenth-century eclecticism.

The leading exponent of Neo-Classicism in Italy and an unabashed promoter of ancient Roman architecture was Giovanni Battista Piranesi (1720–1778), a man known

not so much for his architectural designs as for his 3000 or so engravings of architectural subjects. Piranesi even made a large-scale map of ancient Rome, including both actual buildings and imaginary projects composed of complex geometric shapes. From the mid-1750s until the end of his life, he issued a series of engravings titled *Vedute di Roma*, or *Views of Rome*. These views of ancient ruins rising enigmatically and provocatively from the accumulated detritus and Renaissance and Baroque buildings designed by the masters of those ages sparked the imaginations of artists and architects throughout Europe. Perhaps even more provocative were Piranesi's *Carceri*, or *Prisons*, a series of fourteen plates made in 1745, and reissued in around 1760, depicting vast spaces teeming with unidentified toilers whose labors are illuminated by obscure light sources (Fig. 13.6). The scale is gigantic, of the magnitude of the great Roman baths, while the spatial organization is even more complex. Arches, vaults, and staircases rise in the gloom and are revealed by shafts of light that perhaps mimic the spotlighting of partly excavated rooms in Pompeii and Herculaneum, where archaeologists tunneled into them from above. Because they were inexpensive, produced in large quantities, and easily transported, Piranesi's engravings were widely distributed across Europe in his own time, and they continue to impress architects and artists today.

## ROBERT ADAM AND WILLIAM CHAMBERS

An Englishman who traveled to Rome and became friends with Piranesi was the Scottish-born Robert Adam (1728–92). At the age of twenty-six he met and accompanied Charles-Louis Clérisseau to Nîmes. Together they traveled to Split, Croatia, where they made measured drawings, which Adam published in 1764 as *Ruins of the Palace of the Emperor Diocletian at Spalato, in Dalmatia*. Adam was initially as interested in Vitruvius as the Palladians, but during a trip to Italy, which lasted from 1754 to 1758, he became aware that, while the greatest archaeological interest followed Vitruvius in focusing on the religious architecture of antiquity, little thought was being given to the houses. Adam devoted his attention to what little was known about ancient residential design and interior detailing, in part because he realized that his architectural practice, like that of his father and brothers, would rely on clients who required homes, not temples or churches, based on the classical styles.

Architecturally successful but financially disastrous was his Adelphi scheme (1768–72) fronting on the river Thames in London. It was partially demolished in the 1930s, but a few pieces remain. The Adelphi consisted of brick town houses with stone and terracotta trim facing four streets, two parallel and two perpendicular to the river. Mimicking a typical palatial façade, the eleven houses facing the river had central and end pavilions and

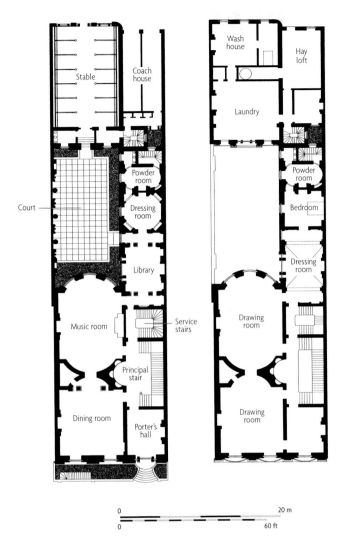

**13.7a** Robert Adam, Plans of the Williams-Wynn House, London, 1772.

On a long, narrow site, Adam disposed a variety of spatial types, including apsidal and double-apsidal rooms, rectangles, and polygons, without a trace of awkwardness. Not unrelated to developments in French hôtels, such residential designs provided a context for Adam's interior-ornamentation inventions.

**13.7b** Robert Adam, Williams-Wynn House interior ornament, London, 1772.

This drawing illustrates Adam's delicate, net-like ornament inspired by his investigations of ancient Rome and ancient-Roman inspired Renaissance wall paintings.

tall façade proportions, but not the bold pilasters or columns of an earlier age. Instead Adam introduced decorative panels filled with Greek acroteria. The interior decoration was similar, with Greek vine motifs on wall panels complementing the thin, flat geometric designs of the ceilings.

Adam's Williams-Wynn House at 20 St. James's Square in London (1772) demonstrates his dexterous planning and extraordinary system of interior design. On a narrow site he ingeniously arranged a variety of room shapes in a fashion akin to the French designers of Parisian **hôtels** (Fig. 13.7a). He employed a distinctive graphic method for representing interior elevations, arranging them orthographically around a room's plan as if they were walls folded down. Thus he could study five related interior surfaces simultaneously. The unified results are evident in the Williams-Wynn House where Adam spread a thin "net" of stucco ornament (Fig. 13.7b), inspired by Raphael's and Giulio Romano's inventive grotesques based on the sixteenth-century excavations at Nero's Golden House, and introduced colors taken from the excavations at Herculaneum and Pompeii. Adam claimed, and probably rightly, that his elegant, attenuated decorations brought about a revolution in English architectural taste.

Adam's work on country houses often consisted of remodeling or adding to late Elizabethan and Jacobean structures. An exception is his Luton Hoo, Bedfordshire, built in 1767–69 but damaged by fires and rebuilt twice in the nineteenth century. While Adam conceived the exterior to be rather plain, dominated on its west elevation by a full-width colonnade and a central temple front preceding a Pantheon-like dome and on the east by an attenuated hexastyle portico, his interior planning is ingenious. Primary circulation occurs along cross axes, with the longitudinal axis passing through an elongated oval expanded by niches, a rotunda with a ring of interior columns, and a rectangle with apse and lateral tripartite column screens—an overall arrangement remniscent of Roman baths. To either side, Adam arranged rectangular and double-apsidal rooms until he reached the end pavilions, where he returned to the rotunda and column-screen motifs. The spatial experience for someone moving along

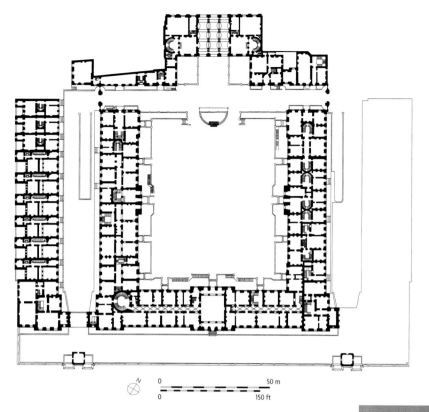

**13.8** William Chambers, Plan of Somerset House, London, 1776–86.

Unlike most Englishmen, William Chambers went to Paris for his architectural education. The scale and rigor of his plan reflect the French tradition of J. F. Blondel and the Ecole des Beaux-Arts.

**13.9** William Chambers, Somerset House river-front façade, London, 1776–86.

Along the Thames, Chambers created a façade organized in the French manner, with pavilions punctuating highly textured expanses of masonry walls. At the highly rusticated base, he inserted thermal windows and below them huge arches with prominent voussoirs, like something from Piranesi's etchings of grand remains in ancient Rome or Ledoux's gatehouses.

the axes or through the enfilade arrangement of banks of rooms must have been extraordinary before the many subsequent modifications.

The other major figure in English architecture of the last half of the eighteenth century was Sir William Chambers (1723–1796). His work says much about the strengths and weaknesses of English designers of the period. Chambers spent four years in Rome as an extension of his studies with J. F. Blondel in Paris. He produced an influential *Treatise on Civil Architecture* (1759) and even published *Designs of Chinese Buildings* (1757) as a result of his travels in China while a young merchant seaman. Chambers's great work is Somerset House on the north bank of the Thames in London, done while he served jointly with Robert Adam as architect to the King. Here Chambers was called upon to centralize the English government offices. After proposing a number of complex schemes, he settled on a rigorous C-shaped plan (Fig. 13.8), some 500 feet square, with a freestanding entry block along the Strand, the road running parallel to the river. It is comparable in formal conception to the many green residential squares developed throughout London. One can only imagine the cleverness and diplomacy required of Chambers in satisfying the myriad political fiefdoms, each determined to have the most prominent and desirable locations within the complex. Along the Thames the façade rises from a great rusticated, Piranesian arcade to linked pavilions reflecting Chambers's French training but marred by an undersized dome that reflects the English difficulty with monumentality (Fig. 13.9). Sculpted figures and groups arrayed throughout the complex celebrate England's maritime prowess.

## ETIENNE-LOUIS BOULLÉE AND CLAUDE-NICOLAS LEDOUX

In France the Neo-Classical movement developed somewhat differently than in England. French Enlightenment architects were interested in the primary geometric solids of the cube, sphere, and pyramid as the logical basis for architectural expression, an approach that paralleled the work of contemporary French philosophers, who were exploring rationality as a basis for human affairs. While there is some similarity in this approach to the early Renaissance interest in the circle, square, and triangle, the Neo-Classical designers of France went beyond previous geometric investigations to propose entire buildings dominated by the geometries of elementary volumes.

The most inventive French Neo-Classicists were Etienne-Louis Boullée (1728–1799) and Claude-Nicolas Ledoux (1736–1806), both of whom designed many hypothetical projects as well as real ones. Boullée's imaginary schemes give prominence to spheres, cylinders, hemispherical domes, pyramids, and cones, most often at a gigantic scale. His design for a **cenotaph** for Sir Isaac Newton, the discoverer of the laws of classical mechanics, is a hollow sphere 500 feet in diameter, the top half of which represents the dome of heaven, perforated with holes to give the impression of stars and the moon when viewed from the interior (Fig. 13.10). Suspended inside the sphere is a giant lamp representing the sun. Boullée explained his concept of the design in a tribute to Newton contained in his *Treatise on Architecture*: "Sublime mind!

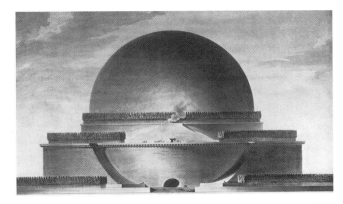

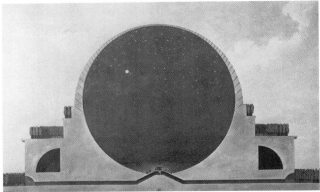

**13.10** Etienne-Louis Boullée, Cenotaph for Sir Isaac Newton, 1784.

The most striking feature of Boullée's design is certainly its intended vast scale, with the width of the sphere some 500 feet in diameter. The selection of Newton as the figure to be honored expresses Enlightenment admiration for reason through a celebration of the discoverer of the clock-like universe.

**13.11** Claude-Nicolas Ledoux, Plan of Chaux, 1775–79. Engraving.

In the center of the plan is the Director's House, with buildings for salt production flanking it and workers' housing in the surrounding oval.

Vast and profound genius! Divine Being! Newton! Accept the homage of my weak talents. . . . I conceive the idea of surrounding thee with thy discovery, and thus, somehow, surrounding thee with thyself." Another project by Boullée, this one for a national library, houses books inside an enormous semicylinder lit by an equally enormous skylight cut into the coffered vaulting. The vault is supported by stoa-like files of columns, and the columns are in turn supported by terraces of bookstacks working their way down to the main floor so that the books can be lowered from level to level by attendants, rationally obviating the need for hazardous step ladders.

Ledoux's designs for Chaux (1775–79) reveal his vision for an ideal town to include a saltworks (Fig. 13.11). Significantly, while completely Neo-Classical in their architectural language, the designs explore the phenomenon of eighteenth-century industrialization. In plan the community is organized in a great oval of workers' houses, with the buildings for salt-making placed across the lesser diameter. Outside the oval are gardens, recreational facilities, and various communal buildings. Through its integration of planned open space with residential and industrial development, the design for Chaux anticipated the Garden City movement of the late nineteenth century, which was similarly concerned with providing a healthy environment for city-dwellers. In architectural terms the linkage of man and nature at Chaux is expressed in basic geometries. The cemetery building is a sphere, symbolizing the eternal cosmos, and the wheelwright's house is identified by large circles incorporated into its façade. Ledoux's design for the Inspector's House at the Source of the River Loüe (Fig. 13.12) is shaped like a hollow cylinder set horizontally on a podium, with the stream flowing through the lower half of the cylinder and the rooms of the building arranged in buttress-like rectangular blocks along its tunnel sides.

None of these highly symbolic projects was constructed, although portions of the plan of Chaux were built between the towns of Arc and Senans. Ledoux's executed designs make use of simplified versions of the classical orders realized in heavily rusticated masonry. The authority of the director of the saltworks is stated emphatically by the heavy banded columns of his house. Under the portico of the main entry gatehouse, with its baseless Tuscan columns, a heavily rusticated apse beneath huge rusticated voussoirs becomes a grotto, and the windows of this building take the form of urns spilled over on their sides to disgorge petrified water. The severity of the composition reflects the state's jealous monopoly of salt production.

Ledoux's Hôtel de Thelluson in Paris (1778–83) is a remarkable exercise in the manipulation of three-dimensional space, both externally and internally. His composition for a newly developing residential section of Paris begins with a massive triumphal-arch gateway sunken into the ground as if it were a half-buried monument in ancient Rome (Fig. 13.13a). Entry is made through this arch, then along a two-part elevated carriageway over landscaped gardens, then through the corps-de-logis; a service court stands to the rear (Fig. 13.13b). A full appreciation of Ledoux's achievement can only be had by examining a longitudinal building section cut along the central axis, where his skill in modulating the ceiling plane and creating various lighting conditions is apparent (Fig. 13.13c). On the second or piano-nobile floor, one moves along the principal axis through the curving colonnade—treated like part of an embedded circular temple—into a grand oval salon lit from high windows by means of a truncated dome, then into an octagonal antechamber lit by a roof lantern, then into a square antechamber with enfilade connections along the rear wall.

Ledoux also built a series of tollgates for the city of

**13.12** Claude-Nicolas Ledoux, Inspector's House at the Source of the River Loüe, published 1804.

This surprising structure illustrates Ledoux's conception of an *architecture parlante*, or a speaking architecture. Here the river-keeper lives, appropriately, in a house through which water constantly flows.

**13.13a** Claude-Nicolas Ledoux, Hôtel de Thelluson, Paris, 1778–83, engraving.

In the foreground, Ledoux placed a gateway like an ancient Roman, half-buried triumphal arch. A walkway at the second level then leads back to the corps-de-logis, or main block of the house, with its central motif appearing as an embedded trabeated circular temple.

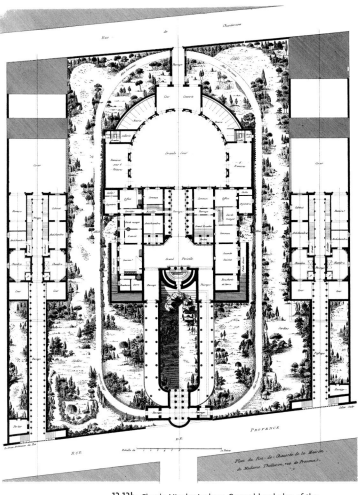

**13.13b** Claude-Nicolas Ledoux, Ground-level plan of the Hôtel de Thelluson, Paris, 1778–83, engraving.

Built in a developing Parisian suburb, this hôtel was placed on an open site. Consequently, Ledoux had room to combine house, courts, gardens, and systems of pedestrian and vehicular circulation.

**13.13c** Claude-Nicolas Ledoux, Longitudinal section through the Hôtel de Thelluson, Paris, 1778–83. Engraving.

Perhaps this section gives the most informative view of Ledoux's hôtel. It reveals the bi-level organization, the situation of the building components in the landscape, and the extreme manipulation of the ceiling plane in the corps-de-logis.

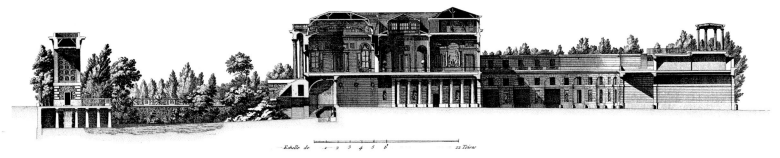

Paris, most of which have now been demolished. While they were despised by the Parisian people as symbols of tyrannical taxation and criticized at the time of their construction by other architects as inappropriate interpretations of the classical language, they have come to be seen as remarkably successful variations on a common theme: the urban gateway inserted at intervals in a circumferential city wall. Ledoux first argued for a set of triumphal arches based upon those of ancient Rome or the Propylaea leading into the ancient Athenian Acropolis. However, because his tollgates had to include rooms on one or more floors,

Ledoux was forced to conceive of new types, drawing upon both ancient and Renaissance precedents. His forms include gable-roofed temples, circular temples akin to Bramante's Tempietto, several variations on Palladio's Villa Rotonda, pavilions with banded columns like the Director's House at Chaux, and even some compositions that appear, like images from Piranesi, to be half-buried. The still-extant Barrière de la Villette (1784–89) is composed of a cylinder, without a dome but ringed with Serlianas, rising out of a low square block. The massing and the masonry, including baseless, square Tuscan columns, are so handled as to convey a sense of ponderousness befitting the structure's tollgate function. Taken as a group, these gates can be compared to Wren's city churches as evidence of fertile architectural minds.

## FRENCH ARCHITECTS AND THE AGGRANDIZEMENT OF THE STATE

During the eighteenth century, most French architects still worked for the government, as did Ledoux. Consequently, their buildings were most often intended to serve public functions and to aggrandize the state. In 1771–77, the architect, theorist, and teacher J. F. Blondel set forth his ideas about architecture in his *Cours d'architecture* (*Lectures on Architecture*), really the lecture notes from his own teaching. His writing explains in detail the essential elements of good architecture and the hierarchy of buildings, from common residences to those associated with the king. Blondel discussed *l'art de la distribution*, which involved arranging the plan, and *l'art de la décoration*, which involved composing a façade. Both were governed by **ordonnance**, **convenance**, and **bienséance**. Ordonnance referred to the correct relationship of parts to one another and to the whole. Convenance and bienséance concerned appropriateness and the correct form of a building relative to its purpose and social rank. Another influential writer of the period was the Abbé Marc-Antoine Laugier. In his *Essai sur l'architecture* (*Essay on Architecture*), he argued that all proper architecture was traceable to a single prototype in prehistory: the primitive hut. This pure building type, Laugier believed, was entirely rational, composed of columns, lintels or entablatures, and a sloping roof or pediment. Laugier's theories resonated in the Enlightenment architectural mind.

The architect Jacques-Gabriel Soufflot set out to build a structure according to Laugier's dictates that would exemplify the rich tradition of French architecture since the Middle Ages: the church of Ste.-Geneviève, first dedicated to the patron saint of Paris, since secularized, and now called the Panthéon (1757–90). Soufflot traveled to Rome and farther south to the dramatic ruins at Paestum in the company of the Marquis de Marigny, and it was the Marquis who secured for him the Panthéon commission. The Panthéon's central plan, deftly lengthened at the choir and portico, follows in the tradition of Bramante and Michelangelo at St. Peter's and of Wren's "Great Model" for St. Paul's. However, Soufflot based his design on Laugier-inspired freestanding columns and lintels rather than the traditional piers with pilasters and arches, and he experimented with concealed flying buttresses to stabilize the dome (Figs. 13.14–13.15). Openwork structure had been preferred by such highly regarded French architects as François Mansart and his nephew J.-H. Mansart, who were inspired by the spaciousness of local Gothic cathedrals. Like François Mansart at the central pavilion of his

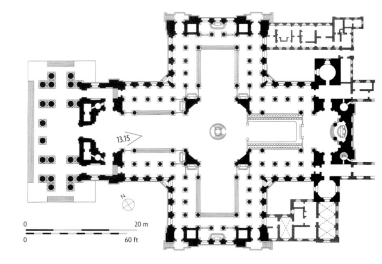

**13.14** Jacques-Gabriel Soufflot, Plan of the Panthéon, Paris, 1757–90.

Like the exterior, the interior of Soufflot's building, designed as a church, has been altered: the piers of the crossing have been modified, as the original columns began to fail. The many other columns remain intact, demonstrating Soufflot's interest in lofty Gothic openness.

**13.15** Jacques-Gabriel Soufflot, Panthéon interior, Paris, 1757–90.

As a young man, Soufflot had traveled to Rome and had been much impressed by the scale and monumentality of the ancient ruins. At the Panthéon he re-created this grandeur in a manner that also reflects his admiration for the great seventeenth-century French architect François Mansart.

**13.16** Ange-Jacques Gabriel, Petit Trianon, Versailles, 1761–64.

Gabriel's cool classicism represents the end of seventeenth-century French Renaissance developments begun by such men as François Mansart. This rigorous design attitude was never completely lost, even during the period of Rococo extravagances.

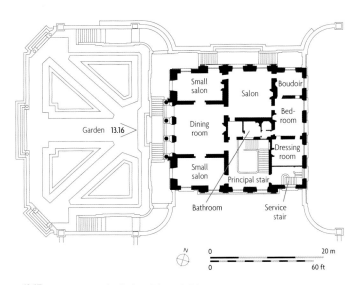

**13.17** Ange-Jacques Gabriel, Plan of the Petit Trianon, Versailles, 1761–64.

Each façade of this building is symmetrical. However, only one set of rooms, that on the west front, is symmetrically distributed. Otherwise the partitions are cleverly arranged to achieve internal convenience without sacrificing external formality.

château at Maisons-sur-Seine, Soufflot placed a columnar building inside a bearing-wall building. However, his skeletal system eventually proved to be too open, and the piers of the crossing had to be modified. In addition, some of his windows have since been infilled to make the building serve as a tomb for French notables, and the original sculptural program has been destroyed. Consequently, the Panthéon does not express the radical views of Laugier to the degree that Soufflot intended.

Ange-Jacques Gabriel (1698–1782) designed the Petit Trianon (1761–64) in the grounds at Versailles as a convenient and comfortable alternative residence to the sprawling palace. It exhibits a cool, chaste classicism and illustrates the cleverness of French domestic planning in the eighteenth century. The tripartite north, or entry, façade has a rusticated basement, Corinthian pilasters, and a prominent balustrade; it is comparable to some English Palladian villas but is at once more grand and more restrained (Fig. 13.16). To the south, the basement level disappears and the piano nobile opens out only a few steps above grade. On the west, freestanding Corinthian columns look out over garden parterres. The east façade offers yet another unique arrangement, having neither columns nor pilasters. These multiple-façade compositions, all symmetrical, in no way compromise the interior planning, where only the larger garden-front rooms are symmetrically placed (Fig. 13.17). Gabriel slid walls about, distributing them around a central service and vertical-circulation core while maintaining spatial order through enfilade connections among the various clusters of rooms. The restrained interior decoration, dominated by rectilinear paneling and mirrors, matches the character of the exterior and looks back to the Versailles interiors created for Louis XIV.

## DESIGNS BY THE PENSIONNAIRES

By the mid-eighteenth century, many French **pension-naires** were spending long periods in Rome examining ancient buildings and using them for inspiration. Their academic exercises often reveal a megalomania and almost obsessive fascination with antiquity that, applied to the realities of site, client, and budget, yielded imposing monumental buildings back in France. Such monumentality was essential in Paris, where the range and scale of public buildings were increasing: these larger buildings often covered their sites completely. Compositions were required that successfully included large expanses of unadorned wall surface, that provided adequate light and ventilation, and that were prominently displayed in the cityscape.

This attitude was given an opportunity for expression in the commission for a royal theater, at a time when the theater as a building type was a particular fascination of French culture. Marie-Joseph Peyre and Charles de Wailly, who had also spent time studying in Rome, designed the Comédie-Française with a Piranesian vision of the ancient city firmly in mind. Influenced perhaps by the ancient Roman insula, the theater had shops on the ground floor at its flanks. The main façade of relentlessly rusticated masonry features a temple front without pediment, the first such form used for a theater (Fig. 13.18). The order is Tuscan, a connection, the architects said, to Apollo, protector of the arts. Peyre and de Wailly presented theatergoers with a social spectacle. From the street, the audience entered into a square vestibule with monumental stairs to either side; de Wailly left a moody drawing of one of the stairs amidst a forest of columns that competes favorably with Piranesi's dramatic perspective scenes. The stairs led

up to a domed vestibule and, in turn, to the theater boxes. The circular arrangement of the theater seating, while controversial at the time, was thought by the architects to be the most intimate arrangement.

Jacques-Denis Antoine (1733–1801) designed the Hôtel des Monnaies, or royal mint (1768–75). His challenge was to house what amounted to a foundry within appropriately dignified quarters. On a triangular site, he cleverly arranged the minting shops and their many support spaces around a main court (Fig. 13.20). At the side wall along the Rue Guénégaud, he employed heavy rustication, as did Sansovino at his Venetian mint (see Fig. 11.58), to indicate the security that he had provided for the activities inside. For the main façade facing the river Seine and the city, he chose to cap a central pavilion with a deep attic story but, as at the Comédie-Française, no pediment and to stretch the wings laterally. In so doing, he produced a strongly horizontal, subdued, and elegant composition appropriate for a building that symbolized the strength of the nation's finances (Fig. 13.19). Spaces on the interior, such as the salon for the School of Mines located on the second floor of the central pavilion, are ornamented with a sumptuous inventiveness traceable to the architect's Roman experiences and his admiration for the work of Ange-Jacques Gabriel.

In 1770–75, Jacques Gondoin (1737–1818) built the Ecole de Chirurgie, or School of Medicine and Surgery. It is characteristic of French Neo-Classicism in its use of decoration to express and even influence societal values. The entrance façade is decidedly un-French, having no end pavilions or central focus, with access provided through a

**13.18** Marie-Joseph Peyre and Charles de Wailly, Elevation of the Comédie-Française, Paris, 1770.

Large theaters were a new phenomenon in eighteenth-century Paris. They were more than venues for entertainment, also being settings for social spectacle and something akin to temples of French drama.

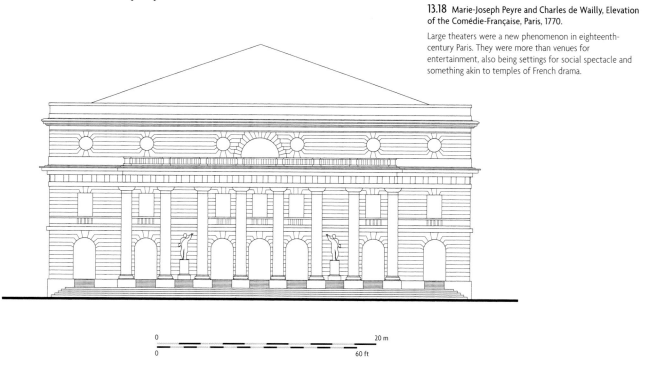

0     20 m

0     60 ft

**13.19** Jacques-Denis Antoine, Hôtel des Monnaies, Paris, 1768–75.

This building has an unusual French façade composition. Its central columns carry no pediment; the wings have no orders; and there are no end pavilions.

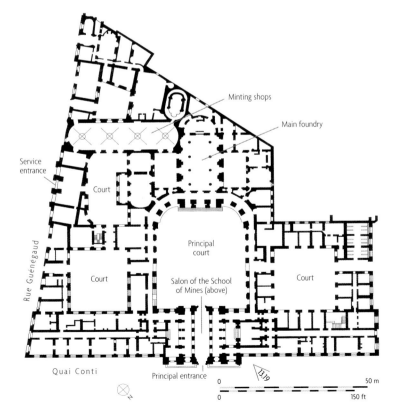

Minting shops

Main foundry

Service entrance

Court

Rue Guénégaud

Principal court

Court

Salon of the School of Mines (above)

Court

Quai Conti

Principal entrance

0    50 m

0    150 ft

**13.20** Jacques-Denis Antoine, Ground floor plan of the Hôtel des Monnaies, Paris, 1768–75.

The public front of this mint faces the Seine, with the principal court behind the center façade. The rooms of the main foundry and minting shops now house a coinage museum.

**13.21** Jacques Gondoin, Ecole de Chirurgie, Paris, 1769–74.

The idea of professional surgeons and a school for them was a new one in eighteenth-century France. At this entry façade, which combines a stoa and a central triumphal-arch-like motif, a sculpted panel includes the goddess of learning, Minerva, the king, and the genius of architecture.

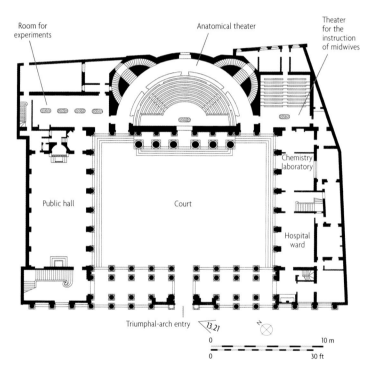

Room for experiments

Anatomical theater

Theater for the instruction of midwives

**13.22** Jacques Gondoin, Plan of the Ecole de Chirurgie, Paris, 1769–74.

In this plan, the entrance façade is at the bottom. Behind it, the court leads to a temple front, then the semicircular anatomical theater.

Chemistry laboratory

Public hall

Court

Hospital ward

Triumphal-arch entry

13.21

N

0        10 m

0        30 ft

triumphal arch-like opening behind a colonnade capped by a deep frieze and balustrade (Fig. 13.21). A sculptural panel shows the king and Minerva, both surrounded by the sick, ordering the construction of the building; the genius of architecture presenting the plan; and the figures of Surgery, Vigilance, and Providence guiding the actions of the king. Together, these images announce the ongoing elevation of French surgeons to the position of medical professionals, a change sanctioned by the French monarchy. Once through the entry, a visitor passes into a court, with a public hall to the left and chemistry laboratory and hospital ward to the right. Opposite the entry, a temple front announces the semicircular anatomical theater behind, its plan based upon the theaters of antiquity and its coffered semidome with oculus comparable to the Pantheon in Rome (Fig. 13.22). Benjamin Henry Latrobe chose this theater as his model for the old House of Representatives chamber in the U.S. Capitol.

## FRENCH ARCHITECTURAL EDUCATION AND THE ECOLE DES BEAUX-ARTS

The famous French architectural school the Ecole des Beaux-Arts has sometimes been presented as a bastion of Neo-Classicism. Actually its teaching was astylar, placing emphasis instead on the architectural-design thought process. Jean-Baptiste Colbert, minister to Louis XIV, founded the Académie Royale d'Architecture in 1671. Its purpose was to direct the arts toward the glorification of the king and, in turn, the state. The academy brought practicing architects together to discuss architectural problems and theories, and it presented public lectures. From 1720 onward, the academy offered regular design competitions for students, but it fell to J. F. Blondel to form the first actual architectural school in 1743. His success encouraged the academy to do the same, and by 1762 Blondel had become one of its professors. By the 1750s students were, of course, spending extended periods in Rome as pensionnaires. While in the Eternal City, they made careful drawings of ancient buildings and made new designs of their own. Architectural teaching was reorganized during the French Revolution and again under Napoleon Bonaparte. By 1819, the Section d'Architecture of the Ecole des Beaux-Arts was well established, with its own faculty and with quarters in a building adapted for its use by Félix Duban (1797–1870). The name "Ecole des Beaux-Arts" became synonymous with architectural education in France, to some extent in England, and eventually in America, and the Ecole continued to operate in this location until 1968.

While details of the educational system changed over time, the general philosophy did not. Would-be students had to pass a challenging qualifying examination that included diverse subjects from drawing to history. Once accepted, a student or **élève** attended a variety of lectures and was examined on those involving technical knowledge. In addition, he had to enter design competitions, or *concours d'émulation*, in the form of either the **esquisse**, a sketch problem, or the **project rendu**, a fully rendered project; they were held in alternate months. Students worked in an **atelier**, or studio, under the supervision of a *patron*, a practicing architect or a member of the Ecole faculty. When a project was issued, the student was given a **précis**, or program describing the essential elements of the project to be designed. He then entered *en loge*, that is, into a cubicle, and worked for twelve hours to produce a proposal. He would then return to his atelier to develop his schematic idea, assisted by comments from his *patron*, until the time of the final submission. At the appointed time, projects were picked up throughout Paris by a cart or *charrette*; students sometimes jumped on board to apply finishing touches, hence the term "**charrette**" used today by architectural students to describe a period of intense work at the end of a project. Comparing the initial sketch to the final solution, a jury would first determine whether the two represented the same idea, in order to ensure the originality of the scheme; then they would award points relative to the project's merits. It was through the accumulation of these points that a student could progress through the Ecole. The highest award given was the *prix*, which eventually became the "Grand Prix de Rome" and which paid the way for a winner to live and study in Rome for an extended period.

## THE CHALLENGE OF THE INDUSTRIAL REVOLUTION

In the minds of many, a great weakness of the Ecole des Beaux-Arts was its apparent lack of concern for developing technologies. Industrial technology advanced in the eighteenth century as inventors and technicians sought more efficient means for accomplishing the various tasks that were necessary to society: the spinning of yarn, the weaving and finishing of cloth, the mining of metallic ores, and so on. Machine work replaced the handwork of men and women, and engines powered by steam supplanted the motive power of men and horses. The changes these new inventions brought to society were many and far-reaching, including an increase in population, the rise of a new urban working class, the substantial growth of factory towns, some redistribution of wealth, and generally improved living conditions.

Among the developments were new and improved methods for making building materials, while scientific advances increased understanding of the how and why of structural design. Structural calculations were first applied to a new design in the building of the Panthéon in Paris; by the middle of the next century, it was possible to predict the behavior of most structural materials under specified loading conditions, freeing engineers and architects from complete reliance on an empirical understanding of what had worked in the past. Another invention, that of descriptive geometry, enabled designers to depict in drawings the shapes of complex three-dimensional objects, so that they could completely describe a building graphically, which relieved them of the necessity of daily attendance at the job site to direct the progress of the work. A related system for representing land contours made more accurate site work possible, as well.

One unfortunate result of these developments was the increasing separation between architecture and engineering. Since the Middle Ages the architect—described by Vitruvius as a man skilled in the design of everything from cities to buildings, mechanical devices, astronomical instruments, and machines of war—had been gradually released from responsibility for mechanical contraptions and items for defense, which passed instead to the newly recognized fields of mechanical and military engineering. Now a growing body of scientific data on materials provided the basis for civil engineering, which was taught at schools organized apart from architectural academies. Civil engineers were charged with the increasing body of utilitarian construction—roads, bridges, mines, factories, warehouses, lighthouses, and canals—while architects were employed on buildings where esthetics and symbolism outweighed pragmatism. Thus it was the engineer who first experimented with the building materials made possible by industrial technology, and it was in utilitarian structures that they were first used.

Of all the construction materials improved or developed

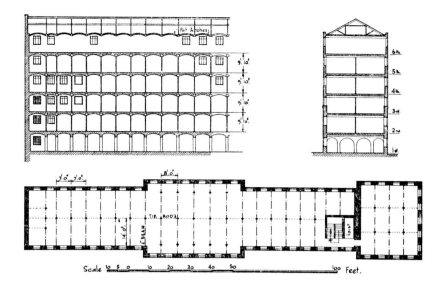

**13.23** William Strutt, Plan of and sections through West Mill, Belper, 1793–95.

With masonry exterior walls and a grid of interior columns, this mill has an open, flexible plan. A challenge for architects during the late nineteenth century would be expressing this internal skeleton on the exterior while covering it with fireproof materials.

during the Industrial Revolution, none was more important than iron. People had been smelting iron from ore since the prehistoric Iron Age, but the quantity of metal produced was small and its quality was highly variable. Therefore, the use of this material in buildings was limited to occasional ornamental work, fasteners, and hardware. Improved means of producing iron were sought by refiners, including Abraham Darby, whose furnace at Coalbrookdale, Shropshire, in England, began production in 1696. In an attempt to advance his work, Darby imported Dutch ironworkers in 1704 and soon succeeded in smelting cast iron for commercial use. Cast iron has a relatively high (3.5 per cent) carbon content and is brittle, though very strong in compression. By 1713 Darby had pioneered a method for producing cast iron by using coal instead of expensive charcoal in his furnace. The structural properties of his cast iron made it a suitable material for columns, where its 80,000–120,000 pounds per square inch (psi) compressive strength could be exploited. When used as a beam, cast iron is comparatively weak, having a tensile strength of only 15,000–30,000 pounds per square inch. If refined iron with a low carbon content (0.4 per cent) is hammered into shape instead of cast, it is known as wrought iron, a material with 70,000–80,000 psi compressive strength and up to 60,000 psi tensile strength. Its superior tensile properties made wrought iron much better than cast iron for beams.

Builders soon found applications for these two types of iron. Darby's furnaces produced wrought-iron railroad ties as early as 1750 and supplied cast iron for the world's first all-metal bridge at Coalbrookdale in 1779. Abraham Darby III, grandson of the pioneering industrialist, collaborated with the architect Thomas Pritchard to design a bridge of five parallel semicircular arches to span 100 feet over the river Severn, a watercourse prone to devastating flooding that could wash out intermediate piers. The bridge cost £6000, a large sum but only about one-third the price of an equivalent masonry span. Its design was conservative but it nonetheless represents the first essay in metal construction for bridges.

The incombustible properties of iron, together with its strength, were exploited in the construction of "fireproof" multi-story textile mills. As early as 1793 the Englishman William Strutt designed and built a six-story calico mill at Derby with cast-iron columns; his West Mill at Belper, constructed the following year, is similar (Fig. 13.23). The dust-laden air of textile mills, combined with coagulated oil and lint on the floors under the machinery and illumination from open flames, created ideal conditions for mill fires in which equipment, raw materials, and workers' lives were lost. To protect the structure, improve sanitation and ventilation, and reduce the opportunities for fire, Strutt and others designed mills with external walls of masonry, cast-iron internal columns, and protected wood beams. An early version of "fireproof" construction had the large wooden floor beams socketed into cast-iron shoes attached to the cast-iron columns. Segmental brick arches spanned from beam to beam, supporting level floors made of sand, screed, and clay tiles, with wrought-iron rods to tie the structure together. Undersides of the wooden members were coated with plaster; with sand on top and plaster below, the wood was protected from fire. Later improvements to this system substituted wrought-iron rails (forerunners of rolled **I-sections**) for the wooden beams: a surviving example of such a structure is the former Benyon, Benyon, and Bage Flax Mill at Shrewsbury in England (1796). Eventually the segmental brick arches at Belper were discarded in favor of other materials, but even with these changes, the metal-frame structure of today remains essentially the same as that built by Strutt in 1793–95.

Bridge designs, rather than building designs, generally exploited the structural properties of cast and wrought iron most directly, and it is there that the new materials were first used eloquently. For example, Darby and Pritchard's work on Coalbrookdale Bridge was soon surpassed by Thomas Telford (1757–1834), who built an iron bridge three miles upstream at Buildwas in 1795–98. Telford's segmental-arch bridge spanned 130 feet, with a rise of twenty-seven feet; he used less than half the iron required to construct the Coalbrookdale Bridge while achieving a longer span. Engineers in the nineteenth century continued to reduce material-to-load ratios and to

**13.24** Lancelot Brown, Blenheim Palace grounds, after 1764.

The English Romantic landscape garden drew some of its inspiration from the garden traditions of China. The English sought to imitate the irregularity of nature rather than artificially ordering natural elements in geometric patterns as in the Italian and French garden traditions.

experiment with systems, such as tensile structures, that were impossible in masonry or timber. These developments will be discussed in the next chapter.

## ROMANTICISM AND THE PICTURESQUE

Industrialization and rapidly developing new technologies hardly pleased everyone. Many saw them as a bane and looked for philosophical positions that would render them unnecessary. Even as Neo-Classical architects and antiquarians were using reason and intellect to reassess the past through archaeological work and scholarly inquiry, a parallel and often overlapping orientation in art and architecture was developing. Its beginnings can be seen in the English landscape movement that accompanied the Neo-Palladians during the first half of the eighteenth century. Developed further and driven by imagination and emotion, it became Romanticism. In some respects Romanticism was a reaction against the order and regularity inherent in Neo-Classicism; in others it was an expression of deeply held religious and moral convictions. Romantics delighted in the asymmetrical and the irregular for their highly picturesque qualities. Contradictory as this may seem at first to the ideals of Neo-Classicism, Romanticism was actually a complementary movement, and a number of established Neo-Classicists designed Romantic works as well. For example, Piranesi's engravings, which were manifestations of Neo-Classicism, fired the Romantic mind. His scenes of fallen vaults and moldering, half-buried monuments populated by enigmatic, tattered beggars expressed the Romantic longing for a perfect place and a perfect time that would remain always remote and unreachable. Ruins in general became a Romantic obses-

sion, as their ruggedness, wildness, and fragmentation illustrated the powerlessness of men and women in the face of irresistible natural forces and the melancholy relentless erosion of their works over time.

The esthetic doctrine of Romanticism was the Picturesque. Edmund Burke wrote about this doctrine in his *A Philosophical Inquiry into the Origins of Our Ideas on the Sublime and the Beautiful* (1756). Here he differentiated between picturesque conditions that were beautiful—possessed of such qualities as delicacy and smoothness—and those that were sublime—possessed of such alternative qualities as power, vastness, and obscurity.

It is clear that Boullée's interest in enormous structures aligns him with the sublime. Looking forward into the nineteenth century, it is equally clear that Romanticism could find fertile ground in an era that would become dominated by new sources of energy and huge machines, as the fruits, both sweet and bitter, of rapid social and technological change altered forever the scale and speed of daily life.

## THE ROMANTIC LANDSCAPE

William Kent's Neo-Palladian landscape creations, including the grounds of Holkham Hall (see Fig. 13.4), are probably more important than his architectural contributions. He is regarded as one of the founders of the English landscape-garden tradition, in which the landscape architect exaggerated and "improved" on natural qualities. Instead of the rigid geometric plantings favored by the French, English garden designers cultivated a certain irregular wildness. They exploited the natural contours of the land, formed trees into apparently natural patterns, and developed seemingly fortuitous, but actually carefully contrived, views of carefully sited buildings. Likewise, equally carefully planned views from the windows of buildings extended beyond nearby clumps of trees into the more distant landscape, where cows grazed as in a landscape painting. A ditch with a fence or hedge at its bottom prevented the cows from encroaching upon the lawns in the immediate vicinity of the house; discovery of this concealed barrier was a surprise, causing one to laugh or exclaim, "Aha!"—thus providing the name **ha-ha** for this landscape device. To the Neo-Palladians, who saw "natural" qualities in the architecture of Palladio and Inigo Jones, there was nothing contradictory in having a symmetrical classical house set in a landscape with naturalistic elements that reflected a painter's vision of the Roman countryside.

Lancelot Brown (1716–83) was the leading promoter of this Picturesque attitude toward landscape architecture. When asked his opinion of any piece of ground, he would say that it had "capabilities," and thus he became known as Capability Brown. He practiced as an architect in the Palladian tradition, but in that field he was a minor figure compared to Kent, for whom he worked as a gardener at Stowe from 1740. However, he knew much more than Kent about horticulture, expressed his ideas with clarity, and followed up his plans with informed supervision if the client requested it. Among his most celebrated works are the relandscaped gardens and park at Blenheim Palace (Fig. 13.24), laid out after 1764 and still extant. This plan included the creation of a serpentine lake and an encircling drive, the planting of tree clusters that still make for a pleasing dappled pattern in the landscape, and intermittent views of the building. Brown's impact on the English

landscape can hardly be overstated. Working throughout the length and breadth of the nation, he transformed large areas of unkempt countryside into the kind of lush parkland for which England has become renowned.

## PICTURESQUE BUILDINGS

Picturesque architecture in England began with follies, the playful use of medieval-inspired structures or ruins of structures as focal points in the layout of gardens. At Hagley Park, Worcestershire, Sanderson Miller built a sham ruin in the Gothic style in 1747, and other landscape designers soon copied the idea. Horace Walpole had his house at Strawberry Hill, Twickenham (Fig. 13.25) near London put up in a medieval manner by a committee of architects and literary friends. Work began in 1748, and the structure soon emerged as an eclectic assortment of Gothic details. The Holbein Room has a chimneypiece adapted from the tomb of Archbishop Wareham at Westminster Abbey; the Long Gallery (page 378) features **pendant vaulting** based on that in the Henry VII Chapel at Westminster Abbey; and the Round Room has ceiling plasterwork inspired by the rose window of old St. Paul's Cathedral. The Rococo chandeliers and purple wallpapers used throughout contribute to a sense of playfulness in this passionate, Picturesque amusement. This early phase of Romanticism in England is often termed "Gothick" (the spelling is deliberately medievalized) to reflect the rather lighthearted character of the work.

While the interior treatments at Strawberry Hill are interesting for their naïve antiquarian enthusiasm, the exterior is equally interesting for its attitude toward Picturesque massing. To understand this condition, it is necessary first to consider the plan, which has virtually no traditional formal order. Certainly there is a clear functional division between Walpole's rooms and those for his servants and other such practical concessions to the activities of daily life. However, to appreciate the house's design fully, one must view it externally and in three dimensions. Here, it becomes clear that Walpole, amateur though he was, intended for Strawberry Hill to present a rich silhouette against the sky, intended that its character should change as one moved around the perimeter, and intended for the ensemble to appear as though it had been built not all at one time, but had grown up randomly over time as had its medieval inspirations. This was a new way of thinking about building composition and one that would be fully exploited in the nineteenth century. Likewise, nineteenth-century scholars would make an intense study of Gothic buildings, establish a chronology of Gothic stylistic development, and master the recomposition of accurately reproduced Gothic elements. And the return of the Gothic would be only one among many such revivals in an era of rampant borrowing from the past, or **eclecticism**.

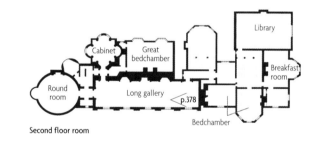

Second floor room

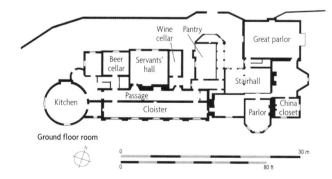

Ground floor room

**13.25** Plan of Strawberry Hill, Twickenham, begun 1748.

No one could call this plan conventionally orderly. However, antiquarian Horace Walpole was little concerned with two-dimensional geometries. Rather, he so arranged a variety of three-dimensional forms that their resulting massing would be varied and irregular and even surprising—in a word: picturesque.

# CONCLUSIONS ABOUT ARCHITECTURAL IDEAS

Historians commonly divide the history of the Western world into three periods: Antiquity, the Middle Ages, and the Modern Age, meaning, in this nomenclature, that the Renaissance represents the beginning of "modernism." While this subdivision is true in the broadest sense, it was the eighteenth-century Enlightenment, with its emphasis on scientific empiricism, evolving secularism, and nascent democratic thinking, and the accompanying Industrial Revolution (which has since become a technological and even informational revolution) that have more specifically ushered in the modern era.

Neo-Classicism arose during the heady years of the Enlightenment's emergence, becoming to some extent synonymous with it. Neo-Palladianism, an early-eighteenth-century English brand of Neo-Classicism, preceded both the Enlightenment and the Industrial Revolution and looked for its inspiration not directly back to ancient Greece or Rome but rather indirectly through Andrea Palladio's and, in turn, Inigo Jones' interpretation of classical style.

Inigo Jones, traveling as he did at the beginning of the seventeenth century, was precocious in journeying south to Italy to make direct contact with classical architecture, but he was far from the last such traveler to do so from England, where it became fashionable to make the Grand Tour. Robert Adam took such a tour in the mid-eighteenth century and was galvanized by what he saw at Herculaneum and Pompeii, where extraordinary evidence of ancient life and art was gradually being unearthed through archaeological excavation. Based on his study of ancient Roman wall paintings, Adam developed a style of interior ornamentation that pushed aside the heavy Palladian taste of the first half of the eighteenth century in England. Adam was also one among many who, after closely studying antique sites in Italy, Greece, and elsewhere, published their findings in an illustrated form and so made knowledge of them widely available. Adam's principal competitor, Sir William Chambers, followed the lead of James Gibbs and actually took up residence in Rome for a period of extended study. In the process, he encountered Piranesi, a contact reflected in his choice of huge, rusticated, Piranesian arches to support Somerset House on its Thames-side elevation (see Fig. 13.9). Chambers also fell into the company of the French pensionnaires, architectural students who had come south as a part of their formal architectural training.

France became the first country in Europe to develop architectural schools, meaning that design training was highly organized and was based on a codified body of architectural theory. J. F. Blondel ranked among the most influential of the French theorist-teachers, and his *Cours d'architecture* laid out the principles for an architecture that responded to the hierarchical ordering of society. Among the many pensionnaires who returned from Italy to work for the French government were Marie-Joseph Peyre and Charles de Wailly, designers of the Comédie-Française (see Fig. 13.18); Jacques-Denis Antoine, designer of the Hôtel des Monnaies (see Figs. 13.19–13.20); and Jacques Gondouin, architect of the Ecole de Chirurgie (see Figs. 13.21–13.22).

More polemical in his writing than Blondel, the Abbé Laugier set forth an ideology for Enlightenment architecture based on the fundamental elements of construction as represented by the supposed rationality of the primitive hut. Jacques-Gabriel Soufflot, subsequent to time spent in Rome, acted upon Laugier's *Essai sur l'architecture* in producing an extravagantly trabeated design for Ste. Geneviève in Paris: the Panthéon (see Figs. 13.14–13.15). While Soufflot necessarily made some compromises in adapting theory to practice, Etienne-Louis Boullée did not, choosing instead to present his architectural ideas in the form of imaginary, often unbuildable projects (see Fig. 13.10). Vast in scale and sweeping in vision, they fired the imaginations of many who saw them. Claude-Nicolas Ledoux produced rhetorical projects of his own but also built both for the Crown and private clients. His Inspector's House at the Source of the River Loüe (see Fig. 13.12) illustrates an *architecture parlante* by overtly expressing function through ideal, abstract forms. Of his barrières, or tollgates, that once ringed Paris, some reflective of the half-buried Roman ruins seen and admired by French architectural students, a few remain to attest to his inventiveness and unique interpretation of the classical language. His Parisian hôtels (see Fig. 13.13a, b, c) verify both the extreme cleverness and efficiency of French domestic planning and the concomitant French skill in manipulating space in three dimensions along the principal path of movement.

The French system of architectural education evolved to become the Ecole des Beaux-Arts. Instructed by a cadre of *patrons*, or teachers of design, some of them practitioners and some strictly academics, and working in ateliers, or open design studios, students learned by means of the *esquisse*, or short-term sketch problem, and the project rendu, a fully rendered building design executed over several months.

Eventually, the methods employed at the Ecole would come into conflict with the radical changes in building technology and emergence of new building types resulting from the Industrial Revolution. Likewise, the potential austerity of classicism and the undesirable effects of industrialization would stimulate the counter-development of Romantic sensibilities based upon the accepted wildness of nature rather the desire for its subjugation, and these polarities, together with burgeoning knowledge of the architectural past, encouraged eclecticism, or the indiscriminate borrowing of forms and motifs. In such issues, we can see the beginnings of those, such as environmental degradation and formalistic confusion, that confound us today. These and other associated conditions will be discussed in the next chapter covering the nineteenth century.

# CHAPTER 14

# NINETEENTH-CENTURY DEVELOPMENTS

Architecture in the nineteenth century was perhaps more varied than ever before. The freedoms introduced by Neo-Classicism and Romanticism encouraged revivals of other historical styles, such as Gothic, Greek, Islamic, Egyptian, Byzantine, and Early Christian, along with inventive new creations, such as the Chinoiserie, Japonais, Moorish, and Hindoo styles. As illustrations of this phenomenon, consider some English and American buildings designed after 1800. Colonial officials returning from India with their fortunes to retire in England built pleasure palaces such as Sezincote in Gloucestershire, its skin designed in the Indian manner in 1805 by Samuel Pepys Cockerell (1754–1827) for his brother Charles. In the same spirit, between 1818 and 1821, John Nash (1752–1835) built the Royal Pavilion at Brighton for the Prince Regent.

In many cases, styles were chosen because of their associations. For instance, the Egyptian style was proposed for buildings related to medicine, which was considered to have originated in the Nile Valley, and to death, since the great monuments of Egypt were erected for the pharaohs and their journey in the afterlife, or wherever suggestions of massiveness or eternity were desired, as in factories, prisons, suspension bridges, and libraries. In the United States, Benjamin Henry Latrobe (1764–1820) proposed an Egyptian-style Library of Congress within the U.S. Capitol, and Henry Austin built Egyptian cemetery gates at New Haven in 1837. Thomas S. Steward selected the Egyptian style for the Medical College of Virginia in Richmond (1854), as also did William Strickland (1788–1854) for the First Presbyterian Church in Nashville (1848). The church has a later but equally remarkable Egyptian interior, including a hypostyle hall painted in perspective on a wall.

Progress in materials science enabled architects and engineers to tackle construction problems in fundamentally new ways, contributing further to the diversity observable in nineteenth-century work. Buildings in Britain and the United States now termed "Victorian" often have little in common with one another, save that they were built during the exceptionally long reign (1837–1901) of Queen Victoria. Amid the stylistic revivals and engineering accomplishments came trends in design that were to have a major impact on twentieth-century architecture. This chapter addresses these developments.

## NEO-CLASSICISM

Three of the Neo-Classicists discussed at length in this chapter—Thomas Jefferson (working in America), Sir John Soane (working in England), and Benjamin Henry Latrobe (working in England and America)—all began producing architectural designs in the decades before the nineteenth

## Chronology

| | |
|---|---|
| Benjamin Henry Latrobe becomes Thomas Jefferson's surveyor of public buildings in Washington, D.C. | 1803 |
| Karl Friedrich Schinkel becomes state architect in Prussia | 1810 |
| A.W.N. Pugin publishes *Contrasts and True Principles of Christian Architecture* | 1836 and 1841 |
| invention of the balloon frame | 1830s |
| Karl Marx publishes the *Communist Manifesto* | 1848 |
| John Ruskin publishes *The Seven Lamps of Architecture* | 1849 |
| Joseph Paxton builds the Crystal Palace | 1851 |
| Charles Darwin publishes *Origin of Species* | 1859 |
| beginning of the Arts and Crafts Movement | ca. 1859 |
| first architectural school in the U.S. established at M.I.T. | 1861 |
| Eugene-Emanuel Viollet-le-Duc publishes *Entretiens sur l'architecture* | 1863–72 |
| Great Fire in Chicago | 1871 |
| H.H. Richardson builds Trinity Church | 1872–77 |
| beginning of Art Nouveau | ca. 1880 |
| invention of the fireproof metal frame for tall buildings | 1880s |
| Gustav Eiffel builds the Eiffel Tower | 1889 |
| Frank Lloyd Wright develops the Prairie House | 1890s |
| Sigmund Freud formulates his theory and method of psychoanalysis | 1892–95 |
| World's Columbian Exposition in Chicago | 1893 |
| Louis Sullivan publishes *The Tall Building Artistically Considered* | 1896 |
| formation of the Viennese Secession | 1898 |

Gustave Eiffel, Eiffel Tower, Paris, 1889.

The Eiffel Tower was seen as a blight on the Parisian skyline when it was built; it was maintained initially in part because of its use as a radio tower. Today it has become a symbol of Paris itself.

century, indeed, as early as the 1770s in the case of Jefferson. While these men could have been part of the preceding chapter, they have been grouped here, for reasons of comparison, with Germany's greatest Neo-Classicist Karl Friedrich Schinkel, who was the youngest of the group and did not begin architectural work on his own until the beginning of the nineteenth century.

## KARL FRIEDRICH SCHINKEL

Nineteenth-century Neo-Classicism in the area equivalent to modern-day Germany is most closely identified with the work of Karl Friedrich Schinkel (1781–1841), who shared some of the formal concerns of Boullée and Ledoux but relied much more on the elements of Greek architecture. Akin to Alberti, Schinkel saw architecture as a means to foster civic consciousness and saw polis-driven Greek classicism as its ideal symbolic language. He joined the Prussian public works office at the conclusion of the Napoleonic Wars, at a time when Prussia was seeking to raise its stature to that of a major European state with Berlin as its capital.

The Neue Wache (1817–18), or Royal Guard House (Fig. 14.1), located on the Unter der Linden, Berlin's most important ceremonial street, celebrated the emerging power of Prussia under King Friedrich Wilhelm III. Schinkel's final proposal placed a Doric portico between heavy pylons, both detailed with such austerity that the building achieves monumentality despite its modest size. Here, Schinkel succeeded in uniting the architectural forms of fortification and civic splendor.

In the summer of 1817, the Prussian national theater in Berlin, designed by Carl Gotthard Langhans in 1800–02, burnt to the ground. By early 1818, Schinkel had produced a new design for the Schauspielhaus (Fig. 14.2) to sit atop the old foundations between existing French and German churches. Schinkel treated the space captured by them and by his new structure as a great vestibule and placed the monumental entry stair on the outside, unlike the practice in Neo-Classical France where the stair

**14.1** Karl Friedrich Schinkel, Neue Wache, Berlin, 1817–18.
Here Schinkel projected a classical temple front forward from a pylon-like block. While modest in size, it is made monumental by Schinkel's skillful handling of proportions.

**14.2** Karl Friedrich Schinkel, Schauspielhaus, Berlin, 1818–21.

For this theater, Schinkel chose a wall treatment of superimposed pilaster strips that anticipates the grid-like façades of twentieth-century skyscrapers. He illustrated it and his other work in his book *Sammlung Architektonischer Entwurfe* (*Collection of Architectural Designs*).

became part of the initial, dazzling interior space. Schinkel's stair leads to a building at once monumental, taut, and planar. The entire structure is raised on a high base and is dominated by an Ionic portico with receding masses to either side articulated by plain pilasters and precise, shallow moldings that appear to have been stretched tightly over an internal skeleton. The plan is equally clever and precise, effortlessly uniting multiple room sizes within a symmetrical distribution.

Easily Schinkel's most famous structure is Berlin's Altesmuseum, or Old Museum (Fig. 14.3) (1823–28), the first public art museum in Europe. He sited it opposite the existing palace and arsenal to the south, creating a great civic court with a wall of trees along its east side. The museum's façade is a giant Ionic colonnade raised on a high base and stretching the full width of the building. Its orthogonal simplicity both creates a sense of urban dignity and pre-pares the visitor for the clever rigor of the plan behind (Fig. 14.4). Here, Schinkel placed a central rotunda flanked by open courts that are surrounded by flexible gallery spaces. Read as an interlocking set of classical prototypes, the museum is like the Pantheon caught between two temples both fronted by a stoa. From the second-floor stair landing, a viewer can look back through the double file of columns for a panoramic view of Schinkel's Berlin.

**14.3** Karl Friedrich Schinkel, Altesmuseum, Berlin, 1823–28.

Schinkel carefully planned for his museum along the banks of the River Spree. He also designed a loggia on the second level at the central entry to act as a viewing platform to the urban landscape outside.

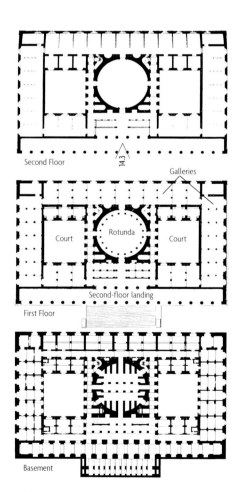

**14.4** Karl Friedrich Schinkel, Plans of the Altesmuseum, Berlin, 1823–28.

At the first- and second-floor levels, Schinkel combined a stoa along the front façade with a central rotunda, or pantheon of art, beyond, flanked by twin temples, their cellas' courtyards, and their prostyle columns part of the stoa front.

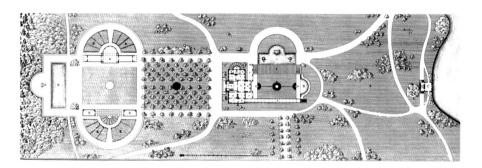

**14.5a** Karl Friedrich Schinkel, Plan of Charlottenhof, Potsdam, 1829–31. Engraving.

Schinkel was also skilled in planning such asymmetrical compositions as this one. He manipulated architecture, landscape, and water features to achieve calculated vistas and panoramas.

FAÇADE GEGEN DIE TERRASSE.

FAÇADE NACH DEN PFLANZENHÄUSERN.

**14.5b** Karl Friedrich Schinkel, Charlottenhof, Potsdam, 1829–31. Engraving.

Shown here from the *Sammlung* are two views of the temple-fronted villa that Schinkel made by remodeling a small eighteenth-century farmhouse into a formal ancient Roman villa rustica, or elaborate farmhouse.

Schinkel was equally deft in manipulating the Picturesque vocabulary of Romanticism. At the Charlottenhof near Potsdam (1829–31), he placed individually symmetrical, classically inspired buildings (Fig. 14.5a) in an informal but carefully conceived landscape setting that includes water features and level changes (Fig. 14.5b), certainly inspired by Schinkel's travels through the Italian countryside as a student.

## SIR JOHN SOANE

The leading exponent of Neo-Classicism in England at this time was Sir John Soane (1753–1837), an idiosyncratic architect whose work also has Romantic qualities. His building complex in London for the Bank of England (1788 and later; now destroyed except for its perimeter walls) used daylight in imaginative ways, since bank secu-

rity required absolutely blank exterior walls (Fig. 14.6). Soane met the challenge with courtyards, clerestories, and skylights that, when coupled with the pure forms of the rotundas and vaulted spaces of the interior, seem inspired by Piranesi engravings, and indeed Soane may have met Piranesi when traveling in Italy. Decoration was incised into the stone rather than sculpted out of it; detailing is generally linear, simple, and minimal. Soane's own

**14.6** John Soane, Bank of England rotunda, London, begun 1788. Drawing by J.M. Gandy.

Gandy was an architect in his own right, but is more celebrated for his many moody renderings of Soane's buildings, some shown complete, some shown during the process of construction, some even shown as ruins. In this drawing, Gandy illustrates Soane's preference for top-lighting, made necessary in the Bank of England by its many densely packed spaces with little if any exposure along the perimeter walls.

**14.7** John Soane, The Colonnade, 13 Lincoln's Inn Fields (Sir John Soane's Museum), London, 1812–37. Drawing by J.M. Gandy.

Soane made the rear portion of his own house into a museum. Here he collected paintings by Hogarth, etchings by Piranesi, and shards from classical and medieval sites visited by him or his friends.

**14.8** John Soane, Breakfast Room, 13 Lincoln's Inn Fields, London 1812–37.

The vault in this small room is the type preferred by Soane: low-slung arches springing directly from elegant columns or piers supporting a billowing, ribbed dome. His ornament was most often incised, or cut into the surface, in order to emphasize spatial volumes.

London house (now a museum) at 13 Lincoln's Inn Fields contains a diverse array of spaces and levels, lit by clerestories and top lights, articulated by layered wall planes, and reflected by both flat and convex mirrors (Fig. 14.7). Such a unique design does not fit easily into any one stylistic category, although one can detect traces of Neo-Classicism in the form of the shallow saucer-domed breakfast room (Fig. 14.8), where daylighting is brilliantly handled by means of a central lantern and lateral light monitors.

### BENJAMIN HENRY LATROBE AND THOMAS JEFFERSON

Soane's contemporary in the United States was Benjamin Henry Latrobe (1766–1820), who was born in England, educated there and in Europe, and practiced as an architect and engineer in and around London, before emigrating to America to become the country's first professional archi-tect. In 1803 Thomas Jefferson commissioned Latrobe to work on the U.S. Capitol, which had been begun by Dr. William Thornton and continued, sometimes haphazardly, by Stephen Hallet and George Hadfield. Latrobe completed both the north and south wings, introducing into the work his own designs for American orders: tobacco-leaf capitals in the rotunda of the Senate chamber and corncob capitals in the north basement vestibule. He also used capitals based on those of the archaic Greek temples at Paestum in the Supreme Court chamber.

In Philadelphia Latrobe designed the Bank of Pennsylvania (1799), combining there Greek Ionic porticoes front and back and a central dome with oculus that covered the monumental banking space. Late in his life, Latrobe was commissioned to design the Roman Catholic cathedral in Baltimore (Figs. 14.9–14.10). For this project he supplied two alternative schemes for the same plan, one based on

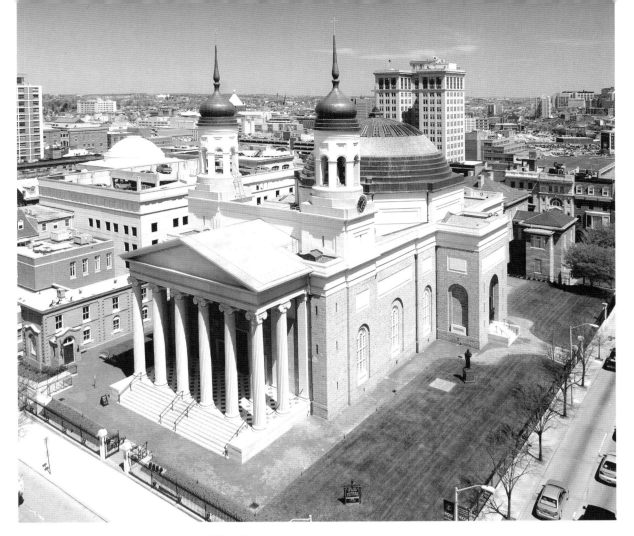

**14.9** Benjamin Henry Latrobe, Roman Catholic cathedral, Baltimore, 1805–18.

Latrobe presented both Gothic and Neo-Classical designs of this church to his client. The classical proposal was selected but did not include the towers seen here; they were added by the architect's son, John H. B. Latrobe. Notice the skylights at the top of the dome.

**14.10** Benjamin Henry Latrobe, Roman Catholic cathedral interior, Baltimore, 1805–18.

This building reopened in 2006 after a radical restoration. The interior now has its original paint colors, white marble floor, and largely white pews.

Gothic precedent and one on Roman. The latter version was selected by the client, resulting in a building of remarkable clarity, with a dome sixty-five feet in diameter at the crossing.

The only other American Neo-Classical architect who was as versatile and talented as Latrobe was the Roman Revivalist Thomas Jefferson (1743–1826), who also penned the Declaration of Independence and served as the country's third president. The son of a land surveyor and a graduate of William and Mary College, Jefferson trained to be a lawyer, yet he made contributions in many fields. He was a statesman, philosopher, scientist, educator, economist, inventor, and gentleman architect—in short, a personification of the Renaissance ideal of an educated man. While serving as minister to France in 1785, Jefferson was asked to propose a design for the State Capitol of Virginia

**14.11** Thomas Jefferson, Virginia State Capitol, Richmond, Virginia, 1785–89.

Jefferson based this temple design on the ancient Roman Maison Carrée in Nîmes, which he had seen and much admired while minister to France. Initially designed to stand on open ground, it is now surrounded by additions and high-rise government and office buildings. The flanking wings are not Jefferson's.

(Fig. 14.11). The model he prepared in response was based on the Maison Carrée in Nîmes, a building he knew then only through the architectural treatise of Colen Campbell. Jefferson converted the relatively small Roman temple into a two-story legislative building, with a circular domed assembly room that is not expressed on the exterior. He changed the Corinthian order of the Maison Carrée to the Ionic for Richmond because he feared American stonecarvers would lack the skill to handle the more complex Corinthian capitals.

Jefferson began his own home, Monticello (Figs. 14.12–14.13), in 1770 and used it almost as an architectural laboratory, continuing to evolve it until his death more than fifty years later. At first he envisioned a Palladian villa with two-story portico, but the final realization documents Jefferson's experience abroad as a minister to France

and his admiration for the new Parisian hôtels. More than any single influence, however, Monticello reveals his extraordinary powers of synthesis. In its final form, the house's central block is two stories tall above the basement, but through clever placement of fenestration appears to be a single story. The house is crowned by an octagonal dome, not apparent on the interior except as an isolated attic room, and is connected to the landscape by two walkways atop basement spaces that extend to enclose the rear lawn. Here Jefferson placed the service functions—kitchens, storage, the icehouse, stables, and so on—below the grade of the lawn, so that they remained close at hand yet out of sight. The walkways, which capture rainwater and channel

**14.12** Thomas Jefferson, Plan of Monticello, Charlottesville, Virginia, begun 1770.

This plan shows the ground floor of the central block and the basement level of the wings.

**14.13** Thomas Jefferson, Monticello, Charlottesville, Virginia, begun 1770.

For his own house Jefferson turned the familiar Palladian five-part organization backward in order to focus the complex on spectacular mountain views. This view from the front shows that Jefferson disguised the two-story elevation to appear as only one story.

**14.14** Thomas Jefferson, University of Virginia lawn, Charlottesville, Virginia, 1817–26.

Still the most admired example of campus planning in America, the University of Virginia was called an "academical village" by Jefferson. Seen here at the far left is Pavilion IV, then VI, VIII, and X, all connected by the colonnade.

**14.15** Thomas Jefferson, Pavilion VII, University of Virginia, Charlottesville, Virginia, 1817–26.

This pavilion design was suggested to Jefferson by William Thornton, winner of the competition for the design of the U.S. Capitol. It is the only pavilion façade given an arcade of arches on piers.

**14.16** Thomas Jefferson, Plan of the University of Virginia campus, Charlottesville, Virginia, 1817–26.

Extending from the library at the top of the scheme are the two files of five pavilions each connected by the walkways fronting dormitory rooms or what Jefferson called "ranges." Behind the pavilions are gardens and behind them more ranges as well as dining halls.

it to a cistern, terminate at the Honeymoon Cottage (above the "Brewins room"), where Jefferson and his wife first lived, and Jefferson's law office (above "Fodder storage"). The house's interior details testify to the sometimes idiosyncratic inventiveness of its owner. A clock in the entrance hall operates on a mechanism driven by cannonball weights that disappear through a hole in the floorboards. Wind direction can be determined indoors from a weather vane set on a tripod atop the east portico. Double doors between the hall and the drawing room open together even if only one is pushed because of a mechanism under the floor. Jefferson's bed separates his study and sleeping quarters, and its narrowing of space between the two rooms gives greater velocity to summer breezes.

In his later years Jefferson turned his architectural talents to the design of the campus of the University of Virginia at Charlottesville (1817–26), an institution that he had done much to establish and for which he served as rector after its opening in 1825 (Fig. 14.14). His early plan for the campus consisted of a U-shaped distribution of student rooms, linked by colonnades and punctuated by larger pavilions serving as lecture halls and faculty residences. Jefferson planned for the design of each pavilion to serve a didactic purpose, informing students about the best of architecture from antiquity. He called this extraordinary complex an "academical village," and he solicited

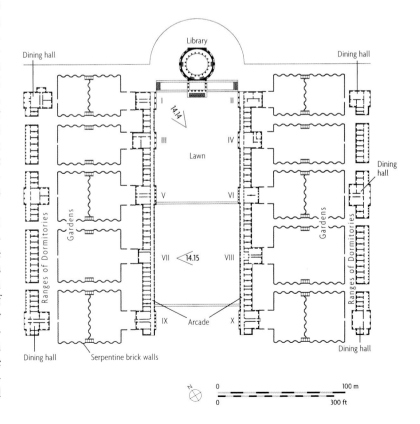

comments on the site plan and pavilion designs through correspondence with William Thornton and Latrobe. Thornton contributed a suggested design for Pavilion VII (Fig. 14.15); Latrobe contributed at least two and also recommended that the site plan should have a dominant focal element, an idea that Jefferson had originally rejected because of his opposition to centrality in government. The compositional improvement inherent in such a focus became obvious, however, and Jefferson designed a library based on the Pantheon (at half-scale) to serve as the head of the scheme (Fig. 14.16).

# THE GOTHIC REVIVAL

## A. W. N. PUGIN

Romanticism acquired a more serious tone with the widespread emergence of the ecclesiastical Gothic Revival. In England the leading Gothic Revivalist was Augustus Welby Northmore Pugin (1812–1852), a convert to Catholicism who regarded the Gothic as an embodiment of proper

moral and religious values from the past that he felt were all but absent in his own time. Unlike the "Gothick" designers, Pugin was well versed in the realities of medieval buildings, having worked with his father as a draftsman in preparing a four-volume study of Gothic ornament. It was another book by Pugin that brought him into the public eye, however. In 1836 he published (second edition, 1841) *Contrasts; or, A Parallel Between the Noble Edifices of the Fourteenth and Fifteenth Centuries, and Similar Buildings of the Present Day; Shewing the Present-Day Decay of Taste*, a brief volume whose long title sums up the author's message. Pugin compared his view of medieval and modern conditions by means of drawings (Fig. 14.17). The "Catholic Town in 1440" had fifteen church spires and a guildhall tower marking its skyline, while "The Same Town in 1840" had factory smokestacks as the dominant element in an industrial townscape; Protestant chapels of a vaguely classical form had replaced Catholic churches, and many spires had had their tops lopped off.

Pugin's comparison of public charity past and present was even more damning. The medieval "residence of the poor" was shown as a monastery where the almoner received the needy with kindness; fed them a hearty diet of beef, mutton, ale, cider, milk, porridge, bread, and cheese; robed them in clean garments; preached a sermon to enforce discipline; and provided them with a decent Christian burial. By contrast, the "modern poor house" was a prison-like walled building with a temple-front portico. The poor here were kept shackled in cells; fed a diet of small amounts of oatmeal, potatoes, gruel, and bread; cruelly beaten to enforce discipline; and loaded in a box labeled "for dissection" after death. Pugin was of course overstating the virtues of medieval institutions while detailing all the evils of his own time, but to him the medieval town was a total visual and religious environment, while the industrial town, with its vested interests and greedy capitalists, was a detestable degradation of human existence.

In 1841 Pugin published *The True Principles of Pointed or Christian Architecture,* in which he enumerated his ideals: "First, that there should be no features about a building which are not necessary for convenience, construction, and propriety, and second, that all ornament should consist of the enrichment of the essential construction of the building." He regarded the Gothic as the "only correct expression of the faith, wants, and climate" of England and advocated its use for all buildings, including modern secular ones such as railroad stations.

While writing treatises and giving lectures, Pugin was also busy as a designer. He collaborated with Sir Charles Barry on the competition-winning design for rebuilding the Houses of Parliament, which had been destroyed by fire in 1834. The overall conception of the building was Barry's (Fig. 14.18), while the profusion of lively and historically correct detail, inside and out, was Pugin's contribution.

**14.17** A.W.N. Pugin, Ancient and modern towns compared, from *Contrasts*, second edition, 1841.

In the lower view, the benign medieval town appears in urban harmony, announcing its values through the silhouettes of its church towers. In the upper view, the malignant nineteenth-century city is a deplorable cacophony of prison, factories, and almost-obscured churches.

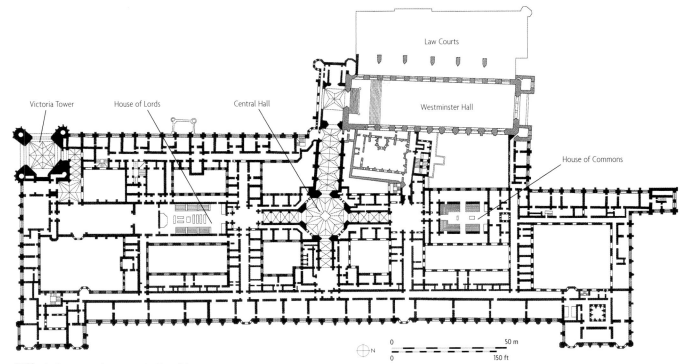

**14.18** Charles Barry and A.W.N. Pugin, Plan of the Houses of Parliament, London, 1836–68.

The long façade faces the Thames. Behind it, the dominant spaces are the House of Commons and the House of Lords. At the rear of the site is Westminster Hall, saved from the fire of 1834. The rigor of the plan belies the complex's picturesque massing.

## THE ECCLESIOLOGICAL MOVEMENT IN ENGLAND AND AMERICA

During the 1830s, the intellectual force of the Oxford Tractarian Movement and the Cambridge Camden Society led to reforms in Anglican church architecture. The resulting Ecclesiological Movement sought a return to forms of medieval ritual that had been swept away by the tide of the Reformation. Architects, clerics, and antiquarians exhaustively examined Gothic buildings and sought to identify features of churches and furnishings that contributed to liturgical and symbolic functions of the worship service and to develop rules governing church design. Pugin was viewed with suspicion by the Ecclesiologists because of his conversion to Roman Catholicism, but his buildings conformed to their views.

The full force of the Ecclesiological Movement in the United States was felt at the Episcopal church of St. James-the-Less in Philadelphia (1846–48) (Fig. 14.19). Drawings for the church were sent directly by the Cambridge Camden Society, which had based the design on the thirteenth-century church of St. Michael Longstanton in Cambridgeshire. St. James-the-Less was constructed entirely of natural materials, not superficial applications such as plaster, and its small **bellcote** became a typical feature of modest Episcopal churches in the U.S.

Richard Upjohn (1802–78) was the first American architect to follow Pugin's principles, although Upjohn was Episcopalian rather than Catholic and built only Episcopal churches as a result of his sincere belief that it was the only acceptable denomination. His first major commission was

**14.19** St. James-the-Less, Philadelphia, Pennsylvania, 1846–48.

St. James-the-Less was modeled specifically on the English church of St. Michael Longstanton. Drawings for it were sent to the United States by the Cambridge Camden Society.

**14.20** Richard Upjohn, Trinity Church, New York City, 1839–46.

Trinity Church has been dwarfed by skyscrapers, which once included the now-destroyed World Trade Center. In 1846 the church was a prominent landmark.

E. GUILLAUMOT.

**14.21** Eugène-Emmanuel Viollet-le-Duc, Iron-frame assembly hall from the *Entretiens*, 1863–72. Drawing.

Viollet-le-Duc was more successful as a theorist than as a practitioner. Interpreting Gothic structure as a highly rational response to the problem of load and support, he proposed the substitution of iron members as a logical use of the products of the Industrial Revolution.

for Trinity Church in New York City (1839–46), which was designed for a growing and wealthy congregation. Upjohn used Decorated Gothic for the church, which features an extended chancel, raised altar, and ceiling vaults constructed of wood and plaster rather than stone (Fig. 14.20).

### EUGÈNE-EMMANUEL VIOLLET-LE-DUC

The leading proponent of the Gothic Revival in France was Eugène-Emmanuel Viollet-le-Duc (1814–1879), an architect who shared Pugin's enthusiasm for medieval works. However, the moral and religious views that so strongly colored Pugin's writings were not shared by Viollet-le-Duc, who was more interested in the rational basis of medieval structure. He saw the system of rib vault, pointed arch, and flying buttress as analogous to nineteenth-century iron framing, and he aspired to a modern architecture based on engineering accomplishments that would have the integrity of form and detail found in medieval works (Fig. 14.21). His theoretical writings—especially the two volumes of *Entretiens sur l'architecture* (*Discourses on Architecture*), published between 1863 and 1872—stress the importance of rationality in design.

Much of Viollet-le-Duc's time was spent opposing the French architectural establishment's denial of all medieval styles. The only government-sponsored school for architects, the Ecole des Beaux-Arts, was dominated by architects working in classical styles, and efforts by Viollet-le-Duc and others to have its courses include the study of Romanesque and Gothic buildings met with little success. However, the extended controversy identified Viollet-le-Duc as an architect knowledgeable about medieval architecture, and from 1840 onward he was involved in scores of restoration projects for the major historical monuments of France, including Notre-Dame Cathedral and the Sainte-Chapelle in Paris; the abbey church of St. Denis; St. Sernin at Toulouse; Ste. Madeleine at Vézelay; the ramparts of Carcassonne; and the cathedrals of Reims, Amiens, and Beauvais. Out of this rich experience in dealing first-hand with medieval projects came the ten-volume *Dictionnaire raisonné de l'architecture française du XIe au XVIe siècle* (*Encyclopedia of French Architecture from the Eleventh to the Sixteenth Centuries*) (1858–65), which remains an important scholarly resource for medievalists. Twentieth-century architectural preservationists shudder at Viollet-le-Duc's philosophy of restoration—"to restore a building is not only to preserve it, to repair it, or to rebuild, but to bring it back to a state of completion such as may never have existed at any given moment"—which is quite the opposite of current attitudes toward this sort of work. Nevertheless, one must acknowledge that many of the buildings restored by Viollet-le-Duc might not have survived into the twentieth century without his intervention. For better or worse, his work marks the beginning of scholarly attempts at historic preservation. While the architectural projects he designed as original undertakings are not particularly distinguished, his theories had a major impact on the development of nineteenth-century rationalism and twentieth-century Modernism.

## THE ECOLE DES BEAUX-ARTS

The French school of architecture, the Ecole des Beaux-Arts, remained highly influential in France throughout the nineteenth century, principally producing public work, and had a profound effect on American architecture in both the public and private sectors in the second half of the nineteenth century. Ecole students learned to read closely a précis, or program, understand the hierarchical relationships of the various spaces, and distribute these spaces symmetrically along first major, then minor, axes, with an emphasis on the **marche** or movement through the spaces along these axes and in three dimensions. It was this system for ordering space that represented the best of the Ecole's methodology, not the eclectic skin that it allowed to be applied afterward, almost as an afterthought. However, the extraordinary skills of delineation fostered at the Ecole have sometimes made its designers seem more concerned with superficial appearance than with matters of structure and construction. This complaint played a major role in the supplanting of Ecole principles by those of European Modernism in the early twentieth century.

The elaborate system of Ecole instruction was unmatched in the rest of Europe and in the United States, where apprenticeship in the office of a practicing architect was the norm for architectural education during most of the nineteenth century. Some technical universities in Germany offered architectural studies as part of engineering programs, but it was American landgrant colleges that were to lead the world in placing architecture in the university curriculum. M.I.T. established a School of Architecture in 1861, and fifteen other universities had followed suit before the end of the century. Their curricula were all based on that of the Ecole des Beaux-Arts. Architectural graduates of American universities seeking additional polish would attend the Ecole in Paris, although they were not eligible for the Grand Prix competition, and American universities sought to hire Frenchmen from the Ecole to

**14.22** Richard Morris Hunt, The Breakers, Newport, Rhode Island, 1892–95.

Richard Morris Hunt was the first American to attend the Ecole des Beaux-Arts in Paris. The knowledge he gained there of academic planning and monumental design made him the architect of choice among the late nineteenth-century American elite.

direct their studies in architectural design. As a result of this cultural exchange, and the economic prosperity and westward expansion that occurred in the United States after the Civil War, the country has far more Beaux-Arts-influenced architecture than France.

### RICHARD MORRIS HUNT AND THE WORLD'S COLUMBIAN EXPOSITION

The first American to attend the Ecole des Beaux-Arts was Richard Morris Hunt (1827–1895), who entered the school in 1846. He had lived in Paris since 1832, when his family had moved there after the death of his father. Returning to New York after his education, Hunt established a practice that prospered greatly until his own death. Newly rich industrial magnates wanted houses that imitated the ancestral mansions of European nobility, and of all American architects Hunt was best able to provide the designs desired. His work for the Vanderbilt family—a town house on Fifth Avenue; a "cottage" called The Breakers at Newport, Rhode Island (Fig. 14.22); and Biltmore, their chateauesque country mansion at Asheville, North Carolina—are well known, but he also designed the base for the Statue of Liberty (1880) and the central portion of the Fifth Avenue façade of the Metropolitan Museum of Art in New York (1895).

Perhaps Hunt's greatest impact on American architecture came through his involvement with the 1893 World's Columbian Exposition in Chicago. Landscape architect Frederick Law Olmsted developed the site plan and a committee of the country's most important architects was formed under the leadership of Daniel H. Burnham to design the temporary buildings for the fair. Hunt used his influence as the profession's leading practitioner to direct the entire plan along Beaux-Arts lines. The principal

**14.23** Richard Morris Hunt, Administration Building, World's Columbian Exposition, Chicago, Illinois, 1893.

Hunt's Administration Building stands at the head of the Court of Honor and its lagoon. The "White City" captivated the American public. Using widespread exterior electric lighting for the first time, it started a movement that produced proposals for new civic cores in cities nationwide.

buildings, assigned to different architectural firms, were disposed around a large Court of Honor, with the domed Administration Building (Fig. 14.23) by Hunt at its head and an open peristyle by Charles B. Atwood terminating the vista out to Lake Michigan. To ensure unity around the Court of Honor, it was agreed that all designs would be based on the precedent of the Italian Renaissance; would use a common material, stucco (plaster), painted white; and would maintain a uniform sixty-foot-high cornice line. The effect was stunning. Visitors named it the "White City" and went away greatly impressed by the dramatic spectacle. The 1893 fair did much to advance the ornate and monumental Beaux-Arts style as the appropriate one for important American buildings and civic designs. Train stations, art museums, city halls, post offices, and churches were built across the country in emulation of the White City.

In their enthusiasm for Beaux-Arts architecture, fair visitors completely overlooked the truly innovative buildings in Chicago, the tall metal-framed buildings downtown. Louis Sullivan, an architect who participated in the design of the fair, later remarked that it set the cause of American architecture back by fifty years. His observation is a biased one, however, made late in his life when his career had gone into decline. The construction of great Beaux-Arts buildings was only finally terminated by the economic hardships of the Great Depression, but in truth the fair did no damage to the architects, including Sullivan, who formed the American avant-garde of the late nineteenth century.

## McKIM, MEAD, AND WHITE

Among American practitioners following Ecole principles, none was more successful than the firm of McKim, Mead, and White. One author has metaphorically described the careful Mead as the keel, the esthete McKim as the hull, and the flamboyant White as the sail of an imaginary ship in this, the first great architectural partnership in America.

William Rutherford Mead (1848–1928) was born into a family of painters and sculptors and began his professional life working in New York for German-trained architect and critic Russell Sturgis, whose Victorian Gothic buildings reflected the influence of architectural critic John Ruskin. Subsequent to travel and study in Europe, he returned to America and met Charles Follen McKim (1849–1909), then working in the office of H. H. Richardson. Always interested in construction, Mead provided the technical and business acumen needed in a large, complex architectural firm.

McKim's parents were Quaker abolitionists; their spirit of idealism remained with him throughout his life. Growing up in a hotbed of mid-century avant-garde culture, Llewellyn Park near New York City, McKim had contact with such luminaries as William Cullen Bryant, Horace Greeley, Henry David Thoreau, and landscape architect Frederick Law Olmsted. McKim attended Harvard's Lawrence Scientific School, worked briefly for family friend Russell Sturgis, then set out for Paris and the Ecole des Beaux-Arts. In 1870 he returned to work for Richardson, where he met Mead. In mid-1872 Mead and McKim set up a practice of their own.

Stanford White's (1856–1906) father was an art and music critic for literary magazines. Among his contacts were the architect Calvert Vaux, the painter John LaFarge, and Frederick Law Olmsted. Through Olmsted, White

**14.24** McKim, Mead, and White, Villard Houses, New York City, 1882–85.

The firm of McKim, Mead, and White established the model for the large-scale American architectural practice. They based this residential structure on Roman palazzi such as the Palazzo Farnese.

**14.25** McKim, Mead, and White, Boston Public Library, Boston, Massachusetts, 1887–95.

Charles McKim looked back to Henri Labrouste's Bibliothèque Ste.-Geneviève for his façade composition. He made numerous studies, including full-scale mock-ups of the cornice, before settling on his final design.

became a precocious apprentice to H.H. Richardson without the benefit of any formal architectural training. In 1878 White left to travel in Europe, and in 1879 returned to enter into partnership with Mead and McKim. He became legendary for his prodigious output of work and indeed for his appetites in general. The firm would eventually have more than 100 employees and produce almost 1000 commissions.

McKim, Mead, and White designed the Villard Houses (Fig. 14.24) in New York City in 1882–85. Consisting of

six separate houses arranged around a central courtyard, the building takes on the appearance of a single Roman palazzo. The Villard Houses are large, grand, chaste, and refined, and presented a face of civic decorum in a city then taking its place among world capitals, providing their owner, shipping tycoon Henry Villard, with instant credibility among his nouveau-riche associates.

Charles McKim was largely responsible for the Boston Public Library (Fig. 14.25) (1887–95), which faces H. H. Richardson's Trinity Church across Copley Square. Then housing the largest public collection of books in the United States, it symbolized Boston's cultural heritage. Its form has layers of precedent, the most recent being Henri Labrouste's Bibliothèque Ste.-Geneviève in Paris (see Figs. 14.31–14.33), itself based upon the lateral walls of Alberti's San Francesco in Rimini (see Fig. 11.15), a church that drew inspiration from both the nearby Arch of Augustus and the Tomb of Theodoric in Ravenna. McKim organized the library around a central court, placing the public reading room and elaborate entry sequence to the front of the site. The structure is faced with Milford granite but includes advanced technology such as thin-shell vaults. Sculpted panels above the entry were designed by Augustus St. Gaudens and the bronze entry doors by Daniel Chester French.

Back in New York City, the firm produced the vast Pennsylvania Station (1902–11) (Figs. 14.26a,b) which covered some eight acres on three levels but was tragically demolished in the 1960s. Based upon the model of Roman baths, the station provided a grand portal to the city as it brought in passengers some forty-five feet below the ground level and covered them with monumental vaulted spaces lit by great thermal windows; it brilliantly manipulated the hordes of people passing through each day.

## DEVELOPMENTS IN STEEL

In seeking to expand the market for iron and improve the desirable qualities of the material, nineteenth-century ironmakers experimented with new methods for manufacturing steel, which is an alloy of low-carbon iron and trace amounts of other metals. Small quantities of steel had been manufactured in India as early as 1500 BCE, and Celtic peoples in Austria, Spain, and Britain had made and worked the material at sites where iron ore containing manganese occurred in natural deposits. Blacksmiths, knifesmiths, and swordmakers could work the extracted iron and make steel, which was greatly respected for its ability to hold a superior cutting edge. Industrialization of this process required reducing the carbon content of the molten iron and using less charcoal in the furnace because that fuel was becoming scarce and expensive.

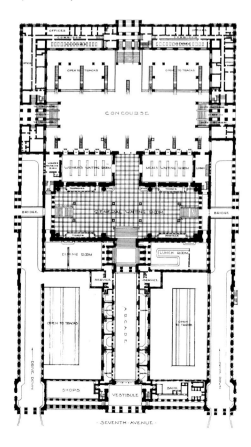

**14.26a** McKim, Mead, and White, Plan of Pennsylvania Station, New York City, 1902–11.

Of all of McKim, Mead, and White's planning accomplishments, none is more impressive than this train station. Here they looked to the Roman baths for inspiration in managing the huge crowds that passed through these vast spaces each day.

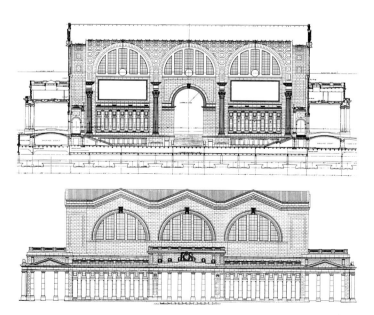

**14.26b** McKim, Mead, and White, Section and elevation of Pennsylvania Station, New York City, 1902–11.

Like the plan, McKim, Mead, and White's elevation and section were inspired by the Roman baths. The dominant features were the great thermal windows that lit the groin-vaulted waiting area. The destruction of this terminal must be considered a tragedy for American architecture.

**14.27** J.A. and W.A. Roebling, Brooklyn Bridge, New York City, 1869–83.

No suspension bridge has been more celebrated than this one connecting Manhattan to Brooklyn across the East river. Its steel cables were not raised intact but were woven by a spider-like machine that passed repeatedly from bank to bank.

An American ironmaker, William Kelly (1811–1888), was the first to develop a converter that burnt off excess carbon with a blast of air. He constructed seven of them at his works in Eddyville, Kentucky. When he was ready to apply for a patent on his pneumatic process in 1856, however, he found that the Englishman Henry Bessemer (1813–1898) had just been granted one for the same idea. Although Kelly's prior claim to the process was subsequently demonstrated, he received neither the recognition nor the financial rewards that should have been his. Bessemer became known as the inventor of the converter that made reliable quantities of steel efficiently and affordably. From 1875 onward, steel began to replace both cast and wrought iron in construction because its compressive and tensile strengths exceeded those of iron and it was cheaper to produce.

Steel was first used for railroad ties and in engineering works. The first steel bridge built in the United States was the Eads Bridge (1869–74) over the Mississippi river at St. Louis. Its designer, Captain James B. Eads (1820–1887), had been a riverboat captain and salvage operator on the river, and despite his complete lack of engineering training (he was assisted by capable engineers and mathematicians who provided the technical abilities he lacked) he was able to gain the confidence of local businessmen who backed the construction of the bridge. Eads understood the behavior of the Mississippi and insisted that the bridge foundations extend to bedrock, which lay under fourteen feet of water and eighty-one feet of sand. The bridge required four stone piers to support three segmental-arched steel spans of 502, 520, and 502 feet; the arches were fabricated of eighteen-inch-diameter cast-steel tubes, interconnected by triangulated bracing to form an integrated unit. Construc-

tion was accomplished by sinking pneumatic **caissons** for pier foundations and then cantilevering the arch sections out from each pier until the arch could be closed; using centering to support the arch in construction would have interfered with navigation on the river.

Steel was also employed for the major suspension bridge of the nineteenth century, the Brooklyn Bridge, connecting Manhattan and Brooklyn over the East river with a 1600-foot clear span (Fig.14.27). The bridge was designed by John Augustus Roebling (1806–1869) and constructed under the supervision of his son, Washington Augustus Roebling (1837–1926). They sank two gigantic caisson foundations for the bridge towers, and spun galvanized steel wire for the two main cables that supported the roadway. Each cable contains over 5000 strands of wire, compacted and wrapped with a continuous spiral of softer steel. Diagonal stays radiating from the towers provide wind bracing and are probably strong enough to carry the bridge's loads by themselves should the main cables break, while a stiffened deck checks any tendency the bridge might have to develop destructive vibrations resulting from wind loads. One of the most enjoyable experiences in New York City is to walk the pedestrian level of the bridge from Brooklyn Heights back toward Manhattan and its skyline.

# THE COMING OF THE RAILROAD

by Mark Reinberger

**14.28** W.P. Frith, *The Railway Station*, 1866. Engraving.

No single development had a greater impact on life in the nineteenth century than the railroad. After the first line opened from Stockton to Darlington in England in 1825, this new means of transportation spread with astonishing rapidity. By the 1840s railroads reached all parts of England. In the 1830s lines were begun in France, Germany, Ireland, Russia, and Italy. The first American line was the Baltimore and Ohio, which began operations in 1830. Ten years later the country had 3000 miles of track, and by the outbreak of the Civil War, 30,000 miles had been laid. In 1869, the first American transcontinental line linked the east and west coasts.

More than any other invention, the railroad linked all regions of countries together, creating unified nations and leading to more integrated economies and the century's stronger sense of nationalism. Regional differences in consumption, fashion, and architecture lessened in the wake of the railroads, which made possible rapid, long-distance mail delivery, the rapid spread of news, and the easier distrib-

ution of products including building materials.

The growth of the railroads spurred, and in turn was dependent upon, nineteenth-century industrialization. A large-scale railroad network was unthinkable without such elements of a modern industrial economy as a large and mobile labor force, the creation of steel for rails capable of withstanding heavy loads, the standardization of tools and machinery, finer tolerances in manufacturing, new structural capabilities for bridges and tunneling, and a prodigious amount of mining for coal. All of these industries, in turn, provided jobs for millions of workers.

Railroads also made possible the modern extended city, and allowed more than just the upper and upper-middle classes (who could afford a carriage) to live in suburbs. Subways and streetcars also made possible denser concentrations of businesses in city centers, necessitating the development of the tall office building late in the century. In America, railroads also helped open up remote areas to

mining and settlement and were responsible for much town-founding. They also tied together colonialized countries abroad, allowing international powers such as Britain to extract resources more economically and exercise closer control over places such as India.

The accompanying engraving (Fig. 14.28), painstakingly composed by W.P. Frith, depicts Paddington Station in London in 1866. The artist's acknowledged goal was the portrayal of modern urban life with its crowds, its mixture of social classes, and its greater bustle. He aimed to create a kind of literary tableau in the spirit of Dickens, then England's most popular author. He also lovingly portrayed the iron-and-glass architecture of a new building type—the railroad station—and the details of the train. The many tender family scenes in the image remind us that the train allowed for greater communication between friends and family, and diminished the isolation of rural areas. In both cities and country, the railroad station to some degree replaced the town square as the center of social intercourse.

## ARCHITECTURAL APPLICATIONS OF IRON AND STEEL CONSTRUCTION

Iron and steel were not admired for their architectural qualities in the nineteenth century: prevailing Neo-Classical and Romantic attitudes looked to past ages when buildings had always been of load-bearing masonry construction. Everything that architects and their clients admired and felt comfortable with could be constructed by using traditional materials and methods. Thus architects were slow to exploit the possibilities of iron and steel, which were first used in industrial utilitarian buildings, such as textile mills, warehouses, and greenhouses.

Iron was most elegantly employed in landscape gardening. Victorian England, prosperous from the wealth of its empire, had a fascination with the tropical plants that were brought back from India, Africa, and the Far East. Keeping these specimens alive in the cool, overcast climate of Britain required structures that could reproduce the humid heat of their native countries, so builders and gardeners set about erecting greenhouses large enough to contain palm or banana trees. Unfettered by ancient prece-

**14.29** Decimus Burton and Richard Turner, Palm House, Kew Gardens, London, 1845–47.

Greenhouses provided an impetus for the design of lightweight, quickly constructed, transparent structures. Between the iron arches, the glass frames were folded in alternate ridges and furrows, which provided rigidity.

dent, the builders turned to lightweight iron framing systems with glass infill panes. The Palm House at Kew Gardens, London (1845–47) by Decimus Burton and Richard Turner (Fig. 14.29) is an example of this kind of work, as is the Conservatory at Chatsworth House (1836–40) by Burton and Joseph Paxton. The strength of the building at Chatsworth derived from its glass-and-iron skin, which was arranged in alternating ridge-and-furrow-like folds.

### JOSEPH PAXTON

Joseph Paxton (1801–1865) was a landscape gardener by training, acquiring through experience his skill at building with glass and iron for greenhouses. He revolutionized architecture with the unsolicited design he submitted for a building in Hyde Park, London, to house the first modern world's fair in 1851. The building committee for the London exhibition had received 245 designs of all sorts, none of which was entirely suitable, so it had decided to produce its own, a great domed structure with a brick drum and adjacent walls. Even this traditional structure could probably not have been built rapidly enough and within the £300,000 budget. These circumstances made Paxton's tardy submission in July of 1850 all the more attractive (Fig. 14.30a). His design proposed an 1851-foot-long structure of glass and iron at an estimated price of £150,000; and through negotiations with the

manufacturers who would supply the materials, Paxton could guarantee completion on time. His scheme was accepted. In constructing the building, the contractors Fox and Henderson made one of the first large-scale demonstrations of prefabrication. The repeated iron-and-glass sections required a limited number of individual components, which meant that supplying factories could easily mass-produce the tremendous quantity of material required for the eighteen-acre building: 3800 tons of cast iron, 700 tons of wrought iron, twenty-four miles of rainwater guttering, 900,000 square feet of glass, and 600,000 cubic feet of wood (Fig. 14.30b). Materials arrived at the site preassembled into subsections, and final assembly proceeded at an unprecedented rate. Once the exhibition opened, the building was visited by about one-quarter of the population of England and was universally acclaimed for its vast, airy interior space. Journalists dubbed it the Crystal Palace, a name it has retained. The construction success and public praise for the Crystal Palace had much to do with the increasing acceptance of a larger amount of glass and iron in buildings designed by architects. After the

exhibition ended, the building was dismantled and reerected in a park at Sydenham, outside London, where it remained until it was destroyed by fire in 1936.

## HENRI LABROUSTE

Designers in France soon took up the techniques of glass-and-iron construction as well. Henri Labrouste (1801–1875) made a fine architectural use of cast iron in the Bibliothèque Ste. Geneviève (1842–50) in Paris. On the exterior (Fig. 14.31) the building presents a correct Neo-Classical façade recalling Italian Renaissance palace and church designs; but on the interior at the second-floor level one finds for that time an unprecedentedly great reading room (Fig. 14.32) which extends the length and width of the building, covered by light semicircular cast-iron arches. Sixteen slender cast-iron columns, with proportions previously found only in Pompeiian wall paintings, divide the long space into two barrel-vaulted halves. The ceiling vaults, consisting of interlaced wires covered with plaster, rest on the delicately scrolled cast-iron arches.

**14.30a** Joseph Paxton, Crystal Palace, London, 1851. Lithograph.

Joseph Paxton designed a building with prefabricated parts that could be mass-produced and erected rapidly. It stood in stark contrast to traditional, massive stone constructions.

**14.30b** Joseph Paxton, Crystal Palace interior, London. Lithograph.

Such a structure as this one was not considered to be "architecture" by theorist and critic John Ruskin because it lacked permanence. However, its lightweight, skeletal, transparent construction pointed toward the future.

In 1854 Labrouste was named architect of the Bibliothèque Nationale (the French National Library), an institution with a rapidly growing collection of books and inadequate quarters in which to house them. Labrouste worked on the buildings for the library for the next

**14.33** Henri Labrouste, Bibliothèque Nationale central reading room, Paris, 1858–68.

Labrouste's reading room for this library lies in the center of the plan. While the attenuated proportions of the cast-iron columns were new, the domical vaults were based on traditional masonry forms.

twenty-one years, designing around existing structures to create a central reading room (Fig. 14.33) and a separate bookstack, the first to be provided in a library. As in the Bibliothèque Ste. Geneviève, Labrouste used masonry for the Neo-Classical exterior walls and iron for the interior. The most spectacular use of iron is in the reading room, where nine domes, each nearly thirty-five feet in diameter, rest on a grid of sixteen slender iron columns. Illumination for the space comes from clerestories and oculus windows in each dome. Equally important, but less celebrated, is the iron framing of the bookstacks. Here there are six floors of shelving and aisle space, top-lit by skylights and light-wells. The grillwork of the floors and the columns supporting the shelf units form a structural framework independent of the enclosing masonry walls.

### GUSTAVE EIFFEL

The most famous French designer using iron in the second half of the nineteenth century was Gustave Eiffel (1832–1923). This engineer gained fame for his graceful bridge designs, such as the Garabit Viaduct over the river Truyère (1880–84) in southern France (Fig. 14.34), and then used his experience with iron construction to build the world's tallest tower, the 1010-foot-high Eiffel Tower, erected for the Paris International Exposition of 1889 (page 400). Not until the completion of the Chrysler Building in New York was Eiffel's tower exceeded in height, and it remains the largest iron construction in the world, for steel was rapidly becoming the preferred material for metal framing. Eiffel's tower design was derided by the artistic elite of France before and during construction, but Parisians of all classes were thrilled by the magnificent views from its top, and they soon adjusted to its gigantic silhouette being cast against the skyline. The opening of the tower in 1889 also provided the first large-scale demonstration of the passenger safety elevator, a model designed by the American Elisha Graves Otis.

### THE FIRST SKYSCRAPERS

American builders were to become the primary innovators in metal-frame construction for buildings. From about 1865 onward, architects in New York and then Chicago developed an original building type, the skyscraper, on a scale and at a level of sophistication unmatched by European designers. Tall buildings were a response to rising urban real-estate values and the desire of businesses to remain close to established centers of commerce. A whole range of technical improvements—including mass-pro-

**14.34** Gustave Eiffel, Garabit Viaduct over the river Truyère, Garabit, France, 1880–84.

Eiffel made the steel-frame bridge into an art form. Striking even today in its grace and lightness, this structure was considered absolutely shocking in the late nineteenth century.

**14.35** Cast-iron façade, Richmond, Virginia, ca. 1870.

Such cast-iron store fronts were attached to buildings with perimeter bearing walls of brick and internal, heavy-timber columns and beams. The cast-iron designs were often based on palazzo façades from Renaissance Venice.

**14.36** William Le Baron Jenney, Home Insurance Company Building, Chicago, Illinois, 1883–85.

William Le Baron Jenney was only one of the many architects searching for effective ways to fireproof steel-frame construction for late nineteenth-century buildings. His Home Insurance Company Building was among the first successful solutions.

duced structural components, the safety elevator, and fireproofing techniques—made them feasible, and their structural systems were most logically executed in steel frame, laterally braced to withstand wind loads.

Pre-Civil War building technology included the first structural use of iron for buildings in the cast-iron fronts and building frames that were mass-produced by men such as James Bogardus (1800–1874) and Daniel Badger (1806–1884) in New York and shipped as far as steamships traveled (Fig. 14.35). Cast iron was favored for its strength, fire-resistance, and plastic qualities. The classical detail desired for commercial structures could be economically cast from molds and repeated for as many bays and stories as desired, and the finished façade could be painted to resemble stone or other materials. The simplicity of construction appealed to many businessmen, who built increasing numbers of cast-iron structures from 1849 onward. Whole districts of them, such as SoHo in New York City, sprouted when extensive fires destroyed the previous timber-framed buildings.

In most instances cast-iron buildings lacked the wind bracing essential to high-rise construction, so they cannot be considered the first skyscrapers. However, James Bogardus introduced the European iron I-section, now universally employed as wide-flange sections for steel framing, and his concept of an all-iron building must have encouraged others to think more seriously about the alternatives to masonry bearing-wall construction. In the process of rebuilding the business district of Chicago, largely destroyed by fire in 1871, a number of inventive men perfected fireproofed metal-frame construction for high-rise buildings and thus created the skyscraper. William Le Baron Jenney (1832–1907), the designer of the Home Insurance Company Building (1883–85), is generally credited with the early development of the skyscraper, although the building is not entirely metal-framed as the first floor contains sections of masonry bearing wall (Fig. 14.36). Above the ground floor the masonry exterior was supported on shelf-angle supports attached to the frame, and steel rather than iron was employed for the structure above the sixth-floor level. The second Rand McNally Building (1889–90) by Daniel H. Burnham (1846–1912) and John Welborn Root (1850–1891) had all the elements of the modern skyscraper, including a completely steel frame designed by the structural engineering firm of Wade and Purdy, even though its external appearance looked

**14.37** Daniel H. Burnham and John Welborn Root, Monadnock Building, Chicago, Illinois, 1890–91.

The front portion of this building—back to the projecting cornice— is original. Built using traditional masonry bearing walls, rather than the new steel frame, it is highly expressive in its use of materials. The need for economy precluded external ornament. As handsome as it is, the Monadnock Building signaled the end of the bearing-wall skyscraper because its thick walls were not economical.

**14.38** Daniel H. Burnham and John Welborn Root, Reliance Building, Chicago, Illinois, 1894–95.

The Reliance Building's external skin of terracotta and glass clips onto an internal steel skeleton. This construction method anticipated the curtain walls of the 1950s and '60s.

backward rather than forward. Even where masonry bearing walls were retained, as in Burnham and Root's Monadnock Building (1890–91), an internal iron frame provided lateral bracing through riveted girder-column connections (Fig. 14.37).

Architects who produced the high-rise buildings of Chicago dating from 1875 to 1925 are collectively termed the Chicago School, indicating their common design attitudes and construction technologies. Innovative as the structures of these buildings are, they do not necessarily express their metal frames on the outside; most are clad in masonry, which gives the impression that this is the structural material. Their façades are derived from classical precedents, which, however, offered very few buildings in which the vertical elements dominated the horizontal, and nothing that even approximated their scale of multi-floor construction. Designers solved the problem in a variety of ways. The decorative terracotta cladding on the

Reliance Building (1894–95) repeats the same exterior elevation from the third floor to the attic story, expressing in the process the slenderness of its metal-frame columns and the depth of the beams supporting the floors (Fig. 14.38). Other Chicago School buildings were composed by grouping floors in three or four horizontal layers, which could then conform to the proportioning of columns and entablatures and the whole idea of streetscape established by Renaissance architects.

## SKELETAL CONSTRUCTION IN CONCRETE AND WOOD

The ancient Romans had, of course, built using concrete. But this material had fallen into disuse for some 1400 years before Joseph Aspdin developed Portland cement in 1824. As early as 1774, the English engineer John Smeaton had experimented with a mixture of quicklime and clay that hardened under water for his famous Eddystone Lighthouse. By the late nineteenth century, designers in America and Europe were using concrete reinforced with steel, most notably Ernest Ransome (1844–1917) and François Hennebique (1842–1921). Ransome, whose father had patented a "concrete stone," made innovations in both reinforcing steel and formwork that enabled him to produce a true concrete frame by 1900. Hennebique developed a system that he licensed to others, resulting in the construction of some 40,000 reinforced concrete structures by 1921. By 1894, Anatole de Baudot, a student of Henri Labrouste, had constructed the Parisian church of St.-Jean de Montmartre with a **ferroconcrete** skeleton, which expresses the theories of Viollet-le-Duc with whom Baudot was associated.

Another innovative system of skeletal construction developed in the nineteenth century, this time in wood, was the **balloon frame** (Fig. 14.39). Traditional wood-frame construction had involved heavy timbers shaped by hand and assembled using mortise-and-tenon joints held together by wooden pegs. While it inspired a high level of craftsmanship, it was an inefficient method of construction and one which had only a minimum of lateral bracing in the form of diagonal members. In the nineteenth century, the appearance of dimensioned lumber, that is lumber produced in standard sizes in water- or steam-driven sawmills, and the development of machines to mass-produce nails, made possible a radical change. The balloon frame consists of a sill plate from which rise long studs, placed at fairly close intervals, that are received by a top plate. These wooden members are nailed in place and braced laterally with diagonal studs. It only remained for plywood to appear in the twentieth century, which provided a lateral-bracing diaphragm as a result of diagonal nailing. Balloon framing eventually evolved into platform framing, where the first floor rises to a platform and the skeletal construction is repeated, eliminating the need for two-story-tall studs.

## THE ARTS AND CRAFTS MOVEMENT

The rapid pace of industrialization in nineteenth-century England created a new social order based on investment in mechanized and trading enterprises. Factory-made goods from soap to steel were widely distributed and generally raised the material standard of living. Yet the picture was not entirely a rosy one. For instance, factory towns, surrounded by long rows of dreary housing for workers, grew up in the Midlands, where water power and coal were readily available. We have already seen how the unrestrained capitalist system affected individuals such as A.W.N. Pugin, who was dismayed by the decline of the moral and spiritual values that he associated with the Middle Ages. Others were becoming concerned about the decline of artistic standards in manufactured goods because trained designers were not involved in creating such wares for industrial production.

### JOHN RUSKIN

These two issues—social values and the artistic quality of manufactured products—were at the heart of the Arts and Crafts Movement, which flourished from about 1850 to 1900 in Britain and later (1876–1916) in the United States. Originating in Victorian England, its ideas spread to Europe and finally found a "modern" resolution in postwar Weimar Germany. John Ruskin (1819–1900), a prolific critic of art and society, may be regarded as the originator of Arts and Crafts ideals. In Ruskin's view, the Industrial Revolution was a grievous error exerting a corrupting influence on society. Ruskin avoided technological progress whenever possible, insisting, for example, on coach transport rather than traveling on the railroads and vigorously advocating a return to the handicrafts, where the work produced reflected the shape of the tool and the passage of the worker's hand. Like Pugin before him, Ruskin associated high moral values with certain historical styles in which he believed truth and beauty in building were to be found. Ruskin had only contempt for those who hoped to teach industrial design to students. He wrote:

> The tap-root of all this mischief is in the endeavor to produce some ability in the student to make money by designing for manufacture. No student who makes this his primary object will be able to design at all; and the very words "School of Design" involve the profoundest of art fallacies. Drawing may be taught by tutors, but design only by Heaven; and to every scholar who thinks to sell his inspiration, Heaven refuses his help.

**14.39** Balloon-frame construction, 19th century.

The origin of the term "balloon" for wood framing remains unverified. This new method of building using mass-produced materials transformed building in wood from a craft practiced by highly skilled labor to an industry.

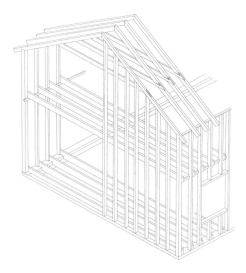

In *The Stones of Venice* (1851–53), Ruskin wrote about an architecture reflective of craftsmen's devotion to building. In *The Seven Lamps of Architecture* (1849), he laid out seven "lamps" or principles of great architecture. The Lamp of Sacrifice is dedicated to the craft of building and asks "Was it done with enjoyment. . .?" The Lamp of Truth expresses the moral quality necessary for exemplary building. The Lamp of Power explores the esthetic force of the sublime, the Lamp of Beauty extols nature as the source of architectural order, and the Lamp of Life demands outward expression of the human mind, while the Lamp of Memory argues for an architecture of permanence. Finally, the Lamp of Obedience urges that no new styles should be created, but that the Pisan Romanesque and the Gothic of northwestern Italy should serve as the only proper models.

## WILLIAM MORRIS

Ruskin's speeches and writings had a tremendous influence on a younger generation of sensitive men, who put many of Ruskin's ideals into practice. The leader of this activist group in England was William Morris (1834–1896), an Oxford divinity student who abandoned theology and studied both architecture and painting after encountering Ruskin's teachings. After his marriage Morris could find no house that met his standards of design, so he commissioned his architect friend Philip Webb (1831–1915) to design what became known as the Red House at Bexleyheath (1859–60), a redbrick structure that harkened back to the medieval domestic vernacular (Figs. 14.40–14.41). Its straightforward approach to structure and its undisguised use of materials surprised contemporary visitors, as did its elaborate use of decorative detail on the interior. Partly as a result of collaborating with his artist friends in the work on the Red House, Morris founded the firm of Morris, Marshall, Faulkner and Company in 1862, establishing workshops where artist-craftsmen created wallpaper, textiles, stained glass, utensils, furniture, and carpets using handicraft techniques. Morris's firm reflected his philosophy of dignity and joy through honest craftsmanship.

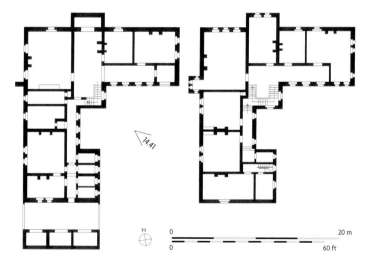

**14.40** Philip Webb, first floor (left) and second floor (right) plans of Red House, Bexleyheath, Kent, 1859–60.

The plan seems even less exceptional than the exterior appearance. However, its direct response to light and ventilation and to everyday needs anticipates the functionalism of twentieth-century Modernists.

**14.41** Philip Webb, Red House, Bexleyheath, Kent, 1859–60.

This house near London appears to be no more than a comfortable composition using forms familiar in the mid-nineteenth-century English countryside. What sets it apart is Webb's attempt to produce a design true to its materials and means of construction and expressive of the site and local culture.

It was intended to be an alternative to the factory system, where mass-produced elements were assembled by workers who had become little more than cogs in a machine and had no interest in, control over, or love for the goods produced. Morris believed that the provision of well-designed, handcrafted products in the homes of ordinary working-class people would raise them above the level of disinterested bread-winning employment. His concern for the welfare of the working class extended to his enthusiastic and active espousal of Socialism, and architectural historian Nikolaus Pevsner has argued that Morris's social consciousness represents one of the origin points for the development of European Modernism, with its casting of the architect as a molder of society. Unfortunately the output of Morris's workshops was insufficient to meet the needs of a broad market, and the price of his well-made objects tended to be higher than comparable factory-made goods, so his vision of supplying quality furnishings to ordinary people was never realized. The establishment of his firm, however, marks the first attempt to address the inferior quality of manufactured goods and the dehumanizing aspects of industrial production, a problem that would remain for others to solve. For instance, the writings of John Ruskin and the firm of William Morris and his partners inspired Elbert Hubbard to create his Roycrofters Workshops in East Aurora, New York; Hubbard's work was much admired by the young Frank Lloyd Wright.

## RICHARD NORMAN SHAW, C.F.A. VOYSEY, AND HERMAN MUTHESIUS

While in no way a social revolutionary, Richard Norman Shaw (1831–1912) made significant contributions to the development of Arts and Crafts architecture in England. Pugin's Gothic Revivalism impressed him as a youth. After traveling in Europe, he worked for Gothicist George Edmund Street, whom he considered his mentor. Shaw's early buildings are rationally conceived, as are Street's, but picturesque. Leyswood (1870) (Fig. 14.42) in Sussex has been much published in the form of Shaw's dramatic bird's-eye-view perspective. Its façades of "Old English" character, based upon Shaw's sketchbook studies of medieval buildings in Sussex, are carefully wrapped around a central court and produce a rich silhouette of clustered chimney stacks, multiple steeply sloping gable roofs, and a straightforward use of natural building materials. Much more ornamental, but equally rigorous and attuned to English precedents, is his New Zealand Chambers (1871–73) (Fig. 14.43), which looks back to the red brick and stone trim of the Queen Anne buildings of the early eighteenth century. Shaw designed it to be extremely efficient, including some eighty small offices and a suite for the owners, and composed the façade using tall **oriel windows** and lush wood, plaster, and stone ornament. Shaw's work influenced the development of the Queen Anne and Shingle styles in the United States.

**14.42** Richard Norman Shaw, Leyswood, Sussex, 1870. Drawing.

Richard Norman Shaw trimmed away the excesses of the Victorian Gothic to produce a rural vernacular known as "Old English." Picturesque Leyswood looks as if it grew over time in response to functional needs and the exigencies of its site.

**14.43** Richard Norman Shaw, New Zealand Chambers, London, 1871–73.

Shaw looked back to both the seventeenth and eighteenth centuries in creating his "Queen Anne" style for urban buildings. Characteristics include red brick, white window sash, and carefully controlled ornament.

Of the English architects influenced by the Arts and Crafts Movement, the most notable was Charles Francis Annesley Voysey (1857–1941), whose early commissions included wallpaper designs that owe much to Morris. He seldom used wallpaper or ornament in the houses he designed, however, preferring instead the purity of white plaster walls or unfinished oak paneling. Because of this omission, he was considered by others (he did not accept the label) as a pioneer Modernist. Voysey's houses, such as The Orchard in Chorleywood (1899) or Greyfriars near Guildford, Surrey (1896), are informal and reminiscent of the medieval vernacular. They feature wide, overhanging eaves; steeply pitched roofs; broad and bold chimneys; leaded casement windows; and either white-washed masonry or stone walls. Their interiors feature natural-finish materials, such as slate flooring and untreated oak paneling; Arts and Crafts furniture, some of

it designed by Voysey himself; and the evidence of hand-crafting in both ornamental and functional fittings, including carpets, pottery, clocks, candlesticks, hinges, and latches. Voysey created a bold but simple scheme in his design for Broadleys (1898), a vacation house on Lake Windermere for A. Currer Briggs (Figs. 14.44–14.45). Three bowfront windows extend through the two stories of the house, interrupting the roofline, to provide views over the lake to the west. The house is constructed of local stone, laid two feet thick in the walls, and is capped by a slate roof with a series of iron brackets supporting the overhanging eaves. The overall composition is asymmetrical yet dignified. With this design and other residential commissions from 1890 to 1905, Voysey helped set the style for much suburban housing built in England and the United States before 1930.

The spirit of Arts and Crafts design was carried to

**14.44** C.F.A. Voysey, Broadleys, Lake Windermere, Cumbria, 1898.

Early chroniclers of the Modern Movement saw C.F.A. Voysey as one of its pioneers. However, he eschewed such an attribution, considering his work to be instead in the tradition of yeoman buildings in the southern English countryside.

**14.45** C.F.A. Voysey, Plan of Broadleys, Lake Windermere, Cumbria, 1898.

Broadleys was planned to take advantage of views out over the lake. The great bowfront windows light each of the principal rooms, while bedrooms and service spaces stretch out to the rear.

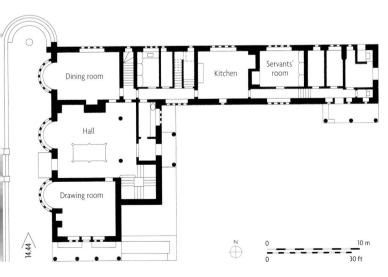

Germany by Herman Muthesius, a representative of the Board of Trade attached to the German embassy in London from 1896 to 1903. Germany was experiencing the same absence of good design in industrial products that had been noted earlier in Britain, and Muthesius was assigned the task of reporting on the state of English architecture and design, by then very highly regarded on the continent. The result was a three-volume report, *Das Englische Haus* (*The English House*), which documented all aspects of late Arts and Crafts work, from architecture to plumbing fixtures. On his return to Germany in 1903, Muthesius was appointed head of the Board of Trade, where he was responsible for selecting notable designers to teach in schools of arts and crafts. The impetus for the formation of the German design school called the Bauhaus can be traced to the work of the men he chose, including Peter Behrens, Hans Poelzig, and Bruno Paul, although a more complete discussion of that development must wait for the next chapter.

## ART NOUVEAU

A new and highly decorative style arose during the era known as "La Belle Epoque" (about 1880 to 1905). Nurtured by a variety of sources, including Late Baroque and Rococo, the Gothic Revival, the Arts and Crafts movement,

**14.46** Arthur Mackmurdo, Title page of *Wren's City Churches*, 1883.

The Art Nouveau style is characterized by the long, sinuous curve seen here. Mackmurdo was sympathetic to the writings and work of William Morris, John Ruskin, and Richard Norman Shaw.

**14.47** Victor Horta, Tassel House, Brussels, 1892–93.

At the end of the century, designers throughout Europe were looking for new ideas. In urban houses such as this one, Horta explored the tensile and ductile potential of iron.

the Celtic Revival, and the arts of China and Japan, it was a widely practiced style that was given different names in different countries. It was known as Art Nouveau in France, England, and the Low Countries, "Stile Liberty" or "Stile Floreale" in Italy, and "Jugendstil" in Germany. Whatever its name, it abandoned the multiple, backward-looking late Victorian styles and attempted to produce something excitingly new. The linear, sinuous lines found in Late Baroque and Rococo work were developed into free-flowing compositions based loosely on plant and animal forms. In fact, a parallel can be drawn with Celtic art or the Animal Style of the early Middle Ages, although Art Nouveau curves have a freedom to change width and direction that exceeds medieval practice.

One finds the earliest examples of florid ornament in England, although the fullest expression of the style was to come elsewhere. As early as 1876–77, James MacNeill Whistler (1834–1903), an American painter with strong English ties, created the Peacock Room for Frederick Leyland's London mansion, a design marked both by Japanese delicacy and by exotic peacocks, which represented the designer and his client feuding over the fee! (The Peacock Room is now installed at the Freer Gallery in Washington, D.C.) Arthur Mackmurdo's (1851–1942) swirling linear design for the title-page of *Wren's City Churches* (1883) is commonly cited as the first true Art Nouveau piece (Fig. 14.46), but its influence was limited. Wallpapers and carpets designed by William Morris at

about the same time share its linearity, as do the illustrations and decorative flourishes included in the Kelmscott Press editions of books published by Morris after 1890. Other illustrators, especially Aubrey Beardsley, made woodcuts that exhibit the lively, curving Art Nouveau line.

If one looks beneath the florid surface of Art Nouveau work, however, there are more substantive forces at work. On the one hand, Art Nouveau architecture manifested through its slender iron construction the kind of direct, expressive, skeletal structure advocated by the rationalist Viollet-le-Duc. On the other, there are moments in Art Nouveau interiors when space itself seems to flow and openness dominates, anticipating the more radical spatial experiments of such early twentieth-century architects as Adolf Loos.

### VICTOR HORTA AND HECTOR GUIMARD

Art Nouveau architects turned structural necessity into a language of organically derived curves. The earliest architectural innovator was Victor Horta, a Belgian architect

**14.48** Victor Horta, Hotel Van Eetvelde interior, Brussels, 1897.

On his interiors, Horta used iron for columns, ceilings, windows, and handrails. Here he made the stairwell a brilliantly lighted core in the constrained urban environment.

**14.49** Hector Guimard, Métro entrance, Paris, 1899–1904.

Guimard's Métro stations still cover the entries into several of Paris's subway stations. In this example, plant-like iron members support a fan-like canopy.

and the designer of the Tassel House in Brussels, built in 1892–93 (Fig. 14.47). Horta incorporated swirling tendril designs not only in surface patterning on floors, walls, and ceilings, but also in structural elements such as the staircase, balustrades, and balcony railings. Historian Sigfried Giedion celebrated Horta's "flexible" groundplan with its levels and half-levels and interior light-wells, seeing it as the forerunner of the subsequent spatial investigations by Modernists such as Adolf Loos and Ludwig Mies van der Rohe. The interior of Horta's Hotel Van Eetvelde (1897) in Brussels exhibits these same qualities (Fig. 14.48). His later Maison du Peuple (1896–99) exploited its structural relationship to plant forms, particularly in the upper-floor auditorium, where undulating iron ceiling trusses merged with upright supports in the manner of branches leaving a tree trunk. Even the balcony was sculpted into a curvilinear form, its delicate supports terminating as protective railings. While the expressive linearity of iron construction was masterfully handled in this, the first iron-and-glass

façade building in Belgium, the plan was quite traditional, with a central axis and cross axis on the ground floor.

Hector Guimard (1867–1942) was the French architect most celebrated for his Art Nouveau designs. The most famous of his works were made from 1899 to 1904 for the entrances to the Métropolitain, or Métro, the Paris subway system (Fig. 14.49). These are canopies over staircases that descend from the sidewalk, and Guimard provided several designs that employ wrought-iron swirls and curves, some of which support glass roofs. The unity of these little projects is remarkable, for all the elements are deftly integrated in the plant-like forms. Lighting standards (upright supports) are terminated by bud-shaped electric bulbs, while patterns derived from vegetable leaves are used as infill on the railings. Guimard's other architectural projects reflect his ability to blend the decorative with the functional, as can be seen at the Castel Béranger (1894–98), an apartment building in Paris, where latent medievalism is nicely balanced by free-flowing asymmetrical decoration in iron and ceramic to form a unified whole.

**14.50** Antonio Gaudí, Façade of the Nativity, Church of the Sagrada Familia, Barcelona, begun 1882.

Partly inspired by the Catalan Gothic, showing traces of Cubism, and commonly associated with Art Nouveau, the Sagrada Familia fits into no single stylistic category. Like many before him, Gaudí drew upon nature and exploited local methods of workmanship.

## ANTONIO GAUDÍ

In Spain, Art Nouveau reached its most idiosyncratic expression in the work of Antonio Gaudí (1852–1926), a Catalan influenced by the writings of Ruskin who began as a Gothic Revivalist. Because of his interest in medieval styles, he was asked in 1884 to take charge of construction of the Sagrada Familia (the Expiatory Temple of the Holy Family) in Barcelona, begun two years earlier by another Gothic Revivalist and still incomplete to this day. In the course of work on the Sagrada Familia and on the Colònia Güell Chapel, where he hung sandbags on ropes and covered them with canvas to determine ideal vault cross sections, Gaudí moved away from the Gothic Revival style to an intensely personal one that he used for apartment buildings, houses, and landscape designs as well as ecclesiastical works. While his three-dimensional curvilinear forms, floral decoration, and plastic, flowing plans link it

more closely with Art Nouveau than any other stylistic movement, Gaudí's work ultimately resists categorization. The Sagrada Familia, for example, retains Gothic structural overtones, yet has such a heavy, towering, sculptural presence, enriched with lovingly crafted details, that it is clearly not Gothic. Its Façade of the Nativity is an array of grotto-eroded elements flowing together, with four great spires towering above (Fig. 14.50).

Gaudí's design for Casa Milá (1905–07), a large apartment house in Barcelona (Fig. 14.51), has an undulating plasticity in its façade and a curvilinear plan that is made possible by its expressive exterior load-bearing wall. There are no bearing walls inside, giving the designer the freedom to sculpt individual, non-orthogonal spaces, no two alike. His designs for the Parc Güell (1900–14), a real-estate development situated on a hillside west of Barcelona, allowed an extensive merging of naturalistic

**14.51** Antonio Gaudí, Casa Milá, Barcelona, 1905–07.

This apartment block is so massive and so apparently natural in its use of stone that it is referred to locally as the "stone quarry." The iron railings were made from salvaged material, and at one spot, the roof sculpture creates a framed view of the Sagrada Familia.

**14.52** Antonio Gaudí, Parc Güell viaduct colonnade, Barcelona, 1900–14.

Using ropes, sandbags, and canvas, Gaudí experimented empirically with the transfer of forces in vaulted construction. One of the results was sloping columns that responded empirically to force vectors, in this case produced by the centrifugal force of cars making turns on the viaduct above.

forms into walkways, stairways, and seating. Vaulting leans at oblique angles in a grotto walkway (Fig. 14.52); stairs flow downward like lava; and benches, conforming to the irregular curves of the seated human form, wind sinusoidally along the upper-level plaza edge. Ceramic-tile finishes and details contribute durable surfaces and an appropriate touch of whimsy. The informal, amorphous, and rambling park is a skillfully inventive total design.

## CHARLES RENNIE MACKINTOSH

Gaudí's highly individualistic interpretations of Art Nouveau have a Scottish parallel in the work of Charles Rennie Mackintosh (1868–1928), a gifted designer whose architectural career was brief. Mackintosh and a small circle of friends worked primarily in Glasgow, developing a unique style that is related to Art Nouveau in its use of curves derived from natural forms. Other influences are detectable in Mackintosh's work as well, including the massive forms of Scottish baronial architecture and the delicate interlacing decoration of Celtic art. His architecture tends to have bold massing deftly composed, with light and airy interiors accented by subtle attenuated curves or linear patterns that are usually symmetrical. Like Art Nouveau architects, Mackintosh was greatly concerned with furniture, light fixtures, and details such as window hardware.

The Glasgow School of Art (1897–1909) was Mackintosh's first and largest commission (Fig. 14.53). Located on the north side of a sloping site, the building presents three elevations to the perimeter streets. The main entrance façade on Renfrew Street is a tight monolithic mass domi-nated by two rows of large, north-facing studio windows and a heavily sculpted central-entry composition, while the later west façade along Scott Street rises austerely as the hill drops, in the manner of medieval fortifications. This elevation, expressing the library, is a bold design broken by the three twenty-five-foot-high windows along the upper section of wall. The library interior is the most celebrated space (Fig. 14.54). Mackintosh designed its furniture and light fixtures to harmonize with the dominant pattern of horizontals and verticals in the windows and mezzanine balcony. A more fluid linearity is found in other rooms, and the southern rear attic level has simple arched openings that are reminiscent of Romanesque work. To the rear or south and facing the railroad yard, the façade (Fig. 14.55) is seemingly perfunctory, with windows punched wherever interior spaces required them. However, Mackintosh so manipulated these simple openings in an otherwise plain, cliff-like wall as to produce a composition of power, variety, and conviction that has few equals.

Other Mackintosh commissions include Windyhill (1900–01), located outside Glasgow at Kilmacolm; Hill House (1902–04) at Helensburgh; and the Scotland Street School (1904–06) in Glasgow. Hill House (Fig. 14.56), designed for a Glasgow publisher, stands like a castle on rising ground, reflecting the influence of the Scottish vernacular in its turrets, expressive chimneys, and dominant roof. The monolithic character of the exterior is achieved by **pebble-dash** stucco. Its plan (Fig. 14.57) is logically compartmentalized into functional areas: the library and cloakroom near the entrance, for the easy conducting of business, followed by the drawing and dining rooms and

**14.53** Charles Rennie Mackintosh, Glasgow School of Art, Glasgow, 1897–1909.

This is the main façade on Renfrew Street. The huge windows gather northern light for painting and design studios. The central entry includes motifs drawn from Glasgow's medieval vernacular.

**14.54** Charles Rennie Mackintosh, Library interior, Glasgow School of Art, Glasgow, 1897–1909.

The supporting columns are heavy timber with a dark finish typical of late nineteenth- and early twentieth-century interiors. Mackintosh designed the reading tables and light fixtures as well.

**14.55** Charles Rennie Mackintosh, rear elevation of the Glasgow School of Art, Glasgow, 1897–1909.

While the north elevation provides the proper public face, this rear elevation is no less powerful a composition. Its reliance on the simple but deft application of windows as figures on the plain field of the masonry walls is comparable to Mackintosh's concern for figure–ground relationships in his watercolor drawings from nature.

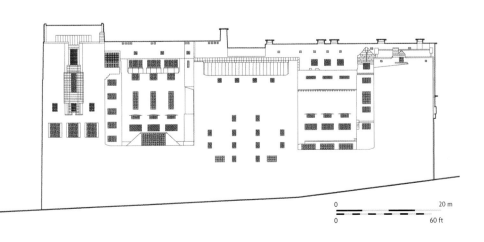

0        20 m

0                  60 ft

**14.56** Charles Rennie Mackintosh, Hill House, Helensburgh, 1902–04.

The picturesque silhouette and massing of Hill House are very expressive of nineteenth-century sensibilities. The stark, unornamented wall surfaces, however, have received much attention from those tracing the origins of twentieth-century Modernism.

**14.57** Charles Rennie Mackintosh, first floor (*below*) and second floor (*above*) plans of Hill House, Helensburgh, 1902–04.

These plans could not be more straightforward in their functional organization, but the building's perimeter was obviously determined with three-dimensional expression in mind. Notable are the circular stairs that notch into a reentrant (internal, or inside) corner, and the stair that projects outward in the form of a semicircular landing.

a servants' wing at the end. Upstairs are the bedrooms, with the nursery and servants' bedrooms over the service wing. All interiors are handcrafted in the Arts and Crafts tradition, with custom-designed carpets, light fixtures, stencil decorations, and furniture (Fig. 14.58). Dark wood-work contrasts with pastel colors on floor and wall surfaces. A barrel-vaulted ceiling in one bedroom becomes a canopy over the bed.

Art Nouveau designers in various parts of Europe were aware of one another's work through international publications. Mackintosh's entry in the 1901 German competition to design the "House of an Art Lover" brought him second prize, and his project drawings became known through inclusion in a publication edited in Darmstadt.

**14.58** Charles Rennie Mackintosh, Hill House interior, Helensburgh, 1902–04.

On the interior, Mackintosh designed Hill House to have both regimented orthogonals and Art Nouveau curves.

Darmstadt had become a center of the Jugendstil in 1899, when Ernst Ludwig, Grand Duke of Hesse, established an artists' colony in the suburb of Mathildenhöhe, attracting artists from Munich and Vienna. While the colony's life as an art center was brief, the houses built in the Mathildenhöhe district remain today a preserve of Jugendstil architecture. Major buildings in the Jugendstil included a house for Ernst Ludwig designed by Joseph Maria Olbrich (1867–1908), who came from the Viennese Secessionists, and an elaborate and expensive residence (1899) built for his family by the young German painter Peter Behrens— Behrens quickly outgrew the Jugendstil and went on to figure prominently in the development of modern architecture in Germany. On the whole, the Jugendstil is a late manifestation of Art Nouveau, and its architectural manifestations tend to be linear but less free than comparable work in Belgium or France.

## THE VIENNESE SECESSION

Art Nouveau architects in Austria were members of the Viennese Secession, an association primarily of artists formed in 1898. The oldest member of the group, although not one of its founders, was Otto Wagner

(1841–1918), a Neo-Classical architect who was promoted to the post of professor of architecture at the Vienna Academy of Fine Arts in 1894. Upon his appointment to academic life, Wagner seems to have undergone a philosophical shift away from archaeologically correct architecture to a more rational, modern expression suited to current-day requirements. The Viennese Secession movement was formed by some of his most outstanding students, and Wagner soon joined them in espousing Art Nouveau ornament.

Wagner's most notable designs in this mode were thirty-six stations for the Vienna subway system, the Stadtbahn (1894–1901). While not as exuberant as Guimard's work for the Paris Métro, Wagner's designs do employ the characteristic stylized ornament in cast and wrought iron. After 1900, Wagner's enthusiasm for Art Nouveau waned, and he abandoned the style completely for his masterpiece, the Postal Savings Bank (1904–06 and 1910–12) in Vienna (Figs. 14.59–14.60). Within an irregularly shaped block, Wagner placed a grand staircase leading up to a

**14.59** Otto Wagner, Postal Savings Bank, Vienna, 1904–12.

Marble veneer attached by means of aluminum-capped bolts creates the pattern of Wagner's façade. Aluminum also appears at the columns and the roof supports of the entry canopy.

**14.60** Otto Wagner, Postal Savings Bank interior, Vienna, 1904–12.

Wagner originally intended for the glazed vault of the banking room to be suspended from masts and cables above it. Today, a rain-shedding, two-level gable roof protects the glazing. Against the rear and right-side walls are cylindrical aluminum air-supply standards.

wide vestibule, then into the central banking room, which he surrounded with offices. He faced the front façade with white Sterzing marble in shingle-like panels. He attached these panels to the superstructure by means of bolts covered with aluminum caps that create a distinctive grid. Using more aluminum, a radical choice at the time, he created an elegant entry canopy supported by thin aluminum columns with cantilevered arms. Passing through this canopy to the banking room, one enters a space filled with light brought in through a glass-vaulted ceiling that Wagner originally intended to support with cables hung from aluminum masts. Some of the light passes through glass-brick floor panels to illuminate the rooms below. Within the banking room, two files of columns create a basilican plan, with the tellers' counters in the "aisles" and

with cylindrical aluminum air-supply standards around the perimeter. As at the façade, connections are everywhere made prominent, from the bases of the aluminum-cladded columns to the newel posts of the handrails.

Wagner's talented pupil, Josef Maria Olbrich, became the leading architect of the Viennese Secession, influenced in part by the work of Mackintosh. Like Mackintosh, Olbrich found an essentially orthogonal basis for his architectural forms, embellishing them with the controlled vegetation of Art Nouveau. His first major commission was from the Secessionists themselves, a small building for meetings and exhibitions of art. The Secession Hall (1898–99) is a Neo-Classically inspired mass, crowned by a pierced metal dome (Fig. 14.61). Along the exterior walls between high windows Olbrich set low-relief ornament based on plants and flowers. Compared to French or Belgian work, Olbrich's designs seem rather heavy and symmetrical, but publication of this building brought widespread acclaim to its architect, and the Grand Duke of Hesse, Ernst Ludwig, invited Olbrich to join his artists' colony at Darmstadt.

**14.61** Josef Maria Olbrich, Secession Building, Vienna, 1898–99.

Olbrich covered his dome with a laurel motif symbolic of Apollo, god of poetry, music, and learning. The building served as a meeting and exhibition space for the Secession.

From 1899 until his death from leukemia in 1908, Olbrich worked at Darmstadt, erecting numerous houses, studio buildings, entrance gates, and a Wedding Tower or Hochzeitsturm (1907–08) to commemorate the Duke's marriage. The tower is a symbolic structure, rising above the colony with an arched and paneled gable that recalls the shape of organ pipes. It is built of brick and trimmed with contrasting stone around doors and windows. These windows are all the more unusual for wrapping around the corner of the tower, seeming to defy the mass required there for strength at the junction of the walls. This feature was to reappear on Modernist buildings in the 1920s and 1930s.

## THE SEARCH FOR AN AMERICAN STYLE

A recurring theme in American architectural history is the search for a proper "American" style of building. Jefferson advocated the use of Roman architecture because it symbolized the greatness of the Roman republic, which he saw as a worthy model for the new republic of the United States. Proponents of the Greek Revival cited similar desirable symbolic linkages with the democratic government of ancient Athens, while Gothic Revivalists drew parallels between the Christian values of medieval times and those of the present day. Two American architects of the nineteenth century contributed to the search for a truly American expression in architecture, not by reviving past styles, but by evolving a fresh approach to the materials and building problems presented by life in the United States. Their accomplishments have had a lasting effect on the course of American design.

### HENRY HOBSON RICHARDSON

Henry Hobson Richardson (1838–1886) was the first American after Richard Morris Hunt to attend the Ecole des Beaux-Arts in Paris. Born to a wealthy Louisiana family, Richardson completed the course at the Lawrence Scientific School of Harvard University before enrolling at the Ecole in 1860. The onset of the Civil War cut off his financial support from home, forcing him out of school and into the Paris office of Théodore Labrouste (brother of Henri), where he worked until 1865, when he returned to New York. After a few years, he moved his office to Boston and gained national acclaim for his competition-winning design for Trinity Church (1872–77) in Copley Square, Boston.

Trinity Church (Fig. 14.62) was to become the most celebrated building of its age; a national poll of architects in 1885 identified it as the best building in the United States. What was it that designers (and the general public) admired so much about this church? In many respects the design is a pastiche, very much in the tradition of nineteenth-century eclecticism. The plan (Fig. 14.63) is based on a stubby Latin-cross basilica, and the polychrome stonework and general massing come from French Romanesque churches of the French Auvergne; the triple-arched portal is derived from St. Gilles-du-Gard in Provence (see Fig. 8.48); and the great crossing tower reflects the tower of the Old Cathedral in Salamanca, Spain. Despite these borrowings, an abundance of original thinking gives Trinity Church its distinctive character. Richardson conceived of the building as a polychrome church, both inside and out, and his design shows a true flair for scale and texture. Ashlar stonework in warm gray

**14.62** Henry Hobson Richardson, Trinity Church, Boston, Massachusetts, 1872–77.

It was Stanford White, then working in H.H. Richardson's office, who designed the church's tower, basing it on the Romanesque Salamanca Cathedral. With its three arched openings, the base is quite similar to the Romanesque church of St. Gilles-du-Gard in Provence.

**14.63** Henry Hobson Richardson, Plan of Trinity Church, Boston, Massachusetts, 1872–77.

Richardson's plan is remarkably simple. Its vaults are ornamented with murals by John LaFarge. Connected to the chancel end of the church is the parish house, laid up in the same polychromatic stone.

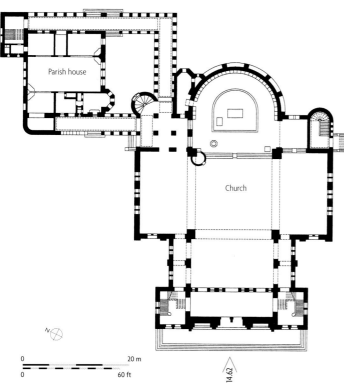

Parish house

Church

N

| 0 | 20 m |
| 0 | 60 ft |

14.62

contrasts with the red-brown sandstone trim, and slate roofs on the parish house set off the red clay tiles prominent on the tower roof. Murals painted by John LaFarge and his pupil Augustus Saint-Gaudens enrich the plaster walls inside, and William Morris and Edward Burne-Jones made the stained-glass windows, an artistic collaboration that was entirely in accordance with Arts and Crafts ideals. The success of Trinity Church assured the prosperity of Richardson's career, while atoning for the less satisfactory design of his earlier Brattle Square Church (1870), which proved on completion to have faulty acoustics in the nave.

The design of Trinity Church also established what was to become Richardson's characteristic architectural style: an intelligent and personal interpretation of the Romanesque. This was far from a slavish imitation, however, so his work is designated "Richardsonian" to indicate that this was not merely a revival. His adoption of the Romanesque was in fact the starting point in his search for an appropriate American building tradition, for, while he had seen and been impressed by medieval buildings in Europe, he had not been instructed in any medieval modes at the Ecole des Beaux-Arts. Richardson was a romantic who was inspired by the abundant stone of New England, and he worked to evolve a style worthy of its

**14.64** Henry Hobson Richardson, Marshall Field
Wholesale Store, Chicago, Illinois, 1885–87.

There has been no more satisfying composition in American
architecture than this one. Notice the vertical unity of each
window bay, which begins with a rectangular opening
lighting the basement, and terminates with four vertical
rectangles over two round-headed windows. Unfortunately,
the building has long since been destroyed.

rugged massiveness and load-bearing capacities (technical
advances in glass and metal construction had little impact
on his work). A chronicle of his major commissions illustrates the progressive development of his thinking about
the expression of masonry. In 1878 he designed Sever Hall
for his alma mater, Harvard University. It is a classroom
building, executed in brick to harmonize with existing
structures in the Harvard Yard, but the expression that
Richardson gave to the material, built into a low arch at
the entrance and modeled into bowfronts that resemble
turrets, conveys a feeling of solidity, quite a contrast to the
rather delicate Georgian buildings that are its neighbors.
Two years later Richardson designed nearby Austin Hall to
house the law school, an almost symmetrical stone struc-

ture that was a free and romantic reinterpretation of
Romanesque forms.

In 1885 Richardson designed two projects in Chicago,
the Glessner House for a wealthy industrialist and the
Marshall Field Wholesale Store (Fig. 14.64). The store,
since demolished, was a revelation to architects in the
city, providing a dignified and simple treatment for a six-
story block. Richardson eschewed ornamentation and
historical trappings, leaving the unadorned rusticated
masonry and the great arched openings to convey power
and monumentality. It has been proposed that Richardson's model for the broad arches of the central stage of
the store may have been the Roman aqueduct at Segovia,
Spain, a construction included in Richardson's collection
of photographs. Whatever his inspiration, Richardson succeeded in creating a design as bold and monumental as
the Roman engravings of Piranesi. Behind the articulated
stone bearing walls of the store was an internal and unex-
pressed structural skeleton of iron. The Glessner House
(Figs. 14.65–14.66) is similarly restrained and austere on

**14.65** Henry Hobson Richardson, Glessner House, Chicago, Illinois, 1885.

This was Richardson's smaller commission in Chicago. The most impressive feature of the front (south) façade is the huge semicircular arch made of rock-faced voussoirs. The large opening to the left is the carriage portal.

**14.66** Henry Hobson Richardson, Plan of the Glessner House, Chicago, Illinois, 1885.

This plan occurs at the level of the front-façade doorway and carriage portal. The outside walls of this U-shaped plan are laid up in rock-faced stone, while the walls of the inner court are brick. The scale change is striking, but appropriate. Compare the projecting stairs and bays in the court to the work of Charles Rennie Mackintosh.

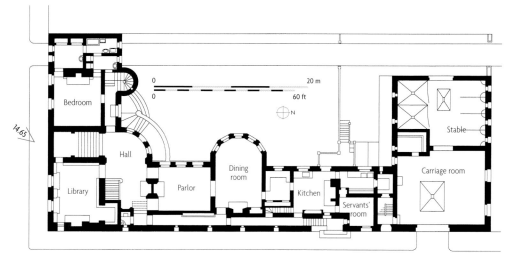

the exterior. Rooms open outward onto the public streets and inward onto an interior courtyard sheltered from street noise and dirt by the building's U-shaped plan. While the courtyard walls are laid up in brick, the street-front façades are constructed in varied courses of rock-faced stone interspersed with orthogonal windows, grills, and a massive semicircular arch.

In his residential commissions Richardson also did much to create what became known as the "Shingle Style." Built with wooden frames, these houses were covered with wooden shingles on the wall and roof planes, providing a sense of both volume and simplicity. His design for the Watts Sherman House (1874) in Newport, Rhode Island, has rusticated stone on the ground-floor walls and shingles on the upper-floor walls and roof, stretched like a membrane over the dormers and bay windows that articulate the façade (Fig. 14.68). Great overhanging eaves at the steeply pitched roof and substantial chimneys present an irregular, picturesque profile against the sky. A later design for the Stoughton House (Fig. 14.67) in Cam-

bridge, Massachusetts (1882–83) shows how far Richardson had gone toward simplifying the rather complex forms of the Sherman House. Here, the shingle skin covers a bold composition of geometric solids atop an L-shaped plan. Although the design owes something to the forms of early Colonial houses in New England, it transcends any one period or style, being as devoid of applied ornament as the slightly later Marshall Field Wholesale Store. The interior of the Stoughton House features a two-story living hall, an element originated in Pugin's design for his own house at Ramsgate.

## LOUIS HENRI SULLIVAN AND THE TALL BUILDING

Richardson's scheme for the Marshall Field Wholesale Store was particularly influential on the work of Louis Henri Sullivan (1856–1924), a Chicago architect who has already been mentioned as a participant in the design of the World's Columbian Exposition of 1893, where he was responsible for the design of the Transportation Building.

**14.67** Henry Hobson Richardson, Stoughton House, Cambridge, Massachusetts, 1882–83.

Here Richardson drew partly upon the New England Colonial vernacular to produce a building completely clad in shingles. Particularly effective is the curving shingle-covered wall of the projecting stair.

**14.68** Henry Hobson Richardson, Watts Sherman House, Newport, Rhode Island, 1874.

Richardson also worked in wood, in this case assisted by Stanford White. Close observation of the textures created by the mock-heavy timber and the shingles of the roofs and gables reveals the similarity in feeling to Richardson's compositions in stone. The treatment of the wood members is also comparable to the Queen Anne style of Richard Norman Shaw in England.

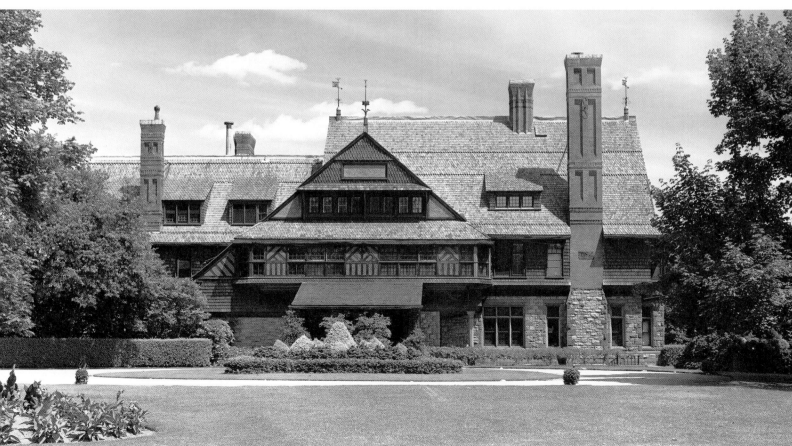

**14.69** Dankmar Adler and Louis Sullivan, Auditorium Building, Chicago, Illinois, 1886–90.

Obviously Sullivan was influenced by Richardson's Marshall Fields Wholesale Store. The projecting block above the triple arches is the hotel lobby.

**14.70** Dankmar Adler and Louis Sullivan, Plan of and longitudinal section through the Auditorium Building, Chicago, Illinois, 1886–90.

The so-called Auditorium Building is actually a hotel and an office building that surrounded an auditorium. It was certainly the cleverest plan composition that Sullivan (together with Adler) ever produced.

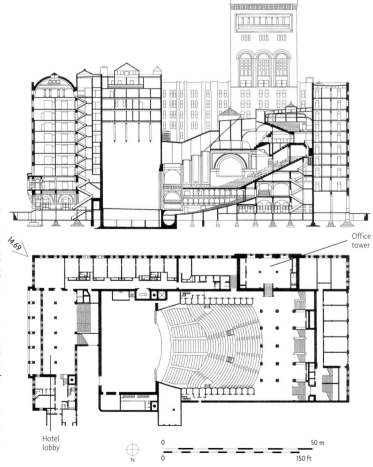

At the time that the Marshall Field Wholesale Store was being completed, Sullivan, then in practice with Dankmar Adler (1844–1900), was designing the Chicago Auditorium Building (1886–90) (Fig. 14.69). After seeing Richardson's masterpiece, he simplified his design, giving greater emphasis to the arches above entrance doors and arches used for wall articulation.

Sullivan was as original an architect as Richardson. While traces of Neo-Classicism and Romanticism appear in his work, he engaged directly the rapidly emerging building technologies of Chicago and expressed them architecturally. Born in Boston, the young Sullivan spent much of his childhood on his grandfather's farm north of the city, where he became acquainted with the natural plant forms that would later be incorporated in his architectural ornament. Determined to become an architect, Sullivan spent a year in the newly created architectural program at M.I.T.

and then worked briefly in the offices of Frank Furness in Philadelphia and William Le Baron Jenney in Chicago. He went to Paris in 1874 to study at the Ecole des Beaux-Arts, where he found the teaching uninspiring. After a year there, he traveled in Italy before returning to Chicago and joining the office of Dankmar Adler and Company in 1879. Adler's engineering and managerial expertise complemented Sullivan's artistic inclinations, and in 1881 the firm name changed to Adler and Sullivan.

Adler's understanding of acoustics gained the firm the commission to design the Chicago Auditorium Building, one of the most complex multi-use buildings constructed in the country up until that time. Its name derives from the huge 4237-seat concert hall located at its center, but the building also contained a ten-story hotel and a seventeen-story office tower, with additional offices at the rear (Fig. 14.70). Erecting such a structure on the muddy subsoil of Chicago challenged the engineering talents of Adler, who also made sure that the sightlines and acoustics were excellent for every seat in the auditorium. Sullivan's task was to give architectural harmony to the diverse elements of the building, and in the process he was influenced, as has already been noted, by the Marshall Field Wholesale Store.

Romantic that he was, Sullivan turned to classical precedent for inspiration when he tackled the problem of artistic expression appropriate to a tall building. In 1890 a commission from a St. Louis brewer, Ellis Wainwright, gave Adler and Sullivan their first opportunity to design a skyscraper, and Sullivan's treatment of the exterior became the exemplar for much of later high-rise construction (Fig. 14.71). Rather than a layering of horizontal elements drawn from one or more historical periods, the Wainwright Building has a base, a middle section, and a top. Sullivan, in his essay "The Tall Building Artistically Considered" (1896), explained his reasons for this organization. He expressed the ground floor (where easy access could be made from the street into banks, shops, or the like) and mezzanine or second floor (still easily reached on foot) as a unit; he placed stacked offices on the third through top floors, where repetitive windows illuminated floor areas that could be subdivided to suit the requirements of various tenants; and he located the mechanical systems, from tanks and pumps to elevator machinery, behind a deep cornice. Sullivan liked nothing better than to discover a general principle, what he characterized as "a rule so broad as to admit no exceptions." His most famous dictum was "form follows function," which was not actually original to him. Sullivan's buildings, however, are generally poor examples of this principle in operation. The Wainwright Building, for instance, has a steel frame with riveted columns behind its red granite, brick, and terracotta exterior cladding. The form of the exterior only partially reflects the structural function of the steelwork, for every second vertical pier is a dummy, covering no steel but necessary for flexible internal planning arrangements

**14.71** Dankmar Adler and Louis Sullivan, Wainwright Building, St. Louis, Missouri, 1890.

In his essay "The Tall Building Artistically Considered," Sullivan called for two walk-in, walk-up stories, repetitive office floors, and a cap containing mechanical equipment. Here are his theories at work, with terracotta ornament in the spandrel panels and at the deep cornice. The steel frame is obscured because of fireproofing requirements, but its presence is expressed on the exterior.

and for the visual effect Sullivan desired, and the elaborate, flowing frieze adorns nothing more important than the mechanical floor.

It is better to think of Sullivan's work not in terms of any one maxim such as "form follows function," then, but in terms of the original contributions he made to design. In addition to finding an unashamedly vertical expression for tall buildings, Sullivan evolved a characteristic ornamental style derived from natural plant forms. In fact, this aspect of his work can be considered part of Art Nouveau, although he seems neither to have been directly influenced by, nor to have had a direct influence on, contemporary developments in Europe. Ornament for Sullivan was an integral part of the building's design, and his swirling circular patterns were generally designed for ease of production from a master mold or cast in terracotta, iron, or plaster. The Wainwright Building has ornate terracotta **spandrels** under each window and repetitive patterns on the frieze and roof **fascia**. Sullivan used essentially the same formula in the design of the Guaranty Building (1894) in Buffalo, New York (Fig. 14.72).

With allowance for changing architectural fashions,

**14.72** Dankmar Adler and Louis Sullivan, Guaranty Building, Buffalo, New York, 1894.

This office structure exhibits the same tall-building composition as the Wainwright Building. Even more dramatically displayed here is Sullivan's cast ornament that illustrates his principle of organic growth.

Sullivan's conception of the skyscraper's composition remains valid today. In place of the brick and terracotta infill panels that Sullivan used, subsequent high-rise construction makes extensive use of glass **curtain walls**, where the lightweight frames holding the glass are brought forward of the structural columns, a technique first used by

W. J. Polk in the Halladie Building (1918) in San Francisco.

Under New York's zoning code of 1916, skyscraper façades were required to be tiered back from the street in relation to their height, producing the characteristic stepped profile of landmarks like the Chrysler Building (see Fig. 15.33) and the Empire State Building (see Fig. 15.38). Inspired by the Seagram Building (1958) (see Fig. 15.70) in New York, with an elegant public open space at its base, more recent codes have permitted unbroken vertical façades if a portion of the site is given over to a pedestrian plaza. Unfortunately, this has often resulted in lifeless

**14.73** Louis Sullivan, Carson Pirie Scott Department Store, Chicago, Illinois, 1899–1904.

At the Wainwright and Guaranty buildings, Sullivan chose to emphasize the vertical. Here he balanced horizontals and verticals and inserted "Chicago windows," windows that have large fixed panes between operable sash.

plazas at other midtown towers. The proper massing, density, and location of high-rise buildings remains a very controversial subject for architects, urban planners, and the general public.

Sullivan used more florid and three-dimensional ornament for the main entrance of the Schlesinger and Mayer Store, now the Carson Pirie Scott Department Store (1899–1904), in Chicago, a building that represents the maturity of Sullivan's design ideas for tall buildings (Fig. 14.73). Here, the large windows are set in wide bays, articulated by white terracotta cladding on the steel columns and spandrel panels. The overall effect of the building is more horizontal than vertical. Display windows on the ground floor are terminated by cast-iron ornamental panels that can be readily viewed from the street level. The ornament becomes far more exuberant around the heads of the doorways, thereby giving emphasis to the entrance, which is further defined by its location at a slightly projecting radiused (i.e. 90° of curvature) corner. Upper-level windows have slender ornamental frames. Thus, the building provides visual rewards from several vantage points. From a distance, its austere white frame reads as a cleanly subdivided rectangular grid resting on a dark base; from a medium distance, the articulated entrance can be easily distinguished; and from a close view, one can appreciate the abundant detail around windows and doorways. With the Carson Pirie Scott Department Store, Sullivan achieved an integration of uninterrupted line and decorative detail that has seldom been equaled.

Having reached its apogee, Sullivan's architectural practice declined precipitously. The Carson Pirie Scott Department Store was to be his last major commission. He and Adler dissolved their partnership in 1895, and neither prospered separately. Within a year Adler proposed rejoining forces, but Sullivan turned him down. Sullivan's misanthropy and growing alcoholism estranged him from his family, his wife, his professional colleagues, and most prospective clients. Between 1907 and 1924 he had only thirteen minor commissions, the most impressive of which was the National Farmers' Bank (1907–08) in Owatonna, Minnesota.

## CONCLUSIONS ABOUT ARCHITECTURAL IDEAS

Neo-Classicism, Romanticism, and eclecticism in general, as well as materials-science and engineering advances accompanying the on-going Industrial Revolution have been central to the preceding discussion of the nineteenth century. However, nineteenth-century architectural circumstances appeared in such profusion that it is difficult to produce a summary that ties the diverse individuals and events together with the kind of unified sense of direction, results, and conclusions seen in earlier chapters. Perhaps this is just as well, as circumstances only further diversified

in the twentieth century, as did interpretations of them, culminating with the current twenty-first-century "post-modern" condition wherein there is a lack of faith among some that even an approximation of the truth about the past is possible.

Certainly Karl Friedrich Schinkel was not plagued by any such dilemma. His governmental and institutional buildings for Berlin are models of lucidity, as confident in their connection to antiquity and to their own time as the Prussian government was of its right to power. But conditions were already bi-polar, as Schinkel was equally adept at composing picturesque compositions, and Prussian militarism led to two cataclysmic world wars.

In England, Sir John Soane's mature work was equally sophisticated but more idiosyncratic. The moody interiors of his own house at 13 Lincoln's Inn Fields and the Bank of England, especially as seen in J.M. Gandy's renderings, reflect a somewhat self-conscious, skeptical personality and a disinterest in the capacity of classical forms to make incarnate the world's larger truths.

The Neo-Classicism that arrived in America had more the spirit of Schinkel than Soane, as it became the instrument for outward expression of the optimism afoot in the world's newest democracy. Beginning at Monticello and ending at the University of Virginia campus, Thomas Jefferson gave a Neo-Classical architectural face to his dream for an agrarian republic composed of noble farmers. Jefferson found Benjamin Henry Latrobe soon after his emigration from England and made him the architect of the deteriorated President's House and the incomplete U.S. Capitol. Latrobe's nearby Baltimore Cathedral has been restored as the serene, simplicity-informed, light-filled expression of Enlightenment rationalism that he intended it to be.

Back in England at mid-century, A.W.N. Pugin, through his publication of *Contrasts*, was making a scathing indictment of industrialization's effect on nineteenth-century architecture and cities. Accompanying his condemnations was an interest in picturesque composition, given particularly dramatic form as the ever-changing, irregular silhouette of the Houses of Parliament on which Pugin worked both early and late in his career.

Neither Soane, nor Latrobe, nor Pugin benefited from institution-based architectural education in England, as there was none. Across the English Channel in Paris, however, the Ecole des Beaux-Arts exercised a profound influence not only in France but also throughout Europe and, by the 1860s, even in America. The Ecole had become such an academic juggernaut that it was able largely to ignore the presence of industrialization (and the related proposals for reform by Viollet-le-duc), allowing its lumbering teaching system to continue on for another 100 years.

An Ecole virtue was certainly its prescriptive design process. Among those trained to use it, the truly gifted could do extraordinary things and those whose talents were at best modest could at least produce consistent competency. The first Americans to study in Paris were among the gifted: Richard Morris Hunt, architect to the Gilded Age set; Henry Hobson Richardson, who developed a personal style that became an American style; and Charles McKim, who, together with partners William Rutherford Mead and Stanford White, formed the first modern architectural office.

By mid-century, few European architects had taken readily to the newly available materials, abdicating their roles as innovators in favor of engineers and even greenhouse designers, as it was the landscape gardener Joseph Paxton who created the Crystal Palace. Its rapidly mass-produced and assembled skeletal construction represented a sea-change not only in how buildings were to be built but also how they were to be perceived, as did Gustav Eiffel's tower and bridges.

Some architects did begin gradually exploiting the new technologies. At his Bibliothèque Nationale, Henri Labrouste inserted spindly iron reading-room columns inside a traditional masonry armature and used "transparent" iron construction for the stack area (concealed from the public) of his Bibliothèque Ste. Geneviève. And European designers were simultaneously taking the first steps toward exploiting the skeletal potential of steel-reinforced concrete, while American builders were doing so for the wooden balloon-frame.

At the largest scale, that of the tall office building, it was Chicagoans who would be the innovators after the city's great fire in 1871. The Monadnock Building illustrates the economic limitations of bearing-wall construction, while experiments from William LeBaron Jenney's Home Insurance Building to Burnham and Root's Reliance Building took functionality and structural rationalism to the level of art in the form of the steel-frame skyscraper.

Back in England, counter currents to industrialization had become, if anything, more pronounced. Cultural critic John Ruskin set down a philosophy in his *Seven Lamps of Architecture* that deplored what he considered to be amoral industrial production and demanded a rebirth of what he saw as the morally healthy craft tradition. Responding to Ruskin's call, designers like William Morris offered as an alternative the Arts and Crafts Movement, so forward-looking in its honest appreciation of materials that Arts-and-Crafts architect C.F.A. Voysey, actually inspired by English yeoman cottages, became a proto-Modernist in the minds of those later searching for the sources of twentieth-century Modernism. Others working within the Arts and Crafts tradition, like Richard Norman Shaw, produced compositions that had more to do with suave eclecticism than ideology or reform. German cultural attaché Herman Muthethius so admired the work of Voysey and his contemporaries that he assembled their domestic work in *Das Englische Haus*, a book that would have implications for the rise of Modernism in Germany.

Fueled by a desire for "newness" at the end of the nineteenth century, designers sought to exploit the plastic capabilities of iron in a movement that became known as the Art Nouveau. Victor Horta in Belgium, Hector Guimard in France, and Antonio Gaudí in Spain (his work being by far the most exotic of the three) produced buildings with flowing, organic lines as their principal characteristic. Charles Rennie Mackintosh in Scotland has been associated by some with the Art Nouveau, but his work has perhaps more in common with the Arts and Crafts, and it was also admired by members of the Viennese Secession. An elder statesman among these Secessionists, Otto Wagner dabbled in the Art Nouveau but settled on a tectonic architecture exploitative of new materials, including aluminum, but maintained classical ordering principles. Wagner's pupil Joseph Olbrich designed everything from garments to automobiles to buildings, with overt linearity being a formal constant in his work.

In America, barely a century old as a country, the search was on for a national style, and H.H. Richardson had taken the lead by producing the Richardsonian Romanesque. At his Marshall Fields Store in Chicago, he explored the expressive qualities of massive stone masonry, appropriate in its aggressiveness for a young country still on the make. His Glessner House displays a similar tectonic grammar, while his Watts Sherman House, as much a product of the mind and pencil of employee Stanford White as Richardson, and the Stoughton House near the Harvard campus owe something to the Arts and Crafts Movement but also to the New England Colonial architecture then being chauvinistically reinterpreted by American architects for the first time.

But it was the skyscraper that best expressed the energy and ingenuity of the nation subsequent to its centennial. And it was Louis Sullivan who elegantly summarized this new building type's proper organization in his essay "The Tall Building Artistically Considered." Along with his partner Dankmar Adler, he gave form to his ideas at the Auditorium Building in Chicago, and ever more dramatically at the Wainwright Building in St. Louis and the Guaranty Building in Buffalo, New York, before beginning a downward spiral personally and professionally that saw him reduced to designing small but exquisite Midwestern banks by the early twentieth century. It was Sullivan's protégé Frank Lloyd Wright who would become the most famous American architect of the twentieth century, and his work, along with that of other Modernists, is covered in this book's final two chapters.

# CHAPTER 15

# THE TWENTIETH CENTURY AND MODERNISM

The development of "modern" architecture has been complicated, an inescapable condition in the twentieth century. Evaluating this complexity has been made more difficult by the polemical nature of much writing by those advocating or disparaging the Modern Movement or European Modernism. While a superficial look at Modernist buildings may suggest that this work is reductivist or stripped of all but its essential parts and, some would say, left with little or no meaning, such is not the case. The founders of Modernism intended that their buildings should be didactic; they intended for them to instruct. But benefiting from this instruction often requires an awareness not only of what can be seen, but also of what cannot, that is, of what has been eliminated from the architecture that preceded Modernism and to which the Modernists were reacting.

## THE IDEA OF A MODERN ARCHITECTURE

In the wake of the horrors of World War I, many young architects shared a general disillusionment, indeed a sense that European culture had failed and would have to be replaced by a transformed society; they believed that architecture could and should become an instrument of this transformation. They also believed in the power of rational thought, and ultimately in its handmaidens, economy and functionality, and they believed that their rational designs could best be produced through mechanization, yielding efficient, somehow machine-made buildings. As a corollary, and following nineteenth-century social and architectural critics like John Ruskin, they revered the direct expression of building materials and their processes of assembly.

Adding to the difficulty in understanding individual buildings from the formative period of Modernism has been the general absorption of Modernist buildings into the broader architectural scene and their construction outside the geographical and social context in which they originated. Frequently Modernist utopianism has given way to mass culture, economy to parsimony, and honesty to banality. Ironically, this modern architecture, with its often Socialist roots, was appropriated by corporate America, most dramatically for the glass-and-steel towers that became companies' headquarters and projected their capitalist images. In order to begin making our way through these potentially confusing circumstances and to begin exploring Modernism's principal themes, let us identify the authors who have written about it and cast a critical eye on what they have had to say.

## Chronology

| | |
|---|---|
| Albert Einstein publishes *General and Special Theories of Relativity* | 1905 |
| Pablo Picasso and George Braque create Cubism | 1908–12 |
| Filippo Marinetti publishes the *Futurist Manifesto* | 1909 |
| beginning of federal income tax in the United States | 1913 and 1916 |
| Henry Ford fully mechanizes mass production of automobile | 1914 |
| World War I | 1914–18 |
| Dada art movement | ca. 1915 |
| Bolshevik Revolution in Russia | 1917 |
| Theo van Doesburg begins the journal *De Stijl* | 1917 |
| Mussolini founds the Fascist Party in Italy | 1919 |
| Walter Gropius founds the Weimar Bauhaus | 1919 |
| women granted the right to vote in the United States | 1920 |
| Le Corbusier articulates his "five points of architecture" | 1926 |
| Joseph Stalin assumes power in the Soviet Union | 1926 |
| Werner Heisenberg formulates his Uncertainty Principle | 1927 |
| New York Stock Market crashes, beginning the Great Depression | 1929 |
| Adolf Loos develops the *Raumplan* | 1930 |
| invention of air conditioning | 1932 |
| *The International Style: Architecture Since 1922* exhibition opens at New York City's Museum of Modern Art | 1932 |
| World War II | 1939–45 |
| atomic bomb dropped at Hiroshima | 1945 |
| first computer assembled | 1945 |
| Francis Crick and James Watson discover DNA | 1953 |
| *Brown v. Board of Education* rules that racial segregation is illegal in United States schools | 1954 |
| Rachel Carson publishes *Silent Spring*, beginning the environmental movement | 1962 |

Ely Jacques Kahn, Number Two Park Avenue, New York City, 1927.

Ely Jacques Kahn was probably the most prominent practitioner of Art Deco in New York City. While ignored in all accounts of the development of twentieth-century Modernism, he had an extraordinarily productive career that stretched over fifty years.

In 1927, Gustav Platz published *Die Baukunst der neuesten Zeit* or *The Architecture of the New Age*. This German word *Zeit* is an important one, as the notion of *Zeitgeist*, or the Spirit of the Age, had been assembled from it by nineteenth-century German art historians. *Zeitgeist* combines the notions of newness, inherited from Art Nouveau, and style that somehow together encapsulate the aspirations and accomplishments of an era as did, some have argued, the Gothic in France or the High Renaissance in Italy. The publication of Platz's book was sandwiched between Le Corbusier's *Vers une architecture* (1923), usually translated as *Toward a New Architecture*, and Frank Lloyd Wright's *Modern Architecture* (1931) and Walter Gropius's *The New Architecture and the Bauhaus* (1935). In each of these publications, the author sought to promote his own design philosophy; this had been done before, but, encouraged by the escalating power of the media, it would be done with a vengeance in the twentieth century. In fact, by the 1970s, many architects would begin publishing monographs about their work before they had built anything of significance, a trend that continues today.

In 1932, architectural historian Henry-Russell Hitchcock and his protégé Philip Johnson, in support of the recently held exhibition at the Museum of Modern Art (MoMA) in New York City that they had organized with the museum's director, Alfred Barr, Jr., produced a thin volume entitled *The International Style: Architecture Since 1922*. Here, they announced that European Modernism was a new style and dubbed it international since it had already been transplanted from Europe to America (and would be exported elsewhere). Historians immediately went to work searching for the origins of the newly announced phenomenon, showing the same zeal and promoting the same confusion that had accompanied Baker and Speke's nineteenth-century search for the source of the Nile. None was more persuasive at the beginning than Nikolaus Pevsner. In his *Pioneers of the Modern Movement: From William Morris to Walter Gropius* (1936), Pevsner identified William Morris, as the title suggests, and his circle of Arts and Crafts designers in England, with Herman Muthesius as a connection to Germany, as the forerunners of the *Neue Sachlichkeit* or, as it is often translated, the "New Objectivity," and he saw the various late nineteenth-century art movements as having established a new set of ideals. He discussed developments in iron, steel, and concrete, spent considerable time on Art Nouveau, and concluded with an examination of work in Vienna, including that of Adolf Loos, and of Peter Behrens and his Werkbund associates in Germany. While Pevsner mentioned Futurism, he completely ignored Constructivism, De Stijl, and Expressionism, movements that did not fit neatly into his narrative.

Sigfried Giedion took a not dissimilar view in *Space, Time, and Architecture* (1941), a book so persuasive that many Modernist schools of architecture adopted it as a textbook in architectural history classes in the 1940s, '50s, and '60s. Delivered originally as a series of lectures, the text has serious disjunctures, but Giedion wrote with such authority and conviction that these lacunae serve to intensify, if sometimes confuse, the narrative. His principal themes are truth and honesty, the force of technology, and the so-called space-time conception in art and architecture, all presented in a *Zeitgeistian* context. It is at once a spectacular and insidious book as a result of Giedion's professed method of selecting pertinent materials. In explaining this method, he spoke of constituent and transitory facts, the former being "tendencies which, when they are suppressed, inevitably reappear" and the latter as trends which "lack the stuff of permanence and fail to attach themselves to a tradition." Giedion's critics have seen this differentiation simply as a facile way for him to include those historical events that supported his arguments while ignoring those that did not.

The Pevsner–Giedion Modernist vision held sway almost completely until 1960, when Reyner Banham, in *Theory and Design in the First Machine Age*, argued that the two scholars had got it wrong. He quickly dispensed with the German and Austrian developments in the first section of his book; he spent the entire second section on Futurism, and the entire third section on the De Stijl movement and Expressionism in Holland and Germany, then concluded in part four with Le Corbusier, Gropius, and Mies van der Rohe. Six years later, Dennis Sharp published *Modern Architecture and Expressionism* (1966), an entire book devoted to buildings that Pevsner and Giedion had seen as inconsequential only thirty years before. The year 1966 also saw the publication of Robert Venturi's iconoclastic *Complexity and Contradiction in Architecture*, a publication that both thrilled and shocked students of the time and announced the end of Modernist dominance in education and practice; more will be said about it in the next chapter.

What does this series of publishing events tell us? For young students, perhaps, it presents something destabilizing and even frightening: historical truth does not seem to be a constant; and, indeed, it is not. Things change, human perspectives change, ideals change, and so our view of history, and therefore history itself, changes. Students should not be discouraged, however; in fact quite the opposite is true. History is not dead; it is like a living organism.

Early Modernists were also militant; they sought to annihilate by any means available their revivalist enemies, including the entire Ecole des Beaux-Arts. They assumed ultimate power in the role of designers and design teachers for better than thirty years; some of them still linger on. In some cases they behaved badly, arrogantly, even ignorantly, and their architecture sometimes showed it, but many of the so-called Post-Modernists (another term to be dealt with in the next chapter) who replaced them or wrote about those who replaced them in the 1960s and afterward would have us believe that these Modernists were reprobates. How can this be? Can so many, so committed for so long, have been completely wrong? The answer is this: it is just not that simple!

Modern architecture was conceived during a time of tremendous upheaval in Western culture, including a world war and a revolution in Russia and developments in art and science that transformed our fundamental views about, among other things, both time and space. Designers in the first decade and a half of the twentieth century sought to come to terms with new ways of seeing, analyzing, and understanding, with tremendous advances in technology, and with the perceived necessity to create a modern art. Subsequent to World War I, the dominant issue became the desperate need for housing. As Modernists competed with traditionalists, the most extreme among them moved toward the New Objectivity, arguing that modern work was more efficient and cost-effective, which in some cases it was. However, their efforts to make modern architecture appear, if not in fact be, machine-producible and to render it functional and expressive of that functionality, led, in the eyes of many, to a reductivistic architecture, one short on character, symbolism, and even "livability." Still, whatever the final assessment, one can only admire the zeal and conviction with which Modernists took to the task at hand.

## ADOLF LOOS

Early in his career, Adolf Loos (1870–1933) was affiliated with the Vienna Secession, but he soon became estranged from it. After completing his architectural education, he worked and traveled in the United States in 1893–96, where he saw the buildings of the Chicago School and encountered the writings of Louis Sullivan, such as his essay "Ornament in Architecture" (1892). Sullivan had written: "I shall say that it would be greatly for our esthetic good if we should refrain entirely from the use of ornament for a period of years, in order that our thought might concentrate acutely upon the production of buildings well formed and comely in the nude." Apparently the young Loos took the statement to heart for, when he returned to Europe to settle in Vienna, he soon began to speak against the inclusion of ornament on buildings. This was a difficult position to maintain within the Viennese Secession, for Art Nouveau has nothing if not a highly refined sense of ornament. Some historians have theorized that Loos's turning against the prevailing Viennese school was a response to losing the commission to decorate and furnish the Secession council chamber. In any case, he set out on an exploration that would lead him to posit a new method of spatial composition: the *Raumplan*.

### ORNAMENT AND CRIME

Loos's theoretical writings were extremely influential. The most famous was published in 1908 under the title *Orna-*

*ment and Crime*. Here he took Sullivan's suggestion to abandon ornament in architecture a step further, proposing that the tendency to decorate surfaces was a sign of primitive culture or infancy. In advanced societies or in adults, he said, the urge to ornamental design was a sign of dependency or criminality. He wrote polemically:

> *Children are amoral, and so, by our standards, are Papuans. If a Papuan slaughters an enemy and eats him, that doesn't make him a criminal. But if a modern man kills someone and eats him, he must be either a criminal or degenerate. The Papuans tattoo themselves, decorate their boats, their oars, everything they can get their hands on. But a modern man who tattoos himself is either a criminal or a degenerate. Why, there are prisons where eighty per cent of the convicts are tattooed, and tattooed men who are not in prison are either latent criminals or degenerate aristocrats. When a tattooed man dies at liberty, it simply means that he hasn't had time to commit his crime. . . . I have therefore evolved the following maxim, and pronounce it to the world: the evolution of culture marches with the elimination of ornament from useful objects.*

This was a radical message indeed, and after its original publication in the German art periodical *Der Sturm* (*The Storm*), it was translated into French and published in *Les Cahiers d'aujourd'hui* (*The Notebooks of Today*) in 1913. Loos became the darling of avant-garde artists in Paris, and he moved there in the early 1920s. By extolling the virtues of architecture without ornament, he addressed an issue that had been of general concern to designers in various places around the turn of the century. His writings led to admiration of the simple vernacular forms of undecorated peasant architecture and the rather plain, functional constructions of engineers, both types of buildings previously considered to have no particular esthetic merit. Furthermore, Loos's admonition to build without ornament suggested a way to build in a style appropriate to a mechanized age.

### THE RAUMPLAN AND LOOS'S BUILDINGS

Loos's architectural designs are largely absent of ornament, befitting his theories. Moreover, unlike many revolutionaries, who only identify what to eliminate, Loos had proposals for what should be added too. A sequence of his house designs may illustrate his contributions. His Steiner House of 1910 (Fig. 15.1a) in Vienna is an unadorned white cubical mass with plain modest window openings and a streetfront façade that pays at least lip service to the more traditional surrounding residences. Its plan is straightforward and largely symmetrical, and its section (Fig. 15.1b) shows layered floor slabs of equal height. Its interior offers a slightly richer set of experiences, with considerable use of wood for wainscots, door and window

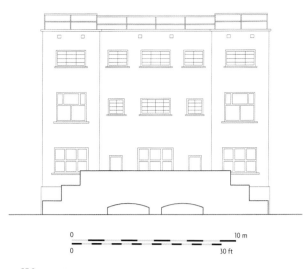

0    10 m
0    30 ft

**15.1a** Adolf Loos, Rear elevation of the Steiner House, Vienna, 1910.

Orthogonal massing, punched-out windows, a pipe-rail balustrade, and an absolute lack of ornament announce the nature of Loos's radical architectural proposals. At the front elevation, he made concessions to the surrounding residential context that he would not make again.

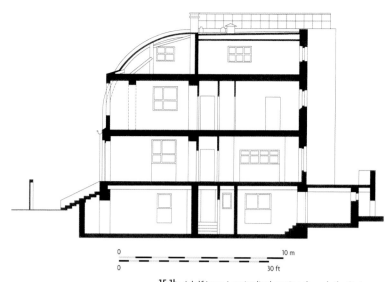

0    10 m
0    30 ft

**15.1b** Adolf Loos, Longitudinal section through the Steiner House, Vienna, 1910.

Neither Loos's plan nor section yet suggests the investigations of spatial interpenetrations that will appear in his mature houses.

0    10 m
0    30 ft

**15.2** Adolf Loos, Rear elevation of the Moller House, Vienna, 1930.

Gone is the symmetry of the Steiner House. Even more dramatically used are the simple window frames and the linear railings. The space on the inside has become the dominant element of the composition.

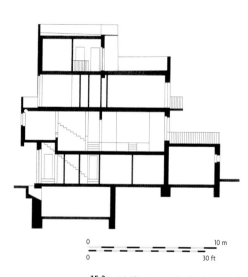

0    10 m
0    30 ft

**15.3a** Adolf Loos, Longitudinal section through the Moller House, Vienna, 1930.

In this section, Loos has begun to manipulate the floor heights and to cantilever floor plates. Rather than being stacked, the floors are spatial units displaced horizontally across one another.

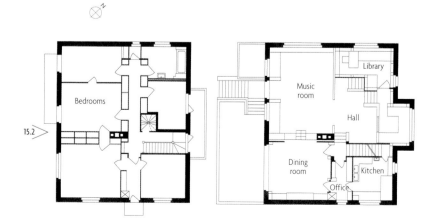

Bedrooms

15.2

Library

Music room

Hall

Dining room

Kitchen

Office

**15.3b** Adolf Loos, Second-floor (*right*) and third-floor (*left*) plans of the Moller House, Vienna, 1930.

Above the ground floor Loos inserted few full-height walls. However, his plans never had the horizontal spatial interactions of Frank Lloyd Wright's residential designs of the turn of the century.

casings, and ceiling grids; but this interior is not unlike the work of many others during this period. His Moller House of 1930 shows several dramatic advances. The exterior mass (Fig. 15.2) is still without conventional ornament, but each element—doors, windows, handrails, parapets, cantilevered slabs—becomes a distinctive and carefully disposed part within an asymmetrical but balanced whole. The plan (Fig. 15.3b) is also asymmetrical, with some rooms interconnected spatially by large door openings or low-walled apertures. The section (Fig. 15.3a) is more dramatic than that of the Steiner House in its spatial explorations, as the floor levels vary in height and some become mezzanines. On the interior, the materials are plain but rich by virtue of their natural character, conspicuously grained wood in particular. Of the Müller House (1930) the same can be said of its exterior massing and plans, but the section is even more adventurous, with multiple ceiling heights and an overt use of stairs to unify space vertically. Likewise, the interior materials are richer, particularly the use of marble without moldings such that its grain alone is left to provide scale and detail. Finally, in his earlier but more experimental (and unbuilt) villa on the Lido in Venice (1923), Loos demonstrated the full potential of his style of spatial composition, his *Raumplan*. The section (Fig. 15.4) is the most revealing drawing—multiple ceiling heights, mezzanine levels, and bold openings among spaces. Here Loos accomplished spatially what Giedion could only claim for Victor Horta and prepared the way for Le Corbusier's Modernist spatial compositions based upon his five points and Mies van der Rohe's meticulous compositions using stainless steel, onyx, marble, glass, and water.

**15.4** Adolf Loos, Section through the Lido villa, Venice, 1923.

Ceiling heights vary, and the two adjacent shafts of space have been displaced vertically producing multiple floor levels.

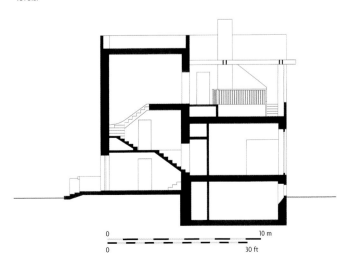

0                    10 m

0                    30 ft

## THE MODERN MASTERS

Three twentieth-century architects are sometimes termed the masters of modern architecture; the first two certainly fit the profile of the heroic figure battling often Philistine forces in the name of their art. They are Frank Lloyd Wright, Le Corbusier, and Ludwig Mies van der Rohe. Walter Gropius is often added to the group, although his most significant contributions were made in the field of architectural education. None of these architects developed their ideas in a vacuum; all were influenced by earlier architects, the use of new construction materials, and other artistic movements. For example, it would be difficult to conceive of Wright without the influence of Richardson, Sullivan, and the Arts and Crafts movement. Through the Wasmuth portfolios, Wright's work influenced the Dutch De Stijl movement, which had an effect on Gropius and the Bauhaus. Both Mies and Le Corbusier admitted their indebtedness to Wright, and in some respects they emulated his designs. In addition to his borrowings from Wright, Mies looks back to Schinkel through the eyes of his master, Peter Behrens, while Le Corbusier is tied into developments in concrete construction by August Perret and the ideas of city planning espoused by Tony Garnier.

## FRANK LLOYD WRIGHT

Louis Sullivan's architectural career profoundly influenced Frank Lloyd Wright (1867–1959). Wright was born in Wisconsin, the son of a domineering Welsh mother and an itinerant preacher-musician father, and he grew up in a variety of locations until his mother moved back near her family in Wisconsin when Wright was eleven. There he worked on his uncle's farm and attended school sporadically, all the while involving himself in drawing, crafts, painting, and printing. Wright's mother had decided before his birth that her son would become an architect, so she encouraged his interest in artistic and spatial investigations. After his parents divorced in 1885, Wright dropped out of high school and worked as an office boy for a professor of civil engineering at the University of Wisconsin. He later entered the university's evening school as a special student, taking one semester of descriptive geometry and failing to complete a class in French. At the age of nineteen, he went to Chicago and found employment in the architectural office of Joseph Lyman Silsbee, a friend of his uncle's. Wright's ambition, however, was to work for Adler and Sullivan, and he practiced drawing Sullivanesque ornament so that he could make a favorable impression at the job interview.

In 1888 he landed a job there, demonstrating his graphic skill to Sullivan's satisfaction and gaining a five-year contract as draftsman. With an advance on his salary Wright started construction of his own house (1889) in

**15.5** Dankmar Adler and Louis Sullivan, Charnley House, Chicago, Illinois, 1891.

For this composition Frank Lloyd Wright, then working in the Adler and Sullivan office, obviously drew upon the Auditorium Building (see Figs. 14.69–70). The projection of the lobby there became a loggia off the central stair hall in the Charnley House.

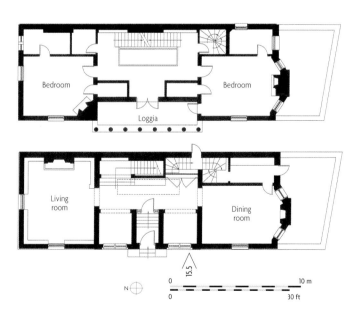

**15.6** Dankmar Adler and Louis Sullivan, Plans of the Charnley House, Chicago, Illinois, 1891.

These carefully balanced plans only hint at Wright's subsequent interior-space designs. The cross axes on both floors intersect at the two-story space of the stair opening.

the Chicago suburb of Oak Park. The house began as a modest two-story building, with a Serliana in the shingle-covered gable end turned to the street. Over the years, the house was greatly enlarged and reworked to provide space for Wright's six children and his mother. In the office of Adler and Sullivan, Wright was sometimes given a free hand with residential commissions, such as that for the James Charnley House (1891), a two-story structure on a narrow city lot in Chicago (Figs. 15.5–15.6). Wright's symmetrical design has a central doorway with carved Sullivanesque ornament below a second-level loggia with Doric columns.

## DEVELOPING THE PRAIRIE HOUSE

Wright soon began designing other houses outside of office time, a practice Sullivan denounced as a violation of Wright's contract with the firm. As a result, Wright was fired and established his own practice, which he based in a studio built onto his Oak Park house. It was the newly developing Chicago suburbs for the rising middle class, like Oak Park, that Wright would use as his first architectural laboratory. While his clients wanted value for money, they were frequently willing to allow Wright to experiment. His early years of independent practice were characterized by explorations of many styles of domestic

**15.7** Frank Lloyd Wright, Winslow House, River Forest, Illinois, 1893.

This is another case where Wright looked to Sullivan for inspiration. The ornamental frontispiece echoed such compositions as Sullivan's Getty Tomb.

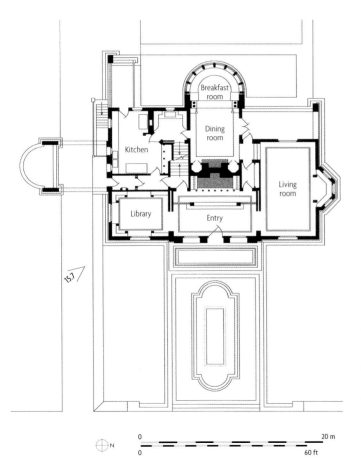

**15.8** Frank Lloyd Wright, Plan of the Winslow House, River Forest, Illinois, 1893.

Wright often spoke of "breaking the box." That process had begun here, where the front rooms are self-contained and axially connected, while the side and rear rooms project as a porte-cochère and as semicircular and semipolygonal bays, and the terraces are defined by platforms and projecting walls.

architecture—Colonial, Tudor, Georgian, Shingle Style, and Queen Anne—although Wright later edited his body of work to include only those designs that obviously contributed to the development of his Prairie Style. Among these was his first independent commission, a house for William H. Winslow (1893) in River Forest, Illinois (Figs. 15.7–15.8). Like the Charnley House, the Winslow House is symmetrical with Sullivanesque ornament. In common with the later Prairie houses, the Winslow House is organized around a central fireplace and dominated by horizontal lines. The hipped roof overhangs the second floor at the level of the window heads, and the apparent height of the ground floor extends to the second-floor windowsills, effectively reducing the perceived volume of the upper level and creating the impression that the building hugs the ground. Wright even broadened the chimney mass to emphasize the horizontal aspect rather than the vertical.

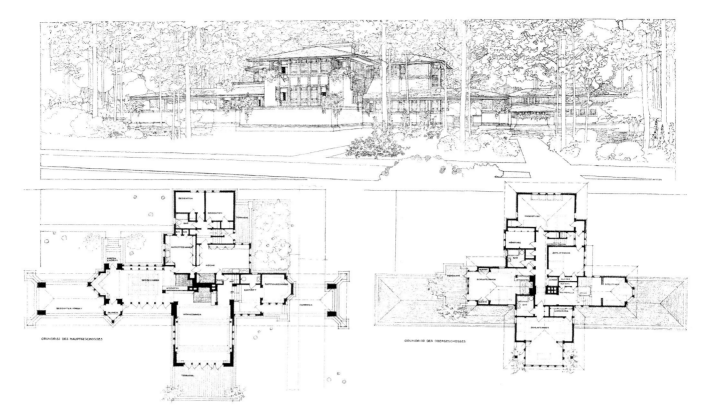

**15.9** Frank Lloyd Wright, Plans and perspective of the Ward Willits House, Highland Park, Illinois, 1901. Drawing.

Ten years after the Charnley House, Wright had devised a new kind of residence. In it, the center is solidly anchored by a great hearth, and the rooms project out aggressively into space, covered by long, low, hovering roofs. His distinctive perspective-drawing technique was influenced by an interest in Japanese prints.

With the design of the Ward Willits House (1901) in Highland Park, Illinois, Wright abandoned the compact composition of the Winslow House for a cruciform plan (a commonly used plan in many houses of the period 1900–10) of four arms extending out into the landscape from the central chimney mass (Fig. 15.9). Again the horizontal line dominates the exterior, accentuated by the overhanging eaves of the roofline and the extension of the transverse axis of the house to form a porte-cochère (a covered drive-through for vehicles) at one end and a covered porch at the other. The exterior stucco is banded by continuous horizontal strips of dark wood marking the first-floor level and the windowsill line. By lowering the eaves to the level of the window heads and diminishing the chimney's height, Wright again minimized the vertical component of this two-story house.

Wright developed the Prairie house out of his search for an appropriate regional expression for American homes, especially in the Midwest. Taking his cue from the gently rolling land of the prairie, he designed houses that sat close to the ground and seemed to be tied organically to the landscape. The prevailing eclectic Victorian styles, which he had tried and discarded, Wright now dismissed as "pimples" on the land. He also responded to the prevailing materials of construction, including brick and wood cut in standard sizes by sawmills, by trying to devise uses for them that were sympathetic to them and their modes of fabrication.

Environmental factors also affected his designs. The broad overhanging eaves shielded the windows from the hot Chicago sun while permitting the lower winter rays to enter and warm the interior. The central fireplace mass gave warmth to the heart of the home, both functionally and symbolically. All major rooms were oriented to provide cross-ventilation. Some of the most remarkable aspects of the Prairie houses are evident on the interiors, where living spaces flow smoothly from one area to another, creating an integrated spatial experience that was to have a profound influence on early Modernist architects in Europe. Wright's Prairie houses are said to "break the box" because neither the external form nor the internal spaces are contained in tight rectangular units. Even the windows wrap around corners as if to deny the traditional structural corner post. Wright extended the spatial freedom of the two-story living hall used by Richardson and Pugin to the entire interior and gave corresponding freedom to the exterior as it embraced the landscape.

Wright incorporated all these features on even the most difficult of sites, such as the narrow suburban lot of Elizabeth Gale, an Oak Park neighbor for whom he designed a house in 1909. Hemmed in by Victorian hulks on either side, the Gale House had little opportunity to spread out to the landscape, so Wright provided the visual link between interior and exterior through a series of balconies cantilevered off the major living spaces. He would return to this idea later when faced with the far more dramatic hillside site of the Kaufmann House (1935–36) called Fallingwater. The last and by far the most celebrated of the early Prairie houses was built for Frederick Robie on two small

**15.10** Frank Lloyd Wright, Robie House, Chicago, Illinois, 1909.

This is the most celebrated house from the first phase of Wright's career. It is a "Prairie house" that acknowledges the horizontality of the Midwestern landscape.

**15.11** Frank Lloyd Wright, Plans of the Robie House, Chicago, Illinois, 1909.

The client owned a small lot on a busy street and had young children. Wright responded with a very compact plan. The front section is very open, while the rear service section consists of more conventional, self-contained rooms, principally for servants and children.

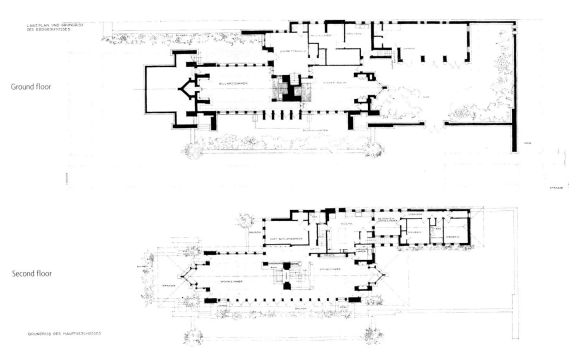

Ground floor

Second floor

corner lots in south Chicago in 1909 (Figs. 15.10–15.11). Robie was a self-made man, a manufacturer who had an interest in engineering, and he and Wright got along exceedingly well. Robie requested a house where he could have privacy from the street and separation from the noise of his small children at play. Wright's response was a three-story design, with the garage, playroom, and service functions on the ground floor, the living and dining areas on the second floor, and bedrooms on the third. A low wall in front of the house shields the ground floor from passers-by, and the elevated windows of the second floor, protected by a balcony, give the privacy Robie desired. A horizontal element was created by the long lines of the walls and balconies, but especially by the great roof of the second floor, which cantilevers daringly at either end of the house. Welded steel beams made this structural bravura possible, and their employment in the Robie House marked the first use of welded steel in residential construction. Bricks for the house, as for other Prairie houses, were custom-made in St. Louis. Shaped like long, thin Roman bricks, they were laid with wide horizontal mortar joints that were sharply raked to cast a horizontal shadow.

In plan the house is organized around the chimney mass. The entrance is off the short side-street frontage into the rear of the house, and the staircase that leads to the second floor is integrated into the masonry of the chimney. The living room and dining room are in effect one continuous space, interrupted only partly by the fireplace, so that the great linear space, illuminated by long bands of windows on either side of the living space, is airy and unified. Wright designed all the interior fittings to complement the space—the light fixtures, furniture, carpets, and even clothes for Mrs. Robie to wear when entertaining. All this was very much in the Arts and Crafts tradition, except for the fact that the designs, especially for the furniture, were based on primary geometric forms and crisp, uncompromising right angles. This made the chairs and tables fit the space well, but all too often Wright's furniture did not fit the non-orthogonal human body.

One of the architects working in Frank Lloyd Wright's circle was Marion Mahoney (1871–1962), the second woman to receive an architectural degree from M.I.T. Ironically, Mahoney's design career may have suffered from her brilliance as a delineator, which meant that she spent much of her time producing presentation-quality renderings. A close comparison of Wright's drawings made before 1895 with those made after Mahoney began working in the office (frequently initialing her work) suggests that she had at least as much influence on the celebrated style of Wright's pages in the Wasmuth portfolios as did Wright himself. No one has successfully isolated her other contributions as a designer of furnishings, mosaics, stained glass, and murals for Wright's Prairie style houses, but they are likely manifold. After she and her husband, the architect Walter Burley Griffith, struck out on their own, Mahoney continued her production of superb renderings, most notably for their entry in the international design competition for Canberra, Australia. More collaborative work followed after the couple relocated "down under", but again attribution of specific work to Mahoney has proved difficult.

Wright's early years as an architect were not entirely devoted to residential commissions. Two notable designs, the Larkin Building in Buffalo, New York, and Unity Temple in Oak Park, illustrate his approach to public buildings. The Larkin Building (1904) (Figs. 15.12a,b) contained offices for a company that sold packaged soap with coupons printed on the labels. Consumers could save these coupons and redeem them for small gifts, a novel practice at the turn of the century. The Larkin Building was populated by rows of young women carrying out clerical tasks and even more rows of filing cabinets holding paperwork. For them Wright designed a frankly vertical six-story building with a full-height skylit atrium at the center (Fig. 15.12c). He placed banks of filing cabinets in partitions or against the exterior wall with windows above them; light from the atrium balanced the illumination on each floor.

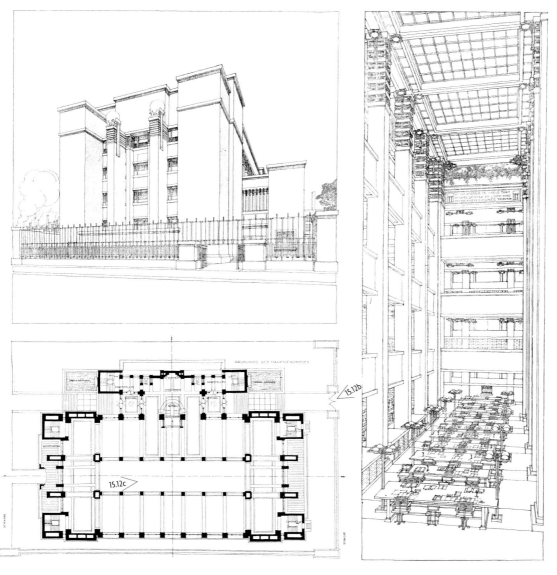

**15.12a,b** Frank Lloyd Wright, Plan (far left, below) and perspective view (far left, above) from the street of the Larkin Building, Buffalo, New York, 1904.

Unfortunately, the Larkin Building has long since been destroyed. Its innovations were many, including central air-conditioning and built-in filing cabinets, which are visible in Fig. 15.12c.

**15.12c** (left) Frank Lloyd Wright, Interior atrium of the Larkin Building, Buffalo, New York, 1904.

A comparison of this perspective with the view from the street shows the continuity. Notice as well the Wright-styled furniture and light fixtures in this top-lit space surrounded by galleries.

**15.13** Frank Lloyd Wright, Unity Temple, Oak Park, Illinois, 1906.

It is remarkable to consider that this landmark work is almost 100 years old. Built for a congregation of modest means, its early use of poured-in-place concrete was an economy-driven innovation.

**15.14** Frank Lloyd Wright, Plan of Unity Temple, Oak Park, Illinois, 1906.

To the left is the sanctuary; to the right is the Sunday-school wing. Entry occurs between the two. Notice the way that Wright breaks away the corners from each volume.

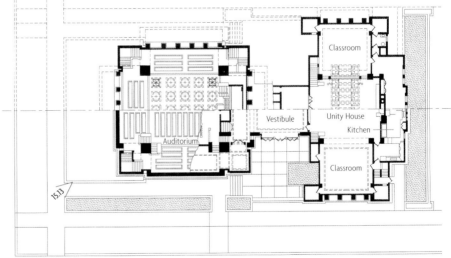

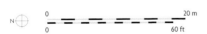

Massed plantings at either end of the atrium introduced the natural environment into the work space, and uplifting moralizing inscriptions, such as "Honest labor needs no master. Simple justice needs no slaves," were cast in the spandrels and placed around the exterior fountains to inspire the workforce. The custom-designed metal furniture used throughout included chairs connected to the desks, so that, after office hours, the back would fold down on the seat and the entire chair would swing out of the way of the cleaning crew's mops. The exterior of the building was rather austere, rising as an uninterrupted vertical brick mass to the height of a thin string course carefully placed to mark the parapet wall around the rooftop recreation space. The stairs, located in all four corners, rose as towers distinct from the building mass, leaving the walls in between to be articulated by repetitive bands of windows. As an office building design, the Larkin Building was forward-looking. Entirely ventilation-controlled, with filtered air intake and extract ducts in the stair towers, it was planned for modular furnishings and flexibility, while provisions made for employee recreation anticipated the corporate health clubs of the present day. It became one of Wright's most widely published designs, especially in Europe, where it was emulated by various designers, making it all the more unfortunate that the City of Buffalo demolished the building in 1949 to create a parking lot.

A happier fate has been visited upon Unity Temple (Figs. 15.13–15.14), built in 1906 for the Unitarian-Universalist congregation of Oak Park. The site was on the corner of two particularly busy thoroughfares, so Wright turned the building inward to reduce the impact of street noise. The two major elements of the church, the worship space, called an auditorium in Wright's drawings, and the unity house containing classrooms and a kitchen, are connected by a common vestibule, neatly solving at once the problems of entrance and separation of the noise of Sunday-school classes from adult worship. The worship space is an articulated cube with two levels of balconies on three walls facing the pulpit on the fourth. It is a rich and glowing interior. Light from leaded-glass windows high in the wall balances that from the deeply coffered, amber-colored skylights over the major congregational seating in the center of the main floor. Insofar as possible, the interior trim consists of orthogonal geometries composed of thin strips of wood. The lights, also designed by Wright, are either spheres or cubes of glass suspended from wooden frames.

Equally remarkable is the exterior, which is constructed entirely in poured-in-place concrete. Unity Temple was Wright's first essay in concrete, and it was also one of the first attempts anywhere to design straightforwardly with that material, instead of covering it or disguising the surface to resemble stone. Wright designed discrete geometric ornament in the formwork of the piers between the high windows, and gave the same treatment to the smaller and lower unity house. The church stands today, carefully restored, and still serving its original functions.

## THE FLIGHT FROM AMERICA

By 1908 Wright was well established as an architect, and his reputation had spread abroad. Public and professional acceptance did not bring happiness, however, and he felt increasingly hemmed in by family responsibilities and office routine. When an offer came from Ernst Wasmuth, a prestigious Berlin publisher, to prepare a portfolio of his work for publication, Wright saw the chance to escape. Abandoning his wife and six children, he took with him instead the wife of a client and neighbor, Mamah Borthwick Cheney, who left her husband and three children, and together they traveled to Europe in September of 1909. For the next twenty-five years, Wright's turbulent personal life seriously interfered with his professional work, and he built very little. The publication of the Wasmuth portfolios, *Frank Lloyd Wright: Ausgeführte Bauten* (*Executed Buildings*) (1910/11) and *Ausgeführte Bauten und Entwürfe von Frank Lloyd Wright* (*Executed Buildings and Projects*) (1911), gave European architects access to his work, but the press in the United States was principally interested in the scandal in Wright's private affairs.

In this difficult period the only major commission Wright received was for the Imperial Hotel in Tokyo (1916–22), remembered now chiefly for its ingenious foundations and cantilevered structural system. The very muddy subsoil conditions of the hotel site prompted Wright to float the foundations instead of digging further

for bedrock. The whole of Japan is prone to earthquake hazard, so Wright sought to balance the building in sections on central concrete pile clusters with a cantilevered concrete slab on top, much as a waiter balances a tray on raised fingertips. The hotel was designed around courtyards with a pool of water in front of the entrance, both for beauty and for firefighting in case of earthquakes. Its form was complex and its decorative program equally so. Looking to create a language of modern Japanese ornament, Wright began with the elementary geometries of circles and squares, but eventually softened them in favor of a personal adaptation of traditional Japanese forms. Beyond decoration, the structural system worked as intended in the severe earthquake of 1923, one of the few triumphs Wright could record in that unfortunate year. Over subsequent years, differential settlement, aided by a lowering of the water table under the area, caused large cracks in the building, and the demand for more spacious, air-conditioned hotel accommodations made Wright's structure increasingly obsolete. It was demolished in the late 1960s to make room for a high-rise.

The architectural career of Frank Lloyd Wright was not over, however, for he would enter another phase of great productivity in the mid-1930s. Those works will be discussed later in this chapter along with other projects of the same period.

## PETER BEHRENS AND THE DEUTSCHER WERKBUND

Previous discussion of the English Arts and Crafts movement included reference to the German Herman Muthesius, who was sent to England in 1896 to report on all aspects of English architecture, design, and manufacture, with the intention that his research should prove useful in raising the design standards of German products. Muthesius's subsequent appointment of eminent designers to leadership positions at German arts and crafts schools was one result of the reform process begun after his return to Germany. In 1907 another significant step came when Muthesius, together with sympathetic manufacturers and designers, formed the Deutscher Werkbund. (This German title does not translate easily. Perhaps "German products association" would be an appropriate English equivalent.) The Werkbund encouraged fine design in industrially manufactured goods. The motive was primarily economic: Muthesius and others were very much concerned that German products would not be competitive in domestic or international markets unless they could equal the standards set by other countries, especially England. Just what artistic direction the Werkbund would take was the subject of considerable debate in the early years, but the word "quality" was used with great frequency. The Werkbund increasingly urged the merits of abstract forms for manufactured products and standardized parts for production

**15.15** Peter Behrens, Poster design for AEG, 1908.

As artistic consultant to AEG, Behrens sought to create a graphic image for a large corporate client. He produced letterheads and advertising graphics as well as trade images such as this one.

**15.16** Peter Behrens, AEG Turbine Factory, Berlin, 1909.

Many have commented on the barn-like aspect of this structure's massing and roof profile, suggesting vernacular inspirations. However, the more relevant features for twentieth-century Modernism are the exposed steel supports and the huge, screen-like end-wall glazing set between massive corner piers.

ease, and demanded that esthetic quality should be evaluated separately from manufacturing quality. All these ideas were to be of great importance to postwar designers.

Another important event of 1907 was the hiring of Peter Behrens (1868–1940), a member of the Werkbund, by the Allgemeine Elektricitäts-Gesellschaft (AEG), or General Electric Company. Behrens was responsible for all aspects of design for the firm—including its letterhead, electric-light fixtures, and production facilities—a brief embracing the modern fields of graphic design, product design, and architecture (Fig. 15.15). The man entrusted with this work was originally trained as a painter, but he was also influenced by the arts and crafts teachings of William Morris.

The buildings Behrens designed for AEG have a quality of stripped classicism. While they are forceful, bold statements, representing the first architectural attempts to deal with industrial facilities, they are also symbols of the new industrial order arising in Germany. The most famous is the Turbine Factory in Berlin (1909), where the polygonal profile of the roof truss over the large manufacturing assembly hall is reflected on the exterior (Fig. 15.16). Behrens avoided applied ornament entirely and gave the structural materials direct expression. The steel frame is exposed along the side walls, where large windows open up between the supports, while concrete panels, slightly battered and articulated in large rectangular coursings, dominate the end elevations. The large front window projects slightly from the concrete mass as if to emphasize its non-loading-bearing status. A lower two-story factory block to the left of the turbine hall has banks of vertical windows framed by a concrete surround closely following classical proportions, but treated here without classical detail.

Perhaps because of his AEG work, Behrens's office soon became known as one of the most progressive in Europe, and a number of the young designers who came to work for him became postwar leaders of the architectural profession. Walter Gropius met his first collaborator, Adolf Meyer, when they worked for Behrens; both Mies van der Rohe and the young Le Corbusier were also employed by Behrens before the outbreak of World War I.

## FUTURISM AND CONSTRUCTIVISM

Two fairly short-lived movements that had an influence on the development of European Modernism were Futurism in Italy and Constructivism in Russia. The ideas of Futurism were laid down primarily by Filippo Marinetti (1876–1944), who published a foundation manifesto in 1909—the same year that Frank Lloyd Wright was abandoning the United States for Europe. Marinetti was passionate in his belief that Italian culture, including Italian architecture, was in a stupor of decrepitude. He called for a radical transformation of the Italian landscape—his plans included paving the canals of Venice! He praised speed, danger, audacity, and even war as a cleanser of society, and he announced the end of traditional space and time. Around this fiery rhetoric coalesced both artists and sculptors, but they had no appropriate graphic means for expressing themselves. By 1912, they had visited Paris and met with Braque and Picasso. The Cubism they saw

**15.17** Antonio Sant'Elia, Project for a Milan power station, 1913.

Antonio Sant'Elia died young as a result of trauma suffered in World War I. His extraordinary perspective drawings made him the best-known exponent of Futurism.

**15.18** Antonio Sant'Elia, La Città Nuova detail, 1914.

Sant'Elia explored the possibilities of a dynamic city dominated by multiple means of transportation. Particularly dramatic here are the tall elevator towers connected to building flanks by leaping bridges.

there suggested ways in which they could represent episodic experiences, energy, and motion in paintings and sculpture, which they did in works such as Umberto Boccioni's *Bottle Evolving in Space*. The most celebrated Futurist architect was Antonio Sant'Elia (1888–1916) but with his death Futurist architecture lost its momentum. Sant'Elia is best known for his "Città Nuova" ("New City") exhibition of 1914 and its accompanying publication, *Messagio*, which became the manifesto for Futurist architecture. Using a dramatic perspective technique, he pro-

posed designs for airship hangars, apartment blocks, transportation centers, hydroelectric plants, and power stations (Figs. 15.17–15.18). All were characterized by bold massing without ornamentation, verticality and battered or stepped-back walls, multiple levels of horizontal circulation, external elevators, and exposed power-production facilities.

In revolutionary Russia, Constructivists were in an equally heady mood, but they were doomed to succumb to stultified Stalinist classicism. In a vast land where many

**15.19** (left) Vladimir Tatlin, Model of the *Monument to the Third International*, 1919.

This tower project, with its dramatic proposal for the use of new materials and construction methods, strongly influenced young Russian designers. Gone are solid walls in favor of a technologically efficient, open frame.

**15.20** (right) Viktor and Alexandr Vesnin, Pravda Newspaper Building, Moscow, 1924. Drawing.

Features such as exterior elevators and huge changeable graphics did not become common on modern buildings until the second half of the twentieth century. Equally portentous are the diagonal braces that were to give rigidity to the slender structural frame.

**15.21** (below) Konstantin Melnikov, Soviet Pavilion, Exposition des Arts Décoratifs, Paris, 1925.

Melnikov achieved this dynamic form through the use of a deformed planning grid intersected by a diagonal stair-concourse. Melnikov's structure appeared in the same Paris exhibition that included the display of Friedrich Kiesler's Cité dans l'Espace (see Fig. 15.43).

in the countryside still lived in environments little changed since the Middle Ages, Constructivists envisioned a Soviet republic with an architecture driven forward by the forces of industrialization, but many of their ideas exceeded the technical capabilities of a backward country in total flux. They sought to exploit modern building materials such as steel, concrete, and large expanses of glass. Like the Futurists, they proposed the dramatic use of external transportation systems, and they added monumental external graphics, prefiguring today's huge digital displays.

Vladimir Tatlin (1885–1953) designed the *Monument to the Third International* (Communist Congress) in 1919 (Fig. 15.19). This tower was to be a fantastic, dynamic double spiral some 1300 feet tall, with revolving cone and cylinders that would have housed governmental and propaganda offices. It was unbuildable, but the vision caught the attention of the world. In 1924, the Vesnin brothers, Viktor (1882–1950) and Alexandr (1883–1959), produced the Pravda Newspaper Building (Fig. 15.20), complete with a loudspeaker system, to house the primary instrument of Soviet propaganda, the *Pravda* newspaper. To its exposed, skeletal frame of steel, including X-bracing, they attached external elevators and a clock with digital readouts, and atop it all they placed a searchlight as a metaphor for the Communist experiment. Konstantin Melnikov (1890–1974) designed the Soviet Pavilion (Fig. 15.21) for the 1925 Exposition des Arts Décoratifs. Its rhomboidal volumes and cantilevered structure emphasized dynamism, and its interconnected spaces expressed the still-open agenda of Soviet Communism. Melnikov's

**15.22** Konstantin Melnikov, Rusakov Workers' Club, Moscow, 1927–28.

Melnikov's club not only demonstrates the kind of dramatic use of structure aspired to by the Constructivists; it also housed the kind of collective activity made necessary by the Russian Revolution. However, within a few years, the progressive Constructivist mentality was replaced by the crushing control of Stalin.

Rusakov Workers' Club in Moscow (1927–28) (Fig. 15.22) shows the same fascination with dramatic structure, in this case through bold cantilever seating constructed of reinforced concrete.

## DUTCH AND GERMAN EXPRESSIONISM

Between 1900 and 1914, painters of the German Brücke (Bridge) and Blaue Reiter (Blue Rider) groups revolted against academic naturalism and sought to express emotions, thoughts, and feelings directly in their paintings. Subsequent to World War I, Expressionist artists and architects reacted passionately to the grinding horrors of trench warfare, as society attempted to come to terms with the guilt, angst, and estrangement of the postwar period. Expressionism in architecture has sometimes been characterized as anti-rationalistic, a twentieth-century continuation of nineteenth-century Romantic sensibilities, and has sometimes been defined by default as everything that did not conform to International Style standards, but its two principal guises—Dutch Expressionism (or Wendigen) and German Expressionism—are better understood by what they were and were for, than by what they were not or what they were against.

The members of Wendigen lived and worked in Amsterdam. Their designs owed much to the work of H.P. Berlage (1856–1934) and stressed the handicraft process of building, the revelation of structure, and the resulting high level of construction-process-related, sometimes fantastic detail. Berlage is best known for his Amsterdam Stock Exchange (1897–1903) (Fig. 15.23), a brick and stone bearing-wall structure of medieval inspiration, but one with a skylit iron-truss roof over the stock-exchange floor (Fig. 15.24). While the Stock Exchange was conceived quite rationally by Berlage, following the precepts of German architect and esthetic theorist Gottfried Semper—about whom Berlage had learned while a student in Zurich—and P.J.H. Cuipers—a designer in the brick tradition of Amsterdam with connections to the thinking of Viollet-le-Duc, its Ruskinian expression of building materials, particularly through the colors and textures of its carefully composed wall surfaces, provided a starting point for Wendigen explorations.

In 1901 Berlage was commissioned by the City of Amsterdam to lay out residential neighborhoods in the area called Amsterdam South. His proposals for two-storey walk-ups of brick, with the street as the primary organizing element, provided the environment for buildings by such designers as Piet Kramer (1881–1961) and Michael de Klerk (1884–1923). Kramer, an outgoing personality with an interest in the occult as well as Communist sympathies, designed his units for the De Dageraad housing association in 1918–23 (Fig. 15.25). He used brick to make taut planar and bulging curvilinear walls, inserted grid-like windows with avian overtones, and applied roof tiles and copings to produce aggressive, prickly silhouettes. De Klerk was perhaps the most talented and original of the Dutch Expressionists. His project for the Eigen Haard housing association (1913–21) (Fig. 15.26) is more plastic than Kramer's work, its silhouette more irregular, and its detailing more highly textured. De Klerk's abilities went well beyond the treatment of surfaces, however, as his housing on the Henrietta Ronnerplein (1921) demonstrates. Here, he manipulated battered walls, linking chimneys, and composite windows to produce a three-dimensional architecture that is among the most original and provocative of the early twentieth century.

German Expressionism was more diverse than the Dutch, concerned with both form and utopianism. Central to much German Expressionist thinking was the writing of Paul Scheerbart and his vision for a glass or crystalline architecture that would somehow ameliorate the repressive opacity of modern culture. In part a reaction against the directions being pursued by the state-run

**15.23** H.P. Berlage, Amsterdam Stock Exchange, Amsterdam, 1897–1903.

Berlage drew upon the longstanding brick building tradition in Holland. The brickwork of the Stock Exchange is enriched by the use of polychromatic stone both inside and out.

**15.24** H.P. Berlage, Amsterdam Stock Exchange interior, Amsterdam, 1897–1903.

On the interior, not only is there brick and stone, but also iron in the form of arched trusses. The material that had once been considered appropriate only for such structures as greenhouses and train sheds had by now become acceptable in institutional buildings.

**15.25** Piet Kramer, De Dageraad housing project, Amsterdam, 1918–23.

The Dutch Expressionist movement, called Wendigen, included such highly imaginative works as this one by Piet Kramer. Inspired by the brick masonry investigations of Berlage, its members sought to be expressive through the natural use of materials in the handicraft tradition.

Deutsche Werkbund, the counter-proposals of German Expressionism appeared dramatically at the 1914 Werkbund exhibition in Cologne where Henri Van de Velde's Werkbund Theater explored the theme of *Kunstwollen*, or the will to form, in contrast to the mechanistic type-form precepts of mainstream Werkbund thinking, and Bruno Taut's Glass Pavilion (Fig. 15.27) gave physical reality to Scheerbart's proclamations. This variety of approaches illustrates the internal stresses at work within the Werkbund: rationality attuned to industrial mass-production versus self-expression made possible by the handicrafts, and, as a corollary to the latter, utopian collectivism and individual romanticism. Taut's Glass Pavilion was quite formal in its organization: a circular concrete base with central, axial stair; a circular rotunda; and a dome. However, Taut so thoroughly exploited the possibilities of glass that the building became a kind of walk-in prism (Fig. 15.28). Glass walls, glass treads and risers, glass panels in the dome, all filtered and reflected light and color to produce a space intended at once to display glass as a product of industrial production and to nourish the human spirit.

Perhaps the most idiosyncratic of all built German Expressionist work was the Goetheanum designed by an amateur, Rudolf Steiner (1861–1925). A philosopher, scholar, and student of the occult, Steiner founded the Anthroposophical Society in 1912 and set out to build a "free high school for spiritual science," which he called the Goetheanum and so connected his thinking to the writings of German literary giant Johann Wolfgang von Goethe. There were, in fact, two Goetheanums, both in

**15.26** Michael de Klerk, Eigen Haard housing project, Amsterdam, 1913–21.

The exotic quality of projects such as this one should not obscure their designers' concerns for making them good places to live. These two-story walk-ups include common areas and landscaped courts.

**15.27** Bruno Taut, Glass Pavilion, Cologne, 1914.

This pavilion was on display at an exhibition organized by the German Werkbund, an organization dedicated to the improvement of German manufactured products. Taut sought to dramatize the potential uses of glass as a building material.

**15.28** Bruno Taut, Glass Pavilion interior, Cologne, 1914.

Taut's obsession with glass began with his so-called "glass chain" writings in which, following the lead of philosopher Paul Scheerbart, he celebrated a vision of culture made less repressive through the use of the transparent material.

Dornach, just across the German border in Switzerland, the first built of wood in 1913 and destroyed by fire at the end of 1922, and the second of concrete, which opened in 1928 (Fig. 15.29). Goetheanum I can be compared to Van de Velde's Werkbund Theater; it was dominated by curvilinear shapes, many that seemed melted and deformed. Underlying this deformity, however, was a symmetrical plan composed of interlocking circles, and the roofs were not unlike many traditional German profiles intended to shed snow. Goetheanum II, which is also systematic in plan, is at once more sculptural and faceted, with the most fantastic part of the complex being the boilerhouse with its vegetal chimney stack.

The Einstein Tower in Potsdam (1920–21) (Fig. 15.30) and the design for a hat factory in Luckenwalde (1921–23) by Erich Mendelsohn (1887–1953) offer yet another

**15.30** (laft) Erich Mendelsohn, Einstein Tower, Potsdam, 1920–21.

Actually quite modest in size, the Einstein Tower possesses a monumentality befitting its function as a laboratory named for one of the twentieth century's foremost scientists. Intended to be made of concrete, it was constructed of stucco over brick for reasons of economy.

**15.31** Erich Mendelsohn, Einstein Tower, Potsdam, Drawings.

Here is evidence of Mendelsohn's extraordinary conceptual thinking. Rapidly executed and energetic, these sketches capture not only the form but also the spirit of the Einstein Tower.

**15.32** Hans Poelzig, Water tower, Posen, 1911.

Hans Poelzig was a highly respected member of the Werkbund; today he would be called a corporate man. Even so, he was comfortable producing this evocative design based upon faceted polychromatic panels. Some of the exterior panels carry over to the interior amid a skeleton of trussed columns.

Expressionistic approach to architecture. The dynamic qualities of the Einstein Tower, built of brick covered with stucco, demonstrate Mendelsohn's interest in streamlined forms, with little connection to the Italian Futurists, but certainly a kinship to Van de Velde's Werkbund Theater and with the Secessionist productions of Joseph Maria Olbrich. The bold graphic technique of Mendelsohn's sketches for it (Fig. 15.31) and related works displays the powerful and often poetic hand of someone forcefully influenced by the act of drawing itself. The appropriateness of dynamism to the activities of a scientist exploring space and time is obvious. Mendelsohn also exploited metaphorical qualities in his hat factory design; here he produced, upon a foundation of rational decisions, a scheme appropriate both to the realities of industrial manufacturing and the spirit of German economic aspirations. The administration building has a De Stijl quality, with its asymmetrical composition of orthogonal shapes, but in the production facilities Mendelsohn exploited structural and mechanical systems to produce logical but highly provocative forms. The rigid frame supporting the workshop inspired a rhythmic composition of triangles on the exterior, and the ventilating hoods of the dye vats are both purposeful and evocative.

Another much-published German Expressionist monument is Hans Poelzig's (1869–1936) water tower at Posen (now Poznan, Poland) (1911) (Fig. 15.32). Here Poelzig, a stalwart member of the Werkbund, orchestrated a collision of seemingly heterogeneous functions and an almost hallucinogenic industrial esthetic. The skin of the tower is faceted and highly textured, with disparate masonry and glazing patterns. On the inside, set in a skeletal structure comparable to that seen in Fritz Lang's Expressionist film *Metropolis* and beneath the water reservoir, Poelzig designed an exhibit space that he planned to be converted into a market hall. The tower is a remarkable amalgamation of purpose and fantasy.

## ART DECO

Some have found a kinship between Art Deco and Expressionistic work. Art Deco is a slippery term describing a diverse design idiom that encompassed everything from graphics to ceramics, furniture, and architecture. Art Deco decorative arts, then known as *l'art moderne*, thrived in France from 1910 or so, and Art Deco architecture continued to be popular in America, especially for skyscrapers and theaters, through the 1930s. As a style, it has only been recognized since the 1960s and so did not even make it into Reyner Banham's *Theory and Design in the First Machine Age* (1960); thus evaluation of the work remains incomplete.

Art Deco designers consistently preferred sumptuous materials and produced objects of supple elegance. Like Art Nouveau and various other Modernist investigations, Art Deco was a movement in search of newness for a new century. However, its inspirations were eclectic in the extreme. From Cubism it drew overlapping and faceted shapes, from Russian Constructivism the language of mechanization, and from Futurism a fascination with motion. Add to these sources motifs drawn from ancient Egypt, Africa, the Orient, and elsewhere such as stylized flowers, coiled tendrils, faceted geometries including chevron patterns, and stylized, idealized, heroic human figures. In France, *l'art moderne* produced lavish ornamentality, so much so that at the 1925 Exposition des Arts Décoratifs in Paris, it succumbed to the tide of European Modernism and its reductivist, mass-production esthetic championed by designers such as Adolf Loos and Le Corbusier.

Ironically, there were abundant French examples of Art Deco architecture at the 1925 exposition, but they were razed at the end of the event. In England, Art Deco designers sought modernity through the expression of function and economy, so the style was considered appropriate for such buildings as power stations, airports, and movie theaters. In the United States, architects of the 1920s were searching for a decorative vocabulary applicable to skyscrapers, which had previously been modeled on everything from campaniles to ziggurats. At a time when European Modernism had not yet taken the field in America, Art Deco ornament was seen as modern, stylish, and appropriate for machine production, making it a viable substitute for the historicism of Gothic-inspired towers such as the Woolworth Building (1913) by Cass Gilbert (1859–1934) in New York City, and reproducible in terracotta, brass, and aluminum. Art Deco offered, if not a machine-age esthetic, a means to celebrate both art and technology.

The most famous Art Deco skyscraper is the Chrysler Building, also in New York (1928) (Fig. 15.33), designed by William Van Alen (1883–1954). Its crown-like dome of stainless steel, with tiered arches filled with sunbursts and capped with a spire, remains a classic for skyline-makers. Its other notable ornamental features include

**15.33** William Van Alen, Chrysler Building, New York City, 1928.

There is still no more distinctive silhouette on the New York skyline than the stainless-steel crown of the Chrysler Building. Long ignored by Modernists, this aspect of tall-building design reemerged as almost a fetish in the 1970s and '80s.

**15.34** Raymond Hood, New York Daily News Building, New York City, 1929–30.

Contemporary with the Chrysler and Empire State buildings, the New York Daily News Building approaches International Style minimalism but displays incised decorative panels of Art Deco inspiration.

**15.35** Raymond Hood, New York Daily News Building incised ornament, New York City, 1929–30.

The Art Deco Style made its appearance at the base of the tower. The sources for Art Deco ornament were many, from Pre-Columbian imagery to forms responding to the period's penchant for speed.

eagle **gargoyles** and the famous radiator-cap acroteria and adjacent frieze of abstracted car wheels.

New York's most prolific Art Deco designer was Ely Jacques Kahn (1884–1972), whose career spanned some fifty years. Representative of his output is the building at Number Two Park Avenue (1927) (page 450), with its wealth of faceted and geometric detail both inside and

**15.36** Reinhard and Hofmeister, Corbett, Hood, Fouilhoux, and others, Rockefeller Center, New York City, begun 1929.

While the individual buildings are distinctive, it is the urban ensemble they create and the space they define that has caused the Rockefeller Center to be so celebrated. For many, it is the very heart of Manhattan. At the center of the complex, the tallest tower, with its distinctive setbacks, is the RCA Building.

**15.37** Wallace K. Harrison, Radio City Music Hall foyer, New York City, 1933.

Within Rockefeller Center, no single interior space is better known than this one. Its plush furniture, opulent materials, and dramatic lighting capture the spirit of New York City in the 1920s and '30s.

out. In 1929–30, Raymond Hood (1881–1934) designed the New York Daily News Building (Fig. 15.34) in New York, which in some ways approaches the minimalism of the International Style but also displays incised decorative panels of Art Deco inspiration (Fig. 15.35) and includes a subtle color palette of greens and terracottas—colors outside the range of European Modernist dicta. Hood and Fouilhoux, along with other firms, designed the complex of buildings comprising the Rockefeller Center (begun 1929) (Fig. 15.36) and located within it a significant body of public art, including Art Deco sculpture by a variety of artists and the famous Diego Rivera fresco that was destroyed soon after completion because of its sympathetic treatment of communism. An artwork in itself is Radio City Music Hall (Fig. 15.37), with its plush furniture and lush materials and lighting. The tallest structure of the period was, of course, the Empire State Building (1931) (Fig. 15.38) by Richmond Shreve (1877–1946), William Lamb (1883–1952), and Arthur Harmon (1878–1958). Its Art Deco ornament includes a vast number of sandblasted aluminum spandrel panels with zigzag ornamentation.

In Los Angeles, Art Deco buildings took two forms: the so-called "Zig-Zag Moderne" and the "Streamline Moderne." The Wiltern (1931) and Pantages (1929) theaters have façades of stepped-back vertical pylons interspersed with ornamental spandrel panels (Fig. 15.39). Their interiors are a riot of sunburst and faceted geometric motifs, including prism-like mirrors and prismatic fan vaults. The Coca-Cola Bottling Plant (1936) (Fig. 15.40) by Robert Derrah (1895–1946), actually a remodeling, illustrates the streamline mode. It includes nautical motifs such as porthole windows, hatch-like doorways, and offices reached by way of a "promenade deck."

A particularly rich body of Art Deco work can be found at Miami Beach, Florida, where the international idiom was fused with a local color palette and adapted to the subtropical climate (Fig. 15.41). These modestly scaled buildings are painted in vivid pinks, greens, peaches, and lavenders that would be garish inland but are delightful here, and are often outfitted with strongly horizontal sunscreens and balconies and punctuated with dramatically vertical entry bays and stair towers. Decoration includes stock Art Deco motifs such as sunbursts, but extends to local flora and fauna, including the ubiquitous Miami palms and flamingos.

**15.38** Richmond Shreve, William Lamb, and Arthur Harmon, Empire State Building, New York City, 1931.

This building would be famous even if the only popular image of it were King Kong batting at airplanes from its summit.

**15.39** B. Marcus Priteca, Pantages Theater, Hollywood, California, 1929.

Theaters offered an opportunity for flights of fancy. The Art Deco office building was tame compared to outrageous Mayan-, Byzantine-, and Egyptian-inspired environments that were created in buildings where illusion was the principal commodity.

**15.40** (above) Robert Derrah, Coca-Cola Bottling Plant, Los Angeles, California, 1936.

A variation on the already diverse Art Deco was the "Streamline Moderne" style. This production facility, with its sleek curves and porthole windows, was actually a remodeling of an existing building.

**15.41** Anton Skislewicz, The Breakwater, Miami Beach, Florida, 1939.

The most popular massing compositions for Art Deco buildings in Miami combine several horizontal floors with a tall, central feature, here a hotel sign and stair tower.

# DE STIJL

The De Stijl movement in Holland had two phases, both of them guided by the painter, designer, typographer, critic, writer, and rabble-rouser Theo Van Doesburg (1883–1931). The origins of the movement can be traced to the work of the painter Piet Mondrian (1872–1944) and the architect H.P. Berlage (discussed earlier in this chapter in the context of Dutch Expressionism). Both men sought a modern expression in their work, Berlage through a moralistic search for truth in building and Mondrian through a reductivism that, he believed, would reveal and subject to criticism the essence of early twentieth-century culture. As Dutch Expressionists tended to be extremely figurative and attuned to handicraft means of building production, so De Stijl designers sought in equal and opposite measure to be ultra-rational, abstract, and mechanistic.

An art student in Amsterdam from age twenty, Mondrian moved to Paris in 1911 and was immediately influenced by Cubism. Back in Holland during World War I, he met Theo Van Doesburg, and they founded the journal *De Stijl* (*The Style*) in 1917. Here, Mondrian set out his doctrine of Neo-Plasticism, influenced by the writings of esoteric mathematician-philosoper M.H.J. Schoenmaekers, who believed that the world functioned with absolute regularity and that this regularity could be expressed through "plastic" mathematics. Mondrian returned to Paris and, following his published philosophy, began a gradual process of abstraction that led him to produce frameless panels laid out in grids, with squares and rectangles painted in only the three primary colors.

Berlage was certainly not an abstractionist, but his writings espoused what he considered to be elementary truths: the primacy of space, the wall as the creator of form, and the need for systematic proportions. It was also Berlage who brought Frank Lloyd Wright to the attention of Dutch designers following the publication of his work by Ernst Wasmuth in 1910–11.

In 1921 Van Doesburg began the first phase of De Stijl, which included as participants Mondrian, several other Dutch painters, and the architects Rob van t'Hoff (1887–1979) and J.J.P. Oud (1890–1963). The group advocated the creation of forms that were universal, spatially unbounded, and attuned to modern technology. Van t'Hoff, who had been to Oak Park, produced a house in Huis ter Heide (1916) that is a convincing adaptation of Wright's work, with its strong horizontals, including clusters of windows, and cantilevered roof and floor slabs. Oud, though never fully committed to De Stijl principles, produced a significant body of related work before he returned to a more staid traditionalism later in his career; the early buildings eventually earned him stature as a first-generation European Modernist. His Hook of Holland housing project (1924) (Fig. 15.42), while not very experimental spatially, is highly reductivist, with its long, seem-

**15.42** J.J.P. Oud, Hook of Holland housing project, Rotterdam, 1924.

The contrast between Oud's housing and that of the Dutch Wendigen designers is almost shocking. Oud had made contact with members of the Dutch De Stijl movement and at the Hook of Holland housing displayed the latter's reductivist desire to de-emphasize applied ornament.

ingly extruded white stucco walls on a base of red and yellow brick, large expanses of glass with plain metal window frames, and details painted in primary colors—a remarkable contrast to the work of Kramer and de Klerk of about the same period.

In 1921–22, the roster of De Stijl participants changed significantly, becoming much more international in profile. Mondrian departed, but Van Doesburg remained as the catalyst. New on the scene were the Russian Constructivist El Lissitzky (1890–1941), Friedrich Kiesler (1890–1965) from the Berlin G Group (which included the young Mies van der Rohe), the planner Cor Van Eesteren (born 1897), and the Dutch architect and furniture-maker Gerrit Rietveld (1888–1964). De Stijl work remained abstract and mechanistic, but became more Constructivist and radical in its exploitation of space in three dimensions. A case in point is Kiesler's Cité dans l'Espace (Fig. 15.43), exhibited at the 1925 Exposition des Arts Décoratifs in Paris. Relieved of the responsibility of serving as a conventional building, this was a three-dimensional grid of linear elements suspended in and organizing infinite space. Likewise, in 1923 Van Eesteren and Van Doesburg collaborated on studies for a house in which they used axonometric drawings and a model by Rietveld to show planar spatial compositions in neutral space affected only minimally by any form of context, including gravity. In his furniture designs, Rietveld developed his own idiom,

called Elementarism, in which he so assembled individual elements that each maintained its individual integrity, and the completed assembly made clear the entire process of construction. His much celebrated Red-Blue Chair (1917–18) (Fig. 15.44) is still in production today. Rietveld's Schroeder House in Utrecht (1924) (Fig. 15.45) is most often cited as the quintessential De Stijl building, but it is limited by the realities of habitation. From the exterior, it looks like one of Van Eesteren and Van Doesburg's house compositions: planes in various orthogonal orientations intersecting and interconnected by linear steel sections. The interior (Fig. 15.46) is somewhat disappointing—very open, dominated by linear, Elementarist components and primary colors, but hardly an investigation of infinite space as defined by Mondrian.

**15.43** Friedrich Kiesler, Cité dans l'Espace, Exposition des Arts Décoratifs, Paris, 1925.

While only an exhibit piece and not a building, Kiesler's composition succeeds in translating Mondrian's two-dimensional ideas into three dimensions. Kiesler was a member of De Stijl in its later stages, when it had reached out to German and Russian designers.

**15.44** Gerrit Rietveld, Red-Blue Chair, 1917–18.

This chair is still produced. Its apparent construction from discrete elements explains Rietveld's description of his work as "Elementarism."

**15.45** Gerrit Rietveld, Schroeder House, Utrecht, 1924.

It is not hard to imagine the shock felt by neighbors in their traditional brick houses when this unfamiliar composition appeared on their street. It had been some twenty years since Adolf Loos first stripped a house of its applied ornamentation.

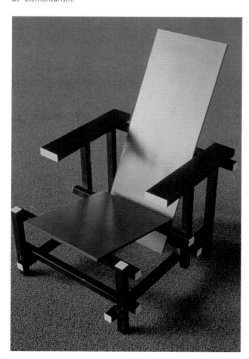

**15.46** Gerrit Rietveld, Schroeder House interior, Utrecht, 1924.

Such an interior shows that it was not easy to translate Mondrian's paintings or Van Doesburg's planar compositions into livable spaces. There is, however, a rigor and, not apparent here, a palette of primary colors like those preferred by Mondrian.

## EXPLOITING THE POTENTIAL OF CONCRETE

The development of the open plan depended ultimately on the availability of materials that could be used for post-and-beam structural systems with **moment connections** between columns and beams or slabs. Just as the development of metal-frame construction was one of the major engineering contributions of the nineteenth century, the development of reinforced concrete has been an important aspect of twentieth-century engineering. Although the idea of reinforcing concrete with metal rods originated in the late nineteenth century, the technique was not extensively exploited for building construction until the twentieth century.

Robert Maillart (1872–1940), a Swiss engineer, explored the possibilities of steel-reinforced concrete. After positioning the reinforcing rods to resist various loads, he allowed the concrete to follow their shape. Through such a rational act of engineering, he was able to exploit the plastic potential of concrete and to produce extremely expressive forms. He also developed a system of mushroom or flared columns supporting flat slabs that eliminated the need for beams, and used it for a warehouse in Zurich, Switzerland, in 1910. Maillart is most famous for his reinforced-concrete bridge designs, which unified load-bearing arches and the horizontal surface of the roadway. The first of these was the Tavanasa Bridge of 1905 (destroyed in a landslide in 1927) and perhaps the most dramatic is the Salginatobel Bridge of 1930 near Schiers in eastern Switzerland, which seems to leap across the valley below it.

In France Auguste Perret (1874–1954) built numerous apartment houses, commercial buildings, and churches,

**15.47** Auguste Perret, Notre Dame interior, Le Raincy, 1922–23.

Auguste Perret was a pioneer in the architectural use of ferroconcrete. Here thin columns support a low-slung longitudinal vault and short transverse ones, all surrounded by a lattice-like enclosing skin.

**15.48** Auguste Perret, 25 bis Rue Franklin, Paris, 1902.

Perret's clever design replaced the conventional Parisian interior light-well with a U-shaped plan that increased the percentage of daylight-lit exterior walls. He cast ornament into the building's concrete skin.

such as Notre Dame, Le Raincy (1922–23) (Fig. 15.47), in reinforced concrete. His earliest notable work was the Paris apartment house at 25 bis Rue Franklin (1902), in which the concrete frame allows an irregular disposition of rooms to reflect the fact that the walls are not load-bearing (Fig. 15.48). This same freedom is reflected in the disposition of the windows, which are closer together than would be possible in a structure with load-bearing walls. In response to neighbors' complaints about the "rudeness" of the material, the exterior concrete was scored to resemble stone. The young Le Corbusier worked for Perret and gained from him his interest in and knowledge of reinforced concrete, a material he would use extensively throughout his career.

## LE CORBUSIER

Charles Edouard Jeanneret-Gris, better known as Le Corbusier, is remembered for his architectural mastery of form and light. Le Corbusier (1887–1965) was born in the Swiss watchmaking town of La Chaux-de-Fonds, and he received his formal art instruction in the local arts and crafts school, which trained its students to do fancy engraving for watch cases. Recognizing his artistic talents, his teachers encouraged him to consider more ambitious goals than a job in the watch industry. His architectural education came from experience garnered in the offices of Auguste Perret (1908–09) and Peter Behrens (1910), sandwiched between sketching trips throughout the Mediterranean, including the Greek islands. He returned to La Chaux-de-Fonds in 1912, taught in the art school, and designed a few houses.

### THE DOM-INO AND CITROHAN HOUSES

From Perret he acquired a firm understanding of reinforced concrete, and from Behrens he learned about designing for industry. He combined these two strains in his first noteworthy project, the Dom-ino House (1914), made in response to the outbreak of World War I. Anticipating that destruction caused by the fighting would increase the demand for rebuilding when hostilities ended, Le Corbusier proposed a mass-produced housing scheme that reduced components to a minimum: floor slabs, regularly spaced piers for vertical support, and stairs to connect the floors (Fig. 15.49). Inherent in the design was the possibility of factory fabrication of these parts near the construction site and rapid erection of the frame by crane. The subdivision of the interior and precise weatherproof enclosure (the walls) of the exterior would be left to the discretion of the builders so that local preferences could be observed.

In 1916 he moved to Paris. It was at this time that he adopted the pseudonym of Le Corbusier, a name taken from his mother's family, for his architectural projects. (He continued to paint under his given name.) With the war still raging, there was not much work for an unknown young Swiss architect, and Le Corbusier occupied his time with painting, writing, and drawing projects. In 1920 he and the poet Paul Dermée began a small journal, *L'Esprit*

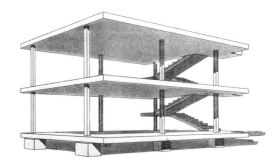

**15.49** Le Corbusier, Dom-ino House, 1914. Drawing.

With this system, Le Corbusier separated structure from enclosure. The results were the free plan, with its flexible distribution of walls, and the free façade, which could take on any desired configuration.

**15.50** Le Corbusier, Citrohan House, 1922. Drawing.

This house's name was a play on words taken from the Citroën automobile and connecting it to Le Corbusier's conception of a "machine for living." The largely blank lateral bearing walls show that it was really envisioned as one unit within a multi-unit block.

*nouveau* (*The New Spirit*), which covered all the visual arts, music, and the esthetics of modern life in its three years of publication. A collection of Le Corbusier's essays on architecture that first appeared in the pages of *L'Esprit nouveau* was reprinted as a book, *Vers une architecture* (translated as *Toward a New Architecture*) in 1923. In it Le Corbusier's tendency for poetic overstatement is indulged in the best traditions of Romanticism, and the book is still illuminating to read for the flavor it gives of the arts in Paris during the early 1920s. "Architecture is the masterly, correct, and magnificent play of masses brought together in light," he proclaimed, as he endorsed the design of buildings based on the esthetics of the machine. In anticipation of eventual mass-production on a modular basis, he also advocated the use of dimensions derived from both a Golden Section-based system of proportions and the size of an average man, for all elements in a building.

Among the projects illustrated in *Vers une architecture* was the Citrohan House (1922), Le Corbusier's attempt to design a modest dwelling that would be as affordable as the Citroën automobiles then being manufactured in France (Fig. 15.50). The house is built of reinforced concrete, raised off the ground by piers or **pilotis**, with a garage and service-storage rooms on the lowest level. The second floor, in the tradition of the piano nobile, has the living and dining rooms, maid's room, and kitchen; the third floor has the master bedroom overlooking the two-story living room; and children's rooms and a roof garden fill the fourth level. Many of Le Corbusier's later houses would incorporate a two-story living room with overlooking balcony. Fenestration consists of simple punched openings filled with industrial windows that divide the exterior into horizontal bands extending continuously with little regard for the location of interior partitions.

## THE VILLA STEIN AND THE VILLA SAVOYE

Later in the decade, Le Corbusier was given the opportunity to build a number of modest and not-so-modest houses, putting his design theories into practice. At Garches he designed the Villa Stein (1927) (Fig. 15.51). As with the Citrohan House, the main living floor is at the piano-nobile level, and the roof becomes an elegant terrace. The regularly spaced structural piers permit freely curving interior partitions, while continuous bands of horizontal windows extend across both the north and south façades. (The end elevations are largely blank, for Le Corbusier was considering this as a prototype for rather narrow suburban lots, where the neighboring houses would create party walls.) The major building proportions were based on Palladio and determined by the Golden Section, the "regulating traces" being included in the published elevation drawings.

More expressive was the Villa Savoye (1929–31) at Poissy, outside Paris (Figs. 15.52–15.54), designed as a weekend house for an art-loving family. The curving ground-floor wall is determined by the turning radius of the motor car that would convey the family here from Paris. The driveway extends under the house, between the pilotis, and continues past the main entrance to a three-car garage and the maid's quarters. From the ground-level entrance hall the visitor has the choice of climbing the sculptural stair or ascending the ramp (which links all three levels) to the second floor. Here, from the main

---

**15.51** Le Corbusier, Plans of the Villa Stein, Garches, 1927.

Here are the results of the dom-ino system in a suburban villa. The walls do not necessarily align with the column bays, and the perimeter wall can be penetrated at any point. The ground floor is at the far right.

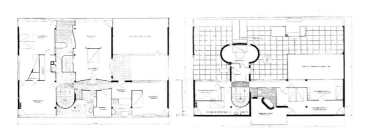

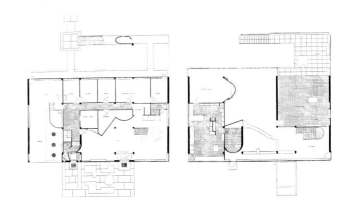

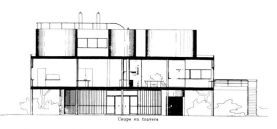

Coupe en travers

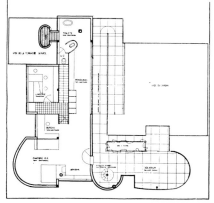

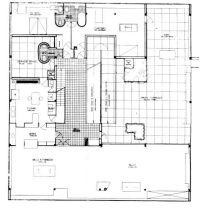

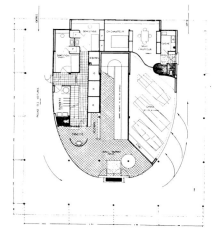

**15.52** Le Corbusier, Plans of and section through the Villa Savoye, Poissy, 1929–31.

The three free-plan floor layouts (ground floor at the right) have almost no correspondence to one another. Continuity is provided by the columnar structural system and by the ramp—an extension of the accomplishments of Adolf Loos.

**15.53** Le Corbusier, Villa Savoye, Poissy, 1929–31.

This view reveals the thin enclosing planes made possible by Le Corbusier's dom-ino system of columns and floor slabs.

**15.54** Le Corbusier, Villa Savoye interior, Poissy, 1929–31.

The dining area (right) and the living area (left) form a single long, narrow space lit by almost continuous ribbon windows.

living floor, one obtained an unobstructed view over the clearing in which the house sits to the forested hills enclosing the site. The large living room is separated by an enormous sliding glass door from the exterior patio and the ramp that continues to the upper-level terrace with its sculptural windscreen walls. The appearance of regularity is carefully maintained on the exterior. All four elevations are essentially identical, consisting of a horizontal ribbon of windows at the second-floor level in a wall plane supported by regularly spaced, recessed pilotis. In fact, the house is a good deal more complex than this simple exterior skin implies, for a close study of the plan reveals that the structural system is *not* a regular grid, as both Le Corbusier's theoretical writings and the façade would lead one to believe. Regular spacing would have made it next to impossible to park cars in the garage, and it would have inconvenienced interior spaces on the second floor as well. Nevertheless, Le Corbusier scrupulously avoided having interior partitions coincide with columns.

Le Corbusier's choice of interior finishes and fittings reflects his enthusiasm for industrial products and his admiration for the functional aspects of oceanliners. The entrance hall alone has unglazed ceramic tile flooring; simple pipe rails, painted black; a pedestal washbasin, freestanding in the hallway; and industrial light fixtures, directed upward to provide reflected light. Skylights, painted intense blue, provide softly colored light reflecting off the white wall surfaces on the second floor, where the master bath has a particularly famous lounging recliner and tub in ceramic tiling. The artful incorporation of varied spatial experiences and light within a simple geometric container testifies to the mastery of form Le Corbusier had achieved by 1930.

## LE CORBUSIER'S "FIVE POINTS"

By 1926 Le Corbusier had articulated his "Five Points Toward a New Architecture":

1. The supports (pilotis) are precisely calculated, spaced regularly, and used to elevate the first floor off the damp ground.
2. The flat roof or roof garden is used for domestic purposes such as gardening, play, and relaxation—thereby recovering all the built-upon ground for outdoor activities.
3. The interior walls, independent of the support system, can be arranged in a free plan.
4. The horizontal windows, made possible by the support system, assure even illumination from wall to wall and admit eight times as much light as a vertically placed window of equal area.
5. The façade, also independent of the structural supports, can be freely designed.

Some of these points are not logical. Concerning point 4, for example, the amount of light coming through a given area of glass is the same regardless of window orientation, but other conditions in the room, such as color and reflective surfaces, do have a great deal to do with the spatial effect of light in a room. It is also unlikely that the rooftop recreations advocated in point 2 would be equivalent to what was possible on the ground. All the points taken together, however, defined a new esthetic for building design, which Le Corbusier followed in most projects until the mid-1950s. His later works will be treated with contemporary developments later in this chapter.

**15.55** Eileen Gray's home at Roquebrune, France, 1926–29.

Few women broke into the ranks of male-dominated European Modernism. Lilly Reich worked with Ludwig Mies van der Rohe on his interiors, but only Eileen Gray produced International Style houses on her own. Interestingly, its plain, white walls are quite consistent with the traditional architecture of the Mediterranean coast and islands.

Within the circle of Parisian Modernists that included Le Cobusier, Eileen Gray (1878–1976) had a unique position. She began as an artist, making lacquer-finish objects from ceramics to furniture, then moved on to interior design, then to architecture. In the early 1920s, she opened a gallery called Jean Désert and had a complete issue of *Wendigen* dedicated to her work. In 1926–29, she built a house for herself in Roquebrune on the rugged south coast of France (Fig. 15.55). Displaying a complete Modernist vocabulary, it is distinguished by the specificity of its response to site, intelligent use of sunscreens, private settings within an open plan, original furniture designs, and varied systems of built-in storage. Gray built another nearby residence for herself in the 1930s and a final, small summer house in the 1950s and left a number of other projects unbuilt.

## WALTER GROPIUS

Prior to World War I, thoughtful architects and designers in the United States, England, Austria, Italy, France, and Scotland were struggling with the problem of finding an esthetic expression appropriate to the industrial world. The war brought a temporary halt to these investigations, but shortly after the termination of hostilities, an approach to the vexing problem of industrial production and artistic expression was proposed by the founding of the Bauhaus, a new school of design in Weimar, Germany. Its students, faculty, methods of teaching, and designs

**15.56** Walter Gropius and Adolf Meyer, Fagus Shoe-Last Factory, Alfeld-an-der-Leine, 1911.

Gropius and Meyer did not intend to create a new style with their rigorously functional esthetic. However, the strips of steel-frame windows and related spandrels and flat roofs created a type used in the United States not only for factories but also for schools and even gas stations.

were to strongly influence the Modern Movement that spread worldwide.

### BUILDING DESIGNS

Walter Gropius, the founder of the Bauhaus, was unusual among the masters of the Modern Movement in being the product of a thoroughly academic architectural education at the universities of Berlin and Munich. The son of an architect, Gropius (1883–1969) obtained valuable practical experience from 1907 to 1910 in the office of Peter Behrens and then set up an independent practice with Adolf Meyer (1881–1929). Their first major project, the Fagus Shoe-Last Factory at Alfeld-an-der-Leine (1911), is still considered a landmark in the history of modern architecture because it used elements that later characterized the International Style: glass curtain walls between expressed steel supports, corners left free of solid masonry, and simple rectangular massing with a flat roof (Fig. 15.56). Having received the commission after a previous designer had already begun construction on the complex, Gropius gave most of his attention to one wing of the factory, where he was able to express his ideals most clearly.

Like Behrens, Gropius was a member of the Werkbund. For its exhibition in Cologne in 1914, Gropius and Meyer designed a model factory to demonstrate the possible architectural expression of a hypothetical manufacturing plant with an attached office block. In consultation with local industry, Gropius devised the building's program to answer the needs of a medium-sized business. The rear of the office block was a glass curtain wall, which extended dramatically around the sides and around the circular stair towers on the front corners, while the front façade was windowless and clad with limestone made to look like brick. Symmetry governed the entire ensemble; the central entrance was placed on axis; and the stair cylinders were overshadowed by tower elements containing roof-level dancefloors connected by a covered restaurant. Separating the office block from the manufacturing plant was a large open courtyard, which led axially to the industrial area, a large basilican hall, itself divided into thirds by the supports for its double-pitched skylit roof. It was far more daring and complex than anything that had yet been constructed for German industry. On the strength of this design, the Grand Duke of Sachsen-Weimar-Eisenach asked Gropius to assume direction of the ducal arts and crafts school.

### THE BAUHAUS IN WEIMAR AND DESSAU

The outbreak of World War I delayed implementation of the Grand Duke's invitation as Gropius served from 1914 to 1918 in the German army on the western front. At the conclusion of the war the German nobility lost their domains, but the Grand Duke's offer was renewed by the new civic authorities, and in 1919 Gropius combined the

# A RUSSIAN PAINTER AT THE BAUHAUS

by Jay C. Henry

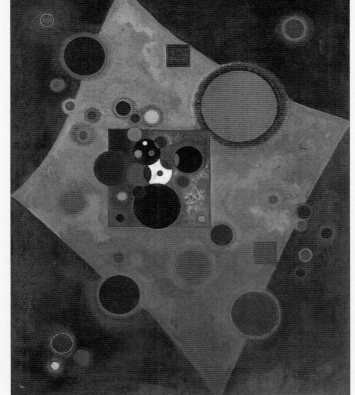

**15.57** Wassily Kandinsky, *Accent in Pink*, 1926. Oil on canvas, 100.5 x 80.5 cm. Musée National d'Art Moderne, Centre Georges Pompidou, Paris.

Abstraction has been a fundamental principle of twentieth-century art, and with the exception of Pablo Picasso, Wassily Kandinsky stands as the most influential abstract artist of the century. Picasso, however, never totally eschewed representation. *Les Demoiselles d'Avignon* (1907) and *Guernica* (1937) remain images with narrative themes. Conversely Kandinsky, by the time he was teaching at the Bauhaus (1922–33), had evolved to the point of total abstraction. *Accent in Pink* (Fig. 15.57) represents nothing but itself—it is pure form and color. And one can appreciate why a painter who viewed art as pure form without extrinsic content would be a valued teacher at a school like the Bauhaus where design was taught as an abstract discipline. It is this rapprochement between an international abstract art and an international modern architecture that makes the Bauhaus and its extraordinary faculty so vitally relevant to the history of twentieth-century design.

Wassily Kandinsky was born in Russia in 1866, making him a contemporary of Frank Lloyd Wright (born 1869) and other figures of the first Modernist generation. His early interest in Russian folk art establishes a common context with national Romantic movements elsewhere in Europe. In 1896 he moved to Munich to study art, where he fell under the influence of the arts and crafts wing of the German Jugendstil. This exposure to William Morris's ideas—for instance, that craftsmanship and design were just as much fine arts as painting, sculpture, and architecture—may have conditioned Kandinsky's ultimate role as teacher in the century's most important design school. Unlike Behrens or Van de Velde, who matured in the same Jugendstil environment, Kandinsky remained fundamentally a painter, and in 1913 he joined the Blaue Reiter group of German Expressionists and published his essay "On the Spiritual in Art" ("Über die Geistliche in der Kunst"), one of the most influential twentieth-century treatises on art. It argued, among other things, that form and color convey emotional and spiritual values beyond mere representation of images.

As an enemy alien, Kandinsky was forced to return to Russia in 1914 and eventually took up a teaching position in one of the new Soviet art schools of the early 1920s, establishing connections with Constructivists. In 1922 he returned to Germany on a visit and accepted Walter Gropius's invitation to teach at the Bauhaus, where he remained until the school's dissolution in 1933. Fleeing the Nazis, he died in exile in Paris in 1944.

By the time Kandinsky joined the Bauhaus faculty in 1922, Expressionism was a waning influence in German art and architecture. His age and conservative temperament made him something of a father-figure and a stabilizing influence following the departure of the eccentric Expressionist Johannes Itten. Kandinsky joined Paul Klee and László Moholy-Nagy, among other new faculty, and, after 1925, the junior masters Marcel Breuer, Josef Albers, and Herbert Bayer, in the move to Dessau in 1926, where his sixtieth birthday was celebrated with a commemorative exhibition. One of Breuer's seminal pieces of Bauhaus metal-tube furniture, the Wassily chair, was named for him.

former Grossherzoglich Sachsen Weimarische Hochschule für Angewandte Kunst (Ducal School of the Applied Arts) and the Grossherzoglich Kunstakademie (Ducal Art Academy) in Weimar into the Staatliches (State, or Public) Bauhaus Weimar. (Bauhaus can be literally translated as "House of Building.")

In joining the former ducal arts and crafts school with the fine-arts academy, Gropius created a new type of institution dedicated to training students in all aspects of design. In the early years most of the faculty were painters from Berlin and Vienna whom Gropius had known before the war. Dominant at the beginning was the Viennese painter Johannes Itten, who taught the *Vorkurs*, or introductory course. Itten's radical, anti-authoritarian philosophy, austere lifestyle, and eccentric mode of dress spread to the students and eventually created friction with the community. The model used for organizing the curriculum was the medieval guild: students were called apprentices and graduated with journeyman's certificates. Gropius was firmly convinced that fine art came through mastery of craft, and he arranged the teaching program so that students were given manual instruction in one of the many craft workshops (wood, metal, weaving, pottery, mural painting) and were led in theoretical studies in principles of form by separate instructors, most often painters such as Paul Klee and Wassily Kandinsky. As Gropius wrote in an essay in 1923:

> By depriving handicrafts and industry of the informing services of the artist, the academies drained them of their vitality, and brought about the artist's complete isolation from the community. Art is not one of those things that may be imparted. Whether a design be the outcome of knack or creative impulse depends on individual propensity. But if what we call art cannot be taught or learnt, a thorough knowledge of its principles and of sureness of hand can be. Both are as necessary for the artist of genius as for the ordinary artisan.

Gropius, himself a product of the European academic system of architectural education, saw the curriculum of the Bauhaus as a sharp break with Beaux-Arts training, and he had harsh words for the older methods:

> The besetting vice of the academy schools was that they were obsessed by that rare "biological" sport, the commanding genius; and forgot that their business was to teach drawing and painting to hundreds and hundreds of minor talents, barely one in a thousand of whom could be expected to have the makings of a real architect or painter. In the vast majority of cases, this hopelessly one-sided instruction condemned its pupils to the lifelong practice of a purely sterile art. Had these hapless drones been given a proper practical training, they could have become useful members of society.

"The ultimate aim of all visual art is the complete building!" Thus began the 1919 prospectus advertising the Bauhaus to students. Through involvement in its workshops, students would become skilled in a craft, learn drawing and painting, and receive instruction in science and theory. It was envisioned that workshop projects would attract outside support, in the form of commissions or production licenses, and that the Bauhaus might soon become self-supporting. Collaboration was stressed from the beginning.

In 1921 Gropius received a commission from Adolf Sommerfeld to design a house, and he saw this as an opportunity to give practical (and paid) experience to some of his apprentices in the woodworking shop. Gropius (with Adolf Meyer) designed the structure, while the Bauhaus apprentices were given a rather free hand to design and furnish the interior. The result was unusual, to say the least. Postwar Germany, saddled with enormous reparation payments to the Allies, had chronic shortages of just about everything. So, to assemble building materials, Sommerfeld, a contractor, purchased a dismantled navy ship for the teakwood it contained, and this wood was used for almost every element. In elevation the house has an affinity with Wright's Winslow House, with due allowance for the peculiarities of its teakwood construction. The interior has been described as "a riot of styles and contemporary clichés," owing to Gropius's encouragement of individual approaches among his students.

As the Bauhaus matured, the thrust of its program, which began with the idea of handicraft as a means to art, shifted to handicraft as a means of making prototypes for industrial production. This adjustment had been made by 1923, in response to three main influences: outside pressure created by growing scandal about flamboyant faculty members and the bohemian lifestyles of the students; the Dutchman Theo van Doesburg's presence and haranguing of these students; and Gropius's own interests in mass production. Moreover, the anticipated support from trade groups or industrial concerns had not materialized, which left the Bauhaus in bad financial straits. If designs could be sold to manufacturers, the income would help alleviate the financial situation. More importantly, in placing emphasis on design for industrial production the Bauhaus had found an appropriate resolution of the relationship of art to the machine. Rather than seeing the two as adversaries, as had Ruskin and the Arts and Crafts Movement, the Bauhaus saw the integration of art with mechanized production as the great challenge for the twentieth-century designer, and it organized its teaching to address this issue.

Despite these changes, the position of the school in Weimar became increasingly difficult. Gropius removed the most eccentric members of faculty and requested that the students wear ordinary clothes, but the radio and newspaper attacks on the Bauhaus continued. At Easter in 1925 the progressive mayor of Dessau offered assistance, and the Bauhaus moved to temporary quarters there. By

15.58 Walter Gropius, Bauhaus, Dessau, 1926.

The plan of this building is a pinwheel, reaching out into space like a Mondrian painting. The workshop wing seen here is a concrete column-and-slab frame enclosed by a glass curtain wall. Considered decadent and expressive of Communist values, the building was shut down by the Nazis in 1932.

December 1926 the school was established in a new home designed by Gropius in buildings that rank among the finest expressions of the emerging Modern Movement (Fig. 15.58). The reinforced-concrete-frame structures consist of four major elements, arranged freely on the flat site so that there is no "front" in the customary sense. The workshop wing, four stories tall, is the largest mass, containing behind its glass curtain wall the studio spaces for preliminary instruction and workshops for printing, carpentry, dyeing, sculpture, weaving, and wall painting, in addition to exhibition and lecture spaces. A road (added by Gropius) runs through the site beside the workshop building, requiring an enclosed bridge to connect it to the separately administered trade school. In the bridge were administrative offices for the Bauhaus and Gropius's private architectural office. Parallel to the road and extending behind the workshop wing is the low dining hall and auditorium building, equipped with a stage between the two spaces and provided with movable walls for maximum flexibility. Beyond this is a five-story student dormitory with twenty-eight rooms and related facilities.

What made this building complex so remarkable? Several characteristics can be identified. The asymmetrical, sprawling composition represented a break with the typical monumental disposition employed for educational facilities. Separate articulation was given to each element of the program, resulting in an abstract, sculptural treatment for the whole, and the introduction of a road and bridge reinforced the sense of free-moving space. Bauhaus workshops designed and executed all the interiors, with the metal workshop responsible for lighting fixtures and the tubular steel furniture (designed by Marcel Breuer), the printing workshop for the graphics, and so on. Thus, the building was a total work of art, a unity of architecture and related crafts. Its industrial construction materials, concrete and glass, were employed without ornament, and circulation

was clearly expressed in the layout.

Gropius also designed a series of seven dwelling units—one detached house and three duplex houses—for Bauhaus faculty. The duplex units are identical, yet by changing their orientations and making one the mirror image of the other Gropius obtained the effect of three different designs. Thus, standardization was combined with variety. Like the Bauhaus buildings, these houses are flat-roofed and were originally painted white with industrial-looking pipe-rail details on the balconies.

The Bauhaus in Dessau continued to emphasize design for industrial production and licensed a number of products to German manufacturers. Gropius began to offer specific architectural instruction to advanced workshop students, marking the first time building design had been taught in the curriculum. Bauhaus designs, whether for architecture, graphic design, or products, tended to favor primary geometric shapes and solids, coupled with linear elements, to achieve an appearance of simplicity. The forms of finished goods reflected both the nature of the material and the manufacturing process required for fabrication. Although Gropius always denied that there was a Bauhaus "style," there is a strong visual affinity among many of the student projects and faculty designs created there.

These designs became widely known through exhibitions and publications, gaining general acclaim for the school throughout Europe. The facilities in Dessau provided workspace superior to anything the Bauhaus had had in Weimar, and it seemed that the turmoil that had marked the school's early years was past. This was not to be, however. Financial problems, while greatly reduced, were not entirely solved, and the reactionary political forces accompanying the rise of Nazism were gaining strength in the provinces around Dessau. In hopes of diminishing criticism of the Bauhaus, criticism he interpreted as being directed at him personally, Gropius resigned as head of the school in April 1928 and returned to his private architectural practice.

A young architect, Hannes Meyer, was appointed to succeed Gropius. Meyer set about enlarging the architectural program, adding courses in mathematics and engineering and emphasizing through lectures and studio projects the social responsibilities of architects. The other workshops were urged to increase production, and more designs than ever were licensed to industry, bringing increasing royalties to the school. But Meyer also encouraged students to become active in politics, a courageous, if imprudent counsel in the deteriorating political climate of the time, and in the summer of 1930 the authorities asked him to resign. His replacement was Mies van der Rohe, an architect long active in the Deutscher Werkbund, whose reputation was by then international.

Mies moved to stabilize the school by flatly prohibiting any political activity and insisting on the highest possible standards of work. More powerful political forces were gathering, however, and in 1932 the Nazis gained control of Dessau. One of their first acts was to move against the Bauhaus, which to them symbolized Communism, decadence, and subversion; in October 1932 they closed the school. Shortly afterward Mies managed to reopen the Bauhaus as a private institution in Berlin, but in April 1933 the building was raided by the Gestapo, and it finally closed its doors in July 1933.

## LUDWIG MIES VAN DER ROHE

Ludwig Mies van der Rohe (1886–1969) was the son of a stonemason, and he received practical experience in construction from his father, later working as an apprentice in the office of furniture designer Bruno Paul. From 1908 to 1911, Mies worked in the office of Peter Behrens. His early designs as an independent architect show the influence of Karl Friedrich Schinkel, as can be seen in the projected house for Mrs. Kroller-Müller (1912), which was a symmetrical rectangular solid with a stripped classical colonnade across the front.

After World War I Mies worked on a series of projects that were to have an enormous impact on later architecture even though they were never constructed. The first was a competition entry for an office building above the Berlin Friedrichstrasse station (1919), a twenty-story skyscraper completely sheathed in glass. In 1920–21 Mies carried the concept of a transparent skyscraper a step further in a project for a thirty-story tower, again wrapped entirely in glass, with a highly irregular perimeter and two circular elevator-stair cores. Mies's idea was to capitalize on the varying reflections. The irregular curves of the walls were actually composed of short line segments, representing the width dimension of the curtain-wall panels, so the entire building was to be a highly faceted, shimmering shaft. Its internal structure was provided by reinforced concrete slabs, can-

tilevered to a thin edge at the outside wall. However, because material science and construction techniques in 1920 were inadequate to construct these designs, the first completely glazed office building was not built until 1950–52: Lever House on Park Avenue in New York City, designed by Gordon Bunshaft of Skidmore, Owings, and Merrill. Its curtain-wall construction includes horizontal strips of plate glass with dark-green spandrel glass covering the floor construction, both set in stainless-steel frames.

Two other projects from the early 1920s show that Mies was thinking about materials other than glass. His project for a concrete office block (1922) has seven floors, each a great horizontal tray with cantilevers. The height of the tray edge was determined by the vertical dimension of filing cabinets; windows above ran in a continuous horizontal strip in a plane recessed from the outer edge of the concrete. If one recalls the Larkin Building, which had incorporated the same idea on its office floors, one can perhaps detect the influences of Wright's Wasmuth publications. The ideas of De Stijl and the free plans and flowing spaces of Wright's early Prairie houses also affected Mies's designs. His 1923 project for a brick country house, with its walls extending as vertical planes out into the landscape, seldom intersecting one another but effectively defining space, is an early example. Some of this freedom would reappear in his 1929 masterpiece, the Pavilion of the Deutscher Werkbund for the International Exposition in Barcelona.

### THE BARCELONA PAVILION AND THE TUGENDHAT HOUSE

The Barcelona Pavilion (Figs. 15.59–15.60) has become one of the most celebrated architectural designs of the twentieth century, even though until recently it was known to most people only through photographs, since after the exposition was over, the building was dismantled and its materials sold at auction; a replica of the pavilion has recently been built on the original site. It is a small structure, and unlike most exhibition buildings, it contained no displays. Aside from the stainless-steel tables, stools, and chairs designed by Mies specifically for the building, the only object on view was a sculpture of a dancing girl by Georg Kolbe, carefully placed in a reflecting pool at one end of the building.

The influence of the Barcelona Pavilion derived not from what it contained but from the building itself. Mies intended that it should stand for quality design, materials, and craftsmanship. The design is at once simple and sophisticated. Raised on a low podium, as if to elevate it above the frenzy of the fair, the pavilion was a one-story jewel box. Most of its ground plane was occupied by an exterior courtyard, dominated by the large reflecting pool lined with black glass. Eight cruciform columns supported a horizontal roof slab that appeared to hover, independent of the vertical walls (Fig. 15.61). The walls

**15.59** Ludwig Mies van der Rohe, Barcelona Pavilion, Barcelona, [1929] 1986.

Mies's building was dismantled at the end of the Barcelona exhibition. However, it has recently been rebuilt, using stone from the original quarries, so that Mies's ideas can be personally experienced once again. The image seen here is of the reconstruction of 1986.

**15.60** Ludwig Mies van der Rohe, Plan of the Barcelona Pavilion, Barcelona.

Compare this plan to the early work of Frank Lloyd Wright or the dom-ino houses of Le Corbusier. All sought a new means of spatial expression, which was the most significant area of study among twentieth-century Modernists.

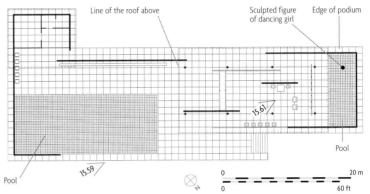

Line of the roof above • Sculpted figure of dancing girl • Edge of podium

Pool

15.61

15.59

Pool

0   20 m
0   60 ft

N

**15.61** Ludwig Mies van der Rohe, Barcelona Pavilion interior, Barcelona, 1929.

While Mies was not a member of De Stijl, his spatial conceptions certainly corresponded to those of the movement. The materials he used were onyx for the floors, marble veneer for the partitions, and stainless steel for the columns. The stools and chairs are also his designs.

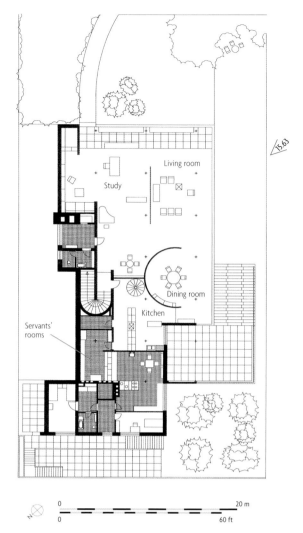

**15.63** Ludwig Mies van der Rohe, Tugendhat House rear view, Brno, 1930.

The private terrace to the rear is surrounded by a retaining wall of rock-faced masonry. The glass walls offer unobstructed views out into the natural landscape.

**15.62** Ludwig Mies van der Rohe, Plan of the Tugendhat House, Brno, 1930.

Mies's spatial experiments could be applied to day-to-day living conditions. The family space lies to the top in the plan and is only minimally subdivided. The service spaces are much more enclosed.

were not incorporated in or aligned with the column grid; in this way, Mies deliberately expressed a separation between structure and enclosure while conforming both to the same orthogonal geometry. The columns were shiny chromium-plated steel; the walls were polished book-matched marble in deep shades of green and red; the floors were Roman travertine; and the onyx and gray-tinted glass contributed to the feeling of sophisticated taste and luxury. The Barcelona chairs and stools were chrome-plated steel with white kid upholstery. Mies's collaborator, Lilly Reich, shares credit with him for the interior design, particularly for the deep-red velvet curtain that hung over the front glass wall.

Influences on the pavilion's architecture can be identified: Schinkel for the podium and formality of the com-position; Wright for the flowing spatial qualities and great horizontal sweep of the roof; and De Stijl for the almost abstract composition of solid, void, and line. The master-ful integration of these diverse influences into a new archi-tectural synthesis remains the great accomplishment of Mies van der Rohe.

Mies used his concepts from the Barcelona Pavilion in a residential commission of 1930, the Tugendhat House (Fig. 15.62) in Brno, Czech Republic. The same regular grid of chromium-steel cruciform columns supports the roof, and polished slabs of marble serve as walls to define interior spaces in an open plan. Because of the hilly site, the Tugendhat House has two stories, set firmly within a series of terraces cut into the slope; but thanks to its largely glass walls, the predominant view is out to the surround-ing landscape (Fig. 15.63). Color on the interior is subdued, confined to the natural hues of the finish mate-rials and a white linoleum floor, so that the changing light and colors of the outside world determine much of the color inside the house.

By the mid-1920s progressive architects in many Euro-pean countries were working in a manner that reflected a new admiration for industrial materials and products, respect for rational, straightforward architectural expres-sion devoid of applied ornament, and an accompanying interest in the purity of simply geometric forms and planar surfaces. For want of a better term, this is still called the "Modern Movement," although eventually we will need to develop a more descriptive label (perhaps even more than one) to reflect the diverse currents in architectural design since 1920.

**15.64** Ludwig Mies van der Rohe, Weissenhof Siedlung blocks of flats, Stuttgart, 1927.

Mies developed the site plan for this exposition and built his apartment block on the highest ground. Notice the mass-produced windows and pipe-rail balconies like those used twenty years earlier by Adolf Loos.

**15.65** Le Corbusier, Weissenhof Siedlung housing unit, Stuttgart, 1927.

Le Corbusier composed his housing unit using by-now-familiar elements: supporting columns or pilotis, an unornamented façade, horizontal ribbon windows, and a roof garden.

## THE WEISSENHOF SIEDLUNG AND THE INTERNATIONAL STYLE

In 1925 the Deutscher Werkbund proposed that an exhibition be held in 1927 to demonstrate the latest thinking about housing design, interior fittings, and construction technology. The City of Stuttgart and various materials suppliers contributed land and money for the construction of thirty-three permanent buildings on a hillside on the outskirts of the city. Mies, as vice-president of the Werkbund, was placed in charge of the enterprise; he developed the master plan and contributed the design of a block of flats. With characteristic generosity he invited participation by sixteen leading architects from across Europe, assigning them sites for detached houses, duplexes, or row houses. The permanent buildings became known as the Weissenhof Siedlung (or model housing estate at Weissenhof).

The concept behind the exhibition was to design modestly scaled, modern dwelling units suitable as prototypes for mass production. A variety of approaches were adopted by the individual designers, but it was the elements their designs had in common that were crucial in

the development of Modernism. All the buildings were painted white; they had "functional" windows that emphasized the horizontal; and almost all had flat roofs, some with garden terraces. Industrial character was expressed in the cylindrical pipe railings on balconies, the major decorative element on the exterior. Window trim was minimal, and there were no cornices. In a manner recalling the Cité Industrielle of Garnier, Mies had originally planned to keep cars on the perimeter, with only pedestrian access to the housing area; but the city authorities, who wanted to resell the units as individual dwellings after the exhibition, requested that the land be divided into plots with separate access. Mies was able to retain his basically sculptural conception of the overall form of the site, with the tallest and largest building, his own four-story block, set on the highest portion of the hill (Fig. 15.64).

Mies's building included standard elements—a kitchen-bathroom core, prefabricated partitions, and storage walls—that allowed each of the twenty-four units to be arranged differently in plan. Standardization and rational planning, together with a steel frame, made this flexibility possible. The roof terrace provided recreational facilities, and each apartment has a small balcony. Horizontal strip windows facilitated cross ventilation for each dwelling unit.

Walter Gropius built two detached houses, but neither remains. Continuing the approach being studied at the Bauhaus, he designed in close collaboration with several manufacturers, and both houses were constructed entirely of prefabricated panels. The module of the panels could readily be seen inside and out, and the interior was furnished with the products designed by Marcel Breuer and produced in the Bauhaus workshops. It is interesting to note that, after coming to the United States in 1937, Gropius continued his interest in prefabricated housing but failed to interest American manufacturers in the idea. When he built his own home at Lincoln, Massachusetts (1938), in collaboration with Breuer, Gropius turned instead to the building components already available in light-industrial construction and artfully incorporated them as the major elements of the house.

Le Corbusier also contributed two designs, one a single-family dwelling in reinforced concrete and the other a duplex with a steel frame (Fig. 15.65), a realization of the Citrohan concept. The latter was one of the most controversial structures at the exhibition, in part because of its unorthodox interior proportions. The main circulation spine is a corridor that runs the length of the house, with dimensions and windows that suggested a train more than a residence, particularly as some bedrooms were narrow, like the sleeping compartments of European trains. Le Corbusier was, in fact, fascinated by the functional designs of oceanliners and airplanes, so it is possible that railway cars also inspired his architecture.

The common thread of rational or functional design could be detected in all buildings at the Weissenhof Siedlung, and the projects of German architects were not dissimilar in appearance to those produced by designers from other countries. This esthetic affinity and a book, *Internationale Architektur* (1925) by Walter Gropius, led Alfred H. Barr of the Museum of Modern Art in New York to call the modern architecture of the late 1920s the International Style.

European architectural developments were a major focus of the MoMA show (mentioned at the beginning of this chapter) organized by Barr, Henry-Russell Hitchcock, and Philip Johnson in 1932. For the first time the American public and American architects were made aware of postwar advances in Germany, France, Holland, and Belgium, as works like Gerrit Rietveld's Schroeder House were displayed alongside early Wright designs such as the Winslow House, and the abstract rationalism of De Stijl appeared alongside the work of Mies, Gropius, and Le Corbusier.

According to the definition devised by Barr, the International Style was characterized by "emphasis upon volume—space enclosed by thin planes or surfaces as opposed to the suggestion of mass and solidity; regularity

**15.66** George Howe and William Lescaze, Philadephia Savings Fund Society Building, Philadelphia, Pennsylvannia, 1929–32.

George Howe brought William Lescaze from Europe to inform his office about the new International Style. The vertical articulation masks stacked horizontal ribbon windows and spandrels.

as opposed to symmetry or other kinds of obvious balance; and, lastly, dependence upon the intrinsic elegance of materials, perfection, and fine proportions, as opposed to applied ornament." Hitchcock later revised this statement to include the articulation of structure in the place of the point about ornament. Even allowing for this adjustment, it is apparent that the architecture of the Weissenhof Siedlung was succinctly described by Barr's definition.

**15.67** Ludwig Mies van der Rohe, Crown Hall, I.I.T. Chicago, Illinois, 1956.

"God is in the details," said Mies. At I.I.T. he demonstrated his mastery of detailing in steel, glass, and brick. The steel skeleton of Crown Hall is completely exposed, including the plate girders that rise above the roof.

As an indication of the strength of Beaux-Arts classicism and Art Deco in the United States in the 1920s, only a handful of American buildings were included in Hitchcock and Johnson's book, *The International Style*, which was based on material in the MoMA exhibition. The largest American International Style building included was the Philadelphia Savings Fund Society Building (1929–32) by George Howe (1886–1955) and William Lescaze (1896–1969) (Fig. 15.66). The entire Market Street façade was cantilevered beyond the column line, allowing the windows to wrap in a horizontal band around the corner to glorify the freedom from structural constraint. No towers quite so bold as this would be built in the United States for the next decade, in part because of the Great Depression and World War II. Smaller structures that were built according to the dictates of the International Style, or at least in imitation of it, were often seen as cheap because they lacked presumably expensive ornament or because they were simply bad imitations of the European originals.

## LATER WORK OF MIES VAN DER ROHE

By making visible the modern architecture of Europe, the MoMA show did much to increase awareness of the International Style. The impact would be greater still when the leading architects of Germany, fleeing Nazi intolerance of their work (called "Arab" by Hitler), emigrated across the Atlantic. Walter Gropius arrived in 1937, after a period of professional practice in England, to direct the Department of Architecture at the Graduate School of Design at Harvard University; Marcel Breuer, a pupil and teacher at the Bauhaus, also taught under Gropius at Harvard; and Mies van der Rohe came to Chicago in 1938 to head the Architecture School at the Armour Institute of Technology (soon to merge with the Lewis Institute and become the Illinois Institute of Technology [I.I.T.]).

### PLANNING AND BUILDING AT I.I.T.

In his twenty years at I.I.T. Mies had the opportunity to plan the new campus, design many of its buildings, and influence the architectural education of a whole generation of students. The curriculum laid down by him stressed clarity, rationality, intellectual order, and discipline, and progressed from building in wood to stone, brick, concrete, and finally steel. Once students understood the materials, they studied problems of design. The highest standards of draftsmanship and precision were expected at all levels, and the essence of architecture was reduced to skin and bones—the glass spandrel panels or brickwork (skin) set in the structural frame (the bones).

The master plan Mies made for I.I.T. reflects the order and rationality of the curriculum. A square grid subdivides the rectangular site, and the buildings are all conceived as rectangular masses conforming to the grid, creating a continuous series of interlocking courtyards and exterior walks. Mies saw that steel was the major American industrial building material (labor costs for formwork often made concrete less economical), so he set about designing the purest, most elegant steel expressions achieved up until that time. For the I.I.T. campus he designed Crown Hall (1956) (Fig. 15.67) to house the School of Architecture. It is a one-story building raised above a high basement. Four deep panel girders straddle the building, supporting the roof and leaving the entire interior free of columns. Except for the stairs and toilet rooms, which are fixed, the possible locations of subdividing walls are not hindered by the architectural container. As in his other projects, Mies was designing for flexibility and change, so that other, unforeseeable uses might easily be accommodated within the building at a later time.

In his office Mies designed a range of other projects. On a beautiful site in downtown Chicago overlooking Lake Michigan, he built a pair of apartment towers known

15.68 Ludwig Mies van der Rohe, 860 Lake Shore Drive, Chicago, Illinois, 1949–51.

Notice that Mies designed the blinds to be positioned up, down, or halfway between, and in no other positions. His reductivist mentality made accommodation of individual tastes impossible.

by their address, 860 Lake Shore Drive (1949–51), the first glass-and-steel high-rise residential construction in the United States (Fig. 15.68). Twenty-six stories tall, they are the realization of the concept he first proposed in the glass-tower schemes of 1919–21. During the interval, technological capabilities had come up to the level required to construct a glass tower. The 860 Lake Shore Drive buildings are framed in steel, made fireproof by a masonry casing. Mies was able to express the actual structural material only by welding additional non-structural steel to the exterior of the frames. To increase the vertical appearance of the buildings, thinner I-beams run continuously up the building as window mullions. This exterior steel serves no structural function, of course, but Mies judged it necessary to make the building "look right."

As early as 1946 Mies was at work designing an all-glass house for Dr. Edith Farnsworth, to be located on land near the Fox river in Plano, Illinois. Design and construction took six years, during which time Philip Johnson built a glass house for himself (1949) in New Canaan, Connecticut. The Farnsworth House (1950–52), raised off the ground because the Fox river occasionally flooded the site, sits as a simple white frame in the landscape, as elegant an expression of skin-and-bones architecture as could be imagined (Fig. 15.69). The glass walls can be screened with white curtains when privacy is desired, but the play of light as it reflects off the glass and the immediacy of the natural surroundings viewed through the walls are more effective unscreened. Thus, it is an expression of an architectural ideal rather than a model for everyday

15.69 Ludwig Mies van der Rohe, Farnsworth House, Plano, Illinois, 1950–52.

Whatever the complaints about Mies's reductivism, the formal results are elegant, almost timeless. In fact, the Farnsworth House can be interpreted as a classical temple, its stylobate or base slid forward to create an arrival sequence.

**15.70** Ludwig Mies van der Rohe, Seagram Building, New York City, 1958.

There is no more celebrated Miesian skyscraper than this one. Unlike Crown Hall and the Farnsworth House, but like 860 Lake Shore Drive, this high-rise structure was required by building codes to have all of its steel structure covered with fireproofing. The steel frame expressed on the outside is therefore structurally redundant.

as in Crown Hall; and the longest spans would have a steel space-frame, as in the Nationalgalerie in Berlin (completed 1968).

## LATER WORK OF FRANK LLOYD WRIGHT

The previous discussion of Wright concluded with his design of the Imperial Hotel. While his architectural practice in the 1920s suffered because of his personal difficulties, he did manage to do some work, notably in California. There he built a series of so-called textile-block houses, which were not of cloth but of patterned concrete block, made to his own designs, laid in a stacked bond, and held together by internal steel reinforcing bars. One such house, built in Pasadena for Alice Millard (1923), illustrates the group. The use of concrete block imposed an orthogonal geometry on the design, although Wright, as usual, created an open and flowing plan, with balconies and terraces to link the house to its hillside site. The custom-designed pattern molded into each block contributes an overall texture to the exterior and reinforces the sense of surface integrity in both a structural and an artistic sense. As in Unity Temple and the Imperial Hotel, one can detect influence from Maya art in the massing and ornamental detail.

Toward the end of the decade, Wright's chaotic private life became more orderly. He was still hounded by the press and pursued by creditors (his home at Spring Green, Wisconsin—Taliesin East—was almost forcibly sold for nonpayment of taxes), but in his third wife, Olgivanna Lazovich, he found a steadying influence. To rescue him from financial pressures, a group of loyal friends incorporated Wright and paid off the mortgages on Taliesin, counting on his future earnings to repay their investment. Wright formed the Taliesin Fellowship in 1932 for young men and women who wished to work under his tutelage, charging them a fee for the experience. It became a highly personal school of architecture, reflecting Wright's disdain for the formal trappings of educational enterprises. Students, called apprentices, participated in all aspects of life and work at Taliesin, from helping with farm and kitchen chores, to constructing the ever-expanding physical plant, to performing in musicals or theatrical events, and even to assisting Wright in the drafting room. With Olgivanna's encouragement, Wright also began to write; the first edition of his *Autobiography* dates from 1932.

### BROADACRE CITY

Just as Wright was again becoming a productive architect, the national economy took a nosedive into the Great Depression. There was little work for anyone to do, so Wright and his apprentices turned their attention to a utopian scheme that Wright christened Broadacre City. It illustrated many of Wright's ideals about the proper

family living; it carries the concepts of the Tugendhat House to their logical conclusion, losing in the process a certain degree of practicality.

Mies evolved a thoroughly rational approach to architecture, designing "universal" spaces enclosed in rectangular containers, the most easily used of geometries. From the beginning, he designed with later modification and reuse in mind by making painstaking studies of the exterior architectural expression to ensure a timeless and elegant character. Mies used one of a selection of several steel-framing systems depending on the maximum clear span required. Short spans would use ordinary columns and beams, as in the Farnsworth House, 860 Lake Shore Drive, and the Seagram Building (1958) in New York City (Fig. 15.70); moderate spans would employ plate girders,

manner of living in America. The single-family house, set in about one acre of land, was the basic dwelling unit. The urban center was rather small and dispersed, for Wright anticipated that efficient communications and high-speed transportation would largely eliminate the need for the congestion associated with city life and business. (Heavy industry seems to have been conveniently overlooked.) In some respects Broadacre City looked backward to the nineteenth century and to the small, largely agrarian towns that characterized much of the United States then. Small, self-sufficient communities clustered around cultural and recreational facilities conjure up romantic visions of a past that probably never existed. In other respects Wright's scheme was farsighted, for it seemed to incorporate enduring American attitudes: a mistrust of bigness, a love of the land and open air, and the opportunity for individual expression. The phenomenal suburban growth around American cities after 1945 reflects in part the popular interpretation of concepts embedded in Broadacre City.

All of Wright's later buildings were designed to fit into a setting like Broadacre City. For residences, Wright developed the Usonian House as an ideal, and he constructed many actual examples across the country from the mid-1930s until the late 1950s. Usonian houses differed from Prairie houses in several respects. They were generally smaller, reflecting the reduced size of the American family and middle-class budgets, and they were designed for families without household servants. Their designs provided easy access by automobile, and interior activities could be easily supervised from the kitchen, identified as the principal workstation of the housewife. The interior opens up to outdoor spaces away from the street, either to the side or the rear. Wright was a master of site planning, generally managing to locate the house so that it appeared to rise naturally (organically, as he would describe it) from the land.

As has already been mentioned, buildings by Wright were included in the 1932 MoMA show on modern architecture, although not in the book illustrating the International Style. Wright had scathing comments to make about the leading Internationalists and their designs, remarking with a characteristic lack of humility to Henry-Russell Hitchcock, "Not only do I fully intend to be the greatest architect who has yet lived, but the greatest who will ever live. Yes, I intend to be the greatest architect of all time." But by International Style standards, Wright's work in the 1920s was loaded down with fussy detail and excessive ornament. Seeing the 1932 exhibition in New York must have influenced him to a certain degree, for afterward he started to design in a much less ornate way, producing several masterpieces in the 1930s.

## FALLINGWATER

One of the young men who came to Taliesin as an apprentice was Edgar Kaufmann, Jr., son of a wealthy Pittsburgh department-store owner. Hearing that his father was contemplating the construction of a vacation house in the mountains of western Pennsylvania, young Edgar persuaded E.J. Kaufmann, Sr., to employ Wright as architect. The result was Fallingwater (1935–37), perhaps the most famous house not built for royalty anywhere in the world (Figs. 15.71–15.72). (Fallingwater is now open to the public under the trusteeship of the Western Pennsylvania Conservancy.) Wright took the major natural feature of the site, a rocky outcropping where a small stream falls over a series of ledges, and planted the house beside the stream, letting the reinforced concrete balconies cantilever dramatically out over the stream. In order to see the waterfall, one must go outside, below the house, where the falls and the house can be seen together in the classic view that Wright planned, and he did a rendering from just that point to measure the effect before construction.

Stone quarried on the site was laid in irregular horizontal courses to form the four great piers supporting the living room, the fireplace mass, and the remaining bearing walls. The balconies, which form the dominant and dramatic elements of the design, cantilever in two directions and are stiffened at their edges by the upturned parapet wall. Large expanses of glass float between slate floors and stuccoed ceilings, minimizing the distinction between interior and exterior. Fallingwater's planar treatment of surfaces and abstract fragmentation of volumes suggest a debt to the European Modernists. It is cultural historian Lewis Mumford's assessment that, in Fallingwater, Wright "created a dynamic multidimensional composition that made Le Corbusier's buildings seem flat cardboard compositions." At age sixty-eight, Wright was just beginning his second great period of creativity.

## THE GUGGENHEIM MUSEUM AND TALIESIN WEST

Wright continued to explore the possibilities of circular forms, especially those involving continuous ramps. A project for an observatory atop Sugar Loaf Mountain in Maryland (1925) may have first set his mind to the idea, and the concept reappeared in the V.C. Morris Gift Shop (1949) in San Francisco, and in a car park proposed for Pittsburgh. The notion was brought to full realization in the Guggenheim Museum (1957–59) in New York City (Figs. 15.73–15.74), where a quarter-mile-long ramp spirals around a six-story interior sculpture court. The Guggenheim has extensive holdings of twentieth-century art, and it has been suggested that, by designing a museum with a continuously sloping floor and outward leaning, curving walls, Wright was expressing his scorn for modern art. Display possibilities are certainly restricted by the design, and no artist can single-handedly compete with the strong three-dimensional spatial experience Wright has created on the interior.

As he grew older, Wright preferred the warm weather of the desert southwest to the cold, blustery Wisconsin winters, so the Fellowship moved south to avoid the cold,

**15.71** (above) Frank Lloyd Wright, Edgar Kaufmann House, "Fallingwater," Ohiopyle, Pennsylvania, 1935–37.

A stream runs under the house and the stratified stone walls appear to grow from the landscape as they support cantilevered balconies. Part of Wright's genius was to place the house atop the waterfall rather than situating it on adjacent ground with views to the falling waters.

**15.72** (below) Frank Lloyd Wright, Plan of Fallingwater, Ohiopyle, Pennsylvania, 1935–37.

Wright had set out to "break the box" while at work in Oak Park forty years earlier. In this plan, the service spaces are more enclosed to the rear, while the living spaces in front break out dramatically onto the landscape. Compare it to Mies's Tugendhat House plan.

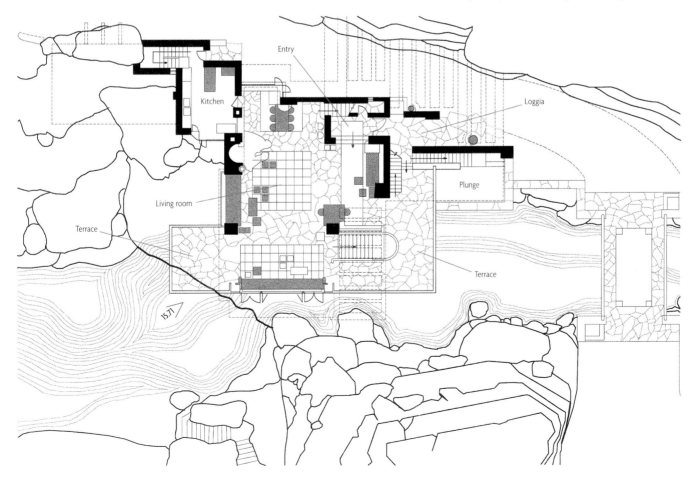

**15.73** (above) Frank Lloyd Wright, Guggenheim Museum, New York City, 1957–59.

The Guggenheim is considered one of the great buildings of the twentieth century. Visitors can take the elevator to the top, then walk down the spiraling ramp; among the problems for art lovers are the limited viewing distance and the constant slope.

**15.74** Frank Lloyd Wright, Guggenheim Museum interior, New York City, 1957–59.

This view shows clearly Wright's fascination with geometry; the art housed within the building was incidental. Such circular (as well as triangular, and polygonal) geometries dominated Wright's work in what was the third phase of his long career.

returning to Wisconsin only in the spring. Near Phoenix, Arizona, Wright began construction of Taliesin West (1938 onward), a sprawling encampment set in the rugged spareness of the desert, to replace the wood-and-canvas Ocotillo desert camp dating from 1927. He used materials taken from the locale. He combined adobe and desert boulders, redwood beams, and canvas panels to create a shaded interior that moderated the sun's heat and glare.

## WRIGHTIAN PROTÉGÉS

Austrians Richard Schindler (1887–1953) and Richard Neutra (1892–1970) knew Adolf Loos. They both immigrated to America where they met in the studio of Frank Lloyd Wright before moving on to Los Angeles. Long on spatial intuition and short on concern for detailing and craftsmanship, Schindler produced the much-publicized Lovell Beach House at Newport Beach (1926) for Richard and Leah Lovell. A more instructive example of Schindler's work, however, is his own Kings Road House (1921–22), which he claimed to be the first Modernist residence in the United States. Crudely built using tapered, tilt-up, concrete slabs with glass seams between them and movable partitions and trimmed out in wood, it displays extraordi-

nary relationships between interior and exterior spaces and a layered landscape of native plant material.

Neutra, a fine technician as well as a gifted designer, took detailing seriously. None of his projects has been more admired than the steel-stud-construction, so-called "Health House" (1927–29), that he designed for the same Lovells for whom Schindler built the beachfront home. He also designed an extraordinary desert house (1946) in Palm Springs for the same Edgar Kaufmann, Sr. for whom Wright had created Fallingwater. Both Neutra designs are rational and strongly connected to the landscape, in the case of the desert house to a level of sublimity. Perhaps most interesting in terms of Modernist intentions transported to America was Neutra's own residence (built in 1932, burned in 1963, and rebuilt by his son Dion). This so-called V. D. L. Research House (Fig. 15.75) was relatively cheaply constructed, exquisitely proportioned, and open to views from front-facing rooms, balconies, and a roof-top solarium out across a sweeping reservoir and to the rear into an atrium. Though modest in size, it was replete with innovations from a variety of materials obtained from local building suppliers to mirrors so positioned as to extend apparent space as in the seventeenth-century Rococo.

**15.75** Richard Neutra, V. D. L. Research House, Los Angeles, 1932 (burned and rebuilt in 1963).

This is not the building that Neutra constructed, but a more-or-less exact replica that his son Dion rebuilt after fire destroyed the original. Its site is part of a subdivision that includes other Neutra designs and looks out onto a panoramic water reservoir.

## LATER WORK OF LE CORBUSIER

Just as Wright designed his later works to fit into Broadacre City, Le Corbusier conceived of his later works as elements of an ideal city he called La Ville Radieuse (The Radiant City). His first opportunity to build an apartment block came after World War II, when the mayor of Marseille invited Le Corbusier to construct the first Unité d'Habitation, or Unified Dwelling House (1946–52) (Figs. 15.76–15.77). Some critics consider the Unité a masterpiece, both for its bold sculptural forms and its novel approach to the problems of apartment living. The Unité block is set in a landscaped park and raised on pilotis. The apartments are ingeniously designed to have frontage on both the east and west sides of the building, making possible cross-ventilation, a desirable trade-off for their long, narrow plans. Balconies, integrated into **brises-soleil** or sunscreens, give each side exterior living space. As a consequence of the apartment design, the elevator stops only on every third floor. The building originally featured a two-story shopping floor (grocery store, beauty shop, repair services, etc.) halfway up, and the roof levels were devoted to extensive recreational and health facilities: a gymnasium, running track, movie theater, health club, nursery school, sun terraces, and the like. The concrete work throughout is forceful. Patterns resulting from the carpentry formwork can be regarded as surface ornament disciplined by the fabrication process. Le Corbusier created the building's proportions using a system that he called "Le Modular," based upon the height of an average person repeatedly subdivided using the Golden Section ratio (approximately 5:8). Ship imagery characterizes the rooftop ventilation stacks, elevator housing, and recreational facilities, for here Le Corbusier could exercise his formal repertoire quite freely. Above all, the concept of sunlight, air, and green open space for all 1600 residents guided the design.

Le Corbusier's critics have pointed out that the scheme is essentially anti-urban, turning its back on the architectural and street patterns of Marseille. Even the provision of shops (which were a financial failure) was attacked,

**15.76** Le Corbusier, Unité d'Habitation, Marseille, 1946–52.

Not visible here are the pilotis that support this ferroconcrete structure. The exterior walls are faced with brises-soleil (sun screens) that modulate light entering the apartments. The continuous vertical baffles about halfway up and toward the rear shield the ill-fated "shopping street" that was to provide for tenants' every need.

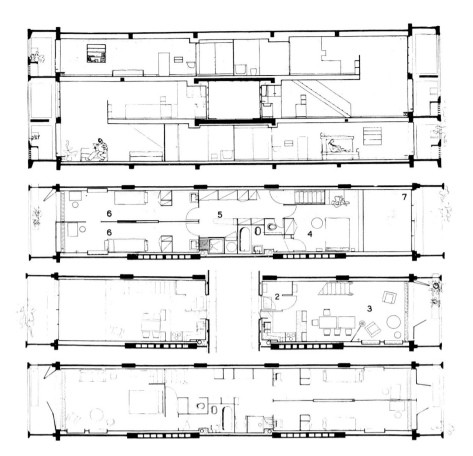

**15.77** Le Corbusier, Section through and plans of the Unité d'Habitation, Marseille, 1946–52.

The apartments are obviously very narrow, particularly when they are divided into hall-like bedrooms. The section shows that each unit has a two-story living space with an overlooking balcony.

because it meant the residents would have little need to associate with the commercial life of the town, and grocery shopping, done daily in France, is a great socializing opportunity. Rather than an affront to Marseille, however, the Unité must be seen as a design in harmony with Le Corbusier's idealized city, a world that was quite different from any existing urban setting.

## RONCHAMP AND SAINTE-MARIE-DE-LA-TOURETTE

In the east of France, not far from the Swiss border, Le Corbusier designed the pilgrimage chapel of Notre-Dame-du-Haut at Ronchamp near Belfort (1951–55) (Figs. 15.78–15.79), to replace a previous church destroyed by artillery fire during World War II. This small building allowed him to give maximum expression to the sculptural possibilities of architectural form. The rationalism of earlier works was laid aside—no proportional system, no five points, no pilotis!—and a dramatic, highly symbolic design emerged. Even the structure is non-rational: a metal frame is made to look like massive masonry. The walls are rough-textured stucco painted white, and the roof is a great billowing sail of board-formed concrete that rolls over the east wall to provide protection for the exterior pulpit. Large crowds attend services out of doors, sitting on the lawn; the interior provides seats for only fifty people, although there is standing room for more. The spectacular south wall has exaggerated thickness and an array of splayed windows inset with hand-painted colored glass. From the outside, they look like an irregular series of small apertures, but from the interior, the wall turns into a glowing light sculpture, as moving in its own way as the

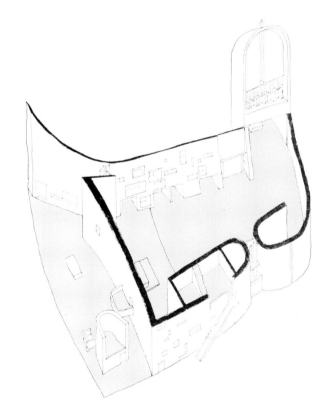

**15.78** Le Corbusier, Axonometric view of Notre-Dame-du-Haut, Ronchamp, 1951–55.

Built as a pilgrimage site for worshipers, Ronchamp (near Belfort, France) has become as much a pilgrimage site for architects and architectural students. The tower lights an altar below. Services can be held inside or held outside on the concrete apron to the left.

**15.79** Le Corbusier, Notre-Dame-du-Haut, Ronchamp, 1951–55.

The chapel is built of brick covered with stucco. The random window openings in the east wall to the left contain glass decorated with Le Corbusier's painted images. The principal entry lies between this wall and the tower, with a secondary entry in the rear between the two smaller towers.

windows of Chartres Cathedral. A very thin strip of clear glass intervenes between the walls and roof, which seems to float. Meditation chapels underneath the towers have top illumination from high clerestories on the wall behind the worshipers. The light from an unseen source spilling softly over the rough-textured red stucco powerfully conveys a sense of humanity's essential loneliness.

Southwest of Lyon is the small town of Eveux-sur-l'Arbresle, outside of which Le Corbusier was commissioned to design a Dominican monastery, Ste. Marie-de-la-Tourette (1956–60) (Figs. 15.80–15.81). Here he accomplished a modern reworking of the medieval monastic program. The church, a simple rectangular solid with sculptural subsidiary chapels in the crypt, is located on the

northwest side of an open courtyard, crisscrossed by enclosed passageways connecting the church to other parts of the monastery. The remaining monastic quarters are arranged in three wings: the refectory on the level of the church; the library, study rooms, and an oratory on the second level; and two floors of monks' cells around the upper levels.

All the work is in concrete. Le Corbusier returned to the use of pilotis and "regulating traces" of his proportioning system, although the sculptural freedom found at Ronchamp is present here, too. With a master's hand, he manipulated light in dozens of different ways to enrich the experience of the basically simple forms within the building simply by taking into account the movement of the sun from day to day and season to season. Window mullions vary according to a harmonic rhythm; scoops catch the light and direct it through colored conical sections to focus on altars in the crypt; long horizontal ribbons provide even illumination for the corridors on the dormitory floor; each monk's room has a virtual wall of glass looking out over the balcony brise-soleil to the distant horizon; and a truncated pyramidal roof with a skylight provides an ethereal glow for the oratory.

## CHANDIGARH

Despite his numerous city-planning projects on paper, Le Corbusier was invited only once to design an actual town. In 1951 the government of India asked him to work on the design of Chandigarh, the new capital of the state of Punjab in northern India (Figs. 15.82–15.83). Le Corbusier made a master plan, while the design of individual sectors and most buildings was left to others. However, Le

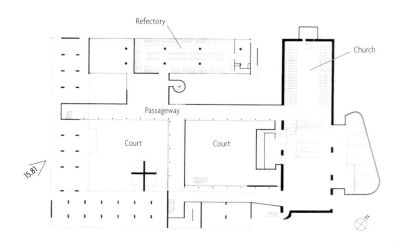

**15.80** Le Corbusier, Plan of Ste. Marie-de-la-Tourette, Eveux-sur-l'Arbresle, 1956–60.

Here, Le Corbusier transformed the traditional monastic plan. Ramps and a small chapel inhabit the traditional interior cloister, with the latter's functions moved to the roof. This arrangement was never found acceptable by the monks, who chose to meditate in the wooded areas nearby.

**15.81** Le Corbusier, Ste. Marie-de-la-Tourette, Eveux-sur-l'Arbresle, 1956–60.

Monks' cells rise about the pilotis on the south façade. The rooms have sunscreens like those used in the Unité (Fig. 15.76).

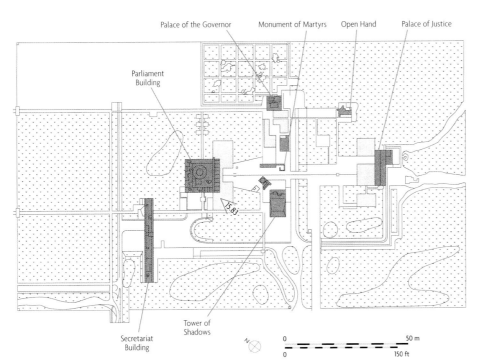

Palace of the Governor    Monument of Martyrs    Open Hand    Palace of Justice

Parliament
Building

Tower of
Shadows

Secretariat
Building

0        50 m
0        150 ft

**15.82** Le Corbusier, plan of Chandigarh, Punjab, 1951–59.

This master plan illustrates Le Corbusier's preference for large buildings set wide apart within a garden-like landscape.

**15.83** Le Corbusier, Parliament Building, Chandigarh, Punjab, 1951–59.

Here Le Corbusier continued to explore ways to manipulate sunlight. The poured-in-place concrete structure is sculpted along one side and cut away sunscreen-fashion along the other. His goals were certainly in part environmental, but he also sought to celebrate the state by associating it with the sun.

Corbusier designed the symbolic governmental buildings, which he located on the highest ground at the head of the scheme with the majestic foothills of the Himalayas beyond, in a manner that recalls the Acropolis in Athens. He grouped four major buildings around a great ceremonial plaza: the palace of the governor (not built), the Secretariat Building (1951–57), the Parliament Building (1956–59), and the Palace of Justice (1951–56). All of these buildings blend the rational discipline so evident in his early works with the sculptural freedom of his later projects. The Parliament Building, for example, is almost square in plan, with stacked rows of offices around two sides. The legislative chamber is circular, located at the base of a truncated hyperbolic surface of revolution (a hyperbolic curve rotated about a central axis) equipped with monitors at the top to filter the intense Indian sun. Control of light was of great importance, for with shade

comes coolness. The *brises-soleil* were designed to introduce indirect sunlight and to provide views. Concrete, Le Corbusier's favorite material, was well suited to the Indian context. It is labor-intensive but inexpensive to produce. Its mass also buffers climatic extremes.

## THE CONTINUATION OF TRADITIONAL ARCHITECTURE

The level of originality among these traditionalists varied considerably. The Englishman Edwin Lutyens was born in 1869 (d. 1944), the same year as was Frank Lloyd Wright. While his work was consistently eclectic, his interpretations were inventive, clever, even ambiguous and idiosyncratic. Lutyens organized his plans by means of a profusion of interlaced axes that often extend out into

**15.84** Edwin Lutyens' Heathcote House interior, Ilkley, Yorkshire, 1906.

This view of a typically intricate, even tricky, Lutyens interior includes two Serliana, their arches defining the hall's principal cross axis (with a parallel enfilade). The varied spacing of double, paired, green-marble columns to each side amplifies the room's complex spatial ordering.

**15.85** Stockholm Public Library, 1918–27.

Asplund produced a somewhat abstracted and cool but extremely approachable form of classicism. Here he juxtaposed an oversized, shouldered doorway with a planar façade and a rising cylinder that announces the location of the bookstacks inside.

gardens designed by his longtime collaborator Gertrude Jekyll, and it is safe to say that he would not have risen to the level of achievement that he did without her contributions. Typically working for the newly monied classes, Lutyens manipulated his houses within their settings to make them appear larger than they were. Internally, he delighted in denying selected axes, turning enfilades in one room into a central axis in another (and vice versa), and creating layers of space by manipulating the apparent thickness of walls and inserting bands of carefully placed columns (Fig. 15.84—Heathcote, Ilkley, Yorkshire, 1906). Externally, he ascribed to the honest expression of materials advocated by practitioners of the Arts and Crafts and developed his ability to create picturesque compositions by closely studying vernacular structures in the English countryside. While his reputation declined in the mid-twentieth century, it rose abruptly in the 1970s, when he was celebrated in print for his "mannerist" tendencies, to the point that a retrospective of his work appeared at New York's Museum of Modern Art in 1978.

Eric Gunnar Asplund (1885–1940) and his like-minded colleagues brought Modernism to the fore in Sweden at the Stockholm Exhibition of 1930, and Asplund had apparently rejected classicism two decades earlier when he and Sigurd Lewerentz and four other students abandoned education at the Royal Academy of Art in

favor of attending the short-lived, atelier-driven Klara School. These events are misleading, however, for while a few of Asplund's commissions, notably the Bredenberg Department Store in Stockholm (1933–35), display overtly Modernist features, most do not.

Intent on producing an architecture that spoke of its time yet had both the graceful authority of classicism and the authenticity of the regional vernacular favored by the contemporary National Romanticists, or Realists, Asplund, as have the best of architects, produced original work. Two of his commissions, the Stockholm Public Library (1918–27) (Fig. 15.85) and the Woodland Cemetery, illustrate his personal vision.

The library's plan is one of extreme clarity: a circle within a square that is open on one side. In three dimensions, the circle rises as a cylinder containing the bookstacks, and the sides of the square hold support spaces. While an early scheme had a dome, Asplund eliminated it and everything else that seemed superfluous, achieving a kind of distillation to essence that can only be compared to Claude-Nicholas Ledoux's Barrière de la Villette. In a manner suggesting entry into the tomb of some mythical Nordic king, access to the circular, central lending hall is made through tall shouldered doorways; beyond, a cloud of light inside the rising drum illuminates the three levels of stacks. The effect is as crisp and clear as a cloudless, wintry Swedish night.

In 1915, Asplund collaborated with his former classmate Sigurd Lewerentz to win the competition for the design of the Woodland Cemetery, which took twenty-five years to complete. Part of a broad burial-reform effort in Sweden, it takes on meaning through the longstanding

**15.86** Eric Gunnar Asplund, Woodland Cemetery, 1915 and after.

To the left, alongside the flagstone path is a stone wall that accompanies visitors to the top of the hill and the crematorium-columbarium-chapel. Asplund and Leverentz reclaimed this serene, noble landscape from the ravages of a gravel quarry, something of a metaphor for the cycle of birth, death, and rebirth.

Nordic affinity for nature. The site plan does little to explain the architects' efforts to express the connection of the dead to the living and to acknowledge the necessity for mourning. Understanding the extraordinary landscape resurrected from abandoned gravel pits must come from ground-level experience. A canted semicircle at street-side announces the cemetery's shielded existence. Upon entering, a visitor experiences not a formal axis but a serene panoramic view up to a stone cross and a hillock with a grove of weeping elms, then proceeds up along a sloping stone path, compared by some to Rome's Appian Way (Fig. 15.86). To the left and parallel to this approach runs a rock-faced stone wall that glistens with a constant film of water, then beyond it noble buildings: a columbarium, a crematorium, and a chapel called Mount Hall—a building of classical essences with a square-columned, projecting portico. In front of the chapel, hidden from view from below, lies a flat sheet of blueness in the form of a lily pond. Within the surrounding forest the burial plots are informally distributed among the tall trees. Axes cut through them lead to additional structures, including Asplund's Woodland Chapel, a Laugier-esque columnar pavilion with a hemispherical dome covered by a pyramidal roof. Asplund treated the children's cemetery like a sunken garden, with ranks of delicate crosses surrounded by vertical pines. The entire setting speaks of humility and humanity and spirituality.

## CONCLUSIONS ABOUT ARCHITECTURAL IDEAS

Anyone looking for the apparent safety of a conveniently single and inevitable historical path welcomed this chapter's presentation of European Modernism as the product of energetic, frantic, even desperate investigations that became a single-minded architectural juggernaut of design sensibilities. However, the triumph was to be relatively brief, and in the next chapter Modernism will be ripe for a fall.

Modernist motivations were often noble, frequently heroic, and perhaps too often utopian. After the cataclysm that was World War I, many European architects saw building design as a potential instrument of societal transformation. In chaotic economies desperately in need of housing, they chose as their principal concerns utility and efficiency and a related mechanization of the building industry, but leavened their pragmatism with advanced spatial conceptions then current in the visual arts. These emerging Modernists saw themselves in a winner-take-all conflict with the obstructionist forces of bourgeois traditionalism. Armed with arguments of rationality and prepared to speak and write polemically, they set out to win the battle among the avant garde, in the architectural media, and, they hoped, in the hearts and minds of the larger population—which they never did.

There was no scarcity of new ideas: Adolf Loos and his attack on "decadent" ornamentation and his development of the *Raumplan*; Frank Lloyd Wright and his determination to invent a unique American domestic type, which he did with his Prairie-style houses, and his technical innovations like central air-conditioning at the Larkin Building and economical poured-in-place concrete at Unity Temple; and the German experience wherein Peter Behrens and others like him founded the Deustcher Werkbund in an effort to raise the general quality of manufactured goods and Walter Gropius developed a new system of design education at the Bauhaus, first in Weimar, then in Dessau, before its dissolution by the Nazis. Add to this yeasty mix the radical proposals, frequently drawn but less frequently built, for dynamism by the Italian Futurists, for infinite-space modulations by the De Stijl designers, and for radical material assemblies by the Russian Constructivists. In the end, space was the stuff of Modernism. This can be seen consistently, if in differing interpretations, in the works of the triumvirate of modern "masters": Le Corbusier, Walter Gropius, and Ludwig Mies van der Rohe (with Frank Lloyd Wright as a constant American competitor and even antagonist).

In addition to all these happenings, there were concurrent advances in building technology, especially the use of steel and steel-reinforced concrete, and new visions of the city as a place of modern industry and modern systems of transportation and as a place of physical and emotional health, even a place of utopian ideals. And if this were not enough, remember that most built architecture of the period did not fit the Modernist prescriptions, from the alternative forms of the Dutch and German Expressionists to the hybrid forms of the Art Deco to the latent forms of continuing eclecticism, which in terms of sheer numbers of built works still held the field. And if this were still not enough, the situation in the late twentieth century and beyond would only become more complex and unresolved, as will be seen in the final chapter.

# CHAPTER 16

# MODERNISMS IN THE MID- AND LATE TWENTIETH CENTURY AND BEYOND

This final chapter still concerns Modernism, but also addresses reactions to it and against it, and takes the architecture into the twenty-first century. With so little historical distance, it is more a report on current events than a history, as the canon has not yet been firmly established. Categorizations exist for the contemporary architecture discussed in this chapter, but they must be viewed as conveniences of the moment for these designations will be subjected to scrutiny, as will the merits of some of the individuals and buildings within them.

Beginning in 1928, an organization with the acronym CIAM (Congrès Internationaux d'Architecture Moderne) promoted modern architecture and addressed pressing building design and city planning issues. Le Corbusier was a principal figure, but most of the Modernist luminaries participated, like Walter Gropius and the younger Alvar Aalto, whose work is discussed in this chapter. After World War II, the organization attempted to reformulate its goals, but it soon became clear that a new generation of designers found the Modernist doctrine constraining. In 1953, at a meeting in southern France, a loosely organized group calling itself Team-X ("X" being the Romal numeral ten) was given responsibility for planning the next conference, which they did, only to see CIAM dissolved.

Team-X included husband and wife Peter (1923–2003) and Alison (1928–93) Smithson and Ralph Erskine (1914–2005), all three from England, and Aldo Van Eyck (1918–1999) from Holland. Their thinking differed from that of main-line Modernists, particularly in being less obsessed with pure rationalism, more attuned to the problems of the postwar era, and more interested in matters of regional and local context.

The Smithsons' work, dubbed Brutalism, certainly owes a debt to Le Corbusier and is best illustrated by their long, multi-story, concrete housing units. Constructed as late as 1972, Robin Hood Gardens in London is tough and gritty (or brutal) in its outward appearance, but was intended as a sympathetic response to modern English working-class urban life and included "street-decks," or generous elevated walkway-bridges, that were to be social-izing mechanisms as well as new urban symbols.

Ralph Erskine subsequently produced his own solution to urban living for workers by developing an inclusive design process for the long Byker Wall Housing (Fig. 16.1) in Newcastle-upon-Tyne (1969–75) that involved a close dialogue with future users. One high face of his oscillating housing slab looks north onto a highway, and so is fortress-like, while the opposite face is a riot of picturesque, multi-colored heavy-timber and wood-lattice balconies and brickwork.

Aldo Van Eyck moved even further toward the intuitive and even the spiritual, as in his Orphanage in Amsterdam (1957–60), where he organized space to stimulate imagination and play and sought to imbue his forms with deep meanings and values. Rather than the spirit of the age, Van Eyck wished to express that which is intrinsic and timeless.

The work of these four designers suggests some of the diversity arising at mid-century. In order to examine these conditions more carefully, consider the careers of: Alvar Aalto, Eero Saarinen, and Louis Kahn.

## ALVAR AALTO

Alvar Aalto (1898–1976) was a native of Finland and spent most of his career there. He studied architecture at the Helsinki Polytechnic Institute; during his formative years, Finnish architects were trying to develop a regional identity, experimenting with a Nordic version of Neo-Classicism and a nationalistic Romanticism associated

## Chronology

| | |
|---|---|
| development of Post-Modern architecture | 1960s |
| Vietnam War | 1965–73 |
| Robert Venturi publishes *Complexity and Contradiction in Architecture* | 1966 |
| assassination of Martin Luther King | 1968 |
| Apollo astronauts land on the moon | 1969 |
| first Earth Day celebration | 1970 |
| creation of the Internet | ca. 1981 |
| introduction of the personal computer | 1982 |
| fall of the Berlin Wall | 1989 |
| dissolution of the Soviet Union | 1991 |
| Al Qaeda terrorist attacks destroy World Trade Center | 2001 |
| beginning of the war in Iraq | 2003 |

Frank Gehry, Guggenheim Museum Bilbao atrium, Bilbao, 1997.

With its walls, glass, railings, and steel frame all twisting as they rise, the atrium offers an exhilarating sense of dynamic space. Inhabiting the structure makes manifest the previously impossible: entering and moving through a building-size piece of free-form sculpture.

with chauvinistic myths and respected local building traditions. Aalto developed, apparently independently, a functional approach that closely paralleled the Deutscher Werkbund architects of the same period, but with overtones of both classicism and Romanticism. In 1924, he traveled to Italy, but after returning north never lost his enthusiasm for traditional Italian architecture, particularly its hilltowns. In 1927, he won the competition to create a municipal library for Viipuri (now Vyborg, Russia) (Figs. 16.2–16.3) with a design of such a thoroughly modern cast that conservative local forces delayed its construction until 1930–35. Its carefully proportioned form might be described as stripped classicism; but this apparent reductivism is tempered by a poetic sensitivity to both materials and occupancy. For instance, the building includes an auditorium at ground level with an undulating wooden ceiling and custom-designed bentwood stools. Elsewhere, the reading-room walls are bathed in indirect lighting

**16.1** Ralph Erskine, Byker Wall Housing, Newcastle-upon-Tyne, 1969–75.

Among the concerns of Team-X members ("X" being the Roman numeral ten) in the post-World War II period was the sensitive response to context, or localized site conditions. In designing this housing project, Ralph Erskine sought to take contextualism one step further by responding directly to the suggestions of multiple end-users.

**16.2** Alvar Aalto, Municipal Library, Viipuri, 1930–35.

Early in his career, Aalto was strongly influenced by European Modernism. Even then, however, his work had moments of lyricism, such as this elegantly ascending stair, that set it apart from much of the International Style.

**16.3** Alvar Aalto, Ground-story plan of the Municipal Library, Viipuri, 1930–35.

This configuration, with one rectangle slid against another, was used frequently in the twentieth century. Two other notable examples are Frank Lloyd Wright's Robie House (see Figs. 15.10–15.11) and Mies van der Rohe's Farnsworth House (see Fig. 15.69).

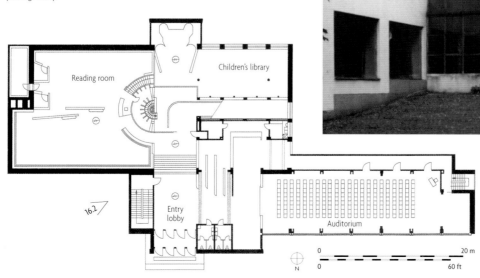

**16.4** Alvar Aalto, Municipal Library interior, Viipuri, 1930–35.

Aalto consistently manipulated the ceiling plane in inventive ways. Here a field of skylights illuminates the main reading room. The ceiling of the theater in the adjacent rectangle is an undulating plane of matched boards that is both sculptural and acoustically beneficial.

**16.5** Alvar Aalto, Tuberculosis Sanatorium, Paimio, 1929–33.

None of Aalto's commissions has been more celebrated as an International Style icon than this one. Notable features are the long strip windows and related spandrels and the extensive balconies for convalescing patients.

from deep, glare-free skylights (Fig. 16.4).

Aalto's design for the Tuberculosis Sanatorium (1929–33) at Paimio brought him international acclaim, both for its overall planning and its attention to detail. Located on a hilltop surrounded by evergreens, the sanatorium rises dramatically in the landscape (Figs. 16.5–16.6). Like Walter Gropius at the Bauhaus, Aalto articulated each component. The block of south-facing patients' rooms, a long, thin, six-story wing, dominates the grouping, connecting via an entrance and doctors' wing to the public rooms, kitchen and services building, garage, and boilerhouse. In order to conform to the topography

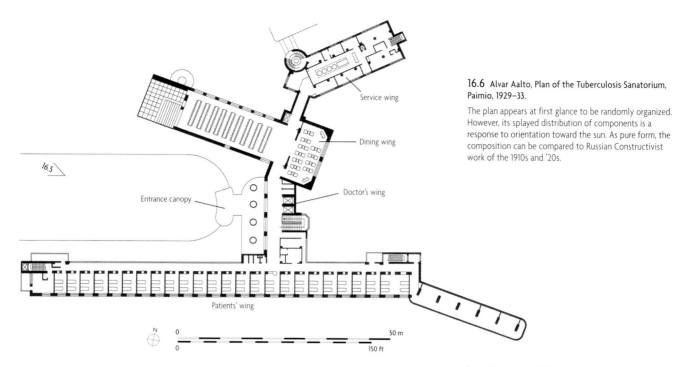

**16.6** Alvar Aalto, Plan of the Tuberculosis Sanatorium, Paimio, 1929–33.

The plan appears at first glance to be randomly organized. However, its splayed distribution of components is a response to orientation toward the sun. As pure form, the composition can be compared to Russian Constructivist work of the 1910s and '20s.

Service wing

Dining wing

16.5

Entrance canopy

Doctor's wing

Patients' wing

N

0                     50 m

0                     150 ft

**16.7** Alvar Aalto, Cellulose Factory, Sunila, 1936–39.

This composition shows Aalto's moving away from the regimentation of the International Style and toward more Romantic massing and the use of undulating forms as major exterior features. He was much impressed by the irregular silhouettes of the hilltowns in Italy and integrated his experiences there into his own design work.

**16.8** Alvar Aalto, Baker House, M.I.T., Cambridge, Massachusetts, 1947–49.

Aalto's only project in the United States faces the Charles river. He used the undulating plan here to provide the dormitory rooms with views up and down the river. He placed support spaces in orthogonal rooms to the rear. The low-rise element on the left is the dining room and lounge.

and the sun's path, these units are not always related orthogonally (as at the Bauhaus), which introduces an expressive angularity to the site plan that is suggestive of Russian Constructivist work.

Furniture design interested Aalto throughout his career. Finland's greatest natural resource is wood, and Aalto used the material in innovative ways. Through experimentation, he developed a technique for bending and laminating thin wood veneers to form plywood sheets of any desired curvature. In 1932 he designed his first chair with a one-piece plywood seat and back supported by a tubular metal frame. Subsequent designs were fabricated entirely in wood, and many of these are still available on the commercial market.

In the 1930s Aalto's largest commission was for the Sunila Cellulose Factory (1936–39, with later expansion in 1951–57) at Karhula, including the design of workers' housing nearby. The factory is a carefully composed array of repetitive rectangular forms, animated by the diagonal

lines of conveyors and the vertical thrust of a smokestack (Fig. 16.7).

After World War II, Aalto's mature style moved away from the white rectangular masses and linear pipe railings of International Style architecture. Brick, timber, and copper became his favorite building materials, and he worked them into harmonious compositions that frequently included great curving walls, single-pitched roofs, and imaginative daylighting. During a teaching appointment at M.I.T. in the late 1940s, he designed Baker House (1947–49), a campus dormitory (Fig. 16.8). Located on a site parallel to the Charles river, the seven-story brick building has its riverfront plan arranged in a sinusoidal curve, permitting oblique views from the dormitory rooms up or down the river. As far as possible, Aalto placed service and common rooms at the rear on each floor, with the dining hall and lounge in a low wing at the front.

A more ambitious program was involved in the commission for a "Town Hall" for Säynätsalo (1951–52),

**16.9** Alvar Aalto, Roof-and-courtyard-level plans of the Town Hall, Säynätsalo, 1951–52.

Aalto's plan *parti* also suggests the kind of spontaneous design found in Italian hill towns. The roughly square courtyard has one of its sides slid away just far enough to allow a slightly deflected path through the complex. One stair is orthogonal, while the other cascades out of the plaza over grass-covered treads as seen in Fig. 16.10.

**16.10** Alvar Aalto, Town Hall, Säynätsalo, 1951–52.

Aalto's complex exhibits multiple scales. It rises two stories on the outside, but only one story in the courtyard over which the tower of the council chamber stands. This view suggests that Aalto was still being influenced by his travels in Italy almost thirty years before.

designed as a group of buildings around a grassy courtyard (Figs. 16.9–16.10). In fact, it provides the entire civic center for this small community, housing the municipal offices, council chamber, public library, and retail shops. Within a basically orthogonal layout, the brick volume of the council chamber dominates the ensemble, its sloped-roof profile reflecting a graceful wooden fan truss inside. The Town Hall is entered by a set of either brick or turf stairs. The building's scale, which seems appropriately monumental from without, becomes almost diminutive within the courtyard. Here and throughout all his work Aalto took a humanistic approach to architecture that is perhaps unmatched in the twentieth century, one that grew out of his own temperament as well as the distinctive place where he lived and worked.

## EERO SAARINEN AND HIS OFFICE

The works of Eero Saarinen (1910–1961) are eclectic, reflecting a wider range of sources than those of Aalto. However, a constant in his career was a relentless, exploratory, inventive attitude toward new materials and technologies. Like Aalto, Saarinen was of Finnish ancestry; his architect father, Eliel, created the exquisite campus at Cranbrook Academy outside Detroit, Michigan, after relocating the family to the United States in the 1920s. After studying sculpture in Paris and completing his architectural education at Yale in 1934, Eero practiced with his father until 1950.

In the General Motors Technical Center (1948–56) at Warren, Michigan, Saarinen took an apparently Miesian approach, setting modular steel-and-glass-walled rectangular volumes in a campus-like park; the orthogonal theme is broken only by a circular auditorium and a metallic sphere water tower that gives verticality to a composition of otherwise horizontal, seemingly mass-produced objects. However, closer observation reveals that the skins of his reductivist objects possess a sensuality unknown in Mies's work; one sees the hand of the fine artist leavening the mix of the technician.

For the Trans World Airlines (TWA) Terminal (1956–62) at Kennedy Airport in New York City, Saarinen abandoned the orthogonal General Motors esthetic in favor of a fluid, sculptural form expressive of flight (Fig. 16.11). Forsaking metal in favor of viscous concrete, he created thin-shelled vaults supported by free-form, poured-in-place concrete piers. The terminal's billowing roof resembles a great bird alighting; it has also been compared to the swooping tail fins of 1959 Chevrolet automobiles, which Saarinen may have seen in developmental form at the General Motors Technical Center. Inside, the flowing space is dramatic but intimate. Most fittings were custom-designed to match the spirit of the building, for

**16.11** Eero Saarinen, TWA Terminal, Kennedy International Airport, New York City, 1956–62.

Saarinen died while still in his early 50s. He had not yet established a single direction for his architectural development. Here, he explored the potential of poured-in-place concrete to create expressive shapes and dynamic spaces.

ordinary furniture looks out of place in a space where curves dominate the walls and ceilings, and ramps generate motion in the floor plane. A later design for Dulles Airport (1958–62), outside Washington, D.C., drew its inspiration from early sketches done by the German Expressionist architect Erich Mendelsohn. Outward-leaning concrete pylons rise on the exterior to support the concrete-panel-covered cable-hung roof, which provides a clear span inside. The effect of the building in the landscape is noble, but the interior is a disappointment, for the orthogonal clutter of partitions and a central roof drain that violates the untouched ceiling negate the curving geometries of the building's enclosure. In 1997, the firm of Skidmore, Owings, and Merrill doubled the length of the terminal by replicating Saarinen's profile of pylons and catenary cables.

Architect Charles Eames (1907–1978) and sculptor and painter Ray Eames (1912–88) created the prototype for all those fiberglass-reinforced plastic airport chairs familiar to travelers throughout the world. The two designers met at the Cranbrook Academy outside of Detroit at a time when Eero Saarinen was its director. Charles subsequently entered Saarinen's office, where experimentation with new building materials and technologies was so fundamental to the design process. As part of a competition promoting Modernism and industrialization in architecture, the Eameses, initially working with Saarinen, produced a Case Study House, in which they used lightweight structural steel and off-the-shelf, pre-fabricated parts. As built in 1945–49, this project became the Eameses' residence in Pacific Palisades, California. It has unified interior space and strong interior–exterior relationships, both Modernist signatures, but also the kind of inviting warmth—achieved through the generous introduction of furniture, fabrics, plants, and other fittings—more characteristic of well-designed traditional architecture. When

their architectural ideas were not embraced by the public, Charles and Ray Eames focused their attention on furniture and exhibition design and film.

## LOUIS I. KAHN

The work of Louis I. Kahn (1901–1974) represents the fusion of seemingly contradictory sources. In 1905 Kahn immigrated to Philadelphia from the small Russian island of Saarama, in the Baltic Sea. He received a Beaux-Arts-influenced architectural education at the University of Pennsylvania, where he acquired the concept of served and servant spaces that would affect nearly all his buildings. Moreover, he learned to create symmetrical, hierarchically arranged compositions and to produce monumentality, even in everyday circumstances. In so doing, he was able to render the common uncommon, and the uncommon transcendent. Giving new life to a largely inert design tradition, he achieved timelessness where others resorted to historicism.

Medieval vernacular forms from Italian hilltowns inspired Kahn in his design for the Richards Medical Research Building (1957–61) at the University of Pennsylvania (Fig. 16.12). In plan the building is a model of rationalism. The medical laboratories are square, open-plan, glass-walled spaces stacked into towers. Pairs of columns set on each side support the structural grid of each floor, while ducts, mechanical services, elevators, and stairs are set in attenuated brick shafts. By wedding straightforward functional planning with a picturesque massing, Kahn created one of the most influential architectural compositions of the 1960s. Purists note that one of the service shaft towers is a dummy, included for artistic effect rather than functional necessity, and scientists using the building have found the flexibility of the lab spaces to be less than

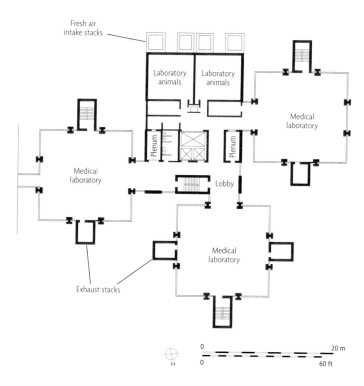

Fresh air
intake stacks

Laboratory animals | Laboratory animals

Medical laboratory

Plenum | Plenum

Medical laboratory

Lobby

Medical laboratory

Exhaust stacks

0        20 m
0        60 ft
N

**16.12** Louis Kahn, Plan of the Richards Medical Building, University of Pennsylvannia, Philadephia, 1957–61.

This plan illustrates Kahn's conception of servant and served spaces. The medical laboratories are served by the stairtowers and fume exhaust stacks, or plenums. The functional towers and stacks all become elements in a picturesque composition.

**16.13** Louis Kahn, Salk Institute for Biological Sciences plaza, La Jolla, California, 1959–65.

As much a poet—or even a mystic—as an architect, Louis Kahn was interested in expressing the eternal rather than the transitory. Here in La Jolla, California, he did so by framing the plane of the earth, an axial water channel, and an expanse of sky between rhythmically receding concrete towers.

the designer imagined and have been forced to install sun shades where glare and heat gain have been a problem.

Kahn also absorbed some Modernist principles, particularly from the work of Le Corbusier; and he traveled in Europe, where Greek temples, ancient Roman construction systems, vernacular townscapes, and the works of Brunelleschi created lasting impressions on him. The simple geometries of Neo-Classicism also influenced his architectural conceptions. Kahn admired the works of Boullée and Ledoux, considering them to have been as important to architecture as Johann Sebastian Bach was to music. Among Kahn's often poetic writings, one finds the following: "Spirit in will to express/ can make the great sun seem small./ The Sun is/ Thus the Universe./ Did we need Bach/ Bach is/ Thus music is./ Did we need Boullée/Boullée is/ Did we need Ledoux/ Ledoux is/ Thus Architecture is." Inspired by such poetic visions and by a high regard for rational construction, particularly the heavy vaulting of ancient Rome, Kahn imbued structural forms such as the arch and vault with a mystical, even sublime quality and enabled them to become metaphors for the human condition.

Probably no twentieth-century building has become more of a pilgrimage site for admiring architects than Kahn's Salk Institute for Biological Sciences (1959–65) in La Jolla, California. A unique situation for him where his client Dr. Jonas Salk had as profound a vision as did the architect, the project began with a *parti* split between laboratories at one end and a place for community at the other. It evolved to have a configuration not unlike Thomas Jefferson's University of Virginia campus (see Fig. 14.16), with the lawn becoming a paved plaza between canted, concrete faces of laboratory towers, all of them ennobled by a narrow, linear seam of water leading to the ocean and the horizon (Fig. 16.13). It is a scene with connections less to other modern buildings and more to timeless ritual settings, but with scientists replacing the ancient priests.

The influence of Neo-Classicism in general and Piranesi in particular is manifest in Kahn's designs for the National Assembly of Bangladesh in Dacca (1962–74). The building is composed of ideal geometric forms, circles and squares, expressed volumetrically as prisms, and its layering of spaces recalls buildings at Hadrian's Villa, while its interiors are as grand and somber as images in Piranesi's *Carceri* engravings. A similar treatment is found inside the library of Phillips Exeter Academy (1967–72) in Exeter, New Hampshire, where the essentially square building is dominated by a cubical volume at the center (Fig. 16.14). Huge circular cutouts provide vistas into the library stacks on the surrounding floors in a manner reminiscent of Piranesi's engravings of imaginary prisons. Individual study carrels surround the stacks on each floor, and the windows against which they fit provide a regular articulation for the brick exterior, which is treated rather like the nineteenth-century mill buildings of nearby Manchester, New Hampshire.

**16.14** Louis Kahn, Library interior, Phillips Exeter Academy, Andover, New Hampshire, 1967–72.

Kahn admired imperial Roman architecture and here sought to capture both the period's monumentality and the rich layering seen in such complexes as Hadrian's Villa.

Kahn was never more successful than in his design for the Kimbell Art Museum in Fort Worth, Texas (1966–72). In his site plan, one enters into a court through a grove of trees, with reflecting pools to each side. He chose as his spatial and structural unit an apparently barrel-vaulted bay, which is actually covered by a pair of cantilevers meeting at a continuous skylight (Figs. 16.15–16.16). Kahn placed sixteen of these units side by side in three ranks (Fig. 16.17), combining many spatially by replacing the load-bearing walls with longitudinal beams. As materials he chose poured-in-place concrete, travertine, oak, and stainless steel, all bathed in natural light, with much of it reflected by baffles beneath the skylights, so that the interiors have a consistent luminescence. The spaces are ancient Roman in their monumentality, gravity, and exquisite finishes. Yet their scale and general sense of humanity make them both neutral enough to serve as proper galleries and flexible enough to provide a rich spatial experience.

In contrast to his contemporaries, Kahn was a late bloomer, emerging as an original voice in American architecture only in the late 1950s. His buildings reflect Beaux-Arts principles, tenets of Modernism, and a respect for historical values in a highly original synthesis. Both his works and his teaching at the University of Pennsylvania encouraged a generation of younger architects to explore

**16.15** Louis Kahn, Kimbell Art Museum, Fort Worth, Texas, 1966–72.

Almost sepulchral in character, the apparently barrel-vaulted units house the museum galleries. Where necessary, Kahn opened them up, as in the external passage or porch in the foreground.

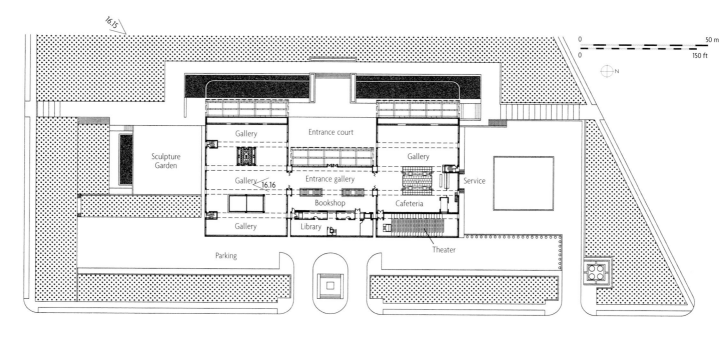

**16.16** Louis Kahn, Kimbell Art Museum interior, Fort Worth, Texas, 1966–72.

Kahn's modular units are not really barrel-vaulted, as the summit of each intrados is a void into which a baffled skylight has been inserted. The structural system is actually repetitive double-cantilevered butterfly canopies.

**16.17** Louis Kahn, Plan of the Kimbell Art Museum, Fort Worth, Texas, 1966–72.

One would hardly anticipate the spatial richness of Kahn's interiors from the simple geometry of his plan. This richness is amplified by the elegance of the building materials: silver-gray concrete, travertine, natural-finish wood, and stainless steel.

alternatives to the orthodoxies of the International Style. His preference for articulating individual rooms in plan, rather than employing the space-flow characteristics of much modern architecture, ties him to earlier eras, but his use of materials such as exposed concrete is modern in every way. Looking at his body of work, one can make the argument that he was the most original architect of the twentieth century. Kahn's son has produced and directed a film on his father titled *My Architect* (2003), which sheds much light on Kahn's life and serves as a kind of parallel universe to his work.

If Aalto's, Saarinen's, and Kahn's wide range of architectural interests were to be distilled to a single feature for each man, they might be construction methods for Aalto, form for Saarinen, and circumstance for Kahn. Aalto always maintained certain Modernist predilections, but tempered them according to his Nordic sensitivity toward site conditions. Eero Saarinen approached architecture through technology, sometimes meaning structural systems and always meaning materials and their assemblies. Louis Kahn was certainly concerned with materials, particularly weighty ones like brick and concrete, but this concern was driven by a personal, spiritual search for transcendent architectural form. The three categories these designers represent do not quite conform to the Vitruvian "firmness" (structure and materials), "commodity" (function), and "delight" (beauty), as discussed in this book's introduction, but they are close enough, and they will be useful in organizing the discussion that follows, beginning with the interlude called Post-Modernism.

## ROBERT VENTURI'S RADICAL COUNTER-PROPOSAL TO MODERNISM

As we have seen, the monolith of Modernism began to show hairline cracks after World War II. Members of Team-X surveyed the architectural field and found the terrain to be changing. Those like Aalto, Saarinen, and Kahn sought new, if not iconoclastic, directions. To others, however, the despised eclecticism to which Modernists had reacted so vehemently thirty or forty years earlier now seemed less important, and for some even appeared to offer welcome diversity. Add to this mix an increasing concern for the environment and conditions were right for a radical, if transitory, change.

The 1960s saw the emergence of Post-Modernism, a way of thinking about architecture that turns on its ear the approach of International Style designers. As did many earlier twentieth-century design movements, Post-Modernism began with a treatise, published in 1966 under the title *Complexity and Contradiction in Architecture* and hailed by Vincent Scully as "the most important writing on the making of architecture since Le Corbusier's *Vers une Architecture* of 1923." The author, Robert Venturi (born 1925), a student of Louis Kahn, made the case for non-straightforward, multivalent architecture. Using a style that echoed the phraseology of earlier manifestos, he observed:

> Architects can no longer afford to be intimidated by the puritanically moral language of orthodox Modern architecture. I like elements which are hybrid rather than "pure," compromising rather than "clean," distorted rather than "straightforward," ambiguous rather than "articulated," perverse as well as impersonal, boring as well as "interesting," conventional rather than

"designed," accommodating rather than excluding, redundant rather than simple, vestigial as well as innovating, inconsistent and equivocal rather than direct and clear. I am for messy vitality over obvious unity. I include the non sequitur and proclaim the duality.

The book extolled the ambiguities, inconsistencies, and idiosyncracies of Palladio, Michelangelo, Nicholas Hawksmoor, John Soane, Edwin Lutyens, Aalto, and Le Corbusier, and glorified Mannerist and Baroque architecture generally. Venturi went on to equate the atmosphere, lighting effects, and theatrics of Las Vegas casinos with Counter-Reformation art. By celebrating the "ugly and ordinary" aspects of twentieth-century buildings, as exhibited in roadside strip developments, neon advertising signs, and billboards, Venturi discarded the orderly purity and pristine character of Modernism in favor of pluralistic, often anonymously designed, and eminently practical populist work, dubbed by some detractors as the New Banality. Venturi wittily restated the Miesian dictum "Less is more" as "Less is a bore." Roots for this shift in architectural thinking can be found in the cultural diversity manifested in political and social movements of the period; increased attention to vernacular architecture, stemming in part from Bernard Rudofsky's "Architecture Without Architects" exhibition at the MOMA in 1964; British Brutalism; and the unique work of Venturi's mentor, Louis Kahn.

When *Complexity and Contradiction in Architecture* was published, Venturi had built very little, although he had placed well in architectural competitions. His largest completed commission was the ninety-one-unit Guild House (1960–63) (Fig. 16.18), an apartment block for the elderly in Philadelphia, in which common building elements

**16.18** Robert Venturi and John K. Rauch, Guild House, Philadelphia, Pennsylvania, 1960–63.

The architects celebrated the ordinary in this housing unit for the elderly. From the mundane signage to the false, gold-anodized television antenna and aluminum window frames, the building presents itself as an unapologetic product of mass culture.

were used in pragmatic yet unconventional ways. Double-hung windows were overscaled; a gold-anodized, roof-mounted, fake television antenna demarcated the central axis of the symmetrical façade; a single polished granite column denoted the entranceway and contrasted with the white glazed brick around the door, dignifying the building's institutional character. Interiors were thoughtfully designed with the well-being of the tenants in mind. A majority of the apartments were oriented to the south and overlooked activity on the street, while the corridors were offset to avoid the tedium of long hallways.

More famous, perhaps, is Venturi's 1962 house for his mother, Vanna, in Chestnut Hill, Pennsylvania (Fig. 16.19). In this modest dwelling, he combined simplicity of external form with complexity of interior layout, and conventional symbols and elements with contradictory arrangements. For example, the location of the central recess for the door is obvious, but the double-doors themselves are concealed and are much too grand for the cramped vestibule into which they open. Stairs to the second floor are set behind the chimney mass and compete with it for space; they widen as they ascend, then abruptly narrow to a minimum passage around the firebox. The fireplace and mantel are overscaled for the size of the living room, and the original furniture was of mixed ancestry rather than all being Bauhaus-inspired modern. On the outside the house presents a bold gable end to the street, in the manner of a Shingle Style house, yet its landlord-green color and stucco finish bear no resemblance to such buildings.

Venturi, working with his wife, Denise Scott-Brown (born 1931), has continued to make controversial proposals. In 1986–91, their firm placed an addition, known as the Sainsbury Wing, on the National Gallery in London. They erected this building on a difficult site in Trafalgar Square near James Gibbs's St. Martin-in-the-Fields (see Fig. 12.56). It is highly erudite and somewhat self-effacing and much more complex internally than its principal façade would lead one to believe. It projects east from the existing museum to face Pall Mall East and acknowledges William Wilkins's 1830 museum building, itself competent at best, by means of an accordion-like series of Corinthian reentrant pilasters; then other pilasters and an attached column more widely spaced; a related entablature and balustrade/parapet; various openings, some blind, some with surrounds; a discontinuous molding; and a grid of more-modern windows, looking all in all to detractors like a bad remodeling. On the other hand, even critics must acknowledge that the complex functional program and circulation and viewing requirements on the interior were handled extremely successfully and reflect generous amounts of both pragmatism and artfulness. In the end, the façade has been seen by many as presenting the same dilemma as much modern art: being self-consciously contrived and maddeningly hermetic and thereby rendering the public unable to assimilate it.

## INTELLECTUAL INSPIRATIONS FOR POST-MODERNISM

Understanding the various ideas that led to Post-Modernism in architecture and understanding the meaning of Post-Modernism in society at large (and these are two quite different phenomena) requires a brief survey of twentieth-century methods of inquiry in both the humanities and sciences. At the turn of the century, the humanities still took exclusively the hermeneutic approach, that is, the interpretation of texts from the point of view of their authors; those critical of this method argued that it "privileged" or placed far too much emphasis on these authors. At the same time, scientific inquiry was based on positivism, the view that science could address all questions about the world through the establishing of facts and the relationships among them. An alternative to these two approaches was put forward by the philosopher Edmund

**16.19** Robert Venturi, Vanna Venturi House, Chestnut Hill, Pennsylvania, 1962.

Robert Venturi built this house for his mother. The modest building is loaded with allusions to prior architecture, from the arch-like molding above the entry to the split-pediment-like massing of the full block.

Husserl (1859–1938). He created phenomenology, which he based upon a systematic investigation of human consciousness, as both a critique of and a means to combine humanistic and scientific endeavors. In the mid-twentieth century, at a time when phenomenology was losing ground in other fields, some architectural thinkers, disillusioned with what they considered to be the inhumane results of International Style principles, turned to it as a means for emphasizing people, values, belief systems, and motivations, and for privileging subjectivity over objectivity.

In the early twentieth century, however, it had been quantum physics in science and language in the humanities that had taken center stage. Physicists discovered a whole new world of subatomic particles that did not behave according to the laws of Newtonian mechanics. Einstein's theories of General and Special Relativity are the best-known results, but more important here are the uncertainties that these scientists uncovered and that, incidentally, Einstein never accepted. Werner Heisenberg's Uncertainty Principle says that it is impossible to know simultaneously both the position and velocity of a subatomic particle. It began to appear that ultimate truths about the natural world were ungraspable, and with this realization a sense of apprehension began to settle over not only the sciences but also the humanities. In the humanities, the philosopher Ludwig Wittgenstein (1889–1951) argued that language has limits and, therefore, that the task of philosophy is to "make us see what cannot be said, through clearly displaying the logic of propositions." In the 1920s and early 1930s, the so-called Logical Positivists in Vienna proposed that philosophy should focus its attention on why science works, ruling out esthetics entirely as a field of inquiry. Wittgenstein responded with the idea of linguistic analysis, whereby one could seek clarity through a critique of language and establish accurate means for analyzing information.

For those who found the empiricism of science inadequate for their needs, but who found phenomenology to be too mystical, linguistic analysis offered an alternative; the form of linguistic analysis known as Structuralism matured after World War I and reached its peak of influence in the mid-1960s. Created by individuals such as linguist Ferdinand de Saussure (1857–1913) and philosopher and anthropologist Claude Lévi-Strauss (born 1908), Structuralism looked at the world in terms of structures, that is, parts and the relationships among those parts within a system, with its goal being the discovery of universal principles that govern the human mind.

The line of Structuralist thinking that was most followed by architects and by architectural critics and theorists was semiotics. Semioticians saw the hermeneutic attempt to recover an author's intentions as impossible. They looked to the text, not the author, for meaning, specifically in the form of embedded signs and symbols. Buildings, they argued, carried layers of meaning too, and took on meanings never intended by their designers.

In the late 1960s Structuralism gave way to Post-Structuralism, whose developers included Jacques Derrida (1930–2004) and Michel Foucault (1926–84). A loosely organized group, they argued that no philosophical system could arrange and explain man's knowledge and that there were no absolute standards in any field of inquiry, a kind of literary uncertainty principle. As a means for addressing the relativism they had created, the Post-Structuralists focused on the text as discourse. Discourses, they argued, contained within them their own criteria for judgment, while signs and symbols, they said, only pointed to other signs and symbols. One could deconstruct a text so that it spread out in a never-ending network of uncertainties. A text could be interpreted in any number of ways by any number of people; interpretations were relative.

With this intellectual background in mind, we can now return to a discussion of Post-Modernist architectural practice. The term "Post-Modernist" was created to identify new directions in architecture after Modernism. It did not describe what these directions were, only what they were not. Subsequent to its introduction in an architectural context, it has taken on a counter-meaning in the broader culture, suggesting a Post-Structuralist fragmentation and distrust of any attempt to build systems of thought on firm foundations. One strain of Post-Modernist architecture has connections to Structuralism, specifically to semiotics. Authors like Geoffrey Broadbent and particularly Charles Jencks have been interested in architecture as a language and have written about signs and symbols as a way of reading the buildings of such designers as Philip Johnson, Charles Moore, and particularly Michael Graves. Jencks set out this position in *The Language of Post-Modern Architecture* (1977). Here he speaks of "double-coding": creating forms that carry meaning for both the elite, as he says the Modernists did, and for the man on the street—the vernacular message. Jencks appropriated the terms "univalent" and "multivalent" to describe the efforts of Post-Modernists to move beyond Modernist reductivism. Univalent, in his lexicon, means "an architecture created around one (or a few) simplified values." Multivalent means layers of values including historicism, revivalism, the vernacular, contextualism, and ecological issues, among others. The source for this coding has been a highly informed, some would say pedantic and esoteric, type of eclecticism with a high degree of relativity since, Jencks says, "all revivals are possible and each depends on an argument from *plausibility*, since it certainly can't be proved as necessary."

## PHILIP JOHNSON

No twentieth-century architect received more attention for his historicism than Philip Johnson (1906–2000), nor did

**16.20** Philip Johnson, Boissonas House, New Canaan, Connecticut, 1956.

By the late 1950s, Johnson had begun to move away from the Miesian tendencies of his early work. Among his experiments was this house, which was influenced by the domestic projects of Louis Kahn.

**16.21** Philip Johnson and John Burgee, American Telephone and Telegraph Headquarters, New York City, 1984.

With this building and its references to architectural styles of the past, Philip Johnson broke completely with the Miesian tradition. In fact, his client had said emphatically that the company did not want another glass box.

any architect practice or, indeed, live longer than he, nor did any architect have a more varied or controversial career. Johnson was dogged, for instance, by allegations that he had been a Nazi sympathizer. When a twenty-six-year-old graduate of Harvard with a degree in philosophy, he co-authored *The International Style: Architecture Since 1922* (discussed in the previous chapter) to accompany the 1932 MOMA exhibition on the International Style. While the exhibition was only modestly successful at the time, it eventually assumed the stature of myth, foreshadowing the persona that Johnson would create for himself later in the century. In 1938 he entered the Harvard Graduate School of Design, then headed by Walter Gropius, and, once graduated, opened his own office, with the most prominent result being his own Miesian house in New Canaan, Connecticut, mentioned in the previous chapter. By the late 1950s, however, he was moving away from his strongly Miesian, International Style tendencies, and producing a series of projects traceable to various sources, such as his Boissonas House in New Canaan (1956) (Fig. 16.20), which owes much to some of Louis Kahn's domestic work. His 1963 Museum for Pre-Columbian Art at Dumbarton Oaks in Washington, D.C. was overtly iconoclastic, with rooms defined by huge marble columns and covered by domes. But it was twenty-one years later, in 1984, that Johnson took the center of the Post-Modernist stage, with his American Telephone and Telegraph Headquarters in New York City (Fig. 16.21), designed in partnership with John Burgee. At its base is a giant Serliana, which has been compared by some to the façade of Brunelleschi's Pazzi Chapel, and at its crown a broken pediment, which has been compared to a grandfather clock or eighteenth-century highboy. Johnson has received less than consistent critical acclaim. Rather than his ability as a designer, it often seems to have been his cleverness in garnering media attention and his role as a power broker in the awarding of commissions and the selection of participants in exhibitions that ensured his fame.

## CHARLES MOORE

Charles Moore (1925–1993) brought to Post-Modernism a gentle but studied playfulness that made his buildings immediately accessible to the public and professionals alike. Moore took pleasure in historical allusions, but with large doses of whimsy. His critics have called his work superficial and ephemeral; his supporters have called it refreshing and ironic. In 1963–65, at a time when he was practicing as a partner in Moore, Lyndon, Turnbull, and Whitaker (MLTW), he was a principal designer for Sea Ranch I (Fig. 16.22), a set of ten contiguous condominium units on the coast north of San Francisco. On the exterior, the complex combines the massing of Aalto's Villa Carré near Paris with the rough-hewn, redwood wall surfacing of the Bay Area vernacular to produce a serene early comment on regionalism and building in visual harmony with the environment. On the interior, each cubic unit is organized around an aedicula—four columns supporting a roof—that produces lighthearted and convivial, yet complex, spaces.

Moore's Piazza d'Italia (Fig. 16.23) in New Orleans (1975–79), done in collaboration with Perez Associates, consists of a flamboyant, sometimes irreverent, neon-outlined, wildly Neo-Classical, scenographic backdrop for a contour map of Italy set in a pool of water that is demarcated by concentric rings of marble paving. It is as much

**16.22** Charles Moore et al, Sea Ranch condominiums, north of San Francisco, California, 1963–65.

Moore's living units are an early example of modern contextual design. The irregular massing reflects the topography and changing winds, and the redwood siding appears almost as camouflage.

**16.23** Charles Moore, Piazza d'Italia, New Orleans, Louisiana, 1975–79.

Moore's work took on an almost carnival aspect with projects like this one, a fountain with backdrop for a developing New Orleans public space. Here, the classical language has become a medium for wit and glibness, as in the Mannerist compositions of sixteenth-century Italy.

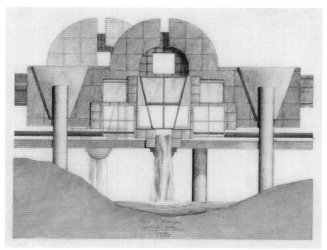

**16.24** Michael Graves, Elevation of the central portion of the Fargo-Moorhead Cultural Center Bridge, 1977.

Graves's projects and drawing style were influential long before he had constructed many buildings. Here he created his version of Claude-Nicolas Ledoux's eighteenth-century river-keeper's house (see Fig. 13.12).

spectacle as architecture, and its many details, such as the portrait of Moore's face in stainless steel spouting water like the fountain masks at the Villa d'Este near Rome, exhibit the wit that became his personal and professional trademark. The whole complex also seems to be an unintentional satire on Italian government, since its lights and fountains hardly ever work. Moore's academic appointments at Yale, U.C.L.A., and the University of Texas in Austin, as well as his indefatigable teaching and lecturing elsewhere, influenced myriad students from the 1960s onward.

## MICHAEL GRAVES

No Post-Modernist architect has been more agreeable to semioticians than Michael Graves (born 1934). Graves describes his work as "figurative," with the figural elements traceable to "classical and anthropomorphic sources." His earliest projects, particularly house additions in Princeton, New Jersey, were neo-Corbusian, but he soon began to explore new ground. Grave's unbuilt Fargo-Moorhead Cultural Center Bridge (1977) (Fig. 16.24) contains broadcasting facilities and a concert hall on one bank and a history museum on the other, all linked by an art museum spanning from Fargo, North Dakota, to Moorhead, Minnesota, over the Red river. At the conceptual level, imagery for the bridge is traceable principally to Ledoux's design for the Inspector's House at the Source of the River Loue (see Fig. 13.12), but details such as keystones were transformed into windows and roof drains through a clever manipulation of the classical language. Graves's beautiful colored-pencil rendering of the bridge exhibits a lyricism that has become a constant in his work. The built Portland Building in Portland, Oregon (1980), is equally famous as a rendered elevation. It is replete with quotations from the classical language: the temples

**16.25** Michael Graves, Portland Building, Portland, Oregon, 1980.

It becomes almost a game with compositions such as this one to count all of the quasi-classical elements. Some of the appurtenances in Graves's published designs for the building, such as a flying figure and a roof-top village, were never realized.

on the roof (never built), the giant keystone beneath them, the pair of fluted pilasters of indeterminate order, and the tiered stylobate at street level (Fig. 16.25). Graves was also a force in reintroducing color into twentieth-century architecture, as here with the green base, terra-cotta-colored columns, and tan flanking walls punctured by square windows. His Swan and Dolphin hotels (1987) at Disney World in Orlando, Florida demonstrate Graves's ability to design at all scales from building to flatware. He first developed a master plan for the area, then designed the hotels to be placed around a crescent-shaped lake. The mass of the Swan Hotel seems relatively unimportant among the tent-lined approach causeway, palm trees, giant swan and clamshell sculptures, and even the hotel's own camouflage-like, wave-pattern paint scheme. Once inside, the visitor confronts more tents, a fountain, and wall murals, and Graves designed carpets, light fixtures, wallpapers, even placemats and plates. His style seems to fit perfectly the surreptitiously controlled environment of Disney World. The Dolphin Hotel has an equally diverse set of appurtenances in addition to its central Boullée-having-fun triangular façade (Fig. 16.26) and Napoleonic-Empire-one-better tented rotunda lobby. While only a pedant or an unreconstructed Modernist could fail to enjoy the place, one can question whether it has the staying power of the grand resort hotels of the late nineteenth and early twentieth centuries such as the Belleview-Biltmore in Belleair, Florida, or the Grand Hotel on Mackinac Island, Michigan.

**16.26** Michael Graves, Dolphin Hotel, Disney World, Orlando, Florida, 1987.

Here Graves brings Boullée to a theme-park environment. While the rooms are modest, the designed context of water, causeways, cabanas, and palm-lined promenades makes for fun.

**16.27** Robert Stern, Lang House, Washington, Connecticut, 1973–74.

This house in the country has a cowboy-storefront-like façade, over which extended label moldings have been added like piped-on cake icing. This is Stern's early brand of classical allusionism.

## ROBERT A. M. STERN

Graves's work conforms nicely to the attributes of Post-Modernism defined by the architect and architectural historian Robert A. M. Stern (born 1939): contextualism, allusionism, and ornamentalism. Contextualism refers to connections between the building and its setting as Post-Modernist architects attempt to link their buildings to established patterns, geometries, and possibilities for future growth, rather than conceiving each design as an isolated object in the landscape, as many would argue that Modernists did. As an architect, Stern has often quarried New England sources, producing for instance many convincing neo-Shingle Style houses. Less convincing but much-published at the time of its construction is his Lang House (1973–74) (Fig. 16.27) in Connecticut with its pencil-thin, classically motivated **label moldings** applied almost like piping on the sleeve of a garment. His Newport Bay Club Hotel at Disneyland Resort Paris (1988–92) was successfully derived from classic resorts such as the Michigan Grand Hotel mentioned above. Stern has written at length about classicism, calling it the "fulcrum about which architectural discourse balances," and has built in a variety of traditional styles.

## DECONSTRUCTION

Post-Modernism has also included within it work described as Deconstructivist. In *Deconstructivist Architecture* (1988), which accompanied an exhibition at MOMA in New York City, the argument is made that, even though the terminology is the same, Deconstruction in architecture means something quite different from literary Post-Structuralist endeavors to deconstruct written texts in order to locate their hidden meanings:

> *A deconstructive architect is therefore not one who dismantles buildings, but one who locates the inherent dilemmas within buildings. The deconstructivist architect puts the pure forms of the architectural tradition on the couch and identifies the symptoms of a repressed impurity. The impurity is drawn to the surface by a combination of gentle coaxing and violent torture: the form is interrogated.*

The MOMA exhibition, assembled by the perceptive and wily Philip Johnson, was fraught with controversy even before it opened and was showered with constant criticism afterward because of the vagaries of Deconstruction's meaning and relevance.

Some practitioners, notably Bernard Tschumi (born 1944) and Peter Eisenman (born 1932), argue that their buildings are indeed Derridian; Tschumi says that his Parc

**16.28** Bernard Tschumi, *Folie*, Parc de la Villette, Paris, 1982–85.

The Parc de la Villette is intended to be an open-air cultural center with space for workshops, gymnasium and bath facilities, playgrounds, exhibitions, concerts, and more. Each *folie* is an undifferentiated, neutral object in the landscape where designated activities can take place.

**16.29** Peter Eisenman, House III, Lakeville, Connecticut, 1969–71.

In the 1960s, Peter Eisenman explored the abstract possibilities of rotated grids. Spaces became an effect caused by the manipulation of selected elements according to a set of rules.

de la Villette in Paris (1982–85) (Fig. 16.28) explores the disjunctures in culture, emphasizing fragmentation and dissociation rather than traditional unity and synthesis. Frank Gehry, on the other hand, has seemed quite content to "dismantle," beginning with the design for his own house in Los Angeles (see Fig. 16.32), and today has a thriving practice driven to a great extent by the ability of computer technology to make his irregular and often intersecting geometries understandable to builders. Charles Jencks sums up his view of Deconstruction this way, describing it as principally iconoclastic:

> Deconstruction . . . always depends for its meaning on
> that which is previously constructed. It always posits an
> orthodoxy which it "subverts," a norm which it breaks,
> an assumption and ideology which it undermines.
> And the minute it loses this critical role, or becomes
> a dominant power itself (as in so many academies),
> it becomes a tyrannical bore. The same is true of
> Deconstructionist architecture: it works best as an
> exception within a strongly defined norm.

Some have seen such arguments as erudite castles in the air made by professional designers envious of the intellectual depth found in the humanities. Others have supported these arguments, saying that they promote a serious and necessary criticism of unbridled consumer culture and media-driven hyper-reality.

## PETER EISENMAN

The work of Peter Eisenman certainly fits Jencks's description. He is an architect who has reinvented himself more times than Philip Johnson, and like Johnson has exhibited a genius for self-promotion. In a career driven by an almost maniacal extraction of ideas from the then-current cultural milieu in fields as diverse as the linguistic investigations of Foucault and the potential geometries created by fractals, Eisenman has honed his image as a provocateur and man of intellect among lesser minds. Some criticize his work as contrived and opportunistic, while others see it as endlessly investigative and serious to the point of tragedy. He first became known for the series of houses, most of them unbuilt, that he designed in the late 1960s and early 1970s (Fig. 16.29). While they respond to complex programs based upon both individual and societal issues, they are outwardly formalistic experiments using colliding and interlocking geometries that seem only self-referential; Eisenman touted them as linguistic-architectural inquiries into the basic grammar and syntax of space. In his Biocentrum in Frankfurt am Main, Germany (1987), "DNA is used as a model of a logical sequence with infinite possibilities for expansion, change, and flexibility." Here, the collision of geometries remains, overlaid with biological metaphor, certainly more apparent to the designer than the casual passer-by.

## COOP HIMMELBLAU

The firm of Coop Himmelblau (Himmelblau meaning sky-blue) was formed in 1968 by the Austrian Wolf Dieter Prix (b. 1942) and the Polish Helmut Swiczinsky (b. 1944). Intensely urbanistic and alert to its responsibility in the public realm, their architecture has always proceeded from intense discussions directly to a conceptual sketch, which, when fully developed, reveals little change from the original idea. Such was the case with their law-office Rooftop Remodeling for a firm then operating out of an undistinguished, two-story building in Vienna. Prix and Swiczinsky broke through the roof, then attached an assemblage of largely transparent planes in a kind of free-form polygon, perhaps suggestive of the flight of a falcon (as the building faces the Falkstrasse, or Falcon Street). While critics writing about Deconstruction included this design in their discussions, the architects were simply following the on-going trajectory of their work. The remodeling's fractured quality cannot but be compared to Hans Hollein's Viennese jewelry shop façade (discussed below).

## ZAHA HADID

Zaha Hadid (born 1950), Iraqi and female and a short time ago only the creator of fantastic, unbuilt, and perhaps unbuildable projects that existed only as translucent layers of computer graphics and that seemed disassembled (and so, to some, Deconstructivist), has now become an international architectural star laden with real commissions. The Vitra Fire Station (1993) and Bergisel Ski-jump in Innsbruck, Austria demonstrate her originality. Her first built project, the fire station in Wiel am Rhein, Germany, is a projectile-like construction of concrete and metal that figuratively slashes through space, as much sculpture as architecture. Eventually made unnecessary by changes in local fire-districts, the station became a display space for the Vitra furniture company's chairs, acknowledging its museum-like, open, compelling spatial organization.

The Bergisel Ski-jump (Fig. 16.30) has a square, concrete shaft capped by a cantilevered, helmet-like, metal-and-glass summit that accommodates a café as well as waiting athletes and looks out from its mountaintop site over the Tyrolean Alps and down upon Innsbruck.

**16.30** Zaha Hadid, Bergisel Ski-jump, Innsbruck, Austria, 2002.

At a time when women are assuming greater prominence on the international architectural scene, none is more celebrated than Iraq-born Zaha Hadid. Designing a ski-jump afforded her the opportunity to explore her interests in speed, change, and related angularities of form.

**16.31** Zaha Hadid, Rosenthal Center for Contemporary Arts, Cincinnati, 2003.

On the interior of this downtown Cincinnati building, Hadid made a bold but relatively conventional gesture to the urban street edge. On the interior, however, she continued her intense enquiry into the nature of dynamic space.

Evolving in space like a piece of Futurist sculpture, from tight turn to a straight run, the metal ski-ramp figuratively uncoils before reaching down into the sloping landscape.

Hadid's Rosenthal Center for Contemporary Arts (Fig. 16.31) in downtown Cincinnati (2003) has been criticized by some as too tame relative to her previous work and lionized by others, not only for connectedness to its urban surroundings but also for its raising the standards for urbanism in this often-ignored Midwestern city. This is not to say that Hadid's preferred angular geometries and dramatic means of vertical circulation are absent. In exhibition space designed to accommodate only temporary shows, walls soar, light penetrates dramatically, stair-ramps leap, and floors bend. If space can be considered the stuff of modern architecture, then this museum is a classic modern building.

## FRANK GEHRY

Frank Gehry (born 1929) has succeeded in having a host of designs that would seem destined to remain as models or conceptual drawings actually built. He has been strongly influenced by artists, many of whom are his close friends. Early in his career he realized, as have many other architects, that he often preferred buildings in an incomplete state of construction to the finished products. While most would have left it at that, however, Gehry began to design new buildings, with an obvious kinship to Russian Constructivist work, that seem frozen in a state of becoming. His own much-published house in Santa Monica, California (1977–78) (Fig. 16.32) is a case in point. Its ribbed metal siding, chain-link fencing, and unpainted wood, all pouring forth from a seemingly confused early twentieth-

century bungalow behind, make the composition look as much like an active construction site as an occupied structure. Afterward, Gehry began to explode buildings, breaking them up into discrete volumes in a way that, to some, reflects the fragmentation in modern society. His Winton Guest House in Wayzata, Minnesota (1983–86) (Fig. 16.33) stands adjacent to a main house designed in 1952 by Philip Johnson. Gehry somewhat awkwardly but powerfully arranged a set of very sculptural forms—one vault-like, one a shed-roofed box, the others boxes with flat roofs—around a central truncated pyramid. His objective, he said, was to create a building with a "certain amount of humor and mystery and fantasy." His Team Disneyland Administration Building in Anaheim, California (1996) can be compared organizationally to Aalto's Baker House.

**16.32** Frank Gehry, Gehry House, Santa Monica, California, 1977–78.

Frank Gehry began modestly, making additions to his own bungalow that fall somewhere between sculpture and industrial residue. As with Peter Eisenman, Gehry eventually needed the computer to build fantastical structures that he could at first only imagine.

**16.33** Frank Gehry, Winton Guest House, Wayzata, Minnesota, 1983–86. Model.

Gehry was always as interested in sculpture as architecture. Here simple, recognizable volumes collide. His sheathing materials are stone, Finnish plywood, and copper.

**16.34** Frank Gehry, Team Disneyland Administration Building, Computer rendering, Los Angeles, California, 1996.

Only computer technology made it possible to build such distorted forms. On the inside, Gehry's plans exhibit a much more conventional ordering.

Seen from the freeway, its flat, quilted sheet-metal façade appears to be quite conventional, its regularity broken only by slight offsets in the stacking of windows and the mottled color scheme. To the rear (Fig. 16.34), however, the building's massing becomes curvilinear, warped, even delusional, as canary-yellow walls bend, lean forward, and lean back, their canopies equally disfigured, as if the result of a recent seismic event. On the interior, the same wildly sculptural unconventionality holds sway at the main stair, with its compound curves, and in the theater, where walls are formed by overlapping sheets of plywood shaped in response to acoustical requirements. Even more urbanistically aggressive is Gehry's Nationale Nederlander office building in Prague, in the Czech Republic, known locally as "Fred and Ginger" (1997) (Fig. 16.35). Here, within a historic context, Gehry took movement as his theme for a corner building that twists and projects in space with an energy expressive of the opening up of eastern Europe since the dissolution of the Soviet Union. Economic constraints called for one more floor than in neighboring buildings, but accommodated within the same cornice height. In order to resolve the conflict, Gehry lowered and camouflaged the floor levels by means of fishscale-like undulating layers of cement plaster and more displaced windows. The entrance tower of concrete columns bundled in glass seems to sway as if part of an urban choreography in step with the surrounding buildings and space, hence the "Fred and Ginger" nickname. The result, though idiosyncratic, is surprisingly contextual, acknowledging adjacent medieval towers and Baroque façades and domes.

Gehry's Guggenheim Museum Bilbao (opened 1997) in Bilbao, Spain (page 506 and Figs. 16.36–16.37), has aroused a kind of popular and critical interest equaled by few other twentieth-century constructions. His exhilarating structure replaced dock facilities on a site adjacent to the Nervión river in a gritty manufacturing city. Out of a four-story mass blossom "pleated petals" of titanium attached to a steel frame. The museum acts as a mirror,

**16.35** Frank Gehry, Nationale Nederlander ("Fred and Ginger"), Prague, 1997.

Taken out of context, this building perhaps appears shocking. However, it actually fits quite well among its neighbors. The nearby curving gables, spiky towers, and richly textured façades convey the same energy and urban liveliness as Gehry's intervention.

**16.36** Frank Gehry, Guggenheim Museum Bilbao, Bilbao, 1997.

No recent building has garnered more attention in the popular press or been a more popular site for architectural pilgrimages. Visitors love to touch its shiny skin of titanium.

**16.37** Frank Gehry, Guggenheim Museum Bilbao in its urban context, Bilbao, 1997.

The effect of the sculpted, quilted titanium surfaces at the end of the Calle de Iparragguirre is startling. The play of light on the facets of the metal causes the character of the building to change dramatically with the changing position of the sun and changing atmospheric conditions.

reflecting and absorbing the city, reflecting and absorbing itself. Giving off a metallic luminescence, it hovers and shimmers at the end of hard-edged urban vistas (Fig. 16.37). Visitors have come to Bilbao in droves, more to see the building than its contents. They want to be in it and around it, and they want to touch it. In the complex first-floor plan, where the only orthogonal spaces house mechanical systems, the loading dock, and storage and exhibition-preparation rooms, a towering central atrium connects to an auditorium and galleries, one of them a trapezoid, one L-shaped, and the largest one a long and narrow boat-like giant that passes beneath the Puente de la Salve, the major road through Bilbao, as it reaches out to the east beside a free-form water garden. On the second and third floors, the plan becomes more regular, including a series of square galleries placed *en enfilade*. The space inside the atrium (page 506) is enormous, half as tall again as Wright's Guggenheim rotunda, with bowing steel, angular stone-faced walls, and undulating masses cut away to admit light; it is the fulfillment of a Baroque spatial dream made possible by modern building and computer technology.

## REM KOOLHAAS

When the Dutch architect Rem Koolhaas (born 1944) published *Delirious New York* in 1978, he established himself as a thinker about urbanism with a highly original, intellectualized, and edgy view of the architectural scene. For those interested in Rockefeller Center, the influential delineator Hugh Ferris, and Le Corbusier's view of the Big Apple, as well as case studies of buildings infrequently included in standard architectural histories, such as the Waldorf-Astoria Hotel and the New York Athletic Club and all of Coney Island, this book will be found both insightful and amusing. Koolhaas's own imaginary designs for the city, such as his Hotel Sphinx (Fig. 16.38), show him to have been little concerned then with construction but fascinated with modern culture, conditions that have not changed significantly.

In Rotterdam, he founded the Office of Metropolitan Architecture (OMA), wherein he operates more as a philosopher and visionary than as a traditional designer. Called Modernist works by some, Deconstructivist by others, many of his projects exist only on paper, and only now have a sufficient number of them been built to allow for a proper evaluation of Koolhaas's style.

In 1992, Koolhaas completed the KunstHal, or Art Hall, in Rotterdam, taking advantage of a sloping site located between a basalt dike and a new Museum Park. The south elevation has a relatively low, horizontal profile, not without connections to Rotterdam's De Stijl Movement of the period during and after World War I, while the east elevation boldly displays an auditorium behind

**16.38** Rem Koolhaas, graphic rendering of Hotel Sphinx, as published in *Delirious New York* (1978).

Koolhaas brought a cerebral European perspective to the study of that most reinvented of places: New York City. It has taken him more than a quarter of a century to transform his published urban visions into radical, built realities.

**16.39** Rem Koolhaas, Seattle Central Library, Seattle, Washington, 2004.

It is not difficult to connect the inventor of the Hotel Sphinx with the creator of the Seattle Central Library, but it is hard to imagine a building with more dramatic cantilevers, unless it is Koolhaas's CCTV building (Fig. 16.80). Some have questioned whether his concern for materials assemblages and detailing matches his penchant for conceptualization.

extensive glazing. The building's interiors owe something to the spatial investigations of Le Corbusier, with a penetrating north–south street that runs tangent to the auditorium. Materials most often eschew elegance in favor of tough-minded translucencies, in the form of metal-grid floors and corrugated plastic sheeting.

Opened to the public in 2004, Koolhaas's Seattle Central Library covers an entire city block (Fig. 16.39). On the outside, it is a reflective prism with glazing in a diamond-grid exoskeleton that is ideally viewed in the Seattle mist. The huge interior volume, part hotel atrium, part space station, with cantilevered floor levels connected by a giant ramp or "Books Spiral," aspires to be the city's living room, a true public domain and a techno-sphere where hard-copy books and the digital world can be good neighbors.

## PERSEVERENCE OF THE CLASSICAL TRADITION

The discussion of classical architecture—be it that of ancient Greece and Rome or any of its later reinventions from fifteenth-century Italy to eighteenth-century Enlightenment Europe and North America—has consumed much of this book. The popularity of classical compositions among both the most knowing and innovative designers and the broader public speaks of the expressiveness, flexibility, and nuance of the classical language. But can it or should it thrive in a modern or post-modern world? Some architects like those discussed below argue yes.

### ALLAN GREENBERG

No one embraced classicism in the twentieth century more completely and less apologetically than Allan Greenberg (born 1934). He argues that classicism is modern because it expresses "eternal human values" and is "rooted in the physiology and psychology of the individual human being." Even those who disagree with his philosophy, and there are many, must admit that his detailing and appointments are exquisite and his compositions, if not original, are supple and confident. His Treaty Room Suite for the U.S. Department of State was inserted into the State Department Building (1941, 1958) that stands north of the Mall in the vicinity of the Lincoln and Vietnam memorials in Washington, D.C. T-shaped in plan, it consists of an elevator lobby with paired Doric columns and a coffered ceiling in the form of a shallow vault, leading to the elliptical treaty room with anterooms to each end. The ellipse contains paired Corinthian columns supporting a full entablature above a floor pattern inspired by the paving of Michelangelo's Campidoglio in Rome.

### ANDRES DUANY AND ELIZABETH PLATER-ZYBERK

In 1981, Andres Duany and Elizabeth Plater-Zyberk produced Seaside (Fig. 16.40), a coastal residential community in the Panhandle of Florida. Their instrument of control was the design standard, what they called a "Traditional Neighborhood Development Ordinance," with an emphasis on the "Traditional." With this project, they established a design philosophy that has become known as the New Urbanism (meaning, somewhat ironically, an

**16.40** Andres Duany and Elizabeth Plater-Zyberk, Seaside coastal residential community, Florida, 1981.

Following the wishes of developer Robert Davis, Andres Duany and Elizabeth Plater-Zyberk sought an architecture based on local building traditions for their planned town called Seaside. To this end, they created detailed design guidelines but did not impose a specific architectural style. Some critics, however, have seen this unity as artificial and divorced from reality.

urbanism drawn from historical patterns), allying them with the likes of Allan Greenberg, as well as Robert A. M. Stern (discussed previously and again below) and Léon Krier (discussed below). Duany and Plater-Zyberk have become lightning rods for urbanistic controversy, with opinions on their design proposals diverging wildly. Some have accused them of social engineering because of the prescriptive nature of their ordinances. Others dismiss their architectural ensembles as lived-in Disneyworlds: artificial, nostalgic villages for the well-to-do. While both views contain elements of truth, few will argue that Modernism has produced more than its share of ugly, failed urban environments, and since Jane Jacobs's *Death and Life of Great American Cities* appeared in 1961, with a stinging criticism of Modernism and its handmaiden urban renewal, few have pretended there was not a problem. Duany and Plater-Zyberk press on with their solution to this dilemma and have now designed more than two hundred communities.

### CELEBRATION, FLORIDA

Beyond Seaside, the New Urbanism has been much publicized for such community designs as Kentlands in Maryland and Laguna West in California. However, the project with the most force behind it is surely the Walt Disney Company's new town of Celebration near Disney World. Laid out by Robert A. M. Stern and Jaquelin Robertson, it includes not only residences in compact neighborhoods but also a town center facing a lake. Housing styles are strictly traditional, in what are designated as classical, Victorian, colonial revival, coastal, Mediterranean, and French patterns, all of them controlled by a strict design code. Many American architects discussed in this chapter (Philip Johnson, Robert Venturi and Denise Scott-Brown, Charles Moore, etc.) have done work here, but as unlikely as it seems, so has the Italian Rationalist Aldo Rossi (1931–1997), hired by the Disney Development

Company to lay out an office complex and design its initial buildings. Shorn of the palimpsestic Italian urban context, however, his buildings hardly seem distinguishable from the ubiquitous, often banal, developer structures covered with drivit, or synthetic stucco, that already appear so frequently in the American landscape.

### ALDO ROSSI

Rossi's Italian buildings forego any sense of their construction in favor of a Platonic universalism of form. Modern in the sense that he eschewed ornament, Rossi approached architecture through distinctive drawings that evoke a sense of mystery and timelessness as well as fantasy. His competition-winning design for the Cemetery of San Cataldo in Modena (Fig. 16.41), on which he worked from 1971 to 1984, consists of a large rectangular plot surrounded by a gable-roofed arcade, with repetitive, square openings in its frieze-like upper reaches. Along the cemetery's central axis running the short dimension of the rectangle lies first a shrine in the form of a cube with an unbroken grid of windows in all four façades, all atop a subterranean columbarium (depository for ashes of cremated bodies), then a series of planar ossuaries (depositories for the bones of the dead) that form a triangle in both plan and section, and, finally, a truncated cone above the common grave of the homeless and abandoned. Rossi's 1972–76 elementary school in Fagnano Olona near Varese shares some of the cemetery's enigmatic sense of solitude yet somehow seems to be an appropriate setting for teaching the young. Rossi also received much attention for his analysis of urbanism in *The Architecture of the City* (1966).

### LÉON KRIER

Léon Krier was born in Luxembourg in 1946. He has championed the abandonment of consumer-driven, automobile-dominated sprawl, the "disposable, adaptable,

**16.41** Aldo Rossi, graphic rendering of Cemetery of San Cataldo, Modena, 1971–84.

Working in a country where the remains of the ancient Roman and Renaissance pasts lie around in abundance, it is not surprising that Italian architects continue to respect and reinterpret classicism. In Aldo Rossi's case, he sought not architectural fashion but a world of archetypal forms that aspire to display larger truths.

**16.42** Luis Barragán (1902–88), El Bebedero (drinking trough and fountain), Las Arboledas, Mexico City, 1959–62.

Water is a precious commodity in arid places like much of Mexico, and water has associations with life and rebirth and renewal, meaning that though designated a "drinking trough," this mirror-like pool and its garden surroundings become an introspective landscape of reflection and contemplation. Compare this scene to Islamic or Moorish work such as the Court of Myrtle Trees at the Alhambra in Spain (see Fig. 7.37).

plug-in" city advocated by the Metabolists (discussed below), and the zoned Modernist city, promoted by the likes of Le Corbusier, in favor of the city as a "document of intelligence, memory, and pleasure." In 1988, on 400 acres of land owned by the Duchy of Cornwall, Prince Charles (an architectural dilettante or savior of the built landscape, depending on which critic you ask) chose Krier to design the model new town of Poundbury in the southern English county of Dorset. It was to be a socially inclusive and sustainable village of 5000 residents, with its architecture following traditional Dorset models and its scale conducive to walking. Opened to occupancy in 2000, it has roads that gently curve and meander, as well as courts and squares that invite community interaction. A Poundbury Building Code ensures the continuity of traditional materials and forms and an appropriately humane scale.

## MODERN REGIONALISM

Some modern architects have followed the path defined by members of Team-X and have sought to develop a contemporary idiom by responding to more localized conditions. This effort can, in part, be interpreted as a reaction against the cultural homogenization produced by easier communications, increased and more rapid travel, and the pervasiveness of mass media. The most gifted regional designers have grounded themselves in local values, building traditions, and form languages and have remained sensitive to local site conditions, while leavening their design proposals with the yeast of modern compositional principles, new technologies, and a broad social conscience.

### LUIS BARRAGÁN

Luis Barragán (1902–1988) from Guadalajara, Mexico pursued a poetic vision of place-intensive design that incorporates traditional Mexican building materials and uses water so advantageously that it can stand comparison to Moorish work at the Alhambra in Spain (see Fig. 7.37). The many lava-wall houses that he designed for his own subdivision called El Pedregal (1945–50) are composed using both white and intensely colored planes that provide privacy, often frame the sky, and unite interior space with the landscape. Modern in its results, Barragán's work is ultimately timeless and intensely personal. The focused simplicity of his El Bebedero (1959–62) in Las Arboledas (Fig. 16.42) produces a level of quietude rarely equaled.

**16.43** Mario Botta, 1973 House, Monte San Giorgio, Switzerland, 1973.

Building in such a spectacular setting presents a challenge to any designer, especially when the building is so modest in size. Botta responded by planting the elementary geometry of a cube in the sloping landscape and making it accessible by a delicate, skeletal bridge.

**16.44** Álvaro Siza, Galician Center of Contemporary Art, Santiago de Compostela, Spain, 1985–92.

First, Siza related his building to the road, then he united the older convent, cloister, and church with his new museum by means of their shared landscapes, including monastic gardens. Just as there is a carefully shaped seam of space between the two structures, there is a corridor and interior court inside the museum and between the galleries.

## MARIO BOTTA

With connections to the rationalism of Aldo Rossi, Mario Botta (born 1943) has produced a body of work in which houses have been prominent. Seen here is one of his early successes (Fig. 16.43), the 1973 House (really a villa in the traditional sense) in Monte San Giorgio in the Ticino region of Switzerland. A true "machine in the garden," it is a heavy masonry cube reached by a light, interpenetrating steel-girder bridge and stands within a snow-peaked Swiss Alps landscape. Elementary in its Platonic geometry, it is supple in its detailing.

## ÁLVARO SIZA

Portuguese architect Álvaro Siza (born 1933) developed a plan for the Galician Center of Contemporary Art (1985–92) in Santiago de Compostela, Spain that incor-

porates the Modernist fusion of space, prevalent since architecture's early-twentieth-century instruction by Cubist, Futurist, and Constructivist artists, and Adolf Loos's invention of the *Raumplan*. However, as a tangible object, the Center speaks to its particular situation in a town whose rich pilgrimage tradition goes back to the Middle Ages. The museum stands on a down-slope below a seventeenth-century Baroque monastery (Fig. 16.44), of which Siza allowed glimpses from selected points within his building. While he abstractly composed his masses by paring them into simple volumes, intersecting them, celebrating their connections, and leaving a seam of circulation in their midst, he also gave them materiality, using local granite applied in a brindled pattern that speaks sympathetically to adjacent, lichen-covered, masonry walls. This affinity for site is amplified by the great care that Siza took in preserving, restoring, and supplementing the remains of the monastic gardens.

He has also designed a number of structures for the Portuguese port town of Leça da Palmiera. On a coastline where grassy slopes erupt at the water's edge into craggy rock formations, Siza has built in concrete, stucco, wood planking, and heavy timber, with terracotta for roof tiles. The contrast of cool, white planar surfaces and warm interior finishes can be compared to Alvar Aalto's houses of the 1930s and Siza's organic site placements to those of Frank Lloyd Wright or of Charles Moore at Sea Ranch (see Fig. 16.22).

## SAMUEL MOCKBEE AND THE RURAL STUDIO

Samuel Mockbee (1944–2001) took his architecture conceptually and geographically to a place not chosen by anyone else, a place not even considered by anyone else. Imagining buildings through revelatory drawings and paintings, he transferred his architectural practice from Jackson, Mississippi to the middle of nowhere: Hale County in West Central Alabama. Here he conjured up from his collective teaching experiences the "Rural Studio," gave it a social conscience, gathered Auburn University architectural students around him, and led them in the production of a small universe of authentic and even noble buildings, often using unorthodox, even salvaged building materials, and, unlikely as it seems, became famous doing it.

Hale County was found decades ago, when Walker Evans took pathos-evoking Great Depression-era photographs of it and James Agee wrote sympathetic but censorious prose about the conditions among its sharecropper poor, both black and white. Since that time, local grinding poverty has been mitigated only marginally, so it is hard to imagine a less likely place for an architect to seek out clients; but cobbling together university funding, state social-services assistance, and private and foundation contributions, and teaching and inspiring his students and making use of his own gift for turning life into art, Mockbee somehow did the undoable.

The Rural Studio's building types and construction methods include a hay-bale-wall residence; student housing constructed of compressed corrugated cardboard and partially clad in old license plates; a baseball field, a playground, a children's center, a boys-and-girls club; the list goes on, all the construction somehow both anonymous and intensely personal, all of it designed and built by the privileged without being patronizing or condescending. The question of individual authorship, that is, Mockbee's contributions versus those of his students, has been little talked about and appropriately so, as he seems to have accepted and encouraged the creative sensibilities of all those who were drawn to him.

Both the Mason's Bend Community Center (2000) in New Bern and the Yancey Chapel (1995) in Sawyerville illustrate these conditions. Like all of Samuel Mockbee's buildings, their plans are of little consequence, meaning that they are rarely shown in publications of Rural Studio work.

**16.45** Samuel Mockbee, Mason's Bend Community Center, New Bern, Alabama, 2000.

When Samuel Mockbee died in 2001 at the age of fifty-seven, the world lost one of its most original artist–architects. As modest evidence of this fact, the walls of this building are made of automobile windshields overlapped like shingles.

The community center (Fig. 16.45), built by four thesis students, has walls made of rammed earth and a faceted roof of tin and Chevrolet Caprice windshields. It looks like an excavated archaeological site with a new protective canopy, or like something from the minds of Coop Himmelblau's Wolf Prix and Helmut Swiczinsky transported from urban Austria to Black Belt Alabama.

The chapel, built by three students, is situated on a bluff, has a sway-back roof inspired by those on local collapsing barns and, as its principal wall material, donated tires packed with earth and reinforcing rods, wrapped in wire mesh, laid up like masonry, and covered with stucco. After passing by an existing cattle trough transformed by its altered context into an art installation, visitors proceed through a dimpled tire-canyon before entering the longitudinal chapel that is covered by a skeletal wooden roof, not without similarity to the chapel frames of Arkansas architect Faye Jones. Above the floor of scavenged slate, with a narrow channel of water running along one side, light enters at the ridge through a continuous skylight, and at the far end, beyond an altar assembled from scrap steel, the space extends out into the landscape, like a pier into a calm sea. The whole building cost $15,000.

## MODERNISM AND JAPAN

Traditional Japanese architecture was discussed in Chapter 4. A perusal of the images reproduced there makes clear two of its limitations: a reliance on wooden construction and a scarcity of large buildings. While these conditions had changed to some extent by the end of World War II, it became clear to Japanese architects that they were presented with a challenge: how to synthesize traditional Japanese values and principles with modern political, economic, and technological realities.

### KENZO TANGE

Kenzo Tange (1913–2005) achieved early notice with his competition-winning design for the Hiroshima Peace Center in 1949. Working most often with reinforced concrete (in a country plagued by earthquakes) and with obvious early affinities for the work of Le Corbusier, he evolved a personal style by the time of his Kurashiki City Hall (1957–60) that expressed both continuity and newness and addressed the communal reconstruction of his country along democratic lines. His St. Mary's Cathedral and Olympic Sports Complex (Fig. 16.46) in Tokyo, the latter built for the 1964 games, are suspension structures in which Tange was able to define entry and movement sequences and create soaring spaces through logical

responses to the laws of physics, while still acknowledging Japan's traditional, formal architectural language. Later in his career, he explored a kind of mechanistic architecture capable of growth and change. A group of younger Japanese architects, calling themselves the "Metabolists," further pursued this line of enquiry and proposed vast utopian schemes dependent on transcendent technologies such as large-scale standardized components plugged into enormous organizing infrastructures.

### FUMIHIKO MAKI

To some extent a rationalist and a student of Tange, Fumihiko Maki (born 1928) has embraced the scale of the individual, Japan's history-laden modern condition, and the fractured, noble incompleteness of the contemporary world view. In a manner that must be compared to the Woodland Cemetery in Stockholm (see Fig. 15.86), his Kaze-no-Oka (Hill of the Winds) Crematorium rises gently out of the ground on its site near the small southern-Japan city of Nakatsu. Already extant there was a

**16.46** Kenzo Tange, Olympic Sports Complex, Tokyo, 1964.
The dragon-like apperception of this building is created by steel-reinforced-concrete walls and a roof supported by steel cables. The plan is a spiral, with arriving viewers drawn in along the perimeter of the unwinding, dynamic geometry.

**16.47** Arata Isozaki, Fujima Country Club, Oita, Japan, 1974.

While vaulted roofs like these became something of a fashion in the 1980s, they were quite original, even exotic, in Japan in the 1970s. That Isozaki insinuated Andrea Palladio into his design sources says something about today's "global village."

**16.48** Tadao Ando, Museum of Wood, Mikata-gun, Hyogo, Japan, 1994.

Seen from the air, this striking composition of circle, line, and square nested in a forest seems more like a monastery than a museum. The Japanese have a long history of expert woodworking, as can be seen in Chapter 4.

cemetery and some ancient burial mounds. In their midst, Maki added his building containing a reception area with offices, the crematorium, and a hall for vigils and funeral services. The hall is a tilted brick octagon situated at the front of the overall structure and adjacent to a porte-cochère and forecourt, while the entrance vestibule behind it has a triangular plan created by Maki's conceptually swinging out the front wall of the crematorium. A placid courtyard with a reflecting pool and tall, surrounding concrete walls provides a serene core for the crematorium and its adjacent spaces.

### ARATA ISOZAKI

Arata Isozaki (born 1931) worked for Tange from 1963 to 1973, encountered Metabolism, but did not embrace radical new technologies, and over the course of his career has pursued his own, sometimes idiosyncratic, sometimes ironic, interpretation of Modernism. His Kamioka Town Hall (1976–78) appears as an alien spacecraft landed in this remote town in north-central Japan. His Fujima Country Club in Oita (1974) has a porte-cochère elevation that alludes to Palladio's Villa Poiana and an enveloping copper roof with a form that would become almost his signature: the barrel vault (Fig. 16.47). For the Museum of Contemporary Art in Los Angeles (1981–86), he chose to repeat the barrel vault, add pyramids, and employ the Golden Section as a means, he said, for expressing the integration of Eastern and Western cultures on the West Coast. Still present are references to Palladio and highly refined detailing.

### TADAO ANDO

Tadao Ando (born 1941) is self-taught, never having studied architecture in a school or served an apprenticeship. Through a long process of external investigation and personal introspection, he has become one of the most successful form makers of his generation. Consider, for instance, his Museum of Wood (1994) in the Mikata-gun forest northwest of Osaka. Here, a long spine-like wooden path through a pristine forest connects a hollow, truncated cone, containing an exhibition hall and having its inner and outer faces covered with horizontal, lapped boards, with a rotated concrete cube attached to a gate-like baffle-plane (Fig. 16.48). The heavy-timber construction inside the hall acknowledges traditional Japanese carpentry practices.

Ando applied the same kind of elemental geometries to his Awaji-Yumebutai, or Awaji Island, project west of Osaka (1999). Like Asplund and Lewerentz at the Woodland Cemetery, he was given a site that had been mauled by prior development, in this case through the removal of an entire mountaintop of earth to be used elsewhere as fill. Ando reclaimed the land as the location for a hotel and conference center that looks more like a modern monastery and added a "100 Step Garden"—a grid of walled terraces filled with dazzling "pools" of flowering plants.

Ando's Modern Art Museum of Fort Worth, which opened in 2002, stands 100 yards northeast of Louis Kahn's Kimbell Art Museum (see Figs. 16.15–16.17) and a short ride from Renzo Piano's Nasher Sculpture Gallery (discussed below) in Dallas. While it hardly seems obvious from the finished building, Ando's conceptual sketches suggest that he used the Kimbell's building section as a starting point for his design process. He did finally produce a series of side-by-side pavilions, but their parallel-ness seems unimportant when viewed on-site, and the area between his and Kahn's building is sympathetic to neither structure. Ando's museum works best where it addresses the large, L-shaped pool of water on its northeast side. Within the building, there are many gratifying moments, including the long, concrete stairwells covered with curving, baffle-like ribs and sky-lit. Without doubt, it is seen most advantageously at night, when its inner core of concrete walls becomes cella-like and the surrounding, glazed, metallic skeleton suggests the peripteral columns of an ancient Greek temple.

## FORM-MAKING IN THE UNITED STATES

Le Corbusier wrote that "Architecture is the masterly, correct, and magnificent play of masses brought together in light." While the work in this next section certainly resulted from a broad range of concerns, and the buildings are commensurately diverse, all of them display an abiding concern for "masses brought together in light," or, put more simply: form. Some architects, like Richard Meier, have even been described as "formalists," meaning that they have been concerned with form for its own sake. Most architects, however, have made form an outward expression of inward societal circumstances and values.

### THE BOSTON CITY HALL

In the late 1960s, no building made a greater impact on the American architectural scene than the Boston City Hall (Fig. 16.49), its 1962 competition-winning design sub-

**16.49** Gerhard Michael Kallmann, Noel Michael McKinnell, and Frank Knowles, Boston City Hall from across plaza, Boston, 1968.

This building is now almost old enough to be eligible for listing on the National Register of Historic Places. It may need such a designation of significance, as much of the public has remained skeptical about modern architecture to the point that some now advocate the City Hall's demolition.

mitted by Gerhard Michael Kallmann (born 1915) and Noel Michael McKinnell (born 1935) together with Frank Knowles, the former two then a faculty member and student, respectively, at Columbia University. Somewhat shocking today in its aggressive posture facing the figuratively cowering eighteenth-century Faneuil Hall, it presents an immediately legible façade composition. Three-part, like a classical column or a sonata, it absorbs pedestrians at a largely transparent lower level, ensconces government officials and bodies in a middle range of sculptural protrusions, and fixes workers in repetitive bays of offices defined by vertical fins and collectively producing a terminating cornice.

### THE VIETNAM VETERANS MEMORIAL

It can be said with certitude that no built object in the twentieth century has received greater initial condemnation or greater ultimate acclaim than Maya Lin's Vietnam Veterans Memorial (1982) in Washington, D.C. (Fig. 16.50). Now more than two decades after its construction and more than three after the end of the Vietnam War, it has become a symbol, indeed an instrument, of national

**16.50** Maya Lin, Vietnam Veterans Memorial, Washington D.C., 1982.

No photograph can capture the emotional experience of arriving at the west end of the Mall in the shadow of the Lincoln Memorial, walking down the ramp carved into the earth, and being confronted by this extraordinary construction. The wall material is highly polished black granite.

reconciliation. Lin (born 1959), a landscape-architecture student at the time of the competition for the memorial, made the names of those Americans who died or went missing in Vietnam between 1959 and 1975 not simply visible, as required in the competition brief, but the essence of her winning submission. Carving a walkway down into the earth and raising a black-granite-veneered retaining wall inscribed with the names above it, she simultaneously created a sepulcher and a safe harbor and proved that an abstract setting can be nationally cathartic. Anyone who has ever arrived on the west end of the Mall; been drawn down the sloping ramp; and passed by, fixated upon, reached out and touched, or even knelt at this disarmingly simple, planar construction will attest to its nobility and poignancy. As a corollary, so many objects, offerings really, have been left here by visitors, be they flowers inserted into the seams between the stone panels, a relinquished purple heart, or entire nurses' uniforms left pressed and folded, that they are collected every night by the National Park Service and some of them displayed in the National Museum of American History.

## THE UNITED STATES HOLOCAUST MEMORIAL MUSEUM

The architect I.M. Pei (born 1917), principal in the firm of Pei Cobb Freed, has built widely, including the East Wing of the National Gallery in Washington, D.C. and the underground expansion of the Louvre in Paris, which is announced on the surface by a glazed pyramid. His firm designed and built the United States Holocaust Memorial Museum located south of the Mall in the Capitol, with James Ingo Freed (1930–2005) as the partner-in-charge. The museum opened in 1993. Freed's intention was to embody the cold deliberateness and disquieting efficiency with which the "final solution" was carried out. The museum's principal façade displays a kind of Spartan Neo-Classicism, which Freed intended to give a "premonition of loss." A hexagonal structure at the back of the site contains a theater and the Hall of Remembrance. Beyond the principal entry, the large, foyer-like Hall of Witness (Fig. 16.51), wrapped by display spaces and a learning center, is an industrial-character mixture of steel, brick, and glass intended to remind visitors of German industry's enthusiastic collusion with the Nazi regime. Some have criticized

**16.51** Pei Cobb Freed, Hall of Witness interior, U.S. Holocaust Memorial Museum, Washington, D.C., 1993.

Called the Hall of Witness, this space serves as the building's lobby. It is an embarkation point for one of the most intense museum experiences in the world.

the space for being too airy and elegantly detailed. Certainly conveying so grotesque an event as the Jewish Holocaust in a moving way, while using familiar forms, presented a daunting design challenge. Perhaps the building can be didactically compared to the Vietnam Veterans Memorial and to Daniel Libeskind's Jewish Museum and

**16.52** Kevin Roche and John Dinkeloo, Ford Foundation Building, New York City, 1963–68.

Various gestures toward urban amenity were made during the 1960s. Here Roche and Dinkeloo created a huge botanical-garden-like atrium inside one of the more expensive buildings of the period.

**16.53** Manhattan looking east along 56th Street, 1984.

Left to right, one sees Trump Tower by Der Scutt, Swanke, Hayden and Connell; the AT&T Building (now Sony Plaza) by Johnson/Burgee; and Citicorp by Hugh Stubbins Associates. This forest of skyscrapers is supported by the bedrock underlying Manhattan Island.

Peter Eisenman's challenging Memorial to the Murdered Jews in Europe (2005), the latter two in Berlin and all three much more abstract in their formal conceptions.

## TALL BUILDINGS IN NEW YORK CITY

The Ford Foundation Building (1963–68) (Fig. 16.52), designed by Kevin Roche (born 1922) and John Dinkeloo (1918–1981), successors to the firm founded by Eero Saarinen, reflects the great social liberal confidence of the early 1960s. Set between 42nd and 43rd streets on a nearly square site within a Manhattan block near the United Nations Building, the Ford Foundation's offices enframe an eleven-story greenhouse that occupies about half the ground floor. Additional planted terraces on the third, fourth, and fifth floors extend the greenery above the entrance level, and the office spaces either share the view into the court or have outside windows. The building's principal materials—weathering steel, granite, bronze, and glass—establish a neutral dark ground for the natural light and vegetation that characterize the interior. Richness and elegance reign in a building that cost four times as much as Kahn's Kimbell Art Museum.

Despite its extravagance, or perhaps because of it, the Ford Foundation headquarters became one of the most influential buildings of the third quarter of the twentieth century. Aside from providing a handsome working envi-

ronment for the foundation's employees, it also created a pedestrian link through the long side of one of Manhattan's 200-by-400-foot blocks, and this idea of an enclosed walkway was taken up by the Office of Midtown Development as a solution to preserving pedestrian access within New York City. Zoning incentives encouraged developers to include ground-floor public passageways in new high-rise buildings. The idea was not new. The splendid nave of the Crystal Palace had inspired many glass-roofed commercial arcade buildings in Europe and the United States, of which the best-known example is the Galleria Vittorio Emanuele (1865–77) in Milan, Italy, designed by Giuseppe Mengoni (1829–1877) to connect the Piazza del Duomo to La Scala, the opera house a block away.

Major New York buildings that benefited from these zoning incentives include the Citicorp Building (1974–77), set between 53rd and 54th streets on Lexington Avenue. Hugh Stubbins, the architect, designed a six-story podium for the building and dedicated it to retail shops opening off a central atrium and then placed the fifty-nine-floor office tower astride a sunken plaza at the Lexington Avenue end. The IBM Center by Edward Larrabee Barnes (1984) and Trump Tower by Der Scutt with Swanke, Hayden, and Connell (1984), both seen in Figure 16.53, provide ground-level amenities with enclosed atrium spaces containing informal seating, food services, gallery displays, ornamental planting, and handsomely presented boutiques.

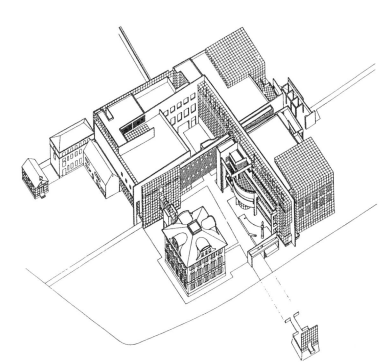

**16.54** Richard Meier, Axonometric drawing of the Museum für Kunsthandwerk, Frankfurt, 1980–83.

Meier graduated from Cornell University at a time when its design studios were dominated by the compositional manipulations celebrated in Colin Rowe and Fred Koetter's *Collage City*. This building seems to be ideally viewed in a bird's-eye axonometric drawing such as this one.

## RICHARD MEIER

Richard Meier (born 1934) has continued the early traditions of Modernism. While Meier's architecture owes an obvious debt to Le Corbusier's houses of the 1920s, as in his use of cubical massing relieved by gentle curves, he also claims to have been influenced by the spatial layering and light quality of Baroque interiors and by such works as Frank Lloyd Wright's Guggenheim Museum. Qualities abstracted from these and other sources include columnar systems of planning grids with a clearly expressed skin enclosing volumetric space; planar elements that slice through the building and penetrate one another; and impeccable white-panel exteriors comparable to the late works of Hoffman and Wagner.

The results of this approach can be seen in Meier's design for the Museum für Kunsthandwerk (Museum of Decorative Arts) in Frankfurt, Germany, which won a limited competition in 1980 and was completed in 1983 (Fig. 16.54). Although nominally an addition to an old villa containing the existing museum, Meier's building is nearly ten times larger than the Neo-Classical original, and, except for a second-floor glass-enclosed connector, it stands free of it in an L shape. The position of the villa and the angle of the frontage road paralleling the river Main prompted Meier to indulge in two overlapping grid systems set at an angle of 3.5 degrees to one another. While such a minor shift is imperceptible in reality (unless the museum-goer commonly notes slight misalignments in normally orthogonal building materials), the two grids are distinctly seen in the plan drawings, and their interaction obviously inspired Meier to employ room shapes that would otherwise have seemed arbitrary. Le Corbusier-style regulating traces were overlaid on elevation studies to show that both the villa and the new building have similar proportions; a module derived from the older building relates to basic quadrants in the addition. Panels cover the exterior and align with square mullions in the generously sized windows. Interior circulation is organized by a system of switchback ramps linking axial corridors on all floors, while the exhibits are displayed in galleries created by partial-height walls set within the structural bays, establishing a domestic scale appropriate to the museum's collections. Despite the clashing geometries of the building's plan, spaces merge gracefully into one another, and abundant natural light reflecting off shiny white surfaces is welcome in the habitually overcast Frankfurt climate.

Meier employed a similar vocabulary in the High Museum (1981–84) in Atlanta, Georgia (Fig. 16.55). He

**16.55** Richard Meier, High Museum, Atlanta, Georgia, 1981–84.

This art museum stands along Peachtree Street. The ramp in the foreground takes visitors to the bulging entry vestibule, then into the three-story, switchback-ramped rotunda that gives access to the gallery floors.

**16.56** Antoine Predock, American Heritage Center and Art Museum, University of Wyoming, Laramie, Wyoming, 1993.

Designing a building for the stern and frequently hostile landscape of Wyoming offers a special set of challenges. Everything about this building's form, from the canted cone to the low, windowless wing, speaks of protection from the elements.

disengaged the continuous ramp of the Guggenheim Museum and made it the dominant circulation path around the circumference of a quarter-cylinder glass-enclosed atrium, off which he arranged more conventional orthogonal galleries with artificial illumination. Whereas the ramp in the Frankfurt museum is immediately adjacent to gallery displays, in the Atlanta museum their separation isolates the art from the building's most interesting architectural feature. The conditions most curators demand for the display of paintings are in part responsible for this decision. Strong sunlight quickly deteriorates pigments, so works of art need to be kept in controlled lighting conditions.

Meier's billion-dollar Getty Museum (1984–97) in West Los Angeles, spreads out in the form and at the scale of a Modernist hilltown. For the outside walls, he combined his signature modular porcelain-enameled panels with equally modular but textured stone. A circular garden by Robert Irwin suggests the island enclosure at Hadrian's Villa.

### ANTOINE PREDOCK

Antoine Predock (born 1936) has created a body of work with a decidedly spiritual-become-extra-terrestrial quality, none of it more arresting than his American Heritage Center and University Art Museum in Laramie, Wyoming (Fig. 16.56), a place where winds have been known to topple semi-trailers and temperatures casually plunge to negative numbers. Only with this context in mind does the appropriateness of Predock's building become clear. As seen from the parking lot, a truncated cone rises up, evoking multiple associations: a hogan or tipi, the surrounding mountain peaks, a space ship. It is egg-shaped in plan, contains a reception area and myriad other small spaces, and is connected to a long, orthogonal wing that houses galleries, a library, and offices. When experienced from within and at its base, with mountains seen through broad windows in panorama, the building evokes a sense of geological time, and the skin of the cone, made of black-patinated copper, is penetrated by apertures that align with the cardinal points and certain astronomical phenomena, evoking even a sense of cosmic time.

### STEVEN HOLL

Steven Holl (born 1947) has established himself as a contemporary master of natural-light manipulation. Nowhere is this more apparent than his Chapel of St. Ignatius (1997) in Seattle, what he calls (based on an early conceptual drawing) a "stone box, containing seven bottles of light." The stone box is a puzzle-like assemblage of monochromatic concrete panels, and the bottles are roof-top, tubular-steel-frame monitors (their effects mimicked by artificial light at night) that direct sunlight down through multi-hued glass lenses, where it bathes the worship spaces in a highly specific atmosphere of glowing color. The effect has been found by visitors, even the unchurched, to be one of enveloping spirituality. The main sanctuary is surprisingly formal in an era of religious informality, with central-aisle directionality and fixed pews, but both conditions were requested by the student users. Holl drew upon local Seattle artisans for such appointments as blown-glass pendant lights and gold-leaf prayer text embedded in layers of beeswax.

**16.57** Steven Holl, Simmons Hall dormitory, M.I.T, Cambridge, Massachusetts, 2002.

This massive block with huge cut-outs and a seemingly endless grid of windows looks like a dormitory for the digital age. On the inside, in the free-form lobbies, Holl took the opportunity to display his skill in introducing natural light.

On an M.I.T. campus where Alvar Aalto built a celebrated dormitory (see Fig. 16.8) in 1947–49, exemplary architecture has generally been in short supply. Here Holl has chosen to repeat Aalto's theme of the wall, but with different emphases and building at an unapologetically huge size. The giant, variable-height cliff-face (Fig. 16.57) that is his Simmons Hall dormitory (2002) has a gridded, screen-like façade of anodized aluminum cladding behind which lighting conditions, volume cut-outs, and splashes of color make for a level of energy consistent with modern student life. Because the hundreds of windows all operate, their individually chosen positions make for a lively, constantly changing appearance as well as a non-hermetic living environment. Inside, the ranks of orthogonal rooms are literally carved into by free-form stair lobbies, with their goal being spontaneous interaction among occupants. Whether this theory works better in practice than the shopping street in Le Corbusier's Unité in Marseilles (see Fig. 15.76) awaits post-occupancy evaluation.

## MORPHOSIS

The Los Angeles firm called Morphosis (meaning "manner of formation") began with Thom Mayne and (until 1991) Michael Rotundi as partners and with strong connections to the Southern California Institute of Architecture, of which they were both founders. The body of their early work, much of it unbuilt, is striking for its adventurous use of computer modeling; dramatic expression of structural elements; transparencies and translucencies; and the related disintegration of traditional enclosure systems—a kind of Futurism, De Stijl, Constructivist collision conceived for the nowhere urbanism of Southern California in which a building has to fight for its life.

For the Diamond Ranch High School in Los Angeles, Mayne did not allow a modest budget to deter him from the kind of spatial experimentation for which he has become well known. Using corrugated metal as a wall material, he created a central, linear student mall flanked by angular, leaning, sometimes cantilevered building masses. One mass with a secondary circulation spine alternates classrooms and courtyards and culminates with an outdoor theater and gymnasium. Opposite this aggressive assemblage, more classrooms sit atop parking and alternate with dramatic ramps adjacent to bulging courtyards. The project has been celebrated for both its internal civic nature and its external integration into the freeway sprawl around its steeply sloping site. Morphosis's newly completed San Francisco Federal Building (2005) signals that the firm has moved into the mainstream without abandoning its avant garde tendencies.

## TOD WILLIAMS AND BILLIE TSIEN

There is an almost unnerving intensity in the work of Tod Williams (born 1943) and Billie Tsien (born 1949). Because the site for their Neurosciences Institute in La Jolla, California (1995) is located less than a mile from Louis Kahn's Salk Institute (see Fig. 16.13), the architects felt obliged to "confront" but certainly not "mimic" it. A "monastery for science," their facility houses a small number of visiting fellows in an environment designed to allow constant interaction and the constant exchange of ideas (Fig. 16.58).

Williams and Tsien set out to make every experience, even the smallest moments, potentially meaningful. They had the hilltop site excavated in order to provide space for a modern cloister defined by a U-shaped building that houses a Theory Center and laboratories. At the open end of the U, they largely denied a distant view to the mountains by inserting an auditorium that rises from a low berm, and so located a switch-back ramp that it becomes a viewing promontory. Their chosen building materials contribute to a sense of timelessness: fossil-implanted limestone, sand-blasted glass and concrete, redwood, and stainless steel. Given that their client, Dr. Gerald Edelman, has argued for a nuanced, Darwinian-evolutionary, environmentally interactive development of the individual human brain, it seems most appropriate that Williams and Tsien sought to acknowledge this theory architecturally by

**16.58** Tod Williams and Billie Tsien, Neurosciences Institute, La Jolla, California, 1995.

Being so understated and contemplative in its site development, this monastery-like building ensemble comes close to being unphotographable. In this vignette, looking from the Theory Center to the auditorium, the reference to Louis Kahn's nearby Salk Institute (see Fig. 16.13) is unmistakable. However, Williams and Tsien have downplayed views to the mountains (not the ocean) and have set their pool (not channel) of water at an angle (not on the principal axis), emphasizing the skydome as the enframed feature and creating a metaphor for the complex, nuanced activities of the human brain and its creative powers that are studied here.

creating an environment of random episodic incidents and encounters that can be experienced in myriad sequences and combinations and results in a unique, cumulative awareness for each participant.

Their Museum of American Folk Art (2001) stands just west of the entrance to the Museum of Modern Art on 53rd Street in New York City. Almost menacing, with white-bronze panels hanging like giant shields on the outside, its eight stories rise as a narrow canyon on the interior. It is difficult to imagine a better fit between architects and museum contents, which here oscillate between the polarities of hard-edged, sometimes disturbing, reality and romantic longing. It is also difficult to imagine what the construction documents looked like, as the compressed complexity of detailing is as dizzying as the internal spatial manipulation. Materials choices suggest the same kind of indestructibility seen on the exterior, and include iron-like wood from long-submerged Douglas-fir logs, bush-hammered concrete, cold-rolled steel, and aged Italian limestone. The architects have compared the rich and varied experience of moving through their building to that at Sir John Soane's 13 Lincoln's Inn Fields (see Figs. 14.7–14.8), and the comparison is valid, as both contain tall, top-lit spaces and make virtues of their designers' obsessions.

## MACK SCOGIN AND MERRILL ELAM

Difficult to characterize—part 1950s drive-in restaurant, part Russian Constructivism, part art installation, part (sometimes by economic necessity) local hardware store—the early work of Atlanta architects Mack Scogin (born 1943) and Merrill Elam (born 1943) speaks with the voice of authenticity in the language of originality. Their eclectic inspirations seemed to know no bounds, be they the Mannerist Villa Giulia in Rome or a thrown-together barbecue stand in some forgotten corner of the South, and in the potentially spirit-numbing architectural marketplace, they have somehow retained their sense of wonder about the process of building.

Long before the computer made it possible to more easily define irregular geometries and so to emphasize building enclosure systems, Scogin and Elam moved the selection of external cladding materials outside the realm of the familiar and into that of admirable strangeness. The Branch Library in Clayton County (1989) outside Atlanta looks like a miniature airplane hangar wrapped in the mottled cover of an outlandishly oversized composition book (actually made by camouflage-painting corrugated sheet metal). When the facility opened, patron numbers soared.

In 2000, they completed their design for Knowlton Hall that houses the architectural school at The Ohio State University; the building opened in 2004. The earliest plans looked like collages of overlapping trapezoidal planes, with their lines responding to the campus's pedestrian traffic pattern (a more site-specific take on Daniel Libeskind's Jewish Museum discussed below). Because of budgetary constraints and concerns for internal orientation, a second scheme became completely orthogonal, with studio spaces and faculty offices to each side of a "system of inclined [circulation] planes" (not unlike Álvaro Siza's museum in Santiago de Compostela; see Fig. 16.44). Eventually, the architects gave their gridded plan dynamism—by exposing it to the original set of pedestrian traffic patterns—and nuance—by expanding it to the limits of the irregularly shaped site. Commensurately, the building's cladding became as aggressive as the site-generated lines of force. Highly textured expanses of marble

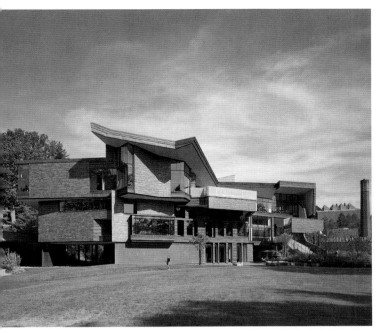

**16.59** Mack Scogin and Merrill Elam, Wang Campus Center, Wellesley College, Wellesley, Massachusetts, 2006.

As something of a metaphor for the freewheeling and varied student organizations at Wellesley College, this building moves up, in, out, cants, and torques. An appreciation of the diversity of the interior spaces will require a visit.

shingles (their patterning inspired by quarrying practices but, given the architects' lexicon of Southern inspirations, perhaps comparable to a masonry armadillo) present a hovering curtain in front of set-back glazing. Canyon-like, transparent, landscaped courts and a huge, almost intimidating, carved-out, corner entry and interior spaces where architectural intentions never seem to end, make for a building that demands engagement.

At Wellesley College, southwest of Boston, Scogin and Elam got to take the architectural gloves off, so to speak, with their design for the Wang Campus Center (Fig. 16.59). The Wellesley buildings are strewn across an almost wild landscape that works its way down to a lake. The jaggedly-massed Campus Center looks like something geological, powerfully carved and then deposited here during the last period of glaciation. Wellesley has long prided itself on diversity, before the word became politicized jargon, and on educating students to think for themselves, which means that the right institution and the right architects have met.

The Center stands at the heart of the campus and has a plan outline that looks like a New England decapod crustacean, claws extended and making its way across the landscape. The program called for spaces to support Wellesley's multifarious student organizations as well as a bookstore, pub, café, and a big room for varied events. Consequently, the wildly angular plan contains only a limited number of identifiable rooms, being made up instead of "unowned spaces" and banks of lockers that invite student groups to gather up what they need and appropriate a place of their liking.

Taken to three dimensions, the building becomes lived-in sculpture, not the Frank Gehry type, where flamboyant exterior form sometimes gives way to conventional interior planning, but a spatial plurality that befits the program and the institution. As for comparable thinking, the work of Hans Scharoun comes to mind, but also Herbert Greene's bird-like prairie houses and the unlikely, fluid-space investigations of Friedrich Kiesler for his "endless house." But comparison could just as easily be made to grown-up-over-time buildings in back-alley Boston or in rural Georgia. All this contextual and historical energy notwithstanding, the Wang Campus Center is artfully composed without being overwrought and, with its "geological" layers of copper-shingle cladding, could even speak coherently to a 1970s Roman-brick subdivision house. It is another building from the minds of Mack Scogin and Merrill Elam that could not have been conceived without modern art, the computer, and steel erectors who appreciate a challenge.

### DANIEL LIBESKIND

Daniel Libeskind was born in Poland in 1946 but studied architecture in England and the United States. At one time labeled a Deconstructivist, he is perhaps better described as someone intent upon expressing ideas and happening to use architecture as his means of communication. His working method has involved typography and collage. In urban circumstances, he has explored the palimpsestic nature of the city, as in his winning design for the City-Edge competition in Berlin (1987). He created the plan of his Jewish Museum in Berlin by means of determinants ranging from the geographical plotting and connecting of addresses for notable Jewish Berliners, to a close reading of the texts for Arnold Schoenberg's unfinished opera *Moses and Aaron* and art critic Walter Benjamin's *One Way Street.* Needless to say, connecting the physical reality of the building with such myriad, some would say arcane, inspirations requires perseverance, if not clairvoyance, on the part of an observer. Supporters say that only through such rarefied means can such an extreme circumstance as the Holocaust even be approached, never mind understood, and that Libeskind has accomplished exactly that. His building is an extended, zigzagging, concrete box covered with a metallic skin in which angular openings have been left in a variety of shapes and patterns. The poured-concrete interior has the quality of a three-dimensional maze, more akin to a house of illusions or the set for a Kafka play than a conventional museum.

Libeskind won the international competition for the World Trade Center after Minoru Yamasaki's towers (see Fig. 14.20) were tragically destroyed by terrorist-piloted airliners in 2001. The intensely political and emotional circumstances surrounding this commission and the many overlapping jurisdictions and economic interests on a site at the base of Manhattan have led to co-authorship with David C. Childs and significant revisions in his proposal that included an angular, faceted, spiky, 1776-foot-tall "Freedom Tower." Additional towers are being designed by Fumihiko Maki (discussed earlier in this chapter) and by Richard Rogers and Norman Foster (both discussed below). Jean Nouvel (also discussed below) received a tower commission as well, but this is now in doubt. Frank Gehry (discussed earlier in this chapter) is designing an associated performing arts center and Santiago Calatrava (discussed below) is responsible for a PATH train station on the site.

### THE DIA: BEACON

Among America's museums, none can be found in a more unexpected place than the DIA Center for the Arts (2003) nor takes a more iconoclastic position toward the architect as a design presence or the museum as an architectural monument. At the DIA, located in tiny Beacon, New York on the Hudson River north of New York City, artist Robert Irwin (born 1928), the architectural firm OpenOffice, and the Arup engineering firm (discussed below with Norman Foster) transformed a 1920s printing plant into vast galleries for post-World War II European and American art. The professionals had an ironic charge: rendering their contributions—primarily environmental control, life-safety, and fire-safety systems—invisible, which they largely did. Irwin also let the original building speak for itself, adding only a modest temple-like entry and adjacent gardens on the river side and making a few changes in window openings and floor heights. With almost 300,000 square feet of interior space, most of it lit by ranks of saw-tooth skylights and tall clerestories, the museum has a consistently sun-illuminated spaciousness. Because of its remote location and huge floor-plates, a visitor can lounge about on couches in the middle of the huge galleries and view some of the late twentieth century's most celebrated art in virtual isolation. Also because of its size, the DIA could permanently install works so large that they would otherwise be relegated to storage. The museum's Andy Warhol materials alone would fill the display space in many other venues.

### THE MUSEUM OF MODERN ART

The Museum of Modern Art (MOMA) in New York City is arguably the most well known institutional advocate of Modernism in the world. It has figured prominently in this book, with, for instance, its 1932 exhibition on the International Style. Its facilities located just south of Central Park have been designed over time by modern architects from Edward Durrell Stone (1902–1978) to Phillip Johnson. Most recently, Yoshio Taniguchi (born 1937) was asked to radically increase the museum's size, while maintaining its atmosphere of cool modernity. Most critics agree that he succeeded, though the vast expanses of drywall seem to have explored this material's architectural

limits. When readers visit any other of the many museums discussed in this chapter, most of them intended as overt symbols of newness and change in their respective cities, they can compare them to the MOMA, where confidence about both institutional stature and image made monument-building unnecessary.

### ELIZABETH DILLER AND RICARDO SCOFIDIO

The development of modern architecture has been intertwined with modern painting since the beginning of the twentieth century. While painting has given way to various other media in the art world, the connections between art and architecture are still strong, and nowhere more so than in the work of Elizabeth Diller (born 1954) and Ricardo Scofidio (born 1954). Anyone examining the exhibition of their various installations at the Whitney Museum of American Art in 2003 would have been impressed by their use of moving images, robotic systems, translucent materials, sophisticated assemblies, and transferred technologies, as well as their pursuit of a host of artistic themes.

The application of their art-thinking to architecture can be seen to advantage in their Brasserie restaurant (2000) located within the base of Mies van der Rohe's Seagram Building in New York City. Necessarily hermetic because it lies below grade, it demanded the creation of an artificial environment. Diller and Scofidio introduced a backlit wall of apparently floating bottles behind the bar, above which a strip of video screens displays images of entering patrons. A perforated metal ceiling becomes a wall, becomes the seating within a space that seems to glow from within. The artist-architects' Blur Building (really a large installation) in Lake Neuchâtel in Yverdon-les-Bains, Switzerland (2002) took transparency and luminosity a step further and to a much larger scale, being a lightweight metal frame from which a fine mist of water was sprayed, creating a localized environment like a cloud descended to earth.

Diller and Scofidio's Slither Housing (2000) in Kitagata, Japan applies translucency to the problem of low-income, urban living. Here, fifteen modular towers are set at slight angles to one another, creating a gentle arc in plan and allowing the perforated, metal façade panels to overlap at their edges. As in the Brasserie, the detailing of handrails, cantilevered sunscreens, and internal sliding durable-plastic panels seems to be a logical extension of assembly investigations in their art installations. It remains to be seen whether they can successfully translate the scale and intentions of their art into larger, more complex, and more varied building types.

### FORM-MAKING ELSEWHERE

As in America, modern architects throughout the rest of the world have explored the expressive potential of archi-

**16.60** Jørn Utzon, Sydney Opera House, Sydney, 1957.

With downtown Sydney in the background, the sail-like roofs of the Opera House rise above tiered platforms on a paved peninsula. No modern building has become a more visible architectural symbol for a country than this one.

tectural form. As fully compressive masonry construction gave way to concrete in combination with steel reinforcing and to the steel frame, beginning in the nineteenth century, much of what had been impossible to build has become possible. However, the architects in the section that follows have subordinated structural expression to the expression of surface and spatial enclosure.

## JØRN UTZON

When the Dane Jørn Utzon (born 1918) won the competition for the Sydney (Australia) Opera House (Fig. 16.60) in 1957, he immediately became one of the world's most well-known architects. However, immense problems with its construction and associated cost overruns stigmatized him on the international scene, even though the completed building, with its "billowing" sail-like, parabolic, post-tensioned, concrete shells set atop platforms of Pre-Columbian inspiration, has become virtually the symbol for Australia. Utzon should not be known, however, only as the originator of one profound building idea, as a survey of his larger body of work makes clear. Particularly successful is his Bagsvaerg Church (1976), with its disciplined orthogonal plan, oscillating, thin-shell-concrete ceiling, exquisite masonry detailing, and Nordic luminosity. Utzon, now in his 80s, continues to practice, as with his design for the Dunker Cultural Center (2002) in Helsingborg, Sweden, and has recently received renewed media attention for a lifetime of architectural accomplishments.

## ARTHUR ERICKSON

The Canadian architect Arthur Erickson (born 1924) sought to move beyond ideological Modernism and to make buildings into sensory experiences, livable places, and part of larger landscapes. His Museum of Anthropology in Vancouver, British Columbia (1972) is abstract and yet contextual. Straddling World War II gun emplacements, it faces a shallow pond then the tidal shore, and finally glacial mountain, a site condition, Erickson said, partially inspired by Haida Indian tribal villages. Much of the building is sunken below grade, meaning that, while the galleries are suitably generous to celebrate the museum's collection of enormous carvings, including giant totem poles, its dramatic, set-back profile does not overwhelm the surroundings.

## HANS HOLLEIN

The Austrian Hans Hollein executed the small Viennese Schullin Jewelry Shop in 1972–74. Questioning both classicism and Modernism, the building's stone façade with strategically placed gold outlining that suggests a rich vein inside the earth, speaks with the kind of wit advocated by Robert Venturi. On the inside, however, Hollein meticulously integrated structural and mechanical systems, display devices, surfacing materials, and light in a manner that can stand comparison to the *Gesamtkunstwerk*, or complete work of art, of fellow Austrian Joseph Hoffman (1870–1956) in the period before World War I.

## CESAR PELLI

Argentinian Cesar Pelli (born 1926) has proved himself particularly adept at creating dramatic profiles for tall buildings, including the giant Petronas Towers in Kuala

**16.61** Justus Dahinden, Mityana Pilgrims Shrine, Uganda, 1983.

Conceptually, this building could once have been a hemisphere, its sections now disengaged to reveal its inner workings. Built of concrete, it can nonetheless be interpreted within Africa's long tradition of adobe construction (see for instance Figs. 10.56 and 10.57).

Lumpur, Malaysia (1998). Known to visit a distant site, then sketch multiple ideas on note cards during the flight back home, Pelli responded to the Malaysian heritage by adopting an intricate pattern of abstract forms in a largely Islamic country where this means of articulation has a long tradition. Tight geometric manipulations extend to each tower's plan, which includes interlocking squares forming an eight-pointed star. The two reinforced-concrete structures rise like telescoping, attenuated temples with faceted surfaces. A dramatic sky-bridge atop angled struts more than forty stories above the ground announces the arrival of advanced technology and accompanying Modernism on the Malaysian peninsula.

## JUSTUS DAHINDEN

If architects in Japan have been challenged by the need to maintain continuity with historical traditions while addressing modern issues, architects working in Africa have been even more so. A particularly successful result of such an effort is the Mityana Pilgrims Shrine (1983) in Uganda, north of Lake Victoria, designed by the Swiss architect Justus Dahinden (born 1925). His use of tinted, poured-in-place concrete recognizes the long-established African adobe building tradition, as do the relatively unarticulated but dramatic building volumes (Fig. 16.61). The complex building program included a parish hall, presbytery, and Carmelite convent as well as a school and social center. Because the church is dedicated to three African martyrs, Dahinden raised up three, tall segments of spheres, each based on a quadrant-of-a-circle plan, housing a chapel, a confessional, and a baptistery. The central worship space is covered by a horizontal volume with a ribbon window and a skylight above the altar. It would be hard to imagine this precise and rational but slightly mysterious building existing anywhere other than Africa. While firmly planted there, it reflects Dahinden's eclectic influences, from the Japanese Metabolists to the German Expressionist Rudolf Steiner to African Bantu-tribe religious structures.

## HERMAN HERTZBERGER

Herman Hertzberger was born in the Netherlands in 1932. His Chassé Theater in Breda is dominated by an undulating roof that conceals two tall fly-towers. Along one flank, a common area includes a foyer and a café, and within it an irregular grid of columns demarcates space as it supports the roof. Bridges, broad walkways, and balconies at the second level energize the interior space and encourage spontaneous social interaction—a particular concern of Hertzberger's in what he sees as an increasingly fragmented and consumer-driven society—and make the building's entry sequence an updated version of the promenade, or procession, used so effectively by Ecole des Beaux-Arts designers like Charles Garnier at his Paris Opera.

## CHRISTIAN DE PORTZAMPARC

Christian de Portzamparc was born in 1944 in Casablanca and graduated from the Ecole des Beaux-Arts in 1969, at about the time of its dissolution. His Cité de la Musique (1984–90) in Paris occupies a site at the southern extremity of Bernard Tschumi's Parc de la Villette (see Fig. 16.28). A teaching and performance center for both music and dance (with a second stage of construction now being completed), its U-shaped distribution of multiple, connected buildings is arranged around a paved and landscaped court, some of it sunken, altogether producing a neighborhood-like character. Each façade of the Cité consciously addresses its context in a unique way, an expression of de Portzamparc's desire for site-specific urban pluralism.

## HERZOG AND DE MEURON

Eschewing any form of representation, the Swiss architects (Jacques) Herzog and (Pierre) de Meuron (both born in 1950) aspire to an "immediate, visceral impact" with their buildings, meaning that they have paid particular atten-

tion to enclosure systems. Their Rue de Suisse Housing in Paris (2000) is a long concrete box fixed on three sides with outriggers supporting a diagonal grid of rope that, in turn, serves as a trellis. On the fourth side, rippling expanses of roll-down wooden shutters protect balconies.

Herzog and de Meuron designed their Laban Center for Movement and Dance (2002) for a site in Deptford, a great London naval center beginning in the early sixteenth century but a place where former glories have largely vanished. Their building stands adjacent to an unimpressive stream that flows into the Thames and is surrounded by mediocre urban development (Fig. 16.62). Into this largely characterless scene, the architects inserted a kind of warehouse of their own, a glowing one sheathed in durable plastic panels, some of them painted on their inner faces in pastel shades of lime, magenta, and turquoise. The building's plan is trapezoidal, with its shorter base deformed in a gentle concave arc that responds in kind to the area's most notable building: Thomas Archer's Church of St. Paul (1712–30) on Deptford High Street, with its circular tower rising from a semi-circular portico. At the center's core sits a windowless auditorium, and around it and lit by skylights run corridors of constantly changing widths, with reflecting pools below on the ground floor. Interior spatial character varies from corporate mechanistic to New Age ethereal. Dancers' forms appear as moving apparitions to those in Deptford viewing the building at night, and carefully selected window placements provide occupants with intermittent connections to their surroundings.

As an object in the city, Herzog and de Meuron's Prada Tokyo store is Mies van der Rohe's glass skyscraper project of 1922 become a pleated crystal of diamond-shaped, concave, convex, and flat glass panels. At night, as seen from the street, vertical steel elevator shafts and plenums rise like tree trunks, with their limbs being horizontal

tubes used as dressing rooms, all made homogenous through the application of creamy hues of acrylic paint. Adjacent to the angular tower lies a plaza, an anomaly within Tokyo's dense urbanism.

## RAPHAEL MONEO

Raphael Moneo (born 1937) worked at one time for Jørn Utzon, before returning to his native Spain. In 1986, he completed the National Museum of Roman Art in Mérida in a form that merges antique and modern forms as well as construction methods. Built using load-bearing brick walls and arches that support reinforced-concrete floors, it stands directly atop archaeological remains in a city founded by the Emperor Augustus. On the exterior, Moneo employed large expanses of Roman-brick relieving arches, more as wall articulation than as a method for transferring loads. On the interior, arched openings arranged *en enfilade* are braced by the floor plates, their huge scale broken down only by linear steel handrails. The effect is comparable to that in the Baths of Diocletian in Rome, where vast, vaulted interior spaces house Roman antiquities (and a church; see Fig. 5.25) in a setting that is spare yet rich in visual experiences.

Moneo's Roman Catholic Cathedral of Our Lady of the Angels opened in Los Angeles in 2002. It has been met with more than a little criticism, which demonstrates how much the public remains skeptical about the on-going Modernist program. Even some in the architectural press have found it to have awkward moments and to be inconsistently successful in making the traditional cathedral a modern monument—a tall order. As for successes, its tawny shingle-patterned exterior walls of carefully formed, poured, and cured concrete welcome the brilliant Southern California sunlight and more than hold their own adjacent to a depressed but roaring freeway and near to

**16.63** Raphael Moneo, Cathedral of Our Lady of the Angels interior, Los Angeles, California, 2002.

While this would seem to be a conventional view from the narthex, entry into this church is actually made at the far altar end and to the right of the visible frame. Tapestries hang on the sidewalls.

Frank Gehry's highly aggressive and reflective Disney Concert Hall. The plan of the nave looks like a much larger and more symmetrical Ronchamp (see Fig. 15.78) but is wrapped in a U-shaped, reverse-oriented ambulatory. This configuration is made necessary by Moneo's unorthodox but highly successful decision to have the faithful enter on the eastern end, adjacent to but obscured from the chancel, then move down a wide, limestone-floored corridor, alongside chapels on the right and a tall concrete exterior wall on the left, until reaching an imported Baroque retable, or decorative altar screen, then turn right to enter the nave or move beyond and down the opposite corridor. Within the nave (Fig. 16.63), the wooden ceiling suggests the suspended hull of a ship, with clerestory lighting to each side beneath it, and still lower, depicting "everyday parishioners," hang photo-realistic tapestries that possess an undeniable gravity even if some have criticized them as near-kitsch. Built in a well-known earthquake zone, the whole building sits atop rubber and steel isolators introduced, along with other measures, to dampen the effects of a major seismic event.

### FOREIGN OFFICE ARCHITECTS

In 1995, London's Foreign Office Architects (FOA) won the competition for the Yokohama International Port Facility, which opened in 2002. Partners Farshid Moussavi (born 1965), from Iran, and Alejandro Zaero-Polo (born 1963), from Spain, averaged only thirty years of age and had built nothing large, never mind super-large. Developing a plan more than 1400 feet long and 200 feet wide, they conceived the Yokohama facility as an extension of the city, with parking at the lowest level and an undulating roof that becomes a new landscape of broad, oscillating promenades interspersed with green expanses and an outdoor theater. Flowing spaces inside offer multiple

routes through three interior levels that are made dramatic by a ceiling of visible, folded-steel plates spanning the transverse dimension, with a concealed system of steel girders above them. The completed building can only be compared to a berthed ship, and because of its size, the construction process was actually akin to shipbuilding.

## EUROPEAN ARCHITECTS AND TECHNOLOGY

While advances in technology have affected buildings everywhere, they have had the most dramatic effects among Europeans, whose work runs the gamut from the craftsman-level technologies demanded by the work of Carlo Scarpa to the dazzling technological eloquence of Renzo Piano to the high-tech engineering-become-art of Santiago Calatrava or Nicholas Grimshaw. Common to it all, however, is a transcendent expressiveness and an overt celebration of the process of making.

### CARLO SCARPA

Venetian architect Carlo Scarpa (1902–1978) embraced European Modernism in general and Italian Rationalism in particular in the 1940s. However, his idiosyncratic search for expression through materials and their assemblage set him apart from those ideologies with which he initially identified. His unfinished Brion Cemetery (begun 1969) in the village of San Vito near Venice includes a pavilion, sacristy, chapel, Brion family tombs, and pools of water. It sits adjacent to the village cemetery and is surrounded by the flat ground of the Veneto that extends to distant mountains. Scarpa's construction is executed largely in concrete and prominently displays somewhat enigmatic geometric motifs, such as interlocking circles and repeatedly-set-back planes that present themselves both as highly personal statements and expressions of the mystery inherent in the human condition. Scarpa oversaw construction on the site constantly as he sought to translate hundreds of his delicate colored-pencil drawings into a physical yet poetic reality.

## JAMES STIRLING

In the 1960s the English architect James Stirling (1926–1992) used the theme of industrial assemblage in his commissions for the Engineering Building at Leicester University (1964) and the History Faculty Building at Cambridge University (1968), both of which were startling for their sculptural and unconcealed use of standard building materials. Aluminum-framed commercial greenhouse windows were set in the industrial brick walls of the Engineering Building's office tower and were also employed to wrap completely the walls and ceiling of its attached laboratory wing, where sawtooth skylights are treated as prismatic solids as they terminate at the edge of the building. In the History Faculty Building (Fig. 16.64), which contains a library on the lowest levels and faculty offices in the L-shaped block that rises on two sides, industrial glazing systems were used to cover the library and enclose the long exterior walls of the offices. A giant cascade of glass brings abundant light (and solar greenhouse-effect heat build-up in summer) to scholars working in the fan-shaped library. Stirling's Staatsgalerie (Figs. 16.65–16.66) in Stuttgart, Germany (1977–83)

shows that he moved toward Post-Modernism and beyond in his mid-career. It owes much to Schinkel's Altesmuseum in Berlin (see Fig. 14.4), contains a host of historical allusions, and responds to its site in a fashion somewhere between the search for a *genius loci*, or peculiar character of a place, and literal deconstruction. The building contains galleries in a U shape around a central, open rotunda, hence the Schinkel connection. Stirling made the rotunda a sculpture garden and part of a public walkway designed in homage to an established pedestrian path through the site. As for the allusions, which range from Greek or Roman pediments to Egyptian **cavetto** cornices to displaced stonework like that used by the Mannerist Giulio Romano, Stirling said that he was "sick and tired of the boring, meaningless, non-committed, faceless flexibility and open-endedness of the present architecture," meaning that he had moved on from his high-tech phase. At the interrupted side of the U in his plan, he set out a sculpture-like display of ramps, platforms, and a sinusoidal-curve lobby. The walls are laid up throughout in a striated coursing of variegated stone that gives the impression of an excavated classical site.

**16.64** James Stirling, History Faculty Building, Cambridge University, Cambridge, England, 1968.

Stirling's use of dramatic, exposed structural elements can be compared to Russian Constructivist explorations of the early twentieth century. Offices occupy the tower, with a library in the cascade of glass.

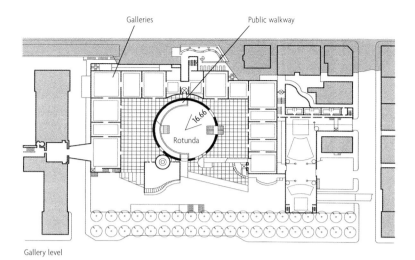

Galleries    Public walkway

16.66

Rotunda

Gallery level

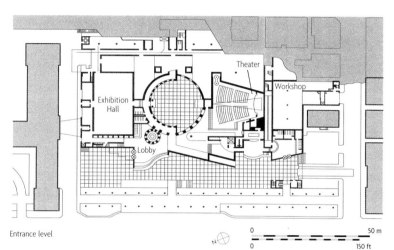

Theater

Workshop

Exhibition
Hall

Lobby

Entrance level

N

0          50 m
0          150 ft

**16.65** James Stirling, Plans of the Staatsgalerie, Stuttgart, 1977–83.

By this stage of his career, Stirling had forsaken dramatic technology for an almost archaeological-dig historicism combined with spatial manipulations derived from the European Modernists.

**16.66** (below) James Stirling, Staatsgalerie rotunda, Stuttgart, 1977–83.

Stirling presents this space almost as a ruin. Elsewhere, he left stone blocks strewn on the ground as though dislodged over time.

## RENZO PIANO

It is hard to say what is more impressive about Italian architect and contractor's son Renzo Piano (born 1937): the geographic coverage of his practice or the consistently exceptional quality of his work. While technological innovation seems, at least superficially, to be his primary interest, it is really technology's benefits, paid out in the currency of free-flowing space, a sense of shelter, and quality of craftsmanship that invigorate his process of design enquiry. The same can be said for his contextualism, as environmental benefits accrue naturally from his concern for quality of light and immediacy of inhabitants with the natural world. In his 1998 acceptance speech for the Pritzker Prize, he compared himself to Robinson Crusoe, "an explorer capable of surviving in foreign lands," and described himself as someone "ignoring boundaries between disciplines" and "taking risks and making mistakes."

Along with Richard Rogers, Piano designed the Pompidou Center (1976) in the Beaubourg area of Paris (Fig. 16.67), not far from the former site of Les Halles. The principal architectural features hang on the outside of the building, where the white web of diagonally braced steel framing, bright blue air-handling ducts, red exhaust stacks, and exterior escalator snaking up the front façade encase a multi-story glass rectangular solid. The galleries contained inside are unremarkable when compared with the exterior, and the building's bristling mechanics are curiously out of place in its nineteenth-century neighborhood.

In 1982, Piano designed the Menil Collection Museum in Houston, Texas as a low-slung, light-articulated box. He wrapped a series of reinforced-concrete, light-modulating, baffles, with apostrophe-shaped cross-sections, around a cella-like core of galleries. On the interior, he suspended extended versions of the baffles from a series of steel-lattice girders and distributed a grid of square steel columns between them and a black wooden floor. The light modulators create a rhythmic wave effect, not unlike that of the saw-toothed skylights at the DIA in Beacon, but at a much smaller scale, and they anticipate the ceiling conditions at Piano's Nasher Sculpture Center discussed below.

Piano was one among an international group of architects (including his former partner Richard Rogers, Arata Isozaki, and Raphael Moneo, all three discussed above) that contributed to rebuilding around Berlin's Potsdamer Platz, an area laid to waste at the end of World War II. On what had been a no-man's-land for half a century, Piano brought a triangular pool of water in from the Landwehrkanal to the south and responded to Hans Scharoun's expressionistic State Library (1967–72; completed 1978) to the west. Between the library and his new "B1" and "Debis" office towers and the new Marlene Dietrich Platz, Piano located a casino and theater, clad with anodized aluminum that harmonizes with Scharoun's work and capped with a series of suspended metallic roofs. It is an altogether inclusive design in a long-fragmented city.

**16.67** Renzo Piano and Richard Rogers, Pompidou Center, Paris, 1976.

The innards of a building (structural skeleton, mechanical systems and piping, etc.) that had long been concealed or downplayed are allowed to become the principal architectural expression. The site quickly became one of the most visited in Paris.

**16.68** Renzo Piano, Jean-Marie Tjibaou Cultural Center, Nouméa, New Caledonia, 1991.

More like wispy sculpture or part of the local flora than buildings, these tall, unconventional constructions announce the conventional galleries below them. The finger-like vertical members are made of laminated wood.

**16.69** Renzo Piano, Nasher Sculpture Center interior, Dallas, Texas, 2003.

At the beginning of this chapter, Eero Saarinen was identified as an architect still searching for his "style" when he died in 1961 at the age of fifty-one. Renzo Piano's buildings are as diverse as Saarinen's but are in no way immature. Piano also shares Saarinen's intense concern for innovative building materials. This view looks through one of the galleries and into the rear court.

Piano is the only architect in this book to have designed a cruiseship: the Regal Princess (1987–91). Streamlined in a form that updates the 1930s Moderne style of industrial designer Raymond Loewy (1893–1996), it evolved from the form of a dolphin, but this could as easily have been a bird, as the vessel's skin is expressively aerodynamic. As with his buildings, Piano sought to make the ship modest and humane, in this case by connecting the passengers as much as possible with the sights, sounds, smells, and feelings of the sea.

No work of any living architect is more lyrical than Piano's 1991 design for the Jean-Marie Tjibaou Cultural Center in Nouméa, New Caledonia (Fig. 16.68). He placed a series of tall, perforated, sail-like structures along a forested ridge between a lagoon and the ocean, their forms based on local huts but reaching dramatically skyward like attenuated fingers. The "huts" are constructed of double layers of laminated wooden uprights atop hinge-connection bases and are stabilized by cable-and-strut wind bracing and partially covered with wooden staves. Adjacent to them lie more conventional galleries and support spaces, some below grade, that share a high level of detailing and

craftsmanship with Piano's other work. At once technologically innovative and grounded in local building traditions, the ensemble is stunning when seen from a distance and engaging when entered to view the artifacts.

In 2003, Piano completed the Nasher Sculpture Center on a site in downtown Dallas, Texas. The collection of twentieth-century artworks is housed indoors and in a quiet rear court, which includes a sky-viewing installation by James Turrel. Acknowledging Louis Kahn's Kimbell Art Museum in nearby Fort Worth (see Figs. 16.15–16.17), Piano created five, long, narrow, parallel pavilions, but there the similarity ends. The lateral walls of his pavilions have unctuous travertine on their interior faces, while shorter end walls are completely glazed (Fig. 16.69). Above, stainless-steel rods support slightly arching steel ribs that, in turn, support low-iron-content (and therefore extremely clear) glass atop an aluminum mesh, its complex pattern of oblique holes developed by the Arup engineering firm to allow in abundant but only indirect sunlight. In the basement, Piano placed light-sensitive works, research and conservation facilities, an auditorium, and offices.

**16.70** Santiago Calatrava, Milwaukee Art Museum addition, Milwaukee, Wisconsin, 2001.

While this roof could easily be a large piece of sculpture, it is actually a kinetic sunscreen. Eero Saarinen, mentioned in the previous caption, designed the original museum to which Calatrava made this distinctive addition.

## SANTIAGO CALATRAVA

Born in Spain in 1951, Santiago Calatrava is both an architect and an engineer and, arguably, a sculptor. Exploiting new technologies, particularly those capable of producing long spans and dramatic cantilevers, he has pursued a course like countryman Antonio Gaudí's a century before, using structural logic and metaphorical references to forms found in nature to produce his buildings. His Stadelhofen Railway Station (1990) in Zurich, Switzerland makes dramatic use of bridges and roof extensions above an organic, vaulted, underground arcade. Like Gaudí's Güell Chapel and Güell Park viaduct (see Fig. 14.52), the station walls and roof become an organic whole, reaching upward like the trunk and branches of trees.

In 2001, Calatrava completed an addition, largely in concrete, to the Milwaukee Art Museum. It appears as an avian creature about to take flight, its most prominent element being a soaring, kinetic brise-soliel, or sun-control device, that tempers the environment in the museum's glazed reception area (Fig. 16.70). Beneath this fantastic contrivance, the low-slung galleries run north–south, seemingly extruded from the base of the brise-soliel, until they reach the War Memorial Art Gallery built in the 1960s by Eero Saarinen. Finally, a pedestrian bridge supported by a leaning mast and cables reaches back to the east and downtown Milwaukee.

## JEAN NOUVEL

In ancient Roman times, Némausus was the name for modern-day Nîmes. Here, in 1994, Jean Nouvel (born 1949) completed his Némausus, two parallel, bull-nosed housing blocks made from the kind of relatively inexpensive materials usually associated with industrial construction. Rejecting historicism but also Le Corbusier's specific brand of Modernism, Nouvel has sought through technology and a close reading of contemporary culture to produce buildings decidedly of their time. In Nîmes, he chose to build with raw concrete, corrugated aluminum sheeting, commercial glazed partitions, and perforated aluminum for continuous, projecting balcony shields that represent a metallic version of Le Corbusier's brise-soliel. Adjacent parking, landscaped with plane trees, is sunken, leaving the ground level free as a conceptual sea, through which the ship-like Némausus volumes appear to ply. Despite this Romantic sensibility, Nouvel's forms more than hold their own among surrounding industrial construction and warehouses.

## NORMAN FOSTER

The Englishman Sir Norman Foster (born 1935) met Richard Rogers at Yale, subsequently partnered with him, before forming Foster Associates with his wife, Wendy Cheesman Foster. An admirer of R. Buckminster Fuller (discussed below), whom Foster credits with giving him early direction both in construction innovation and what has become known as sustainable design, he has explored

**16.71** Norman Foster, Hong Kong Bank, Hong Kong, 1986.

Like an insect, this high-rise bank has an exoskeleton. Its long sides orient to views, while mechanical and service functions close off the short east and west elevations.

the potentialities of twentieth and now twenty-first-century technologies, but with a concomitant concern for the environment.

In designing the international headquarters for the Hong Kong Bank (1986) (Fig. 16.71), Foster responded to a site which has splendid views of Hong Kong harbor (to the north) and Victoria Peak (to the south), by creating a forty-seven-story rectangular prism with its long sides oriented to the views while mechanical and service functions close off the short east and west elevations. The most public banking areas are housed in the third through twelfth floors, which are grouped around a central atrium lit by mirrors attached to a south-facing "sunscoop" (an adjustable apparatus with mirrors to track the sun's path) hung outside the building. Save for mechanical rooms, structure, and elevator lobbies, the ground level is devoted entirely to an open plaza from which paired escalators rise through a glass ceiling to the atrium above. Construction detail gives character to the exterior; eight steel-truss towers comprise the "legs" from which the floors are suspended in five modules of diminishing height. Thus a column-free interior is obtained with a structural system that acts like five superimposed bridges suspended from horizontal trusses. Each horizontal truss occupies a double-height story containing meeting rooms, recreation

**16.72** Norman Foster, Reichstag interior, Berlin, 1993.

Around the perimeter of this rotunda, figures ascend and descend on the circumferential ramp. Below is the legislative chamber and rising within is the inverted cone that reflects light downward and channels heat upward.

areas, and food services, and each has exterior terraces that serve as refuge areas in case of fire. The truss floors divide the building into zoned layers housing related functional units of the bank, and floors within each zone are linked with escalators rather than elevators to establish spatial continuity. Setbacks at the upper levels conform to building codes, and a penthouse at the top provides space for the bank's officers with its roof serving as a helicopter landing pad.

In 1993, Foster won a competition for the redevelopment of the century-old German Reichstag, left in ruins after a suspicious fire in 1933 amid the Nazi party's grab for power and further mutilated when Allied and Russian armies entered Berlin in 1945. In close proximity to the Berlin Wall, it was largely ignored until reunification of East and West Germany in 1989. Intervening within the remains of the nineteenth-century structure, Foster added a transparent dome and spiral exterior ramp above the legislative chamber and an internal faceted cone that reflects light downward and channels heated air upward like a chimney. The symbolism of a phoenix rising from the literal ashes is obvious (Fig. 16.72).

Standing near the vertically expressive Tower Bridge, Foster's incongruously leaning London City Hall bows toward the south as if to announce that once unchallengeable paradigms are no longer so. Arrived at as a simultaneous solution to problems of form and performance, this deformed-egg-shaped, yet elegant building has a minimum surface area (for its enclosed volume) exposed to direct sun; includes horizontal sunscreens at its overhanging orientation; and incorporates triple glazing and operable sash. On the north side, wedding-cake layers of glazed triangles open up the Assembly Chamber to public view from the outside. Vertical circulation occurs within a spiral stair that provides a dynamic rotunda for this chamber and can only be compared in its combined functionality and beauty to the structure of a chambered nautilus.

The City Hall is only one project among many in this chapter where the firm now known as Arup Associates provided the engineering services. In an era when the lion's share of a project's costs pays only for "systems," the need for engineers determined to produce "delight" as well as "firmness" and to do so innovatively is undeniable. Arup Associates is arguably the best in the world at what they do, with projects discussed in this chapter that go back as far as the Sydney Opera House. Founded in 1946 by Danish engineer Sir Uve Arup (1895–1988), the firm stresses close engineer-architect cooperation in a highly creative, open-minded environment and places an emphasis on breadth as well as depth of knowledge.

### NICHOLAS GRIMSHAW

The Waterloo International Terminal (1994) in London by Sir Nicholas Grimshaw (born 1939) receives trains that have come through the English Channel Tunnel. It succeeds at the scale of both urban image and construction intricacy. A descendant of nineteenth-century iron-and-glass train sheds, it has an undulating 1312-foot-long plan that snugs up to the existing Waterloo Station. Like a giant insect, perhaps a centipede given its plan, Grimshaw's construction has an exoskeleton of pin-connected, three-dimensional, bow-string arches and is glazed on its west side and largely covered with rippled stainless-steel decking on the east. Much time was spent addressing the problems of expansion, contraction, and displacement associated with temperature change, train movements, and wind loading.

**16.73** R. Buckminster Fuller, Geodesic dome, U.S. Pavilion, Montreal International Exposition 1967.

In the 1960s, Buck Fuller traveled far and wide, wearing watches from three time zones (one each for where he was, where he had been, and where he was going) and lecturing to every student who would listen. Within his multi-hour presentations were detailed discussions of his geodesic domes illustrated by his hand drawings.

Grimshaw's Ljburg Bridges opened in Amsterdam in 2001. Beginning like the tail of a whale raised above the waterline, pylons give way to triple, oscillating steel arches, laterally braced by triangular clusters of spars, that support cables and, in turn, the deck below. Grimshaw allowed extreme engineering rationality to produce a dynamic structural grace not seen since the bridges of Robert Maillart. Like the Brooklyn Bridge (see Fig. 14.27), the span accommodates motorized vehicles, bicycles, and pedestrians along separate, protected paths.

## SUSTAINABLE DESIGN

The subject of sustainable design, meaning architecture that has the least possible negative impact on the environment, ideally none at all, is a difficult and often paradoxical one. It involves not only a building's effects on its site during and after construction, but the repercussions of gathering and processing the building materials, providing the required energy for on-going use, and much more. Architects, some more than others, have always been concerned with environmental issues, but the scale of concerns such as dwindling energy supplies, global warming, widespread destruction of habitat and extinction of species, and over-population have pushed these issues to the fore. General cultural and governmental responses have as yet been sporadic and incomplete (more aggressive in Europe than the United States), and architectural responses can only be described as immature. It seems obvious, however, that environmental degradation will become one of the most important issues, if not the single most important, facing coming generations.

### R. BUCKMINSTER FULLER

R. Buckminster Fuller (1895–1983) can only be categorized as uncategorizable. With wildly divergent influences, such as family connections back to New England transcendentalists and Navy experience in applied engineering, he became to some a visionary savant of advanced technologies and an early proponent of global resource conservation, but to others, more of a showman and gadfly. In any case, he streaked like a meteor through the architectural sky on an oblique trajectory of cosmic-scale predictions and universal design strategies. At least conceptually, his Dymaxion House, a low-cost living unit suspended from a central mast and intended to be placed on sites by sky-cranes, was certainly a more mass-producible "machine for living" than anything offered up by a European Modernist architect. Most of his built structures were **geodesic domes**, or domes made of light, straight structural members held largely in tension. The best known of these was constructed in 1967 for the Montreal International Exposition, or Expo '67 (Fig. 16.73).

### MVRDV

A building that speaks raucously about sustainability, even though providing few solutions to related problems, was designed by the Dutch firm MVRDV as their country's pavilion at the Expo 2000 in Hanover, Germany. Conceived by architects from a place that has always highly valued land, because it is scarce and much of what there is has been reclaimed from the sea by diking systems, the pavilion is a layer cake of disparate floor plates, each of them representing an earth condition: subterranean, open fields, mechanical artificiality, forest land, and sky at the top, where windmills supply electricity.

### GLENN MURCUTT

The Australian architect Glenn Murcutt (born 1936) has pursued a personal line of inquiry that emphasizes both form-making and adaptation to environment. Among the early influences on him were Mies van der Rohe, particularly his Farnsworth House, and Richard Neutra and Craig Ellwood in California, both of whom produced elegant post-and-beam frames like Mies. Murcutt was also imbued with a reverence for site by the so-called Sydney School of designers at work in Australia in the late 1950s and early 1960s. He became interested in lightweight, permeable structures, building upon his experiences with a father who exposed him to the Australian agricultural buildings of wood and corrugated metal and who sensitized him to the act of making. Murcutt tends to design units that are long and narrow, with their long sides

**16.74** Glenn Murcutt, Douglas Murcutt House interior, Sydney, 1969–72.

Here is a subtle essay on interior and exterior space and the transition between the two. The structure is Farnsworth House-like, with thin, box columns supporting a hovering roof.

**16.75** Glenn Murcutt, Local History Museum and Tourist Office, Kempsey, New South Wales, 1976, 1979–82, 1986–88.

Murcutt has drawn upon the local vernacular for many of his forms, but has reinterpreted them in terms of modern materials and methods of construction. The exhaust turbines on the roof become important formal elements.

facing north and south in order to assure proper ventilation and respond to the path of the sun. He extrudes their cross sections, but gives them complex profiles responding to sun and wind as well as to human habitation. He then details these skins to accept louvers and screens that both modulate climatic forces and articulate their surfaces. Subsequent to contact with the Mexican architect Luis Barragán, Murcutt has made pools of water a significant feature in many of his projects.

The Douglas Murcutt House in Sydney (1969–72) (Fig. 16.74) is Farnsworth House-like but lowered to the ground and merged with nature, in the form of a courtyard planted with native vegetation. The Ball-Eastaway House (1980–83), located northwest of Sydney, consists of a tubular-steel-frame pavilion, minimalist in its structure and minimal in its environmental impact. Sited in a forest of acacias, eucalyptuses, and banksias, it has a vaulted cross section with walls almost completely covered by louvers and a downspout system that is akin to sculpture. In Kempsey, New South Wales, Murcutt designed a Local History Museum and Tourist Office (1976, 1979–82, and 1986–88) (Fig. 16.75) that is equally subtle and overt in its responses to environmental forces. He placed non-bearing brick walls atop a brick base, insulated them, then covered them with zinc alloy panels; the corrugated metal roof is supported by a separate tubular-steel frame. Ventilation

**16.76** Glenn, Murcutt, Local History Museum and Tourist Office interior, Kempsey, New South Wales, 1976, 1979–82, 1986–88.

Environmental control elements are important parts of the interior of every Murcutt design. Venetian blinds both alter light and provide scale-giving elements. Below them, wooden transoms can be opened for ventilation.

**16.77** Glenn Murcutt, Magney House, Bingi Point, New South Wales, 1982–84.

Beneath the slab of this house, Murcutt placed cisterns to collect rainwater. The apparently eccentric roof form actually responds both to the path of the sun and to prevailing winds.

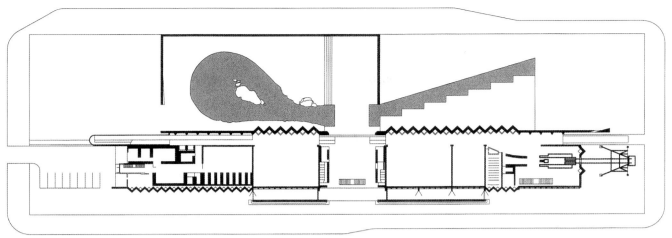

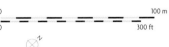

**16.78** Glenn Murcutt, Plan of the Minerals and Mining Museum, Broken Hill, New South Wales, 1987–89.

Many of Murcutt's plans are long and narrow, like this one, in order to take advantage of orientation and cross ventilation. The skin, separate from the structural grid, seems alive in its sensitivity to its context.

**16.79** Glenn Murcutt, Simpson-Lee House, Mount Wilson, New South Wales, 1989–94.

This project combines a Spartan, mechanistic elegance with a sincere yet practical response to passive climate control. The result approaches art.

occurs in the seam between the systems (Fig. 16.76) and is enhanced and dramatized by roof monitors. The rich textures of the walls and ceiling, and the light qualities they allow, belie their straightforward construction origins. The Magney House at Bingi Point, New South Wales (1982–84) (Fig. 16.77) is a Miesian box no more. Its asymmetrical butterfly roof, metal cladding, louvers, and down-

spout system leading to subterranean cisterns come together in a metallic organism finetuned to its windswept environment and its purpose as a vacation house for clients who had long visited and admired the site.

As a metaphor for Australian mining structures, Murcutt's unbuilt Minerals and Mining Museum in Broken Hill, New South Wales (1987–89) (Fig. 16.78) exaggerates both the frame and the skin, yielding something akin to but more explicable perhaps than the work of the Deconstructivists. Rammed-earth walls outfitted with wind traps of Egyptian inspiration keep the interior space ten degrees centigrade cooler than the outside air without the benefit of mechanical air-conditioning. Finally, the Simpson-Lee House in Mount Wilson, New South Wales (1989–94) (Fig. 16.79) possesses an equipoise that results from the placement of each piece—frame-constructed pavilions, linear walkway, and pool of water—in a kind of environmental equilibrium. Movement along the walkway, past the studio, and alongside the pool and the living quarters is calculated to give the occupants a sense of gradual withdrawal into a private realm with almost monastic qualities.

## THE CENTER FOR MAXIMUM POTENTIAL BUILDING SYSTEMS

Truly sustainable design remains far removed from conventional architectural practice, existing instead in oases of future-thinking like The Center for Maximum Potential Building Systems in Austin, Texas. Directed by architect Pliny Fiske and Gail D. A. Vittori, its program of building design, planning, and policy development has as its goal the creation of environments that are in harmony with themselves throughout their full life-cycles. Among the Center's concerns are renewable energy sources, on-site rainwater conservation and harvesting, wastewater treatment and recycling, materials recycling, and an equilibrium of atmospheric chemistry. They accept contemporary construction methods but look to merge them with indigenous ones proven over time to be sympathetic to their locales. The Center's immediate architectural products are intended to encourage a broader program of sustainable construction and one that can be institutionalized as governmental policy.

## ARCHITECTS WORKING IN CHINA

The first requisite for architectural practice is to "get the work," and currently the most work is being done in China, so architects are flocking to this emerging global economic juggernaut. No Chinese project has assumed a higher profile than Rem Koolhaas and his Office of Metropolitan Architects' office building for CCTV, China's billion-viewer-strong broadcasting company (Fig. 16.80). Remembering that Koolhaas has been imagining high-rise castles in the air since his 1978 publication of *Delirious New York*, it is not surprising to find him still infatuated with buildings that seem to defy gravity and are large enough (in this case 760 feet tall and enclosing 4.4 million square feet of floor space) to become cities unto themselves. The connection of Koolhaas's design to modern sculpture (the work of David Smith [1906–65]

comes to mind) is obvious, as was the need for the ubiquitous Arup firm to make Koolhaas's unorthodox configuration structurally sound. Its rambling form suggests that something like the 100-story John Hancock Center in Chicago, braced externally by a diamond-shaped steel grid, has been bent—once, twice … five times—then base and top reconnected, producing, among other things, the world's largest cantilever. The CCTV headquarters are perhaps the most dramatic but far from the only attempt by the Chinese to use radical architecture as an announcement of their country's optimism on the eve of the 2008 Olympic Games in Beijing.

Among the architects discussed in this chapter and now working in China, Steven Holl has designed eight linked apartment towers with façades not unlike his Simmons Hall at M.I.T. (see Fig. 16.57); Zaha Hadid has proposed a new opera house that looks so aerodynamically responsive that it could be mistaken for the next generation of stealth bomber; and even lesser-known designers have gotten into the act. The nascent Atlanta firm of Plexus r + d, with partners Jordan Williams and Erik Lewitt, won a competition in 2005 for the Beijing Zhongguanchun Life Science Park. Using the kind of slick computer graphics long the stock in trade of Chinese architectural students seeking graduate degrees in the United States, they both represented their ideas convincingly and, they contend, better predicted and will better control construction costs.

## CONCLUSIONS ABOUT ARCHITECTURAL IDEAS

The lion's share of buildings discussed in this final chapter are accessible, at least in part, to the public, including the many museums, and this emphasis was placed by design. Reading about architecture while studying drawings and photographs is one good way to get some architectural education, but as a vicarious activity it has its limits. Architecture needs to be walked through, touched, and used; it needs to be experienced, and the authors hope that this is what will happen.

The principal conclusion to be drawn from this chapter must be that there is no main line of development in building design at the beginning of the twenty-first century. Post-Modernism has come and gone, and Deconstruction has proved to be more of a label than a direction. Like culture in general, and for better or for worse, pluralism best describes the current situation. There are some new forces at work, perhaps the most obvious being the computer. Electronic drafting programs and the internet have made it much easier for architects, architectural offices, and multiple offices to cooperate. Numerous individuals, including engineers, can now have access to drawings simultaneously, and changes in them can be made

**16.80** Rem Koolhaus, CCTV Headquarters, Beijing.

This 760-foot-tall convoluted structure needs all of the X-bracing that it can get, given the outlandish cantilever. The Dutch author of *Delirious New York* (written as part of his architectural studies at the Architectural Association School in London) is now trying to build this tower as the largest structure in China.

easily and universally with little concern for geography. In addition, the ability of the computer to rapidly draw polygons and curvatures and represent the three-dimensional results in a form that is now approaching photo-realism has made complex shapes more conceivable and more buildable and so more fashionable and, in tandem with new construction technologies, has encouraged wide-ranging investigations of new building-enclosure systems, meaning exterior walls or skins.

Finally, it is also impossible to imagine that the twin issues of environmental degradation and dwindling energy supplies are not going to radically alter daily life world-wide, sooner rather than later. That well-known view from space of the third planet from the Sun—our beautiful but finite and fragile blue orb, or as R. Buckminster Fuller enjoyed saying, "spaceship Earth"—is being despoiled at an alarming rate. This book is replete with cultures that variously degraded their environments, some, like the Pre-Columbian Maya, to a point where they were unlivable; but this was only a regional catastrophe. The issue is now global and will demand global solutions of which architecture must be a part.

# GLOSSARY

**Abacus** On a classical column, the stone set directly over the capital.

**Abbey** A monastery governed by an abbot.

**Acanthus** A plant used as a model for decoration on Corinthian and Composite capitals.

**Acropolis** Literally "high city". In Greek city-states, the acropolis was the location of the most important temples and religious shrines.

**Acroterion** An upright ornament placed at the apex and eaves of gabled roofs in Greek architecture.

**Adobe** A wall-building material made from sun-dried clay or clay-like earth.

**Agora** In Greek cities, the term applied to the area of markets and city government.

**Aisle** In a basilican church, the portion set parallel to the nave, generally separated from it by columns or piers.

**Allée** A linear garden walk defined by trees on both sides.

**Ambulatory** The curving passageway behind the choir of a church, often used to connect the radiating chapels.

**Amphitheater** An arena with raked seating arranged around a circular or oval floor.

**Aniconic** Ornamentation that is symbolically suggestive rather than literally representational.

**Anta** A pilaster-like thickening of the wall edge or jamb of a wall opening that responds to an adjacent column.

**Apadana** An audience hall in Persian palace architecture.

**Appartements** A suite of rooms (French).

**Apse** The termination of the nave of a basilica or the choir in a basilican church.

**Aqueduct** A pipe for conducting water under gravity flow. The term is often applied to the arched structure built to support the pipe across valleys.

**Arcade** A series of arches carried on columns or piers.

**Arch** A curved element that spans an opening and supports the structural loads above it. Most often, arches are made of small, wedge-shaped masonry elements called voussoirs. The profile of an arch may vary from semicircular to pointed to almost flat.

**Architrave** In classical architecture, the bottom portion of an entablature.

**Arris** The intersection of two curved surfaces, most commonly applied to the line formed when the flutes of a Doric column join.

**Ashlar** Smooth stone masonry laid so that the joints are visible.

**Atelier** An architect's studio or workplace.

**Atrium** The central space of a Roman house, open to the sky and serving as a source of light and fresh air. In Early Christian churches, the atrium was a large open courtyard, surrounded by covered galleries, which preceded the entrance to the church.

**Attic** The story built above the cornice of a building, sometimes used to conceal the roof.

**Axis** A line at the end of which movement terminates at a significant feature and thereby divides a composition into two equal parts.

**Balcony** A platform cantilevered from a wall, generally surrounded by a railing or balustrade.

**Baldachin** or **Baldacchino** An elaborate canopy erected over an altar.

**Balloon framing** A wooden framing system composed of vertical studs extended unbroken from bottom sill to top plate even in multistory construction.

**Baptistery** A building, generally octagonal, used for the Christian rite of baptism.

**Barrel vault** A semicircular vault over a rectangular space.

**Base** The lowest part of a column or pier, often broader than the sections above to spread the load to the foundation.

**Basilica** Literally, "king's hall". In Roman architecture, a hall used for public administration. The term generally refers to a rectangular building that has a central section with a higher roof (the nave if a church) flanked by lower aisles on both long sides. A semicircular projection, the apse, was often set at one or both of the shorter ends. Early Christians adapted the form as a basis for church design, replacing one apse with the main entrance and establishing a processional axis the length of the building. The altar was placed in the apse at the end.

**Bastide** A medieval new town founded both for defense and economic development of an unsettled region.

**Bay** A building module defined by the repetition of an element such as a column or pier.

**Bazaar** A covered market in Islamic cities.

**Beam** A horizontal element that carries structural loads between upright supports.

**Bellcote** A modest belfry located astride the ridge of a church roof or made as a narrowed extension upward of the principal gabled façade.

**Belfry** The tower or steeple in which bells are hung.

**Beltcourse** A projecting horizontal board or projecting course(s) of brick or stone that define a floor level on the inside.

**Belvedere** An elevated room or structure situated to afford a fine view or capture breezes.

**Bienséance** Concerned with appropriateness and the correct form of a building relative to its purpose in eighteenth-century French architectural theory.

**Blind opening** A framed element like a window applied to a wall but lacking an opening to the outside.

**Bochki** Reverse curve gables seen in Russian architecture.

**Boiserie** Interior wood paneling enriched by carving, gilding, painting, or inlay.

**Book-matched** Side-by-side sheets of veneer arranged to have symmetrical graining about their common joint.

**Bosco** A dense grove of trees.

**Bouleterion** In classical Greek architecture, a building used for senate or council meetings.

**Bracket set** Elaborate interlocking supports in Chinese architecture that produce a roof overhang.

**Brise-soleil** A screen attached to a building to shade windows from the sun.

**Buttress** Masonry reinforcement applied to a wall to provide additional strength.

**Caisson** An airtight box or chamber used for work on river bottoms.

**Caldarium** The hot or sweating bath chamber in Roman baths or thermae.

**Campanile** In Italy, the name given to a freestanding belltower.

**Cantilever** A beam firmly anchored on one end and unsupported at the other end.

**Capital** In classical architecture the termination of a column, generally given decorative carving.

**Caravanserai** Accommodation for traveling merchants, usually built around a large open court and provided with stables for animals, secure storage for cargo, and an inn for travelers.

**Cardo** In Etruscan and Roman cities, the principal north-south road.

**Carolingian** The term applied to buildings constructed under the influence of the emperor Charlemagne, who reigned from 792 to 814.

**Cartouche** A boldly decorated frame hung above doorways.

**Caryatid** A pier carved in the form of a standing woman and used in place of a column.

**Castrum** A Roman military camp or garrison (pl. *castra*).

**Cathedral** The church that serves as seat of a bishop. (The bishop's chair is called a cathedra.)

**Cavetto** A concave molding, usually a quadrant of a circle and often used for cornices.

**Cella** The shrine room in the center of a temple.

**Cement** The binding component of concrete. Natural cements occur in areas of former volcanic activity, as around Puteoli in Italy, where the Romans exploited deposits they called pozzolana. Artificial cements have been made since 1824, when Joseph Aspdin discovered a process for heating limestone, clay, and sand to a very high temperature and then grinding the results.

**Cenotaph** A monument erected in memory of someone who is not interred within it.

**Centering** The wooden scaffold or form required to support a masonry vault or arch while under construction.

**Chaitya** In India, a traditional village memorial erected over the grave of an honored person. A structure built to enclose such a memorial and permit circulation around it is known as a chaitya hall.

**Chancel** The east end of a church, in which the main altar is placed.

**Chapter house** An assembly room in a monastery, generally located off the cloister, where the monks and abbot gathered daily for reading a chapter of the Rule by which monastic life was governed.

**Charrette** A period of intense work on an architectural project at its conclusion. The term is derived from the cart, or charrette, used to pick up Ecole des Beaux-Arts student projects throughout Paris.

**Château** The French word for castle. In Renaissance France, the term is generally applied to a large country residence without any military pretentions.

**Chatra** A triple-tiered umbrella form set atop a stupa, symbolic of the Bodhi tree under which Buddha gained enlightenment.

**Chigi** In Shinto architecture, upward extensions of bargeboards at gable ends of the shrine, forming an X-shape.

**Choir** The eastern end of a basilican church, where the divine service was sung.

**Classical language of architecture** The architectural grammar based on the classical orders of ancient Greece and Rome.

**Clerestory** Windows placed high in a wall, generally above lower roof elements.

**Cloister** In a monastery, the covered walk surrounding a quad-rangular court that connects the domestic buildings and the church.

**Cloister vault** A dome with groined surfaces rising from a square or octagonal base. Also known as a domical vault.

**Coffers** Ceiling recesses set in a geometric pattern.

**Colonnade** A linear series of columns with entablature.

**Column** In classical architecture, the upright structural element consisting of a base, shaft, and capital.

**Composite** A Roman order combining features of the Ionic and Corinthian.

**Concrete** A plastic building material consisting of sand, water, cement, and aggregate, which hardens to a stone-like consistency.

**Console** A bracket, generally decoratively curved, that supports a cornice or projecting element.

**Convenance** Concerned with appropriateness and the correct form of a building relative to its purpose in eighteenth-century French architectural theory.

**Coquille** A seashell-like organic form.

**Corbel** Masonry that projects slightly from a wall and serves as a support.

**Corbeled vault** Construction, without true arching action, made by shifting opposing courses slightly and regularly inward until they meet.

**Corinthian** The order that features acanthus-leaf capitals atop a fluted shaft.

**Cornice** The uppermost element of an entablature, which projects beyond the plane of the exterior wall; more generally, the overhanging molding atop any building.

**Corps-de-logis** The main, freestanding unit in a French building complex.

**Cortile** In Italian architecture, the term applied to an open courtyard inside a building.

**Crockets** Decorative bud-like protrusions on the angles of Gothic stonework, especially on spires and towers.

**Crossing** In a basilican church, the space where transepts, nave, and choir intersect.

**Cross-in-square** Another name for the quincunx plan.

**Cross vault** The vault formed by two intersecting barrel vaults. Also known as a groin vault.

**Crypt** The basement level of a church, originally used for burial.

**Cupola** A dome. The term is also applied to the lantern on any roof structure, and is generally used to describe the structure over the oculus of a dome.

**Curtain wall** In medieval castles, a section of defensive walling between projecting towers. In modern construction, a nonstructural exterior surface hung from metal framing.

**Cyclopean masonry** Walls made of very large stones, only minimally shaped.

**Decorated period** Phase of the English Gothic following the Early English, sometimes divided into the Geometric and subsequent Curvilinear; its features include elaborated tracery and lierne and tierceron ribs.

**Decumanus** In Etruscan and Roman cities, the principal east–west road.

**Dentil** A type of cornice molding composed of rectangular blocks set in a row like teeth; hence the name.

**Diagonal rib** A rib crossing a bay diagonally from pier impost to pier impost.

**Dome** A continuously curved roof over a polygonal or circular plan, generally having a semicircular or elliptical section.

**Domical vault** A dome with groined surfaces rising from a square or octagonal base. Also known as a cloister vault.

**Domos** The principal space in a megaron.

**Doric** The Greek order that has a fluted shaft, no base, and an echinus molding supporting the abacus. Roman Doric columns have a base.

**Dormer** A window that projects above the slope of a roof.

**Drum** The cylindrical volume supporting a dome.

**Early English period** First phase of the English Gothic, more or less equivalent to the French High Gothic.

**Eave** The edge of the roof plane that projects over the exterior wall of a building.

**Echinus** The curved cushion-like molding that, together with the abacus, forms the capital in the Doric order.

**Eclecticism** The selection and combination of architectural elements from a variety of styles.

**Egg-and-Dart** An egg-shaped ornament alternating with a dart-shaped one.

**Élève** An entering student at the Ecole des Beaux-Arts.

**Enfilade** The aligning of a series of doors through a series of adjacent rooms.

**En suite** A series of rooms arranged side by side.

**Entablature** In classical architecture, the horizontal elements supported by columns, consisting (in ascending sequence) of the architrave, frieze, and cornice.

**Entasis** The slight outward curve of a column, which then tapers toward the top of the shaft.

**Esquisse** A preliminary sketch or quickly drawn design solution expressing the germinal idea in the Ecole des Beaux-Arts design process.

**Exedra** A semicircular niche, often used as a seat of honor or place for a statue.

**Façade** The exterior elevation of a building.

**Faïence** A mainly quartz and sand (non-clay), glazed, ceramic material, usually light blue-green in color with subtle surface variations.

**Fan vault** In English Perpendicular Gothic buildings, vaults with ribs having the same curvature and radiating or fanning out from the springing of the vault.

**Fascia** Horizontal bands in the architrave of the Ionic and Corinthian orders; more generally, the end board of a roof at the eaves.

**Feng shui** The Chinese art of adjusting a design to site-specific conditions so as to promote harmony in accordance with Daoist principles.

**Ferroconcrete** Concrete with embedded steel wire or rods. The combination takes advantage of the compressive strength of the former and the tensile strength of the latter.

**Fillet** The flat vertical face between the flutings of a column shaft.

**Fluting** Vertical grooves incised in the shaft of a classical column.

**Flying buttress** In Gothic architecture, the combination of external buttress pier and slender arch, which attaches to a wall just below the springing of the vaulting in order to resist lateral thrust.

**Forum** In Roman towns, the open space near the center used for commerce and civic life.

**Fresco** A painting executed on wall surfaces by working pigments into wet plaster.

**Frieze** The horizontal element above the architrave and below the cornice in an entablature.

**Frigidarium** The cold-water baths in a Roman thermae.

**Frontispiece** An elaborated door surround at the front façade of a building.

**Gable** The pedimented end of a classical temple; more generally, the triangular space at the end of a double-pitched roof.

**Galilee** A porch or chapel at the west end of medieval churches.

**Gallery** The passage over the aisle in medieval churches.

**Garbhagriha** The "womb chamber" or shrine room at the heart of a Hindu temple.

**Gargoyle** A decorative rainwater spout, often carved to resemble a fanciful animal.

**Geodesic dome** A grid-like structure that takes the form of a dome and is composed only of small, linear elements, most of them held in tension.

**Gopura** In Hindu architecture, a monumental gateway erected on axis with the temple.

**Grand salon** The major living space in a Venetian palace, usually extending from front to back of the house.

**Greek-cross plan** A plan in the form of a cross having arms of equal length.

**Groin vault** The vault formed by two intersecting barrel vaults. Also known as a cross vault.

**Ha-ha** A ditch used to control the movement of livestock, which is not visible in a planned landscape.

**Half-timbering** Wall construction with heavy-timber members carrying the structural load and made weather-tight with infill materials.

**Hall church** A basilican church where the nave and aisles are of similar height.

**Hammerbeam** A bracketed cantilevered beam used as support for a timber roof truss.

**Haram** Literally, "private" or "sacred". Used to describe the sanctuary in a mosque and the family living quarters in an Islamic house.

**Harmika** The square railing at the top of a stupa.

**Hemicycle** A semicircular room or recess.

**Hipped roof** A roof built with inclined gables on all four sides.

**Hôtel** A French urban domestic building.

**Huaca** An ancient Peruvian sacred artifact, animal, or land form inhabited by a god or spirit.

**Hypostyle hall** A large hall composed of many columns placed close together to support the roof.

**Iconostasis** A screen in Byzantine churches that divides the nave from the chancel and that is used as a support for devotional images or icons.

**Imperial stair** A stair that rises up a central flight to a landing then doubles back on either side to complete its ascent.

**Impluvium** In Roman houses, the shallow pool that collected rainwater draining from the atrium roof.

**In antis columns** Columns in the plane of a wall and often between antae.

**Insula** A Roman apartment house.

**Intarsia** Mosaic inlay in wood.

**Intercolumniation** The space between columns.

**Ionic** The order that features volutes in the capital; the shaft is usually fluted.

**I-section** A structural member with an I-shaped cross section; its horizontal members are called flanges and its vertical member a web.

**Iwan** Roofed or vaulted chamber open on one side, often facing the courtyard of a mosque.

**Jetty** A short wooden cantilever supporting an upper wall section, most commonly found on timber houses of the medieval period.

**Jian** A module used in Chinese wooden architecture, particularly houses, measuring about twelve by twenty feet.

**Katsuogi** Short horizontal elements set atop the ridge of Shinto shrines; probably used originally to hold down the thatch roof.

**Keep** The central enclosed tower of a medieval castle.

**Keystone** The central voussoir of an arch.

**Ki** A brush-and mud-covered domical structure built by indigenous tribes in the American southwest.

**Kiva** A ritual or assembly space in the Ancestral Pueblo culture, often circular, and usually sunken into the ground.

**Kodo** In Japanese Buddhist architecture, the name given to the lecture hall.

**Külliye** The Turkish word for a mosque and its related buildings, typically including educational, charitable, medical, and commercial facilities.

**Label molding** A molding that extends horizontally across an opening, then returns vertically for a short distance down each side.

**Labyrinth** A building with, or arrangement of, winding or confusing pathways.

**Lantern** A tower with windows rising above the roofline or above the oculus of a dome.

**Lierne** A decorative, nonstructural supplementary rib added to Gothic vaulting.

**Linga** An upright stone in traditional Indian shrines symbolic of the male element.

**Lintel** Any horizontal member that spans an opening.

**Loggia** An open porch, generally raised above the ground floor and covered by a roof.

**Lombard bands** Decorative wall detailing composed of corbeled arches and pilasters.

**Long-and-short work** Quoin-like masonry corners with units oriented alternately horizontally and vertically.

**Long gallery** A wide and long passageway in English and French Renaissance houses used for living purposes.

**Lunette** The semi-circular or crescent-shaped projection of a window opening into a vaulted ceiling.

**Lustral basin** A pool used for ritual purification.

**Machicolation** In medieval fortifications, a corbeled stone gallery projecting in front of a defensive wall, open at the bottom to allow materials to be dropped on those below.

**Madrasa** Islamic college for theological, legal, and literary studies.

**Mandala** The geometrical diagram based on a subdivided square that is used to generate proportions for Hindu temple designs.

**Mandorla** An almond-shaped frame surrounding the image of a saint, used to indicate divinity.

**Maqsura** In early mosques, an area in front of the mihrab reserved for officials and sometimes given extra ornamentation (unusual vaulting or a dome) or special screening for security.

**Marché** Movement along a defined architectural path.

**Martyrium** A building associated with a Christian martyr.

**Masjid** A district or neighborhood mosque.

**Mastaba** An Egyptian tomb with a flat top and sloping sides, built over a grave shaft.

**Mausoleum** An elaborate tomb, named after the tomb of King Mausoleus.

**Medallion** An ornamental plaque, frequently oval or square.

**Megalith** Large stones or boulders used in prehistoric architecture.

**Megaron** In Mycenaean architecture, a rectangular room having a central hearth and four columns supporting a roof with an atrium opening. More generally, the term applies to a single-cell house in the Aegean region.

**Metope** An element of the Doric frieze, set alternately with triglyphs. Metope panels contain low-relief carvings.

**Mihrab** A niche in the qibla wall indicating the direction of Mecca.

**Minaret** In Islamic architecture, the tower associated with a mosque from which the faithful are called to prayer.

**Minbar** In a mosque the pulpit from which the imam leads prayers.

**Minka** Wooden Japanese folk houses, typical of rural communities.

**Moat** A broad surrounding ditch, sometimes filled with water, constructed for defense.

**Modillion** Another word for console, sometimes applied to a series of ornamental brackets supporting a cornice.

**Moment connection** A connection between two elements, usually beam and column, that is capable of resisting a bending force.

**Monastery** A religious institution providing living accommodations and worship space for monks.

**Mortise** A rectangular opening, or socket, prepared to receive a tenon, usually in wooden construction.

**Mosaic** A floor, wall, or ceiling decoration composed of small pieces of colored glass or stone that form designs.

**Mosque** An Islamic house of prayer.

**Motte-and-bailey** Medieval castle with a mound (motte) and yard (bailey) defined by a ditch and wall.

**Muqarna** Islamic vault treatment that fragments the surface into many concave segments. Muqarnas may be built in masonry or suspended as elements from an overhead structure.

**Mutules** A block beneath the soffit of a Doric cornice, usually decorated with cylindrical or truncated conical elements.

**Naos** The sanctuary of a Greek temple.

**Narthex** The entrance porch or chamber before the nave of a church.

**Nave** The western arm of a basilican church.

**Newel** The center post around which a circular stair winds or a straight stair turns.

**Niche** A wall recess.

**Nymphaeum** A room or building with a fountain or spring and intended for relaxation.

**Obelisk** A stone monolith, square in plan, with sides tapering toward a pyramidal top.

**Oculus** The circular opening at the apex of a dome.

**Opisthodomos** The enclosed room at the back of a Greek temple, often used as a treasury.

**Opus incertum** Roman walls built of irregularly shaped stones facing a concrete core.

**Opus listatum** Roman walls constructed of stone and brick in alternate courses.

**Opus quadratum** A Roman wall built of squared masonry.

**Opus reticulatum** A Roman wall formed of pyramidal stones, their points set inward and their square heads set to form a diagonal grid.

**Opus testaceum** Roman walls constructed of brick facing on a concrete core.

**Orangery** A building used to protect ornamental shrubs and trees in cold weather.

**Orchestra** In a Greek theater, the circular floor used for dancing.

**Orders** The trabeated systems of architecture developed by the Greeks and extended by the Romans. The Greek orders—Doric, Ionic, and Corinthian—differ slightly from the Roman orders. The Romans developed the Tuscan and Composite orders.

**Ordonnance** Correct relationship of parts to one another and to the whole in eighteenth-century French architectural theory.

**Oriel window** A corbeled bay window in English medieval architecture.

**Pagoda** A tapering tower with multiple roof levels, built by Buddhists particularly in China and Japan. The word derives from the Sanskrit dagoba, meaning stupa.

**Palaestra** A Roman building used for exercise; a gymnasium.

**Palazzo** A palace type; in the Italian Renaissance, a four-square block with central court or cortile and the main floor on the second or piano nobile level.

**Palladian motif** A central arched opening with lower trabeated openings to each side.

**Parapet** A low wall at the perimeter of a roof.

**Parterre** An ornamental, geometrical arrangement of flat, planted beds.

**Pavilion** A prominent feature in a façade composition, usually at the center or at the ends and typically set forward, raised higher, and capped with a distinctive roof form.

**Pebble dash** A stucco wall given a pitted texture by throwing pebbles against it.

**Pediment** The gable end of a temple, framed by cornices.

**Pendant vaulting** Vaults with suspended, decorative elements hanging from their ribs.

**Pendentive** A spherical triangle that transforms a square bay into a circle for the springing of a dome.

**Pensionnaires** French architectural students who spent an extended period studying in Rome.

**Peripteral columns** Columns placed around all sides of a building.

**Peristyle** A colonnaded court or garden.

**Perpendicular period** Final phase of the English Gothic characterized by strongly vertical panel tracery and fan vaults.

**Piano nobile** The main living floor of a house, generally raised a story above ground level.

**Piazza** An open space surrounded by buildings; in nineteenth-century American architecture, the term is sometimes applied to a porch on a house.

**Pier** A structural element, square or rectangular in plan, that supports an arch.

**Pietra serena** A gray stone used extensively in Renaissance Florence for architectural details.

**Pilaster** A rectangular column, engaged in a wall, which is sometimes articulated as an order.

**Pilotis** Freestanding posts or supports for an upper-level structure; the term was most commonly used by Le Corbusier.

**Pit house** A semi-subterranean structure with its one-room excavated space roofed by an earth-covered wood frame.

**Plank house** Similar to the shed house, a rectangular, post-and-lintel structure covered on its walls and roof with hand-split wood planks.

**Pointed arch** A two-centered arch, pointed at its apex.

**Polis** The ancient Greek city-state.

**Polychromy** The decorative use of colored stone, seen primarily in medieval architecture.

**Pomochi** In Russian wooden architecture, a series of stacked cantilevers.

**Porte-cochère** A projecting canopy or carriage porch.

**Portico** A colonnaded porch.

**Post** An upright structural member; a column.

**Pozzolana** A volcanic ash containing silicon and aluminum, which will harden as a cement when ground fine and mixed with lime and water.

**Precis** A brief or short, precise building program describing the essential elements to be designed that was issued at the Ecole des Beaux-Arts at the beginning of a design competition.

**Prodomos** See pronaos.

**Projet rendu** A fully rendered or highly developed and closely detailed design solution at the Ecole des Beaux-Arts.

**Pronaos** The vestibule or antechamber to the shrine room (naos) of a Greek temple.

**Proskenion** The area directly in front of the skene in the ancient Greek theater.

**Prostyle** A portico of columns on the front of a building.

**Pueblo** A communal house or group of houses built of adobe or stone.

**Putti** Representations of plump, naked, often winged young children in paintings or sculptures.

**Pylon** A massive entrance to an Egyptian temple, with sloping walls and a central opening.

**Qasr** An Arabic word for castle.

**Qibla** The direction of Mecca, indicated in a mosque by the mihrab; by extension, the wall in which the mihrab is placed.

**Quadripartite vault** A vault over one bay divided by diagonal ribs into four parts.

**Quatrefoil** A four-lobed (or foiled) pattern seen frequently in Gothic architecture.

**Quincunx** Five objects arranged in a square, with one in the center. Byzantine churches with a quincunx plan typically have five domes, the center one being balanced by four domes at the corners.

**Quoin** A brick or piece of stone used to give strength or visual prominence to an external corner.

**Ramada** A flat-roofed rectangular post-and-lintel structure roofed with brush.

**Ratha** A wheeled cart or chariot. In Hindu architecture, the stone building form carved or constructed to resemble such a chariot.

**Rayonnant** Thirteenth- and fourteenth-century French Gothic tracery that is characterized by radiating lines.

**Rib** A raised molding applied to the arris of a vault.

**Rib vault** A vault where ribs ride below and usually support the vault web.

**Rocaille** Eighteenth-century scroll ornament based upon water-worn elements such as rocks and seashells.

**Roundel** A small circular panel or opening.

**Rustication** Rough stonework with exposed joints.

**Sahn** An open courtyard in a mosque.

**Salient** A projecting element, particularly an arrowhead-shaped projection from the walls of a fort.

**Semidome** A surface representing one-fourth of a sphere and often covering an apse.

**Serdab** In Egyptian tombs, an above-ground chamber where offerings to the deceased were placed.

**Serliana** A central arched opening with lower trabeated openings to each side. Also sometimes called a Palladian or Serlian motif.

**Sexpartite vault** A vault over two bays divided by diagonal ribs and a transverse rib into six parts.

**Shaft** The vertical element above the base and below the capital in an architectural order.

**Shatyor** Tent-roof forms used on Russian churches.

**Shed house** Similar to the plank house, a flat- or gable-roofed, post-and-lintel structure covered with wood planks.

**Shikhara** The tall curving roof, often with a parabolic profile, that rises like an artificial mountain over the garbhagriha in a Hindu temple.

**Sipapu** A fist-sized depression in Ancestral Pueblo Kivas, perhaps intended as a portal to the spirit world.

**Skene** The backdrop building in a classical theater.

**Spandrel** A wall surface, ornamented or unornmented, between major architectural elements such as windows or arches.

**Sphinx** A mythological creature with the body of a lion and a male human head.

**Squinch** A corbeled arch used to transform a square bay into an octagon for the springing of a dome.

**Stave** A tall post, generally a peeled tree-trunk, used in construction.

**Stele** An upright slab, often carrying images or inscriptions.

**Stereotomy** The art of carving stone in complex, three-dimensional forms.

**Stoa** In Greek architecture, a linear building with one or more rows of columns. Stoas could be used for shops, meetings, or exhibitions.

**Stupa** In Buddhist architecture, the mound of earth and stones erected over relics of the Buddha or, by extension, over the remains of a holy person.

**Stylobate** The base, usually having steps, on which a colonnaded temple sits.

**Superimposed orders** Orders placed atop one another.

**Suq** A street in an Islamic market.

**Tablero** The vertical, often ornamented, plane in Pre-Columbian pyramid construction, comparable to the frieze in ancient Greek architecture.

**Tablinium** In Roman atrium houses, a reception area, usually on axis with the entrance.

**Talud** The inclined plane in Pre-Columbian pyramid construction.

**Tatami** Mats woven of rice straw, approximately three by six feet, that establish the module for room dimensions in traditional Japanese houses.

**Tenon** A usually wooden knob or tongue prepared for insertion into a mortise.

**Tepidarium** The warm-water chamber in Roman baths or thermae.

**Terracotta** Unglazed fired clay, often used for ornamental purposes.

**Thermae** Roman baths, usually containing rooms for hot-, warm-, and cold-water bathing.

**Tholos** A dome over a circular-plan building, or more generally the building itself.

**Totem pole** The popular name for large cedar posts carved with effigies by Native Americans in the northwest.

**Tierceron** In Gothic vaulting, a secondary rib extending from the support to the crown of the vault.

**Tokonoma** In Japanese houses, an alcove in the vestibule of a house where treasured objects are displayed.

**Torana** An elaborate entrance gate into a Buddhist shrine.

**Torii** An elaborate post-and-lintel gateway into Buddhist shrines in Japan.

**Torus** Convex, roughly semi-circular molding often seen at the base of a classical column.

**Tracery** The stonework divisions in Gothic windows.

**Transept** The north and south arms of a basilican church.

**Transfer beam** A heavy beam that distributes (transfers) loads from the structure above to supports that are not directly aligned below.

**Transom** An opening above a door for light and/or ventilation.

**Transverse arch** An arch spanning across a long hall or nave.

**Trefoil** A three-lobed (or foiled) pattern seen frequently in Gothic architecture.

**Triclinium** A dining room in Roman houses and palaces.

**Triforium** In Gothic churches, the narrow passage below the clerestory corresponding to the lean-to roof over the aisle.

**Triglyph** A channeled block set between metopes in a Doric frieze.

**Trilithon** Two upright stones supporting a lintel stone.

**Triumphal arch** In Roman architecture, a gateway structure, with one or three arched openings, built to celebrate the return of a conquering army.

**True arch** A curving, often semi-circular arch composed of voussoirs.

**Truss** A structural frame composed of relatively short elements, typically configured into triangles, used to form a bridge or span a roof.

**Tuscan** An order based on Etruscan architecture, employing unfluted columns and simplified capitals.

**Tympanum** A panel, generally semicircular, over the lintel and under the arch of a doorway. Also, the central triangle of a pediment.

**Vault** An arched ceiling or roof of brick or stone.

**Verdika** Fence surrounding a stupa.

**Vestibule** An antechamber before a major space.

**Vihara** A Buddhist monastery.

**Villa** The Roman word for a farm. By extension, the term used during the Renaissance and afterward for a rural house, often of extensive size.

**Villa rustica** A Roman agricultural establishment that included living quarters for family members and slaves as well as stalls, store rooms, etc.

**Volute** A decorative spiral found in Ionic, Corinthian, and Composite capitals.

**Voussoir** A wedge-shaped masonry unit set to form an arch.

**Wall pillar** Space-shaping, pilaster-faced cross walls providing lateral stability for nave vaults in German Baroque churches.

**Wandfeiler** See wall pillar.

**Westwerk** The narthex, chapels, and towers set at the entrance end of churches of the Carolingian and later periods.

**Yoni** Concentric circles surrounding the linga and representing the female principle in traditional Indian architecture.

**Ziggurat** A stepped pyramid form used in ancient Mesopotamia as the platform for a religious building.

# BIBLIOGRAPHY

## Chapter 1

Arnold, Dieter. *Building in Egypt: Pharaonic Stone Masonry.* New York: Oxford University Press, 1991. A summary of what is known from archaeology about methods used in Egyptian monumental stonework, from quarrying to transport to erection.

Arnold, Dieter. *The Encyclopedia of Ancient Egyptian Architecture.* Princeton: Princeton University Press, 2003. Use as a reference volume.

Bourdier, Jean-Paul and Trinh T. Minh-Ha. *Drawn From African Dwellings.* Bloomington, IN, 1996. Covers a wide variety of housing types and is amply illustrated.

Burenhult, G. (ed.) *Old World Civilizations: The Rise of Cities and States.* New York: Harper Collins, 1994. An illustrated overview of history and artifacts of the ancient world.

Denyer, Susan. *African Traditional Architecture.* New York: Africana Publishing Company, 1978. General introduction to the vernacular architecture of Africa.

Duly, Colin. *The Houses of Mankind.* London: Thames and Hudson, 1979. Includes a section on Africa.

Fagan, Brian M. *The Seventy Great Mysteries of the Ancient World.* London: Thames and Hudson, 2001. For anyone curious about the unanswered questions surrounding early civilizations and peoples, this is a treat. Summaries of current knowledge are presented straightforwardly by international experts.

Guidoni, Enrico. *Primitive Architecture,* trans. Robert Erich Wolf. *History of World Architecture* series. New York: Harry N. Abrams, 1978. Worldwide survey with substantial discussion of traditional architecture in Africa.

Gurney, Oliver Robert. *The Hittites.* London: Folio Society, 1999.

Hawkes, Jacquetta. *The Atlas of Early Man.* New York: St. Martin's Press, 1993. In measured time frames, developments across the world are presented through text, maps, and drawings.

Hawkins, Gerald. S. *Stonehenge Decoded.* Garden City: Doubleday, 1965. This is the pioneering study that demonstrated how Stonehenge was used.

Isler, Martin. *Sticks, Stones and Shadows: Building the Egyptian Pyramids.* Norman, OK: University of Oklahoma Press, 2001. Isler looks at practical issues associated with cutting, moving, and placing very large stones, advancing the idea that staircases may have been used instead of ramps in constructing the great pyramids. Compare this book with Arnold's study.

Lerner, Mark. *The Complete Pyramids.* New York: Thames and Hudson, 1997. Well-illustrated and concise text on all aspects of the pyramids, from religion to construction.

Lloyd, Seton, Hans Wolfgang Müller, and Roland Martin. *Ancient Architecture: Mesopotamia, Egypt, Crete, Greece.* New York: Abrams, 1973. Dry text but good illustrations, especially for reconstructions of now-ruined buildings.

Mellaart, James. *Catal Hüyük: A Neolithic Town in Anatolia.* New York: McGraw-Hill, 1967. Mellaart led the excavations at Catal Hüyük, and this book presents what he found there.

Nnanmdi, Elleh. *African Architecture: Evolution and Transformation.* New York: McGraw-Hill, 1997. A reasonably comprehensive survey that includes a variety of building types.

Oliver, Paul. *Shelter in Africa.* New York: Praeger Publishers, 1971. Very useful but the coverage is spotty, subject to the interests of the contributor.

Renfrew, Colin. *Before Civilization.* Harmondsworth, England: Penguin, 1973.

Rudofsky, Bernard. *Architecture Without Architects.* New York: Doubleday, 1964. Discussed in the text.

Smith, Earl Baldwin. *Egyptian Architecture as Cultural Expression.* Watkins Glen: American Life Foundation, 1968. Somewhat dated text, but the line illustrations are well done.

Smith, W.S. *The Art and Architecture of Ancient Egypt.* New Haven, CT: Yale University Press, 1998.

Soffer, Olga. *The Upper Paleolithic of the Central Russian Plain.* Orlando, FL: Academic Press, 1985. One of the few sources in English on the prehistoric settlements in Ukraine.

Wilkinson, Richard H. *The Complete Temples of Ancient Egypt.* New York: Thames and Hudson, 2000. Covers not only the temples themselves, but also places these monuments in context of history, religion, and society. Excellent illustrations.

## Chapter 2

Camp, John M. *The Athenian Agora: Excavations in the Heart of Classical Athens.* New York: Thames and Hudson, 1998. Clear documentation of the Agora's development from earliest times through the Roman period, based on work undertaken by the American School of Classical Studies in Athens, with plans and reconstruction views for buildings no longer extant.

Coulton, J.J. *Ancient Greek Architects at Work.* Ithaca, NY: Cornell University Press, 1977.

Hoepfner, Wolfram and Ernst-Ludwig Schwandner. *Haus und Stadt im klassischen Griechland.* Munich: Deutscher Kunstverlag, 1994. Although written in German, this book is still valuable for its extensive illustrations. It is the most recent book to report on field work at sites associated with the Classical city-states.

Lawrence, Arnold Walter. *Greek Architecture.* New Haven, CT: Yale University Press, 1996. Part of what was originally the generally excellent Pelican series on the history of art.

Marinatos, Nanno. *Minoan Religion: Ritual, Image, and Symbol.* Columbia, SC: University of South Carolina Press, 1993. Excellent study of Minoan religious practice, impeccably researched and clearly presented.

Rhodes, Robin Francis. *Architecture and Meaning on the Athenian Acropolis.* Cambridge, England: Cambridge University Press, 1995. A lively examination of the cultural references incorporated in the architecture on the Acropolis.

Robertson, Donald Struan. *Greek and Roman Architecture.* Cambridge, England: Cambridge University Press, 1969. Dry but thorough.

Scully, Vincent. *The Earth, the Temple, and the Gods.* New Haven, CT: Yale University Press, 1979. Studies at a somewhat intuitive level of the specific relationship of individual Greek temples to their settings.

Tzonis, Alexander and Phoebe Giannisi. *Classical Greek Architecture: The Construction of the Modern.* Flammarion, 2004. A comprehensive study in which the authors attempt to shed new light on engrained perceptions of often-studied structures.

Wycherley, Richard Ernest. *How the Greeks Built Cities.* New York: Norton, 1976.

## Chapter 3

Deva, Krishna. *Khajuraho.* New Delhi: Archaeological Survey of India, 2002. Well-illustrated account of the temples at Khajuraho, setting the monuments in cultural and historic perspective.

Grover, Satish. *Buddhist and Hindu Architecture in India.* New Delhi: CBS Publishers and Distributors, 2003. A general text, written for Indian architecture students. Good diagrams and clear explanations of culture and terms.

Huntington, Susan L. *The Art of Ancient India: Buddhist, Hindu, Jain.* New York: Weatherhill, 1985. A summary text for art as well as architecture.

Johnson, Gordon, general editor. *The New Cambridge History of India: Architecture and Art of the Deccan Sultanates.* Cambridge: Cambridge University Press, 1999. A huge project intended to eventually include more than thirty volumes. Those already published include Catherine Asher's *Architecture of Mughal India* and George Mitchell's *Architecture and Art of Southern India.* Coverage extends to the present day and includes social and economic issues as well as architecture.

Michell, George. *The Hindu Temple: An Introduction to Its Meaning and Forms.* Chicago, IL: University of Chicago Press, 1988. Clearly written volume that provides religious and cultural background needed to understand Hindu temple design.

Michell, George and Mark Zebrowski. *The New Cambridge History of India: Architecture and Art of the Deccan Sultanates.* Cambridge: Cambridge University Press, 1999.

Miksic, John. *Borobudur: Golden Tales of the Buddhas.* London: Bamboo Publishing, 1990. Handsome illustrations of and extensive narration on the architecture and iconography of the monument.

Rowland, Benjamin. *Art and Architecture of India: Buddhist, Hindu, Jain.* Harmondsworth, England: Penguin, 1953. One of the generally excellent volumes in the Pelican History of Art series.

Stierlin, Henri. *Hindu India: From Khajuraho to the Temple City of Madurai.* Cologne: Taschen, 1998. Part of a projected forty-volume set on world architecture, this book contains many color illustrations to support the text.

Tadgell, Christopher. *The History of Architecture in India: From the Dawn of Civilization to the End of the Raj.* London: Architecture Design and Technology Press, 1990. A more complex text than some, this book has good illustrations.

**Chapter 4**

Boyd, Andrew. *Chinese Architecture and Town Planning, 1500 BC—AD 1911.* Chicago, IL: University of Chicago Press, 1962. This volume is older than most, but its text is still worth reading closely. As "a very small book on a very large subject," it carries off the presentation exceptionally well.

Bussagli, Mario. *Oriental Architecture. History of World Architecture* series. New York: Harry N. Abrams, 1973. Another volume in the *History of World Architecture* series, this book covers not only China, Japan, and India, but also Sri Lanka, Vietnam, Cambodia, Thailand, Tibet, and Korea, among others.

Chinese Academy of Architecture. *Ancient Chinese Architecture.* Hong Kong: Joint Publishing Company and Beijing: China Building Industry Press, 1982. Remarkable for demonstrating how the writing of history can also be a political statement. Good color photographs are juxtaposed with a collectively written text intended for English-speaking audiences. Among other things, readers are informed that "[t]he Great Wall is a masterpiece of ancient China. It manifests the tough, determined, and unwavering spirit of the Chinese, and the brightness of the wisdom of the working people."

Chinese Academy of Sciences, Institute of the History of Natural Sciences. *History and Development of Ancient Chinese Architecture.* Beijing: Science Press, 1986. A massive book, methodically treating the subject with concise text, clear illustrations, and a minimum of political commentary. It includes separate coverage of buildings by China's ethnic minorities.

Frankfort, Henri, Michael Roaf and Donald Matthews. *The Art and Architecture of the Ancient Orient.* New Haven, CT: Yale University Press, 1996.

Isozaki, Arata. *Katsura Villa: Space and Form.* New York: Rizzoli, 1987. A thoughtful text with extensive and beautiful photography.

Jinghua, Ru and Peng Hualiang. *Palace Architecture. Ancient Chinese Architecture.* Vienna: Springer-Verlag, 1998. A volume in the extensive *Ancient Chinese Architecture* series. Beautifully illustrated.

Kawashima, Chuji. *Minka: Traditional Houses of Rural Japan.* Tokyo: Kodansha International, 1986. Clearly written and handsomely illustrated study of the great variety of minka, with particular attention paid to construction techniques and design features.

Liu, Laurence G. *Chinese Architecture.* New York: Rizzoli, 1989. A well-written account supplemented with clear photographs and plans.

Nishi, Kazuo and Kazuo Hozumi. *What Is Japanese Architecture?* Tokyo: Kodansha International, 1985. A concise text illustrated with line drawings showing the basic characteristics of traditional Japanese buildings.

Qijun, Wang. *Vernacular Dwellings. Ancient Chinese Architecture.* Vienna: Springer-Verlag, 2000. Another volume in the *Ancient Chinese Architecture* series.

Suzuki, Kakichi. *Early Buddhist Architecture in Japan.* New York: Kodansha International, 1980.

Tange, Kenzo and Noboru Kawazoe. *Ise: Prototype of Japanese Architecture.* Cambridge, MA: M.I.T. Press, 1965. Features beautiful photographs by Yoshio Watanabe taken after the 1953 rebuilding of the shrines and offers views not normally available. Separate essays by Tange and Kawazoe cover architecture and cultural context.

Xinian, Fu, Guo Daiheng, Liu Xujie, et al, Nancy S. Steinhardt, ed. *Chinese Architecture. The Culture and Civilization of China* series. New Haven and Beijing: Yale University Press and New World Press, 2002. The best available general survey of architecture in China.

Zhu, Jianfei. *Chinese Spatial Strategies: Imperial Beijing.* London: RoutledgeCurzon, 2004. A specialized study based on a dissertation, this book explains Chinese planning in terms of court life, rituals, authority, etc.

**Chapter 5**

Grant, Michael. *Cities of Vesuvius.* Harmondsworth, England: Penguin, 1976.

MacDonald, William L. *The Architecture of the Roman Empire.* New Haven, CT: Yale University Press, 1982.

——— *The Pantheon: Design, Meaning, and Progeny.* Cambridge, MA: Harvard University Press, 1976.

——— and John A. Pinto. *Hadrian's Villa and Its Legacy.* New Haven, CT: Yale University Press, 1995. This is a very readable account of the villa and its place in architectural history.

Packer, James E. *The Forum of Trajan in Rome: A Study of the Monuments.* Berkeley, CA: University of California Press, 1997. A monumental, three-volume study of this forum, including new restoration drawings based on excavations.

Richardson, Lawrence. *Pompeii: An Architectural History.* Baltimore, MD: Johns Hopkins University Press, 1988.

Sear, Frank. *Roman Architecture.* Ithaca, NY: Cornell University Press, 1992. A useful text with good illustrations, this book includes substantial coverage of Roman works outside Italy, in Africa, the Middle East, and Europe.

Taylor, Rabun. *Roman Builders: A Study in Architectural Process.* Cambridge: Cambridge University Press, 2003. A detailed study that takes the reader sequentially through the Roman building process using selected structures such as the Colosseum and Pantheon. Considerable speculation about the Roman use of construction cranes.

Vitruvius, M. *The Ten Books on Architecture.* New York: Dover, 1960. English translation of the only complete surviving architectural treatise from antiquity.

Ward-Perkins, John B. *Roman Imperial Architecture.* Harmondsworth, England: Penguin, 1981.

**Chapter 6**

Brumfield, William Craft. *A History of Russian Architecture.* Cambridge, England: Cambridge University Press, 1993. Text and photographs covering all aspects of Russian architecture, including the churches considered here.

Krautheimer, Richard. *Early Christian and Byzantine Architecture.* Harmondsworth: Penguin, 1986. Part of the generally excellent Pelican History of Art series.

——— *Rome: Profile of a City, 312–1308.* Princeton, NJ: Princeton University Press, 1980. A fascinating account of Rome from the Early Christian period through the medieval period.

Lowden, John. *Early Christian and Byzantine Art.* London: Phaidon Press, 1997. A beautifully illustrated and lucid book that covers selected monuments in detail, placing them firmly in their historical context.

Mainstone, Rowland J. *Hagia Sophia: Architecture, Structure, and Liturgy of Justinian's Great Church.* New York: Thames and Hudson, 2001. A detailed examination of this masterpiece church. Clear text and ample illustrations.

Opolovnikov, Alexander and Yelena Opolovnikova. *The Wooden Architecture of Russia: Houses, Fortifications, Churches.* New York: Abrams, 1989. The best available source in English for information about wooden buildings in Russia, which vastly outnumber structures in masonry.

**Chapter 7**

Aftullah, Kuran. *Sinan: The Grand Old Master of Ottoman Architecture.* Istanbul and Washington, D.C: Institute of Turkish Studies and ADA Press, 1987. A complete study of the architect who took Hagia Sophia as a point of departure for designing Istanbul's domed mosques.

Armstrong, Karen. *Islam, A Short History.* New York: The Modern Library, 2002. A short, readable account of the history and current status of Islam in the world.

Dazhang, Sun. *Ancient Chinese Architecture: Islamic Buildings.* New York: Springer-Verlag, 2003. A beautiful book that covers Islamic work not addressed in this chapter.

Esposito, John L., ed. *The Oxford History of Islam.* Oxford: Oxford University Press, 1999. A reliable reference source.

Grabar, Oleg. *The Alhambra.* Cambridge, MA: Harvard University Press, 1978. Even though almost 30 years old and without color images, this book places the Alhambra in its broader context.

Hillenbrand, Robert. *Islamic Architecture.* New York: Columbia University Press, 1994. Comprehensive study by categories: mosques, minarets, mausoleums, caravanserai, and palaces.

Hoag, John D. *Islamic Architecture.* New York: Harry N. Abrams, 1977. Thorough and well illustrated coverage of North Africa, Spain, the Middle East, Egypt, Turkey, and India.

Jairazbhoy, R.A. *An Outline of Islamic Architecture.* New York: Asia Publishing House, 1972.

Kostoff, Spiro. *A History of Architecture: Settings and Rituals.* New York: Oxford University Press, 1995. See pages 454–68 on Istanbul.

Mitchell, George, ed. *Architecture of the Islamic World and Its History and Social Meaning.* New York: William Morrow, 1978. This survey of building types includes sections on craftsmen, construction methods, decoration, and traditional housing.

Petersen, Andrew. *Dictionary of Islamic Architecture*. New York: Routledge, 1999. Only lightly illustrated but a very useful companion to narrative histories.

Stierllin, Henri. *Islam*, vol. 1: *Early Architecture From Baghdad to Corboda*, Cologne: Taschen, 1996. A volume in Taschen's *World Architecture* series. It covers Islamic architecture from its inception through to the thirteenth century.

Yeomans, Richard. *The Story of Islamic Architecture*. New York: New York University Press, 1999. Large format with plenty of color illustrations.

## Chapter 8

Braunfels, Wolfgang. *Monasteries of Western Europe: The Architecture of the Orders*. Princeton, NJ: University Press, 1980. Clear explanation of Western monasticism and its architectural manifestations.

Calkins, Robert. *Medieval Architecture in Western Europe*. New York: Oxford University Press, 1998. A readable and comprehensive guide to architecture from 330 to 1500.

Conant, Kenneth John. *Carolingian and Romanesque Architecture, 800–1200*. New Haven, CT: Yale University Press, 1978. A basic guide to this period, originally part of the excellent Pelican History of Art series.

——— *Cluny: Les églises et la maison du chef d'ordre*. Macon: Imprimerie Protat Freres, 1968. The culmination of a lifetime of scholarly work. Although the text is in French, the extensive illustrations are universally understandable.

Horn, Walter, and Ernest Born. *The Plan of St. Gall*. Berkeley, CA: University of California Press, 1979. A model of research and scholarship, this beautiful three-volume work traces the impact of antique building on Carolingian architecture and the influence of the Plan of St. Gall on later buildings.

Kinder, Terryl N. *Cistercian Europe: Architecture of Contemplation*. Grand Rapids, MI: Cistertian Publications, 2002. Specialized study of one of the principal monastic organization of the Middle Ages. Splendid illustrations.

Kubach, Hans Erich. *Romanesque Architecture*. New York: Abrams, 1975. An extensive review of Romanesque architecture.

Male, Emile. *Religious Art in France: The Twelfth Century*. Princeton, NJ: Princeton University Press, 1978. An excellent guide to understanding the medieval mind and religious symbolism in Romanesque sculpture.

Shaver-Crandell, Annie and Paula Gerson. *The Pilgrim's Guide to Santiago de Compostela: A Gazetteer*. London: Harvey Miller, 1995. Includes a translation of the twelfth-century "Pilgrim's Guide" and an alphabetical guide to the sites as they would have appeared to a contemporary traveler.

Stalley, Roger. *Early Medieval Architecture*. New York: Oxford University Press, 1999. Lucid text, good photographs: highly recommended.

## Chapter 9

Beresford, Maurice and John Hurst. *Wharram Percy: Deserted Medieval Village*. New Haven, CT: Yale University Press, 1991. For anyone interested in the ordinary buildings of the medieval period, this book serves as a readable introduction to the complex and tentative nature of our knowledge of non-monumental architectural history.

Bony, Jean. *French Gothic Architecture of the Twelfth and Thirteenth Centuries*. Berkeley, CA: University of California Press, 1983. Notable for its thorough treatment of Gothic churches in France, together with clear photographs and many building plans.

Coldstream, Nicola. *Medieval Craftsmen: Masons and Sculptors*. London: British Museum Press, 1991. A concise summary of the builders and building processes of medieval times.

Erlande-Brandenburg, Alain. *Cathedrals and Castles: Building in the Middle Ages*. New York: Harry N. Abrams, 1995. Well-illustrated account of the entire medieval building process, including translations of selected historic documents related to building sites and construction matters.

James, John. *Chartres: The Masons Who Built a Legend*. London: Routledge and Kegan Paul, 1982. James's detailed studies of the physical fabric of Chartres lead him to conclude that eight teams of master masons worked simultaneously on different parts of the cathedral. His thesis is not universally accepted, but his book provokes thought.

Mark, Robert. *Experiments in Gothic Structure*. Cambridge, MA: M.I.T. Press, 1982. The author considers engineering problems posed by Gothic buildings through analysis of models using polarized light.

Taylor, Arnold. *The Welsh Castles of Edward I*. London: Hambledon Press, 1986. A concise account from documentary sources of the construction of seventeen castles in Wales, this book demonstrates what surviving records tell us about the process of castle-building.

White, John. *Art and Architecture in Italy, 1250 to 1400*. New Haven, CT: Yale University Press, 1993. Originally part of the excellent Pelican series on the History of Art, this volume is particularly interesting for its extended summary of the debates over the design of Milan Cathedral.

Wilson, Christopher. *The Gothic Cathedral: The Architecture of the Great Church, 1130–1530*. New York: Thames and Hudson, 1992. Discusses cathedrals and large churches across Europe, including lesser-known examples.

## Chapter 10

Andrews, G.F. *Maya Cities: Placemaking and Urbanization*. Norman, OK: University of Oklahoma Press, 1975. Contains an introductory section on city components, then a city-by-city survey.

Broda, Johanna, David Carrasco, and Eduardo Matos Moctezuma. *The Great Temple of Tenochtitlán: Center and Periphery in the Aztec World*. Berkeley: University of California Press, 1987. These essays by scholars in different disciplines offer interpretations of the principal Aztec shrine.

Driver, H.E. *Indians of North-America*, 2nd revised edition. Chicago, IL: University of Chicago Press, 1969. Broad discussion of Indian cultures.

Gasparini, G. and L. Margolis. *Inca Architecture*. Bloomington, IN: Indiana University Press, 1980. A good place to begin when doing research on the Incas. Abundant images accompany the text.

Heyden, D. and P. Gendrop. *Pre-Columbian Architecture of Meso-America*. New York: Abrams, 1975. Part of the Abrams series on Western architecture. It covers Mexico and Central America and is filled with black-and-white photographs and drawings.

Kosok, P. *Life, Land and Water in Ancient Peru*. New York: Long Island University Press, 1965. This book emphasizes the Inca manipulation of the land, especially their extraordinary systems of irrigation. It includes material culture as well as architecture.

Miller, Mary E. *Maya Art and Architecture*. New York: Thames and Hudson, 1996. Covers sculpture, mural painting, ceramics and small objects, as well as architecture.

Moctezuma, Eduardo Matos and Felipe Solis Olguin, eds. *Aztecs*. London: Royal Academy Books, 2003. Beautifully illustrated exhibition catalog that concentrates on the art of royalty.

Morgan, W.N. *Ancient Architecture of the Southwest*. Austin, TX: University of Texas Press, 1994. Covers Native American sites in Utah, Colorado, Arizona, and New Mexico. Maps and some drawings, but no photographs.

Moseley, Michael. *The Incas and Their Ancestors: the Archaeology of Peru*. London: Thames and Hudson, 1992. Broad survey that places the architecture in a larger cultural context.

Nabokov, P. and R. Easton. *Native American Architecture*. New York: Oxford, 1989. An excellent survey with plenty of photographs and drawings. This is the first book to look at for an introduction to Native American building in North America.

Robertson, D. *Pre-Columbian Architecture*. New York: Braziller, 1963. A short but very useful look at ancient building practices from Mexico to Peru.

Various editors. *Handbook of North American Indians*. 17 vols. Washington, D.C.: Smithsonian Institution, beginning 1978. Offers in-depth information on Native-American cultures. Volumes 4–11, 15 and 17 have so far appeared.

von Hagen, Adriana and Craig Morris. *The Cities of the Ancient Andes*. London: Thames and Hudson, 1998. Comprehensive, well illustrated survey of Inca and pre-Inca cultures.

## Chapter 11

Ackerman, J.S. *Palladio*. New York: Penguin, 1986. A very readable account by the foremost American scholar on Palladio.

——— *The Architecture of Michelangelo*. Baltimore: Penguin, 1971. A thoroughly illustrated account of Michelangelo's building designs.

Alberti, L.B. *On the Art of Building in Ten Books*. Cambridge, MA: M.I.T. Press, 1988. Alberti's fifteenth-century treatise expressing his ideas and theories about architecture.

Bruschi, Arnaldo. *Bramante*. London: Thames and Hudson: 1977. A focused, understandable and well-illustrated study. The line drawings are particularly useful.

Burckhardt, J. *The Architecture of the Italian Renaissance*. London: John Murray, 1985. A classic text first published in 1860. Much of the information has been superseded, but a comparison with later works provides insights into changing attitudes about the period.

Heydenreich, L.H. and W. Lotz. *Architecture in Italy, 1400 to 1600.* Harmondsworth, England: Penguin, 1974. Another volume in the useful and workmanlike Pelican *History of Art* series.

Howard, Deborah and Sarah Quill. *The Architectural History of Venice.* New Haven, CT: Yale University Press, 2002. A readable account of the broader architectural trends in a city that participated in Eastern as well as Western traditions.

Murray, P. *Renaissance Architecture.* New York: Abrams, 1971. Peter Murray offers the best general survey of Renaissance buildings. The text is accessible to the undergraduate and is supported by ample illustrations.

Norberg-Schulz, C. *Intentions in Architecture.* Cambridge, MA: M.I.T. Press, 1965. Architectural history written from the existential point of view.

Palladio, A. *The Four Books of Architecture.* New York: Dover, 1965. Palladio's highly influential treatise that includes illustrations of his own work.

Saalman, H. *Filippo Brunelleschi: The Buildings.* University Park, PA: Pennsylvania State University Press, 1993. Saalman wrote extensively on Brunelleshi throughout his career, eventually yielding this thorough account.

Serlio, S. *The Five Books of Architecture.* New York: Dover, 1982. The first Renaissance treatise to contain a significant number of illustrations.

Shepherd, J.C. and Geoffrey Alan Jellicoe. *Italian Gardens of the Renaissance.* New York: Princeton Architectural Press, 1993. The beautiful watercolor plans and sections alone make this book worth thumbing through.

Summerson, J. *Inigo Jones.* Harmondsworth, England: Penguin, 1966. The literature on Jones is almost uniformly dull. Much of this can be traced to inadequate knowledge of his life. Summerson's account is the most readable.

Wittkower, R. *Architectural principles in the Age of Humanism.* London: Academy, 1988. Theories of proportion from Alberti to Palladio. A strong influence on twentieth-century archiecture.

## Chapter 12

Blunt, A. *Art and Architecture in France, 1500–1700.* New Haven, CT: Yale University Press, 1999. Sir Anthony Blunt is equally known as an architectural historian, as director of the Courtauld Institute of Art, and as a Communist spy. Originally another volume in the Pelican *History of Art* series.

——— *Borromini.* Harmondsworth, England: Penguin, 1979. A good place to begin on Borromini for whom much of the literature has not been translated from the Italian.

Braham, A. *François Mansart.* London: Zwemmer, 1973. While Braham's separating of this work into a volume of text and a volume of illustrations makes using them slightly inconvenient, they are well researched and well written.

Hibbard, H. *Bernini.* Harmondsworth, England: Penguin, 1965. A short but useful text.

Meek, H. A. *Guarino Guarini and His Architecture.* New Haven, CT: Yale University Press, 1988. A relatively brief and to the point study of this architect-engineer.

Norberg-Schulz, C. *Baroque Architecture.* New York: Abrams, 1971.

——— C. *Late Baroque and Rococo Architecture.* New York: Abrams, 1971. These volumes cover all aspects of Baroque architecture throughout Europe. The two offer the best starting point for undergraduate research on the subject.

Pommer, R. *Eighteenth-Century Architecture in Piedmont.* New York: New York University Press, 1967. Pommer treats Guarini, Vittone, and Juvarra in their development of Late Baroque architecture in Italy.

Portoghesi, P. *Rome of Borromini; Architecture as Language.* New York: Braziller, 1967. Portoghesi is not the most readable source on Borromini, but the illustrations, especially Borromini's drawings, are splendid.

Summerson, J. *Architecture in Britain 1530–1830.* New Haven, CT: Yale University Press, 1993. Sir John Summerson wrote particularly well. All of his books, article and essays are worth spending some time with. Originally part of the Pelican *History of Art* series.

Walton, G. *Louis XIV's Versailles.* Chicago, IL: University of Chicago Press, 1986. Just as there are monographs on individual architects, there are works dedicated to individual buildings. Intended for the non-specialist, this book tries to explain why Versailles took the form that it did.

Wittkower, Rudolf, Joseph Connors and Jennifer Montagu. *Art and Architcture in Italy, 1600–1750.* New Haven, CT: Yale University Press, 1999. Originally another volume in the comprehensive Pelican *History of Art* series. Wittkower was one of the most

eminent European scholars to emigrate to America as a result of events leading to World War II.

## Chapter 13

Bergdoll, Barry. *European Architecture, 1750–1890. Oxford History of Art.* Oxford: Oxford University Press, 2000. A volume in the *Oxford History of Art* series. Clearly written and well illustrated. Perhaps the best current survey of the period.

Braham, A. *The Architecture of the French Enlightenment.* Berkeley, CA: University of California Press, 1980. The most comprehensive and up-to-date source for French Neo-Classicism in the eighteenth century.

Honour, H. *Neo-Classicism.* Harmondsworth, England: Penguin, 1977. Honour emphasizes painting and sculpture, but includes architecture in what he intended as a study of "all manifestations of the Neoclassical style."

Kalnein, W.G. and M. Levy. *Art and Architecture in Eighteenth-Century France.* Harmondsworth, England: Penguin, 1972. Penguin's effort to deal with the eighteenth century offers significant doses of painting, sculpture, and architecture.

Kaufmann, E. *Architecture in the Age of Reason: Baroque and Post-Baroque in England, Italy, and France.* New York: Dover, 1968. Kaufmann was the first scholar to write comprehensively on the period. Others have superseded him in many areas, but his book is still worth studying.

## Chapter 14

Benton, Charlotte, Tim Benton, and Ghislaine Wood, eds. *Art Deco, 1910–1939.* London: V&A Publications, 2003. A series of essays collected to accompany an exhibition at the Victoria and Albert Museum in London.

Clark, K. *The Gothic Revival: An Essay in the History of Taste.* London: J. Murray, 1962.

Condit, Carl. *American Building Art—The Nineteenth Century.* New York: Oxford University Press, 1960. A survey of developments in wood framing, iron framing, iron bridge construction, and concrete.

——— *The Chicago School of Architecture: A History of Commercial and Public Building in the Chicago Area, 1875–1925.* Chicago, IL: University of Chicago Press, 1990s. A place to start in understanding the development of the Chicago School skyscraper.

Drexler, A. (ed.). *The Architecutre of the Ecole des Beaux-Arts.* Cambridge, MA: M.I.T. Press, 1977. Published to coincide with an exhibition at the Museum of Modern Art in New York City, this volume includes a series of essays and reproductions of many drawings made by the Ecole's students.

Greenhalgh, Paul, ed. *Art Nouveau, 1890–1914.* London: V&A Publications, 2000. A series of essays collected to accompany an exhibition at the Victoria and Albert Museum in London.

Hitchcock, H.R. *Architecture: Nineteenth and Twentieth Centuries.* New Haven, CT: Yale University Press, 1987. An encyclopedic survey, long on description and short on analysis. Many photographs. Originally a volume in the Pelican *History of Art* series.

Middleton, R. and D. Watkin. *Neoclassicism and 19th-Century Architecture.* London: Faber, 1987. The best place to begin for a survey of Neo-Classicism throughout Europe.

Scully, V. *The Shingle Style and the Stick Style.* New Haven, CT: Yale University Press, 1971. Written as Scully's doctoral dissertation, this lively volume sheds much light on the complex architectural developments in late nineteenth-century America. It deals primarily with domestic buildings.

Stanton, P. *Pugin.* New York: Viking, 1971. Some have traced the roots of Modernism to the kind of passionate search for truth or at least honesty promoted by Gothic Revivalist Augustus Welby Northmore Pugin.

Twombly, R. *Louis Sullivan: His Life and Work.* New York: Viking, 1986. One of many monographs on the man that Frank Lloyd Wright called his master.

Woods, Mary N. *From Craft to Profession: The Practice of Architecture in Nineteenth-Century America.* Berkeley: University of California Press, 1999. A discussion of the American architectural profession from the time of Benjamin Henry Latrobe at the end of the 18th century to the present.

## Chapter 15

Banham, R. *Theory and Design in the First Machine Age.* New York: Praeger, 1967. Early revisionist writing on Modernism, challenging the arguments made by such scholars as Pevsner and Giedion.

Benevolo, L. *History of Modern Architecture.* Cambridge, MA: M.I.T.

Press, 1971. Comprehensive history by an author who emphasizes city planning and urban development.

Boesiger, W. (ed.). *Le Corbusier and Pierre Jeanneret: Oeuvre Complète*. Zurich: Girsberger, 1935–65. These volumes provide the opportunity to view a life's work by one of the principal European Modernists.

Collins, P. *Changing Ideals in Modern Architecture, 1750–1950*. Montreal: McGill-Queens University Press, 1998. A book about ideas that have influenced modern architecture, so few illustrations.

Colquhoun, Alan. *Modern Architecture. Oxford History of Art*. Oxford: Oxford University Press, 2002. Another volume in the *Oxford History of Art* series. Covers the period from the Art Nouveau through the 1960s.

Doordan, Dennis P. *Twentieth-Century Architecture*. Upper Saddle River, NJ and New York: Prentice Hall and Harry N. Abrams, 2002. A concise, readable, well-illustrated survey.

Frampton, K. *Modern Architecture: A Critical History*. London: Thames and Hudson, 2003. A thoughtful, comprehensive survey, but a little dense for anyone just beginning a study of the period.

Giedion, S. *Space, Time, and Architecture*. Cambridge, MA: Harvard University Press, 1980. A classic of polemical writing that purports to examine the roots of Modernism. Giedeon hobnobbed with many of the great architectural talents of the mid-twentieth century and was an unabashed proponent of European Modernism.

Gropius, Walter. *The New Architecture and the Bauhaus*. London: Faber and Faber, 1965. In this book first published in 1937, Gropius relates the radical experiment in design education at the Bauhaus to the "new architecture" then being produced in Europe.

Hayden, Delores. *Building Suburbia: Green Fields and Urban Growth 1820–2000*. New York: Pantheon Books, 2003. A critique of the sprawling residential development that has accompanied the disintegration of the modern American city.

Hitchcock, H.R. *In the Nature of Materials: The Buildings of Frank Lloyd Wright, 1887–1941*. New York: Duell, Sloan, and Pierce, 1942. The literature on Wright is almost endless. This book, by a scholar who wrote on a broad variety of architectural-history topics, accompanied an exhibition on Wright at the Museum of Modern Art in 1940.

——— and P. Johnson. *The International Style: Architecture Since 1922*. New York: Norton, 1932. This small book accompanied the exhibition of European and American Modernism mounted at the Museum of Modern Art in New York City. A 1995 edition is now also available.

Jordy, W.H. *American Buildings and Their Architects: The Impact of European Modernism in the Mid-Twentieth Century*. Garden City, NY: Anchor Press/Doubleday, 1976. A readable author's interpretation of Modernism in America through the close study of six seminal buildings.

Le Corbusier. *Towards a New Architecture*. New York: Praeger, 1972. Le Corbusier's ideas about architecture, first published in 1923.

Le Corbusier, Pierre Jeanneret, Willy Boesiger, Oscar Stonorov and Max Bill. *Oeuvre Complète*. Zurich: Editions d'Architecture Erienbach, 1946–1970 (8 vols). Le Corbusier's publication of his work showing his drawing style.

Paperny, Vladimir. *Architecture in the Age of Stalin: Culture Two*, trans. by John Hill and Roann Barris. Cambridge: Cambridge University Press, 2002. While not ideal for the beginning student, this text does explore architecture in a setting that has long been ignored.

Pevsner, Nicholas. *Pioneers of Modern Design: From William Morris to Walter Gropius*. Harmondsworth, England: Penguin, 1975. When this book was first published in 1936, Pevsner was among the first to look for the sources of European Modernism. While he later admitted that he should have been more inclusive, his small book does illuminate many of the principles that Modernists held dear.

Schulze, F. *Mies van der Rohe: A Critical Biography*. Chicago, IL: University of Chicago Press, 1985. A thorough study but with limited illustrations.

Sharp, D. *Modern Architecture and Expressionism*. New York: Braziller, 1966. The first work to focus on a large part of twentieth-century architectural production that was not intensely "rational" and so at odds with the fundamental tenets of Modernism.

Tafuri, M. and F. Dal Co. *Modern Architecture*. New York: Rizzoli, 1986. Modernism interpreted from the Marxist perspective.

Wingler, Hans Maria and Joseph Stein. *The Bauhaus: Weimar, Dessau, Berlin, Chicago*. Cambridge, MA: M.I.T. Press, 1983. A history of the Bauhaus in its various manifestations. Large format with abundant illustrations.

Wright, F.L. *Modern Architecture*. Princeton, NJ: Princeton University Press, 1931. Some of Wright's ideas about architecture and his answer to the polemics of Le Corbusier.

Note: Also see monographs on individual architects.

**Chapter 16**

Curtis, William J.R. *Modern Architecture Since 1900*. London: Phaidon, 1996. An excellent, very readable, well-illustrated world-wide survey with many color images.

Drexler, A. (ed.). *Five Architects: Eisenman, Graves, Gwathmey, Hejduk, Meier*. New York: Oxford University Press, 1975. This thin, overtly promotional publication advanced five careers and gave the false impression that their work was alike.

Jencks, C. *Modern Movements in Architecture*. New York: Penguin, 1985. Charles Jencks explores the demise of Modernism and the then-emerging pluralism that he saw as taking its place.

——— *Late-Modern Architecture*. London: Academy Editions, 1991. Jencks's first effort (when first published in 1980) to pull together his ideas about the "end" of Modernism.

——— *The New Paradigm in Architecture: The Language of Post-Modern Architecture*. New Haven, CT: Yale University Press, 2002. One among many volumes by the high priest of Post-Modernism. Like Sigfried Giedion for Modernism, Jencks has been a tireless promotor as well as a reporter and analyst.

Klotz, H. *The History of Post-Modern Architecture*. Cambridge, MA: M.I.T. Press, 1988. The most complete survey of the various architectural directions that have been lumped into the category of Post-Modernism.

*The Phaidon Atlas of Contemporary World Architecture*. New York: Phaidon Press, 2004. This behemoth includes entries on more than one thousand buildings by over five hundred architects practicing around the world.

Venturi, R. *Complexity and Contradiction in Architecture*. New York: Museum of Modern Art, 1990. Robert Venturi's iconoclastic work (first published in 1966) announced the crumbling of the edifice of Modernism.

Wigley, M. and P. Johnson. *Deconstructivist Architecture*. Boston, MA: Little, Brown, 1988. Published by the Museum of Modern Art in New York City to accompany an exhibition of the same name.

The monographs on individual architects are too numerous to list here, but there are many worthy and well illustrated volumes. Another essential sources is architectural journals such as *Architectural Record* (US) and *The Architectural Review* (UK) and many others published in various countries and languages. Journals are usually the first place where buildings are published after they have been completed, and they are often the only place to find plan, elevation, and section drawings and even site plans.

# PICTURE CREDITS

The authors and Laurence King Publishing Ltd thank the sources of photographs for supplying and granting permission to reproduce them. Every effort has been made to contact all copyright holders, but should there be any errors or omissions Laurence King Publishing Ltd would be pleased to insert the appropriate acknowledgment in any subsequent printing of this publication.

0.01, 0.03, 0.04, 0.06, 0.07, 0.09, 0.10 Marian Moffett; 0.02 Ronald Scott, 0.05 R. Bruce Moffett; 1.00, 1.17 Robert Harding World Imagery; 1.04, 1.07 Marian Moffett; 1.05 Jason Hawkes/Corbis; 1.08 Kimbell Art Museum/Corbis; 1.09 Courtesy of The Oriental Institute of The University of Chicago; 1.13 Hirmer Fotoarchiv; 1.18 R. Bruce Moffett; 1.19 Michael Fazio; 1.21 © Paul M.R. Maeyaert; 1.24 Photo Spectrum/HIP/Scala, Florence; 1.26 Raiford Scott; 1.29 Ancient Art & Architecture Collection; 1.33 Charles & Josette Lenars/Corbis; 1.34 C. Murray Smart, Jr; 2.00 Robert Harding World Imagery; 2.02 Rachel McCann; 2.03 akg-images/Herbert Kraft; 2.04, 2.33 Ancient Art & Architecture Collection; 2.05, 2.13, 2.14 Marian Moffett; 2.08, 2.34 Craig & Marie Mauzy, Athens; 2.10 The Art Archive/Gianni Dagli Orti; 2.11, 2.30 Hirmer Fotoarchiv; 2.20 J William Rudd; 2.21 Kenneth Moffett; 2.23, 2.24, 2.39 Michael Fazio; 2.25 Sonia Halliday Photographs; 2.27 British Museum, London; 2.29 Alison Frantz Archive, American School, Athens; 2.37 J. Allan Cash Ltd, London; 2.41 BPK, Berlin; 3.00, 3.04, 3.06, 3.19 A.F. Kersting; 3.02, 3.21 Robert Harding World Imagery; 3.07, 3.14 Lawrence Wodehouse; 3.10 akg-images/Paul Almasy; 3.12, 3.13 Dinodia; 3.16, 3.17 Ancient Art & Architecture Collection; 3.18 akg-images/Jean-Louis Nou; 3.23 Bob Krist/Corbis; 3.24 Gerald Anderson; 4.00 Liu Liqun/Corbis; 4.02, 4.24, 4.26, 4.30, 4.37 Gerald Anderson; 4.03, 4.04 Orientphoto; 4.07, 4.08, 4.10 Chinapix; 4.15 Robert Harding World Imagery; 4.16, 4.19 Robert Craig; 4.20 Kin Cheung/Reuters/Corbis; 4.22, 4.25, 4.36 Embassy of Japan; 4.23 Ancient Art & Architecture Collection; 4.28 Courtesy of Jingu Administration Office; 4.31 akg-images; 4.33 Lawrence Wodehouse; 4.34 Robert Holmes/Corbis; 5.00 © Paul M.R. Maeyaert; 5.03, 5.31 Alinari; 5.05 Ancient Art & Architecture Collection; 5.08, 5.10, 5.16, 5.18, 5.19, 5.29, 5.34, 5.38 © Vincenzo Pirozzi, Rome; 5.13, Photo Scala, Florence - courtesy of the Ministero Beni e Att. Culturali; 5.15, 5.17 Fototeca Unione; 5.20 © Christie's Images/The Bridgeman Art Library; 5.23 akg-images; 5.28 Lawrence Wodehouse; 5.32, 5.33 Robert Harding World Imagery; 6.00, 6.23, 6.28 akg-images /Erich Lessing; 6.01, 6.02 6.05 6.06, 6.10, 6.11, 6.26, 6.29, 6.30 Marian Moffett; 6.07 Lawrence Wodehouse; 6.08 © Vincenzo Pirozzi, Rome; 6.09 Mary Evans Picture Library; 6.12 Turkish Tourist Office; 6.14 Kenneth Moffett; 6.16 The Art Archive; 6.17, 6.20 A.F. Kersting; 6.18 Alinari; 6.22 Marvin Trachtenberg, New York; 7.00, 07.16, 7.19, 7.35 Robert Harding World Imagery; 7.01 Kazuyoshi Nomachi/Corbis; 7.02, 7.09, 7.20, 7.31 A.F. Kersting; 7.04 Gyori Antoine/Corbis Sygma; 7.05 Zainal Abd Halim/ Reuters/Corbis; 7.08 Charles & Josette Lenars/Corbis; 7.10, 7.11, 7.12 Lawrence Wodehouse; 7.15, 7.17 R. Bruce Moffett; 7.21, 7.24 Sonia Halliday Photographs; 7.23 Vanni / Art Resource, NY; 7.26 Foto Marburg; 7.29 Nevada Wier/Corbis; 7.30 Ludovic/Maisant/ Corbis; 7.37, 7.38 © Paul M. R. Maeyaert; 7.39 Spectrum Colour Library; 7.40 Adam Woolfitt/Corbis; 8.00, 8.02, 8.07, 8.17, 8.20, 8.46, 8.47, 8.48, 8.49, 8.51, 8.52 © Paul M.R. Maeyaert; 8.03 Ancient Art & Architecture Collection; 8.10, 8.12 akg-images/Erich Lessing; 8.04, 8.15, 8.31, 8.32, 8.33, 8.34, 8.38, 8.39, 8.40, 8.44, 8.53, 8.56 Marian Moffett; 8.05 Michael Fazio; 8.13 J. Allan Cash, London; 8.19, 8.25, 8.57 A.F. Kersting; 8.21, 8.54 Bildarchiv Foto Marburg; 8.22 © Studio Fotografico Quattrone, Florence; 8.24 Massimo Listri/Corbis; 8.26, 8.27 Giancarlo Costa; 8.29 Serge Chirol; 8.41, 8.42 Robert Craig; 9.00, 9.04, 9.05, 9.18, 9.25 © Paul M.R. Maeyaert; 9.02, 9.07, 9.22, 9.27, 9.29, 9.30, 9.32, 9.33, 9.36 A.F. Kersting; 9.06, 9.10, 9.17, 9.28, 9.34, 9.38, 9.39, 9.49, 9.51, 9.59, 9.63 Marian Moffett; 9.09 Art Resource; 9.11 Musée de Notre Dame de Paris; 9.12, 9.20, 9.31 Angelo Hornak; 9.16 James Austin; 9.21 Sonia Halliday Photographs; 9.41 Alinari; 9.42 Bridgeman Art Library/Giraudon; 9.48 Corbis; 9.53, 9.55 Kenneth Moffett; 9.57 Francesco Venturi/Corbis; 9.61 akg-images; 9.62 Cameraphoto Arte, Venice; 10.00 A.F. Kersting; 10.02, 10.03, 10.04, 10.11 Smithsonian Institution; 10.05, 10.12, 10.17, 10.18, 10.19, 10.21, 10.22, 10.23, 10.24, 10.25, 10.26, 10.30, 10.39 Michael Fazio; 10.06 Wolfgang Kaehler/Corbis; 10.10 Jamen Berk; 10.15, 10.36 Tony Morrison/South American Pictures; 10.27, 10.28 Ronald Scott; 10.29 Justin Kerr, New York; 10.32 Alamy/Robert Fried; 10.35 Kathy Jarvis/South American Pictures; 10.37 Hulton-Deutsch Collection/Corbis; 10.38 Charles & Josette Lenars/Corbis; 10.40 Jack Dabaghian/Reuters/Corbis; 10.41 EP.0.0.820, collection MRAC Tervuren; photo C. Zagourski / © DACS 2007; 10.42 Scheufler Collection/Corbis; 10.43 Dave G.Houser/Corbis; 10.44 Bettmann/Corbis; 10.46 Robert Harding World Imagery/Alamy; 10.48 musée du quai Branly/Scala, Florence; 10.49 Copyright: Frobenius Institute, Frankfurt am Main; 10.50 Yann Arthus-Bertrand/Corbis; 10.51 David Wall/Alamy; 10.52, 10.55 Robert Harding World Imagery; 10.54 Brian A. Vikander/Corbis; 10.56 Gavin Hellier/JAI/Corbis; 10.57 Michel Gounot/Godong/Corbis; 11.00 akg-images/Erich Lessing; 11.02, 11.09, 11.37 © Studio Fotografico Quattrone, Florence; 11.03, 11.06, 11.25, 11.34, 11.57, 11.69 A.F. Kersting; 11.11, 11.13, 11.14, 11.42, 11.47 Alinari; 11.15, 11.72 Lawrence Wodehouse; 11.16 R. Lieberman and Laurence King Publishing Archives; 11.19 James Austin; 11.22, 11.50, 11.54 Marian Moffett; 11.27, 11.40, 11.62 © Vincenzo Pirozzi, Rome; 11.32, 11.35, 11.46, 11.51, 11.55, 11.73 Michael Fazio; 11.43 James Morris, London; 11.48 Ancient Art & Architecture Collection; 11.58, 11.59 Cameraphoto Arte, Venice; 11.63, 11.64, 11.66, 11.67 Paul M.R. Maeyaert; 11.65 Spectrum Colour Library; 11.71 Country Life Picture Library; 11.75 RCHM; 11.77 Robert Harding World Imagery; 12.00, 12.26, 12.28, 12.34 Paul M.R. Maeyaert; 12.01, 12.12, 12.13, 12.15, 12.17, 12.18, 12.19, 12.21 © Vincenzo Pirozzi, Rome; 12.04 Photo Spectrum/HIP/Scala, Florence; 12.08, 12.31 Michael Fazio; 12.10 Araldo De Luca, Rome; 12.20 Peter Kent; 12.22 akg-images; 12.25 akg-images/Erich Lessing; 12.29 akg-images/Stefan Drechsel; 12.30, 12.33, 12.45, 12.50, 12.52, 12.55 A.F. Kersting; 12.36, 12.40 Pamela Scott; 12.41 Private Collection; 12.42 Roger-Violet; 12.43 J. William Rudd; 12.48 Angelo Hornak; 12.51 RCHM; 13.00, 13.02 A.F. Kersting; 13.04 Lawrence Wodehouse; 13.05 Private Collection; 13.09 Peter Kent; 13.15, 13.16 Pamela Scott; 13.19, 13.21 Roger-Viollet; 13.24 Ronald Scott; 14.00, 14.31, 14.49, 14.60, 14.61 Paul M.R. Maeyaert; 14.01 akg-images/Erich Lessing; 14.02 akg-images, London/Dieter E Hoppe; 14.03 akg-images; 14.06, 14.07 Courtesy John Soane Museum; 14.08, 14.29, 14.34 A.F. Kersting; 14.09, 14.10 Property of the Basilica of the Assumption Historic Trust, Inc; 14.11 The Library of Virginia; 14.13, 14.35, 14.52, 14.56, 14.62 Marian Moffett; 14.14, 14.15, 14.41, 14.53 Michael Fazio; 14.19 Lawrence Wodehouse; 14.20 Leo Sorel; 14.22, 14.25, 14.65 J. William Rudd; 14.23, 14.38, 14.64 Chicago Historical Society; 14.24 New York Historical Society; 14.27 Getty Images; 14.28 Science & Society Picture Library; 14.32, 14.33 James Austin; 14.37 Library of Congress; 14.43, 14.44, 14.58 RCHM; 14.47 Bastin & Evrard/© DACS 2007; 14.48 Bastin & Evrard; 14.50 © Inigo Bujedo Aguirre, London; 14.51, 14.72 R. Lieberman and Laurence King Publishing Archives; 14.54 Glasgow School of Art; 14.59 Bildarchiv Foto Marburg; 14.67, 14.68, 14.69, 14.71 Esto/Wayne Andrews; 14.73 Wayne Andrews; 15.00, 15.70, 15.71 Esto; 15.05 Pamela Scott; 15.07, 15.29, 15.44, 15.48, 15.64, 15.75 Michael Fazio; 15.08, 15.09, 15.11, 15.12a, 15.12b, 15.12c, 15.14, 15.72, 15.74 © ARS, NY and DACS, London 2007; 15.10, 15.62, 15.45 15.56, 15.65, 15.79 Marian Moffett; 15.13 Wayne Andrews; 15.16 Courtesy AEG; 15.20, 15.60, 15.62 © DACS 2007; 15.21 Musée des Arts Décoratifs; 15.22 Canadian Center for Architecture, Montreal; 15.23 akg-images /Stefan Drechsel; 15.24 Courtesy Beurs van Berlage, photo Jan Derwig, Amsterdam; 15.25 Jeff Elder; 15.26 Netherlands Architecture Institute; 15.27, 15.28 Bildarchiv Foto Marburg; 15.30, 15.58, 15.63, 15.67, 15.73 J. William Rudd; 15.31 BPK; 15.32 Plansammlung Technische Universitätsbibliothek, Berlin; 15.33, 15.35 Peter Mauss/Esto; 15.34 Ezra Stoller/Esto; 15.36 Courtesy The Rockefeller Group; 15.37, 15.41 Peter Aaron/Esto; 15.38 Museum of the City of New York; 15.39 Robert Craig; 15.40 Courtesy of the Coca Cola Company; 15.46 Courtesy Centraal Museum, Utrecht; 15.47 Paul M.R. Maeyaert; 15.49, 15.50, 15.51, 15.52, 15.54, 15.77, 15.78, 15.80, 15.82 © FLC/ADAGP, Paris and DACS, London, 2007; 15.54 Peter Kent; 15.55 Reproduced with kind permission of the National Museum of Ireland; 15.57 RMN/©ADAGP, Paris and DACS, London 2007; 15.59 akg-images/Erich Lessing; 15.61 akg-images/Erich Lessing/© DACS 2007; 15.66 G.E. Kidder Smith, New York; 15.68 Chicago Historical Society; 15.69 Lawrence Wodehouse; 15.76 Anderson & Low, London; 15.81 RIBA; 15.83 Mark DeKay; 15.84 Country Life Picture Library; 15.85 ©F.R. Yerbury/ Architectural Association; 15.86 Världsarvet Skogskyrkogården, Kyrkogårdsförvaltningen Stockholms stad; 16.00 © FMGB Guggenheim Bilbao Museoa/ Erika Barahona Ede; 16.01 Colin Dixon/ arcaid.co.uk; 16.02, 16.04, 16.05, 16.07 Courtesy Alvar Aalto Museum; 16.08 photo by Donna Coveney, MIT; 16.10 Kenneth Moffett; 16.11, 16.15, 16.52, 16.55 J. William Rudd; 16.13 Peter Aprahamian/Corbis; 16.14 Steve Rosenthal; 16.16 Kimbell Art Museum, Fort Worth, Texas; 16.18 Robert Craig; 16.19, 16.28 Marian Moffett; 16.20, 16.22 Ezra Stoller; 16.21 Peter Mauss/Esto; 16.23, 16.32, 16.26, 16.66 Michael Fazio; 16.24, 16.41 DIGITAL IMAGE © 2007, The Museum of Modern Art /Scala, Florence; 16.27 Ed Stocklein; 16.29 Eisenman Architects; 16.30, 16.68 Architekturphoto/ arcaid.co.uk; 16.31, 16.69 John Edward Linden/arcaid.co.uk; 16.33, 16.35 Frank Gehry; 16.34, 16.45, 16.53, 16.56, 16.59 © Timothy Hursley; 16.36 The Solomon R. Guggenheim Foundation, New York, photo David Heald; 16.37 Richard Bryant/arcaid.co,.uk; 16.38 Image courtesy of the Office for Metropolitan Architecture (OMA) 1975/© DACS 2007; 16.39 Floto + Warner/ arcaid.co.uk; 16.40, 16.58 Michael Moran; 16.42 © 2007 Barragan Foundation/DACS 2007; 16.43 Mario Botta; 16.44 Centro Galego de Arte Contemporánea; 16.46 Angelo Hornak/Corbis; 16.47 Arata Isozaki & Associates/Yasuhiro Ishimoto; 16.48 Tadao Ando & Associates/Mitsuo Matsuoka; 16.49, 16.70 Joseph Sohm/Visions of America/Corbis; 16.50 akg-images; 16.51 Kelley Mooney Photography/Corbis; 16.57 ©Andy Ryan; 16.60 James Marshall/Corbis; 16.61 Professor Dr Justus Dahinden; 16.62 ©Dennis Gilbert/ VIEW; 16.63 Art on File/Corbis; 16.64 John Donat; 16.67 A.F. Kersting; 16.71 Ian Lambot; 16.72 Rudi Meisel/Architects: Norman Foster + Partners; 16.73 Tibor Bognar/Corbis; 16.74, 16.75, 16.76, 16.77 Max Dupain; 16.79 Anthony Browell; 16.80 Office for Metropolitan Architecture (OMA).

# INDEX

*Page numbers in bold refer to captions.*

Aachen (Germany)
  Charlemagne's palace 178, **178**
  Palatine Chapel 178–80, **179**, **180**, 210
Aalto, Alvar 507–12, **508**, **509**, **510**, **511**, **512**, 516, 517
abambars (urban cisterns) 175
acanthus leaves 55
Acropolis
  Athens 47, **48**, 50–3, **52**, 52–3, 58
  Tepe Gawra, Sumer 16, **16**
  Tikal, Guatemala 263, **264**
Adam, Robert 383, 384–6, **385**, 399
Adena culture 253–5
Adler, Dankmar 444, **444**, 445, **445**, **446**, 448, 449, 455, 456, **456**
adobe structures 257, 269
  Africa 275, 276, **278**, 278, 282
  China 92
AEG Turbine Factory, Berlin (Behrens) 463, **463**
Aegean cultures 35–44
Afghanistan 65
Africa 274–82, 283
  adobe structures 275, 276, 278, **278**, 282
  courtyard houses 276, **276**, 280, **280**
  granaries **277**, 277–8
  palaces 280, 280–1
  tower houses 275, **276**
Agora, Athens 58, **58**
Agra (India), Taj Mahal 168–9, **169**
Aihole (India), Ladkhan Temple 72, **72**, 78
airports (Eero Saarinen) 512–13, **513**
Ajanta (India), cave temples 68
Akbar, Mughal emperor 163
Akbar al-Isfahani, Ali 162
Akhenaten (Amenophis IV), pharaoh 32
Akhetaten (Tell-el-Amarna) (Egypt) 32–3, **33**
Akkadians 16–17
Albers, Josef 485
Alberti, Leon Battista 292–7, 336
  churches 293–4
  ideal city 295–7
  Palazzo Rucellai, Florence 293, **293**
  S. Andrea, Mantua 294, **295**, 336
  S. Francesco, Rimini 5, 293–4, **294**
  S. Maria Novella, Florence 294, **294**
  S. Sebastiano, Mantua 294, 295, **295**
  writings 292–3
Alen, William Van **472**, 472–3
Aleuts, Alaska 255
Alexander the Great 20, 21, 54, 65
Alfeld-an-der-Leine (Germany), Fagus Shoe-Last Factory (Gropius and Meyer) 484, **484**
Alhambra palace, Granada (Spain) **172**, 172–5, **173**, **174**
Alonquin tribes 253
ambulatories 194–5, 198
Amenophis IV see Akhenaten
America, Pre-Columbian 251–74, 282–3
American Heritage Center, University of Wyoming (Predock) 544, **544**
American style 439–48
American Telephone and Telegraph Headquarters, New York (Johnson and Burgee) **520**, 520–1
Amiens Cathedral (France) 412

amphitheaters, Roman 112, 124, **124**, 124–5, **125**
Amsterdam (Holland)
  De Dageraad housing project (de Klerk) 466, **468**
  Eigen Haard housing project (de Klerk) 466, **468**
  Henrietta Ronnerplein (de Klerk) 466
  Libung Bridges (Grimshaw) 560
  Orphanage (Van Eyck) 507
  Stock Exchange (Berlage) 466, **467**
Anasazi see Ancestral Pueblo
Anatolia, Catal Hüyük, prehistoric settlement 10, **10**
Ancestral Pueblo (Anasazi) 257–8
Ancy-le-Franc (France), château (Serlio) 328
Ando, Tadao **539**, 539–40
Angkor Wat (Cambodia) 78, 79
Anglo-Saxon architecture 184, 185–6, 208, 210
Angloulème, Cathedral of St. Pierre **204**
Animal Style ornament 184, 187
Anthemius of Tralles 140, 143
Antoine, Jacques-Denis 392, **393**, 399
Apollodoros of Damascus 115
apses 121, 134
aqueducts, Roman 108–9
Aquitaine (France), Romanesque churches 202–3
Arapaho tribe 252
Arch of Augustus, Perugia 106, **107**
Arch of Constantine, Rome 116, **116**
Archaic period 44–7
arches 2, **3**, 240
  Carolingian, horseshoe **181**, 182
  centering 3
  corbeled 3, **194**, 211, **240**
  diaphragm 192
  Gothic 213, 214
  horseshoe 3, 158, **181**, 182, **240**
  Islamic **4**, 158, 163, **163**
  Lombard bands **194**, 211
  Roman 3, 106, **107**, 108, 115–16, **116**, 290
  Romanesque 198–201, 203, 210
  segmental **240**
  semicircular 3, 188–9, 201, 290
  squinch **240**
  true arch 72, 108
  Tudor **240**
  *see also* pointed arches; triumphal arches
architects 1, 5
  and civil engineering 395
  education 394–5, 399, 413, 448–9 (*see also* Bauhaus)
  Renaissance 285–6
Arctic tribes 255–6
Arles (France), St. Trophîme 205, **205**
Arnolfo di Cambio 287
arris 47
Art Deco 472–5, 493, 505
Art Nouveau 429–37, 445, 449
Artaxerxes 20
Arts and Crafts Movement 425–9, 449, 455
Arup Associates 548, 559, 564
Aryans 65
Asam, Cosmas Damian 361
Asam, Egid Quirin 361
Ashanti (Asante) people (Ghana) 275–6, **276**

ashlar 110
Asklepios, Sanctuary of see Epidauros
Asoka, Indian emperor 65, 67
Asoka columns 65, 67
Aspdin, Joseph 424
Asplund, Eric Gunnar **504**, 504–5, **505**
Assyria and Assyrians 18
Athens 47, 54, 111
  Acropolis 47, **48**, 50–3, **52**, 52–3, 58
  Agora 58, **59**
  bouleterion 58
  Choragic Monument of Lysikrates 55–6, **56**
  Erechtheion 46, **52**, **53**, 53–4, 56
  Great Panathenaic Procession 51, **51**
  Hephaisteion temple 58
  Metroon 58
  Older Parthenon 47
  Panathenaic Way 58
  Parthenon 46, 47–50, **48**, **49**, 53, 61
  Propylaea **50**, 52, 54
  Royal Stoa 58
  Stoa of Attalos 58
  Temple of Athena Nike **48**, **50**, 53
  Temple of Athena Polias **52**, 53, 54
  Theater of Dionysos 57
Atlanta, Georgia, High Museum (Meier) 543–4, **544**
atria 106
  Early Christian basilicas 134
  Roman 125–6
Attalid Dynasty 60
Attalos of Pergamon **60**
Atwood, Charles B. 414
Augustus Caesar 108, 113–14
Austin, Henry 401
Autun (France), St. Lazare 202, **202**
Awaji-Yumebutai conference center, Japan (Ando) 540
axonometric drawings 7, **7**
Aztecs 268–9, 283

Babylon and Babylonians 18, 117
Bacon, Edmund 343
Badger, Daniel 423
Baghdad (Iraq)
  Islamic houses **170**
  National Museum 15
Bagnaia (Italy), Villa Lante (Vignola) 324, **325**
Bagsvaerg (Denmark), church (Utzon) 549
Baker House, M.I.T. School of Architecture (Aalto) 511, **511**
baldachin 55, 343–5
ball courts 259, 261, **261**, 262, 264
balloon frame construction 425, **425**, 449
Baltimore, Mass., Roman Catholic cathedral (Latrobe) 406–7, **407**, 448
Bamiyan (Afghanistan), colossal Buddha 70, **70**
Banham, Reyner 452
Bank of England (Soane), London 405, **405**, 448
banks 405, **405**, **437**, 437–8, **438**, 448, **558**, 558–9
Banpo (China), Neolithic houses 81, **82**
Banqueting House (Inigo Jones), London **334**, 335
baptisteries, Christian 133, 135
barabaras, Aleutian 255

Barbaro, Daniele and Marcantonio 317
Barcelona (Spain)
    Barcelona Pavilion (Mies van der Rohe)
        488–90, **489**
    Casa Milá (Gaudí) 433, **433**
    Church of the Sagrada Familia (Gaudí)
        **432**, 433
    Colònia Güell Chapel (Gaudí) 433
    Parc Güell (Gaudí) 433–4, **434**
Barma (architect) 150
Barnes, Edward Larrabee 542
Baroque architecture 339–77, 379
    Central Europe 357–61
    and colonial America 377
    England 369–76, 377
    France 363–9, 377
    Italy 339–55, 376–7
Barozzi da Vignola, Giacomo see Vignola,
    Giacomo Barozzi da
Barr, Alfred 492
Barr, Alfred, Jr. 452
Barragán, Luis 535, **535**, 561
barrel-vaults **240**
    Baroque 357
    Byzantine basilicas and churches 140, 143,
        144, 146
    Carolingian 178
    Roman 109, 110, **110**, 121, 130–1
    Romanesque **177**, 189, 196
Barry, Charles 410, **411**
basilicas
    Byzantine 139–43
    Early Christian 134–5, 192
    Palladio 316, **316**
    Roman 112, 120–1, **121**, 151
    Romanesque 190
Bassai, Temple of Apollo Epicurius 45, **54**,
    55
bastides 245, 245–6, **246**, 249
Bath (England) 123
Baths of Diocletian, Rome **122**, 123
baths (thermae), Roman 121–3
Baudot, Anatole de 425
Bauhaus 429, 455, 484–8, 492, 505
    building at Dessau (Gropius) 487, **487**
Bavaria, church of Die Wies (Zimmerman)
    359–60, **360**, 377
Bayer, Herbert 485
bazaars, Islamic 170, 171, **171**
Beacon, New York, DIA Center for the Arts
    (Irwin, OpenOffice, Arup) 548
beams 2
Beardsley, Aubrey 430
Beauvais (France), St. Pierre Cathedral **221**,
    249, 412
Behrens, Peter 429, 437, 452, 455, 463, **463**,
    480, 484, 505
Beijing (China) 88–90, **89**, 92, 103
    CCTV Headquarters (Koolhas) 564, **565**
    Fragrant Hills Hotel (Pei) 91
    Hall of Supreme Harmony 89–90, **90**
    Zhongguanchun Life Science Park (Plexus r
        + d) 564
belfries 180
bellcotes 411
Belper (England), West Mill (Strutt) 396, **396**
Benedictines 182
    see also St. Gall monastery
Beni Hasan (Egypt), rock-cut tombs 28, **28**
Benin architecture
    palaces of the Abomey 281
    pole-frame houses 275
Bergisel Ski-jump, Innsbruck, Austria
    (Hadid) **526**, 526–7
Berlage, H.P. 466, **467**, 477

Berlin (Germany)
    AEG Turbine Factory (Behrens) 463, **463**
    Altesmuseum (Schinkel) 403, **404**
    Jewish Museum (Libeskind) 541–2, 547
    Memorial to the Murdered Jews in Europe
        (Eisenman) 542
    Nationalgalerie 495
    Neue Wache (Schinkel) 402, **402**
    Potsdamer Platz, rebuilding 555
    Reichstag (Foster) 559, **559**
    Schauspielhaus (Schinkel) 402–3, **403**
Bernard of Clairvaux, St. 205, 207, 237
Bernini, Gianlorenzo 343, 354, 363, 370,
    377
    Piazza del Popolo, Rome 352, **352**
    Piazza Navona, Rome 350, 350–1
    Piazza of St. Peter's, Rome 345, **345**
    S. Andrea al Quirinale, Rome 346, **346**, 376
    S. Maria dei Miracoli, Rome 352, **352**
    S. Maria in Montesanto, Rome 352, **352**
    St. Peter's, Rome 343–5, **345**
Bessemer, Henry 417
Bethlehem, Church of the Nativity 135, **136**
Bhagavad Gita 65
Bhitargaon (India), Vishnu Temple 72, 72–3
Bhubaneshwar (India), temples 73, **73**, 78
Bibliothèque Nationale, Paris (Labrouste)
    421–2, **422**, 449
Bibliothèque Ste. Geneviève, Paris
    (Labrouste) 5, 420, **421**, 449
Bilbao, Guggenheim Museum (Gehry) **507**,
    529–31, **530**, **531**
Biltmore, Asheville, North Carolina (Hunt)
    413
Bingi Point (Australia), Magney House
    (Murcutt) **562**, 563
Blackfoot tribe 252
Blenheim Palace (Vanbrugh), Oxfordshire
    (England) 374, **375**, 379
    grounds (Brown) **397**, 398
Blois, château (France) 326, 326–7
Blondel, J.F. 386, 390, 395, 399
Blur Building, Yverdon-les-Bains
    (Switzerland) (Diller and Scofidio) 548
Boffrand, Germain 379
Bogardus, James 423
boiserie 379
Boissonas House (Johnson), New Canaan
    520, **520**
Bolivia 269, 272
Borgund (Norway), stave church **186**, 187,
    **187**
Born, Ernest 182, 184
Borobudur (Java), stupa 79
Borromeo, Charles 357
Borromini, Francesco 346
    Piazza Navona, Rome 350, **350**
    S. Agnese, Rome 350–1, **351**
    S. Carlo alle Quattro Fontane, Rome **347**,
        347–8, **348**, 376
    S. Ivo della Sapienza (Rome) **348**, 348–50,
        **349**
bosco 324
Bossi, Antonio 362
Boston, Mass.
    Boston City Hall (Kallman, McKinnell, and
        Knowles) 540, **540**
    Brattle Square Church (Richardson) 440
    Public Library (McKim, Mead, and White)
        5, 293–4, **415**, 416
    Trinity Church (Richardson) 439–40, **440**
Botammariba tribe (Togo) 275, **276**
Botta, Mario 536, **536**
bouleterion, Athens 58
Boullée, Etienne-Louis **387**, 387–8, 397, 399

Bourges (France), St. Etienne Cathedral **221**,
    222–3, **223**, 224, 238, 249
Boyle, Richard see Burlington, third Earl
Bramante, Donato 298, 299–304, 326
    Belvedere Courtyard, Rome **303**, 303–4,
        324, 336
    House of Raphael, Rome 304, **304**
    S. Maria delle Grazie, Milan 299, **299**
    S. Maria presso S. Satiro, Milan **230**, 299
    St. Peter's, Rome 302, **302**
    Tempietto, Rome **301**, 301–2, 336
Breakers, The, Newport, Rhode Island
    (Hunt) 413, **413**
Breakwater, The, Miami Beach, Florida
    (Skislewicz) **476**
Breda (The Netherlands), Chassé Theater
    (Hertzberger) 550
Bremerhaven (Germany), medieval
    longhouse **241**
Breuer, Marcel 485, 487, 492, 493
brick 2
    Byzantine 143
    China 83, 92
    Sumerian 16
    Wright 459
bridges
    concrete 479
    Graves 522, **522**
    Grimshaw 560
    iron and steel 396–7, 417, **417**, 422, **422**
    Post-Modernist (Graves) 522, **522**
    Roman 4
    suspension 4, **5**
    trusses 4, **4**
Brighton (England), Royal Pavilion (Nash)
    401
Brno (Czech Republic), Tugendhat House
    (Mies van der Rohe) 490, **490**
Broadacre City (Wright) 495–6
Broadbent, Geoffrey 519
Broadleys, Cumbria (England) (Voysey) 428,
    **429**
broken barrel vaults 198
Broken Hill, New South Wales, Minerals and
    Mining Museum (Murcutt) **563**, 563–4
Brooklyn Bridge, New York (Roebling) 417,
    **417**
Brown, Joseph 375–6
Brown, Lancelot (Capability) **397**, 398
Brunelleschi, Filippo 286–91, 292, 336
    Florence Cathedral dome 5, 120, 287, 288,
        **288**, 336
    Ospedale degli Innocenti, Florence 288–9
    Pazzi Chapel, S. Croce, Florence **285**, 290,
        291, 336
    S. Lorenzo, Florence 289, **289**, 290–1
    S. Maria degli Angeli, Florence **290**, 291
    S. Spirito, Florence 289, 289–90
Brussels (Belgium)
    Hotel Van Eetvelde (Horta) 431, **431**
    Tassel House (Horta) 430, 431
Brutalism 507
Bryant, William Cullen 414
Buddha, the (Siddhartha Gautama) 66
Buddhism 66, 71
    China 66, 81–2
    India 65, 66
    Pure Land Buddhism 96
    Sri Lanka 66
Buddhist monasteries
    China 83–4
    India 66, 68
    Japan 95–6
Buddhist shrines, India 66–71
Buddhist temple halls, China 86

Buddhist temples, Japan 94–6, 101
Buffalo, New York
   Guaranty Building (Adler and Sullivan)
      445, **446**, 449
   Larkin Building (Wright) **460**, 460–2, 505
Buildwas, Shropshire (England), bridge
   (Telford) 396
Bukhara (Uzbekistan), Tomb of Ismail the
   Samanid 168, **168**
Bullant, Jean **328**, 329
Bunshaft, Gordon 488
Burgee, John **520**
Burgundy (France) 177
Burke, Edmund 397
Burkina Faso, Bobo-Dioulasso Mosque 282,
   **282**
Burlington, Richard Boyle, third Earl 380,
   **381**
Burlington House, London 380
Burne-Jones, Edward 440
Burnham, Daniel H. 423, 424, **424**
Burton, Decimus 419, **419**
Byker Wall Housing, Newcastle-upon-Tyne
   (Erskine) 507, **508**
Byzantine architecture 164
   basilicas 139–43
   centrally-planned churches 143–6
   churches in Russia 146–51

cables 4
Cades Cove, Tennessee, barn **3**
Caen (France), abbey church of St. Etienne
   208, **208**
Cahokia, Illinois 255
Calatrava, Santiago 548, 557, **557**
caldarium 123
California (northern), tribes 256–7
Cambridge, Cambs. (England)
   History Faculty Building (Stirling) 553, **553**
   King's College Chapel **228**, 234–5, **235**,
      249, 331
   Pembroke College Chapel (Wren) 370
Cambridge, Mass. (USA), Stoughton House
   (Richardson) 442, **443**, 449
   see also M.I.T. School of Architecture
Camden Society 411
campaniles 180, **193**, 194
Campbell, Colen 380, **380**
Canigou see St. Martin at Canigou
Canterbury Cathedral, Kent (England) 208,
   226–7, **228**
cantilever construction 2, 3, **3**, 5
capitals, Romanesque **199**, 200, **200**, 202
Caral, Peru 269
caravanserai 165
Carcassonne (France) **244**, 244–5, **245**, 249,
   412
cardo 105, 113
Carleton, Ken 254
Carnac (France), megalith tomb **10**, 11
Carolingian architecture 178
   horseshoe arches 182
   masonry construction 178–82
   monasteries 182–4
   westwerks 178–80
caryatids **52**, 53–4
cast iron 396, 420, **423**
Castle Howard, Yorks. (England) (Vanbrugh)
   374, **374**
castles
   Japan, timber **100**, 100–1
   medieval 242–3, 249
castra (military camps), Roman 105, 113
catacombs, Rome 133

Catal Hüyük (Anatolia), prehistoric
   settlement 10, **10**
cathedrals 135
   early Gothic 216–19
   High Gothic 220–4
   Norman 208–10
   see also individual cathedrals
cave-temples
   China 83
   India 68–71
   see also rock-cut temples
Cawston, Norfolk (England), St. Agnes's
   church 229, **229**
CCTV Headquarters (Koolhas), Beijing
   (China) 564, **565**
Celebration, Florida (Stern and Robertson)
   534
cellas 50, 55
cemeteries and crematoria
   cemetery gates, New Haven (Austin) 401
   Cemetery of San Cataldo, Modena (Rossi)
      534, **534**
   Kaze-no-Oka Crematorium, Nakatsu
      (Maki) 538–9
   Woodland Cemetery, Sweden (Asplund)
      504–5, **505**
Center for Maximum Potential Building
   Systems 564
centering (arches) 3
Cerro Blanco (Peru), temple mounds **271**,
   271–2
Certosa monastery, Pavia (Italy) 326
Chaco Canyon (New Mexico) **257**
   Pueblo Bonito 258, **258**
chaitya halls, India 66, 68
Chambers, William 383, 386, **386**, 399
Chambord (France), château (Cortona) **327**,
   327–8
Chan Chan (Peru) 272, **273**
Chandigarh (India) (Le Corbusier) 502–3,
   **503**
Chandragupta 20, 65
Chang'an (modern Xian) (China) 87–8, **88**
chapter houses 231
charette 395
Charlemagne, Holy Roman Emperor 178,
   210
Charles Martel 153
Charleston, S. Carolina, St. Michael's
   (Harrison) 376
Charlottenhof, Potsdam (Schinkel) **404**, 405
Charlottesville, Virginia
   Monticello (Jefferson) **408**, 408–9
   University of Virginia (Jefferson) 120, **409**,
      409–10
Charnley House, Chicago (Adler and
   Sullivan) 456, **456**
Chartres (France), Notre-Dame Cathedral
   **213**, **220**, 220–2, **221**, **222**, 223–4, 240,
   249
Chassé Theater, Breda (Hertzberger) 550
châteaux
   Baroque 365–6
   Renaissance 326–8, 337
chatra 66
Chatsworth House (England), Conservatory
   (Burton and Paxton) 419
Chaux (Ledoux) **387**, 388, **388**
Chavín de Huántar (Peru) 270–1, **271**
Chelles, Jean de 218
Chenonceau (France), château (Orme and
   Bullant) 328, **328**, 329
Cheops see Khufu
Chephren see Khafre

Chestnut Hill, Penn., Vanna Venturi House
   (Venturi) 518, **518**
Cheyenne, the 252
Chicago, Illinois
   860 Lake Shore Drive (Mies van der Rohe)
      494, **494**
   Auditorium Building (Adler and Sullivan)
      444, **444**, 445, 449
   Carson Pirie Scott Department Store
      (Sullivan) **447**, 448
   Charnley House (Adler and Sullivan) 456,
      **456**
   Crown Hall, I.I.T. (Mies van der Rohe) 493,
      **493**, 495
   Glessner House (Richardson) 441–2, **442**,
      449
   Home Insurance Building (Jenney) 423,
      **423**, 449
   Marshall Field Wholesale Store
      (Richardson) 441, **441**, 442–4, 449
   Monadnock Building (Burnham and Root)
      424, **424**, 449
   Rand McNally Building (Burnham and
      Root) 423–4
   Reliance Building (Burnham and Root)
      424, **424**, 449
   Robie House (Wright) 458–9, **459**
   World's Columbian Exposition, 1893
      (Hunt) 413–14, **414**
Chicago School 424
Chichén-Itzá (Mexico) 267, 282–3
   Caracol 267, **267**
chickees, Native American 255
Childs, David C. 547–8
Chimor Kingdom 272
China 4, 81, 153
   architects working in 564
   architectural principles 84–6
   brick structures 83, 92
   Buddhism 66, 81–2
   cave temples 83
   city planning 87–90
   color schemes 86
   garden design 81, 91, 92–3
   Great Wall **81**, 81–2
   Hellenistic art 83
   houses **84**, 84–5, 90–2, **92**, 93, **93**
   jian (modular unit) 84
   monasteries/temples 83, **83**, 83–4, **84**, 85,
      **85**, 86, **86**, 87
   Neolithic houses at Banpo 81, **82**
   pagodas **82**, 83, 83–4
   watchtowers 84
Chinoiserie style 401
Chinook tribe 256
Chippewa, the 253
Chiswick House, London (Lord Burlington)
   380, **381**
Choctaws, the 254, 283
Choragic Monument of Lysikrates, Athens
   55–6, **56**
Chorleywood (England), The Orchard
   (Voysey) 428
Christian architecture see Early Christian
   architecture
Chrysler Building, New York (Van Alen) 446,
   **472**, 472–3
CIAM (Congrès Internationaux
   d'Architecture Moderne) 507
Cincinnati, Rosenthal Center for
   Contemporary Arts (Hadid) 527, **527**
Cistercian order/monasteries 237, 240, 249
Cité dans L'Espace (Kiesler) 477, **478**
Citeaux monastery (France) 208

cities, medieval 244–8
Citrohan houses (Le Corbusier) 481, **481**
Città Nuova, La (Sant'Elia) 464, **464**
city and town planning
  Athens 58
  Aztec 268
  China 87–90
  Etruscan 105
  grid systems 87–8, 111, 131, 245–6
  Harappan 63
  Hellenistic 59–61
  Islamic 170–1
  Italian medieval 246–8
  Japan 103
  Le Corbusier 502–3
  medieval 244–8
  New Urbanism 533–4
  Poland 246
  Poundbury, Dorset 535
  Renaissance 292, 329–30
  Roman 105, 111–16, 131, 341–2, 350–2, 376
  *see also* ideal towns and cities
ciudadelas 272
Classical period *see* Greece
Clayton County, branch library (Scogin and Elam) 546
Clement VII (Giulio de' Medici), Pope 305, 308
Clérisseau, Charles-Louis 382
Cloaca Maxima, Etruscan/Roman sewer 106, 108, 113
cloister vaults 178
cloisters 184
Cluny (France), medieval house **242**
Cluny monastery (France) **198**, 198–202, **199**
Coalbrookdale Bridge (Darby III and Pritchard), Shropshire (England) 396
Coca-Cola Bottling Plant, Los Angeles (Derrah) 475, **476**
Cockerell, Samuel Pepys 401
Coducci, Mauro 321
Colbert, Jean-Baptiste 394–5
Coleshill, Berks. (England) (Pratt) 372, **373**, 377
Cologne (Germany), Glass Pavilion (Taut) 468, **469**
colonists' houses, early 6, **6**, **7**
colonnettes 196, 211, 213
color
  China 86
  Greek temples 54
Colosseum *see* Rome
column-and-beam construction *see* post-and-lintel construction
Comanche, the 252
compression, of structural materials 2
concrete 2
  concrete and wood construction 424–5
  ferroconcrete 425
  reinforced 425, 449, 479–80, 505
  Roman 110, **110**, 117, 120
  Wright's use of 462
Confucius and Confucianism 81, 86, 87, 384
Connecticut, colonial houses 6, **6**, **7**
Conques (France), St. Foy **196**, 196–7, **197**, 211
Constantine, emperor 133, 134, 135, 144
Constantinople (Istanbul), Turkey 133, 153, 164, 177
  *see also* Istanbul
Constructivism 463, 464–6, 505
Coop Himmelblau 526

Copán (Honduras) **261**, **264**, 264–5, 282
corbeled construction 2, **2**, 3, **240**
  Egypt 24
  Mayan **2**, 264
  Mycenae 42, **42**
  Romanesque **194**, 211
  Tiryns 43, **43**, 44
Córdoba (Spain), Great Mosque **157**, 158, **159**
Corinthian order 45, **46**
  Baroque 346, 375
  Greece 45, **45**, 54, 55, **55**, 56
  Modernism 533
  Palladio mannerist 320, 321
  Roman 118, 125, 290
  Romanesque 192, 205
Cortona, Domenico da **326**, 327
Cortona, Pietro da **351**, 351–2
country houses, England
  Baroque 372–4, 374, 377
  Elizabethan 331–3
  Lutyens 504
  Neo-Classical 385
  Neo-Palladian 380–2
courtyard houses
  Africa 276, 280
  China 93
  Mesopotamia 17
  Morocco 280
  Renaissance 297
Cranbrook Academy, Detroit (Eliel Saarinen) 512
Creek tribe 255
Crete 35, 36
  *see also* Knossos; Minoans
Crow tribe 252
Crown Hall, I.I.T., Chicago (Mies van der Rohe) 493, **493**, 495
Crystal Palace, London (Paxton) 419–20, **420**, 449, 542
Cubism 463–4, 472, 477
Cuipers, P.J.H. 466
curtain walls 446
Cuvillés, Françoise 379
Cuzco (Peru) 273, **273**
cyclopean construction
  Inca 273, **273**
  Mycenae 39
Czech Republic (Bohemia) 359, 363

Dacca (India), National Assembly of Bangladesh (Kahn) 514
Dahinden, Justus 550, **550**
Dahshur (Egypt), pyramids **24**, 25
Dallas, Texas, Nasher Sculpture Center (Piano) 556, **556**
Damascus (Syria), Great Mosque 157, **157**
Daniell, Thomas 384
Daoism 81, 86, 92
Darby, Abraham 396
Darby III, Abraham 396
Darius 19, 47
Darmstadt (Germany) 437
  Wedding Tower (Olbrich) 439
De Dageraad housing project, Amsterdam (de Klerk) 466, **468**
De Stijl 452, 455, 477, 488, 492, 505
dead loads 2
Deconstructivist architecture 524–33, 564
decumanus 105, 113
Deir-el-Bahari (Egypt)
  Hatshepsut's mortuary temple **29**, **30**, 30–1, 33
  Mentuhotep's tomb and temple 28, **28**

Delhi (India), tomb of Humayun 168
Delian League 47, 54
Dengfeng (China), Songyue Pagoda 83
dentils 46
Dermée, Paul 480–1
Derrah, Robert 475, **476**
Derrida, Jacques 519
Dessau (Germany), Bauhaus building (Gropius) 487, **487**
Detroit, Michigan, Cranbrook Academy (Eliel Saarinen) 512
Deutscher Werkbund 462–3, 468, 484, 491, 505
DIA Center for the Arts, Beacon, New York (Irwin, OpenOffice, Arup) 548
diaphragm arches 192
Dientzenhofer, Christoph 359, **359**, 377
Dientzenhofer, Kilian Ignaz 359
Dientzenhofer brothers 359
Diller, Elizabeth 548
Dinkeloo, John 542, **542**
Disney World, Swan and Dolphin hotels, Orlando, Florida (Graves) 523, **523**
Djenne (Mali), Great Mosque **281**, 281–2
Djoser, pharaoh 23
Doesburg, Theo Van 477, 486
Dogon people (Mali), villages 278, **279**
Dom-ino House (Le Corbusier) 480, **480**
Dome of the Rock, Jerusalem 154–6, **155**
domes 3, **240**
  Baroque 346, **349**, 350, 355, **356**, 357, **368**, 369, 370, **371**
  Byzantine 139–46
  Carolingian 180
  geodesic 560, **560**
  Islamic **4**, 153, 158, 161, 163, 165, 167, 168, 169, 175
  Neo-Classical 385
  onion domes 150
  "pumpkin vault" 143, **143**
  Renaissance 287, **288**, 302, 308, 313–14
  Roman 108, 118–20
  Romanesque 202, 203
  Russian churches 147, 150
domical vaults 237
Dominicans 237
Donatello 286, 292
Dorians 44
Doric order 45
  Greece 45, **45**, 46, 47, **49**, 54–5, 58
  Mannerist 307, 316
  Modernism 533
  Roman 124, 125
Dornach (Switzerland), Goetheanum buildings (Steiner) 468–9, **469**
drawings, architectural 5–7
Duany, Andres **533**, 533–4
Duban, Félix 395
Dulles Airport, Washington D.C. (Saarinen), 513
Dumbarton Oaks, Washington D.C., Museum for Pre-Columbian Art (Johnson) 520
Dunker Cultural Center, Helsingborg (Utzon) 549
Dur-Sharrukin (Khorsabad) (Assyria) 18
Durham (England), St. Cuthbert's Cathedral 208–10, **209**, **210**, 211, 249
Dutch Expressionism (Wendigen) 466, 477, 505
Dymaxion House (Fuller) 560

Eads, James B. 417
Eads Bridge, St. Louis 417

Eames, Charles and Ray 513
Eanna, Sumer, temples 16
Early Christian architecture 133–4
  basilicas 134–5, 192
  martyria 135
  mausolea 135–9
earth lodges, Plains tribes 253
earth mounds, Native American 253–5, 254, **254**, 255, **255**, 282
eaves 3
Ecclesiological Movement 411–12
eclecticism 398, 448
Ecole des Beaux-Arts 394–5, 399, 412, 413–14, 414, 439, 445, 448–9, 452, 493
Edirne, Selimiye Mosque (Sinan) 167, **167**
Eesteren, Cor Van 477
Egret's Castle, Himeji (Japan) **100**, 100–1
Egypt 14, 20–33
  building materials 117
  and Islam 153
  *see also* hypostyle halls; mortuary temples; obelisks; pyramids; tombs
Egyptian style (Revival) 382, 401
Eiffel, Gustave **401**, 422, **422**, 449
Eigen Haard housing project, Amsterdam (de Klerk) 466, **468**
Einsiedeln, abbey church of (C. and J. Moosbrugger) 361
Einstein, Albert 519
Einstein Tower, Potsdam (Mendelsohn) **470**, 470–1
Eisenman, Peter 525, **525**, 542
El Pedregal, lava-walled houses (Barragán) 535
Elam, Merrill 546–7
Elementarism 478
elevations 6, **6**, **7**
Elgin, Lord 50
Elizabeth I, Queen 331
Ely Cathedral (England) **233**, 233–4, **234**
Empire State Building, New York (Shreve, Lamb, and Harmon) 446, 475, **475**
Enfant, Pierre L' 343
England
  Anglo-Saxon architecture 184, 185–6, 208, 210
  Art Deco 472
  Arts and Crafts Movement 425–8
  Baroque 369–76
  Ecclesiological Movement 411
  Gothic Revival 410
  Neo-Classicism 384–6, 405–6
  Neo-Palladian 380–2
  Renaissance 330–6
  *see also* country houses
English Gothic 249, 330
  Decorated period 226, 230–1, 233, 249
  Early English 226, 249
  Perpendicular 226, 227, 249, 330
Enlightenment, the 379, 399
entablature 45
entasis 47, 49
Ephesus (Greece)
  Library of Celsus **2**
  Temple of Artemis 44
Epidauros (Greece)
  Sanctuary of Asklepios, tholos 55, **55**
  theater **57**, 57–8
Er-Mané, Carnac (France), megalith tomb **10**, 11
Erickson, Arthur 549
Eridu, Sumer, shrine 16
Erskine, Ralph 507
Eskimos *see* Inuits

Este family 324–5
Ethiopian churches 281, **281**
Etruscans 105–7, 111
Eusebius of Caesarea 138, **138**
Evans, Sir Arthur 36
Evelyn, Sir John 369
Eveux-sur-l'Arbresle (France), Ste.-Marie-de-la-Tourette (Le Corbusier) 502, **502**
exedrae 123
Exeter, New Hampshire, Phillips Exeter Academy library (L.I. Kahn) 514, **515**
Exposition des Arts Décoratifs, Paris 465, **465**, 477, **478**
Expressionism 466–71, 505
Eyck, Aldo Van 507

Fagnano Olona, elementary school (Rossi) 534
Fagus Shoe-Last Factory, Alfeld-an-der-Leine (Gropius and Meyer) 484, **484**
Fairfield, Connecticut, Ogden House **7**
Fajda Butte, Chaco Canyon (New Mexico) 258
Fali tribe (Cameroon) 277, **277**
fan vaults, English Gothic 226, 227
Fargo-Moorhead Cultural Center Bridge (Graves) 522, **522**
Farnsworth House, Plano (Mies van der Rohe) **494**, 494–5
Fasil Ghebbi (Ethiopia) 280
Fatehpur Sikri (India), Friday mosque **162**, 163, **163**
feng shui 86
ferroconcrete 425
feudal system 177
Fiesole (Italy), Medici Villa (Michelozzo) 324, **324**
Fillmore, Lavius 376
"fireproof" buildings 396, 423, 494
Fischer von Erlach, Johann Bernhard 357, **358**, 377
Fiske, Pliny 564
Flemish influences 331
Florence (Italy) 113, 285
  Cathedral, dome (Brunelleschi) 5, 287, 288, **288**, 336
  Laurentian Library (Michelangelo) 308–9, **309**
  Ospedale degli Innocenti (Brunelleschi) 288–9
  Palazzo Rucellai (Alberti) 293, **293**
  Pazzi Chapel, S. Croce (Brunelleschi) **290**, 291, 336
  S. Lorenzo: (Brunelleschi) 289, **289**, 290–1; (Michelangelo) 289, 308–10, **309**
  S. Maria degli Angeli (Brunelleschi) 290, 291
  S. Maria Novella 237, 237–8; (Alberti) 294, **294**; (Masaccio fresco) 286, **287**, 336
  S. Miniato al Monte 192, **192**, **193**
  S. Spirito (Brunelleschi) 289, 289–90
  Uffizi (Vasari) **306**, 306–7
flying buttresses 238
  Gothic 213–14, 217, 218, 220, **223**, 230, 237
  Roman 115
Fogong Monastery, Shanxi, China **83**, 83–4, **85**, **86**
follies 398
Fontana, Domenico 343, 350, 376
Fontenay abbey (France) **206**, 207, **207**
fora, Roman **111**, 111–15, **112**, 113–15, **114**
Ford Foundation Building, New York (Roche and Dinkeloo) 542, **542**
Foreign Office Architects (FOA) 552

Fort Worth, Texas
  Kimbell Art Museum (Kahn) 15, 515, **515**, **516**
  Modern Art Museum (Ando) 540
Fossanova monastery (Italy) 208
Foster, Norman 548, 557–9, **558**, **559**
Foucault, Michel 519
Fouilhoux 474
France 153, 177
  architects and the aggrandizement of the state 390–1
  l'art moderne (Art Deco) 472
  Baroque architecture 363–9, 377
  Gothic architecture 326, 327
  Gothic Revival 412–13
  Neo-Classicism 387–90, 392–4, 422
  pensionnaires 392–4, 399
  Renaissance 326–30, 337
  *see also* châteaux
Francis I of France 326, **326**, 327, 329
Franciscans 237, 238
Frankfurt (Germany)
  Biocentrum (Eisenman) 525
  Museum für Kunsthandwerk (Meier) **543**, 543–4
Freed, James Ingo 541
frigidarium 123
Frith, W.P., *The Railway Station* (eng.) 418, **418**
Fujima Country Club, Oita (Japan) (Isozaki) 539
Fulani people (Burkina Faso) 274, **275**
Fuller, R. Buckminster 560, **560**, 565
Futurism 452, 463–4, 505

Gabriel, Ange-Jacques 391, **391**
Galician Center of Contemporary Art, Santiago de Compostela (Siza) 536, **536**
Garabit Viaduct (Eiffel) 422, **422**
Garches (France), Villa Stein (Le Corbusier) 481, **481**
garden design
  China 81, 91, 92–3
  English Romantic 397–8
  Islamic 169, 172, 324
  Mannerist 324–5
  Renaissance 324
  Zen stone gardens 103
Garnier, Tony 455
Gaudí, Antonio **432**, 433, 433–4, **434**, 449
Gedi (Kenya) 280, **280**
Gehry, Frank **507**, 525, **528**, 528–31, **529**, **530**, **531**, 548
General Motors Technical Center, Warren (Saarinen) 512
Genghis Khan 70
geodesic domes 560, **560**
geometry
  descriptive 395
  medieval 240
  Neo-Classical 387
  Renaissance 286
German Expressionism 466–71, 505
Germany
  Arts and Crafts Movement 425, 429
  Baroque in 357, 363
  Deutscher Werkbund 462–3, 468, 484, 491, 505
  Gothic architecture 235, 249
  Jugendstil 430, 437
  medieval longhouse **241**
  Neo-Classicism 402–5
  Romanesque (Ottonian) architecture 190, 210
  *see also* Bauhaus

Germigny-des-Près (France), Oratory 180–2, **181**, 210
Getty Museum, Los Angeles (Meier) 544
Ghiberti, Lorenzo 286, 292
Giacomo della Porta 314, 340, **340**, **341**, **348**
Gibbons, Grinling 370–2
Gibbs, James 375, **376**, 377, 399
Giedion, Sigfried 431, 452
Gilbert, Cass 472
Giovanni da Udine 305
Giulio Romano 304, **307**, 307–8
Giza (Egypt)
　Khafre's (Chephren's) pyramid and mortuary temple 24, 25, **25**, **26**, 26–7, **27**
　Khufu's (Cheop's) pyramid 24, **25**, 25–6, **26**, 27
　Menkaure's (Mycerinus's) pyramid 24, 25, **25**, 26, **26**
　pyramids 24, **25**, 25–7, **26**, 29
Glasgow (Scotland)
　School of Art (Mackintosh) 434, **435**
　Scotland Street School (Mackintosh) 434
glass and iron construction 419–20, 431
Glass Pavilion, Cologne (Taut) 468, **469**
Goetheanum buildings, Dornach (Steiner) 468–9, **469**
Goharshad Mosque, Mashhad (Iran) 4
Gondoin, Jacques 392–4, **394**, 399
Gonzaga family 294, 307
Gothic architecture
　basic elements 213–14
　Czech Republic 236
　early Gothic 214–19
　English Gothic 249, 330; (Decorated period) 226, 230–1, 233, 249; (Early English) 226, 249; (Perpendicular) 226, 227, 249, 330
　France 326, 327
　Germany 235, 249
　High Gothic 220–6
　Italy 237–9, 249, 285, 287
　Venetian 248, 249, 321
Gothic Revival 410–13, 439
Gothick style 398
Goujou, Jean 329
granaries, Africa **277**, 277–8
grass houses, Plains tribes 253
Graves, Michael 519, 522–3, **523**
Gray, Eileen 484
　home at Roquebrune **483**, 484
Great Buddha style, Japan 96
Great Plains/Great Lakes tribes 251–3
Great Wall of China **81**, 81–2
Great Zimbabwe 280
Greece 35
　Aegean cultures 35–44
　Archaic period 44–7
　Classical period 47–54
　Hellenistic period 54–8, 59–61
Greek-cross plans
　Byzantine 143–5, 151
　Carolingian 180
　Islamic tombs 168
　Romanesque churches 202
Greek Revival Style 439
Greeley, Horace 414
Greenberg, Allan 533, **533**
greenhouses 419, **419**
Greensted (England), Anglo-Saxon church 186
Greyfriars, Surrey (England) (Voysey) 428
Griffith, Walter Burley 460
Grimshaw, Nicholas 559–60

groin vaults 189, 213, **240**
　Byzantine 146
　Romanesque 189, 190, **194**, 201
Gropius, Walter 452, 455, 463, 484–8, 505, 507, 520
　Bauhaus building, Dessau 487, **487**
　Fagus Shoe-Last Factory, Alfeld-an-der-Leine 484, **484**
　home in Lincoln, Mass. 492
　Weissenhof Siedlung 492
Guaranty Building, Buffalo, New York (Adler and Sullivan) 445, **446**, 449
Guarini, Guarino 158, 355, **355**, 377
Guggenheim Museum, Bilbao (Gehry) **507**, 529–31, **530**, **531**
Guggenheim Museum, New York (Wright) 496, **498**
Guidoni, Enrico 277
Guild House, Philadelphia (Venturi and Rauch) **517**, 517–18
Guimard, Hector 431, **431**, 449
Gunzo (architect) 198
Guti, the 17

ha-has 398
Hadfield, George 406
Hadid, Zaha **526**, 526–7, **527**, 564
Hadrian, emperor 5, 118
Hadrian's Villa, Tivoli 129–30, **130**
Hagia Sophia, Istanbul (Anthemius and Isidorus) 140–3, **141**, **142**, 151, 164, 214
Hagley Park, Worcs. (England), sham ruin (Miller) 398
Haida tribe 256
half-timber construction **241**, 241–2, 249
hall churches 235–6, 238
Halladie Building, San Francisco (Polk) 446
Hallet, Stephen 406
hammerbeam roofs 229, 234, **234**, 331
Hammurabi, king 18
Hampton Court Palace (England) 331
haram (covered prayer hall) 153, 165, 167, 175
Harappan culture 63–5
Hardwick Hall, Derbyshire (Smythson) **332**, 333
harmika 66
Harmon, Arthur 475, **475**
Harrison, Peter 376
Harrison, Wallace K. **474**
Harvard University, Sever Hall and Austin Hall (Richardson) 441
Hatshepsut, Queen 30, 31
Haussmann, Baron Eugène Georges 343
Hawkins, Gerald 13–14
Hawksmoor, Nicholas 374–5, **375**, 377
Heathcote House, Ilkley, Yorks. (England) (Lutyens) 504, **504**
Heisenberg, Werner 519
Hellenistic period
　and China 83
　Greece 54–8, 59–61
　and Roman architecture 109, 130
Helsingborg (Sweden), Dunker Cultural Center (Utzon) 549
Hennebique, François 425
Henry IV, king of France 329
Henry VIII, king of England 229, 234, 330, 331
Herculaneum (Italy) 382, 385, 399
hermits 182
Hertzberger, Herman 550
Herzog, Jacques **501**, 550–1
Hesse, Ernst Ludwig, Grand Duke of 437, 438

Hézelon 198
Hidatsa earth lodges 253
High Museum, Atlanta, Georgia (Meier) 543–4, **544**
High Renaissance 302, 304, 336
Highland Park, Illinois, Ward Willits House (Wright) 458, **458**
Hildesheim (Germany), St. Michael 190, **191**
Hill House, Helensburgh (Mackintosh) 434–6, **436**
Himeji (Japan), Egret's Castle **100**, 100–1
Hindoo style 401
Hindu temples 71–5, 77, **77**, 78, **78**, **79**
Hinduism, in India 65, 66
Hippodamus of Miletus 59–60
Historic American Buildings Survey 6, **7**
Hitchcock, Henry-Russell 452, 492, 496
Hittites 18
Hofmeister **474**
hogans, Navajo 258, **258**
Hohokam, the 257
Holkham Hall, Norfolk (England) 382, **382**
Holl, Steven 544–5, **545**, 564
Holland see De Stijl; Dutch Expressionism
Hollein, Hans 549
Holocaust Memorial Museum, Washington D.C. (Pei Cobb Freed) **541**, 541–2
Home Insurance Building, Chicago (Jenney) 423, **423**, 449
Homer 36
Hong Kong Bank (Foster) **558**, 558–9
Hood, Raymond 473, **474**, 475
Hook of Holland housing project, Rotterdam (Oud) 477, **477**
Hooke, Robert 369
Hopi, the 258
Horjuyi temple complex, near Nara (Japan) **94**, 95, **95**
Horn, Walter 182, 184
horseshoe arches 3, 158, **181**, 182, **240**
Horta, Victor **430**, 430–1, **431**, 449
Hosios Loukas (Greece), monastery churches **141**, 146, **146**
Hôtel Amelot, Paris (Boffrand) 379
Hotel Sphinx (Koolhas) (graphic rendering) 532, **532**
House of the Prophet, Medina 156, **156**
houses
　Benin 275
　China 84, 84–5, 90–2, **92**, 93, **93**
　Etruscan 106
　Islamic 170, **170**
　Japan 98, 98–100, **99**
　medieval 240–2, **241**, **242**, 249
　Mohenjo-Daro 63
　Mycenae 43, **43**
　Native American 253, 256–8, **257**
　Neolithic 81, **82**
　Roman 125–7, 128–30
　see also country houses; courtyard houses; longhouses; saltbox houses; tower houses
Houston, Texas, Menil Collection Museum (Piano) 555
Howe, George 492, 493
Hsüan-tsang 70
Huaca de los Reyes (Peru) 270, **270**
Hubbard, Elbert 427
humanism 285–6
Humayun, tomb of, Delhi 168
Huni, pharaoh 24
Hunt, Richard Morris **413**, 413–14, **414**, 449
Hupa tribe 256
Hurley, William 234
Husserl, Edmund 518–19

huts, prehistoric 10
"hydraulic" civilizations 21
Hyksos, the 29
hypostyle halls
   Egyptian **9**, 19, 31
   Nashville (Strickland) 401
   Persepolis 19

I-sections 423
IBM Center, New York (Barnes) 542, **542**
iconostasis (screen) 150
ideal towns and cities
   Alberti 295–7
   Le Corbusier 500–1
   Ledoux 388
   Sant'Elia 464
   Wright 495–6
idgabs 153
iglus, Inuit 256, **256**
Iktinos 47, 55
Ilkley, Yorkshire (England), Heathcote House
   (Lutyens) 504, **504**
Illinois Institute of Technology (I.I.T.) 493
   Crown Hall (Mies van der Rohe) 493, **493**,
      495
Imhotep 23, **23**
imperial stairs 362
impluvium 126
Incas 272–4, 283
India 65–75, 153
   Buddhism 65, 66
   Buddhist monasteries 66, 69
   Buddhist shrines 66–71
   cave-temples 68–71
   chaitya halls 66, 68
   domed chamber tombs 168–9
   Hindu temples 71–5, 78
   Hinduism 65, 66
   mosques 162, 163
   shikhara roofs 72–3
   stone (masonry) construction 65, 67, 68,
      71–2, 75
   stupas 66–8
Indonesia 153
Indus Valley 63–5
Industrial Revolution 379, 395–7, 399, 448
Innocent X, Pope 354
Innsbruck, Austria, Bergisel Ski-jump
   (Hadid) **526**, 526–7
Inspector's House (Ledoux) 388, **388**
insulae (apartment blocks), Roman 128,
   **128**, 131
International Style 496
Inuits (Eskimos) 255–6
Ionians 44, 47
Ionic order 45, **46**
   Baroque 346
   Greece 45, **45**, 46, **46**, 52, 53, 54, 55, 58
   Mannerist 316
   Neo-Palladian 380
   Roman 124, 125
Iran 153, 175
   *see also* Persepolis
Iraq 153
Ireland
   megalith tombs **10**, **11**, 11–13
   monasticism 182
iron 2, 449
   bridges 396–7
   cast iron 396, 420, **423**
   Eiffel Tower 422
   glass and iron construction 419–20, 431
   Industrial Revolution 419
   wrought iron 396

Iroquois longhouses 253
Irwin, Robert 544, 548
Ise Shrine, Uji-Yamada (Japan) **97**, 97–8, 103
Isfahan 171
   bazaar 171, **171**
   city planning 171
   Friday Mosque **153**, **160**, 161–2
   Maidan-i-Shah **170**
   Masjid-i-shah **160**, **161**, 162, **162**, 171
   Sheikh Lutfullah Mosque 171
Isidorus of Miletus 140, 143
Islamic architecture 153–75
   abambars (urban cisterns) 175
   Alhambra palace and garden 172–5
   arches 4, 158, 163, **163**
   bazaars 170, 171, **171**
   city planning 170–1
   domes 4, 153, 158, 161, 163, 165, 167,
      168, 169, 175
   garden design 169, 172, 324
   houses 170, **170**
   ornament 154, 161–2, 162, 175
   palaces 172–5
   shrines 154–6
   Spain 153, 172–5, 177
   *see also* mosques
Isozaki, Arata 539, **539**, 555
Istanbul (Constantinople), Turkey
   Church of the Holy Apostles 144
   Hagia Sophia (Anthemius and Isidorus)
      140–3, **141**, **142**, 151, 164, 214
   Mosque of Süleyman the Magnificent
      (Sinan) 165–7, **168**
   S. Irene 139–40, **140**
   SS. Sergius and Bacchus **141**, 143, **143**, 144
   Shehzade Mosque (Sinan) **164**, 165, **165**
   *see also* Constantinople
Italy
   Baroque architecture 339–55, 376–7
   Futurism 463–4, 505
   Gothic architecture 237–9, 249, 285, 287
   medieval houses 242, **242**, 249
   Renaissance 296, 297–336
   Romanesque churches 190–4
   *see also* Etruscans
iwans 160

Jacobs, Jane 534
Jahan, Shah 168, 169
Jainism 65–6
Japan 94
   Buddhist monasteries/temples 94–6, 101
   castles **100**, 100–1
   city planning 103
   Great Buddha style 96
   houses 98, 98–100, **99**
   Modernism 538–40
   pagodas 95, **95**
   Shinto shrines 97–8
   tatami 99
   tea houses 101–3, **102**, **103**
   Zen Buddhist architecture 101–3
Japonais style 401
Jean-Marie Tjibaou Cultural Center, Nouméa
   (Piano) 556, **556**
Jefferson, Thomas 120, 401–2, 406, 407–10,
   **408**, **409**, 439, 448
Jekyll, Gertrude 504
Jencks, Charles 519, 524, 525
Jenney, William Le Baron 423, **423**
Jericho (Israel), prehistoric settlement 10
Jerusalem
   Dome of the Rock 154–6, **155**
   pilgrimages 194

Jesuits 339, 346, 376, 384
jetty (of a building) 3
Ji Cheng 91
jian (modular unit), China 84
Jinci temple complex, Taiyuan (China) 86,
   **87**
John Graves House, Madison **6**
Johnson, Philip 452, 492, 519–21, **520**, 524,
   528, 534, 548
Jones, Faye 537
Jones, Inigo 333, 337, 380, 399
   Banqueting House, Whitehall, London
      **334**, 335
   Covent Garden, London **335**, 335–6
   Queen's House, Greenwich **333**, 333–5,
      **334**
   St. Paul's, London 336
journeymen 239
Jugendstil 430, 437
Julius II, Pope 302, 336, 341, 342
Julius III, Pope 324
Justinian, emperor 139, 144

Kabah (Mexico), arch **2**
Kahn, Ely Jacques **451**, 473–5
Kahn, Louis I. 513–16, **514**, **515**, **516**, 517
Kallikrates 47, 53
Kallmann, Gerhard Michael 540, **540**
Kamioka Town Hall, Japan (Isozaki) 539
Kandinsky, Wassily 485, **485**
*Kao Gong Ji* 87, 103
Karli (India), cave-temple **69**, 69–71
Karnak (Egypt), Great Temple of Amun 31, **31**
   Hypostyle Hall **9**
Karok tribe 256
Katsura Imperial Villa, Kyoto **101**, 101–3,
   **102**, **103**
Kaufmann House, "Fallingwater," Ohiopyle
   (Wright) 458, 496, **497**
Kaze-no-Oka Crematorium, Nakatsu (Maki)
   538–9
Kekrops, king of Athens 53
Kelly, William 417
Kempsey (Australia), History Museum and
   Tourist Office (Murcutt) 561–3, **562**
Kent, William 380, 382, **382**, 397
Kentlands, Maryland 534
Kew Gardens, London, Palm House (Burton
   and Turner) 419, **419**
keystones 108
Khafre (Chephren) pyramid and mortuary
   temple 24, 25, **25**, **26**, 26–7, **27**
Khajuraho (India)
   Kandariya Mahadeva Temple **63**, **74**, 78
   Lakshmana Temple **73**, 73–4, **74**, 78
Khan, 'Abd al-Karim Ma'mur 169
Khan, Makramat 169
Khmer architecture 77
Khorsabad (Assyria), palace and ziggurat 18,
   **19**
Khufu's (Cheop's) pyramid 24, **25**, 25–6, **26**,
   27
ki, southwest tribes 257
Kickapoo, the 253
Kiesler, Friedrich 477, **478**
Kiev (Russia) 150
   St. Sophia 150
Kimbell Art Museum, Fort Worth, Texas
   (Kahn) 15, 515, **515**, **516**
King's Road House, West Hollywood, Calif.
   (Schindler) 499
Kiowa-Apache 253
Kitagata (Japan), Slither Housing (Diller and
   Scofidio) 548

kivas 258
Kizhi (Russia)
  Church of the Raising of Lazarus 147, **147**, **148**
  Church of the Transfiguration **148**, **149**, 149–50, **150**
Klee, Paul 485
Klerk, Michael de 466
Knossos, palace of King Minos **36**, 36–9, **37**, **38**
Knowles, Frank 540, **540**
Knowlton Hall, Ohio State University (Scogin and Merrill) 546–7
Knoxville, Tennessee, railroad bridge 4
Koolhas, Rem **532**, 532–3, 564
Korea 94
Kos, Sanctuary of Asklepios 56, **56**
Kraków (Poland) 246, **246**, **247**
Kramer, Piet 466
Krier, Léon 534–5
Kuala Lumpur, Petronas Towers (Pelli) 549–50
Kuba tribe (Zaire) 274, **275**
Kutná Hora (Bohemia) St. Barbara 236, **236**
Kyoto (Japan), Katsura Imperial Villa **101**, 101–3, **102**, **103**

La Jolla, Calif.
  Neurosciences Institute (Williams and Tsien) 545–6, **546**
  Salk Institute for Medical Sciences (L.I Kahn) 514, **514**
La Venta, Tabasco (Mexico) 259, **259**
Laban Center for Movement and Dance, Deptford (Herzog and de Meuron) 551, **551**
Labrouste, Henri 5, 420–2, **421**, **422**, 449
labyrinths 36, 37
Ladkhan Temple, Aihole (India) 72, **72**, 78
LaFarge, John 414, 440
Laguna West, Florida 534
Lahawri, Ahmad 169
Lakeville, Connecticut, House III (Eisenman) 525, **525**
Lakota Sioux 251
Lakshmana Temple, Khajuraho (India) **73**, 73–4, **74**, 78
Lamb, William 475, **475**
landscape design, Romantic **397**, 397–8
Lang House, Washington, Connecticut (Stern) 524, **524**
Langhans, Carl Gotthard 402
Laon (France), Notre-Dame Cathedral **215**, 216–17, **217**, 221
Laotzu 81
Laramie, Wyoming, American Heritage Center (Predock) 544, **544**
Larkin Building, Buffalo (Wright) **460**, 460–2, 505
Latrobe, Benjamin Henry 394, 401, 406–7, **407**, 410, 448
Laugier, Marc-Antoine 390, 399
Laurana, Luciano 297
Le Corbusier 452, 455, 463, 472, 480–4, 500–3, 505, 507, 540
  Chandigarh, India 502–3, **503**
  Citrohan houses 481, **481**
  Dom-ino House 480, **480**
  "Five Points" 483
  La Ville Radieuse 500–1
  "Le Modular" 500
  Notre-Dame-du-Haut, Ronchamp **501**, 501–2, **502**
  Ste.-Marie-de-la-Tourette 502, **502**

Unité d'Habitation, Marseille **500**, 500–1, **501**
Villa Savoye, Poissy 481–3, **482**
Villa Stein, Garches 481, **481**
Weissenhof Siedlung housing unit **491**, 492
Le Nôtre, André 366–7, **367**
Le Raincy (France), Notre Dame (Perret) **479**, 480
Le Vau, Louis 363, **364**, 366, 377
Lebrun, Charles 363, **364**, 368, 377
Leça da Palmiera (Portugal), buildings by Siza 537
Ledoux, Claude-Nicolas 387, **387**, **388**, 388–90, **389**, 399
Lemercier, Jacques 329, **329**, 363
Leo X, Pope 349
Leonardo da Vinci 298, 299
  *Vitruvian Man* 286, **286**
Leoni, Giacomo 380
Leptis Magna, Hunting Baths 123
Lescaze, William **492**, 493
Lescot, Pierre 329, **329**
Lever House, Park Avenue, New York (Bunshaft) 488
Lévi-Strauss, Claude 519
Lewerentz, Sigurd 504
Lewitt, Erik 564
Leyswood, Sussex (England) (Shaw) 427, **427**
Libeskind, Daniel 541–2, 547–8
Library of Celsus, Ephesus 2
Lido villa (Loos) 455, **455**
lierne ribs 226
light wells 37, 38
Ligorio, Pirro 324–5, 325, **325**, 348
Limoges (France), St. Martial 195
Lin, Maya 540–1, **541**
Lincoln Cathedral, Lincs. (England) 208, **228**, 232, 232–3, 249
linear perspective 286, 299
lintels 3
Lissitzky, El 477
live loads 2
loads 2
log construction
  Navajo 258, **258**
  Russia, horizontal 147, 149
  *see also* stave churches
loggias 285
Lombard bands 190, **194**
Lombardo, Martino and Tullio 321
London (England)
  Adelphi scheme (Adam) 384–5
  Bank of England (Soane) 405, **405**, 448
  Banqueting House, Whitehall (Jones) **334**, 335
  Burlington House 380
  Chiswick House 380, **381**
  Christ Church, Spitalfields (Hawksmoor) 374–5, **375**
  City Hall (Foster) 559
  Covent Garden (Jones) **335**, 335–6
  Crystal Palace (Paxton) 419–20, **420**, 449, 542
  Houses of Parliament (Barry and Pugin) 410, **411**
  Laban Center for Movement and Dance, Deptford (Herzog and de Meuron) 551, **551**
  New Zealand Chambers (Shaw) 427, **428**
  Palm House, Kew Gardens (Burton and Turner) 419, **419**
  Queen's House, Greenwich (Jones) **333**, 333–5, **334**

Robin Hood Gardens (P. and A. Smithson) 507
Sainsbury Wing, National Gallery (Venturi and Scott-Brown) 518
St. Dunstan-in-the-East (Wren) 370
St. Martin-in-the-Fields (Gibbs) 375, **376**, 377
St. Mary-le-Bow (Wren) 370
St. Paul's Cathedral: (Jones) 336; (Wren) 5, 370–2, **371**, 377
St. Stephen Walbrook (Wren) **369**, 370
Soane's Museum, Lincoln's Inn Fields 406, **406**, 448, 546
Somerset House (Chambers) 386, **386**
Tower of London (White Tower) 243, **243**
Waterloo International Terminal (Grimshaw) 559
Westminster Abbey 330
Westminster Hall 234, **234**
Williams-Wynn House (Adam) 385, **385**
Wren's replanning 369, 370
longhouses
  Iroquois 253
  medieval 240, **241**
Longhua Pagoda, Shanghai 83
Loos, Adolf 430, 452, 453–5, **454**, 472, 505
Lorsch (Germany), abbey gatehouse 180, **180**
Los Angeles, Calif.
  Art Deco buildings 475, **476**
  Cathedral of Our Lady of the Angels (Moneo) 551–2, **552**
  Coca-Cola Bottling Plant (Derrah) 475, **476**
  Diamond Ranch High School (Mayne) 545
  Gehry House, Santa Monica (Gehry) 525, 528, **528**
  Getty Museum (Meier) 544
  Lovell Health House (Neutra) 499
  Museum of Contemporary Art (Isozaki) 539
  Pantages Theater (Priteca) 475, **476**
  Team Disneyland Administration Building (Gehry) 528–9, **529**
  V. D. L. Research House (Neutra) 499, **499**
  The Wiltern theater 475
Louis IX, king of France 224, 244
Louis VII, king of France 214, 216
Louis XII, king of France 326
Louis XIV, king of France 363
Lowell Beach House, Newport Beach, CA. (Schindler) 499
lustral-basins, Knossos 39
Luton Hoo, Bedfordshire (England) (Adam) 385–6
Lutyens, Edwin 503–4, **504**
Lysikrates, monument 55–6, **56**

Machu Picchu (Peru) **251**, 274
Mackintosh, Charles Rennie 434–7, **435**, **436**, 449
McKim, Charles Follen 414, 416, 449
McKim, Mead, and White 5, 414–15
  Boston Public Library 5, 293–4, **415**, 416
  Pennsylvania Station, New York 416, **416**
  Villard Houses, New York **415**, 415–16
McKinnell, Noel Michael 540, **540**
Macmurdo, Arthur, *Wren's City Churches* (title page) 430, **430**
Maderno, Carlo 314, 346
Madison, John Graves House **6**
madrasas 162
Magney House, Bingi Point (Australia) (Murcutt), **562**, 563

Mahabalipuram (India), temples (rathas) 75, **75**
Mahoney, Marion 459–60
Maiano, Giovanni da 330
Maidu tribe 258
Maillart, Robert 479
Maisons-sur-Seine, château (Mansart) 365–6, **366**
Major, Thomas 382
Maki, Fumihiko 538–9, 548
Malatesta, Sigismondo 293
Malcontenta (Italy), Villa Foscari (Palladio) 318, **319**
mandalas 71
Mandan earth lodges 253
Mannerism (Late Renaissance) 304–23, 336
  garden design 324–5
manor houses, medieval 241, **241**
Mansart, François 5, **364**, 364–6, **365**, **366**, 377, 390
Mansart, Jules-Hardouin 367–9, **368**, 390
Mantua (Italy)
  Palazzo del Te (Romano) **307**, 307–8
  S. Andrea (Alberti) 294, **295**, 336
  S. Sebastiano (Alberti) 294, 295, **295**
maqsura 153
marble 46, 61, 117, 211
Marinetti, Filippo 463–4
Mark, Robert 223
Marseille (France), Unité d'Habitation (Le Corbusier) **500**, 500–1, **501**
Marshall Field Wholesale Store, Chicago (Richardson) 441, **441**, 442–4, 449
martyria, Early Christian 135
Marzabotto (Italy) 105, **106**
Masaccio 292
  *The Trinity* 286, **287**, 336
Maser (Italy), Villa Barbaro (Palladio) 317–18, **318**
Mashhad (Iran), Goharshad Mosque **4**
masjids 153
Mason's Bend Community Center, New Bern, Alabama (Mockbee) 537, **537**
mastaba tombs, Egypt 21, **21**
master builders, medieval 239, 240
mausolea, Early Christian 135–9
Maya, the **2**, 262–7, 282, 283
Mayne, Thom 545
Mead, William Rutherford 414, 449
Mecca
  Ka'ba 156, **156**
  Mosque of the Prophet **154**
Medes 19
Medical College of Virginia, Richmond (Steward) 401
Medici family 285, 308, 324, 336
Medici, Cosimo de' 298
Medici Villa (Michelozzo), Fiesole 324, **324**
medieval architecture 177
  castles 242–3, 249
  cities 244–8
  construction 239–40
  geometry 240
  housing 240–2, **241**, **242**, 249
  *see also* Carolingian architecture; Gothic architecture; Norman architecture; Vikings
Medina, House of the Prophet 156, **156**
megalithic constructions
  Stonehenge **12**, **13**, 13–14
  tombs **10**, **11**, 11–13
megarons 41
  Minoan, at Knossos 39, 61
  Mycenaean 41, **43**, 44
Mehmet II, Sultan 164

Meidum (Egypt), pyramid **24**, 24–5
Meier, Richard **543**, 543–4, **544**
Meissonier, J.A. 379
Meledo (Italy), Villa Trissino (Palladio) 320, **320**
Melk abbey (Austria) 357–9, **359**
Melnikov, Konstantin **465**, 465–6, **466**
Mendelsohn, Erich **470**, 470–1, 513
Menes, king of Egypt 21
Mengoni, Giuseppe 542
Menil Collection Museum, Houston, Texas (Piano) 555
Menkaure (Mycerinus), pharaoh, pyramid at Giza **24**, 25, **25**, 26, **26**
Mentuhotep II, tomb and temple 28, **28**, 33
Mereworth Castle, Kent (Campbell) 380, **380**
Mérida (Spain), National Museum of Roman Art (Moneo) 551
Mesa Verde, Colorado 257, **257**, 258
Mesopotamia (Iraq) 14–20
Metabolists 538
Métro entrances, Paris (Guimard) 431, **431**
Meuron, Pierre de **501**, 550–1
Mexico, Pre-Columbian 259–69, 282, 283
Mexico City, El Bebedero (Barragán) 535, **535**
Meyer, Adolf 463, 484, **484**, 486
Meyer, Hannes 488
Mi Fu 91
Miami Beach, Florida, Art Deco buildings 475
  The Breakwater (Skislewicz) **476**
Michelangelo Buonarroti 123, 304, 308–15, 341
  Campidoglio, Rome **310**, 310–11, **311**
  Laurentian Library, Florence 308–9, **309**
  Palazzo Farnese, Rome 312, **312**
  Porta Pia, Rome **314**, 315, 341
  S. Lorenzo, Florence **289**, 308–10, **309**
  St. Peter's, Rome 5, **312**, 312–14, **313**
  Sforza Chapel, S. Maria Maggiore, Rome 315, **315**, 336
Michelozzo di Bartolomeo 336
  Banco Mediceo, Milan 298
  Medici Villa, Fiesole 324, **324**
Micmac, the 253
Mies van der Rohe, Ludwig 100, 235, 452, 455, 463, 477, 488–90, 492, 493–5, 505
  Barcelona Pavilion 488–90, **489**
  Crown Hall, I.I.T. 493, **493**, 495
  Farnsworth House, Plano **494**, 494–5
  860 Lake Shore Drive, Chicago 494, **494**
  Seagram Building, New York 495, **495**
  Tugendhat House, Brno 490, **490**
  Weissenhof Siedlung, block of flats **491**, 491–2
mihrabs 153, 158
Milan (Italy) 298, 326
  Banco Mediceo (Michelozzo) 298
  Cathedral 224, **237**, **238**, 238–9, 249
  Galleria Vittorio Emanuele (Mengoni) 542
  S. Ambrogio **192**, 194, **194**, 211
  S. Maria delle Grazie (Bramante) 299, **299**
Miletus (Asia Minor) 59–60
mill buildings 419
  English textile mills 396, **396**
Miller, Sanderson 398
Milwaukee Art Museum (Calatrava) 557, **557**
minarets 157, 165, 167, 169
minbars 153
Minerals and Mining Museum (Murcutt), Broken Hill (Australia) **563**, 563–4
minka (wooden folk houses), Japan 99, 99–100
Minoans 36–9, 61

Mirande (France), bastide 245, **245**
Mississippi River basin, tribes 253–5
M.I.T. School of Architecture, Cambs. Mass. 413
  Baker House (Aalto) 511, **511**
  Simmons Hall dormitory (Holl) 545, **545**
Mitla, Oaxaca (Mexico) 262, **262**
Mityana Pilgrims Shrine, Uganda (Dahinden) 550, **550**
Miwok tribe 258
Mixtecs 262
Mnesikles 52
moats 242, 244
Moche culture 271–2
Mockbee, Samuel 537, **537**
Modena, Cemetery of San Cataldo (Rossi) 534, **534**
Modern Movement 490
Modernism 427, 451–505, 507–16
  classical tradition in 533–5
  form-making 548–52; (USA) 540–8
  Japan 538–40
  modern regionalism 535–7
  sustainable design 560–5
  technology and 552–60
  Venturi's counter proposal 517–18
  *see also* Post-Modernism
Mogollan, the 257
Mohenjo-Daro (Indus Valley) 63, **64**
Moholy-Nagy, László 485
Moller House, Vienna (Loos) **454**, 455
monasteries 177
  Benedictine (*see* St. Gall)
  Carolingian 182–4
  China 83–4, 85, 86
  Cistercian 205–8
  Cluny **198**, 198–202, **199**, 211
  Early Romanesque 188–9
  India, Buddhist (viharas) 66, 68
  Japan 95–6
  Le Corbusier 502, **502**
  Romanesque 188–9
  *see also* Buddhist monasteries
Mondrian, Piet 477
Moneo, Raphael 551–2, **552**, 555
Mongols 146, 150
Monpazier (France), bastide 245, **245**, **246**
Monte Albán (Mexico) 261, **261**
Monte San Giorgio (Switzerland), 1973 house (Botta) 536, **536**
Montefeltro, Federigo da 297
Monticello, Charlottesville (Jefferson) **408**, 408–9
Montreuil, Pierre de 218
*Monument to the Third International* (Tatlin) 465, **465**
Moore, Charles 519, **521**, 521–2, **522**, 534
Moorish style 401
Moosbrugger, Caspar 361
Moosbrugger, Johann 361
Morocco
  courtyard houses 280
  kasbahs 278–80, **279**
  tents 274, **275**
Morphosis 545
Morris, William **426**, 426–7, 430, 440, 449, 452
mortise-and-tenon joints 13
mortuary temples, Egyptian 28, **28**, 30–2
mosaics 110, 135, 139, 144, 146, 151, 182
Moscow (Russia) 150
  Kremlin 150
  Pravda Newspaper Building (V. and A. Vesnin) 465, **465**

Rusakov Workers' Club (Melnikov) 466, **466**

St. Basil the Blessed (Cathedral of the Intercession of the Moat) (Barma and Posnik) 150–1, **151**

mosques
 columnar/hypostyle 157–8, 175
 conception of 156–7
 iwan 157, 160–3, 175
 multi-domed 164–7
 *see also* individual mosques

motte and bailey castles 242–3, **243**
mounds *see* earth mounds
Moundville, Alabama 255, **255**
Mount Wilson (Australia), Simpson-Lee House (Murcutt) **563**, 564
Moussavi, Farshid 552
Mozarabic churches 182
Mumford, Lewis 496
muqarnas vaults 154, 172, **174**, 175
Murcutt, Glenn 560–4, **561**, **562**, **563**
Museum for Pre-Columbian Art (Johnson), Dumbarton Oaks 520
Museum für Kunsthandwerk, Frankfurt (Meier) **543**, 543–4
Museum of American Folk Art, New York (Williams and Tsien) 546
Museum of Anthropology, British Columbia (Erickson) 549
Museum of Contemporary Art, Los Angeles (Isozaki) 539
Museum of Wood, Osaka (Ando) **539**, 539–40
Mussolini, Benito 342–3
Muthesius, Herman 429, 449, 452, 462
MVRDV 560
Mycenae 39–43, **40**
 houses 43, **43**
 Lion Gate 39–40, **41**
 palace 40–1
 tombs (tholoi) 41–2
 Treasury of the Atreus **41**, 41–2, **42**
Mycenaeans 36, 39
Mycerinus *see* Menkaure

Nakatsu (Japan), Kaze-no-Oka Crematorium (Maki) 538–9
Nanchan Monastery, Shanxi, China **84**, 85, 86
Nanih Waiya mound, Mississippi 254, **254**
Napoleon 382, 395
Narmer, Pharoah 21
Nash, John 401
Nasher Sculpture Center, Dallas (Piano) 556, **556**
Nashville, Tennessee
 First Presbyterian Church (Strickland) 401
 Tennessee State Capitol (Strickland) 56
Naskapi, the 253
Nasrid Dynasty 172
Natchez tribe 255
National Assembly of Bangladesh, Dacca (Kahn) 514
National Farmers' Bank, Owatonna (Sullivan) 448
Native Americans 251–8, **252**, 283
Navajo nation 258, 283
naves 134
Nazca, the 272
Neo-Classicism 379–80, 383, 397, 399, 401–2, 419, 448
 England 384–6, 405–6
 France 387–90, 392–4, 422
 Germany 402–5

United States 406–10
Neo-Palladianism 380–2, 398, 399
Neo-Plasticism 477
Neo-Sumerian period 17
Neolithic period, Banpo, houses 81, **82**
Neumann, Johann Balthasar **339**, 361, 361–3, **362**, 377
Neurosciences Institute, La Jolla (Williams and Tsien) 545–6, **546**
Neutra, Richard 499, **499**
New Bern, Alabama, Mason's Bend Community Center (Mockbee) 537, **537**
New Canaan, Connecticut, Boissonas House (Johnson) 520, **520**
New Haven, cemetery gates (Austin) 401
New Orleans, Louisiana, Piazza d'Italia (Moore) 521–2, **522**
New Urbanism 533–4
New York City
 American Telephone and Telegraph Headquarters (Johnson and Burgee) 520, 520–1
 Brooklyn Bridge (Roebling) 417, **417**
 Chrysler Building (Van Alen) 446, **472**, 472–3
 Citicorp Building (Stubbins) 542, **542**
 Daily News Building (Hood) **473**, 475
 Empire State Building (Shreve, Lamb, and Harmon) 446, 475, **475**
 Ford Foundation Building (Roche and Dinkeloo) 542, **542**
 Guggenheim Museum (Wright) 496, **498**
 IBM Center (Barnes) 542, **542**
 Lever House, Park Avenue (Bunshaft) 488
 Metropolitan Museum of Art 413
 Museum of American Folk Art (Williams and Tsien) 546
 Museum of Modern Art (MOMA) 548
 Number Two Park Avenue (E.J. Kahn) **451**, 473–5
 Pennsylvania Station (McKim, Mead, and White) 416, **416**
 Radio City Music Hall (Harrison) **474**, 475
 Rockefeller Center **474**, 475
 Seagram Building (Mies van der Rohe) 446, 495, **495**, 548; Brasserie (Diller and Scofidio) 548
 Trinity Church (Upjohn) 412, **412**
 Trump Tower (Der Scutt et al) 542, **542**
 TWA Terminal, Kennedy Airport (Saarinen) 512–13, **513**
 Villard Houses (McKim, Mead, and White) **415**, 415–16
 Woolworth Building (Gilbert) 472
 World Trade Center, design competition 547–8
Newcastle-upon-Tyne (England). Byker Wall Housing (Erskine) 507, **508**
Newgrange, Co. Meath (Ireland), passage grave **11**, 11–13, 33
Newport, Rhode Island
 The Breakers (Hunt) 413, **413**
 Watts Sherman House (Richardson) 442, **443**, 449
Newport Bay Club Hotel, Disneyland Resort (France) (Stern) 524
Newport Beach, Calif., Lowell Beach House (Schindler) 499
Newton, Sir Isaac, cenotaph (Boullée) **387**, 387–8
Nez Perce, the 256
Nicholas V, Pope 302, 341
Nimes (France)
 Némausus (Nouvel) 557

Pont du Gard aqueduct **105**, 109
Temple of Diana 110, **110**
Nineveh (Kuyunjik) 18
Nördlingen (Germany), St. George Church 235, **235**, **236**
Norman architecture 208–10, 211
Northeastern tribes, Native American 253
Northwestern tribes, Native American 256–7
Norway, stave churches 184–7, **185**, **186**, **187**
Nouméa, New Caledonia, Jean-Marie Tjibaou Cultural Center (Piano) 556, **556**
Nouvel, Jean 548, 557
Novgorod (Russia), Church of the Nativity of the Virgin **148**, 149
number ratios 285–6, 290
Nymphenburg Castle (Germany), pavilion (Cuvillés) 379

Oak Park, Illinois
 Gale House (Wright) 458
 Unity Temple (Wright) 460, **461**, 461–2, 505
obelisks
 Egypt 21, 33
 Vatican Obelisk 343, 350, 352, **352**, **353**
Ogden House, Fairfield, Connecticut 7
Ohio State University, Knowlton Hall (Scogin and Merrill) 546–7
Ohiopyle, Penn., Fallingwater (Kaufmann House) (Wright) 458, 496, **497**
Olbrich, Joseph Maria 437, 438–9, **439**, 449
Olmecs, the 255, 259, 282
 stone heads 259, **259**
Olmsted, Frederick Law 413, 414
Olympia, Temple of Hera 44, 45, **45**
Olympic Sports complex, Tokyo (Tange) 538, **538**
onion domes 150
open-plan buildings 479
OpenOffice 548
opus incertum 109, 110
opus listatum 111
opus quadratum 109
opus reticulatum 110
opus testaceum 110
Orchard, The, Chorleywood, Herts. (Voysey) 428
orders of architecture **45**, 45–6, **46**, 105–6
 *see also* Corinthian order; Doric order; Ionic order; Tuscan order
oriel windows 427
Orme, Philibert de l' **328**, 328–9
orthographic projections 5–6, 385
Osaka (Japan), Museum of Wood (Ando) **539**, 539–40
Ostia, insula 128, **128**
Ottonian architecture 190, 210
Oud, J.J.P. 477, **477**
Owatonna, Minnesota, National Farmers' Bank (Sullivan) 448
Oxford (England), Sheldonian Theater (Wren) 369–70

Paestum (Italy) 59, **60**, 382, 390
 Temple of Hera **45**, 46–7, **47**
pagodas
 China **82**, **83**, 83–4
 Japan 95, **95**
Paimio (Finland), Tuberculosis Sanatorium (Aalto) **509**, 509–11
palaces
 Africa **280**, 280–1
 Assyria 18, **19**
 Baroque **361**, 361–3

Carolingian 178, **178**
Islamic **172**, 172–5, **173**, **174**
Khorsabad 18, **19**
Mayan 266, **266**
Minoan 36, 36–9, **37**, **38**
Mycenae 40–1
Persepolis 19–20, **20**
Roman, urban 129, **129**
Teotihuacán (Mexico) 261, **261**
Palatine Chapel, Aachen 178–80, **179**, **180**, 210
Palenque (Mexico) 265, **265**, 282
Palladio, Andrea 304, 315–21, 336–7, 376, 399
  basilica in Vicenza 316, **316**
  churches in Venice 320–1
  and the English Renaissance 333
  *I quattro libri dell'architettura* 315–16, **316**
  Palazzo Chiericati, Vicenza 316, **317**, 334
  Palazzo Valmarana, Vicenza 316
  S. Giorgio Maggiore, Venice **320**, 320–1
  Teatro Olimpico, Vicenza 321, **321**
  Villa Barbaro, Maser 317–18, **318**
  villa designs in the Veneto 317–20
  Villa Foscari, Malcontenta 318, **319**
  Villa Rotonda (Villa Americo-Capra), Vicenza 318–20, **319**
  Villa Trissino, Meledo 320, **320**
  *see also* Neo-Palladianism
Panini, Giovanni Paolo, *The Interior of the Pantheon* **120**
Pantages Theater, Los Angeles (Priteca) 475, **476**
Pantheon, Rome 5, 118–20, **119**, **120**, 131
Papago tribe 257
Paris (France)
  Arc du Triomphe 115–16
  Barrière de la Villette (Ledoux) 389–90
  Bibliothèque Nationale (Labrouste) 421–2, **422**, 449
  Bibliothèque Ste. Geneviève (Labrouste) 5, 420, **421**, 449
  Castel Béranger (Guimard) 431
  Cité de la Musique (Portzamparc) 550
  Comédie-Française (Peyre and Wailly) 392, **392**
  Ecole de Chirurgie (Gondoin) 392–4, **394**
  Eiffel Tower (Eiffel) **401**, 422
  Exposition des Arts Décoratifs 465, **465**, 477, **478**
  Hôtel Amelot (Boffrand) 379
  Hôtel de Monnaies (royal mint) (Antoine) 392, **393**
  Hôtel de Thelluson (Ledoux) 388, **389**
  Louvre: (Bernini) 363; (Lemercier) 329, **329**, 363; (Lescot) 329, **329**; (Pei) 541; (Perrault, Lebrun and Le Vau) 363–4, **364**, 377
  Métro entrances (Guimard) 431, **431**
  Notre-Dame Cathedral 217–19, **218**, **219**, 249, 412
  Panthéon (Ste.-Geneviève) (Soufflot) **390**, 390–1, 395
  Parc de la Villette, *Folie* (Tschumi) **524**, 524–5
  Place Royale (Place des Vosges) 330, **330**
  Pompidou Center (Piano and Rogers) 555, **555**
  Roman baths, Cluny Museum 123
  Rue de Suisse Housing (Herzog and de Meuron) 550–1
  Rue Franklin apartment house (Perret) 480, **480**
  Sainte-Chapelle 224–6, **225**, **226**, 249, 412

St.-Jean de Montmarte (Baudot) 425
St. Louis-des-Invalides (J.-H. Mansart) **368**, 368–9
Ste. Marie de la Visitation (Mansart) 364, **364**
Soviet Pavilion, Exposition des Arts Décoratifs (Melnikov) 465, **465**
tollgates (Ledoux) 388–90, 399
Val-de-Grâce (Mansart) 5, 364–5, **365**
Parler, Johann 236
Parthenon, Athens 46, 47–50, **48**, **49**, 53, 61
Pasadena, house for Alice Millard (Wright) 495
Pasti, Matteo de' 294
Paul, Bruno 429, 488
Paul III, Pope 310, 313, 341
Pavia (Italy), Certosa monastery 326
Paxton, Joseph 419–20, **420**, 449
pebble-dash 434
Pei, I.M. 91, 541
Pelli, Cesar 549–50
pendant vaulting 398
pendentives 143, 196, 202
Pennsylvania Station, New York (McKim, Mead, and White) 416, **416**
Penobscot, the 253
pensionnaires (France) 392–4, 399
Pergamon 60
  Great Altar of Zeus 60–1, **61**
Périgueux (France), St. Front 202–3, **203**
peristyle 126
Perpendicular Gothic 226, 227, 249, 330
Perrault, Claude 363, 364, **364**, 377
Perret, Auguste 455, **479**, 479–80, 480
Persepolis, Persia (Iran) 19–20
Persia/Persian Empire 19–20, 47, 59
perspective, linear 286, 299
perspective drawings 6–7, **7**
Peru 269, 270–2, 282, 283
Perugia (Italy), "Arch of Augustus" 106, **107**
Peruzzi, Baldassare 313
Peter the Great of Russia 151
Petronas Towers, Kuala Lumpur (Pelli) 549–50
Pevsner, Nikolaus 427, 452
Peyre, Marie-Joseph 383, 392, **392**, 399
phenomenology 519
Phidias, sculptor 50
Philadelphia, Penn.
  Bacon's redevelopment 343
  Bank of Pennsylvania (Latrobe) 406
  Guild House (Venturi and Rauch) **517**, 517–18
  Philadelphia Exchange (Strickland) 56
  Philadelphia Saving Fund Society Building (Howe and Lescaze) 492, **493**
  Richards Medical Research Building, University of Pennsylvania (Kahn) 513–14, **514**
  St. James-the-Less 411, **411**
Philip of Macedon 54
Phillips Exeter Academy library, New Hampshire, (L.I. Kahn) 514, **515**
Phoenix Hall, Uji (Japan) 96, **96**
Piano, Renzo **555**, 555–6, **556**
Piazza d'Italia, New Orleans (Moore) 521–2, **522**
Picturesque, the 397, 398
Pienza (Italy) 296, **296**
pilgrimage road churches 194–7, 363
Pima tribe 257
Piranesi, Giovanni Battista 383, **383**, 384, **384**, 397, 399, 405
Pisa (Italy), Cathedral and Campanile

(Leaning Tower) **192**, 192–4, **193**
pit houses, Native American 256–8, **257**
Pittsburgh, Penn., Seventh Street Bridge **5**
Pius II, Pope 296
Pius IV, Pope 341
Plan of St. Gall (manuscript) *see* St. Gall
plank houses, northwestern tribes 256
Plano, Illinois, Farnsworth House (Mies van der Rohe) 494, **494**–5
plans, architectural 5–6, **6**
Plater-Zyberk, Elizabeth **533**, 533–4
platform framing 425
Plato 35, 285
Platz, Gustav 452
Plexus r + d 564
Pliny the Elder 117
Pliny the Younger 303
Poelzig, Hans 429, 471, **471**
pointed arches 3, **240**
  Gothic 213, 214
  Norman 210
  Romanesque 198–201, 203, 210
Poissy (France), Villa Savoye (Le Corbusier) 481–3, **482**
Poland, city planning 246
Polk, W.J. 446
Polykleitos 55, 57
Pompeii (Italy) **111**, 111–13, **112**, 382, 385, 399
  amphitheater 112, 124, **124**
  basilica 112–13, 120–1
  baths 111, 123, **123**
  forum **112**, 112–13
  houses 125–7, **126**, **127**, 128–9, **129**
  streets **127**, 127–8
  temples 112, 113
  triumphal arch 112, **116**
Pompidou Center, Paris (Piano and Rogers) 555, **555**
Pontelli, Baccio 297–8
Porta, Giacomo della *see* Giacomo della Porta
Portland Building, Portland, Oregon (Graves) 522–3, **523**
Portland cement 424
Portzamparc, Christian de 550
Posen (Germany), water tower (Poelzig) 471, **471**
Posnik (architect) 150
post-and-beam construction, China 84
post-and-lintel (column-and-beam) construction 2, **2**
  Catal Hüyük 10
  earth lodges 253
  hogans 258
  Japan 94
Post-Modernism 452, 517, 518–33, 564
Post-Structuralism 519
Potsdam (Germany), Einstein Tower (Mendelsohn) **470**, 470–1
Potsdamer Platz, Berlin, rebuilding 555
Poundbury, Dorset (Krier) 535
Poverty Point site, Louisiana 255
pozzolana 110, 117
Praeneste (Palestrina), Sanctuary of Fortuna Primigenia 109, **109**
Prague (Czech Republic)
  Müller House (Loos) 455
  Nationale Nederlander office (Gehry) 529, **530**
  St. Nicholas on the Lesser Side 359, **359**
Prairie houses (Wright) 456–9, 505
Prandtauer, Jacob 357–9, **358**, **359**
Pravda Newspaper Building, Moscow (Vesnin) 465, **465**

Pre-Columbian Americas 251–74, 282–3
Predock, Antoine 544, **544**
prefabrication 420
prehistoric settlements 10–14
Pritchard, Thomas 396
Priteca, B. Marcus **476**
Prix, Wolf Dieter 526
Procopius of Caesarea 141
proportion, Greek system of 35, 61
Provence (France) 211
  St. Gilles-du-Gard 203–5, **204**
  Sénanque monastery 208
Providence, Rhode Island, Baptist church
  (Brown) 375–6
Ptolomies 54
Pueblo *see* Ancestral Pueblo
Pueblo Bonito, Chaco Canyon (New
  Mexico) 258, **258**
pueblos 258
Pugin, A.W.N. 410, 411, **411**, *425*
  *Contrasts* 410, **410**, 448
"pumpkin vaults" 143, **143**
putti 323, 346
Putún culture 267
pylon gateways, Egypt 31–2, **32**
pyramids
  Aztec 268
  Bolivian 272
  Egyptian 21, 23–7, **24**, **25**, **26**, 29, 33
  Khmer 77
  Mayan 263–4, **264**, 265, **265**, 267–8
  Olmec 259, **259**, **260**
  Peru 269, 270, 271
  Toltecs 267, 268
  Zapotecs **261**, 261–2
Pythagoras 35, 285

qasr storage fortresses 278, **278**
qiblas 153, 175
quadripartite vaults 220
quatrefoils 226
Queen Anne style 427, **428**
Queen's House, Greenwich (Jones) **333**,
  333–5, **334**
Quinault tribe 256
quincunx plans, Byzantine 144–6, 151

Rabirius 129
Radio City Music Hall, New York (Harrison)
  **474**, 475
railroads 418
Rainaldi, Carlo 350, **351**, 352, **352**
ramada, southwest tribes 257
Ramesses II 31
rancherías 257
Rand McNally Building, Chicago (Burnham
  and Root) 423–4
Ransome, Ernest 425
Raphael 304, 312
  House of Raphael, Rome (Bramante) 304,
  **304**
  Villa Madama, Rome 305–6, **306**, 324
rathas (temples) 75, **75**
Rauch, John K. **517**
Ravenna (Italy)
  Baptistery of the Orthodox 135, **137**
  S. Apollinare in Classe 139, **139**, **140**
  S. Apollinare Nuovo **134**, 135
  S. Vitale **141**, 143, 144, **144**, 210
  Tomb of Theodoric 5
Red Blue Chair (Rietveld) 478, **478**
Red House (Webb), Bexleyheath 426, **426**
Reich, Lilly 490
Reims Cathedral (France) 412

reinforced concrete 425, 449, 479–80, 505
Reinhard 474
Rejsek, Matej 236
Reliance Building, Chicago (Burnham and
  Root) 424, **424**, 449
Renaissance architecture 285–337
  city planning 292, 329–30
  domes 287, **288**, 302, 308, 313–14
  England 330–6
  France 326–30, 337
  gardens and landscapes 324
  High Renaissance 302, 304, 336
  Italy 296, 297–336
  orders of architecture 46
Revel (France), bastide 245, **245**
Revett, Nicholas 382
Rhodes, street **3**
rib vaults
  Gothic 213, 215
  Norman 209–10
  Romanesque 194
Richards Medical Research Building, Univ. of
  Pennsylvania (L.I. Kahn) 513–14, **514**
Richardson, Henry Hobson 439–42, **440**,
  **441**, **442**, 449, 455
Richmond, Virginia
  cast-iron façade **423**
  Medical College of Virginia (Steward) 401
  State Capitol of Virginia (Jefferson) 407–8,
  **408**
Ried, Benedikt 236
Rietveld, Gerrit 477–8, **478**, 479
Rimini (Italy), S. Francesco (Alberti) 5,
  293–4, **294**
River Forest, Illinois, Winslow House
  (Wright) 457, **457**, 492
Robbia, Luca della 292
Robertson, Jaquelin 534
Robie House, Chicago (Wright) 458–9, **459**
Roche, Kevin 542, **542**
rock-cut temples, India 71
  *see also* cave-temples
rock-cut tombs, Egyptian 28, **28**, 29–30
Rockefeller Center, New York **474**, 475
Rococo style 379, 398
Roebling, John Augustus 417, **417**
Roebling, Washington Augustus 417
Rogers, Richard 548, 555, **555**
Roman architecture 107–8, 121–3
  amphitheaters 112, 124, **124**, 124–5, **125**
  aqueducts 108–9
  arches 3, 106, **107**, 108, 115–16, **116**, 290
  barrel-vaults 109, 110, **110**, 121, 130–1
  basilicas 112, 120–1, **121**, 151
  baths (thermae) 121–3
  bridges 4
  building materials 110, 117, 121, 128, 130,
  1120
  building techniques 108–11
  castra (military camps) 105, 113
  city planning 105, 111–16, 131, 341–2, **342**,
  350–2, 376
  domes 108, 118–20
  flying buttresses 115
  fora 111, 111–15, **112**, 113–15, **114**
  houses 125–7, 128–30
  insulae (apartment blocks) 128, **128**, 131
  temples 118–20
  theaters 123–4, **124**
  triumphal arches 112, 113, 115–16
  urban palaces 129, **129**
Romanesque architecture
  Aquitaine and Provence 202–5
  early Romanesque 188–9

Holy Roman Empire 190–4
  pilgrimage road churches 194–7
  structural techniques 188–9
  *see also* Cluny monastery; Ste. Madeleine;
  Vézelay
Romanticism 383, 397–8, 419, 448
Rome (Italy) 106, 107, 108, 111, 177, 194
  Arch of Constantine 116, **116**
  Arch of Septimus Severus 116
  Baroque replanning 341–2, **342**, 350–2,
  376
  Basilica Nova 121, **121**
  Basilica of Constantine 131
  Basilica Ulpia 115, 121
  Baths of Diocletian **122**, 123
  Belvedere Courtyard (Bramante) **303**,
  303–4, 324, 336
  Campidoglio (Michelangelo) **310**, 310–11,
  **311**
  Castel Sant'Angelo 341
  catacombs 133
  Colosseum 107, 125, **125**, 130–1
  Forum of Augustus 115
  Forum of Trajan (Apollodorus of
  Damascus) 115, 131
  Forum Romanum 113, **114**
  House of Raphael (Bramante) 304, **304**
  Il Gesù (Vignola and Giacomo della Porta)
  339–41, **340**, 341, 357, 376
  Nero's Golden House 385
  obelisk 343, 350, 352, **352**, 353
  Palace of Domitian (Rabirius) 129, **129**
  Palazzo Farnese (Michelangelo and
  Sangallo the Younger) 312, **312**
  Pantheon 5, 118–20, **119**, **120**, 131
  Piazza del Popolo 342, 352, **352**, 353
  Piazza Navona (Bernini and Borromini)
  **350**, 350–2, 354, **354**
  Piazza of St. Peter's (Bernini) 345, **345**
  Porta Pia (Michelangelo) **314**, 315
  S. Agnese (Borromini and Rainaldi) 350–1,
  **351**
  S. Andrea al Quirinale (Bernini) 346, **346**,
  376
  S. Bernardo 123
  S. Carlo alle Quattro Fontane (Borromini)
  **347**, 347–8, **348**, 376
  S. Costanza (Constantia's mausoleum)
  **136**, 136–9, **137**
  S. Ivo della Sapienza (Borromini) **348**,
  348–50, **349**
  St. John Lateran 135
  S. Maria degli Angeli (Michelangelo) 123
  S. Maria dei Miracoli (Rainaldi and
  Bernini) 352, **352**
  S. Maria della Pace (Cortona) **351**, 351–2
  S. Maria in Montesanto (Rainaldi and
  Bernini) 352, **352**
  S. Maria Maggiore, Sforza Chapel
  (Michelangelo) **315**, 315
  St. Peter's 302, 342–3, **344**; (Bernini)
  343–5, **345**; (Bramante) 302, **302**;
  (Giacomo della Porta) 314, **344**;
  (Maderno) 314, **344**; (Michelangelo) 5,
  **312**, 312–14, **313**, 336, **344**; (Sangallo the
  Younger) 313; (Vignola) **344**
  St. Peter's, Old 135, **136**
  Sforza Chapel, S. Maria Maggiore
  (Michelangelo) **315**, 315, 336
  Spanish Steps (Francesco de Sanctis) 352,
  **353**
  Tempietto (Bramante) **301**, 301–2, 336
  Temple of Fortuna Virilis 118, **118**
  Temple of Vesta 118

Theater of Marcellus 124, **124**
Trajan's Column 115
Trajan's markets 115, **115**, **116**, 131
Vatican Obelisk 343, 350, 352, **352**, **353**
Villa Giulia 324
Villa Madama (Raphael) **305–6**, **306**, 324
Ronchamp (France), Notre-Dame-du-Haut
  (Le Corbusier) 500–2, **501**, **502**
roofs
  Chinese 83, 84, 85
  hammerbeam 229, 234, **234**, 331
  "hidden" structure, Japan 101
  hipped, Native American 255
  shatyor (tent roofs) **148**, 149, 150
  shikhara 72–3
  space frame construction 4
  trusses 4
Root, John Welborn 423, 424, **424**
Roquebrune (France), Eileen Gray's home
  **483**, 484
rose windows 215, 218
Rosenthal Center for Contemporary Arts,
  Cincinnati (Hadid) 527, **527**
Rossellino, Bernardo **296**, 302
Rossi, Aldo 534, **534**
Rotterdam (Holland)
  Hook of Holland housing project (Oud)
    477, **477**
  KunstHal (Koolhas) 532–3
Rotundi, Michael 545
Roycrofters Workshop 427
Rudofsky, Bernard 9, 251, 277, 517
Rural Studio, the 537
Rurik 146, 184
Rusakov Workers' Club, Moscow (Melnikov)
  466, **466**
Ruskin, John 414, 425–6, 427, 449, 451
Russia
  Byzantine churches 146–51
  Constructivism 463, 464–6, 505
  horizontal log construction 147, 149
  prehistoric settlements 10
  shatyor (tent roofs) **148**, 149, 150

S. Gimignano (Italy), tower houses 242, **242**,
  249
Saarinen, Eero 512–13, **513**, 516, 517, 557
Saarinen, Eliel 512
Sabines 106
sahns 157, 163, 165, 175
Sainsbury Wing, National Gallery, London
  (Venturi and Scott-Brown) 518
Saint-Gaudens, Augustus 440
St. Denis abbey church (France) 214–16,
  **215**, **216**, 412
St. Gall mosastery (Plan of St. Gall) 182–4,
  **183**, **184**, 207, 210, 240
St. Gilles-du-Gard, Provence (France) 203–5,
  **204**
St. Luke's, Isle of Wight County, Virginia 248
St. Martin at Canigou, monastery 188, **188**,
  **189**
St. Martin at Tours (France) 195
St. Paul's Cathedral *see* London
St. Peter's *see* Rome
St. Savin-sur-Gartempe, hall church 235
Ste.-Marie-de-la-Tourette, Eveux-sur-
  l'Arbresle (Le Corbusier) 502, **502**
Salginatobel Bridge, Switzerland (Maillart)
  479
Salisbury, Wilts. (England), Cathedral **228**,
  **230**, 230–1, **231**, 249
Salk Institute for Medical Sciences, La Jolla,
  Calif. (L.I Kahn) 514, **514**

saltbox houses 6, **6**, **7**
saltworks (Ledoux) **387**, 388
Samarkand (Uzbekistan)
  Bibi Khanum Mosque 160, **160**
  Gur-i-Amir 168, **168**
Samarra (Iraq), Great Mosque of al-
  Mutawakkil 157–8, **158**
Samuel Daggett House, Connecticut 6
San Francisco, Calif.
  Halladie Building (Polk) 446
  San Francisco Federal Building
    (Morphosis) 545
  Sea Ranch I (Moore) 521, **521**
  V.C. Morris Gift Shop (Wright) 496
Sanchi (India)
  Great Stupa **67**, 67–8, **68**, **69**
  temples 68, 71
Sanctis, Francesco de 352, **353**
Sangallo, Giuliano da 312
Sangallo the Younger, Antonio da 312, 313
Sanmichele, Michele 323
Sansovino, Jacopo **322**, 323, **323**
Santa Monica, Calif. *see* Los Angeles
Sant'Elia, Antonio 464, **464**
Santiago de Compostela (Spain)
  Galician Center of Contemporary Art (Siza)
    536, **536**
  St. James's church 194–5, 195, 197, 211
Saqqara (Egypt), Djoser's funerary complex
  and pyramid **23**, 23–4, **24**
Saqsaywaman, fortress of (Cuzco) 273, **273**
Saussure, Ferdinand 519
Sawyerville, Alabama, Yancey Chapel
  (Mockbee) 537
Säynätsalo (Finland), Town Hall (Aalto)
  511–12, **512**
Scamozzi, Vincenzo 321, **321**, 323, 331
Scharoun, Hans 555
Scheerbart, Paul 466
Schindler, Richard 499
Schinkel, Karl Friedrich **402**, 402–5, **403**,
  **404**, 448, 455, 488
Schliemann, Heinrich 39
Schroeder House, Utrecht (Rietveld) 478,
  **478**, **479**, 492
Scofidio, Ricardo 548
Scogin, Mack 546–7
Scott-Brown, Denise 518, 534
Sea Ranch I, San Francisco (Moore) 521, **521**
Seagram Building, New York (Mies van der
  Rohe) 446, 495, **495**, 548
Seaside, Florida **533**, 533–4
Seattle, Washington D. C.
  Chapel of St. Ignatius (Holl) 544
  Seattle Central Library (Koolhas) **532**, 533
Sechin Alto (Peru) 270, **270**
sections 6, **6**
segmental arches **240**
seismic loads 2
Seleucids 54
Selimiye Mosque, Edirne (Sinan) 167, **167**
Semioticians 519
Semper, Gottfried 466
Senmut 30
Sens Cathedral (France) 213, **227**
Serliana 316, 323
Serlio, Sebastiano 316, 328, 331, 337
sexpartite vaults 217
Sezincote, Glos. (England) (Cockerell) 401
Sforza, Francesco 298
Sforza family 326
Shanghai (China), Longhua Pagoda 83
Shanxi province (China)
  Fogong Monastery **83**, 83–4, **85**, 86

Nanchan Monastery **84**, 85, 86
shatyor (tent roof) **148**, 149, 150
Shaw, Richard Norman 427, **427**, **428**, 449
shed houses, northwestern tribes 256, **256**
Shepseskaf, pharaoh 26
shikhara roofs, India 72–3
Shingle Style 427, 442
Shinto 94
  shrines 97–8
Shreve, Richmond 475, **475**
Shrewsbury, Shropshire (England), flax mill
  396
shrines
  Buddhist, in India 66–71
  Canterbury, St. Thomas à Becket 227
  Islamic 154–6
  Mityana Pilgrims Shrine, Uganda
    (Dahinden) 550, **550**
  Shinto 97–8
  Sumerian 16
Siena (Italy) 246–8, **247**
  Palazzo Pubblico **247**, 248
Silsbee, Joseph Lyman 455
Simmons Hall dormitory, M.I.T. School of
  Architecture (Holl) 545, **545**
Simone da Orsenigo 238
Simpson-Lee House (Murcutt), Mount
  Wilson **563**, 564
Sinan, Koca 164–5
  Mosque of Süleyman the Magnificent,
    Istanbul 165–7, **168**
  Selimiye Mosque, Edirne 167, **167**
  Shehzade Mosque, Istanbul **164**, 165, **165**
sipapus 258
Sixtus IV, Pope 341
Sixtus V, Pope 304, 341–2, 343, 352, 376
Siza, Álvaro **536**, 536–7
Skidmore, Owings, and Merrill 513
skin-coverings
  prehistoric huts 10
  subarctic tupik 256
Skislewicz, Anton **476**
skyscrapers
  Art Deco 472–5
  first 422–4, **423**, **424**, 445–7, 449
Slither Housing, Kitagata (Diller and
  Scofidio) 548
Smeaton, John 424
Smithson, Peter and Alison 507
Smythson, Robert 331, **331**, 333
Sneferu, pharaoh 24
Soane, Sir John 401–2, **405**, 405–6, **406**,
  448, 546
Songyue Pagoda, Dengfeng 83
Soufflot, Jacques-Gabriel **390**, 390–1, 399
Southwestern tribes, Native American 257–8
space frame construction 2, 4
Specchi, Alessandro 352
Speyer Cathedral (Germany) 190, **190**, **191**
Sphinx, Giza **26**, 27, **27**
squinches 146, 196, **240**
St. Louis, Missouri
  Eads Bridge 417
  Wainwright Building (Adler and Sullivan)
    445, **445**, 449
stained-glass windows 215, 222, 224–6
staircases
  Baroque **339**, 362
  Renaissance 303, 304, 310
stave churches 184–7, **185**, **186**, **187**
steel 2, 416–17, 419, 423, 459
Steiner, Rudolf 468–9, **469**
Steiner House, Vienna (Loos) 453–4, **454**
stelae 263, **264**, 272

stereotomy 202, 211
Stern, Robert A.M. 524, **524**, 534
Steward, Thomas S. 401
"Stile Floreale" 430
"Stile Liberty" 430
Stirling, James 553, **553**, **554**
stoas 56, 109
Stock Exchange, Amsterdam (Berlage) 466, **467**
Stockholm (Sweden)
  Bredenberg Department Store (Asplund) 504
  Stockholm Public Library (Asplund) 504, **504**
Stone, Edward Durrell 548
stone (masonry) construction 2, 3, 210
  Cambodia 77
  Carolingian 178–82
  Egypt 27
  Greek 44, 46–7, 61
  India 65, 67, 68, 71–2, 75
  pre-Columbian Bolivia 272
  Russia 150
Stonehenge, Wilts. (England) **12**, **13**, 13–14
stonemasons 177
Stornoloco, Gabrielle 238
Stoughton House, Cambridge (Mass.) (Richardson) 442, **443**, 449
Strawberry Hill, Twickenham (Walpole) **379**, 398, **398**
Streamline Modern 475, **476**
Street, George Edmund 427
Strickland, William 56, 401
structural systems, classification 2–5
Structuralism 519
Strutt, William 396, **396**
Stuart, James 382
Stubbins, Hugh 542, **542**
stupas, India **66**, 66–8
Sturgis, Russell 414
Stuttgart (Germany)
  Staatsgalerie (Stirling) 553, **554**
  Weissenhof Siedlung **491**, 491–2
stylobate 49
Suger, Abbot 220, 226, 248
Süleyman the Magnificent, mosque and tomb, Istanbul (Sinan) 165–7, **166**
Sullivan, Louis Henri 414, 442–8, 449, 453, 455, 456
  Auditorium Building, Chicago 444, **444**, 445, 449
  Carson Pirie Scott Department Store, Chicago **447**, 448
  Charnley House, Chicago 456, **456**
  Guaranty Building, Buffalo 445, **446**, 449
  National Farmer's Bank, Owatonna 448
Sumerians 14–16
Sunila (Finland), Cellulose Factory (Aalto) **510**, **511**
Suryavarman II, king of Cambodia 77
suspension bridges 4, **5**
sustainable design 560–5
Suzhou (China), garden **92**, 93, **93**
Swahili tribe (Kenya) 280
Swiczinsky, Helmut 526
Sydney (Australia)
  Ball-Eastaway House (Murcutt) 561
  Douglas Murcutt House (Murcutt) 561, **561**
  Opera House (Utzon) 549, **549**
Syria and Syrians 153

tablinum 126
Taihu rocks 91, **91**
Taj Mahal, Agra (India) 168–9, **169**

Talenti, Francesco 287
Taliban, the 70
Taliesin Fellowship 495, 496–8
talud and tablero motifs 259, 262, **262**, 263–4, **266**, 268
Tange, Kenzo 538, **538**
Taniguchi, Yoshio 548
Tanjore (India), Brihadesvara Temple 75, **76**, 78
Tassel House, Brussels (Horta) **430**, 431
tatami, Japan 99
Tatlin, Vladimir, *Monument to the Third International* 465, **465**
Taut, Bruno 468, **469**
Tavanasa Bridge (Maillart) 479
tavertine 125
tea houses, Japan 101–3, **102**, **103**
Team-X 507, 517, 535
Teatro Olimpico (Palladio and Scamozzi), Vicenza 321, **321**
teepees **252**, 252–3, 283
Telford, Thomas 396
Temple of Artemis, Ephesus 44
Temple of Athena Nike *see* Athens
Temple of Athena Polias *see* Athens
Temple of Edfu, Egypt **32**
temples
  Buddhist 94–6, 101
  China 83, 86, **87**
  Egyptian, mortuary and valley 28, **28**, 30–2
  Etruscan 105–6, **106**
  Greek 36, 45–50, 52, 53–4, 55, 58, 61
  Hindu 71–5, 77, **77**, 78, **78**, **79**
  Jain 66
  Japan 94–6, 101
  Roman 118–20
  Sumerian 16, 17
  *see also* cave-temples; rock-cut temples
Tennessee State Capitol, Nashville (Strickland) 401
Tenochtitlán (Mexico) 268, **268**, 269
tensile construction 2, 4
tension, of structural materials 2
tents, Moroccan 274, **275**
Teotihuacán (Mexico) 259–61, **260**, **261**, 282
Tepe Gawra, Sumer (Iraq), temple 16, **16**
tepidarium 123
textile-block houses (Wright) 495
textile mills 396, **396**, 419
thatch/thatch roofs 44, 65, 81, 99, 275, **276**
theaters 550
  Art Deco **474**, 475
  French Neo-Classical 392, **392**
  Greek 57–8
  Modernist 550
  Roman 123–4, **124**
Theodoric, king 135
thermae *see* baths, Roman
t'Hoff, Rob van 477
tholoi 55, 58
Thomas of Hoo 227
Thoreau, Henry David 414
Thornton, William 406, 410
Thutmose I, pharaoh 30, 31
Thutmose II, pharaoh 30
Thutmose III, pharaoh 30, 31
Tiepolo, Giovanni Battista 362, 377
tierceron ribs 226
Tijou, Jean, ironmonger 370, 372
Tikal (Guatemala) **263**, 263–4, **264**, 282
Tikar tribe (Cameroon) 275, **276**
Tillamook tribe (Native American) 256
Timgad (Algeria), Roman city 113, **113**
Timur the Lame 160, 163

Tiryns **40**, **43**, 43–4, **44**
Tivoli (Italy)
  Hadrian's Villa 129–30, **130**
  Temple of the Sibyl 118
  Villa d'Este garden (Ligorio) 324–5, **325**
Tiwanaku (Bolivia) 272, 283
Todaiji, Nara (Japan), monastery 95–6, **96**
Todi (Italy), S. Fortunato 238
togunas, Dogon 278, **279**
tokonoma 103
Tokyo (Japan)
  Imperial Hotel (Wright) 462
  Olympic Sports complex (Tange) 538, **538**
  Prada store (Herzog and de Meuron) 551
Tolowa tribe 256
Toltecs 267–8
tombs
  Egyptian: (mastaba) 21, **21**; (rock-cut) 28, **28**, 29–30
  Islamic 168–9
  Mayan 265, **265**
  megalithic **10**, 11–13
  Mycenaean (tholoi) 41–2
  Theodoric, Ravenna 5
  toranas (entrance gates) 68, **68**
Torrigiani, Pietro 330
totem poles 256
Toulouse (France), St. Sernin **195**, 195–6, 197, 211
Tournus (France), St. Philibert, monastic church 194–5
Tours (France), St. Martin 195
tower houses
  African adobe 275, **276**
  medieval 242, **242**
towers
  Carolingian 178–80
  Ottonian 210
  Romanesque 198
town planning *see* city and town planning
Tractarian Movement 411
Trajan, emperor 113
Trans World Airlines Terminal, Kennedy Airport, New York (Saarinen) 512–13, **513**
transepts 135, 151
trefoils 226
triclinium (dining room) 126
Trier (Germany) 113
trilithons 13
triumphal arches 112, 113, 115–16
trusses 2, 3–4, **4**, 5
Tschumi, Bernard **524**, 524–5
Tsien, Billie 545–6, **546**
Tudor arches 240
Tugendhat House, Brno (Mies van der Rohe) 490, **490**
Tula (Mexico), pyramid and temple **267**, 267–8, 283
tulou houses, China 93, **93**
Tuni, Badi' al-Zaman 162
tupiks, subarctic region 256
Turin (Italy)
  Cappella della SS. Sindone (Guarini) 355, **355**
  S. Lorenzo (Guarini) 355, **356**, 377
Turner, Richard 419, **419**
Tuscan order 106, 392
tympana 196, **197**, 201–2, 202, **202**, 215, 222

Uffizi, Florence (Vasari) **306**, 306–7
Uganda, palace of the chiefs 280–1
Uji-Yamada (Japan), Ise Shrine **97**, 97–8, 103

Ukraine, prehistoric huts 10
Unité d'Habitation, Marseille (Le Corbusier)
    **500**, 500–1, **501**
United States of America
    African influences 275
    American style 439–48, **449**
    architectural university education 413
    Art Deco 472–5, 493
    Arts and Crafts Movement 425, 427
    Baroque influences 377
    Ecclesiological Movement 411–12
    English influences 372, 375–6, 377
    Native Americans 251–8, **252**, 283
    Neo-Classicism 406–10, 448
    railroads 418
    saltbox houses 6, **6**, **7**
Unity Temple, Oak Park (Wright) 460, **461**,
    461–2, 505
University of Pennsylvania, Richards Medical
    Research Building (Kahn) 513–14, **514**
University of Virginia, Charlottesville
    (Jefferson) 120, **409**, 409–10
University of Wyoming, American Heritage
    Center (Predock) 544, **544**
Upjohn, Richard 411–12, **412**
Uppark, Sussex (Talman) 372–4, **373**, 377
Ur, Mesopotamia (Iraq) 17, **17**, **18**
Urban VIII, Pope 349
Urbino (Italy) **297**, 297–8
Urnes (Norway)
    carved portal **186**, 187
    stave church 184–6, **185**, **186**, **187**
Uruk, Sumer, White Temple 16, **16**
U.S. Capitol
    Latrobe 401, 406
    Walter (dome) 5
Usonian houses 496
Utrecht (Holland), Schroeder House
    (Rietveld) 478, **478**, **479**, 492
Utzon, Jorn 549, **549**
Uxmal (Mexico) 266
    Govenor's Palace 266, **266**
    Nunnery 266, **266**

V. D. L. Research House, Los Angeles
    (Neutra) 499, **499**
Valadier, Giuseppe 352, **353**
Van de Velde, Henri 468
Vanbrugh, Sir John 374, **374**, **375**, 377
Vasari, Giorgio 304, 313
    Uffizi, Florence **306**, 306–7
vaults 2, 3, **240**
    domical 237
    fan 226, 227
    muqarnas 154, 172, **174**, 175
    pendant 398
    "pumpkin" 143, **143**
    quadripartite 220
    Roman 108
    sexpartite 217
    *see also* barrel-vaults; groin vaults; rib
        vaults
Vaux, Calvert 414
Vedas, the 65
Veneto, villa designs by Palladio 317–20
Venice (Italy)
    Ca' d'Oro 248, **248**
    Doge's Palace 248, **248**
    Gothic architecture 248, 249, 321
    La Zecca (Sansovino), mint 323, **323**
    Library of S. Marco (Sansovino and
        Scamozzi) **322**, 323
    Palazzo Grimani (Sanmichele) 323, **323**
    Palazzo Vendramini-Calergi (Coducci) 321

    Palladio in 321–3
    Piazza S. Marco 321, **322**
    S. Giorgio Maggiore (Palladio) **320**, 320–1
    S. Marco **133**, **141**, 144, **145**, 202, **203**
    Scuola di S. Marco 321
Venturi, Robert 452, **517**, 517–18, **518**, 534
verdika (fence) 67, 68
Versailles (France)
    château 366–8, **367**, 379
    Petit Trianon (Gabriel) 391, **391**
Vesnin, Viktor and Alexandr 465, **465**
Vespasian 115
Vézelay (France), Ste. Madeleine **177**, **201**,
    201–2, 412
    Mystic Mill capital 200, **200**
Vicenza (Italy)
    basilica (Palladio) 316, **316**
    Palazzo Valmarana (Palladio) 316
    Teatro Olimpico (Palladio and Scamozzi)
        321, **321**
    Villa Rotonda (Villa Americo-Capra)
        (Palladio) 318–20, **319**
Victorian style 401
Vienna (Austria)
    Karlskirche 357, **358**, 377
    Moller House (Loos) **454**, 455
    Postal Savings Bank (Wagner) **437**, 437–8,
        **438**
    Schullin Jewelry Shop (Hollein) 549
    Secession Hall (Olbrich) 438, **439**
    Stadtbahn (subway system) stations
        (Wagner) 437
    Steiner House (Loos) 453–4, **454**
Viennese Secession 437–9, 449
Vierzehnheiligen (Germany), church
    (Neumann) **362**, 363, 377, 379
Vietnam Veterans Memorial, Washington
    D.C. (Lin) 540–1, **541**
Vignola, Giacomo Barozzi da 324, 331, **340**,
    340–1, **341**
viharas (monasteries) 66, 68
Viipuri (Vyborg), Municipal Library (Aalto)
    **508**, 508–9, **509**
Viking architecture 184–7, 210
    Animal Style ornament 184, 187
    and monasteries 182, 208
    *see also* Norway; stave churches
Villa Barbaro, Maser (Palladio) 317–18, **318**
Villa d'Este, Tivoli, garden (Ligorio) 324–5,
    **325**
Villa Foscari, Malcontenta (Palladio) 318,
    **319**
Villa Giulia, Rome 324
Villa Lante, Bagnaia (Vignola) 324, **325**
Villa Madama, Rome (Raphael) 305–6, **306**,
    324
Villa Rotonda, Vicenza (Palladio) 318–20,
    **319**
Villa Savoye, Poissy (Le Corbusier) 481–3,
    **482**
Villa Stein, Garches (Le Corbusier) 481, **481**
Villa Trissino, Meledo (Palladio) 320, **320**
Villard de Honnecourt 217
    notebooks **239**, 239–40
Villard Houses, New York (McKim, Mead,
    and White) **415**, 415–16
villas, Roman **128**, 128–30, **130**
Villefranche-de-Rouergue (France), bastide
    245, **245**
Viollet-le-Duc, Eugène-Emmanuel 218, **412**,
    412–13, 425, 430, 448
Virgin Mary 216, 220
Virginia State Capitol (Jefferson) 407–8, **408**
Vishnu Temple, Bhitargaon **72**, *72–3*

Visigoths 244
Vitruvius (Marcus Vitruvius Pollio) 1, 45, 46,
    53, 110, 380
    *Ten Books of Architecture* 108, 285, 292
Vittori, Gail D. A. 564
volutes (scrolls), Ionic 46
voussoirs 3, **3**
Voysey, Charles Francis Annesley 428, **429**,
    449
Vries, Hans Vredman de 331, 333

Wade and Purdy 423
Wagner, Otto **437**, 437–8, **438**, 449
Wailly, Charles de 383, 392, **392**, 399
Wainwright Building, St. Louis (Adler and
    Sullivan) 445, **445**, 449
Walpole, Horace 379, 398
Walter, Thomas U. 5
wandpfeilers (wall pillars) 357, 361
Wang Campus Center, Wellesley College
    (Scogin and Merrill) 547, **547**
Ward Willits House, Highland Park (Wright)
    458, **458**
Warren, Michigan, General Motors Technical
    Center (Saarinen) 512
Warren trusses 4, **4**
Washington, Connecticut, Lang House
    (Stern) 524, **524**
Washington D.C.
    Holocaust Memorial Museum (Pei Cobb
        Freed) **541**, 541–2
    Treaty Room Suite, State Department
        Building (Greenberg) 533
    Vietnam Veterans Memorial (Lin) 540–1,
        **541**
Wasmuth, Ernst 462, 477
Wastell, John 227, 234
watchtowers, China 84
water tower, Posen (Poelzig) 471, **471**
Watts Sherman House, Newport, Rhode
    Island (Richardson) 442, **443**, 449
Wayzata, Minnesota, Winton Guest House
    (Gehry) 528, **528**
Webb, Philip 426, **426**
Weissenhof Siedlung, Stuttgart **491**, 491–2
Wellesley College, Mass., Wang Campus
    Center (Scogin and Merrill) 547, **547**
Wendigen (Dutch Expressionism) 466, 477,
    505
westwerks, Carolingian 178–80
Whistler, James MacNeill 430
White, Stanford 414–15, 449
Wiel am Rhein (Germany), fire station
    (Hadid) 526
wigwams 253, **253**
wikiups 253
William of Sens 226–7
William the Conqueror 208, 211, 243
William the Englishman 227
Williams, Jordan 564
Williams, Tod 545–6, **546**
Winchester Cathedral, Hampshire (England)
    208
wind-eyes 185
wind loads 2
window tracery, Gothic (plate and bar) 214,
    221, **227**
Windyhill, Kilmacolm, Scotland
    (Mackintosh) 434
Winnebago, the 253
Winslow House, River Forest, Illinois
    (Wright) 457, **457**, 492
Winton Guest House, Wayzata (Gehry) 528,
    **528**

Wittgenstein, Ludwig 519
Wittkower, Rudolf 294
Wollaton Hall, Notts. (England) (Smythson) **331**, 331–3, **332**
Wolsey, Cardinal Thomas 330–1
wood 2
  China 84–5
  English hammerbeam Gothic roofs 234, **234**
  Japan 94, **100**, 100–1
  *see also* log construction
Wood, Robert 382
Woodland Cemetery (Sweden) (Asplund) 504–5, **505**
wool churches 229
Woolworth Building, New York (Gilbert) 472
World Trade Center, New York, design competition 547–8
World's Columbian Exposition, Chicago, 1893 413–14, **414**
Wren, Christopher 369, 377
  London replanning 369, 370
  Pembroke College Chapel, Cambridge 370
  St. Dunstan-in-the-East, London 370
  St. Mary-le-Bow, London 370
  St. Paul's Cathedral, London 5, 370–2, **371**, 377
  St. Stephen Walbrook, London **369**, 370

Sheldonian Theater, Oxford 369–70
Wright, Frank Lloyd 91, 100, 427, 449, 452, 455–62, 477, 495–9, 505
  Broadacre City 495–6
  early public buildings 460–2
  Fallingwater (Kaufmann House), Ohiopyle 458, 496, **497**
  Gale House, Oak Park, Illinois 458
  Guggenheim Museum, New York 496, **498**
  Imperial Hotel, Tokyo 462
  Larkin Building, Buffalo **460**, 460–1, 505
  Prairie houses 456–9, 505
  Robie House, Chicago, Illinios 458–9, **459**
  Taliesin West 499
  textile-block houses 495
  Unity Temple, Oak Park 460, **461**, 461–2, 505
  Usonian houses 496
  V.C. Morris Gift Shop, San Francisco 496
  Ward Willits House, Highland Park, Illinois 458, **458**
  Winslow House, River Forest, Illinois 457, **457**, 492
wrought iron 396
Würzburg Residenz (Neumann) **339**, **361**, 361–3, 377, 379

Xerxes 47
Xuanzang 70

Yakima, the 256
Yancey Chapel, Sawyerville (Mockbee) 537
yin and yang 81, 92
*Yingzao-fashi* 85–6, 103
Yokohama (Japan), International Port Facility (FOA) 552
Yoshimura House, near Osaka (Japan) **98**
Yungang (China), cave-temples 83
Yurok tribe 256
Yverdon-les-Bains (Switzerland), Blur Building (Diller and Scofidio) 548

Zaero-Polo, Alejandro 552
Zapotecs 261–2
*Zeitgeist* 452
Zen Buddhist architecture 101–3
Zig-Zag Moderne 475
ziggurats
  Egypt 33
  Khorsabad 18, **19**
  Mesopotamia 17, **17**
Zimmerman, Dominikus 359–60, **360**, 377
Zimmerman, Johann Baptist 360, 377, 379
Zuni, the 258
Zurich (Switzerland), Stadelhofen Railway Station (Calatrava) 557